Scripting with Objects

Scripting with Objects

A Comparative Presentation of Object-Oriented Scripting With Perl and Python

Avinash C. Kak
Purdue University

WILEY
A John Wiley & Sons, Inc., Publication

Published by John Wiley & Sons, Inc., Hoboken, New Jersey.
Published simultaneously in Canada.

For general information on our other products and services or for technical support, please contact our Customer Care Department within the United States at (800) 762-2974, outside the United States at (317) 572-3993 or fax (317) 572-4002.

Wiley also publishes its books in a variety of electronic formats. Some content that appears in print may not be available in electronic format. For information about Wiley products, visit our web site at www.wiley.com.

Library of Congress Cataloging-in-Publication Data:

Kak, Avinash C.
Scripting with objects : a comparative presentation of object-oriented scripting with Perl and Python / Avinash C. Kak.
p. cm.
ISBN 978-0-470-39725-1
1. Object-oriented programming (Computer science) 2. Scripting languages (Computer science) 3. Perl (Computer program language) 4. Python (Computer program language) I. Title.
QA76.64.K3555 2008
005.1'17—dc22 2007035480

To

my daughter

Carina

Contents in Brief

Contents

Preface

During the last several years, scripting languages have become just as important as systems programming languages. Thus it felt natural to follow my *Programming with Objects (PWO)* with *Scripting with Objects. Programming with Objects* was a comparative presentation of C++ and Java, two dominant languages of that genre. In the same vein, *Scripting with Objects* is a comparative presentation of Perl and Python, two dominant languages of the genre that these languages represent.

Scripting with Objects is based on the same overall philosophy as *PWO*, that, in addition to its syntax, it is essential to depict a programming language through its applications in order to establish fully its beauty and power. Teaching a programming language divorced from its applications would be akin to teaching English through its grammar alone.

This book is not intended for a reader who wants to acquire quickly the rudiments of a scripting language for solving some problem that the he or she has in mind. Rather, this book is designed for a reader who desires to acquire a more comprehensive and expansive perspective on scripting by simultaneous exposure to two languages.

There is an adage that says that you can never understand one language until you understand at least two.[1] This adage goes straight to the heart of becoming a good programmer these days and developing a good sense of the range of programming ideas that are out there. While learning a single language will equip you with the

[1] Attributed to Ronald Searle, artist (1920-).

syntax, it will not necessarily give you an appreciation for all of the nuances associated with the usage of that syntax. Learning two languages (and, if at all possible, multiple languages) that are at once similar and different is perhaps the most effective way to appreciate those nuances. In the old days, the more serious students of English literature would often learn Latin as well as a number of other Romance languages such as French, Italian, and Spanish. This was certainly true of all of the noted British poets, novelists, and playwrights of the eighteenth and nineteenth centuries. Learning multiple languages gave them the ability to create literary and linguistic effects in their native tongue that otherwise would not have been possible.

However, learning two languages at the same time does create its own challenges, especially when the languages are as large as Perl and Python. A beginner can easily become confused as to which syntactical construct belongs to what language. Additionally, certain habits one quickly acquires in one language (such as terminating every Perl statement with a semicolon and using just indentations for indicating block termination in Python) can reflexively manifest themselves in the other language. With regard to the first difficulty, note that practically all modern programming requires that you keep the documentation page open in one window as you are programming in another window. All of the major modern languages have become so large that it is impossible to commit to memory all of the functionality in all the modules of a language. So, if you really think about it, working with two programming languages in this day and age should be no different than working with one programming language. In either case, you will be looking up the documentation as you are writing your program or script. The second issue — the data entry habits of one language interfering with the writing of programs in the other language — is a more significant problem, but one that can nevertheless be overcome with practice.

Organization of the Book

This book's treatment of Perl and Python is mostly comparative, all the way from the basic syntax of the two languages to writing application-level scripts. By comparative, I mean that similar scripting concepts in the two languages are explained with identical examples in most cases. In many chapters, I have followed a Perl presentation of a scripting concept with a Python presentation of the same concept. In other chapters, it seemed more appropriate to present first all of the Perl-related notions, followed by the corresponding Python-based notions.

The book begins in Chapter 1 with the presentation of a multilanguage view of modern application development and the importance of scripting languages (and their differences from the mainstream systems programming languages). The basic Perl syntax is reviewed in Chapter 2, and the basic Python syntax in Chapter 3. Chapter 4 then provides a review of regular expressions and how to use them in Perl and Python. Chapter 5 presents the notion of a reference in Perl. These five chapters constitute the basic scripting material in the book.

With Chapter 6, we begin the presentation of object-oriented scripting, the focus of that chapter being on the notion of a class in Perl. Chapter 7 then follows with a similar discussion but in Python; this chapter also introduces the reader to the new-style classes in Python. Chapter 8 discusses inheritance and polymorphism in Perl, with Chapter 9 doing the same for Python. Chapter 10 is devoted to the topic of exceptions in Perl and Python. Throwing and catching exceptions have become central to object-oriented programming and scripting, so much so that now you see them being used even for affecting certain forms of flow of control. Chapter 11 shows how to define abstract classes and methods in Perl and Python. Abstract classes and methods play a very important role in object-oriented programming in general. They can be used as mixin classes to lend specialized behaviors to other classes and, by serving as root classes, they can help to unify the other classes into meaningful hierarchies. Chapter 12 goes into the issues that deal with memory management and garbage collection.

Application-level scripting starts with Chapter 13 where we take up the subject of writing scripts for creating graphical user interfaces. Chapter 14 presents multithreaded scripting. Multithreading plays an important role when scripts are written for graphical user interfaces and network applications. We take up the topic of network programming with Perl and Python in Chapter 15. Chapter 16 shows how to write scripts for interacting with databases. Finally, Chapter 17 presents scripting for processing XML. This chapter is one of the longest chapters in the book because the world of XML has literally exploded during the last few years. In addition to becoming the technology of choice for representing document content in a manner that is independent of how the document is displayed, XML is also emerging as the *lingua franca* for the interoperability needed for the rapidly emerging business of web services.

For a more in-depth description of each chapter, see Section 1.2 of Chapter 1.

Intended Audience

The book is designed both for a one-semester undergraduate course on advanced scripting (this would be for students with prior background in the basics of Perl and Python), and a two-semester undergraduate program for students who will be experiencing scripting for the first time. When used in a one-semester advanced scripting course, the recommended starting point in the book would be Chapter 6. For such a course, the first five chapters are intended to serve as basic reference material. When used for a two-semester educational program in scripting, my recommendation would be to cover roughly the first 500 pages in the first semester and the rest in the second semester.

Figure 0.1 is a recommendation for the use of the book for a one-semester undergraduate course on advanced scripting. Note that there are definite advantages to having all of the reference material needed for advanced instruction in the text itself. Chapter 12 is optional and depends on the degree to which the instructor wants to emphasize memory management issues. After Chapter 12, all of the application chapters can be taught in any order. In longer chapters, such as Chapter 17 on XML, the instructors may wish to only address the material they would like to emphasize.

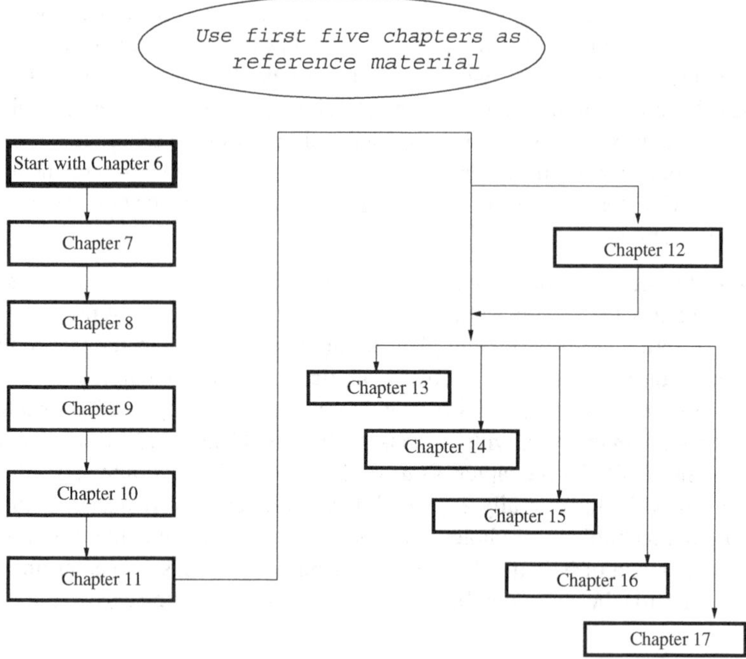

Fig. 0.1 *For a One-Semester Undergraduate Course on Advanced Scripting*

Figure 0.2 outlines the recommended use of the book for a two-semester program of instruction in scripting. I believe that a two-semester program would result in a quicker rate of learning, thus making it possible to accommodate a sophisticated project in the latter half of the second semester.

Finally...

I will be glad to share my teaching materials with the prospective instructors planning to use this book as a text. I would also appreciate hearing from the readers about any typos and other errors they may find. All corrections received will be posted at `www.scripting-with-objects.com` and the authors of the corrections duly acknowledged. The corrections and other feedback can be sent to me directly at `kak@purdue.edu`. I would also love to hear from the readers if I have slipped up

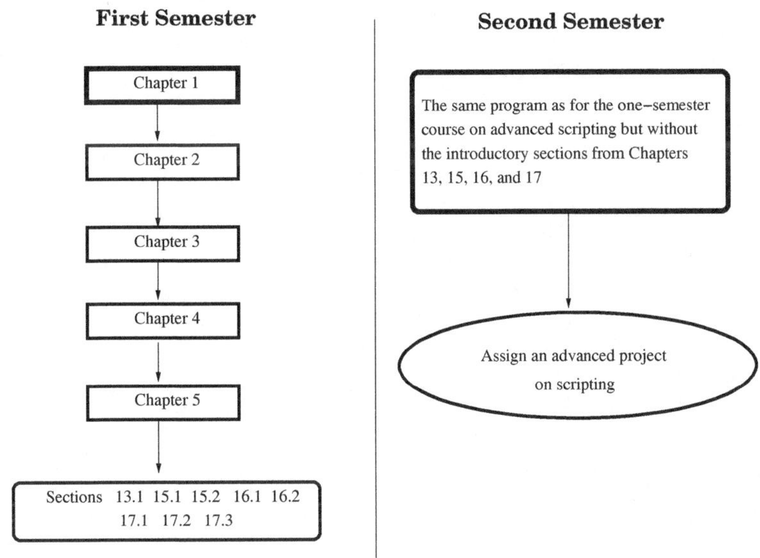

Fig. 0.2 *For a Two-Semester Program of Courses Devoted to Scripting*

in making proper attributions to other authors. When an example script in this book was inspired by some material I saw elsewhere, I have acknowledged the author of that material in a footnote or in the "Credits and Suggestions for Further Reading" section at the end of the chapter.

Before ending, I would also like to add that this book should be useful for those who are making a transition from Perl to Python or vice versa.

Avinash C. Kak

West Lafayette, Indiana

Acknowledgments

I'd like to thank my editor George Telecki at John Wiley whose experience and expertise have guided me through yet another book. George is the quintessential editor who is as much in tune with the human side of what it takes to write and produce a book as with the scientific and technological dimensions of the work involved.

Many of the example scripts and the explanations presented in this book evolved through my teaching object-oriented scripting and computer security courses at Purdue. The students who sat through these classes deserve special mention for providing valuable feedback.

Several of the core object-oriented ideas presented here for Perl and Python were refined though a tutorial given at the 2006 Open Source Convention; many thanks to the organizers of that conference for giving me the opportunity. I also owe thanks to the tutorial participants who endured my experiments with a comparative presentation of two languages in a time-limited format.

Special thanks to Malcolm Slaney, now a Principal Scientist at Yahoo Research, for his feedback on several of the chapters. You could call Malcolm a natural-born "computationalist." He is a well of knowledge whose waters run deep and wide.

It is a challenge to ensure that a large volume such as this is as error-free as possible. Much help toward that end was provided by John Mastarone who was brave enough to wade through the entire manuscript. Copy-editing help was also provided by others who looked at various sections of the manuscript. I owe all my gratitude. Obviously, whatever errors remain, typographical or otherwise, are mine to fix in hopefully future printings of the book.

Special thanks to Amy Hendrickson, Wiley's Latex expert, for her help with the formatting of the book.

Finally, my deepest and most pleasurable thanks go to Stacey for her loving support of an exhausting project that we both thought was never going to end. I also owe her much for contributing her language skills to the smoothing out of the text at many places in the book.

A. C. K.

1

Multilanguage View of Application Development and OO Scripting

We now live in a world of multilanguage computing in which two or more languages may be used simultaneously in an application development effort.

Increasingly, application development efforts are thought of as exercises in high-level integration over components that may be independent. Often each component is programmed using a systems programming language and these components are integrated using a scripting language. Although systems programming languages like C and C++ provide type safety,[1] speed, access to existing libraries, fast bit-twiddling capabilities, and so on, scripting languages such as Perl and Python allow for rapid application-level prototyping, easier task-level reconfigurability, automatic report generation, easy-to-use interfaces to built-in high-level data structures such as lists, arrays, and hashes for analysis and documentation of task-level performance, and so forth.

What is important is that at both ends — the component end and the integration end — more and more software development is being carried out using object-oriented concepts. The reasons for this are not surprising. The software needs that are driving the object-oriented (OO) movement in the systems programming languages are the same as the needs for scripting languages: code extensibility, code reusability, code modularization, easier maintenance of the code, and so forth. As software becomes increasingly complex, whether for the programming of the individual components or

[1]An example of type safety is static type checking by the compiler that can catch many programming errors and that can reduce, if not eliminate, run-time type errors. Run-time type errors are, in general, more expensive to handle than compile-time errors.

for systems integration, it cries out for solutions that in many cases are provided by OO.

In other words, the fundamental notions of OO — encapsulation, inheritance, and polymorphism, exception handling, and so on — are just as useful for scripting languages as they are for systems programming languages. Since much of the evolution of OO programming took place in the realm of systems programming languages, the aforementioned fundamental concepts of OO are widely associated with those languages. This association is reinforced by the existence of hundreds of books that deal with OO for systems programming languages. Less well known is the fact that, in recent years, OO has become equally central to scripting languages.

You can, of course, get considerable mileage from scripting languages without resorting to the OO style of programming.[2] The large number of non-OO-based Perl and Python scripts available freely on the internet bears a testimony to that. But the fact remains that much of today's commercial-grade software in both of these languages is based on OO. Additionally, in Python, even if one does not directly use the concepts of subclassing, inheritance, and polymorphism in a script, the language uses the OO style of function calls for practically everything. That is, you invoke functions on objects, even when the objects are not instances constructed from a class, as opposed to calling functions with object arguments.[3] In Perl also, even when you choose not to use the concepts of subclassing, inheritance, and polymorphism, you may nonetheless run headlong into OO when you make use of language features such as tying a variable to a disk-based database file. The simple act of assigning a value to such a variable can alter the database file in any desired manner, including automatically storing the value of the variable on the disk.

Scripting languages did not start out with object-oriented features. Originally, their main purpose was to serve as tools for automating repetitive tasks in system administration. You would, for example, write a small shell script for rotating the log files in a system; this script would run automatically and periodically at certain times (under cron in Unix environments). But over the years, as the languages evolved to incorporate easy-to-use facilities for graphical user interface (GUI) programming, network programming, interfacing with database managers, and so on, the language developers resorted to object orientation.

---

[2] By OO style of programming we mean programming that makes use of subclassing and programming that exploits inheritance, polymorphism, and object-oriented exception handling.

[3] In comparing Perl and Python, this language feature of Python has caused some authors to claim that everything in Python is an object, implying that not everything in Perl is an object. On the contrary, both Perl and Python are on the same footing regarding the "objectification" of the languages. In other words, everything in Perl is also an object although the low-level syntax features do not make that apparent.

1.1 SCRIPTING LANGUAGES VERSUS SYSTEMS PROGRAMMING LANGUAGES

Many people today would disagree with the dichotomy suggested by the title of this section, especially if we are to place Perl and Python in the category of scripting languages.

Scripting languages were once purely interpreted. When purely interpreted, code is not converted into a machine-dependent binary executable file in one fell swoop. Instead, each statement, consisting of calls either to other programs or to functions provided specially by the interpreter, is first interpreted and then executed one at a time. An important part of interpretation is the determination of the storage locations of the identifiers in the statements. This determination is generally carried out afresh for each separate statement, commonly causing the interpreted code to run slower than the compiled code. Languages that are purely interpreted usually do not contain facilities for constructing arbitrarily complex data structures.

Yes, Perl and Python are not purely interpreted languages in the sense that is described above. Over the years, both have become large full-blown languages, with practically all the features that one finds in systems programming languages. Additionally, both have a compilation stage, meaning that a script is first compiled and then executed.[4] The compilation stage checks each statement for syntax accuracy and outputs first an *abstract syntax tree* representation of the script and then, from that, a *bytecode file* that is platform independent.[5] The bytecode is subsequently *interpreted* by a virtual machine. If necessary, it is possible to compile a Perl or Python script directly into a machine-dependent binary executable file — just as one would do with a C program — and then run the executable file separately, again just as you would execute an `a.out` or `a.exe` file for C. The main advantage of first converting a script into an abstract syntax tree and then interpreting the bytecode is that it allows for the intermixing of the compilation and interpretation stages. That is, inside a script you can have a string that is actually another script. When this string is passed as an argument to an evaluation function, the function compiles and executes the argument at run time. Such evaluation functions are frequently called `eval`.

Therefore, we obviously cannot say that Perl and Python are interpreted languages in the old sense of what used to be meant by "interpreted languages." Despite that, we obviously cannot lump languages like C and C++ in the same category as languages

---

[4]Nevertheless, the Perl executable *perl* and the Python executable *python*, both normally installed in `/usr/bin` or `/usr/local/bin`, are commonly referred to as *interpreters*.

[5]On the other hand, the compilation-linking phase, through which a program written in a systems programming language must always be taken, yields an optimized binary executable that is specific to the machine architecture. Despite this difference, many of the compiler optimizations for a program written in a scripting language are the same as the optimizations carried out for a systems programming language. Also note that the bytecode output in the case of scripting languages may be thought of as the assembly code of a hypothetical virtual machine.

like Perl and Python. What we have now is an interpreted-to-compiled continuum in which languages like the various Unix shells, AppleScript, MSDOS batch files, and so on, belong at the purely interpreted end and languages like C and C++ belong at the purely compiled end. Other languages like Perl, Python, Lisp, Java, and so on occupy various positions in this continuum.

While compilation versus interpretation may not be a sound criterion to set Perl and Python apart from the systems programming languages like C and C++, there are other criteria that are more telling. We will present these in the rest of this section. The material that follows in this section draws heavily from (and sometimes quotes verbatim from) an article by Ousterhout, creator of the `Tcl` scripting language [51].

Closeness to the machine: To achieve the highest possible efficiencies in data access, data manipulation, and the algorithms used for searching, sorting, decision making, and so on, a systems programming language usually sits closer to the machine than a scripting language.

Purpose: Starting from the most primitive computer element — a word of memory — a systems programming language lets you build custom data structures from scratch and then lets you create computationally efficient implementations for algorithms that require fast numerical or combinatorial manipulation of the data elements. On the other hand, a scripting language is designed for gluing together more task-focused components that may be written using systems programming languages. Additionally, the components utilized in the same script may not all be written using the same systems programming language. So an important attribute of a scripting language is the ease with which it allows interconnections between the components written in other languages — often systems programming languages.

Strongness of data typing: Fundamentally speaking, the notion of a data type is not inherent to a computer. Any word of memory can hold any type of data, such as an integer, a floating-point value, a memory address, or even an instruction. Nevertheless, systems programming languages are strongly typed in general. When you declare the type of a variable in the source code, you are telling the compiler that the variable will have certain storage and run-time properties. The compiler uses this information to detect errors in the source code and to generate a more computationally efficient executable than would otherwise be the case. As an example of compile-time error checking on the basis of types, the compiler would complain if in C you declare a certain variable to be an integer and then proceed to use it as a pointer. Similarly, if you declare a certain variable to be of type `double` in Java and then pass it as an argument to a function for a parameter of type `int`, the compiler would again complain because of possible loss of precision. Using type declarations to catch errors at compile time results in a more dependable product as such errors are caught before the product is shipped out the door. On the other hand, a run-time error would only invite the wrath of the user of the product.

Regarding binary code optimization, which the compiler can carry out using the type information for systems programming languages, if the compiler knows, for example, that the arguments to a multiplication operator are integers, it can translate that part of the source code into a stream of highly efficient assembly code instructions for integer multiplication. On the other hand, if no such assumption can be made at compile time, the compiler would either defer such data type checking until run time, which would extract some performance penalty at run time, or the compiler would make a default assumption about the data type and simply invoke a more general (albeit less efficient) code for carrying out the operation.

Data typing is much less important for scripting languages. To permit easy interfacing between the components that are glued together in a script, a scripting language must be as typeless as possible. When the outputs and the inputs of a pair of components are strongly typed, their interconnection may require some special code if there exist type incompatibilities between the outputs of one and the inputs to the other. Or it may become necessary to eliminate the incompatibilities by altering the input/output data types of the components; this would call for changing the source code and recompilation, something that is not always feasible with commercially purchased libraries in binary form. However, in a typeless environment, the output of one component can be taken as a generic stream of bytes and accepted by the receiving component just on that basis. Or, as is even more commonly the case with scripting languages because string processing is the main focus of such languages, the components can be assumed to produce character streams at their outputs and to accept character streams at their inputs.

Compile-time type checking versus run-time type checking: When a variable is typeless at compile time, the compiler must generate additional code to determine at run time that the value referenced by the variable is appropriate to the operation at hand. For example, if an operation in a script calls for two strings to be concatenated with the + operator applied to operands whose types are not known to the compiler, the compiler must generate additional instructions so that a run-time determination about the appropriateness of the operands for string concatenation can be made. For obvious reasons, this will extract run-time performance penalties; but for scripting languages that is not a big issue since the overall performance of an application is determined more by the speed of execution of the components that are glued together by a script than by the workings of the script itself.

High level versus low level: Compared to systems programming languages, scripting languages are at a higher level, meaning that, on the average, each line of code in a script gets translated into a larger number of machine instructions compared to each line of code in a program in a systems programming language. The lowest-level language in which one can write a computer program is, of course, the assembly language — the assembler translates each line of the assembly code into one machine instruction. It has been estimated that each line of code in a systems programming language translates into five machine instructions on the average. On the other hand, each line of a script may get translated into hundreds or thousands of machine instructions. For example, an innocuous looking script statement may call for substring substitution in a text file. The actual work of substring substitution is likely to be carried out by a sophisticated regular expression engine under the hood. The point is that the primitive operations in a script often embody a much higher level of functionality than the primitive operations in a systems programming language.

Programmer productivity: It was observed by Boehm [3] that programmers can write roughly the same number of lines of code per year regardless of the language. This implies that the higher the level of a language, the greater the programming productivity. Therefore, if a task can be accomplished with equal computational efficiency when programmed in a systems programming language or a scripting language, the latter should be our choice since scripting languages are inherently higher level. But, of course, not all tasks can be programmed in a computationally efficient manner in a scripting language. So for a complex application, one must devise a component-based framework in which the components themselves are programmed in systems programming languages and in which the integration of the components takes place in a scripting language.

Abstraction level of the fundamental data types: The fundamental data types of scripting languages include high-level structures. On the other hand, the systems programming languages use only fine-grained fundamental data types. For example, both Perl and Python support hash tables for storing and manipulating associative lists of `(key, value)` pairs. Both languages also support flexible arrays for storing dynamically alterable lists of objects. On the other hand, C's fundamental data types are `int`, `float`, `double`, and so on. It takes virtually no programming effort to use the high-level data types that are built into scripting languages.

Ability to process a string as a snippet of code: As previously mentioned, many scripting languages provide an evaluation function, usually named `eval`, that takes a string as an argument and then processes it as if it were a piece of code. The string argument may or may not be known at compile time; in other words, it may become available only at run time. A systems programming language like C or C++ cannot provide such a facility because of the distinct and separate compilation and execution stages. After a C or a C++ program is compiled and subject to run-time execution, the compiler cannot be invoked again (at least not easily). Therefore, you cannot construct a string of legal C code and feed the string as an argument to some sort of an evaluation function. Since compilation in a scripting language essentially consists of checking the correctness of each statement of the script and, possibly, transforming it into a parse tree independently of the other statements, compilation and execution can be intermixed. If needed, the run time can invoke the compiler on a string if the string needs to be subsequently interpreted as a piece of code, followed by the execution of the code.

Function overloading or lack thereof: High-level systems programming languages like C++ and Java allow the same function name to be defined with different numbers and/or types of arguments. This allows for the source code to be more programmer-friendly, as when a class is provided with multiple constructors, each with a different parameter structure. To elaborate, a class constructor in C++ and Java has the same name as the name of the class. So if a class is to be provided with multiple constructors, because there is a need to construct instance objects in different ways, it must be possible to overload the class name when used as a constructor. Scripting languages like Perl and Python do not allow for function overloading. If multiple definitions are provided for the same function name, it is the latest definition that will be used, regardless of the argument structure in the function call and regardless of the parameter structure in the function definition. So in the following snippet of Perl code,

```
foo(1);                        # second foo called         #(A)

sub foo {                                                  #(B)
    my $arg = shift;
    print "first foo called with arg equal to $arg\n";
}

foo(1);                        # second foo called         #(C)

sub foo {                                                  #(D)
    print "second foo called\n";
}

foo();                         # second foo called         #(E)
foo(1);                        # second foo called         #(F)
```

it is the definition in line (D) that will be invoked in response to all four function calls in lines (A), (C), (E), and (F) even though there is a better "match" between the function calls of lines (A), (C), and (F) with the function definition in line (B).[6] [7]

Execution speed versus development speed: Scripting languages sacrifice execution speed for development speed, meaning that if we actually wrote an entire application first in a scripting language and then in a systems programming

---

[6]If you run a Perl script with the warning switch -w turned on, you will at least get a warning that you are redefining a function.

[7]We should also mention that, for the example shown, the same result would be obtained regardless of when a function call is made in relation to the multiple function definitions for the same function name in the source code.

language, the software development cycle for the former is likely to be shorter. However, the latter would mostly likely run faster. In actual practice, scripting languages are not used for developing an application from scratch. As previously mentioned, they are used for plugging together the components that are often written in other languages, with the understanding that the components may require fine-grained data structures and complex algorithmic control that are best implemented in a systems programming language. For complex applications programming that involves both scripting and systems programming languages in the manner indicated, the overall speed of execution would be determined primarily by the speed at which the components are executed.

Figure 1.1 shows graphically the relationship between assembly languages, systems programming languages, and scripting languages with regard to the level at which the languages operate and the extent of data typing demanded by the languages. As mentioned previously, scripting languages, as higher level languages, give rise to many more machine instructions per statement than the lower level systems programming languages.

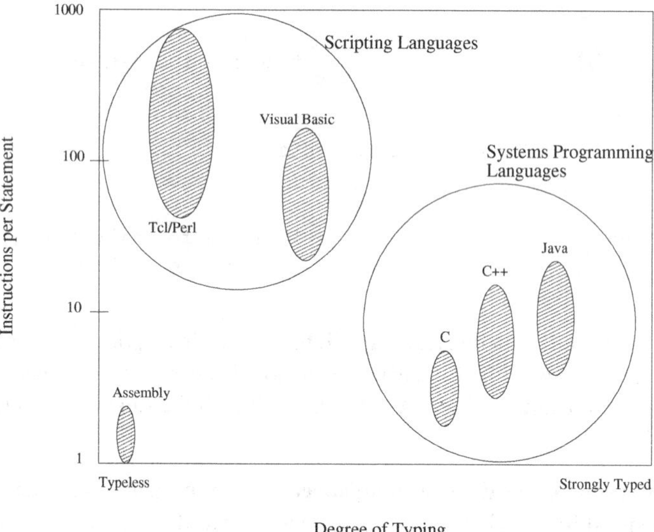

Fig. 1.1 *A comparison of various systems programming languages, scripting languages, and assembly languages with respect to two criteria: the degree of typing required by each language and the average number of machine instructions per statement of the language. (From Ousterhout [51].)*

1.2 ORGANIZATION OF THIS BOOK

We will now provide the reader with an overview of the layout of this book. First we review the basics of Perl in Chapter 2 and the basics of Python in Chapter 3. Considering that both Perl and Python are large languages and that entire books have been devoted to each, our reviews here are by necessity somewhat terse and intended primarily to aid the explanations in the rest of the book.

Chapter 4 presents a review of regular expressions. Text processing is a major preoccupation of scripting languages and regular expressions are central to text processing. Regular expressions in both Perl and Python work the same way, although the precise syntax to use for achieving a desired regular-expression-based functionality is obviously different.

Chapter 5 then goes into the concept of a reference in Perl. Class type objects in Perl are manipulated through references (blessed references, to be precise). References are also needed in Perl for constructing nested data structures, such as lists of lists, hashes with values (for the keys) consisting of lists or other hashes, and so on. A reference is essentially a disguised pointer to an object. When comparing Perl with Python, it is interesting to note that whereas the use of a reference in Perl is optional, in Python *all* objects are manipulated through their references (although in a manner that is transparent to the programmer).

Chapter 6 presents the basic syntax of a class definition in Perl. Also in this chapter are other key Perl OO notions, such as instance variables and instance methods, class variables and class methods, object destruction, and so on. Chapter 7 does the same for Python. Chapter 7 also goes into the fact that Python associates attributes with *all* objects, attributes that are accessed through the dotted-operator notation common to object-oriented programming. An instance constructed from a user-defined class comes with system-supplied attributes just as much as the class itself. Chapter 7 also discusses in detail the differences between the classic classes and new-style classes in Python.

Chapter 8 first discusses what is meant by inheritance in Perl OO, though the same arguments also apply to Python OO, and then goes on to show how the definitions presented earlier in Chapter 6 can be extended to form subclasses. Also included in this chapter is a discussion on how inheritance is used to search for an applicable method in a class hierarchy, and so on. Chapter 9 treats similar topics in Python. Chapter 9 also goes into the details of what every new-style class in Python inherits from the root class `object` and into issues related to subclassing the built-in classes of Python. Chapter 9 also includes a discussion of the Method Resolution Order (MRO) in Python (this is the order in which the inheritance graph is searched for an applicable method) and the differences in MRO between the classic classes and the new-style classes in Python.

Chapter 10 reviews exception handling in Perl and Python. Software practices of today demand defensive programming. Software that involves network communications, database accesses, GUI interactions, and so on, cannot be made foolproof against every conceivable run-time eventuality. For example, when expecting an answer from a human during a GUI session, it is not possible to account for all possible invalid answers from the user. Similarly, when network communications are involved, it is not possible to write a separate `if/else` block for all possible network conditions arising from dropped connections, delayed communications, and so on. Even with software that needs no connections with the outside world, there can be run-time contingencies created by conditions such as insufficient memory, nonexistent files, wrong type of data in files, version incompatibilities, and so on. In old times, such run-time errors would frequently result in core dump — an unceremonious abrupt termination of an application. Now, modern languages provide special exception handling mechanisms to deal with such unforeseen run-time errors. If desired, these mechanisms — often in the form of `try-catch` or `try-except` blocks — can be used to transfer the flow of control to other software packages for initiating new and possibly remedial threads of execution.

Chapter 11 talks about the abstract classes and methods in Perl and Python. Abstract classes play an important role in object-oriented programming in general. It is not so common to see them in Perl and Python scripts that use object-oriented concepts. That could change as developers start tackling more and more complex problems with multilevel object hierarchies. In general, abstract classes are used to lend organization to other classes in a class hierarchy. Abstract classes are also useful for building implementations incrementally and, as mixin classes, to lend specialized behaviors to other classes.

Chapter 12 delves into memory management issues in Perl and Python. The chapter discusses the reference-counting-based garbage collection that is carried out in both languages. The chapter also presents the notion of *weak references* supported by both languages. An object pointed to by a strong reference gets scooped up by the garbage collector when there are no variables holding references to the object. On the other hand, an object pointed to by a weak reference may be scooped up if there is pressure on the memory — even when there are variables holding references to the object. Weak references are useful for memory-intensive applications.

Starting with Chapter 13, the book goes into the applications of object-oriented scripting. Chapter 13 shows how you can write Perl and Python scripts for creating graphical user interfaces. Both languages provide local wrappers for the `Tk` GUI toolkit. The commonly used Perl wrapper is the `Perl/Tk` module and the commonly used Python wrapper is the `Tkinter` module.

Chapter 14 takes on multithreaded scripting. Modern applications, especially if they involve user interaction, require multithreaded implementations. With a multithreaded implementation for its front end, a database server can assign each client request to a separate thread while it goes back to monitoring the network for new incoming calls. By the same token, a multithreaded GUI can download a video clip in a separate thread while the main thread remains responsive to further user interaction. As this chapter demonstrates, multithreading requires care when different threads share data objects.

Chapter 15 delves into scripting for network programming. Practically all of this sort of scripting is based on the client-server model of communications. Within the client-server framework, there are fundamentally two different types of communication links that can be established through a port: those that are commonly based on the Transmission Control Protocol (TCP) and those that commonly use the User Datagram Protocol (UDP). TCP gives us a one-to-one, open and continuous connection that employs handshaking, sequencing, and flow control to ensure that all of the information packets sent from one end of a link are received at the other end. On the other hand, UDP gives us a simpler, and, not surprisingly, faster, one-shot messaging link that does not use any handshaking, but that nevertheless plays an important role in internet communications. This chapter shows how one can write Perl and Python scripts for both types of links. This chapter also discusses broadcasting and multicasting with the UDP protocol.

How to write Perl and Python scripts to interact with databases is the goal of Chapter 16. This chapter considers three types of databases of increasing levels of complexity: flat-file databases, disk-based hash tables, and the commercial-strength relational databases (as exemplified by the open-source MySQL database management system). This chapter also explains how to use Perl's tie mechanism that allows the program variables to be stored in a transparent manner on a disk. The tie mechanism binds a variable to a class type object so that any subsequent accesses to the variable are automatically translated under the hood into method calls on the object.

Finally, Chapter 17 addresses the now very large world of XML (eXtensible Markup Language) and how Perl and Python scripts can be written for many of the different tasks that can be accomplished with XML. The chapter starts out with showing scripts for extracting information from simple XML documents. We then talk about more complex regular-expression-based processing for decomposing an XML document into its constituent parts. This is followed by a discussion of validating and nonvalidating parsers for XML documents. The chapter then takes up the important and very current topic of XML for web services. Under this heading, we discuss scripting that uses the XML-RPC and the SOAP (Simple Object Access Protocol) protocols for constructing servers and clients for web services. The last part of the chapter examines XSL (eXtensible Style Language) that is used for writing style sheets for transforming XML into HTML (HyperText Markup Language), for instance.

1.3 CREDITS AND SUGGESTIONS FOR FURTHER READING

As mentioned already, much of the material on the comparison between systems programming languages and scripting languages was based on an article by Ousterhout

[51]. Many of the statements that were made in the comparison were drawn verbatim from that article. The "claim" that each line of code in a systems programming language translates into five machine instructions on the average was attributed by Ousterhout to a study by Capers Jones [36]. The "Programming Language Table" mentioned in the citation [36] is unfortunately no longer available at the listed URL. With regard to comparing languages with quantitative measures, the reader may also want to look at the report by Lutz Prechelt [52].

2

Perl — A Review of the Basics

This chapter uses a tutorial-style presentation to review the basic features of Perl.[1]

As was mentioned in Chapter 1, Perl is interpreted — but not literally so, since there is a compilation stage that a Perl script goes through before it is executed. The executable `perl`, normally installed in `/usr/bin/` or `/usr/local/bin`, when invoked on a script first converts it into a parse tree, which is then translated into a bytecode file. It is the bytecode that is interpreted by `perl`. The process of generating the bytecode is referred to as compilation. This compilation phase goes through many of the same optimization steps as the compilation of, say, a C program — such as elimination of unreachable code, replacing of constant expressions by their

[1]For further information regarding the language features presented in this chapter, the reader should consult Perl's online documentation, commonly referred to as `perldoc`. Enter

```
perldoc -h
```

in a window of a terminal to see all of the different ways in which the `perldoc` command can be used to search through the online documentation. More detailed information regarding how to use `perldoc` can be seen with the command `man perldoc` or the command `perldoc perldoc`. For example, to see the documentation on the module `DBD::mysql`, you'd use the command `perldoc DBD::mysql`. To see all of the contents of the main module file, including the implementation code, you'd say `perldoc -m DBD::mysql`. (If your system has the man pages installed, you may also be able to use the command `man DBD::mysql` to see the stored documentation on this module.) With `perldoc` you can also see the documentation on the built-in functions by using the `-f` option. For example, to see the documentation on the `print()` function, you'd say `perldoc -f print`. And to see all of the question-answer entries in the Perl FAQs for which the questions contain a particular keyword, you'd say `perldoc -q keyword`.

Scripting with Objects. By Avinash C. Kak

values, loading in of library definitions for the operators and the built-in functions, etc.

For those who are steeped in systems programming languages like C, C++, Java, C#, etc., perhaps the biggest first surprise that Perl throws at you is that it is typeless.[2] By that we mean that a variable in Perl is not declared as being of any specific type before it is assigned a value. A variable that was previously assigned a number can next be assigned a string and vice versa. In fact, *any* scalar variable in Perl can be assigned at any time one of three different kinds of values: a *number*, a *string*, or a *reference*.[3] Numbers, strings, and references represent Perl's data objects at their most atomic level.

We will start in Section 2.1 by reviewing numbers and strings in Perl. [Since the notion of a reference is the cornerstone of object-oriented scripting in Perl, we will review references separately in Chapter 5.] That will then allow us to review in Section 2.2 the three different kinds of variables in Perl — *scalar*, *array*, and *hash* — that provide us with three different storage mechanisms for holding data. This will be followed in Section 2.3 with a discussion of the scoping rules that apply to Perl's lexical and global variables.

The rest of this chapter can be divided roughly into three parts: (1) Basic language issues, such as the built-in facilities for I/O, functions, control structures, conditional evaluation, etc., — these are covered in Sections 2.6 through 2.10. (2) Packaging issues related to the design of modules and how to import them into scripts, etc., — these are covered in Section 2.11. And, finally, (3) Language facilities for interacting with the platform and its operating system — these are covered in Sections 2.16, 2.17, and 2.18. Additional topics, equally important, that are covered in this chapter include in Section 2.14 the `eval` operator that plays a critical role in advanced scripting; the ever-useful functional programming tools like the built-in `map()` and `grep()` functions in Section 2.15; and so on.

2.1 SCALAR VALUES IN PERL

A *scalar value* is an individual unit of data. Perl allows for three different kinds of scalar values: *numbers*, *strings*, and *references*. This section will provide a quick review of the first two, leaving references to Chapter 5.

[2]As we will see in Chapter 3, Python is also typeless in the same sense as Perl.

[3]A variable can also be made "undefined" by assigning to it the special object `undef`. You can think of `undef` as Perl's null object.

2.1.1 Numbers

Internally, a number in Perl can be stored in any of the following four forms:

- As a signed integer
- As an unsigned integer
- As a double-precision floating-point value
- As a numeric string

By a *numeric string*, we mean a character string that would correspond to the print representation of a number. What a "signed integer," an "unsigned integer," and a "double-precision float" mean to Perl is whatever they mean to the C compiler used for building the Perl executable.[4] So, on most machines today, when a number is stored as a signed integer, 4 bytes are allocated for the value. The same is the case when a number is stored as an unsigned integer. Eight bytes are allocated for a number if it is stored as a double-precision float.

It is interesting to note that these representations are hidden from the programmer for the most part. Magnitude permitting, Perl will use the signed integer representation for a number. However, if a positive integer is too large to be stored as a signed integer, Perl will try to store it as an unsigned integer. With native 4-byte integers, the range of a signed integer is from -2^{31} to $2^{31}-1$ and that of an unsigned integer from 0 to $2^{32}-1$. If a number is too large to be represented as an integer, or if a number has a floating-point value, Perl will store it as a double-precision float. As already mentioned, on most modern machines 8 bytes are allocated for such a number. The precision of such numbers is close to 16 decimal digits and the range corresponds to the decimal exponent taking a value between -304 and $+304$. Obviously, the range and the precision are determined by the number of bits reserved for the exponent and for the fraction parts.

Line (A) of the next script, `Integer.pl`, uses a hexadecimal representation to assign to the variable `$num` the largest positive integer that can be represented with the commonly used 4-byte signed integer representation.[5] The underscores in

---

[4] What these representations mean to the C compiler used for building Perl are referred to as the *native representations*.

[5] As already mentioned, the numerical value of this integer is $2^{31}-1$. But, depending on the implementation, it may prove erroneous to use Perl's exponentiation operator `**` in the statement

```
$num = 2 ** 31 - 1;
```

in order to create the largest possible signed 4-byte integer value. The reason has to do with the fact that, when using a signed integer representation, the most significant bit is reserved as a sign bit. As a consequence, the integer value 2^{31} cannot be accommodated as a positive integer within 4 bytes, since the binary representation of this value calls for all the bits to be zero except for the most significant bit, which must be 1. The largest positive value that can be accommodated within 4 bytes is indeed $2^{31}-1$, but the

the hexadecimal value in line (A) are purely for human readability and are ignored by Perl when interpreting the number. Line (B) calls on Perl's built-in function `print()` to print out the value of this number. Line (C) does the same with the help of Perl's `printf()` function. This function, like C's `printf()`, takes a format string containing *conversion specifiers* as its first argument and the objects to be printed out for the remaining arguments. The conversion specifier `%d` used in line (C) is for printing out a signed integer that is presented to `printf()` in a decimal format.

Line (D) adds 1000 to the number value stored for `$num` in line (A). Since the new number returned by the right-hand side in line (D) is now too large to be stored as a signed integer, Perl stores it away as an unsigned integer. It can now be printed out by the `%u` conversion specifier in the `printf()` invocation, as we show in line (E). However, as shown in line (F), if we try to print out the number with the `%d` conversion specifier in the format string supplied to `printf()`, we get a wrong answer. As mentioned earlier, the conversion specifier `%d` is for outputting signed integers. We also get the correct output by using `print()` directly in line (G). Since `print()` is aware of the internal representation of the value of `$num`, it does the correct thing automatically.

The multiplication on the right of the assignment in line (H) results in a number that is too large to be stored as an integer, even an unsigned integer. Therefore, it is stored as a double-precision float. Note that the conversion specifiers `%d` in line (I) and `%u` in line (J) both produce the wrong output because the number is no longer either a signed integer or an unsigned integer. However, we get the correct output in lines (K) and (L), in the first case by using the exponential-format conversion specifier `%e`, and in the second by depending on the fact that `print()` implicitly knows the correct representation of the scalar it prints out.[6]

---

computation entailed by the above statement first requires that 2^{31} be evaluated as a positive integer and only subsequently it be decremented by one. Also note that, compared to what we have shown in line (A) of the script, a more portable way to generate the largest possible value for a signed integer is

```
$num = - (1 + sprintf "%d", -1e100);
```

This relies on the fact that the conversion specifier `%d` will extract the largest possible negative integer from the very large negative floating-point value `-1e100`. For a 4-byte integer representation, this value is -2^{31}, with the binary representation corresponding to the hexadecimal `0x80_00_00_00`. The call to `sprintf()` returns the print representation of this numeric value, which would be the negative number -2^{31}. The operation of addition inside the parentheses converts this numeric string back into a number. Adding 1 to this number yields the binary word `0x80_00_00_01`. Finally, to take the negative of this, we use the two's complement representation of negative integers; this calls for inverting all the bits and adding 1. Inverting the bit pattern yields `0x7f_ff_ff_fe`. When we add 1 to this pattern, we get `0x7f_ff_ff_ff`, which is the bit pattern for the largest possible positive 4-byte integer. This portable approach for generating the largest possible positive integer value on a platform was suggested by Ilya Zakharevich in the `comp.lang.perl.moderated` newsgroup in response to a query posted by the author.

[6]We should also mention that, ordinarily, we can also use the `%f` conversion specifier to print a floating-point value in a decimal format. For all of the conversion specifiers shown, we can include flags between the symbol `%` and the conversion letter such as `d`, `u`, `f`, `e`, etc. These flags can be used to exercise

The rest of the script, in lines (M) through (W), shows some of the other operators that Perl provides for numbers in general. Line (N) shows the exponentiation operator; the result obtained by this operator on the number of line (M) is shown in line (O). Line (P) shows the *compound assignment* version of the *exponentiation operator.* This statement does the same thing as

```
$num = $num ** 0.5;
```

Perl possesses all of the usual arithmetic operators and for each there exists a compound assignment version. Line (R) shows the compound assignment version of the *remainder operator,* also known as the *modulus operator.* This statement does the same thing as

```
$num = $num % 9;
```

The remainder operator returns the remainder when the left operand is divided by the right operand. Line (T) shows the compound assignment version of the division operator. Finally, lines (V) and (W) show the postfix and the prefix versions of the autoincrement operator. As expected, the postfix version in line (V) changes the value of the argument after it is evaluated for the function `print()`. So while the number printed out in line (V) is 1.75, the value of the variable `$num` when the flow of execution goes past line (V) is 2.75. On the other hand, the prefix version of the increment operator in line (W) first increments the value of `$num`; the new value is then supplied to `print()`. This explains the output in line (W). Perl also has the postfix and the prefix versions of the decrement operator `--`.[7]

```
#!/usr/bin/perl -w

### Integer.pl

$num = 0x7f_ff_ff_ff;             # max for signed 4-byte int       #(A)
print $num, "\n";                 # 2147483647                       #(B)
printf "%d\n", $num;              # 2147483647                       #(C)

$num = $num + 1000;                                                  #(D)
printf "%u\n", $num;              # 2147484647                       #(E)
printf "%d\n", $num;              # -2147482649   (WRONG)            #(F)
print $num, "\n";                 # 2147484647                       #(G)

$num = $num * $num;                                                  #(H)
printf "%d\n", $num;              # -1            (WRONG)            #(I)
```

---

additional control over how exactly the output is displayed and whether or not an integer is displayed in a decimal, octal, or hexadecimal format. See the entries under `sprintf` in the `perlfunc` document page.

[7]The example code shown is for Unix-like operating systems. For other operating systems, in most cases the only change necessary would be to the first line. In some cases, you would not need that first line. You would instead call the script from a command line by supplying it as an argument to `perl`.

```
printf "%u\n", $num;               # 4294967295    (WRONG)        #(J)
printf "%e\n", $num;               # 4.611690e+18                 #(K)
print $num, "\n";                  # 4.61169030910072e+18         #(L)

$num = 16;                                                        #(M)
$num = $num ** 2;                                                 #(N)
print $num, "\n";                  # 256                          #(O)
$num **= 0.5;                                                     #(P)
print $num, "\n";                  # 16                           #(Q)
$num %= 9;                                                        #(R)
print $num, "\n";                  # 7                            #(S)
$num /= 4;                                                        #(T)
print $num, "\n";                  # 1.75                         #(U)
print $num++, "\n";                # 1.75                         #(V)
print ++$num, "\n";                # 3.75                         #(W)
```

Since the focus of the above script was on demonstrating how integer values are represented in Perl, we glossed over some of the beginning syntax before line (A). The incantation in the first line of the script

```
#!/usr/bin/perl -w
```

invokes the "sh-bang"(`#!`) mechanism to inform the operating system that the script to follow is to be executed by the program that comes next, that is, by `/usr/bin/perl`. This way of executing scripts works only in Unix-like systems. This syntax for the first line of a script also assumes that the Perl executable resides in the directory `/usr/bin`. If not, that pathname string would need to be changed accordingly. The `-w` switch in the first line asks the compiler to turn on a large number of execution time warnings, such as for accessing uninitialized variables, finding a string where a number is expected, redefining a subroutine, attempting to write to a stream that is opened only for reading, and so on. These warnings can also be turned on by invoking the *warning pragma* by

```
use warnings;
```

and turned off by

```
no warnings;
```

In general, a *pragma* is a stricture issued to the compiler. Pragma declarations in Perl have *lexical scope*,[8] meaning that when warnings are turned off or on, that condition applies from the point of the declaration to the end of the lexical scope in which the

[8] Section 2.3.1 explains what is meant by *lexical scope*.

pragma is invoked. After exiting from the scope, the warnings will be treated as specified by the outer enclosing block.[9]

After the `#!` incantation at the beginning of the first line in a script, the symbol `#` signifies the start of a comment. The comment then extends to the end of the line. Therefore, the second line of the above script is a comment showing the name of the disk file that contains the script. In almost all the scripts shown in this book, the commented-out second line will show the name of the file containing the script. The suffix `.pl` for the file name is usually not necessary, but it may be desirable for informing your text editor that you are creating a Perl file. Smart text editors are capable of providing many useful facilities like autoindentation, syntax coloring, detection of unbalanced parenthesis, and so on, if they know what type of file you are creating.[10]

The next script shows examples of floating-point numbers and some operations on such numbers. Both the lines (A) and (B) use the decimal format for the floating-point values on the right side of the assignment operator. But note that line (B) also uses the underscore. As already mentioned, Perl permits programmer-specified numbers in source code to contain underscores for better readability by humans. So the number on the right of the assignment in line (B) is the same as `1234.000000000003`. Line (C) uses `print()` to output the result of multiplying `$x` and `$y`. Line (D) does the same with `printf()` with the `%.3e` conversion specifier to limit to 3 the number of digits after the decimal point. Line (E) uses the exponential format, more commonly known as *scientific notation*, for specifying the floating-point number on the right side of the assignment. Line (F) shows the output from the multiplication in the argument to `print()`. This is the same output we obtained in line (C) because the two numbers being multiplied remain unchanged. Lines (G) and (H) show the result of a division.

```
#!/usr/bin/perl -w

### Float.pl

$x = 0.000000000003;                                                    #(A)
$y = 1_234.000_000_000_003;                                             #(B)
print $x * $y, "\n";                    # 3.70200000000001e-09          #(C)
```

---

[9]We should also mention that the flag `-W` unconditionally enables the warnings throughout a script, ignoring any `no warnings` declarations no matter where they show up. The flag `-X` does the exact opposite of `-W` by disabling all warnings in the script.

[10]After you have created and tested a script, you will, in most cases, want to get rid of the file-name suffix `.pl` to make for cleaner syntax for script invocation. We should also mention that to execute the script file `Integer.pl` shown here, all you have to do is say in the command line

```
Integer.pl
```

provided you remembered to make the file executable by changing its permissions with a command like

```
chmod +x Integer.pl
```

```
printf "%.3e\n", $x * $y;                 # 3.702e-09                  #(D)

$y = 1234 + 3.00e-12;                                                  #(E)
print $x * $y, "\n";                      # 3.70200000000001e-09       #(F)

$z = 1e50;                                                             #(G)
print $x / $z, "\n";                      # 3e-62                      #(H)
```

As mentioned earlier, a number can also be specified by a numeric string, meaning a string all of whose characters are digits. Consider the initialization of the variable `$x` in the script shown next. We initialize it with the double-quoted string[11] consisting of the digit characters 1, 2, 3, and 4, with the decimal-point character between the last two. This string is interpreted as the print representation of a number[12] in line (B) where it is added to another number to produce the result shown in the commented-out portion of line (C). If we wanted to, we could, of course, treat the value of `$x` as a genuine string, as we do in the string concatenation operation in line (D).[13] A numeric result from a numeric operation, such as what is stored in `$y` in line (B), can also be treated as a string if so required in its role as an operand. Line (F) shows the numeric value stored in `$y` being used for string concatenation. The interesting thing to note in this example is that, whereas the value of the variable `$x` is stored as a string object, the value of `$y` — a value derived from that of `$x` — is stored as a number. Perl is obviously quite comfortable treating strings and numbers interchangeably, but this interchangeability cannot be pushed too far. For example, given that the value of `$w` will be stored as a string, the statement in line (H) produces an error because some of the characters in the string value of `$w` are not digits. Lines (I) through (L) show floating-point values being specified as numeric strings.[14]

```
#!/usr/bin/perl -w

### NumericString.pl

$x = "123.4";                                                          #(A)
$y = $x + 8;                                                           #(B)
```

[11]The next subsection reviews the two different kinds of strings supported by Perl — the single quoted and the double quoted.

[12]Internally, Perl uses something like the C library's `atof(3)` function to convert a string to a number. To convert a number to a string, it does the equivalent of `sprintf(3)` with the format set to `%.14g` on most machines [68, pp. 59].

[13]Perl's various string operators, including the concatenation operator "`.`", are presented in the next subsection.

[14]All constant values specified in source code are called *literals*. The value `jello` in line (F) of the script under discussion is a string literal, as is the value `123.4` in line (A). On the other hand, the number 8 in line (B) is an integer literal. We have already seen various forms of number literals in the scripts we have shown so far, such as the numbers `0.000000000003`, `1_234.000_000_000_003`, `3.00e-12`, etc.

```
print $y, "\n";                          # 131.4               #(C)

$z = $x . "hello";                                              #(D)
print $z, "\n";                          # 123.4hello          #(E)

$w = $y . "jello";                                              #(F)
print $w, "\n";                          # 131.4jello          #(G)

#my $a = $w + 8;                         # ERROR               #(H)

$x = "1.23e100";                                                #(I)
$y = "0.0000000003";                                            #(J)
$z = $x * $y;                                                   #(K)
print $z, "\n";                          # 3.69e+90            #(L)
```

2.1.2 Strings

A string is a sequence of characters. Unlike a C string, a Perl string does not need to be terminated in the null character; Perl knows how long a string is because it internally keeps track of the number of characters in the string. Perl supports three different kinds of strings:

- Single-quoted strings
- Double-quoted strings
- Version strings

Of these, the two that you are most likely to use in a script are the single-quoted and the double-quoted strings. The version strings are used for a very narrow and specific purpose — to denote the version number associated with a script.

The main difference between single-quoted and double-quoted strings is that, with two exceptions, the former does not permit any special meanings to be associated with any of its characters. The two exceptions are when you want to use a single quote inside a single-quoted string, say as an apostrophe, and if you want to use a backslash as a backslash character.

In the next script, `SingleQuotedStrings.pl`, line (A) shows an ordinary single-quoted string on the right of the assignment. The single-quoted string we have in line (B) wants to use a single quote as an apostrophe. So we escape the special meaning of a single quote in such strings by backslashing it. Line (C) shows that it is okay for a single-quoted string to contain backslashes as individual characters — as long as they are not used as escapes.

Line (D) wants to use two backslashes together, but as the printout of the string in the next line shows, it does not work. That is because the first backslash after `C:` is used for escaping the special meaning of the second backslash that comes next. As a result, only one backslash is left between the substrings `C:` and `My`. If we really want to have two backslashes between `C:` and `My`, we must use three backslashes together, as shown in line (E). Now the first backslash is used to escape the special meaning of a backslash as the escape character. As a result, the second backslash now becomes an ordinary backslash. The third backslash, because its meaning is no longer escaped by a previous backslash, remains also as an ordinary character. So we get the result shown in the printout after line (E).

Line (F) wants to use backslashes as ordinary characters throughout, but that does not work for the last backslash in the string because it wants to escape the string-termination meaning of the single quote that comes next. The correct way to write the single-quoted string of line (F) is shown in line (G). Now the first of the two backslashes together at the end will suppress the escape meaning of the second backslash. The second backslash will therefore be used as an ordinary character, as shown by the printout in the next line.

Lines (H) and (I) show that the characters `$` and `@` have no special meanings inside a single-quoted string. As we will show later, these two symbols have a very special role in double-quoted strings — they allow other strings to be interpolated into double-quoted strings.

Lines (J) and (K) show that the commonly used escape sequences, `\n` for newline and `\t` for horizontal tab, are treated as ordinary two-character sequences inside a single-quoted string.[15]

When we talk about double-quoted strings, we will show that the character escapes `\U`, `\u`, `\L`, `\l`, and `\E` can be used to control the case of the characters that follow in the string. However, as shown in line (L), these character escapes lose their special meaning in a single-quoted string. Line (M) shows that even a double-quote loses its special meaning inside a single-quoted string.

As we will show for double-quoted strings, the numeric escape sequences used in line (N) — `\x68`, `\x65`, `\x6c`, and `\157` — represent the ASCII codes for the letters h, e, l, and o. The first three are in hexadecimal form and the last in octal.

[15] An *escape sequence* is ordinarily a backslash followed by one or more designated characters such that the entire sequence stands for a single character. Many of the escape sequences when sent to an output device can be used to control the position of the cursor for the next piece of information to be displayed. Commonly used examples of escape sequences are: `\n` for newline, `\r` for carriage return, `\t` for horizontal tab, `\a` for bell, `\f` for form feed, `\b` for backspace, and so on. Such escape sequences are also known as *character escapes*. These are to be distinguished from *numeric escapes*. The numeric escapes come in two forms: hexadecimal and octal. An example of a "hex" escape is `\x68` which stands for the letter h, since the decimal value of the hex 68 is 104, the ASCII code for h. The octal numeric escape for the same letter is `\150`. For a complete ASCII table that shows the decimal values and the corresponding hex and octal representations for the various characters, visit `www.asciitable.com`.

When placed inside double-quoted strings, these escapes will actually insert the corresponding letter in the string. However, as line (N) shows, inside a single-quoted string they lose their special meaning.

Finally, line (O) demonstrates that single quotes can act as delimiters for multiline strings.

```
#!/usr/bin/perl -w

### SingleQuotedStrings.pl

# A single-quoted string:
$str = 'hello';                                                     #(A)
print $str, "\n";                      # hello

# A single-quoted string with a single quote
# mark inside:
$str = 'Trillian\'s puppy';                                         #(B)
print $str, "\n";                      # Trillian's puppy

#Backslashes unless followed by a single
# quote are no problem:
$str = 'C:\My Files\Cats\Temp';                                     #(C)
print $str, "\n";                      # C:\My Files\Cats\Temp

# This does NOT give us two backslashes
# together:
$str = 'C:\\My Files\Cats\Temp';                                    #(D)
print $str, "\n";                      # C:\My Files\Cats\Temp

# But this does:
$str = 'C:\\\My Files\Cats\Temp';                                   #(E)
print $str, "\n";                      # C:\\My Files\Cats\Temp


# A backslash that comes just before a
# single quote, if needed as a character,
# must be escaped:
#$str = 'C:\My Files\Cats\Temp\';      # WRONG                      #(F)
$str = 'C:\My Files\Cats\Temp\\';                                   #(G)
print $str, "\n";                      # C:\My Files\Cats\Temp\

# The symbol $ inside a string has
# ordinary meaning:
$how_much = 200;
$str = 'Price: $how_much';                                          #(H)
print $str, "\n";                      # Price: $how_much
```

```
# The symbol @ inside a string has ordinary
# meaning:
@nospam = ("ham", "yam", "bam");
$str = 'mailto: me@nospam.com';                                    #(I)
print $str, "\n";                     # mailto: me@nospam.com

#Even \n loses its special meaning:
$str = 'hello\nthere\nhow are you!';                               #(J)
print $str, "\n";                     # hello\nthere\nhow are you!

# The tab character \t also loses its
# special meaning:
$str = 'name\tage\tweight';                                        #(K)
print $str, "\n";                     # name\tage\tweight

# The operators \U, \u, etc. also lose
# their special meanings:
$str = '\Uname\t\uage\t\Lweight';                                  #(L)
print $str, "\n";                     # \Uname\t\uage\t\Lweight

# You can even have double quotes inside a
# single-quoted string:
$str = 'Names: "peter", "paul", "mary"';                           #(M)
print $str, "\n";                     # Names: "peter", "paul", "mary"

# Numeric escapes do NOT work in single-quoted
# strings:
$str = '\x68\x65\x6c\x6c\157';                                     #(N)
print $str, "\n";                     # \x68\x65\x6c\x6c\157

# You can create multiline strings with
# single quotes:
$str = 'This is a successful attempt at
        creating a multiline string with
        single quotes';                                            #(O)
```

As the above script demonstrates, `\'` and `\\` are the only character escapes recognized inside a single-quoted string, and that the nonalphanumeric symbols `$` and `@` do not possess any special meanings inside such strings. In what follows, we will now show that the backslash has a lot more "power" in a double-quoted string. Unless it itself is escaped by another backslash, Perl will try to think of a backslash and the next character as a possible escape sequence. The symbols `$` and `@` will also now carry very special meanings: the former will allow for what is known as *variable interpolation* and the latter *array interpolation* in a double-quoted string.

Contrast the previous script with the one shown next where we present examples of double-quoted strings. For each single-quoted string in the previous script, the next script shows a corresponding double-quoted string.[16]

Line (A) of the next script depicts an ordinary double-quoted string. Line (B) shows that a single quote is an ordinary character inside a double-quoted string.

What is shown in line (C) is important in the sense that it demonstrates that Perl thinks of every backslash in a double-quoted string as the start of an escape sequence. So if we replaced the double backslashes in line (C) with single backslashes, Perl will complain since it will not be able to recognize what would look like escape sequences: `\M`, `\C` and `\T`. So we have no choice but to escape each backslash with an additional backslash if we want to create a string as shown in the commented-out portion of the next line.

Line (D) is a failed attempt to create two backslashes together between `C:` and `M` in the double-quoted string shown. Of the three backslashes shown together, the first acts as an escape for the second, which then becomes an ordinary character. This causes the third backslash to be construed as the beginning of what looks like an escape sequence — `\M`. But since Perl cannot recognize this sequence as a valid escape sequence, it issues a warning to that effect. If you ignore the warning, Perl will ignore the backslash that comes just before `M`.

Line (E) shows that if you really want two backslashes between `C:` and `M`, you have to use four. The first escapes the special meaning of the second, which then becomes an ordinary backslash character in the string. The third does the same to the fourth.

Line (F) shows that a backslash just before the terminating double quote will prevent the double quote from terminating the string unless the backslash is escaped.

Lines (G) and (H) show a most important feature of double-quoted strings in Perl — *variable interpolation*. When a scalar variable is present in a double-quoted string, the print representation of the value of the variable is substituted into the string, as shown by the example in line (G). For an array variable in a double-quoted string, as in the string in line (H), the array is first evaluated in a list context; this evaluation should return a list of the elements in the array. White-space separated print representations of these elements are then substituted into the double-quoted string.

Lines (I) and (J) illustrate that, inside a double-quoted string, the commonly-used character escapes are interpreted as expected for controlling the position of the cursor as the string in question is displayed.

---

[16]The correspondence between the single-quoted strings of `SingleQuotedStrings.pl` and the double-quoted strings of `DoubleQuotedStrings.pl` is only at the level of similarity of examples. Since character escaping and the special symbols like `$` and `@` work differently in the two cases, the actual strings produced would be different for each.

Line (K) demonstrates the roles played by the special character escapes `\U`, `\u`, `\L`, `\l`, and `\E` in a double-quoted string. The character escape `\U` causes all of the succeeding characters to become uppercase until the character escape `\E` is encountered, which effectively ends the conversion-to-uppercase action initiated by `\U`. The character escape `\L` does the same except that it starts the conversion-to-lowercase action that continues until the ending `\E` is encountered. The character escape `\u` converts only the next character to uppercase (if it is not already so) and `\l` makes it lowercase (if it is not already so).

Line (L) shows that if you want to include double quotes inside a double-quoted string, you must backslash the interior double quote.

Line (M) demonstrates that the characters inside a double-quoted string can be specified as numeric escapes. The string being created in that line is `hello`. We have used hex forms of the numeric escapes for the letters h, e, and l, and the octal form of the numeric escape for the letter o.

Finally, line (N) shows that you get a multiline string if you write a double-quoted string in multiple lines. As we showed earlier, we can do the same with single-quoted strings. However, with double-quoted strings, it is more common to create multiline strings by embedding one or more instances of the newline character escape `\n` inside the string, as we did in line (I).

```
#!/usr/bin/perl -w

### DoubleQuotedStrings.pl

# A double-quoted string:
$str = "hello";                                                    #(A)
print $str, "\n";                      # hello

# No need to escape an interior single quote:
$str = "Trillian's puppy";                                         #(B)
print $str, "\n";                      # Trillian's puppy

# Now the backslashes must be escaped by backslashes:
$str = "C:\\My Files\\Cats\\Temp";                                 #(C)
print $str, "\n";                      # C:\My Files\Cats\Temp

# This does NOT give us two backslashes
# together between C: and M
$str = "C:\\\My Files\\Cats\\Temp";    # WARNING                   #(D)
print $str, "\n";                      # C:\My Files\Cats\Temp

# But this does:
$str = "C:\\\\My Files\\Cats\\Temp";                               #(E)
print $str, "\n";                      # C:\\My Files\Cats\Temp
```

```
# A backslash that come just before a double quote,
# if needed as a character, must be escaped:
$str = "C:\\My Files\\Cats\\Temp\\";                         #(F)
print $str, "\n";                       # C:\My Files\Cats\Temp\

# The symbol $ inside a string now has
# special meaning unless backslashed:
$how_much = 200;
$str = "Price: \$$how_much";                                 #(G)
print $str, "\n";                       # Price: $200

# The symbol @ inside a string now has
# special meaning:
@nospam = ("ham", "yam", "bam");
$str = "mailto: me@nospam.com";                              #(H)
print $str, "\n";                       # mailto: meham yam bam.com

# \n now stands for newline:
$str = "hello\nthere\nhow are you!";                         #(I)
print $str, "\n";                       # hello
                                        # there
                                        # how are you!
# \t will now introduce horizontal tabs:
$str = "name\tage\tweight";                                  #(J)
print $str, "\n";                       # name    age     weight

# The operators \U, \u, etc. now
# carry special meanings:
$str = "\Uname\E\t\uage\t\LweIght\E";                        #(K)
print $str, "\n";                       # NAME    Age     weight

# Double quotes inside a string must be
# backslashed; single quotes ok as they are:
$str = "Names: \"peter\", 'paul', 'mary'";                   #(L)
print $str, "\n";                       # Names: "peter", 'paul', 'mary'

# Numeric escapes work:
$str = "\x68\x65\x6c\x6c\157";                               #(M)
print $str, "\n";                       # hello

# You can create multiline strings with
# double quotes:
$str = "This is a successful attempt at
        creating a multiline string with
        double quotes";                                      #(N)
```

We will now use the next script, `StringOps.pl`, to present some of the more commonly used built-in functions and operators that work with strings. Please note that there are many other operations that may be carried out on strings with the help of regular expressions. Those we will review in Chapter 4.

Line (A) of the next script shows the binary concatenation operator for joining the two strings supplied to it as operands. As with practically all binary operators, we can chain multiple concatenation operations together, as shown in line (B). Line (C) demonstrates the compound concatenation operator "`.=`", also known as the *append operator*. It replaces the string value of the variable on the left with a concatenation of that value with the string value on the right.

Line (D) demonstrates the function `uc()` that can be used to convert all the letters in an argument string to uppercase. Obviously, the function leaves unchanged the characters that have no uppercase equivalents or that are already uppercase. The function `lc()` in line (E) does the same but in the opposite direction; it converts all the nonlowercase letters in a string to lowercase.

Line (F) shows the use of the built-in function `length()` for calculating the length of a string, meaning the number of characters in a string. When supplied with a number argument, as we do in line (H), it returns the length of the print representation of the number in the decimal form. So if we had specified a number as `1.2e10`, the value returned by `length()` would be 11.

Line (I) shows the use of the `x` operator for replicating a string a specified number of times. All of the replicated strings are joined with the original string and the result is returned as a new string.

Lines (J) through (M) show different ways of invoking the `substr()` function for extracting a substring from an argument string. The syntax in line (J)

```
substr("hello there", 6)
```

returns the portion of the string in the first argument that begins at the position whose index is specified by the second argument. The substring returned goes to the end of the argument string. If the second argument is a negative integer, as shown by the following syntax in line (K):

```
substr("hello there", -5)
```

the starting position of the substring returned is counted from the end of the argument string. The negative index of the last character is -1. Lines (L) and (M) show calls to a three-argument version of `substr()`. The third argument is the number of the characters returned from the starting location specified by the second argument.

Line (N) shows the `index()` function for locating the first occurrence of a substring inside the string that is supplied as the first argument to the function. Line (O) does the same but with a three-argument version of the function. The last argument specifies the starting location for searching for the second-argument substring. This function returns -1 if the second-argument substring cannot be found in the first-argument string.

In line (P) we set the global variable `$\` known as the *output record separator* to the newline character. Whatever character is stored in this global variable is used by Perl's `print()` to terminate its output. Unless explicitly defined, this global variable does not contain any specific value by default. Up to this time, whenever we wanted to show in a separate line the argument(s) given to `print()`, we explicitly provided the newline at the end of those arguments. But now by setting `$\` to newline, we will not have to do so any more.

Line (Q) shows the use of `sprintf()` to construct a string with the help of a format string, which is supplied to `sprintf()` as its first argument. The format string includes conversion specifiers, each specifier consisting of the `%` character followed by various formatting flags and terminating in the *conversion specification symbol.* Default formatting is used if the flags between the character `%` and the conversion specification symbol are not provided. Some of the commonly used conversion specification symbols are: `d` for interpreting the argument as a signed integer in decimal form, `u` for interpreting the argument as an unsigned integer in decimal form, `o` for interpreting the argument as an unsigned integer in its octal representation (base 8), `x` and `X` for interpreting the argument as an unsigned integer in hexadecimal representation (base 16), `f` for interpreting the argument as a floating-point value in decimal notation, `e` and `E` for interpreting the argument as a floating-point value in scientific notation, and so on.[17]

Another built-in function that also constructs a string from multiple items of data is `pack()`. The main feature that distinguishes `pack()` from `sprintf()` is that the former can be made to produce fixed-length strings regardless of the size of the data. As we will show in Chapter 16, this makes `pack()` useful for creating strings for fixed-length record-oriented databases in which each record is supposed to occupy the same number of bytes in a disk file. Consider the call to `pack()` in line (R). The first argument to the function is usually called the *template,* although it could also be called a format string, as for `sprintf()`. The template consists of format letters that may be followed by an integer value whose significance depends on the format letter. In our case, the format `a5` in the template means a 5-character-long ASCII string. If the number of characters supplied in the corresponding argument — which in our case is the string `hello there` — is more than 5, only the first five will be used in the string returned by `pack()`. And if the number of characters in the argument string is less than 5, then null characters will be inserted where

---

[17]The previous subsection on numbers invoked the function `printf()` at a number of places to display the results of operations on numbers. According to the `perlfunc` manpage, the call

```
printf FILEHANDLE FORMAT, LIST;
```

is equivalent to

```
print FILEHANDLE sprintf(FORMAT, LIST);
```

The parameter `FILEHANDLE` will ordinarily be returned by a call to `open`, as we will explain later in Section 2.6. As stated in that section, a filehandle is the name of an I/O connection.

characters were expected. The second part of our template has the format letter `I`, which generally means a 4-byte binary representation of an unsigned integer. The number 2 that follows this letter indicates a *repeat count* of 2 for the integer. With this understanding of the format letters inside the template, we look again at our call to `pack()` in line (R):

```
pack( "a5 I2", "hello there", 555819297, 589505315 )
```

In this case `pack()` will return a 13-character string. The first 5 of these will be the first 5 ASCII characters from the argument string `hello there`. The next 4 characters will be the ASCII characters corresponding to the 4 bytes in the 4-byte binary representation of the integer 555819297. The final 4 characters in the string will correspond similarly to the integer 589505315. As to why we chose these large and strange-looking integer values, it was for the ASCII characters corresponding to each byte in the 4-byte representations of these two integer values. The hex form of the 4-byte representation of 555819297 is

```
0x21212121;
```

So each byte is the same with a hex value equal to 21, which is decimal 33. The corresponding ASCII character is "`!`". Similarly, the 4-byte representation of the second integer, 589505315, is given by the hex

```
0x23232323;
```

Here the hex value of each byte is 23, which is decimal 35. The corresponding ASCII character is "#". Therefore, it should be no surprise to see what we get when we print out the length of the string returned by `pack()` in line (S) and the string itself in line (T).

A string created by `pack()` can be unpacked to retrieve the data by invoking `unpack()`, as shown in line (U). For obvious reasons, you will want to supply the same template to `unpack()` that was used by `pack()` originally.[18]

```
#!/usr/bin/perl -w

### StringOps.pl
```

[18]Perl allows for a large number of format letters in the template supplied to `pack()`. The integer that is allowed to follow these letters carries a meaning that depends on the format letter. The invocation of `pack()` shown in line (R) of the `StringOps.pl` script consumes only the first five characters of the argument string `hello there`. The following invocation, which uses the format `a*` as opposed to `a5`, will consume an argument string that is arbitrarily long:

```
$str = pack( "a*", "hello there");
```

See the `perlfunc` manpage for all details concerning `pack()`, `unpack()`, and how to specify the templates for these functions.

```
# Concatenation operation:
$str = "he" . "llo";                                              #(A)
print $str, "\n";                        # hello
$str = "he" . "llo" . " THERE";                                   #(B)
print $str, "\n";                        # hello THERE
$str .= "!\n";                                                    #(C)
print $str;                              # hello THERE!

# Uppercasing a string:
print uc( $str );                        # HELLO THERE!           #(D)

# Lowercasing a string:
print lc( $str );                        # hello there!           #(E)

# Finding the length:
print length($str), "\n";                # 13                     #(F)
$x = 123.456;                                                     #(G)
print length($x), "\n";                  # 7                      #(H)

# Replicating a string:
print "ab_" x 5, "\n";                   # ab_ab_ab_ab_ab_        #(I)

# Extracting substrings:
print substr("hello there", 6), "\n";    # there                  #(J)
print substr("hello there", -5), "\n";   # there                  #(K)
print substr("hello there", 6, 3), "\n"; # the                   #(L)
print substr("hello there", -5, 3), "\n"; # the                  #(M)

# Locating the first occurrence of a substring:
print index("hello there", "lo"), "\n";   # 3                    #(N)
print index("hello there", "e", 6), "\n"; # 8                    #(O)

# Set output record separator:
$\ = "\n";                                                        #(P)
# Using a format string to construct a new string:
$str = sprintf "he%s the%s a %d times", "llo", "re", 10;          #(Q)
print $str;                              # hello there a 10 times

# Create a string by packing data into a template:
$str = pack( "a5 I2", "hello there", 555819297, 589505315 );      #(R)
print length( $str );                  # 13                       #(S)
print $str;                            # hello!!!!####            #(T)

# Extract the data from a string produced by pack():
($s1, $num1, $num2) = unpack( "a5 I2", $str );                    #(U)
print $s1;                             # hello
print $num1;                           # 555819297
print $num2;                           # 589505315
```

All of the string operations shown above may also be carried out on single-quoted strings, as demonstrated by the following script. Obviously, any escape sequences in the operand strings — such as the commonly used newline character \n — must not be within single-quoted strings.

```
#!/usr/bin/perl -w

### StringOpsSingleQuoted.pl

# Concatenation operation:
$str = 'he' . 'llo';                                             #(A)
print $str, "\n";                        # hello
$str = 'he' . 'llo' . ' THERE';                                  #(B)
print $str, "\n";                        # hello THERE
$str .= "!\n";                                                   #(C)
print $str;                              # hello THERE!


# Uppercasing a string:
print uc( $str );                        # HELLO THERE!          #(D)

# Lowercasing a string:
print lc( $str );                        # hello there!          #(E)

# Finding the length:
print length($str), "\n";                # 13                    #(F)
$x = 123.456;                                                    #(G)
print length($x), "\n";                  # 7                     #(H)

# Replicating a string:
print 'ab_' x 5, "\n";                   # ab_ab_ab_ab_ab_       #(I)

# Extracting substrings:
print substr('hello there', 6), "\n";    # there                 #(J)
print substr('hello there', -5), "\n";   # there                 #(K)
print substr('hello there', 6, 3), "\n"; # the                   #(L)
print substr('hello there', -5, 3), "\n"; # the                  #(M)

# Locating the first occurrence of a substring:
print index('hello there', 'lo'), "\n";   # 3                    #(N)
print index('hello there', 'e', 6), "\n"; # 8                    #(O)

# Set output record separator:
$\ = "\n";                                                       #(P)

# Using a format string to construct a new string:
$str = sprintf 'he%s the%s a %d times', 'llo', 're', 10;         #(Q)
```

```
print $str;                                   # hello there a 10 times

# Create a string by packing data into a template:
$str = pack( 'a5 I2', 'hello there', 555819297, 589505315 );        #(R)
print length( $str );                        # 13                   #(S)
print $str;                                  # hello!!!!####        #(T)

# Extract the data from a string produced by pack():
($s1, $num1, $num2) = unpack( 'a5 I2', $str );                      #(U)
print $s1;                                   # hello
print $num1;                                 # 555819297
print $num2;                                 # 589505315
```

2.2 PERL'S VARIABLES: SCALARS, ARRAYS, AND HASHES

In Perl, a variable may hold a single scalar value, in which case it is called a *scalar variable*, or it may hold a sequence of scalar values, in which case it is called an *array variable*, or it may hold a collection of key-value pairs, in which case it is called a *hash variable*. For the last case, a key must be a string, whereas a value may be any scalar value.

A scalar variable may be referred to as a *scalar* for short. Similarly, an array variable may be referred to as an *array*, and a hash variable as a *hash* for short.

Scalars, arrays, and hashes may also be thought of as Perl's built-in *containers*. Obviously, a scalar can only hold a single value, which is often referred to as a *scalar value*, an array a sequence of scalar values, and a hash a collection of key-value pairs, where keys and values are scalar values with certain stipulations on what types can be used for the keys and the corresponding values.

In the rest of this section, we will discuss separately these three different types of variables in Perl.

2.2.1 Scalar

A scalar variable's value can be a string, a number, or a reference.[19] The prefix marker $ used in the names of the variables $x and $y in statements such as

```
$x = 4;
```

[19] We will discuss Perl references in Chapter 5.

```
$y = "hello";
```

means that these variables are scalars. More precisely, the prefix `$` stands for the fact that *we expect the variable to return a scalar value.* The next subsection explains in greater detail what is meant by "expecting a variable to return a scalar value."

If a scalar variable is left uninitialized at its first use in a script, its value is set automatically to Perl's null object `undef`.

A scalar can be *interpolated* into a double-quoted string. Interpolation means that the *print representation* of the value that the scalar variable is holding will be substituted at the location of the scalar variable. For example, we can say

```
$x = "Trillian";
$y = "Good morning to $x";
```

This will cause the value of `$y` to become the string `Good morning to Trillian`. Recall from the previous section that only the double-quoted strings can be interpolated into.

2.2.2 Array

An array is a sequence of scalars. The name of an array variable must be prefixed by the marker `@` as in the following statement that defines an array named `@arr` consisting of the four scalar values shown:[20]

```
@arr = (1, 2, 3, "hello");
```

What we have on the right in the above assignment is a *list literal,* in this case consisting of the four comma-separated scalar values shown. A *list* in general is an ordered sequence of scalar values and an *array* is a variable whose value is a list.

If an array variable is left uninitialized at its first use in a script, its value is set to the empty list `()`.

[20]The actual name of this array variable is just `arr`, the marker `@` serving as a *qualifier*. So, strictly speaking, it is perfectly okay to have a scalar variable, an array variable, and a hash variable of the same name:

```
$x = 1;
@x = (1, 2, 3);
%x = ( a => 1,
       b => 2,
     );
```

Perl recognizes that each of these three variables is different with the help of *typeglobs,* a concept we will review in Section 2.13. With regard to what can be used for a user-defined name after the markers `$`, `@`, and `%`, any sequence of letters, digits, and the underscore symbol works. The usual constraint on an identifier that it begin with either a letter or an underscore does not apply to the names for user-defined variables in Perl.

As mentioned, an array element is always a scalar. An individual element of an array can be accessed through an index in the following manner:

```
print "$arr[1]\n";              # will output 2 and then a newline

$arr[3] = "jello";              # the value of the array element
                                # at index 3 will change from
                                # "hello" to "jello"
```

These accesses are for the same `@arr` array that we defined earlier. The first statement shows us retrieving the second element of the array and the second statement assigning a new value to the fourth element. The important thing to note here is that since we expect an array element to be a scalar value, we access it with the same `$` prefix that we use for accessing the value of an ordinary scalar variable. Of course, the `$` prefixed name must be followed by a `[]`-enclosed integer index if the intent is to access an array element.

The first statement above also illustrates again the notion of *interpolating a scalar into a double-quoted string*. The array element `$arr[1]` is a scalar that happens to be a number. The decimal print representation of this scalar value is interpolated into a string that terminates in a newline.

The list that is used to initialize an array is allowed to contain expressions for its elements. When that happens, each such expression is evaluated in what is known as the *list context* (see Section 2.8 for what is meant by the *list context*), and the result returned by such evaluation is interpolated into the list. To explain what we mean by this interpolation, consider the following example in which the list being assigned to the array `@arr` contains a nonscalar element — an array to be precise. When Perl executes the second statement below, the array `@friends` is evaluated in a list context in accordance with the explanation in Section 2.8. This evaluation returns the list of scalar elements shown on the right in the first statement. Each element returned by the evaluation of `@friends` is *inserted* into the list on the right of the assignment operator in the second statement. As a result, the list assigned to `@arr` will be `(1, 2, 3, "harry", "sally", "monica", "joe", 4)`. The operator `qw//`, also known as the *quote word* operator, causes its argument to be broken into a list of strings with the intervening white spaces as string delimiters. It returns the list of strings so formed.[21]

```
@friends = qw/ harry sally monica joe /;
@arr = (1, 2, 3, @friends, 4);
```

An important aspect of Perl arrays is that it is not an error to access an element outside the range dictated by the list used for initializing the array variable. Such

[21] Important things to bear in mind about the `qw//` operator: Instead of `//`, you can also use any other nonalphanumeric character as a delimiter. However, for symbols that come in matched pairs, such as `()`, `{}`, `[]`, etc., the beginning and the terminating delimiters must correspond to the opening and the closing elements of the pair. The `qw//` operator does its work at compile time.

access will simply return Perl's null object `undef`. It is also not an error to assign a value to an array element whose index is outside the range specified by the list used for initialization. Like all variables in Perl, an array element, no matter what its index, will spring into existence simply by assignment.[22] When that happens, each intervening array element, if previously nonexistent, is given the value `undef`. In that sense, Perl arrays are limitless in size — bounded of course by the available memory.

A small array is usually displayed by interpolating it directly into a string as follows:

```
@arr = ('one', 'two', 'three', 'four');
print "@arr\n";                  # one two three four
```

The interpolation causes the array variable to be evaluated in a list context.

For a given array `@arr`, the index of the last element can be retrieved through the scalar `$#arr`. So the size of an array `@arr` is always equal to `$#arr + 1`. As we will show in Section 2.4, we can also retrieve the size of an array `@arr` by evaluating `@arr` in a *scalar context*.

It is possible to manipulate the size of an array `@arr` by making assignments to the scalar `$#arr`. Let an array `@arr` be initialized as follows:

```
my @arr =  (0, 1, 2, 3, 4);
```

Now if we make the assignment

```
$#arr = 2;
```

the array `@arr` will only retain the first three elements. In other words, if we print out the contents of `@arr` after the above assignment, we will get

```
print "@arr";                    # 0 1 2
```

For a given array `@arr`, an assignment to the scalar `$#arr` can also be made to extend the array indefinitely. For example, if for the above example, we say

```
$#arr = 9;
```

Perl will now make `@arr` 10 elements long; the last 7 elements will be set to the null element `undef`.

Perl also allows negative indices for accessing array elements, starting with the index -1 for the last element, -2 for the next to the last, and so on. So for an array `@arr`, the last element may be referred to either by `$arr[$#arr]` or by `$arr[-1]`.

---

[22]This property of Perl — an array element or a hash element springing into existence merely by the act of assigning to the element — is known as *autovivification*.

While all array elements can be accessed by indexing into them, Perl has specially designated functions for insertion/extraction operations at the two ends of an array. These operations can be used to treat arrays as stacks and queues.

The operations for the front end are `shift` and `unshift`.[23] The former extracts the first element of an array, shuffles the remaining elements toward the front, shrinking the size of the array by one. The latter takes a list as a second argument (the array is the first argument) and inserts the elements from that list into the array at its front end. Whereas `shift` returns the value of the element extracted from the front end of the array, `unshift` returns an integer that is the size of the lengthened array.

The corresponding operations for the back end of an array are `pop` and `push`. The `pop` operator returns the last element of an array and shortens the length of the array by one. The `push` operator takes a list as a second argument, inserts each item in the list at the back end of the array, and returns the number of items inserted into the array.

The next script, `Array.pl`, illustrates how an array can be initialized and modified by the various operators mentioned above.[24] Line (A) shows that a one-element array can be initialized with a single scalar. The scalar on the right of the assignment operator in line (A) is evaluated in a list context, which causes it to get *promoted* to a list of the scalar value. So, in effect, the statement in line (A) is equivalent to[25]

```
@arr = ('a');
```

Line (C) uses the `qw//` operator — in this case actually `qw{}` — to return a list of three strings that initializes the array `@arr`. (See the footnote comment made earlier in this section about the `qw//` operator.) Line (D) shows a single element of this array by interpolating it into a double-quoted string argument to `print()`. Line (E) displays all of the elements of the array. Line (F) evaluates the array `@arr` in a scalar context, which returns the size of the array. Line (G) prints out the size.

---

[23]Many of the Perl's built-in functions can be also be called as operators. That is, Perl allows many of its built-in functions to be called with and without the function call operator `()`. Therefore, functions like `shift` and `unshift` can be called with parenthesized arguments or with arguments without the enclosing parenthesis, as we show in the next script. Therefore, the operations at the front end of an array may be shown either as `shift` and `unshift`, or as `shift()` and `unshift()`. The same applies to virtually all other built-in functions of Perl. Section 2.7 talks further about the distinction between functions and operators and when it is safe to use a function as an operator.

[24]The reader will notice in the first line of the script that we did not use the `-w` switch to turn on the warnings. As was mentioned earlier, this switch asks the compiler to turn on a large number of execution-time warnings. One of these warnings relevant to the discussion at hand is accessing uninitialized variables. Since we want to demonstrate autovivification for arrays — array extensions of arbitrary length coming into existence simply by the mechanism of assignment to one or more elements — we can end up with intervening array elements that would be uninitialized. If the warnings were turned on with the `-w` switch, printing out an array with uninitialized elements could fill up a screen with warning messages, one for each uninitialized element.

[25]This is a general property of Perl that a scalar evaluated in a list context returns a list of the scalar value. See Section 2.8 for Perl's evaluation contexts.

Line (H) changes the value of the scalar `$#arr`. As mentioned earlier, this scalar holds the index value of the last element of the array. Since array indices are zero-based by default, the value of `$#arr` is one less than the size of the array. This means that line (H) extends the size of the array to five elements — as demonstrated by the output in line (K). The two additional elements created by the assignment in line (H) are given the null value `undef`. Since the print representation of `undef` is an empty string, we get the same printout for the extended array in line (I) as we did for the original array in line (E).

Line (L) shows how multiple array elements can all be assigned new values in a single statement.[26] Line (L) is not actually putting anything new into the array since the values of `$arr[3]` and `$arr[4]` are already `undef`. But what line (L) demonstrates via line (M) is that the print representation of `undef` is indeed an empty string.

Lines (N) through (Q) show autovivification for an array. The assignment shown in line (N) causes a new array element at index 6 to come into existence. In general, such an assignment will cause an array to grow to whatever size is needed for accommodating the new element. Any new intervening elements created through such an extension are given the null value `undef`.

Line (R) shows that an array name can appear inside a list on the left side of the assignment operator. For the syntax shown in line (R), the variables `$x` and `$y` that appear inside the list on the left of the assignment operator will be given the values 1 and 2, respectively. The rest of the values on the right will be placed in the array `@arr`, as borne out by the print statement in line (S).

Line (T) again shows how you can bring a new array into existence simply by invoking an operation on it that creates one or more of its elements. The `unshift` operator in line (T) inserts the string `hi` into a previously nonexistent array `@barr`. Line (U) shows a statement modifying an array by using its previous value on the right side of the assignment.

Lines (W) through (Z) demonstrate array *slicing*. A slice of an array is composed of a selection of elements that are in the same sequential order as in the original array. The subscript `[0,2]` in line (W) causes `@arr[0,2]` to return a list consisting of two elements, one at index 0 and the other at index 2. On the other hand, the use of the Perl's range operator `..` inside the subscript operator `[]` in line (Y) returns all elements whose indices span the range 0 to 2, both ends inclusive.[27] Note that

---

[26]This is the same syntax as in the assignment of a list of scalar values to a list of scalar variables:

```
($x, $y) = ('a', 'b');
```

which will cause the value `a` to be assigned to the scalar variable `$x` and the value `b` to be assigned to the scalar variable `$y`.

[27]In general, the range operator returns a list of numbers starting from the left scalar operand and incrementing it repeatedly by one until the value reaches the right operand.

in lines (W) and (Y) the array `@barr` is composed of the list `(hi hi)`, as set previously in line (U).

Line (b) shows the use of slice subscripting for switching array elements. Switching elements around in this manner can be carried out for more than two elements at a time. For example, we could have said

```
@arr[0,1,2] = @arr[1,2,0];
```

This works because an array slice expressed with the syntax `@arr[0,1,2]` is equivalent to the list `($arr[0], $arr[1], $arr[2])`. So the above statement is equivalent to the assignment

```
( $arr[0], $arr[1], $arr[2] ) =  ( $arr[1], $arr[2], $arr[0] );
```

Lines (d) through (q) demonstrate the `shift` and the `unshift` operators that structurally modify the front end of an array. As previously mentioned, the `shift` operator, shown in lines (d) through (h), extracts the first element of the array, shuffles all other elements down with regard to their indices, and shrinks the size of the array by one. A call to `shift` returns the value of the element extracted from the front end of the array. On the other hand, the `unshift` operator, as shown in lines (i) through (n), inserts a list of scalar values at the front end of an array. The items inserted into the array are kept in the same order in which they appear in the second argument to `unshift`. Index 0 now begins with the first of the new elements inserted. As mentioned previously, the `unshift` operator returns an integer that is the size of the array after it is lengthened by `unshift`. A more common call to `unshift` is shown in line (o) where the second argument consists of a scalar that is inserted into the front end of the array. The commented-out line (q), if uncommented, elicits an error from Perl because the `unshift` argument needs an array for its first argument, and not a list.[28]

As shown in lines (r) through (zb), what `shift` and `unshift` do at the front end of an array is accomplished at the back end by `pop` and `push`. As the reader would expect, the call to `pop` in line (r) removes and returns the last element in an array, shrinking the size of the array by one. On the other hand, as shown in line (x), `push` is able to insert a list of items at the back end. Line (y) shows this operator returning the size of the array after it is made larger in line (x). A more common call to `push` inserts a single scalar into the back end of the array, as shown in line (zc).

Line (ze) shows the use of the built-in `reverse()` function for reversing the order in which the elements are stored in an array. A call to `reverse()` *returns* the reversed list; the original list supplied as the argument is left unchanged.

Lines (zg) and (zh) show how an array can be sorted by invoking the built-in `sort()` on it. The default behavior of `sort()` treats the array as a collection of

---

[28] This is true of all array modification operators — `shift`, `unshift`, `pop`, and `push` — that each requires an array for its first argument.

strings and sorts the elements in a lexicographic order on the basis of the ASCII codes associated with the characters comprising the string elements. This default behavior can be changed by supplying separately to `sort()` the criterion to be used for comparing elements. We will illustrate how to do that in Sections 2.4 and 2.5 of this chapter.

Lines (zi) through (zr) show experiments with the built-in `splice()` function. Depending on how this function is called, it can splice one array into another array or just erase a portion of an array. The call in line (zj) uses only two arguments and the second is an integer of value 4. This call will cause `splice()` to delete all elements of the first-argument array that are indexed 4 and higher.[29] This is made evident by the output in line (zk).

If `splice()` is called with two integer arguments after the first array argument, as shown in line (zm), the number of elements deleted equals the value of the integer in the third argument. The starting index for the deletion of the elements corresponds to the second argument. So the call in line (zm) will delete just two elements, at index values 4 and 5.

To splice one array into another, `splice()` needs to be called as shown in line (zq). In this four-argument version of `splice()`, the last argument is the array that needs to be spliced into the first-argument array. Splicing begins at the index corresponding to the second argument. But, before splicing, starting at the second-argument index Perl deletes from the first-argument array a number of elements equal to the third argument. This explains the output shown in line (zr). Note that the three elements of the array `@brr` have replaced the two deleted elements of the array `@arr`.

Finally, we show in lines (zs) through (zu) what happens when `chomp` is invoked on an array of strings, as we do in line (zs).[30] If any of the strings in the array terminates in the newline character, `chomp` gobbles up the newline character.

```
#!/usr/bin/perl

### Array.pl
```

---

[29]We have chosen to ignore the value returned by `splice()` in all the examples shown, though it is useful to know that this function returns the last element deleted in a scalar context and a list of all the elements deleted in a list context.

[30]Strictly speaking, the end-of-the-string character that (when present) is deleted by `chomp` is whatever the value of the special variable `$/` happens to be. As previously mentioned in the explanations related to the last two scripts of Section 2.1.2, this variable, known as the *input record separator*, stores the character(s) that represent the line breaks in character files on a given platform. For Unix-like platforms, a line break is the character represented by the escape `\n`. On the other hand, a line break on a Windows machine is the pair of characters `\r\n`. On Macs, a line break is the character `\r`. Also note that most internet protocols require the line breaks to be indicated by `\r\n`, as we will see in Chapter 15.

```
# Initialize array with a scalar:
@arr = 'a';                                                      #(A)
print "@arr\n";                          # a                     #(B)

# Initialize array with a list:
@arr = qw{0 1 two};                                              #(C)
print "$arr[2]\n";                       # two                   #(D)
print "@arr\n";                          # 0 1 two               #(E)
$size = @arr;                                                    #(F)
print "$size\n";                         # 3                     #(G)

# Extend the array:
$#arr = 4;                                                       #(H)

# The new array:
print "@arr\n";                          # 0 1 two               #(I)
$size = @arr;                                                    #(J)
print "$size\n";                         # 5                     #(K)

# Explicitly undef the new elements:
($arr[3], $arr[4]) = (undef, undef);                             #(L)
print "@arr\n";                          # 0 1 two               #(M)

# Try autovivification:
$arr[6] = 6;                                                     #(N)
print "@arr\n";                          # 0 1 two    6          #(O)
$size = @arr;                                                    #(P)
print "$size\n";                         # 7                     #(Q)

# Slice an array out of a longer list:
($x, $y, @arr) = ( 1, 2, 'zero', 'one', 'two' );                 #(R)
print "@arr\n";                          # zero one two          #(S)

# A "funny" way to make an array:
unshift @barr, 'hi';                                             #(T)
@barr = (@barr, @barr);                                          #(U)
print "@barr\n";                         # hi hi                 #(V)

# Insert a slice of one array into another:
@carr = (@barr, @arr[0,2]);                                      #(W)
print "@carr\n";                         # hi hi zero two        #(X)

# Use range operator for slicing:
@carr = (@barr, @arr[0..2]);                                     #(Y)
print "@carr\n";                         # hi hi zero one two    #(Z)

# Switch elements:
print "@arr\n";                          # zero one two          #(a)
@arr[0,1] = @arr[1,0];                                           #(b)
```

```
print "@arr\n";                         # one zero two           #(c)

# The shift operator extracts the first
# element of the array:
$first = shift @arr;                                             #(d)
print "$first\n";                       # one                    #(e)
print "@arr\n";                         # zero two               #(f)
$size = @arr;                                                    #(g)
print "$size\n";                        # 2                      #(h)

# The unshift operator pushes elements in at the
# front end of the array:
@new_stuff = (0, 1);                                             #(i)
$x = unshift @arr, @new_stuff;                                   #(j)
print "$x\n";                           # 4                      #(k)
print "@arr\n";                         # 0 1 zero two           #(l)
$size = @arr;                                                    #(m)
print "$size\n";                        # 4                      #(n)

# A more common call to unshift:
$x = unshift @arr, 'three';                                      #(o)
print "@arr\n";                         # three 0 1 zero two     #(p)
#$x = unshift qw/zero one/, 'three';    # WRONG                  #(q)


# The pop operator works at the back of
# the array:
$y = pop @arr;                                                   #(r)
print "$y\n";                           # two                    #(s)
print "@arr\n";                         # three 0 1 zero         #(t)
$size = @arr;                                                    #(u)
print "$size\n";                        # 4                      #(v)


# The push operator works at the back of
# the array:
@new_stuff = qw/a b/;                                            #(w)
$x = push @arr, @new_stuff;                                      #(x)
print "$x\n";                           # 6                      #(y)
print "@arr\n";                         # three 0 1 zero a b     #(z)
$size = @arr;                                                    #(za)
print "$size\n";                        # 6                      #(zb)

# A more common call to push:
push @arr, 'c';                                                  #(zc)
print "@arr\n";                         # three 0 1 zero a b c   #(zd)

# Reverse an array:
my @rev = reverse @arr;                                          #(ze)
```

```
print "@rev\n";                          # c b a zero 1 0 three  #(zf)

# Sort an array:
my @sorted = sort @rev;                                          #(zg)
print "@sorted\n";                       # 0 1 a b c three zero  #(zh)


# Experiments with splicing:

@arr = (0, 1, 2, 3, 4, 5, 6);                                    #(zi)
splice(@arr, 4);                                                 #(zj)
print "@arr\n";                          # 0 1 2 3               #(zk)

@arr = (0, 1, 2, 3, 4, 5, 6);                                    #(zl)
splice(@arr, 4, 2);                                              #(zm)
print "@arr\n";                          # 0 1 2 3 6             #(zn)

@arr = (0, 1, 2, 3, 4, 5, 6);                                    #(zo)
@brr = ('a', 'b', 'c');                                          #(zp)
splice(@arr, 4, 2, @brr);                                        #(zq)
print "@arr\n";                          # 0 1 2 3 a b c 6       #(zr)


# chomp invoked on an array of strings:
@names = ( "peter\n", "paul", "mary\n" );                        #(zs)
chomp @names;                                                    #(zt)
print "@names\n";                        # peter paul mary       #(zu)
```

We are not completely done with the subject of arrays in Perl. Section 2.4 presents the different forms of syntax one can employ to display the contents of an array in Perl.

2.2.3 Hash

Another important built-in data structure in Perl is *hash*. It is used for storing associative data in the form of key-value pairs. The name of a hash is prefixed with the symbol %, as in the following statement that defines %phone_book as a hash that contains the three key-value pairs shown:

```
%phone_book = ( zaphod       =>  3456789,
                beetlegeuse  =>  0123456,
                trillian     =>  0001111 );
```

What we have on the right-hand side of the assignment operator above is a list, although this time it is shown with a big arrow (=>) between pairs of items to make it easier to see the keys and their associated values. Use of the big arrow in the manner shown also makes it possible to display the keys as *barewords*. We have the option of initializing a hash with a regular list containing comma-separated items. In that case, Perl will construe every odd-numbered element of the list as a key and every even-numbered element as a value. If we choose to use such a list literal for initializing a hash, it would be necessary to quote the keys that must always be strings, as we mention below. The big arrow implicitly quotes the key to its left.

Only strings, or expressions that evaluate to strings, can be used for hash keys. Furthermore, there can only be one key corresponding to a given string.[31] In other words, all the keys in a hash are strings and they are all distinct. Hash keys are also immutable, meaning that a key cannot be modified after a key-value pair is created. Of course, a given key-value pair can be deleted and a new pair inserted. A value, on the other hand, can be any scalar, and a given value can appear any number of times in a hash. To be more specific, a value for a given key could be a number, a string, or a reference.[32] A value can also be the null value `undef`.

The scalar value corresponding to a key in a hash can be accessed by using the `$` prefix, as for any ordinary scalar, and by enclosing the key in braces. For example, we would invoke

```
$phone_book{ zaphod }
```

to retrieve the value associated with the key `zaphod` in the `%phone_book` hash. An ordinary identifier within braces is always treated as a string and therefore does not have to be quoted. If we wanted to change the value associated with this key, we could say

```
$phone_book{ zaphod } = 7893456;       # will change the value
                                       # associated with the
                                       # key zaphod from
                                       # 3456789 to 7893456
```

This syntax for fetching a hash value can be used directly for interpolating such values in a double-quoted string. For example, we could say

```
$key = "zaphod";
print "$key's phone number is $phone_book{$key}\n";
```

Perl gives us two functions, `keys()` and `values()`, that when invoked on a hash in a list context[33] return, respectively, a list of all the keys and a list of all the values. For example, with the hash `%phone_book` initialized as shown previously, if we say

[31] As we will see in Chapter 5, a Perl reference can also serve as a key in a hash. However, it is the string representation of the reference that is actually used as a key.

[32] We will discuss Perl's references in Chapter 5.

[33] See Section 2.8 for evaluation contexts in Perl.

```
@k = keys %phone_book;
@v = values %phone_book;
```

the list of keys returned by the `keys()` function will be placed in the array `@k` and the list of values returned by `values()` in the array `@v`. The keys and the values are returned in the order in which they happen to be stored in the hash. Each operation on a hash that either inserts a new key or deletes an existing key is potentially capable of changing the order in which the elements of a hash are stored. The keys and the values that are returned by the operators[34] `keys` and `values` are copies of the actual items contained in the hash. So modifying one or more elements of the arrays `@k` and `@v` will not change the contents of the `%phone_book` hash.

When `keys()` and `values()` are invoked in a scalar context, you will simply get the number of elements — meaning the number of key-value pairs — in a hash. For the same `%phone_book` hash we have used so far, if we say

```
$how_many = keys %phone_book;                # 3
$how_many = values %phone_book;              # 3
```

the scalar `$how_many` will be set to the number 3 in each case. The fact that, in a scalar context, the `keys` operator applied to a hash returns a scalar can be used to set the number of buckets preallocated to the hash. A single bucket of a hash table holds the value for one key. So if we say

```
keys %phone_book = 1000;
```

the memory management system will typically preallocate for the hash the number of buckets that is the next power of 2. For the above invocation, that number would be 1024. Without such preallocation, the number of buckets will usually increase incrementally as new entries are made into a hash. Such incremental changes to the allocated memory could entail moving the entire hash from one location in memory to another if the hash is not allowed to grow in place because of other objects in adjoining segments of memory. This migration of a hash in memory would obviously extract a performance penalty if it happens too frequently. Preallocating memory in the manner indicated could prove important in performance-critical applications.

Whereas a new key-value pair is inserted into a hash merely by assignment, as in

```
$phone_book{ arther_denton } = 34521;
```

an existing key-value pair may be removed from a hash by using the `delete()` function:

```
delete $phone_book{ arthur_denton };
```

[34] Recall an earlier footnote in the previous subsection where we talked about our interchangeable use of "operator" and "function" for many of Perl's built-in functions. Section 2.7 talks about the distinction between the two and when it is safe to use a function as an operator.

Whether or not a key-value pair for a given key exists in a hash may be ascertained by invoking the function `exists()` on the key, as in

```
exists $phone_book{ arther_denton }
```

This invocation will return true[35] if the `%phone_book` hash contains a key-value pair for the `arthur_denton` key.

It is often the case that one needs to scan a hash, element by element. This is also referred to as *iterating* over a hash. The function `each()`, when invoked on a hash will return the next key-value pair. So we could use `each()` in a `while` loop in the following manner:

```
while ( ($name, $number ) = each %phone_book ) {
    print "$name => $number\n";
}
```

Another way to iterate over a hash is to first fetch all the keys by using the `keys()` function in the manner already described and then to use the `foreach` control structure to iterate over the keys. We will show examples of this and other approaches in Section 2.5.

The next script brings together several of the hash-related notions presented above and some additional ones. In going through the script, we urge the reader to ignore for now the syntax used for the `display_hash()` subroutine, defined in lines (a) through (d), and the syntax used for calling this subroutine in lines (B), (D), (F), and so on.

Line (A) of the script shows that a hash can be brought into existence merely by the act of assigning a value to a key. So the assignment in line (A) creates a hash with a single key-value pair, the key being `a` and the value 100. We display this hash by calling `display_hash()` in line (B).

Line (C) shows a hash being initialized by a list whose items are alternately meant to be keys and values. The initialization in line (C) works the same as the one shown in the statement that ends in line (E), except that the latter is easier to read by a human as an association list. As mentioned already, the big-arrow notation used in the statement that ends in line (E) allows for barewords to be used as keys.

Line (G) shows a key-value pair being deleted from a hash by invoking `delete()`. The `delete()` function returns the value part of the key-value pair it deletes. And line (I) shows how the `exists()` function can be used as a conditional that checks for the existence of a key-value pair in a hash.

Lines (K) and (M) show, respectively, the `keys()` and the `values()` built-in functions being invoked in list contexts for retrieving the keys and the values in a

---

[35] It actually returns the number 1 on success (which evaluates to true when treated as a Boolean in the conditional of, say, an `if` statement) and 0 on failure, which evaluates to false.

hash. On the other hand, the same functions when invoked in scalar contexts in lines (O) and (Q) return the number of keys and the number of values.

The commented-out lines (S) and (T) show that it is not possible to use an uninitialized access to a new key in a hash with the hope that the corresponding value would be default initialized to, say, `undef`.

Lines (U), (V), and (W) show how a slice of a hash can be deleted at once. Similarly, lines (X), (Y), and (Z) show us inserting a new slice into a hash.

```
#!/usr/bin/perl

# Hash.pl

# Bring a hash into existence by autovivification:
$h{a} = 100;                                                #(A)
&display_hash( \%h );                   # a => 100          #(B)

# Initialize a hash with a list:
%h = ('a', 1, 'b', 2, 'c', 3);                              #(C)
&display_hash( \%h );                   # c => 3            #(D)
                                        # a => 1
                                        # b => 2
# Initialize a hash with a list using the big arrow notation:
%h = ( a => 1,
       b => 2,
       c => 3,
       d => 4);                                             #(E)
&display_hash( \%h );                   # c => 3            #(F)
                                        # a => 1
                                        # b => 2
                                        # d => 4
# Delete a key-value pair:
delete $h{c};                                               #(G)
&display_hash( \%h );                   # a => 1            #(H)
                                        # b => 2
                                        # d => 4
# Check for the existence of a key-value pair:
if ( exists $h{a} ) {                                       #(I)
    print "yes\n";                      # yes               #(J)
}

# Retrieve all keys:
@keys = keys %h;                                            #(K)
print "@keys\n";                        # a b d             #(L)

# Retrieve all values:
@values = values %h;                                        #(M)
```

```
print "@values\n";                          # 1 2 4                  #(N)

# The keys() function in a scalar context:
$how_many_keys = keys %h;                                            #(O)
print "$how_many_keys\n";                   # 3                      #(P)

# The values() function in a scalar context:
$how_many_values = values %h;                                        #(Q)
print "$how_many_values\n";                 # 3                      #(R)

#$h{e};                                     # ERROR                  #(S)
#$h{f};                                     # ERROR                  #(T)

# Deleting a slice of the hash:
my @some_keys = qw/a b/;                                             #(U)
delete @h{@some_keys};                                               #(V)
&display_hash( \%h );                       # d => 4                 #(W)

# Inserting new key-value pairs as a hash slice:
my @new_keys = qw/e f/;                                              #(X)
@h{@new_keys} = (15, 16);                                            #(Y)
&display_hash( \%h );                       # e => 15                #(Z)
                                            # d => 4
                                            # f => 16
#The display_hash subroutine:
sub display_hash {                                                   #(a)
    ($r) = @_;                                                       #(b)
    while ( ($name, $number ) = each %$r ) {                         #(c)
        print "$name => $number\n";                                  #(d)
    }
}
```

We are not completely done with the subject of hashes in Perl. As mentioned earlier in the explanation of the above script, Section 2.5 will go more deeply into the various forms of syntax one can use to display the contents of a hash in Perl.

2.3 LEXICAL SCOPE, LEXICAL VARIABLES, AND GLOBAL VARIABLES

Once a variable is defined, the following important question arises: Where will it be visible in the rest of the script and, when visible, through what naming convention? The basic distinction to be made here is between *lexical variables* and *global variables*. Lexical variables, also known as `my` variables, are the local variables of

Perl. After the point of its declaration, a lexical variable is visible only in its *lexical scope* — a notion we will explain further in this section. With regard to the global variables, it helps to make a distinction between the following two different kinds:

- System-supplied truly global variables
- Package variables

The system-supplied global variables, such as Perl's default variable `$_`, can be accessed anywhere in a script without any special prefixes. So the system-supplied global variables can be considered to be truly global. On the other hand, a package variable is visible everywhere after its declaration, provided it is called with a package-qualified name. As we will explain shortly, it is possible to call a package variable directly, that is, without its package qualification, under certain conditions. But, first, in the next subsection, we will start with a discussion of lexical variables.

2.3.1 Lexical Variables

A lexical variable is defined with a `my` declaration, as in

```
my $x = 4;
my $y = "hello";
my @arr = (1, 2, 3, "four");
my %phone_book = undef;
```

Lexical variables have *lexical scope*. That means such variables are visible from the point of their declaration only until the end of the lexical scope. A lexical scope (also known as *static scope*) will generally correspond to a brace-delimited block of code. However, it can also correspond to the string argument given to the `eval` operator.[36] For lexical variables declared outside a braces-delimited code block, the lexical scope will cover the rest of the script file. For those steeped in systems programming languages like C, C++, and Java, the lexical scope of Perl amounts to a combination of the block scope in all three languages and the file scope in C and C++. But note that, in addition to the block and the file scopes, Perl's lexical scope also includes the scope corresponding to the argument supplied to the `eval` operator.

Lexical variables of the same name may be defined in *nested scopes*, as we do with the variable `$x` in the following scriplet:

```
my $x = 2;
my $y = 100;
print "$x, $y \n";                    # 2 100
{
```

[36]The `eval` operator is presented in Section 2.14.

```
        my $x = 4;
        print "$x, $y \n";                          # 4 100
        {
            my $x = 8;
            print "$x, $y \n";                      # 8 100
        }
        print "$x, $y \n";                          # 4 100
    }
    print "$x, $y \n";                              # 2 100
```

What this shows is that an outer lexical scope covers all inner lexical scopes and that a lexical variable in an inner scope hides its outer scope definition. Upon exit from the inner scope, the outer scope definition of such a variable is restored.[37]

Multiple variables may simultaneously be declared as lexical by placing them all in parentheses, as in

```
my ($x, @arr, %phone_list);
$x = 4;
@arr = (1, 2, 3, "four");
%phone_list = ( peter => 123, paul => 234, mary => 345 );
```

One or more scalars and an array may also be initialized at the same time they are declared to be lexical in a single statement like

```
my ($x, $y, @arr ) = (1, 2, 3, 4, 5);
print "$x\n";                                   # 1
print "$y\n";                                   # 2
print "@arr\n";                                 # 3 4 5
```

Similarly, one or more scalars and a hash can be initialized at the same time that they are declared to be lexical. This can be done in a single statement, as in

```
my ($x, $y, %h ) = (1, 2, "a", 3, "b", 4);
print "$x\n";                                   # 1
print "$y\n";                                   # 2
my @k = keys %h;
print "@k\n";                                   # a b
my @v = values %h;
print "@v\n";                                   # 3 4
```

[37]Each lexical scope provides its own namespace dictionary in the form of a hash table. This namespace dictionary is also known as the *local scratchpad*. When a new name is added in a scope, a corresponding entry is made in the dictionary. The name then stays visible until the end of the scope, at which time the dictionary for that scope is destroyed. Lexical scoping should be distinguished from *dynamic scoping*. While the visibility of a name in both cases ends with the end of the innermost enclosing block, the enclosing block is defined dynamically at run time for dynamic scoping. The keyword `local` defines a dynamically scoped variable. See Section 2.12 for further details concerning this declaration.

When variables of different types are simultaneously declared and initialized in the manner shown, the scalar variables must come before the array or the hash variables.

2.3.2 Package Variables

There are three different ways of creating a package variable:

- By using package-qualified naming syntax
- Through an `our` declaration
- Through a `use vars` declaration

Since a package variable is global, it is accessible everywhere after its declaration, *provided it is called with a package qualified name.*[38] A package variable may also be called directly — that is, without being qualified with its package name — but under restrictions that depend on how the package variable was created. As we will see in this section, an `our` variable is accessible without package qualification throughout its lexical scope — just like a lexical variable. On the other hand, a `use vars` variable, when called without its package qualification, is accessible only within its own package. A package variable created originally with full package-qualified naming syntax cannot be accessed directly anywhere without the package qualification. At the same time, any package variable, no matter through which of the three methods it was created, can be accessed directly without its package qualification in another package, provided it is *imported* into the destination package using the special `use package` syntax, as we will see later in Section 2.11.2.

It is important to bear in mind that, *when called without the package qualified naming syntax*, exactly the same scoping rules apply to an `our` variable as to a `my` variable with regard to its visibility. That is, unless called with its package-qualified name, an `our` variable is not visible outside of the lexical scope in which it is defined. Thus, if an `our` variable is defined inside a braces-delimited block, it will not be accessible without its package qualification outside the block. Remember, the lexical scope may also correspond to the entire file, or to an `eval` block.

All package variables are stored in a namespace dictionary separately for each package. Like all dictionaries in Perl, the namespace dictionary is a hash in which the name of each package variable must be unique. A namespace dictionary, known as a *symbol table hash*, is more briefly referred to as a *stash*.

The thread of execution inside a Perl script is *placed* in a *package namespace* by invoking the `package` declaration, as in lines (I), (O), (R), (T), (a), and (c) of

---

[38] On the other hand, a lexical variable, meaning a `my` variable, is simply not accessible by any means outside of its lexical scope.

the next script, PackageNames.pl. Once the execution starts in a namespace, it continues in that namespace until another package declaration is seen. However, if a package declaration is within a separate lexical scope, as is the case with the braces-delimited package declaration in line (T), the thread of execution will revert to the namespace of the enclosing lexical scope at the end of the inner lexical scope. Therefore, in the following script, once the thread of execution hits the right brace in line (Y), the currently operational namespace will revert back to Pack1 because of the declaration in line (R).

We will now provide further insights into the behavior of package variables by going line-by-line through the script PackageNames.pl.

At the beginning, before the invocation of any package declaration, the operating namespace is the main namespace. This is where the story of the PackageNames.pl script begins. Line (A) declares a lexical variable. The name of this variable is stored away in the scratchpad dictionary corresponding to the top-level lexical scope that is associated with this script. Obviously, at this time, the lexical scope encompasses the entire file, so it is the same thing as file scope. Thus, the lexical scalar variable $a will be visible throughout the file, unless it is masked by our variables of the same name, or by a lexical variable of the same name but in a nested scope.

Line (B) uses the package-qualified syntax

```
$main::x = 100;
```

to declare the scalar variable $x as a package variable in the main package. The name of this variable will be recorded in the namespace dictionary corresponding to the main package. Line (C) shows another way to declare a package variable — with the our declaration shown below:

```
our $y = 101;
```

This declaration does two things simultaneously: It introduces the variable $y into the currently operational namespace, main, and it *imports* this name into whatever namespace is in effect at the point of the our declaration. This difference between the declaration in line (B) and the one in line (C) is subtle but important. Whereas both declarations introduce the target names into the package namespace main, the our declaration makes it possible to use the name without the package qualification. This is demonstrated by the print statements in lines (E) through (H). Uncommenting the commented-out print statement in line (E) elicits an error report from Perl because we are not allowed to access the package variable $x directly, that is, without its package-qualified name. On the other hand, we have no such trouble with the package variable $y in line (F). Of course, as shown in lines (G) and (H), we can access both these variables using the package-qualified naming syntax.

Line (I) uses the package declaration

```
package Pack1;
```

to change the operational namespace from `main` to `Pack1`. Any subsequent `our` declarations, prior to any further changes in the operational namespace, will inject variables into the package `Pack1`. Line (J) declares another lexical variable, `$b`. Being lexical, this variable will be recorded in the same scratchpad namespace as the lexical variable `$a` of line (A). Like `$a`, this variable also has file scope.

The `our` declaration of line (K) introduces the variable `$x` into the namespace for the package `Pack1` and, at the same time, makes it possible to access this variable directly, that is, without a package-qualified name for it, as we do in the print statements in lines (M) and (N). Using the package-qualified naming syntax, line (L) introduces the variable `$y` into the namespace `Pack1`. Line (M) shows what can happen when you try to directly access a package variable that was injected into the namespace with package-qualified syntax. What we get for `$y` in line (M) is not the variable defined in line (L), but the variable `$y` of the `main` namespace, as declared in line (C). Note the use of the package-qualified naming syntax for accessing `Pack1`'s `$y` in line (N).

The next few lines show that you can go back and forth between the different namespaces in the same script. Line (O) changes the package namespace in effect from `Pack1` to `Pack2`. Lines (P) and (Q) then declare a lexical scalar variable, `$c`, and a global variable `$x` specific to the `Pack2` namespace. In line (R), the operational namespace reverts back to `Pack1` from `Pack2`.

Remaining within the namespace `Pack1` that began in line (R), line (T) switches to the namespace `Pack3` that is enclosed within the braces in lines (S) and (Y). The result of putting the `Pack3` namespace within braces is that, when the thread of execution goes past the right brace in line (Y), the operational namespace automatically reverts back to what it was before the left brace of line (S), that is, `Pack1`. So the `our` variable `$z` of line (Z) belongs to the `Pack1` namespace. Also note that while we are within the `Pack3` namespace inside the braces, we can access and, if we wish, declare new variables in any of the other namespaces with the appropriate syntax. For example, line (W) introduces a new variable, `$y`, in the namespace of `Pack2`. We then switch back to the `Pack2` namespace in line (a) and declare a new `our` variable `$z` in this namespace in line (b). Finally, in line (c), we change back to the `main` namespace; this is the namespace in which the execution of the script began. Line (d) then introduces a new variable, `$z`, into this namespace.

Lines (e), (f), and (g) show that a `my` variable hides a global variable of the same name. Line (f) introduces a `my` variable `$z`, which has the same name as the global `our` variable `$z` of line (d).[39] We are allowed to access the `$z` of line (d) without namespace qualification, but when we do so in line (g), what we get is the `my` variable of line (f). Note that we had no trouble accessing the global version of `$z` in line (e).

---

[39]Since this script is executed with the warnings turned on, the statement of line (f) will result in a warning message to the effect that the `my` variable is masking an earlier declaration in the same scope.

Line (h) displays the values of all four lexical variables declared in the script. Line (i) displays the value of the variable named `$x`. This value corresponds to the declaration of `$x` as a `Pack2` package variable in line (Q). Note that this value of the global variable `$x` does *not* correspond to the assignment in line (U). That version of `$x` was created in the lexical scope of the braces in lines (S) and (Y); this value can only be accessed through the package-qualified syntax, as we see in line (m).

With the help of the print statements, lines (j) through (m) show the values of the `$x`, `$y`, and `$z` package variables in the four different namespaces, `main`, `Pack1`, `Pack2`, and `Pack3`.

```
#!/usr/bin/perl -w

### PackageNames.pl

use strict;

my $a = 10;                                                  #(A)
$main::x = 100;                                              #(B)
our $y = 101;                                                #(C)
print "$a \n";                           # 10                #(D)
#print "$x \n";                          # ERROR             #(E)
print "$y \n";                           # 101               #(F)
print "$main::x \n";                     # 100               #(G)
print "$main::y \n";                     # 101               #(H)

package Pack1;                                               #(I)
my $b = 20;                                                  #(J)
our $x = 1000;                                               #(K)
$Pack1::y = 1001;                                            #(L)
print "$x $y \n";                        # 1000 101          #(M)
print "$x $Pack1::y \n";                 # 1000 1001         #(N)

package Pack2;                                               #(O)
my $c = 30;                                                  #(P)
our $x = 2000;                                               #(Q)

package Pack1;                                               #(R)
{                                                            #(S)
    package Pack3;                                           #(T)
    our $x = 3000;                                           #(U)
    $Pack3::y = 3001;                                        #(V)
    $Pack2::y = 2001;                                        #(W)
    $Pack3::z = 3002;                                        #(X)
}                                                            #(Y)
our $z = 1002;                                               #(Z)
```

```
package Pack2;                                                          #(a)
our $z = 2002;                                                          #(b)

package main;                                                           #(c)
our $z = 102;                                                           #(d)

# A "my" variable hides a global of the same name:
print "$z \n";                                  # 102                   #(e)
my $z = 40;                                     # WARNING               #(f)
print "$z \n";                                  # 40                    #(g)

# Show values of all variables in this script:
print "$a $b $c $z \n";                         # 10 20 30 40           #(h)
print "$x \n";                                  # 2000                  #(i)
print "$main::x $main::y $::z \n";              # 100 101 102           #(j)
print "$Pack1::x $Pack1::y $Pack1::z \n";       # 1000 1001 1002        #(k)
print "$Pack2::x $Pack2::y $Pack2::z \n";       # 2000 2001 2002        #(l)
print "$Pack3::x $Pack3::y $Pack3::z \n";       # 3000 3001 3002        #(m)

# Show all names in Pack1 stash:
print join "\n", keys %Pack1::;                                         #(n)
                                                # x
                                                # y
                                                # z
# Show all names in main stash:
print join "\n", keys %main::;                  # STDOUT                #(o)
                                                # STDIN
                                                #  ...
                                                # x
                                                # y
                                                # z
                                                #  ...
```

The above script also shows in lines (n) and (o) how you can print out the names stored in a namespace dictionary.[40] In line (n), we print out the names stored in the `Pack1` namespace. Note that the name of the hash in which the package names of `Pack1` are stored is `%Pack1::`. Line (o) shows the same for the `main` namespace. Of course, as you would expect, this namespace, stored in the hash `%main::`, has a large number of entries in addition to those that we may enter into it.[41]

[40] See Section 4.12.1 of Chapter 4 for a more detailed explanation of `join`. As explained there, the first argument to `join` acts like glue and is inserted between the successive elements of the array.

[41] This syntax for printing out the names in a package namespace was posted by Charles Huff in the `comp.lang.perl.moderated` newsgroup in response to a query from the author.

As mentioned at the beginning of this section, another mechanism for injecting package variables into a namespace is through the `use vars` declaration. Such package variables are global in the same sense as the package variables created through the other two naming conventions. As long as the flow of execution stays within the same namespace — that is, within the same package — a `use vars` variable can be accessed directly without its package-qualified name, just like an `our` variable. However, whereas an `our` variable, when called without its package-qualified name, is visible everywhere throughout its lexical scope (and this scope may cross package boundaries within the same file), a direct access to a `use vars` variable cannot cross package boundaries. Therefore, even within the same lexical scope, if you cross namespace boundaries, because you have crossed package boundaries, you have to use a package-qualified name to access a `use vars` variable.

This distinction between the `use vars` and `our` package variables is illustrated with the help of the script `PackageNamesUseVars.pl` shown next. Note the following `use vars` declaration in line (B) of the `Pack1` namespace:

```
use vars qw/$u $v/;
```

This creates two variables named `$u` and `$v` in the `Pack1` package. Subsequently, we assign values to them in lines (C) and (D). We also define two `our` package variables, `$x` and `$y`, in `Pack1` package in lines (E) and (F). Line (G) defines yet another package variable, `$z`, for `Pack1`, but now we use the package-qualified naming syntax for the variable. Using the usual syntax, meaning direct calls to `our` and `use vars` variables and package-qualified call to a variable created with package-qualified naming syntax, we access the values of `$x`, `$y`, and `$z` in lines (H) and (I).

We then switch to a nested namespace, `Pack2`, in line (J). Note the differences between the behaviors of `$u` and `$v`, on the one hand, and `$x`, `$y`, and `$z`, on the other. Comparing lines (H) and (K), we are now unable to access the `use vars` variables `$u` and `$v` in the namespace of `Pack2` in line (K). However, we can still access them through their package-qualified naming syntax, as we show in line (L). On the other hand, we can access `$x`, `$y`, and `$z` in exactly the same manner in line (M) as we did earlier in line (I).

We now want to point out that the `our` and `use vars` variables behave differently outside the lexical scope in which they are first created. We declare an `our` variable, `$w`, and a `use vars` variable, `$t`, in the lexical scope corresponding to the braces in lines (O) and (S). The `our` variable `$w` can only be accessed through its package-qualified name outside the lexical scope, as we show through lines (U) and (V). The `use vars` variable can, however, be accessed directly outside the lexical scope as long as we remain in `Pack2`'s namespace, as we show in line (W). When we change the namespace to `main` in line (Y), we are no longer able to access `$t` directly in line (a).

```
#!/usr/bin/perl -w

# PackageNamesUseVars.pl

use strict;

package Pack1;                                                          #(A)
use vars qw/$u $v/;                                                     #(B)
$u = 2000;                                                              #(C)
$v = 2001;                                                              #(D)
our $x = 1000;                                                          #(E)
our $y = 1001;                                                          #(F)
$Pack1::z = 1002;                                                       #(G)
print "$u $v \n";                           # 2000 2001                 #(H)
print "$x $y $Pack1::z \n";                 # 1000 1001 1002            #(I)

package Pack2;                                                          #(J)
#print "$u $v \n";                          # ERROR                     #(K)
print "$Pack1::u $Pack1::v \n";             # 2000 2001                 #(L)
print "$x $y $Pack1::z \n";                 # 1000 1001 1002            #(M)
print "$Pack1::x $Pack1::y $Pack1::z \n";   # 1000 1001 1002            #(N)
{                                                                       #(O)
    our $w  = 3000;                                                     #(P)
    use vars qw/$t/;                                                    #(Q)
    $t = 4000;                                                          #(R)
}                                                                       #(S)
print "$x $y $Pack1::z \n";                 # 1000 1001 1002            #(T)
#print "$w \n";                             # ERROR                     #(U)
print "$Pack2::w \n";                       # 3000                      #(V)
print "$t \n";                              # 4000                      #(W)
print "$Pack2::t \n";                       # 4000                      #(X)

package main;                                                           #(Y)
print "$Pack2::w \n";                       # 3000                      #(Z)
#print "$t \n";                             # ERROR                     #(a)
print "$Pack2::t \n";                       # 4000                      #(b)
```

To summarize, both `our` and `use vars` declarations create global variables of the package variety that can be accessed without the package qualification syntax under different types of restrictions. When called without package qualification after the point of its declaration, an `our` variable is visible throughout its own lexical scope, even when the lexical scope crosses namespace/package boundaries in the same file — just like a `my` variable. And when called without package qualification after the point of its declaration, a `use vars` variable is visible only within its own package/namespace. Of course, when their names are qualified with the package names, both the `our` and the `use vars` variables are accessible everywhere after their points of declaration — unlike the `my` variables.

We have yet to explain the purpose of the following *pragma declaration* in the third line of the previous two scripts:

```
use strict;
```

This pragma is a shorthand for the following three strictures to the compiler:

```
use strict "refs";
use strict "vars";
use strict "subs";
```

The first of these — `use strict "refs"` — triggers an error if a script uses a symbolic reference, a topic discussed in Chapter 5.

With the second pragma declaration — `use strict "vars"` — from that point on if you call a variable without package qualification, that variable had better be a previously declared `my` variable; or a previously declared `our` variable; or a previously declared `use vars` variable in the same package; or a variable that was defined originally in another module and that was imported into the current scope by using the syntax explained in Section 2.11.2; or one of Perl's truly global variables such as `$_` and `@ARGV`. If that is not the case, your script will elicit an error from the compiler.

The last of the three pragma declarations shown above — `use strict "subs"` — disallows the use of barewords, meaning unquoted strings, in a script unless the meaning of such words can be inferred from the script processed up to that point or if such a word is used as a key in a hash.

As with the `use warnings` pragma mentioned earlier, all of the `strict` pragmas have lexical scope. The `use strict` pragma can be turned off by the declaration `no strict`. The `use strict "refs"` can be turned off by `no strict "refs"`. The same is the case for turning off the other two `strict` pragmas listed above.

2.4 DISPLAYING ARRAYS

One frequently wants to display the contents of an array. What is interesting is that seemingly slight variations in the syntax used for printing out an array can cause large variations is what is actually displayed in the output. The purpose of this section is to show these small variations in the print syntax and what these do to the output.

Line (A) of the script shown next, `DisplayingArrays.pl`, defines an array `@arr` consisting of the four string elements shown there. Now note that line (B), lines (C) and (D), and line (E) are all trying to do essentially the same thing: to print whatever is returned by evaluating the array `@arr` followed by the printing out of the newline. As the reader can see, the output produced is dramatically different depending on the precise syntax used. Why these differences arise will be explained in greater detail in Section 2.8 where we talk about context dependency of evaluation. Suffice it to say here that, for the purpose of string interpolation in line (B), `@arr` is evaluated in a list context and spaces interposed between the elements of the array. The evaluation of `@arr` in line (C) also takes place in a list context, but this time it is *not* for the purpose of interpolation in a string. So the elements of the array are printed out one after the other without any spaces in between. On the other hand, the evaluation of `@arr` in line (E) takes place in a scalar context; the context is scalar because we expect `@arr` to return a single value whose print representation can be concatenated with what comes after the dot operator in line (E). In other words, the scalar context in line (E) for the evaluation of `@arr` is supplied by the concatenation operator. Since the scalar evaluation of an array returns just the number of elements in the array, we get the number 4 for the output, as shown in the commented-out portion of line (E).

Line (F) shows the syntax for the interpolation of one array element in a double-quoted string.

As the reader knows from our earlier explanation in Section 2.2.2, associated with each array definition is a special variable whose value is the zero-based index of the highest element in the array. The name of the variable is the hash mark followed by the identifier in the name of the array. So associated with the array `@arr` is the scalar variable `$#arr` whose value is 3, as shown in line (G), since there are exactly four elements in the array. As was also shown by the example in Section 2.2.2, we can expand or shrink an array by merely altering the value of this variable. This is demonstrated in line (H) where we have expanded the array to contain 10 elements. But, as stated earlier, these additional elements will remain uninitialized. If an array `@arr` is either uninitialized or empty, `$#arr` will return -1.

Lines (I) through (N) show a loop for displaying the contents of the expanded array. The `foreach` looping structure in line (I), explained further in Section 2.9, places each element of the array in Perl's special variable `$_`. Through the invocation of the `defined()` function on the implicit argument `$_`, the conditional of the `if` statement in line (J) checks whether or not this element of the array is initialized. If uninitialized, we print out `undef` for that element. This explains the output in the commented-out portion of line (N).

The `for` loop of lines (O) through (T) shows another way of iterating through the array, testing whether or not an element is initialized, and printing out a value accordingly. The two dots together in the header of the `for` statement in line (O) constitute the range operator, an example of which was shown earlier in Section 2.2.2. As mentioned there, the invocation

```
0..$#arr
```

returns a list consisting of the integer elements

```
0 1 2 3 4 5 6 7 8 9
```

The `for` loop iterates over this list and uses the indices to reach into the array `@arr`. The call in line (P), `defined($arr[$i])`, then tells us whether or not the `i`-*th* element of the array is initialized.

Line (U) shows that, except when supplied as an argument to `defined()`, it is an error to access an uninitialized array element. If you uncomment this statement, the runtime will come back with the warning message, "Use of uninitialized value in print at ...." if you invoked the interpreter with the `-w` flag, as we do in the very first line of the script. The same thing happens if you try to evaluate the expanded array in line (V) as an argument to `print()`.

The rest of the script shows how to display sorted arrays. As mentioned briefly in Section 2.2.2, ordinarily when you invoke `sort()` on an array, the sorting routine assumes that the elements of the array are all strings — even when that is not the case — and orders them lexicographically on the basis of the ASCII codes associated with the characters. This behavior of `sort()` is illustrated in lines (W), (X), and (Y) of the script below. Note the sorted order produced in line (Y).

The default behavior of `sort()` can be changed by supplying it with a subroutine that compares the elements in the desired manner. This subroutine, which may either be supplied by name or in the form of a braces-delimited block of code just before the array to be sorted, must tell `sort()` how to compare any two elements of the array. This subroutine must return one of three possible values: -1 if the first element is less than the second element, 0 if the two elements are equal, and +1 if the first element is greater than the second element. In Perl, such a subroutine is known as the *sort subroutine* or the *comparison subroutine*. Perl makes it convenient to specify such subroutines with the help of two system-defined variables `$a` and `$b`. This is demonstrated by the different examples in lines (Z) through (1) of the script.

Note the call to `sort()` in line (Z):

```
sort {$b <=> $a} @arr;
```

The comparison subroutine, specified in the form

```
{$b <=> $a}
```

uses the binary operator `<=>` that returns one of three possible integers, -1, 0, or 1, depending on whether the left operand is numerically less than, equal to, or greater than the right operand. Both the operands supplied to `<=>` must be numbers. As mentioned earlier, the variables `$a` and `$b` in this definition are system-defined. When the left operand mentions `$a` and the right operand `$b`, the sorted order is ascending with respect to the meaning of the "less than" operator being used. Otherwise, it is descending. The `<=>` operator is also known as the *spaceship operator*.

What <=> does for numbers, the operator `cmp` does for strings. The operator `cmp` gives us a three-valued comparison of a pair of strings on the basis of their lexicographic ordering as dictated by the ASCII codes associated with the characters. Note the call to `sort()` in line (g):

```
sort {$a cmp $b} @arr;
```

If the lexicographic order dictates that the string bound to `$a` must come before the string bound to `$b`, `cmp` will return -1. If they are both the same string, `cmp` will return 0. Otherwise, it will return +1. When `sort` is called without a comparison subroutine, it uses the `cmp` operator by default. This is illustrated by the call to `sort()` in lines (e) and (g). They both produce the same sorted order. The advantage of using `cmp` explicitly is that we can modify the values of the special variables `$a` and `$b` to alter the comparison criterion. Note the call to `sort()` in line (i):

```
sort {"\L$a" cmp "\L$b"} @arr;
```

This call shows how the inline comparison function supplied to `sort` can be modified for a case-insensitive string comparison. This comparison function

```
{ "\L$a" cmp "\L$b" }
```

uses the operator `\L` to modify the string values bound to the variables `$a` and `$b`. As shown in Section 2.1.2, the operator `\L`, when used inside a double-quoted string, interpolates into the string a lowercase version of the argument. The operator `\U` used in line (k), on the other hand, turns its argument into all uppercase. The same effect could also have been achieved by using the built-in functions `uc()` and `lc()`. The former returns an all-uppercase version of its string argument, and the latter an all-lowercase version.

It is important that the comparison subroutine supplied to `sort` not modify the values bound to the variables `$a` and `$b`. That is because `$a` and `$b` serve as aliases for the actual elements in the container being sorted. Any modifications to the values bound to `$a` and `$b` will change the elements in the container.

```
#!/usr/bin/perl -w

### DisplayingArrays.pl

use strict;

my @arr = ('one', 'two', 'three', 'four');                          #(A)

print "@arr\n";             # one two three four                    #(B)

print @arr;                 # onetwothreefour                       #(C)
print "\n";                                                         #(D)
```

```
print @arr . "\n";          # 4                                         #(E)

print "$arr[1]\n";          # two                                       #(F)

print $#arr. "\n";          # 3                                         #(G)

$#arr = 9;                  # expand the array to 10 elements           #(H)

# For printing out the contents of the expanded array:
foreach (@arr) {                                                        #(I)
    if (defined) {                                                      #(J)
        print $_ . " ";                                                 #(K)
    } else {                                                            #(L)
        print "undef ";                                                 #(M)
    }
}       #  one two three four undef undef undef undef undef undef       #(N)

print "\n";

# Another way to print out the contents of the expanded array:
for my $i (0..$#arr) {                                                  #(O)
    if (defined($arr[$i])) {                                            #(P)
        print $arr[$i] . " ";                                           #(Q)
    } else {                                                            #(R)
        print "undef ";                                                 #(S)
    }
}       #  one two three four undef undef undef undef undef undef       #(T)

print "\n";

# print $arr[7];                      # WARNING                         #(U)

# print "@arr\n";                     # WARNING                         #(V)

#Sorting experiments:

@arr = (94, 7, 34, 87, 5);                                              #(W)
my @sorted = sort @arr;                                                 #(X)
print "@sorted\n";                    # 34 5 7 87 94                    #(Y)

@sorted = sort {$a <=> $b} @arr;                                        #(Z)
print "@sorted\n";                    # 5 7 34 87 94                    #(a)

@sorted = sort {$b <=> $a} @arr;                                        #(b)
print "@sorted\n";                    # 94 87 34 7 5                    #(c)

@arr = ("hello", "JELLO", "hELLO", "JELlo", "yello");                   #(d)
my @sorted = sort @arr;                                                 #(e)
print "@sorted\n";                    # JELLO JELlo hELLO hello yello #(f)
```

```
@sorted = sort {$a cmp $b} @arr;                                  #(g)
print "@sorted\n";                  # JELLO JELlo hELLO hello yello #(h)

@sorted = sort {"\L$a" cmp "\L$b"} @arr;                          #(i)
print "@sorted\n";                  # hello hELLO JELLO JELlo yello #(j)

@sorted = sort {"\U$a" cmp "\U$b"} @arr;                          #(k)
print "@sorted\n";                  # hello hELLO JELLO JELlo yello #(l)
```

2.5 DISPLAYING HASHES

Although their storage mechanisms are completely different, from a purely usage perspective it is not a stretch to think of arrays and hashes as being similar. Whereas the different elements of an array are indexed by integers, the different values stored in a hash are indexed by the symbolic names that are used as keys. Just as one can talk about a slice of an array, meaning the elements whose indices fall in a specified range, one can talk about a hash slice, which consists of the key-value pairs for which the keys belong to a specified set.

As with an array, there are different ways to output a hash. One can output just the keys, or just the values, or both the keys and the values separately, or both the keys and the values together. Again, as with arrays, a seemingly small difference in the syntax used for outputting all or some aspect of a hash can produce a completely different result. The next script, `DisplayingHashes.pl`, shows examples of the different ways of examining the contents of a hash.

Line (A) of the script defines `%hash` as a hash. Line (B) demonstrates that you cannot display the contents of a hash by interpolating it into a double-quoted string. The output produced by line (B) is simply the string `%hash`.[42]

Line (C) shows what happens if we invoke the print command directly on a hash. As we will mention in Section 2.8 where we discuss the different evaluation contexts of Perl, `print()` causes its arguments to be evaluated in a list context. The list context evaluation of `%hash` in line (C) returns a simple list whose alternate entries are the keys and the values. As the reader has already seen in the previous section, when `print()` is supplied with a list of scalar values, it simply prints out the

[42]What this means is that the character `%` does not possess any special meaning inside a double-quoted string, unlike the characters `$` and `@`, which cause, respectively, a scalar and a vector to be interpolated into the string.

values one after another without any spaces in between. That is what we see in the commented-out output in line (C).

Except for the newline, the output produced by line (D) is identical to what we get from line (C). Line (D) supplies two comma-separated arguments to `print()`. Each comma-separated argument to `print()` is evaluated in a list context.

However, line (E), which differs from line (D) only by the presence of a period where there was a comma before, produces an entirely different output. That is because the period is the string concatenation operator. This operator has a higher precedence compared to `print` when treated as an operator. The concatenation operator supplies a scalar context for the two operands on its either side. So in this case, `%hash` is evaluated in a scalar context. When a hash variable, such as `%hash` here, is evaluated in a scalar context, it returns a nonzero number for hashes that have at least one key-value pair. This number is usually a ratio of the number of buckets occupied to the number of buckets allocated in the hash table.

Line (F) shows the syntax for interpolating one hash value in a double-quoted string.

In lines (G) and (I), and in the commented-out lines (H) and (J), we experiment with the print syntax in which we invoke the `keys` and the `values` operators[43] in the first argument to `print`. This does not work when we have a period separating the invocation of `keys` (or of `values`) and a substring that consists of just the newline character. The reason for this is not difficult to understand. Since the concatenation operator, meaning the period, in line (H) has a higher precedence compared to `keys`, the parse of the syntax in line (H) presents to the `keys` operator not the argument `%hash`, but a tree rooted at the concatenation operator. This, for obvious reasons, causes the compiler to complain.

Lines (K) through (N) show a variation on the syntax in lines (G) through (J). Instead of invoking `keys` and `values` as operators, we now invoke them as functions. Note that we do not run into the same parsing problems in lines (L) and (N) that we did earlier in lines (H) and (J). But also note the rather unexpected output produced by the lines (L) and (N). The reason is that the concatenation operator causes the output of `keys()` and `values()` to be evaluated in a scalar context. What we get back in the scalar context is the just the number of keys and the number of values, as already mentioned in Section 2.2.3. This is confirmed in lines (O) and (P) that explicitly supply scalar contexts for the evaluation of `keys` and `values`.

Lines (Q) and (R) illustrate the use of the `each` operator for iterating over a hash. As described in Section 2.2.3, each application of this operator fetches the next key-value pair from the hash. Another method of iterating over a hash is with the `foreach` control structure in lines (S) through (W). Line (T) shows the use of the `exists` predicate to check whether a hash element exists for a given key.

---

[43]The distinction between operators and functions will become clear in Section 2.7.

Lines (X) through (a) show another way to iterate over a hash. We again use a `while` loop to iterate over the hash, but this time we pop the arrays `@keys` and `@values` as we go along.

The example in lines (b) and (c) shows how you can scan a hash in a key-sorted manner. The default behavior of the built-in `sort` function in line (m) is to order the keys according to the lexicographic order dictated by the ASCII codes associated with the characters. Recall that only string objects are allowed for hash keys.

Lines (d) and (e) show how one can scan a hash in a value-sorted order. Now it is necessary to alter the default behavior of `sort` by supplying it with a comparison subroutine. As mentioned in the previous section, this subroutine, which may either be supplied by name or in the form of a braces-delimited block of code, tells `sort` how it should compare any two elements of the container that is being sorted. Note the syntax of this comparison function in line (d):

```
{ $hash{$b} <=> $hash{$a} }
```

Recall from the previous section that the binary operator `<=>` returns one of three possible integers, -1, 0, or 1, depending on whether the left operand is less than, equal to, or greater than the right operand. Both operands supplied to `<=>` must be numbers. Also recall that the variables `$a` and `$b` in a comparison function supplied to `sort` are system-defined. In accordance with our earlier explanation, since the left operand mentions `$b` and the right operand `$a`, the sorted order will be descending with respect to the meaning of the "less than" operator being used.

The example in lines (f), (g), and (h) demonstrates displaying the hash in case-insensitive key-sorted order. This is accomplished by using the following comparison subroutine in the call to `sort()`:

```
{ "\L$a" cmp "\L$b" }
```

which uses Perl's `cmp` operator for a three-valued comparison of a pair of strings on the basis of lexicographic ordering dictated by the ASCII codes associated with the characters. See Section 2.4 for further explanation on the `cmp` operator and on the `\L` operator used here for case-insensitive comparison of strings.

```
#!/usr/bin/perl -w

# DisplayingHashes.pl

use strict;

my %hash = (a => 11, b => 12, c => 13 );                           #(A)

print "%hash\n";                        # %hash (NOT WHAT YOU WANT) #(B)

print %hash;                            # c13a11b12                 #(C)
```

```
print "\n";

print %hash, "\n";                        # c13a11b12             #(D)

print %hash . "\n";                       # 3/8                   #(E)

print "$hash{b}\n";                       # 12                    #(F)

print keys %hash, "\n";                   # cab                   #(G)
#print keys %hash . "\n";                 # ERROR                 #(H)
print values %hash, "\n";                 # 131112                #(I)
#print values %hash . "\n";               # ERROR                 #(J)

print keys(%hash), "\n";                  # cab                   #(K)
print keys(%hash) . "\n";                 # 3                     #(L)
print values(%hash), "\n";                # 131112                #(M)
print values(%hash) . "\n";               # 3                     #(N)

print scalar keys %hash, "\n";            # 3                     #(O)
print scalar values %hash, "\n";          # 3                     #(P)

# For printing out each key-value pair in a separate line:
while ( my ($k, $v ) = each %hash) {                              #(Q)
    print "$k => $v\n";                                           #(R)
}                                         # c => 13
                                          # a => 11
                                          # b => 12

# Another way to print out each key-value pair in a separate line:
foreach my $kee ( keys %hash ) {                                  #(S)
    if ( exists $hash{$kee} ) {                                   #(T)
        print "$kee => $hash{$kee}\n";                            #(U)
    } else {                                                      #(V)
        print "NO ENTRY FOR THIS KEY\n";                          #(W)
    }
}                                         # c => 13
                                          # a => 11
                                          # b => 12

# Yet another way to iterate over a hash:
my @keys = keys %hash;                                            #(X)
my @values = values %hash;                                        #(Y)
while (@keys) {                                                   #(Z)
    print pop(@keys), ' => ', pop(@values), "\n";                 #(a)
}                                         # b => 12
                                          # a => 11
                                          # c => 13

# Iterating over a hash in a key-sorted manner:
```

```
foreach my $key (sort(keys %hash)) {                                    #(b)
    print $key, ' => ', $hash{$key}, "\n";                              #(c)
}                                              # a => 11
                                               # b => 12
                                               # c => 13

# Iterating over a hash in a value-sorted manner:
foreach my $key (sort { $hash{$b} <=> $hash{$a} } keys %hash) {        #(d)
    printf "%2d <= %s\n", $hash{$key}, $key;                            #(e)
}                                              # 13 <= c
                                               # 12 <= b
                                               # 11 <= a

# Iterating over a hash in a case-insensitive key-sorted manner:
%hash = qw( cat 1 CAT 2 DOG 3 dog 4 );                                  #(f)
foreach my $key (sort { "\L$a" cmp "\L$b" } keys %hash) {               #(g)
    printf "%s => %s\n", $key, $hash{$key};                             #(h)
}                                              # CAT => 2
                                               # cat => 1
                                               # dog => 4
                                               # DOG => 3
```

2.6 TERMINAL AND FILE I/O

Perl provides three streams: STDIN for standard input, STDOUT for standard output, and STDERR for standard error. During the execution of a script, these streams, usually called *filehandles* in Perl parlance, are attached to files or devices as dictated by the process in which the script is running. Ordinarily, the stream STDOUT sends its output to the terminal screen, the stream STDIN reads input from the terminal screen, and the stream STDERR also sends its output error messages to the terminal screen.[44]

[44] In addition to being redirectable by the process executing a script, these standard streams may also be redirected inside a script with the open command, as by the invocation:

```
open STDIN, "/usr/share/dict/words";
```

The input information read through STDIN would now be fetched from the file /usr/share/dict/words.

2.6.1 Terminal I/O

Information that is available at the STDIN input stream can be read into a script using the *line input operator* <>, also known as the *diamond operator*. The next script, TermIO.pl, shows three ways of accomplishing this. The invocations of the line input operator in lines (B) and (E) explicitly mention the STDIN stream through the syntax <STDIN>. The invocation of the same operator in line (H) does not mention STDIN. Nevertheless, it will also read from STDIN implicitly, provided the script is called with no command-line arguments. If the script were to be called with command-line arguments in the following manner:

```
TermIO.pl data1.txt data2.txt
```

the arguments data1.txt and data2.txt would be placed in the system-supplied array @ARGS. The line input operator <> would then read from these files named in the array.[45]

All of these invocations of the line input operator in the script are in the scalar context supplied by the conditional of the while loops.[46] That means that only one line at a time will be read from STDIN. In the first loop, the input line is placed in the scalar $input. On the other hand, the input line in the second loop is read into Perl's default variable $_. The same thing happens in the third loop.

When reading from a terminal, the line input operator <> returns the null object undef when the user hits Ctrl-D on the keyboard. As we will mention in Section 2.9.3, the value undef evaluates to false in the conditional of a while loop. So each while loop in the script below will continue to execute as long as the user does not enter Ctrl-D on the keyboard. An entry of Ctrl-D will transfer control to the next while loop of the script. An entry of Ctrl-C at any time will terminate the script immediately. While the entry of Ctrl-D causes <> to return undef, the entry of Ctrl-C is handled differently, in that the default behavior of the Perl virtual machine is to trap the signal issued by the operating system for the Ctrl-C entry and abort immediately.

```
#!/usr/bin/perl -w

### TermIO.pl

use strict;
```

[45]Note that unlike the argc and argv of C, only the command-line *arguments* are stored in Perl's @ARGV. The name of the script itself is stored in the special variable $0. Perl also comes with a scalar variable $ARGV whose value is the name of the file from which the line input operator <> is currently reading. If the line input operator is reading from the standard input, the value of $ARGV is the symbol - that is used in Unix for denoting the standard input. For example, in Unix, the command cat - causes cat to read from the standard input, while sending its output to the standard output.

[46]See Section 2.8 for the context dependencies of Perl's operators and functions.

```
# All loops below do the same thing.  Enter Ctrl-D
# to switch from one loop to the next.  The third
# entry of Ctrl-D will terminate the script.

print "Starting first loop:\n";                               #(A)
while ( my $input = <STDIN> ) {                               #(B)
    print "FIRST LOOP:  You said =>    $input";               #(C)
}

print "Starting second loop:\n";                              #(D)
while ( <STDIN> ) {                                           #(E)
    print "SECOND LOOP:  You said =>    $_";                  #(F)
}

print "Starting third loop:\n";                               #(G)
while ( <> ) {                                                #(H)
    print "THIRD LOOP:  You said =>    $_";                   #(I)
}
```

The above script also shows examples of output to STDOUT, the standard output stream. The print commands in lines (C), (F), and (I) will, by default, send their outputs to STDOUT, which, unless redirected, is the terminal window in which the script is invoked. An output statement such as the one shown in line (C) is equivalent to

```
print STDOUT "FIRST LOOP:  You said =>    $input";
```

Note that there is no comma after STDOUT in this statement. If we wanted to send the information to the standard error stream, we would have said

```
print STDERR "FIRST LOOP:  You said =>    $input";
```

As already mentioned, ordinarily both STDOUT and STDERR send their output to the terminal window in which the script is invoked. But they can be redirected independently, as demonstrated by the script `StdErr.pl` shown next. This script echos back each line you enter in the terminal window after prefixing it with the `You said:` string. The echo is sent to the standard output STDOUT. The script also determines the length of the string you entered in each line. The value of this length is sent to the standard error stream STDERR. In some Unix shells (for example, bash), if you call this script with the invocation

```
StdErr.pl 2> length_log
```

the STDERR stream will be redirected to write into the file `length_log`, whereas the STDOUT stream will echo the user-entered strings to the terminal window. The shells that allow for such command-line redirection of the standard streams associate the file descriptor 0 with the standard input, the file descriptor 1 with the standard output, and the file descriptor 2 with the standard error.

```
#!/usr/bin/perl -w

### StdErr.pl

use strict;

while ( my $input = <STDIN> ) {                                  #(A)
    print STDOUT "You said =>    $input";                        #(B)
    my $len = length $input;                                     #(C)
    print STDERR "$len\n";                                       #(D)
}
```

2.6.2 File I/O

Perl provides us with the built-in function `open()` that can be used in a script to attach a stream, or, synonymously, a filehandle, with a disk file, an output device, another process, etc., through an invocation like

```
open( FILEHANDLE, filename );
```

or, for defensive scripting, through the syntax

```
open( FILEHANDLE, filename )
        or die "unable to open file: $!";
```

which depends on the fact that, upon failure, `open()` returns the null object `undef`, which evaluates to false in a Boolean context.[47] Upon success, `open()` returns a nonzero value, which evaluates to true. The identifier `FILEHANDLE` is any programmer chosen name for the stream; by common practice it is usually all uppercase. The `or` operator will cause `die` to be invoked upon failure of `open`. The string argument given to `die` is output to the `STDERR` stream.[48] [49]

[47] See Section 10.1 of Chapter 10 for the four ways in which `die` can be called for immediate termination of a script should something go wrong.

[48] When `die`-like action for script termination is needed inside a subroutine, it is often more useful to use `croak()` from the `Carp` module. When `croak()` gets invoked, the system will also print out the identity of the calling function. On the other hand, with `die`, only the location of the line containing the `die` statement is printed out when the script is terminated. The same applies to the built-in `warn()` vis-à-vis the `carp()` function provided by the `Carp` module.

A filehandle that is opened with a call to `open()` is, by default, meant for reading from a file. To make it explicit that you want to read from a file, you can say

```
open( FILEHANDLE, "< data.txt" )
        or die "unable to open file: $!";
```

To open a filehandle for writing, you need to reverse the direction implied by the angle bracket above:

```
open( FILEHANDLE, "> data.txt" )
        or die "unable to open file: $!";
```

To open a file in the append mode, that is, when you don't want to clobber the existing file, you say

```
open( FILEHANDLE, ">> data.txt" )
        or die "unable to open file: $!";
```

To open a filehandle for both reading and writing operations, you say

```
open( FILEHANDLE, "+< data.txt" )
        or die "unable to open file: $!";
```

which assumes that the file `data.txt` already exists on the disk. If you want to create a new file for read/write access, you can say

```
open( FILEHANDLE, "+> data.txt" )
        or die "unable to open file: $!";
```

If you want to take advantage of both modes simultaneously, that is, open an existing file if it is there or create a new one if the specified file does not exist, you will use the following syntax:

```
open( FILEHANDLE, "+>> data.txt" )
        or die "unable to open file: $!";
```

When a filehandle is opened for both reading and writing, the built-in function `seek()` sets the position of the file pointer for the next read/write operation. The next call to `read()` will start from this position onwards and the next call to `print()` will start writing from that position, assuming that the read and the write operations are invoked on the filehandle that is supplied as the first argument to `seek()`. A call to seek typically looks like

```
seek(FILEHANDLE, $pos, 0)
```

[49]Note that the argument supplied to the `die` in the examples shown has the special scalar variable `$!` embedded in it at the end. Upon failure of a system call, Perl sets this variable to an internally generated error message substring which often holds a clue as to why the system call may have failed. On Unix systems, the error message stored in the variable `$!` would be the same as retrieved by the C function `perror`. See Chapter 10 for further details regarding this.

which would cause the file pointer to be positioned at `$pos` bytes from the beginning of the file. The other possible values for the third argument are 1 and 2, the former for setting the file pointer relative to the previous position and the latter for positioning the pointer with respect to the end of the file. Obviously, for the last case, the value of the second argument must be negative.

To close a filehandle, you say

```
close FILE_HANDLE;
```

or, even more safely, by

```
close( FILEHANDLE )
        or die "unable to close file: $!";
```

Closing a stream will flush any input/output buffers associated with the stream. Reopening a previously opened stream resets the stream to point to the beginning of the file; it is as if the stream was closed and then opened again. Exiting a script will also automatically close an open stream and flush the buffers associated with the stream.

We can also use `open()` to launch a process and to then stay in communication with the same. This will be explained in greater detail in Section 2.17.5.

2.6.2.1 I/O for Text Files

The script `TextFileIO.pl` shown next wants to write information into a text file called `data_out.txt`. The call to `open()` in line (A) associates the filehandle `FILEOUT` with the file. The source of what is written into the file depends on which `while` loop is executed — the one in lines (D), (E), and (F), or the one in lines (J), (K), and (L). The selection of the `while` loop is determined by how the script is called. If the script is called with one or more command-line arguments, as in

```
TextFileIO.pl data1.txt data2.txt
```

Perl will store the file names in the command line in the special array `@ARGV`. In this case, the conditional of the `if` statement in line (C) will evaluate to true. The line input operator `<>` in line (D) will then read one line at a time from all of the files in the array `@ARGV` into the default variable `$_`. Line (E) will output to the standard output the current value of this variable, and line (F) will write out this value to the stream `FILEOUT`.

On the other hand, if the script is invoked without any command-line arguments, as in

```
TextFileIO.pl
```

the array `@ARGV` will now be empty. As a result, the code in lines (H) through (L) will be executed. This code first opens the file `data.txt` for reading in line (H).

The call to the line input operator in line (J) then reads this file one line at a time, the line being deposited in the default variable `$_`. The current value of `$_` is output to the terminal window in line (K) and written out to the file `data_out.txt` in line (L).

```
#!/usr/bin/perl -w

### TextFileIO.pl

use strict;

open FILEOUT, ">data_out.txt"                                           #(A)
        or die "unable to open file: $!";                               #(B)

if (@ARGV) {                                                            #(C)
    while (<>) {                                                        #(D)
        print;                                                          #(E)
        print FILEOUT;                                                  #(F)
    }
} else {                                                                #(G)
    open FILEIN, "data.txt"                                             #(H)
        or die "unable to open file: $!";                               #(I)
    while (<FILEIN>) {                                                  #(J)
        print;                                                          #(K)
        print FILEOUT;                                                  #(L)
    }
}
```

Any file reading that the script `TextFileIO.pl` carries out is done one line at a time. That is because all the invocations of the line input operator `<>` in this script take place in the scalar context supplied by the conditional of a `while` loop.[50] If we try to read the output of `<>` directly into an array, thus providing the operator `<>` with a list context, we can read an entire file all at once. This is shown in the next script, `Slurp.pl`. If any file names are specified in the command line, this script will execute the lines (D) through (F). Otherwise, the lines (H) through (L) will be executed. In either case, we read from the line input operator into an array. For the invocation in line (D), we read *all* of the files named in the command line at once into the array `@all_of_it`, with each line stored in a separate element of the array. The invocation of the line input operator in line (J) does the same thing — it reads the file `data.txt` all at once into the array `@all_of_it`, again storing each line

[50]The different evaluation contexts of Perl are discussed in Section 2.8.

in a separate element of the array. (Another way to slurp in an entire file all at once is presented in Section 2.9.4.)

Note also how we write the lines stored in the array `@all_of_it` all at once into the output file `data_out.txt` in lines (F) and (L) of the script.

```
#!/usr/bin/perl -w

### Slurp.pl

use strict;

open FILEOUT, ">data_out.txt"                                   #(A)
        or die "unable to open file: $!";                      #(B)

if (@ARGV) {                                                    #(C)
    my @all_of_it = <>;                                         #(D)
    print @all_of_it;                                           #(E)
    print FILEOUT @all_of_it;                                   #(F)
} else {                                                        #(G)
    open FILEIN, "data.txt";                                    #(H)
        or die "unable to open file: $!";                      #(I)
    my @all_of_it = <FILEIN>;                                   #(J)
    print @all_of_it;                                           #(K)
    print FILEOUT @all_of_it;                                   #(L)
}
```

2.6.2.2 I/O for Binary Files

The previous subsection dealt with I/O for text files. What about the files that contain object code, images, video clips, and so on? I/O operations related to such files are important for copying them byte-by-byte from one file system to another on the same machine or from one machine to another on a network. Byte-level I/O operations for such files are also useful for peering into the files for diagnostic purposes.

Before we delve into byte-level I/O for binary files, let's first see how one would write out an integer to a file in its binary form as opposed to in its print representation. Let us say that the integer that a script wants to write to a file is the decimal 825373492. We choose this rather strange looking integer because its binary form is printable. Most modern machines use 4 bytes to store an integer. In the big-endian representation used by the Sparc family of processors, the internally stored 4-byte representation of the integer 825373492 when expressed in hexadecimal form is 31323334. This 4-byte bit pattern translates into an ASCII print-out of 1234. (Hex 31 maps to the character 1, hex 32 to the character 2, hex 33 to the character 3, and hex 34 to the character 4.) So if the integer 825373492 was actually written out to a file in its binary form (and *not* in its print representation), and if we subsequently read the file in the character mode, we should see 1234 in the file. Note that in the big-endian representation, the most significant byte is at the leftmost end of a bit pattern. On Windows machines that use the x86 family of processors, the 4-byte integer 825373492 would be stored in the little-endian form where the most significant byte is at the rightmost end. Now the hex form of the decimal 825373492 would be 34333231 — this would be the bit pattern stored in the memory of the computer. If this pattern were to be written out to a file in the binary mode and the file read in the character mode, we should see 4321 in the file.

To write out the decimal 825373492 in its binary form to a file, we obviously cannot say

```
$x = 825373492;
print( FILEHANDLE  $x );
```

since that would output the 9-byte print representation of the decimal integer and not its 4-byte binary representation. We could try the other not-uncommonly used output function used in Perl, `syswrite()`:

```
$x = 825373492;
syswrite( FILEHANDLE, $x, length($x) );
```

that also outputs just the print representation of the integer. To output the binary form of what is contained in `$x`, we must first invoke the `pack()` function discussed earlier in Section 2.1.2 to gain access to the binary representation of the integer, as shown below:

```
$x = 825373492;
$bin = pack( "I", $x );
syswrite( FILEHANDLE, $bin, length($bin) );
```

The last statement will write to the file a bit pattern whose print presentation will be 1234 on a big-endian machine and 4321 on a little-endian machine. Instead of `syswrite()`, we could also have called `print()` to achieve the desired output.

Let's now talk about the I/O for binary files. If the goal is simply to read a binary file from a source and to copy it over to some destination, one can use a `while` loop that makes repeated calls to `sysread()` and `syswrite()`:

```
open FROM, "source_file";                                      #(A)
open TO, ">destination_file";                                  #(B)
binmode( FROM );                                               #(C)
binmode( TO );                                                 #(D)
my $buf;                                                       #(E)
while (sysread(FROM, $buff, 1024)) {                           #(F)
```

```
        syswrite(TO, $buff, length($buf));                          #(G)
    }
```

The call in line (F) will try to read 1024 bytes from the source attached to the filehandle `FROM` into the scalar `$buff`. If fewer than 1024 bytes are found remaining in the file, it will go ahead and read however many bytes there are in the file into the scalar. The size of the scalar expands or shrinks depending on how many bytes are actually read by `sysread()`. The function returns the actual number of bytes read. The returned value is zero if nothing is read from the file. If there is an error during reading, `sysread()` will return `undef`. Therefore, it is appropriate to use the returned value as a Boolean in the conditional for the `while` loop, as we show above in line (F). After however many bytes are read into the scalar `$buff` by `sysread()`, they are written out to a destination file attached to the filehandle `TO` by the call to `syswrite()` in line (G). If we wanted to carry out a byte-by-byte copy in the `while` loop shown above, one can also use a two-argument version of `syswrite()`:

```
    syswrite( TO, $buff )
```

Both `sysread()` and `syswrite()` also support a four-argument call in which the last argument is for supplying an offset for the read and write operations; the offset determines the exactly position in a file for the I/O operation. The calls to the `binmode` function in lines (C) and (D) above are for old systems that distinguish between binary and text streams; most modern systems do not. The calls set the streams to binary mode.

While the code we showed above works fine for byte-by-byte copying of a binary file, what if we want to read the binary data into a script and extract some sort of information from it? Toward that end, our next script, `BinaryFileIO.pl`, shows how to create a hex dump of a binary file. The raw bytes of a binary file cannot all be displayed for obvious reasons — since not all the bytes will possess printable character representations. However, if it is necessary to peer into a binary file for diagnostic reasons, we can print out the hex representation of each byte, as we show in the next script.

The next script creates two outputs from the input file whose name is supplied as a command-line argument. One output consists of a hex dump of the input file. Each byte of the input file, treated as an unsigned integer between 0 and 255, is converted into its hexadecimal representation. This representation is output into a file called `out.hex`. The other output consists of simply a byte-by-byte copy of the input binary file. The name of this output is `out`. The script is called with a command-line invocation:

```
    BinaryFileIO.pl input_file_name
```

Line (A) of the script ensures that the command line has exactly one argument. Line (B) opens the input file for reading. Lines (C) and (D) open two output files for writing, `dump.hex` for the hex dump and `out` for the byte-by-byte copy. Line (E) then reads one byte at a time. The value stored in the scalar `$byte` will be the unsigned integer representation of the one byte read from the file. Line (F) creates a string representation of the 1's and 0's from this number. The symbol `b` in the format string `%vb` in line (F) tells `sprintf()` that the supplied argument needs to be converted into the binary representation of an unsigned integer. The flag `v` in the format string tells `sprintf()` that the supplied string, bound to `$byte`, should be treated as a vector of integers — one integer for each character in the string.

Now we can invoke the `bin2dec()` function from the Perl Cookbook [7] to convert the "stringified" bit pattern returned in line (F) into a decimal integer. The definition of this function `bin2dec()` is shown in lines (K) and (L). It basically calls on the `unpack()` function with the `"N"` template to convert the stringified bit pattern into a decimal integer. The prepending of 32 zeros to the left of the supplied bit string and then extracting the last 32 elements of the augmented bit string is to take care of the fact that line (F) deletes any leading zeros from the bit string. So the concatenation with zeros from the left and the extraction of the last 32 bits restores the leading zeros if needed.

With the unsigned decimal integer representation of the byte read now available to us, we can output its hex representation as shown in line (H). The conversion specifier in that line, `%x`, puts out the hexadecimal representation of an unsigned integer value. (In case the reader is wondering why we did not supply `$byte` directly as the third argument to `printf()` in line (H), that does not work because `printf()` in that statement wants its third argument to be an unsigned integer, a condition that, in general, will not be fulfilled by the value of `$byte`.

To create a byte-level copy of the input file, we call on `pack()` in line (I) with the `"I"` template string to create a 4-byte binary word. We then output the least significant byte from this word in line (J).

The script shown below also includes the other bit-pattern to decimal number conversion function from the Perl Cookbook [7]. This function, `dec2bin()`, shown in lines (M) through (P), does the opposite of what we used `bin2dec()` for. The function `dec2bin()` returns a bit string for a given decimal integer.

```
#!/usr/bin/perl -w

### BinaryFileIO.pl

use strict;

die "Needs one command-line argument" unless @ARGV == 1;              #(A)

open FILEIN, shift @ARGV or die "unable to open file: $!";           #(B)
open FILEOUT, ">out" or die "unable to open file: $!";               #(C)
open FILEDUMP, ">dump.hex" or die "unable to open file: $!";         #(D)

my $byte;
```

```
while ( sysread FILEIN, $byte, 1 ) {                              #(E)
    my $str = sprintf "%vb", $byte;                               #(F)
    my $x = bin2dec( $str );                                      #(G)
    printf FILEDUMP "%x ", $x;                                    #(H)
    my $bin = pack("I", $x);                                      #(I)
    syswrite FILEOUT, $bin, 1;                                    #(J)
}

#From "Perl Cookbook"
sub bin2dec {                                                     #(K)
    return unpack("N", pack("B32", substr("0" x 32 . shift, -32)));#(L)
}

#From "Perl Cookbook"
sub dec2bin {                                                     #(M)
    my $str = unpack("B32", pack("N", shift));                    #(N)
    $str =~ s/^0+(?=\d)//;                                        #(O)
    return $str;                                                  #(P)
}
```

In the previous example, we read one byte at a time from a binary file. But what if we wanted to read, say, 8 bytes at a time, our goal being to produce 64-bit long bitstrings? We can use the same call to `sysread` as before, except that now the last argument must be set to 8 for the 8 bytes we want to read in one go. However, placing the bits read into a bitstring with a call to `sprintf()` requires some care. Consider the following code snippet that tries to read 8 bytes at a time. Pay attention to the conversion specifier in line (F): `%*v08b`. The number 8 before the flag `b` assigns a field width of 8 for each element of the contents of `$buff` when it is interpreted as a vector of integers, one integer corresponding to each byte. The number 0 before 8 says to use zeros as a filler for left-justifying the contents in each 8-position field. Without this 0, the leftmost 0's of the binary representation of the integers in `$buff` would be discarded. The flag `v` before 0 tells `sprintf()` that *each character* of the string bound to `$buff` should be thought of as an integer. Finally, the flag `*` that precedes the flag `v` tells `sprintf()` that the value of what comes before the flag `v` is to be taken from the next argument to `sprintf()`.

```
open FROM, "junk.txt";                                            #(A)
binmode( FROM );                                                  #(B)
my $buff;                                                         #(C)
sysread( FROM, $buff, 8 );                                        #(D)
print "$buff\n";                                                  #(E)
my $str = sprintf "%*v08b", " ", $buff;                           #(F)
print "$str\n";                                                   #(G)
print length( $str ), "\n";                                       #(H)
```

The following output is produced by this snippet for a text file that contains only the string `A hungry brown fox` followed by the newline character:

```
A hungry
01000001 00100000 01101000 01110101 01101110 01100111 01110010 01111001
71
```

where the first line, produced by the print statement of line (E), shows the 8 characters read into the scalar `$buff`. The second line, output by the print statement in line (G), is the corresponding bitstring stored in the scalar `$str`. The last line is the total length of the bitstring. If we change the call to `sprintf()` in line (F) so that its second argument is now an empty string:

```
my $str = sprintf "%*v08b", "", $buff;
```

we get the output:

```
A hungry
0100000100100000011010000111010101101110011001110111001001111001
64
```

which is what we want. If we choose not to supply the second argument to `sprintf()` and, at the same time, not to use the symbol `*` before the flag `v`, we get

```
A hungry
01000001.00100000.01101000.01110101.01101110.01100111.01110010.01111001
71
```

since the default behavior of the conversion specifier `%vb` introduces a dot between the elements of the third argument when it is interpreted as a vector of integers.

For writing production quality scripts that involve bit processing, a popular module to use is `Bit::Vector`. To demonstrate just a few features of this large module, we will now show a simple exercise in block encryption of a data file. We want to read the file in blocks of 64 bits and replace each block with a randomly permuted block. In order to keep the script small, we will keep the permutation order fixed for all the blocks. This permutation order then becomes the encryption key. On the decryption side, we will then use the same permutation key to decrypt the encrypted file.

The script `BlockEncrypt.pl` shown next reads a data file in binary mode with programmer-specified `BLOCKSIZE` bits at a time. `BLOCKSIZE` must be a multiple of 8 because `sysread()` only reads in multiples of bytes. There is, of course, no reason to assume that the size of a file will always be an exact multiple of `BLOCKSIZE`. When the file size in bits is not a multiple of `BLOCKSIZE`, extra bytes are attached at the end of the file in lines (O) and (P) of the script. The extra characters added consist of the number `0`, repeated as many times as necessary.

Encryption takes place by first randomly permuting an array of integers from 0 through `BLOCKSIZE-1` in lines (J) and (K). This permutation key is saved away in a file in line (L) and later used for permuting the plaintext blocks in line (T).

As to why we need the `Bit::Vector` module, the problem is that the information that is read by `sysread()` is in units of bytes. Let's say you are asking `sysread()` to read 64-bit blocks. When `sysread()` deposits this bit block into the scalar that serves as the buffer, `$buff`, the bit block can only be decomposed into individual bytes. But a byte-level decomposition is not sufficient for us because we want to carry out permutation at the bit level and NOT at the byte level. Note that byte-level permutation of a text file would be no different from alphabetic permutation — a method of encryption that is most easily broken by statistical analysis of the encrypted output, such as by making a simple histogram of the encrypted text and searching for the most frequently occurring characters, etc. That is where `Bit::Vector` comes to our rescue. Lines (Q) and (R) construct a bit vector from the scalar into which `sysread()` writes the bits it extracts from the input file. Note the use of `Bit::Vector->Store($bitstring)` to create a bit vector from a string representation of all the bits. Subsequently, when we invoke `$bitvec->to_Bin()` in line (S), what that returns is a bitstring.

Perhaps the best way to state the difference between the `BLOCKSIZE` bits in `$buff` and the `BLOCKSIZE` bits in what is returned by `$bitvec->to_Bin()` is that the former stores a bytestring and the latter stores a bitstring. So if we had applied `split()` directly to the contents of `$buff`, we would have obtained a character-level decomposition. On the other hand, applying `split()` to the bitstring returned by `$bitvec->to_Bin()` gives us a truly bit-level decomposition that is subsequently permuted in line (T).

We feed the permuted array back into a `Bit::Vector` object in line (V). There is a most important reason for why we do not want to write the permuted array directly into the output: The left-to-right order of the bits stored in a `Bit::Vector` object may not correspond to how the bits appear in an input data file. In fact, it could be the opposite, depending on the underlying architecture. So by having the `Bit::Vector` write out the information to the output file, we cancel out any ordering effects introduced at the data input time.

This script expects to be called with the command line:

```
BlockEncrypt.pl  in_file_name  out_file_name
```

where the command line arguments have obvious meanings. The script deposits the encryption key in a file named `keyfile.txt`.

```
#!/usr/bin/perl -w
use strict;

###  BlockEcrypt.pl

use Bit::Vector;                                                    #(A)
use constant BLOCKSIZE => 64;                                       #(B)
```

```
die "Needs two command-line arguments for in file and out file"        #(C)
    unless @ARGV == 2;                                                  #(D)

open FROM, shift @ARGV or die "unable to open file: $!";               #(E)
open TO, ">" . shift @ARGV or die "unable to open file: $!";           #(F)
open KEYFILE, "> keyfile.txt";                                          #(G)
binmode( FROM );                                                        #(H)
binmode( TO );                                                          #(I)

my @permute_indices = 0..BLOCKSIZE-1;                                   #(J)
fisher_yates_shuffle( \@permute_indices );                              #(K)
print KEYFILE "@permute_indices";                                       #(L)

while (1){                                                              #(M)
    my $num_of_bytes_read = sysread( FROM, my $buff, BLOCKSIZE/8 );     #(N)
    if ($num_of_bytes_read < BLOCKSIZE/8) {                             #(O)
        $buff .= '0' x (BLOCKSIZE/8 - $num_of_bytes_read);              #(P)
    }
    my $bitvec = Bit::Vector->new(BLOCKSIZE);                           #(Q)
    $bitvec->Block_Store( $buff );                                      #(R)

    my @data_arr = split //, $bitvec->to_Bin();                         #(S)
    my @permuted_array = permute( \@data_arr, \@permute_indices );      #(T)

    my $permuted_bit_string = join "", @permuted_array;                 #(U)
    my $out_vector = Bit::Vector->new_Bin(BLOCKSIZE,
                                      $permuted_bit_string);            #(V)
    my $out_buff = $out_vector->Block_Read();                           #(W)
    syswrite( TO, $out_buff, BLOCKSIZE/8 );                             #(X)
    last if $num_of_bytes_read < BLOCKSIZE/8;                           #(Y)
}                                                                       #(Z)

sub fisher_yates_shuffle {                                              #(a)
    my $arr =  shift;                # ref to array to be shuffled      #(b)
    my $i = @$arr;                                                      #(c)
    while (--$i) {                                                      #(d)
        my $j = int rand( $i + 1 );                                     #(e)
        @$arr[$i, $j] = @$arr[$j, $i];                                  #(f)
    }
}

sub permute {                                                           #(f)
    my $ref1 = shift;            # ref to the array to be permuted      #(g)
    my $ref2 = shift;            # ref to the permutation array         #(h)
    my @data_arr = @$ref1;                                              #(i)
    my @permute_arr = @$ref2;                                           #(j)
    my @permuted_output;                                                #(k)
    for my $i (0..$#permute_arr) {                                      #(l)
```

```
        push @permuted_output, $data_arr[$permute_arr[$i]];          #(m)
    }
    return @permuted_output;                                         #(n)
}
```

Shown below is a script that decrypts the output produced by the above script. Since the output of `BlockEncrypt.pl` is always a multiple of `BLOCKSIZE` number of bits, we do not need to worry about having to read a fraction of `BLOCKSIZE` number of bits. This allows the call to `sysread()` to be placed directly in the condition of the `while` loop in line (H). As shown in lines (I) and (J), how we create a ṽerb+Bit::Vector+ object from a block of `BLOCKSIZE` bits is exactly the same as in the `BlockEncrypt.pl` script. When we invoke `$bitvec->to_Bin()` on the bit vector, we get a bitstring, as opposed to the bytestring that is stored in the buffer `$buff`. In lines (K) and (L), we send the bit array constructed from the bitstring to the `unpermute()` subroutine that undoes the permutation carried out by the encryption algorithm. This script is called with the command line:

```
    BlockDecrypt.pl  encrypted_file_name  out_file_name
```

The script assumes that the permutation order used by the encryption script is stored in a file called `keyfile.txt`.

```
#!/usr/bin/perl -w
use strict;

###  BlockDerypt.pl

use Bit::Vector;
use constant BLOCKSIZE => 64;

die "Needs two command-line arguments for in file and out file"
    unless @ARGV == 2;

open FROM, shift @ARGV or die "unable to open file: $!";             #(A)
open TO, ">" . shift @ARGV or die "unable to open file: $!";         #(B)
open KEYFILE, "keyfile.txt";                                         #(C)
binmode( FROM );                                                     #(D)
binmode( TO );                                                       #(E)

chomp( my $permute_indices = <KEYFILE> );                            #(F)
my @permute_indices = split / /, $permute_indices;                   #(G)

while ( sysread( FROM, my $buff, BLOCKSIZE/8 ) ) {                   #(H)
    my $bitvec = Bit::Vector->new(BLOCKSIZE);                        #(I)
    $bitvec->Block_Store( $buff );                                   #(J)
```

```
    my @data_arr = split //, $bitvec->to_Bin();                               #(K)

    my @decrypted = unpermute( \@data_arr, \@permute_indices );               #(L)

    my $decrypted_bit_string = join "", @decrypted;                           #(M)
    my $out_vector = Bit::Vector->new_Bin(BLOCKSIZE,
                                      $decrypted_bit_string);                 #(N)
    my $out_buff = $out_vector->Block_Read();                                 #(O)
    syswrite( TO, $out_buff, BLOCKSIZE/8 );                                   #(P)
}

sub unpermute {
    my $ref1 = shift;             # ref to the array to be unpermuted         #(Q)
    my $ref2 = shift;             # ref to the permutation array              #(R)
    my @data_arr = @$ref1;                                                    #(S)
    my @permute_arr = @$ref2;                                                 #(T)
    my @unpermuted_output;                                                    #(U)
    for my $i (0..$#permute_arr) {                                            #(V)
        $unpermuted_output[ $permute_arr[$i] ] = $data_arr[$i];               #(W)
    }
    return @unpermuted_output;                                                #(X)
}
```

2.7 FUNCTIONS, SUBROUTINES, AND FUNCTIONS USED AS OPERATORS

A user-defined function in Perl is called a *subroutine*. Built-in functions like `print()` and `chomp()` are referred to synonymously as functions or subroutines. In this book, when discussing Perl, we will use the terms *function* and *subroutine* interchangeably, whether user-defined or built-in. (Since a Perl function is defined with the keyword `sub`, it sometimes seems more natural to call it as a subroutine.)

2.7.1 Using a Function as an Operator

A function or a subroutine in Perl may also be referred to as an *operator*. While operators like &&, +, ++, and so on, are not to be thought of either as functions or subroutines, a function may be thought of as an operator when it can be called without a *parenthesized list* of empty or nonempty arguments.

Since many of Perl's built-in functions can be used as operators, from a notational standpoint, built-in function like `print()`, `chomp()`, `keys()`, etc., may also be displayed as print, chomp, keys, etc., [that is, without the accompanying function call operator symbol ()] to highlight their usage as operators.

The following script calls Perl's built-in chomp() as a function in line (C) and as an operator in lines (D) and (H). The invocation in line (C) is a function call as we have supplied chomp() with a parenthesized argument. On the other hand, the calls to chomp in lines (D) and (H) carry operator semantics since the arguments in those statements are unparenthesized. The purpose of chomp() [which is the same thing as chomp] is to get rid of the newline character, if one is present, at the end of a string. Note that what chomp accomplishes, it does so as a side effect.[51]

```
#!/usr/bin/perl -w

### Chomp.pl

use strict;

my $line1 = "My name is IRobot\n";                                      #(A)
my $line2 = "My name is IDruid\n";                                      #(B)

chomp( $line1 );                                                        #(C)
chomp $line2;                                                           #(D)

print $line1 . " --- " . $line2 . "\n";                                 #(E)
                        # My name is IRobot --- My name is IDruid

my @many_lines = ("hello\n", "yello\n", "mello\n", "jello\n");          #(F)

print "@many_lines\n";                                                  #(G)
                        # hello
                        #  yello
                        #  mello
                        #  jello
chomp @many_lines;                                                      #(H)
print "@many_lines\n";  # hello yello mello jello                       #(I)
```

[51] chomp() returns an integer that equals the number of deleted newline characters. This number will ordinarily equal 1 when chomp() is invoked separately on each line of text that is read from a text file. When chomp() is invoked on a list of strings, as we do in line (H) of the script, the returned integer could be greater than 1, depending on how many of the strings in the list terminate in the newline character. For the example in lines (G) and (H), the returned value equals 4.

When a function is called as an operator, meaning with its arguments unparenthesized, one must pay attention to the precedence properties of all other operators in the same statement. For example:

```
print 1 + 2 + 3;
```

will print out 6 because the operator `+` binds tighter than the operator `print`. But the following invocation:

```
print(1 + 2) + 3;
```

will only print out 3, as `print` would be invoked as a function on its parenthesized argument. When invoked as a function, the white space between the function name and the left parenthesis is immaterial. Therefore, the following call:

```
print (1 + 2) + 3;
```

will also print out just 3. However, note that the seemingly small variation on the previous call:

```
print +(1 + 2) + 3;
```

will again print out 6 since `print` is being invoked again as an operator. For `print` to act as a function there can only be white space, if anything at all, between the function name and the left parenthesis of the pair of parentheses that surround its arguments.

When used as an operator, a function name may act like a *unary operator* or a *list operator*. As you might expect, as a unary operator, the operator will work on only the first argument even if there are what look like additional comma-separated arguments following the name of the function. As a unary operator, a function name supplies a scalar context[52] for the evaluation of the argument, which will be the first argument that follows the function name. As a list operator, a function name may supply either a list context or a scalar context for the evaluation of each of the arguments that follow the function name, or it may do both. When a function name used as an operator supplies both kinds of contexts, it supplies the list context only to the last argument; the other arguments are provided with scalar contexts.

In the following example, `print` considers everything that comes after it as a list and therefore evaluates all nonscalar arguments in a list context. The call to `print` then prints each item of the list one after another, without any intervening spaces. This should explain the output shown in the commented-out portion of the third line below. The call to `print` supplies a list context for each of the first two arguments that needs an evaluation.

```
@arr1 = (1, 2, 3);
@arr2 = (4, 5, 6);
```

[52]See Section 2.8 for a more detailed discussion on the different evaluation contexts of Perl.

```
print @arr1, @arr2, 7, 8;                # 12345678
```

2.7.2 User-Defined Functions

In general, a subroutine is defined with the keyword sub, as in line (C) of the script GetName.pl shown next, and called with the ampersand & prefix, as in line (A). It is possible to call a subroutine without the ampersand prefix, provided Perl can figure out at compile time that you are making a subroutine call. Obviously, if a subroutine call has a parenthesized list of arguments, which may be empty, following the name of the subroutine, Perl knows unambiguously that a function call is being made and you can ignore the ampersand prefix. A subroutine called in this manner does not have to be defined before it is called. If a subroutine is defined beyond the point of its call, it is best to call it with the ampersand prefix.

In the script below, lines (D) and (F) of the subroutine get_name prompt the user for his/her first name and last name. The names entered by the user are retrieved by the line input operator <> in lines (E) and (G). As mentioned previously in Section 2.6.1 and 2.6.2, this operator ordinarily reads sequentially from all the files that are stored in the special array variable @ARGV used for capturing all the command-line arguments supplied when a script is run. However, when @ARGV is empty, it reads from the standard input. Line (E) is yet another illustration of chomp for getting rid of the newline character that the line input operator fetches for each line entered by the user.

Note in line (H) of the following script how the subroutine returns a list that is constructed in that line. In general, a Perl subroutine always returns whatever is obtained by the last evaluation in the body of the subroutine. To exit a subroutine earlier, say because a particular condition was satisfied, one can use the return operator to bring that about. If return is used with no expressions to evaluate, the subroutine will return undef in a scalar context and an empty list in a list context.[53]

```
#!/usr/bin/perl -w

### GetName.pl

use strict;

my @name = &get_name;                                          #(A)

print "@name\n";                                               #(B)

sub get_name {                                                 #(C)
```

[53] See Section 2.8 for what is meant by a scalar context and by a list context.

```
    print "Enter your first name: ";                              #(D)
    chomp( my $first = <> );                                      #(E)
    print "Enter your last name: ";                               #(F)
    chomp( my $last = <> );                                       #(G)
    ($first, $last);                                              #(H)
}
```

As our example above demonstrates, Perl does not require a subroutine to be defined before it is called in a script. If it is defined before it is called, you can call the subroutine without the & prefix, just like a built-in function. If you do not wish to define a subroutine before it is called in a script, and at the same time you do not wish to use the prefix & in a subroutine call, you have to make the call look like a function call, as we mentioned earlier in this section. This is shown in the following replacement for line (A) in the above program:

```
my @name = get_name();
```

2.7.3 Passing Arguments to Functions

We will now talk about passing arguments to a subroutine. To illustrate the idea, we will use the script PassArgs.pl shown next, where the subroutine takes two arguments, a scalar and an array. The purpose of the subroutine is to return the index of the scalar in the array if the scalar is found to be identical to one of the elements of the array. Whenever the value of the scalar is not found in the array, we want the subroutine to return undef.

All arguments are passed to a subroutine through a special internally defined array variable @_ that is local to the subroutine.[54] [55] Inside the subroutine, one can extract the elements of this array to access each of the arguments. Note the call to the subroutine find_index in line (B) of the PassArgs.pl script. We have intentionally not used & as a prefix when we called the subroutine in line (B) because the name of the subroutine is followed by a parenthesized list of arguments. The arguments to this subroutine are the string mello and the array @arr that is initialized with a call to the qw// operator in line (A). As was mentioned previously in Section 2.2.2, the qw// operator, working at compile time, takes a string argument

[54]Note that, in accordance with our explanation in Section 2.2.2, the actual name of this array is just the _ symbol, the prefix @ serving merely as a qualifier.

[55]The fact that the array variable @_ acts local to the subroutine is important for nested subroutine calls. When one subroutine calls another subroutine (or even the same subroutine in a recursive call), you obviously do not want the @_ for the inner call to interfere with the @_ for the outer call. So when a subroutine is called, Perl temporarily puts away the current value stored in @_ while the called subroutine is executed. The original value of @_ is restored upon exit from the called subroutine.

between two delimiters and returns a list of the words obtained by splitting the string on white space. Seeing line (B), Perl constructs a single list from the argument `mello` and all of the elements in the array argument `@arr`, places all the elements from the resulting list in the special array `@_`, and makes the array available inside the subroutine `find_index`.

Inside the subroutine, line (E) retrieves the first argument — `mello` — by applying the `shift` operator to the argument array `@_`. As explained in Section 2.2.2, the `shift` operator extracts the first element of the array and causes the rest of the elements to get shuffled toward the beginning of the array.

Now let's examine the `foreach` loop in lines (F) through (H) of the script. Recall that the purpose of the script is to figure out the index of the first argument to the subroutine in the array that is its second argument. The syntax of `foreach`, explained in greater detail in Section 2.9, uses Perl's special variable `$_` as the loop control variable. The value of this variable is set, in turn, to each element of the list that follows the `foreach` keyword in line (F). That list is returned by the range operator `..` and consists of all integers between 0 and `$#_`, both ends inclusive. As mentioned in Section 2.2.2, given an array of name `@array_name`, the call `$#array_name` returns the zero-based index of the last element of the array. Since the unqualified name of the argument array is just the `_` symbol, the scalar `$#_` returns the index of the last element of the array `@_`. When the subroutine `find_index()` is first called, the argument array `@_` supplied to the subroutine has five elements in it, one for the argument `mello` and four for the elements in the array `@arr`. Shifting the first element out in line (E) causes the size of the array `@_` to change from five to four. Therefore, the value of the scalar `$#_` in line (F) will be 3, since that will be the index of the last element of a four-element array. The list supplied to `foreach` in line (F) will therefore be `(0, 1, 2, 3)` and the loop control variable `$_` will be set first to 0, then to 1, then to 2, and, finally, to 3.

Let us now see what is going on in the conditional of the `if` statement[56] in line (G). From line (E), the scalar `$arg` will be set to the string `mello`. So the conditional compares for equality the string `mello` with what is returned by `$_[$_]`. Recall that the unqualified name of the argument array is just the `_` symbol, with `@` acting as a qualifier. So `$_[$_]` returns the element that is at index `$_` in the argument array `@_`. As explained in Section 2.1.2, the operator `eq` in line (G) does for two strings what the operator `==` does for numbers — it tests for equality of value.

[56]The different control structures of Perl, including the `if` control structure used in line (G), are reviewed in Section 2.9.

```
#!/usr/bin/perl -w

### PassArgs.pl

use strict;

my @arr = qw/ hello mello yello jello /;                               #(A)

my $index = find_index( "mello", @arr );                               #(B)

print "$index\n";                      # output: 1                     #(C)

sub find_index {                                                       #(D)
    my $arg = shift @_;                                                #(E)
    foreach (0..$#_) {                                                 #(F)
        if ( $arg eq $_[$_] ) {                                        #(G)
            return $_;                                                 #(H)
        }
    }
    undef;                                                             #(I)
}
```

Arguments are passed by reference to a subroutine. What that implies is that any changes made to the arguments inside a subroutine are visible in the argument object outside the subroutine after the thread of control has exited the subroutine. This is demonstrated by the following script. The subroutine `test` of line (E) takes each of its argument objects and concatenates it with itself. Going into the subroutine, the first argument object is the string `hello`, as specified in line (A). But when we print out this argument object in line (D) after the control has returned from the subroutine, we get `hellohello` for the first element of the array.

```
#!/usr/bin/perl -w

### ArgRef.pl

use strict;

my @arr = qw/ hello mello yello /;                                     #(A)

print "@arr\n";                  # hello mello yello                   #(B)

test( @arr );                                                          #(C)
```

```
print "@arr\n";                 # hellohello mellomello yelloyello        #(D)

sub test {                                                                 #(E)
    foreach (@_) {                                                         #(F)
        $_ = $_ . $_;                                                      #(G)
    }
}
```

2.7.4 Functions Can be Called with Keyword Arguments

Sometimes a function has a large number of parameters. When calling such a function, it is often difficult to remember the positional order of the parameters and easy to make errors in sequencing the arguments correctly. For such cases, a function can be defined with *named parameters* and the function called with an argument list that consists of keyword-argument pairs. By the same token, if a function returns a large number of different values in the form of a list, and if it is difficult to remember the order in which the different values appear in the returned list, one can get a function to return keyword-value pairs.

Note the call to the function `volume_calc()` in lines (A), (B), and (C) of the script `NamedParam.pl` shown next. If we were to write this call in a single line, it would look like:

```
volume_calc( length => 10, width  => 5, height => 8 );
```

The script `NamedParam.pl` would behave the same whether we called the arguments in the order shown above or with any permutation of that order. The above call to `volume_calc()` is equivalent to the following call:

```
volume_calc( height => 8, length => 10, width => 5 );
```

In accordance with what we mentioned earlier about how Perl interprets the big arrow symbol `=>`, the call

```
volume_calc( length => 10, width  => 5, height => 8 );
```

is equivalent to

```
volume_calc( 'length', 10, 'width', 5, 'height', 8 );
```

So, in effect, the function `volume_calc()` is called with six arguments, although a more usual implementation of this function would need only the three numbers. Supplying the additional keywords helps us to read the whole argument list into a local hash, as we do in line (F) of the function. What is important to realize is that the correct values for the length, the width, and the height will be read into the variables in lines (G), (H), and (I) regardless of the order in which keyword-argument pairs are supplied in a function call.

Notice how the function `volume_calc()` returns the results in line (L). That statement is equivalent to

```
return ('area', $area, 'volume', $volume);
```

This list, when received in line (A), can be read directly into a hash, as we show there. The individual elements of the results can then be extracted as shown in line (D).

```
#!/usr/bin/perl -w

### NamedParam.pl

use strict;

my %result = volume_calc( length => 10,                              #(A)
                          width  => 5,                               #(B)
                          height => 8 );                             #(C)

print "Area: $result{area} and Volume: $result{volume}\n";           #(D)
                                        # Area: 50 and Volume: 400

sub volume_calc {                                                    #(E)
    my %args = @_;                                                   #(F)
    my $length = $args{length};                                      #(G)
    my $width = $args{width};                                        #(H)
    my $height = $args{height};                                      #(I)

    my $area = $length * $width;                                     #(J)
    my $volume = $area * $height;                                    #(K)

    return (area => $area, volume => $volume);                       #(L)
}
```

2.7.5 Default Values for Function Arguments

It is possible to specify default values for one or more of the trailing arguments expected to be seen by a subroutine in Perl. As we mentioned, a subroutine in Perl can be called with an arbitrary number of arguments. Unless one specifically checks for the number of arguments supplied, if the number of arguments supplied is fewer than what is expected, the subroutine will set the rest, at least initially, to `undef`.

On the other hand, if the number of arguments is greater than what the subroutine expects, the rest will simply be ignored.

The script shown below, DefaultArgs.pl, defines a subroutine setUserInfo() for setting values for the global parameters $name, $age, $position, and $gender declared in line (A) of the script. Lines (J), (L), (N), and (P) call this subroutine with different argument lists. In each case, Perl will use the arguments supplied to assign values to the subroutine "parameters" starting from the leading end of what the subroutine expects to see. When the supplied arguments are are all used up, Perl will resort to the default action specified in lines (E) through (H). So, for the call in line (J), the variables $name, $age, and $gender will be set to the values in the subroutine call. However, the variable $position will be set according to the statement in line (H).

By the same token, the call in line (L) will cause the variables $name and $age to be set according to the arguments in the call. The variables $gender and $position, though, will be set according to the statements in lines (G) and (H). Similarly, for the call in line (N).

Notice what happens when we make the no-argument call in line (P). Now the default action for the variable name, which is the most leading variable for value assignment in the subroutine setUserInfo(), is to call croak() from the Carp module. This causes the script to be aborted and the error message shown in the commented-out section just below line (P) to be printed out.

The script DefaultArgs.pl also points to an interesting difference that occurs between Perl and Python when a default value for an argument is specified through a variable. The issue concerns the value of the variable at the point of a function call versus its value at the point of a function definition. For example, the value of the variable $position_default is Staff at the point of the function definition in line (C). However, this value is MemberStaff at the points of the function calls in lines (J), (L), (N), and (P). In Perl, it is the value at the point of the function call that is used in the function in line (H), but, as we will see in Section 3.6.3 of Chapter 3, in Python it is the value at the point of the function definition that is used.

```
#!/usr/bin/perl -w

### DefaultArgs.pl

use strict;
use Carp;

our ($name, $age, $gender, $position);                              #(A)

my $position_default = 'Staff';                                     #(B)

sub setUserInfo {                                                   #(C)
```

```
    ($name, $age, $gender, $position) = @_;                          #(D)
    croak "illegal call --- must supply name" if !defined $name;     #(E)
    $age = 'unknown' if !defined $age;                               #(F)
    $gender = 'unknown' if !defined $gender;                         #(G)
    $position = $position_default if !defined $position;             #(H)
}

$position_default = 'MemberStaff';                                   #(I)

setUserInfo( 'Trillian', 96, 'female' );                             #(J)
print "$name $age $gender $position\n";                              #(K)
                    # Trillian 96 female MemberStaff

setUserInfo( 'Trillian', 96 );                                       #(L)
print "$name $age $gender $position\n";                              #(M)
                    # Trillian 96 unknown MemberStaff

setUserInfo( 'Trillian' );                                           #(N)
print "$name $age $gender $position\n";                              #(O)
                    # Trillian unknown unknown MemberStaff

setUserInfo();                                                       #(P)
        # illegal call --- must supply name at DefaultArgs.pl line 16
        # main::setUserInfo() called at DefaultArgs.pl line 35
```

2.8 WHAT IS RETURNED BY EVALUATION DEPENDS ON CONTEXT

Perl has this unique feature that what is returned by evaluating an expression depends on the context in which the evaluation takes place. The two primary contexts in Perl are the *scalar context* and the *list context*, although one may also talk about the *Boolean context* and the *void context*.

As one expects, the evaluation of an expression in a scalar context returns a scalar. By the same token, the evaluation of an expression in a list context returns a list. When a given array is evaluated in a scalar context, it only returns a single number that is equal to the number of elements in the array. And when the same array is evaluated in a list context, the process of evaluation returns a list of the elements of the array, as demonstrated by the following script which we will go through in some detail.

In lines (A), (B), and (C) of the script `Context.pl` shown next, we first initialize an array `@friends` in line (A). Since this array is one of the elements of the list used to initialize another array, `@arr`, in line (B), the array `@friends` is evaluated in a list context. The list of items returned by the evaluation of `@friends` is inserted into the enclosing list on the right of the assignment in line (B). This insertion is on an item-by-item basis so that the inserted items are on par with the original items.

Line (D) shows the array `@friends` being evaluated in a list context again, but what is printed out is quite different from what was printed out for the list evaluation of the same array in line (B). To understand what happens in line (D), recall what we mentioned in Section 2.6 about the behavior of `print`. This function considers all of the arguments that are sent to the output as a single list; any nonscalar items in this list are evaluated in a list context. The final list of items thus obtained is printed out one item after another without any intervening spaces. Therefore, the array `@friends` in line (D) will be evaluated in the list context. This array returns the list of four quoted words that were used to initialize the array in line (A). The call to `print` in line (D) then prints them out one after another, without any spaces in between, as shown in the commented-out portion of that line.

Line (E) also evaluates the array `@friends` in a list context, but the printed output obtained is different from the previous list-context evaluation of the same array. When the result obtained by a list context evaluation of an array are interpolated in a double-quoted string, a blank space is inserted between the successive elements of the array by default. So the output of line (E) is `My friends are harry sally monica joe.`

In line (F), we supply a comma-separated sequence of items to `print`. This sequence of expressions is interpreted as a list argument by `print`. Perl prints out each item of this list as the item is encountered. If an item happens to be an expression, it is evaluated in a list context and each entity thus returned printed out without any intervening spaces. So when `print` advances to `@friends` in line (F), it evaluates the array in a list context and prints out each item of this array without any spaces in between. As a result, the output of line (F) is `My friends are harrysallymonicajoe.`

Line (G) shows the array `@friends` being evaluated in a scalar context. The context in this case is provided by the nature of the variable on the left side of the assignment. Since the variable to which the assignment is being made is a scalar, it stands to reason that the right-hand side should return a scalar. Since in a scalar context an array returns the number of elements in the array, the output in line (H) is just the number 4.

Line (I) shows a scalar context for the evaluation of the array `@friends`. Since the concatenation operator binds tighter than the operator `print`, what is supplied as an argument to `print` is the output of the concatenation operator.[57] The concatenation

[57]The reader might ask as to which of the two applications of the concatenation operator in line (I) supplies the concatenated string to `print`. This operator is left associative. Therefore, the expression `A.B.C` will be parsed as the `(A.B).C` expression. This implies that the right application of the concatenation operator in line (I) will supply the final argument string to `print`.

operator supplies scalar context for the evaluation of its operands. As a consequence, the array `@friends` is evaluated in a scalar context, which yields the number 4. Therefore, the output produced in line (I) is `I have 4 friends`.

Line (J) forces the array `@friends` to be evaluated in a scalar context by invoking `scalar` on the array. This forced scalar evaluation returns 4 for the number of elements in the array. As a result, line (J) also outputs `I have 4 friends`.

Like (K) is straightforward. It interpolates the scalar value returned for the array element into the double-quoted string. The output is `My third friend is monica`.

Line (L) evaluates the array element again in a list context — in this case the list has only one item and this item is displayed as such, with the same output as for line (K).

```
#!/usr/bin/perl -w

### Context.pl

use strict;

my @friends = qw/ harry sally monica joe /;                         #(A)

# List context for the evaluation of @friends; the
# items returned by the evaluation are interpolated
# into the list that is assigned to @arr:
my @arr = (1, 2, 3, @friends, 4);                                   #(B)
print "@arr\n";                                                     #(C)
                                 # 1 2 3 harry sally monica joe 4

# List context for @friends; will print out the
# items one item after another without any spaces
# in-between; the output has the appearance of a
# single string:
print @friends, "\n";            # harrysallymonicajoe              #(D)

# List context for the evaluation of @friends;
# for the purpose of interpolation into the
# double-quoted string, the items are separated
# by blank space:
print "My friends: @friends\n";                                     #(E)
                                 # My friends: harry sally monica joe

# List context for @friends; the items of the
# array @friends will be output one item after
# another without any intervening spaces, giving
# the appearance of a single string to the output:
```

```
print "My friends: ", @friends, "\n";                          #(F)
                                # My friends: harrysallymonicajoe

# Scalar context for @friends:
my $num_friends = @friends;                                    #(G)
print $num_friends, "\n";       # 4                            #(H)

# Scalar context for @friends; the scalar value
# returned will be a print representation of
# the scalar evaluation of the array @friends:
print "I have " . @friends ." friends\n";                      #(I)
                                # I have 4 friends

#Scalar context for @friends
print "I have ", scalar @friends, " friends\n";                #(J)
                                # I have 4 friends

# Scalar context for the scalar element $friends[2]:
print "My third friend is $friends[2]\n";                      #(K)
                                # My third friend is monica

# List context for the scalar $friends[2], but
# the list consists of only one item which is
# displayed as such (without parentheses):
print "My third friend is ", $friends[2], "\n";                #(L)
```

Our discussion so far in this section has focused on how an array variable is evaluated in a scalar context and in a list context. Exactly the same considerations apply to any expression that is capable of returning a list in the list context and a scalar in the scalar context. But note that one can encounter expressions that return a list in the list context but do not return anything in the scalar context. The `sort` function, for example, returns a sorted list in a list context. But what it returns in a scalar context is undefined, as demonstrated by:

```
@arr = qw{ hello yello mello jello };
print sort @arr;            # hellojellomelloyello
print "\n";
print scalar sort @arr;     # prints out an error message saying that
                            # print is being asked to output an
                            # uninitialized value.
```

Our discussion above deals primarily with the context dependency of evaluating expressions that return a list. What about the context dependency of evaluating an expression that only returns a scalar. What if the context demanded that the expression return a list? If an expression only returns a scalar and is not programmed to return a list in a list context — meaning that the expression does not have a *list value*, it only has a *scalar value* — the scalar value is *promoted* to a list by forming a one-element list. Suppose we say

```
$x = "hello";
```

and then invoke

```
@y = $x;
```

Perl will construct a one-element list out of the value of `$x` and assign that list to the array variable `@y`.

We will now talk about how one may write a subroutine that can be made to return different values depending on the context in which the subroutine is invoked. This is done with the help of the `wantarray` predicate in a sûbroutine. When a subroutine is called in a list context, this predicate evaluates to true. On the other hand, in a scalar context, the predicate evaluates to false. In the following script, the function defined in lines (E) through (I) uses this predicate to return the list `(miss bo peep)` in the list context of line (A) and just the string `peep` in the scalar context of line (C).

```
#!/usr/bin/perl -w

### WantArray.pl

use strict;

my @x = &func;                                                          #(A)
print "@x\n";                          # miss bo peep                   #(B)

my $y = &func;                                                          #(C)
print "$y\n";                          # peep                           #(D)

sub func {                                                              #(E)
    if ( wantarray ) {                                                  #(F)
        return qw/miss bo peep/;                                        #(G)
    } else {                                                            #(H)
        return "peep";                                                  #(I)
    }
}
```

With regard to the context dependency of the various Perl operators, of particular note is the behavior of the line input operator `<>`. As mentioned earlier in Section 2.6, this operator ordinarily reads one line at a time from each file whose name appears in the array `@ARGV`, or from the standard input if `@ARGV` is empty. But this only happens when the operator is invoked in a scalar context. In a list context, the operator will return all of the lines in all of the files listed in @ARGV in one fell swoop.

To illustrate this context dependency of the <> operator, we will have it input text from two files data1.txt and data2.txt. The contents of these two files are

```
data1.txt:              hello
                        jello yello

data2.txt:              mello
```

We now consider the following script in which we first provide a scalar context and then a list context for <> for reading from the same set of files. The file names are placed in the array @ARGV in line (A). The conditional of the while loop in line (B) provides a scalar context for <>. So, in line (B), one line at a time is read from the files listed in @ARGV. As a result, the output of the print statement in line (C) is as shown in the commented-out section just below the while loop. Line (D) then reinitializes @ARGV array.[58] Line (E) supplies a list context for the <> operator in that line. So all of the lines from both the text files listed in @ARGV are read all at once into the array @all_data. Just for variety, in this case we now invoke chomp on the array. As the reader should know from our earlier script Chomp.pl, this causes any newline terminators to be dropped from each of the strings stored in the array @all_data. So the output now looks like what is shown in the commented-out portion of line (F).

```
#!/usr/bin/perl -w

### ContextDependency.pl

@ARGV = qw/data1.txt data2.txt/;                                        #(A)

# Read one line at a time:
while ( my $line = <> ) {                # scalar context for <>       #(B)
    print $line;                                                        #(C)
}                                        # hello
                                         # jello yello
                                         # mello

# Read all lines all at once, but first
# reinitialize @ARGV:
@ARGV = qw/data1.txt data2.txt/;                                        #(D)
```

[58]The reinitialization of @ARGV is made necessary by the fact that each file name is "unshifted" out of the @ARGV array and a filehandle implicitly attached to the file for carrying out the read operation. So by the time all the files in @ARGV have been read, this array is empty. That will be the situation after the flow of execution has exited the while loop of line (B).

```
chomp( my @all_data = <> );            # list context for <>             #(E)

print "@all_data";                     # hello jello yello mello         #(F)
```

In the above script, in the scalar context in line (B), we read the output of `<>` into an explicitly specified scalar variable `$line`. This was done to highlight the scalar nature of the context provided to the `<>` operator. It is important to realize that the conditional of a `while` loop all by itself also provides a scalar context for the evaluation of the conditional expression. So another way of writing the lines (A), (B), and (C) would be

```
@ARGV = qw/data1.txt data2.txt/;
while ( <> ) {
    print;
}
```

As before, the operator `<>` will still be invoked in a scalar context. Therefore, it will still read one line at a time, but this line will now be read into the default scalar variable `$_`. The invocation of `print` in the next line will output whatever is the current value of `$_`.

In addition to the list and the scalar contexts, it is also possible to talk about the *void context*. A typical situation corresponding to the void context is when a function is called for its side effects only and not for its returned value. Obviously, if a function is expected to return a list, we have a list context for function evaluation, and if a function is expected to return only a scalar, the evaluation context is scalar. But if a function that is capable of returning a list in a list context and a scalar in a scalar context is called without expectation of any return, — that is, when such a function is called in a void context — in what context should the function be evaluated? Perl uses the rule that, when called in a void context, a function is evaluated in a scalar context. This is illustrated by the following variation on the `WantArray.pl` script shown earlier. The function `func()` of line (C) returns a list in line (E) when the function is called in a list context and just the scalar in line (H) when called in a scalar context. But when invoked in line (A) without any expectation of any return value, it is evaluated in the scalar context, as verified by the output of line (A). Note that the evaluation context for a function call is established at compile time.

```
#!/usr/bin/perl -w

### VoidContext.pl

use strict;

&func;                      # scalar context invoked                   #(A)
```

```
sub func {                                                    #(B)
    if ( wantarray ) {                                        #(C)
        print "list context invoked\n";                       #(D)
        return qw/miss bo peep/;                              #(E)
    } else {                                                  #(F)
        print "scalar context invoked\n";                     #(G)
        return "peep";                                        #(H)
    }
}
```

2.9 CONDITIONAL EVALUATION AND LOOP CONTROL STRUCTURES

Perl has all of the common *control structures* for both the conditional and the repeated execution of a portion of code.

Perl has the `if/else` and `unless` control structures for conditional evaluation of a block of code. The `if/else` control structures works in the same way as in all computer languages — a block of code is evaluated subject to what is known as a *conditional* or a *controlling expression* being true. The `unless` control structure works in a reverse fashion — a block of code is evaluated subject to the conditional of the `unless` construct being false.

Perl also gives us the `while`, `until`, `foreach`, and `for` control structures for setting up loops for iterative and conditional evaluation of a block of code. Whereas the `while` control structure continues to loop through a block of code as long as the conditional of the `while` construct is true, the `until` control structure only loops through a block of code as long as the conditional is false.

With regard to the Perl's control structures for loops, it is important to understand the role played by the default variable `$_` that Perl may use implicitly as the *loop control variable* in the absence of a user-defined loop control variable. The other important issue relates to when an expression is considered to be true and when false. In what follows, we will first illustrate the syntax of the different control structures, while shedding light on the role played by `$_`. Sections 2.9.2 and 2.9.3 will then address the question of how Perl figures out when something is true or false.

Looping with `while`:

Here is an an example that illustrates both the `while` control structure for conditional looping through a block of code and the `if` control structure for conditional evaluation of one or more statements. The example asks the user to enter one number per line and then press Enter in a blank line when done. When the user has finished data entry, the script prints out the sum of the numbers entered.

```
#!/usr/bin/perl -w

### WhileIf.pl

use strict;

print "Enter numbers, one per line. When done, just press Enter\n"; #(A)

my $sum;                                                               #(B)

while (<>) {                                                           #(C)
    if (/^\s*$/) {                                                     #(D)
        printf "Sum of numbers is: %d\n", $sum;                        #(E)
        last;                                                          #(F)
    }                                                                  #(G)
    $sum += $_;                                                        #(H)
}
```

As explained earlier in Section 2.6, the line input operator `<>` in line (C) will read one line at a time from the standard input into the Perl's special variable `$_`. About the condition specified for the `if` construct in line (D), the statements in lines (E) and (F) will be executed only if the condition, commonly referred to as the *conditional*, checks out to be true. The string within the two forward slashes in the conditional, reproduced below:

```
/^\s*$/
```

is a *regular expression*, *regex* for short. If the regex can be successfully matched with the value stored in the Perl's special variable `$_`, the conditional will test out to true. Otherwise, the conditional will test out to false. As will be explained in considerable detail in Chapter 4, the regex shown contains, at the beginning and at the end, two anchor metacharacters, `^` and `$`. These denote, respectively, the beginning and the end positions of the string contained in `$_`. The rest of the regex, `\s*`, stands for any number of repetitions, including zero, of what are known as the *white-space characters*, these being the newline, the horizontal tab, the carriage return, and the form feed. Since regular expressions are discussed in detail in Chapter 4, all we want to say here is that the conditional shown in line (D) will test out to true if the user presses the Enter key on the keyboard while the screen cursor is on a blank line.

A variation on the `while` loop is the `while-continue` loop we show in the next script whose purpose is to again elicit numbers from a user, but to now print out separately the sums of the even integers and the odd integers. The script asks the user to enter integers, one per line, in response to the prompt `Number:` that is first printed out in line (C) and that is subsequently printed out by the `continue` statement in line (L). After the first iteration through the body of the `while` loop in lines (E) through (K), the code in the continue block in line (L) is executed just before the evaluation of the conditional in line (D) at the end of each iteration of the loop. As for the rest of the code in this example, in line (E) we make sure that the entry is composed of numerical digits only and that the number is even. Line (F) does the same for odd numbers. The operator `%` in both of these lines carries out a modulo division. If the user does not enter any information before hitting the Enter key, the `elsif` block in lines (G) through (J) prints out the result and terminates the loop by calling the *loop control operator* `last` that is explained next in this section. The structure of the regexes used in lines (E), (F), and (G) will be clear after the reader has gone through Chapter 4.

```
#!/usr/bin/perl -w
use strict;

### WhileWithContinue.pl

print "Enter numbers, one per line. When done, just enter return\n"; #(A)

my ($sum_even, $sum_odd) = (0,0);                                    #(B)

print "Number: ";                                                    #(C)
while (<>) {                                                         #(D)
    if ( $_ =~ /^\d+$/ && $_ % 2 == 0 ) { $sum_even += $_ }          #(E)
    elsif ( $_ =~ /^\d+$/ &&  $_ % 2 != 0 ) { $sum_odd += $_ }       #(F)
    elsif (/^\s*$/) {                                                #(G)
        printf "Sum of even numbers is: %d\n", $sum_even;            #(H)
        printf "Sum of odd numbers is: %d\n", $sum_odd;              #(I)
        last;                                                        #(J)
    } else { print "Entry not recognized. Try again.\n" }            #(K)
} continue { print "Number: "; }                                     #(L)
```

`last`, `next`, and `redo` *for loop control*:

Line (J) of the script above shows the *loop control operator* `last` for terminating the `while` loop when the conditional in line (G) evaluates to true. The other loop control operators of Perl are `next` and `redo`. The `next` operator abruptly shifts the flow of control to the end of the loop block, without the evaluation of the intervening statements. The `redo` operator causes the current iteration to be executed again, without the loop conditional being tested again.

`if-else` *for flow control*:

Whereas the script `WhileIf.pl` illustrated how to use an `if` clause by itself for flow control, the script `WhileWithContinue.pl` showed how flow-control can be orchestrated with a series of `elsif` clauses and a final `else` clause. The general form of this control structure can be displayed as:

```
if ( conditional ) {
    code ...
} elsif ( conditional ) {
    code ...
} elsif ( conditional ) {
    ...
    ...
} else {
    code
}
```

Note that, in contrast with C, the block of code that is to be executed conditionally, which is the code that follows the conditional, whether in the `if` clause or in the `elsif` clause or in the `else` clause, *must* be enclosed by braces even if this block of code consists of a single statement.

Looping with `foreach`:

Another looping mechanism in Perl, provided by the `foreach` control structure, is convenient for walking through an array. When using `foreach`, the loop control variable is set to the consecutive elements of the array in each iteration. This is illustrated by the following example where, as mentioned previously in Section 2.2.2, the `qw//` operator — in this case, it is actually the `qw{}` operator — working at compile time, takes a string argument between two delimiters and returns a list of the substrings obtained by splitting the string on white space.[59]

```
#!/usr/bin/perl -w

### Foreach.pl

use strict;

my @files = qw{/home/kak/perl/perl-run
               /home/kak/perl/perl-functions};                    #(A)
```

[59] By placing the items of the argument to the `qw//` operator in two different lines, line (A) also shows that you can use the white space characters as needed in the argument supplied to the `qw//` operator in order to make your script visually easier to read.

```
foreach (@files) {                                                    #(B)
    print "$_ looks like a text file and is readable\n" if -r && -T;#(C)
}
```

The foreach control structure in line (B) uses the Perl's default variable $_ as the loop control variable. Perl sets $_ to each element of the list argument supplied to foreach and then processes the block of code that follows. In the example shown, for the first iteration, the variable $_ will be set to the file name shown in the first argument to qw. The statement in line (C) will then apply the *file tests* -r and -T to this file. The former test checks whether the permission bits set for the file make it readable by whomever is running the Perl script and the latter checks to see if the file is a text file. Perl provides a large number of file tests for testing the various attributes of files and directories. We will briefly revisit the subject of file tests in Section 2.16.2.

Also note in line (C) the backward form of the if statement. What follows if in line (C) is the condition that must evaluate to true for what comes before if to be executed. So the statement in line (C) is identical to the following if block:

```
if (-r && -T) {
    print "$_ looks like a text file and is readable\n";
}
```

When if is used in the backward manner shown in line (C) of the script, it is called a *modifier*. The other modifiers are unless, until, while, and foreach. So there is a modifier for each of the control structures.

Since a loop control variable was not mentioned explicitly in line (B) of the above script, it was set implicitly to the default $_. We can, of course, supply the loop control variable explicitly, as demonstrated by the following version of the above script.

```
#!/usr/bin/perl -w

### Foreach2.pl

use strict;

my @files = qw{/home/kak/perl/perl-run
               /home/kak/perl/perl-functions};                        #(A)
foreach my $file (@files) {                                           #(B)
    print "$file looks like a text file and is readable\n" if -r $file
                                                       && -T $file;#(C)
}
```

Note that now line (B) mentions `$file` as a loop control variable; the value of this variable will be set to each element in the list argument supplied to `foreach`. The file tests in line (C) are now being carried out on whatever is bound to the variable `$file`. Also note that the loop control variable has been declared as a `my` variable to comply with the strictures imposed by the `strict` pragma. If we had chosen a previously declared variable as the loop control variable in line (B) of the above script, its value prior to the invocation of `foreach` would be restored after the thread of execution exits the `foreach` loop. Also note that when the loop control variable is assigned an item from the argument list it is walking through, what the loop control variable gets is the item itself and not a copy of the item. So if you happen to modify the current value of the loop control variable inside a loop, that change would be reflected in the argument list also.

Looping with `until` and `unless`:

As stated earlier, the control structure `unless` reverses the sense in which the condition must succeed in an `if` statement, and the loop control structure `until` plays the same role vis-à-vis `while`. The following script illustrates both `until` for setting up a loop and `unless` for the conditional evaluation of a block of statements. The goal of the script is to report on the occurrences of a specified string within a longer string. The longer string is supplied in lines (A) and (B). Note the use of the dot operator in line (A) that joins the quoted strings in lines (A) and (B). Line (C) specifies the substring whose occurrences we want the script to search for in the string supplied through lines (A) and (B).

```
#!/usr/bin/perl -w

### UntilUnless.pl

use strict;

my $string = "The difference between reality and fiction?" .            #(A)
             "The fiction has to make sense";                            #(B)

my $str = "fiction";                                                     #(C)

my $where = 0;                                                           #(D)
until ( $where == -1 ) {                                                 #(E)
    $where = index( $string, $str, $where );                             #(F)
    unless ( $where == -1 ) {                                            #(G)
        print "$where\n";                                                #(H)
        $where++                                                         #(I)
    };
}
```

The actual substring search in the script is carried out by the `index()` function call in line (F). This function returns -1 if the substring supplied via the second argument is not found in the string supplied via the first argument. If the substring is found, the value returned is the zero-based index of the first character in the long string that matches the first character of the substring. The search starts at the position indexed by the value supplied through the last argument. The reason for incrementing the `$where` variable in line (I) is that, after the current location of the substring is found, we must start the search immediately to the right of where the substring was last found in order to locate the next occurrence of the substring. The above script returns the values:

```
35
47
```

In the above script, note how the `until` loop will continue to iterate through the lines (E) through (I) as long as `index()` does not return -1. Also note the role played by `unless` in line (G). Lines (H) and (I) will not be executed if the substring is not found in the long string.

Looping with `for`:

That brings us to the `for` control structure, which works just like the `for` in C, as shown by the following example:

```
#!/usr/bin/perl -w

### For.pl

use strict;

for (my $i = 0; $i < 10; $i++) {
    printf "square of $i is %d\n", $i * $i;
}
```

which produces the following output:

```
square of 0 is 0
square of 1 is 1
square of 2 is 4
 ....
 ....
```

The above example illustrates again the `printf()` function for the formatted output. As mentioned previously, it works like C's `printf()` function.

It is also possible to use `for` as an abbreviation for `foreach`. What is shown below is really a `foreach` loop written with `for`:

```
#!/usr/bin/perl -w

### For2.pl

use strict;

for (0..9) {                                                    #(A)
    printf "square of $_ is %d\n", $_ * $_;                     #(B)
}
```

The range operator `..` in line (A), as already explained in Section 2.2.2, creates a list of values starting from the left scalar, incrementing it repeatedly by 1, until the value equals the right scalar. So the construct `(0..9)` returns the list (0,1,2,3,4,5,6,7,8,9). Just as would be the case for a `foreach` loop, Perl's default variable `$_` is used for loop control in the above example. This variable is set successively to the values in the list (0,1,...,9).

2.9.1 Controlling an Outer Loop from an Inner Loop

When a script contains nested loops, Perl offers a convenient feature — a loop label — for controlling an outer loop from an inner loop. The next script, `Label.pl`, illustrates the idea. This script scans a file, reading one line at a time, and looks for the first occurrence of the word `blue`. When and if this word is found, the script terminates and, if the word was found, prints out the line number containing the word.

This is accomplished with the help of two loops, a `while` loop in line (B) and a `foreach` loop in line (C). The `while` loop uses the line input operator to read in one line at a time from the standard input. The `foreach` loop invokes the `split()` function, which is further explained in Section 4.12 of Chapter 4, to split each line at the white space between the words. (This is the default behavior of `split`.) Line (D) then matches each word with the word `blue` using the following forward-slash delimited regular expression

```
/\b$word\b/
```

Note the two occurrences of `\b`. As explained in Section 4.4 of Chapter 4, `\b` is known as the *word boundary anchor metacharacter*. It matches any word to not-word and not-word to word transition in an input string. What that means is that we are looking for the word `blue` all by itself in a file and not as a substring of longer words like `jetblue`, `blues`, etc. It will be okay for `blue` to show up as a part of a hyphenated word as in:

```
A hungry dog
jumped over a
lazy blue-colored
fish.
```

With regard to the script shown next, note that the outer `while` loop has the label `FIND_BLUE` associated with it in line (B) and how we supply this label as an argument to the loop control operator `last` in line (D). The behavior of `last` when supplied with a label is the same as its behavior for the non-nested loop case. When the condition stated in line (D) is satisfied, that will terminate the outer loop labeled `FIND_BLUE` — that is, the `while` loop in line (B).

```
#!/usr/bin/perl -w

### Label.pl

use strict;

my $word = "blue";                                                   #(A)

FIND_BLUE: while (<>) {                                              #(B)
    foreach (split) {                                                #(C)
        last FIND_BLUE  if /\b$word\b/;                              #(D)
    }
}

print "The word '$word' makes its first appearance" .
                    " in line $. of $ARGV\n";                        #(E)
```

Notice Perl's special variable `$.` in line (E) of the script. As the line input operator in line (B) writes each line from the input file into the variable `$_`, it stores the corresponding line number in the `$.` variable. As mentioned previously, the special variable `$ARGV` stores the name of the file from which data was last read.[60] When this script is run with the text file `data.txt` supplied as a command-line argument,

[60] As mentioned in Section 2.6, the scalar variable `$ARGV` is different from the array variable `@ARGV` that is used for storing the command-line arguments. Both `$ARGV` and `@ARGV` are used in the `Label.pl` script, the latter because the script is called using a command-line like

```
Label.pl data.txt
```

where `data.txt` is the text file in which the word search is carried out. With this command line, the array `@ARGV` will consist of a single item, the file name `data.txt`.

the file containing the `A hungry dog ...` text shown above, the following output is produced:

```
The word 'blue' makes its first appearance in line 3 of data.txt
```

As with the loop control operator `last` in line (D) of the script above, you can also supply a loop label to the other two loop control operators — `next` and `redo` — with predictable effects.

We should also mention that, by convention, a loop label is written all uppercase. As to which characters may be used for a label, they are the same as for any identifier, meaning any combination of letters, digits, and underscores, as long as the first character is not a digit.[61]

2.9.2 When Is a Conditional True or False?

We will now address the question of when an expression in the conditional of a control structure evaluates to true and when it evaluates to false. In general, Perl examines the value returned by an expression and makes a decision about its truth value on the basis of the following criteria:

- The null object `undef` evaluates to false. All scalar variables that are not explicitly initialized by a programmer are default-initialized to the null object `undef`. The value of `undef` is also returned by the line input operator `<>` when either the end-of-file condition or some error condition is encountered. The null value `undef` is also returned by many built-in functions and operators upon failure. When so desired, the function `defined()` can be used to test whether its argument evaluates to `undef`. The following script, another way of writing the script `WhileIf.pl` that we showed at the beginning of Section 2.9, illustrates the use of `defined()`.

```
#!/usr/bin/perl -w

### Defined.pl

use strict;

print "Enter numbers, one per line. " .
        "Enter Ctrl-d to indicate the end of data entry.\n";   #(A)
my $sum;                                                        #(B)
```

[61] Unlike a label in, say, C or Fortran where a label marks a target point, a label in Perl names the entire block.

```
while ( defined( my $entry = <> ) ) {                          #(C)
    $sum += $entry;                                            #(D)
}

print "Sum = $sum\n";                                          #(E)
```

In comparison with the earlier `WhileIf.pl` script, the above script asks the user to enter Ctrl-d to indicate the end of data entry. Entering Ctrl-d causes the end-of-file condition to be read from the input stream attached to the keyboard. Since the end-of-file condition corresponds to the special value `undef`, the argument to `defined()` in line (C) will evaluate to false when the user enters Ctrl-d, causing the termination of the `while` loop.

- When tested for its truth value, an expression that evaluates to either 0 or 0.0 is considered to be false. An expression that evaluates to any other number is considered to be true.

- When tested for its truth value, an expression evaluating to a single-quoted or a double-quoted empty string is considered to be false. In other words, the empty strings `''` and `""` are false as conditionals. All other strings are true except for the two special cases of `'0'` and `"0"` that evaluate to false. The reason for this has to do with the already-mentioned fact that Perl, being typeless, is able to interpret a string as a number (and vice versa) if the context demands that interpretation. So the strings `'0'` and `"0"` must evaluate to false in order to be consistent with the number 0 evaluating to false.

2.9.3 Complex Conditionals

The examples we have shown so far for the conditionals in the various control structures used simple expressions. In other words, each conditional we have shown so far consisted of a single Boolean element — meaning a single expression that could be tested for its truth value. As with other languages, one can also use more complex conditionals in the control structures. These would be *logical expressions* built using the *numeric relational operators* (<, <=, >, and >=), the *numeric equality operators* (== and !=), the *string relational operators* (lt, le, gt, and ge),[62] the *string equality operators* (eq and neq), the *binary logical operators* (&& and ||), and the *unary logical negation operator* (!).

[62]The string relational operator `lt` stands for *less than*, `le` for *less than or equal to*, `gt` for *greater than*, and `ge` for *greater than or equal to*. The default behavior of the string relational operators is based on the lexicographic orderings of the strings as dictated by the ASCII codes associated with the characters. A string `s1` is *less than* a string `s2` if the former occurs earlier in the lexicographic order.

Should the operands supplied to any of the numeric equality and relational operators (==, !=, <, <=, >, >=) happen to not be numeric, Perl will try to "cast" them into numbers. Whereas this numeric interpretation of the operands will obviously work for some strings that are print representations of numbers (see Section 2.1.1), in general an operand may not be convertible into a numeric value for these operators to work. If Perl is called upon to interpret a non-numeric operand as a number for these operators, it is because the programmer made an error in the script. By the same token, if the operands supplied to any of the string equality and relational operators (`eq`, `neq`, `lt`, `le`, `gt`, `ge`) happen to be nonstrings. Perl will try to interpret the operands as strings.

When a logical expression in a conditional has two or more Boolean elements connected by either the `and` operator `&&` or the `or` operator `||`, Perl carries out a *short-circuit evaluation* of the logical expression. Given a logical expression of the form:

```
A && B
```

short-circuit evaluation means that if `A` is evaluated to be false, Perl will ignore `B` since the Boolean value of the entire logical expression will be false anyway. Similarly, in a logical expression of the form:

```
A || B
```

if `A` evaluates to true, Perl will ignore `B` since the Boolean value of the entire expression will be true no matter what the value of `B`.

When a logical expression `A && B` is true or when `A || B` is false (meaning that when both the operands are evaluated), it is the value of the right operand that is returned. This can be useful for assigning default values to variables, as in the example below. This example expects a user to provide at most five command-line arguments in the form of numbers. The script computes the average of the numbers in line (E) and prints out the average. When the number of command-line arguments provided by a user is fewer than 5, it penalizes the user by assuming a default of -10 for each missing entry. This is accomplished by the logical expression in line (C). In this expression, first the left operand of the `||` operator is evaluated. This is done by using the `shift` operator to extract the first element stored in the `@ARGV` array and examining the resulting value. Recall that the command-line arguments are all stored in the `@ARGV` array. If what is returned by `shift` is undefined, the left operand of the `||` operator will evaluate to false. The short-circuit evaluation procedure for logical expressions will now cause the right operand of `||` to be evaluated, which returns the true value of -10.

```
#!/usr/bin/perl -w

### DefaultWithOr.pl

use strict;
```

```
die "Too many command-line args\n" unless @ARGV <= 5;                #(A)

my $sum;

foreach ( 1..5 ) {                                                    #(B)
    my $entry = shift @ARGV || -10;                                   #(C)
    $sum += $entry;                                                   #(D)
}

my $avg = $sum / 5.0;                                                 #(E)

print "The average over five entries is $avg\n";
```

Also note in line (A) of the above example a demonstration of the very commonly used `die` function to terminate a script immediately should certain conditions not be fulfilled. Earlier, we used `die` in Section 2.6 to terminate a script upon failure of `open` to return a filehandle. As mentioned there, `die` and the different ways of using it are presented in detail in Chapter 10.

Perl also allows you to use the keyword `and` for the `&&` operator and the keyword `or` for the `||` operator. Although the operators `and` and `or` are logically identical to the operators `&&` and `||`, respectively, they differ in one very important manner: The precedence levels of `and` and `or` are much lower compared to the precedence levels of `&&` and `||`. As a result, the `and` and the `or` operators do not stick to their operands as tightly as the `&&` and `||` operators, creating a reduced need for parentheses for the grouping of the operands. The following script illustrates the use of `or` in line (A):

```
#!/usr/bin/perl -w

### Or.pl

use strict;

open( FILE, "< data.txt" )  or die "Unable to open file: $!";        #(A)
local $/ = undef;                                                     #(B)
my @all_words = split /\s+/, <FILE>;                                  #(C)
my $num_of_words = @all_words;                                        #(D)
print "Number of words in the text file: $num_of_words\n";           #(E)
close FILE;                                                           #(F)
```

There is another interesting Perl feature illustrated in this script: Line (B) illustrates the use of `local` declaration for a language-supplied global variable. As explained further in Section 2.12, when such a global variable is declared `local`, its value is temporarily put away until the end of the scope of the `local` declaration. The reason for why this declaration is named `local` is that it temporarily *localizes* the otherwise global definition of the variable. As the thread of execution exits that scope, the original value of the global variable is restored. The language-supplied global variable `$/` holds, as was stated in Section 2.1.2, the input record separator, which tells Perl when to recognize the end of a line as it is reading from an input stream. The input record separator is ordinarily the newline character `\n`. By setting its value to `undef` in line (B), the line input operator in line (C) will no longer be able to separate the individual lines in the text file. Instead, the line input operator will read all of the text file as a *single* string.[63] Subsequently, as explained in greater detail in Section 4.12 of Chapter 4, the `split` operator in line (C) breaks up the long string read in according to the white space separating the words. The upshot is that a single statement, as shown in line (C), deposits a list of words in the array `@all_words`.

2.10 FUNCTIONS SUPPLIED WITH HERE-DOC ARGUMENTS

Perl comes with *here documents* — a way of providing arguments to functions that has proved useful when writing scripts for CGI programming[64] and for creating formatted reports. When the argument to a function starts with the symbol <<, the actual argument to the function is the text material that starts in the next line and ends at the next occurrence of the same string that was placed immediately after <<. This text material is known as the "here document," or "here-doc" for short. The following example illustrates the notion:

```
print <<END;                                                #(A)
hello jello
yello
END
                                # hello jello
                                # yello
```

The syntax in line (A) specifies that the string `END` that immediately follows << is meant to be used as the end-of-text indicator for the here-doc material beginning in the next line. So, for the example shown, the argument to `print` becomes the string

[63]The script `Or.pl` is obviously another way of reading a file in the slurp mode that we talked about in Section 2.6 of this chapter. See the script `Slurp.pl` in that section for the way mentioned earlier.

[64]CGI stands for *Common Gateway Interface*. CGI scripts, frequently written in Perl or Python, are automatically executed by a web server for processing the data returned by a browser. Additional information concerning CGI can be found in Problem 6 in the Homework section of Chapter 4.

hello jello\nyello, which includes the newline character between jello and yello. The output produced by the above call to print is shown in the two commented-out lines below the here-doc.

With regard to the *terminating* appearance of the end-of-text indicator, important constraints are that the indicator must always be unquoted and, starting at the beginning of the line, it must be the only string in that line. That line is not allowed to have even white space after the indicator.

In the above example of a here-doc, the opening appearance of the end-of-text indicator was left unquoted in line (A). In general, in its opening appearance, the end-of-text indicator can be quoted. In fact, it must be quoted with single quotes or double quotes if there exists any white space between << and the indicator. An unquoted end-of-text indicator in its opening placement is the same as a double-quoted indicator.

When quoted, the quote marks used for the end-of-text indicator carry meaning, in the same sense that they carry meaning for regular Perl strings. A here-doc constructed with a double-quoted end-of-text indicator allows for string interpolation in the same sense as a double-quoted string. On the other hand, a here-doc constructed with a single-quoted end-of-text indicator forces all the characters inside the here-doc to be taken literally, as with any single-quoted string in Perl. To illustrate, whereas the here-doc shown below allows the interpolation of the array @arr:

```
my @arr = qw(mello cello);
print << "END";
hello jello @arr
END
                    # output:  hello jello mello cello
```

the here-doc shown below with single-quoted end-of-text indicator does not:

```
my @arr = qw(mello cello);
print << 'END';
hello jello @arr
END
                    # output:  hello jello @arr
```

The next script, HereDoc.pl, presents eight examples with different usages of here-docs. The first, starting in line (A), invokes a one-argument function, joiner(), with the argument being supplied as the text in the next two lines. As the definition of joiner() at line (W) shows, this function joins up all the words entered in the here-doc into a single string while discarding any newline characters that may be present in the here-doc. The call to split() with the white-space character as its first argument is special-cased to eat up *all* white-space characters, including the newline character.[65]

The next example, starting in line (C), shows a function call where multiple arguments, in this case two, are supplied as here-docs to a function called `mingler()` that is defined in line (X). This function returns a string obtained by interleaving the words in its two arguments. By the way, if multiple arguments in a function call are here-docs, they do not need to be consecutive in the function call syntax. For example, the first argument can be a here-doc, as per our Example 2, the second argument a regular something, and the third argument again a here-doc.

Example 3 in lines (E) through (H) shows how one can use a format string to produce a formatted output. The function `formline()` takes two arguments, the first of which is a format string containing special symbols that act as place-holders for the different fields and for controlling the display of those fields. The second is a list of values to be inserted into the format string. The formatted output is placed in the special global variable `$^A`, also named `$ACCUMULATOR` in the `English` package.[66] In Example 3, the first argument to `formline()` is supplied in the form of a here-doc. We print out the contents of the accumulator in line (G) and then zero out the accumulator in line (H). We see that the last field spit out by the accumulator is truncated. That is for reasons explained in Problem 8 in the Homework section of Chapter 4. Just to show another way of calling `formline()`, our Example 4 parallels Example 3, with the difference being that we now ask for the argument values to be substituted for the variables in the call to `formline()` in line (L). Our format string now allows for all of the second field to be printed out, as shown in the output in the commented-out portion of line (M).

Example 5 in lines (O) through (P) shows a common way to emit HTML in a CGI script that is written in Perl. As briefly explained in the statement of Problem 7 in the Homework section of Chapter 4, a CGI script is used on the server side to process the information returned when a remote user fills out an HTML form in a browser window and then hits the "Submit" button in the form. Whatever the CGI script writes to its standard output is sent back to the remote browser for display. Example 5 shows us using a here-doc to write some HTML to the standard output.

---

[65]The syntax used in the definition of `joiner()` will become clear after we have discussed Perl references in Chapter 5. Suffice it to say here that the definition shown is equivalent to the slightly more verbose

```
sub joiner {
    my @words = split( ' ', join( ' ', @_ ) );
    return "@words";
}
```

The `split()` and `join()` functions are presented in greater detail in Section 4.12 of Chapter 4.

[66]See Problem 8 in the Homework section of Chapter 4 for a brief explanation of the symbols in the format string.

Example 7, to be contrasted with Example 6, shows that when the here-doc end-of-text indicator is quoted with backtics, each line in the here-doc will actually be executed in a separate process. Whatever these processes write to the standard output is captured by the variable `$str` for the example in line (S).[67] On the other hand, with the forward tics (the usual single quote) used for quoting the end-of-text indicator in line (Q) in Example 6, the string value stored in `$str` is literally what is in the here-doc.

Our last example, Example 8, shows a here-doc being used to specify the input string needed for a substring "search and replace" operation. Such operations are discussed in greater detail in Section 4.13 of Chapter 4.

```
#!/usr/bin/perl -w

### HereDoc.pl

use strict;

#                                EXAMPLE 1

my $res = joiner( <<END );                                              #(A)
hello jello mello
pillow yellow
END
print $res, "\n";             # hello jello mello pillow yellow         #(B)


#                                EXAMPLE 2

$res = mingler( <<END1, <<END2 );                                       #(C)
abra babra cabra dabra
libra zebra
END1
kiki
yucky
ziki
END2
print $res, "\n";                                                       #(D)
          # abra kiki babra yucky cabra ziki dabra  libra  zebra


#                                EXAMPLE 3
```

[67]The use of backtics to launch external processes in Perl and to capture their output is explained in greater detail in Section 2.17.2.

```
use English;                                                         #(E)

formline <<END, "hello", "jello", "melloyellow";                     #(F)
        @<<<  @|||  @>>>
END
print "$ACCUMULATOR\n";          #        hell  jell  mell           #(G)
$ACCUMULATOR = "";                                                   #(H)



#                               EXAMPLE 4

my $item1 = "silly";                                                 #(I)
my $item2 = "hillbilly";                                             #(J)
my $fmt = '     @<<<<      @>>>>>>>>>';                              #(K)
formline($fmt, $item1, $item2);                                      #(L)
print $ACCUMULATOR, "\n";        #      silly       hillbilly        #(M)
$ACCUMULATOR = "";                                                   #(N)



#                               EXAMPLE 5

print <<ENDHEADER;                                                   #(O)
<HEAD><TITLE>My Guestbook</TITLE></HEAD>
<BODY bgcolor=dcdcdc>
<CENTER>
<H1>My GUESTBOOK</H1>
<A HREF=guestbook.cgi>[Post a message]</A>
</CENTER>
<H2>Prior Messages</H2>
ENDHEADER
                 # output: exactly as it appears in the              #(P)
                 #         "here document" above


#                               EXAMPLE 6

my $str = << 'END';                                                  #(Q)
ls -al
END
print $str, "\n";                # ls -al                            #(R)


#                               EXAMPLE 7

$str = << `END`;                                                     #(S)
```

```
ls -al
END
print $str, "\n";                                                          #(T)
                  # output: a listing of the items in your
                  #         current directory



#                              EXAMPLE 8

($str = <<END)  =~ s/hello/jello/g;                                        #(U)
  one hello is like another hello
END
print $str, "\n";              # one jello is like another jello           #(V)


#---------------------- Subroutines used above -----------------------

sub joiner {                                                               #(W)
    return "@{[ split( ' ', join( ' ', @_ ) ) ]}";
}

sub mingler {                                                              #(X)
    my @arr1 = split ' ', shift;
    my @arr2 = split ' ', shift;
    my $mingled;
    my $i = 0;
    while ($i <= (($#arr1 > $#arr2) ? $#arr1 : $#arr2) ) {
        $mingled .= ($arr1[$i] or "")
                  . ' '
                  . ($arr2[$i++] or "")
                  . ' ';
    }
    return $mingled;
}
```

2.11 MODULES AND PACKAGES IN PERL

A great deal of functionality that you may desire from Perl has already been programmed in the form of modules that come either prepackaged with the Perl distribution or can easily be downloaded from the web. Also, when you create nontrivial scripts that you want to share with others, you would want to write them in the form of modules.[68]

A Perl *module* is an extension of the core language. Most frequently, a module consists of a single file of Perl code with the file name ending in the suffix .pm, and with the first statement in the file being

```
package module_name;
```

Perhaps the most important property of a module is that it defines a separate *namespace*. The namespace modularization is achieved by using the package declaration, which, as discussed previously in Section 2.3.2, is the primary mechanism in Perl for creating separate namespaces. The reason for the distinction between a *package* and a *module* in Perl is that a single module file can contain multiple package declarations, and, hence, multiple namespaces.

Let us say that you have created a namespace with a package declaration for a module and now you want to access the global names in the namespace in another module. Ordinarily, you'd need to use the package-qualified naming syntax

```
package_name::identifier_name
```

for that purpose. As was mentioned in Section 2.3.2, the top level, meaning your own script into which you may want to load other modules and which does not start with a package declaration, also defines a separate namespace — the namespace main. So, while most commonly you'd refer to a locally defined identifier that is *not* a my variable only by its name at the top level, it does have a package-qualified name also, which is

```
main::identifier_name
```

that is allowed to be abbreviated to just

```
::identifier_name
```

If a name is defined in the global namespace without a package being explicitly active at the time of the definition, then that name is global by default in the implicitly defined package main. Also note that the built-in variables such as $_, @_, etc. are defined in the implicitly defined package main. As variables that belong to the package main, these are special in the sense that they may be accessed in any namespace without the main:: prefix.

[68]To quickly determine whether or not a given module is available on your system, execute the following as a command line:

```
perl -e "use module_name"
```

where module_name stands for the name of the module you are looking for. If the module is not installed, you will get a "Can't locate" error.

2.11.1 Creating Your Own Module

Shown below is a user-defined module that sits in a file called `HelloModule.pm` in a directory named `MyModules`.[69] Line (A) of the script declares a new namespace named `HelloModule`. Lines (B) and (C) then define two subroutines in this namespace. Finally, line (D) takes care of the fact that when a module is incorporated in a script by either the `use` or the `require` directive, the directive must return a Boolean denoting either the success or the failure of the requested operation. A directive is considered to have succeeded when it returns a nonzero value. The directives `use` and `require` return whatever is returned by the last executable statement of a module. Ordinarily, the last statement of a module will be either `return` 1 or just 1, as in the example below in line (D).

```
# HelloModule.pm

package HelloModule;                                              #(A)

sub say_loud_hello {                                              #(B)
    print "HELLO!!! HOW ARE YOU!!!\n";
}

sub say_soft_hello {                                              #(C)
    print "hi dear! how are you this morning!\n";
}

1                                                                 #(D)
```

Let's assume that this module is stored in the following file:

```
/home/kak/MyModules/HelloModule.pm
```

We will now show how this module can be used in a script. A module is loaded into a script by either the `use` or the `require` directive. (The reader has already many examples of our employing the `use` directive in the various scripts shown so far.) Loading a module into a script achieves roughly the same result as `#include` in C or C++; that is, the source code in the module is pulled into the current file.[70]

[69]By convention, the name of a user-defined module should begin with an uppercase letter. Module names that are all lowercase are reserved for the Perl core. These are typically pragma modules like `strict` or `integer`. As mentioned earlier in this chapter, a pragma, as in `use strict`, is a compiler directive.

[70]This analogy with `#include` in C or C++ is only approximate since the `use` and `require` directives not only pull in the code, but also execute it.

When you load a module into your current file with either the `use` or the `require` directive, Perl looks for that module in the directories whose pathnames are stored in the global array `@INC`. The pathnames for all the modules that come with the standard Perl distribution[71] will already be in this array.[72] To make Perl aware of your own modules in nonstandard locations, you have to insert those locations into the array. This can be accomplished with a statement like

```
unshift @INC, "pathname_to_directory_containing_your_module";
```

As to when this `unshift` operation must be executed, note that before a Perl script is executed, it goes through a compilation stage when every statement is parsed and tested for the correctness of syntax. During this compilation scan, there is only one statement that is actually executed — the `use` statement. So, if during the parsing of the script, the following statement is encountered:

```
use HelloModule;
```

Perl will immediately look for `HelloModule` at all the locations specified in the array variable `@INC`. So if you have the following combination of statements in your file:

```
unshift @INC, "pathname_to_HelloModule";
use HelloModule;
```

the first of these will only be tested for syntax correctness during the compilation phase and the second will be actually executed. Obviously then, you would get a compilation error since Perl would not be able to find `HelloModule` in any of the locations it already knows about through `@INC`.

To resolve this dilemma, Perl provides a special keyword `BEGIN`.[73] Any code that is in a block named `BEGIN` is executed during the compilation phase itself. So the above problem can be fixed as follows:

```
BEGIN {
    unshift @INC, "pathname_to_HelloModule";
}
use HelloModule;
```

---

[71] The most basic Perl package that is always installed on a machine if it has Perl at all is referred to as the *core Perl*. Then there is the *standard distribution Perl*. The standard distribution consists of the Perl core and the additional modules that have been *officially* approved as extending the language. These modules may or may not already be installed on your machine. They are, however, readily downloaded and installed from `www.cpan.org`. In addition to the modules that are officially included in the standard distribution, there also exist at `www.cpan.org` and other sites thousands of other modules that are not officially included in the language but can nonetheless be used for specialized functionality.

[72] The pathnames in this array for an installed Perl distribution can be seen by invoking the following command in a terminal window:

```
perl -V
```

[73] `BEGIN` is actually a built-in name for a subroutine with a predefined behavior. See Section 2.11.5 for further details.

Now Perl will be able to locate HelloModule during the compilation phase itself.

Earlier we mentioned that both use and require can be used for loading a module into a script.[74] The main difference between the two is that while use loads in a module at compile time, require does the same at execution time. Additionally, use treats its argument as a module name, which it expects to see as a bareword ending in the .pm suffix. On the other hand, require wants its argument as a quoted string and does not insist that it end in the .pm suffix. So you could gather up a bunch of subroutines in, say, a .pl file and pull them into your script with a require directive. As is the case with the use directive, any file pulled in with a require directive must also return true to the calling script. For that reason, library files used for require directives end in the statement that consists of just the number 1 that always evaluates to true.

To summarize the above discussion, shown below is a Perl script that uses the module HelloModule defined at the beginning of this subsection.

```
#!/usr/bin/perl -w
use strict;

###  UsingHelloModule.pl

BEGIN {
    unshift @INC, "/home/kak/MyModules/";
}

use HelloModule;

&HelloModule::say_loud_hello();

&HelloModule::say_soft_hello();
```

For Unix-like pathnames to modules, it is also possible to use the lib pragma to achieve the same effect as what is accomplished by the BEGIN construct shown above. That is, in the above script we could have replaced

```
BEGIN {
    unshift @INC, "/home/kak/MyModules/";
}
```

by

[74] As we will see shortly, under the hood, the use directive actually employs the require directive. So, contrary to appearances, the two are not "independent" directives.

```
use lib "/home/kak/MyModules/";
```

Perl does not strictly enforce the privacy of a namespace corresponding to a module. A namespace may be expanded upon and modified in other namespaces. To demonstrate this, the code shown in the following example belongs to the namespace `main`. Nonetheless, in line (C) we are allowed to define a new subroutine, `say_mild_hello`, in the namespace of `HelloModule`. Subsequently, in line (F) we can invoke this new subroutine in a manner that is no different from the other subroutines that were defined originally for `HelloModule`.

```
#!/usr/bin/perl -w
use strict;

### UsingHelloModuleNoPrivacy.pl

BEGIN {                                                         #(A)
    unshift @INC, "/home/kak/MyModules/";
}

use HelloModule;                                                #(B)

sub HelloModule::say_mild_hello {                               #(C)
    print "Hi, How are you!\n";
}

&HelloModule::say_loud_hello();                                 #(D)

&HelloModule::say_soft_hello();                                 #(E)

&HelloModule::say_mild_hello();                                 #(F)
```

When you add to the definitions of namespace A while you are in namespace B, it does not mean that you are writing into the file that contains the hard-coded definitions for namespace A. It only means that, while you are active in namespace B, you shall see a version of namespace A that is larger than what is provided by the disk file in which the module corresponding to namespace A resides.

Is it possible to keep hidden in a module some of the code defined therein? Yes. We will show later how to do that after introducing the notion of a Perl reference in Chapter 5.

2.11.2 Importing Names from a Module

Ordinarily, when you load a module into the active namespace with the `use` directive, all the global names in that module become available in the active namespace, provided they are accessed by using their fully qualified names, meaning with the prefix `package_name::`.

Always having to use the `package_name::` prefix for a name defined in a module can become tiresome. In that event, we can `import` the name into the current namespace. An imported name can be used directly, without the prefix `package_name::`. An imported name acts as if it was locally declared.

However, before a name can be imported from another module, that module must permit its export. Choosing which names are allowed to be exported by a module can be controlled by a special module, `Exporter`. To demonstrate how `Exporter` is used to specify the names that are allowed to be imported by other modules, shown below is a rewrite of our `HelloModule` presented earlier. We will refer to this version of the module as `HelloModule2`.

Line (B) of `HelloModule2` loads in the `Exporter` module. Line (C) declares the current module to be a subclass of the `Exporter` module.[75] Line (D) then declares which names will be exported by `HelloModule2`. Not all of these names have to be imported by another module, but the names imported will always be a subset of the those declared in line (D). If the list on the right-hand side in line (D) is left empty, `Exporter` will NOT allow any names to be imported from `HelloModule2`. Note also that if the declaration in line (D) mentions the array `@EXPORT` (as opposed to the array `@EXPORT_OK`) followed by a list of names, all of those names (and only those names) will be exported into the calling module. If nothing follows `@EXPORT` in such a statement, by default that causes all of the names to be exported into the calling module.

```
# HelloModule2.pm

package HelloModule2;                                                    #(A)

use Exporter;                                                            #(B)

@ISA = ( 'Exporter' );                                                   #(C)

@EXPORT_OK = ( 'say_loud_hello', 'say_soft_hello' );                     #(D)

sub say_loud_hello {                                                     #(E)
```

[75] Subclassing is an object-oriented notion that for Perl will be explained in detail in Chapter 8. Suffice it to say here that, because of the `ISA` declaration in line (C), if a function cannot be found in the `HelloModule2` module, it will be searched for in the `Exporter` module.

```
    print "HELLO!!! HOW ARE YOU!!!\n";
}

sub say_soft_hello {                                                  #(F)
    print "hi dear! how are you this morning!\n";
}

1
```

Shown below is a script that uses `HelloModule2` and its export facility. Note the new syntax for the `use` directive in line (B):

```
    use module_name ( 'name1', 'name2', 'name3', .... );
```

The names to be imported from `HelloModule2` are in the list that follows the name of the module. In this particular example, we want only one name, `say_loud_hello`, to be imported. Subsequently, this name can be called without its namespace qualification, as shown in line (C). On the other hand, as shown in line (D), we must use the full package qualified name for `say_soft_hello` because it is not in the list in line (B) — and despite the fact that this name is on the export list of `HelloModule2`.

```
#!/usr/bin/perl -w
use strict;

### UsingHelloModuleWithImport.pl

BEGIN {                                                               #(A)
    unshift @INC, "/home/kak/MyModules/";
}

use HelloModule2 ( 'say_loud_hello' );                                #(B)

say_loud_hello();                                                     #(C)

&HelloModule2::say_soft_hello();                                      #(D)
```

In general, the `use` directive

```
    use module_name ( 'name1', 'name2', 'name3', .... );
```

is equivalent to[76]

```
BEGIN {
    require module_name;
    module_name->import( 'name1', 'name2', 'name3', .... );
}
```

where BEGIN causes the *compile-time execution* of the block that comes next. The require directive immediately pulls in the source code from the designated module file into the memory and then executes it to create bindings for the subroutine names and the global variables in the module.[77] The import() statement that comes next then decides which of the names of the module file just pulled in can be accessed directly (that is, without package qualified syntax) in the current namespace. Note that the definition of import() that will be used comes from the same module that was just pulled in by the require directive. [It is this import() that will often be inherited by a module from the Exporter module.]

If a module that was loaded in by the require directive does not supply import(), the call to import() following the call to require() is simply ignored. In that case, all the subroutine and other global names in the module file pulled in by require become available in the current script without package qualification. If a module does come with import() but it needs to be ignored, that can be achieved by supplying an empty list as a second argument to the use directive, as in

```
use Some_Module ();
```

This call is exactly equivalent to

```
BEGIN { require some_module; }
```

which would ensure that no names at all are imported from the module into the current script. Now these names will only be accessible with package-qualified syntax.

Note that nothing prevents a module from defining its own import() that will then be employed by any script that wants to load this module. Chapter 11 shows examples of user-defined implementations for import() for eliciting specialized behavior from modules at load time.

---

[76]Chapter 5 explains the arrow operator used in the second statement in the BEGIN block. What we are trying to do here is to call import() function as a static method directly on the module. Static methods of Perl are explained in Section 6.6 of Chapter 6.

[77]This should lend credence to the claim we made in an earlier footnote in this section that the use directive depends on the require directive for a part of what the former directive accomplishes.

2.11.3 "Nesting" of Modules

Strictly speaking, you cannot nest modules in Perl because all namespaces created by the `package` declaration are equally global in scope. However, for the purpose of organizing the modules, you can create an illusion of nesting by storing a set of modules hierarchically in a directory structure. For example, let's say that a set of related modules is organized in a directory structure that looks like

```
top_directory                                                  #(A)
    sub_directory                                              #(B)
        sub_sub_directory                                      #(C)
            module.pm            (file)                        #(D)
```

If the paths included in the array `@INC`, where Perl looks for modules, contain the path to the top-level `top_directory` listed above, then in a script using the `module.pm` file, the namespace corresponding to the module can be represented by the notation:

```
top_directory::sub_directory::sub_sub_directory::module
```

In other words, if your script includes the following `use` directive:

```
use top_directory::sub_directory::sub_sub_directory::module;
```

the Perl compiler will expect to see a directory structure like the one shown in lines (A) through (D) above.

2.11.4 The Autoloading Feature

Let us say that you have loaded in a module with the `use` directive and that you are now calling a nonexistent subroutine from the module. When that happens, ordinarily you would get a compile-time error. But not so if the module provides implementation for a subroutine called `AUTOLOAD`.

Consider the following module, `HelloModule3`, that was placed in the same directory as the `HelloModule` and `HelloModule2` modules shown earlier. Note the implementation for the subroutine `AUTOLOAD` in line (A) of this module:

```
# HelloModule3.pm

package HelloModule3;

sub say_loud_hello {
    print "HELLO!!! HOW ARE YOU!!!\n";
}
```

```
sub say_soft_hello {
    print "hi dear! how are you this morning!\n";
}

sub AUTOLOAD {                                                      #(A)
    print "Message from HelloModule3:\n",                           #(B)
          "The function you called does  \
                    not exist in HelloModule3.\n";                  #(C)
}

1
```

The script shown next loads HelloModule3 in line (A) and invokes its two subroutines in lines (B) and (C). However, in line (D) it invokes a subroutine that does not exist in HelloModule3. The output for this invocation is the message shown above in the implementation of the AUTOLOAD subroutine in lines (B) and (C) of HelloModule3.

```
#!/usr/bin/perl -w
use strict;

### UsingHelloModuleWithAutoload.pl

BEGIN {
    unshift @INC, "/home/kak/MyModules/";
}

use HelloModule3;                                                   #(A)

&HelloModule3::say_loud_hello();                                    #(B)

&HelloModule3::say_soft_hello();                                    #(C)

&HelloModule3::say_friendly_hello();                                #(D)
```

When invoking AUTOLOAD, Perl stores the name of the actual method called in the scalar variable $AUTOLOAD in the namespace of the package on which the method is called. In Chapter 6, we will show how this feature can be used to prevent AUTOLOAD from being invoked if it is not meant to be called for certain intentionally missing methods in a package.

2.11.5 Package Constructors and Destructors

The four subroutine names — BEGIN, CHECK, INIT, and END — are assigned special roles in a package. The first three are generally referred to as package *constructors* and the last, END, as a package *destructor* on account of the order in which they are executed in relation to the run-time execution of the script that loads in the package.[78] Here are their behaviors:

BEGIN: As a package is being loaded into a script, a subroutine that is named BEGIN is executed as soon as its definition is complete. Therefore, a BEGIN subroutine can be used to pull in definitions and implementation code from other sources and these can then be made available to the rest of the script as the loading process continues. A package can contain any number of BEGIN subroutines; they will be executed in the order in which they appear in the package. As soon as a BEGIN subroutine is executed, it is undefined and any memory allocated during its execution freed up. This prevents a BEGIN subroutine from being called as a free-standing function later.

CHECK: A subroutine named CHECK is executed as soon as the compilation phase of a package is complete and just prior to the start of the run-time execution of the script pulling in the package. A package can contain any number of subroutines named CHECK; these will be executed in the reverse order of their appearance in the package.

INIT: If a package contains a single INIT subroutine — which is probably the most common case as far as this subroutine is concerned — it is executed *before* the run-time execution of the script that is loading in the package. If a package contains multiple such subroutines, they are executed in the order of their appearance, but all prior to the run-time execution of the script loading in the package.

END: A subroutine named END from a loaded-in package is executed as late as possible during the execution of a script. In other words, this subroutine will be taken up for execution just prior to the interpreter coming to a halt. A very important thing to note here is that END from a loaded-in package will be run even if the run-time execution of the script loading in the package is aborted by, say, a die function.[79] If a package contains multiple END subroutines, they are taken up for execution in the reverse order of their appearance in the package. An END subroutine is allowed to use the special global variable $? for specifying the exit status of the script.

---

[78]The use of sub is optional when defining a subroutine that is named either BEGIN, CHECK, INIT, or END.

[79]However, the END subroutines will not be executed if an error is encountered during the compilation of the script loading in the package.

To illustrate these behaviors of the package constructors and destructors, consider the following module in which we have two definitions for each of the four subroutines:

```
### PackageConstDestr.pm

package PackageConstDestr;

print "executing the top-level of PackageConstDestr module\n";

BEGIN {
    print "executing the first BEGIN subroutine\n";
}
BEGIN {
    print "executing the second BEGIN subroutine\n";
}
END {
    print "executing the first END subroutine\n";
}
END {
    print "executing the second END subroutine\n";
}
CHECK {
    print "executing the first CHECK soubroutine\n";
}
CHECK {
    print "executing the second CHECK soubroutine\n";
}
INIT {
    print "executing the first INIT subroutine\n";
}
INIT {
    print "executing the second INIT subroutine\n";
}
1;
```

The following script loads in the above module:

```
#!/usr/bin/perl -w
use strict;

### TestPackageConstDestr.pl
```

```
BEGIN {
    unshift @INC, "/home/kak/MyModules/";
}

use PackageConstDestr;

print "Perl runtime has begun execution\n";

die "Execution aborted\n";
```

We have the following output:

```
executing the first BEGIN subroutine
executing the second BEGIN subroutine
executing the top-level of PackageConstDestr module
executing the second CHECK soubroutine
executing the first CHECK soubroutine
executing the first INIT subroutine
executing the second INIT subroutine
Perl runtime has begun execution
Execution aborted
executing the second END subroutine
executing the first END subroutine
```

As the reader can see, the `BEGIN` subroutines of the module are executed in the order of their appearance in the package, the `CHECK` subroutines in the reverse order of their appearance, the `INIT` subroutines in the order of their appearance, and `END` in the reverse order. The `CHECK` subroutines are invoked after the main body of the imported package is executed, and just after the compilation phase of the script importing the package is complete. The `INIT` subroutines are invoked just before the run-time execution of the script that has loaded in the package. The `END` subroutines are invoked just before the interpreter is about to come to a halt — in this example because of the exception thrown by the main body of the script.

2.12 TEMPORARILY LOCALIZING A GLOBAL VARIABLE

As briefly mentioned in Section 2.9.4, when a global variable is declared `local`, its value is temporarily put away until the end of the scope in which the `local` declaration is made. When the flow of execution exits that scope, the previous value of the global variable is restored. As we will show in this section, this property of global variables, especially the built-in global variables whose names consist of the prefix `$` followed by a nonletter character, can be taken advantage of to elicit altered — and sometimes useful — behavior from the various operators and functions of Perl.

The next script consists of two examples. The first example, in lines (A) through (F), simply demonstrates what we mean by temporarily localizing a global variable. Line (A) initializes a user-defined global variable `$x`.[80] Line (B) begins a new block scope that ends in line (E). Line (C) declares the global scalar `$x` to be `local`, causing its previous value to be temporarily put away, and assigns a value of 200 to the variable. When we print out the value of this variable in line (D), we get 200, as one would expect. However, when print out the value of the same variable in line (F) after exiting the block in line (E), we get the original value as set in line (A).

The second example, in lines (G) through (U), shows the same application of localizing a global variable that we did in the script `Or.pl` in Section 2.9.4. By localizing and then "undefing" the value of the built-in variable `$/`, we cause the line input operator <> to read an entire text file in one fell swoop, as opposed to reading the file one line at a time. Ordinarily, as was mentioned in Section 2.9.4, the value of the global `$\` is whatever it takes to recognize a new line of text in a text file. Typically, this value is the newline character. Line (L) declares this variable `local` and makes its value `undef`. With this change in the value of `$\`, the line input operator <> becomes blind to the role of the newline character as a line-delimiting character in an input text file. So the invocation of the <> operator in line (M) will read the entire file all at once into a single string. This string becomes the second argument to the `split` function in the same line. The `split()` function breaks the string into individual words using white space, which includes blank space, newlines, tabs, and so on, as the word delimiter.[81] When the input file contains the following text:

```
A hungry dog
jumped over a
lazy blue-colored
fish.
```

the slurp mode reading of the file in line (M) places the following words into the array `@all_words`:

```
A hungry dog jumped over a lazy blue-colored fish.
```

On the other hand, when we read the same file with the same operator in lines (Q) and (R), we get the following words into the array `@all_words`:

---

[80]The syntax we have used for declaring the global variable in line (A) is only one of the three different ways for doing the same. All three ways are described in Section 2.3.2. Also note that, as mentioned previously, a top-level script such as the one shown here is implicitly in the package `main`. So a package-qualified name for a global variable at the top level would carry the `main::` prefix.

[81]As pointed out in Section 4.12 of Chapter 4, the following invocation of split:

```
split ' ', astring;
```

is special syntax for invoking this function. Ordinarily, the first argument to this function is a regular expression that specifies word boundaries. Any characters that match the regular expression are swallowed up by the splitting process and separate the preceding and the following word. When the first argument is just the blank character shown above, it is a signal to `split` that it should use all white space characters for word separation, and, additionally, if there are any white space characters at the beginning of the second-argument string, it should ignore them too.

```
A hungry dog
```

This occurs because, after the flow of execution has exited the local block in line (O), the value of the global `$\` reverts back to the newline character. So the operator `<>` again reads only one line at a time.

```
#!/usr/bin/perl -w
use strict;

### LocalizeGlobal.pl

# EXAMPLE 1:

$main::x = 100;                                                    #(A)
{                                                                  #(B)
    local $main::x = 200;                                          #(C)
    print "$main::x\n";                         # 200              #(D)
}                                                                  #(E)
print "$main::x\n";                             # 100              #(F)


# EXAMPLE 2:

my $file = "data.txt";                                             #(G)
my @all_words;                                                     #(H)
{                                                                  #(I)
    open FILE, $file                                               #(J)
        or die "Can't open $file: $!";                             #(K)
    local $/ = undef;                                              #(L)
    @all_words = split ' ', <FILE>;                                #(M)
    close FILE;                                                    #(N)
}                                                                  #(O)
print "@all_words\n";                                              #(P)
                # A hungry dog jumped over a lazy blue-colored fish.

open FILE, $file                                                   #(Q)
    or die "Can't open $file: $!";                                 #(R)
@all_words = split ' ', <FILE>;                                    #(S)
close FILE;                                                        #(T)
print "@all_words\n";                           # A hungry dog     #(U)
```

2.13 TYPEGLOBS FOR GLOBAL NAMES

As we mentioned earlier, in all names such as `$xvar`, `@words`, `%phone_book`, etc., the actual name of the variable is what follows the first nonletter prefix, the prefix serving as a qualifier for the name. As the reader has already seen, in addition to such names, Perl uses names without any nonletter prefixes for filehandles and formats. Perl allows different usages of the same name within the same scope, yet Perl recognizes them to be distinct and independent of one another. For example, all of the following six uses of the name `xvar` are distinct (in the sense that each use does not conflict with the other uses), and simultaneously valid:

```
$xvar      -->   used as a scalar

@xvar      -->   used as an array

%xvar      -->   used as a hash

&xvar      -->   used to call a subroutine

xvar       -->   used as a filehandle

xvar       -->   used as a format
```

How does Perl keep track of the different uses of the same name? For global names,[82] Perl accomplishes this with the help of an internal data structure called *typeglob*. Perl associates one typeglob with each name in the global scope. In the rest of this section, we will first briefly talk about Perl's symbol tables, where the names are interned, and then review the typeglob data structure for how it can be used to create name aliases in a script.

As previously mentioned in Section 2.3.2, Perl interns each global name in a symbol table that is implemented as a hash.[83] Each name is a key in a key-value pair in the symbol table. Since no duplicate keys are allowed in a hash, there can only be one entry for the six uses of the same name shown above. The value associated with a key is a pointer to a typeglob data structure. It is the typeglob structure that has six slots for the six different uses that a name can be put to. So when you call, say, `$xvar` in a script, Perl reaches into its symbol table and retrieves the typeglob associated with the name `xvar`. The prefix `$` then causes Perl to seek out the pointer in the first slot of the typeglob associated with `xvar`. This pointer leads to the value of the scalar `$xvar`. The same procedure is invoked for all other uses of the name `xvar`. Of course, if each name is used uniquely in a script, likely to be

---

[82]Names declared `my` — that is, the lexical names — are kept track of separately. As described in Section 2.3, each local scope has associated with it a *scratchpad* for keeping track of the lexical names.

[83]As was also mentioned previously in Section 2.3.2, the symbol table hash of Perl is also called a *stash*.

the case in a well-written script, only one of the six slots of a typeglob will have a non-null pointer.

The typeglob associated with a name is accessible through the prefix `*`. Therefore, the typeglob associated with the name `xvar` is `*xvar`. Typeglobs can be assigned, stored as values in data structures, passed as arguments, and so forth. You can even create "local" versions of them.

What do we achieve by assigning a typeglob? The answer is simple: Name aliases that are convenient when programming perspicuity requires that you use a long and meaningful name for, say, a subroutine inside a module, but you not subject the user of that module to have to directly type in the long name in his/her calls to the subroutine. To illustrate how name aliasing can be achieved with typeglob assignment, suppose we declare the following uses for the name `xvar` in a script:

```
$xvar = 10;
@xvar = (1, 2, 3, 4);
%xvar = (a => 5, b => 6);
open xvar, "info.dat";
sub xvar {
     print "hello\n";
}
```

Now if we make the following assignment:

```
*yvar = *xvar;
```

The symbol-table entry for the name `yvar` will point to the same typeglob as the symbol table entry for the name `xvar`. Since the typeglobs associated with the names `xvar` and `vyar` are the same, `$yvar` will be synonymous with `$xvar`, `@yvar` with `@xvar`, `%yvar` with `%xvar`, etc. Indeed, if we say

```
print $yvar;
```

we will see 10 for the output of `print` because that is the value of `$xvar`. And if we say

```
print "@yvar\n";
```

we will get

```
1 2 3 4
```

since those are the elements in the array `@xvar`. The same would be true for other uses of the names `xvar` and `yvar`.

The next script, `TypeGlobAssign.pl`, is a working demonstration of this discussion. Since we have used the `strict` pragma, all global names must carry package qualifications.[84] That is why the global names in the script carry the `main::` prefix. Lines (A) through (G) establish different uses for the name `xvar`. It is a scalar in line (A), an array in line (B), a hash in line (C), a filehandle in line (D), and, finally, a subroutine name in line (E). Line (H) uses typeglob assignment to establish `yvar` as an alias for `xvar`. The fact that `yvar` is indeed acting as an alias for `xvar` is established by the commented-out outputs shown in lines (I) through (P), where we make all our accesses through the `yvar` name. The file `data.txt` referred to in line (D) has the following text in it:

```
A hungry dog
jumped over a
lazy blue-colored
fish.
```

Lines (Q) through (T) show how the name aliasing effect created by a typeglob assignment can be localized in a script — localized in the sense that the alias is effective only inside a block. Line (Q) declares and initializes a new global variable `zvar`. But then, inside a block in line (R), we make `zvar` local and assign to the typeglob `*zvar` the typeglob `*xvar`. This causes `$zvar` in line (S) to act as an alias for `$xvar`, as seen by the value output by the print command. However, upon exiting the block, the original meaning of the identifier `zvar` is restored, causing the original value of `$zvar` to be printed out in line (T).

We mentioned earlier in Section 2.3.2 that if you do not use the `strict` pragma, you can declare global variables without package qualifications. Now, apparently, there can be name conflicts between a global name and a similar lexical name. Any such name conflicts are resolved by using the rule that the lexical meaning will hide the global meaning. This is depicted with the help of lines (U) through (Y) of the script. We first countermand the `strict` pragma by the `no strict` directive in line (U). Now it is not necessary to use package qualifications for the global variables. So when we directly access the variable `$xvar` in line (V), we get its global definition. Line (W) then declares a lexical variable of the same name and initializes it to 10000. When we access the variable `$xvar` in line (X), we see its lexical definition. The global definition of this variable can only be accessed by using package qualification, as we do in line (Y).[85]

Recall that Perl allows you to replace the prefix `main::` in the package qualified name of a global variable by just the `::` prefix. Therefore, the lines (A) through (G) of the following script could also have been written as

```
$::xvar = 10;
@::xvar = (1, 2, 3, 4);
%::xvar = (a => 5, b => 6);
```

---

[84] Unless, of course, we use `our` or `use vars` variables, as explained in Section 2.3.2.

[85] Earlier in Section 2.3.2 we showed a `my` variable hiding the meaning of an `our` variable of the same name.

```
open(::xvar, "data.txt");
sub ::xvar {
    print "hello\n";
}
```

Here is the script:

```
#!/usr/bin/perl -w

### TypeglobAssign.pl

use strict;

# Assign values for the different uses of the name 'xvar':
$main::xvar = 10;                                                       #(A)
@main::xvar = (1, 2, 3, 4);                                             #(B)
%main::xvar = (a => 5, b => 6);                                         #(C)
open(main::xvar, "data.txt");                                           #(D)
sub main::xvar {                                                        #(E)
    print "hello\n";                                                    #(F)
}                                                                       #(G)

# A typeglob alias for the name 'xvar':
*main::yvar = *main::xvar;                                              #(H)

# Process 'yvar' as if it is 'xvar':
print "$main::yvar\n";                       # 10                       #(I)
my @arr = @main::yvar;                                                  #(J)
print "@arr\n";                              # 1  2  3  4               #(K)
my @for_print = %main::yvar;                                            #(L)
print "@for_print\n";                        # a  5  b  6               #(M)
&main::yvar;                                 # hello                    #(N)
my $string_from_file = <main::yvar>;                                    #(O)
print "$string_from_file\n";                 # A hungry dog             #(P)

# Name aliasing by typeglob assignments can be localized:
$main::zvar = 100;                                                      #(Q)
{
    local *main::zvar = *main::xvar;                                    #(R)
    print "$main::zvar\n";                   # 10                       #(S)
}
print "$main::zvar\n";                       # 100                      #(T)

# "my" name hides global name:
no strict;                                                              #(U)
print "$xvar\n";                             # 10                       #(V)
my $xvar = 10000;                                                       #(W)
```

```
print "$xvar\n";                              # 10000                   #(X)
print "$main::xvar\n";                        # 10                      #(Y)
```

The typeglob assignment creates a general alias in the sense that all uses of one name amount to the corresponding uses of the other name. In other words, if we say

```
*yvar = *xvar;
```

then `$yvar` will become an alias for `$xvar`, `@yvar` will become an alias for `@xvar`, and so on. It is also possible to create name aliases on a selective basis. For example, if you say

```
*yvar = \$xvar;
```

only the name `$yvar` will serve as an alias for `$xvar`. If we want to create an alias for the `@` prefix for the `xvar` name, we must write

```
*yvar = \@xvar;
```

and so on.

2.13.1 Creating Global Variables by Direct Assignments to Typeglob Slots

Let us imagine we want to create a global scalar `$foo` in the namespace `main`. As the reader has already seen, it is done quite easily by assignment syntax like[86]

```
$main::foo = "hello";                                                   #(A)
print "$main::foo\n";                       # hello                     #(B)
```

Line (A) causes a typeglob for the name `foo` to be created and for the scalar slot of this typeglob to point to the value `hello`.

However, there is a way to bring into existence a global scalar that more directly involves the creation of the underlying typeglob. Consider the following syntax:

```
${*foo} = "hello";                                                      #(C)
print "$main::foo\n";                       # hello                     #(D)
```

[86]As already pointed out, we can also use the more abbreviated syntax:

```
$::foo = "hello";
print "$::foo\n";                    # hello
```

Now, in line (C), we are directly accessing the typeglob `*foo` in the current namespace, `main`, and are asking that the scalar slot of this typeglob be made to point to the value `hello`.

Just as a scalar was placed in the typeglob's scalar slot by directly accessing the typeglob in line (C), so, too, can we place an array in the array slot of a typeglob:

```
@{*foo} = ( 'one', 'two', 'three' );
print "@{*foo}\n";                    # one two three
```

2.14 THE eval OPERATOR

There are two entirely different ways to use `eval` in Perl:

- Use `eval` for evaluating a string if the string is a snippet of Perl code.
- Use `eval` to evaluate a block of code to trap run-time errors and, if they occur, to place the errors in a special variable `$@`.

In both cases, if the argument to `eval` is executed without error, the value returned by `eval` is whatever was returned by the last expression processed in the argument to the operator. The expression that is processed for its return value is evaluated in the same context that applies to `eval` itself. If the argument string (or the argument block of code) to `eval` cannot be parsed and compiled successfully into a piece of valid Perl code, `eval` returns `undef`.

To see how `eval` is used for evaluating a string argument, consider the following code snippet:

```
my $str = '$a / $b';                                          #(A)
my $a = 10;                                                   #(B)
my $b = 20;                                                   #(C)
print eval $str, "\n";                   # 0.5                #(D)
```

The right-hand side of line (A) defines a single-quoted string. As it is single-quoted, no substitutions for any variables are allowed in this string. So as things stand at the end of line (A), `$str` is just a string of 7 characters. When we invoke `eval` on this string in line (D), Perl literally thinks of the contents of the string argument as a block of code. It parses the string into Perl statements, executes each of those statements, and, as with any block of code, returns the output of the last statement executed.

Now, with the help of the following two scenarios, we will demonstrate the second type of usage for `eval` — this use allows `eval` to trap run-time exceptions. Here are the two scenarios:

SCENARIO 1:

Say we are reading a file one line at a time and checking each line for a pattern match:

```
my $pattern = 'hello';
while (<>) {
    if (/$pattern/) {
        print;
    }
}
```

As explained earlier in Section 2.9, the conditional of the `if` statement, `/$pattern/`, will be tested for its truth value by invoking the regular-expression engine to match the pattern bound to the scalar `$pattern` with the input string that is currently stored in the default variable `$_`.[87] If the name of this script file is `Test.pl` and we invoke it by:

```
Test.pl a.txt
```

where `a.txt` is the name of a text file, the script will print out the lines of text in the text file that can be successfully matched with the pattern.

There is no strong reason to use `eval` to trap run-time errors in the above script because the pattern is known at compile time. So the compiler will make certain that the program syntax is right and that the pattern forms a legal regex. The same would be the case even if the pattern was supplied as a command-line argument, since Perl would know about it at the time of scanning the lines of Perl code.

SCENARIO 2:

Now consider the situation when we want a user *to interact with a script on a continuous basis*, each interaction consisting of the user entering a regular-expression pattern in the terminal window and the script coming back with all the lines in the disk file that can be matched with the pattern. In this case, it will not be possible to check at the compile time that the pattern entered by the user is a legal regular expression. So if the pattern entered is an illegal regular expression, the script will simply abort — unless you make a pattern match inside an `eval`, as shown in the script below. The `eval` will trap any errors arising at run time and report on them through the special global variable `$@`. The loop for doing this would look something like what is shown in lines (G) through (S) of the following script:

[87] This notation for string matching is explained in Chapter 4. We also used it earlier in the `WhileIf.pl` script in Section 2.9.

```
#!/usr/bin/perl -w

### TestRegex.pl

use strict;

print "Press ENTER twice to end session\n\n";                    #(A)

my $file = "data.txt";                                            #(B)

open FILE, $file                                                  #(C)
    or die "Cannot open $file: $!";                               #(D)

my @all_lines =  <FILE>;                                          #(E)

while (1) {                                                       #(F)
    print "Enter a pattern: ";                                    #(G)
    chomp (my $pattern = <STDIN>);                                #(H)
    last if $pattern =~ /^\s*$/;          # end session           #(I)
    my @matched_lines = eval {                                    #(J)
        grep /$pattern/, @all_lines;                              #(K)
    };
    if ($@) {                                                     #(L)
        print "Error in your pattern: $@";                        #(M)
        next;                                                     #(N)
    }
    if (!@matched_lines) {                                        #(O)
        print "no match\n";                                       #(P)
    } else {                                                      #(Q)
        map "$_\n", @matched_lines;                               #(R)
        print @matched_lines;                                     #(S)
    }
}
```

To describe the above script, line (A) informs the user how to end the session with the script. We name a text file in line (B). Lines (C) and (D) open a filehandle to this text file. Line (E) slurps in the entire file into an array in a single step by reading from the <> operator in a list context. Each line of the text file will be stored in a separate element of the array `@all_lines`.[88] In line (G), we ask the user to supply us with a pattern that could be an illegal regular expression. Line (I) tests for the session

[88] Slurping in the file is not essential to the working of this script whose main focus is to demonstrate how `eval` can be used to trap run-time errors. The essential point of this script could have been made even when a file is read one line at a time.

termination condition, which occurs when the user presses the Enter key when there are no other characters in the line of the terminal window where the screen cursor is currently situated.

Lines (J) and (K) use Perl's built-in `grep()` function, explained further in the next section, to match the pattern of line (H) simultaneously with all of the text-file lines stored in the array `@all_lines`. This pattern matching is carried out inside an `eval` block for trapping any errors in the supplied pattern.

In lines (L), (M), and (N) we check for any errors encountered during the execution of the code block supplied to `eval` in line (J). In this manner, even if the pattern supplied by the user is an illegal regular expression, we are able to continue the interaction between the user and the script; the user is asked to enter the pattern again at the next go-around through the `while` loop. The loop control keyword `next` in line (N), as mentioned already in Section 2.9, skips to the next iteration of the `while` loop when the `if` conditional in line (L) evaluates to true.

Lines (O) through (S) check whether the call to `grep()` in line (K) returned any matching text-file lines at all. The `if` conditional in line (O) will evaluate to true if the array `@matched_lines` is empty. If this array is indeed empty, a message to that effect is printed out. Otherwise, the matched lines are displayed. Notice how we use Perl's built-in `map()` function to place a newline at the end of each string in the array `@matched_lines`. The next section explains how `map()` works.

Trapping run-time exceptions with `eval` is discussed in greater detail in Chapter 10. That chapter addresses specifically the trapping of programmer-defined exceptions raised with the `die` operator.

2.15 grep( ) AND map( ) FUNCTIONS

The second example in the previous section also illustrated Perl's built-in functions `grep()` and `map()` that are frequently invoked on lists. Whereas `grep()` selects items from a list on the basis of a specified criterion, `map()` modifies every item of a list on the basis of a specified rule. In a list context, both `grep()` and `map()` return lists, the former a list of the items selected and the latter a list composed of the modified versions of the items in the original list.[89]

The following script, `Grep.pl`, shows the different ways of calling `grep()`. Basically, there are two ways. You could make the following call:

```
grep some_expression, a_list
```

[89] The name `grep` is believed by some to be an abbreviation for "generalized regular expression parser" and by others an abbreviation for "global regular expression print". The latter view is probably based on the fact that `grep` does the same thing as the command `g/re/p` in the Unix command-line editor `ed`. In this `ed` command, `g` stands for "global," `re` for "regular expression," and `p` for "print."

where some_expression is evaluated for each element of the second-argument list. All elements of a_list that return true are included in the output list returned by grep(). Or, you could make the following call:

```
grep { block_of_code } a_list            # no comma after first arg
```

where the first argument consists of a brace-delimited block of statements that are evaluated for each item in a_list. All items for which the last executed statement inside the braces returns true are included in the output list returned by grep. Note that it is a syntax error to place a comma after the first argument in this case.

In both modes of invocation described above, as each item from the second-argument list is chosen for testing, its value is placed in the Perl's default variable $_.

The first kind of call to grep is illustrated by lines (B) and (D) of the next script, Grep.pl. The call in line (B) selects all the words in @arr that end in the letter w. Exactly the same is done by the call in line (D), except that now our first argument to grep() is a call to the subroutine selector() defined in lines (F) and (G). Note that this subroutine uses the assumption that the list item under test is in $_. Inside this subroutine, the regular expression testing in line (G) is against the value stored in the global variable $_.

The second kind of call to grep() is illustrated by lines (H) and (J). Now we use a braces-delimited block of code as the first argument to grep(). Placing each item of the second-argument list in the special variable $_, grep evaluates the code inside the braces. If the last executed statement inside the braces returns true, the item is placed in the output list. The first argument block in line (H) has only one statement, which tests true for all strings of length 5. To show that it is only the last executed statement in the first argument block that matters regarding what is selected from the second-argument list, the first-argument block in the example in lines (J) through (M) contains two statements. The first merely prints out the message hi and the second does the job of selecting an item.

A call to grep() returns a list of the selected items, but only in a list context. In a scalar context, the function returns the number of items selected. This is illustrated by the call in line (P). This invocation of grep() is the same as in line (B) except for the fact that now we call grep() in a scalar context. So, in line (P), grep() returns 3, the number of items selected from the second-argument list.

We should also point out the value of the special variable $_ is an actual item in the second-argument list. So if per chance we should modify $_, that will alter the second-argument list. This is something to be avoided because it can result in buggy code. If the goal is to modify the elements of a list, Perl provides the function map() for that. We will discuss that function after showing the following script:

```
#!/usr/bin/perl

### Grep.pl

my @arr = qw/ hello mellow jelloh yellow pillow bello /;             #(A)

my @selections = grep /w$/, @arr;                                    #(B)
print "@selections\n";                   # mellow yellow pillow      #(C)

@selections = grep &selector, @arr;                                  #(D)
print "@selections\n";                   # mellow yellow pillow      #(E)

sub selector {                                                       #(F)
    /.*w$/;                                                          #(G)
}

@selections = grep { length( $_ ) == 5 } @arr;                       #(H)
print "@selections\n";                   # hello bello               #(I)

@selections = grep {                                                 #(J)
                      print "hi ";                                   #(K)
                      length( $_ ) == 5;                             #(L)
                  } @arr;                                            #(M)
                                         # hi hi hi hi hi hi         #(N)
print "\n@selections\n";                 # hello bello               #(O)


# Invoking grep in a scalar context returns only the
# number of items matched:
my $x = grep /w$/, @arr;                                             #(P)
print "$x\n";                            # 3                         #(Q)
```

The built-in function `map()` works on a list in much the same way as `grep()`, in the sense that it examines every element of its second-argument list. But whereas `grep()` returns a selection of the list items based on some criterion, `map()` returns a list composed by modifying each element from its second-argument list.

The following script, `Map.pl`, shows examples of calls to `map()`. As with `grep()`, there are two kinds of calls. The first has the following syntax:

```
map an_expression, a_list
```

In this call, `map` supplies to `an_expression` each item of `a_list` by binding the item to the default variable `$_`. Whatever is returned by `a_expression` is placed in the output list returned by map. The second kind of call to map takes the following form:

```
map { block of code } a_list         # note no comma after first arg
```

Now map supplies each item of a_list as a value for the variable $_ to the block of code inside the curly braces. Whatever is returned by the last executed statement in that block of code is placed in the output list returned by map.

In the next script, Map.pl, the first kind of a call to map() is shown in line (B). In that invocation, map applies the length operator to each item of the second argument list and returns what is shown in the commented-out portion of line (C).

Let us say that you want to use map to modify each word in a list of words, and we will assume that the modification you want is to replace a terminating o with a oo. If you are writing a script in a hurry, you may think that the way to do it would be as shown in line (D). After all, the expression in the first argument to map does call for carrying out exactly the string substitution we want.[90] But the result is evident in the output of the print statement in line (E). The array @new_list, as returned by map in line (D), holds the following elements:

```
1 undef undef
```

which explains the commented-out printout in line (E). What is happening is that map places in the output list whatever is *returned* by the first-argument expression. As we will explain in Chapter 4, the substitution operator returns 1 if it can make the substitution called for and undef if it cannot. So the output list constructed in line (D) contains 1 for the first element hello of @arr and undef for the other two. When we print out @new_list in line (E), we only see the number 1 because, as mentioned earlier in this chapter, the print representation of undef is an empty string. The fact that @new_list contains three elements is evident by the printout shown in line (F).

We next use the same @arr in the call to map() in line (G) as in line (D).[91] The invocation of map() in line (G) does something similar to what the programmer tried to do in line (D) without success. Note that the call to map() in line (G) is of the second kind — when the first argument consists of a braces-delimited code block. As mentioned earlier, whatever is returned by the last statement of the code block will be placed in the output list for each item of @arr. Whereas line (D)

---

[90] If the reader is not already familiar with regular expressions, this will become clear after the reader has gone through Section 4.13 of Chapter 4. The first argument to map() in line (D), s///, is the Perl's string substitution operator. This operator replaces the portion of an input string that matches the pattern placed between the first two forward slashes with the string placed between the second and the third forward slashes.

[91] The items in the array @arr did get modified by the call to map in line (D), although the output produced in line (E) does not tell us so directly.

turned an ending `o` into `oo`, line (G) turns an ending `w` into `wish`. The overall result is what is shown in the commented-out portion of line (H).

The call to `map()` in line (I) is again of the first kind. The expression in the first argument is a call to a separately defined subroutine in lines (K) through (M). This subroutine carries out a string substitution on the strings stored in the variable `$_`. As mentioned already, `map` places each item successively in that variable as it scans the second-argument list.

Finally, lines (N) and (O) show that `map` behaves the same as `grep` when called in a scalar context — it returns the number of items in the output list.

```
#!/usr/bin/perl

### Map.pl

my @arr = qw/ hello mellow yellow /;                                  #(A)

my @new_list = map length $_, @arr;                                   #(B)
print "@new_list\n";                        # 5 6 6                   #(C)

@new_list = map s/(o)$/$1$1/, @arr;         # POSSIBLY NOT WHAT YOU WANT #(D)
print "@new_list\n";                        # 1                       #(E)
print @new_list . "\n";                     # 3                       #(F)

@new_list = map {s/(w)$/$1ish/; $_;} @arr;                            #(G)
print "@new_list\n";                        # helloo mellowish yellowish #(H)

@new_list = map &modifier, @arr;                                      #(I)
print "@new_list\n";                        # hello mellow yellow     #(J)

sub modifier {                                                        #(K)
    s/o$|ish$//;                                                      #(L)
    $_;                                                               #(M)
}

# Invoking map in a scalar context returns the number of elements
# in the new list:
my $x = map length $_, @arr;                                          #(N)
print "$x\n";                               # 3                       #(O)
```

2.16 INTERACTING WITH THE DIRECTORY STRUCTURE

One frequently wants to determine the *current working directory*, meaning the directory in which the script is currently executing its statements, as opposed to the directory in which the script was originally launched. When a script is first invoked, Perl stores the pathname to the current working directory as the value for the `PWD` key in the `%ENV` hash. But, for obvious reasons, for a script engaged in scanning a directory, the initial value stored for the `PWD` key will not reflect the current working directory. A convenient module that comes in handy for quickly figuring out the current working directory is the `Cwd` module that comes preloaded with the standard Perl distribution. This module contains the function `cwd()` that returns the full pathname to the current working directory. So if you say

```
use Cwd;
print cwd;     # full pathname to the current working directory
```

The built-in command `chdir` can be used to switch to a directory that is different from the current working directory. If its argument begins with a forward slash, the pathname to the target directory is interpreted relative to the root of the directory tree. Otherwise, `chdir` considers the argument string to be a pathname relative to the current directory. So

```
chdir "foo";
```

means to move into the subdirectory `foo` of the current directory. If `chdir` is called without any arguments, Perl will try to set the current working directory to the user's home directory.

After you have switched to a given directory, probably the next thing you would want to do is to list all the items, files and subdirectories, in the current directory. The built-in function `glob()`[92] comes in handy for that. For listing all of the items in the current directory, you will say

```
@all_items = glob "*";
```

and for listing all the files whose names end in, say, `.tex`, you will say

```
@all_tex_files = glob "*.tex";
```

Now that we know how a script can list all the items in a directory, we may wish to remove some of them. In Unix, files are commonly removed with the `rm` command. The same is accomplished in Perl by the `unlink` operator through the syntax:

```
unlink file_name
```

[92]This function is named after the *globbing* operation commonly performed by Unix shells. A Unix shell carries out a globbing operation when it expands a *file name pattern*, such as `*.tex`, into a list of all the file names that match the pattern using `*` as a wildcard.

where again file_name may either be an absolute pathname to a file or a name that is relative to the current working directory. By supplying the output of the glob operator to unlink, we can remove multiple items at a time, as in

```
unlink glob "*~";
```

which will delete all files whose names end in a tilde. The unlink operator will only delete files.

While unlink deletes files, a call to link creates a hard link to a file elsewhere in the same file system. And a call to symlink creates a symbolic link to either a file or a directory anywhere that is accessible in a networked environment:

```
link $pathname_to_existing_file, $link_name_in_current_dir
    or warn "Can't link to $pathname_to_existing_file: $!";

symlink $pathname_to_existing_item, $link_name_in_current_dir
    or warn "Can't soft link to $pathname_to_existing_item: $!";
```

A call to link basically declares just another name for the same file. That is, both the original name and the new link name refer to the same *inode* on the disk. A call to link increments the *link count* associated with that inode. Link count is the number of names associated with the same inode on a disk. Any number of hard links to a file is allowed. Invoking a file delete operation with unlink either on the original name or on one of its link names only removes the corresponding name from a directory. The inode continues to hold the file as long as the link count associated with the inode is greater than zero. Of course, invoking a file delete operation on all of the names associated with a given inode will cause the inode's link count to go down to zero. That inode on the disk will then become available for allocation to some other file in the future. A symbolic link, on the other hand, is just a special entry in a directory that points to another location where a given file or a directory is to be found. Of course, this other location could itself be a symbolic link to yet another location, and so on. A symbolic link does not increment the link count associated with an inode. As is the case with hard links, invoking unlink on a symbolic link removes only the link.

Perl provides rename to change the name of a file:

```
rename $old_name, $new_name;
```

To delete an empty directory, you must use the rmdir operator, as in

```
rmdir $directory_name;
```

for deleting a specific empty directory, or

```
rmdir glob "$foo/*.d";
```

for deleting all empty directories whose names terminate in the .d suffix under the directory name stored in the variable $foo. As you would expect, the opposite of rmdir is accomplished with the mkdir operator. You invoke mkdir to create a new directory:

```
mkdir $new_directory_name, 0644;
```

where the second argument, in this case the octal 0644, is the initial permission setting for the new directory.[93]

The permissions on a file or a directory can be changed with the chmod operator, as in

```
chmod 0755, glob "*.pl";
```

where the first argument, an octal number, specifies the permissions, and the rest of the arguments, in this case generated by glob, specify a list of the files and directories whose permissions are to be modified.

To change the user and group ownerships of a file or directory, there is the chown operator. Unlike the Unix command of the same name, the Perl chown operator only takes numeric user-ID (UID) and group-ID (GID) values. If these numeric IDs are not known, you'd need to call the getpwnam() and getgrnam() functions to first convert the symbolic names into the numeric IDs:

```
defined( my $uid = getpwnam("zaphod") )
                        or die "user not known";
defined( my $gid = getgrnam("galactica_touring_group") )
                        or die "unknown group";
chown $uid, $gid, glob "*.tex";
```

Embedding the invocations of getpwnam() and getgrnam() within calls to defined ensures that these two functions do not return undef, which they will for invalid user and group names.

Perl provides the utime operator for changing the timestamp of a file. Operating systems commonly associate three timestamps with a file: *last access time* which could be for the purpose of, say, reading or copying a file; *last modification time*, which could correspond to when the file was modified last; and what's referred to as *ctime*. The last timestamp, used primarily for incremental backups, is always set to *now* for any interaction of the system with the file. The utime operator can be used to change the first two timestamps associated with a file. For example, if we wanted to update both the access time and the modification time for all items in our directory to the current time, we'd say

```
my $current_time = time;
```

[93]Leaving out the leading zero will cause the second argument to mkdir to be interpreted as a decimal, which would correspond to strange and most likely unacceptable permissions. The same thing occurs if the second argument is supplied via a string-valued variable. When a string needs to be interpreted as a number, it is only interpreted as a decimal number. In such cases, it is important to first feed the string value to the oct operator for conversion to an octal number.

```
utime $current_time, $current_time, glob "*";
```

where the first argument to `utime` is for setting the last-access timestamp and the second for setting the last-modification timestamp. The function `time` usually returns the value of the current time as measured in seconds from the *epoch*, which is typically the start of January 1, 1970, according to the Universal Time.

2.16.1 Directory Handles

Another way to list all the items in a specified directory is through what is known as a *directory handle* that is created by the `opendir()` function:

```
opendir DIRHANDLE, directory_name;
```

If you wish to obtain a directory handle for the current working directory, you would say

```
opendir DIRHANDLE, ".";
```

Subsequently, one can use the `readdir()` function to list the directory items:

```
@all_items = readdir DIRHANDLE;
```

You can call `readdir()` on a directory handle in the following manner if you want to do something to each item in a directory:

```
opendir DIRHANDLE, directory_name;
foreach $item ( readdir DIRHANDLE ) {
    next if / regex to select directory items /;
    do something with the selected item;
}
close DIRHANDLE;
```

2.16.2 File Tests

Perl makes it convenient to test whether a given item is a plain file, a directory, a symbolic link, a socket (Unix-domain sockets only), a pipe, a block-special file (corresponding to a mountable disk), a character-special file (corresponding to an I/O device), etc. Perl can also tell us with great reliability whether a file is a text file or a binary file. These and many other attributes of a file can be tested by using simple syntax, such as

```
-X $filename
```

where `X` is a single character that designates a test. For example, if we need to know whether the size of a file is nonzero, we can use `-s` for the test, as in

```
die "file $filename has zero size\n" if -s $filename;
```

The `-s` test also returns the size of a file in bytes. For another example, if we do not want to create a new file with a given name because one already exists under that name, we can use the test:

```
die "file $filename already exists\n" if -e $filename;
```

To check whether an item returned by, say, `glob` is an actual file or a subdirectory, we can either use the `-d` test, which returns true for a directory item, or the `-f` test, which returns true for an actual file. To check whether an item is merely a symbolic link in a directory, we can use the `-I` test; it returns true for a symbolic link. There is the `-x` test for checking whether a file is executable by the user running the script.

See the `perlfunc` documentation page for a listing of all possible file tests. In all, Perl gives us 27 tests for testing the various attributes of files and directories.

2.16.3 Taking Advantage of Shell's Globbing

Let us say you want to use a Perl script to do something to all the files (or to multiple files of a certain type) in a directory. This does not always require Perl to create a listing of the contents of the directory. It is possible to write a Perl script in such a way that all of the work of obtaining all the files on which to invoke the script is done by the shell in which the script is invoked. A *shell*, frequently referred to as a *command-line interpreter*, is a continuously running process that reads user input and executes commands. However, if the user input contains certain special characters, known as the *shell metacharacters*, the shell may modify the human-entered command according to those characters, carry out any indicated I/O redirection, and decide whether or not to launch a separate process or separate multiple processes to execute the command.

The shell metacharacter of particular interest to us in this section is `*`. When a file-name argument given to a command in a shell contains `*`, it causes the shell to *glob* that argument into a list of all the directory items that match the rest of the argument. For example, the file-name argument `*.pdf` will be globbed by the shell interpreter into all the directory items whose names terminate in the suffix `.pdf`.

To illustrate how Perl can take advantage of a shell's globbing ability, let's say we want to send to the printer all the files in a directory whose names end in the suffixes `.pdf` or `.ps`. The following script does the job. It is written to send just one file to the printer, but when we invoke it in a command line with

```
PrintFiles.pl *.pdf *.ps
```

the shell globs the patterns `*.pdf` and `*.ps` into a list of all the matching file names. This list, interpreted by the shell as the command-line arguments for the invocation of `PrintFiles.pl`, is stored by Perl in the array `@ARGV`. The script uses the loop in lines (B) through (H) to send each file to the printer. For each file, we use Perl's `system()` function in line (E) to launch in a separate child process[94] an external ghostview[95] application corresponding to the command

```
gs -q -dPrinted -dNOPAUSE -sOUTPUTFILE=- -sDEVICE=pswrite $_ -c quit
```

where `$_` is set to the name of the file. The output of the `ghostview` process is piped into a printer process in which the following command is executed:

```
lp -d elt339
```

where `elt339` is the name of the printer.

```
#!/usr/bin/perl -w

### PrintFiles.pl

use strict;

die "requires at least one file name"
    unless @ARGV;                                                    #(A)

foreach (@ARGV) {                                                    #(B)
    die "Only pdf and ps files can be printed out\n"                 #(C)
        unless /\.ps|(df)$/i;                                        #(D)
    system "/usr/local/bin/gs -q -dPrinted -dNOPAUSE ".             #(E)
           "-sOUTPUTFILE=- -sDEVICE=pswrite ".                       #(F)
           "$_ -c quit ".                                            #(G)
           " | lp -d elt339";                                        #(H)
}
```

2.16.4 Scanning a Directory Tree

Scanning a directory tree recursively is no more difficult than examining the contents of a single directory. To show an example of a recursive search in a directory tree, we will now present a script that searches for either a single word or for a serial combination of words in a single line in all the text files in a directory tree.[96] This

[94] Section 2.17.1 explains in considerable detail the workings of the `system()` function.

[95] Ghostview is a viewer for postscript documents.

[96] You may think of `findword` as a poor man's version of the much fancier and much more feature-laden Unix `grep` utility.

Perl script does *not* search through symbolic links and files whose names end in `.out`, `.ps`, `.pdf`, and so on. The script is run with a command line:

```
findword word
```

or:

```
findword word1 word2
```

if you want to locate a phrase consisting of multiple words. When you search for a phrase, the script reports back correctly only if all the words are in a single line of the text file.

Line (A1) of the script is for printing out the message shown and then aborting further execution if the script is called with no words to search for. Line (A2) tells us what the current working directory is. Initially it will the directory in which the script is invoked. Line (A3) declares a scalar whose value will be set to the pattern to search for in the text files.

Lines (A4) through (A9) check whether the user has supplied a single word or a sequence of words to search for. For the former case, the search pattern in line (A4) is set to the word supplied. For the latter, line (A8) joins all the words together with a single blank space between every pair of consecutive words. The concatenated string then becomes the search pattern.

The main work of the script is carried out by the two subroutines: `search_in_directory()` and `search_in_file()`. The job of `search_in_directory()` is to open a directory, ignore all files that have unacceptable suffixes, invoke `search_in_directory()` recursively on all the subdirectories, and invoke `search_in_file()` on all the text files.

To understand the coding of `search_in_directory()`, line (B3) changes the current working directory to the directory in which the search is to be conducted. Since it is possible that the argument supplied to `chdir` in line (B3) will be relative to the upper-level directory, line (B4) gets the full path to the current working directory. The `glob "*"` operation in line (B5) returns all the items in the current working directory.

The file test `-d` in the conditional in line (B6) succeeds for directory items while the negated file test `!(-l)` succeeds when an item is not a symbolic link. For all those items returned by the `glob` that pass the two tests in line (B6), we invoke the code in lines (B7), (B8), and (B9). Basically, this code consists of a recursive invocation of `search_in_directory()` on the subdirectories in line (B7). Since each such invocation will change the script's sense of the current working directory, line (B8) resets the value of the current working directory for the next recursive invocation of `search_in_directory()` in line (B7).

The goal in lines (B10) through (B19) is to ship off the search to the individual files in the directory, but only those files that are readable [the file test `-r` in line

(B10)]; that are most likely to be text files [the file test `-T` in line (B11)]; whose modification age[97] is at least one second ago [the file test `-M` in line (B12)];[98] that are not symbolic links [the file test `!-l` in line (B13)]; and that are not the files whose names end in `.ps`, `.pdf`, etc. [the tests in lines (B14) through (B19)].

Regarding the subroutine `search_in_file()`, the main work of finding a matching text line for the search pattern is carried out by the regular expression matching operation in line (C5).[99] The purpose of the code in lines (C6) through (C12) is to construct a path string to the file in which a pattern match is scored. You see, for each match, the output of `findword` is an abbreviated path string to the file in which a match is scored; this pathname ends in the name of the file. The pathname is followed by the number of the line that contains matching text, and then followed by the text in the line. For deeply nested files, a full path string to a file can become much too long and create too much visual clutter in the output. So the pattern match in line (C7) helps us extract the path string relative to the directory in which `findword` is invoked. The regular expression syntax in line (C7) and the use of the backreference `$1` in line (C10) will be clear after the reader has covered Chapter 4. Line (C13) synthesizes and then displays the output string for each match with a line of a text file.

```
#!/usr/bin/perl

### findword

use strict;

use Cwd;

die "$0 requires one argument, which is a target string \n
     to search for.  If you supply multiple arguments, they are
     concatenated together to form a single search pattern.\n"
    unless @ARGV;                                                   #(A1)

my $search_dir = cwd;                                               #(A2)

my $pattern;                                                        #(A3)

if (@ARGV == 1) {                                                   #(A4)
    $pattern = shift;                      # the word to search for #(A5)
    &search_in_directory( $search_dir );                            #(A6)
} else {                                                            #(A7)
```

---

[97]The modification age as measured by the `-M` test is in days, hence the number 0.00001 in line (B12).

[98]This is to prevent searching for words in the same file into which the operating system may have directed the output of the script `findword`.

[99]How this regular-expression-based matching works is explained in Chapter 4.

```
    $pattern = join ' ', @ARGV;                                          #(A8)
    &search_in_directory( $search_dir );                                 #(A9)
}

sub search_in_directory {                                                #(B1)
    my $dir = shift @_;                                                  #(B2)
    chdir $dir or die "Unable to change directory to $dir: $!";         #(B3)
    $dir = cwd;                                                          #(B4)
    foreach ( glob "*" ) {                                               #(B5)
        if ( -d and !(-l) ) {                                            #(B6)
            &search_in_directory( $_ );                                  #(B7)
            chdir $dir                                                   #(B8)
                or die "Unable to change directory to $dir: $!";        #(B9)
        } elsif (-r _ and                                               #(B10)
                 -T _ and                                               #(B11)
                 -M _ > 0.00001 and  #modify age is at least 1 sec#(B12)
                !( -l $_ ) and                                          #(B13)
                !m{\.ps$} and                                           #(B14)
                !m{\.pdf$} and                                          #(B15)
                !m{\.eps$} and                                          #(B16)
                !m{\.out$} and                                          #(B17)
                !m{~$} ) {                                              #(B18)
            &search_in_file( $_ );                                      #(B19)
        }
    }
}

sub search_in_file {                                                     #(C1)
    my $file = shift @_;                                                 #(C2)
    open IN, $file;                                                      #(C3)
    while (<IN>) {                                                       #(C4)
        if (/\b$pattern/io) {                                            #(C5)
            my $pwd = cwd;                                               #(C6)
            $pwd =~ m{$search_dir.?(\S*)$};                              #(C7)
            my $file_path_name;                                          #(C8)
            unless ( $1 eq "" ) {                                        #(C9)
                $file_path_name = "$1/$file";                           #(C10)
            } else {                                                    #(C11)
                $file_path_name = $file;                                #(C12)
            }
            printf( "%s at line %d:    %s\n", $file_path_name, $., $_ );
        }                                                               #(C13)
    }
    close( IN );
}
```

2.17 LAUNCHING PROCESSES

When you run a program in a Unix-like environment, it is executed in a process.[100] In a typical Unix-like environment, there will be tens and sometimes hundreds of processes running simultaneously, each executing a specific program. Every process is assigned its own program counter and its own address space. Each process is also assigned a non-negative decimal integer for identification. This integer is known as the *Process ID* and abbreviated `PID`.

The operating system interacts with a process by sending it *signals*. The signals may convey to a process such information as the user wanting to terminate the program immediately, the program trying to access prohibited regions of memory, etc. A process typically has default behavior for dealing with the different signals. This default behavior can be overridden by incorporating *signal handlers* in your program.

Since a program can ask the operating system to launch another program, this means that a process can launch another process. This leads to the notions of *child processes*, *parent processes*, and *process hierarchies*. A child process will typically inherit the attributes of the parent process. These attributes include the standard input, output, and error streams, any overriding signal handlers in the parent process, etc. Of course, a child process can change for itself and its children any attributes inherited from the parent process. Associated with each process is a positive decimal integer called its *Parent Process ID*, abbreviated `PPID`. The `PPID` of a process is the `PID` of its parent.

Related processes are usually grouped together into *process groups*. For example, the four processes launched by the following chained command-line in Unix:[101]

```
ls -fl | grep -e '\.pl$' | sort -k 9b | more
```

[100]Stevens [63, p. 9] defines a *program* as an executable file on a disk and an executing instance of a program as a *process*.

[101]In the command line shown, `ls -fl` produces an unsorted listing of all the files in a directory, with the output for each item in the following long format:

```
-rwxr-xr-x   1  kak    kak     3518    May 5  14:33  System.pl
```

where the different fields are for file permissions, user name, group name, etc. The process in which `ls -fl` is executed writes to its standard output, where it is read by the standard input for the second command in the chained invocation shown, `grep -e '\.pl$'`. The `grep` process applies the regular expression `\.pl$` as a filter to the listings produced by `ls`. Therefore, the `grep` will write to its standard output only the Perl files. Finally, we ask `sort` to take incoming data on its standard input, sort it alphabetically using the ninth field as the sort key (which is where the name of the file is), and finally write the sorted entries to the standard output, where it will be picked by the standard input of `more`. The pipe, represented by the symbol | between the individual commands, ensures that whatever the process on the left writes to its standard output will be picked up by the process on the right on its standard input. Such chained commands are also referred to as *shell pipelines*. See Section 2.17.5 for further discussion on shell pipelines.

will be grouped together in the same process group. Processes are also grouped together for more efficient distribution of signals emanating from the operating system. What we mean is that the operating system can directly signal a process group, causing the signal to be sent automatically to all the processes in the group. Each *process group* has a designated *group leader*. For group identification, each process is assigned a positive decimal integer called the *Process Group ID*, abbreviated `PGID`. The `PGID` of a process is the `PID` of its group leader. Obviously, then, the `PGID` of a group leader will be the same as its `PID`. By default, a newly created process joins the process group of its parent. A process can also designate itself as a group leader with respect to its child processes.

A process may be run under the direct control of a terminal. Such a process can be made responsive to the signals triggered by certain special user inputs, such as Ctrl-C for terminating a process immediately. Such a process is known as a *foreground process*. A *background process*, on the other hand, runs independently of any terminal. A background process is also known as a *daemon process* or just a *daemon*.[102] In general, all of the processes launched from a terminal session will consist of a single foreground process group and one or more background process groups. A signal generated by a user input like Ctrl-C is sent to all the processes in the foreground process group.

When a foreground process is launched from a terminal, we say that the process has associated with it a *controlling terminal*. In general, multiple processes may be launched from the same terminal, some in the foreground and some in the background. Or, from a larger perspective, multiple groups of processes may be launched from a terminal, with one group in the foreground and the rest in the background. This leads to the notion of a *session*. A session is by definition a group of process groups. A foreground process that is associated with the controlling terminal is designated as the *session leader* for all the processes in a session. The terminal process corresponding to the session leader is also referred to as the *controlling process*. When a new process is created and designated as a session leader, it automatically becomes a group leader at the same time.

A session is identified by a positive decimal integer called the *Session ID*, abbreviated `SID`. The `SID` of all the processes in a session is the `PID` of the session leader. Obviously, then, the `PID`, the `PGID`, and the `SID` of a session leader are the same. A newly created process joins the session of its parent.[103]

---

[102]Daemon started out being an abbreviation for *Disk And Execution Monitor*. Now it is commonly thought of as just a spelling variant of "demon."

[103]To understand the usefulness of `SID`, suppose you close a terminal while the processes launched by it are still running. The operating system will identify all the affected foreground processes by comparing their `SID`s with the `PID` of the terminal process. If the two are the same, it will send all the affected processes the `SIGHUP` signal, which ordinarily will cause those processes to terminate immediately.

So far we have talked about the PID, PPID, PGID, and the SID identifiers associated with a process.[104] Also associated with a process is UID, a positive decimal integer that identifies the user responsible for creating the process. In Unix-like systems, every user account has a unique UID associated with it. The UID of 0 is special; it indicates a superuser. A superuser process has special privileges with regard to file permissions, etc. Also associated with a process is GID, a positive decimal integer that identifies the group ID of the user responsible for the process.[105] Two additional attributes associated with a process are the *root directory* and the *current working directory*. These are used for resolving the pathname searches.

The PIDs of 0 and 1 are special. The PID of 0 is reserved for the process scheduler, also known as the *swapper*. This is the only process for which there is no corresponding disk-based executable program. For Unix-like operating systems, it is a part of the kernel and is known as a *system process* [63]. The PID of 1 is reserved for the init process, the *initialization process*. All other processes are derived from init by *forking*, a notion we will explain later. Therefore, init is the ancestor of every process except for the process whose PID is zero. When a Unix-based system is first booting up and after the kernel is bootstrapped, it is init's job to read the system initialization files that are usually stored in one or more "rc" files[106] and subdirectories in the /etc directory, and to then bring up the operating system in the desired state (single-user, multi-user, etc.). Another important function served by init has to do with the cleanup of the otherwise dead processes that have become orphaned. How that works will be explained in a later section of this chapter.

---

[104]The ps command that we will use in the next subsection may also show a TPGID entry, for *terminal process* GID. Although listed separately for each process, this is not a property of a process. On the other hand, TPGID is a property of the terminal in which the ps command is invoked. It is the PGID if the foreground process group that has the controlling terminal. This value of TPGID is shown for all the processes in a session, foreground and background, if the session includes the foreground process group that has the controlling terminal. Otherwise, the value is shown as -1.

[105]Unix-like operating systems actually make a distinction between *real* UID and *effective* UID, and between *real* GID and *effective* GID. Often the two will be the same. That is, the real UID will be the same as the effective UID, and the real GID will be the same as the effective GID. The real and the effective ID's are different for a process when either the set-user-ID bit, also referred to as the setuid bit, or the set-group-ID bit, also referred to as setgid bit, is set. Ordinarily, the permissions accorded a process correspond to the user launching the program and not to the owner of the program. An example of a user launching a program being different from the owner of the program is passwd in Unix that is used for changing a password. This program is owned by root but should be executable by all. For such programs, the permissions can be made to correspond to those allowed for the owner of the program by setting the setuid bit or to those allowed for the group associated with the program by setting the setgid bit. On Unix-like systems, the syntax for setting the setuid and setgid bits is:

```
chmod u+s filename
chmod g+s filename
```

Said succinctly, when an executable file has its setuid bit set, the effective UID of the process in which the executable is run is set to the owner of the file. This calls for extra care in setting the other permissions when an executable is setuid to root. For example, you would not ordinarily want the executable to possess the group and world read and write permissions.

[106]The abbreviation "rc" stands for "runnable commands."

2.17.1 Launching a Child Process with system()

Perl's built-in function `system()` launches a new child process. For example, if we say in a script:

```
system "ls";
```

this will launch a child process in which the Unix command `ls` is executed. The main process, one in which Perl is running, suspends any further execution until the child process returns successfully. As mentioned, a child process inherits all the standard streams from the parent process. So when the Unix `ls` command sends a list of files in the current directory to the standard output in the child process, it is the same standard output — most likely to be a window on your terminal screen — that is associated with the original process running Perl. A call to `system()` returns 0 if the command supplied to it as the argument completed successfully; otherwise, what is returned is a value derived from the exit code of the child process that failed and the circumstances of the failure. More specifically, what `system()` returns is the value stored in the special variable `$?`.

The launching of a child process by `system` becomes slightly more complex if its argument contains any shell-interpretable characters, such as `*`, `&`, `|`, etc.[107] In this case, Perl actually launches a command-line shell and hands over the argument to the shell.[108] The shell interprets the special characters in the command string and launches the processes as necessary. So if a Perl script contains a statement like:

```
system 'ls *.pl';
```

Perl will first launch a shell process as a child of the process in which the executable `perl` is running. The shell will glob the string `*.pl` and expand it into a list of all the file names with the suffix `.pl`. The shell will then launch another child process for executing the `ls` command. So, when the argument supplied to `system` contains shell metacharacters, the commands in the argument are actually executed in a grandchild of the process running Perl. This grandchild process may be either a foreground process or a background process. If it is a foreground process, the original Perl process and the shell process will both wait until the grandchild process has terminated. On the other hand, for an invocation like:

```
system 'ls *.pl&';
```

the grandchild process will be a background process on account of the terminating `&` in the argument string presented to `system`. Now the shell process terminates as soon as it has launched a child process for executing the `ls` command. So the original Perl process will execute the next statement in the script. In this case, the Perl process will know nothing about the grandchild process executing `ls`.

---

[107] These are also referred to as *shell metacharacters*, as mentioned in Section 2.16.3.

[108] As stated in Section 2.16.3, a shell is a special kind of process for command-line interpretation and job control. A shell launches a process for each executable command.

So far we have talked about two different ways of using Perl's `system()` function: (1) We can supply it with a single string argument with no shell metacharacters, in which case it launches a child process for processing the argument string. (2) We can supply `system()` with a single string containing shell metacharacters, in which case it first launches a shell process for interpreting the metacharacters. The shell subsequently launches a child process or processes for executing the commands in the argument string.

There is a third way to use `system` — by supplying it with a list of string arguments. But now the shell is not invoked regardless of the presence of any shell metacharacters in any of the arguments. What that implies is that the following call to `system()`

```
my @command = qw/grep hello *.pl'/;
system @command;                              # ERROR
```

will not work. In this case, since the argument supplied to `system()` is a list of strings, Perl does not launch a shell where the shell metacharacter `*` could be globbed. So the child process in which Perl tries to execute the command `grep` looks for a nonexisting file named literally `*.pl`. On the other hand, the following invocation works:

```
my @command = qw/grep hello SayHello.pl'/;
system @command;                              # OK
```

because now we have no need for a shell, as no shell-interpretable metacharacters are involved in the arguments supplied to `system()`.

Our next script, `System.pl`, calls `system()` in line (A) to dump the output produced by the following call to the Unix command `ps`:[109]

```
ps -j -U kak
```

[109]We have used the call `ps -j -U kak` to illustrate the workings of the Perl's `system()` function because it produces a small output, since it only shows the processes whose `UIDs` correspond to the username `kak`. In general, the command `ps`, which stands for *process status*, prints out information about the currently active processes in Unix-like environments. It takes a large number of optional flags that control the amount of detail and the display format to use for the information that is returned. The `-j` option causes the `PID` and `PGID` to be printed out for each process that `ps` reports on. The option `-U kak` causes only those processes to be listed for which the `UID` corresponds to the user `kak`. More common calls to `ps` during code development are `ps ax`, `ps ajx`, `ps aux`, `ps -AH`, etc., in Linux-based environments, and `/bin/ps -ef`, `/bin/ps -efj`, etc., in Solaris-based environments. In the options supplied, the letters `e` and `A` are meant to show all the processes, the letter `a` all the processes attached to the terminal, the letter `x` the processes with a controlling terminal, the letter `H` for showing the process hierarchy, etc. Solaris-based machines usually include multiple versions of `ps`. To see all of the different versions of `ps` on a Solaris platform — for that matter, to see all the different versions of any command in a Unix-like environment — use the `whereis` utility:

```
whereis ps
```

This very useful utility can search not only for executables, but also for libraries, manpages, and configuration files, by looking into all of the standard locations on your platform.

into a temporary text file called `temp`.

As mentioned already, the call to `system()` returns a value that is based on the exit code of the launched shell child process. This returned value is 0 if the shell was launched successfully and some nonzero value indicating the error condition encountered otherwise.[110] Note that the exit code returned by `system()` does not tell us whether or not the commands executed by the shell ran successfully.

Line (B) prints out the `PID` of the process in which the Perl script is being executed. The positive decimal integer value of this `PID` is stored in the special variable `$$`. The function call `getpgrp $$` in line (C) returns the `PGID` associated with the `PID` stored in `$$`. As shown in the commented-out portions of lines (B) and (C), since both the `PID` and the `PGID` of the process running the Perl script are the same, that makes this process a group leader.

Line (E) slurps in all the contents of the file `temp` into an anonymous array, with one line from `temp` in each element of the array, and then invokes the `map` operator to remove any white space before the first data character in each line. This cleaned up data is stored in the array `@all`. Line (F) gets rid of the terminating newline for each item stored in `@all`.

Line (G) uses `grep` to extract from the array `@all` those `ps`-produced lines that contain at least one mention of the `PID` of the process that is running the Perl script. For a given run of the script, this output of `grep` is reproduced below:

```
  PID  PGID   SID  TTY          TIME      CMD

12716 12716  2976  pts/2    00:00:00  System.pl
12717 12716  2976  pts/2    00:00:00  sh
12718 12716  2976  pts/2    00:00:00  ps
```

The first line above is for the process in which the Perl script `System.pl` is running. We see that since both the `PID` and `PGID` of this process are the same, it is a group leader. The `SID` of 2976 is the `PID` of the terminal process. The second line is for the shell that is launched as a child process by the statement in line (A). And the third is for the child process launched by the shell for executing the `ps` command. As shown above, all three processes belong to the same group and the same session.

The `for` loop in lines (J) through (O) extracts all the group leaders and all the session leaders currently active under the username `kak`. Lines (P) through (S) sort

---

[110]Line (A) of the script could also have been written in the following form that shows you can ask Perl to interpolate inside a double-quoted string argument before launching a shell for executing the command in the argument:

```
my $user_login = 'kak';
my $exit_status = system( "ps -j -U $user_login  > temp" );
```

But what if the command string supplied to `system` needs to use the `$` prefix for some shell variable? Those uses of the symbol `$` must be backslashed. Another alternative is to use single-quoted argument strings, but then you would not be able to carry out the sort of variable interpolation we have shown.

the group and session leader arrays in ascending numerical order and then display these lists.

Lines (T) through (Z) are for answering questions like: "Which group leaders are session leaders also?" and "Which group leaders are not session leaders?" Both these questions call for set operations on the lists stored in the arrays `@group_leaders` and `@session_leaders`. The first question can be answered by finding the intersection of the two lists, thought of as sets, and the second by finding the difference set. While the set operations cannot be carried out directly on arrays, one can come close by first defining hashes, as we do in lines (T) and (U), and then using `grep` creatively, as shown in lines (V) and (Y).

```
#!/usr/bin/perl -w

### System.pl

use strict;

my $exit_status = system( 'ps -j -U kak  > temp' );                  #(A)
print "$exit_status\n";                                  # 0

print $$, "\n";                                          # 12716     #(B)
print getpgrp $$, "\n";                                  # 12716     #(C)

open IN, "temp";                                                     #(D)
my @all = map {$_ =~ s/^\s*(.+)/$1/; $_} <IN>;                       #(E)
chomp @all;                                                          #(F)

print join "\n", grep /\b$$\b/, @all;                                #(G)
                  #  PID   PGID   SID  TTY        TIME     CMD
                  # 12716 12716  2976  pts/2    00:00:00  System.pl
                  # 12717 12716  2976  pts/2    00:00:00  sh
                  # 12718 12716  2976  pts/2    00:00:00  ps

print "\n\n";

my @group_leaders;                                                   #(H)
my @session_leaders;                                                 #(I)

for (1..$#all) {                                                     #(J)
    my @arr = split /\s+/, $all[$_];                                 #(K)
    #Is PID the same as GID?
    if ($arr[0] == $arr[1]) {                                        #(L)
        push @group_leaders, $arr[0];                                #(M)
    }
    #Are PID, GID, and SID the same?
    if ($arr[0] == $arr[1] && $arr[1] == $arr[2]) {                  #(N)
```

```
        push @session_leaders, $arr[0];                              #(O)
    }
}

#Sort group leader PIDs (ascending order):
@group_leaders = sort {$a <=> $b} @group_leaders;                    #(P)

#Sort session leader PIDs (ascending order):
@session_leaders = sort {$a <=> $b} @session_leaders;                #(Q)

print "Group leaders: @group_leaders\n\n";                           #(R)
             # Group leaders: 2526 2585 2820 2931 2934 2976 3017 \
             # 3371 3627 7223 7265 12716 19577 20128 20647 20757 \
             # 21111 21562 27149 29501 31205 31566 31756

print "Session leaders: @session_leaders\n\n";                       #(S)
             # Session leaders: 2585 2820 2931 2934 2976 3371 \
             # 7223 19577 20128 20647 20757 21111 27149 31756

#Form group leaders set:
my %group_leaders = map { $_ => 1 } @group_leaders;                  #(T)

#Form session leaders set:
my %session_leaders = map { $_ => 1 } @session_leaders;              #(U)

#Form intersection set:
my %common_leaders = map { $_ => 1 }
              grep { $session_leaders{$_} } keys %group_leaders;     #(V)

my @common_leaders = sort {$a <=> $b} keys %common_leaders;          #(W)

print "Group leaders that are also session " .
                            "leaders: @common_leaders\n\n";          #(X)

             # Group leaders that are also session leaders: 2585 \
             # 2820 2931 2934 2976 3371 7223 19577 20128 20647   \
             # 20757 21111 27149 31756

my @diff_array =
      grep { ! exists $session_leaders{$_} } keys %group_leaders;    #(Y)

print "Group leaders that are NOT session leaders: @diff_array\n";   #(Z)
             # Group leaders that are NOT session leaders: 12716 \
             # 21562 2526 31566 3627 31205 29501 7265 3017
```

2.17.2 Launching a Child Process with Backticks

Perl provides another mechanism for invoking a process — via backticks. A string placed between two backticks is understood to be a command to be executed in one or more child processes. Whatever is returned by the process (or the processes if multiple processes are launched) on its standard output is returned by the backticks to Perl in the form of either one string or a list of strings, depending on the context in which the backticks are invoked. If the backticked string launches multiple processes, the usual shell job-control rules apply to them in order to determine whose standard output is captured by the backticks. If the command executed by the backticks fails for some reason, the exit status of the failed process and the error condition encountered can be obtained by examining the value of the special variable `$?`. The value of this variable is set to 0 when a backticked command executes successfully.

Regarding the nature of what can go between the backticks, the backtick mechanism works just like `system()` for the case when `system()` is supplied with a single double-quoted argument. That means you can do the usual string interpolation into a backticked string before the string is used for launching a process.

The next script, `Backticks.pl`, shows two ways of using backticks for launching processes and capturing their output. The usage in line (A) invokes backticks in a scalar context and the usage in line (E) in a list context. When backticks are used in a scalar context, whatever is made available on their standard outputs by the launched processes is returned by the backticks in the form of a single string — even if the output made available is in the form of multiline text. On the other hand, when backticks are invoked in a list context, if multiline text is placed by the launched processes on their standard outputs, the backticks will return a list of strings, with one line in each separate element of the list. It would obviously be the case that if there is only one line of text to be read at the standard output, the backticks will return a list consisting of only one string.

The backticks in line (A) call the Unix utility `uname` that returns on the standard output some basic white-space separated information about the system, such as the name of the operating system, the name of the host machine, operating system version, etc. The option `-a` means "all" of the information in Linux and just the "basic" information in Unix. This information, made available on the standard output of the process that is executing `uname`, is read by the Perl virtual machine on its standard input as a single string that becomes the value of the variable `$result_string`. Line (B) extracts the first three pieces of information from the string stored in `$result_string`‘ and displays the result in line (C).

How the backticks are used in line (E) shows that you can do variable interpolation in the sequence of characters between the backticks. It also shows that you can use shell metacharacters, just as you can do with a double-quoted string argument supplied to `system()`. The Unix command that will be executed by the backticks in line (E) is:

```
ls *txt; ps -j -U kak
```

Since this command string contains a shell metacharacter, Perl will first launch a shell for the interpretation of this character, and then the shell will launch the child processes needed for the execution of the commands. For our example, the shell will first glob the string `*txt` into a list of all file names that end in the suffix `.txt`. The shell will then launch a process for executing the `ls` command on this list of file names. The shell will also launch another process for executing the `ps` command. The outputs from both the `ls` process and the `ps` process will be placed at the respective standard outputs where they will be read by the standard input of the Perl process and placed in the array `@all`. Each separate line from the `ls` and the `ps` commands will be in a separate element of `@all`.

Line (G) then extracts from `@all` all those lines that mention the current process whose `PID` is stored in the variable `$$`. The output shown below line (G) shows three processes, the one running the script `Backticks.pl`, the shell process, and the shell's child process for executing the command ps. We do not see a process for executing `ls` because that process would already have terminated by the time `ps` is executed.

```
#!/usr/bin/perl -w

### Backticks.pl

use strict;

my $result_string = `uname -a`;                                      #(A)

my ($os_name, $host_name, $os_version) =
                                split / /, $result_string;          #(B)

print "Operating System: $os_name \n" .
      "Host Name: $host_name      \n" .
      "OS Version: $os_version    \n";                               #(C)

my $usr_name = 'kak';                                                #(D)
my @all_lines = `ls *txt; ps -j -U $usr_name`;                       #(E)

chomp( my @all = map {$_ =~ s/^\s*(.+)/$1/; $_} @all_lines );        #(F)

print join "\n", grep /\b$$\b/, @all;                                #(G)
            # PID   PGID   SID  TTY        TIME      CMD
            # 30398 30398  2976 pts/2    00:00:00 Backticks.pl
            # 30400 30398  2976 pts/2    00:00:00 sh
            # 30402 30398  2976 pts/2    00:00:00 ps
```

2.17.3 exec( ) for Transferring Control to a Process

Another function that Perl provides for launching a process is `exec()`. However, once Perl hands control over to the process that is launched by `exec()`, it cannot get it back. Often it is the case that before `exec()` is invoked, you'd first want to set up the system environment variables for the command to be executed by `exec()`. Perl makes all the environment variables available inside a script through a special hash `%ENV`. So by assigning values to or changing the existing values of the different environment variables stored as the keys in `%ENV`, one can create the conditions needed for executing another program.

The next script first demonstrates Perl's hash `%ENV` where all the environment variables are stored as the keys. Line (A) prints out all the variables currently in this hash when the execution of the script first starts. The output produced by line (A) looks like

```
BACKSPACE BROWSER BSNUM CLASSPATH COLORTERM CXX DISPLAY GROUP HOME
HOST HOSTNAME HOSTTYPE INPUTRC JAVA JAVA_HOME LANG LANGUAGE
LC_COLLATE LC_CTYPE LC_MESSAGES LC_MONETARY LC_NUMERIC LC_TIME
....
....
```

Line (B) demonstrates how we augment the current value of the `PATH` environment variable. The directory pathnames that are stored in this variable are used to locate a command that we may wish to run with `exec()` or `system()` or with the backticks. Line (C) shows that you are free to create and define your own environment variables in a script. The statement in that line creates an environment variable `ACK_MSG` whose value is a short string for acknowledging the message entered by a user in a terminal.

Finally, line (D) invokes `exec()` to hand the control over to a child process for executing the shell script that is in the argument to that function. The shell script consists of an infinite loop that reads the message entered by a user at the standard input. The shell script then writes this message back to the standard output after prefixing it with the `You said:` string. Note how the shell script uses the programmer-specified environment variable `ACK_MSG`. The constructs `while`, `do`, `echo`, and `done` inside the shell script are the shell built-in commands. When you fire up this script, the following sort of interaction with the script will ensue:

```
hello
You said: hello
I like jello
You said: I like jello
...
...
```

```
#!/usr/bin/perl -w

### Exec.pl

use strict;

print map {$_ . " "} sort keys %ENV;                                   #(A)
print "\n\n";

$ENV{PATH} .= '/home/kak/myscripts/';                                  #(B)

$ENV{ACK_MSG} = "You said: ";                                          #(C)

exec('while a=a; do read MYINPUT; echo $ACK_MSG $MYINPUT; done');     #(D)
```

2.17.4 Launching a Child Process with fork()

The `system()`, `exec()`, and the backticks are all high-level mechanisms for launching processes. They execute the commands supplied to them as arguments but do not give you any direct control over the launched processes. For a finer level control over the launched processes, Perl provides `fork()`.[111]

A call to `fork()`[112] creates a new process. The newly created process is usually called the *child process*, and the process in which `fork()` is called the *parent process*. As freshly created, a child process is identical to the parent process. For this reason, the child process created by `fork()` is also referred to as a *clone* of the parent process. A child process, being a copy of the parent process, gets a *copy* of the parent's data space, heap, and stack. That is, a child and its parent do not share these portions of memory. So any child-process-instigated modifications made to a data object declared prior to the invocation of `fork()` will not be visible in the parent process. A parent process can call `fork()` multiple times and thus become the parent of multiple child processes. However, a child process can have only one parent. A child process inherits from its parent various *process attributes* such as the parent's `GID`, `UID`, environment variables and their values, current working directory, root directory, controlling terminal, and so forth.

[111] Forking off a child process from a parent process has its roots in Unix. A similar idea in Windows machines is referred to as *spawning* a process.

[112] As functions go, `fork()` is unusual in the sense that it is a *call once and return twice* function. A call to `fork()` returns 0 in the child process and the `PID` of the child process created in the parent process.

After a child process is created by `fork()`, the rest of the code is executed in both of the processes — the parent process and the child process. Despite the fact that all of the code that follows `fork()` is available for execution in both the processes, one can nonetheless use the value returned by `fork()` to specify blocks of code that would be executed in one or the other of the processes. As mentioned, a call to `fork()` returns 0 in the child process and the `PID` of the child process in the parent process.[113] If `fork()` is unsuccessful at creating a child process, it returns `undef`. So by the mere expedient of testing the value returned by `fork()` in the conditional of an `if/else` statement, one can specify blocks of code that would be executed in only one or the other of the two processes.

The script shown next illustrates using `fork()` to create a child process. Line (A) invokes `fork()`. So the rest of the script after line (A) will be executed in the parent process as well as in the child process. If `fork()` returns successfully, the value of `$child_pid` in line (A) will be set to the child's `PID` in the parent process, and to the number 0 in the child process itself. If `fork()` is not able to create a child process, because of, say, the system is running out of memory, it returns `undef`. So we have the statement in line (B) to make sure that `fork()` was successful. Line (C) sets the variable `$str` to the string `hello`. We will use this variable to demonstrate that the child process does not share the parent's data memory.

The conditional in line (D) ensures that the code in the `if` block in lines (E) and (F) only gets executed in the child process. By the same token, the code in the `else` block in lines (H), (I), and (J) will only be executed in the parent process. In line (H), we put the parent to sleep for one second to give the child process a chance to finish up (so that the outputs produced on the terminal do not get intermixed between the two processes).[114] In line (J) we check the value of the variable `$str` to see if the assignment of line (F) had any effect on it.

The output of this script is:

```
I am a child process with PID 21536

        I am the parent process
        My own PID is 21535
        My child's PID is 21536
        hello
```

[113]It is important to realize that the value of 0 returned by `fork()` in a child process is *not* a `PID`. It is merely the number 0. As mentioned previously in the introduction to Section 2.17, the `PID` of 0 is special and is reserved for the process scheduler, which is always in operation. This special process, along with the other special process, `init`, whose `PID` is 1, are created by the kernel when the system is bootstrapped.

[114]Barring explicit process synchronization, we cannot say which of the two processes — the parent or the child — will start executing first after a call to `fork()`. That depends on the scheduling algorithm used by the process scheduler.

As the reader can see, the PID of the child process is distinct from the parent's PID. Also, the value of $str in the parent process is unaffected by the assignment to this variable in the child process.

```
#!/usr/bin/perl -w

### ForkBasic.pl

use strict;

my $child_pid = fork();                                              #(A)

die "Unable to fork: $!" unless defined $child_pid;                  #(B)

my $str = "hello";                                                   #(C)

if ($child_pid == 0) {                                               #(D)
    # Execute in child process:
    print "I am a child process with PID $$\n\n";                    #(E)
    $str = "jello";                                                  #(F)
} else {                                                             #(G)
    # Execute in parent process:
    sleep(1);                                                        #(H)
    print "      I am the parent process\n".                         #(I)
          "      My own PID is $$\n".
          "      My child's PID is $child_pid\n";

    print "      $str\n";              # hello                       #(J)
}
```

Since a child process is executed concurrently with the parent process, the following questions arise with regard to their simultaneous execution:

- What happens if the parent process runs to termination before the child process has come to its end?
- What happens if a child process runs to termination before the parent process has terminated?
- Can the parent process be made to wait on a child process to finish execution?

A running child process becomes orphaned if its parent has already run to termination. All orphaned processes are inherited as child processes by the init process whose

PID equals 1.[115] It then becomes the duty of the init process to perform any cleanup work required after a previously orphaned child process terminates.

When a child process terminates, the operating system sends the CHLD (named SIGCHLD in Unix) signal to the parent process. Upon receipt of this signal, a parent can immediately check on the exit status of the child process through the invocation of functions like wait() and waitpid(). However, if the parent does not invoke either of these functions, a small record of the exit status of the child process, along with its PID and the CPU time consumed, is stored away in memory in the form of a *zombie process*. The idea is that a zombie should remain in memory until the parent has had a chance to check on its child.

When a parent process invokes wait() in response to the receipt of the SIGCHLD signal, wait() returns immediately with the PID of the terminated child process. However, if a parent process invokes wait() without having received the SIGCHLD signal, the parent process waits until the signal is received. So we can say that wait() *blocks* until a child process — any child process if multiple child processes were launched — terminates. To make a parent process wait on a specific child process to terminate, we can use the waitpid() function.

The next script, ForkWait.pl, illustrates the presence of a zombie process after a child process has terminated and before the parent process has called wait() on it. Line (A) creates a child process. Subsequently, line (D) will only be executed in the child process and the lines (F) through (J) in only the parent process. The child process invokes the print_processes() function to display the launched processes at that point in the flow of execution.

The parent process also calls the print_processes() function to display the launched processes, but it does it twice: once before invoking wait() in line (G) and then again in line (I) after invoking wait(). A run of this script produced the following output on a Linux machine:

```
[child ] [18:17:45] [25123]    PID TTY          TIME CMD
[child ] [18:17:45] [25123] 10783 pts/8     00:00:00 tcsh
[child ] [18:17:45] [25123] 25122 pts/8     00:00:00 ForkWait.pl
[child ] [18:17:45] [25123] 25123 pts/8     00:00:00 ForkWait.pl
[child ] [18:17:45] [25123] 25124 pts/8     00:00:00 ps


[parent] [18:17:47] [25122]    PID TTY          TIME CMD
[parent] [18:17:47] [25122] 10783 pts/8     00:00:00 tcsh
[parent] [18:17:47] [25122] 25122 pts/8     00:00:00 ForkWait.pl
[parent] [18:17:47] [25122] 25123 pts/8     00:00:00 ForkWait.pl <defunct>
[parent] [18:17:47] [25122] 25125 pts/8     00:00:00 ps
```

[115] We talked about the init process in the introduction to Section 2.17. When an orphaned process terminates, it does not turn into a zombie process (the next paragraph explains what that means) because init is programmed to immediately check on the exit status of a child process as soon as it terminates.

```
[parent] [18:17:47] [25122]   PID TTY          TIME CMD
[parent] [18:17:47] [25122] 10783 pts/8    00:00:00 tcsh
[parent] [18:17:47] [25122] 25122 pts/8    00:00:00 ForkWait.pl
[parent] [18:17:47] [25122] 25126 pts/8    00:00:00 ps

Returned by wait: 25123
```

The leftmost field shows whether an output line came from the parent process or the child process. The next field shows the clock time when the `ps` command was executed inside the `print_processes` function. The third field shows the `PID` of the process in which the function `print_processes()` function was invoked. The rest of the fields are supplied by the `ps` command.

Let's now focus on the two lower blocks of the output shown above; these are produced by the parent process. The first of these two lower blocks shows two entries in the third and the fourth lines for the two processes running the `ForkWait.pl` script. The first, of `PID` 25122 is the parent process, and the second, of `PID` 25123 is the child process. Notice how the child process is shown as `<defunct>`. That is because it is a zombie process. By the time the parent gets to calling `print_processes()` in line (G) after having slept for 2 seconds, the child process has already terminated and turned into a zombie. The last block in the output displayed above, produced by the parent process after the call to `wait()`, shows the zombie process as absent because it was cleaned up by the call to `wait()` in line (H).

The last line of the output is produced by line (J) where we display what is returned by the call to `wait()`. The script `ForkWait.pl` follows:

```
#!/usr/bin/perl -w

### ForkWait.pl

use strict;

my $child_pid = fork();                                              #(A)

die "Unable to fork: $!" unless defined $child_pid;                  #(B)

if ($child_pid == 0) {                                               #(C)
    # Execute in child process only:
    print_processes( 'child ' );                                     #(D)
} else {                                                             #(E)
    # Execute in parent process only:
    sleep(2);                                                        #(F)
    print_processes( 'parent' );                                     #(G)
    my $zid = wait();                                                #(H)
    print_processes( 'parent' );                                     #(I)
```

```
    print "Returned by wait: $zid\n";                                  #(J)
}

sub print_processes {                                                  #(K)
    my ($child_or_parent) = @_;                                        #(L)
    my ($now) = (localtime =~ /(..:..:..)/);                           #(M)
    print "\n";
    print map { "[$child_or_parent] [$now] [$$] $_" } `ps`;            #(N)
    print "\n";
}
```

2.17.5 open( ) for Interprocess Communications

If the goal is to launch a child process and then to stay in continuous, albeit unidirectional, communication with it, one can do so with a call to `open()`.

Ordinarily, as the reader saw in Section 2.6.2, `open()` associates a filehandle with a file. But if we prefix or postfix the pipe symbol | to the name of an executable file, Perl will launch a separate child process for executing the file and maintain a continuous communication link with it. For example, the declaration, where we have prefixed the pipe symbol | to the name `executable_file`:[116]

```
open FILEHANDLE, "|executable_file"
```

will launch `executable_file` in a child process and associate `FILEHANDLE` with the standard input of this child process. Thereafter, whenever Perl tries to write to `FILEHANDLE` it will be available to `executable_file` on its standard input. This interaction between the Perl process and process executing `executable_file` may be referred to as the Perl process using `FILEHANDLE` to *write into a pipe* that at the other end is connected to the standard input of `executable_file`.

By the same token, the following declaration, where we have postfixed the symbol | to the name of an executable file:

```
open FILEHANDLE, "executable_file|"
```

will again launch `executable_file` in a separate child process, but this time `FILEHANDLE` will be associated with the standard output of the child process. Thereafter, whatever the child process puts out on its standard output will be read by the Perl process through the filehandle `FILEHANDLE`. So we can say that the Perl process is

[116]A call to `open()` for opening a pipe is referred to as *piped open*. When a piped open does not succeed because the operating system failed to fork off a child process, the error condition is stored in the variable `$!`. If a child process fails to launch for other reasons, that error condition is stored in the variable `$?`.

using FILEHANDLE to *read from a pipe* that at the other end is receiving information from the standard output of executable_file.

One may chain together a series of processes for such unidirectional input/output. A chain of processes linked in this manner on their standard outputs and inputs is known as a *pipeline*.

The child processes launched in a pipeline are independent of the parent Perl process. In other words, they do not automatically die when the parent Perl process terminates, unless, of course, the termination of the Perl process creates a condition that would also cause the child processes to die. When the process at one end of a pipe exits while the process at the other end is still reading from the pipe, the reading process will see the end-of-file condition as the last item in the input buffer. And when the process at one end of a pipe terminates while the process at the other end is still writing into the pipe, the writing process immediately receives the SIGPIPE signal from the operating system. The SIGPIPE signal is issued to all the processes in a pipeline when a pipe breaks unexpectedly.

We next show two scripts, OpenIPC1.pl and OpenIPC2.pl, that execute concurrently through the pipeline established by the piped open call in line (C) of OpenIPC1.pl. Just to show that we can have multiple processes chained together through their standard outputs and inputs, our call links together three processes:

```
open WRITE_TO_PIPE, "|cat -A |OpenIPC2.pl 2>/dev/null"
```

The filehandle WRITE_TO_PIPE in OpenIPC1.pl will write to the standard input of a child process executing cat -A, whose standard output will write to the standard input of a child process executing the script OpenIPC2.pl. As it is, when not supplied with a file name, the cat command reads from its standard input and writes to its standard output. The -A option to cat stands for "show all," meaning that we want cat to also output all nonprintable characters using the ^ and M- notation and to show the line ends with the $ symbol. For example, the -A option will cause cat to show a tab by ^I.

The while loop in lines (G), (H), and (I) of OpenIPC1.pl accepts user input, one line at a time, on a continuous basis from the standard input of the Perl process — the keyboard. It then does two writes of the message supplied by the user: line (H) prints out the message on the user's terminal to show what is about to be transmitted into the pipeline and line (I) writes the message out to the pipeline.

The OpenIPC2.pl also includes a while loop, in lines (R) and (S), for reading one line at a time from the standard input of that process and then writing out the message to the standard output of the same, which will again be the user's terminal.

If you fire up the script OpenIPC1.pl, a typical interaction with the script will look like:

```
Started OpenIPC1 process with PID 6167
Started OpenIPC2 process with PID 6170
```

```
hello   jello   mello
PARENT WRITES INTO PIPELINE: hello      jello   mello
MESSAGE RECEIVED FROM PIPELINE: hello^Ijello^Imello$

for an armadello
PARENT WRITES INTO PIPELINE: for an armadello
MESSAGE RECEIVED FROM PIPELINE: for an armadello$

....
....
```

where we have introduced vertical space to make it easier to see the different lines of text entered by the user. In the first block of three lines, the first line is what the user entered in the terminal; these are three tab-separated words. The second line is produced by line (H) of `OpenIPC1.pl`. The third line is produced by the print statement in line (S) of `OpenIPC2.pl`. As the reader can see, on account of the `cat -A` command in the pipeline, the tabs are replaced by `^I` and the line ends by `$`.

```
=====================   Filename: OpenIPC1.pl   =======================
#!/usr/bin/perl -w

### OpenIPC1.pl

use strict;
use IO::Handle;             # for autoflush()                          #(A)

print "Started OpenIPC1 process with PID $$\n";                        #(B)

open WRITE_TO_PIPE, "|cat -A |OpenIPC2.pl 2>/dev/null"                 #(C)
    or die "Cannot fork: $!";                                          #(D)

local $SIG{PIPE} = sub { die "pipe has broken" };                      #(E)

WRITE_TO_PIPE->autoflush(1);                                           #(F)

while (<>) {                                                           #(G)
    print "PARENT WRITES INTO PIPELINE: $_";                           #(H)
    print WRITE_TO_PIPE;                                               #(I)
}

close WRITE_TO_PIPE;                                                   #(J)

die "Non-zero exit of $?" if $?;                                       #(K)
```

```
====================   Filename: OpenIPC2.pl   ======================
#!/usr/bin/perl -w

### OpenIPC2.pl

use strict;                                                         #(P)

print "Started OpenIPC2 process with PID $$\n";                     #(Q)

while (<>) {                                                        #(R)
    print "MESSAGE RECEIVED FROM PIPELINE: $_";                     #(S)
}
```

To explain the rest of the scripts above, the inclusion of the string `2>/dev/null` with the command `OpenIPC2.pl` in line (C) tells the operating system that the standard error (whose file descriptor is 2) of the `OpenIPC2.pl` process is to be directed into `/dev/null`, meaning that we want all error messages produced by `OpenIPC2.pl` to be ignored.

Line (E) defines a signal handler for the `PIPE` signal that the operating system will issue to the Perl process should the pipeline break unexpectedly. This could happen if, say, the `OpenIPC2.pl` process is "killed" inadvertently while the pipeline is still open from the `OpenIPC1.pl` end. The next section explains the syntax used for the signal handler.

The invocation of `autoflush()` in line (F) is critical to the proper working of the pipeline. The arrow syntax used causes `autoflush()` to be invoked on the object that is to the left of the arrow. This is object-oriented syntax that will become clear in Chapter 6. The invocation of `autoflush()` causes the characters placed in the buffer used by the `WRITE_TO_PIPE` filehandle to be flushed out at once into the standard input of the next process in the pipeline. Otherwise, depending on the platform, the buffer may hold on to them until it is full or until it receives a newline character. The function `autoflush()` is defined in the package `IO::Handle`, hence its inclusion in line (A).

Line (J) closes the filehandle to the pipeline. Closing a pipeline in this manner does not automatically mean that the child processes launched by the piped open will also terminate at the same time. As mentioned already, the child processes ordinarily are independent of the Perl process that starts up the pipeline. But in our case, closing the pipeline in `OpenIPC1.pl` will send the end-of-file condition out to the standard input of the `cat` command, bringing the `cat` process to termination. At its last act before dying, `cat` will put out the end-of-file condition to the standard input of `OpenIPC2.pl`. This would cause the line input operator in line (R) to return `undef`. That would terminate the `while` loop in `OpenIPC2.pl`. So the flow of execution in `OpenIPC2.pl` will proceed beyond the `while` loop and bring that process to termination also. Line (K) checks on the exit status of the last process terminated in this manner.

Earlier we showed a snippet of an interactive session with `OpenIPC1.pl`. The session started with the following output produced by lines (B) and (Q) of the script:

```
Started OpenIPC1 process with PID 6167
Started OpenIPC2 process with PID 6170
```

In case the reader is wondering as to what happened to the two other processes with intervening `PID`s, the first of these, of `PID` 6168, corresponds to the shell that is invoked for interpreting the command

```
cat -A |OpenIPC2.pl 2>/dev/null
```

The shell then launches a child process of `PID` 6169 for executing the `cat` command and a child process of `PID` 6170 for executing `OpenPIC2.pl`.

2.18 SENDING AND TRAPPING SIGNALS

The operating system sends a signal to a process that is executing a script if something out of the ordinary should happen. For example, if a human tries to interrupt a script running as a foreground job by entering Ctrl-C on the keyboard, the operating system sends the signal `SIGINT` to the process. Ordinarily, the process in which the script is being executed will trap the signal and bring the script execution to a halt. But a programmer can provide his/her overrides for the default behavior of a process. Scripting languages generally make it easy to specify this override response to a signal. In Perl, all that a programmer has to do is make a key-value entry into a special hash called `%SIG`.

For example, if we want our Perl script to specify how the process (in which the script is being executed) should respond to the signal sent by the operating system when a human presses Ctrl-C on the keyboard, we could make the following entry in the `%SIG` hash:[117]

```
$SIG{ INT }  =  name_of_the_subroutine
```

where the subroutine named on the right-hand side of the assignment expresses the action we want to take and where `INT` is a reserved signal name that Perl uses to identify the `SIGINT` signal that corresponds to the Ctrl-C entry on the keyboard. Perl uses the same signal names as Unix except for the missing prefix `SIG`.

[117]Instead of directly naming the signal handler subroutine in the `%SIG` hash, one can also use a reference to the subroutine. Perl references are presented in Chapter 5.

To see all the signal names that are known to Perl, execute the following code fragment:

```
use Config;
print $Config{sig_name};  # sig_name is a global identifier     #(A)
```

This will output the following signal names:

```
ZERO HUP INT QUIT ILL TRAP ABRT BUS FPE KILL USR1   \
SEGV USR2 PIPE ALRM TERM STKFLT CHLD CONT STOP TSTP \
TTIN TTOU URG XCPU XFSZ VTALRM PROF WINCH IO PWR SYS\
RTMIN NUM33 NUM34 NUM35 NUM36 NUM37 NUM38 NUM39     \
NUM40 NUM41 NUM42 NUM43 NUM44 NUM45 NUM46 NUM47     \
NUM48 NUM49 NUM50 NUM51 NUM52 NUM53 NUM54 NUM55     \
NUM56 NUM57 NUM58 NUM59 NUM60 NUM61 NUM62 RTMAX IOT \
CLD POLL UNUSED
```

where the backslash at the end of each line indicates that all of the displayed lines actually constitute a single logical line in the output. Instead of the invocation shown in line (A), we can also call:

```
print $Config{sig_num};  # sig_num is also a global identifier #(B)
```

This will return an integer associated with each of the signals:

```
0 1 2 3 4 5 6 7 8 9 10 11 12 13 14 15 16 17 18 19 20 \
21 22 23 24 25 26 27 28 29 30 31 32 33 34 35 36 37 38\
39 40 41 42 43 44 45 46 47 48 49 50 51 52 53 54 55 56\
57 58 59 60 61 62 63 6 17 29 31
```

So associated with the signal `ZERO` is the integer 0, with the signal `HUP` the integer 1, with the signal `INT` the integer 2, etc. Note that Unix has the same integer identifiers for the various signals.

Here is a list of all the Unix signals, what causes a signal to be issued by the operating system to a process, and the default behavior of the process when a signal is received. This list is from the `signals.h` header file:

```
Signal Name      What Triggers the Signal              Default Action
-----------      ------------------------              --------------
  SIGHUP         Terminal-line hangup (from,           Terminate process
                 say, the hanging up of a modem
                 or the closing of an Xterm)

  SIGINT         Interrupt program with, say,          Terminate process
                 ctrl-C

  SIGQUIT        Quit program                          Core dump

  SIGILL         Illegal instruction                   Core dump
```

SIGTRAP	Trace trap	Core dump
SIGABRT	Call abort()	Core dump
SIGEMT	Emulate instruction executed	Core dump
SIGFPE	Floating-point exception	Core dump
SIGKILL	Intentionally kill program	Terminate process
SIGBUS	Bus error	Core dump
SIGSEGV	Segmentation violation	Core dump
SIGSYS	System call given invalid arg	Core dump
SIGPIPE	Write to a pipe with no reader	Terminate process
SIGALRM	Real-time timer expired	Terminate process
SIGTERM	Software termination signal	Terminate process
SIGURG	Urgent condition present on socket	Ignore signal
SIGSTOP	Stop (cannot be caught or ignored)	Stop process
SIGSTP	Stop signal generated from keyboard	Stop process
SIGCONT	Continue after stop	Ignore signal
SIGCHLD	Child status has changed (meaning that a child process has either terminated or stopped) (also note that if the action for the SIGCHLD is set to SIG_IGN, the child processes of the calling process will not be transformed into zombie processes when they terminate)	Ignore signal
SIGTTIN	Background read attempted from controlling terminal	Stop process
SIGTTOU	Background write attempted to controlling terminal	Stop process
SIGIO	I/O to a descriptor	Ignore signal
SIGXCPU	CPU time limit exceeded	Terminate process

SIGXFSZ	File size limit exceeded	Terminate process
SIGVTALRM	Virtual time alarm goes off	Terminate process
SIGPROF	Profiling time alarm goes off	Terminate process
SIGWINCH	Window size change	Ignore signal
SIGINFO	Status request from keyboard	Ignore signal
SIGUSR1	User-defined signal 1	Terminate process
SIGUSR2	User-defined signal 2	Terminate process

Sending the signal `ZERO` to a process does not affect the target process, but it can be used to find out if the target process is alive.

We will now return to the subject of how you can specify in a Perl script a subroutine that would be invoked when the process executing the script receives a signal from the operating system. Let us say that we want to specify our own subroutine for the handling of the `SIGINT` signal that the operating system sends to our Perl process when a user presses Ctrl-C on the keyboard. We can do it as shown in the next script.

We define a signal handler in lines (A), (B), and (C), and then enter in the `%SIG` hash the name of the subroutine as the value for the `INT` key in line (D).[118] Note that `kill` in line (C) is a Perl function, not to be confused with the `kill` of Unix. Its first argument is the identity number of the signal to be sent to a destination process and the second argument the `PID` of the destination process. As mentioned previously, the special variable `$$` in Perl holds the `PID` of the process running the current Perl script. The signal ID 9 kills the destination process because it corresponds to `SIGKILL`, as should be clear from the Perl-generated signal names and signal numbers shown previously in this section. So the invocation in line (C) will kill the current process running the Perl script. Without this invocation of `kill`, the entry of Ctrl-C by a user will not kill the current script; it will only result in the printing out of the message of line (B). The `while` loop in line (F) parks the control in an infinite loop so that one can play with the Ctrl-C input.

```
#!/usr/bin/perl -w
use strict;

### SigHandler.pl
```

[118] We could also have entered a reference to the subroutine as the value in the `%SIG` hash, as shown by the commented-out syntax in line (E). The concept of a reference in Perl is discussed in Chapter 5.

```
sub ctrl_c_handler {                                          #(A)
    print "Ctrl C pressed\n";                                 #(B)
    kill 9, $$;                                               #(C)
}

$SIG{ "INT" } = 'ctrl_c_handler';                             #(D)

#$SIG{ "INT" } = \&ctrl_c_handler;                            #(E)

while (1) {}                                                  #(F)
```

2.19 CREDITS AND SUGGESTIONS FOR FURTHER READING

The most authoritative source for all aspects of Perl is the book by the creator of the language, Larry Wall, and his collaborators Tom Christiansen and Jon Orwant [68]. Another book that makes for easy and fun reading if this is your first exposure to Perl is by Randal Schwartz and Tom Phoenix [56]. See [61] for some of the more specialized issues addressed in this chapter, which include how to use typeglob aliases for creating filehandles that can be assigned and that can therefore be passed to functions as arguments. Also see [61] for how to create read-only constants through the mechanism of selective aliasing that is possible with typeglobs. The set operations on array data that we showed in Section 2.17.1 are based on a web posting by Steven McDougall [49]. The Unix shell script incorporated in the Perl script `Exec.pl` in Section 2.17.3 was suggested by Guilherme DeSouza.

2.20 HOMEWORK

1. What is the output of the following script? Note that the last line of the script is commented out. Will the script run if we uncomment this line (and make no other changes to the script)? Explain your answer in terms of lexical variables, global variables, lexical scopes, etc.

```
#!/usr/bin/perl -w
use strict;

my $x = 10;
print $x, "\n";
{
    my $x = 20;
    my $y = 30;
}
```

```
print $x, "\n";
#print $y, "\n";
```

2. What is the output of the following variation on the script of the previous problem? Note that now we do not enforce the `strict` pragma and the last line of the script is now uncommented.

```
#!/usr/bin/perl -w

$x = 10;
print $x, "\n";
{
        $x = 20;
        $y = 30;
}
print $x, "\n";
print $y, "\n";
```

3. The following script produces no output. Why?

```
#!/usr/bin/perl
@arr = (100, 200, 300);
$str = 'my @data = @arr';
eval $str;
print "@data\n";
```

But the following version of the above script works fine. Why?

```
#!/usr/bin/perl
@arr = (100, 200, 300);
$str = '@data = @arr';
eval $str;
print "@data\n";
```

4. Consider a "flatfile" database in which each line consists of the following colon-separated fields:

```
last_name:first_name:age:gender:phone_number:email_address
```

Assume that the name of this file is `contacts.txt`. Now write a Perl script that does the same as the following command line in a Unix shell:

```
cat contacts.txt  |  awk -F: '{print $1}'  |  sort  |  uniq
```

where `awk` is a line-oriented editor that automatically splits each line made available at its standard input into fields on the basis of the separator character specified by the `-F` option. (The default field separator is blank spaces and/or tabs.) What comes between the single quotes after that consists, in general, of a *pattern-action* statement, where the action part enclosed in curly braces is invoked on only those lines at the input that match the pattern. In the invocation of `awk` shown above, we have not specified any pattern; so the action `print $1` will be applied to every input line. The `print $1` action will cause `awk` to output the first field of each input line. This field is the last name in the `contacts.txt` file. The `sort` command sorts the lines at its standard input and sends the sorted lines to the standard output. The `uniq` command eliminates any duplicates in the sorted lines made available at its standard input. The above command line will therefore print out a sorted list of the unique last names in the `contacts.txt` file.

5. Write a Perl script that does the same thing as the following Unix command line:

```
awk -F: '{print $5}' /etc/passwd  |  uniq  |  wc -l
```

In Unix-like systems, each line of the file `/etc/passwd` typically consists of seven colon-separated fields, as in the following example

```
kak:x:568:52:Avi Kak:/home/kak:/bin/tcsh
```

The first field here consists of the user name, the second field is just the letter `x` these days,[119] the third field the user ID (`UID`), the fourth field the group ID (`GID`), the fifth field the actual name of the user, the sixth field the home directory of the user, and, finally, the last field the shell used by the user. The command `awk -F: '{print $5}'` extracts the fifth field from each line, meaning the actual user name field. (In general, the variable `$n` refers to the n-*th* field of the input line in the argument to `awk`. The variable `$0` refers to the whole line.) The `wc` command with the `-l` option prints out to the standard output the number of lines at its standard input. So the Unix command line for this question will print out the actual number of users listed in the `/etc/passwd` file. A user with multiple account names would be counted only once.

[119]It used to be the encrypted password in old days. The password information is now placed in the just root-readable file `/etc/shadow` in Unix-like systems.

6. Write a Perl script that extracts from the output of the Unix `w` command a sorted list of unique user names currently logged into the system. The output of the `w` command typically looks like

```
  2:50pm  up 109 day(s),  7:18,  15 users,  load average: ......
User     tty            login@  idle   JCPU   PCPU  what
aghosh   pts/8          Thu 8am 2days  2:35      3  -bash
dobert   pts/15         24May04 2days  7:37     37  -ksh
ruwanda  pts/16         Fri 1pm 2days     1         -sh
...      ...            ...     ...    ...    ...   ...
```

The following Unix command-line does the job that your Perl script is supposed to carry out:

```
w -h | awk '{print $1}' | sort | uniq
```

where the option `-h` to the `w` command suppresses the two header lines shown above in the output of the `w` command (since these lines will only add extraneous information to the desired output).

7. As an exercise[120] in the use of `push`, `pop`, and `shift` operators, write a Perl script that produces a randomly shuffled version of an array of 10 integers. So, if we start with an array like

```
my @arr = (0, 1, 2, 3, 4, 5, 6, 7, 8, 9);
```

its randomly shuffled version may look like

```
7 6 3 2 9 8 1 5 0 4
```

Of course, each run of your script will result in a different order for the elements.

8. Write a Perl script that shows `map()` returning a list that has more elements in it compared to the number of elements in the second-argument list (meaning the list on which `map` operates).

[120] Use the Fisher-Yates shuffle algorithm shown in Perl FAQ4 for a much more efficient approach to randomizing an array. A key step of this algorithm is in-place swapping of pairs of randomly chosen elements of the array.

9. The following piece of Perl code is famous in its own right. It is frequently referred to as the *Schwartzian Transform* after Randal Schwartz, author of widely used books on Perl.

```
@sorted_array = map  { $_->[0] }
                sort { $a->[1] <=> $b->[1] }
                map  { [ $_, -M $_ ] }
                @files_array;
```

Explain what it does. Using this example, write a Perl script for sorting an array of strings on the basis of the length of each string.

10. Autovivification is one of the reasons Perl is so flexible and why it lends itself to writing compact code. But the price one pays for this convenience is that in a large script this feature of the language can introduce difficult-to-locate bugs — even under the `strict` pragma and even with the warning flag `-w` turned on. Keeping this in mind, what could potentially be wrong with the following scriplet? It compiles and executes without any error reports.

```
#!/usr/bin/perl -w
use strict;
my %hash = ( horizParam          =>  2.3,
             verticalDeg         =>  89,
             freqOfUse_adults    =>  3,
             freqOfUse_children  =>  10 );
$hash{vertDeg} = 90;
$hash{freqOfUse_adult}++;
```

11. This is a test of whether you believe that a loop control variable is directly an element of the collection you are iterating through or a copy of the element. In the following script, if the loop control variable `$ele` was a copy of the actual element in the array, setting it to `undef` in line (A) would not change the array at all. On the other hand, if `$ele` is the array element itself, the third element of the array would get nulled. What do you think happens?

```
my @arr = qw/a b c d e f/;
for my $ele (@arr) {
    if ($ele eq 'c') {
        $ele = undef;                                        # (A)
    }
}
no warnings;
print "@arr\n";
```

3

Python — A Review of the Basics

In the same manner as we did for Perl, the goal of this chapter is to review the basics of Python.[1]

As with Perl, when you invoke the executable `python` on a Python script, the script is first taken through a compilation phase in which it is parsed to construct a parse tree and the parse tree used to emit bytecode.[2] The executable `python` subsequently interprets this bytecode.

When you first start programming with Python, what takes some getting used to — especially if you are primarily a C, C++, Java, or Perl programmer — is the fact that Python statements do not terminate in semicolons[3] and that Python code blocks are not delimited by braces. The traditional statement terminating role of a semicolon is played by the line separator in Python and the role of braces by a combination of a colon and indentation. This is illustrated by the following script which plays a guessing game with the user. The script first generates a random integer between 0

[1]As with Perl, Python comes with excellent documentation that can be downloaded from `www.python.org`.

[2]Strictly speaking, this two-step approach to bytecode generation is no longer true for versions 2.5 and higher of Python. Bytecode is now generated by the following sequence of steps: (1) the source code is parsed to construct a parse tree; (2) the parse tree is transformed into an *abstract syntax tree* (AST); (3) the AST is transformed into a *control flow graph* (CFG); and, finally, (4) the bytecode is emitted by the CFG. See [6] for details.

[3]Python does have semicolons, but they are used to separate multiple statements in the same line. So a statement that terminates in a semicolon with nothing that follows will be acceptable to Python for obvious reasons. But, unless you really want to place multiple statements in one line, the standard practice is to not use a semicolon as a statement terminator.

and 10, both inclusive, in line (D). The `while` block between lines (E) and (M) then asks the user to make a guess for this integer. Note the structure of the `while` loop. It has a header in line (E) that ends in a colon. The body of the `while` block, in lines (F) through (M), is known as a *suite*. What groups all the statements together in the suite is that they all have the same indentation vis-à-vis the header of the `while` loop in line (E). As is shown by the `if` clause in line (G), the `elif` clause in line (I), and the `else` clause in line (L), a suite can contain its own compound statements, each beginning with a colon-terminated header and an indented suite.

```
#!/usr/bin/env python

### Guess.py

import random                                                          #(A)
import sys                                                             #(B)

ran = random.Random()                                                  #(C)

num = ran.randint(0,10)                                                #(D)

while 1:                                                               #(E)
    guess = int( raw_input('Guess an integer between 0 and 10: ') ) #(F)
    if num == guess:                                                   #(G)
        print "YOU WIN! Your guess is correct!"                        #(H)
        sys.exit(0)                                                    #(I)
    elif guess < num:                                                  #(J)
        print "Your guess is on the low side. Try again."              #(K)
    else:                                                              #(L)
        print "Your guess is on the high side. Try again."             #(M)
```

As to the functions called by the above script, `raw_input()` in line (F) first writes to the standard output (without a trailing newline) the message that is supplied to it as its argument. It next reads a line from the standard input; this would be the entry made by the user in response to the message displayed on the terminal. The user's answer read by `raw_input()` is returned in the form of a string that consists of the ASCII characters entered by the user (but without the terminating newline produced by the user hitting the Enter key). The call to `int()` in the same line subsequently converts this string into a decimal integer.

The calls to `print` in lines (H), (K), and (M) of the above script send to the standard output a print representation of the argument in each case. The function `print` automatically adds a newline at the end of whatever it is asked to print out.[4]

The very first line of the above Python script

```
#!/usr/bin/env python
```

first searches for the `python` executable at the locations stored in the `PATH` environment variable. The rest of the script is then executed by the executable thus found.[5] Again as with a Perl script, after the first line, the character `#` denotes the start of a comment that extends to the end of the line. We will use the same convention in our Python scripts that we chose for our Perl scripts: The commented-out second line will show the name of the file containing the script. As with Perl, the file extension `.py` for a Python filename is usually not necessary, but it may be desirable for informing your text editor that you are creating a Python file. As mentioned before, smart text editors are capable of providing many useful code-specific facilities like autoindentation, syntax coloring, detection of unbalanced parentheses, and so on.[6]

To run the script, all you have to do is to say in a command line

```
Guess.py
```

after you make the file executable by changing its permissions with a command like

```
chmod +x Guess.py
```

In addition to the "look and feel" of Python that hopefully was conveyed by the previous script, another noticeable thing about Python is that the language is just as

---

[4]To suppress this feature of `print`, place a comma at the end of the last argument supplied to it. So, whereas

```
print "hello"
```

will place the output cursor at the start of a new line after the string `hello` is printed out, the statement

```
print "hello",
```

will leave the cursor in the same line just after the `hello` string. We should also mention that another default behavior of `print` is to insert a blank space between the successive arguments that it prints out.

[5]This use of the `sh-bang` (`#!`) mechanism to inform the operating system as to how to process the code in the file was seen earlier for Perl in the previous chapter where, instead of first calling `/usr/bin/env`, we directly called the `perl` executable. We could have used the same `/usr/bin/env` mechanism to make the Perl scripts shown earlier more portable. But note that, by common usage, the first line of a Perl script is either `#!/usr/bin/perl -w` or `#!/usr/local/bin/perl -w` on Unix-like systems. This syntax calls for passing the switch `-w` to the Perl executable. Since the `/usr/bin/env` program sometimes has difficulty passing these switches to the named executables, in order to create a more portable version of a Perl script you would need to replace the first line by the following two lines:

```
#!/usr/bin/env perl
use warnings;
```

[6]For production scripts, as with Perl, you would in most cases want to get rid of the file extension `.py` to make for cleaner syntax for script invocation.

typeless as Perl. That is, it is not necessary to declare the type of a variable when it is first introduced in a scope. So a variable can be assigned a number at some point in a script and a string — or any other object — at the next point, as demonstrated by the following lines of code. First we assign to the variable `x` an integer of value 123, and then the string literal `hello`, and then the list `[1, 2, 3]`, and finally the tuple `("one", "two", "three")`:[7]

```
x = 123
print x                                  # 123

x = "hello"
print x                                  # hello

x = [1, 2, 3]
print x                                  # [1, 2, 3]

x = ("one", "two", "three")
print x                                  # ('one', 'two', 'three')
```

We will now list some differences between Perl and Python, not from the standpoint of deep-level issues related to language design, but from the perspective of writing quick throw-away scripts for everyday tasks:

- The sometimes very convenient and fun-to-use (that, as mentioned in Chapter 2, can also become a source of hidden bugs in a script) autovivification feature of Perl has a much more limited role in Python. For example, if you make the following assignment in Perl

  ```
  $arr[5] = 100;
  ```

  Perl will immediately create a 6-element array named `@arr`, store the null value `undef` in the first five elements and the value 100 in the last element.[8] This you cannot do in Python. In other words, unless we previously declared `arr` to be a tuple or a list that could hold six or more elements, the following statement would be illegal in Python:

  ```
  arr[5] = 100
  ```

[7] Python's lists and tuples are reviewed in Section 3.3.

[8] In Perl this works as long as the `strict` pragma is turned off. With the `strict` pragma on, you could use the following snippet of code to demonstrate autovivification in Perl

```
my @arr;
$arr[5] = 100;
print "@arr\n";
```

Note also that if the `warning` pragma is turned on, the print statement will cause warnings to be printed out for the uninitialized values being output for the first five elements of the array. This is in accordance with the explanation in Section 2.1 of Chapter 2.

Even telling Python that `arr` is a list won't suffice. That is, even the following statements are illegal

```
arr = []
arr[5] = 100
```

Now Python will complain that the assignment in the second statement is indexing an out-of-range element of the list.

- Perl allows for the interpolation of the print representations of scalars and arrays into double-quoted strings. Python does not permit such interpolations. For example, all of the following are legal constructs in Perl:

```
$x = "hello";
$y = "jello";
print "$x is not $y";                    # hello is not jello

@arr = ("hello", "jello");
print "@arr $arr[0] $arr[$#arr]\n";  # hello jello hello jello

%h = ( k1 => 'hello', k2 => 'jello' );
print "$h{k1} $h{k2}\n";                  # hello jello
```

But similar constructs do not exist in Python.[9]

- The autoincrementing and autodecrementing operators do not work in Python. In Perl, it is common to see constructs such as `$x++`, `$x--`, `++$x`, and `--$x` for incrementing and decrementing the number value held by a scalar. So whereas in Perl you can say

```
$x++;
```

in Python, you would say

---

[9]However, similar effects can be achieved in Python with the `%` operator when it follows a format string containing conversion specifiers, as demonstrated by the following examples:

```
x = "hello"
y = "jello"
print "%s is not %s" % (x,y)                  # hello is not jello

arr = ("hello", "jello")
print "%s %s %s" % (arr, arr[0], arr[len(arr)-1])
                                  # ('hello', 'jello') hello jello

h = { 'k1' : 'hello', 'k2' : 'jello' }
print "%s %s" % (h['k1'], h['k2'])                  # hello jello
```

The various constructs we have shown for the Python code above will be made clear in Sections 3.3 and 3.4 of this chapter. Suffice it to say here that `arr` is a tuple and `h` a dictionary.

```
x += 1
```

- The frequently used ternary operator `?:` in Perl that is semantically equivalent to an `if-else` statement does not work in Python. Here is a legal construct in Perl:

  ```
  $x = 4;
  print $x < 0 ? 'negative' : 'non-negative', "\n";
  ```

  that causes the word `non-negative` to be printed out. Being an operator, `?:` can be used within any Perl expression. Python requires you to use an `if-else` statement for such conditional action.[10]

- Vis-à-vis Perl, a lot more happens at run time in Python than at compile time. This creates interesting differences between how the two languages behave with regard to the order in which the different objects are created in a script. As an example of this difference, when we use a variable to specify a default argument for a function parameter, the value used for the variable is as it exists at the point of function definition, as opposed to at the point of function call. This will be illustrated in Section 3.8.3 of this chapter.

Before leaving this section, we should mention that, as for Perl, the standard Python interpreter is written in C and that every action in a Python script is carried out by some piece of C code.

3.1 LANGUAGE MODEL: PERL VERSUS PYTHON

The language model underlying Perl makes a distinction between the different types of scalar values, on the one hand, and the different types of data storage mechanisms on the other. The scalar values in Perl can be either numbers, or strings, or references. And the storage mechanisms that the language provides are scalars, vectors, and hashes.

Python uses a more uniform language model in which no particular distinction is made between the different types of values that can be assigned to a variable or stored in the different types of storage mechanisms. Every variable in Python can be viewed as a scalar variable that holds a scalar value which is always a reference to some data object. It is true that in many cases when a variable is directly evaluated, what the system returns is the data object itself to which the variable is holding a reference (or, in some cases, some print representation of the data object). Nonetheless, a variable

[10] Python 2.5 permits a variation on the usual ternary operator for conditional evaluation. The allowed syntax is `X if C else Y`. See [67] for further information.

is to be thought of as holding a reference to an object, as opposed to holding the object directly. This is analogous to a variable in C holding a pointer to a number, as opposed to holding the number directly.

So, in Python, there is no difference between a variable to which is assigned a single number and a variable to which is assigned a list of numbers. In both cases, what the variable actually holds is a single "scalar," which is a reference to a number in the first case and a reference to a list of numbers in the second. On the other hand, Perl uses very different storage mechanisms for holding a single value and for holding a list of values; the former is held by a scalar variable and the latter by a vector variable. If, for the sake of discussion, we wanted to force Perl into the Python mold, a list of numbers in Perl would be stored in an anonymous array whose reference would be held by an ordinary scalar variable.

A reference to a data object in Python is very much like a reference in Java or a pointer in C++, or, for that matter, a reference in Perl. Python puts references to good use in the dotted-attribute object-oriented notation for achieving much of the functionality associated with different kinds of data objects. We should also mention that this causes some aficionados of the language to claim that Python is more object-oriented than Perl. But, looking at object-oriented programming and scripting from a more fundamental perspective, that is evidently not the case. A language derives its object-oriented power from the facilities it provides for inheritance, polymorphism, access control, abstract types, and so on. As we will see in the later chapters of this book, with regard to these criteria for assessing the degree of object orientation of a language, there is not that much difference between Perl and Python.

Every data object in Python has three properties: (1) an identity, which can be retrieved by using the built-in function `id()`; (2) a type, which can be retrieved by using the built-in function `type()`; and (3) a value, which is automatically returned when the object is evaluated. The following script illustrates the retrieval of these three properties associated with an integer object and with a string object. In line (A), we create a numeric object of value 100. Line (C) prints out its identity. The identity number returned by the `id()` function is related to the memory location where the object resides.[11] Line (D) retrieves the type of the object. What is returned by `type()` in line (D) is itself an object — of typename `TypeType`. What is printed out in line (E) is the print representation of this `TypeType` object. Finally, line (F) prints out the value of the object created in line (A). Lines (G) through (L) show the retrieval of the same three properties for a string object created in line (G). As presented in Section 3.3.1, a string object is endowed with a number of attributes through which we can determine the various properties of a string. Line (M) illustrates the invocation of the `count()` method on the string object created in line (G); this function returns the number of occurrences of the argument substring in the string on which the method is invoked. (The function call syntax used in line (M) will become clear after the reader has gone through the beginning sections of

[11]The identity of an object as returned by `id()` never changes after the object is created.

Chapter 7.) Line (N) shows the use of another built-in function, `len()`, defined for sequences, for determining the number of characters in a string.

```
#!/usr/bin/python

### IdTypeVal.py

x = 100                                                      #(A)
iden = id( x )                                               #(B)
print iden                          # 134601696              #(C)
tipe = type( x )                                             #(D)
print tipe                          # <type 'int'>           #(E)
print x                             # 100                    #(F)


x = "hello"                                                  #(G)
id = id( x )                                                 #(H)
print id                            # 134818504              #(I)
tipe = type( x )                                             #(J)
print tipe                          # <type 'str'>           #(K)
print x                             # hello                  #(L)

print x.count( 'l' )                # 2                      #(M)
print len( x )                      # 5                      #(N)
```

3.2 NUMBERS

Python has the following options for representing a number:

- Plain integer
- Long integer
- Floating-point number
- Complex number

With regard to the maximum size of a plain integer, it is the same as a signed `long` integer as recognized by the underlying C library. A `long` integer in Python is different from its corresponding counterpart in C; Python's `long` integers have unlimited range (subject, of course, to virtual memory limitations).[12] How an integer is stored internally depends on its magnitude, as in Perl. Ordinarily, Python will try to use the `plain` integer representation. But if the value is too large for that representation, Python will automatically switch to its `long`.

The Python script `Integer.py` that follows — it parallels the Perl script `Integer.pl` in Section 2.1.1 of Chapter 2 — demonstrates that the manner in which Python automatically changes the internal representation of an integer is different from Perl. Perl switches the internal representation of an integer from signed to unsigned to floating-point as the integer gets larger and larger. But not in Python. An integer in Python always stays an integer regardless of its size.

In line (A), the script `Integer.py`[13] uses the hexadecimal representation[14] to assign a plain integer value to a variable. This is the same value that was assigned as a signed integer in line (A) of the Perl script `Integer.pl` in the previous chapter. But note that since a plain integer in Python is based on the underlying C library's *signed long* integer, the value shown in line (A) of the Python script `Integer.py` will typically *not* be the largest possible for Python's plain integers. Line (B) calls on Python's `print` to print out the decimal value of this number. This call to `print` converts each argument object into its string representation (using rules specific to that object) and outputs the strings thus obtained to the standard output. The default behavior of `print` is to place a blank space between successive pairs of output strings and to output the newline character after the last string, as mentioned earlier in our explanation of the script `Guess.py` script.

Line (C) shows another call to `print`, but this time it acts like the `printf()` of Perl and C. As mentioned in a footnote in the introduction to this chapter, when the argument supplied to Python's `print` contains the symbol `%` after a first-argument quoted string, the quoted string serves the role of a format string containing conversion specifiers. The arguments following the `%` symbol are then evaluated and substituted into the format string, as in C and Perl. The output produced by the `%d` conversion specifier in line (C) is what you would expect — the actual decimal value of the integer.

Paralleling the Perl script `Integer.pl`, we now add to the value stored in the variable `num` in line (D). When we did the same thing in Perl, the internal representation of the integer was changed from a signed integer to an unsigned integer. Python, on the other hand, keeps the internal representation unchanged because of the much larger range allowed for its plain integers. Note particularly,

---

[12]A negative `long` integer acts as if it has an infinite number of sign bits toward the left. The bit pattern for a negative integer, in general, is obtained by taking a 2's complement of the unsigned integer. The leftmost bit in the bit pattern thus obtained is the sign bit. This bit will always be 1 for a negative integer.

[13]As mentioned already, the educational value of this script lies in its line-by-line comparison with the Perl script `Integer.pl` in Section 2.1.1 of Chapter 2.

[14]Note that Python does not allow the use of underscores in its numeric literals.

that the values output by both the conversion specifiers `%u` and `%d` in lines (E) and (F) remain the same. Compare this with what happened in the Perl script `Integer.pl`. As the representation of the number changed internally to the *unsigned* type, its output produced by the `%d` conversion specifier was incorrect.[15]

The multiplication shown in line (H) results in an integer that, for the case of Perl in `Integer.pl`, was too large to represent as an integer, signed or unsigned. But Python, with its unlimited-precision `long`, has no such trouble. So the very large number returned by the multiplication in line (H) is represented as Python's `long` integer. In a formatted output, this value is printed out correctly by both the `%d` and the `%u` conversion specifiers in lines (I) and (J). As the reader can see from the output shown for `Integer.pl` in the previous chapter, Perl had to convert the number to its floating-point representation which could then be printed out correctly only by the conversion specifiers meant for that representation. Line (K) shows the output for this number with the exponential-format conversion specifier. Line (L) shows the output with a simple call to `print`.

As with the Perl script, the rest of the script below shows some of the Python's operators for numbers. As you would expect, Python possesses all of the usual arithmetic operators and their *compound assignment* versions. Lines (N) and (O) show the exponentiation operator applied to the number of line (M). The result of exponentiation is displayed in line (O). Lines (P) and (Q) show the compound assignment version of the exponentiation operator. Lines (R) and (S) show the compound assignment version of the remainder operator (also called the modulus operator) and lines (T) and (U) the compound assignment version of the ordinary division operator.

With regard to the division operation shown in line (T), it is important to realize that when both operands are integers, Python carries out an integer division and returns an integer for the answer. The integer answer thus returned bears a "round toward negative infinity" relationship to the floating-point answer. So `1/2` returns 0 and `(-1)/2` returns `-1`. This is also referred to as the "flooring" of the result. Python also provides another division operator, `//`, that always returns the floor of the quotient for all three cases of purely integer operands, purely floating-point operands, and mixed operands.[16]

When the operands supplied to an arithmetic operator are of mixed number representations, the *narrower* representation is automatically converted to its *wider* form before applying the operator. The result is then returned in the wider representation. Therefore, when multiplying an integer with a floating-point value, the integer will first be converted to its floating-point equivalent and the result returned as a floating-

---

[15]See the explanation associated with the script `Integer.pl` in the previous chapter for the roles assigned to the different conversion specifiers in a format string.

[16]Note that starting with Python 3.0, the meaning of the regular division operator `/` will change; it will then reflect "true division," that is, the result will not be floored [70].

point number. Such conversions are also used when comparing numbers in different representations.

The commented-out lines (V) and (W) show that the autoincrement operators do not work in Python, whereas, as shown in `Integer.pl`, they do in Perl.

Lines (X) and (Y) show that if we want to force Python to use the wider `long` representation for an integer that might otherwise be represented as `plain`, you must append the letter `L` to the integer literal. It is also possible to use the lowercase `l`, but that can create readability problems because it is not visually so distinguishable from the character `1` for the number one. Another way to force Python to use `long` for representing an integer is by a call to the `long()` constructor,[17] as shown in line (Z).

Lines (a) and (b) show the Python's built-in `abs()` function for obtaining the absolute value of a number, that is, the value obtained by discarding the sign if any associated with the number.

Lines (c) through (k) demonstrate the built-in function `int()` that converts a string or a number into an integer. When supplied with a floating-point argument, the function simply drops off the fractional part (that is, truncates the number toward zero) and returns the rest as an integer, as demonstrated by lines (c), (d), and (e). However, when supplied with a string argument, the string must be the print representation of an integer. That explains why uncommenting the commented-out line (g) would give rise to an error. On the other hand, the string of line (h) works fine for the call to `int()` in line (i).

When called with two arguments, `int()` assumes that the first argument is the string representation of a literal that can be converted into an integer using the second argument as a radix. The second argument must obviously be an integer, its value between 2 and 36, both inclusive. This is demonstrated by lines (k), (l), and (m).

What lines (c) through (m) show for `int()`, lines (n) through (x) show for `long()`. Whereas `int()` returns a `plain` integer, `long()` returns a `long`. As evident from the output shown for the case of `long()`, both `int()` and `long()` possess identical behaviors, except for the internal representations of the integers returned.

```
#!/usr/bin/env python

### Integer.py

# Since Python uses C's long for plain integers, this will
# typically NOT be the largest value for a plain integer:
num = 0x7fffffff                                                    #(A)
```

[17] As to what is meant by a constructor call will become clear in Chapter 7.

```
print num                          # 2147483647                     #(B)
print "%d" % num                   # 2147483647                     #(C)

num = num + 1000                                                    #(D)
print "%u" % num                   # 2147484647                     #(E)
print "%d" % num                   # 2147484647                     #(F)
print num                          # 2147484647                     #(G)

# A very large integer:
num = num * num                                                     #(H)
print "%d" % num                   # 4611690309100714609            #(I)
print "%u" % num                   # 4611690309100714609            #(J)
print "%e" % num                   # 4.611690e+18                   #(K)
print num                          # 4611690309100714609            #(L)

# Show some math operators:
num = 16                                                            #(M)
num = num ** 2                                                      #(N)
print num                          # 256                            #(O)
num **= 0.5                                                         #(P)
print num                          # 16.0                           #(Q)
num %= 9                                                            #(R)
print num                          # 7.0                            #(S)
num /= 4                                                            #(T)
print num                          # 1.75                           #(U)
#print num++                       # Error                          #(V)
#print ++num                       # Error                          #(W)

# Force the 'long' representation:
num = 123456L;                                                      #(X)
print num;                         # 123456                         #(Y)

# Another way to force the 'long' representation:
num = long(123456)                                                  #(Z)

# The abs() function:
num = -123                                                          #(a)
print abs(num)                     # 123                            #(b)

# Demonstrate the int() constructor:
x = 123.45678                                                       #(c)
y = int( x )                                                        #(d)
print y                            # 123                            #(e)

x = "123.45678"                                                     #(f)
#y = int( x )                      # Error                          #(g)

x = "123"                                                           #(h)
y = int( x )                       # now okay                       #(i)
```

```
print y                              # 123                              #(j)

x = "10101010"                                                          #(k)
print int( x, 2)                     # 170                              #(l)
print int( x, 3)                     # 2460                             #(m)

# Demonstrate the long() constructor:
x = 123.45678                                                           #(n)
y = long( x )                                                           #(o)
print y                              # 123                              #(p)

x = "123.45678"                                                         #(q)
#y = long( x )                       # Error                            #(r)

x = "123"                                                               #(s)
y = long( x )                        # now okay                         #(t)
print y                              # 123                              #(u)

x = "10101010"                                                          #(v)
print long( x, 2)                    # 170                              #(w)
print long( x, 3)                    # 2460                             #(x)
```

Our next script, `Float.py`, shows examples of floating-point numbers in Python and some operations on such numbers. For storing floating-point numbers, Python uses the double-precision float as understood by the underlying C library. As mentioned in the previous chapter, most modern machines will allocate 8 bytes for such numbers. The precision and the maximum/minimum size of such numbers is determined by how many bits are reserved for the exponent and how many for the fraction part. Usually, the precision is 17 decimal digits and the range corresponds to the decimal exponent between -304 and +304.

Lines (A) and (B) of the next script use the decimal format for the floating-point values on the right of the assignment operator. Line (C) uses `print` to output the result of multiplying the two floating-point values. By default, Python presents its scientific-notation output with only three digits after the decimal point, whereas Perl shows all of the digits up to the precision of the representation of a double-precision float. Of course, with additional flags in the conversion specifier, Python is happy to supply the additional digits, as shown in line (G).

Line (D) does the same as line (C) except that it specifically calls for the scientific-notation conversion specifier with three digits after the decimal point. Line (E) uses the exponential format (also called the *scientific format*) for specifying the floating-point number on the right side of the assignment. Line (F) shows the output from the multiplication in the argument to `print;` this is the same output we obtained in line (C) because the two numbers being multiplied are the same in value. Line (G) shows the same result at the full limit of the precision of a double-precision float. Lines (H) and (I) show the result of a division.

The rest of the script demonstrates the built-in conversion function `float()` that returns the floating-point representation of a number or a string if the latter is the print presentation of a number. Lines (J) and (K) really don't do anything since the argument in each case is a floating-point number and the returned value is a floating-point number of exactly the same value. Lines (L) and (M), on the other hand, show something useful. When supplied with a string that is the print representation of a floating-point number, `float()` returns a value that *is* the floating-point number.

```
#!/usr/bin/env python

### Float.py

x = 0.000000000003                                               #(A)
y = 1234.000000000003                                            #(B)
print x * y                         # 3.702e-09                  #(C)
print "%.3e" % (x * y)              # 3.702e-09                  #(D)

y = 1234 + 3.00e-12                                              #(E)
print x * y                         # 3.702e-09                  #(F)
print "%.14e" % (x * y)             # 3.70200000000001e-09       #(G)

z = 1e50                                                         #(H)
print x / z                         # 3e-62                      #(I)

print float(x)                      # 3e-12                      #(J)
print float(y)                      # 1234.0                     #(K)

x = "1234.5678"                                                  #(L)
print float( x )                    # 1234.5678                  #(M)
```

An important issue related to floating-point numbers is that what you see in the output produced by a script may be ever so slightly different from what is actually stored in the memory of the computer. This is illustrated by the code fragment shown below. Line (A) assigns the floating-point value 0.1 to the variable x. The problem with this innocuous assignment is that the decimal fraction[18] 0.1 cannot be represented exactly with a binary fraction.[19] For example, just as the value to be associated with the decimal fraction 0.1 is given by 1×10^{-1}, the value to be

[18]Meaning a fraction in base 10 number representation.

[19]Meaning a fraction in base 2 number representation, the only representation that can be stored in the computer.

associated with the binary fraction 0.0001 is given by $0 \times 2^{-1} + 0 \times 2^{-2} + 0 \times 2^{-3} + 1 \times 2^{-4}$, which is equal to the decimal 0.065. Adding another digit to this binary fraction, we can show that 0.00011 equals the decimal 0.09375. We can keep on adding binary digits to the binary fraction, choosing each digit on the basis of whether or not it takes us closer to the target value of 0.1, and show that eventually we will end up with an infinitely repeating binary pattern that *approaches* but never exactly equals the decimal number 0.1.[20]

This problem with the storage of the decimal 0.1 assigned to `x` in line (A) becomes evident in lines (B) and (C) when we try to print out `repr(x)`. The purpose of the built-in `repr()` function is to return a string representation of the argument object so that when `eval()` is invoked on the string returned by `repr()`, you will get back the original object. That is, it must be the case that `eval(repr(x)) == x`. When `x` stores a floating-point value, this equality must hold up for no less than 17 significant digits after the decimal point (in order to conform to the IEEE 754 Floating Point Standard). What that implies is that if we were to use `eval()` to recreate the floating-point object from the string returned by `repr()`, we would get a binary representation in the memory that would be identical to the binary representation we had originally stored for 0.1 up to an accuracy of 17 significant digits.[21]

Lines (D) and (E) show that, in contrast with the behavior of `repr()`, `str()` returns a string that looks exactly like our original entry for the floating-point number in line (A). That is because `str()`'s purpose is to create a "nice" printable representation of the argument object. Therefore, when `str()` is invoked on a floating-point value, it rounds it earlier for a cleaner print representation. Calling `print` directly on `x`, as in line (F), implicitly calls `str()` on the argument object. So we should expect `print x` to create the same display as `print str(x)`.

```
x = 0.1                                                  #(A)
y = repr( x )                                            #(B)
print y                     # 0.10000000000000001        #(C)
z = str( x )                                             #(D)
print z                     # 0.1                        #(E)
print x                     # 0.1                        #(F)
```

The next script, `Complex.py`, shows how complex numbers are created and manipulated in Python. In algebra, a complex number is the sum of a real number and an imaginary number. Imaginary numbers in Python are specified by appending `j` or `J` to a numeric literal, as we show in lines (A) and (B). The real and the imaginary parts of a complex number `z` can be retrieved separately through the read-only attributes `real` and `imag` through the calls `z.real` and `z.imag`, respectively, as we show in line (C). The double-precision float representation of the

---

[20] For the case of decimal 0.1, this infinitely repeating binary fraction looks like [29]:

`0.00011001100110011001100110011001100110011......`

[21] It is for this reason that `repr()` uses the `%.17g` format to construct the output string for floating-point numbers.

underlying C library is used for storing the real and the imaginary parts of a complex number.

In general, a complex number is created by the constructor call[22] `complex()`, as shown in lines (D), (E), and (F). Line (F) shows us retrieving the real and the imaginary parts separately of the number returned by `complex()`. A complex number may also be specified by directly adding real and imaginary parts, as we do in line (G).

Python supports all the usual math operators that one uses on complex numbers. Examples of these are shown in lines (H), (I), and (J).

```
#!/usr/bin/env python

### Complex.py

z = 123J                                                          #(A)
print z                                 # 123j                    #(B)
print z.real, z.imag                    # 0.0 123.0               #(C)

z = complex( 3, 4 )                                               #(D)
print z                                 # (3+4j)                  #(E)
print z.real, z.imag                    # 3.0 4.0                 #(F)

t = 1 +  2j                                                       #(G)

print z * t                             # (-5+10j)                #(H)

print z / t                             # (2.2-0.4j)              #(I)

print z ** 0.5                          # (2+1j)                  #(J)
```

3.3 PYTHON CONTAINERS: SEQUENCES

These built-in containers of Python allow sequential access to the elements stored in the containers via integer index offsets that can be either positive or negative. Python has the following sequence types:

- String

[22]What that means will become clear in Chapter 7.

- Unicode string
- Tuple
- Xrange
- List

Of these, only Lists are *mutable*, meaning that they can undergo in-place modifications, as, for example, by the insertion of a new element at the beginning, in the middle, or at the end. All other sequence types are *immutable*. All sequences support the operations shown in Table 3.1.

operator/ function	***operand/ argument types***	***call***	***value returned***
in	sequence x, sequence s	x in s	True if an item of s equals x, False otherwise
not in	sequence x, sequence s	x not in s	False if an item of s equals x, True otherwise
+	sequence s, sequence t	s + t	Concatenation of s and t
*	sequence s, integer n	s*n or n*s	Concatenations of n shallow copies of s
[]	sequence s, integer i	s[i]	Item at index i in sequence s
[:]	sequence s, integer i, integer j	s[i:j]	Slice of s from index i to index j-1
[::]	sequence s, integer i, integer j, integer k	s[i:j:k]	Slice of s from i to j-1 in steps of k
len	sequence s	len(s)	The number of elements in s
min	sequence s	min(s)	The smallest element in s
max	sequence s	max(s)	The largest element in s

Table 3.1

With regard to the replication operator * in Table 3.1 for concatenating multiple copies of a sequence, the copies used are *shallow*. What that means is that if the original sequence holds a reference to a Python object (let's call it the target object), all of the copies used in the concatenation will hold references to the same target object. If the target object were to change subsequently, that will affect all replications in the concatenation previously returned by the `*` operator.

In the fifth row of the table, the index `i` used for accessing an element, as in `s[i]`, is allowed to be negative. A negative index is interpreted relative to the end of a sequence, with the last element accessible via the index `-1`. The index `-(n+1)` represents the first element, where `n` is the number of elements in the sequence.[23]

The call `s[i:j]` in the sixth row of the table is for fetching a slice of a sequence. The returned elements are consecutively indexed starting at `i` and ending at `j-1`. And in the call `s[i:j:k]` in the next row, the elements returned are within the same range as before, but in steps of `k`. If the slicing operation is supposed to fetch all elements above an index `i`, one can leave unspecified the upper bound, as in the notation `s[i:]`. By the same token, if one wishes to fetch all the elements up to but not including the element at index `i`, the notation `s[:i]` would work. The syntax `s[:]` is special-cased to return a copy of the original sequence. So any changes made to the elements of `s[:]` will not be visible in the original sequence. On the other hand, any changes made to `s[i:j]`, with specific values for `i` or `j` or both, will directly affect the original sequence.

Python provides the following built-in functions (actually constructor calls[24]) for converting a data object from one sequence type to another:

`list()`: When supplied with a sequence-type data object as the argument, this function returns a list version of the argument object. If the argument object itself is a list, the returned object is a copy of the list.

`str()`: This function returns a print representation of the argument data object.

`tuple()`: When supplied with a sequence-type data object as the argument, this function returns a tuple version of the argument object. If the argument object itself is a tuple, the returned object is the argument tuple itself.

The operations listed in Table 3.1 are supported by all sequence containers — immutable and mutable. Table 3.2 shows the operations that are specific to mutable containers, of which the list container is currently the only example in the language.

With regard to the notation shown in Table 3.2, as was the case with the notation in Table 3.1, a negative index used for accessing an element, as in `s[-i]`, is interpreted relative to the end of a sequence, with the last element accessible via the index `-1`.

[23] The ostensibly negative index `-0` is the same as `0`, meaning that `s[-0]` and `s[0]` point to the same element — the very first element of the sequence.

[24] Chapter 7 explains what is meant by a constructor call.

operation on a mutable sequence s	*result*
`s[i] = x`	Replace `i`-th element of `s` with `x`
`s[i:j] = t`	Replace the indicated slice by object `t` (`t` may be a single element or a sequence)
`del s[i:j]`	Delete the indicated slice
`s[i:j:k] = t`	Replace the indicated slice with t (the size of `t` must be same as the indicated slice)
`del s[i:j:k]`	Delete the indicated slice
`s.append(x)`	Append new element `x` at the end of `s`
`s.count(x)`	Return the number of elements with `s[i] = x`
`s.index(x)`	Return smallest index `i` for which `s[i] = x`
`s.index(x,j,k)`	Returns smallest index `i, j<=i<k`, so that `s[i] = x`
`s.insert(i,x)`	Insert a new element `x` at index `i`
`s.pop()`	Delete and return last element
`s.pop([i])`	Delete and return element at index `i`
`s.remove(x)`	Delete the first occurrence of `x` in `s`
`s.reverse()`	Reverse in place the order of elements in `s`
`s.sort()`	Sort the items of `s` in place
`s.sort(compFunc)`	Sort items in place using `compFunc` for comparing pairs of elements

Table 3.2

As before, the index `-(n+1)` represents the first element, where `n` is the number of elements in the sequence. The notation `s[i:j]` for accessing a slice of a container is again to be understood as before, as is also the case with the notation `s[i:j:k]` for accessing a slice but in steps of `k`.

All operations shown in Table 3.2, except `index()` and `count()`, cause structural modifications to the underlying container. In other words, they are *mutating operations*. Note in particular that even the operations that are specified through a container slice — there are four such operations — cause changes to the underlying container.

The `reverse()` and `sort()` operations listed in Table 3.2, meant to be invoked *on* a list, work in place. As we will show in the next section, there is also the built-in stand-alone function `sorted()` that *returns* a sorted list.

3.3.1 Strings

A Python string is similar to a Perl string in the sense that it does not need a terminating null character. But that is where the similarity ends. Probably the most significant difference between the two is that you cannot interpolate inside a Python string of any kind, whereas string interpolation plays a hugely important role in scripting with Perl.[25]

Python allows for the following different ways to delimit a sequence of characters for the purpose of defining a string literal:

- By a pair of matching single quotes
- By a pair of matching double quotes
- By a pair of matching triple single quotes
- By a pair of matching triple double quotes
- As a raw string in which character escapes lose their special meaning

As we will see in the script to follow, all quoting styles are equivalent with regard to how the characters composing a string are understood by Python. This applies particularly to any special backslashed escaped characters that are commonly used as control characters for controlling the position of the cursor in an output device, for drawing the attention of the user, and so on. These include `\n` for linefeed, `\t` for horizontal tab, `\a` for bell, `\b` for backspace, etc. This equivalence between the different quoting styles also applies to any embedded numeric escapes. The only difference between single-quoted and double-quoted string literals, on the one hand, and triple-quoted string literals, on the other, is that the latter allows the literals to be specified in multiple lines of a script.[26]

---

[25]There is a single exception to this rule in Python. As we showed through examples in a footnote in the introduction to this chapter, when a Python string is followed by the character `%`, the character acts as an interpolation operator and the string to the left of `%` is construed to be a *format string*. Now if this string contains conversion specifiers, Python will look for objects following the character `%` whose print representations can be used to replace the conversion specifiers in the format string. If there is more than one conversion specifier in the format string, the corresponding values must be presented in the form of a tuple after the `%` character.

[26]This makes triple quoting a common tool for rendering nonoperational a portion of a script during code development — provided, of course, the portion does not contain any triple-quoted strings with the same quote mark. *For this reason, some Python programmers take to reserving one of the two quote*

If, except for the multiline feature of triple quoting, all the quoting styles work the same, how does one choose between them? When choosing between single quoting and double quoting, the main reason for using a particular quoting style would be that you may want to use the other for setting off a portion of the string literal. This saves you the bother of having to escape the embedded quote marks. And the main reason for using triple quotes as string delimiters is that your literal needs to be specified in multiple contiguous lines. You choose the single-quote marks or the double-quote marks for the triple-quote delimiters depending on which quote marks are embedded inside the string literal. If a multiline string literal does not contain any quote marks, it matters not as to which style of triple quoting you use.

As mentioned already, single-quoted, double-quoted, and triple-quoted Python strings are equivalent with regard to any embedded escaped characters and other special nonalphanumeric symbols. This is unlike what happens in Perl. In Perl, as shown in the previous chapter, special nonalphanumeric characters allow you to carry out variable interpolation in double-quoted strings (but not in single-quoted strings). Additionally, all characters except for the backslash take on their literal meanings inside a single-quoted string. This makes single-quoted strings ideal for specifying regular expressions in Perl.

If all the quoting styles work the same with regard to the embedded nonalphanumeric symbols and backslashed escaped characters, how does one represent regular-expression strings in Python? Python gives us what are known as raw strings for that purpose. Simply by prefixing a string literal with the letter `r` or `R`, you get essentially the same effect as by single quoting in Perl.

The script `SpecifyingStrings.py` shown next presents the different ways of specifying a string literal in Python. Lines (A) through (H) of the script demonstrate

---

marks for rendering nonoperational portions of a script during debugging. In terms of its usefulness during script debugging, using triple-quotes in this manner is similar to what can be achieved in Perl by the `=` and `=cut` tokens. That is, a portion of a Perl script can be rendered nonoperational by inserting a line that starts with, say, `=for later` just before the portion and a line that starts with, say, `=cut back to Perl` just after. (What follows `=` in the opening token and `=cut` in the ending token can be any sequence of characters; so it is useful to choose a mnemonic word or phrase.) If the code section to be rendered nonoperational is toward the end of a script file, in Perl it is more common to use the token `__END__` to immediately halt further compilation/execution in a script. A direct analog of what `__END__` accomplishes in Perl would be to call `sys.exit("some message here")` in Python. This call raises the `SystemExit` exception. An even more direct way to halt further execution in a Python script is to insert the statement `raise SystemExit` in a script. Yet another way to halt further execution in a Python script is to insert the following statements where you want the execution halted:

```
import pdb
pdb.set_trace()
```

where `pdb` is the debugger module that comes with the standard distribution. The advantage of this approach is that it lets you examine the data objects that are in scope at the point where the above two statements are inserted. To examine these data objects, you must first enter `n` for the next line subsequent to the above two statements that place the execution of the script in the debugging mode.

that string literals using any of the allowed quoting styles behave the same with regard to the embedded newline and tab character escapes.

If you need to specify a string literal in multiple physical lines, you must use triple quotes, as shown by lines (I) and (J).

Lines (K) through (P) present the reason as to why you would want to use one or the other of the allowed quoting styles in single-line or multiline formats. You may not need to escape the embedded quote marks in a string if you choose wisely for the string delimiting quote marks.

Lines (Q) through (T) demonstrate that when a backslash is not performing duty in an escape sequence inside a quoted string, its meaning is taken literally. That is, it becomes an ordinary character in the string.

Lines (U) through (X) show that if you want two contiguous backslashes together in a string literal, just placing the two together in the string literal at the definition time doesn't cut it. We still get a single backslash in the string literal that is created. That is because the first backslash is used for escaping the special meaning of the second backslash, which causes the second backslash to be taken as an ordinary character. Of course, in the example shown, the second backslash, since it does not precede any recognizable escape sequence, would have been taken to be an ordinary character anyway [as demonstrated by lines (Q) through (T)], but that is besides the point.

If you want two backslashes together in a string literal, you must either use three together at the definition time, as shown in lines (Y) through (b), or four together, as shown in lines (c) through (f). With three together, the first backslash suppresses the special meaning of the second backslash, which causes the second backslash to be accepted as an ordinary character. The third backslash in a three-backslash sequence is accepted as an ordinary character anyway in the example shown because it is not recognized as start of an escape sequence. Obviously, the safest way to get two backslashes together in a string literal is to use four together at the definition time. Now the third backslash will suppress the special meaning of the fourth backslash regardless of what follows the last backslash.

Lines (g) through (j) show the use of a backslash to escape the quote mark when it needs to be included in a string literal.

Lines (k) through (n) show that a string literal can include the numeric escape sequence representation[27] for any character, printable or nonprintable. The escape sequences can be either in hexadecimal form (`\xdd`, where `d` is a hex digit), or the octal form (`\ddd`, where `d` is an octal digit), or the Unicode form (either as `\udddd` for 16-bit Unicode or as `\udddddddd` for 32-bit Unicode, where `d` is again a hexadecimal digit). In the string literal shown in lines (k) through (n), the characters for the words `hi` and `how` are in hex and the characters for the word `are` in octal.

[27] A footnote in Section 2.1.2 of Chapter 2 explains the difference between character escapes and numeric escapes.

If you want to suppress the special role of the backslash character inside the definition of a string literal, you need to use Python's *raw string*. As shown by the examples in lines (o) through (r), a raw string literal is defined the same way as a regular string literal except for the prefix that must either be `r` or `R`. If it is desired to create a string literal whose internal representation would consist of Unicode characters, one must either use the prefix `u` or `U`, as shown in line (s) for the case of a double-quoted string. Raw versions of Unicode strings can be created by combining the two prefixes, as shown in line (t). In such combined use of the prefixes, the Unicode prefix must appear before the raw-string prefix. The last example, in line (u), shows us creating a Unicode tripled-quoted string literal.

```
#!/usr/bin/env python

### SpecifyingStrings.py

# Embedded '\n' causes newlines in the output in all cases:
print 'hi! \nhow are you'                 # hi!                  #(A)
                                          # how are you

print "hi! \nhow are you"                 # hi!                  #(B)
                                          # how are you

print '''hi! \nhow are you'''             # hi!                  #(C)
                                          # how are you

print """hi! \nhow are you"""             # hi!                  #(D)
                                          # how are you

# Tab works for all cases:
print 'name\tage\tweight'                 # name    age    weight  #(E)
print "name\tage\tweight"                 # name    age    weight  #(F)
print '''name\tage\tweight'''             # name    age    weight  #(G)
print """name\tage\tweight"""             # name    age    weight  #(H)

# Only triple-quoted strings are allowed to be specified in
# multiple lines:
print '''hi!
  how are you'''                          # hi!
                                          #   how are you      #(I)
print """hi!
  how are you"""                          # hi!
                                          #   how are you      #(J)

# Single-quoted strings can include embedded double quotes:
print 'I "am" okay!'                      # I "am" okay!         #(K)

# Double-quoted strings can include embedded single quotes:
```

```
print "I 'am' okay!"                          # I 'am' okay!           #(L)

# Triple-quoted strings can included embedded single and double quotes:
print '''I 'am' "okay"!'''                    # I 'am' "okay"!         #(M)
print """I 'am' "okay"!"""                    # I 'am' "okay"!         #(N)

# Triple-quoted strings can also include triple quotes using the
# other quote mark:
print '''I """am""" okay!'''                  # I """am""" okay!       #(O)
print """I '''am''' okay!"""                  # I '''am''' okay!       #(P)

# Backslashes when not used for character escapes show up as
# backslashes:
print 'C:\My Files\Cats\Temp'                 # C:\My Files\Cats\Temp  #(Q)
print "C:\My Files\Cats\Temp"                 # C:\My Files\Cats\Temp  #(R)
print '''C:\My Files\Cats\Temp'''             # C:\My Files\Cats\Temp  #(S)
print """C:\My Files\Cats\Temp"""             # C:\My Files\Cats\Temp  #(T)

# This does NOT give us two backslashes together:
print 'C:\\My Files\Cats\Temp'                # C:\My Files\Cats\Temp  #(U)
print "C:\\My Files\Cats\Temp"                # C:\My Files\Cats\Temp  #(V)
print '''C:\\My Files\Cats\Temp'''            # C:\My Files\Cats\Temp  #(W)
print """C:\\My Files\Cats\Temp"""            # C:\My Files\Cats\Temp  #(X)

# But this does:
print 'C:\\\My Files\Cats\Temp'               # C:\\My Files\Cats\Temp #(Y)
print "C:\\\My Files\Cats\Temp"               # C:\\My Files\Cats\Temp #(Z)
print '''C:\\\My Files\Cats\Temp'''           # C:\\My Files\Cats\Temp #(a)
print """C:\\\My Files\Cats\Temp"""           # C:\\My Files\Cats\Temp #(b)

# However, this is a safer way if you want two backslashes together:
print 'C:\\\\My Files\Cats\Temp'              # C:\\My Files\Cats\Temp #(c)
print "C:\\\\My Files\Cats\Temp"              # C:\\My Files\Cats\Temp #(d)
print '''C:\\\\My Files\Cats\Temp'''          # C:\\My Files\Cats\Temp #(e)
print """C:\\\\My Files\Cats\Temp"""          # C:\\My Files\Cats\Temp #(f)

# Backslash used to escape the special meaning of the string
# delimiter quote mark:
print 'Trillian\'s puppy'                     # Trillian's puppy       #(g)
print "Z's love: \"Trillian\""                # Z's love: "Trillian"   #(h)
print '''Trillian\'s puppy'''                 # Trillian's puppy       #(i)
print """Z's love: \"Trillian\""""            # Z's love: "Trillian"   #(j)

# Numeric escapes work as expected in all cases:
print '\x68\x69! \x68\x6F\x77 \141\162\145 you'                        #(k)
                                              # hi! how are you
print "\x68\x69! \x68\x6F\x77 \141\162\145 you"                        #(l)
                                              # hi! how are you
print '''\x68\x69! \x68\x6F\x77 \141\162\145 you'''                    #(m)
```

```
                                           # hi! how are you
print """\x68\x69! \x68\x6F\x77 \141\162\145 you"""            #(n)
                                           # hi! how are you

# Specifying raw ASCII strings:
print r'hi! \nhey \there'                  # hi! \nhey \there   #(o)
print r"hi! \nhow \there"                  # hi! \nhey \there   #(p)
print r'''hi! \nhey \there'''              # hi! \nhey \there   #(q)
print r"""hi! \nhey \there"""              # hi! \nhey \there   #(r)

# Specifying a Unicode string:
print u"hi! \nhey \there"                  # hi!                #(s)
                                           # hey     here

#Specifying a Unicode raw string:
print ur'hi! \nhey \there'                 # hi! \nhey \there   #(t)

# Specifying a Unicode multiline string:
print u'''hi!
  all done.'''                             # hi!
                                           #   all done.        #(u)
```

The next script, `StringOps.py`, demonstrates many of the more common operations that are carried out on strings. The operations shown include those that are listed in Table 3.1 for sequence-type containers, and some additional ones that are specific to the string type.

Lines (A), (B), and (C) of `StringOps.py` show the `in` and `not in` predicates that test whether or not a substring is contained in a string. The substring to search for is the left operand to these predicates and the string in which to carry out the search the right operand. These predicates, like all predicates in Python, return the Boolean constants `True` or `False`, depending on the truth value of the predicate.

Line (D) of the script shows the concatenation operator `+` for joining together strings.[28] While the Perl's concatenation operator automatically converts its arguments into their string representations (assuming they do not evaluate to strings to begin with), Python expects the arguments to evaluate to strings. So, whereas Perl would have automatically converted the number 123 in line (D) into its ASCII string representation, in Python you have to invoke the `str()` constructor explicitly. Line (E) shows Python's replication operator `*`. The operator returns a string that is an `n`-fold concatenation of the string operand, where `n` is the integer operand.

---

[28] A variation on the concatenation operator `+` is the operator `+=` for compound concatenation that works the same way as any compound assignment operator.

Line (G) of the script shows that a character at a specific location in a string can be retrieved through the subscript operator `[]` via an index offset. What is actually returned by this indexed access is in reality not a character, but a string containing only one character. *The difference between the two is crucial because Python does not contain a character type. A character in Python can only be considered as a string containing just one character.*

Lines (H) through (J) show how a substring from a string can be extracted by the slicing operator whose behavior was explained earlier when we talked about Python's sequence containers in general. Line (H) returns a substring consisting of all characters starting at a position whose index is at the left of the `:` symbol. Line (I) returns a substring starting at the beginning but ending at a positional index one short of the integer at the right of the `:` symbol. Line (J) returns a substring starting at the index whose value is the first integer, ending at the index one short of the second integer, and in steps corresponding to the third integer. So the slicing operator `[1:4:2]` will return the characters at the indices 1 and 3. The commented out line (K) shows that, because a string is an immutable sequence type, you cannot change its characters after the string is created.

Line (L) shows that the built-in function `len()` can be used to determine the length of a string. The `min()` function in line (M) returns the smallest character in a string on the basis of the integer ASCII code values associated with the characters. The `max()` function in line (N) returns the largest character using the same criterion.

Lines (O) through (W) show the various predicates and functions one can invoke on a string. Note that all these invocations are in the style of object-oriented syntax where you invoke a method on an object.[29] The predicate `isalnum()` of line (P) returns `True` if the string it is invoked on consists entirely of alphanumeric characters. The predicate `isalpha()` of line (Q) returns `True` if the string consists of just alphabetic characters. In our case, that is obviously false. The predicate `islower()` returns `True` if the characters in a string are all lowercase. The method `find()` of line (S) returns the index that corresponds to the start of the argument substring in the string on which the method is invoked. If the argument substring cannot be found, it returns -1, as shown in line (T). The predicate `endswith()` of line (U) returns `True` if the string ends in the argument substring. The method `replace()` of line (V) returns a new string that is obtained from the old string by replacing the first-argument substring with the second-argument substring. Finally, the method `upper()` of line (W) returns a new string all of whose characters are uppercase versions of the characters in the string on which the method is invoked.

Lines (X) through (c) show how the `split()` and `join()` methods can be invoked, the first to split up a string into substrings on the basis of specified matching

---

[29] If the reader is not already familiar with this style of function invocation, it is explained in Chapter 7 for Python. Although the distinction between *functions* and *methods* will be explained in Chapters 6 and 7, suffice it to say here that when we invoke a function *on* a string with the dot operator, we refer to the function as a method.

intervening characters, and the second to join up a list of strings into a longer string. Line (X) shows that when `split()` is invoked without an argument on a string, it uses the white-space characters as separators for creating the splits. Multiple adjoining white-space characters count the same as a single white-space character. Now note the behavior of `split()` when it is actually supplied with an argument in line (Y). This argument is used as the separator for creating the splits. The method creates a split wherever there is a match with the separator; the characters matched with the separator do not become a part of any of the substrings output by `split()`. Also, whenever there are two consecutive matches with the separator, `split()` spits out an empty substring for the output. That should explain why we see an empty string in the second element in the commented out output shown in line (Y).

Line (Z) shows how the `join()` method works. The string on which it is invoked acts like glue for joining together the substrings in the tuple supplied as an argument to `join()`. Note that `join()` does not modify the substrings in the argument tuple itself; it constructs and returns a new string. It is interesting to see the invocation of `join()` in line (c). Treated as a sequence, the argument string `123` is composed of the items `1`, `2`, and `3`, and the glue for joining these together is the string `jello`.

Lines (d) through (h) show how the `rstrip()` method can be used to strip off one or more of the trailing characters in a string. The call in line (e) strips off the trailing newlines in the string defined in line (d). Note that the cleaned up string is a new string that is constructed from the string on which the method is invoked; the original string is not affected. When `rstrip()` is called without any arguments — as in line (g) — it strips off the trailing white space from a string. This is verified by the call to `len()` in line (h).[30]

Line (i) demonstrates a Boolean string comparison with the `<` operator. The default behavior of this and the other relational operators (`>`, `<=`, `>=`, `==`, and `!=`) is to compare strings on the basis of their lexicographic ordering as established by the ASCII codes associated with the characters in the strings.[31]

Line (j) shows the use of the built-in `cmp()` function for comparing two strings. In general, `cmp(x,y)` returns one of three possible values: -1 if `x<y` is true, 0 if `x==y` is true, and +1 if `x>y` is true.

---

[30] When called with a string argument, `rstrip()` is capable of deleting every *trailing* character if it is present in the argument string. There is also the method `lstrip()` that does at the leading end of a string what `rstrip()` accomplishes at the trailing end. Yet another method along the same lines is `strip()` that strips off characters at both ends of a string.

[31] All relational operators can be invoked on any pair of objects in Python, complex numbers being the only exception to this rule. Objects of different types are never considered to be equal. For the purpose of responding to the `<` and the `>` operators, objects of different types are ordered by their typenames. This rather arbitrary ordering has only one benefit — it makes the response of the relational operators consistent. Objects of the same type are ordered by their memory addresses. When the operands are class instances, what is returned by a relational operator depends on the implementation of the `__comp__()` method for the class.

Lines (k), (m), and (o) show single-quoted, double-quoted, and triple-quoted empty strings. The Boolean value of an empty string is always `False`.[32] That explains the output shown in lines (l), (n), and (p).

Earlier we showed Python's string concatenation with the `+` operator. Lines (q) through (t) show that adjacent quoted strings, even when they appear in separate lines, are also concatenated together. However, concatenation achieved by simply placing string literals one after another works differently from string concatenation achieved by the `+` operator; the former works at compile time and the latter at run time. The compile time concatenation is useful for breaking long string literals into smaller segments for better readability of a script and for possibly commenting each segment separately. As shown by the example in lines (q) through (t), the different strings literals in such concatenations are allowed to be quoted differently.

Line (v) shows the use of `del` operator to delete a string. It would obviously be an error to access a deleted string, as we show in line (w).

```
#!/usr/bin/env python

### StringOps.py

s = "abracadabra"                                                    #(A)

# The 'in' and 'not in' operators:
print "bra" in s                          # True                     #(B)
print "bra" not in s                      # False                    #(C)

# String concatenation and replication:
print "hello" + "jello" + str( 123 )      # hellojello123            #(D)
print "hello" * 3                         # hellohellohello          #(E)

# The subscripting and slicing operators:
x = "hello"                                                          #(F)
print x[1]                                # e                        #(G)
print x[1:]                               # ello                     #(H)
print x[:3]                               # hel                      #(I)
print x[1:4:2]                            # el                       #(J)
#x[0] = "j"                               # WRONG                    #(K)

# Anciliary functions:
print len(x)                              # 5                        #(L)
print min(x)                              # e                        #(M)
print max(x)                              # o                        #(N)
```

[32]Every object in Python has a truth value associated with it. Empty strings always evaluate to `False` when tested for their truth values. See Section 3.9.1.

```
# String predicates:
w = "abc" + str(123)                                                #(O)
print w                               # abc123
print w.isalnum()                     # True                        #(P)
print w.isalpha()                     # False                       #(Q)
print w.islower()                     # True                        #(R)
print w.find( "12" )                  # 3                           #(S)
print w.find( "45" )                  # -1                          #(T)
print w.endswith( "123" )             # True                        #(U)
print w.replace( "123", "def" )       # abcdef                      #(V)
print w.upper()                       # ABCDEF                      #(W)

# String splitting and joining:
print "pel mel    del".split()        # ['pel', 'mel', 'del']       #(X)
print x.split( 'l' )                  # ['he', '', 'o']             #(Y)
print ' '.join( ('hi', 'fi', 'xi') )  # hi fi xi                    #(Z)
y = "jello"                                                         #(a)
z = 123                                                             #(b)
print y.join( str(z) )                # 1jello2jello3               #(c)

# To strip off trailing newlines:
x = "abcdefghi\n\n\n\n\n"                                           #(d)
print x.rstrip( "\n" )                # abcdefghi                   #(e)

# To strip off trailing whitespace:
x = "abcdefghi           "                                          #(f)
print x.rstrip()                      # abcdefghi                   #(g)
print len( x.rstrip() )               # 9                           #(h)

# Boolean string comparison:
if (x < y): print 'hello is less than jello'                        #(i)
                                      # hello is less than jello
# Three-valued string comparison:
if ( cmp(x, y) ): print 'hello is less than jello'                  #(j)
                                      # hello is less than jello
# Single-quoted empty string:
empty1 = ''                                                         #(k)
if (not empty1): print 'empty1 is an empty string'                  #(l)
                                      # empty1 is an empty string
# Double-quoted empty string:
empty2 = ""                                                         #(m)
if (not empty2): print 'empty2 is an empty string'                  #(n)
                                      # empty2 is an empty string
# Triple-quoted empty string:
multiline = """"""                                                  #(o)
if (not multiline): print 'multiline is an empty string'            #(p)
                                      # multiline is an empty string
# Compile time string concatenation:
```

```
x =   ('hi!'                          # single-quoted                #(q)
       "how"                          # double-quoted                #(r)
       '''are'''                      # triple-quoted                #(s)
       """you""")                     # triple-quoted also           #(t)
print x                               # hi!howareyou                 #(u)
del x                                                                #(v)
#print x                              # WRONG                        #(w)
```

One frequently wants to sort a sequence of strings.[33] The built-in `sorted()` comes in handy for that, as we show in the script `BuiltinSorted.py` presented next.[34] When called with just the sequence, as we have done in line (B), the default criterion for sorting the sequence is ascending ASCII, as demonstrated by the output in line (C). In addition to the sequence that needs to be sorted as its first argument, the function `sorted()` can be supplied with three optional *keyword arguments*.[35] The keywords associated with the three arguments are: `cmp`, `key`, and `reverse`. The argument supplied for the `cmp` keyword is the comparison criterion to be used for sorting; this criterion tells `sorted()` what it means for one item to be greater than, equal to, or smaller than the other item in a pairwise comparison. The argument supplied for the keyword `key` is the property that characterizes each object for the purpose of sorting. We may, for example, wish to sort a list of strings on the basis of their lengths. In this case, the string length becomes the argument that would be supplied via `key`. The keyword *reverse* in the arguments supplied to `sorted()` is for reversing the order in which sorting is carried out in relation to the comparison criterion used.

If only one additional argument is supplied to `sorted()` and it is not a keyword argument, the argument is assumed to be the value of the `cmp` keyword, as demonstrated by the call syntax used in line (D). Here the second argument to `sorted()` is a lambda function[36] that calls the built-in `cmp()` function with the two arguments that are the uppercase versions of whatever two values the sorting routine will be comparing for the purpose of determining their relative positions in the sorted order. Note that all sorting routines compare values on a pairwise basis. By a sorting criterion one usually means a function that takes two arguments and returns -1 if the first argument is less than the second, 0 if the two arguments are equal, and +1 if the

---

[33]The material to follow on sorting is best read after the reader has worked his/her way through Section 3.10.

[34]Any *iterable* object can be sorted by calling the built-in `sorted()`. Although we show sort results on tuples, we would have obtained identical results on lists. The built-in `sorted()` always returns a list. The behavior of `sorted()` that we demonstrate here is identical to that of the `sort()` method when invoked on a list, the major difference being that whereas `sorted()` always *returns* a list, *invoking* `sort()` *on* a list modifies the list in place.

[35]See Section 3.8.5 for what is meant by a keyword argument and the restrictions on their use.

[36]Lambda expressions are discussed in Section 3.8.7.

first argument is greater than the second. The crucial question here is as to what is meant by less than, equal to, and greater than. For strings, the meaning is derived, by default, from the ASCII values associated with the characters and by assuming the strings to be lexicographically ordered. This is the meaning supplied by the built-in `cmp()` function, which is what is used by default if you call `sorted()` without a user-defined criterion for comparing the objects to be sorted. Line (D) supplies a user-defined comparison criterion in the form of a lambda function. This lambda function calls the built-in `cmp()` function with arguments that are *not* directly the strings to be compared, but their uppercase versions.

The call syntax in line (D) is not efficient because the sorting routine is called upon to compute the uppercase versions of the argument strings for every pairwise comparison. A more efficient way to bring about the same result as we show in line (D) is through the `key` option that will be explained shortly.

Line (F) shows how we can use the `reverse` keyword in calling `sorted()`. The result is an ASCII descending order for the output strings; this order is exactly opposite of what was shown in lines (B) and (C). Note that this is only one way to reverse the order of sorting. Another way, albeit a less efficient one, would be to supply a reversed comparison criterion to `sorted()`. Yet another way would be to reverse the sequence after it is sorted.

Line (H) shows how we can specify a key for sorting. Now we do not want the strings to be sorted on the basis of the characters in each string, but on the basis of their lengths. So we use a lambda function to return the length of each string. This length is the "key" supplied to the sorting routine. We could have achieved the same result by embedding the length calculation inside a user-defined comparison function, but that would be inefficient as the same length calculation would be carried out repeatedly on a string as it is compared with other strings. By using the syntax in line (H), the lengths of all the strings would be precomputed before any sorting is carried out.[37] Line (J) demonstrates another example of us using the `key` argument for sorting a list of strings on the basis of the second character in each string.

Lines (M) demonstrates the use of the `cmp` key for supplying a user-defined comparison criterion. Note that unless you are also using one of the other keyword arguments, it is not necessary to use the keyword `key` since the second argument will be taken to be a comparison function by default. In this case, we want to sort a tuple of numbers not on the basis of their values but on the basis of how long their print representations are. But, as was mentioned before, what we have in line (M)

[37]Efficient sorting routines typically need to carry out only $O(NlogN)$ pairwise comparisons for sorting a list of N items. Therefore, when sorting is to be carried out on the basis of a computed property, the additional computation burden would amount to the same factor. However, with precomputation, this additional computational burden reduces to just $O(N)$. By asking Python to precompute the keys for the object to be sorted, we achieve the same efficiency as obtained by using the *Schwartzian Transform* in Problem 9 of the Homework section of Chapter 2. As the reader will recall, Schwartzian Transform consists of explicitly precomputing the keys for all the objects to be sorted and then calling up the sorting routine on the keys.

is a computationally inefficient call. A more efficient version of the same is shown in line (O) where we now use the `key` argument. This line also demonstrates why it might become necessary to also use the `reverse` argument when you are using the `key` argument. When a key is used for sorting, the sorted output will still be in the ascending order with respect to the key, since all Python does in this case is to invoke the built-in `cmp()` function for comparing the keys. If you also wanted to reverse the output at the same time you supply a comparison key, you would need to set the `reverse` key to `True`, as shown in lines (O) and (P). Lines (Q), (R), and (S) demonstrate that if you call `sorted()` directly on a string, it is the characters in the string that will get sorted. That is because, as mentioned earlier, a string is a sequence container unto itself, the container holding the characters of the string.

```
#!/usr/local/bin/env python

### BuiltinSorted.py

words = ( 'hello', 'armadello', 'JELLO', 'JAYLO' )                        #(A)

# Sort in the default (ascending ASCII) order:
sortedwords = sorted( words )                                             #(B)
print sortedwords     # ['JAYLO', 'JELLO', 'armadello', 'hello']         #(C)

# For sorting, consider the strings to be all uppercase:
sortedwords = sorted( words, lambda x,y: cmp(x.upper(), y.upper() ) )#(D)
print sortedwords     # ['armadello', 'hello', 'JAYLO', 'JELLO']         #(E)

# Sort in descending ASCII order:
sortedwords = sorted( words, reverse=True )                               #(F)
print sortedwords     # ['hello', 'armadello', 'JELLO', 'JAYLO']         #(G)

# Sort strings on the basis of their lengths
sortedwords = sorted( words, key = lambda x: len(x) )                     #(H)
print sortedwords     # ['hello', 'JELLO', 'JAYLO', 'armadello']         #(I)

# Sort strings on the basis of the second character:
sortedwords = sorted( words, key=lambda x: x[1]  )                        #(J)
print sortedwords     # ['JAYLO', 'JELLO', 'hello', 'armadello']         #(K)

# Sort numbers by lengths of their print representations:
nums = (1, 100, 10)                                                       #(L)
sortednums = sorted(nums, \
                cmp=lambda x,y: cmp(len(str(y)),len(str(x))))            #(M)
print sortednums      # [100, 10, 1]                                      #(N)

# A more efficient way:
sortednums = sorted(nums, key=lambda x: len(str(x)), reverse=True)       #(O)
print sortednums      # [100, 10, 1]                                      #(P)
```

```
# A string by itself is a sequence:
string = 'jellomello'                                              #(Q)
sortedchars = sorted( string )                                     #(R)
print sortedchars     # ['e','e','j','l','l','l','l','m','o','o']  #(S)
```

The string type supports a large number of functions in addition to those shown in this section. These additional functions help out with tasks such as coding and decoding of strings, case conversion, centering within a given text field, etc. The reader is referred to the online documentation for these.

3.3.2 Tuples

Like strings, tuples are also immutable. A tuple is defined by the comma operator, as long as it is not used inside square brackets, *with or without the enclosing parentheses.* Line (A) of the next script, `TupleOps.py`, shows us defining a tuple with just the comma operator and without the enclosing parentheses. Its print representation is shown in the commented out portion of line (B). More typically, a tuple is created by using the comma operator within enclosing parentheses, as in line (C).

That a tuple can hold disparate types of objects[38] is illustrated by testing the types of the first and the third elements of the `x` tuple of line (A) in lines (E) and (F). As shown in the commented-out portions of those lines, Python reports the first element to be of type string and the third element to be of type integer.

Lines (G) and (H) illustrate the `in` and `not in` predicates to test for the presence or absence of a specified element in a tuple. Lines (I) and (J) demonstrate using the + operator to join two tuples to create a larger tuple.

The commented-out line (K) demonstrates the fact that since a tuple is immutable, its elements cannot be changed. When nested data-structures are involved, one must, however, remember the fact that even though the elements of a tuple cannot be changed at the top-level, it may still be possible to modify the interior structure of those elements. This is illustrated by the code in lines (L) through (O). The tuple created in line (L) has a list for its first element. While, of course, the tuple itself is immutable, its list element is certainly mutable. So when we change the first element of this list in line (N), the result is as shown in line (O).

Application of the replication operator `*` to a tuple is shown in lines (P) and (Q), and applications of the slicing operator in lines (R), (S), and (T). They work as

[38]This should not come as a surprise in light of the discussion in Section 3.1.

expected and in accordance with our earlier explanations of the syntax of the slicing operator.

Line (U) shows us invoking the built-in function `len()` to determine the number of elements in a tuple. Lines (V) and (W) report back the minimum and the maximum elements, respectively, in the tuple. As mentioned earlier, for the purpose of making comparisons, Python orders elements of the different types by their typenames and elements of the same type by their memory addresses. (Of course, when comparing elements of the same type for which comparison operators are explicitly defined, those operator definitions are used.) This is the logic used for returning the values shown in lines (V) and (W).

Line (X) shows that the `del` operator can be used to delete from memory the argument tuple. Obviously, as shown in line (Y), if you try to access the same tuple later, you'll get an error.

We will now show that while the enclosing parentheses are optional when creating a tuple through assignment, as in line (A), leaving them out in other contexts may produce unintended effects. Consider first the print statement in line (Z). As expected, the output of the statement is a tuple, as shown in the commented out portion of that line. However, when we leave out the enclosing parentheses in a similar looking statement in line (a), what is output by `print` is not a tuple but simply a display of three separate items in the same line of the output. This is because of the special behavior of `print` vis-à-vis the comma supplied for separating the arguments. The `print` gets to work on each of those arguments sequentially, printing out the result, one item at a time, with a blank space separating the consecutive outputs. The effect is the same as shown by the three consecutive invocations of `print` on three separate items individually in line (b).[39] [40] [41]

Line (c) shows how to specify a singleton tuple, that is, a tuple containing only one element. The syntax requires that the single element have a trailing comma, as shown in that line. That comma suppresses the other meaning of a matching pair of parentheses — as a grouping operator. Finally, line (e) shows how to specify an empty tuple.

---

[39] As shown in line (b) and as mentioned at the beginning of this chapter, semicolons can be used in Python to chain simple statements in a single line.

[40] In comparing the output in line (Z) with what is produced in lines (a) and (b), also note that when `print` displays a string in a tuple, it shows it single-quoted. On the other hand, when `print` is asked to display a string individually, as in lines (a) and (b), it shows the string without any quoting.

[41] A further thing to note about `print` as used in line (b) is that when its argument terminates in a comma, it does not implicitly add a newline at the end of the argument. This feature of `print` was mentioned earlier in the introduction to this chapter.

```
#!/usr/bin/env python

### TupleOps.py

# Comma operator defines a tuple:
x = 'zero', 'one', 2, 3                                            #(A)
print x                             # ('zero', 'one', 2, 3)        #(B)

# A more common way to create a tuple:
y = (0, 1, 'two', "three")                                         #(C)
print y                             # (0, 1, 'two', 'three')       #(D)

# A tuple can hold disparate items:
print type( x[0] )                  # <type 'str'>                 #(E)
print type( x[2] )                  # <type 'int'>                 #(F)

# For testing for membership:
print 'one' in x                    # True                         #(G)
print 4 not in y                    # True                         #(H)

# Joining together two tuples:
z = x + y                                                          #(I)
print z           # ('zero', 'one', 2, 3, 0, 1, 'two', 'three')    #(J)

# Illegal, tuple is immutable:
#x[0] = 0                           # WRONG                        #(K)

# Immutability may not apply to interior structors:
w = ([1, 2, 3], 4, 5)                                              #(L)
print w                             # ([1, 2, 3], 4, 5)            #(M)
w[0][0] = 100                                                      #(N)
print w                             # ([100, 2, 3], 4, 5)          #(O)

# Replication operator:
x = 1,2                                                            #(P)
print x * 3                         # (1, 2, 1, 2, 1, 2)           #(Q)

# Slicing operations:
print z[4:]                         # (0, 1, 'two', 'three')       #(R)
print z[:4]                         # ('zero', 'one', 2, 3)        #(S)
print z[1:6:2]                      # ('one', 3, 1)                #(T)

# Some utility functions:
print len(w)                        # 3                            #(U)
print min(w)                        # 4                            #(V)
print max(w)                        # [100, 2, 3]                  #(W)
```

```
# To delete an entire tuple:
del w                                                         #(X)
#print w                              # WRONG                 #(Y)

# The role of comma again:
print ("4", 5, '''six''')             # ('4', 5, 'six')       #(Z)
print "4", 5, '''six'''               # 4 5 six               #(a)
print "4",; print 5,; print "six"     # 4 5 six               #(b)

# Singleton tuple:
singleton_tuple = (1,)                                        #(c)
print singleton_tuple                 # (1,)                  #(d)

# Empty tuple:
empty_tuple = ()                                              #(e)
print type(empty_tuple)               # <type 'tuple'>        #(f)
```

3.3.3 Lists

Whereas a tuple is constructed with the comma operator, a list is constructed with a pair of matching square brackets containing a comma-separated sequence of items, as shown in line (A) of the following script, `ListOps.py`. The fact that, in contrast with a tuple, a list is mutable is illustrated by line (C) of the script where we assign a new two-element list to a two-element slice of the list `x`. This assignment causes the 0-th element to change from `zero` to 0 and the 1st element to change from `one` to 1, the last element remaining unchanged. The resulting list `x` is shown in line (D).

Although already clear from the outputs shown in lines (B) and (D), lines (E) and (F) further establish that a list can hold items of different types.[42] Lines (G), (H), and (I) show that two lists can be joined by the `+` operator to create a larger list. And lines (J) and (K) demonstrate the membership predicates `in` and `not in`.

Lines (L) and (M) show a new list constructed by applying the replication operator `*` to a slice of the list `x`. The copies that are used in such replication are shallow, in the sense that the each copy that is replicated is still pointing to the same locations in memory as the original data. This issue can become important for nested lists, as in a list of lists. If such a data structure is replicated by the `*` operator, any changes made to one of interior lists will affect all of its replications.

Lines (N), (O), and (P) illustrate how some of the functions defined for the sequence type can be used to infer various properties of a list, such as its length, the value of its

[42] As with tuples, this should not be surprising in light of the discussion in Section 3.1.

maximal element, and the value of its minimal element. For returning the max and min values, any two items of a list are compared on the same basis as for sorting.

This brings us to operations that modify a list structurally. The method `remove()` invoked in line (Q) removes the first occurrence of its argument object from the list.[43] Line (S) shows how a new element can be inserted into a list at a position that corresponds to the index supplied as the second argument.

Line (U) shows the use of the `del` operator to remove a slice of a list. Note that we are using the `[i:j:k]` version of the slice operator in line (U) in which the index `j` has been left unspecified. Therefore, the second index will default to the end of the list. The call in line (U) will therefore remove every second element starting at index 3 in the list.

Line (W) shows how a portion of a list can be altered by direct assignment. In this case, we want to change in one go the last three elements of the list to the null object `None`. We use line (Y) to make the list shorter for the rest of the script.

Line (a) demonstrates using `append()` to push a new item into a list from the right. Line (c) invokes `reverse()` to reverse the order of elements in a list. This reversal occurs in place and not as a side effect. Line (e) shows us popping off the last element of a list, thus shortening its length by one. The function `pop()` returns the element that comes off the list.

Line (g) illustrates the invocation of `sort()` on a list. As for the cases of `min()` and `max()` functions, unless a comparison function is supplied to `sort()`, Python orders objects on the basis of ASCII codes for strings, ASCII codes for class names for class-type objects, typenames for all other objects when comparing objects of dissimilar types, and memory addresses for comparing objects of the same type. We will have more to say about the `sort()` method when we show the script `ListSorting.py` later in this section.

Line (i) illustrates the `count()` method that when invoked on a list returns the frequency of occurrence of the argument object. Line (j) shows how the `index()` method can be used to determine the index of the first occurrence of the argument object in a list.

We mentioned at the beginning of Section 3.3 that the syntax `s[:]`, where we do not place an index either before or after the colon, is special-cased to return a copy of the original sequence and that any changes made to this copy do not alter the original sequence. This is illustrated by line (k). In this line, the copy of the entire list returned by `z[:]` would be treated as a separate temporary object. Changing the first element of this temporary object to 1000 does not affect the list `z`, as is clear from the output displayed in the next line.

---

[43] If the object to be removed is not found in the list on which `remove()` is invoked, the method throws the `ValueError` exception that if not caught will cause the program to abort.

Line (m) shows how a list can be eliminated all at once by using the `del` operator. For obvious reasons, any subsequent references to the deleted list would give rise to error, as indicated by the commented out line (n).

Line (o) shows how a single list is created; no need for a comma here as was the case for a singleton tuple. Line (q) shows how an empty list is specified.

Lines (s) through (x) illustrate the use of *list comprehensions* in Python for generating lists. The call to the built-in `range()` function in line (s) returns a list of integers starting from 0 and ending at one less than the argument provided.[44] Each successive iteration of the `for` loop in the manner shown in lines (s) and (u) yields a new element for the list. A fancier example of the same is shown in lines (w) and (x) where each element of one list multiplies every element of the second list. However, if it is the element-on-element operation that is desired, then one can use the sort of syntax that is shown in lines (y) and (z). Using the list comprehension syntax, one can also construct a list of lists or a list of tuples by drawing elements from one or more lists.

```
#!/usr/bin/env python

### ListOps.py

#Define a list:
x = ['zero', 'one', 2, 'three']                                    #(A)
print x                     # ['zero', 'one', 2, 'three']          #(B)

#Show list is mutable:
x[0:2] = [0, 1]                                                    #(C)
print x                     # [0, 1, 2, 'three']                   #(D)

#A list can hold disparate types:
print type( x[0] )          # <type 'int'>                         #(E)
print type( x[3] )          # <type 'str'>                         #(F)

#Joining two lists:
y = [4, 5]                                                         #(G)
z = x + y                                                          #(H)
print z                     # [0, 1, 2, 'three', 4, 5]             #(I)

#Test for membership:
print 1 in z                # True                                 #(J)
print 'five' not in z       # True                                 #(K)
```

[44] When `range()` is called with two arguments, the returned list starts at the first argument and ends at one less than the second argument. This function can also be called with three arguments, in which case the third argument becomes the step between the consecutive numbers.

```
#Replication operator:
z = x[0:3] * 3                                                      #(L)
print z                        # [0, 1, 2, 0, 1, 2, 0, 1, 2]        #(M)

print len(z)                   # 9                                  #(N)
print min(z)                   # 0                                  #(O)
print max(z)                   # 2                                  #(P)

#Deleting an element by value:
z.remove( 2 )                                                       #(Q)
print z                        # [0, 1, 0, 1, 2, 0, 1, 2]           #(R)

#Inserting an element by value:
z.insert( 2, 'two' )                                                #(S)
print z                        # [0, 1, 'two', 0, 1, 2, 0, 1, 2]    #(T)

#Deleting a slice:
del z[3::2]                                                         #(U)
print z                        # [0, 1, 'two', 1, 0, 2]             #(V)

#Replacing a slice:
z[3:] = [None] * (len(z) - 3)                                       #(W)
print z                        # [0, 1, 'two', None, None, None]    #(X)

#Make the list shorter for the
#rest of the script:
del z[3:]                                                           #(Y)
print z                        # [0, 1, 'two']                      #(Z)

#Appending element at the end:
z.append( 'two' )                                                   #(a)
print z                        # [0, 1, 'two', 'two']               #(b)

#Reversing a list in place:
z.reverse()                                                         #(c)
print z                        # ['two', 'two', 1, 0]               #(d)

#Pop off the value at the end:
print z.pop()                  # 0                                  #(e)
print z                        # ['two', 'two', 1]                  #(f)

#Sort in place:
z.sort()                                                            #(g)
print z                        # [1, 'two', 'two']                  #(h)

#Count the number by elemnt value:
print z.count( 'two' )         # 2                                  #(i)

#Find lowest index by element value:
```

```
print z.index( 'two' )            # 1                                    #(j)

#A slice accessed on its own for
#its elements acts as a separate
#object:
z[:][0] = 1000                                                           #(k)
print z                           # [1, 'two', 'two']                    #(l)

#Delete the entire list:
del z                             # deletes the list z from memory       #(m)
#print z                          # WRONG                                #(n)

#A singleton list:
singleton_list = [1]                                                     #(o)
print singleton_list              # [1]                                  #(p)

#An empty list:
empty_list = []                                                          #(q)
print type(empty_list)            # <type 'list'>                        #(r)

#Generating a list compactly:
z = [ x * 2 for x in range(5) ]                                          #(s)
print z                           # [0, 2, 4, 6, 8]                      #(t)

#Another example:
z = [ x * 3 for x in ['a', 'b', 5] ]                                     #(u)
print z                           # ['aaa', 'bbb', 15]                   #(v)

#A fancier example:
z = [ x*y for x in [1,2,3] for y in [4,5,6] if x*y > 8 ]                 #(w)
print z                           # [10, 12, 12, 15, 18]                 #(x)

#Element-on-element operation:
x = [2, 3, 4]
y = [7, 8, 9]
z = [ x[i]*y[i] for i in range(len(x)) ]                                 #(y)
print z                           # [14, 24, 36]                         #(z)
```

As mentioned earlier, the list container comes with its own sorting method, `sort()`, that sorts a list in place. The next script, `ListSorting.py`, illustrates this method. With regard to the keyword arguments that can be supplied to this method and the effects achieved by those arguments, it behaves in exactly the same manner as the built-in sorting function `sorted()` presented in Section 3.3.1 of this chapter. But note that, as previously mentioned, whereas the built-in `sorted()` *returns* a sorted list, `sort()` orders *in place* and through side effect the list on which it is invoked. The call to `sort()` does not return anything, as illustrated by line (A1) of the next script. So if we insist on catching the value returned by `sort()`, we get meaningless output.

Lines (B) through (P) of the script demonstrate that the `sort()` method takes the same keyword arguments as the built-in function `sorted()`. These lines parallel the similarly labeled lines in the `BuiltinSorted.py` script shown earlier in Section 3.3.1. For example, as in that earlier script, lines (B) and (C) show the default behavior of the sorting routine, which is to order the sorted strings in ASCII ascending order. Lines (D) and (E) demonstrate how we can supply a user-defined comparison criterion to `sort()`.[45] Lines (F) and (G) show how the optional argument supplied via the `reverse` keyword can be used for in-place descending-order sorting. Lines (H) and (I) show how we can designate the object property to be used for sorting — by providing a function argument for the keyword `key`. With the sorting key as shown in line (H), the list will be sorted in ascending order on the basis of the *lengths* of the strings. Lines (J) and (K) demonstrate in-place sorting on the basis of the second character in each string. Lines (L), (M), and (N) show the use of the `cmp` keyword for supplying a comparison function for sorting. Since there is only one argument being supplied to `sort()` in this case, it is not necessary to use the keyword `cmp`; by default, if `sort()` is supplied with just one argument, that argument is taken to be the comparison criterion. Finally, line (O) shows a more efficient way to do the same sort as in line (M). The reason the call syntax in line (O) results in a more efficient sort was presented earlier in the explanation associated with the `BuiltinSorted.py` script.

```
#!/usr/local/bin/env python

### ListSorting.py

words = [ 'hello', 'armadello', 'JELLO', 'JAYLO' ]                    #(A)

print words.sort()    # None                                          #(A1)

# Sort in the default (ascending ASCII) order:
words.sort()                                                          #(B)
print words          # ['JAYLO', 'JELLO', 'armadello', 'hello']       #(C)

# For sorting, consider the strings to be all uppercase:
words.sort( lambda x,y: cmp(x.upper(), y.upper() ) )                  #(D)
print words          # ['armadello', 'hello', 'JAYLO', 'JELLO']       #(E)

# Sort in descending ASCII order:
words.sort( reverse=True )                                            #(F)
print words          # ['hello', 'armadello', 'JELLO', 'JAYLO']       #(G)
```

---

[45] The syntax of the lambda expressions used in lines (D), (H), (J), (M), and (O) is explained in Section 3.8.7. As mentioned there, lambda expressions allow small anonymous functions to be embedded in a script.

```
# Sort strings on the basis of their lengths
words.sort( key = lambda x: len(x) )                                    #(H)
print words            # ['hello', 'JELLO', 'JAYLO', 'armadello']       #(I)

# Sort strings on the basis of the second character:
words.sort( key=lambda x: x[1]  )                                       #(J)
print words            # ['JAYLO', 'JELLO', 'hello', 'armadello']       #(K)

# Sort numbers by lengths of their print representations:
nums = [1, 100, 10]                                                     #(L)
nums.sort( cmp=lambda x,y: cmp(len(str(y)),len(str(x))))                #(M)
print nums             # [100, 10, 1]                                   #(N)

# A more efficient way:
nums.sort( key=lambda x: len(str(x)), reverse=True)                     #(O)
print nums             # [100, 10, 1]                                   #(P)
```

3.3.4 Xrange Sequences

An Xrange sequence is generated by the `xrange()` function. The generated sequence — known as a *range* — is an arithmetic progression of integers, starting at the first argument to `xrange()`, terminating just before the second argument, and incrementing according to the third argument — assuming, of course, that `xrange()` is called with all three arguments. So the sequence corresponding to the call

```
xrange(0, 10, 2 )
```

will be

```
0 2 4 6 8
```

When the third argument is not supplied, it is assumed to be 1. Also, when `xrange()` is called with a single argument that is assumed to be the end of the range, the beginning of the range is assumed to be 0 in this case. The entire sequence of numbers generated by `xrange()` is not actually stored anywhere in the memory — the numbers are generated on an as-needed basis. This behavior of `xrange()` is different from the closely related function `range()` that simply returns a list of all the numbers. So `range(1000000)` will actually need to store a million integers in the memory somewhere. On the other hand, `xrange(1000000)` will spit out each number in the range only as it is needed. Therefore, contrary to what happens with `range()`, an `xrange` object always takes the same amount of memory, regardless of the size of the range.

The following script shows examples of calls to `xrange()`. Note the difference in behavior between a direct call to `xrange()` in line (D) and a direct call to `range()` in line (F). When we print out the value of `xr` in line (E), we get the function call `xrange(4)`. On the other hand, when we print out the value of `r` in line (G), we get the list spit out by the `range()` function in line (F).

Line (H) shows that even though what is returned by a call to `xrange()` is not the actual range, but one integer at a time on an as-needed basis, applying the built-in `len()` to the range object returns what one would expect — the number of elements in the range. For comparison, we have invoked `len()` on the range sequence returned in line (F).

```
#!/usr/local/bin/env python

### Xrange.py

for i in xrange( 4 ): print i*i, ' ',              # 0 1 4 9             #(A)
print

for i in xrange(1, 4): print i*i, ' ',             # 1 4 9               #(B)
print

for i in xrange(4, 1, -2): print i*i, ' ',         # 16 4                #(C)
print

xr = xrange( 4 )                                                         #(D)
print xr                                           # xrange(4)           #(E)

r = range( 4 )                                                           #(F)
print r                                            # [0, 1, 2, 3]        #(G)

print len( xr )                                    # 4                   #(H)

print len( r )                                     # 4                   #(I)
```

3.4 PYTHON CONTAINERS: DICTIONARIES

What a hash is to Perl, a dictionary is to Python. Like a hash, a dictionary in Python stores key-value pairs. All keys must be unique. Any immutable object can serve as a key. A dictionary is stored in the form of a hash table in the memory. This means that, in general, the key-value pairs will not be stored in any particular order. The exact order of storage depends on the hash function that translates each key into a location for storing the corresponding value. A dictionary is a mutable container. A dictionary is specified by the following syntax:

```
my_dict =  { key1 : value1,
             key2 : value2,
             key3 : value3,
             ....
             ....
           }
```

The value corresponding to a key may subsequently be retrieved by key-based array-like subscripting as in

```
my_dict[ key1 ]
```

The same access syntax can also be used to create a new key-value pair in a dictionary:

```
my_dict[ key4 ] = value4
```

This will insert the pair `(key4,value4)` into the dictionary.

In the rest of this section, we will show many of the Python functions that can be used to examine and manipulate dictionaries. This we will do with the help of the next script, `DictOps.py`. Line (A) of the script demonstrates again the syntax that is used for creating a new dictionary — by comma-separated `key:value` pairs enclosed by braces. Since a dictionary acts very much like a phone book in which every name appears only once, the name `ph_book` for the dictionary in line (A) is appropriate. Note that when the dictionary is printed out in line (B), the key-value pairs appear in the output not in the same order in which they were specified when the dictionary was created in line (A). This is to be expected in light of the statements we have made previously about how a dictionary is stored in the memory.

A list of all the keys in a dictionary can be obtained by invoking the method[46] `keys()` on the dictionary, as in line (C), and a list of all the values by invoking `values()`, as in line (D). The method `items()`, shown in line (E), returns a list of tuples, one tuple for each key-value pair in the dictionary. The predicate `has_key()` when invoked on a dictionary, as in line (F), tells us whether or not a key, supplied as the argument to the predicate, exists in the dictionary. Line (G) shows using the `len()` function to determine the number of key-value pairs in a dictionary.

Lines (H) through (J) demonstrate the purpose served by the `update()` method when invoked on a dictionary. It updates the dictionary on which it is invoked according to the key-value pairs in the argument dictionary. The updating can consist of either changing the value of a key, if such a key already exists in the invoking hash, and, otherwise, adding a new key-value pair to the invoking hash. The output

[46]The distinction between *method* and *function* will become clear in Chapters 6 and 7. For now, suffice it to say that when we invoke a function *on* an object, the function is a method.

line after (J) shows the `x` dictionary after it is updated with the `y` dictionary. Note that whereas the invoking dictionary, `x` in this case, gets modified, the argument dictionary, `y`, remains unchanged.

Lines (K) and (L) demonstrate the behavior of the `del` operator when invoked on a specific key-value pair, as in line (K), and when invoked on an entire dictionary. In the former case, it deletes that key-value pair from the dictionary. In the latter case, the entire dictionary get erased from the memory. A subsequent reference to a dictionary deleted in this manner, as in the line after line (L), would elicit an error message.

Line (M) shows how a new key-value pair can be inserted into a dictionary. The same syntax can be used to modify the value associated with an existing key. Line (N) shows how an empty dictionary can be specified by a matching pair of braces with nothing inside.

The rest of the script shows how one can traverse a dictionary by using an iterator object. An iterator object in this case is essentially a list of tuples, each tuple containing a key-value pair from the dictionary.[47] An iterator object supports the `next()` method that at the first call returns the first key-value pair stored in the object and, upon subsequent calls, returns the next such pair. The `next()` method throws the `StopIteration` exception when it runs out of key-value pairs in the dictionary.

The first example of iterating through a dictionary, in lines (O) and (P), first constructs an iterator object by invoking the `iteritems()` method of the dictionary. By iterating through the items, each of which is a tuple containing one key-value pair, line (P) then prints out the list of tuples with the values and the keys reversed.

The second example of iteration, in lines (Q) through (S), uses a `for` loop to walk through a dictionary and to select only certain key-value pairs based on some decision criterion. Only those key-value pairs are selected whose values exceed the number 3. The output of this loop is shown in the two commented out lines just below line (S).

The last example of iteration, in lines (T) through (Y), uses a `while` loop and the `next()` method defined for iterator objects to walk through the dictionary. The `next()` method is called inside a `try-except` block to trap the `StopIteration` exception to detect the end of the dictionary. The `try-except` syntax used is explained in Chapter 10.

Lines (Z) through (o) show various other ways of displaying the contents of a dictionary. The example in lines (Z) through (d) shows what is probably the most

[47]Recall that there is a randomness to the order in which the key-value pairs are stored in a hash table. So the order in which the iterator object returns the key-value pairs will, in general, not correspond to the order in which the pairs were entered into a dictionary. Additionally, any modification to the dictionary caused by the insertion of a new key or by the deletion of an existing key will alter the order of storage of the key-value pairs.

common way to display the contents of a dictionary in a key-sorted manner. Using the `keys()` method, we retrieve the keys in the form of a list in line (a). In line (b), we then invoke the `list`'s `sort()` method to carry out an in-place sorting of the list of keys. Subsequently, the `for` loop in lines (c) and (d) prints out the key-value pairs in a key-sorted manner.

Line (e) shows another way to construct a key-sorted list of the key-value pairs stored in the dictionary. The call `mydict.items()` returns a list of two-element tuples, each tuple consisting of a key-value pair. The built-in function `sorted()` returns a sorted version of this list using for sorting the comparison criterion supplied as a lambda function in line (e).[48] This lambda simply says that any two tuples in the list returned by `items()` are to be compared on the basis of what is returned by applying `cmp()` to the first elements — that is, the keys — of the tuples. As shown in line (g), this syntax can be easily modified to yield a value-sorted list of the tuples. As shown in line (k), if we want the list returned by the built-in `sorted()` to be reverse-ordered in relation to the comparison action specified by the lambda, all we have to do is to set the flag `reverse` to `True`. As a result, the syntax in lines (j), (k), and (l) value-sorts the tuples returned by `items()` but does so in decreasing order for the values.

Line (m) shows yet another way to retrieve a key-sorted list of values from a dictionary. The main idea here is to ask `map()` [49] to invoke the `mydict.get()` method on every key in the sorted list returned by `sorted(mydict.keys())`. A call to `mydict.get()` with a key supplied as the argument to `get()` will return the value associated with that key. If we wanted to print out just a sorted list of the values (sorted according the data type used for the values), we can, of course, use the simpler syntax shown in line (n). As the reader would expect, just calling `mydict.values()`, as in line (o), returns a list of values stored in the dictionary, but, in general, there will be no particular order to the values returned.

```
#!/usr/bin/env python

### DictOps.py

ph_book = { 'yuki' : 3211234, 'xeno' : 5671290, 'trilo' : 342 }      #(A)
print ph_book     # {'xeno': 5671290, 'trilo': 342, 'yuki': 3211234} #(B)

print ph_book.keys()                  # ['xeno', 'trilo', 'yuki']     #(C)

print ph_book.values()                # [5671290, 342, 3211234]       #(D)

print ph_book.items()                                                 #(E)
```

[48] Python's lambda expressions for embedding small anonymous functions in a script are presented in Section 3.8.7.

[49] Python's `map()` function is presented in Section 3.13.

```
          # [('xeno', 5671290), ('trilo', 342), ('yuki', 3211234)]

print ph_book.has_key( 'xeno' )       # 1                          #(F)

print len( ph_book )                  # 3                          #(G)

x = {'a' : 1, 'b' : 2}                                             #(H)
y = {'b' : 3, 'c' : 4}                                             #(I)
x.update( y )                                                      #(J)
print x                               # {'a': 1, 'c': 4, 'b': 3}

del y['b']                                                         #(K)
print y                               # {'c': 4}
del y                                                              #(L)
#print y                              # ERROR

x['d'] = 100                                                       #(M)
print x       # {'a': 1, 'c': 4, 'b': 3, 'd': 100}

empty_dict = {}                                                    #(N)
print type( empty_dict )              # <type 'dict'>

iter = x.iteritems()                                               #(O)
print [(value, key) for (key, value) in iter]                      #(P)
                        # [(1, 'a'), (4, 'c'), (3, 'b'), (100, 'd')]
iter = x.iteritems()                                               #(Q)
for item in iter:                                                  #(R)
    if item[1] > 3: print item                                     #(S)
                                      # ('c', 4)
                                      # ('d', 100)

iter = x.iteritems()                                               #(T)
while ( 1 ):                                                       #(U)
    try:                                                           #(V)
        item = iter.next()                                         #(W)
    except StopIteration: break                                    #(X)
    if item[1] > 3: print item                                     #(Y)
                                      # ('c', 4)
                                      # ('d', 100)

# Dictionary example used in the rest of the script:
mydict = {'a': 10, 'c': 4, 'b': 9, 'd': 100}                       #(Z)

# Key-sorting dictionary contents for display:
keys = mydict.keys()                                               #(a)
keys.sort()                                                        #(b)
for key in keys:                                                   #(c)
    print "%s  %d" % (key, mydict[key])                            #(d)
                                      # a  10
```

```
                                    # b  9
                                    # c  4
                                    # d  100

# Another way to key-sort the dictionary contents:
for item in sorted( mydict.items(), lambda x,y: cmp(x[0], y[0]) ):  #(e)
    print item                                                      #(f)
                                    # ('a', 10)
                                    # ('b', 9)
                                    # ('c', 4)
                                    # ('d', 100)

# A value-sorted display of dictionary content:
for item in sorted( mydict.items(), lambda x,y: cmp(x[1], y[1]) ):  #(g)
    print item                                                      #(h)
                                    # ('c', 4)
                                    # ('b', 9)
                                    # ('a', 10)
                                    # ('d', 100)

# Reverse sorting of dictionary contents by value:
for item in sorted( mydict.items(),                                 #(i)
                    lambda x,y: cmp(x[1], y[1]),                    #(j)
                    reverse=True ):                                 #(k)
    print item                                                      #(l)
                                    # ('d', 100)
                                    # ('a', 10)
                                    # ('b', 9)
                                    # ('c', 4)

# Print out a key-sorted list of the values:
print map( mydict.get, sorted( mydict.keys() ) )                    #(m)
                                    # [10, 9, 4, 100]
# Print out a value-sorted list of the values:
print sorted( mydict.values() )                                     #(n)
                                    # [4, 9, 10, 100]
# Print out a list of the values:
print mydict.values()                                               #(o)
                                    # [10, 4, 9, 100]
```

3.5 BUILT-IN TYPES AS CLASSES

In actuality, the built-in types of Python are all classes.[50] What that implies is that you can subclass them to create more specialized types for a particular application. In this section, we will consider as classes two of the built-in types: string and integer. However, the discussion in this section applies to all other built-in types also. In the next section then we will show how one can subclass the built-in types.[51]

3.5.1 String Type as a Class

The Python strings we have shown so far are all instances of the built-in class `str`. When we create a string by

```
s = "hello";
```

we get `s` as an instance of the `str` class.[52] We could have been more explicit in invoking the string constructor by making the call

```
s = str( "hello" )
```

We may examine this instance in the following manner:

```
print s.__class__                           # <type 'str'>          #(A)

print isinstance( s, str )                  # True                  #(B)

print isinstance( s, object )               # True                  #(C)

print isinstance( s, (int, float, str) )    # True                  #(D)

print isinstance( s, int )                  # False                 #(E)
```

As should be evident from the statement in line (A), `__class__` is a system-supplied data attribute for instance objects. (Chapter 7 explains what that means.) When we query this attribute of `s` in line (A), we get the name of the class of which `s` is an instance, as shown in the commented-out portion of that line. Lines (B) through (E) show different invocations of the `isinstance()` function. This function returns

---

[50]For readers with no prior exposure to object-oriented notions in Python, it is best to read this section after scanning through the introductory material presented in Chapters 7 and 9. The basic idea of a Python class is presented in Chapter 7 and the notion of subclassing in Chapter 9

[51]Of the various built-in types, `number`, `string`, `code`, `type`, and `xrange` are considered to be the *atomic types*. An atomic type object is never duplicated. Multiple usages of an atomic type object are kept track of through the mechanism of reference counting, a topic that is presented in Chapter 12.

[52]More precisely, the variable `s` will hold a reference to an instance of the `str` class.

true or false depending on whether the first argument object is an instance of the type name supplied as the second argument. When the second argument is a tuple of type names — as is the case in line (D) — the function returns true if the first argument object is an instance of any of the types mentioned in the tuple.

Note the call to `isinstance()` in line (C) where we have queried whether `s` is an instance of `object`. As will be discussed in greater detail in Chapters 7 and 9, `object` is the root class of what are known as the new-style classes in Python. All built-in classes in Python,[53] of which the string class `str` is an example, are new-style classes. It is a fundamental tenet of object-oriented programming that an instance constructed from a class is also considered to be an instance of all the superclasses of that class; hence the answer `True` shown in the commented-out portion of line (C).

3.5.2 Numeric Types as Classes

As mentioned previously, each of the numeric types, `int`, `long`, and `float`, is in actuality a class. We show below an instance of an `int` in line (A), an instance of a `float` in line (G), and an instance of a `long` in line (M). We can examine these instances by querying their classes via the `__class__` attribute, as we do in lines (B), (H), and (N), and by calling `isinstance()` on them, as we show in the rest of the lines. As already mentioned for the case of strings, all the built-in classes are subclassed from the root class `object`. So all the instances we show below are also instances of the `object` class.

```
x = 100                                                       #(A)
print x.__class__                    # <type 'int'>           #(B)
print isinstance(x, int)             # True                   #(C)
print isinstance(x, long)            # False                  #(D)
print isinstance(x, float)           # False                  #(E)
print isinstance(x, object)          # True                   #(F)

x = 100.00                                                    #(G)
print x.__class__                    # <type 'float'>         #(H)
print isinstance(x, int)             # False                  #(I)
print isinstance(x, long)            # False                  #(J)
print isinstance(x, float)           # True                   #(K)
print isinstance(x, object)          # True                   #(L)

x = 12345678901234567890                                      #(M)
```

[53]The built-in classes of Python that are important for scripting are `int`, `long`, `float`, `complex`, `str`, `unicode`, `tuple`, `list`, `dict`, and `type`. Instances can be constructed from each of these classes by calling the class name as a function, followed by zero or more arguments within parentheses. If a class name is called as a function with no arguments, the instance constructed will be a zero of the appropriate kind. For example, the call `str()` returns an empty string.

```
print x.__class__                   # <type 'long'>         #(N)
print isinstance(x, int)            # False                 #(O)
print isinstance(x, long)           # True                  #(P)
print isinstance(x, float)          # False                 #(Q)
print isinstance(x, object)         # True                  #(R)
```

The statements shown above created instances of the numeric built-in types by directly assigning numeric values to variables. We could also have constructed those instances by calling on the constructors of the respective classes, as we do in the following lines:

```
x = int( 100 )
print x.__class__                   # <type 'int'>

x = float( 100 )
print x.__class__                   # <type 'float'>

x = long( 100 )
print x.__class__                   # <type 'long'>
```

3.6 SUBCLASSING THE BUILT-IN TYPES

As mentioned already, one of the main advantages of the built-in types being classes is that they can be subclassed into more specialized classes. In this section,[54] we will show two examples of such subclassing, first for the string class `str` and then for the integer class `int`.

3.6.1 Subclassing the String Type

Let's say that we want a "silly" string class with the following behavior: (1) It should always construct a palindrome from the argument string literal, and (2) when the class is called without arguments, it should return the string `@@@@`. If we name this string class `silly_string`, a call such as

```
silly_string( "ma" )
```

should return the string `maam`, and a call like

```
silly_string()
```

[54] As with the previous section, this section is best read after the reader has gone through the introductory material in Chapter 7 where we introduce the notion of a class in Python. A preliminary read of Chapter 9 would also be helpful for understanding this section.

should return the string `@@@@`. Both these properties are exhibited by the extension of the string class `str` shown in the script `SubclassingStrClass.py` presented next. As we will explain in Chapters 7 and 9, the syntax in line (A) of the script:

```
class silly_string( str )
```

means that our `silly_string` class will be a subclass of the base class `str`. Again as explained in Chapters 7 and 9, this means that, unless overridden, all of the methods defined for the built-in class `str` will be directly available in the subclass `silly_string`.

Lines (B) through (F) show `silly_string`'s override definition for the method `__new()__`. To understand the reason for this override definition, you have to understand how Python constructs instances from a class — a topic discussed in greater detail in Chapter 7. Python's instance construction is based on the notion that the creation of an instance should be separated from its initialization. A class must have available to it a *static method*[55] called `__new__()` for constructing an instance from the class definition and an instance method called `__init__()` for the initialization of the instance returned by `__new__()`. We may provide a class with either or both of `__new__()` and `__init__()` by directly defining these methods in the body of the class. When not defined directly in the class, a class may acquire one or both of these methods by inheritance from one of the parent classes. When a subclass needs data attributes over and above what its parent classes provide, these can be defined in the override definition of the `__init__()` for the subclass. And when a subclass needs a customized approach to how instances are created — which would generally be case when an immutable type is subclassed — we would need to provide the subclass with an override for `__new__()`. Chapter 7 delves deeper into when to provide an override for `__new__()` and when to do so for `__init__()`.

The `silly_string` class needs to override its parent class's `__new__()` because it needs to modify the string itself that will be stored in a `str` instance. For the purpose of instance initialization, the `silly_string` class will use the `__init__()` method inherited from its parent class `str`. Since it does not need any data attributes of its own, the `silly_string` class does not need to override its parent's `__init__()` with its own implementation for this method.

In the definition of `__new__()` in lines (B) through (F) of the script, in the header

```
def __new__( cls, arg = "@@" )
```

the parameter `cls` is set to the class whose instance will be constructed by this method.[56] The second parameter, `arg`, will be set to the string literal from which a

[55] As described in Chapter 7, a method is declared to be static with the help of the `staticmethod()` declaration, or, equivalently, with the `@staticmethod` decorator. This declaration is not necessary for `__new__()` as it is considered to be implicitly static.

silly_string instance is to be constructed. It is default initialized[57] to the string literal @@ to meet one of the two requirements on the class silly_string that we stated at the beginning of this subsection.

The code in the body of __new__() is based on the rationale that a string of type str is immutable, meaning that it cannot be modified in place. Line (C), therefore, first converts the string into a mutable object, a list. Therefore, if arg is set to the string literal cat, the call in line (C) will return the list ['c','a','t']. The list, being mutable, is then reversed by the call in line (D). The reversed list is converted back into a string by the call to join() in line (E).[58] Finally, line (F) invokes the parent class str's __new__() to return an instance of silly_string. Note that the first argument in the call to str.__new__() in line (F) will be set to silly_string and not str as we want __new__() to return an instance of silly_string and not an instance of str.

That brings us to the test code in lines (G) through (T). We first construct an instance s1 of silly_string in line (G). The calls to isinstance() in lines (I), (J), and (K) inform us that, as should be expected, s1 is an instance of the class silly_string and all its parent classes. Line (L) constructs another instance from silly_string. In line (N), we invoke the parent class str's definition of the + operator to join two silly_string strings. The result, as is to be expected and as shown by the output in lines (O) and (P), is a string of type str, but not of type silly_string. If we wanted the binary operator in line (N) to return a string of type silly_string, the class silly_string would need to provide an override definition for the operator.[59] Finally, line (Q) calls the silly_string constructor with no arguments, with the output conforming to one of the requirements on this class.

```
#!/usr/bin/env python

### SubclassingStrClass.py

#-----------------------  class silly_string  -----------------------
class silly_string( str ):                                        #(A)
    def __new__( cls, arg = "@@" ):                              #(B)
        l = list( arg )                                          #(C)
        l.reverse()                                              #(D)
```

[56]As will be elaborated on in Chapter 7, ordinarily, by convention, the first parameter of a method is named self. Such methods are typically *instance methods*. When such a method is invoked on an instance, the parameter self is implicitly set to the instance. The method __new__(), on the other hand, is meant to be a static method. When the system invokes __new__() for constructing a new instance from a class, the class itself is provided to the method as its first argument.

[57]Default initialization of function arguments is discussed in Section 3.8.3.

[58]The syntax for using join() in line (E) is explained in Section 4.12.1 of Chapter 4.

[59]Operating overloading for Python classes is discussed in Section 7.11 of Chapter 7 and Section 9.11 of Chapter 9.

```
        arg = arg + "".join(l)                                  #(E)
        return str.__new__( cls, arg )                          #(F)

#---------------------------- Test Code ------------------------------
s1 = silly_string( "hello" )                                    #(G)
print s1                              # helloolleh              #(H)
print isinstance( s1, silly_string )  # True                    #(I)
print isinstance( s1, str )           # True                    #(J)
print isinstance( s1, object )        # True                    #(K)

s2 = silly_string( "jello" )                                    #(L)
print s2                              # jelloollej              #(M)

s3 = s1 + s2                                                    #(N)
print s3                              # helloollehjelloollej    #(O)
print isinstance( s3, silly_string )  # False                   #(P)
print isinstance( s3, str )           # True                    #(Q)
print isinstance( s3, object )        # True                    #(R)

s = silly_string()                                              #(S)
print s                               # @@@@                    #(T)
```

3.6.2 Subclassing the Integer Type

We will now show[60] how one can go about subclassing the built-in integer type `int`. The next script, `SubclassingIntClass.py`, presents `size_limited_int`, a new class that is derived from the built-in class `int`. The class `size_limited_int` is meant to represent range-limited integers. We want the constructor for this new class to raise an exception if an attempt is made to construct an integer instance whose value is outside the range permitted by the class. We also want to provide the class with an override definition for the `+` operator that would allow us to add two instances of type `size_limited_int`, with the summation also being of type `size_limited_int`. As with the string subclass example shown earlier, the following syntax for the class header in line (A)

```
class size_limited_int( int )
```

ensures that `size_limited_int` will be considered to be a subclass of `int`. Line (B) then declares `maxSize` to be a static data attribute for the class. This is where we will store the maximum size allowed for the absolute value of the integer that is allowed to be represented by an instance of type `size_limited_int`.

[60] As with the previous two subsections, a basic understanding of the material in Chapter 7 is necessary to fully appreciate the discussion that follows.

The class `size_limited_int` overrides the static method `__new__()` of the base class in lines (C) through (G). As was mentioned in the previous subsection, every class must possess, either by direct definition in the body of the class or by inheritance, a static method `__new__()` and an instance method `__init__()` for the creation/initialization of instances from the class. The previous subsection also explained briefly the different roles played by `__new__()` and `__init__()` (and pointed the reader to Chapter 7 for a more detailed discussion on instance creation).

About the body of the code in the override for `__new__()`, line (D) assigns a value, if supplied in the call to the constructor, to the default-initialized static data attribute `maxSize`.[61] Line (E) checks whether the second argument to the constructor is within acceptable bounds. If not, an exception is raised in line (F). Finally, in line (G), the subclass's `__new__()` calls on the parent's `__new__()` to construct and return as instance of type `size_limited_int`. As explained in the previous subsection, the first argument in this call to the parent class's `__new__()` must be the subclass if this call is to return an instance of the subclass. Since a constructor call will set the parameter `cls` in line (C) to the subclass `size_limited_int`, the subclass will be passed to the parent class's `__new__()` in line (G).

In order to override the parent class's definition for the `+` operator, the subclass implements the `__add__()` method[62] in lines (H) though (K). A crucial part of this code is the `super` statement in line (I). One makes a call to `super` in Python OO if you want to invoke a method from the parent class.[63] The syntax used for the call to `super` in line (I):

```
res = super( size_limited_int, self ).__add__( arg )
```

causes the parent class's `__add__` to be invoked for the addition operation. This syntax also ensures that if this operation were to return any object at all, it will be an instance of the subclass type, that is of type `size_limited_int`.[64] Finally, line (J) forces a range check on the result returned by the addition operation in line (I).

Lines (K) through (Y) show some experiments with the new integer type. We first construct an instance of the new integer type in line (K). Lines (M), (N), and (O) show

[61] The parameter `size` for `__new__()` is default initialized to 100. So if the constructor is called with only one explicit argument, `size` will be set automatically to 100. Section 3.8.3 talks about the syntax for specifying default arguments for function parameters.

[62] Section 7.11 of Chapter 7 discusses in detail how various operators can be overloaded for a user-defined class.

[63] A call to `super` actually initiates a search for an applicable method definition in the inheritance tree that converges on the subclass in question. The precise algorithm that is used for this search is presented in Section 9.8 of Chapter 9.

[64] We should also mention that we could also have used the following syntax in line (I):

```
res = int.__add__( self, arg )
```

but now the object returned by the addition operation would be of type `int` as opposed to `size_limited_int`.

that the new instance is correctly recognized as being of type `size_limited_int`, `int`, and `object`, all at the same time.

In line (Q) we try to make another instance of the new integer type, but this time with a value that is outside the maximum permitted. Since this call is expected to raise an exception, we make this call inside a `try-except`[65] block in lines (P) through (S). The result is the commented-out message displayed in line (S).

To test the subclass's override of the addition operator, we construct another instance of the new integer type in line (T). Lines (U) through (Y) demonstrate that the result returned by the addition operation in line (U) is recognized to be of type `size_limited_int`.

```
#!/usr/bin/python

### SubclassingIntClass.py

#----------------------  class size_limited_int  ----------------------

class size_limited_int( int ):                                         #(A)

    maxSize = 100                                                      #(B)

    def __new__( cls, intValue, size = 100 ):                          #(C)
        cls.maxSize = size                                             #(D)
        if intValue < -cls.maxSize or intValue > cls.maxSize:          #(E)
            raise Exception( "out of range")                           #(F)
        return int.__new__( cls, intValue )                            #(G)

    def __add__( self, arg ):                                          #(H)
        res = super( size_limited_int, self ).__add__( arg )           #(I)
        return size_limited_int( res, self.maxSize )                   #(J)

#--------------------------  Test Code  -----------------------------

n1 = size_limited_int( 5 )                                             #(K)
print n1                                      # 5                      #(L)
print isinstance( n1, size_limited_int )      # True                   #(M)
print isinstance( n1, int )                   # True                   #(N)
print isinstance( n1, object )                # True                   #(O)

try:                                                                   #(P)
    n2 = size_limited_int( 1000 )                                      #(Q)
except Exception, error:                                               #(R)
    print error                               # out of range           #(S)
```

[65]Python's `try-except` syntax for exception handling in presented in Chapter 10.

```
n3 = size_limited_int( 10 )                                     #(T)
n4 = n1 + n3                                                    #(U)
print n4                                    # 15                #(V)
print isinstance( n4, size_limited_int )    # true              #(W)
print isinstance( n4, int )                 # True              #(X)
print isinstance( n4, object )              # True              #(Y)
```

3.7 TERMINAL AND FILE I/O

As with Perl, Python provides three standard streams: `stdin` for standard input, `stdout` for standard output, and `stderr` for standard error.[66] All three are made available through the `sys` module that comes prepackaged with the Python distribution. During the execution of a script, these file objects will be attached to a file or a device as dictated by the process in which the script is running. Ordinarily, `stdout` will send its output to the terminal screen, `stdin` will read input from the terminal screen, and `stderr` will also send its output error messages to the terminal screen.[67]

3.7.1 Terminal I/O

Information available through `stdin` can be pulled into a script in a couple of different ways, as shown in the next script, `TermIO.py`. The script also shows examples of how the information residing in a script can be pushed out to the output stream `stdout` and the error stream `stderr`.

The script `TermIO.py` contains two different `while` loops for doing the same thing: Each loop reads from the standard input the string entered by a user in a terminal window and then echos it back to the terminal. The echoed string includes at the beginning an acknowledgment substring, which is "`FIRST LOOP: You said =>`" for the first loop and "`SECOND LOOP: You said =>`" for the second loop.

---

[66] Stream objects in Python are usually called file objects, because they are objects of type `file`. As mentioned in the previous chapter, stream objects in Perl are usually referred to as filehandles.

[67] These standard streams may also be redirected inside a script with the `open()` command, as by the invocation

```
open( sys.stdin, "/usr/share/dict/words" )
```

The input information read through `stdin` would now be fetched from the file `/usr/share/dict/words`.

The first loop explicitly uses in line (D) the stream object `sys.stdin` for input from the terminal window and in line (F) the stream object `sys.stdout` for output. Let's now focus on the call to `readline()` in line (D):

```
input = sys.stdin.readline()
```

The method `readline()`, defined for file objects, reads one line at a time from `stdin`, retaining the terminating newline character if it exists. The end-of-file (EOF) indication takes place when `readline()` returns an empty string.[68]

The echo-back in the first `while` loop takes place by a call to `writelines()` that is defined for the file objects. This function takes a sequence of strings as its argument and outputs them to the file object on which the function is invoked.

The second `while` loop uses the built-in function `raw_input()` in lines (H) through (L) to fetch the user-entered information from `stdin`. This is a more common way to fetch information from a terminal in Python. [A special feature of `raw_input()` is that it first outputs a prompt, which is a string that is provided to it as its argument, before fetching what the user enters in response to that prompt, as illustrated by the example in lines (M) and (N).] For the use in line (J), we make a no-argument call to `raw_input()` since our goal here is to merely fetch from the terminal whatever is entered there by the user and to then echo it back to the terminal. For the echo-back, we use the built-in `print` as shown in line (L).

There are two important ways in which the read functions for file objects, `readline()` being a case in point, differ from the built-in `raw_input()` when fetching text from `stdin`. First, the file-object read functions retain the newline character at the end of a line of text, whereas `raw_input()` strips off the newline character if it is there. Additionally, the read functions return an empty string when encountering the end-of-file condition, whereas `raw_input()` throws the `EOFError` exception. In order to provide for a graceful exit out of the `while` loop of line (H), we therefore invoke `raw_input()` in line (J) inside a `try-except` block.[69]

We have another invocation of `raw_input()` in lines (M) and (N). Now we provide this function with an argument string that serves as a prompt to be displayed on the terminal.

Line (P) invokes `sys.exit()` with an exit code of 0. This will cause immediate termination of the script, the exit code 0 indicating to the operating system a successful execution of the script.

---

[68]Compare this to Perl where the end-of-file is indicated by the stream object evaluating to false. All read functions defined for stream objects in Python return an empty string upon encountering EOF. This behavior is not compliant with POSIX standards. When a Python script is run in a POSIX compliant mode, the read functions return the null object `None` upon encountering EOF. POSIX stands for *Portable Operating System Interface*. It can be thought of as a portable subset of Unix-like operating systems.

[69]Chapter 10 explains in greater detail the syntax for throwing and catching exceptions in Python.

Line (R) demonstrates the script writing explicitly to the standard error stream `stderr`, which unless redirected by the operating system will also be the terminal window in which the script is called. The call to `sys.exit()` in line (S), since it has a noninteger argument, first sends the argument string to `stderr` and then implicitly invokes `sys.exit(1)`.

```
#!/usr/bin/env python

### TermIO.py

# Both loops below do the same thing.  Enter Ctrl-D
# to switch from one loop to the next.

import sys                                                         #(A)

print "Starting first loop:"                                       #(B)
while 1:                                                           #(C)
    input = sys.stdin.readline()                                   #(D)
    if (input == ''): break                                        #(E)
    sys.stdout.writelines( ("FIRST LOOP: You said => ", input) )   #(F)

print "Starting second loop:"                                      #(G)
while 1:                                                           #(H)
    try:                                                           #(I)
        input = raw_input()                                        #(J)
    except EOFError: break                                         #(K)
    print "SECOND LOOP:  You said =>  %s" % input                  #(L)

final_input = raw_input( "Are you really done? "                   #(M)
                         "Enter 'yes' or 'no': ")                  #(N)

if ( final_input == "yes" ):                                       #(O)
    sys.exit(0)                                                    #(P)
else:                                                              #(Q)
    sys.stderr.writelines( "sorry\n" )                             #(R)
    sys.exit("sorry again\n")                                      #(S)
```

As already mentioned, ordinarily both the standard output and the standard error streams will send their output to the terminal window in which the script is invoked, but they can be redirected independently, as demonstrated by the script `StdErr.py` shown below. This script echos back each line you enter in the terminal window after prefixing it with the string "`You said:`." The echo is sent to the standard output `sys.stdout`. The script also determines the length of the string entered by the user in each line. The value of this length is sent to the standard error stream `sys.stderr`. In some Unix shells (for example, bash), if you call this script with the invocation

```
StdErr.py 2> length_log
```

the `sys.stderr` stream will be redirected to write into the file `length_log`, whereas the `sys.stdout` stream will echo the user-entered strings to the terminal window. The shells that allow for this sort of command-line redirection of the standard streams associate the file descriptor 0 with the standard input, file descriptor 1 with the standard output, and the file descriptor 2 with the standard error.

```
#!/usr/bin/env python

### StdErr.py

import sys                                                    #(A)

while 1:                                                      #(B)
    try:                                                      #(C)
       input = raw_input()                                    #(D)
    except EOFError: break                                    #(E)
    print "You said =>    %s" % input                         #(F)

    length = len( input )                                     #(G)
    sys.stderr.writelines( str(length) + "\n" )               #(H)
```

3.7.2 File I/O

Let's now talk about I/O operations for disk files. A file I/O stream is created with the built-in function `open()`, which is actually an alias for the newer built-in `file()`, that returns a `FileType` object, referred to informally as a *file* object. A file object is used in the same manner as a filehandle in Perl. A general call to `open()` is

```
open( name_of_file_or_device, mode )
```

where `mode` specifies whether the file object returned by `open` is for reading, writing, or appending.[70] Reading is specified by the letter `r` for `mode`, writing by `w`, and appending by `a`. When `mode` is set to `r+`, the file is opened for both reading

[70]Python will throw an `IOError` exception if for some reason a file cannot be opened for writing or appending. If that were to happen, the error message printed out will contain the failed `open()` statement from the script and the reason for failure. The most common reason for such failure is that the named file does not exist in the directory.

and writing. When `mode` is not supplied, `r` is assumed by default. The meaning of what is meant by *appending* is derived from the underlying operating system. In most cases, this mode would cause the new information to be inserted at the end of the current file. However, in some cases, it could also mean that the new information would be inserted starting at the current `seek` position of the file pointer.

A more general call to `open()` has the following syntax

```
open( filename, mode, buffsize )
```

where the last argument specifies the buffer size to use for the I/O operations on the file. Ignoring this argument means to use the system default. The same is implied by a negative value for this argument. A value of 0 means to use no buffering. Otherwise, a buffer of roughly the size `buffsize` will be used.

When Python is built with *universal newline support*, using the additional character `U` in the mode string causes the text file line terminations to be always seen as `\n` — which is the Unix end-of-line convention — even when the actual line terminations are `\r` (the Macintosh convention) or `\r\n` (the Windows convention). The value of the newline used for a file is stored in the attribute `newlines` of the file object returned by `open()`.

A file object supports the following methods:[71] [72]

`read(number_of_bytes):` reads *number_of_bytes* from the disk file provided no end-of-file condition is encountered; otherwise will read the maximum number of bytes possible. *This function will read the entire file in one fell swoop if the argument is left out.* The bytes read are returned in the form of a string, with each character of the string corresponding to one byte in the disk file. If a call to this function runs immediately into the end-of-the-file condition, the function returns an empty string.

`readline():` reads one line at a time from the file object attached with a text file. The function returns a string for the line read. Also, the function retains the newline character at the end of the line, unless the string being returned is the last line in a file that does not end in a newline. This implies that a blank line in an source text file will always be returned as a newline character by `readline()`. This also implies that when `readline()` returns an empty string, that indicates the end-of-file condition.

[71]We show only the more commonly used methods defined for file objects, and those too with only the more commonly used argument structure. The other supported methods are `flush()` for flushing the internal buffers, `fileno()` for getting hold of a file descriptor integer, `isatty()` that returns true if a file is connected to a tty or a tty-like device, and `next()` that is used internally when a file object acts as an iterator. See Section 2.2.8 of the Python Library Reference for further details.

[72]The difference between *function* and *method* will be made clear in Chapters 6 and 7. Suffice it to say for now that, for the case of Python, when a function is called *on* an object with the dot operator, we refer to the function as a method.

`readlines()`: reads all the lines all at once from the file object attached to a text file and returns a list of strings, with each string representing all the characters in a single line. Trailing newlines are retained in the strings.

`write(`*`string`*`)`: writes out to the stream object the string supplied as the argument. Nothing is returned. Due to buffering, the string that is written out may not show up at its destination until the buffer is flushed.

`writelines(`*`sequence_of_strings`*`)`: writes out a sequence of strings, typically a list of string, to the stream object. Nothing is returned.

`seek(`*`offset`*`)`: moves the file pointer to a place specified by its argument. There is also a two-argument version of this function that can position the file pointer relative to, say, the current position.

`close()`: closes the file. It is not an error to close the same file more than once. The exception `ValueError` is thrown when a method is invoked on a closed file if that method is meant to be invoked only on open files. Closing a file object will flush the buffers associated with the stream.

3.7.2.1 I/O for Text Files

In the next script, `TextFileIO.py`, we demonstrate various ways of reading from and writing to a text file. The first block, in lines (A) through (D), makes a no-argument call to the `read()` method to read in all of the source-file bytes in one go. All of these bytes are returned in the form of *a single string object* by `read()`. This string is then written out to the destination file by the call to `write()`. Since the `write()` method buffers the output, the bytes it writes out may not show up in the destination file until either `close()` or `flush()` is invoked on the file object. In line (D) we invoke `close()` on the file object to close the stream.[73]

Another way of reading from a text file and writing out text to a file is shown in lines (E) through (H). Now we invoke the `readlines()` method to read all the lines in the source text file into a list of strings. The call to `writelines()` then writes out this list of strings to the output file.

Yet another way of reading from and writing to text files is shown in lines (I) through (O). Now we read one line at a time by calling `readline()` until the end-of-file condition is detected in line (M) in the form of a returned empty string. As mentioned earlier when we talked about Python's standard streams, the

---

[73]Actually the script would work perfectly fine without the calls to `close()` in lines (D), (H), (O), and (U). That is because when the script terminates, all of the streams would be flushed and closed by Python automatically. The reader will also notice that we did not call `close()` on the input-stream file object `filein`. We can get away with that because when you open a file, any previous file objects attached to that file are automatically closed. Nonetheless, it is always a good idea to close an open file object when you are done with I/O on the file.

readline() method retains any newline characters at the end of each line and returns an empty string upon encountering the end-of-file condition. Line (N) of this approach to text file I/O also shows another way of using the print built-in function. Usually referred to as "print chevron," a call to print>>() expects the first argument to evaluate to a file object. It subsequently writes out the rest of the arguments to this file object. Should the first argument evaluate to None, the rest of the arguments are written out to the standard output.

Our next way of doing text file I/O is illustrated in lines (Q) through (U). The approach shown uses the fact that a file object, since it comes equipped with a method called next(), is its own iterator. The syntax for item in file_object used in line (S) implicitly invokes the next() method of the file object to iterate through all the lines in the source text file, one line at a time. Also shown in line (T) of the same code block is a formatted output of each source-file line. The formatted output consists of two columns. The entry in the first column is just a series of chevrons, >>>>, and the entry in the second column the text lines read from the source file. Additionally, the entries in the second column are right-justified in a field that is 20 characters wide. This formatting is accomplished by calling string.rjust().[74]

```
#!/usr/bin/env python

### TextFileIO.py

# Slurp in all of the input file in a single call to read()
# and write it out to the output file in a single call to write:
filein = open( "data_in.txt" )                                      #(A)
fileout = open( "data_out1.txt", 'w' )                              #(B)
fileout.write( filein.read() )                                      #(C)
fileout.close()                                                     #(D)

# Slurp in all lines of the input file in a single call to
# readlines() and write them all out to the destination
# file in a single call to writelines():
filein = open( "data_in.txt" )                                      #(E)
fileout = open( "data_out2.txt", 'w' )                              #(F)
fileout.writelines( filein.readlines() )                            #(G)
fileout.close()                                                     #(H)

# Read input file one line at a time and write it out one
# line at a time:
filein = open( "data_in.txt" )                                      #(I)
fileout = open( "data_out3.txt", 'w' )                              #(J)
while 1:                                                            #(K)
```

[74] This should explain why we had to import the string module in line (P). Python's modules and their import in a script are discussed in greater detail in Section 3.10.

```
    line = filein.readline()                                    #(L)
    if (line == ''): break                                      #(M)
    print>> fileout, line,                                      #(N)
fileout.close()                                                 #(O)

import string                                                   #(P)

# Use the fact that a file object is its own iterator.
# Therefore, the 'for' loop below will implicitly call
# repeatedly the next() method defined for file objects
# in order to iterate through a text file.
filein = open( "data_in.txt" )                                  #(Q)
fileout = open( "data_out4.txt", 'w' )                          #(R)
for each_line in filein:                                        #(S)
    print>> fileout, ">>>>", string.rjust(each_line, 20),       #(T)
fileout.close()                                                 #(U)
```

3.7.2.2 I/O for Binary Files

Note that, ordinarily, you would not need to make a distinction between binary files and text files. However, if such a distinction is important to the underlying operating system, or if such a distinction is needed for documentation purposes, the mode strings in the calls to `open()` become `rb`, `wb`, `ab`, and `r+b`, where the letter `b` denotes binary. If you use the letter `b` in this manner, but the system does not need to differentiate between the text and the binary files, the letter is ignored.

To keep the binary I/O discussion in this section parallel to our treatment of the same topic in Perl (see Section 2.6.2.2 of Chapter 2), we will first address the issue of how we would write out an integer to a file in its binary form, as opposed to its print representation. That is, if the integer to be written out to a file is, say, 82537349, we want the actual output to the file to consist of 4 bytes whose hex representation is `31323334`.[75] In Perl this was accomplished by the `pack()` function. It produced a byte stream that was the binary representation of its argument. The same thing in Python can be accomplished with the `pickle` module if its version is 1 or higher.[76]

---

[75]If we insisted on reading this file in text mode on a big-endian platform, we should see the string `1234` since `31` is the ASCII code in hex for the character 1, `32` the ASCII code in hex for the character 2, `33` for 3, and `34` for 4. On a little-endian machine, a text-mode reading of the file should produce `4321`.

[76]The basic purpose of the `pickle` module is *serialization* of complex data structures. Serialization consists of converting a data structure, which may be hierarchical in nature (such as a list of lists), into a byte stream for the purpose of transmission over a communication link to a different machine or for long-term storage.

For the goal at hand, the `pickle` module comes with two methods, `dump()` and `load()`, the former for serialization and the latter for deserialization. When the target object is a simple integer, serialization produces essentially a binary representation of the integer, with some additional bytes for informing `load()` how to reconstruct the integer object from the byte stream. Shown below in line (E) is a call to `pickle.dump()` to output the binary representation of the value of variable `x` to the output stream `FILE`:

```
import pickle                                                        #(A)
import sys                                                           #(B)
FILE = file( "outdata", 'w' )                                        #(C)
x = 825373492                                                        #(D)
pickle.dump( x, FILE, 1 )                                            #(E)
FILE.close()                                                         #(F)
```

If we were to examine what is deposited in the output file, we would get the following sequence of bytes:

```
4a 34 33 32 31 2e
```

which, apart from the one extra byte at the beginning and one at the end, is exactly what we want. To read this binary data back into a script, we can use the following statements:

```
FILE = file( "outdata" )                                             #(G)
y = pickle.load( FILE )                                              #(H)
print y                                  # 825373492                 #(I)
FILE.close()                                                         #(J)
```

Paralleling again the Perl discussion in Section 2.6.2.2 of Chapter 2, we will now talk about the I/O for binary files. Our next script, `BinaryFileIO.py`, does three things:

- It reads the input binary file in the slurp mode, meaning all at once, into a single string. This string, obviously containing many unprintable characters, is then written out to an output file named `out1`, again all at once.

- It reads the input binary file, one byte at a time, and writes this byte out to the destination file, again one byte at a time. The name of this destination file is `out2`.

- As it reads the input binary file one byte at a time, it writes out the two-character hexadecimal representation of the byte to an output *text* file called `out.hex`. Recall our mention in Section 2.6 of Chapter 2 that it is sometimes useful to peer into binary files for diagnostic reasons. Since a binary file obviously cannot be printed out, a convenient way to peer into such a file is to create a hex dump of the file. The hex dump can then be read as a text file. For the hex dump, the script shown below treats each byte of the input binary file as an unsigned integer between 0 and 255, and converts it into its hexadecimal representation.

The script shown next is called with a command-line invocation like

```
BinaryFileIO.py input_file_name
```

Lines (C) and (D) of the script ensure that the command line has exactly one argument, the name of the input binary file.[77] Line (E) opens the input binary file for reading and line (F) the destination file for copying. The call to `read()` in line (G) reads the entire input binary file all at once into a single string. The call to `write()` in the same line then writes out this string to the destination file.

The second part of the script, in lines (J) through (Z), does two things simultaneously: it reads the input binary file one byte at a time by invoking `read(1)` inside a `while` loop in line (P). Line (V) then prints out a hex representation of this byte to the hex-dump output file. And line (W) outputs the raw byte directly to another destination file.

About the complicated looking syntax in line (V) and the preamble in lines (O) through (U) before the output actually takes place, note that our goal is to output the hex for 10 bytes per line. Additionally, we want the hex representation for each byte to be right-justified in a field of four characters. The index `i` helps us keep track of how many bytes we have output in each line of the dump file. When this count reaches 10, we also output a newline. This is done in lines (S) and (U) by assigning either a space or a newline to the variable `spacer`. In line (V), the value of `spacer` is inserted between the hex outputs for the successive bytes.

Note also how in line (V) we convert each byte into its hex representation. To understand this conversion, bear in mind that `read()` called in line (P) will always return a string of one character from the binary file. When `ord()` is called on a one character string in line (V), it returns an integer which is the ASCII code associated with the character. Calling `hex()` on this character then returns the hex representation of the byte.

The hex dump produced by this script looks like:

```
0xff  0xd8  0xff  0xe1  0x3d  0x6a  0x45  0x78  0x69  0x66
 0x0   0x0  0x49  0x49  0x2a   0x0   0x8   0x0   0x0   0x0
 0xc   0x0   0xe   0x1   0x2   0x0  0x20   0x0   0x0   0x0
0x88   0xb   0x0   0x0   0xf   0x1   0x2   0x0  0x18   0x0
....
....
```

[77]Python stores its command line arguments in the list attribute `argv` of the `sys` module. The name of the script called from the command line is stored in the first element of the list, that is, in `sys.argv[0]`, the first command line argument in `sys.argv[1]`, and so on.

Note that we have three spaces between the hex representations of the successive bytes (when the hex representation occupies the maximum of four character positions assigned to it). One of these spacings comes about from the value of `spacer` in line (U). The other spacing is produced by the `print` statement in line (V). One additional spacing comes from the call to `string.rjust()`. Its last argument, 4, means that the output of this function will be *at least* four characters wide. In our case, it uses a width of 5 character positions in which it right-justifies the hex representation.

Here is the script:

```
#!/usr/bin/env python

### BinaryFileIO.py

import sys                                                              #(A)
import string                                                           #(B)

# This script must be called with
# exactly one argument, the name of
# the input binary file:

if len(sys.argv) != 2:                                                  #(C)
    sys.exit( "call syntax: script_name input_file_name" )              #(D)


# Copy the binary file by reading in
# the slurp mode:

filein = open( sys.argv[1], 'rb' )                                      #(E)
fileout = open( "out1", 'wb' )                                          #(F)
fileout.write( filein.read() )                                          #(G)
filein.close()                                                          #(H)
fileout.close()                                                         #(I)


# Copy the binary file by reading it
# one byte at a time.  At the same
# time,   also create its hex dump:

filein = open( sys.argv[1], 'rb' )                                      #(J)
fileout = open( "out2", 'wb' )                                          #(K)
filedump = open( "out.hex", 'w' )                                       #(L)

i = 0                                                                   #(M)
while 1:                                                                #(N)
    i = i + 1                                                           #(O)
```

```
    byte = filein.read(1)                                                 #(P)
    if (byte == ''): break                                                #(Q)
    if ( i % 10 == 0 ):                                                   #(R)
        spacer = '\n'                                                     #(S)
    else:                                                                 #(T)
        spacer = ' '                                                      #(U)
    print>> filedump, string.rjust( hex( ord(byte) ), 4 ), spacer,        #(V)
    fileout.write(byte)                                                   #(W)

filein.close()                                                            #(X)
fileout.close()                                                           #(Y)
filedump.close()                                                          #(Z)
```

3.8 USER-DEFINED FUNCTIONS

As the following script illustrates, a user-defined function is created by the keyword `def` followed by the function name, which in turn is followed by a parenthesized list of the function parameters.[78] The body of the function begins in the next line. Lines (A) through (D) of the script define a function called `get_name()` whose purpose is to ask the user for his/her first name and last name. The first line of the body of a function — line (B) in our example — is typically a documentation string, referred to as *docstring*. By convention, a documentation string should be concise, should begin with an uppercase letter, and should end in a period. The `get_name()` function uses the previously discussed system-supplied `raw_input()` function to elicit from the user his/her first name and last name in lines (C) and (D). The function returns a tuple of the two names. Line (F) calls this function and line (G) prints out what is returned by the function. In line (H), we print out the type of the object `get_name`.

```
#!/usr/bin/env python

### Function_Basic.py

def get_name():                                                           #(A)
    "Get from the user his/her first and last names"                      #(B)
    first = raw_input( "Enter your first name: " )                        #(C)
    last = raw_input( "Enter your last name: " )                          #(D)
```

[78] It is important to note that the function definition is bound to the name of the function only at the program execution time. That is the main reason why the definition of a function must appear before a call to the function in a Python script. Binding a function definition to a name in Python is no different from assigning an integer value to a variable. The semantics of both operations are the same at execution time.

```
    return (first, last)                                              #(E)

full_name = get_name()                                                #(F)
print full_name                                                       #(G)

print type( get_name )                # <type 'function'>             #(H)
```

3.8.1 A Function Is an Object

A user-defined function is like any other object. It can be assigned to a variable, placed in a container, compared to other objects, passed as an argument to another function, and so on.[79] When assigned to a variable, a function can be invoked using that variable, as shown by the following example. We define a function `foo()` in line (A). This function object is assigned to the variable `bar` in line (C), which in turn is assigned to the variable `baz` in line (E). Invoking `bar()` in line (D) and `baz()` in line (F) is equivalent to invoking `foo()`.

Line (G) of the script makes a list of the three function objects, `foo`, `bar`, and `baz`. As shown by the lines (H) and (I), we can loop through this list and invoke each function in turn via the loop control variable. The output of this looping action is shown in the three commented out lines immediately after line (I). Lines (J), (K), and (L) show what is returned when function names are evaluated as objects, that is, when they are called without the associated function-call operator `()`. As shown by the commented out output in these lines, all three names — `foo`, `bar`, `baz` — refer to exactly the same function, `foo`, located at exactly the same place in the memory. Finally, lines (M), (N), and (O) show that all three names — `foo`, `bar`, and `baz` — are objects of type `FunctionType`, which the `type()` function writes out as `<type 'function'>`.

```
#!/usr/bin/env python

### FuncAsObject.py

def foo(x, y):                                                        #(A)
    print max( x , y )                                                #(B)

bar = foo                                                             #(C)
bar( 3, 4 )                           # 4                             #(D)
```

[79]These properties of Python functions are summarized by saying that Python function objects are *first-class objects*, implying that everything you can do to a data object can also be done to a function object.

```
baz = bar                                 # 8                          #(E)
baz( 8, 7 )                                                            #(F)

myfuncs = [foo, bar, baz]                                              #(G)

for item in myfuncs:                                                   #(H)
    item( 2, 3 )                                                       #(I)
                                          # 3
                                          # 3
                                          # 3

print foo                                 # <function foo at 0x804f664>#(J)
print bar                                 # <function foo at 0x804f664>#(K)
print baz                                 # <function foo at 0x804f664>#(L)

print type( foo )                         # <type 'function'>          #(M)
print type( bar )                         # <type 'function'>          #(N)
print type( baz )                         # <type 'function'>          #(O)
```

3.8.2 The Object Returned by a Function Call

A Python function always returns a single object. If no return objects are specified in a function, the null object `None` is returned implicitly.

If it is desired to return multiple objects, they can always be packaged into a tuple or a list and returned as a single object. The following script defines a function `swap()` in line (A). From line (B), it seems like this function returns two values, but it does not. What it returns is a tuple of the values supplied as the arguments to `return`. We show two invocations of this function, one in line (C) and the other in line (D). Line (E) shows the type of what is returned by `swap()` in line (D) — it is obviously a tuple.

Starting in line (G), the script also shows a slightly more sophisticated function — `histogram()`. When supplied with a tuple of integers, this function returns a histogram indicating the frequency of occurrence of each integer in the tuple. So given a tuple of integers

```
(2, 2, 2, 4, 4, 4, 4, 4)
```

its histogram would be

```
0 0 3 0 5
```

meaning that the integer 0 occurs zero times in the input tuple, the integer 1 also zero times, the integer 2 three times, the integer 3 zero times, and, finally, the integer 4 five times. The number of "cells" in the histogram equals the value of the largest integer in the input tuple plus one, as calculated by the statement in line (H). Line (I) creates and initializes with zeros a list object for storing this histogram. The actual histogram is then constructed by looping through the input data tuple in lines (J) and (K). Finally, in line (L), we return the list object that is the histogram. Lines (M) and (O) show two example invocations of the `histogram()` function. The histograms produced by these invocations are displayed in lines (N) and (P), respectively.

```
#!/usr/bin/env python

### FuncReturn.py

def swap( x, y ):                                                   #(A)
    return y, x                                                     #(B)

print swap( 'hello', 'jello')          # ('jello', 'hello')         #(C)

t = swap( 3, 4 )                                                    #(D)
print type( t )                        # <type 'tuple'>             #(E)
print t                                # (4, 3)                     #(F)

def histogram( datatuple ):                                         #(G)
    hist_size = max( datatuple ) + 1                                #(H)
    hist = [0] * hist_size                                          #(I)
    for item in datatuple:                                          #(J)
        hist[item] = hist[item] + 1                                 #(K)
    return hist                                                     #(L)

data = ( 1, 1, 1, 1, 1, 1, 1, 1, 1, 1 )                             #(M)
print histogram( data )                # [0, 10]                    #(N)

data = ( 1, 1, 2, 2, 2, 4, 4 )         # [0, 2, 3, 0, 2]            #(O)
print histogram( data )                                             #(P)
```

An interesting difference between a Perl function and a Python function is that the former will return whatever is returned by the last statement of the function, whereas the latter requires that you use a `return` statement explicitly for that purpose. So in a Perl function, you will see `return` only if you want to force an early return based on some condition becoming true. But in Python, every function that must return a value will end in a `return` statement. As mentioned, when a Python function does not explicitly return anything at all, it implicitly returns the null object `None`.

This null object is also returned explicitly when `return` is not supplied with any arguments.

3.8.3 Default Arguments for Function Parameters

It is possible to specify default arguments for one or more of the trailing parameters of a function in Python. The default argument may be a constant object or a variable holding a reference to a constant object. In the `setUserInfo()` function defined in lines (C) through (H) of the following script, the default for the third parameter, `gend`, has been set to the string literal `unknown` and the default for the last parameter, `pos`, to the variable `position_default`.

An interesting question arises when invoking functions whose parameters have been assigned variables as default values: If the value of this variable at the point of function call is different from its value at the point of function definition, which value is used for the default? In the following example, the value of the `position_default` variable at the point of function definition is `Staff`, as set in line (B). On the other hand, the value of the same variable at the point of function call in line (J) is `MemberStaff`, as set in line (I). So which value would be used as default for the parameter `pos` of the function `setUserInfo()` when it is called in (J)? The answer to the question is: *It is the value at the point of function definition that is used as the default.* This is illustrated by the outputs shown in the commented out portions of lines (K) and (M).

```
#!/usr/bin/env python

### DefaultArgs.py

name = age = position = gender = None                                 #(A)

position_default = 'Staff'                                            #(B)

def setUserInfo( aname, years, gend = 'unknown', \
                                  pos = position_default ): #(C)
    global name, age, position, gender                                #(D)
    name = aname                                                      #(E)
    age = years                                                       #(F)
    position = pos                                                    #(G)
    gender = gend                                                     #(H)

position_default = 'MemberStaff'                                      #(I)

setUserInfo( 'Trillian', 96, 'female' )                               #(J)
print name, age, gender, position       # Trillian 96 female Staff   #(K)
```

```
setUserInfo( 'Trillian', 96 )                                       #(L)
print name, age, gender, position        # Trillian 96 unknown Staff #(M)
```

3.8.4 Functions Can Be Called with Arbitrary Number of Arguments

In the same manner that ellipsis (...) is used in C function definitions, a Python function can be provided with a mechanism for accepting an arbitrary number of arguments. When a function call is matched with a function definition, first all of the position-specific arguments are matched with their corresponding parameters. Subsequently, all the remaining arguments are packaged into a tuple, which as an object is assigned to the remaining parameter *provided that parameter carries the prefix* `*`. In the body of the function, the arguments supplied can be retrieved from the tuple in the usual manner to access the elements of a tuple.

The function in line (A) of the script below has two position-specific formal parameters, `p` and `q`, and the parameter `s` for *absorbing* an arbitrary number of additional arguments if used during a function call. This last parameter is denoted `*s` in the parameter list of the function. The parameter name `s` will be set to a tuple of all these additional arguments. So for the function call in line (F), the parameter `p` gets the value 1, the parameter `q` the value 2, and the parameter `s` the tuple `(3,4)`. On the other hand, for the function call example in line (I), the parameters `p` and `q` get the same values as before, but now the parameter `s` is set to the tuple `(3,4,5,6)`. As shown in lines (D) and (E), one can use the usual tuple-related operators to extract the additional arguments from the tuple that gets bound to the parameter `s`. The commented-out lines shown immediately below the function calls in lines (F) and (H) display the output in each case.

```
#!/usr/bin/python

### VariableArgs.py

def foo( p, q, *s ):                                                #(A)
    print "value of p:", p                                          #(B)
    print "value of q:", q                                          #(C)
    for i in range( len(s) ):                                       #(D)
        print "value of the next arg:", s[i]                        #(E)

foo( 1, 2, 3, 4 )                                                   #(F)
                                   # value of p: 1
                                   # value of q: 2
                                   # value of the next arg: 3
                                   # value of the next arg: 4
foo( 1, 2, 3, 4, 5, 6 )                                             #(H)
```

```
                                          # value of p: 1
                                          # value of q: 2
                                          # value of the next arg: 3
                                          # value of the next arg: 4
                                          # value of the next arg: 5
                                          # value of the next arg: 6
```

3.8.5 Functions Can Be Called with Keyword Arguments

Nothing special needs to be done if you wish to make a function call with keyword arguments using the parameter=value syntax. When a function is called in this manner, the argument positions do not have to correspond to the parameter positions in the function definition. One can also mix regular position-specific arguments with arbitrarily positioned keyword arguments provided all of the former appear *before* any of the latter.

In the following script, note the function call in line (J) where we have supplied three arguments, all in the parameter=value format. Note in particular that the positions of these arguments do not correspond to the positions of the respective parameters in the function definition. The function itself is defined with four parameters in line (C), the last two carrying default values.

As shown by the function call in line (L), it is possible to mix position-specific and keyword arguments in the same function call provided all position-specific arguments come before any keyword arguments. Therefore, the following call

```
setUserInfo(years=96, aname='Trillian', gend ='female', 'HiStaff')
```

would be illegal since the last argument is presumably a value for the last parameter, pos, of the function. This illegal call will elicit the following error message:

```
SyntaxError: non-keyword arg after keyword arg
```

```
#!/usr/bin/python

### KeywordArgs.py

name = age = position = gender = None                                    #(A)

position_default = 'Staff'                                               #(B)
```

```
def setUserInfo( aname, years, gend = 'unknown', \
                                         pos = position_default ): #(C)
    global name, age, position, gender                            #(D)
    name = aname                                                   #(E)
    age = years                                                    #(F)
    position = pos                                                 #(G)
    gender = gend                                                  #(H)

position_default = 'MemberStaff'                                   #(I)

setUserInfo( years = 96, aname = 'Trillian', gend = 'female' )     #(J)
print name, age, gender, position       # Trillian 96 female Staff #(K)

setUserInfo( 'Trillian', gend = 'female', years = 96 )             #(L)
print name, age, gender, position       # Trillian 96 female Staff #(M)
```

Just as we can have an arbitrary number of regular arguments (meaning, nonkeyword arguments) in a function call — provided the parameter list in the function definition ends in a parameter with the * prefix — a function call is also allowed to have an arbitrary number of keyword arguments provided the last parameter in the function definition carries the ** prefix. If a function call needs to be able to specify both an arbitrary number of regular arguments and an arbitrary number of keyword arguments, the *-ed parameter must come before the **-ed parameter, as demonstrated by the following script.

In the script below, the function `foo()` is defined in line (A) with two position-specific regular parameters, `p` and `q`. The parameter list then contains a *-ed parameter `s` for absorbing an arbitrary number of nonkeyword arguments. Finally, the parameter list contains a **-ed parameter `t` for absorbing an arbitrary number of keyword arguments.

In the function call in line (I), the arguments 1 and 2 are assigned to the position-specific parameters `p` and `q`, respectively. The arguments 3 and 4 are packaged into a tuple that is assigned to the parameter `s`. Finally, the keyword arguments, `a=8` and `b=9`, are assigned in the form of a dictionary to the parameter `t`.

In the function call in line (J), on the other hand, all of the arguments after the first two get packaged into a tuple and assigned to the parameter `s`. The parameter `t` in this case will therefore be assigned the object `None`.

Note that the function call in line (I) cannot be replaced by a call such as

```
foo( q=2, p=1, 3, 4, a = 8, b = 9 )
```

because it contains keyword arguments before nonkeyword arguments.

```
#!/usr/bin/env python

### ArbitraryKeywordArgs.py

def foo( p, q, *s, **t ):                                              #(A)
    print "value of p:", p                                             #(B)
    print "value of q:", q                                             #(C)

    # get other non-keyword args
    for i in range( len(s) ):                                          #(D)
        print "value of the next arg:", s[i]                           #(E)

    # get keyword args
    iter = t.iteritems()                                               #(F)
    for item in iter:                                                  #(G)
        print 'the value of the variable', item[0], 'is', item[1]     #(H)


foo( 1, 2, 3, 4, a = 8, b = 9 )                                        #(I)
                                   # value of p: 1
                                   # value of q: 2
                                   # value of the next arg: 3
                                   # value of the next arg: 4
                                   # the value of the variable a is 8
                                   # the value of the variable b is 9
foo( 1, 2, 3, 4, 5, 6 )                                                #(J)

                                   # value of p: 1
                                   # value of q: 2
                                   # value of the next arg: 3
                                   # value of the next arg: 4
                                   # value of the next arg: 5
                                   # value of the next arg: 6
```

3.8.6 Anonymous Functions with Lambda Expressions

Lambda expressions, a concept borrowed from functional programming, allow small *anonymous functions* to be embedded in a script. These are often used as *callback functions*, meaning that the operating system can automatically invoke the functions in response to certain events. For example, in GUI programming, there will usually be a callback associated with a button click.

A lambda expression in Python is specified with the `lamdba` operator. The one-line anonymous functions thus created are also sometimes referred to simply as *lambdas*. The following two lambdas

```
func = lambda x: 4*x
print func(4)                          # 16

evenp = lambda x: x%2 == 0
print evenp(3)                         # False
```

are equivalent to the following two examples, respectively, that use the usual `def` operator to define a function:

```
def func(x): return 4 * x
print func(4)                          # 16

def evenp(x): return x%2 == 0
print evenp(3)                         # False
```

Here is an example that shows a lambda being used as a simple *closure*, a concept presented in greater detail in the next subsection:

```
z = 10
func = lambda x, y=z: x * y
print func(20)                         # 200
```

The lambda in this case retains the value of a variable, `z`, that is defined in the enclosing scope. It is also possible to have a list of lambda functions. Each function can be accessed with the usual subscript operator, as in

```
nums = [1, 2, 3, 4]
lambda_list = [lambda x, y=z: x*y for z in nums]
for i in range(len(nums)):
    print lambda_list[i](5)
```

which prints out 5, 10, 15, and 20, one number per line.

3.8.7 Closures

A *closure* is a function object that has a piece of data attached with it — data that can be initialized at the time the function object is created. As an example, consider the function defined in lines (A) through (D) in the next script. When this function is called, as in lines (E) and (F), it returns a reference to another function, `greeting_generator()`, which is a closure over the lexical variable `whom`.

Therefore, the function to which the variable `greeting_gen1` in line (G) holds a reference has its `whom` variable set to `world`, and the function to which `greeting_gen2` holds a reference has its `whom` variable set to `everyone`. So when we call the functions `greeting_gen1()` and `greeting_gen2()` in lines (G) through (J), we get the outputs shown commented out in those lines.

```
#!/usr/bin/env python

### Closure.py

def make_greeting_generator( whom ):                                    #(A)
    def greeting_generator( greeting ):                                 #(B)
        print greeting, whom                                            #(C)
    return greeting_generator                                           #(D)

greeting_gen1 = make_greeting_generator( 'world' )                     #(E)
greeting_gen2 = make_greeting_generator( 'everyone' )                  #(F)

greeting_gen1('hello')              # hello world                       #(G)
greeting_gen1('good morning')       # good morning world                #(H)

greeting_gen2('hello')              # hello everyone                    #(I)
greeting_gen2('good morning')       # good morning everyone             #(J)
```

3.9 CONTROL STRUCTURES

Python has the `if` control structure for conditional evaluation of a block of code. The block of code that follows the conditional is evaluated subject to the conditional being true. Python gives us `while` and `for` control structures for iterative but conditional evaluation of a block of code.

Looping with `while`:

To parallel the examples in a similarly titled section in the Perl review in the previous chapter, shown below is a Python script that illustrates both the `while` and the `if` control structures. Like the Perl script of the same name, the Python script shown here asks a user to enter numbers, one per line, with each entry indicated by the pressing of the Enter key after the number. The script returns the sum of the numbers. The interaction with the script is terminated by pressing the Enter key without any data in the line. The script accepts any number of blank spaces before you press the Enter key for the purpose of terminating a session.

Each number is read into the script as a string by the call to `raw_input()` in line (D). Line (D) also calls `rstrip()` to strip off any blank spaces that may follow the data in a line of entry. Because of the stripping action in line (D), the condition in line (E) would evaluate to `True` when the user presses the Enter key in a line with no actual data in it, even if this is done after the entry of blank spaces in the same line. Also note the call to the built-in function `float()` in line (H) to convert a user's entry, which is read in as a string by `raw_input()` in line (D), into a floating-point number. If the user was told to enter just integers, we could use the built-in `int()` instead of `float()` in line (H).

```
#!/usr/bin/env python

### WhileIf.py

print "Enter numbers, one per line.  When done, just enter return.";#(A)

sum = 0                                                            #(B)
while 1:                                                           #(C)
    num = raw_input().rstrip()                                     #(D)
    if num == '':                                                  #(E)
        print "Sum of numbers is: ", sum                           #(F)
        break                                                      #(G)
    sum += float( num )                                            #(H)
```

`if-else` *and* `if-elif-else` *for flow control*:

The `if` clause we demonstrated above permits conditional execution of the code in the body of the clause. For conditional execution that is able to choose between two alternative courses of action, one can use the `if` clause together with an `else` clause:

```
    if ( conditional ):
        code ...
    else:
        code ...
```

When multiple alternatives need to be considered, we can use a series of `elif` clauses and a final `else` clause, as shown below:

```
    if ( conditional ):
        code ...
    elif ( conditional ):
        code ...
    elif ( conditional ):
        code ...
    else:
        code
```

Looping with `for`:

In addition to `while`, the other looping mechanism provided by Python is `for`. Shown below is an example that uses this control structure to loop through a sequence of integers as it calculates and prints out the square of each integer in the sequence. The `for` clause includes an `in` subclause to delineate the sequence of permissible values for the loop control variable. As mentioned in Section 3.3.4, the function `range(n)` used in line (A) returns a list of integers with values `0, 1, 2, ..., n-1`.

```
#!/usr/bin/env python

### For.py

for i in range(4):                                                  #(A)
    print "square of", i, "is", i * i                               #(B)
                                        # square of 0 is 0
                                        # square of 1 is 1
                                        # square of 2 is 4
                                        # square of 3 is 9
```

Looping with `for-else`:

A more general form of the `for` control structure in Python is

```
for item in sequence:
    ..code..
else:
    ..code..
```

where the code in the suite of the `else` clause is executed after the sequence in the header of the `for` clause has been completely iterated through.[80] In the following script, line (K) contains the `else` clause that goes with the `for` clause of line (B). The purpose of this script is to iterate through a list of names, discarding each name if it contains more than four characters. Since we want to structurally modify the list through which the `for` loop will be iterating, what we actually iterate through is a copy of the list in line (B). The notation `names[:]` returns a copy of the list of names as a separate object unto itself, as explained previously in Section 3.3.

[80] A `while` loop is also allowed to have an `else` clause in the same manner we show here for the `for` loop. Whereas the `else` clause for the `for` case is executed after the sequence in the `for` header has been completely iterated over, the `else` clause for a `while` loop is executed when the conditional in the `while` header becomes false.

This way we prevent the structural modifications from interfering with the process of stepping through a list.

```
#!/usr/bin/env python

### ForElse.py

names = ['yoyo', 'yuki', 'zaphod', 'xeno', 'trillian', 'tinu']        #(A)

for name in names[:]:                                                  #(B)
    if 1< len(name) <= 3:                                              #(C)
        continue                                                       #(D)
    if len(name) > 4:                                                  #(E)
        names.remove( name )                                           #(F)
    if len(name) == 1:                                                 #(G)
        print "one letter names not allowed -- good bye"               #(H)
        break                                                          #(I)
    print "name is a four-letter word"                                 #(J)
else:                                                                  #(K)
    print names               # ['yoyo', 'yuki', 'xeno', 'tinu']       #(L)
```

`continue` *and* `break` *for loop control*:

The above script also illustrated the `continue` and `break` keywords for controlling the looping action.[81] The `break` keyword causes the flow of control to break out of the loop.[82] The `continue` keyword transfers the flow of control to the next iteration without executing the rest of the statements in the body of the loop.

3.9.1 When Is a Conditional True or False?

The `if` and `while` control structures we have illustrated so far had simple conditionals in their headers. Python allows any object or any expression to be used as a conditional. Every object in Python can be evaluated for its truth value. If a conditional in an `if` or a `while` header returns one of the following objects, the conditional evaluates to false:

---

[81] These keywords work in the same manner in a `while` loop.

[82] In case of nested loops, the `break` statement causes the flow of control to break out of the inner loop to the enclosing loop.

- Null object: `None`
- Numbers: `0, 0.0, 0L`
- Empty strings: `'', "", '''''', """"""`
- Empty tuple: `()`
- Empty list: `[]`
- Empty dictionary: `{}`

As we have already shown in some of the scripts, an `if` or a `while` conditional frequently involves comparing two objects. As briefly mentioned previously in a footnote in Section 3.3.1, Python allows for *any two arbitrary objects* to be compared using the relational operators <, <=, >, and >=, and the equality operators == and `!=`. These operators have the usual meaning when the operands are both either the numeric types or the string types. In general, for class instances, overloading of the `__cmp__()` method tells the system how to compare two such instances. If this method is not overloaded, class instances are considered ordered according to their memory addresses. Objects of different types, when they are neither numeric nor strings, never compare as being equal. Also, when subject to relational comparisons, objects of different types are considered to be ordered by their typenames.[83] Other operators that also return truth values in `if` and `while` conditionals are `is` for testing the identity of an object, and its negation `is not`. Two other operators along similar lines are `in` and `not in` that test for membership in a sequence.

3.9.2 Complex Conditionals

More complex `if` and `while` conditionals can be constructed by using the binary Boolean operators `or` and `and` and the unary Boolean operator `not`. The operands supplied to these Boolean operators can be truth-value-yielding arbitrary expressions

---

[83]Python allows the comparison operators to be *chained* together, in the sense that you can write an `if` header in the following form:

```
if A < B < C :
    ...code...
```

The conditional shown would be interpreted as

```
if ( (A < B) and (B< C)) :
    ...code...
```

except that `B` would be evaluated only once *even when the truth values of both the Boolean components here,* `A<B` *and* `B<C`*, need to be ascertained.* However, due to the short-circuit semantics of Boolean operators (see the next subsection for what means), the second component, `B<C`, may not be needed for the determination of the truth value of the entire conditional. When that happens, `C` would remain unevaluated.

and/or arbitrary objects (since every Python object can be evaluated for its truth value).

When a logical expression in an `if` or a `while` conditional has two or more Boolean elements connected by either `and` or `or`, Python carries out a *short-circuit evaluation* of the logical expression. Therefore, in logical expressions of the form

```
A and B
A or B
```

the second operand, `B`, will be evaluated only if the truth value of the entire logical expression cannot be ascertained directly from the first operand. What that means is that if `A` is false in `A and B`, `B` will not be evaluated. By the same token, if `A` is true in `A or B`, `B` will not be evaluated. *What is returned by the evaluation of a Boolean expression is whatever is returned by the evaluation of the last Boolean component actually tested for its truth value.* Therefore, an evaluation of `A and B` will return the result of evaluating `A` if `A and B` is false on account of `A` being false, and the result of evaluating `B` if `A and B` is true. Similarly, an evaluation of `A or B` will return the result of evaluating `A` if `A or B` is true on account of `A` being true, but the result of evaluating `B` if `A or B` is false.

While on the subject of Boolean operators, we should also mention that the operator `not` has a lower precedence than the relational and the equality operators mentioned earlier. Therefore, a logical expression such as `not A == B` is interpreted as `not(A==B)`.

It is interesting to ponder that whereas the evaluation of a comparison operator (either relational or equality) yields a truth value, meaning that the result of evaluation is either `True` or `False`, the evaluation of the Boolean operators `and` and `or` yields an object corresponding to one of the operands. In the latter case, the object would then be evaluated for its truth value. This, however, is not the case with the unary Boolean operator `not`. This operator directly yields the truth value — which is the negation of the truth value of its operand.

3.10 MODULES IN PYTHON

As with Perl, Python supports the concept of module. One commonly places all the closely related definitions and code in a single physical file whose name typically ends in the suffix `.py`. Such a file is a module, its module name being the name of the file but without the suffix `.py`.

As with Perl, all Python code executes in the context of some module, *even when no module is mentioned explicitly.* For example, the top-level statements in a Python script are executed in the context of the implicit module `__main__`.[84] As to what specific module, implicit or explicit, a given Python statement belongs to has an important bearing on the name binding operations and scoping rules that apply to that statement. For example, all statements executed in the namespace of `__main__` have the interesting property that the *local namespace* is the same as the *global namespace*. Name binding, namespaces, and scoping rules are discussed further in Section 3.11.

To demonstrate a Python module, we will now create a module called `FetchOneOf` that consists of functions for fetching one of a data type from a disk-based text file. By "one of," we mean one of a string, one of an integer, and one of a floating-point number. These functions will have the following names:

```
fetchOneWord( file )
fetchOneInteger( file )
fetchOneFloat( file )
```

where `fetchOneWord()` will return a string, `fetchOneInteger()` an integer, and `fetchOneFloat()` a float, as you would expect. Each function will take one argument, an object of type `file` and return an object of the desired type. Our module will call `read(1)` to read one byte at a time from a disk file, grouping the characters thus read into individual words under the assumption that the words thus formed are separated by either blank spaces or the newline characters.

In the code for the module shown next, the first unassigned string, which is the string in line (A), is the documentation string for the module. It can be retrieved by an invocation such as

```
module_name.__doc__
```

Let's now focus on the function `fetchOneWord()` whose definition starts in line (B). This function reads the first byte of the disk file in line (D). If the read operation runs immediately into the end-of-file condition, it returns an empty string. So we check for the end-of-file condition in line (E). If true, the function also returns an empty string to indicate that there is nothing [or nothing further in an iterative invocation of `fetchOneWord()`] to be read from the file. If the character read in line (D) is a blank space or a newline character, we invoke the `while` loop in lines (G) and (H) to eat away consecutive appearances of such characters. The loop in lines (G) and (H) would be needed when a text file looks like

```
###$
$
$
######hello$
how are you
```

[84] We can also say that the top-level statements are executed in the namespace of `__main__`.

where # stands for a blank space and $ for a newline. After we are done consuming all the consecutively occurring blank spaces and newline characters, we check for the end-of-file condition again in line (I). If the end-of-file condition is encountered, we again return the empty string. If the end-of-file condition is not encountered, then it must be the case that the last character read in the loop of lines (G) and (H) was a word character (assuming a well-formed text file). So in the loop in lines (K) through (N), we form a complete word.

Here is our module `FetchOneOf`:

```
#!/usr/bin/env python

### FetchOneOf.py

'''This module is a collection of read functions for
   reading just one of something in a text file.'''                 #(A)

def fetchOneWord( filehandle ):                                      #(B)
    word = ""                                                         #(C)
    x = filehandle.read(1)                                            #(D)
    if x == '': return ""            # end of file condition          #(E)
    if (x == ' ') or ( x == '\n'):                                    #(F)
        while (x == ' ') or (x == '\n'):                              #(G)
            x = filehandle.read(1)                                    #(H)
    if x == '': return ""            # end of file condition          #(I)
    word = word + x                                                   #(J)
    while (x != ' ') and (x != '\n'):                                 #(K)
        x = filehandle.read(1)                                        #(L)
        if (x != ' ') and ( x != '\n'):                               #(M)
            word = word + x                                           #(N)
    return word                                                       #(O)

def fetchOneInteger( filehandle ):                                   #(P)
    word = fetchOneWord( filehandle )
    return int( word )

def fetchOneFloat( filehandle ):                                     #(Q)
    word = fetchOneWord( filehandle )
    return float( word )

def wordCount( filehandle ):                                         #(R)
    count = 0                                                         #(S)
    while (1 ):                                                       #(T)
        w = fetchOneWord( filehandle )                                #(U)
        if ( not w ): break                                           #(V)
        count = count + 1                                             #(W)
    return count                                                      #(X)
```

```
best_pie = "applepie"                                                  #(Y)

######################     Test code follows     #######################
#
# Test file info.txt:
#
#      how
#
#          are you
#    hello
#
#       123 456
#    789
#
#
# Test file a.data:
#
#    123 456 7890
#    345

if __name__ == '__main__':                                             #(Z)
    handle = open( 'info.txt' )
    newword = fetchOneWord( handle )
    print newword                                      # how
    newword = fetchOneWord( handle )
    print newword                                      # are
    newword = fetchOneWord( handle )
    print newword                                      # you
    handle.close()

    handle = open( 'a.data' )
    num = fetchOneInteger( handle )
    print num                                          # 123
    print type( num )                                  # <type 'int'>
    handle.close()

    handle = open( 'a.data' )
    num = fetchOneFloat( handle )
    print num                                          # 123.0
    print type( num )                                  # <type 'float'>
    handle.close()

    handle = open( 'info.txt' )
    print wordCount( handle )                          # 7
    handle.close()

    print best_pie                                     # applepie
```

Our module `FetchOneOf` looks like any other Python file we have shown before, except for the `if` statement in line (Z). That statement, reproduced below

```
if __name__ == '__main__':
```

allows the module test code to be placed in the module file itself, as shown in the rest of the module file above. When this file is executed on its own, the value of the global variable `__name__` is `__main__`, and therefore the code that follows the conditional of the `if` statement will execute. For the two text files whose contents are shown in the commented-out section above line (Z), the results produced by the test code are displayed in the commented-out portions of the statements below line (Z).

3.10.1 Importing a Module

The definitions laid out in a module are made available in a script through the mechanism of the `import` statement, as we show in the next script in line (A). The `import` statement loads the module into the global namespace of the script that invokes `import`, in the sense that the imported module is actually executed in the global namespace of the script doing the importing. This execution of the module code makes available the names — names that are defined in the global namespace of the module being imported — in the global namespace of the script invoking the `import` statement *provided they are accessed by their module qualified names*, as demonstrated by the calls to the module functions in lines (D) and (F). The module qualified name of the function `fetchOneWord()` that is defined in the module `FetchOneOf` is `FetchOneOf.fetchOneWord()`, and so on, for the other functions defined in the module. Line (I) demonstrates the invocation of the function `FetchOneOf.wordCount()` for counting the number of words in a text file. Before invoking this function, we reset the file pointer in line (H) to the beginning of the disk file.

```
#!/usr/bin/env python

### ModuleTest.py

# This script tests the module FetchOneOf in the same directory.

import FetchOneOf                                                    #(A)

print FetchOneOf.__doc__                                             #(B)

h = open( 'info.txt' )                                               #(C)

w = FetchOneOf.fetchOneWord( h )                                     #(D)
print w                                           # how              #(E)
```

```
w = FetchOneOf.fetchOneWord( h )                                     #(F)
print w                                     # are                    #(G)

h.seek(0)                                                            #(H)

print FetchOneOf.wordCount( h )             # 7                      #(I)

h.close()                                                            #(J)

print FetchOneOf.best_pie                   # applepie               #(K)
```

If a module did not already exist in a byte-compiled form, when a script that imports the module is first run, the module file is automatically byte compiled and the byte-compiled version left in the directory with the suffix `.pyc`.

In general, when you import a module into a Python script, the module is located by searching through the directory pathnames specified by either the environment variable `PYTHONPATH` or the attribute `sys.path`. If there are multiple modules of the same name in a search path, only the first is loaded in. So if multiple versions of a module are available and you want your program to load a particular version, you'd need to position the corresponding directory in the module search path accordingly. This can be done by invoking `insert()` on the list of pathnames that is stored in `sys.path`. If the location of the directory is not important, you can simply add the new directory to the end of the current search path by invoking `append()`, as in

```
import sys
sys.path.append( "/home/kak/new_modules" )
```

A module is loaded in only once. That is the case even if there are multiple import statements for a target module. This fact remains valid even if multiple import statements for a target module are contained in other modules that are imported into a script. *Also note that a Python module is executed when it is loaded in.*

3.10.2 Importing Specific Names from a Module

Importing a module is not the same thing as importing names from a module.[85] Importing a module means that Python has pulled the module code into the current script (by executing the module file), while maintaining the separate namespace identity of the code pulled in. So if you want to access a name in that module, you have to use the namespace qualified syntax for reaching that name. On the other hand, importing names from a module means that those names become a part of the

[85]This subsection will become clearer after the reader has gone through Sections 3.11.2 and 3.11.3 of this chapter.

global namespace that is doing the importing of the names. This is illustrated by the syntax used in line (A) in the following version of the previous script. Now we want the names `fetchOneWord`, `fetchOneInteger`, and `best_pie` to be imported into the global namespace of the `ImportNamesOnly.py` script. Since the names imported in this manner become a part of the global namespace of the current script, you do not have to use the module qualifications for such names. This is illustrated by the function invocations in lines (D) and (F) below. The following version of the `from...import` syntax used in line (A):

```
from module_name import *
```

imports *all* of the names defined in the module namespace dictionary into the current namespace. Now all of those names can be used directly in the current namespace, that is, such names can be used without module qualification.[86]

```
#!/usr/bin/env python

### ImportNamesOnly.py

from FetchOneOf import fetchOneWord, fetchOneInteger, best_pie      #(A)

#print FetchOneOf.__doc__                      # Error                #(B)

h = open( 'info.txt' )                                               #(C)

w = fetchOneWord( h )                                                #(D)
print w                                        # how                  #(E)
w = fetchOneWord( h )                                                #(F)
print w                                        # are                  #(G)

h.close()

h = open( 'a.data' )

i = fetchOneInteger( h )
print i

print best_pie                                 # applepie             #(H)
```

[86]It is *not* a matter of choice whether or not to use the module qualified names when the `from...import` syntax is used. With this syntax, the name of the module itself is not available in the global namespace of the script invoking the import statement. So the dotted notation for accessing the modules names would not work even if we wanted to use that notation. This also explains why we have commented out line (B) in the `ImportNamesOnly.py` script. Since the module name `FetchOneOf` would not be known in the namespace of the script `ImportNamesOnly.py`, uncommenting line (B) would elicit the error report: "`NameError: name 'FetchOneOf' is not defined.`"

3.11 SCOPING RULES, NAMESPACES, AND NAME RESOLUTION

The basic unit of a Python script is a *code block*. Every code block has its own namespace. The following "objects" constitute code blocks:

- Script file
- Module
- Function body
- Class definition

A name is considered to be *bound* in the local namespace of a code block if any of the following *name binding operations* takes place with regard to that name in the code block:

- A name is assigned to.
- A name is used as a function name in a `def` construct.
- A name is used as a class name in a `class` construct.
- A module name used as the target of an `import module_name` statement.
- A name, such as `some_name` below, that is the target of an import statement like

  ```
  from module_name import some_name
  ```

  The name `some_name` is bound in the namespace of the code block containing the `import` statement.
- For code blocks that are function bodies, a name that is a parameter in the function header is bound to the namespace of that function.

A name bound to a code block by any of the name binding operations listed above has *local scope* with regard to that code block. A variable with local scope in a code block is a *local variable* inside that code block. Any assignments made to a local name of any kind will not be visible outside the code block. We can also say that a *local binding for a name hides any bindings for that name in any of the enclosing scopes.*

If a name is *not* bound in the local namespace of a code block *and if the name is not declared* `global`, its binding from the innermost enclosing code block is used. If this immediately enclosing code block does not bind that name, the meaning from the next higher enclosing code block is used. If a name is declared `global`, its meaning corresponds to the module-level binding for that name. We will illustrate this point later with an example. But, remember, that `global` in Python means module level, which for the script file being executed also means at the level of the script file or at the level of `__main__`. The global level is also informally referred to as the *top-level*.

For illustration, in example 1 of the next script, `ScopingRules.py`, lines (A) and (B) initialize two new variables `i` and `j`. These variables are in the enclosing scope of the function `foo()` defined in line (C). The same variable names are used inside the function `foo()` in the commented-out line (D) and in line (E). As variables referenced locally, the call to `i` in line (D) elicits an error report from the compiler, but the call to `j` in line (E) creates no problems. That is because the value of the variable `j` is not changed inside the function `foo()` of line (C), so its global value can be accessed without any problems inside the body of the function. On the other hand, since `i` is assigned to in line (F), it becomes a local variable to the code block in lines (C) through (H). Therefore, accessing it in line (D) is illegal because there it is referenced before any initialization. Subsequently, line (F) initializes this variable to value 100. We invoke the function `foo()` of line (C) in line (I) and print out the value of the variable `i` in line (J). As can be seen, the value printed out in line (J) is what was set in line (A). In other words, the variable `i` defined and used inside `foo()` is invisible outside the function.

By contrast, in example 2 of the script, we redefine the function `foo()` in line (K). We now declare the variable `i` to be global in line (L) of this function. This means that the variable `i` used inside `foo()` of line (K) will be the same *as in the enclosing scope of the function call in line (P)*. Since line (O) sets the value of this variable equal to 500, when we call the function in line (P), it is this value that will be printed out by line (M) of the function. Line (N) of the function will reset the value of `i` to 1000. Because `i` is global, when we print out the value of this variable in line (Q), we get 1000.

The rest of the script, in lines (R) through (Z), shows an example of declaring multiple variables `global` simultaneously inside a function and then examining the values of these variables after the function is called.

```
#!/usr/bin/env python

### ScopingRules.py

# Example 1:
i = 10                                                          #(A)
j = 10                                                          #(B)

def foo():                                                      #(C)
#    print i                                  # ERROR           #(D)
    print j                                   # 10              #(E)
    i = 100                                                     #(F)
```

```
    m = i * j                                                    #(G)
    print m                                # 1000                #(H)

foo()                                                            #(I)
print i                                    # 10                  #(J)


# Example 2:
def foo():                                                       #(K)
    global i                                                     #(L)
    print i                                                      #(M)
    i = 1000                                                     #(N)


i = 500                                                          #(O)
foo()                                      # line (M): 500       #(P)
print i                                    # 1000                #(Q)


# Example 3:
name = age = position = gender = None                            #(R)

def setUserInfo( aname, years, gend, pos ):                      #(S)
    global name, age, position, gender                           #(T)
    name = aname                                                 #(U)
    age = years                                                  #(V)
    gender = gend                                                #(W)
    position = pos                                               #(X)

setUserInfo( 'Zaphod', 125, 'male', 'boss' )                     #(Y)
print name, age, gender, position          # Zaphod 125 male boss#(Z)
```

3.11.1 Nested Namespaces

We will now talk about *nested namespaces* and show that when a name cannot be found in the dictionary corresponding to the local namespace of a code block, the name will be searched for in the namespace corresponding to the innermost enclosing code block. If the name is not found there, it will be searched for in the next higher innermost enclosing code block, and so on. We will use the built-in functions `locals()` and `globals()` to display the namespace dictionaries at different points in the script. But note that the function `globals()` only shows the module-level namespace regardless of where it is invoked in the script. Nonetheless, by printing out the values of the variables not available in the local scope, we will be able to see how Python's name resolution works.

The next script, NestedScope.py, defines two names, x and y, in lines (A) and (B) at the module level, the module being implicitly __main__. Displayed immediately after the calls to print in lines (C) and (D) are the dictionaries for the local and the global namespaces. As we will see, at the module level, both the local and the global namespaces are always identical. In addition to the user-introduced names x and y, the two namespaces contain the system-supplied names: __name__ whose value is __main__; __doc__ with value the null object None; and __builtins__ whose value is the module __builtin__. The module __builtin__ provides direct access to all the built-in functions, such as open(), locals(), globals(), etc., of Python.

The script then contains a function definition statement def starting in line (E). It is important to realize that this statement is an assignment in just the same sense as the assignments in lines (A) and (B), the assignment here being of the body of the function in lines (F) through (U) to the name foo. In other words, the multiline construct in lines (E) through (U) introduces another name into both the local and the global namespaces of the implicit module __main__, the name being foo. We can see this fact when we print out the two namespaces in lines (V) and (W).

The execution of the def statement in line (E) is *not* tantamount to the execution of the body of the function foo() defined in lines (E) through (U). The statements in the body of this function will only be executed when the function foo() is called, as in line (X).

Let's now examine what happens when the body of the function foo() is executed as a result of the call in line (X). The assignments in lines (F) and (G) are name binding operations; therefore, they inject the two names x and z into the local scope of the code block for the function foo(). The print statement of line (H) displays this namespace. On the other hand, when we print out the global namespace in line (I), we get the same dictionary as the module-level global namespace that was printed out earlier by the print statement in line (W).

The function foo() of line (E) contains a nested function, bar(), whose definition begins in line (J) and ends just prior to line (S). The execution of the def statement of line (J) introduces the name bar in the local namespace of the function foo(). This is shown by the output displayed in response to the print statement of line (S). But note that the global namespace at the same point, as shown after line (T), remains the same as printed out earlier in line (W) because that namespace is the module-level namespace.[87]

Let's now see what happens when we call bar() in line (U) as the last statement inside the body of function foo(). At the very outset, as shown by the call to locals() in line (K), the local namespace for bar() is empty because of the absence of any name binding operations. The call to globals() in line (L), on the

[87]Note that at run time line (T) is executed after line (W) because the former is executed as a result of the call to foo() in line (X).

other hand, produces the same result as the earlier call to the same function in line (V).

Line (M) shows what happens if you reference a name that has not yet been assigned to and that will eventually be added to the local namespace of a code block through a name binding operation. Even though the name x belongs to the parent block's namespace available in line (M), that definition of x is not available in line (M) because a local x will subsequently be added to the local namespace through the assignment in line (P).

Contrast the response we elicit from the interpreter in line (M) with the responses in lines (N) and (O). The name in line (N) is resolved by a lookup in the global namespace and the name in line (O) by a lookup in the parent code block's namespace.

That takes us to the assignment in line (P), the source of our earlier difficulty with accessing x in line (M). This assignment introduces the name x into the local namespace of the code block of function bar(), as can be seen by the output produced by the print statement of line (Q). The global namespace produced in the next print statement in line (R) remains the same, because it is always the module-level namespace.

```
#!/usr/bin/python

### NestedScope.py


x = 1                                                               #(A)
y = 1                                                               #(B)

print locals()                                                      #(C)
           # {'__builtins__': <module '__builtin__' (built-in)>,
           #  '__name__': '__main__',
           #  'y': 1,
           #  '__doc__': None,
           #  'x': 1}

print globals()                                                     #(D)
           # {'__builtins__': <module '__builtin__' (built-in)>,
           #  '__name__': '__main__',
           #  'y': 1,
           #  '__doc__': None,
           #  'x': 1}

def foo():                                                          #(E)
    x = 2                                                           #(F)
    z = 2                                                           #(G)
    print locals()                                                  #(H)
           # {'x': 2,
```

```
        #  'z': 2}
    print globals()                                                     #(I)
        # {'y': 1,
        #  'x': 1,
        #  '__builtins__': <module '__builtin__' (built-in)>,
        #  '__name__': '__main__',
        #  'foo': <function foo at 0x805bf1c>,
        #  '__doc__': None}
    def bar():                                                          #(J)
        print locals()                                                  #(K)
        # {}
        print globals()                                                 #(L)
        # {'y': 1,
        #  'x': 1,
        #  '__builtins__': <module '__builtin__' (built-in)>,
        #  '__name__': '__main__',
        #  'foo': <function foo at 0x805bf1c>,
        #  '__doc__': None}
#       print x                   # ERROR                               #(M)
        print y                   # 1                                   #(N)
        print z                   # 2                                   #(O)
        x = 5                                                           #(P)
        print locals()                                                  #(Q)
        # {'x': 5}

        print globals()                                                 #(R)
        # {'y': 1,
        #  'x': 1,
        #  '__builtins__': <module '__builtin__' (built-in)>,
        #  '__name__': '__main__',
        #  'foo': <function foo at 0x805bf1c>,
        #  '__doc__': None}

    print locals()                                                      #(S)
        # {'x': 2,
        #  'z': 2,
        #  'bar': <function bar at 0x804f664>}
    print globals()                                                     #(T)
        # {'y': 1,
        #  'x': 1,
        #  '__builtins__': <module '__builtin__' (built-in)>,
        #  '__name__': '__main__',
        #  'foo': <function foo at 0x805bf1c>,
        #  '__doc__': None}

    bar()                                                               #(U)


print locals()                                                          #(V)
```

```
          # {'y': 1,
          #  'x': 1,
          #  '__builtins__': <module '__builtin__' (built-in)>,
          #  '__name__': '__main__',
          #  'foo': <function foo at 0x805bf1c>,
          #  '__doc__': None}

print globals()                                                    #(W)
          # {'y': 1,
          #  'x': 1,
          #  '__builtins__': <module '__builtin__' (built-in)>,
          #  '__name__': '__main__',
          #  'foo': <function foo at 0x805bf1c>,
          #  '__doc__': None}

foo()                                                              #(X)
```

3.11.2 Name Resolution for Imported Modules

The discussion so far should have made the following points clear to the reader:

- A name binding operation, such as an assignment or a `def` statement, introduces a name into the local scope of a code block.
- If a name is not subject to a name binding operation in a code block, its meaning is resolved using the parent code block's namespace. If the name does not exist in the parent code block's namespace, the search continues to the namespace at the next higher level, and so on.
- If it is necessary for a name to be subject to a name binding operation but the name must be resolved using the namespace at the module level, that name must be declared `global`.

We will now show another script to illustrate the following features of how names are resolved in Python:

- When a module is imported into a script, its names reside in a separate namespace specific to that module. The dictionary holding this namespace can be accessed through the `__dict__` attribute for the module. This dictionary is also referred to as the *module's symbol table*.
- When a name that belongs to an imported module is given a new value in a script, that change is stored in the namespace dictionary specific to that module.

- When a function is called in a script, the names of the parameters of the function are added to the namespace specific to the code block corresponding to the function body.

The `NamespacesWithImport.py` script shown next illustrates these features of namespace resolution. This script imports the module `FetchOneOf` in line (A). This user-defined module was presented earlier in Section 3.10. Line (B) then prints out the symbol table of this module, which is the same thing as the namespace dictionary specific to that module. This dictionary, created when the `import` statement of line (A) is executed, contains all the top-level user-defined names in the module `FetchOneOf` and also all the system-supplied built-in names available inside that module. Recall that the module `FetchOneOf` contains definitions for the functions `fetchOneWord()`, `fetchOneInteger()`, `fetchOneFloat()`, and `wordCount()`, and the variable `best_pie`. All of these user-introduced names make their appearance in the namespace dictionary shown in the commented out section below line (B). This dictionary also contains the names of the attributes `__name__`, `__file__`, and `__doc__` that the system implicitly supplies to every module, with `__name__` storing the name of the module, `__file__` storing the name of the byte-compiled file containing the module, and `__doc__` storing the documentation string for the module.

Line (C) defines a module-level variable `N` and sets its value to 2. [We will use this variable as a "global" variable inside the function `getNthWord()` defined in line (F).] When we now print out the local and the global namespaces associated with the top level in the script, we get what is shown in the commented-out sections after the lines (D) and (E). Note how the `import` statement of line (A) has caused the name `FetchOneOf` to be added to the two namespaces. The value associated with this name is, of course, the module `FetchOneOf`.

Line (F) defines the function `getNthWord()`. The purpose of this function is to fetch the `(N+1)st` word from a text file, with the index 0 designating the first word in the file. The word fetched by this function corresponds to the value of the variable `N` in line (C). For the example shown, since the value of `N` is 2, this function should retrieve the third word from the file `info.txt`.

Invocation of `getNthWord()` in line (W) causes the body of the function in lines (G) through (U) to be executed by the interpreter. Let's now see what happens to the various namespaces as this code block is being executed. When we print out the namespace local to this code block in line (G), we see only one entry in it. This is the entry for the parameter of the function. As demonstrated, the function namespace that is created when a function is called has name entries for all the parameters of the function. This namespace is local to the code block that constitutes the body of the function.

On the other hand, the module-level namespace printed out in line (H) is essentially the same as the module-level namespace printed out in line (E), except for the addition of the entry for the name `getNthWord`. This entry was made in the module-level namespace when the `def` statement in line (F) was seen by the interpreter — something that happened before the invocation of the function `getNthWord()` in line (W).

Next we try to retrieve the value of `N` in line (I), hoping that its global value as set in line (C) would be printed out. But that does not work because of the following reason: Since `N` is assigned to in line (T) in the code block of the function `getNthWord()`, it would ordinarily be added to the local namespace of the code block. But since `N` is declared `global` — but not until line (Q) — it cannot be added to the local namespace and its meaning must be derived from the enclosing code block, but in this case that happens only after the declaration in line (Q).

Let's now see as to what namespace is modified if we alter the value of a name internal to a module. In line (J), we print out the current value of the variable `FetchOneOf.best_pie`. Line (K) changes the value of this variable. When we now print out the symbol table of the module `FetchOneOf` in line (M), we see that value stored for the name `best_pie` reflects the change we made in line (K). In fact, that is the only difference between the module symbol table presented earlier through line (B) and the same shown now through line (M). As shown by the outputs for the lines (N) and (O), the local and the global namespaces at this juncture remain the same as they were earlier in lines (G) and (H).

The main work of the function `getNthWord()` is done in lines (P) through (U). The `while` loop in lines (R) through (T) consumes each word in the text file until the file pointer is at the start of the desired word. The next call to `fetchOneWord()` in line (U) then fetches this word.

Line (Z) demonstrates the fact that any changes made to the assignment of a name internal to a module anywhere in a script — either directly or inside any contained code blocks — will be subsequently visible everywhere.

```
#!/usr/bin/env python

### NamespacesWithImport.py

import FetchOneOf                                                    #(A)

print FetchOneOf.__dict__                                            #(B)
        # {'fetchOneWord': <function fetchOneWord at 0x804e6f4>,
        #  'fetchOneFloat': <function fetchOneFloat at 0x806e71c>,
        #  '__builtins__': {'help': Type help() for interactive help, or
        #                           help(object) for help about object.,
        #                    'vars': <built-in function vars>,
        #                    'pow': <built-in function pow>,
        #                    .......
        #                    .......
        #                    ....... }
```

```
        #  '__name__': 'FetchOneOf',
        #  '__file__': 'FetchOneOf.pyc',
        #  'best_pie': 'apple',
        #  'wordCount': <function wordCount at 0x806018c>,
        #  '__doc__': 'This module ........... '
        #  'fetchOneInteger': <function fetchOneInteger at 0x80663bc>}

N = 2                                                              #(C)

print locals()                                                     #(D)
        # {'__builtins__': <module '__builtin__' (built-in)>,
        #  '__name__': '__main__',
        #  'N': 2,
        #  '__doc__': None,
        #  'FetchOneOf': <module 'FetchOneOf' from 'FetchOneOf.pyc'>}

print globals()                                                    #(E)
        # {'__builtins__': <module '__builtin__' (built-in)>,
        #  '__name__': '__main__',
        #  'N': 2,
        #  '__doc__': None,
        #  'FetchOneOf': <module 'FetchOneOf' from 'FetchOneOf.pyc'>}

def getNthWord( filename ):                                        #(F)
    print locals()                                                 #(G)
        # {'filename': 'info.txt'}
    print globals()                                                #(H)
        # {'getNthWord': <function getNthWord at 0x8066374>,
        #  'FetchOneOf': <module 'FetchOneOf' from 'FetchOneOf.pyc'>,
        #  '__builtins__': <module '__builtin__' (built-in)>,
        #  '__name__': '__main__',
        #  '__doc__': None,
        #  'N': 2}
#   print N                                       # ERROR          #(I)

    print FetchOneOf.best_pie                     # applepie       #(J)
    FetchOneOf.best_pie = "cherrypie"                              #(K)
    print FetchOneOf.best_pie                     # cherrypie      #(L)

    print FetchOneOf.__dict__                                      #(M)
        # {'fetchOneWord': <function fetchOneWord at 0x804e6f4>,
        #  'fetchOneFloat': <function fetchOneFloat at 0x806e71c>,
        #  '__builtins__': {'help': Type help() for interactive help, or
        #                           help(object) for help about object.,
        #                   'vars': <built-in function vars>,
        #                   'pow': <built-in function pow>,
        #                   .......
        #                   .......
        #                   ....... }
```

```
        #  '__name__': 'FetchOneOf',
        #  '__file__': 'FetchOneOf.pyc',
        #  'best_pie': 'cherrypie',
        #  'wordCount': <function wordCount at 0x806018c>,
        #  '__doc__': 'This module ........... '
        #  'fetchOneInteger': <function fetchOneInteger at 0x80663bc>}

    print locals()                                                      #(N)
        # {'filename': 'info.txt'}
    print globals()                                                     #(O)
        # {'getNthWord': <function getNthWord at 0x80663cc>,
        #  'FetchOneOf': <module 'FetchOneOf' from 'FetchOneOf.pyc'>,
        #  '__builtins__': <module '__builtin__' (built-in)>,
        #  '__name__': '__main__',
        #  '__doc__': None,
        #  'N': 2}

    h = open( filename )                                                #(P)
    global N                                                            #(Q)
    while N > 0:                                                        #(R)
        FetchOneOf.fetchOneWord( h )                                    #(S)
        N = N - 1                                                       #(T)
    return FetchOneOf.fetchOneWord( h )                                 #(U)


print N                                            # 2                  #(V)
w = getNthWord( 'info.txt' )                                            #(W)
print w                                            # you                #(X)
print N                                            # 0                  #(Y)

print FetchOneOf.best_pie                          # cherrypie          #(Z)
```

3.11.3 What about the Names Imported with from...import Syntax?

Let's now see how the namespaces created during the execution of a script are affected when names are imported into a script by using the

```
from some_module import name1, name2, ...
```

syntax. As we will see, this syntax behaves very differently from the

```
import some_module
```

syntax. A module symbol table is no longer constructed for the former case. In fact, as we already mentioned in Section 3.10.2, the name of the module from which the names are imported is not even recognized when names are imported with the `from...import` syntax.[88]

In the script that follows, we use the `from...import` syntax to import the names `fetchOneWord` and `best_pie` from the module `FetchOneOf` into the script, meaning into the implicitly defined module `__main__`. When we try to print out the symbol table for the `FetchOneOf` module, we get an error, as pointed out in the commented-out line (B). That's because the new syntax does not directly import the module name into the current scope. This can be seen by printing out the local and the global namespaces (which, of course, would be identical, based on our previous discussion), as we have done via the print statements in lines (C) and (D). Note that the module name, `FetchOneOf`, is not listed in the local or the global namespaces associated with the script that is being executed by the interpreter. However, the imported names, `fetchOneWord` and `best_pie` are listed *as if they were defined locally in the script.*

In conclusion, the `from...import` syntax causes the imported names to behave as if they are locally defined in a script. This is borne out by the listings for the names `fetchOneWord` and `best_pie` in the namespaces shown in the commented out sections after lines (C) and (D).

To further exemplify the same notion, when we open a text file in line (E) and assign a file object to the name `handle`, the name is incorporated into the script-specific namespaces, as illustrated by the output produced by line (F). As far as these namespaces are concerned, there is no distinction to be made between a locally defined name such as `handle` and the imported names such as `fetchOneOf` and `best_pie`. The same applies to the locally defined name `w` in line (G). It is injected into the script-specific namespaces and treated on par with the other locally defined names and the names imported via the syntax in line (A).

```
#!/usr/bin/env python

### NamespacesWithImportedNames.py

from FetchOneOf import fetchOneWord, best_pie                          #(A)

# print FetchOneOf.__dict__                # ERROR                      #(B)

print locals()                                                          #(C)
        # {'fetchOneWord': <function fetchOneWord at 0x8069d74>,
        #  '__builtins__': <module '__builtin__' (built-in)>,
        #  '__name__': '__main__',
```

[88] The discussion here pertaining to the importation of names with the `from...import` syntax obviously also applies to its wild-card form `from some_module import *` that would cause all the top-level names from the named module to be imported into the current scope.

```
        #  '__doc__': None,
        #  'best_pie': 'applepie'}


print globals()                                                    #(D)
        # {'fetchOneWord': <function fetchOneWord at 0x8069d74>,
        #  '__builtins__': <module '__builtin__' (built-in)>,
        #  '__name__': '__main__',
        #  '__doc__': None,
        #  'best_pie': 'applepie'}

handle = open( "info.txt" )                                        #(E)

print locals()                                                     #(F)
        # {'fetchOneWord': <function fetchOneWord at 0x8069d74>,
        #  'handle': <open file 'info.txt', mode 'r' at 0x8092c40>,
        #  '__builtins__': <module '__builtin__' (built-in)>,
        #  '__name__': '__main__',
        #  '__doc__': None,
        #  'best_pie': 'applepie'}

w = fetchOneWord( handle )                                         #(G)

print locals()                                                     #(H)
        # {'fetchOneWord': <function fetchOneWord at 0x8069d74>,
        #  'handle': <open file 'info.txt', mode 'r' at 0x8092c40>,
        #  'w': 'how',
        #  '__builtins__': <module '__builtin__' (built-in)>,
        #  '__name__': '__main__',
        #  '__doc__': None,
        #  'best_pie': 'applepie'}

print w                    # how                                   #(I)
```

3.11.4 Deeply Nested Namespaces and the global Declaration

We mentioned earlier that when a name is bound in a code block, it becomes local to that code block, unless the name is declared to be `global` anywhere in that code block. We now want to reemphasize that `global` does *not* imply the immediately enclosing code block. The `global` declaration for a name causes the module-level definition for that name to be used.

The script below defines a function `foo1()` in line (B). Nested inside `foo1()` is the definition for another function, `foo2()` in line (D). And nested inside `foo2()` is yet another function `foo3()` in line (F). The script contains four code blocks, the top level and the three that are nested one inside the other. The assignment to the name x in line (A) is at the top level, or the script level, or the level of `__main__`, all three standing for the same thing. The assignments to the same name in the lines (C) and (E) are in the nested code blocks corresponding to the function definitions for `foo1()` and `foo2()`, respectively.

Finally, the nested code block for the function `foo3()` declares the name `x` to be `global`. This causes the global definition, meaning the module-level binding, for the name `x` to become visible inside the body of `foo3()`, hiding all other bindings for the same name in any of the enclosing code blocks. This fact is demonstrated by the output produced by the print statement in line (H).

```
#!/usr/bin/env python

### DeeplyNested.py

x = 1                                                           #(A)

def foo1():                                                     #(B)
    x = 2                                                       #(C)
    def foo2():                                                 #(D)
        x = 3                                                   #(E)
        def foo3():                                             #(F)
            global x                                            #(G)
            print x                   # 1                       #(H)
        foo3()                                                  #(I)
    foo2()                                                      #(J)
foo1()                                                          #(K)
```

3.11.5 Python Is Lexically Scoped

All of the decisions as to what namespace a given name should be resolved in are made at compile time. It is the compiler that generated the namespace dictionaries we have shown in the examples presented so far. This is referred to as *static scoping* or *lexical scoping* and we say that Python is either *statically scoped* or *lexically scoped*. We may also refer to the manner in which Python deals with scoping as *statically nested scoping* because if a name cannot be resolved in the namespace of the current scope, the compiler will try to resolve it in the namespace of the nearest enclosing scope that has a binding for that name.

3.12 THE eval() FUNCTION

As described in Section 2.14 of Chapter 2, Perl's `eval()` serves two purposes: It is used for evaluating a string that is ostensibly a piece of Perl code and it is used to trap run-time errors in Perl code. The same function in Python is used for just one purpose — for evaluating a string that is supposedly a snippet of Python code. For trapping run-time errors in Python, you use its `try-except` mechanism presented in Chapter 10.

The script shown next, `Eval.py`, demonstrates Python's `eval()` in action. We ask a user to enter in the command line a polynomial in the variables `x` and `y` using the commonly-employed convention that a variable and an integer occurring together implies a multiplication between them and the symbol `^` stands for exponentiation. Here are some examples:

```
x^6 + y^3 + x - 10y
x^3 - y^3
20y + 10x^3
...
```

The script evaluates the polynomials for `x=3` and `y=4` in the `xy`-plane and prints out the answer. A polynomial expression is evaluated by calling `eval()` in line (D); `eval()` returns the value obtained by evaluating the first argument string as a Python expression. Since we can only feed strings that constitute legal Python expressions for the first argument to `eval()`, we need the substitution operations in lines (C) and (D). The purpose of line (C) is to insert the multiplication operator `*` between the integer part and the variable part[89] in string fragments such as `10x` and the purpose of the string replacement operation in line (D) is to replace the symbol `^` by the exponentiation operator `**`. After the substitutions in lines (C) and (D), a user-entered string such as

```
20y + 10x^3
```

becomes the legal Python expression

```
20*y + 10*x**3
```

Note how the values for `x` and `y` are supplied to the `eval()` function through the dictionary `mydict` defined in line (A). It is possible to call `eval()` with just one argument — the string that needs to be evaluated as a Python expression. In that case, Python will use the global and the local namespaces that hold at the point when `eval()` is called for resolving the names in the string. What that implies is that the following would also work:

```
x = 3
y = 4
```

[89]The syntax used in line (C) will become clear after the reader has gone through Chapter 4.

```
print eval( "x**2 + y**3" )
```

where `eval()` acquires the values for `x` and `y` from the local namespace dictionary applicable at the point of call to `eval()`. In general, `eval()` can be called with one argument as shown above, with two arguments, as shown in the script below, or with three arguments, as in

```
eval( expression_string, dict_globals, dict_locals )
```

When only a single dictionary is supplied in addition to the first argument string, that dictionary is used as both a local namespace and the global namespace for the evaluation of the first argument string. In either case, the dictionary `__builtins__` is implicitly supplied to the namespace used by `eval()`.

```
#!/usr/bin/env python

### Eval.py

import re

mydict = { 'x' : 3, 'y' : 4 }                                          #(A)

entry = raw_input("Enter a polynomial in x, and y."
                  " Use '^' for powers: ")                             #(B)

entry = re.sub( r'\b(\d*)(x|y)', r'\1*\2', entry )                     #(C)

print eval( entry.replace('^', '**'), mydict )                         #(D)
```

3.13 map() AND filter() FUNCTIONS

Python provides three built-in functions, `map()`, `filter()`, and `reduce()`, that are lumped together under the label *functional programming tools*.[90] These take a

[90] The functional approach to programming seeks to compute primarily through the mechanism of function evaluation and without resorting to side-effects during such evaluation. Claiming that a majority of program errors occur because variables obtain unexpected values during program execution, adherents of functional programming seek to eliminate all assignment statements. Functions are treated as *first-class objects* in functional programming, meaning that a function has all of the properties of a data object. For example, a function can be passed around as an argument to other functions. Functional style of programming, as exemplified by Lisp and Scheme, also favors recursion as the primary control structure. Looping is accomplished by processing a list through recursive operations on sublists.

function object as the first argument and a list as the second argument. The function is evaluated on each element of the list.

Comparing Perl and Python with regard to these functional programming tools, what `grep()` does for Perl, `filter()` does for Python. Using `filter()` to invoke a function on a list (or a tuple or a string or any container that supports iteration, for that matter) causes the function to be applied to every element of the list (or whatever the target container is). A call to `filter()` returns a list of only those elements for which the function invocation returns true. In general, the object returned by `filter()` is a list, except when the target container is either a tuple or a string, in which case the output object is the same as the target container.

The built-in function `map()` also works the same way as its counterpart in Perl. We can use `map()` to invoke a function on every element of a list (or any container that supports iteration). A call to `map()` returns an object that is always a list. The output list consists of values returned by the individual invocations of the first argument function on each element of the target container.

The next script, `MapFilter.py`, illustrates the common uses of both `filter()` and `map()`. In lines (C) through (X), the goal of the script is as follows:

1. Allow a user to make a command-line entry of a pattern (which can be a regular expression) in response to a prompt from the script.

2. Check the pattern for its legality. (As we will discuss in Chapter 4, a regular expression must not violate certain rules of syntax for it to be legal.) If the pattern is illegal, ask the user to enter another pattern.

3. Compare the pattern entered with each line of a designated text file. Print out all lines for which matches are scored (very much like the `grep` Unix utility).

4. Terminate a session if the user presses the Enter key without supplying a pattern.

Lines (D) though (H) open the designated text file for reading. Line (I) first calls `read()` to slurp in the whole file into a single string object, and then calls `split()` on the string object to split it into a list of individual lines. Lines (J) and (K) define a one-argument print function that we will invoke via `map()` on a list of text lines. Lines (L) through (X) define an infinite loop for the user interaction. The first thing we do in this loop is to ask the user to enter a pattern in line (M) that we check for non-emptiness (except for white space) in line (N). The entered pattern is then checked for its correctness in the `try-except` construct of lines (P) through (S). If the pattern is illegal, the call to `re.compile()` will throw an exception. [See Chapter 4 for a discussion on `re.compile()`.] By trapping the exception, we are able to let the user try again through the invocation of `continue` in line (S).

Line (T) demonstrates the use of `filter()` to select only those lines that score a match with the user-entered pattern. The first argument to `filter()` is the method `regex.search()` defined for regular expression objects. A call to `regex.search()` will return `None` if there is no match with the string that is provided to the method as its argument. If any matching lines are found at all, line (V) then calls `map()` to invoke our print function `myprint()` on each of those matching lines.

A special feature of the built-in `filter()` is that if the first argument function is `None`, that implies that we want to apply the *identity function* to each element of the target list. That in effect says that we want each element of the target list to be evaluated for its truth value. Thus only those elements that evaluate to `True` are included in the output list. This property of `filter()` is demonstrated in lines (Y) through (a). The list in line (Y) includes many elements that evaluate to false in Python. As seen by the output list printed out in line (a), all of these elements are excluded by `filter()`.

We also want to demonstrate that `map()` can take additional arguments beyond the customary two (which are the function and a target list). Each additional argument to `map()` becomes a source for one more argument to the named function. This effect is illustrated with lines (b), (c), and (d). Line (b) defines a function `func()` of two variables, `x` and `y`. Line (c) asks `map()` to apply `func()` to pairs of arguments, with the first argument taken from the tuple `(1,2,3,4)` and the second from the tuple `(101,102,103,104)`. That is, `map()` will construct function calls like `func(1,101)`, `func(2,102)`, etc.

When `map()` is called with multiple container arguments, the different containers can be of unequal length. When `map()` runs out of the arguments supplied by a container, it uses `None` by default. As was the case with `filter()`, it is also possible to call `map()` with `None` for its first argument. In that case, `map()` returns a list of tuples, each tuple consisting of the elements at the same position in each of the containers. We illustrate both these effects in line (e).

```
#!/usr/bin/env python

### MapFilter.py

import sys                                                          #(A)
import re                                                           #(B)

print "Press ENTER with no input to end session\n"                  #(C)

try:                                                                #(D)
   FILE = open('data.txt', 'r')                                     #(E)
except IOError, e:                                                  #(F)
    print "Unable to open file: ", e                                #(G)
    sys.exit(1)                                                     #(H)

all_lines =  FILE.read().split("\n")                                #(I)
```

```
def myprint(item):                                                  #(J)
    if item: print item                                             #(K)

while 1:                                                            #(L)
    pattern = raw_input( "Enter a pattern: " )                      #(M)
    if pattern.lstrip().rstrip() == '': break                       #(N)
    try:                                                            #(O)
        regex = re.compile( pattern )                               #(P)
    except:                                                         #(Q)
        print "error in your pattern, try again"                    #(R)
        continue                                                    #(S)
    matched_lines = filter( regex.search, all_lines )               #(T)
    if matched_lines:                                               #(U)
        map(myprint, matched_lines)                                 #(V)
    else:                                                           #(W)
        print "no match"                                            #(X)

x = [None, 0, [], (), 1, 2, 3, ('a', 'b'), {}, ('a',), None]        #(Y)
y = filter( None, x )                                               #(Z)
print y                     # [1, 2, 3, ('a', 'b'), ('a',)]         #(a)

def func(x, y): return x**2 + y                                     #(b)
res = map( func, (1, 2, 3, 4), (101, 102, 103, 104) )               #(c)
print res                   # [102, 106, 112, 120]                  #(d)

print map( None, (1, 2, 3), (4, 5), (6,) )                          #(e)
                      # [(1, 4, 6), (2, 5, None), (3, None, None)]
```

3.14 INTERACTING WITH THE DIRECTORY STRUCTURE

In Python, much of the functionality needed for interacting with the system environment is provided by the methods and the data attributes defined for the `os` and the `os.path` modules. This section illustrates the more commonly used methods and data attributes of the `os` module for such interactions. In the subsection that follows, we will focus on the functionality of the `os.path` module.

To determine the current working directory, you would make the following call:

```
cwd = os.getcwd()            # the current working directory
```

Initially, at the start of a script, Python automatically sets the current working directory to the directory in which the script is invoked. If your script is engaged in scanning a directory tree (and if for some reason you do not want to use the functionality provided by `os.path.walk()` that we will discuss in Section 3.14.3), you'd need to call `os.chdir()` as shown below to change the current working directory:

```
os.chdir( pathname_to_new_directory )
```

When supplied with a string argument that does not begin with a forward slash, `chdir()` considers that string to be a pathname relative to the current directory. So

```
os.chdir( "foo" )
```

means to move into the subdirectory `foo` of the current directory.

Python provides the module `glob` for listing either all the items in a directory or all the items that match a given pattern. The method `glob()` from this module returns the names of the items contained in a directory using the same pattern-matching rules as used by globbing in Unix shells. Therefore, the following call will use `*` as a wildcard to return the names of all the items in the current working directory whose names end in the `.tex` suffix:

```
file_list = glob.glob('*.tex')
```

If the string argument given to `glob()` begins with a forward slash, it is treated as an absolute pathname. Pathnames not beginning with a forward slash are interpreted relative to the current working directory. A relative pathname beginning with double dots would ascend the directory tree relative to the current working directory. Another way to pull into a script a list of all the items in the current working directory is to call the `listdir()` method from the `os` module, as in

```
file_list = os.listdir( os.getcwd() )
```

A file may be removed by calling either the `unlink()` method or the `remove()` method of the `os` module:

```
os.remove( file_pathname )
```

or

```
os.unlink( file_pathname )
```

Note that `unlink()` is just another name for `remove()`. A call to `remove()` [or to `unlink()`] deletes only a single file; the function expects a string argument that is the pathname for the file. This is unlike in Perl where a call to `unlink()` with a list argument removes all the files named in the list.

While `unlink()` deletes files, a call to its opposite, that is, to `link()`, creates a hard link to a file elsewhere in the same file system. And a call to `symlink()` creates a symbolic link to either a file or a directory anywhere that is accessible in a networked environment:

```
os.link( name_of_existing_file, hard_link_to_file )
```

```
os.symlink( name_of_existing_file_or_directory, sym_link_name )
```

As was the case with Perl in the previous chapter when we talked about how Perl interacts with a directory structure, a call to `link()` in Python basically declares just another name for the same file. That is, both the original name and the new link name refer to the same *inode* on the disk. When you invoke `os.link()` in Python, you increment the *link count* associated with that inode. Invoking `unlink()` either on the original name or on one of its link names only removes the corresponding name from a directory; the inode continues to hold the file as long as the link count associated with the inode is greater than zero. A symbolic link, on the other hand, is just a special entry in a directory that points to another location where a given file or a directory is to be found. Of course, this other location could itself be a symbolic link to yet another location, and so on. A symbolic link does not increment the link count associated with an inode. As is the case with hard links, invoking `unlink()` on a symbolic link removes only the link.

The `os` module provides the method `rename()` to change the name of a file:

```
os.rename( current_pathname, new_pathname )
```

To delete an empty directory, you have to use the `rmdir` method of the `os` module, as in

```
os.rmdir( empty_directory_pathname )
```

for deleting a specific empty directory. Unlike Perl, Python does not allow for `rmdir()` to be called with a list argument in order to delete multiple empty directories at the same time. Therefore, in Python it is not possible to feed the output of `glob.glob()` to the `os.rmdir()` function.

As you'd expect, the opposite of `rmdir()` is accomplished with the `mkdir()` method. You invoke `mkdir()` to create a new directory:

```
os.mkdir( new_directory_pathname, 0644 )
```

where the second argument, in this case the octal 0644, sets the permissions for the new directory. Forgetting the leading zero when setting the permissions directly with octal digits would cause the second argument to be interpreted as a decimal number, which would in most cases result in weird permissions. The permissions on a file or a directory can be changed with the `chmod()` method, as in

```
os.chmod( file_or_directory_pathname, 0755 )
```

where the first argument is the pathname to the file or directory whose permissions we want to change and the second argument, an integer, specifies the permissions. Note that the argument order is opposite of how it is in Unix and in Perl. Also, the first argument must be a single pathname string, meaning that the permissions can only be changed for one file or one directory in one call to `chmod()`.

The `os` module provides the `chown()` method for changing the user and group ownerships of a file or directory. Like the Perl built-in function of the same name, Python's `os.chown()` only takes numeric user-ID (`UID`) and group-ID (`GID`) values. For example, in the following call

```
os.chown( file_or_directory_pathname,  uid, gid )
```

the arguments `uid` and `gid` must evaluate to the numerical values for the user ID and the group ID.

The `os` module provides the `utime()` method for changing the timestamp of a file. As mentioned when we talked about the `utime` operator in Perl, operating systems commonly associate three timestamps with a file: *last access time* which could be for the purpose of, say, reading or copying a file; *last modification time*, which could correspond to when the file was written into last; and what's referred to as *ctime*. The last timestamp, used primarily for incremental backups, is always set to *now* for any interaction of the system with the file. The `utime()` method can be used to change the first two timestamps associated with a file. For example, if we wanted to update the modification time for a file to the current time and its access time to 30 minutes into the future, we would say:

```
import time
current_time = time.time();
os.utime( file_pathname, (current_time + 1800, current_time) )
```

where the second argument is a tuple consisting of two elements, the first of which will be the new last-access time in seconds and the second the new last-modification time in seconds, both measured from the *epoch*, which is typically the start of January 1, 1970 according to Universal Time. Note the import of the `time` module and the call to `time()` from this module to get the current time, again in seconds from the epoch. Adding 1800 to the first element of the second argument tuple advances the access time to 30 minutes into the future. To verify that the call to `utime()` actually did reset the two times, we can call the Unix utility `stat` on the specified file. Another option would be to call `os.stat(file_pathname)`.

We will now use the next script, `PathAttributes.py`, to demonstrate how the `os` module can be used to retrieve the tokens used by the underlying operating system for separating the pathname components in a directory structure, for line terminators, and so on. When such tokens are specified in a script by their `os`-defined attribute names, you end up with a more portable script. As we have stated earlier, Unix-like platforms use the forward slash `/` as a separator for pathname components, the Windows platforms use the backslash `\`, and the Macintoshes the `:` character. The line terminators are `\n` on Unix-like platforms, `\r` on Macs, and `\n\r` on Windows machines. Different operating systems also use different constant strings for representing the current working directory and the parent of the same. A special thing about the `os` module is that it searches for the Python modules that understand the underlying operating system and imports from them the system-dependent properties and other functionality.

The outputs shown in the commented-out portions of the different lines of the script are for the case when it is run in a Linux environment. The call to `os.name` in line (B) returns the name of the module specific to Linux that Python accesses for general operating-system-dependent information and operations. We invoke `os.path` in line (C) to retrieve the name of the module that `os` accesses for pathname-specific operations under Linux. The call to `os.curdir` in line (D) returns the constant string used by the operating system to refer to the current working directory. This will be the dot for POSIX-compliant systems and the colon for Macintoshes. In line (E), `os.pardir` returns the constant string used by the operating system for the parent directory of the current working directory. This will be `..` for POSIX-compliant systems and `::` for Macintoshes. Line (F) invokes `os.sep` to retrieve the character used by the operating system for separating the components of a pathname in the full name of a directory. Some platforms support an alternate choice for the pathname component separator. As shown in line (G), the Linux platform used for the example does not do so since the call to `os.altsep` returns `None`.[91]

Shown in line (H) is a call to `os.extsep` that returns the character used by the operating system for extensions to the base name of a file. For example, the name of the file that contains the script shown below is `PathAttributes.py`. Its base name is `PathAttributes`, and the extension of the base name `py`, the two being separated by the extension separator, the dot.

The call to `os.pathsep` in line (I) returns the character understood by the operating system for separating the different components of a search path (as opposed to the different components of a pathname, which is returned by `os.sep`). This is usually the colon for POSIX-compliant platforms and the semicolon for Windows platforms.

Line (J) shows the call to `os.linesep` to retrieve the line terminator used for text files. As mentioned earlier, this will be `\n` for POSIX-compliant systems, `\r` for Macintoshes, and `\r\n` for Windows.

Finally, line (K) shows the call to `os.defpath` for retrieving the search path for locating an executable if the operating system does not support the `PATH` environment variable.

```
#!/usr/bin/env python

### PathAttributes.py

import os                                                          #(A)
print "name: ", os.name                     # module: posix        #(B)
print "path: ", os.path                     # module: posixpath    #(C)
```

[91]The Windows platforms will sometimes support `/` for an alternate pathname component separator. This is in addition to the usual `\` on those platforms.

```
print "current dir: ", os.curdir                # .                  #(D)
print "parent dir: ", os.pardir                 # ..                 #(E)
print "pathname separator: ", os.sep            # /                  #(F)
print "alternate path separator: ", os.altsep   # None               #(G)
print "extension separator: ", os.extsep        # .                  #(H)
print "srch path comp separator: ", os.pathsep  # :                  #(I)
print "line separator: ", os.linesep            # \n                 #(J)
print "default search path: ", os.defpath       # :/bin:/usr/bin     #(K)
```

3.14.1 File Tests

Section 2.16.2 of Chapter 2 briefly mentioned the many file tests that Perl provides on a built-in basis for checking whether a given item is a plain file, a directory, a symbolic link, a socket (Unix-domain sockets only), a pipe, a block-special file (corresponding to a mountable disk), a character-special file (corresponding to an I/O device), a text file, a binary file, and so on. Many, but not all, of these tests in Python are provided by the `os.path` module. To illustrate the file tests that can be carried out with the `os.path` module, we will assume that this module has already been imported into a script.

To check if a file at a given pathname really exists, we can test the truth value of the predicate `exists()` in the following manner:

```
if os.path.exists( pathname_to_file ):
    ....
```

As with all other `os.path` predicates shown in this section, the predicate returns `True` upon success and `False` otherwise. This test does the same thing as the `-e` test in Perl.

Another way to check for the existence of a file is to call `getsize()`, which throws the `os.error` exception when the named file does not exist, as in

```
size = None
try:
    size = os.path.getsize( pathname_to_file )
except os.error:
    print "file does not exist"
print "size = ", size
```

Testing for the existence of a file in this manner while also ascertaining its size is akin to the `-s` file test in Perl.

To check that a named directory item is a regular file and not, say, a subdirectory, one can call the `isfile()` predicate. The following scriptlet shows how this test might prove useful for carrying out a keyword search in text files:

```
all_items = glob.glob('*');
for item in all_items:
    if ( not os.path.islink( item ) and os.path.isfile( item ) ):
        search_in_file( item, pattern )
```

This example also illustrates the `islink()` test to determine whether or not what is at the end of a pathname is merely a symbolic link or a genuine item. Perl's uses `-l` for testing whether a named item is a symbolic link and `-f` for whether a named item is a regular file. A related test in Python is `isdir()` that returns true for a pathname that is a directory. Perl's equivalent of this is the `-d` test.

Other tests in the `os.path` module are `isabs()` to test if the argument pathname is an absolute pathname (that is, it begins with a slash) or a relative pathname; `ismount()` to test if the argument is a mount point for a directory that resides in some other file system; and so on. Python — at least, the `os.path` module — does not have file tests that do the same as Perl's `-r` for testing if a file is readable, `-w` for testing if a file is writable, `-x` for testing if a file is executable, `-T` for testing if a file is an ASCII text file, `-B` for testing if a file is a binary file, and so on.

The `os.path` module defines other useful methods in addition to the predicates for file tests. For example, `split()` breaks a pathname into its *tail*, which is the last component of the pathname, and *head*, which is the rest of the pathname. The method `dirname()` returns the name of the directory for a pathname; it is basically the head returned by `split()`. The method `basename()` returns the tail part of what is returned by `split()`. For these and other methods, see the documentation page for the `os.path` module.

3.14.2 Taking Advantage of Shell's Globbing

It is not always necessary for a script to pull in all of the contents of a directory in order to figure out what files the script should work on. One can instead put to work a shell's globbing capability for that purpose. As mentioned in Section 2.16.3 of Chapter 2, the presence of certain metacharacters in a command-line argument causes the shell to first interpret the argument before supplying it to the command. Such interpretation may consist of expanding the provided argument into a list of filenames that meet certain pattern-matching criteria, performing input/output redirection, and so on. In particular, the metacharacter * in a command-line argument is used by the shell to expand the argument into all the filenames that match the rest of the argument.

Shown below is a script that sends to a local printer called "elt339" all `.pdf` and `.ps` files in a directory for printing. The script itself does not need to analyze the contents of the directory in which the script is executed. It depends on the shell to supply it with all the appropriate filenames. Lines (C) through (E) of the script make sure that the shell supplies at least one filename to the script. Note from line (F) that all the command-line entries — *after they are interpreted by the shell* — are available to the script through the list `sys.argv`. The first element of the list, the one with index 0, is always the name of the script itself, as mentioned earlier in this chapter. In line (G) we invoke the `endswith()` method of the string class to accept only those filenames that end in the `.ps` and `.pdf` suffixes. We then synthesize the string for the printer command in lines (H) and (I). Note our use of the string interpolation operator `%` for inserting the value of `item` in the command string in line (H). Finally, we call on `os.system()` in line (J) to execute the printer command.[92]

```
#!/usr/bin/env python

### PrintFiles.py

import sys                          # for argv[], exit()                    #(A)
import os                           # for system()                          #(B)

if len( sys.argv ) < 2:                                                     #(C)
    print "Needs at least one file name as argument"                        #(D)
    sys.exit(1)                                                             #(E)

for item in sys.argv[1:]:                                                   #(F)
    if item.endswith( ('.ps', '.pdf') ):                                    #(G)
        cmd = "/usr/local/bin/gs -q -dPrinted -dNOPAUSE " \
              "-sOUTPUTFILE=- -sDEVICE=pswrite "          \
              "%s" % item                                                   #(H)
        cmd = cmd + " -c quit | lp -d elt339"                               #(I)
        os.system( cmd )                                                    #(J)
```

This script could be called with a variety of command lines to do its job:

```
PrintFiles.py *
PrintFiles.py *.pdf
PrintFiles.py *.ps
PrintFiles.py some_filename.pdf
PrintFiles.py file1.pdf file2.ps file3.pdf ...
...
...
```

[92] See Section 3.15.1 for `os.system()`.

3.14.3 Scanning a Directory Tree

We will now demonstrate how to use the `walk()` method of the `os.path` module to scan a directory tree. As with the Perl script shown in Section 2.16.4 of Chapter 2, we will assume that we want to identify all the text files in a directory tree that contain a particular word or a particular phrase. We wish the search to be carried out over all the files in the directory tree rooted at the directory in which the script is invoked. The script shown next, `FindWord.py`, does the job. We can invoke this script either as

```
FindWord.py  word_to_search_for
```

or as

```
FindWord.py  phrase_to_search_for
```

and it will return all the pathnames, starting from the directory in which the script is invoked, to all the files that yield a match. If there are multiple lines in a text file that match the word or the phrase, the output will include multiple entries for such cases.

The scanning of the directory tree is carried out by the call to `os.path.walk()` in line (O). This call takes three arguments as listed below:

```
os.path.walk( current_directory,  function_name,  arg_to_function )
```

where the first argument is the name of the directory that needs to be scanned. If you invoke the script at the root of the directory that needs to be scanned, this first argument will be set to the current working directory. Unix-like operating systems represent this directory by the `.` symbol. However, a more portable way to designate this directory is by `os.curdir`, as we do in line (O). The second argument is the name of the function that you want invoked on each item of each directory during the scan. In our case, as shown in line (O), the name of this function is `searchInFile`; it is defined in lines (G) through (N).

It is the third argument to `os.path.walk()` that can be a source of some confusion. Python uses this argument as the first element of a 3-element tuple that becomes the argument to the function named in the second. For example, in our case, the second argument function is named `searchInFile`. Python will call this function with the following three arguments:

```
third_argument_to_walk,  directory_name,  directory_items_list
```

Initially, the `directory_name` will be the same as the first argument to `walk()` — most likely to be the current working directory — and `directory_items_list` simply a list of all the items in the directory `directory_name`. Subsequently, these two items will be set to the directories and their contents as they are encountered as `walk()` descends down the directory tree. The scan carried out by `walk()` is depth-first. Basically what that implies is that before scanning all the files in the current directory, `walk()` will first open the subdirectories in the current directory.

Note again the second and the third items shown above are automatically put together by Python for supplying to the function named in the second argument to `walk()`.

Let's now examine the syntax for the function `searchInFile()` in lines (G) through (N). Note, as shown in line (G), this function must be defined with three parameters, which is in accordance with the call syntax explained above for this function. As stated earlier, the parameter `pattern` in line (G) is set to the third argument in the call in line (O). The other two parameters, `dirname` and `filenames`, are provided values automatically by Python during the scan of a directory tree. Line (H) defines the `for` loop to examine the contents of the current directory. Line (I) prepends the pathname associated with the current directory to the name of the directory. To not waste time searching through files inappropriate for the task at hand, in line (J) we eliminate from further consideration all files that are not text files. Lines (K) through (M) then peer into each file and determine whether or not any line matches the string supplied in the command line after the name of the script.

```
#!/usr/bin/env python

### FindWord.py

import os                                    # for curdir()             #(A)
import os.path                               # for join(), isfile()     #(B)
import sys                                   # for argv[], exit()       #(C)

if len( sys.argv ) != 2:                                                #(D)
    print "need a word or a single-quoted phrase to search for"         #(E)
    sys.exit(1)                                                         #(F)

def searchInFile( pattern, dirname, filenames ):                        #(G)
    for name in filenames:                                              #(H)
        name = os.path.join( dirname, name )                            #(I)
        if os.path.isfile( name ) and                   \
          not name.endswith( ('.out','.ps','.eps','.pdf', '~') ):       #(J)
            FH = open( name, 'r' )                                      #(K)
            for eachline in FH:                                         #(L)
                if ( eachline.find( pattern ) != -1 ):                  #(M)
                    print name, ':  ', eachline                         #(N)

os.path.walk( os.curdir, searchInFile, sys.argv[1] )                    #(O)
```

3.15 LAUNCHING PROCESSES

The introductory discussion in Section 2.17 of Chapter 2 applies just as much to launching processes in Python as it does to launching processes in Perl. There we talked about the basics of how an operating system keeps track of the processes through various kinds of IDs [process ID (PID), process parent ID (PPID), process group ID (PGID), session ID (SID), user ID (UID), group ID (GID), and so on] and how it interacts with the processes through signals. We also talked about a process launching child processes and interacting with the progeny. Further discussion in Section 2.17 of Chapter 2 dealt with the notion of process groups for efficient distribution of signals and with the notion of sessions for keeping track of foreground/background processes. There we also talked about process group leaders and session leaders.

3.15.1 Launching a Child Process with os.system( )

The method `system()` defined in the `os` module is a convenient way to start a new child process in Python. Basically, what a call to `system()` does in Perl is accomplished in Python with a call to `os.system()`. For example, the statement

```
os.system( 'ls' )
```

launches a shell, itself a child process of the process in which Python is running, that subsequently launches a child process for executing the Unix `ls` command. So the command `ls` is executed in a grandchild process of the process running the Python script.[93] The main process, the process in which Python is running, suspends any further execution until the child processes launched by it return successfully. As mentioned earlier, a child process inherits all of the attributes of its parent process, including the parent's standard streams. So the output of the `ls` command, even though produced in a child process, goes to the same standard output as defined for the main process in which the Python script was launched. A call to `os.system()` returns the exit code of the child process in which `ls` is launched. This exit code is 0 when the argument command executes successfully.

We will now show a Python script, `System.py`, that parallels the Perl script `System.pl` of Section 2.17.1 of Chapter 2. Our goal here is to examine the output of the `ps` Unix command, extract the processes associated with the user `kak`, and

[93]There is a small difference between how a call to `system()` works in Perl and how `os.system()` works in Python. For simple Unix commands that do not contain shell-interpretable metacharacters, the Perl call will directly launch a child process for executing the command. It is only for more complex commands that Perl will first launch a shell to properly interpret any shell metacharacters and then the shell spawns the child process(es) needed for executing the command. In Python, on the other hand, a call to `os.system()` always launches a shell.

identify the group leaders and session leaders. We also want to find which group leaders are also session leaders.

Line (B) of the script calls on `os.system()` to execute the Unix command

```
ps -j -U kak  > temp
```

in a child process. As mentioned in Section 2.17.1 of Chapter 2, the `-j` option causes `ps` to output both the process parent ID (`PPID`) and the process group ID (`PGID`) of a process. The `-U` option limits the output to just those processes whose user ID (`UID`) is `kak`. The call to `os.system()` returns the exit status of the child process in which the `ps` command is executed. As shown in line (C), when this exit status is 0, that means the Unix command was executed successfully.

Lines (D) through (H) illustrate the `getpid()`, `getppid()`, and `getpgid()` methods of the `os` module. A call to `os.getpid()` returns the `PID` of the process in which the Python script is being executed, as shown in line (D). The method `os.getppid()`, called in line (F), returns the parent process of the process in which the Python script is being executed. For determining the process group ID (`PGID`), there are two ways to call `os.getpgid()`. When called with argument 0, it returns the `PGID` of the process in which the script is running, as shown in line (H). However, this method can also be called with a `PID` argument, as shown in line (G). In that case, the method returns the `PGID` of the argument process.

Our next goal is to read all the information deposited in the file `temp` in line (B) and to extract from it only what is relevant to the process in which the script is running. But first we want to delete any white space at the left margin of each output line produced by the `ps` command. We also want to drop the newline at the end of each output line of the `ps` command. Line (J) calls on `map()` to read all of the contents of the `temp` file into a list and to clean up each line in the manner desired, all at the same time. Alternative syntax for doing the same that does not require the import of the `string` module is shown in the commented-out line (K).

In line (L), we put together the regular expression needed to extract from the output of the `ps` command only those lines that contain the PID of the main process in which the Python script is running. This we do by first converting the `PID` integer obtained in line (D) into a string object and prefixing and postfixing the resulting string with the anchor metacharacter `\b`. As explained in Section 4.4 of Chapter 4, this metacharacter matches a nonword to word or a word to nonword transition.

Line (M) then uses the built-in `filter()` function to extract from the output of the `ps` command only those lines that match the regular expression of line (L). The first argument to `filter()`, as explained in Section 3.13, is the function object to be used for ascertaining which elements to retain from the sequence that is supplied as the second argument. In the lambda-based filtering syntax we have used in line (M):

```
filter( (lambda x: re.search(regex, x)), all )
```

the lambda will return `True` when a line output by `ps` matches the regular expression, and `False` otherwise. This syntax is equivalent to

```
def filt( x ): return re.search( regex, x )
filterout = filter( filt, all )
```

Line (M) also joins together the items selected by the filter by using the newline character as the glue. The join operations on strings are explained in Section 4.12.1 of Chapter 4. Except for the headers, the output produced by line (M) is shown in the commented-out section just below the line and repeated below for convenience:

```
  PID   PGID    SID  TTY          TIME      CMD

29333 29333   2978  pts3       00:00:00  System.py
29334 29333   2978  pts3       00:00:00  sh
29335 29333   2978  pts3       00:00:00  ps
```

The header line shown is for the convenience of the reader and is not output by line (M) of the script.[94] The first line of the output is for the process in which the Python script is running. In accordance with our explanation in Section 2.17 of Chapter 2, this process is also a group leader since its `PID` is the same as its `PGID`. The second line is for the shell that is launched by the invocation in line (B) of the script. The last line is for the child process spawned by the shell in which the `ps` command is being executed.

In the rest of the script, we will identify the group leaders and the session leaders in the output of the `ps` command in line (B). As explained in Section 2.17 and as mentioned above, a group leader is identified by the property that its `PID` is the same as its `PGID` and a session leader by the property that its `PID`, `PGID`, and `SID` are all the same. The `for` loop in lines (P) through (U) of the script examines each line in the output of the `ps` command, splits each line into individual data elements on the basis of the intervening blank space, and tests for the existence of group leaders and session leaders.

Lines (V) and (W) sort the list of group and session leaders in the ascending numerical order of the `PID` values. As mentioned before, the default behavior of `sort()` when invoked on a list is to assume that the sequence elements are strings and to then use lexicographic ordering based on ASCII codes associated with the characters. Since we want the `PID` values to be ordered numerically, note the function object argument supplied to `sort()`:

```
group_leaders.sort( (lambda x,y: cmp(int(x), int(y))) )
```

The lambda supplied tells the sort routine that any pair of elements of the sequence container are to be compared by first converting them into integers. If we wanted the

[94]We could, of course, extract the header line from the output of the `ps` command, but it would not add to the educational value of the script shown.

sorted output to be in a descending order, we would need to switch the two arguments supplied to the built-in comparison function `cmp()`. Lines (X) and (Y) then print out the sorted lists.

Line (Z) figures out which group leaders are also session leaders. Compared to the tortured syntax we had to use in Perl, the `item in sequence` predicate made available by Python makes this set operation a one-liner in the script. Recall from our Perl script `System.pl` of Chapter 2 that we had to convert arrays into hashes to be able to carry out the set operation shown. Line (a) then prints out the list output by line (Z).

Line (b) carries out a set operation that is opposite of what we did in line (Z) — it figures out the group leaders that are not session leaders at the same time.

```
#!/usr/bin/env python

### System.py

import os, re, string                                                    #(A)

exit_status = os.system( 'ps -j -U kak  > temp' )                        #(B)
print exit_status                              # 0                       #(C)

thispid = os.getpid()                                                    #(D)
print thispid                                  # 29333                   #(E)
print os.getppid()                             # 2978                    #(F)
print os.getpgid( thispid )                    # 29333                   #(G)
print os.getpgid( 0 )                          # 29333                   #(H)

IN = open("temp")                                                        #(I)

# Eliminate any white-space chars at the two ends of each line:
all = map( string.strip,  IN.readlines() )                               #(J)

# Alternative syntax for above:
#all = [item.strip() for item in IN.readlines()]                         #(K)

# Construct regex for extracting info related to just thispid:
regex = r'\b' + str(thispid) + r'\b'                                     #(L)

print "\n".join( filter( (lambda x: re.search(regex, x)), all ) )        #(M)
              #  PID  PGID   SID  TTY        TIME      CMD
              # 29333 29333  2978  pts3      00:00:00  System.py
              # 29334 29333  2978  pts3      00:00:00  sh
              # 29335 29333  2978  pts3      00:00:00  ps

group_leaders = []                                                       #(N)
```

```
session_leaders = []                                                #(O)

for eachline in all:                                                #(P)
    arr = eachline.split()                                          #(Q)
    #Is PID the same as GID?
    if (arr[0] == arr[1]):                                          #(R)
        group_leaders.append( arr[0] )                              #(S)
    #Are PID, GID, and SID the same?
    if (arr[0] == arr[1] == arr[2]):                                #(T)
        session_leaders.append( arr[0] )                            #(U)

#Sort group leader PID's (ascending order):
group_leaders.sort( (lambda x,y: cmp(int(x), int(y))) )             #(V)

#Sort session leader PID's (ascending order):
session_leaders.sort( (lambda x,y: cmp(int(x), int(y))) )           #(W)

print "Group leaders: ", group_leaders                              #(X)
             # Group leaders:  ['2205', '2363', '2795', '2796', \
             # '2797', '2798', '2939', '3908', '11862', '12175',\
             # '21002', '29308', '29333']

print "Session leaders: ", session_leaders                          #(Y)
             # Session leaders:  ['2363', '2795', '2796', '2797',\
             # '2798', '11862', '12175', '21002', '29308']

common_leaders = filter( (lambda x: x in session_leaders),
                              group_leaders )                       #(Z)
print "Group leaders that are also session leaders: ",        \
                         common_leaders                             #(a)
             # Group leaders that are also session leaders:  \
             # ['2363', '2795', '2796', '2797', '2798',       \
             # '11862', '12175', '21002', '29308']

diff_leaders = filter( (lambda x: x not in session_leaders),
                                  group_leaders )                   #(b)
print "Group leaders that are not session leaders: ", diff_leaders  #(c)
             # Group leaders that are not session leaders:  \
             # ['2205', '2939', '3908', '29333']
```

3.15.2 os.exec Functions for Launching External Commands

The os module of Python provides eight different exec-type methods for transferring control to an external command. There is one major difference between how the built-in `exec()` works in Perl and how such functions work in Python. Perl's invocation of `exec()` launches the argument command in a new child process, while the process executing the Perl script itself terminates (see Section 2.17.3 of Chapter 2). On the other hand, Python runs the argument command inside the same process in which the script was running. In other words, the calling executable in the same process is replaced by the executable for the called command.[95] So the `PID` of the process executing the command supplied to `exec` remains the same as that of the process in which the script was running. Nonetheless, once the execution of the command supplied to `exec` begins, the control cannot return to the Python script.

All of the `exec` methods in the `os` module take two or three arguments. In all cases, the first argument is the pathname to the command to be executed. For methods named `execl` or `execv`, or their respective extensions `execle` and `execve`, the first argument must be the full pathname to the command. However, if the letter `l` in the name of the method is followed by the letter `p`, the first argument will be just the name of the command. Python will search for this command in the pathnames listed in the `PATH` environment variable.

In all the `exec` methods that contain the letter `l` in the name, the second argument is always just the name of the command. So when the letter `l` is followed by the letter `p`, the first two arguments will be identical.

An `exec` method takes three arguments if the name of the method ends in the letter `e`. The third argument is a dictionary of the environment variables and their corresponding values to be used for executing the external command.

All of the four `os.exec` methods shown below in lines (A) through (D) do the same thing — they execute the Unix `date` command. They all return a string like

```
Fri Jul 23 23:00:29 EST 2004
```

for the current date and time locally. Note that all of the four method calls shown in lines (A) through (D) contain the letter `l` in the name of the methods. So in all cases, the second argument is just the name of the command. The first argument depends on whether or not the letter `l` is followed by the letter `p`. As mentioned earlier, when the letter `l` is not followed by the letter `p`, we must supply through the first argument the full pathname to the command, otherwise we just supply the name of the command again for the first argument, in which case Python will look for the executable in all the pathnames in the `PATH` environment variable. Also note that when the name of the `exec` method ends in the letter `e`, we supply a third argument that is a dictionary for the environment variables to use for executing the command. In the examples shown, we have simply used the dictionary as stored in the `os.environ` attribute, but we are free to modify this dictionary or construct a new dictionary before supplying it as the third argument.

---

[95]The `os.exec` methods of Python may launch new processes in Windows machines, just as is the case for the `exec()` function in Perl.

```
os.execl( '/bin/date', 'date' )                                         #(A)
os.execlp( 'date', 'date' )                                             #(B)
os.execle( '/bin/date', 'date', os.environ )                            #(C)
os.execlpe( 'date', 'date', os.environ )                                #(D)
```

Illustrated below in lines (E) through (H) are the other four `os.exec` methods; these are for commands that need to be executed with optional flags. The methods now include the letter `v` (for *variable* number of arguments) in their names instead of the letter `l` shown above. The letters `p` and `e` carry the same significance as before. The main difference between the `l` versions shown above and the `v` versions shown below is in the nature of the second argument. For the `l` versions, the second argument was just a string that was the name of the command; for the `v` versions, the second argument is a list whose first element is the name of the command and whose subsequent elements are the arguments/flags for the command. In the four examples shown below in lines (E) through (H), we want to do exactly the same thing — execute the `date` command with the optional `-u` flag so that the time would be displayed in UTC (Coordinated Universal Time).

```
os.execv( '/bin/date', ['date', '-u'] )                                 #(E)
os.execvp( 'date', ['date', '-u'] )                                     #(F)
os.execve( '/bin/date', ['date', '-u'], os.environ )                    #(G)
os.execvpe( 'date', ['date', '-u'], os.environ )                        #(H)
```

The output of all four invocations shown above is a string of the following sort:

```
Sat Jul 24 04:32:34 UTC 2004
```

Note that the displayed time is now shown in UTC.

We will now show a Python script that parallels the Perl script `Exec.pl` of Section 2.17.3 of Chapter 2. This script, `Exec.py`, starts out by showing that Python makes all the environment variables and their values accessible through the `os.environ` dictionary. Line (B) of the script retrieves all the keys stored in the dictionary, these being the environment variables, and then line (C) sorts them using Python's default ASCII-based comparison criterion for strings. The output produced by line (D) looks like

```
['BACKSPACE', 'BROWSER', 'BSNUM', 'CLASSPATH', 'COLORTERM', 'CXX',
'DESKTOP', 'DESKTOP_SESSION', 'DISPLAY', 'GCONF_TMPDIR', 'GROUP',
'GS_LIB', 'GTK2_RC_FILES', 'GTK_RC_FILES', 'G_BROKEN_FILENAMES',
'HELP_BROWSER', 'HISTCONTROL', 'HISTFILESIZE', 'HISTSIZE', 'HOME',
....
.... ]
```

Line (E) of the script shows how we can augment the `PATH` environment variable. It is sometimes necessary to do so before handing over the control to the external command supplied to an `exec` method. When the full pathname to the external command is not supplied to a `p`-type `exec` method, Python will search for the command in the directories named in the `PATH` environment variable. If we wanted to examine the new value of the `PATH` variable, we can do so by a call such as

```
print os.environ['PATH']
```

Line (F) demonstrates how you can create additional environment variables simply by assigning to them in the `os.environ` dictionary. In our example, we will utilize the value of the new environment variable `ACK_MSG` in the command string we will supply to the `exec` method. Finally, line (G) shows us calling `os.execv()` to execute the shell script

```
while a=a; do read MYINPUT; echo $ACK_MSG $MYINPUT; done
```

which, in an infinite loop, reads a user's entry of each line in a terminal window and echos back the line to the terminal window after prefixing it with the "`You said:`" string. Note the syntax of the second argument to `os.execv()`:

```
['sh',
 '-c',
 'while a=a; do read MYINPUT; echo $ACK_MSG $MYINPUT; done']
```

Since what we want to see executed by `os.execv()` is not the name of an executable file but a shell script, we need to feed the shell script into the shell interpreter `sh`. Without the option `-c`, `sh` will expect the first name in the shell script to be the name of an executable file and the rest of the names as the positional arguments for the executable. The `-c` option causes `sh` to process the script directly.[96] Here is the script:

```
#!/usr/bin/env python

### Exec.py

import os                                                          #(A)

environ_vars = os.environ.keys()                                   #(B)
environ_vars.sort()                                                #(C)
print environ_vars                                                 #(D)

os.environ['PATH'] += ':/home/kak/myscripts/'                      #(E)

os.environ['ACK_MSG'] = "You said: ";                              #(F)

os.execv('/bin/sh', ['sh', '-c', 'while a=a; do read MYINPUT;     \
                     echo $ACK_MSG $MYINPUT; done'] )              #(G)
```

[96] If we had used `os.system()` to execute the shell script, we could make the simpler call

```
os.system('while a=a; do read MYINPUT; echo $ACK_MSG $MYINPUT; done')
```

but then, of course, we would be spawning a new child process.

3.15.3 Launching a Child Process with os.fork( )

So far we have seen `os.system()` as a high-level method for launching processes in Python and for executing external commands.[97] For finer level control over the creation of new processes and their management, Python comes with the `fork()` method in the `os` module.[98]

All of our introductory discussion in Section 2.17.4 of Chapter 2 regarding the properties of child processes created with `fork()` apply here also, as they do to virtually all languages that come with `fork()`-like functions for creating new processes from existing processes. To summarize that discussion, a call to `fork()` creates a new child process and returns two different values, one in the parent process and the other in the child process. In the parent process, the value returned by `fork()` is the `PID` of the child process. On the other hand, the value returned in the child process is the number 0. Apart from this, the child process is a clone of the parent process. In fact, from the point of the call to `fork()`, the rest of the code is equally visible to both the parent process and the child process and is executed in both processes. Being a clone of the parent process, the child process gets its own copy of the parent's data space, the heap and the stack. An important implication of that is that if a child modifies a variable that was brought into existence before the invocation of `fork()`, the change in the value of the variable would not be visible to the parent.

The basics of the process creation by `os.fork()` are illustrated by the following script, `ForkBasic.py`. In line (A), we import the `os` module, since that is where Python's functionality for process creation and management resides, and the `time` module for its `sleep()` method. Line (B) ascertains the `PID` of the process in which the Python script is running. In line (C), we define and initialize a variable, `message`, that we use later to demonstrate that the child process and the parent process do not share data memory.

Line (D) calls `os.fork()` to fork off a new child process. As mentioned earlier, from this point on, the rest of the code will be executed in both the parent and the child processes. Since `os.fork()` returns different values in the two processes, we can structure the rest of the code in such a way that only certain portions are executed in each of the processes.

In the script shown, lines (F) and (G) will only be executed in the child process because it is in that process that `os.fork()` returns the number 0. Note that we change the value of the variable `message` in the child process in line (G). We will later see that this change is not visible in the parent process.

---

[97]The various `os.exec` methods we discussed in the previous subsection also execute external commands, but they do not create a fresh process for that purpose. As mentioned already, they simply load the executable for the new command into the existing process.

[98]On Windows platforms, a similar idea is referred to as *spawning a process*. Python comes with a number of `os.spawn` methods for spawning processes. On Unix platforms, calling one of the `os.spawn` methods is the same thing as calling `os.fork` followed by `os.exec`.

On the other hand, lines (I), (J), and (K) will only be executed in the parent process. By calling `time.sleep(1)` in line (I) we put the parent process to sleep for 1 second to give the child process a chance to run to completion. If we did not do so, it is possible that the outputs produced by the parent and the child processes would get intermingled. As mentioned in Section 2.17.4 of Chapter 2, barring explicit process synchronization, we cannot say which process — the parent process or the child process — will start executing first after a call to `os.fork()`. A run of the script produced this output:

```
I am a child of process 7883

        I am the parent process
        My own PID is 7883
        My child's PID is 7884

        hello
```

As the reader can see from the last line of the output, the value of the variable `message` in the parent process is unaffected by its change in the child process.

```
#!/usr/bin/env python

### ForkBasic.py

import os, time                                                            #(A)

pid = os.getpid()                                                          #(B)

message = 'hello'                                                          #(C)

child_pid = os.fork()                                                      #(D)

if (child_pid == 0):                                                       #(E)
    # Execute in child process:
    print 'I am a child of process %s\n' % pid                             #(F)
    message = "jello";                                                     #(G)
else:                                                                      #(H)
    # Execute in parent process:
    time.sleep(1);                                                         #(I)
    print "        I am the parent process\n" +                  \
          "        My own PID is %s \n" % pid +                  \
          "        My child's PID is %s\n" % child_pid                     #(J)

    print "        %s\n" % message                    # hello              #(K)
```

As the reader should have surmised from the discussion so far, the parent process and the child process run concurrently after `os.fork()` is called. When the child process runs to completion, the operating system sends the `SIGCHLD` signal to the parent process signifying that the child process has terminated. The default behavior of a parent process is to ignore this signal. If the parent does not respond to the signal immediately, the operating system creates a small record of the termination status of the child process, along with such information as its `PID` and the CPU time consumed, storing it away in the form of what is known as a *zombie process*. If the parent process terminates before the child process has exited, the orphaned child process is inherited by the parent of all user-created processes, `init`. As was mentioned earlier in Section 2.17.4 of Chapter 2, the `init` process is programmed to immediately check on the exit status of all inherited child processes upon receipt of the `SIGCHLD` signal; so no zombies are formed in this case. If the parent process does not check on the exit status of a terminated child process before exiting itself, the left-behind zombie process is checked on by `init` and removed from the memory.

As we did with the Perl script `ForkWait.pl` in Section 2.17.4 of Chapter 2, we now present a Python script, `ForkWait.py`, to demonstrate how a parent process can call `os.wait()` to clean up the zombie process that is left behind after a child process has terminated (and if the parent process does not immediately acknowledge the `SIGCHLD` signal that is sent to it by the operating system when the child process terminates).

The call to `os.fork()` in line (K) forks off a child process as in the previous script. Line (M), which can only be executed in the child process, calls the `print_processes()` function of line (D) to print out a list of the current processes. This call produces the following sort of output

```
child: 12:19:13 24067   PID TTY          TIME CMD
child: 12:19:13 24067  2798 pts3     00:00:00 tcsh
child: 12:19:13 24067 24066 pts3     00:00:00 ForkWait.py
child: 12:19:13 24067 24067 pts3     00:00:00 ForkWait.py
child: 12:19:13 24067 24068 pts3     00:00:00 sh
child: 12:19:13 24067 24069 pts3     00:00:00 ps
```

where the first field simply tells us whether the output is coming from the child process or the parent process. The second field above, generated by the call to `time.strftime()` in line (F), tells us the local time when the statement in line (F) was executed. The third field above is the `PID` of the process in which the function `print_processes()` is being run. The remaining fields are as returned by the ps command. Note how we deploy the `commands.getoutput()` method to run the `ps` command. This method does the same thing as the backticks in Perl — the method returns the output of the external command in the form of a string object. Observe in the output shown above that the process ID number displayed in the third column is the same as the `PID` listed in the fourth row. As mentioned, the fourth through seventh columns of the output are produced by the execution of the `ps` command. As explained earlier in Chapter 2, this command lists all the processes currently running in your system. The PID value of 24066 corresponds to the parent process in which the script ForkWait.py is running. And the PID value of 24067 corresponds to the child process in which the same script is being executed. So it is not surprising that the number shown in the third column, 24067, is the PID of the child process, since it is the invocation of print_processes() in the child process that results in the output shown above.

Let's now go through the lines (O) through (S) of the script that will be executed in the parent process concurrently. The very first thing we do is to call on time.sleep() to put the parent process to sleep for 2 seconds. This we do for basically the same reason as in the previous script, ForkBasic.py. That is, we do not want the outputs from the parent and the child processes to get intermingled. The child process presumably finishes execution during the interval the parent process is asleep. Since the parent process does not process the SIGCHLD signal that the operating system sends it when the child process terminates, the operating system constructs a zombie process for the terminated child process. The existence of this zombie process can be seen from the following output produced by the call to print_processes() in line (P):

```
parent: 12:19:15 24066   PID TTY          TIME CMD
parent: 12:19:15 24066  2798 pts3     00:00:00 tcsh
parent: 12:19:15 24066 24066 pts3     00:00:00 ForkWait.py
parent: 12:19:15 24066 24067 pts3     00:00:00 ForkWait.py <defunct>
parent: 12:19:15 24066 24070 pts3     00:00:00 sh
parent: 12:19:15 24066 24071 pts3     00:00:00 ps
```

The line in which the process name includes the label <defunct> corresponds to the zombie process.

The parent process then calls os.wait() in line (Q). This cleans up the zombie process, as can be seen from the following output by the call to print_processes() in line (R):

```
parent: 12:19:15 24066   PID TTY          TIME CMD
parent: 12:19:15 24066  2798 pts3     00:00:00 tcsh
parent: 12:19:15 24066 24066 pts3     00:00:00 ForkWait.py
parent: 12:19:15 24066 24072 pts3     00:00:00 sh
parent: 12:19:15 24066 24073 pts3     00:00:00 ps
```

The fact that the call to os.wait() returned successfully is indicated in the second element of the tuple shown in the following output produced by the print statement of line (S):

```
Returned by wait: (24067, 0)
```

The first element of this tuple is the PID of the child process whose demise was handled by the call to os.wait().

```
#!/usr/bin/env python

### ForkWait.py

import os                           # for fork, wait                    #(A)
import time                         # for strftime, sleep               #(B)
import commands                     # for getoutput                     #(C)

def print_processes( arg ):                                             #(D)
    child_or_parent = arg                                               #(E)
    now = time.strftime('%X')                                           #(F)
    print "\n"                                                          #(G)
    process_list = commands.getoutput( 'ps' ).split('\n')               #(H)
    for line in process_list:                                           #(I)
        print child_or_parent, str(now), str(os.getpid()), line         #(J)

child_pid = os.fork()                                                   #(K)

if (child_pid == 0):                                                    #(L)
    # Execute in child process only:
    print_processes( 'child:' )                                         #(M)
else:                                                                   #(N)
    # Execute in parent process only:
    time.sleep(2)                                                       #(O)
    print_processes( 'parent:' )                                        #(P)
    zid = os.wait()                                                     #(Q)
    print_processes( 'parent:' )                                        #(R)
    print "\nReturned by wait: %s\n" % str(zid)                         #(S)
```

In the example of `os.wait()` we showed above, this call cleaned up the zombie process that was left behind after the child process ran to completion. In a more common scenario, the thread of control in the parent process will reach the call to `os.wait()` while the child process is still running. When that happens, the parent process suspends itself until all the child processes forked off so far by the parent process have terminated. It is also possible to call `os.waitpid(PID,options)`, where the method is provided with a specific child `PID` as its argument. In this case, the parent process will only wait for that child process to run to completion, or cleanup the zombie of that child process, as the case may be. In such calls, the second argument, `options`, is 0 for normal operations. Another possibility for `options` that one runs into not infrequently is the symbolic constant `WNOHANG` for when we want the parent process to not enter the wait state if the status of the child process is not available.

3.15.4 os.popen( ) for Interprocess Communications

It is not uncommon that we want to execute one or more external commands in a child process and to then stay in continuous communication with that process. As described in Section 2.17.5 of Chapter 2, such continuous communication with a running child process is carried out through the notion of a *pipe*. The parent process first obtains a filehandle (in Python a file object) to a launched child process for the purpose of either writing to the child process or reading from the child process *on an ongoing basis*. If a pipe is created for the purpose of writing into, when the parent process writes into the file object associated with the pipe, the child process reads that information asynchronously at its standard input. On the other hand, if a pipe is created for the purpose of reading from, what the child process writes to its standard output is read asynchronously by the parent process through the file object associated with the pipe.

A child process created through the mechanism of a pipe is independent of the parent process, meaning that the lifetime of one is not predicated directly on the lifetime of the other, unless the death of the process at one end of a pipe creates a condition that would also cause the death of the process at the other end of the pipe. Ordinarily, when the process at one end of a pipe exits while the process at the other end is still in the read mode, the reading process will see the end-of-file condition. And when the process at one end of a pipe exits while the process at the other end is in the write mode, the writing process will be sent the `SIGPIPE` signal by the operating system.

The writing process at one end of a pipe may also initiate the demise of the reading process at the other end by writing certain data into the pipe that the reading process would construe as reason for exiting. For example, in the example of interprocess communication below, when the child process receives the end-of-file condition written into the pipe by the parent process, it terminates.

Python provides the method `popen()` of the `os` module for doing the same thing as what is accomplished in Perl by calling the built-in `open()` with a filename argument that is either prefixed or postfixed with the pipe symbol. A call to `os.popen()` in Python takes two arguments, the first the name of the command to be run in a child process and the second either the symbol `r` for opening access to a pipe in order to read from it, or the symbol `w` for opening access to a pipe in order to write into it. A call to `os.popen()` returns a file object, the same sort of a file object that is returned by `os.open()` or `os.file()`.

The example of interprocess communication shown in the next script consists of two files, `OpenIPC1.py` and `OpenIPC2.py`. The example is run by executing the `OpenIPC1.py` script. Line (D) of this script calls on `os.popen()` to carry out a *piped open* to the child process executing the pipelined commands supplied to it as the first argument. The second argument to `os.popen()` in line (D) is `w` and it means that the returned file object `WRITE_TO_PIPE` is meant for writing into the pipe. What is supplied to `os.popen()` for its first argument is not just a single command, but two commands that can be considered to constitute a pipeline. (See Section 2.17.5 of Chapter 2 for a discussion on pipelines.) The pipelined commands

```
cat -A | OpenIPC2.py 2>/dev/null
```

consist of `cat`, followed by `OpenIPC2.py`. Whatever is written by the parent process to the file object `WRITE_TO_PIPE` will be read by the child process executing `cat` on its standard input, since that is what `cat` is programmed to do by default when it is not provided with an argument. Another default behavior of `cat` is to write to the standard output. As mentioned in Section 2.17.5 of Chapter 2, the option `-A` causes `cat` to also write to the output all nonprinting characters using the `^` and `M-` notation. Whatever `cat` writes to its standard output is read by the child process executing `OpenIPC2.py` on its standard input. As shown in lines (O) through (R), all `OpenIPC2.py` does is to read whatever is coming in on its standard input and write the received message to its own standard output after prefixing it with the string "`RECEIVED BY CHILD FROM PIPELINE:`." The `while` loop of the parent process in lines (E) through (J) reads on its standard input whatever the user enters in the terminal window. Line (G) writes this information to the pipeline and line (I) echos the same back to the terminal window.

When the user enters Ctrl-D in the terminal window, that starts a chain of events that shuts down all the child processes in the pipeline. The Ctrl-D entry causes the variable `input` to be assigned the empty string in line (F). Since an empty string in Python stands for the end-of-file condition, its input into the pipeline in line (G) and its subsequent reading by `cat` causes the exit of the child process running that command. However, before `cat` shuts down, it writes the end-of-file condition to its own standard output, which is read by `OpenIPC2.py` in line (P) as an empty string. This causes the `while` loop of `OpenIPC2.py` to terminate, causing that child process to exit also.

Here is a sampling of a terminal session when you execute the `OpenIPC1.py` script. The first line of each of the two three-line blocks shows what is entered by the user in the terminal window.

```
Started OpenIPC1 parent process with PID 8363
Started OpenIPC2 child process with PID 8366

hickory dickory dock
PARENT WRITES INTO PIPELINE:  hickory dickory dock
RECEIVED BY CHILD FROM PIPELINE:  hickory dickory dock$

the     mouse    ran up the clock
PARENT WRITES INTO PIPELINE: the     mouse    ran up the clock
RECEIVED BY CHILD FROM PIPELINE:  the ^Imouse^Iran up the clock$
....
....
```

In the second three-line block of the output shown, the extra space between the first three words entered by the user corresponds to the tab entries. Notice how the `cat -A` command has translated these into the notation `^I` in the output produced by `OpenIPC2.py`.

```
=======================   Filename: OpenIPC1.py   ====================
#!/usr/bin/env python

### OpenIPC1.py

import os                                 # for popen()                     #(A)
import sys                                # for stdin                       #(B)

print "Started OpenIPC1 parent process with PID", os.getpid()               #(C)

WRITE_TO_PIPE = os.popen( "cat -A | OpenIPC2.py 2>/dev/null", 'w' ) #(D)

while ( True ):                                                             #(E)
    input = sys.stdin.readline()                                            #(F)
    WRITE_TO_PIPE.writelines( input )                                       #(G)
    WRITE_TO_PIPE.flush()                                                   #(H)
    print "PARENT WRITES INTO PIPELINE: ", input,                           #(I)
    if (input == ''): break                                                 #(J)

WRITE_TO_PIPE.close()                                                       #(K)
```

```
=======================   Filename: OpenIPC2.py   ====================
#!/usr/bin/env python

### OpenIPC2.py

import os                                    # for getpid()                 #(L)
import sys                                   # for stdin                    #(M)

print "Started OpenIPC2 child process with PID", os.getpid()               #(N)

while ( True ):                                                             #(O)
    input = sys.stdin.readline()                                            #(P)
    if (input == ''): break                                                 #(Q)
    print  "RECEIVED BY CHILD FROM PIPELINE: ", input                       #(R)
```

We should also point out that invoking `flush()` on the file object `WRITE_TO_PIPE` in line (H) is critical to the operation of the pipeline. This causes the characters placed in the buffer of the file object WRITE_TO_PIPE to be immediately flushed out into the standard input of the next process in the pipeline. Otherwise, depending on the platform, the buffer may hold onto these characters until it is full or until the end of the interaction with the OpenIPC1.py script, whichever comes first.

We will now show how you can establish a bidirectional pipe for communicating with a child process on a continuous basis. Bidirectional communications is made possible by the methods popen2(), popen3(), and popen4() of the os module. Whereas the popen() method we demonstrated in the previous example gives us a file object that can only be used either for writing into a pipe or reading from a pipe, the additional methods named here simultaneously yield file objects for reading from a pipe, writing into a pipe, and, when so desired, reading from the error stream of the child process. In the script below, we will illustrate popen2() that simultaneously yields two file objects: One that writes into the standard input of the child process and one that reads from the standard output of the child process.

As was the case with our previous script, the next example also consists of two files, BidirectIPC1.py and BidirectIPC2.py. The purpose of the latter is simple: It reads the incoming messages in on its standard input and echos them back to its standard output after converting them into all uppercase.

The BidirectIPC1.py script launches a child process for BidirectIPC2.py in line (D) and obtains the two file objects by calling os.popen2(). Subsequently, the while loop reads in line (F) whatever the user enters in the terminal window and writes it out into the pipe in lines (G) and (H). Whatever is echoed back from the child process is read in line (J) and printed out in the terminal window.

When the user enters Ctrl-D, that is read as an empty string in line (F). When the child process reads the empty string in line (P), line (Q) initiates the termination of the child process. The same is done by testing for the empty string in line (I).

```
====================   Filename: BidirectIPC1.py   ====================
#!/usr/bin/env python

### BidirectIPC1.py

import os                                 # for popen2()                    #(A)
import sys                                # for stdin                       #(B)

print "Started BidirectIPC1 parent process with PID", os.getpid()           #(C)

pipe_in, pipe_out = os.popen2( 'BidirectIPC2.py' )                          #(D)

while ( True ):                                                             #(E)
    input = sys.stdin.readline()                                            #(F)
    pipe_in.writelines( input )                                             #(G)
    pipe_in.flush()                                                         #(H)
```

```
    if (input == ''): break                                                  #(I)
    print pipe_out.readline()                                                #(J)

pipe_in.close()                                                              #(K)
pipe_out.close()                                                             #(L)
```

```
====================    Filename: BidirectIPC2.py    =====================
#!/usr/bin/python

### BidirectIPC2.py

import sys                          # for stdin, stdout                      #(N)

while ( True ):                                                              #(O)
    input = sys.stdin.readline()                                             #(P)
    if (input == ''): break                                                  #(Q)
    sys.stdout.writelines( input.upper() )                                   #(R)
    sys.stdout.flush()                                                       #(S)
```

An interactive session with this example of a bidirectional pipe looks like:

```
Started BidirectIPC1 parent process with PID 17452
hello
HELLO

jello
JELLO

yello
YELLO

....
```

3.16 SENDING AND TRAPPING SIGNALS

As described in Section 2.18 of Chapter 2, when the operating system needs to inform a process about the occurrence of some unusual event, it sends a *signal* to the process. How a process responds to a signal depends completely on the process's *signal handler* for that particular signal. If no signal handler is available for a given signal, the default behavior of a process for many of the signals is to ignore the signal. The default behavior of a process to the various signals is shown in a table-like presentation in Section 2.18 of Chapter 2. As that table shows, a process a process will come equipped with default signal handlers for some of the frequently occurring signals, such as those generated by user-entered keyboard interrupts when Ctrl-C is pressed, by terminal line hangups, by the exit of a child process, and so on.

Python's functionality for handling and raising signals in a script is provided through the `signal` module that comes with the standard distribution. The signals themselves are defined as symbolic constants in this module; these symbolic constants carry the same names as those shown for Unix signals in Section 2.18 of Chapter 2. But since they are defined for the module `signal`, they are commonly accessed through the dotted notation such as `signal.SIGINT`, `signal.SIGHUP`, and so on.

A signal handler in Python is created by defining a two-argument function whose first argument is meant to be the Python's symbolic name for a signal and whose second argument is either a frame object or the null object `None`.[99] Once a signal handler is defined, it is registered for a particular signal by using the `signal.signal()` method with the call syntax:

```
signal.signal( signal_name, signal_handler_function )
```

The following script, `SigHandler.py`, shows us defining a signal handler for the `SIGINT` signal that is issued by the operating system to the process executing the script when the user presses Ctrl-C on the keyboard. Lines (C), (D), and (E) define the signal handler. Note the invocation of the `os.kill()` function in line (E). Unlike the built-in `kill()` of Perl, the sole purpose of `os.kill()` is to terminate the process whose `PID` is supplied to the function as its first argument. Line (F) registers the signal handler for the `SIGINT` signal. Finally, line (G) parks the execution in an infinite loop that can be terminated when the user enters Ctrl-C on the keyboard.

```
#!/usr/bin/env python

### SigHandler.py

import signal                                                   #(A)
import os                                                       #(B)

def ctrl_c_handler( signum, frame ):                            #(C)
    print "Ctrl-C pressed"                                      #(D)
    os.kill( os.getpid(), signal.SIGKILL )                      #(E)

signal.signal( signal.SIGINT, ctrl_c_handler )                  #(F)

while (True): pass                                              #(G)
```

---

[99]A *frame object* holds the current state of the computations, in terms of the local and the global variables, the exception caught if any, and other housekeeping information. There is a separate frame for each new scope and each function call.

3.17 CREDITS AND SUGGESTIONS FOR FURTHER READING

The online documentation on Python, authored by the creator of the language, Guido van Rossum, and his editor, Fred L. Drake, Jr., is the ultimate reference for all aspects of the language. The reader is also referred to the detailed expositions of the language by Wesley Chun [9] and Mark Lutz [47]. About the more specialized topics, in Section 3.3.1 we mentioned how you can stop a script from further execution by inserting the statement `pdb.set_trace()` in the script. This statement puts you in the Python debugger `pdb`. To read further about debugging Python scripts, the reader is referred to the article by Stephen Ferg [20].

3.18 HOMEWORK

1. Provide a Python implementation for the homework problem stated in Problem 4 of Chapter 2.

2. Provide a Python implementation for the homework problem stated in Problem 5 of Chapter 2.

3. Provide a Python implementation for the homework problem stated in Problem 6 of Chapter 2.

4. Write a Python version of the following Perl script that calculates the histogram of a text file for the letters of the English alphabet in the file. All the letters are converted to lowercase for the histogram. The script ignores nonalphabetic characters, such as punctuation marks, line breaks, blank spaces, and so on. As shown, the script reads in the text at the standard input. To make it read a text file whose histogram is desired, you'd call it with the following command line:

   ```
   hist.pl  <  name_of_text_file
   ```

   Your Python script should behave the same way. That is, it should read in the text at its standard input and then you can make it read a text file by input-stream redirection as shown above.

```
#!/usr/bin/perl -w
use strict;

### hist.pl

undef $/;
my %hist;
map { $_ =~ /[a-zA-Z]/ ? $hist{"\L$_"}++ : 1; } split //, <>;

foreach my $key ( sort( keys %hist ) ) {
    print "$key\t$hist{$key}\n";
}
```

5. This exercise is about using the `timeit` module for measuring the execution time of code snippets. Use this module to compare the time it takes to create a 1000-element list by[100]

```
mylist = [None]
for _ in xrange(1000): mylist.append(None)
```

and by[101]

```
mylist = [None] * 1000
```

We obviously want this comparison to be fair, in the sense that we do not want our comparison to get skewed by the overhead associated with the `for` loop in the first approach. We are talking specifically about the overhead associating with assigning a value to the loop control variable at each iteration of the loop.

[100]The scriplets shown in this homework problem, including those that illustrate the command-line invocation of the `timeit` module in one of the footnotes for this homework problem are based on the postings by Erik Max Francis and Jeremy Fincher in the `comp.lang.python` newsgroup.

[101]This approach may be thought of as preallocating the memory for a 1000-element list. For most work with Python, you would not need to preallocate memory for a list in this fashion. Python lists expand dynamically to accommodate new elements as they become available. The time complexity of working with such a list (by *work* we mean element access, insert/delete operations, etc.) is *amortized constant time*. That means that most of the time a Python list is highly efficient. Of course, if a large number of additional elements make it necessary for Python to move the list from one location to another, the performance of some of the list operations would suffer momentarily.

If you wish, you can therefore add a dummy `for` loop to the second way of constructing the list:[102]

```
mylist = [None] * 1000
for _ in xrange(1000): pass
```

The `timeit` module defines a class `Timer` with two useful methods for timing the execution of code snippets: `timeit()` and `repeat()`. These methods are invoked on an instance of `Timer`. When a `Timer` instance is constructed, you supply the code snippet as an argument to the constructor. Here is an example[103]

```
snippet = '''
mylist = [None]*1000
for _ in xrange(1000): pass
'''
t = timeit.Timer( stmt=snippet )
print "%.2f usec/per_run" % \
        (1000000 * t.timeit( number=10000 )/10000)
```

Note the argument supplied to the `timeit()` method — it is the number of times you want the code snippet to be executed. Dividing the result returned by `timeit()` by the same number gives us the execution time per pass through the snippet.[104] And multiplying the value thus computed by 1,000,000 makes for easy reading of the value of the execution time in microseconds. Here is a sample of how you can call the `repeat()` method of the `Timer` class for repeating the 10,000-iteration loop 3 times to get a better sense of the

[102]For an even fairer comparison, we should really be using the `for` loop as shown below:

```
mylist = [None] * 1000
for _ in xrange(1000): mylist[_] = None
```

because in practice you'd also need to initialize the array.

[103]The example we show here for the `timeit` module is for a file-based execution of a Python script. You'll, of course, have to import the `timeit` module into your script for that. However, since the `timeit` module was written specifically for small snippets of code, it is frequently invoked in a command line in a shell through the kind of syntax shown below:

```
python /usr/local/lib/python2.3/timeit.py
            'L = [None]*1000' 'for _ in xrange(1000):pass'
```

where all of the syntax is supposed to be in a single line. This invocation runs the `timeit` as a script with default values of the number of times you want the code snippet to be executed and the number of repetitions for the time measurement. The default for the former is 10,000 and for the latter 3. The result returned is the best of the three time measurements.

[104]The time returned by the `timeit()` method is the wall clock time, as opposed to the CPU time. So any other processes running at the same time will be a source of interference with regard to the time returned by `timeit()`. The documentation on the `timeit` module suggests running a loop like the 10,000-iteration loop shown about three times and retaining the least time as the execution time.

execution time in case the other processes running at the same time are a source of interference:

```
snippet = '''
mylist = [None]*1000
for _ in xrange(1000): pass
'''
t = timeit.Timer( stmt=snippet )
time_list = [time*1000000/10000 for time \
                       in t.repeat( 3, 10000 )]
print time_list
```

This will print out a list of three execution times, one for each 10,000-iteration computation of the code snippet.

4

Regular Expressions for String Processing

Regular expressions are basic to string processing in both Perl and Python. String processing in these languages harnesses, on the one hand, the power of regular expressions, and, on the other, the support provided by the languages' I/O facilities, control structures, and so on.[1]

A regular expression helps search for desired strings in text files under flexible constraints, such as when looking for a string that starts with a particular sequence of characters and ends in another sequence of characters without regard to what is in-between. Through a regular expression one can also specify the location of the string to search for in relation to the beginning of a line, the end of a line, the beginning of a file, and so on. Additional constraints that can be built into a regular expression include specifying the number of repetitions of more elemental patterns, whether the matching of the regular expression with an input string should be greedy or nongreedy, and so on. Regular expressions are also extremely useful in search-and-replace operations in string processing, for splitting long strings into shorter substrings based on separators specified by regular expressions, and so on.

[1]It is important to mention for those who are steeped in Unix-like systems that there are significant differences between the regular expressions in Perl and Python, on the one hand, and those in Unix on the other. A lot of what can be accomplished with regular expressions in Perl and Python cannot be done with the regular expressions in Unix command lines and shell scripts. Unix regular expressions are used in `awk`, `sed`, `ed`, `grep`, and other utilities. For a detailed exposition that describes the differences between the various implementations of regular expressions, see the book by Friedl [21].

In this chapter, we will start with the notion of simple word searches in input strings, with and without locational constraints regarding where exactly a word should match in the string. This will set us up to talk about metacharacters in regular expressions. In particular, we will talk about *anchor metacharacters*, which help us constrain the location of a match, *grouping metacharacters*, which help us extract particular substrings from a longer string, and *quantifier metacharacters*, which help us control the number of repetitions of patterns or portions thereof. Other important concepts addressed in this chapter include character classes, specification of alternatives in regular expressions, greedy and nongreedy metacharacters, splitting strings with the help of regular expressions, and so on.

The phrase "regular expression" is frequently abbreviated to *regex* or *regexp*. We will often use *regex* when referring to a regular expression in the rest of the chapter (and the rest of the book).

4.1 WHAT IS AN INPUT STRING?

We will refer to the string that is subject to regex matching as the *input string*. This is simply a device to make it easier to differentiate between the different strings involved in the example scripts showing regex-based processing. The input string will often be read one line at a time from a text file, which justifies *input* in the name *input string*. Note, however, that an entire text file may also be read into a single input string in a script. An input string may also be specified directly in a script.

4.2 SIMPLE SUBSTRING SEARCH

It is not uncommon in the processing of text files (or in the processing of what are known as database flat files containing textual information) to want to know if a line in a file contains a particular substring. In this section, we will see how that can be done with Perl and Python.

Perl:

The most basic syntax for finding a substring in an input string in Perl is through the *match operator* `m//` shown below:

```
"one hello is like any other hello"  =~  m/hello/              #(A)
```

where the prefix `m` in the match operator `m//` stands for matching. Using the regex engine, the match operator `m//` searches an input string for a match with the sequence of characters that is between the two forward slash delimiters. The input string in this example is supplied by the left argument to the *binding operator* =~ in line (A) above. Evaluation of the expression in line (A) in this manner returns true or false depending on the success of the match. In the example here, the returned value will, of course, be true.[2] The sequence of characters between the delimiters // in line (A) above is known generically as a *pattern*. More specifically, when matching is achieved through the mechanism of regular expressions, this pattern is a *regular expression*, or just *regexp* or *regex* for short.[3]

Perl allows for many variations on the m// notation for the match operator. Since it is not uncommon for a regex to include a forward-slash — think of a URL or a Unix pathname — we are allowed to use any nonalphanumeric non-white-space character as a pattern delimiter:

```
m!/usr/bin/perl!
m#http://programmingwithobjects.com#
m{/usr/bin/python}
m[armadello]
...
```

Note from the third and the fourth examples shown above that when using a matched pair of characters, such as {}, as pattern delimiters, the starting and the ending

---

[2]More precisely speaking, the evaluation of the expression in line (A) returns the empty list () upon failure. Exactly what is returned on success depends on the composition of the pattern that is between the forward-slash delimiters and whether the regex matching is carried out in a *scalar context* or in a *list context*. (Perl's evaluation contexts are reviewed in Section 2.8 of Chapter 2.) When this pattern contains no grouping parentheses, the list (1) is returned upon success. In the presence of grouping parentheses and when the evaluation is carried out in a list context, a list of the input substrings successfully matched is returned. Grouping parentheses are discussed in Section 4.8.

[3]With regard to what is returned by the evaluation of

```
"one hello is like any other hello"  =~  m/hello/
```

one may wonder as to which operator is actually doing the returning. A cursory visual examination of the expression would lead one to believe that it is the binding operator =~ that is doing the returning. But that makes no sense because it is the match operator m// that invokes the regex engine, and it is the regex engine that has the job of returning the match results. The role of the binding operator is merely cosmetic, in the sense that it helps us see better the input string that is subject to regex matching. This can be seen by printing out the op tree corresponding to the above expression by executing the following *one-liner* Perl script:

```
perl -MO=Terse -e '"one hello is like any other hello"=~m/hello/'
```

where the flag -MO=Terse tells Perl to use the module Terse and the flag -e tells Perl to execute the single-quoted one-liner script in the rest of the command line. On a given run, this invocation returned

```
LISTOP (0x8059ce8) leave [1]
  OP (0x80bb788) enter
  COP (0x8053140) nextstate
  PMOP (0x8059c80) match /hello/
    SVOP (0x805a130) const  PV (0x8056ecc) "one hello is like any other hello"
```

As the reader can see, the only operator being called is match. This way of examining the role of the match operator vis-à-vis the binding operator was suggested by Simon Cozens in a posting in the comp.lang.perl.moderated newsgroup in response to a query by the author.

delimiter symbols are not identical; they must correspond to the left and the right characters of the matched pair.

Perl also allows you to drop the prefix `m` when using the `//` delimiters for regex matching. So the example we showed earlier in line (A) can be written:

```
"one hello is like any other hello"  =~  /hello/;
```

The Perl script shown below, `WordMatch.pl`, illustrates a simple application of regex matching. This script searches for the word `hello` in a string supplied by the user. Line (D) specifies the regex. Line (E) then asks the user to enter a line of text. This text is pulled into the script by the line-input operator `<>` in line (F) where the entered text becomes the value of the local variable `$input_string`. The `chomp` function invoked in line (F) gets rid of the newline character that will be at the end of the string entered by the user by virtue of his/her pressing the Enter key.

```
#!/usr/bin/perl -w                                                      #(A)

### WordMatch.pl                                                        #(B)

use strict;                                                             #(C)

my $pattern = "hello";                                                  #(D)

print "Enter a line of text:\n";                                        #(E)
chomp( my $input_string = <> );                                         #(F)

# All outputs shown below are for the the case when the
# input string is:  "one hello is like any other hello"

if ( $input_string =~ /$pattern/ ) {                                    #(G)

    # The portion of the line before the match:
    print "$`\n";             # one                                     #(H)

    # The portion of the line after the match:
    print "$'\n";             #  is like another hello                  #(I)

    # The portion of the line actually matched:
    print "$&\n";             # hello                                   #(J)

    # The current line number read by <>:
    print "$.\n";             # 1                                       #(K)

    exit 0;                                                             #(L)
}
print "no match\n";                                                     #(M)
```

The conditional of the `if` statement in line (G) is where the entered text string is matched with the word in `$pattern` through the mechanism of regular expressions.

As mentioned before, the binding operator `=~` in line (G) supplies through its left argument the input string in which the match operator will search for one or more matches for the regex. Evaluation of the conditional of the `if` statement in line (G) is carried out in a scalar context and what it returns is construed as true or false depending on the success or failure of the match operator.

We will now discuss in greater detail how one may *visualize* the string matching operation called for in the conditional of line (G). Recall that the forward-slash-delimited argument on the right of the binding operator is a regex. The regex engine has to compare this regex with the input string that is on the left of the binding operator. The matching process can be visualized by translating the regex `hello` against the string in `$input_string` starting at the left end of the input string as depicted below:

```
input_string:      One hello is like any other hello

regex:             hello ----->
```

For each position of the regex, the input string is compared character-by-character with the regex. If a match is scored for all the characters in the regex, we are done and success is declared. But the very first mismatch in this character-by-character comparison indicates that the current position of the regex is not a matchable position. So the regex is moved over to the right by one character position, as shown below:

```
input_string:      One hello is like any other hello

regex:              hello ----->
```

and the process of character-by-character comparison repeated. The repeated steps of moving the regex to the right by one character position and trying to see if there is a match between the regex and the input string can be visualized as follows:

```
input_string:      One hello is like any other hello

regex:             hello
                    hello
                     hello
                      hello
                       hello
                   (End of search for a match)
```

As the regex is shifted to the right vis-à-vis the input string, the regex engine declares the search for a match to be successful at the very first opportunity. So if the input string happens to contain multiple occurrences of the substring that could be matched with the regex, only the first such substring would be seen by the regex engine. In the above example, the second occurrence of `hello` would not be seen.

It would be good for the reader to reflect for a moment on all the work that is done during regex-based matching: the regex is shifted[4] against the input string and, at each position, subject to a character-by-character comparison vis-à-vis the input string until the first successful match between the input string and the regex.

The script `WordMatch.pl` also demonstrates Perl's special global variables `` $` ``, `$'`, `$&`, and `$.` in lines (H) through (K). After a regex match, the variable `` $` `` contains the portion of the input string just before the match, the variable `$'` the portion just after the match, and the variable `$&` the actual substring from the input string that was matched to the regex. The variable `$.` stores the current line number of what is read by the line-input operator `<>` invoked in line (F) of the script. Since the script shown is asked to read only one line of input, the value stored in `$.` will obviously be the number 1.

The opposite of the `=~` operator is the `!~` operator, in the sense that `!~` returns the logical negation of what would be returned by `=~` in a Boolean context. Therefore, the following expression

```
"one hello is like any other hello"  !~  m/hello/
```

evaluated in a Boolean context would return false.

Python:

Regex matching in Python proceeds in exactly the same way as in Perl. We will now show a Python script that does exactly the same thing as the Perl script shown previously.

Regex matches in Python are carried out with the help of the `re` module. If the goal is to match a regular expression with a string, the following methods of the `re` class are useful for that purpose:

`match()`: This method looks for a match but only at the beginning of the input string. It returns `None` if a match is not found. Otherwise, it returns a `MatchObject` instance.

`search()`: Unlike `match()`, this method *scans* through the entire input string looking for matches with the regex. When successful, it also returns a `MatchObject` instance.

---

[4] Shifting of a regex against the input string makes for convenient imagery that helps understand many aspects of regex matching. Note, however, that the actual algorithm for regex matching would be much too inefficient if it was based on the idea of literally shifting a regex vis-à-vis the input string and comparing the two character by character. For fast matching with input strings, regular expressions are compiled into either *deterministic finite automata* (DFA) or *nondeterministic finite automata* (NDFA) that are implemented as CPU-executable opcodes. When the number of states is not large, DFAs result in more efficient implementations. On the other hand, NDFAs are more compact, but may require backtracking to explore alternative state transitions.

`findall()`: This method returns a list of all the nonoverlapping matches between the regex and the input string.

`finditer()`: The same as `findall()` except that it returns an iterator over all nonoverlapping matches between the regex and the input string.

The script shown next is a simple example of regular expression matching in Python using the `search()` method of the `re` module. Line (B) of the script imports the module. Line (C) defines a variable named `pattern`; the string assigned to this variable will be used as a regex in line (E). Note the use of the prefix symbol `r` in the definition of the regex in line (C):

```
pattern = r'hello'
```

As explained in Section 3.3.1 of Chapter 3, the prefix `r` causes the quoted string that follows to be accepted literally, that is, without interpreting any backslashed characters that may be present. So if the quoted string were to contain what is usually the newline `\n`, it would simply be taken as two separate characters, `\` and `n`, inside the quoted string. For the example here, we could have defined the regex even without the use of this prefix. However, it is a standard practice in Python to use this prefix for strings that are supposed to serve as regular expressions.[5]

Line (D) invokes the `raw_input()` function to prompt the user to enter a line of text. As stated earlier in Chapter 3, the function returns in the form of a constant string the entry made by the user, *but without the trailing newline*.

Line (E) invokes the `search()` method of the `re` class for regex matching. The regex engine uses the first argument to `search()` as a regex and searches for this regex in the input string supplied through the second argument. The `search()` method returns an object of type `MatchObject` at the first match between the regex and the input string. The class `MatchObject` has various methods defined for it that can be employed to figure out the position of the match between the regex and the input string, the groupings of the characters in the input string that match various parts of the regex, etc. The script shown below demonstrates the following methods for a `MatchObject` instance:[6]

`start()`: This method returns a zero-based position index in the input string where the match with the regex was successful.

[5]We can also use the `R` prefix for a string literal to achieve the same effect. As mentioned in Section 3.3.1 of Chapter 3, both `r` and `R` prefixes alter the rules used otherwise for the interpretation of the backslash in a literal. Using either the `r` or the `R` prefix yields what is referred to as a *raw string* in Python, as previously mentioned in Chapter 3.

[6]The descriptions provided are for the case when the methods are called without arguments. All of these four methods can be called with arguments specific to certain groupings of characters inside the regex, as we will see later in this chapter.

`end()`: This method returns an integer that is one plus the ending position index for the match.

`span()`: This is a tuple of the pair of values returned by `start()` and `end()`.

`group()`: This method returns the substring of the input string consumed by the regex match.

Lines (G) through (J) illustrate the values returned by these four methods when the input line of text supplied by the user is "`one hello is like any other hello`."

```
#!/usr/bin/env python

### WordMatch.py                                                    #(A)

import re                                                           #(B)

pattern = r'hello'                                                  #(C)

input_string = raw_input( "Enter a line of text: " )                #(D)

m = re.search( pattern, input_string )                              #(E)

# The outputs shown below are for the case when the user enters
# in the command line the string "one hello is like any other hello"
if m:                                                               #(F)
    # Print starting position index for the match:
    print m.start()                 # 4                             #(G)
    # Print the ending position index for the match:
    print m.end()                   # 9                             #(H)
    # Print a tuple of the position indices that span this match:
    print m.span()                  # (4, 9)                        #(I)
    # print the input strings characters consumed by this match:
    print m.group()                 # hello                         #(J)
else:
    print "no match"                                                #(K)
```

4.3 WHAT IS MEANT BY A MATCH BETWEEN A REGEX AND AN INPUT STRING?

The discussion in the preceding section should have made clear the following meaning of *matching*: A regex matches an input string if there is a character-by-character match between the regex and some substring within the input string. In other words, a match between a regex and an input string does not necessarily require that the match occur from the beginning to the end of both.

As we will see in the next section, it is indeed possible to write down a regex that will cause the regex engine to seek a beginning-to-end match between the regex and the input string. But, in general, a regex will match only a substring of the input string for the matching to be successful.

Another way of describing the matching process is through the notion of the regex engine *consuming* the characters of the input string as the matching between the regex and the input string proceeds. At the very outset, the first character position in the regex coincides with the first character position in the input string. Now the regex engine starts consuming the characters of the input string in accordance with what is needed at each corresponding position in the regex. If the regex engine gets to the end of the regex, having successfully consumed the input-string characters in accordance with the needs of each character position in the regex, we have a successful match between the regex and the input string.

If the matching between the regex and the input string does not work out when the first character of the regex is lined up with the first character of the input string, the regex is shifted to the right by one character position and the entire matching procedure repeated. This shift and match process continues until either a match is scored or any further shifts of the regex are not possible because we run out of room at the trailing end of the input string, in which case the match is declared to be unsuccessful.

4.4 REGEX MATCHING AT LINE AND WORD BOUNDARIES

Regex matching is made flexible by embedding in the regex certain characters, referred to as *metacharacters*, that carry special meaning as to how the regex is to be matched with an input string. Perl and Python use the same set of metacharacters.

This section will focus on those metacharacters that are known as *anchor metacharacters*; these control the location of a match between a regex and an input string. Typically, when position control over matching is needed, you'd want the match to take place either at the very beginning of the input string, or at the very end. Perl and Python use the anchor metacharacter `^` to force a match to take place at the beginning of the input string and the anchor metacharacter `$` to force the match to take place at the end of the input string.

Therefore, the regex `^abra` will match the string `abracadabra`, but not the string `cabradababra`. Similarly, the regex `dabra$` will match the string `abracadabra`, but not the string `dabracababra`.

It is also possible to force a regex to match at the beginning or the end of a word boundary inside an input string that consists of multiple words separated by nonalphanumeric symbols. Both Perl and Python use the anchor metacharacter `\b` to denote the word boundary. The symbol `\b` can stand for either a nonword-to-word transition or a word-to-nonword transition in the input string. So the regex `\bwhat` will match the string "`whatever will be will be free`," but not the string "`somewhat happier than thou`." Similarly, the regex `ever\b` will match the string "`whatever will be will be free`," but not the string "`everywhere I go you go`."

Note that the three anchors, `^`, `$`, and `\b`, do not consume any characters from the input string during the matching operation. While one would expect this to be the case for the line-boundary anchors `^` and `$`, such is not always the case for the word-boundary anchor `\b`.[7]

Perl:

The Perl script shown next demonstrates the use of the anchor metacharacters `^` and `$`. In line (A), we set the variable `$pattern` to the regex `^abra`. The input string is set as shown in line (B). Line (C) calls on the regex engine to match the regex in `$pattern` with the input string in `$input_string`. Owing to the presence of the metacharacter `^` at the beginning of the regex, the regex engine will score a match only if the first four characters of the input string are `a`, `b`, `r`, and `a`. This condition is fulfilled by the input string, which explains the output in the commented-out section of line (C). We then change the input string in line (E), but leave unchanged the regex stored in `$pattern`. Now the regex match in line (F) fails. That explains the output in the commented-out portion of line (G).

The code starting in line (H) shows similar experiments with the `$` anchor metacharacter. These experiments seek to match a regex at the end of the input string. In line (H) we set the regex to `dabra$` and, at the same time, we restore in line (I) the input string to how it was set originally in line (B). The regex match in line (J) succeeds because the ending characters in the input string correspond to the regex. On the other hand, when we change the input string as in line (L), the regex match in line (M) fails.

Lines (O) through (b) show experiments with the word boundary anchor metacharacter `\b`. The regex of line (O), `\bwhat`, matches the input string of line (P) with the start of the input string serving as a nonword-to-word transition. The match of the same regex with the input string of line (S) does not succeed because the input string does not contain a substring `what` that *begins* with a nonword-to-word transition.

[7]The word-boundary metacharacters for `procmail` and `egrep` regular expressions require a match with a specific nonword character.

The regex of line (V) matches the input string of line (W) but not the input string of line (S) for reasons that should be obvious by now.

```
#!/usr/bin/perl -w

## Anchor.pl

use strict;

my $pattern = '^abra';                                                      #(A)

my $input_string = "abracadabra";                                           #(B)
$input_string  =~  /$pattern/ ? print "Yes\n"          # Yes                #(C)
                               : print "No\n";                              #(D)

$input_string = "dabracababra";                                             #(E)
$input_string  =~  /$pattern/ ? print "Yes\n"                               #(F)
                               : print "No\n";         # No                 #(G)

$pattern = 'dabra$';                                                        #(H)

$input_string = "abracadabra";                                              #(I)
$input_string  =~  /$pattern/ ? print "Yes\n"          # Yes                #(J)
                               : print "No\n";                              #(K)

$input_string = "dabracababra";                                             #(L)
$input_string  =~  /$pattern/ ? print "Yes\n"                               #(M)
                               : print "No\n";         # No                 #(N)

$pattern = '\bwhat';                                                        #(O)

$input_string = "whatever will be will be";                                 #(P)
$input_string  =~  /$pattern/ ? print "Yes\n"          # Yes                #(Q)
                               : print "No\n";                              #(R)

$input_string = "somewhat happier than thou";                               #(S)
$input_string  =~  /$pattern/ ? print "Yes\n"                               #(T)
                               : print "No\n";         # No                 #(U)

$pattern = 'ever\b';                                                        #(V)

$input_string = "whatever will be will be";                                 #(W)
$input_string  =~  /$pattern/ ? print "Yes\n"          # Yes                #(X)
                               : print "No\n";                              #(Y)

$input_string = "everywhere I go you go";                                   #(Z)
$input_string  =~  /$pattern/ ? print "Yes\n"                               #(a)
```

```
                    : print "No\n";           # No          #(b)
```

Python:

As previously mentioned, the regex engine in Python uses the same set of anchor metacharacters as those in Perl. That means that the anchor metacharacter that forces the match to start at the beginning of the input string is ^ and the anchor metacharacter that does the same at the end of the input string is `$`. The word boundary anchor metacharacter also remains the same as before, `\b`.

Shown below is the Python version of the Perl script shown above. Line (A) imports the regex module `re` into the script. Line (B) stores the regex `^abra` in the variable `pattern`. And line (C) sets the input string to `abracadabra`. Line (D) invokes `re.search()` for matching the regex with the input string.[8] Since the first character of the regex is `^`, the match in line (D) succeeds only because the first four letters of the input string are `a`, `b`, `r`, and `a`. Recall from our previous Python script that when `re.search()` carries out a successful match, it returns a `MatchObject`, otherwise it returns the null object `None`.

Keeping the regex the same as in line (B), in line (E) we change the input string as shown. Now the attempt at matching in line (F) is unsuccessful. So the call to `re.search()` returns `None`, as indicated by the commented-out output in the `if` block that follows line (F).

In line (G) we change the regex; it now ends in the anchor metacharacter `$`. The match with the input string of line (H) succeeds because that input string terminates in a substring that corresponds exactly to the regex. However, when we change the input string in line (J), the match fails in line (K).

Lines (L) through (T) show regex matching with the word boundary metacharacter `\b` included in the regex. The regex in line (L) matches with the input string in line (M) because the beginning of the input string serves as a nonword-to-word transition. On the other hand, the same regex does not match the input string of line (O) because the latter does not contain the substring `what` that has a nonword character just before `w`. The regex of line (Q) matches the input string of line (R) because the latter contains a substring `ever` that is immediately followed by a word-to-nonword transition. Finally, the regex of line (Q) fails to match the input string of line (R) for reasons that should be obvious by now.

---

[8]To force the regex to match at the beginning of the input string, we could have also called the `re.match()` method, as should be obvious from the description of this method in Section 4.2. Matching with `re.match()` is equivalent to matching with `re.search()` when the anchor metacharacter `^` is the first character in the regex.

```
#!/usr/bin/env python

### Anchor.py

import re                                                              #(A)

pattern = r'^abra'                                                     #(B)

input_string = "abracadabra";                                          #(C)
m = re.search( pattern, input_string )                                 #(D)
if m != None :
    print 'Yes'                             # Yes
else :
    print 'No'

input_string = "dabracababra"                                          #(E)
m = re.search( pattern, input_string )                                 #(F)
if m != None :
    print 'Yes'
else :
    print 'No'                              # No


pattern = r'dabra$'                                                    #(G)

input_string = "abracadabra"                                           #(H)
m = re.search( pattern, input_string )                                 #(I)
if m != None :
    print 'Yes'                             # Yes
else :
    print 'No'

input_string = "dabracababra"                                          #(J)
m = re.search( pattern, input_string )                                 #(K)
if m != None :
    print 'Yes'
else :
    print 'No'                              # No


pattern = r'\bwhat'                                                    #(L)

input_string = "whatever will be will be"                              #(M)
m = re.search( pattern, input_string )                                 #(N)
if m != None :
    print "Yes"                             # Yes
else :
```

```
    print "No"

input_string = "somewhat happier than thou"                          #(O)
m = re.search( pattern, input_string )                               #(P)
if m != None :
    print "Yes"
else :
    print "No"                                  # No


pattern = r'ever\b'                                                  #(Q)

input_string = "whatever will be will be"                            #(R)
m = re.search( pattern, input_string )
if m != None :
    print "Yes"                                 # Yes
else :
    print "No"

input_string = "everywhere I go you go"                              #(S)
m = re.search( pattern, input_string )                               #(T)
if m != None :
    print "Yes"
else :
    print "No"                                  # No
```

4.5 CHARACTER CLASSES FOR REGEX MATCHING

When we specify a regex as

```
hello
```

a successful match between this regex and an input string requires the latter to contain an identical contiguous sequence of characters. In other words, this regex can detect the presence of exactly the same substring in the input string. We could also say that this regex can *extract* from the input string exactly the same contiguous sequence of characters as in the regex.

What if we want more than one choice for an input-string character for a given position in the regex? For example, suppose we want to detect for the presence of *any* of the following words in an input string that contains multiple words:

```
stool  spool  skool
```

Can we write down a single regex for extracting any of these words? In other words, can we specify three alternatives for the second character position in a single regex since that is the only position in which the three words differ? Yes, we can do so with the help of a *character class*. For example, the following regex

```
s[tpk]ool
```

which includes the character class

```
[tpk]
```

will be able to search for any of the three words `stool`, `spool`, and `skool` in an input string. *A character class is simply a set of choices available for a specific character position in a regex.* The most general notation for a character class calls for placing the set of choices inside square brackets as shown. Later we will show other ways of representing character classes inside a regex.

The expressive power of a character class can be enhanced by using special characters; these are metacharacters that carry special meaning inside the delimiting square-brackets. For both Perl and Python, the *character-class metacharacters* are

```
-  ^  ]  \
```

The first of these, `-`, acts as a range operator in a character class. It allows a compact notation for a character class consisting of a sequence of alphabetically contiguous or numerically contiguous characters. For example, the character class

```
[a-f]
```

is simply a compact way of writing

```
[abcdef]
```

Similarly, the character class

```
[3-9]
```

is a compact way of writing

```
[3456789]
```

Here are some other examples of the use of the range operator inside a character class:

```
regex                           matches with
--------                        -----------------------------

var[0-9]                        var0, var1, var2, ....., var9
[0-9a-fA-F]                     a digit or letter in a hex sequence
[nN][oO][pP][eE]                nope, NOPE, Nope, etc.
```

This metacharacter loses its special meaning if it is either the first or the last character inside the square brackets.

Let us now talk about the character-class metacharacter `^`. If this is the first character inside the square brackets, it negates the entire character class. What that means is that any input-string character except those in the character class will be acceptable for matching. The first three rows below show some examples of negated character classes:

```
 regex                          matches with
--------               -----------------------------
[^0-9]                 will match any non-digit character
[^a-zA-Z]              will match any non-alphabetic character
[^c]at                 will match aat, bat, dat, eat, ....
[c^]at                 will match cat, ^at
```

The last example illustrates that if the character `^` appears anywhere except at the beginning of a character class, it loses its special meaning vis-à-vis the character class. *Also, note that a negated character class does not imply a lack of character at that position in the input string.* In other words, some character has to actually exist in order to match at the position that corresponds to a negated character class.

Of the four character-class metacharacters `-`, `^`, `]` and `\`, we have already explained the behavior of `-` and `^`. The metacharacter `]` has special meaning because it marks the end of a character class. The metacharacter `\` is also special because it can be used to escape the special meaning of the next character in a character class. For example, the regex

```
[\^\]]at
```

will match both `^at` and `]at` in an input string.

Whereas the four character-class metacharacters described above work the same in Perl and Python, Perl also accords special meaning to the character `$` inside a character class. This is to allow for string substitution inside a character class. Suppose in Perl a variable $x is set as

```
my $x = "bch";
```

Now we may specify a regex as follows:

```
[$x]at
```

Before using this regex for matching, Perl will substitute in it the value of `$x` to obtain

```
[bch]at
```

This regex will obviously match the words `bat`, `cat`, and `hat`.

We will now show Perl and Python examples of the use of character classes in regexes.

Perl:

The Perl script shown next, `CharacterClass.pl`, demonstrates matching with four regexes, shown in lines (B), (G), (J), and (N). Each regex is matched with a list of input strings generated in line (A) by the following invocation of Perl's `qw//` operator:

```
my @input_strings = qw/hello yello othello Jello melloyello ello/;
```

As mentioned in Chapter 2, the `qw//` operator works at compile time and causes its string argument to be broken into words using the white-space characters as word delimiters.

Our first regex, defined in line (B),

```
^[HhJjMm]ello
```

insists that the first character of the input string be either `H` or `h` or `J` or `j` or `M` or `m`, and that the first character be followed by the substring `ello`. In the `foreach` loop of line (C), the compiler implicitly assumes that Perl's default variable `$_` is the loop control variable and that the string value of this variable is the input string for the pattern match in line (D). At each iteration of the `foreach` loop, the loop control variable `$_` acquires a new value from the list of input strings stored in the array variable `@input_strings`. The output produced by the `foreach` loop is shown commented out just below the block of the code for the loop.

We repeat the above experiment with the regex of line (G), which, as shown below, contains the negated version of the character class in the regex of line (B):

```
^[^HhJjMm]ello
```

So an input string like `yello`, which did not match with the regex of line (B), now matches with the regex of line (G) because the character class in the latter regex admits for the first character position all choices that are not mentioned in the character class.

The other two matching experiments in the script below, one with the regex of line (J) and the other with the regex of line (N), illustrate how to use Perl's scalar variables for injecting characters into a character class. The regex in line (J) is

```
^[$h]ello
```

Perl understands that `$` inside the character class is the prefix symbol for a scalar variable. So, Perl seeks a value for this variable — in this case the variable `$h` — that is then substituted in the regex before any matching takes place. When a scalar variable is used in this manner, Perl assumes that all the characters (alphanumeric and the underscore) that follow `$` constitute the name of the scalar variable. Doesn't this create a problem if we want the name of the variable to be followed by other permissible characters in a character class? This difficulty can be resolved by placing the name of the variable inside braces, as in the regex of line (N). The name of the scalar variable in line (N) is `$hy`. Inside the character class, we want this variable to be followed by the character `y`. That is not a problem when we write the regex as

```
^[{$hy}y]ello"
```

with the name of the variable inside braces. Without the braces, as shown in the commented out line (M), Perl will think that the variable is named `$hyy`. Not finding a value for this variable, the compiler will issue an error report.

```
#!/usr/bin/perl -w

## CharacterClass.pl

use strict;

my @input_strings = qw/hello yello othello Jello melloyello ello/;  #(A)

my $pattern = '^[HhJjMm]ello';                                      #(B)
foreach (@input_strings) {                                          #(C)
    /$pattern/   ?  print "match with $_\n"                         #(D)
                 :  print "no match with $_\n";                     #(E)
}                                                                   #(F)
#                           match with hello
#                           no match with yello
#                           no match with othello
#                           match with Jello
#                           match with melloyello
#                           no match with ello


$pattern = '^[^HhJjMm]ello';                                        #(G)
foreach (@input_strings) {                                          #(H)
    /$pattern/   ?  print "match with $_\n"
                 :  print "no match with $_\n";
}
#                           no match with hello
#                           match with yello
#                           no match with othello
#                           no match with Jello
#                           no match with melloyello
#                           no match with ello


my $h = "h";                                                        #(I)
```

```
$pattern = "^[$h]ello";                                              #(J)
foreach (@input_strings) {                                           #(K)
    /$pattern/    ?   print "match with $_\n"
                  :   print "no match with $_\n";
}
#                             match with hello
#                             no match with yello
#                             no match with othello
#                             no match with Jello
#                             no match with melloyello
#                             no match with ello


my $hy = "h";                                                        #(L)
#$pattern = "^[$hyy]ello";                # ERROR                    #(M)
$pattern = "^[{$hy}y]ello";                                          #(N)
foreach (@input_strings) {                                           #(O)
    /$pattern/    ?   print "match with $_\n"
                  :   print "no match with $_\n";
}
#                             match with hello
#                             match with yello
#                             no match with othello
#                             no match with Jello
#                             no match with melloyello
#                             no match with ello
```

Python:

Shown next is a Python version of the Perl script shown above. Line (B) specifies `input_strings` as a tuple. Line (C) specifies the same regex that we used for our first example in the previous Perl script. The `for` loop in lines (D) through (I) uses `item` as the loop control variable. Inside the `for` loop, in line (E), we invoke the `search()` method of the `re` module for a regex match between the pattern of line (C) and the input string bound to `item`. From the discussion in Section 4.4, the reader will recall that the method returns the null object `None` when the match is unsuccessful.

The output of the `for` loop of lines (D) through (I) is shown commented out below the loop block. It is the same output that we got for the Perl script.

The same experiment as above is repeated with the regex of line (J) which contains a negated version of the character class in the regex of line (C). The output again is as expected and identical to the Perl case.[9]

```
#!/usr/bin/env python

### CharacterClass.py

import re                                                                    #(A)

input_strings = ("hello", "yello", "othello", "Jello",\
                                         "melloyello", "ello")           #(B)

pattern = r'^[HhJjMm]ello'                                                   #(C)
for item in input_strings:                                                   #(D)
    m = re.search( pattern, item )                                           #(E)
    if m != None:                                                            #(F)
        print "match with " + item                                           #(G)
    else:                                                                    #(H)
        print "no match with " + item                                        #(I)

#                           match with hello
#                           no match with yello
#                           no match with othello
#                           match with Jello
#                           match with melloyello
#                           no match with ello


pattern = r'^[^HhJjMm]ello'                                                  #(J)
for item in input_strings:                                                   #(K)
    m = re.search( pattern, item )                                           #(L)
    if m != None:
        print "match with " + item
    else:
        print "no match with " + item
#                           no match with hello
#                           match with yello
#                           no match with othello
#                           no match with Jello
#                           no match with melloyello
#                           no match with ello
```

[9]The Python script shown does not include the experiments with the regexes in lines (J) and (N) of the Perl version. That is because Python does not support string interpolation in the same sense as Perl.

4.6 SPECIFYING ALTERNATIVES IN A REGEX

It is sometimes necessary to specify a list of alternatives for one or more portions of a regex. For example, if `Joe` and `Meera` would work out equally well for a job and you want to see if an input string mentions either name, you could specify a regex as

```
\bJoe|Meera\b
```

with the operator `|`, usually called the "or" operator, creating a choice between what shows up on its left and what shows up on its right. In the above regex, if it is possible that `Joe`'s name could also show up as `Joseph`, we could incorporate that possibility in our regex by rewriting it as

```
\b(Jo(e|seph))|Meera\b
```

where we have used parentheses to make certain that `e` and `seph` are alternatives with regard to `Jo`. If we were to write this regex without the parentheses

```
\bJoe|seph|Meera\b
```

that would match an input string if it contains either `Joe`, or `seph`, or `Meera`. But that is not what we want. We will have more to say about the role of parentheses in regexes in Section 4.8.

When there exist alternatives in a regex for scoring a match with an input string, the regex engine seeks the earliest possible match and, as soon as the engine is successful, stops trying out any remaining alternatives *even if one of the remaining alternatives provides what seems like a better match.* Consider the following example:

```
input_string = "hellosweetsie"
regex  =  h(ey|ello|i)(sweet|sweetsie)
```

Only the `hellosweet` portion of the input string will be used to score a successful match with the regex, even though it would seem that all of the input string would provide a better match, better in the sense of being more complete. Let's see why that happens.

Starting at the first character position in the input string, the regex engine will match `h` of the regex with `h` of the input string. Now there is a triple choice to be made in the regex. Using the left-to-right order in the alternatives available, the engine will first try the character sequence `ey` from the regex. It will score a match for the first character, `e`, but fail at the second character. So the regex engine will backtrack to the last choice-point for the alternatives and choose the next alternative from the regex — the character sequence `ello`. In this case, the regex engine will score a match. So, at least temporarily, it will abandon the third alternative available, the character `i`. Then the regex engine will look at the rest of the regex and see the two alternatives available: `sweet` and `sweetsie`. Taking these up in a left-to-right order, the engine will successfully match the first alternative, `sweet`, and abandon the other alternative, `sweetsie`, even though a match with it would consume more characters from the input string.

This type of search for a successful match is referred to as *backtracking search for matching alternatives.*

In the above example, the match with the input string was successful at the first character position in the input string. But when that is not the case, the regex must be shifted one character position to the right vis-à-vis the input string and the whole process of backtracking search repeated. This "translate the regex and then match with backtracking" is continued until either there is a successful match or it is not possible to translate the regex any further vis-à-vis the input string. When the latter is the case, the match is declared to be unsuccessful.

As the reader might already have inferred from the examples in this section, the precedence level of the `|` operator is lower than that of concatenation. What that means is that in a regex like

```
ab|cd
```

the character `a` will *stick* more tightly to `b` than the latter will stick to the `|` symbol. Similarly, `c` will stick more tightly to `d` on its right than to `|` on its left. So, even without explicit use of parentheses, the above regex is equivalent to

```
(ab)|(cd)
```

4.7 SUBEXPRESSION OF A REGEX

The explanation of some of the regex-related notions in the rest of this chapter is made easier by the informal notion *subexpression of a regex.* Any portion of a regex consisting of a contiguous sequence of regex symbols is a subexpression as long as the portion itself is a regex.[10] For example, in the regex

```
h(ey|ello|i)(sweet|sweetsie)                                    #(A)
```

the following would qualify as subexpressions:

```
h  ey|ello|i  ey  ello  i  e  y  el  ell  .....
```

But note that

```
(ey
```

is not a subexpression of the regex in line (A) because it cannot act as a regex on its own. Parentheses play a special role in regular expressions, as will be clear from the

[10] A regex subexpression is also referred to as an element of a regex.

discussion in the next section. A left parenthesis on its own will not make sense to the regex engine.

4.8 EXTRACTING SUBSTRINGS FROM AN INPUT STRING

As demonstrated in Section 4.6, parentheses in a regex can greatly affect how a match is carried out between a regex and an input string. Parentheses therefore are also metacharacters in a regex. They are known as the *grouping metacharacters.*

In this section, we will show how parentheses can be used to extract desired substrings from an input string on the basis of their match with the parenthesized portions of a regex.

Perl's regex engine stores away the input-string substrings that match the parenthesized portions of a regex in special variables called *match variables.* Perl's match variables are named:

```
$1  $2  $3  $4 ...
```

The value of `$1` is set to the input-string substring that matches the first parenthesized subexpression in a regex, the value of `$2` to the substring that matches the second parenthesized subexpression, and so on. For the following example of an input string and a regex:

```
input string:     hellothere! how are you
regex:            (hi|hello)there
```

The match variable `$1` will be set to `hello`.

Python, on the other hand, makes the matched substrings available through function calls such as

```
m.group(1), m.group(2), m.group(3), m.group(4), ......
```

where `m` stands for the `MatchObject` returned by `re.search()`. For the same example we showed above, `m.group(1)` will return the substring `hello`.

For both Perl and Python, the substrings from the input string that match the parenthesized portions of a regex are made available inside the regex itself through what are known as *backreferences*:

```
\1  \2  \3  \4 .....
```

To see how these backreferences are used, consider the regex

```
(yo|lu)\1(ma|la)\2
```

Note the presence of the backreferences `\1` and `\2` in this regex. This regex will match any of the following input strings:

```
yoyomama   yoyolala   lulumama   lululala
```

Two two regex examples we showed above did not have any nested groupings of subexpressions in the regex. So, when the groupings are nested in a regex, how are the substrings assigned to the match variables for the case of Perl and made available through `m.group()` methods for the case of Python? Consider the following regex which includes nested groupings:

```
(fname: (yo|ho))(lname: (yo|ho))
1       2       3       4
```

where the numbers below the regex indicate which grouping corresponds to which match variable. So, for the case of Perl, scanning the regex from left to right, the grouping corresponding to the first left parenthesis is associated with the variable `$1`, the grouping corresponding to the next left parenthesis is associated with the variable `$2`, the grouping corresponding to the third left parenthesis to the variable `$3`, and so on. For the case of Python, the substrings made available through the different `m.group()` calls with consecutively increasing integer indices parallel the substrings assigned to the match variables in Perl.

One can, of course, ignore the substrings that the regex engine stores away when encountering parenthesized subexpressions in a regex, as we did in the examples provided in Section 4.6. In other words, the grouping parentheses can be used for just that — grouping for the purpose of controlling what is alternated with what and for the purpose of controlling what is repeated with a quantifier, as we explain in Section 4.10.

But the fact remains that when you use parentheses in a regex, the regex engine will store away the value of the matching substring. It becomes a wasted operation by the regex engine if you have no further use for the substrings stored away in this manner. For most ordinary applications of regular expressions, this is not an issue. However, in performance critical applications, one would want to avoid such wasted operations by the regex engine. To take care of this problem, both Perl and Python allow us to specify *nonextracting groupings* (also called *noncapturing groupings*). The role that `()` plays for the groupings that extract substrings is played by `(?:)` for noncapturing groupings, with the symbol pair `?:` attached to the left parenthesis. For example, the regex we wrote earlier as

```
(hi|hello)there
```

can be rewritten using noncapturing groupings in the following form:

```
(?:hi|hello)there
```

In the rest of this section, we will show Perl and Python scripts that should more fully bring to life the grouping ideas discussed above. We will also use the scripts to demonstrated the features of groupings that are specific to each of the languages.

Perl:

The next Perl script, `Grouping.pl`, demonstrates three different examples of how one can use the grouping metacharacters in a regex to extract the matching substrings from an input string. In the example of lines (A) through (D), the regex is set to

```
ab(cd|ef)(gh|ij)
```

Line (C) compares this regex with the input string

```
abcdij
```

Since the regex contains groupings for two subexpressions, the regex engine extracts the input-string substrings matching these subexpressions and places them in the special variables `$1` and `$2`. These substrings are interpolated into the output string in (D) to produce the output that is shown commented out in the same line.

The example in lines (E) through (H) illustrates the fact that while the binding operator (`=~`) returns true/false in a scalar context,[11] in a list context it returns a list of all the substrings extracted from an input string by all the groupings in a regex. The list context in line (G) is supplied by the array variable `@vars` on the left side of the assignment. Therefore, when the regex of line (E):

```
(hi|hello) there(,|!) how are (you|you all)
```

is matched with the input string

```
hello there, how are you.
```

of line (F), the binding operator in line (G) returns all at once a list consisting of the substring `hello`, the single-character substring consisting of just the comma, and the substring `you`. The commented out portion of line (H) shows this output.

The last example, consisting of the lines (I) through (L), shows how backreferences are used within a regex. The regex of line (I)

```
((a|i)(l|m))\1\2
```

contains three groupings. The first grouping starts with the first left parenthesis, the other two are nested inside. As explained earlier, the input-string substring matching the first grouping is placed in the special variable `$1`. This substring is also accessible inside the regex itself through the backreference `\1`. The same applies to the other two groupings, but through the backreferences `\2` and `\3`. Our regex requires that whatever substring matches the first grouping repeat itself in the input string. The two repetitions of this substring are to be followed by whatever matches the second grouping. Consider now the following input string:

```
alala
```

[11] Section 2.8 of Chapter 2 reviews the evaluation contexts of Perl.

Obviously, the substring `al` will be consumed by the first grouping in the regex, with the letter `a` consumed by the second grouping and the letter `l` consumed by the third grouping. Therefore, the substring `al` will be available subsequently through the backreference `\1`, the substring `a` through the backreference `\2`, and the substring `l` through the backreference `\3`. Our regex requires that the substring `al` be followed by what is bound to `\1`, and then followed by what is bound to `\2`. Therefore, the input string `alala` will match the regex shown in line (I).

To explain the rest of the code in the example of lines (I) through (L), line (J) sets the special variable `@ARGV` to a system-supplied file containing a large number of dictionary words.[12] As explained in Section 2.6.2.1 of Chapter 2, when invoked in the conditional of a `while` loop the line-input operator <> reads this file one line at a time into the Perl's default variable `$_`. And, by virtue of the fact that `$pattern` is delimited by forward slashes, line (L) calls on the regex engine to compare the value of `$_` with the regex stored in `$pattern`. The output produced by the `while` loop is shown in the commented out lines just below the loop.

```
#!/usr/bin/perl -w

### Grouping.pl

use strict;

# Demonstrate using match variables:
my $pattern = 'ab(cd|ef)(gh|ij)';                                    #(A)
my $input_string = "abcdij";                                         #(B)
$input_string =~ /$pattern/;                                         #(C)
print "$1 $2\n";                   # cd ij                           #(D)

# Demonstrate the binding op returning a list of matched subgroupings:
$pattern = '(hi|hello) there(,|!) how are (you|you all)';            #(E)
$input_string = "hello there, how are you.";                         #(F)
my @vars = ($input_string =~ /$pattern/);                            #(G)
print "@vars\n";                   # hello , you                     #(H)

# Demonstrate using backreferences:
$pattern = '((a|i)(l|m))\1\2';                                       #(I)
@ARGV = '/usr/share/dict/words';                                     #(J)
while (<>) {                                                         #(K)
    print if /$pattern/;                                             #(L)
}
#                                  balalaika
#                                  balalaikas
```

[12]This file may be in a different location on your machine, possibly at `/usr/dict/words`.

Python:

Shown next is a Python script that does exactly the same thing as the Perl script shown above. The Python script also presents three examples. The first example, in lines (B) through (E), does the same thing as what is accomplished by lines (A) through (D) of the Perl script. Using the raw-string syntax, we specify a regex in line (B). Line (D) then calls on the the `search()` method of the `re` module to compare the regex with the input string of line (C). This method returns a `MatchObject` whose `group()` method when supplied with an integer argument can be used to extract the different substrings corresponding to the different groupings in the regex. The output produced by line (E) is therefore the same as by line (D) of the Perl script. This output is shown commented out in line (E).

The example in lines (F) through (I) does the same thing as the example in lines (E) through (H) of the Perl script, but in a Python way, which is no different from what we described in the previous paragraph. We again use the `search()` method of the `re` module to return a `MatchObject`. Invocation of the `group()` method on this object with different integer arguments yields the desired substrings of the input string.

The last example below, consisting of lines (J) through (U), does the same thing as what is accomplished in lines (I) through (L) of the Perl script. The built-in function `open()` returns a filehandle, an object of type `file`. Line (K) specifies the regex for this example. The rest of the statements for this example read the file `/usr/share/dict/words` one line at a time and try to match the regex with the word in each line. For regex matching, we use the same function as before — `search()`. As explained in Section 3.7.2.1 of Chapter 3, comparing the input line to the empty string in line (O) is a standard idiom in Python for detecting the end-of-file condition. The output produced by the `while` loop in lines (M) through (T) is the same as for Perl. This output is shown commented out at the end of the script.

```
#!/usr/bin/env python

### Grouping.py

import re                                                               #(A)

# Demonstrate using group() for extracting matched substrings:
pattern = r'ab(cd|ef)(gh|ij)'                                           #(B)
input_string = "abcdij"                                                 #(C)
m = re.search( pattern, input_string )                                  #(D)
print m.group(1), m.group(2)                         # cd ij            #(E)

# Another demonstration of the above:
pattern = r'(hi|hello) there(,|!) how are (you|you all)';               #(F)
input_string = "hello there, how are you.";                             #(G)
m = re.search( pattern, input_string )                                  #(H)
```

```
print m.group(1), m.group(2), m.group(3)      # hello , you          #(I)

# Demonstrate using backreferenes:
filehandle = open( '/usr/share/dict/words' )                          #(J)
pattern = r'((a|i)(l|m))\1\2'                                          #(K)
done = 0                                                               #(L)
while not done:                                                        #(M)
    line = filehandle.readline()                                       #(N)
    if line != "":                                                     #(O)
        m = re.search( pattern, line )                                 #(P)
        if ( m != None ):                                              #(Q)
            print line,                                                #(R)
    else:                                                              #(S)
        done = 1                                                       #(T)
filehandle.close()                                                     #(U)
# output of while loop:
#                                               balalaika
#                                               balalaikas
```

Later in Section 4.11.4 we will show how Python allows you to associate a naming tag with a parenthesized portion of a regex and then how that tag can be used to extract the matching substring and/or to create a named backreference to the substring.

4.8.1 Other Uses of Parentheses in Regular Expressions

The usefulness of parentheses in regular expressions goes way beyond what we have shown so far — specifying the alternatives in a regex and extracting input-string substrings that match grouped subexpressions in a regex. Basically, a pair of matching parentheses surrounding a subexpression creates a unit for the following purposes:

- For specifying one of multiple choices, as we saw in Section 4.6.
- For extracting a desired substring from an input string, as we saw in the main part of Section 4.8.
- For being subject to repetition through the use of quantifier metacharacters. Quantifier metacharacters are discussed in Section 4.10.
- For specifying *noncapturing groupings* in regexes, as we discussed earlier in Section 4.8. As mentioned there, parentheses for noncapturing groupings have special notation, `(?: )`, as opposed to the unadorned `( )`. We will present Perl and Python scripts in Chapter 17 that use noncapturing groupings to extract information from XML documents.

- For specifying *lookahead* and *lookbehind assertions*. The parentheses are used in the form `(?= )` for lookahead assertions and `(?<= )` for lookbehind assertions. Lookahead and lookbehind assertions are generalizations of the idea of anchors. In just the same way as the anchor metacharacter `^` insists that the regex be aligned with the beginning of the input string, a lookahead assertion in a regex requires that the assertion be satisfied by the input-string characters that follow. Testing for the assertion itself does *not* consume any characters from the input string. A lookbehind assertion does the same with regard to the input-string characters already scanned. We will not discuss the lookahead and lookbehind assertions in regexes any further in this chapter.

- For embedding *conditional expressions* in regexes. Conditional expressions capture the `if-then` and the `if-then-else` control logic in a regex by using the syntax `((?condition_regex)then_regex)` or the syntax `((?condition_regex)then_regex|else_regex)`. Therefore, when using conditional expressions, the parentheses are used either in the form `((?..)..)` or the form `((?..)..|..)`. This chapter will not discuss conditional expressions in regexes any further.

- For debugging and other purposes, it is sometime useful to embed executable code inside a regex. This can be done by embedding an executable snippet of Perl code, referred to as a *code expression*, inside the delimiters `(?{` and `})`, as in the following regex:

```
HEL(?{print "first L\n"})L(?{print "second L\n"})O
```

  where we have embedded two code expressions in the string `HELLO` for the purpose of "announcing" the occurrence of each of the two `L`'s in an input string, assuming the input string contains the word `HELLO`. As one would expect, an executable statement embedded in a regex does not consume any characters from the input string. Chapter 17 will show an important application of this feature of regular expressions.[13]

[13]Note this feature works only for *precompiled regexes*. A Perl regex can be precompiled with the `qr//` operator. For example, we could say

```
my $pattern = qr/HEL(?{print "first L\n"})L(?{print "second L\n"})O/;
my $input_string = "one HELLO is like any other HELLO";
$input_string =~ /$pattern/;
```

Pattern matching here would cause the following messages to be printed out:

```
first L
second L
```

An alternative to regex precompilation in such cases in Perl is to use the pragma `use re 'eval'`. A Python regex is compiled by calling `re.compile()` with the regex as its argument.

4.9 ABBREVIATED NOTATION FOR CHARACTER CLASSES

Perl and Python support abbreviated notation for the frequently used character classes. These are listed in Table 4.1.

Character Class Notation	*What It Stands For*	*Description*
. (dot)	`[^\n]`	will match any character except the newline
`\d`	[0-9]	will match any digit between 0 and 9
`\D`	`[^0-9]`	same as `[^\d]`, will match any but the digit characters
`\w`	`[0-9a-zA-Z_]`	will match any word character
`\W`	`[^0-9a-zA-Z_]`	same as `[^\w]`, will match any non-word character
`\s`	`[ \t\r\n\f]`	stands for the white space character
`\S`	`[^\s]`	any non-whitespace character

Table 4.1

Note that the three character classes with the uppercase letter designators — `\D`, `\W`, and `\S` — are complements of the corresponding character classes with the lowercase letter designators with regard to the set of all possible characters acceptable to the regex engine.

Of the character classes listed in the table, the class `.` in the first row is probably the most ubiquitous in scripts that use regular expressions. It basically says that you don't care which character appears in a particular position in the input string as long as the conditions specified by the rest of the regex are satisfied. For example, if you tried to match the regex `^foo.` with all the dictionary words, you would be able to isolate all four-letter words whose first three letters are `f`, `o`, and `o`.[14] Considering that the character `.` in a regex has the special meaning explained here, what if you wanted to match specifically with a period in the input string? You'd then need to escape the `.` character, that is, you'd replace this character with `\.` in the regex. So the regex `foo\.` will only match the substring `foo.` in an input string.

The character class `\d` is useful for extracting numerical data from input strings. For example, the regex `\d\d:\d\d:\d\d` can be used to extract the time information

[14]The regex `^foo.` would also match the three-letter word `foo` when it is followed by a blank space.

when it is formatted as `hh:mm:ss`, where `h` stands for the hour, `m` for the minute, and `s` for the second.

The character class `\s` of whitespace characters is very useful for splitting an input string into individual words. The regex engines typically support a `split` function that takes two arguments, the first a regex that specifies how to split an input string and the second the input string itself. The split takes place wherever there is a match with the regex. By using a character class such as `\s` for the first argument to the split function, we are able to break the string into individual words even when the words are separated by tabs.

The character class `\S` comes in handy in those cases when but you need to group together the characters that may include nonalphanumeric characters such as `#`, `/`, `:`, etc.

We will now show some working examples of regexes that use some of the above mentioned abbreviated representations for character classes.

Perl:

The next Perl script shows three examples of regexes containing character classes in their abbreviated representations. In the first example, represented by the lines (A) through (C), the regex is set to

```
\b(\d\d:\d\d:\d\d)\b
```

where, as mentioned earlier, the anchor `\b` stands for the nonword-to-word and for word-to-nonword transitions and where, as Table 4.1 shows, `\d` stands for the character class `[0-9]`. Line (C) calls on the regex engine to match the above regex with the input string of line (B). As mentioned in Section 4.2, ordinarily (that is, in a scalar context)[15] a regex match with the binding operator `=~` returns either true or false. However, in a list context, it returns a list of the substrings that match the various groupings in a regex. In the regex of line (A), the `\d\d:\d\d:\d\d` part of the regex is inside grouping parentheses. Therefore, the part of the input string that can be matched to this portion of the regex will be returned by the binding operator in line (C). In our example, the binding operator in line (C) returns the list `(15:30:00)`. Interpolation of this list into the string that is the first argument to `printf` in line (C) results in the following output:[16]

```
Start time: 15:30:00
```

Let's now talk about the example in lines (D) through (G) of the script below. The regex is now set to

[15] The notions of scalar and list contexts in Perl were reviewed in Section 2.8 of Chapter 2.

[16] See Section 2.1.1 of Chapter 2 for producing formatted output in Perl with `printf()`.

```
(\w\w\w\w)
```

where, as Table 4.1 shows, `\w` is the abbreviated representation of the character class `[a-zA-Z0-9_]`. This regex requires the input string to contain a substring of 4 alphanumeric characters, including possibly the underscore character. In line (F), we call on the regex engine to match the regex with the input string

```
abracadabra is a magical chant
```

The regex match is subject to the modifier `g` that is placed after the second delimiting forward slash for the regex in line (F). As we will explain in Section 4.11.2, the `g` modifier (also referred to as the `//g` modifier) stands for "global," meaning that we do not want regex matching to stop at the first occurrence of a match with the input string. Instead, we want the regex engine to seek out all possible *nonoverlapping* matches between the regex and the input string. This causes all the nonoverlapping matches to be stored in the array `@matched_substrings`. When this list is printed out according to line (G), we get

```
abra cada magi chan
```

That takes us to the third example, in lines (H) and (I) of the script below, where we demonstrate how the `split()`[17] function is frequently used to split an input string into substrings on the basis of separators that match the regex that is the first argument to the function. The regex in line (H) is

```
[\s,-]
```

which is a character class that includes the character class `\s`, the comma character, and the character `-`. Since the character class `\s` stands for the white-space characters, the regex `[\s,-]` will cause the string that is the second argument to `split()` to be split wherever there is a character that is either a white-space character, a comma, or a dash. It is for this reason that the input string

```
apples,oranges mangoes pixie-fruit
```

is split into the words

```
apples   oranges   mangoes   pixie   fruit
```

The last example in the script below, represented by the lines (J) and (K), is the same as the string splitting example we just discussed, except that the regex is now specified by the character class `[\W]`. Since the character class `\W` is the complement of the character class `\w`, the call to `split` in line (J) will cause the string to be split up wherever there is a nonalphanumeric character. So, for the example at hand, the end result is the same as in the example of lines (H) and (I).

[17] See Section 4.12 for a more detailed discussion on the `split()` functions of Perl and Python.

```
#!/usr/bin/perl -w

### CharacterClassAbbrev.pl

use strict;

my $pattern = '\b(\d\d:\d\d:\d\d)\b';                                    #(A)
my $input_string = "The game starts at 15:30:00\n";                      #(B)
printf "Start time: %s\n", $input_string =~ $pattern;                    #(C)
                             # Start time: 15:30:00

$pattern = '(\w\w\w\w)';                                                 #(D)
$input_string = "abracadabra is a magical chant";                        #(E)
my @matched_substrings = $input_string =~ /$pattern/g;                   #(F)
print "@matched_substrings\n";                                           #(G)
                             # abra cada magi chan

my @words = split /[\s,-]/, "apples,oranges mangoes pixie-fruit";        #(H)
print "@words\n";                                                        #(I)
                             # apples oranges mangoes pixie fruit

@words = split /[\W]/, "apples,oranges mangoes pixie-fruit";             #(J)
print "@words\n";                                                        #(K)
                             # apples oranges mangoes pixie fruit
```

Python:

We will now show a Python script that does exactly the same thing as the previous Perl script. The first example in the Perl script is in lines (B) through (F) of the Python script below. Note the use of already mentioned raw-string notation for the regex in line (B). As in our previous Python scripts, the call to `re.search()` in line (D) returns a `MatchObject.` Invoking the `group(1)` method on this object in line (F) returns the substring corresponding to the parenthesized grouping in the regex of line (B).[18] The output produced by the print command in line (F) is shown in the commented-out portion below that line.[19]

[18]The `MatchObject` class also comes with the method `groups()` that returns a tuple of *all* substring matches for all the groups in a regex.

[19]Use of the interpolation operator `%` in the arguments to `print()` for producing formatted output in Python was explained previously in See 3.2 of Chapter 3.

In the example in lines (G) through (K) of the Python script, we use the character class `\w` to construct the regex of line (G). This example also illustrates the use of the `re.findall()` method for achieving the same effect as the match modifier `//g` in line (F) of the Perl script.[20] Recall that the `//g` modifier caused the regex engine to continue to seek additional nonoverlapping matches after the first successful match between the regex and the input string. The call to `re.findall()` in line (I) does the same. It returns a list of all possible nonoverlapping substrings extracted from the input string that match the regex.

Line (L) demonstrates the use of the character class `\s` in a call `re.split()` for the purpose of breaking a long string into words.[21] As with the call to `split()` in line (H) of the Perl script, the string that is the second argument to `re.split()` is split into substrings on the basis of the separator specified by the regex in the first argument. The string characters that are consumed by the regex match at the splitting point are lost, in the sense that they are not a part of the words into which the string is split.

For the input string used, the splitting achieved in line (N) with the `\W` separator is the same as in line (L) with the `[\s,-]` separator, as shown by the commented-out output displayed below line (O).

```
#!/usr/bin/python

### CharacterClassAbbrev.py

import re                                                           #(A)

pattern = r'\b(\d\d:\d\d:\d\d)\b'                                   #(B)
input_string = "The game starts at 15:30:00\n"                      #(C)
m = re.search( pattern, input_string )                              #(D)
if ( m != None ):                                                   #(E)
    print "Start time: %s" % m.group(1)                             #(F)
                # Start time: 15:30:00

pattern = r'(\w\w\w\w)'                                             #(G)
input_string = "abracadabra is a magical chant"                     #(H)
matched_substrings = re.findall( pattern, input_string )            #(I)
if ( matched_substrings != None ):                                  #(J)
    print matched_substrings                                        #(K)
                # ['abra', 'cada', 'magi', 'chan']

words = re.split( r'[\s,-]', "apples,oranges mangoes pixie-fruit" ) #(L)
```

---

[20] Seeking all nonoverlapping matches with `re.findall()` is presented in greater detail in Section 4.11.2.

[21] Python's `re.split()` function is presented in greater detail in Section 4.12.

```
print words                                                              #(M)
              # ['apples', 'oranges', 'mangoes', 'pixie', 'fruit']

words = re.split( r'[\W]', "apples,oranges mangoes pixie-fruit")        #(N)
print words                                                              #(O)
              # ['apples', 'oranges', 'mangoes', 'pixie', 'fruit']
```

4.10 QUANTIFIER METACHARACTERS

A *quantifier metacharacter* is used to control the number of repetitions of the immediately preceding smallest possible subexpression in a regex. Both Perl and Python use the following as quantifier metacharacters:[22]

```
*   +   ?   {}
```

A quantifier metacharacter is placed immediately after the portion of a regex we want to see repeated.

The metacharacter `*` means an indefinite, including zero, repetitions of the preceding portion of the regex, with the stipulation that this portion is a legal regex unto itself. Therefore, the regex

```
ab*
```

will match every one of the following input strings:[23]

```
a
ab
abb
abbb
abbbb

  and so on
```

Obviously, then, it is simple to interpret the behavior of the quantifier `*` when it applies to a single preceding character (that is not a metacharacter), as in the above example where it is applied to the character `b`. But now let's examine the following regex:

```
a[bc]*                                                                   #(A)
```

[22]Quantifier metacharacters are also sometimes referred to as *multipliers*.

[23]The phrase "and so on" at the end of the display that follows (and other such displays in this section) means an indefinitely large number of additional similar examples.

where the quantifier * applies to the character class [bc]. It is best to visualize this regex as a shorthand for writing an indefinitely large number of the following regexes:

```
a
a[bc]
a[bc][bc]
a[bc][bc][bc]
a[bc][bc][bc][bc]

    and so on
```

If there exists a match between the input string and *any* of these indefinitely large number of regexes, the regex engine will declare a successful match between the input string and the regex of line (A) above. Therefore, all of the following input strings would match successfully with the regex of line (A):

```
a
ab
ac
abb
abc
acb
acc
abbb
abbc
abcb
abcc

  and so on
```

Now consider the subexpression .* that is commonly used in regexes. Let's say our regex is

```
a.*b                                                        #(B)
```

This regex is a compact way of writing an indefinitely large number of regexes that look like

```
ab
a.b
a..b
a...b
a....b
a.....b

  and so on
```

Since an input string that matches *any* of these regexes would be considered to be a match for the regex of line (B) above, all of the following input strings would evidently qualify:

```
ab
aab
abb
axb
axyztpqrsb
a  djsl  laskd ?#*& a cdill b
```

So, basically, as long as the character a is followed downstream by the character b in an input string and regardless of what is between a and b (except for the newline character — those are not allowed), the input string will successfully match the regex of line (B) above. If there are no characters between a and b, that is also acceptable for a successful match.

The quantifier metacharacter + again means indefinite repetitions of the preceding subexpression, *but now there must occur at least one occurrence of the subexpression.* For example, the regex

```
ab+
```

will match the following input strings:

```
ab
abb
abbb
abbbb

  and so on
```

As with the * quantifier, it is best to visualize a regex such as

```
a[bc]+                                                    #(C)
```

as a shorthand for writing the following indefinitely large number of regexes:

```
a[bc]
a[bc][bc]
a[bc][bc][bc]
a[bc][bc][bc][bc]

  and so on
```

And, as before, if there exists a match between the input string and any of these indefinitely large number of regexes, the regex engine will declare a successful match between the input string and the regex of line (C) above. Therefore, all of the following input strings would match successfully with the regex of line (C):

```
ab
ac
abb
abc
acb
acc
abbb
abbc
abcb
abcc

  and so on
```

When a subexpression is followed by the ? metacharacter, the subexpression becomes an optional part of the larger regex, meaning that it can appear once or not at all. The regex

```
ab?
```

will therefore match any string that contains either just the character a or the substring ab.

As mentioned, both * and + allow for an indefinite number of repetitions of the preceding subexpression. Whereas, at the low end of the number of repetitions, the former allows for zero appearances of the preceding subexpression, the latter requires at least one. If it is desired to bound the number of repetitions at both the high end and the low end, one can use the {} metacharacters. For example, the regex

```
a{n}
```

with n standing for a specific integer value, means that exactly n repetitions of the character a must occur in the input string. As the reader would expect by now, it must follow that the regex

```
a[bc]{3}
```

is a short way of writing the following regex:

```
a[bc][bc][bc]
```

A variable number of repetitions within specified bounds is expressed in the following manner:

```
a{m,n}
```

where m and n are specific integer values, the former specifying the minimum number of repetitions of the preceding subexpression and the latter the maximum number. Therefore, the regex

```
a[bc]{1,3}                                              #(D)
```

stands for the following regexes:

```
a[bc]
a[bc][bc]
a[bc][bc][bc]
```

So if an input string matches any of these three regexes, it would be considered to match the regex of line (D).

You are allowed to leave unspecified either the value of `m` or the value of `n` inside the `{m,n}` quantifier. That means that an indefinite number of repetitions is allowed at that end of the number of repetitions. Therefore, the regex

```
a[bc]{2,}
```

means that there are to be *at least* two appearances of the subexpression `[bc]` in what is matched with the input string.[24]

4.10.1 Greediness of Quantifiers

The quantifiers shown so far, `*`, `+`, `?`, and `{}`, are all *greedy*. This means a quantifier will consume a maximum number of characters from the input string during the matching process even when a smaller number could have fulfilled the constraints imposed by the quantifier. This greediness is, of course, subject to the entire regex matching the input string successfully.

Let's first consider the greediness of the `?` quantifier. Consider the following regex:

```
a?b
```

Since the character `a` is optional, this regex will match either just the character `b` in the input string, or the character `a` followed by the character `b`. The question now is, which option will be tried first? Being greedy, the regex engine first seeks out the existence of `a` in the input string before attempting a match without `a`.

For an example involving the `*` quantifier, consider the regex:

```
a.*b
```

Let's say we try to match this regex with the the following input string that contains a few blank space characters:

```
a ab cab jab tab bbbb
```

[24] As the reader might have surmised already, it is obviously possible to express the metacharacters `*`, `+`, and `?` in terms of the `{}` notation. The metacharacter `*` is equivalent to `{0,}`, `+` to `{1,}`, and `?` to `{0,1}`.

The match would obviously be successful. But now the questions is, how much of the input string would be consumed by this match? All of it because `*` is greedy.

Here is a regex example that shows how the greediness of `+` can be put to good use:

```
(\w+)\s+\1
```

This will match all double occurrences of the same word in an input string — not an uncommon occurrence when you are drafting a report or a manuscript. The subexpression `\w+` will consume all of a contiguous sequence of alphanumeric characters until there occurs a white-space character. The subexpression `\s+` will then insist that there be at least one white-space character, but it will be happy to consume as many as there are before there is again a word character in the input string. Finally, the backreference `\1` will then insist that what follows the white-space characters be the same as what matched `\w+`. So this regex will match every one of the following three input strings:

```
and that's the the deal, my dear

to run  run for cover when I need it it

but the elephants elephants are smart
```

We will now illustrate the greediness of the `{}` quantifier. Consider the regex

```
a{2,3}\w+                                                    #(E)
```

Given an input string like

```
aaabcdef                                                     #(F)
```

there are the following two ways in which the regex of line (E) could match the input string of line (F):

- the subexpression `a{2,3}` would consume the substring `aa` and the subexpression `\w+` would consume the rest, meaning `abcdef`
- the subexpression `a{2,3}` would consume the substring `aaa` and the subexpression `\w+` would consume the rest, meaning `bcdef`

Since the quantifier `{}` is greedy, it is the second way of matching that is tried first by the regex engine for a successful match in this case.

4.10.2 The Sometimes Unintended Consequence of Greedy Quantifiers

The greediness of the quantifiers can sometimes have unintended consequences, especially when a regex uses multiple such quantifiers. Consider the regex

```
^(.*)(w.*e).*(w.*)
```

and consider the input string

```
whatever will be will be free on the internet -- news report
```

One might think that the second grouping, `(w.*e)`, would extract the first occurrence of `will be` in the input string, allowing the phrase

```
will be free on the internet --- news report
```

to be matched to the last grouping `(w.*)` in the regex. But that is not the case.

In fact, the first grouping, meaning `(.*)`, would try to consume as much of the input string as possible while allowing the rest of the regex to match. The second grouping would behave in the same manner with respect to the remaining portion of the input string, and so on. As a result, this is how the input string would get matched to the three groupings in the regex:

```
(.*)      :     whatever will be
(w.*e)    :     will be free on the internet -- ne
(w.*)     :     ws report
```

and nothing would be consumed by the subexpression `.*` that occurs just before the last parenthesized grouping in the regex.

To see how the above input-string consumption pattern comes about, note that initially, when the matching process begins, the subexpression `(.*)` at the beginning of the regex will consume all of the input string, resulting in the following situation:

```
(.*)      :     <<all of the input string>>
(w.*e)    :     <<unmatchable>>
(w.*)     :     <<unmatchable>>
```

Since this pattern of input-string consumption does not permit any matches to be found for the second and the third groupings in the regex, backtracking is initiated. At some point during backtracking, each backtracking step will assign one less input-string character from the right to the substring consumed by the first grouping `(.*)`. As these backtracking iterations continue, the following pattern of consumption would occur at some point:

```
(.*)      :  whatever will be will be free on the internet -- ne
(w.*e)    :  ws re
.*        :  port
(w.*)     :  <<unmatchable>>
```

Since this leaves the last grouping unmatched, the backtracking iterations would continue, eventually stopping when the substrings consumed by the three different groupings in the regex correspond to what we showed previously for the case of successful overall match. *So we can say that, starting from left to right in a regex, each greedy quantifier consumes the maximum number of characters from the input string that it can, leaving just enough for the other quantifiers on the right to do their job.*

But also recall from our earlier discussion in Sections 4.2 and 4.6 that, unless constrained by the presence of anchor metacharacters, the regex engine seeks the earliest possible match for the regex in the input string even if it is possible to score a better match further down the input string.

To determine what portion of the input string is consumed by each of the subexpressions in a regex, you have to combine the notion of seeking the earliest possible match for the whole regex in the input string with the notion that each quantifier in the regex will consume as many characters as it can while leaving just enough for the rest of the regex to match.

When combining these two notions, the important thing to remember is that *the need to match at the earliest possible position in an input string dominates over the needs of the quantifiers to be greedy.* To illustrate this point, consider the following regexes and the input string:

```
regex1:          (.*)(p{1,2})(.*)

regex2:          (.?)(p{1,2})(.*)

input-string:    peppery peppermint
```

With `regex1`, the first subexpression `.*` can start consuming the input-string characters right from the beginning. Being greedy, it will consume as many characters as it can while still allowing the rest of the regex to match. After all is said and done, this subexpression will consume the `peppery pep` part of the input string. The second subexpression will then consume the string `p`. And, finally, the last subexpression will get the rest, that is `eremint`. So this is how the input string will be consumed by the three groupings in the regex:

```
(.*)           :        peppery pep
(p{1,2})       :        p
(.*)           :        ermint
```

On the other hand, with `regex2`, the greedy first subexpression `.?` will initially consume the first character `p` from the input string. But that would render the next subexpression `p{1,2}` unmatchable. So backtracking would be initiated, which would cause the first subexpression `.?` to be matched to an empty string. Now the second subexpression `p{1,2}` would have to make do with the single `p` that is at the start of input string. The rest of the input string would then be consumed by the third subexpression. So this is how the three groupings within `regex2` will consume the input string:

```
(.?)           :        <<empty string>>
(p{1,2})       :        p
(.*)           :        eppery peppermint
```

If the need to match at the earliest opportunity did not dominate over the needs of the quantifiers to be greedy, the first subexpression `.?` would have consumed the second character `e` of the input string, thus satisfying the greediness of the `?` quantifier, and the second subexpression `p{1,2}` would then have matched the substring `pp`, thus satisfying the greediness of the `{}` quantifier. But that obviously does not happen.

4.10.3 Nongreedy Quantifiers

If the greedy behavior of the quantifiers `*`, `+`, `?`, and `{}` produces undesirable string matching results, one can try the *nongreedy* versions of these quantifiers.[25] The nongreedy quantifiers are

```
*?    +?    ??    {}?
```

So, as far as the notation is concerned, the nongreedy version of each quantifier is the corresponding greedy version with the character `?` attached as a postfix.

As with the `*` quantifier, the quantifier `*?` stands for an indefinite number of repetitions of the preceding subexpression in the regex, *but it will choose as few as possible*. So the regex

```
ab*?
```

will again be able match every one of the following input strings:

```
a
ab
abb
abbb
abbbb

  and so on
```

but, for a successful match, the regex will only consume the letter `a` from the input string, since the fewest possible repetitions for the quantifier `*?` is zero. Compare this to the same example with the greedy quantifier we showed at the beginning of Section 4.10. For the greedy case, the regex `ab*` would consume *all* of the characters in each of the input strings shown above.[26]

Now consider the following regex:

[25] The nongreedy quantifiers are also known as *minimal-match* quantifiers.

[26] While the regex `ab*?` will not consume the letter `b` in any of the strings shown, the regex `ab*?c` will consume *all* of the `b`'s in an input string like `abbbbc`. Therefore, there is no difference between the operation of the greedy `ab*c` and the nongreedy `ab*?c` with regard to an input string like `abbbbc`. What this shows is that whether or not you get different results with a nongreedy quantifier vis-à-vis its greedy version depends on what other constraints are imposed by the rest of the regex.

```
a[bc]+?
```

where we have applied the nongreedy quantifier `+?` to the character class `[bc]`. Like its greedy counterpart, this regex can again be thought of as a shorthand for writing the following indefinitely large number of regexes:

```
a[bc]
a[bc][bc]
a[bc][bc][bc]
a[bc][bc][bc][bc]

     and so on
```

However, now the regex engine will use that regex from the above list that has the fewest possible repetitions of the subexpression `[bc]`, but no fewer than at least one. So given an input string like

```
abbcbccc
```

the regex will only consume the first two letters.

To give an example of the `??` nongreedy quantifier, consider the regex

```
ab??
```

It will consume only the letter `a` from the following input string

```
ab
```

whereas the greedy `ab?` would have consumed all of the two-letter string. Of the two choices that `?` stands for — either zero or one occurrence of the preceding subexpression — being greedy it first goes for the one-occurrence choice. However, the nongreedy `??` first tries for the nonoccurrence of the preceding subexpression.

For an example of the `{}?` nongreedy quantifier, consider the regex

```
a[bc]{1,3}?
```

Like its greedy counterpart, the nongreedy version stands for the following regexes:

```
a[bc]
a[bc][bc]
a[bc][bc][bc]
```

But now the regex engine will try to use the least permissible number of repetitions of the subexpression `[bc]`, as opposed to the most, subject to the bounds specified by the integer values inside the braces. So for an input string like

```
abbb
```

the regex will only consume the substring `ab`.

4.10.4 Perl and Python Example Scripts with Quantifiers

Shown in this subsection are the Perl and Python examples for exercising the quantifier metacharacters presented in the earlier subsections.

Perl:

In the Perl script shown next, `Quantifier.pl`, we construct different regexes by postfixing the string `lulu` with different quantifier metacharacters. For each regex, the script scans the words in the system-supplied file[27] `/usr/share/dict/words` and extracts all the words that can be matched with the regex under consideration.

For the example in lines (A1) through (A4), we use `lulu*` as a regex. The line-input operator `<>` in line (A3) of the script reads from the standard input if the special array variable `@ARGV` is empty. The call to `open()` redirects the standard-input filehandle `STDIN` to read from the file `/usr/share/dict/words` in line (A2). As described in Section 2.6.2 of Chapter 2, each line read by the operator `<>` is deposited in the default variable `$_`. The `if` conditional in line (A4) then matches the regex defined in line (A1) with the string stored in `$_`. Since the `print` command in line (A4) is not supplied with an argument — it is only provided with an `if` condition for its invocation — by default it prints whatever is stored in the variable `$_`. The output of the `while` loop in line (A3) is shown immediately below the `while` block. Let's examine the regex `lulu*` to understand the word selections returned by the `while` loop of (A3). This regex can be thought of as a shorthand notation for the following regexes:

```
lul
lulu
luluu
luluuu
luluuuu

  and so on
```

A match of an input string with any of these regexes is an acceptable match with the regex of line (A1). So in the output words shown, all except `Honolulu` are a result of the matches scored by the regex `lul`. The word `Honolulu` is returned by the regex `lulu`. Evidently, there do not exist words that contain double u's, triple u's, and so on.

The example in lines (B1) through (B4) uses the regex `lulu+` to illustrate the working of the `+` quantifier. The output produced by the `while` loop in line (B4) is

[27] As was mentioned in an earlier footnote in this chapter, a system-supplied file like `/usr/share/dict/words` usually contains a large number of common dictionary words and that makes it useful for testing regexes. Such a file may be at a different location in your system. Another common location for this file is given by the pathname `/usr/dict/words`.

a single entry from the dictionary file: Honolulu.[28] This is obviously not surprising considering the words output in the previous case when the regex was set as in line (A1).

That brings us to the example in lines (C1) through (C4) of the script where we use lulu? as a regex. Surprisingly, or perhaps not surprisingly, the output produced by this example is the same as for the lulu* regex. Once you recognize that the regex lulu? is equivalent to the following two regexes:

```
lul
lulu
```

with a preference for the second since the quantifier is greedy, it is not surprising that the output is the same as for the lulu* regex. The regex lulu* is, of course, capable of returning more words than the lulu? regex, but, as mentioned previously, there apparently are no common words that contain substrings like luluu, luluuu, etc.

We use the regex lulu{1,3} for the example in lines (D1) through (D4). This regex returns only one word — Honolulu — because the dictionary does not contain any words with the substrings luluu and luluuu.

That brings us to the nongreedy quantifier examples in the Perl script. For the first of these, in lines (E1) through (E4), we use lulu*? as the regex. This regex returns the same list of words as the greedy case in line (A1). While the words returned may be the same, the input-string characters consumed by the quantifiers are different, as explained below.

As explained earlier, the nongreedy quantifier *? works the same as the greedy quantifier * except that the former prefers to consume the fewest possible, including zero, characters from the input string subject to the constraints imposed by the rest of the regex. So, whereas for the case of the greedy quantifier the word Honolulu was selected because the regex lulu* consumed the substring lulu from the word, the same word is also selected by the nongreedy lulu*? but now the substring consumed by the regex is only lul.

The example of lines (F1) through (F4) uses the nongreedy lulu+? as a regex. This regex returns only the word Honolulu from the dictionary. This is the same as for the greedy version in line (B1). Since both the greedy and the nongreedy versions insist that there be at least one u at the end of the substring consumed, exactly the same substring will be consumed from the input string in both cases.

The example in lines (G1) through (G4) uses lulu?? as a regex. This regex again returns the same list of words as the greedy version in line (C1). But, in the list of

[28] As explained in Section 2.6.2 of Chapter 2, the call to open in line (B2) closes the filehandle that was opened previously in line (A2) and then reopens it. This sets the file pointer back to the beginning of the file.

words shown in this case, the characters consumed will correspond the subexpression `lul`.

The last example, in lines (H1) through (H5), uses the nongreedy `lulu{1,3}?` as the regex. This regex seeks matches with a substring in the input string that contains `lul` followed by one to three consecutive occurrences of `u`, preferring to keep the number of trailing `u` as few as possible. But since the dictionary contains only one such word — the word `Honolulu` — that word is returned.

```
#!/usr/bin/perl -w

### Quantifier.pl

use strict;

# The greedy '*':
my $regex = 'lulu*';                                                  #(A1)
open STDIN, "/usr/share/dict/words";                                  #(A2)
while (<>) {                                                          #(A3)
    print if /$regex/;                                                #(A4)
}
                              # cellular
                              # cellulose
                              # Honolulu
                              # lull
                              # lullaby
                              # lulled
                              # lulls
                              # multicellular

# The greedy '+':
$regex = 'lulu+';                                                     #(B1)
open STDIN, "/usr/share/dict/words";                                  #(B2)
while (<>) {                                                          #(B3)
    print if /$regex/;                                                #(B4)
}
                              # Honolulu

# The greedy '?':
$regex = 'lulu?';                                                     #(C1)
open STDIN, "/usr/share/dict/words";                                  #(C2)
while (<>) {                                                          #(C3)
    print if /$regex/;                                                #(C4)
}
                              # cellular
                              # cellulose
                              # Honolulu
                              # lull
```

```
                                      # lullaby
                                      # lulled
                                      # lulls
                                      # multicellular
# The greedy '{}':
$regex = 'lulu{1,3}';                                              #(D1)
open STDIN, "/usr/share/dict/words";                               #(D2)
while (<>) {                                                       #(D3)
    print if /$regex/;                                             #(D4)
}
                                      # Honolulu

# The minimal-match '*?':
$regex = 'lulu*?';                                                 #(E1)
open STDIN, "/usr/share/dict/words";                               #(E2)
while (<>) {                                                       #(E3)
    print if /$regex/;                                             #(E4)
}
                                      # cellular
                                      # cellulose
                                      # Honolulu
                                      # lull
                                      # lullaby
                                      # lulled
                                      # lulls
                                      # multicellular

# The minimal match '+?':
$regex = 'lulu+?';                                                 #(F1)
open STDIN, "/usr/share/dict/words";                               #(F2)
while (<>) {                                                       #(F3)
    print if /$regex/;                                             #(F4)
}
                                      # Honolulu

# The minimal match '??':
$regex = 'lulu??';                                                 #(G1)
open STDIN, "/usr/share/dict/words";                               #(G2)
while (<>) {                                                       #(G3)
    print if /$regex/;                                             #(G4)
}
                                      # cellular
                                      # cellulose
                                      # Honolulu
                                      # lull
                                      # lullaby
                                      # lulled
                                      # lulls
                                      # multicellular
```

```
# The minimal match '{}?':
$regex = 'lulu{1,3}?';                                           #(H1)
open STDIN, "/usr/share/dict/words";                             #(H2)
while (<>) {                                                     #(H3)
    print if /$regex/;                                           #(H4)
}
                          # Honolulu
```

Python:

Shown next is a Python version of the Perl script presented above. Lines (A1) through (A11) of the Python script are for selecting words from the dictionary file `/usr/share/dict/words` with `lulu*` as the regex. Invoking `open()` in line (A2) returns a file object associated with the dictionary file. In accordance with our explanation of `open()` in Section 3.7.2 of Chapter 3, we can invoke `readline()` on the file object for reading from the dictionary file one line at a time. This is what we do in the `while` loop of line (A4). As was mentioned in Chapter 3, `readline()` retains the trailing newline character for each line read from the file and it returns an empty string at the end of the file. That explains the condition we test for in line (A6). Line (A7) carries out a regex match between the dictionary word read and the regex of line (A1). When the `MatchObject` returned by `search()` in line (A7) is not null, we know that the regex matches with the word read from the dictionary file. The output produced by this scan of the dictionary file, shown below the `while` block, is the same as for the same regex in the previous Perl script.

The example in the block of code that begins in line (B1) uses `lulu+` as the regex. Note that invoking `open()` again on the dictionary file in line (B2) resets the file pointer so as to point to the beginning of the dictionary file. (It is as if we closed the file object associated with the dictionary file and then opened it again.) The output in this case, shown below the `while` block, consists of the single word `Honolulu` because, as mentioned earlier for the Perl case, there apparently do not exist words that contain substrings line `luluu`, `luluuu`, etc.

The block starting in line (C1) uses `lulu?` for the regex. Its output, shown below the `while` block, consists of all the dictionary words that contain the substrings `lulu` and `lul`. The quantifier used being greedy, the regex matcher would seek a match for `lulu` before seeking a match for `lul`.

The block of script starting in line (D1) uses `lulu{1,3}` for its regex. Since the quantifier used is greedy, the regex matcher would seek a match for `luluuu`, and `luluu`, before settling for a match with `lulu`. Only a single word — `Honolulu` — is returned in this case.

As with the Perl script, the rest of the script below uses the nongreedy versions of the quantifiers. The block beginning in line (E1) uses `lulu*?` as its regex. As with the Perl example, the words returned are the same as for the greedy version of the quantifier. While the words returned are the same, the characters consumed by the matching operations in the two cases are different. (See the explanation for the Perl case.)

The block starting in line (F1) is for the nongreedy version of the example shown earlier in the block starting in line (B1). Both cases return just the word `Honolulu` for reasons that should be clear by now. The blocks starting in lines (G1) and (H1) are the nongreedy versions of the blocks in starting lines (C1) and (D1). In all cases, there is no difference in the selections returned from the dictionary file. However, the number of characters consumed for matching is different between the greedy and the nongreedy cases.

```
#!/usr/bin/env python

### Quantifier.py

import re

regex = r'lulu*'                                                    #(A1)
filehandle = open( '/usr/share/dict/words' )                        #(A2)
done = 0                                                            #(A3)
while not done:                                                     #(A4)
    line = filehandle.readline()                                    #(A5)
    if line != "":                                                  #(A6)
        m = re.search( regex, line )                                #(A7)
        if ( m != None ):                                           #(A8)
            print line,                                             #(A9)
    else:                                                           #(A10)
        done = 1                                                    #(A11)
#                        cellular
#                        cellulose
#                        Honolulu
#                        lull
#                        lullaby
#                        lulled
#                        lulls
#                        multicellular


regex = r'lulu+'                                                    #(B1)
filehandle = open( '/usr/share/dict/words' )                        #(B2)
done = 0
while not done:
    line = filehandle.readline()
```

```
    if line != "":
        m = re.search( regex, line )
        if ( m != None ):
            print line,
    else:
        done = 1
#                           Honolulu


regex = r'lulu?'                                                         #(C1)
filehandle = open( '/usr/share/dict/words' )                             #(C2)
done = 0
while not done:
    line = filehandle.readline()
    if line != "":
        m = re.search( regex, line )
        if ( m != None ):
            print line,
    else:
        done = 1
#                           cellular
#                           cellulose
#                           Honolulu
#                           lull
#                           lullaby
#                           lulled
#                           lulls
#                           multicellular


regex = r'lulu{1,3}'                                                     #(D1)
filehandle = open( '/usr/share/dict/words' )                             #(D2)
done = 0
while not done:
    line = filehandle.readline()
    if line != "":
        m = re.search( regex, line )
        if ( m != None ):
            print line,
    else:
        done = 1
#                           Honolulu


regex = r'lulu*?'                                                        #(E1)
filehandle = open( '/usr/share/dict/words' )                             #(E2)
done = 0
while not done:
    line = filehandle.readline()
```

```
    if line != "":
        m = re.search( regex, line )
        if ( m != None ):
            print line,
    else:
        done = 1
#                         cellular
#                         cellulose
#                         Honolulu
#                         lull
#                         lullaby
#                         lulled
#                         lulls
#                         multicellular


regex = r'lulu+?'                                                    #(F1)
filehandle = open( '/usr/share/dict/words' )                         #(F2)
done = 0
while not done:
    line = filehandle.readline()
    if line != "":
        m = re.search( regex, line )
        if ( m != None ):
            print line,
    else:
        done = 1
#                         Honolulu


regex = r'lulu??'                                                    #(G1)
filehandle = open( '/usr/share/dict/words' )                         #(G2)
done = 0
while not done:
    line = filehandle.readline()
    if line != "":
        m = re.search( regex, line )
        if ( m != None ):
            print line,
    else:
        done = 1
#                         cellular
#                         cellulose
#                         Honolulu
#                         lull
#                         lullaby
#                         lulled
#                         lulls
#                         multicellular
```

```
regex = r'lulu{1,3}?'                                                   #(H1)
filehandle = open( '/usr/share/dict/words' )                            #(H2)
done = 0
while not done:
    line = filehandle.readline()
    if line != "":
        m = re.search( regex, line )
        if ( m != None ):
            print line,
    else:
        done = 1
#                          Honolulu
```

4.11 MATCH MODIFIERS

The matching of a regular expression with a string can be subject to what are known as *match modifiers* that control various aspects of the matching operation. Modifiers are also used to control how a complicated regex is actually laid out in a script.

The modifier flags themselves are not directly a part of a regex. They are a language feature and, therefore, how they are specified is different in Perl and Python. In the subsections to follow, we will review some of the more commonly used modifiers in Perl and Python.

4.11.1 Case-Insensitive Matching

Frequently you want to ignore the case of the letters when you are searching for keywords in a text file.[29] Perl and Python use different approaches for communicating to the regex engine that matching is to be carried out in a case-insensitive manner. Perl uses the match modifier `//i` for this purpose. The same is accomplished in Python by first compiling the regex with a special flag before it is shipped off to the regex engine for matching.

Perl:

Perl uses the modifier `//i` for case-insensitive matching of a regex with a string. The notation `//i` means that you are supposed to place the letter `i` after the right

[29]The default search mode in the Google search engine, for example, is case insensitive.

delimiter for the regex, as can be seen by the usage in line (C) of the script shown next. The script, `IgnoreCase.pl`, asks the user a question in line (A) and then uses the line-input operator `<>` in line (B) to fetch the answer. This answer is compared to the regex[30]

```
^\s*(y(es)?|(no?))\s*$
```

in a case-insensitive manner because of the modifier `i` in line (C) after the right forward-slash delimiter for the above regex. This permits the user to enter his/her answer in any of the following forms:

```
yes  y  Yes  YES  yES  yEs  no  n  No  nO
```

with any amount of blank space before and after the answer. If the user enters some garbage answer, the variable `$answer` will be set to `undef` that evaluates to false in the conditional of the `if` statement in line (D).

Note that in line (C) the binding operator `=~` is invoked in a list context that is supplied by the parenthesized variable on the left of the assignment operator. As a result, the binding operator returns a list of the substrings from the input string that are grouped by the parentheses inside the regex. This would cause the variable `$answer` to be set to one of the legal answers listed above, assuming that the user entered a legal answer.

If the user entered a legal answer, it is checked for whether it is a positive answer in line (G) or a negative answer in line (J), again in a case-insensitive manner.

```
#!/usr/bin/perl -w

### IgnoreCase.pl

use strict;

print "Did you work out today?\n";                                  #(A)
my $input_string = <>;                                              #(B)
my ($answer) = ( $input_string =~ /^\s*(y(es)?|(no?))\s*$/i );      #(C)
```

[30]Unlike our earlier Perl scripts where we needed to process the user-supplied reply, we have not "chomped" the user's entry — meaning that we did not get rid of the trailing newline that will be attached to the string fetched from the user. (The trailing newline would owe its existence to the user having pressed the Enter key on the keyboard to mark the end of his/her answer.) We don't need to chomp the user's reply because the anchor metacharacter `$` matches the end of an input string; it ignores the newline if it is present at the trailing end of the input string. The anchor metacharacter `^` has a similar property with regard to a newline at the beginning of an input string — it matches the beginning of an input string ignoring the newline if one is present at the beginning.

```
if (!$answer) {                                                    #(D)
    print "That was not a legal answer\n";                         #(E)
    exit(1);                                                       #(F)
}

if ( $answer =~ /y(es)?/i ) {                                      #(G)
    print "Great, you were good today\n";                          #(H)
    exit 0;                                                        #(I)
}

if ( $answer =~ /n(o)?/i ) {                                       #(J)
    print "Uh oh! you were bad today\n";                           #(K)
    exit 0;                                                        #(L)
}
```

Python:

Shown next is a Python version of the Perl script shown above. In comparing `IgnoreCase.pl` with `IgnoreCase.py`, note how the match modifier for case-insensitive matching is supplied in lines (E), (H), and (L). If the user enters an illegal answer, meaning not one of the following:

```
yes  y  Yes  YES  yES  yEs  no  n  No  nO
```

the call to `search()` in line (E) will fail and the `MatchObject m` will be set to the null object `None`. If the call to the regex matcher in line (E) succeeds, we first retrieve the answer by invoking `group(1)` on the `MatchObject m`, and then check in lines (H) and (L) whether the answer is positive or negative.

```
#!/usr/bin/env python

### IgnoreCase.py

import re
import sys

input_string = raw_input("Did you work out today?  ")                #(A)

pattern = r'^\s*(y(es)?|(no?))\s*$'                                  #(B)
pattern_yes = r'y(es)?'                                              #(C)
pattern_no = r'n(o)?'                                                #(D)

m = re.search( pattern, input_string, re.IGNORECASE )                #(E)
```

```
if ( m != None ):                                              #(F)
    answer = m.group(1)                                        #(G)
    m1 = re.search( pattern_yes, answer, re.IGNORECASE )       #(H)
    if ( m1 != None ):                                         #(I)
        print "Great, you were good today\n"                   #(J)
        sys.exit(0)                                            #(K)
    m2 = re.search( pattern_no, answer, re.IGNORECASE )        #(L)
    if ( m2 != None ):                                         #(M)
        print "Uh oh! you were bad today\n"                    #(N)
        sys.exit(0)                                            #(O)
else:                                                          #(P)
    print "That was not a legal answer\n"                      #(Q)
    sys.exit(1)                                                #(R)
```

4.11.2 Going Global

As explained earlier, ordinarily, as a regex is translated vis-à-vis the input string during the matching operation, the translation stops at the first possible position in the input string where there is a match with the regex. But if you want the regex engine to continue chugging along and scan the entire input string for all possible positions where there exist matches with the regex, you have to set the global option as explained in this section.

What precisely is returned by the regex engine when you set the global option depends on two factors: (1) Whether or not the regex contains any groupings of subexpressions; and (2) The evaluation context of matching. These notions will be explained below for Perl and Python separately.

Perl:

The Perl script shown next is divided into six cases. In the first case in lines (C) and (D), the call to the regex engine in line (C) uses the notation `//g` to set the global option. (We also use the `//i` option here to ignore the case.) For the input string shown in line (A) and the regex shown in line (B), the regex match in line (C), evaluated in the list context supplied by the array on the left side of the assignment, returns[31] a list consisting of the following substrings extracted from the input string:

[31]Since there are no groupings in this regex, without the `//g` option, the binding operator would only return true/false despite the fact that the regex match is being carried out in a list context —that fact was explained in Section 4.2. On that other hand, when a regex contains one or more groupings of its subexpressions, the regex engine returns a list of all the substrings consumed by those subexpressions

```
cream CREAM Cream cream
```

The second case presented in lines (E) through (M) presents an entirely different way of using the global option. Now we want to count how many times a particular regex can be matched with an input string. The counting itself is done in the subroutine `word_frequency()` that is defined starting in line (G) and that is called in line (E). Note the `while` loop in line (K) that is reproduced below:

```
while ( $string =~ /$word/gi ) {                                    #(K)
    $count++;                                                       #(L)
}
```

Note in particular the `//g` option supplied to the regex engine in the conditional of the `while` loop in line (K) where the evaluation context for the regex match is scalar. Invoking regex matching with the `//g` option keeps on returning true as long as the regex can be matched with the input string as the latter is scanned from the beginning to the end. By incrementing the variable `$count` in the body of the `while` loop in line (L), we can obtain the frequency of occurrence of all the substrings that match the regex. For the regex of line (B) and the input string of line (A), the output produced by line (F) is the number 4, as shown commented out in that line.

Cases 3, 4, and 5 deal with the behavior of the `//g` option when the regex has a single grouping, more than one grouping, and, for comparison, no groupings at all.[32] These cases demonstrate the fact that what the global option causes the regex engine to return depends on whether the regex has one grouping, more than one grouping, or no groupings at all. In Case 3, the regex is `(c)ream` in line (O), in Case 4 it is `(c)(r)eam` in line (R), and in Case 5 the regex is `cream` in line (U). The input string is the same in all three cases, as set in line (N). Nevertheless, the outputs produced by lines (Q), (T), and (W) for the three cases are:

```
CASE 3 output:     c c
CASE 4 output:     c r c r
CASE 5 output:     cream cream
```

This shows that when a regex has a single grouping the output returned by the regex engine in a list context is a list of the substrings consumed by that grouping everywhere in the input string. When the regex has more than one grouping, we get a list of all of the substrings consumed for all match positions in the input string.[33] And, for contrast, when the regex has no groupings at all, as in Case 5, we simply get a list of the substrings consumed by the entire regex for every match position in the input string.

---

in a list context. See the discussion associated with the lines (E) through (G) in the script `Grouping.pl` shown in Section 4.8.

[32]One of the reasons for showing these three cases here is to draw a comparison with the behavior of Python's `re.findall()` for global matching.

[33]Under similar conditions, Python will return a list of tuples, each tuple corresponding to all the substrings consumed for a single match position in the input string.

The last case in the Perl script, Case 6, demonstrates the following additional features of the `//g` match modifier:

1. Previously, in Case 2, we showed how the `//g` modifier can be used in the scalar context provided by the conditional of a `while` statement to hop from one match position to the next in a long input string that contains multiple match positions for the same regex. We will now show that, in a scalar context, the `//g` modifier can also be used without any intent to scan the entire input string with a regex; it may be used to simply provide a value for a special anchor that is denoted `\G`. This anchor can subsequently be used for restarting the scanning of the input string at the position specified by `\G` and, if desired, this subsequent scan can be made with a different regex. *In this manner, one can carry out context dependent processing of an input string.*

2. The `//g` modifier along with the anchor `\G` can be used to return a value for the match position in an input string via the function `pos()`.

To explain these two features, let's reproduce here the scriplet for Case 6:

```
#CASE 6:
$input_string = 'Good night! Torrid dreams.';                    #(X)
if ($input_string =~ /.*good night!/gi) {                         #(Y)
    if ($input_string !~ /\G.+sweet dreams\./i) {                 #(Z)
        print "bad greetings at position ",
                               pos $input_string, "\n";           #(a)
    }
}
```

The goal of this code is to first check that the input string contains the substring "`good night!`." Only if this substring is found, we want to scan the rest of the input string to make sure that the greeting is immediately followed by the substring "`sweet dreams`." So we invoke the `//g` modifier in line (Y), not for any global matching, but just to provide a positional value for the `\G` anchor shown in line (Z). Because of the presence of the `\G` anchor, the regex matching in the input string in line (Z) will begin after the position marked by the anchor. The value of this position can be retrieved by a call to the function `pos()`, as shown in line (a). For the example shown, the output produced by line (a) is

```
bad greetings at position 11
```

as shown in line (b) of the script below.

```
#!/usr/bin/perl -w

### Global.pl

use strict;

my $input_string = "Icecream, YOU SCREAM. Creamy cream. You dream.";#(A)

my $regex = "cream";                                               #(B)

#CASE 1:
my @matches = $input_string =~ /$regex/gi;                         #(C)
#my @matches = $input_string =~ /$regex/i;                         #(C)
print "@matches\n";                  # cream CREAM Cream cream     #(D)

#CASE 2:
my $how_many = word_frequency( $regex, $input_string );            #(E)
print "$how_many" . "\n";            # 4                           #(F)

sub word_frequency {                                               #(G)
    my $word = shift;                                              #(H)
    my $string = shift;                                            #(I)
    my $count = 0;                                                 #(J)
    while ( $string =~ /$word/gi ) {                               #(K)
        $count++;                                                  #(L)
    }
    $count;                                                        #(M)
}

$input_string = "Icecream, you scream.";                           #(N)

#CASE 3:
$regex = "(c)ream";                                                #(O)
@matches = $input_string =~ /$regex/g;                             #(P)
print "@matches\n";                  # c c                         #(Q)

#CASE 4:
$regex = "(c)(r)eam";                                              #(R)
@matches = $input_string =~ /$regex/g;                             #(S)
print "@matches\n";                  # c r c r                     #(T)

#CASE 5:
$regex = "cream";                                                  #(U)
@matches = $input_string =~ /$regex/g;                             #(V)
print "@matches\n";                  # cream cream                 #(W)
```

```
#CASE 6:
$input_string = 'Good night! Torrid dreams.';                            #(X)
if ($input_string =~ /.*good night!/gi) {                                #(Y)
    if ($input_string !~ /\G.+sweet dreams\./i) {                        #(Z)
        print "bad greetings at position ", pos $input_string,"\n"; #(a)
    }
}                                # output: bad greetings at position 11  #(b)
```

Python:

The script shown next is a Python version of the Perl script presented above. What the global option //g does in Perl is achieved by calling `re.findall()` in Python. Whereas the `re.search()` function we used in our earlier Python examples stopped scanning the input string at the first position it scored a match, `re.findall()` scans the entire input string for all possible positions where the regex can be matched. As with the //g operator in Perl, the behavior of `re.findall()` depends on whether the regex contains any groupings.

The Python script presents five of the six cases in the Perl script. The last case — the one for demonstrating the \G anchor — is not included in the Python script because apparently this anchor has not been implemented in Python.

The script starts with a definition for the the `word_frequency()` function in lines (B), (C), and (D). This function is needed for Case 2 where we use it for counting the number of times a regex matches an input string. The behavior of this function will be explained when we present Case 2 below.

We set the input string in line (E), followed by Case 1 in lines (F), (G), and (H). The goal here is to globally search for and match the word `cream` with the input string of line (E) in a case-insensitive manner. Note in particular that in line (F) we must invoke `re.compile()` to construct a compiled version of the regex.[34] This is necessitated by the fact that, unlike the `re.search()` function we used in our previous examples for Python regex matching, the `re.findall()` function we invoke in line (G) for global matching does *not* take any match modifier flags. So the only way to make the matching case insensitive is to compile the regex with the `re.IGNORECASE` option as shown. The function `re.findall()` in this case returns a list of all the nonoverlapping input-string substrings that can be matched with the

[34] Although here we have no choice, in general if a regex will remain unchanged for all its matching operations with a text file, it should be compiled in the manner shown here for Python. The same can be accomplished in Perl by using the //o match modifier. Without explicit programmer-specified compilation, the regex engine will compile it separately into CPU-executable opcodes at each iteration of the regex usage, resulting in reduced performance when matching a regex with a large text file.

regex. This causes line (H) to output the list shown in the commented out portion of that line.

That takes us to Case 2 in lines (I) and (J), and the supporting function in lines (B), (C), and (D). The goal here is to count the number of times a given regex can be matched with a given input string. Since Python does not support the Perl construct in which we can test for a regex match (with the global option set) in the conditional of a `while` loop to hop from match to match, we resort to using `re.findall()` again, as shown in line (C) of the function that actually counts the frequency of matching with a regex. We invoke the built-in function `len()` to tell us the number of tuples returned by `re.findall()`. Since each tuple in the list returned by `re.findall()` corresponds to one regex matching position in the input string, the number of tuples gives us the number of times the regex can be matched with the input string. For the example, the output produced by line (K) is the number 4.

Cases 3, 4, and 5 in lines (L) through (T) of the script below mirror the similarly numbered cases for the Perl script. Case 3 demonstrates that when `re.findall()` is invoked with a regex that has a single grouping, what is returned is a list of all the matches scored with that grouping at *all* matchable positions in the input string. The two occurrences of `c` returned for Case 3 correspond to the first letter of the two occurrences of the substring `cream` in the input string of line (K). Case 4 shows that when `re.findall()` is invoked with a regex that has multiple groupings, it returns a list of tuples, each tuple showing the substrings consumed by each of the groupings at one matchable position in the input string. Finally, for contrast with Cases 3 and 4, Case 5 shows that for the same input string — as specified in line (K) — when the regex contains no groupings at all, the function `re.findall()` returns a list of the input-string substrings consumed by the whole regex at each matchable position.

```
#!/usr/bin/env python

### Global.py

import re                                                                  #(A)

def word_frequency( word, string ):                                        #(B)
    m = re.findall( word, string )                                         #(C)
    return len( m )                                                        #(D)

input_string = "Icecream, YOU SCREAM. Creamy cream. You dream."            #(E)

#CASE 1:
regex = re.compile( r'cream', re.IGNORECASE)                               #(F)
matches = re.findall( regex, input_string )                                #(G)
print matches                        # ['cream', 'CREAM', 'cream', 'Cream']#(H)

#CASE 2:
how_many = word_frequency( regex, input_string )                           #(I)
```

```
print how_many                  # 4                                         #(J)

input_string = "Icecream, you scream."                                     #(K)

#CASE 3:
regex = r'(c)ream'                                                         #(L)
matches = re.findall(regex, input_string)                                  #(M)
print matches                   # ['c', 'c']                               #(N)

#CASE 4:
regex = r'(c)(r)eam'                                                       #(O)
matches = re.findall(regex, input_string)                                  #(P)
print matches                   # [('c', 'r'), ('c', 'r')]                 #(Q)


#CASE 5:
regex = r'cream'                                                           #(R)
matches = re.findall(regex, input_string)                                  #(S)
print matches                   # ['cream', 'cream']                       #(T)
```

4.11.3 Input Strings Consisting of Multiple Lines

All of our discussion so far has dealt with input strings that consisted of single lines, which were either read one line at a time from an input file or were specified directly so in the script. When we say that an input string consists of a single line, we mean that if there is a newline character at all in the string, it occurs only at the end of the line. So what happens if an input string has newline characters in the middle?

Consider the following input string in Perl:

```
$input_string =  "apple\nbanana\npear\n";
```

which has two newline characters in the middle besides the one at the end. Suppose we try to match it with the regex shown at the right below; the regex includes the anchor ^ at the beginning and the anchor $ at the end.

```
$input_string =~   /^apple$/;
```

Would the regex engine return true or false? The regex engine would return false in this case because the default meaning of the anchor metacharacters ^ and $ is that they denote the beginning and the ending of the *entire* input string, regardless of the presence of any newline characters in-between. Does that mean that the following regex match with the same input string as shown above

```
$input_string =~   /^app.*ar$/;
```

would return true? No, because the default behavior of the character class `.` is to *not* match with the newline character.

The default meaning of the anchor metacharacters `^` and `$` and the default behavior of the character class `.` can be changed in both Perl and Python. In Perl, one uses the modifiers `//m` and `//s` for that purpose. In Python, one uses the symbolic constants `re.DOTALL` and `re.MULTILINE` for the same purpose. The Perl and Python scripts we show next illustrate these match modifiers.

Perl:

As mentioned, how Perl deals with input strings containing the newline character is controlled by the `//s` and `//m` match modifiers. The `//s` modifier permits the character class `.` to match the newline character, thus allowing regex subexpressions like `.*` to consume one or more newline characters in the input string. The `//s` modifier does not alter the behavior of the anchor metacharacters `^` and `$`.

On the other hand, the `//m` modifier changes only the behavior of the anchor metacharacters `^` and `$` without altering the default meaning of the `.` character class. With the `//m` modifier, the anchor metacharacter `$` is allowed to match a position that can either be the end of the input string or any position just before any newline character in the interior of the string. By the same token, the option `//m` allows the metacharacter `^` to match any position that is either the beginning of the entire input string or just after any newline character in the input string.

It is possible to use the modifiers `//s` and `//m` together if one needs to match the newline character with `.` and at the same time have the `^` and `$` metacharacters match the newline positions in the interior of the input string.

We will study the `//s` and `//m` match modifiers with the help of the eight cases presented in the script below.

```
#!/usr/bin/perl -w

### MultiLine.pl

use strict;

my $input_string = "abcd\nefgh\nijkl\n";                          #(A)

# CASE 1:
my $regex = 'abcd';                                                #(B)
if ( $input_string =~ /$regex/ ) {                                 #(C)
    print "match successful\n";          # match successful
} else {
```

```
    print "no success\n";
}

# CASE 2:
$regex = '^abcd$';                                                  #(D)
if ( $input_string =~ /$regex/ ) {                                  #(E)
    print "match successful\n";
} else {
    print "no success\n";                   # no success
}

# CASE 3:
$regex = '^ab.*kl$';                                                #(F)
if ( $input_string =~ /$regex/ ) {                                  #(G)
    print "match successful\n";
} else {
    print "no success\n";                   # no success
}

# CASE 4:
$regex = '^ab.*kl$';                                                #(H)
if ( $input_string =~ /$regex/s ) {                                 #(I)
    print "match successful\n";             # match successful
} else {
    print "no success\n";
}

# CASE 5:
$regex = '^abcd$';                                                  #(J)
if ( $input_string =~ /$regex/m ) {                                 #(K)
    print "match successful\n";             # match successful
} else {
    print "no success\n";
}

# CASE 6:
$regex = '^ab.*kl$';                                                #(L)
if ( $input_string =~ /$regex/m ) {                                 #(M)
    print "match successful\n";
} else {
    print "no success\n";                   #  no success
}

# CASE 7:
$regex = '^ab.*gh$';                                                #(N)
if ( $input_string =~ /$regex/sm ) {                                #(O)
    print "match successful\n";             # match successful
} else {
    print "no success\n";
```

```
}

# CASE 8:
$regex = '\Aab.*kl\Z';                                           #(P)
if ( $input_string =~ /$regex/sm ) {                             #(Q)
    print "match successful\n";            # match successful
} else {
    print "no success\n";
}
```

Case 1 in lines (B) and (C) is straightforward, as the regex in line (B) does not use either the character class `.` or the `^` and `$` anchor metacharacters. The match is successful, as evidenced by the commented-out output shown in the `if` block. This case is included simply to make the point that there is no problem with an input string including newline characters in the middle of the string. The entire string defined on the right in line (A) is a single input string.

The match in Case 2 of lines (D) and (E) fails because the anchor metacharacters in the regex require the match to start at the very beginning of the entire input string of line (A) and to end at the very end.

The match failure for Case 3 in lines (F) and (G) is caused by the fact that the character class `.` cannot match the newline characters inside the input string. Case 4 of lines (H) and (I) is the same as Case 3, except that we now use the `//s` modifier that allows the `.` character class to match even the newline character. Therefore, the match succeeds in this case, as can be seen by the output produced by the `if` block.

The match in Case 5 in lines (J) and (K) also succeeds because the `//m` modifier permits the anchors `^` and `$` to match at the newlines in the interior of the input string. However, the match in Case 6 of lines (L) and (M) fails because the `//m` modifier retains the default behavior of the `.` character class — it cannot match the newline character.

The match in Case 7 of lines (N) and (O) succeeds because we are now using both the `//s` and `//m` modifiers. Therefore, it is now possible for `.` to match the newline characters in the interior of the input string. It is also now possible for the metacharacters `^` and `$` to serve as anchors at the newline characters in the interior of the input string.

Given a multiline input string such as the one shown in line (A), what if you wanted to use the `//m` modifier to allow a match to be anchored with respect to the interior newline characters, but, at the same time, you also wanted to retain the ability to anchor a match at the very beginning and at the very end of the multiline input string? Perl provides us with the `\A` and `\Z` anchor metacharacters for that purpose, as demonstrated by the example in Case 8 in lines (P) and (Q).

Python:

What the match modifiers `//s` and `//m` do for Perl is achieved in Python by the optional arguments `re.DOTALL` and `re.MULTILINE` supplied to the `re.search()` function. Shown below is a Python script that parallels the Perl script shown above. Note the use of the optional arguments `re.DOTALL` and `re.MULTILINE` supplied to the `re.search()` function in lines (I), (K), (M), (O), and (Q) of the script. Note especially the combined use of both options in lines (O) and (Q).

Case 1 in lines (B) and (C) is straightforward since the regex of line (B) does not include either the character class `.` or the anchor metacharacters `^` and `$`. This case is included just to illustrate that it is perfectly legal for an input string to have one or more newline characters in the middle. The match in this case is successful.

Case 2 defines a regex in line (D) that uses both the anchor metacharacters `^` and `$`. Since the metacharacter `^` anchors the match at the very beginning of the input string and the metacharacter `$` at the very end, regardless of the presence of any newline characters in-between, the match in line (E) cannot succeed.

Case 3 in lines (F) and (G) uses a regex with the character class `.` and with the `^` and `$` anchors. Since the default behavior of the character class `.` is to *not* match newline characters, the regex of line (F) is unable to consume the entire input string of line (A). So we have an unsuccessful match in this case also.

Case 4 in lines (H) and (I) uses the same regex as Case 3, but we now supply the flag `re.DOTALL` as an argument to the `re.search()` function. This flag changes the default behavior of the character class `.` so that it can also match the newline characters. As a result, the match between the regex and the input string in this case is successful.

Case 5 of lines (J) and (K) uses the same regex as Case 2 of lines (D) and (E). But now we supply the flag `re.MULTILINE` as an argument to `re.search()`. This alters the default behavior of the anchor metacharacters `^` and `$` so that they can now match the newline characters in the interior of an input string. Consequently, whereas the regex match was unsuccessful in Case 2, we have a successful match now.

Case 6 of lines (L) and (M) uses the same regex as in Case 4 of lines (H) and (I). But now, instead of the flag `re.DOTALL`, we supply the flag `re.MULTILINE` to the `re.search()` function. So the character class `.` is unable to consume the newline characters in the middle of the string. This causes the regex match to fail.

Case 7 in lines (N) and (O) shows how both flags, `re.DOTALL` and `re.MULTILINE`, can be supplied to `re.search()`. In this case, the character class `.` will be able to consume the newline characters in the interior of the input string, and the anchor metacharacters will be able to match at the interior newline characters. As a result, the match is successful.

The final case, Case 8 in lines (P) and (Q), demonstrates that the anchor metacharacters `\A` and `\Z` are not yet implemented in Python. Recall from our Perl discussion that `\A` anchors a match at the very beginning of an input string and `\Z` at the very end regardless of any intervening newline characters.

```
#!/usr/bin/env python

### MultiLine.py

import re

input_string = "abcd\nefgh\nijkl\n"                                  #(A)

# CASE 1:
regex = r'abcd'                                                       #(B)
m = re.search( regex, input_string )                                  #(C)
if m: print "match successful"              # match successful
else: print "no success"

# CASE 2:
regex = r'^abcd$'                                                     #(D)
m = re.search( regex, input_string )                                  #(E)
if m: print "match successful"
else: print "no success"                    # no success

# CASE 3:
regex = r'^ab.*kl$'                                                   #(F)
m = re.search( regex, input_string )                                  #(G)
if m: print "match successful"
else: print "no success"                    # no success

# CASE 4:
regex = r'^ab.*kl$'                                                   #(H)
m = re.search( regex, input_string, re.DOTALL )                       #(I)
if m: print "match successful"              # match successful
else: print "no success"

# CASE 5:
regex = r'^abcd$'                                                     #(J)
m = re.search( regex, input_string, re.MULTILINE )                    #(K)
if m: print "match successful"              # match successful
else: print "no success"

# CASE 6:
regex = r'^ab.*kl$'                                                   #(L)
m = re.search( regex, input_string, re.MULTILINE )                    #(M)
if m: print "match successful"
```

```
else: print "no success"                        # no success

# CASE 7:
regex = r'^ab.*gh$'                                              #(N)
m = re.search( regex, input_string, re.MULTILINE | re.DOTALL )   #(O)
if m: print "match successful"                  # match successful
else: print "no success"

# CASE 8:
regex = r'\Aab.*kl\Z'                                            #(P)
m = re.search( regex, input_string, re.MULTILINE | re.DOTALL )   #(Q)
if m: print "match successful"
else: print "no success"                        # no success
```

In the regex examples shown above, we supplied the `re.MULTILINE` and `re.DOTALL` flags to the `re.search()` method. However, in general, these two along with `re.IGNORECASE` are option flags for the `re.compile()` method.[35] We could, for example, have written the lines (H) and (I) of the above script in the following manner:

```
regex = re.compile( r'^ab.*kl$', re.DOTALL )                     #(H)
m = regex.search( input_string )                                 #(I)
```

and the lines (J) and (K) in the following manner:

```
regex = re.compile( r'^abcd$',  re.MULTILINE )                   #(J)
m = regex.search( input_string )                                 #(K)
```

Also, we could have written the lines (N) and (O) in the following manner:

```
regex = re.compile( r'^ab.*gh$', re.MULTILINE | re.DOTALL )      #(N)
m = regex.search( input_string )                                 #(O)
```

This alternative syntax also demonstrates that once you obtain a regular expression object from the `re.compile()` method, you can invoke the `search()` method directly on that object. In general,

```
regex = re.compile( r'my_pattern' )
m = regex.search( input_string )
```

is equivalent to

```
regex = re.compile( r'my_pattern' )
m = re.search( regex, input_string )
```

[35]The script `Global.py` shown previously in Section 4.11.2 called `re.compile()` with the `re.IGNORECASE` option flag.

This is also true for the other regex matching methods: `match()`, `findall()`, and `finditer()`.

4.11.4 Multiline Regular Expressions

Long regular expressions can be painful to read and debug. Both Perl and Python allow a regular expression to be expressed in multiple lines and for trailing comments to be included in the lines.

To demonstrate the convenience of multiline regexes, consider the following problem. Let's say that an XML file contains the following information:[36]

```
<?xml version="1.0"?>
<!-- The name of this XML document is: Phonebook.xml -->
<phonebook>
    <listing>
        <first>John</first>
        <middle>C.</middle>
        <last>Hancock</last>
        <phone type="home">1-800-123-4567</phone>
      </listing>
    <listing>
        <first>Susan</first>
        <last>Anthony</last>
        <phone type="work">1-800-234-5678</phone>
    </listing>
    <listing>
        <first>Zaphod</first>
        <middle> Doubleheaded</middle>
        <last>Beeblecrox</last>
        <phone type="cell">9-000-666-1234</phone>
    </listing>
    <listing>
        <first>Trillian</first>
        <last>Earthling</last>
        <phone type="work">9-000-222-2345</phone>
    </listing>
    <listing>
        <first>Miss</first>
        <last>Importante</last>
        <phone type="cell">0-111-234-8888</phone>
    </listing>
</phonebook>
```

[36]Scripting for processing XML will be presented in considerable detail in Chapter 17 of this book.

And let's say that we want to present the main contents of this XML file to a client in the following more readable format:

```
Anthony, Susan              1-800-234-5678
Beeblecrox, Zaphod          9-000-666-1234
Earthling, Trillian         9-000-222-2345
Hancock, John               1-800-123-4567
Importante, Miss            0-111-234-8888
```

The next Perl script that uses a multiline regex in lines (H) through (K) does the job. The match modifier `//x` in line (K) allows the regex to be expressed in multiple lines that are allowed to include trailing comments as shown. Before we invoke matching with the regex in lines (H) through (K), we first extract the `listing` elements from the XML file in line (F). The `//g` match modifier in line (F) returns an array, each of whose elements is the content of a `listing` element in the XML file. Each `listing` element is subject to the regex matching in lines (H) through (K) for the extraction of the first name, the last name, and the phone number.[37]

```
#!/usr/bin/perl -w

### MultiLineRegex.pl

use strict;                                                             #(A)
use English;                                                            #(B)

die "needs one command line arg, the name of the XML file"
    unless @ARGV == 1;                                                  #(C)

$INPUT_RECORD_SEPARATOR = undef;                                        #(D)

my $the_whole_file = <>;                                                #(E)

my @listings = $the_whole_file =~ /<listing>(.*?)<\/listing>/sg;        #(F)

my %phonelist;                                                          #(G)

map {m/<first>(.*)<\/first>.*?                 # get first name         #(H)
       <last>(.*)<\/last>.*?                   # get last name          #(I)
       <phone.*>(.*)<\/phone>                  # get phone num          #(J)
      /sx; $phonelist{"$2, $1"} = $3 } @listings;                       #(K)

my $template = "@<<<<<<<<<<<<<<<<<<<<<      @>>>>>>>>>>>>>>>";           #(L)
```

[37] The reader is directed to Section 17.2 of Chapter 17 for additional explanation on this script. The name of the this script in that chapter is `ExtractEleInfo.pl`.

```
foreach (sort keys %phonelist) {                                          #(M)
    formline( $template, $_, $phonelist{$_} );                            #(N)
    print $ACCUMULATOR, "\n";                                             #(O)
    $ACCUMULATOR = "";                                                    #(P)
}
```

Multiline regexes in Python are specified with the help of the `re.VERBOSE` flag to the `re.compile()` method for creating a regular expression object, as demonstrated by lines (M) through (P) of the next script. This flag causes all white space within the regex to be ignored unless the white space is inside a character class or is preceded by a backslash. Additionally, in each line, the character `#` is considered to signify the start of a comment, unless this character appears inside a character class or is preceded by a backslash. This script does exactly the same thing as the previously shown Perl script — it extracts, first, the `listing` elements from the XML document in lines (K) and (L) and, subsequently, the first name, the last name, and the phone number from each `listing` element in lines (M) through (U).[38]

```
#!/usr/bin/env python

### MultiLineRegex.py

import sys                                                                #(A)
import re                                                                 #(B)

if len(sys.argv) is not 2:                                                #(C)
    sys.exit( "Name the XML file in the command line")                    #(D)

try:                                                                      #(E)
    FILE = open( sys.argv[1], 'r' )                                       #(F)
except IOError, e:                                                        #(G)
    print "Cannot open file: ", e                                         #(H)
    sys.exit(1)                                                           #(I)

the_whole_file = FILE.read()                                              #(J)

regex = r'<listing>(.*?)<\/listing>'                                      #(K)
matches = re.findall( regex, the_whole_file, re.DOTALL )                  #(L)

regex =  re.compile( r'''<first>(.*)<\/first>.*?     # get first name#(M)
                         <last>(.*)<\/last>.*?       # get last name #(N)
```

[38]Further information on this script is available in Section 17.2 of Chapter 17 where it is named `ExtractEleInfo.py`.

```
                        <phone.*>(.*)<\/phone>''', # get phone num #(O)
                   re.DOTALL | re.VERBOSE )                        #(P)
phonelist = {}                                                     #(Q)
for listing in matches:                                            #(R)
    m = re.search( regex, listing )                                #(S)
    if m is not None:                                              #(T)
        phonelist["%s, %s" % (m.group(2), m.group(1))] = m.group(3) #(U)

for item in sorted( phonelist.items() ):                           #(V)
    print "      %-20s\t%15s" % item                               #(W)
```

As we are on the subject of how to make long regexes more intelligible, this is a good place to mention that Python also allows for symbolic names to be associated with the various capturing groups of a regex as specified with the `()` metacharacters. The block of code in lines (M) through (U) of the above script could, for example, be replaced by the following block that uses named groups:

```
regex =  re.compile( r'''<first>(?P<first>.*)<\/first>.*?  # first#(M)
                         <last>(?P<last>.*)<\/last>.*?     # last #(N)
                         <phone.*>(?P<ph>.*)<\/phone>''',  # phone#(O)
                    re.DOTALL | re.VERBOSE )                     #(P)
phonelist = {}                                                   #(Q)
for listing in matches:                                          #(R)
    m = re.search( regex, listing )                              #(S)
    if m is not None:                                            #(T)
        phonelist["%s, %s" % (m.group('first'), m.group('last'))] = \
                       m.group('ph')                             #(U)
```

Notice we replaced the subexpression `(.*)` by `(?P<first>.*)`. This causes the tag `<first>` to be associated with the input string characters that will be captured by this portion of the regex. Subsequently, as we show in the statement that ends in line (U), they can be retrieved by a more mnemonic syntax `m.group('first')` as opposed to the syntax `m.group(1)` we used previously.

This syntax for naming a grouping inside a regex can also be used in the more commonly employed single-line regexes. When groupings are named in this manner, any backreferences to them inside the same regex uses the `(?P=grouping_name)` syntax.

4.11.5 Other Match Modifiers

So far we have described the following of the Perl's match modifiers: `//i`, `//g`, `//s`, `//m`, `//o`, and `//x`. We have also mentioned that equivalent effects can be achieved in Python by, respectively, the symbolic constant `re.IGNORECASE`, the method call `re.findall()`, the symbolic constant `re.DOTALL`, the symbolic constant `re.MULTILINE`, the method call `re.compile()`, and the symbolic constant `re.VERBOSE`. For the Python case, the symbolic constant `re.IGNORECASE` is supplied as an argument to the method `re.compile()`, and the symbolic constants `re.DOTALL` and `re.MULTILINE` to `re.compile()` or directly to `re.search()`. All of the Python symbolic constants can be supplied as compilation options to `re.compile()`.

Perl also supports the match modifiers `//c` and `//e`. The modifier `//c` is used in conjunction with the modifier `//g` if we do not want a failed match to change the position value stored in the `\G` anchor. The modifier `//e` is used in search and replace operations to evaluate a pattern before it is substituted in the input string, as explained further in Section 4.13.

4.12 SPLITTING STRINGS

Earlier we mentioned that the four most common applications of regex matching are (a) for detecting for the presence or the absence of a given pattern in an input string; (b) for extracting substrings matching all or portions of a pattern; (c) for splitting an input string into substrings based on separators specified as patterns; and (d) for search and replace operations. We have already reviewed in detail the first two applications of regex matching. Now we will talk about how to split an input string into a list of substrings based on the presence of separators between the substrings.

Perl:

Perl provides the function `split()` for splitting an input string into an array of substrings. This function takes two arguments, the first a regex that is used as a separator and the second the input string. Wherever the regex matches the input string becomes a point where the latter is split. The input-string characters consumed by the matches with the separator regex do not appear in the array of words returned by the splitting function. The first argument to `split()` is typically within a matching pair of delimiter symbols that Perl uses for regular expressions, usually `//`. The next script, `Split.pl`, explains the behavior of `split()` by invoking it with different regexes and input strings.

Case 1 in lines (A1) through (A5) shows what is probably the most common use of `split()` in Perl. The separator regex specified in line (A2) matches an arbitrary amount of white space between the words in an input string. For the input string of line (A1), the output produced by the formatting action of lines (A4) and (A5) applied to the result returned by `split()` in line (A3) is shown in the commented-out section below the case block. Line (A4) invokes Perl's `map` function to attach a newline character to each array element so that the individual words returned by `split()` can be displayed vertically.[39]

The input string in line (B1) of Case 2 is meant to demonstrate that the `\s+` separator we used in Case 1 is good enough to consume all white-space characters, including tabs, newlines, etc. The reader is obviously not surprised by this since the character class `\s` stands for all white-space characters. As a consequence, produced by lines (B4) and (B5) is the same as in Case 1.

Case 3 in lines (C1) through (C5) demonstrates the use of `split()` to cleanse the words in an input string of any punctuation marks sticking to them.[40] The output of lines (C4) and (C5) is the same as for Cases 1 and 2.

Case 4 demonstrates what happens if there are instances of the separator pattern at the leading end of the input string. An important property of `split()` is that it creates an element — *even if it is an empty element* — every time it scores a regex match with the separator pattern. The input string in line (D1) is

```
###apples##oranges#bananas###pears
```

where the character `#` denotes a blank space. Since the separator `\s+` of line (D2) can score a match *before* the first word `apples` in the input string, `split()` will create an array element for the output, although this array element will be an empty string. To underscore this point, line (D4) converts every empty string element of the output array into the string `EMPTY`. This explains the output produced by lines (D5) and (D6).

Case 5 demonstrates that the above mentioned property of `split()` does not apply at the trailing end. As shown in line (E1), the input string is now

```
:::apples:oranges:bananas:pears:::
```

and the regex for the separator in line (E2) just the `:` character. Obviously, we have three matches for the separator regex at the leading end of the input string and three matches at the trailing end. However, as can be seen from the output produced, the trailing-end matches with the separator regex are ignored.

Case 6 in lines (F1) through (F5) is merely an application of what we have reviewed so far to an example in which we want to separate the pathname of a file into the names of the directories and the file. The separator pattern here is just the `/` character. Because we also use the same character to delimit the regex, its use for the separator pattern has to be backslashed as shown in line (F2).

Case 7 in lines (G1) through (G4) is meant to show that it is possible to call `split()` without any arguments at all. The no-argument call is equivalent to

[39] If we had displayed them horizontally, the output would look visually similar to the input string.

[40] Cleaning up words in this manner is often a prerequisite to further text processing for the purpose of, say, creating a search tree for fast dictionary lookup of the words.

```
split /\s+/, $_;
```

This comes in handy inside `while` or `foreach` loops when the default `$_` is used as the loop control variable. For the small demonstration in Case 7, we have set the value of `$_` explicitly in line (G1). This is the string that will be split by the argument-less invocation of `split()`, producing the output shown. The no-argument invocation of `split()` has one special property — it ignores any white space at the leading end of the input string.

Finally, Case 8 in lines (H1) through (H4) shows another special case of invoking `split()` when it again ignores any amount of white space at the leading end of an input string. This special case occurs when the separator regex consists of just the blank space character, as in the call to `split()` in line (H2). The input string in line (H1) has five blank space characters at its leading end. So ordinarily, the array returned by `split()` would have five empty elements at the beginning. But that does not happen in this case, as evidenced by the output shown and as can also be confirmed by interposing a statement like the one in line (E4) between lines (H2) and (H3).

```
#!/usr/bin/perl -w

### Split.pl

use strict;

# Case 1:
my $input_string = "apples oranges bananas pears";                #(A1)
my $pattern = '\s+';                                              #(A2)
my @words = split /$pattern/, $input_string;                      #(A3)
@words = map "     $_\n", @words;                                 #(A4)
print @words;                                                     #(A5)
#                                  apples
#                                  oranges
#                                  bananas
#                                  pears

# Case 2:
$input_string = "apples   oranges\nbananas\t    pears";            #(B1)
$pattern = '\s+';                                                 #(B2)
@words = split /$pattern/, $input_string;                         #(B3)
@words = map "     $_\n", @words;                                 #(B4)
print @words;                                                     #(B5)
#                                  apples
#                                  oranges
#                                  bananas
#                                  pears
# Case 3:
```

```
$input_string = "apples,   oranges. bananas;    pears";          #(C1)
$pattern = '[,.;]?\s+';                                            #(C2)
@words = split /$pattern/, $input_string;                          #(C3)
@words = map "     $_\n", @words;                                  #(C4)
print @words;                                                      #(C5)
#                                 apples
#                                 oranges
#                                 bananas
#                                 pears

# Case 4:
$input_string = "    apples  oranges bananas    pears";           #(D1)
$pattern = '\s+';                                                  #(D2)
@words = split /$pattern/, $input_string;                          #(D3)
@words = map { $_ eq "" ? "EMPTY" : $_ } @words;                   #(D4)
@words = map "     $_\n", @words;                                  #(D5)
print @words;                                                      #(D6)
#                                 EMPTY
#                                 apples
#                                 oranges
#                                 bananas
#                                 pears

# Case 5:
$input_string = ":::apples:oranges:bananas:pears:::";              #(E1)
$pattern = ':';                                                    #(E2)
@words = split /$pattern/, $input_string;                          #(E3)
@words = map { $_ eq "" ? "EMPTY" : $_ } @words;                   #(E4)
@words = map "     $_\n", @words;                                  #(E5)
print @words;                                                      #(E6)
#                                 EMPTY
#                                 EMPTY
#                                 EMPTY
#                                 apples
#                                 oranges
#                                 bananas
#                                 pears

# Case 6:
$input_string = "/usr/bin/perl";                                   #(F1)
@words = split /\//, $input_string;                                #(F2)
@words = map { $_ eq "" ? "EMPTY" : $_ } @words;                   #(F3)
@words = map "     $_\n", @words;                                  #(F4)
print @words;                                                      #(F5)
#                                 EMPTY
#                                 usr
#                                 bin
#                                 perl
```

```
# Case 7:
$_ = "apples oranges bananas pears";                         #(G1)
@words = split;                                              #(G2)
@words = map "     $_\n", @words;                            #(G3)
print @words;                                                #(G4)
#                              apples
#                              oranges
#                              bananas
#                              pears
# Case 8:
$input_string = "      apples oranges bananas pears";        #(H1)
@words = split ' ', $input_string;                           #(H2)
@words = map "     $_\n", @words;                            #(H3)
print @words;                                                #(H4)
#                              apples
#                              oranges
#                              bananas
#                              pears
```

Python:

We will now show how we can use the `re.split()` function in Python for splitting an input string when using a regex to specify where the splits should take place.[41] Except for the minor differences we will point out here, `re.split()` produces the same results as the `split()` function of Perl.

Shown next is a Python script that has the Python equivalents of the first six cases from the Perl script. The last two cases cannot be reproduced in Python because the language simply does not allow for those.

The script starts with two functions, `myprint()` and `look_for_empties()`, that are needed to make the output produced by this script look the same as the previous Perl script. As the reader can see, `myprint()`, defined in lines (1) through (3), offsets each word with some empty space and prints it out in a separate line. The function `look_for_empties()`, defined in lines (4) through (8), is used as a first argument to the built-in function `map()` to convert an empty word into the string `EMPTY` so that we can better see the behavior of `re.split()` when an input string has characters at the leading and the trailing ends that match the separator regex.

[41]For simple cases of splitting strings, it is more common in Python to use the `split()` method of the string class, as demonstrated by our scripts `StringOps.py` in Section 3.3.1 and `MapFilter.py` in Section 3.13 of Chapter 3.

The first case, presented in lines (A1) through (A4), is probably the most common invocation of `re.split()` in Python. The separator pattern, specified by the regex in line (A2), causes an input string to be split on the basis of any white-space characters between the words.

Case 2, in lines (B1) through (B4), is basically the same as Case 1, except that the input string now contains newline and tab characters. This case shows that the word separation achieved with the regex in both cases will also absorb white-space characters like tabs, newlines, and so on. Both cases produce the same output, as shown in the commented out lines below the case blocks.

Case 3, in lines (C1) through (C4), shows how any punctuation marks sticking to the words can be removed when an input string is split into separate words.

Case 4, in lines (D1) through (D5), shows what happens when the separator regex is able to match at the very beginning of an input string. The input string in this case has white space at the beginning and the separator regex can match on white space. As with Perl, you will see an empty string for the first word in the output. By invoking `look_for_empties()` in line (D4), we convert each empty string in the output produced by the splitting operation into the word `EMPTY`. Note how Python's built-in `map()` function, reviewed previously in Section 3.13 of Chapter 3, is used in line (D4) to apply `look_for_empties()` to each element of the second argument.

Case 5, in lines (E1) through (E5), considers the case when the separator can match at multiple positions at the leading end and/or at the trailing end of an input string. We again end up with an empty string for the corresponding element in the output of the splitting operation. As in the previous case, we invoke `look_for_empties()` to convert the empty-string words in the output into the more visible word `EMPTY`.

Case 6, in lines (F1) through (F4), shows us invoking `re.split()` on an input string that consists of a Unix pathname. The separator in this case is just the / character.

```
#!/usr/bin/env python

### Split.py

import re

def myprint( words ):                                                     #(1)
    for item in words:                                                    #(2)
        print "    " + item                                               #(3)

def look_for_empties( arg ):                                              #(4)
    if (arg == ""):                                                       #(5)
        return "EMPTY"                                                    #(6)
    else:                                                                 #(7)
```

```
        return arg                                                    #(8)

# Case 1:
input_string = "apples oranges bananas pears"                        #(A1)
regex = r'\s+'                                                        #(A2)
words = re.split( regex, input_string )                               #(A3)
myprint( words )                                                      #(A4)
#                                  apples
#                                  oranges
#                                  bananas
#                                  pears

# Case 2:
input_string = "apples  oranges\nbananas\t    pears"                  #(B1)
regex = r'\s+'                                                        #(B2)
words = re.split( regex, input_string )                               #(B3)
myprint( words )                                                      #(B4)
#                                  apples
#                                  oranges
#                                  bananas
#                                  pears

# Case 3:
input_string = "apples,  oranges. bananas;   pears"                   #(C1)
regex = r'[,.;]?\s+'                                                  #(C2)
words = re.split( regex, input_string )                               #(C3)
myprint( words )                                                      #(C4)
#                                  apples
#                                  oranges
#                                  bananas
#                                  pears

# Case 4:
input_string = "   apples  oranges bananas   pears"                   #(D1)
regex = r'\s+'                                                        #(D2)
words = re.split( regex, input_string )                               #(D3)
words = map( look_for_empties, words )                                #(D4)
myprint( words )                                                      #(D5)
#                                  EMPTY
#                                  apples
#                                  oranges
#                                  bananas
#                                  pears

# Case 5:
input_string = ":::apples:oranges:bananas:pears:::"                   #(E1)
regex = r':'                                                          #(E2)
words = re.split( regex, input_string )                               #(E3)
words = map( look_for_empties, words )                                #(E4)
```

```
myprint( words )                                                  #(E5)
#                                  EMPTY
#                                  EMPTY
#                                  EMPTY
#                                  apples
#                                  oranges
#                                  bananas
#                                  pears
#                                  EMPTY
#                                  EMPTY
#                                  EMPTY

# Case 6:
input_string = "/usr/bin/perl"                                    #(F1)
words = re.split( r'/', input_string )                            #(F2)
words = map( look_for_empties, words )                            #(F3)
myprint( words )                                                  #(F4)
#                                  EMPTY
#                                  usr
#                                  bin
#                                  perl
```

The reader will notice that apart from Case 5, all the other outputs are identical for the Perl and the Python cases. However, for Case 5, Python does the same thing at the trailing end of an input string that Perl only does at the leading end. That is, Python creates an output word every time there is a regex match between the separator pattern and the input string regardless of whether the match takes place before the first text word in the input string, or after the last word. Recall, Perl's `split()` exhibits this behavior only at the leading end of a string, ignoring any characters or substrings at the trailing end if they match the separator regex.

4.12.1 Joining Strings

This subsection really does not belong in a chapter on regular expressions because, unlike what it takes to split a string, there are no regexes involved in joining strings together to form longer strings. Nonetheless, at least from a functional standpoint, splitting and joining do belong together. It is not uncommon that you would first split a long input string on the basis of some separator pattern, select some of the substrings returned by the splitting operation, and then rejoin the selected substrings to form another string.

In the rest of this section, we will demonstrate joining strings in Perl by calling the built-in `join()` function and doing the same in Python with the help of the `join()` method of the string class.

Perl:

Shown below is a Perl script that illustrates how the `join()` function works for creating a string from an array of smaller strings. Line (A) uses the `qw//` operator described earlier in Chapter 2 to deposit a list of words in the array variable `@words`. As shown in line (B), the first argument to `join()` is the "glue" that will be placed between the array elements when they are joined together. The second argument to `join()` is the array containing the strings that need to be joined together. The output produced in line (C) is as shown in the commented-out portion of that line. Lines (D) and (E) show a similar example with the space character as the glue. Note that the output produced by line (E), shown in the commented-out portion of that line, is one continuous string from the beginning letter `h` of `hello` to the ending letter `o` of `jello` and it includes some embedded blank space characters.

```
#!/usr/bin/perl -w

### Join.pl

use strict;

my @words = qw{ hello yello mello jello };                            #(A)

my $string = join ':', @words;                                        #(B)
print "$string\n";                  # hello:yello:mello:jello         #(C)

$string = join ' ', @words;         # hello yello mello jello         #(D)
print "$string\n";                                                    #(E)
```

Python:

To achieve similar string joining effects in Python, we can use the method `join()` that is defined for the string class. Typically, the method is invoked on the string that is meant to be the glue between the words that are supposed to be joined together. This is illustrated by the call syntax in lines (B) and (D).[42] The joining glue in line (B) is the string composed of just the character `:` and the same in line (D) is the string composed of just the blank-space character. Apart from this syntax difference, the end results are the same as for Perl.

[42] The syntax of the function calls in lines (B) and (D) will become clearer after the reader has gone through Chapter 7.

```
#!/usr/bin/env python

### Join.py

words = ["hello", "yello", "mello", "jello"]                          #(A)

string = ":".join( words )                                            #(B)
print string                        # hello:yello:mello:jello         #(C)

string = " ".join( words )                                            #(D)
print string                        # hello yello mello jello         #(E)
```

4.13 REGEXES FOR SEARCH AND REPLACE OPERATIONS

This is the last of the major applications of regex matching we review in this chapter. A search and replace operation is an extension of the matching operation because it calls for surgically altering the input string after a match is found. The alteration consists of replacing the matched portion of the input string with a replacement substring. The input string may be altered either in-place, as is usually the case with Perl, or an altered version of the input string may be returned separately, as is the case in Python.

Perl:

The Perl script shown next demonstrates how the `s///` operator can be used for search and replace operations. The prefix `s` in this operator stands for "switch" or "substitution." The basic syntax for using this operator is illustrated by the following example:

```
"one hello is like any other hello"   =~   s/hello/armadillo/;
```

The `s///` operator searches an input string for the occurrence of a substring that matches the regex between the first pair of delimiters `//` and, when it finds a match, it replaces the substring with the replacement text that is between the second pair of delimiters.[43] The `s///` operator returns an empty string if there does not exist

[43]What is between the second pair of delimiters can, in general, be a Perl expression whose evaluation returns the replacement text. If the replacement is an expression, its evaluation can be carried out with the `//e` modifier as we will explain shortly. The replacement expression is also allowed to contain

a match between the input string and the regex between the first pair of delimiters. Otherwise, it returns a number that equals the number of substitutions made in the input string.

In the above example, the input string is supplied by the binding operator `=~` as its left operand. The binding operator returns false if the `s///` operator fails and true otherwise. If the binding operator is not used for supplying the input string, the substitution operator will carry out the search and replace operations in the string stored in the default variable `$_`.

As with the match operator `m//`, it is not necessary to use the forward slash as the delimiter character when using `s///`. Any nonalphanumeric, non-white-space character can be used as the delimiter. However, since we need a three-part delimiter now, the rules for using delimiters that come in symmetric pairs, such as `{}` and `[]`, are different: Both the pattern and the replacement must be enclosed within such a pair. Moreover, the two pairs of delimiters used in this manner do not have to be identical. Here are some examples of the different ways of expressing the `s///` operator:

```
s/hello/armadillo/
s#\#/#
s{cool}{hot}
s{^}(START: )
...
```

All of the match modifiers we discussed in Section 4.11 for regex matching also apply to the substitution operator `s///`. We want to draw the reader's attention in particular to the `//e` modifier that we mentioned only cursorily as the "evaluation" modifier in Section 4.11.5. As mentioned there, `//e` is particularly useful in search and replace operations where it can be used to evaluate the replacement as a Perl expression before its substitution in the input string. The next script illustrates the use of the `//e` modifier with the help of the following invocation of the `s///` operator:

```
s/^(\S+)/$1 x 3/e;
```

This converts the input string

```
"Ha! You are so funny!"
```

into the string

```
Ha!Ha!Ha! You are so funny!
```

The `//e` modifier causes the replacement pattern `$1 x 3` to be evaluated as a Perl expression. The variable `$1` in this expression supplies the substring matched to the parenthesized subexpression in the regex `^(\S+)` and the Perl's repetition operator

scalar variables with string values. The strings for these variables are interpolated into the replacement expression before substitution.

x causes this substring to be repeated 3 times for the construction of the replacement string.

The rest of the script shown next is self-explanatory. The simplest case is shown in lines (A) through (C) where the modifier //g in line (B) causes every occurrence of hello in the input string to be replaced by armadillo. Without the //g modifier, only the first occurrence of hello would be replaced. The output produced by line (C) is shown commented-out below that line.

The case presented in lines (D), (E), and (F) is a common application of the s/// operator for replacing arbitrarily long white space between the words in a string by a single blank space. Note how the multiple blank spaces, the newline character, and the tab character between the words are all replaced by a single blank space in each case.

The case in lines (G), (H), and (I) shows how one can "filter" an input string by eliminating words on the basis of certain criteria. Here we get rid of the words that have punctuation marks sticking to them. This case also demonstrates that when the substitution operator is invoked without the binding operator, the search and replace operations are carried out on the string stored in the variable $_.

The case in lines (J), (K), and (L) demonstrates using the # character as a delimiter in the s/// operator (so that it now is actually the s### operator).

The case in lines (M), (N), and (O) shows the use of a match variable — in this case the variable $1 — in the replacement expression. Since the search regex is (\ba\w+), the variable $1 will be bound to the substring apples for the input string of line (M). In accordance with the explanation in Section 2.1.2 of Chapter 2, the escape \U then forces this substring to become all uppercase.

We have already explained the effect achieved in the last case, in lines (P), (Q) and (R), with the //e operator.

```
#!/usr/bin/perl -w

### SearchAndReplace.pl

use strict;

my $input_string = "one hello is like any other hello";                  #(A)
$input_string =~ s/hello/armadillo/g;                                      #(B)
print "$input_string\n";                                                   #(C)
#                         one armadillo is like any other armadillo

$input_string = "apples     oranges\nbananas\t    pears";                #(D)
$input_string =~ s/\s+/ /g;                                                #(E)
print "$input_string\n";                                                   #(F)
#                         apples oranges bananas pears
```

```
$_ = "apples oranges, bananas; pears\n";                              #(G)
s/\b(\w+)[.,;:]\s+//g;                                                #(H)
print;                                                                #(I)
#                         apples pears

$_ = "http://programming_with_objects.com";                           #(J)
s#//#//www.#;                                                         #(K)
print "$_\n";                                                         #(L)
#                         http://www.programming_with_objects.com

$_ = "apples oranges bananas pears";                                  #(M)
s{(\ba\w+)}{\U$1}g;                                                   #(N)
print;                                                                #(O)
#                         APPLES oranges bananas pears

$_ = "Ha! You are so funny!";                                         #(P)
s/^(\S+)/$1 x 3/e;                                                    #(Q)
print;                                                                #(R)
#                         Ha!Ha!Ha! You are so funny!
```

Python:

Shown next is a Python version of the Perl script shown above. What was accomplished by the `s///` operator for Perl is now achieved by `re.sub()`. This method is typically called with three arguments: the first argument a regex to search for, the second argument the replacement string, and the third argument the input string.

The script presents the Python equivalents for the first five of the six cases shown in the Perl script. The last case is not included here since Python does not seem to provide evaluation capability for replacement strings.

While the first four cases in the script produce the same results as the corresponding cases for the Perl script, that is, however, not the case for the fifth case in lines (J) and (K). What was achieved by the following invocation of the `s///` operator for Perl

```
s{(\ba\w+)}{\U$1}g;
```

we try to achieve for Python by

```
re.sub( r'(\ba\w+)', r'\1'.upper(), input_string )
```

where we have tried to invoke the method `upper()` defined for the string class to convert whatever is bound to the backreference `\1` into all uppercase. But possibly because of a bug in the system, it does not produce the desired result.[44]

```
#!/usr/bin/env python

## SearchAndReplace.py

import re

input_string = "one hello is like any other hello"                    #(A)
input_string = re.sub( 'hello', 'armadello', input_string )           #(B)
print input_string                                                    #(C)
#                    one armadello is like any other armadello

input_string = "apples     oranges\nbananas\t    pears"              #(D)
input_string = re.sub( r'\s+', ' ', input_string )                   #(E)
print input_string                                                    #(F)
#                    apples oranges bananas pears

input_string = "apples oranges, bananas; pears\n"                     #(G)
output_string = re.sub( r'\b(\w+)[.,;:]\s+', r'\1 ', input_string ) #(H)
print output_string                                                   #(I)
#                    apples oranges bananas pears

input_string = "http://programming_with_objects.com"                  #(J)
print re.sub( r'//', r'//www.', input_string )                        #(K)
#                    http://www.programming_with_objects.com

input_string = "apples oranges bananas pears"                         #(L)
print re.sub( r'(\ba\w+)', r'\1'.upper(), input_string )              #(M)
#                    apples oranges bananas pears

print re.sub( r'(\ba\w+)', r'hello'.upper(), input_string )           #(N)
#                    HELLO oranges bananas pears
```

[44]The problem appears to be with the use of the backreference in combination with the invocation of `upper()`. This is verified by the output shown for the statement in line (N) of the script.

4.14 CREDITS AND SUGGESTIONS FOR FURTHER READING

The book by Jeffrey Friedl [21] is widely acknowledged to be the most authoritative source of information regarding regular expressions. The on-line Perl tutorial "perlretut" (Perl Regular Expressions Tutorial) by Mark Kvale is also excellent and highly recommended. Regular expressions have their roots in the theory of formal languages where they are used for compact representation of *regular languages*, these being languages that are accepted by deterministic finite automata (DFA) and nondeterministic finite automata (NDFA). A practical consequence of this theory is that that regex-based string matching can be carried out very efficiently by compiling a regex into either a DFA or an NDFA and representing the compiled output in the form of machine executable opcodes. For a theoretically inclined reader, Chapter 8 of [16] is an excellent introduction to regular languages, and to deterministic and nondeterministic finite automata.

4.15 HOMEWORK

1. Write Perl and Python scripts that do the same thing as the following Unix command line:

```
awk -F: '/kak/ {print $7}' /etc/passwd
```

   See Problem 4 in the Homework section of Chapter 2 for a brief explanation of what `awk` does. While the example of `awk` shown in that problem used only the *action* part of a single-quoted *pattern-action* pair that was supplied to `awk`, the example shown here specifies both a pattern and the action to be carried out on the line that matches with the pattern. The above command line will therefore print out the 7th field of any line in the `/etc/passwd` file that contains the string `kak`. (See Problem 5 in the Homework section of Chapter 2 for the structure of each line in this file.)

2. Let's say you are given a database flat file called `data.txt` whose contents look like

```
john adams      714-234-3382      38      rockets
sally jones     362-333-1239      37      spartans
hilton jones    213-234-8976      23      jocks
ashton adams    714-333-9876      19      spartans
....
....
```

Each line of this flat file consists of a name, a phone number, age, and the name of the club to which the individual belongs. Let's also say that we want to designate everyone belonging to the `spartans` club as a potential donor to a cause. The following Unix command line does the job:

```
sed '/spartans/s/$/ potential donor/' data.txt >          \
                                      data_with_donors.txt
```

where we have used the text-based line editor `sed` for making the needed changes and writing the output to a new file[45] called `data_with_donors.txt`. The single-quoted string in the above command line consists of four forward-slash delimited parts:

```
address pattern:                spartans
editor command:                 s
regex for substitution:         $
the replacement string:           potential donor
```

The single-quoted string will first seek out all lines that contain the string `spartans`. The string substitution command `s` will then identify that part of the line which matches the regex. The sequence of characters thus identified will then be replaced by the last component of the single-quoted string. In our case, `$` is the regex, meaning that we want the string substitution to take place at the end of the line, the replacement string being "`potential donor`." Therefore, the output file `data_with_donors.txt` will look like

```
john adams      714-234-3382   38   rockets
sally jones     362-333-1239   37   spartans potential donor
hilton jones    213-234-8976   23   jocks
ashton adams    714-333-9876   19   spartans potential donor
```

Write Perl and Python scripts that possess the same functionality as the Unix command line shown.

3. You are given a text file with line breaks that are sometimes in the middle of the words. Here is an example:

[45] If the goal was to just show the changed lines on the terminal screen, we would use the following command line:

```
sed -n '/spartans/s/$/ potential donor/p' data.txt
```

where the `-n` option suppresses the default output that consists of all the lines in the input file regardless of whether they are changed on not. The `/p` option at the end of the single-quoted string prints out just the lines that get changed.

```
They say languages just die, as spo
ken Latin did, and then are rebo
rn as French, Spanish and Italian.
 No big deal. Or, more bluntly, all
 this sentimentalilty about dy
ing languages is just another symp
tom of academe's mewling, politic
ally correct minority-mongering.
 --- The New York Times
```

Assume that when a word is split by a linebreak, the fragment at the beginning of the next line has no white space at its left. Write Perl and Python scripts that first rejoin such words and then store the whole words in an array. (All this can be done with just a couple of statements of Perl that use the `split()` and `join()` functions. The same applies to Python with its own split and join functions as described in this chapter.)

4. What do you think would happen if you use an empty regex for splitting a string, that is, if you call

```
@words = split //, "abracadabra";
```

Along the same lines, try the following for Python

```
words = re.split( r'', "abracadabra" )
```

Is what you get for Perl the same as what you get for Python?

5. The regexes used for splitting a string into substrings usually tend to be simple patterns, basically consisting of whatever characters are meant to delimit the extracted strings. But, at least theoretically, nothing prevents you from supplying a complex looking regex as the first argument to the splitting function. As a step in that direction, what do you think would happen if you include grouping parentheses inside a regex used for splitting a string, as in

```
@words = split /(ab|ba)/, "abracadabra";
```

For Python, give the following a try:

```
words = re.split( r'(ab|ba)', "abracadabra" )
```

6. The goal of this homework problem is to write Perl and Python scripts for extracting the user-supplied information in an HTML form on a web page. This information is sent back to the web server in the form of a single string called the *query string*. The next couple of paragraphs are meant for a reader not familiar with such query strings.

   HTML forms are widely used in web pages to elicit information from users. A user enters the requested information in the designated spaces in a form displayed by a web browser and then clicks on a SUBMIT button. The clicking action causes the information supplied by the user to be sent back to the web server. This information is usually in the form of one long continuous string of characters. To illustrate the nature of this string, let us say that the form displayed by the web browser appears as shown in Fig.4.1. Depending on the

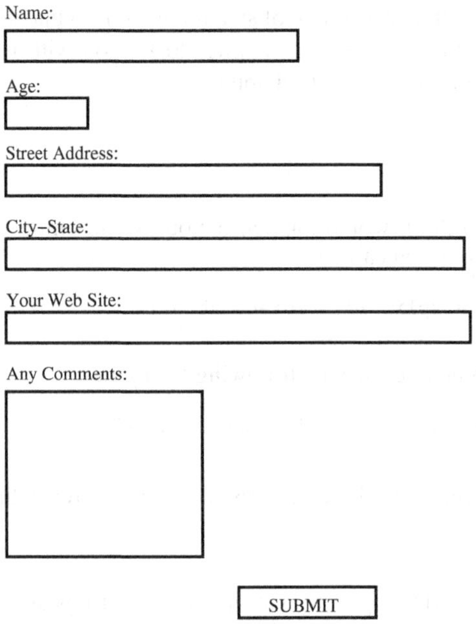

   Name:

   Age:

   Street Address:

   City–State:

   Your Web Site:

   Any Comments:

   SUBMIT

   Fig. 4.1

   entries made by the user, the query string returned to the web server when the user clicks on the SUBMIT button may look like

   ```
   name=Mister+Bigshot&age=39&street=123++Main+Street&city=City+
   of+Joy&website=http%3A%2F%2Fhello.com&comments=This+is+a+
   cool%0D%0Aform.
   ```

   Note that this is supposed to be one continuous string, although it is shown in three separate lines here on account of space constraints. The query string is characterized by the following features:

- The query string consists of `key=value` pairs that are separated by the symbol `&`. The above query string contains the following such pairs:

  ```
  name=Mister+Bigshot

  age=39

  street=123++Main+Street

  city=City+of+Joy

  website=http%3A%2F%2Fhello.com

  comments=This+is+a+cool%0D%0Aform.
  ```

- The key and the value in each `key=value` pair are separated by the = character. This can be seen in the above six examples of such pairs.
- The blank spaces in the values are replaced by the + character. Obviously, for the form and the query string shown above, the user entered `Mister Bigshot` in the space allocated to `Name`. When this name was inserted into the query string, the blank space between `Mister` and `Bigshot` was replaced by the + character.
- Except for the . character, all nonalphanumeric characters in a query string are replaced by the % symbol followed by their hex representations. (This is referred to as *URL encoding* of a string.) As the reader can see, in the value for the `website` key, the colon that comes immediately after `http` in a web site address was replaced by the `%3A` string, and each of the two forward slashes after that by the `%2F` string. The two hex sequences shown in the value for the `comments` key are for the newline after the user-entered word `cool`.

Here is an example of an HTML file that will generate in a web browser the form shown in Fig.4.1:

```
<HTML>
<head>
<TITLE>Personal Info Form</TITLE>
</HEAD>
<BODY bgcolor=white>

<FORM ACTION="testformPARSE.cgi" METHOD="post">

Name:<BR>
<INPUT TYPE="text" SIZE=40 NAME="name"><BR><BR>
Age:<BR>
<INPUT TYPE="text" SIZE=10 NAME="age"><BR><BR>
```

```
Street Address:<BR>
<INPUT TYPE="text" SIZE=40 NAME="street"><BR><BR>
City-State:<BR>
<INPUT TYPE="text" SIZE=40 NAME="city"><BR><BR>
Your Web Site:<BR>
<INPUT TYPE="text" SIZE=40 NAME="website"><BR><BR>
Any Comments:<BR>
<TEXTAREA COLS=40 ROWS=10 NAME="comments"></TEXTAREA><BR><BR>
<CENTER>
<INPUT TYPE="submit" VALUE="SUBMIT">
</CENTER>

</FORM>
</BODY>
</HTML>
```

This HTML file should also explain where the keys shown earlier in the `key=value` pairs come from. The keys are what are specified by the programmer for the `NAME` attribute of the `INPUT` tag. Also, note the `ACTION` attribute of the `FORM` tag. This attribute says that the query string emanating from this form will be fed into a CGI script named `testformPARSE.cgi`.[46] Another attribute of the `FORM` tag is `METHOD`. How exactly a query string is read into the CGI script named for the `ACTION` attribute depends on what is specified for the `METHOD` attribute. When this attribute is `POST`, as is the case in our example, the CGI can receive the query string on its standard input. On the other hand, if the `METHOD` attribute is set to `GET`, then a query string can only be pulled into a CGI script through the `QUERY_STRING` environment variable via a call such as `$ENV{QUERY_STRING}` in Perl.

Your homework consists of writing the CGI script `testformPARSE.cgi` in Perl and Python for extracting the individual values from a query string and then storing them, along with their keys, in a hash for the case of Perl and a dictionary for the case of Python. Your scripts will obviously have to split the query string at the `&` character to separate out the `key=value` pairs, to replace the `+` characters by blank spaces, and to replace the hex representations by the corresponding individual characters.

[46]As mentioned earlier in Chapter 2, CGI stands for *Common Gateway Interface*. CGI scripts, frequently written in Perl or Python, are automatically executed by a web server for processing the data returned by a browser.

7. The primary goal of this Perl homework is to show that you can call up a function inside the pattern match operator `m//` for the purpose of synthesizing a regex on the fly. A secondary goal of the homework is to use the `\G` anchor to start pattern matching at a position set by a prior pattern match controlled by the `//g` modifier used in a scalar context.

   You are given a string that is represented in a Perl script in the following multiline format:

```
my $string = "urls:
                    http://jello.com
                    hoola.org
                    silly.billy.info
                    kelly.telly.biz
                    www.ko.po.cho.ho.org
                    good.old.tv
                    http:///xxxx.com
                    my.nom
                    yours.com";
```

   and you are provided with the following permissible list of domain suffixes:

```
my @suffixes = qw( com biz org edu );
```

   Your goal is to write a Perl script that first uses the `//g` match modifier to position the `\G` anchor past the beginning substring `urls:` and then invokes a single regex pattern match to extract all the top-level domain names that end in one of the permissible suffixes. That is, for the input string shown, the output of your script must be the array

```
jello hoola telly ho xxxx yours
```

   You are not allowed to use a looping construct. Neither can you use the functional programming operators `map` and `grep`. Your pattern match statement is allowed to use the following syntax inside the `m//` operator to construct an or'ed list of the permissible suffixes:

```
@{[join "|", @suffixes]
```

   Note that since the input string is in multiple lines, you may wish to use the `//s` modifier in addition to any other modifiers in your regex match.

8. Write a one-line Perl statement that uses `sprintf()` to output a string consisting of three numbers formatted as follows:

```
120-11:15
```

from an input string of the form

```
"hello, the 120 runners will run at 11::15"
```

The second argument to `sprintf()` must be a regex match that returns the three numbers to be placed in the output string. Any words may appear between the first and the second number in the input string. Also the separator between the second and third numbers may be a double colon as shown, but it can also be a single colon or, for that matter, any other nondigit visually convenient symbol or symbols.

9. As you well know, senders of spam use a variety of subterfuges to conceal their messages. It is especially easy to hide information in HTML-formatted email messages. Here are some of the ploys spammers use, all with the intention of making it harder for keyword-based email filtering programs to do their job:

   - Embed HTML comments into the real content words. So a word like "Viagra" would actually be sent as

     ```
     Via<!-- some meaningless comment -->gra
     ```

   - Use HTML character encodings in the form of numerical character references `&#number;` for some or all of the content. Now a word like "Viagra" may be sent like

     ```
     &#86;&#105;&#97;&#103;&#114;&#97;
     ```

     For US-ASCII characters, the `number` in `&#number;` is simply the decimal ASCII code for a character. For example, the ASCII code for `V` is 86. So `V` is its numerical character reference.

   - Use features of the "quoted-printable" encoding to further obfuscate an HTML email.[47] For example, the sender will override line breaks by

[47]When email is sent in the form of a MIME object, the sender must declare the "Content-Type" and "Content-Transfer-Encoding" headers for the object so the receiver would know how to decode the object. The "Content-Type" header for HTML messages (or the HTML portion of an email that contains different types of MIME objects) will usually be `text/html` and "Content-Transfer-Encoding" header (not uncommonly) `quoted-printable`. The `quoted-printable` encoding is meant for messages that consist mostly of 7-bit US-ASCII characters with an occasional 8-bit character outside this range. With `quoted-printable` encoding, the 8-bit character is represented by a three-character string `=XY` where `XY` is the hex representation of the character. When `quoted-printable` encoding is used, line lengths are not allowed to exceed 76 characters. If longer lines are necessary, the composer of the message can use the `=` character as a soft line break. The email parser joins the lines that are thus broken.

terminating each line in the = character. This would allow the sender to place "Via" portion of "Viagra" at the end of one line, follow that with the soft linebreak character = , and then place "gra" at the beginning of the next line. Recognizing the soft line break, the email reader program will join the two portions "Via" and "gra" into a single word. But a simpleminded email filtering program would obviously be fooled. When using "quoted-printable" encoding, the sender may also try to confuse the receiver by using, say, the encoded string =3D for the = character.

- and so on.

Write Perl and Python scripts that can take the following sort of spam input:

```
<table width=3D100% bgcolor=3Dblack cellpadding=3D3><tr><td colspan=3D3 bg=
color=3Daqua align=3Dcenter><font face=3DVerdana size=3D4><b>Onlin<!-- =
huxley -->e Ph<!-- coronado -->armacy<br><font color=3Dred>No Pr=
<!-- toxin -->ior Prescr<!-- extremal -->iption Nee<!-- =
usurer -->ded!<br><font color=3Ddeeppink>No Ph<!-- monotreme -->y=
sical Ex<!-- substantiate -->am Need<!-- steak -->ed!</td></tr>
<tr><td width=3D100% bgcolor=3Dblueviolet colspan=3D3><p align=3Dcenter><f=
ont face=3DVerdana color=3Dwhite><big><big><b><marquee border=3D1 scrollam=
ount=3D5 scrolldelay=3D1>Va<!-- trash -->lium ... Xa<!-- =
ambush -->nax ... Diazepa<!-- interject -->m ... Amb<!-- =
extraneous -->ien ... &#88;&#101;&#110;&#105;<!-- =
hera -->&#99;&#97;&#108; ... &#86;&#105;&#97;<!-- =
bigelow -->&#103;&#114;&#97; ... And Many Mo<!-- =
destruct -->re</marquee></td><=
/tr>
```

and produce the output that the spammer wants you to see (the output that you could then subject to keyword-based email filtering).

Note that this spam contains only two actual lines of text, all others that terminate in = are soft line breaks that would be ignored by the email reader. Therefore, your first job is to write a subroutine that skips over the soft line breaks and returns the actual lines of text contained in the spam. For this you could write a `nextline()` function that in Perl could look like

```
sub nextline {
    my $line = <>;
    while (defined($line) && $line =~ s/=[\n\r]+$//) {
        last unless (defined($_ = <>));
        $line .= $_;
    }
    return ($line);
}
```

Joining the lines in this manner is important because the spammer has placed a soft line break inside the HTML comments that are embedded inside content words. It is easier to discard these comments wholesale after the lines are joined together at the soft line breaks. However, before you can do so, you'd want to decode any HTML character encodings that are of the form `&#number;` or of the form `&#xnumber;`. To see how this can easily be done, let's continue with our Perl case and say that you have stored the line of text returned by the above function in a variable `$line` by

```
$line = nextline();
```

Now you can invoke replace-substitute operations on this line to replace the character references by the actual characters. In Perl, this can be done with the following sort of syntax:

```
$line =~ s/&#(\d+);/pack('C', $1)/eg;
```

Note the use of the `//e` modifier to evaluate the replacement expression which calls on the built-in function `pack()` to return the ASCII character corresponding to the decimal numerical value stored in the character encoding.[48] It is the format letter `C` supplied as the first argument to `pack()` that causes it to return the ASCII character. But what if the spammer used a hex representation (as opposed to the decimal representation) of the number inside the character encoding? In that case, we would also need to use the following search and replace operation:

```
$line =~ s/&#x([\da-f]+);/pack('C', hex($1))/egi;
```

The call to the built-in `hex()` in the second argument to `pack()` takes a hex representation of a number as its argument and returns its decimal value.

Now we are ready to take out the comments. If a comment is contained entirely within a single line as returned by the call to `nextline()`, in Perl it can be easily eliminated by

```
$line =~ s/<!--.*?-->//g;
```

Note the use of the nongreedy form `*?` for the `*` quantifier. It is essential to use the nongreedy form to deal with the case when there are multiple comment blocks in the same line. *The greedy form will cause the useful information that is between the different comment blocks to also disappear.*

But what if an HTML comment only starts in one physical line as returned by `nextline()` and then ends in some later line that will subsequently be returned by a future call to `nextline()`?[49] To get rid of such a comment, we need to detect the condition when a line as returned by `nextline()` contains only the opening comment tag but not the closing comment tag. This we can do in Perl with the following regex match:

[48] The built-in function `pack()` was discussed previously in Chapter 2.

[49] Note that HTML comments cannot be nested.

```
while ($line =~ /<!--.*(?!-->)/) {
    ....
    ....
}
```

Note the subpattern `(?!-->)` that uses a negated form of a lookahead assertion. The regex will match only if a line with a comment opening tag does not at the same time contain the comment closing tag. Now inside the `while` loop we can call `nextline()` repeatedly, appending the line returned by this function to the current value of `$line`, and eliminating complete comment blocks by search and replace operations.

Although the suggested solution strategy is only for the case of Perl, the reader should easily be able to construct equivalent Python constructs using the language features reviewed in Chapter 3 and this chapter.[50]

[50]The snippets of Perl code shown for this problem are from a posting by Alan Burlison at `http://bleaklow.com/`. That posting was also an inspiration for including this homework problem.

5

References in Perl

Class-type objects in Perl are manipulated through references.[1] References are also central to Perl for constructing and dealing with nested data structures, such as lists of lists, hashes in which the values associated with the keys are lists or even other hashes, and so on. So what is an object reference?

Think of an object reference as a disguised pointer. In fact in Perl, if you try to treat a reference as an integer, its value is the memory address at which the object referred to, known as the *referent*, is located.

It is therefore important to first grasp the general notion of a reference in Perl before delving into how Perl classes are defined and how class-type objects are instantiated from them. In the rest of this chapter, therefore, our focus will be primarily on reviewing the notion of a reference in Perl and how this notion is used in various non-OO contexts. These concepts will then be used in the next chapter in our discussion on Perl classes and class-type objects.

[1] As a point of contrast, note that *all* objects in Python are manipulated through references (although in a manner that is transparent to the user).

5.1 REFERENCING AND DEREFERENCING OPERATORS (SUMMARY)

The reference operator is the backslash. The dereferencing operator depends on what is expected to be returned by dereferencing. If the dereferencing operation is expected to return a scalar, you use `$` as the dereferencing operator. If the dereferencing operation is expected to yield an array, you use `@` as the dereferencing operator. And if the dereferencing operation is expected to yield a hash, you use `%` as the dereferencing operator.

Dereferencing of the individual elements of an array or the individual values in a hash can also be accomplished with the arrow `->` operator. In the construction

```
a->b
```

`a` can be any expression that returns a reference and `b` an index, which for an array is a square-brackets-enclosed positional index and for a hash a braces-enclosed key index. If `a->b` is expected to return a scalar, think of `a->b` as `${a}b`. On the other hand, if `a->b` is expected to return an array, think of `a->b` as `@{a}b`. And if `a->b` is expected to return a hash, think of `a->b` as `%{a}b`. But don't forget that the right-hand side of the arrow must be either an array index of the form `[i]`, or a hash index, of the form `{key}`.

5.2 REFERENCING AND DEREFERENCING A SCALAR

You obtain a reference to a scalar by applying the backslash operator to the scalar, as in

```
$a = 10;
$ref = \$a;          # $ref will now serve as a reference for $a
```

A reference is like any other scalar, amenable to all operations that you can perform on a scalar. You could, for example, push the above reference `$ref` into an array:

```
push @arr, $ref;
```

To dereference `$ref`, we can either say

```
$b = ${$ref};
print $b;                # 10
```

or just

```
$b = $$ref;
print $b;                # 10
```

A reference shows its true colors only when subject to a dereferencing operation. However, depending on the context, a reference may also be treated as a string, or as an integer. When the context requires that a reference behave like a string, the string includes both the type of the referent and its storage location in hex. This is illustrated by the following code snippet in which the print statement causes the reference to be interpreted as a string. The output is shown in the commented out portion of that line.

```
$a = 10;
$ref = \$a;
print $ref, "\n";            # SCALAR(0x804b5f8)
```

On the other hand, when the context causes a reference to be treated like a number, it becomes a decimal integer whose value is the storage location of the referent, as shown below:

```
$a = 10;
$ref = \$a;
print int( $ref ), "\n";     # 134595676
```

The built-in function `int()`, which ordinarily returns the integer portion of its argument, provides a numerical context for the evaluation of `$ref`. So what we get back is the numerical address, in decimal form, of the storage location for the scalar `$a`.

The following working script, `ScalarRef.pl`, pulls these notions together. The script also demonstrates that accessing a scalar directly or via its reference are equivalent. Any changes made to the scalar would be reflected in the value retrieved by dereferencing a reference to the scalar. So when we change the value of the scalar in line (E), that change is reflected in the value returned through the dereferencing operation in line (F). The scalar was defined earlier in line (A) and a reference to the scalar created in line (B).

Lines (G) through (K) demonstrate further the notion that because a reference is just a scalar, you can take a reference to a reference, or a reference to a reference to a reference, and so on. Line (G) causes `$ra` to be a reference to a reference to a reference to the scalar `$a` of line (A), whose value was later changed in line (E). The dereferencing operations in lines (I) and (J) yield references, as can be seen by the commented-out outputs shown in those lines. The triple dereferencing in line (K) finally retrieves the value of the scalar `$a`. Line (L) provides a numerical context for the evaluation of the reference defined in line (G). So, as shown in line (M), we get the decimal value for the storage location for the reference to the reference to the scalar `$a`. To prove this, when we convert the integer returned by the right-hand side in line (M) back into its hex form by using the built-in function `sprintf()`[2] in

[2]The built-in function `sprintf()` was introduced in Section 2.1.2 of Chapter 2.

line (N), we get the same hex string as shown in the output in line (H). The hex string returned by the call to `sprintf()` is shown in line (O).

Finally, lines (P) through (W) show that you can also specify a reference to a literal. But what's interesting is that one would expect there to be only a single copy of a literal to be stored in the memory. But that is not the case, as demonstrated in lines (Q) and (S) for the case of the integer literal 100 and in lines (U) and (W) for the case of the string literal `hello`.

```
#!/usr/bin/perl -w
use strict;

### ScalarRef.pl

# Basics:
my $a = 10;                                                          #(A)
my $ra = \$a;                                                        #(B)
print ${$ra}, "\n";                  # 10                            #(C)
print $$ra, "\n";                    # 10                            #(D)
$a = 20;                                                             #(E)
print $$ra, "\n";                    # 20                            #(F)

# Reference of a reference of a reference to a scalar:
$ra = \\\$a;                                                         #(G)
print $ra, "\n";                     # SCALAR(0x804b5f8)             #(H)
print $$ra, "\n";                    # SCALAR(0x804b514)             #(I)
print $$$ra,"\n";                    # SCALAR(0x8057098)             #(J)
print $$$$ra, "\n";                  # 20                            #(K)
my $int_address = int( $ra );                                        #(L)
print $int_address, "\n";            # 134526456                     #(M)
my $s = sprintf "0x%x", $int_address;                                #(N)
print $s, "\n";                      # 0x804b5f8                     #(O)

# References to literals:
my $r1 = \100;                                                       #(P)
print $r1, "\n";                     # SCALAR(0x805c10c)             #(Q)
my $r2 = \100;                                                       #(R)
print $r2, "\n";                     # SCALAR(0x805c154)             #(S)

my $r3 = \"hello";                                                   #(T)
print $r3, "\n";                     # SCALAR(0x805c1a8)             #(U)
my $r4 = \"hello";                                                   #(V)
print $r4, "\n";                     # SCALAR(0x805c1f0)             #(W)
```

5.3 REFERENCING AND DEREFERENCING A NAMED ARRAY

Practically everything we said in the previous section about the referencing and the dereferencing of scalars carries over to the case of arrays. Shown below is the use of the backslash operator for constructing a reference, `$ref`, to an array named `@arr1`:

```
@arr1 = (10, 20);
$ref = \@arr1;
```

How exactly to dereference an array reference depends on whether we wish to retrieve the entire array or just a single element. To dereference `$ref` in order to retrieve the whole array, we can say

```
@arr2 = @$ref;
print "@arr2\n";                    # 10 20
```

But if we wanted the dereferencing operation to retrieve a single element of the array, we would say

```
$a = $$ref[1];
print "$a\n";                       # 20
```

The same notation can also reset an existing element or create a new element:

```
$$ref[2] = 'thirty';
print "@arr1\n";                    # 10 20 thirty
```

We can also use the arrow operator mentioned in Section 5.1 for accessing an element of the array pointed to by a reference. To access the third element of the array `@arr1`, we can say

```
$a = $ref->[2];
print "$a\n";                       # thirty
```

In addition to pulling together the above definitions in lines (A) through (H), the next script, `ArrayRef.pl`, should give the reader some additional insights into the use of references for arrays.

Lines (I) through (L) of the script show that regardless of whether you manipulate an array directly or through its reference, the end result is the same. Line (I) pushes a new element directly into the array `@arr1`, increasing its size by one. Line (K) also pushes a new element into the same array, but now through the reference `$ref` defined in line (B). We see the longer array when we print it out directly in line (L).

As was mentioned earlier, a reference, regardless of the nature of the referent, is a scalar like any other scalar. So a reference can be an element of an array, as shown in line (M). When we print out this element by itself in line (N), we get the same sort of a string representation of a reference that we showed in the previous section, except that now the type of the referent is ARRAY and not SCALAR. As before, we can dereference a reference element in an array, as in line (O), to either retrieve the entire referent array, as in line (O), or just one element of the referent array, as in line (R).

Nothing prevents an array from containing an element that is a reference to the array itself, as demonstrated by the code in lines (S) through (W). Before changing the array in this manner in line (S), its elements are as shown in the commented-out portion of line (L). When, in line (S), we unshift the reference to this array into the array itself, the array becomes as shown in the commented-out portion of line (T). When we modify this array, as through the pop operation in line (U), that modification will be visible directly, as in line (V), or through the first element of the array, as in line (W).

An example of an array containing a reference to itself as its sole element is shown in lines (X) through (Z).

```
#!/usr/bin/perl -w
use strict;

### ArrayRef.pl

# Basics:
my @arr1 = (1, 2);                                                    #(A)
my $ref = \@arr1;                                                     #(B)
print "@$ref\n";                 # 1 2                                #(C)
print "$$ref[1]\n";              # 2                                  #(D)
$$ref[2] = 'three';                                                   #(E)
print "@arr1\n";                 # 1 2 three                          #(F)

# The arrow notation:
my $a = $ref->[2];                                                    #(G)
print "$a\n";                    # three                              #(H)

# More basics:
push @arr1, 4;                                                        #(I)
print "@arr1\n";                 # 1 2 three 4                        #(J)
push @$ref, 5;                                                        #(K)
print "@arr1\n";                 # 1 2 three 4 5                      #(L)

# An array containing an array reference:
my @arr2 = (5, 6, $ref);                                              #(M)
print $arr2[2], "\n";            # ARRAY(0x805708c)                   #(N)
my @arr3 = @{$arr2[2]};                                               #(O)
print "@arr3\n";                 # 1 2 three 4 5                      #(P)
print "@{$arr2[2]}\n";           # 1 2 three 4 5                      #(Q)
print ${$arr2[2]}[2], "\n";      # three                              #(R)
```

```
# An array containing a reference to itself:
unshift @arr1, $ref;                                                    #(S)
print "@arr1\n";            # ARRAY(0x805708c) 1 2 three 4 5            #(T)
pop @arr1;                                                              #(U)
print "@arr1\n";            # ARRAY(0x805708c) 1 2 three 4              #(V)
print "@{$arr1[0]}\n";      # ARRAY(0x805708c) 1 2 three 4              #(W)

# A donut:
my @donut;                                                              #(X)
unshift @donut, \@donut;                                                #(Y)
print "@donut\n";           # ARRAY(0x805d718)                          #(Z)
```

5.4 REFERENCING AND DEREFERENCING AN ANONYMOUS ARRAY

Ordinarily, as described in Chapter 2, you construct a named array in Perl in the following manner:

```
@arr = (10, 20, 30);
```

where `@arr` on the left is the name of the array and the list `(10, 20, 30)` on the right its initializer. Subsequently, you can form a reference to the array in the manner already discussed. With this approach, you may access the array via either its name or its reference. Either way, the results will be the same.

Perl also gives us *anonymous arrays* that can be manipulated through references without the bother of having to name the arrays. In the following statement, the square brackets on the right construct a new anonymous array containing the elements 10, 20, and 30, and then return a reference to the array, which becomes the value of the variable `$ref` on the left.[3]

```
$ref = [10, 20, 30];
```

We can dereference the reference `$ref` as before:

```
@arr = @$ref;
print "@arr\n";              # 10 20 30
```

and access an element of the anonymous array in the same manner as before

[3]The operator `[]` shown here that returns a reference to an anonymous array and the operator `{}` we will show in Section 5.6 for returning a reference to an anonymous hash are also known as *anonymous constructors*.

```
$a = ${$ref}[1];
print $a, "\n";                    # 20
```

or, using the arrow operator, by

```
$a = $ref->[1];
print $a, "\n";                    # 20
```

Access to an anonymous array through its reference, whether for the purpose of retrieving the entire array or just one of its elements, can be interpolated directly into a double-quoted string:

```
$ref = [10, 20, 30];
print "@$ref\n";                   # 10 20 30
print "$$ref[2]\n";                # 30
print "$ref->[2]\n";               # 30
```

In the next script, `ArrayRefAnon.pl`, line (A) uses the square brackets to create an anonymous array on the right of the assignment operator. A reference to this array becomes the value of the variable `$ref` on the left. Line (B) shows a named array. We will use this array to compare the array access syntax for anonymous arrays and named arrays.

Line (C) shows how you can dereference a reference to an anonymous array for the purpose of retrieving the whole array. The syntax shown here is the same as with references to named arrays. For comparison, we show in line (E) the by now familiar syntax for retrieving a named array. Line (D) shows that Perl allows you to use a block, meaning a code fragment delimited by braces, in place of the array-name identifier, *provided the block evaluates to a reference.*[4]

The syntax for the individual-element dereferencing operations in lines (F), (G), and (H) follow the same rule as before — you replace the array-name identifier, meaning the identifier `arr` in a call like `$arr[i]`, with a reference to yield a construct like `$$ref[i]`. That explains the syntax in line (F) for retrieving the value of the second element of the array. And, as before, the array-name identifier can also be replaced by a brace-delimited block that returns a reference, as shown by the individual-element access in line (G). Line (H) shows the access call for a named array for comparison.

If the goal is to access one of the array elements, the most common way to dereference a reference to an anonymous array is by the use of the arrow operator, as in line (I). As mentioned previously, what shows up on the left of the arrow in a construct like `a->b` can be any expression that evaluates to a reference. It can also be anything that could possibly be obtained by dereferencing a reference. This

[4]As mentioned in Chapter 2, a brace-delimited block of code evaluates to whatever is returned by the evaluation of its last executed statement.

explains why the statement in line (J) works, even though what is on the left of the arrow is not a reference.

Lines (K) through (O) show some operations on the anonymous array of line (A). As with a named array, we are free to include a reference as an element in an anonymous array — as demonstrated by lines (N) and (O).

Line (P) demonstrates that applying the backslash operator to a list of items — in this case a list of strings — does not return a single reference, as you might expect, but an array of references to the items of the list. In other words, the operation

```
\("hello", "yello", "jello", "mello" );
```

is equivalent to the list

```
(\"hello", \"yello", \"jello", \"mello")
```

That should explain the outputs shown in the commented-out portions of lines (Q) and (R).

```
#!/usr/bin/perl -w
use strict;

### ArrayRefAnon.pl

# Constructing an anonymous array:
my $ref = [1, 2, 3];                                              #(A)

# Constructing a named array:
my @arr = (1, 2, 3);                                              #(B)

# Dereferencing to retrieve the anonymous array:
print "@$ref\n";                          # 1 2 3                 #(C)
print "@{$ref}\n";                        # 1 2 3                 #(D)

# Comparison with a named array:
print "@arr\n";                           # 1 2 3                 #(E)

# Dereferencing to retrieve an individual element:
print $$ref[1], "\n";                     # 2                     #(F)
print ${$ref}[1], "\n";                   # 2                     #(G)

# Comparison with a named array:
print $arr[1], "\n";                      # 2                     #(H)

# Dereferencing with the arrow operator:
print $ref->[1], "\n";                    # 2                     #(I)
```

```
# Comparison with a named array:
print @arr->[1], "\n";                    # 2                         #(J)

push @$ref, 4;                                                        #(K)
print "@$ref\n";                          # 1 2 3 4                   #(L)

pop @$ref;                                                            #(M)
push @$ref, $ref;                                                     #(N)
print "@$ref\n";                          # 1 2 3 ARRAY(0x804b514)    #(O)

my @r1 = \("hello", "yello", "jello", "mello" );                      #(P)
print $r1[0], "\n";                       # SCALAR(0x805bde4)         #(Q)
print ${$r1[0]}, "\n";                    # hello                     #(R)
```

We will now show how anonymous arrays can be used to construct arrays of arrays. Recall that, fundamentally, a Perl array can only contain scalar elements. But a reference is a scalar like any other scalar. So by including in an array an element that is a reference to another array, we can construct *nested* or *multidimensional* arrays. The next script, `AoA.pl`, demonstrates the different forms of syntax that can be used to access the elements of the arrays that are nested inside other arrays through references.

Lines (A) and (B) of the script define two arrays, each containing three elements, with each element a reference to an anonymous array. The definition in line (A) gives us an anonymous outermost array and sets the value of `$ref` as a reference to this array. The definition in line (B) creates a named outermost array. We show both definitions here because it is instructive to compare the element access syntax for the two cases. The fact that the outermost arrays in these two lines contain only three scalars each is demonstrated in the outputs shown in the commented out portions of lines (C) and (D).

Line (E) shows the basic syntax for accessing an element of one of the interior arrays for the case when the outermost array is a named array. This syntax, reproduced below, uses a brace-delimited block that returns a reference to an element of the outer array.

```
${$arr[1]}[1]
```

In this case, we are trying to access the second element of the second inner array. As was the case earlier with a one-dimensional array, Perl allows you to replace the block that returns a reference with the reference itself provided you use the arrow notation shown below and used in line (F):

```
$arr[1]->[1]
```

When the arrow shows up between two subscripts, as above, Perl allows you to delete the arrow altogether. So the above syntax acquires a more truly looking multidimensional form shown below:

```
$arr[1][1]
```

This is the form of element access shown in line (G) in the script below.

For comparison, now let's consider the syntax for accessing the individual elements of the interior arrays when the outer array is an anonymous array, as in line (A). The various possible choices are shown in lines (H) through (L). All these choices do the same thing — retrieve the second element of the second interior array. The first choice, shown in line (H) and reproduced below, uses the brace-delimited blocks to return the references at the top-level and at the nested level:

```
${${$ref}[1]}[1]
```

Note that the nesting of the braces is opposite of the nesting of the arrays, which makes intuitive sense, since the goal is to reach from the known top-level memory address to the address of the interior array. So the inner block returns a reference to the outer array, and then its second element, evaluated inside a block, returns a reference to the inner array. The arrow notation can be used to strip away the outer block:

```
${$ref}[1]->[1]
```

This is the form of syntax used in line (I). Recall from our earlier discussion that Perl allows us to ignore the arrow if it appears between two subscripts. So the above form can be replaced by

```
${$ref}[1][1]
```

which is what we have used in line (J).

The logic used for replacing the outer block with an arrowed access that resulted in the syntax `${$ref}[1]->[1]` can be applied to the inner block also, to result in

```
$ref->[1]->[1]
```

which is the form used in line (K). If we again resort to deleting the arrow between two subscripts, we get the form

```
$ref->[1][1]
```

This is the form used in line (L).

If the goal is to not access an individual element of one of the interior arrays, but the whole interior array, one can use the syntax shown in line (M).

```
#!/usr/bin/perl -w
use strict;

### AoA.pl

my $ref = [ [1, 2, 3], ['a', 'b', 'c'], ['hello', 'jello'] ];          #(A)

my @arr = ( [4, 5, 6], ['d', 'e'], ['mello', 'yello'] );               #(B)

# Dereferencing to retrieve the whole array:
print "@$ref\n";
              # ARRAY(0x804b514) ARRAY(0x805c3f4) ARRAY(0x805c430) #(C)
print "@arr\n";
              # ARRAY(0x805704c) ARRAY(0x805c4a8) ARRAY(0x805c4d8) #(D)

# Dereferencing to retrieve a single element from
# an interior array of the named outer array:
print ${$arr[1]}[1], "\n";                  # e                    #(E)
print $arr[1]->[1], "\n";                   # e                    #(F)
print $arr[1][1], "\n";                     # e                    #(G)

# Dereferencing to retrieve a single element from
# an interior array of the anonymous outer array:
print ${${$ref}[1]}[1], "\n";               # b                    #(H)
print ${$ref}[1]->[1], "\n";                # b                    #(I)
print ${$ref}[1][1], "\n";                  # b                    #(J)
print $ref->[1]->[1], "\n";                 # b                    #(K)
print $ref->[1][1], "\n";                   # b                    #(L)

# Dereferencing to retrieve an interior array:
my @arr_interior = @{$ref->[1]};                                   #(M)
print "@arr_interior\n";                    # a b c                #(N)
```

5.5 REFERENCING AND DEREFERENCING A NAMED HASH

As before, a reference to a hash can be created with the backslash operator:

```
%hash = (d => 1, b => 2);
$ref = \%hash;
```

A hash reference may be dereferenced by substituting the name of the reference, `$ref` in our example, for the identifier in the usual access syntax for a hash. So the following is valid syntax for dereferencing the hash reference `$ref` defined above:

```
%$ref
```

which is what we have used in line (C) of the next script, `HashRef.pl`.[5] The identifier in the name of a hash can also be replaced by a brace-delimited block that returns a hash reference, as in

```
%{$ref}
```

This is the dereferencing syntax used in line (D) below. If the goal is to access the value for a given key, we can again use the ploy of substituting the name of the reference, `$ref`, for the identifier that stands for the name of the hash in an expression such as `$hash{key}` to give us

```
$$ref{ key }
```

This is the form used in line (E) of the script below. And, again as before, this reference substitution can occur through what is returned by a block, as in

```
${$ref}{ key }
```

which is the form used in line (F). Line (G) uses the same form as in line (E) to create a new key-value pair in the hash.

Line (H) demonstrates the arrow notation for accessing an individual value of a hash through its reference. The same notation could also be used to create new key-value pairs in the hash.

Line (I) demonstrates that a *value* stored in a hash does not have to be a scalar; it can be a reference. In line (I), the value specified for the key `c` is a reference to an anonymous array. Lines (J) and (K) show that a reference can serve as a key in a hash. It is the string representation of the reference that actually gets used as a key in such cases. Line (J) first creates a reference to an anonymous array; this reference is subsequently used in line (K) as a key to enter a new key-value pair into the hash. As the reader can see from the output produced by the `printhash()` function called after line (K), the hash now contains an array reference for a value (for the key `c`) and another array reference as a key (for which the corresponding value is `ly_sounds`).

Lines (L) through (N) show the different ways you can invoke the `keys()` built-in function that returns an array of the hash keys. In line (L), the function is invoked directly on the hash name. In line (M), we first dereference the reference to the hash and then invoke the `keys()` function. Lines (L) and (M) show the usual rule that you can always substitute a reference, meaning `$ref` here, for the identifier, meaning `hash` here, for gaining access to a hash in the direct syntax of line (L). Line (N)

[5]The `printhash()` function for visualizing the elements of a hash is defined at the end of the script.

shows the other rule that the identifier can also be replaced by a block that returns a reference. What lines (L) through (N) show for the `keys()` function is shown by the lines (O) through (Q) for the `values()` function.

Lines (R), (S), and (T) show different examples for invoking the built-in function `delete()` to erase a key-value pair for a hash. Basically, you have to supply to `delete()` an argument that constitutes a hash access to the key of the key-value pair you want erased. Line (T) uses the arrow notation for the accessing the key-value pair.

Finally, in lines (U) through (X), we show the implementation of the `printhash()` subroutine that was used earlier to display the contents of a hash. This subroutine uses the built-in function `each()`, reviewed previously in Section 2.5 of Chapter 2, in line (W) to iterate through the key-value pairs of the hash.

```
#!/usr/bin/perl -w
use strict;

### HashRef.pl

my %hash = (d => 1, b => 2);                                          #(A)

# Taking a reference to a hash
my $ref = \%hash;                                                      #(B)

# Dereferencing with % to retrieve an entire hash:
printhash(%$ref);                 # b => 2  d => 1                     #(C)
printhash(%{$ref});               # b => 2  d => 1                     #(D)

# Dereferencing with $ to retrieve a single value:
print "$$ref{b}\n";               # 2                                  #(E)
print "${$ref}{b}\n";             # 2                                  #(F)
$$ref{c} = 'three';                                                    #(G)
printhash(%hash);                 # b => 2  c => three  d => 1

# The arrow notation for dereferencing:
my $p = $ref->{b};                                                     #(H)
print "$p\n";                     # 2

# Using a reference for a value
$$ref{c} = ['hello', 'yello', 'mello'];                                #(I)
printhash(%hash);                 # b => 2  c => ARRAY(0x805705c)  d => 1

# Using a reference for a key
my $refkey = ['holly', 'dolly'];                                       #(J)
$$ref{$refkey} = 'ly_sounds';                                          #(K)
printhash(%hash);                 # ARRAY(0x805e2b8) => ly_sounds  b => 2
```

```
                                # c => ARRAY(0x805705c)  d => 1
# The keys() function:
my @keys = keys %hash;                                              #(L)
print "@keys\n";                # b c ARRAY(0x805e44c) d
@keys = keys %$ref;                                                 #(M)
print "@keys\n";                # b c ARRAY(0x805e44c) d
@keys = keys %{$ref};                                               #(N)
print "@keys\n";                # b c ARRAY(0x805e44c) d

# The values() function:
my @values = values %hash;                                          #(O)
print "@values\n";              # 2 ARRAY(0x805705c) ly_sounds 1
@values = values %$ref;                                             #(P)
print "@values\n";              # 2 ARRAY(0x805705c) ly_sounds 1
@values = values %{$ref};                                           #(Q)
print "@values\n";              # 2 ARRAY(0x805705c) ly_sounds 1

# The delete() function:
delete $hash{$refkey};                                              #(R)
delete $hash{c};                                                    #(S)
printhash( %hash );             # b => 2  d => 1
delete $ref->{b};                                                   #(T)
printhash( %hash );             # d => 1


sub printhash {                                                     #(U)
    my %h = @_;                                                     #(V)
    while ( (my $key, my $value) = each %h ) {                      #(W)
        print "$key => $value  ";                                   #(X)
    }
    print "\n";
}
```

5.6 REFERENCING AND DEREFERENCING AN ANONYMOUS HASH

As we will show in this section, a reference to an anonymous hash behaves in the same manner as a reference to a named hash. This section also demonstrates some additional syntax regarding references to hashes, especially when a hash contains values that are themselves references. Also, now we will write a display function, `print_hash_ref()`, for a hash that takes a hash reference for its argument. This function is shown in lines (V) through (Y) of the next script, `HashRefAnon.pl`.

Line (A) of the next script shows how the brace operator can be used to construct an anonymous hash and to return a reference to the hash. To draw comparisons between hash access and hash-element access for the cases of anonymous and named hashes, line (B) shows a named hash with the same key-value pairs.

Line (C) shows us supplying a reference to an anonymous hash as an argument to `print_hash_ref()`. This function retrieves the entire hash by the dereferencing operation in line (X). Line (D) does the same for a named hash, but note that the argument first takes a reference to the hash.

Lines (E) and (F) show the syntax for accessing an individual value from a reference to an anonymous hash. Comparison with the case of a named hash is provided by line (G). Lines (H) and (I) show us doing the same with the arrow operator.[6] Lines (J) and (K) show us using the built-in `delete()` function when its argument is supplied via a reference and directly.

Lines (L) through (U) deal with the case of a nested hash, meaning a hash that contains either hashes or arrays for values. Since a hash value must always be a scalar, the interior hashes and arrays can only be in the form of references. Line (L) sets the value for the key `b` equal to a reference to a new hash consisting of two key-value pairs. The value in the second pair is a reference to an array. Line (M) does the same thing, but for the case of a named outer hash.

Lines (N) through (U) show how to retrieve an interior data element when a hash value itself is either a hash reference or an array reference. Note the syntax used in line (N) for reaching the interior hash for the case when the outer hash is known by its reference:

```
$ref->{b}->{q}
```

As with the arrow between two array subscripts, Perl allows you to drop the arrow between two hash accesses. So, as shown by the usage in line (O), this syntax can be compressed to the more convenient form

```
$ref->{b}{q}
```

When the outer hash is named, the corresponding accesses are

```
$hash{b}->{q}
```

as used in line (P), and

---

[6]The individual element accesses such as those shown in lines (E), (F), and (H) can be interpolated directly into a double-quoted string as in

```
print "$$ref{b}\n";              # 2
print "${$ref}{b}\n";            # 2
print "$ref->{b}\n";             # 2
```

Further examples of the arrow-based individual element accesses interpolated directly into double-quoted strings are shown in lines (N) through (U) of the script.

```
$hash{b}{q}
```

as used in line (Q). Lines (R) through (U) show the syntax for accessing a more deeply nested data element, in this case the data element belongs to an array that is a value for one of the keys in the interior hash. In line (R), we have used the full-blown arrow-based syntax:

```
$ref->{b}->{q}->[0]
```

that is abbreviated to

```
$ref->{b}{q}[0]
```

in line (S). For the case when the outermost hash is named, the same element is reached through the syntax

```
$hash{b}->{q}->[0]
```

in line (T). This can be compressed into

```
$hash{b}{q}[0]
```

as shown in line (U). Finally, lines (V) through (Y) show the implementation for the `print_hash_ref()` function used for displaying the contents of a hash.

```
#!/usr/bin/perl -w
use strict;

### HashRefAnon.pl

# Constructing an anonymous hash:
my $ref = {d => 1, b => 2, c => 4};                              #(A)

# Constructing a named hash:
my %hash = (d => 1, b => 2, c => 4);                             #(B)

# Supplying a hash ref as an argument:
print_hash_ref( $ref );         # b => 2  c => 4  d => 1         #(C)
# Comparison with a named hash:
print_hash_ref( \%hash );       # b => 2  c => 4  d => 1         #(D)

# Dereferencing to retrieve an individual value:
print $$ref{b}, "\n";           # 2                              #(E)
print ${$ref}{b}, "\n";         # 2                              #(F)
# Comparison with a named hash:
print $hash{b}, "\n";           # 2                              #(G)

# Dereferencing with the arrow operator:
print $ref->{b}, "\n";          # 2                              #(H)
```

```
# Comparison with a named hash:
print %hash->{b}, "\n";           # 2                                 #(I)

# The delete() function invoked through a ref:
delete $ref->{d};                                                     #(J)
# Comparison with a named hash:
delete $hash{d};                                                      #(K)

# Setting interior value to a hash ref:
$ref->{b} = {p => 7, q => ['r', 's']};                               #(L)
print_hash_ref( $ref );           # b => HASH(0x805ddd0)  c => 4
# Comparison with a named hash:
$hash{b} = {p => 7, q => ['r', 's']};                                #(M)
print_hash_ref( \%hash );         # b => HASH(0x805de2c)  c => 4

# Retrieving an interior value with arrow:
print "$ref->{b}->{q}\n";         # ARRAY(0x805dcdc)                  #(N)
print "$ref->{b}{q}\n";           # ARRAY(0x805dcdc)                  #(O)
# Comparison with a named hash:
print "$hash{b}->{q}\n";          # ARRAY(0x805de08)                  #(P)
print "$hash{b}{q}\n";            # ARRAY(0x805de08)                  #(Q)

# Retrieving an interior value with arrow:
print "$ref->{b}->{q}->[0]\n";    # r                                 #(R)
print "$ref->{b}{q}[0]\n";        # r                                 #(S)
# Comparison with a named hash:
print "$hash{b}->{q}->[0]\n";     # r                                 #(T)
print "$hash{b}{q}[0]\n";         # r                                 #(U)


sub print_hash_ref {                                                  #(V)
    my $r = shift;                                                    #(W)
    while ( (my $key, my $value) = each %$r ) {                       #(X)
        print "$key => $value  ";                                     #(Y)
    }
    print "\n";
}
```

5.7 REFERENCING AND DEREFERENCING A NAMED SUBROUTINE

Just as you can take a reference to a scalar, to an array, or to a hash, you can also take a reference to a subroutine. Since a reference is like any ordinary scalar, a subroutine reference can be stored in an array or a hash. A reference to a previously defined subroutine is created with the same backslash operator that we used for creating references to scalars, arrays, and hashes. A subroutine reference can be dereferenced by substituting the reference for the identifier that stands for the name of the subroutine in a function call. So, given a named subroutine defined as

```
sub my_subroutine {
    ....code....
}
```

we can obtain a reference to this subroutine in the following manner:

```
$reference = \&my_subroutine;
```

and invoke the subroutine as follows:

```
&$reference( .... args .... );
```

which would be equivalent to the following direct invocation of the subroutine:

```
&my_subroutine( .... args .... )
```

The script shown next, `SubRef.pl`, stores references to three subroutines in an array and then passes a reference to this array to a function that invokes each subroutine in the array on an argument. The three subroutines are defined in lines (A), (G), and (H); these are meant to be predicates for testing whether an argument integer is even, divisible by 3, and divisible by 4, respectively. All of the predicates possess the same implementation except for the modulo division in lines such as (C) and for the messages they print out. We test the three subroutines in lines (I), (J), and (K).

We push references to the three subroutines into the array `@function_array` in lines (L), (M), and (N). Lines (O) through (T) define `apply_funct_array()`, a function that is called with two arguments, as shown in line (U). The first argument to this function is a reference to the array `@function_array` and the second argument any integer to which we want to apply the three predicates defined earlier. In lines (P) and (Q), we locally recover the two arguments that are supplied to `apply_funct_array()`. Lines (R), (S), and (T) then iterate over the array containing the subroutine references and apply each subroutine to the second argument integer.

```
#!/usr/bin/perl -w
use strict;

### SubRef.pl

sub even_p {                                                      #(A)
    my ($number) = @_;                                            #(B)
    if ( $number % 2 == 0 ) {                                     #(C)
        return "$number is even";                                 #(D)
```

```
    } else {                                                        #(E)
        return "$number is not even";                               #(F)
    }
}
sub multiple_of_3_p {                                               #(G)
    my ($number) = @_;
    if ( $number % 3 == 0 ) {
        return "$number is a multiple of 3";
    } else {
        return "$number is not a multiple of 3";
    }
}
sub multiple_of_4_p {                                               #(H)
    my ($number) = @_;
    if ( $number % 4 == 0 ) {
        return "$number is a multiple of 4";
    } else {
        return "$number is not a multiple of 4";
    }
}

print &even_p( 18 ), "\n";              # 18 is even                #(I)
print &multiple_of_3_p( 18 ), "\n";     # 18 is a multiple of 3     #(J)
print &multiple_of_4_p( 18 ), "\n";     # 18 is not a multiple of 4 #(K)

push my @function_array, \&even_p;                                  #(L)
push @function_array, \&multiple_of_3_p;                            #(M)
push @function_array, \&multiple_of_4_p;                            #(N)

# This subroutine takes two arguments, the first a
# reference to an array of function references, and
# the second an integer argument.  Each function
# in the array is invoked on the second argument.
sub apply_funct_array {                                             #(O)
    my $ref_to_array = shift;                                       #(P)
    my $arg = shift;                                                #(Q)
    foreach (@$ref_to_array) {                                      #(R)
        my $answer = &$_( $arg );                                   #(S)
        print $answer, "\n";                                        #(T)
    }
}

&apply_funct_array( \@function_array, 16 );                         #(U)
                                        # 16 is even
                                        # 16 is not a multiple of 3
                                        # 16 is a multiple of 4
```

5.8 REFERENCING AND DEREFERENCING AN ANONYMOUS SUBROUTINE

The previous section showed that we could first define a named subroutine using the syntax

```
sub my_subroutine {
        .... code ....
}
```

and then obtain a reference to the subroutine by

```
$reference = \&my_subroutine;
```

Since a subroutine can be manipulated just as easily through its reference as through its name, Perl provides a way to create a subroutine reference directly without the need for first naming the subroutine. This can be accomplished using the following syntax that yields a reference to a nameless subroutine:

```
$reference = sub {
        .... code ....
};
```

Note the semicolon at the end of the subroutine definition. That is because what is on the right-hand side of the assignment is now an expression that uses the keyword `sub` as an operator to create an anonymous subroutine, in the same sense that we used `[]` as an operator to create an anonymous array and `{}` as an operator to create an anonymous hash. The operator `sub` used in this manner returns a reference to the anonymous subroutine created. In order to invoke the subroutine via this reference, we must dereference the reference. This we are allowed to do by substituting the reference for the identifier in the usual syntax for invoking a subroutine. That is, the following call will dereference the reference created above and invoke the subroutine:

```
&$reference( .... args .... )
```

The substitution for the subroutine name identifier can also occur within a brace-delimited block as long as the block returns a reference to the desired subroutine. Therefore, the following is also legal syntax for invoking a subroutine through its reference:

```
&{$reference}( .... args .... )
```

More commonly, though, one would use the arrow notation for dereferencing and invoking the subroutine in this manner:

```
$reference->( .... args .... )
```

In the script `SubRefAnon.pl` shown next, we define an anonymous subroutine on the right-hand side of the assignment in line (A). The scalar `$ref_to_sub` will hold a reference to this subroutine. Note again that the definition of the anonymous subroutine ends in a semicolon in line (B). Contrast the definition of the anonymous subroutine with that of a regular subroutine that does the same thing in line (C).

Line (E) shows the dereferencing operation to invoke the anonymous subroutine; we substitute the reference for the identifier that would usually come after `&` in a typical subroutine call. Line (F) uses a block for this substitution; the block returns the desired reference. Line (G) shows the arrow operator for the dereferencing operation. Finally, for the sake of comparison, line (H) shows the usual subroutine call for the named subroutine of line (C).

```
#!/usr/bin/perl -w
use strict;

### SubRefAnon.pl

# An anonymous subroutine:
my $ref_to_sub = sub {                                                    #(A)
    my ($number) = @_;
    if ( $number % 2 == 0 ) {
        return "$number is even";
    } else {
        return "$number is not even";
    }
};                                                                        #(B)

# A named subroutine:
sub even_p {                                                              #(C)
    my ($number) = @_;
    if ( $number % 2 == 0 ) {
        return "$number is even";
    } else {
        return "$number is not even";
    }
}                                                                         #(D)

# A subroutine call via its reference:
print &$ref_to_sub( 18 ), "\n";                # 18 is even               #(E)

# A block returning the reference
print &{$ref_to_sub}( 19 ), "\n";              # 19 is not even           #(F)

# The arrow notation for dereference:
print $ref_to_sub->(20), "\n";                 # 20 is even               #(G)

# A regular subroutine call:
print &even_p( 21 ), "\n";                     # 21 is not even           #(H)
```

5.9 SUBROUTINES RETURNING REFERENCES TO SUBROUTINES

A subroutine can return a reference to another subroutine. As we will show, a subroutine returning a reference to another subroutine allows the subroutines to be chained together.

In the script `SubroutineChaining.pl` shown next, the subroutine `funct1()` squares its argument in line (C), prints out the result obtained by the squaring operation in line (D), and returns a reference to another subroutine, `funct2()`, in line (E). If `funct1()` is needed for only its side effect, it can be called all by itself in the following manner:

```
&funct1( 30 );
```

which will print out

```
30 squared gives us 900
```

But since `funct1()` returns a reference to `funct2()`, we are also allowed to make the following invocation, as shown in line (J) of the script,

```
&funct1(30)->(40);
```

With this invocation, after control has returned from `funct1()`, the subroutine `funct2()` will be automatically invoked since what is on the left side of the arrow operator will evaluate to a subroutine reference to `funct2()`. The call to `funct2()` will be made with the argument 40 for the example shown. Now the combined output of the chained invocations of `funct1()` and `funct2()` will be

```
30 squared gives us 900 and 40 cubed gives us 64000
```

An alternative syntax for the chained invocation is shown in lines (K) and (L).

```
#!/usr/bin/perl -w
use strict;

### SubroutineChaining.pl

# The following subroutine squares its arg but
# returns a reference to another subroutine
sub funct1 {                                                  #(A)
    my ($arg) = shift;                                        #(B)
    my $result = $arg * $arg;                                 #(C)
    print "$arg squared gives us $result";                    #(D)
    return \&funct2;                                          #(E)
}
```

```
# This is the other subroutine to which a reference
# is returned by the above subroutine.  This subroutine
# cubes its argument.
sub funct2 {                                                        #(F)
    my ($arg) = shift;                                              #(G)
    my $result = $arg * $arg * $arg;                                #(H)
    print " and $arg cubed gives us $result\n";                     #(I)
}

# One way to chain the two subroutines:
&funct1(10)->(10);                                                  #(J)
        # output: 10 squared gives us 100 and 10 cubed gives us 1000

# Another way to chain the two subroutines:
my $funct_ref = \&funct1;                                           #(K)
$funct_ref->(30)->(40)                                              #(L)
        # output: 30 squared gives us 900 and 40 cubed gives us 64000
```

5.10 CLOSURES

A closure is a reference to an anonymous subroutine that incorporates references to one or more lexical variables in the enclosing scope of the subroutine.

As an example of a closure, consider the subroutine defined in lines (A), (B), and (C) of the script `ClosureBasic.pl` shown next. When this subroutine is invoked, as we do in lines (D), (E), and (F), it returns a reference to the anonymous subroutine of line (C) which *is a closure over the lexical variable* of line (B).

Notice what happens with the three different invocations of the enclosing subroutine `make_offset_counter()` in lines (D), (E), and (F), the first with an argument of 10, the second with 100, and the third with 1000. These three invocations return *three different* counters. When we fire up the first counter in lines (G), (H), and (I), we get a count starting at 10. But when we fire up the second counter in lines (J), (K), and (L), we get a count starting at 100. And when we fire up the third counter in lines (M), (N), and (O), we get a count starting at 1000. *In effect, each counter has its copy of the lexical variable that is incremented independently of the copy of this variable in the other counters.* We can also say that a closure maintains *a lasting reference* to the lexical variable that it is a closure on.

```
#!/usr/bin/perl -w
use strict;

### ClosureBasic.pl

sub make_offset_counter {                                        #(A)
    my $offset = shift;                                          #(B)
    sub { ++$offset; };                                          #(C)
}

my $counter1 = &make_offset_counter( 10 );                       #(D)
my $counter2 = &make_offset_counter( 100 );                      #(E)
my $counter3 = &make_offset_counter( 1000 );                     #(F)

print $counter1->(), "\n";              # 11                     #(G)
print $counter1->(), "\n";              # 12                     #(H)
print $counter1->(), "\n";              # 13                     #(I)

print $counter2->(), "\n";              # 101                    #(J)
print $counter2->(), "\n";              # 102                    #(K)
print $counter2->(), "\n";              # 103                    #(L)

print $counter3->(), "\n";              # 1001                   #(M)
print $counter3->(), "\n";              # 1002                   #(N)
print $counter3->(), "\n";              # 1003                   #(O)
```

It is also possible for different closures to share the same lexical variable from the enclosing scope. When that happens, the changes made in the value of the variable by one closure will be visible through the other closure. This is illustrated by the next script, `ClosureShared.pl`.[7]

Line (A) of the script defines a subroutine that returns a list of two closures. The two subroutines in line (C) result in closures over the same lexical variable, `$offset`, of the enclosing scope. Now let's look at the workings of the pair of counters `$c1` and `$c2` returned in line (D), and the pair of counters `$c3` and `$c4` returned in line (E). As lines (F) through (I) show, the incrementing of the `$c1` counter is visible through the `$c2` counter, and the incrementing of the `$c3` counter is visible through the `$c4` counter. When we trigger `$c1` in line (F), we get 11. And then when we trigger `$c2` in line (G), we get 12, which is one past the count established by the previous trigger of `$c1`.

[7]This script is based on an example that was posted by Benjamin Goldberg in the `comp.lang.perl.moderated` newsgroup in response to a query posted by the author.

```
#!/usr/bin/perl -w
use strict;

### ClosureShared.pl

sub make_two_offset_counters {                                          #(A)
    my $offset = shift;                                                 #(B)
    sub { ++$offset; }, sub{ ++$offset; }                               #(C)
}

my ($c1, $c2) = &make_two_offset_counters( 10 );                        #(D)
my ($c3, $c4) = &make_two_offset_counters( 100 );                       #(E)

print $c1->(), ' ', $c3->(), "\n";              # 11 101                #(F)
print $c2->(), ' ', $c4->(), "\n";              # 12 102                #(G)
print $c1->(), ' ', $c3->(), "\n";              # 13 103                #(H)
print $c2->(), ' ', $c4->(), "\n";              # 14 105                #(I)
```

For another example, the next script, `Closure.pl`, is based on an example provided by Srinivasan [61]. The subroutine defined in lines (A) through (E) returns a subroutine reference that is a closure over the lexical variable `$greeting_target` of line (B). Lines (F) and (G) create two instances of the greeting generator with different targets, `world` and `everyone`. Note the outputs obtained when we fire up the greeting generators in lines (H) through (K). Just for variety, we show in lines (L) through (O) some alternative syntax that can be used for invoking the closures.

```
#!/usr/bin/perl -w
use strict;

### Closure.pl

sub make_greeting_generator {                                           #(A)
    my $greeting_target = shift;                                        #(B)
    sub {                                                               #(C)
        my $salutation = shift;                                         #(D)
        print "$salutation $greeting_target\n";                         #(E)
    };
};

my $greeting_gen1 = make_greeting_generator( "world" );                 #(F)
my $greeting_gen2 = make_greeting_generator( "everyone" );              #(G)
```

```
$greeting_gen1->("hello");            # hello world                #(H)
$greeting_gen1->("good morning");     # good morning world         #(I)
$greeting_gen2->("hello");            # hello everyone             #(J)
$greeting_gen2->("good morning");     # good morning everyone      #(K)

&$greeting_gen1("hello");             # hello world                #(L)
&$greeting_gen2("good morning");      # good morning everyone      #(M)

&{make_greeting_generator("world")}("hello");                      #(N)
                                      # hello world
&{make_greeting_generator("everyone")}("good morning");            #(O)
                                      # good morning everyone
```

5.11 ENFORCING PRIVACY IN MODULES

As discussed in Section 2.11 of Chapter 2, Perl's namespaces are wide open — open from the standpoint of accessibility and modifiability from other namespaces. If you look at the contents of the user-defined modules we used in Section 2.11 of Chapter 2 — HelloModule, HelloModule2, and HelloModule3 — all of the subroutines defined in those module are accessible in any script in any file.

What if you wanted to keep a subroutine defined in a module inaccessible outside the module?

A subroutine can be kept hidden inside a module by having a my variable hold a reference to the subroutine. Since the my variables have nothing to do with the namespaces associated with the packages, their scope never crosses the file boundaries.

Shown below is the code for a new module, HelloModule4, which is a modified version of the original HelloModule used in Chapter 2. Note how we use the my variables in lines (C) and (D) to hide the two subroutines to which they hold references. Through these my variables, these subroutines are accessible only within the module, a fact that we make use of in lines (F) and (G).

```
### HelloModule4.pm

package HelloModule4;                                              #(A)

sub say_loud_hello {                                               #(B)
    print "HELLO!!! HOW ARE YOU!!!\n";
}
```

```
my $very_soft = sub {                                            #(C)
    print "hi sweet thing! how are you this morning!\n";
};

my $not_very_soft = sub {                                        #(D)
    print "hi dear! how are you this morning!\n";
};

sub say_soft_hello {                                             #(E)
    print "How soft?  Say 'very' or 'usual'  :";
    chomp( my $how_soft = <STDIN> );
    $how_soft =~ s/^\s*(\S*)\s*$/$1/;
    if ( $how_soft eq 'very' ) {
        $very_soft->();                                          #(F)
    } elsif ( $how_soft eq 'usual' ) {
        $not_very_soft->();                                      #(G)
    } else {
        die "unrecognized answer\n";                             #(H)
    }
}

1
```

The code shown below uses `HelloModule4`. When we invoke `say_soft_hello()` in line (D), that subroutine in turn invokes one of the two hidden subroutines of `HelloModule4` depending on the answer supplied by the user to the program's query as to how soft.

```
#!/usr/bin/perl -w
use strict;

### UsingHelloModuleWithPrivacy.pl

BEGIN {                                                          #(A)
    unshift @INC, "/home/kak/MyModules/";
}

use HelloModule4;                                                #(B)

&HelloModule4::say_loud_hello();                                 #(C)

&HelloModule4::say_soft_hello();                                 #(D)
```

5.12 REFERENCES TO TYPEGLOBS

It is not infrequently the case that a program needs an internally generated symbolic name. Toward that end, programming languages typically provide a symbol generator that returns a new name that can be used directly as an identifier. Perl also provides a symbol generator function, `gensym()`, in the module `Symbol`. But because, in a figurative sense, a Perl identifier of the global variety is "synonymous" with a typeglob,[8] what `gensym()` returns is not a symbolic name directly, but a reference to an anonymous typeglob. Subsequently, this reference can be dereferenced and values placed in the various slots of the typeglob.

To see what is returned by `Symbol::gensym()`, if you say

```
use Symbol;
$foo = gensym();
print "$foo\n";
```

the print statement produces the output

```
GLOB(0x804b514)
```

which is the string representation of a reference to an anonymous typeglob.

Recall that a reference to a scalar is dereferenced with the prefix `$` used as a dereferencing operator. That is, if `$x` is holding a reference to a scalar, we can use the syntax `$$x` to retrieve the value of the scalar. Similarly, if `$x` is holding a reference to an array, we can use `@$x` to retrieve the array. Along the same lines, if `$x` is holding a reference to a hash, we can use `%$x` to retrieve the hash. Finally, if `$x` is holding a reference to a subroutine, we can use `&$x` to retrieve the subroutine. Analogously, if `$x` is holding a reference to a typeglob, we can use `*$x` to access the typeglob. In other words, a reference to a typeglob is dereferenced with the `*` operator. But note that what we get by dereferencing a typeglob reference is not a printable entity — because it is the typeglob itself. However, the dereferencing operation can be used to fill the various slots of a typeglob created by `gensym()`.

To place a scalar value in the scalar slot of the anonymous typeglob the reference to which is held by `$foo`, we can say

```
${*$foo} = "hello";
print "${*$foo}\n";                 # hello
```

And to place an array in the array slot of the typeglob whose reference is held by `$foo`, we can say

```
@{*$foo} = ('one', 'two', 'three' );
print "@{*$foo}\n";                 # one two three
```

[8]We discussed Perl's typeglobs earlier in Section 2.13 of Chapter 2.

The reference to a typeglob returned by `gensym()` can also be used as a filehandle:

```
open *$foo, 'data.txt'
    || die "cannot open data.txt file: $!";
@all_lines = <$foo>;
close *$foo;
print "@all_lines\n";
```

We can also directly use the typeglob reference returned by `gensym()` as a filehandle, as illustrated by the following script:

```
#!/usr/bin/perl -w
use strict;

### Gensym.pl

use Symbol;

my $bar = gensym;                                                  #(A)
open $bar, 'data.txt'                                              #(B)
    || die "cannot open data.txt file: $!";
my @all_lines = <$bar>;                                            #(C)
close $bar;
print @all_lines, "\n";
```

The scalar `$bar` in line (A) holds a reference to the anonymous typeglob returned by `gensym()`. We use this reference directly as a filehandle in lines (B) and (C).

5.13 THE ref( ) FUNCTION

Perl comes with a very useful built-in function `ref()` that can tell us whether or not an argument scalar is a reference. If the argument is not a reference, the function returns false. Otherwise, it returns one of the following strings:

```
SCALAR
ARRAY
HASH
CODE
GLOB
REF
package_name
```

depending on whether the argument is a reference to a scalar, to an array, to a hash, to a subroutine, to a typeglob, to another reference, or to a *blessed* object in the package `package_name`.[9] To see the usefulness of this function, consider the following complex data object:

```
my %assets = (
  fixed_assets => {
                    real_estate => {house => 100000, farm => 20000},#(A)
                    mobile_prop => {suv => 20000, car => 8000},     #(B)
                    art => {picasso => 8000, matisse => 1500}       #(C)
                  },
  liquid_assets => {bonds => 700, stocks => 800, mut_funds => 900}, #(D)
  cash_on_hand  => [1000, 2000, 3000],     # in different bank accts #(E)
  tax_filing_dates => ["3/1", "6/1", "9/1", "12/1"]                 #(F)
);
```

Let's say that our goal is to find the total worth of the individual whose assets are described in the form of the hash shown above. We assume that all the *numbers* that show up in this hash are dollar amounts representing asset values. We also assume that the exact interior structure of the `%assets` hash can vary from individual to individual.

In order to find the total worth of an individual, we must descend down the assets tree and add up the numbers. But how we process an interior node will depend on the nature of that node. When an interior node is an array of dollar amounts, as in line (E), we can just add all the numbers. But when an interior node is itself a hash, as in lines (A), (B), and (C), we must extract just the values associated with the keys, provided those values are numbers and not strings or references. We must also make sure that certain strings such as those shown in line (F) do not get interpreted as numerical data of any sort.

This problem is best solved with a script that recursively invokes a net-worth finding subroutine called `get_worth` in the code snippet shown below. The subroutine examines each node of the asset tree and acts accordingly. For example, lines (I) through (N) of the code snippet take care of the nodes that are references to arrays, as in lines (E) and (F) above:

```
sub get_worth {                                                     #(G)
    my $ref_node = shift;                                           #(H)
    if ( ref( $ref_node ) eq "ARRAY" ) {                            #(I)
        foreach ( @$ref_node ) {                                    #(J)
            if (ref) {                                              #(K)
                &getWorth( $_ );                                    #(L)
            } elsif (/^\d+$/) {                                     #(M)
                $total_worth += $_;                                 #(N)
            }
```

[9] Chapter 6 explains what is meant by a blessed object.

```
        }
        if ( ref( $ref_node ) eq "HASH" ) {                           #(O)
            ....
            ....
            ....
        }
    }
```

Here `$ref_node` is the node under consideration in the assets tree. Line (I) guarantees that this code snippet will only be invoked if the node is a reference to an anonymous array as in lines (E) and (F) in the assets hash. We dereference the array reference in line (J). The `foreach` loop iterates through the array thus obtained, setting the value of the default variable `$_` to each successive item in the array. Line (K) invokes the `ref()` function on `$_`. If `$_` turns out to be a reference of any sort, we recursively call the `get_worth()` subroutine in line (L). Otherwise, in lines (M) and (N) we first check that the array entries are numbers and if so we add up the numbers to the previously calculated value for `$total_worth`. We will, of course, need to write a similar code snippet for the case when the interior node is a reference to a hash. We leave that as a homework problem for the reader.

5.14 SYMBOLIC REFERENCES

All the references we have talked about so far are also known as *hard references*. We now present *symbolic references*. While hard references allow you to create nested data structures of arbitrary complexity, symbolic references in Perl allow you to create program variables dynamically from strings that may be read either from a data file or from the command line.[10]

Let's say we have a data file with the following contents:

```
two_legged:  man, bird
four_legged: cat, dog, horse, crab
six_legged:  springtail, silverfish
eight_legged: spider, beetle, mite, tick
....
....
hundred_legged: centipede
```

and let's say that when we read this data file into a Perl script, we want the following arrays to come into existence:

[10]To appreciate the difference between a hard reference and a symbolic reference, an analogy with hard links and symbolic links in the naming of Unix files is useful. A hard link points directly to a piece of disk real estate that contains a file. On the other hand, a symbolic link points to another name which will usually be the actual name of the file.

```
@two_legged
@four_legged
@six_legged
@eight_legged
....
....
@hundred_legged
```

We want the entries in each array to be the names of the animal species as shown in the data file. It will be as if the array `@four_legged` was initialized in the following manner inside a Perl program:

```
@four_legged = (cat, dog, horse, crab);
```

What we therefore want is to be able to create certain program variables, such as `@two_legged`, `@four_legged`, etc., whose names would depend on what we find in the data file for each *leggedness*-based category name.

This can be easily accomplished with symbolic references in Perl. To present the basic idea of a symbolic reference, recall that in the following syntax

```
$$ref
```

the scalar `$ref` will ordinarily be taken to be a hard reference created with the backslash operator, in the manner discussed in this chapter so far. But if the most recent binding of the scalar `$ref` is not to a hard reference but to a string, Perl will treat the string as a symbolic reference. That is, if we have

```
$ref = "foo";
$$ref = 1234;
```

then the string `foo` will be treated as a symbolic reference for the variable `$foo`. And the value of this variable, as set via its symbolic reference, will be 1234.

These and other basic ideas about symbolic references are conveyed by the next script, `BasicSymRef.pl`, in which the program variables `$foo` and `@bar` are created dynamically through symbolic references. In line (C), we set a local variable `$x` to the string `foo`. Subsequently, when `$$x=100` is executed in line (D), we can say that effectively it is the value of the scalar `$foo` that is set to 100. In the expression `$$x`, the scalar `$x` is replaced by its symbolic reference `foo`. This is borne out by the output of the print statement in line (F). It is now possible to use the scalars `$$x` and `$foo` interchangeably. For example, when we change the value of `$foo` in line (G), we can see this change through the scalar `$$x` in line (H). And, when we change the value of `$$x` in line (I), we can see the change through the scalar `$foo` in line (J).

For another example, but this time involving a dynamically created array variable, we change in line (K) the string binding of `$x` to `bar`. Subsequently, when we assign to the expression `@$x` in line (L), we effectively create an array of name `@bar`. From this point on, we can use the arrays `@$x` and `@bar` interchangeably.

Line (N) shows the output when we print out the array `@bar`. When we change the array `@bar` by inserting another element in it in line (O), this change can be seen through the array `@$x`, as shown in line (P). By the same token, when we alter the array `@$x` in line (Q), this change can be seen through the array `@bar` in line (R).

The rest of the script, in lines (S) through (X), is meant to show that the program variables created by the mechanism of symbolic references have package scope. In other words, such variables are not lexical. Recall from Chapter 2 that all `my` variables are lexical. As a result, the assignment in line (S)

```
my $foo = 10000;
```

does not at all conflict with the scalar `$foo` as created and manipulated in lines (C) through (J). The scalar `$foo` of line (S) is lexical, whereas `$foo` created through line (D) is global with respect to the package `main` that implicitly corresponds to a top-level script. When we print out the value of `$foo` in line (T), its lexical meaning hides its global meaning. However, we can access the global meaning as set earlier in line (I) through the package qualified call shown in line (U).

The same is true of the lexical `@bar` defined in line (V). In line (W), its lexical meaning hides its global meaning as set in line (Q). However, that global meaning can still be accessed by using the package qualification shown in line (X).

```
#!/usr/bin/perl
use strict;                                                          #(A)

### BasicSymRef.pl

no strict;                                                           #(B)

my $x = "foo";                                                       #(C)
$$x = 100;                                                           #(D)
print $x, "\n";                          # foo                       #(E)
print $foo, "\n";                        # 100                       #(F)
$foo = 200;                                                          #(G)
print $$x, "\n";                         # 200                       #(H)
$$x = 300;                                                           #(I)
print $foo, "\n";                        # 300                       #(J)

$x = "bar";                                                          #(K)
@$x = ('a', 'b', 'c');                                               #(L)
print $x, "\n";                          # bar                       #(M)
print "@bar\n";                          # a b c                     #(N)
$bar[3] = 'd';                                                       #(O)
print "@$x\n";                           # a b c d                   #(P)
$$x[4] = 'e';                                                        #(Q)
print "@bar\n";                          # a b c d e                 #(R)
```

```
my $foo = 10000;                                                        #(S)
print $foo, "\n";                         # 10000                       #(T)
print $main::foo, "\n";                   # 300                         #(U)

my @bar = ('one', 'two', 'three');                                      #(V)
print "@bar\n";                           # one two three               #(W)
print "@main::bar\n";                     # a b c d e                   #(X)
```

The reader will notice that we disabled the usual `strict` pragma in line (B). As mentioned earlier in Chapter 2, the `strict` pragma is a directive that tells the compiler three things: (1) that every variable will either be a lexical variable or will be accessed through its package-qualified name; (2) that there will be no symbolic references in the program; and (3) that no barewords will be used. Obviously then, in order to use symbolic references, you have to turn off the pragma. We could also have simply not used the pragma in line (A). But the invocation in line (A) serves the educational purpose of pointing out why the pragma must be turned off in the manner we have done in line (B). The turning on and off of the `strict` pragma can be done on a selective basis in a block of code. When the pragma is turned off or on, the directive stays in force until the end of the block, as mentioned in Chapter 2.

We will now go back to the situation we presented at the beginning of this section — the need to create program variables whose names correspond to strings read from a text file. The script `SymRef.pl` shown below does exactly that. The script reads in the text file named `datafile.txt` one line at a time. The contents of this file are as shown below:

```
two_legged:  man, bird
four_legged: cat, dog, horse, crab
six_legged: springtail, silverfish
eight_legged: spider, beetle, mite, tick
```

The first string in each line is the name of a category of animals on the basis of the number of legs. We have the animal categories `two_legged`, `four_legged`, `six_legged`, and `eight_legged`. The category name terminates in the `:` character. Following each category name are some of the animal names that belong to that category.

Starting in line (E), the `while` loop of this script reads one line at a time the data file `datafile.txt`. The conditional of the `if` statement in line (H) extracts the animal category name at the beginning of each line of the text file. Line (J) pushes the extracted animal category name into the array named `@all_animal_categories`. Lines (K), (L), and (M) then analyze the rest of the text-file line for the names of the animals in that line. Line (L) gets rid of any white space before the names of the animals (and after the colon). In line (M), we call on `split()` to break up the remaining line on the basis of an intervening (but optional) comma, any optional white space before the comma, and at least one mandatory white space after the comma.

From the standpoint of symbolic references, the important thing to note in line (M) is that we are creating program variables with names `@two_legged`, `@four_legged`, and so on, by using the string binding of the scalar `$animal_category`. Lines (O) through (R) demonstrate that we can treat these program variables just like regular array names. Since the names of these dynamically created program variables are all stored in the array `@all_animal_categories`, we can also use the syntax shown in lines (S) through (V) for accessing them and for examining or modifying their values.

```
#!/usr/bin/perl

### SymRef.pl

my $file = "datafile.txt";                                                      #(A)

open FILE, $file
    or die "Can't open $file: $!";                                              #(B)

my $animal_category;                                                            #(C)
my @all_animal_categories;                                                      #(D)

while (<FILE>) {                                                                #(E)
    chomp;                                                                      #(F)
    next if /^\s*$/;                        # ignore blank lines                #(G)
    if (/^\s*([a-zA-Z_]\w*)\s*:/) {         # extract animal cetegory           #(H)
        $animal_category = $1;                                                  #(I)
        push @all_animal_categories, $animal_category;                          #(J)
    }
    my $str = $';                                                               #(K)
    $str =~ s/^\s*//;                                                           #(L)
    push @$animal_category, split /\s*,?\s+/, $str;                             #(M)
}

print "@all_animal_categories\n";                                               #(N)
                    # two_legged four_legged six_legged eight_legged
print "@two_legged\n";                  # man bird                              #(O)
print "@four_legged\n";                 # cat dog horse crab                    #(P)
print "@six_legged\n";                  # springtail silverfish                 #(Q)
print "@eight_legged\n";                # spider beetle mite tick               #(R)

print "@{$all_animal_categories[0]}\n";                 # man bird              #(S)
print scalar(@{$all_animal_categories[0]}), "\n"; # 2                           #(T)
print "@{$all_animal_categories[3]}\n";                 # beetle mite tick#(U)
print scalar(@{$all_animal_categories[3]}), "\n"; # 3                           #(V)
```

We will now show a small variation on the above script to illustrate an example that uses a mix of symbolic and hard references. The new program variables, instead of holding directly the data read from a text file, will now hold hard references to collections of such data.

The script shown below is basically the same as the one presented above except that now in line (N) we assign to each symbolic reference a hard reference to a temporary array named `@temp`. As shown in lines (P) through (S), the values of the dynamically generated program variables `@two_legged`, `@four_legged`, etc., would now be the corresponding hard references. These new program variables can be dereferenced directly, as in lines (P) through (S), to yield the hard references they hold. And, as shown in lines (T) through (W), we can use the usual dereferencing syntax for hard references to access the arrays themselves. Additionally, we can use the arrow notation to reach the individual elements of these arrays, as shown in lines (X), (Y), and (Z).

```
#!/usr/bin/perl

### SymRefRef.pl

my $file = "datafile.txt";                                          #(A)

open FILE, $file
    or die "Can't open $file: $!";                                  #(B)

my $animal_category;                                                #(C)
my @all_animal_categories;                                          #(D)

while (<FILE>) {                                                    #(E)
    chomp;                                                          #(F)
    next if /^\s*$/;                                                #(G)
    if (/^\s*([a-zA-Z_]\w*)\s*:/) {                                 #(H)
        $animal_category = $1;                                      #(I)
        push @all_animal_categories, $animal_category;              #(J)
    }
    my $str = $';                                                   #(K)
    $str =~ s/^\s*//;                                               #(L)
    push my @temp, split /\s*,?\s+/, $str;                          #(M)
    $$animal_category = \@temp;                                     #(N)
}

print "@all_animal_categories\n";                                   #(O)
                        # two_legged four_legged six_legged eight_legged

print "$two_legged\n";              # ARRAY(0x8057218)              #(P)
print "$four_legged\n";             # ARRAY(0x804b5f8)              #(Q)
print "$six_legged\n";              # ARRAY(0x8057074)              #(R)
```

```
print "$eight_legged\n";              # ARRAY(0x805c564)              #(S)

print "@$two_legged\n";               # man bird                      #(T)
print "@$four_legged\n";              # cat dog horse crab            #(U)
print "@$six_legged\n";               # springtail silverfish         #(V)
print "@$eight_legged\n";             # spider beetle mite tick       #(W)

print $two_legged->[0], "\n";         # man                           #(X)
print $four_legged->[1], "\n";        # dog                           #(Y)
print $six_legged->[2], "\n";         # silverfish                    #(Z)
```

5.14.1 Symbolic References to Subroutines

Just as you can have symbolic references to scalars, arrays, and hashes, you can also have a symbolic reference to a subroutine. As we will show in the following script, a subroutine is also allowed to return a symbolic reference to another subroutine.[11]

In the following script, SymRefSub.pl, the string assignments in lines (A) and (B) will serve as symbolic references to the subroutines named do_squares and do_cubes that are defined in lines (G) and (I), respectively.

Note how a symbolic reference to a subroutine is dereferenced in line (C). Also note the use of the arrow operator for dereferencing a symbolic reference to a subroutine in line (D).

Line (H) shows that a subroutine can return a symbolic reference to another subroutine. In line (H), the subroutine do_squares returns a symbolic reference to the subroutine do_cubes. Since the subroutine do_squares returns a symbolic reference to the subroutine do_cubes, we can chain the subroutine invocations as shown in lines (E) and (F).

```
#!/usr/bin/perl -w

# SymRefSub.pl

my $funct1 = "do_squares";                                            #(A)
my $funct2 = "do_cubes";                                              #(B)

# Dereferencing a symbolic reference to a subroutine:
&$funct1(30);                 # 30 squared gives us 900               #(C)
```

[11] Section 5.9 illustrated a subroutine returning a hard reference to another subroutine.

```
print "\n";

# Dereference the symbolic reference with the the arrow operator:
$funct1->(35);               # 35 squared gives us 1225              #(D)
print "\n";

# Chain the two subroutines:
&$funct1(30)->(40);                                                   #(E)
             # 30 squared gives us 900 and 40 cubed gives us 64000
print "\n";

# Use the arrow for the first subroutine call also:
$funct1->(30)->(40);                                                  #(F)
             # 30 squared gives us 900 and 40 cubed gives us 64000

# Squares its arg but returns a reference to another subroutine:
sub do_squares {                                                      #(G)
    my ($arg) = shift;
    my $result = $arg * $arg;
    print "$arg squared gives us $result";
    # The next statement returns a symbolic
    # reference to another subroutine
    return $funct2;                                                   #(H)
}

# Cubes its argument:
sub do_cubes {                                                        #(I)
    my ($arg) = shift;
    my $result = $arg * $arg * $arg;
    print " and $arg cubed gives us $result\n";
}
```

5.15 CREDITS AND SUGGESTIONS FOR FURTHER READING

The online Perl documentation tutorial `perlreftut` by Mark Jason Dominus is an excellent introductory read on the topic of references in Perl. The online manpage `perlref` (Perl References and Nested Data Structures) has the final word on all issues related to this subject. Two other manpages that show how to use references for creating complex data structures are `perldsc` (Perl Data Structures Cookbook) and `perllol` (Manipulating Arrays of Arrays in Perl), both by Tom Christiansen.

5.16 HOMEWORK

1. You are given the following hash whose keys have associated with them the anonymous arrays shown:

```
my %animals;
$animals{dog} = ["four_legged", "friendly", "protective"];
$animals{cat} = ["four_legged", "friendly"];
$animals{rat} = ["four_legged", "pest", "dangerous"];
$animals{man} = ["two_legged"];
```

   Write Perl scripts that do the following:

   (a) A script to print out all of the attributes associated with a specified animal.

   (b) A script to print out the first attribute associated with each of the animals.

   (c) A script to print out the names of all the animals that are friendly.

2. Write a Perl script to calculate the total worth of an individual whose assets are given by the hash `%assets` shown in Section 5.13. Pretend that you do not know in advance the level of nesting in the hash. You may only assume that all numerical values are asset values and, when they appear in embedded hashes, their associated keys are asset names. You can ignore the strings if they are used as the values associated with the keys.

3. In the previous problem, construct a tabular display in which each asset item is listed in the left column and its value in the right column. Show all the `cash_on_hand` amount together as a single row in this table.

4. Write a Perl script that acts like a *dispatch table*. An example of a dispatch table is a hash whose keys are the different possible command-line arguments to the script and whose values are references to subroutines. Such a dispatch table can be used to select the subroutine to be executed on the basis of the command-line argument supplied. Here is a simple example of a hash that one could use for a dispatch table:

```
my %dispatch_table = (
    key1 => $ref_sub_1,
    key2 => $ref_sub_2,
```

```
        key3 => sub { print "executing an inline sub\n"; },
        key4 => sub { print "executing another inline sub\n"; }
    );
```

The values in the first two key-value pairs in the hash are two previously created references to two subroutines. The values in the next two key-value pairs can be thought of as "inline" subroutines — small subroutines that can be defined in place. Here, as explained in Section 5.8, the keyword `sub` acts as an operator and returns a reference to the anonymous subroutine that follows. In your script, you would obviously need to process the command-line arguments, to select the appropriate subroutine from the hash, and to execute the selected subroutine.

5. Consider the subroutine:

```
sub test {
    my $arg = shift;
    print "inside test\n";
    return 10 * $arg;
}
```

Why is it that the following invocation evokes an error report from the compiler?

```
my $x = \&test(10);
my $result = &$x( 10 );
print "result: $result\n";
```

6. As you well know already, a common way to initialize an array is as follows:

```
my @arr = qw/ a b c d /;
print "@arr\n";
```

But let's say that we wish to use similar initialization syntax for creating a 3x3 "matrix" as follows:

```
my @barr;

$barr[0] = \qw/ 1 2 3 /;
$barr[1] = \qw/ 4 5 6 /;
$barr[2] = \qw/ 7 8 9 /;
```

The compiler refuses to accept this. Why? Note that the compiler is happy with the following attempt at creating such an array:

```
my @barr;

$barr[0] = [1, 2, 3];
$barr[1] = [4, 5, 6];
$barr[2] = [7, 8, 9];

for my $i (0..2) {                    # this prints out the array
    for my $j (0..2) {
        print "$barr[$i][$j] ";
    }
    print "\n";
}
```

If you must use the `qw//` operator for initializing each row of the "matrix," the compiler also has no problem with the following syntax:

```
my @carr;

@{$carr[0]}[0..2] = qw/aa bb cc/;
@{$carr[1]}[0..2] = qw/dd ee ff/;
@{$carr[2]}[0..2] = qw/gg hh ii/;

for my $i (0..2) {                  # this prints out the array
    for my $j (0..2) {
        print "$carr[$i][$j] ";
    }
    print "\n";
}
```

Explain this initialization syntax. As a stepping stone, explain the following syntax for initializing a one-dimensional array:

```
my $darr;
@{$darr}[0..2] = qw/aa bb cc/;
print "@$darr\n";                     # aa bb cc
```

6

The Notion of a Class in Perl

The basic vocabulary of object-oriented programming and scripting consists of: *class*, *encapsulation*, *inheritance*, and *polymorphism*. At a high level of conceptualization, a class can be thought of as a category. We may think of "Cat" as a class. A specific cat would then be an *instance* of this class. For the purpose of writing code, a class is a data structure that is typically endowed with *instance variables* (commonly also called *data attributes*) for representing the various properties of the different instances made from the class, and *methods* for endowing the instances with certain behaviors. For example, a `Cat` class could be defined as:

```
class Cat {
    name;
    weight;
    ## other instance variables

    ## methods:
    meow() {
       ## code for sounding out a meow
    }
    purr() {
       ## code for sounding out a purr
    }
    ## code that would allow a specific cat to be
    ## instantiated from this class, etc.
}
```

In this definition, `name` and `weight` are the instance variables of the class `Cat`, and `meow()` and `purr()` the methods. As this example suggests, the concept of a class helps us pull together the various properties and behaviors important to a certain category of objects.

In object-oriented programming in general, there often arises a need to "hide" some of the implementation detail of a class. If direct access to an instance variable or to a method has the potential of putting an instance in an undesirable or an erroneous state, then obviously you would not allow such direct access. If the implementation code for `meow()` for a `Cat` object requires that we define another method `regulateExhale()`, we probably would not want other objects in a program to access `regulateExhale()` directly. Before invoking `regulateExhale()`, the method `meow()` probably has to place the cat in a state where it has inhaled. An outsider having an unfettered access to `regulateExhale()` could cause the cat to exhale on an empty lung.

Hiding or controlling the access to the implementation-level details in the innards of a class is called *encapsulation*. With appropriate encapsulation, each class will present a well-defined public interface to its clients (the users of the class). A client would only be able to access those instance variables and invoke those methods that are in the public interface.

The other two concepts, *polymorphism* and *inheritance*, rely on us being able to establish a hierarchy of classes for the different types of instances needed in a program or a script. To illustrate the notion of a *hierarchy of classes*, let's start with the class `Animal` which stands for what it means. This class can be extended into a more specialized class `FourLegged` representing just the four-legged animals. The class `Animal` could also be extended to a more specialized class `TwoLegged`. When a class A is extended to create a class B, we say that class B is a *subclass* of class A and that A is a *superclass* of B. We can also say that class A is the *base class* and class B a *derived class* or an *extended class*. A set of classes related through such superclass-subclass relationships forms a *hierarchy*, as illustrated by the example in Fig. 6.1. In particular, a class hierarchy formed in the manner shown in the figure

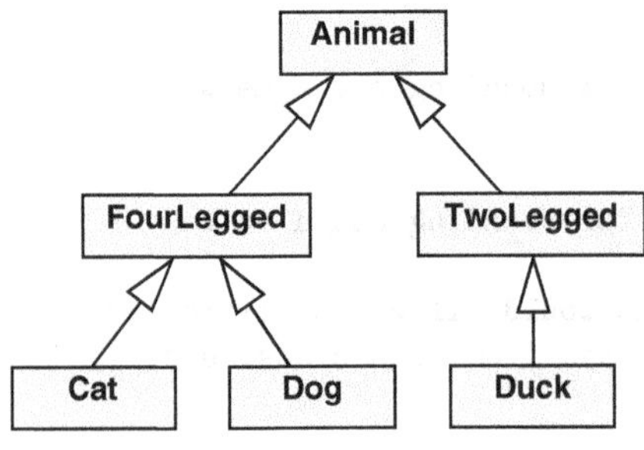

Fig. 6.1

is an *IsA hierarchy*, in the sense every `Cat` IsA `FourLegged`, every `Dog` IsA `FourLegged`, every `FourLegged` IsAn `Animal`, and so on.

Inheritance in object-oriented code allows a subclass to inherit some or all of the attributes, including the methods, of its superclass(es). This is one of the most important reasons why object-oriented code is more easily extendible than other kinds of code. If a vendor-supplied class does not fit the bill exactly, you can extend it by creating a subclass that would inherit the properties and the behavior of the vendor-supplied class and then you can add to it additional properties and behaviors as needed.

That brings us to the notion of polymorphism. Polymorphism basically means that a given instance can exhibit multiple identities at the same time, in the sense that a `Cat` instance can not only behave like a `Cat`, but also like a `FourLegged` and like an `Animal`, all at the same time. Therefore, if we were to make an array like

```
animals = (kitty, fido, tabby, quacker, spot)
```

of cats, dogs, and a duck — instances made from different classes in the `Animal` hierarchy — and if we were to invoke a method named `calculateIQ()` on this list of animals in the following fashion[1]

```
foreach item in animals {
    item.calculateIQ()
}
```

polymorphism would cause the correct implementation code for `calculateIQ()` to be automatically invoked for each of the animals. The method definition invoked for `kitty` would be the `calculateIQ()` defined for the `Cat` class, for `fido` the same method but defined for the `Dog` class, and so on. So polymorphism allows us to treat this diverse group of animals in a uniform manner — since they all are `Animals`, after all — but, at the same time, each animal's real identity in the class hierarchy is taken into account for accessing the most appropriate method definition to be used for that animal.[2]

---

[1]This code fragment is written in no particular language.

[2]In many object-oriented languages, a method such as `calculateIQ()` would need to be declared for the root class `Animal` for the control loop shown to work properly. All of the public methods and data attributes defined for the root class would constitute the public interface of the class hierarchy and each class in the hierarchy would be free to provide its own implementation for the methods declared in the root class. The sort of loop we showed above would constitute manipulating the instances made from the classes in the hierarchy through the public interface defined for the root class. *Polymorphism, in a nutshell, allows us to manipulate the objects constructed from the different classes in a hierarchy through a common interface defined for the root class.* Polymorphism allows for a method of the same name to be implemented differently in the different classes of a hierarchy and for automatic invocation of instance-specific implementations of such methods at run time. This, as we will see later, can lead to great efficiencies in coding.

6.1 DEFINING A CLASS IN PERL

We need to pull together three concepts in order to explain the notion of a class in Perl: (a) packages, discussed already in Chapter 2; (b) references, presented in Chapter 5; and (c) the new notion of *blessing objects into packages* that we will present here. We will start with the notion of what it means to bless an object into a package and what is made possible by the notion of blessing from the standpoint of OO scripting.

6.1.1 Blessing an Object into a Package

A class in Perl is a package that encloses the methods that characterize the behavior of the class and the instances constructed from the class. Upon hearing this, a student of OO would immediately ask: What about the instance variables? How does one encapsulate the instance variables (the same thing as data attributes) needed for representing the state of an instance constructed from a class?

Since, strictly speaking, a package is merely a namespace, it does not allow us to directly incorporate the data variables that can be used on a *per-instance* basis in the same sense that a C++ or a Java class does. (Although, as we will see later, a package does allow us to provide a class with attributes that can be used on a per-class basis, meaning like the static data members in C++ and Java.) This limitation, however, does not prevent us from defining an instance with state. Perl creates stateful instances through the expedient of packaging the instance variables in a standard data structure like a hash and having a constructor return a reference to such a hash as a class instance. It is important to realize that just as much as Perl can use a hash as an instance object, it can also use a scalar or an array. The convenience of a hash is obvious — it gives us named place-holders for the instance variables, just like the data members in a C++ class or a Java class.

So constructing an instance object in Perl is no different from constructing a hash, or an array, or just a scalar. But hashes, arrays, and scalars in Perl are free-standing objects in Perl, meaning they don't ordinarily belong to any particular package. It is indeed true that, in general, a variable inside a package would need to be accessed with its package-qualified name. But if the variable is holding a reference to, say, a hash, that hash itself has no particular package association.

So how does Perl establish the needed association between a data object that is to serve as an instance of a class and the class itself (meaning the package that will be used as a class)? Said another way, how does Perl acquire the notion that a data object is of a certain type? The type labeling is needed if the behavior of the object must correspond to what is specified for that class through its methods.

In Perl, the type association between a data object and a package that is to serve as a class is established through the mechanism of *blessing*. When a data object is blessed into a package, the object becomes tagged as belonging to the package and from that point on can be thought of as an instance of the class corresponding to the package. This is illustrated by the following statements. The variable `$ref` in line (A) holds a reference to an anonymous hash that contains two keys: `name` and `age`. When we invoke the built-in `ref()` function[3] on `$ref` in line (B), the function returns the generic label `HASH`. However, after we have blessed the hash in line (C) into the `Person` package, Perl tells us in line (D) that `$ref` is of type `Person`. From the syntax of the call to `bless()` in line (C), it appears like we are blessing the reference variable `$ref`, but what is actually getting blessed is the *referent* of the reference held by the variable, meaning the hash in this case. It is interesting to note that, for the example code shown below, prior to seeing the statement in line (C), Perl had no knowledge of `Person` being the name of a package. This is yet another example of autovivification in Perl that causes things to spring into existence merely by their use.

```
my $ref = { name => "Trillian", age => 35 };                        #(A)
print ref( $ref ), "\n";                          # HASH            #(B)

bless $ref, Person;                                                 #(C)
print ref( $ref ), "\n";                          # Person          #(D)
```

After an object has been blessed in the manner shown above, a method invoked via the arrow operator on a reference to the object will try to call on the subroutine of that name in the package into which the object was blessed. We illustrate this by the code shown below. Lines (E) through (H) define a package `Person` with a subroutine `get_name()`. In lines (I) through (L), we are back in our top-level namespace `main`, in which we first create a reference to an object in line (J), we bless the object in line (K), and, finally, we invoke the function `get_name()` on the object reference in line (L). Because the *referent* of the variable `$ref`, meaning the object we just created in line (J), is now blessed into the package `Person`, Perl seeks a subroutine named `get_name` in that package and then invokes it.[4]

```
package Person;                                                     #(E)

sub get_name {                                                      #(F)
    my $self = shift;                                               #(G)
    $self->{name};                                                  #(H)
}
```

---

[3]The `ref()` function was discussed previously in Section 5.13 of Chapter 5.

[4]The method call in line (L) could also be written as

```
$ref->get_name
```

that is, without the trailing empty parentheses. Perl allows any subroutine that is not expecting an argument to be called without the trailing empty parentheses. The sans parentheses call shown above is a bit of an extension of that idea since the subroutine `get_name` *is* expecting one argument — a reference to the blessed object — that is supplied implicitly by the arrow operator. When an arrow-based method call is expecting arguments in addition to what is implicitly supplied by the arrow operator, those must be put in parentheses. The reader will recall from Chapter 2 that regular subroutine calls in Perl permit you to leave the arguments unparenthesized.

```
package main;                                                     #(I)
my $ref = { name => "Trillian", age => 35 };                      #(J)
bless $ref, Person;                                               #(K)
print $ref->get_name(), "\n";                   # Trillian        #(L)
```

Subroutines defined for packages that are meant to serve as classes are written a bit differently compared to regular subroutines. For example, the subroutine defined in lines (F), (G), and (H) expects one argument that must be a reference to a blessed object. When this subroutine is invoked without any explicit arguments on a reference to a blessed object, as is the case in line (L), the subroutine invocation is translated by Perl into the following function call:

```
Person::get_name( $ref )
```

which agrees with how the subroutine expects itself to be called. So the local variable `$self` in line (H) becomes a reference to the anonymous hash that was constructed in line (J). Line (H) then returns the value stored for the key `name` in this hash and that's what is returned by the subroutine `get_name()`.

The function call syntax in line (L) follows the object-oriented style of invoking a method on either a class or an instance of a class. In this case, we can think of the arrow operator as invoking the method `get_name()` on the object `$ref`. If we had to speak more precisely, we would say that `get_name()` was being invoked on the object to which the variable `$ref` is holding a reference. Of course, the function call in line (L) could be replaced by the following non-OO syntax to achieve the same result:

```
print Person::get_name( $ref ), "\n";
```

But note that with this non-OO syntax it is not essential for `$ref` to be a blessed reference. In other words, with the definition of the package `Person` as shown previously, the following two statements would first construct an anonymous hash and then fetch us the value of the `name` field in the object constructed:

```
my $ref = { name => "Trillian", age => 35 };
print Person::get_name( $ref ), "\n";
```

But if we tried to do the same by substituting the following two statements for the above two:

```
my $ref = { name => "Trillian", age => 35 };
print $ref->get_name(), "\n";                              # ERROR
```

Perl would come back with the error message:

```
Can't call method ''get_name'' on unblessed reference at ......
```

This error message also points to the fact that although it is a data object like a hash that is blessed into a package, we can loosely talk about a *blessed reference* and an *unblessed reference*. So no harm is done if we say that a call like

```
bless( $ref, package_name )
```

blesses the reference `$ref` into the package whose name is supplied as the second argument. Nonetheless, one should not lose sight of the fact that it is the object to which `$ref` is holding a reference that is being blessed with this call. This fact is made clearer by the following example in which line (E) uses the arrow operator to invoke a method on a reference that appears to be unblessed. The code below blesses the reference `$ref` in line (C), but apparently the reference `$ref2` defined in line (D) is left unreferenced. Nevertheless, both `$ref` and `$ref2` behave the same with regard to the arrow operator in lines (C) and (E). As should be clear already, it is the hash of line (A) that is actually getting blessed into the `Person` package in line (B). Through the assignment operation in line (D), the variable `$ref2` holds a reference to the same blessed hash as the variable `$ref`.

```
my $ref = { name => "Trillian", age => 35 };                              #(A)
bless $ref, Person;                                                       #(B)
print $ref->get_name(), "\n";                          # Trillian          #(C)

my $ref2 = $ref;                                                          #(D)
print $ref2->get_name(), "\n";                         # Trillian          #(E)
```

The examples we showed of blessed references above involved references to hashes. But, as mentioned earlier, any reference in Perl can be blessed. The example code below shows us blessing in line (J) a reference to the anonymous array of line (I). The reference is blessed into the package `StringJoiner` that is defined in lines (A) through (G). Invoking the `wordJoiner()` method on the blessed reference in line (K) calls on the subroutine of line (B) to join up all the strings in the array of line (I). This call returns the joined up string, which as shown is output in line (K).

```
package StringJoiner;                                                     #(A)

sub wordjoiner {                                                          #(B)
    my $self = shift;                                                     #(C)
    my $joinedwords = "";                                                 #(D)
    foreach ( @$self ) {                                                  #(E)
        $joinedwords .= $_;                                               #(F)
    }
    $joinedwords;                                                         #(G)
}

package main;                                                             #(H)

my $ref = ['hello', 'jello', 'mello', 'yello'];                           #(I)
bless $ref, StringJoiner;                                                 #(J)
print $ref->wordjoiner(), "\n";          # hellojellomelloyello           #(K)
```

Note again that because `$ref` was blessed into the `StringJoiner` package in line (J), Perl translates the arrow operator based method call `$ref->wordjoiner()` in line (K) into the following call:

```
StringJoiner::wordjoiner( $ref )
```

which supplies the reference to the array of line (I) as an argument to the subroutine of line (B). The subroutine dereferences the array reference in line (E) and iterates through the elements of the array as shown in lines (E) and (F).

6.1.2 Providing a Class with a Constructor

It is indeed the case that any data object in Perl can be turned into a class instance by blessing the object into the package corresponding to the class. The previous subsection demonstrated this on what were basically arbitrary data objects, like a hash or an array, created outside the packages. These objects got blessed into the packages and thus got turned into class instances.

Now that we have the basic machinery in place for creating an instance of a class, let's focus on some larger issues related to the behavior of a class in OO. In general, a class has a *contract* vis-à-vis the rest of the software. A class's contract is defined in terms of its data attributes whose values are commonly instance-specific, and the methods defined for the class. That is, a class will commonly be provided with a set of methods and a set of instance variables (and possibly other variables, as we will see later).

We now need to bring together the two facts mentioned above — the fact that we can get any data object to act like a class instance through the notion of blessing and the fact that a class is a special data structure that comes equipped with data attributes and methods — into a mechanism to create instances from a specific class. This is done with the help of a specially designated function called a *constructor*. Therefore, in addition to the methods that lend behaviors to a class, a class will also commonly come equipped with one or more constructors. Being internal to a class, one would expect its constructor to know about the storage mechanism for the instance variables (and possibly other attributes). A constructor should therefore be able to acquire the required memory for an instance and to initialize it appropriately.

On the basis of the discussion in the previous subsection, it should be obvious that a constructor for a Perl class must do at least the following:

- Use the prescribed storage mechanism for the instance variables of the class.
- Obtain a reference to the data object created (which will serve as a class instance) from the storage mechanism.
- Bless the data object into the class and return a blessed reference to the object.

There is also the issue of what to call the constructor. While there are constraints on how a constructor is named in Python, as we will see in the next chapter, that is not the case with Perl. However, in Perl, if a class has a single constructor, it will typically be named new. A Perl class is allowed to have any number of constructors, a feature not available in Python.

Shown below is a class Person with a constructor called new:

```
package Person;                                          #(A)

sub new {                                                #(B)
    my ($class, $name, $age) = @_;                       #(C)
    bless {                                              #(D)
        _name => $name,                                  #(E)
        _age  => $age,                                   #(F)
    }, $class;                                           #(G)
}
```

This constructor uses a hash for the class instances. For reasons mentioned previously, that will usually be the case for most classes in Perl. To repeat, a hash gives us the convenience of naming the instance variables, these being the names of the hash keys. Line (C) extracts the arguments from a call to the constructor. Lines (E) and (F) fill up the two slots of an anonymous hash with the arguments supplied. In accordance with our explanation in Chapter 5, the braces in lines (D) and (G) return a reference to an anonymous hash that becomes the first argument to bless(). The function returns the first-argument reference after blessing it into the second-argument class.

The constructor shown above is typically invoked with the following arrow-operator-based syntax:

```
my $person = Person->new( "Zaphod", 114 );
```

Subsequently, the variable $person will hold a reference to an instance of class Person. Note that the arrow operator is now being used to invoke a method on the class itself, as opposed to on a class instance that we showed in the previous subsection. Perl translates this call into

```
my $person = Person::new( "Person", "Zaphod", 114 );
```

whose argument structure conforms to the expectation of the constructor in lines (B) through (G). If we so wanted, we could have used this syntax for constructing an instance of the Person class. But that is not a recommended style for Perl OO because of its ramifications that will become apparent when we talk about constructing instances of the subclasses of a class in Chapter 8.

6.1.3 Data Hiding and Data Access Issues

The reader should also note from lines (E) and (F) of the constructor shown in the previous subsection that the names we used for the attributes started with an underscore. This is just a convention in Perl OO for denoting those names that are internal to a class. Ideally, it should be nobody's business how the various attributes are represented inside a class, not even how they are named. Unlike C++ and Java, there is no way to enforce such privacy aspects of how data is stored in a class in Perl (the same applies to Python). But since it is nonetheless important to honor such privacy, we resort to conventions in Perl (and also in Python). *The convention regarding data hiding is that the names used for the instance variables start with an underscore and that these data attributes be accessed only through the methods designated specifically for that purpose. This convention also applies to the names used for methods that will not be accessed from outside the class — that is, the methods that are meant purely for the internal functioning of a class.*

Shown below is the same class that was presented in the previous subsection, but with access methods added for the two instance variables of the class. The access method for the instance variable `_name` is shown in line (H) and for the instance variables `_age` in lines (I) through (L). In writing these access methods, we have assumed that `_name` is a read-only instance variable, whereas `_age` is a read/write instance variable.

```
package Person;                                              #(A)

sub new {                                                    #(B)
    my ($class, $name, $age) = @_;                           #(C)
    bless {                                                  #(D)
        _name => $name,                                      #(E)
        _age  => $age,                                       #(F)
    }, $class;                                               #(G)
}

sub name { $_[0]->{_name} }                                  #(H)

sub age  {                                                   #(I)
    my ($self, $age) = @_;                                   #(J)
    $self->{_age} = $age if defined $age;                    #(K)
    $self->{_age};                                           #(L)
}
```

Note that the only statement in line (H) for the subroutine `name()` causes this method to return the name of a `Person` instance. This subroutine would typically be invoked as shown in the third statement below:

```
use Person;
my $person = Person->new( "Trillian", 25 );
print $person->name(), "\n";                          # Trillian
```

As discussed previously, the call `$person->name()` is translated by Perl into the call `Person::name($person)`, implying that the variable `$_[0]` in line (H) would be set to the instance reference held by the variable `$person`.[5] This being a blessed reference, Perl will return the value of the `_name` key for the instance. As also mentioned earlier in a footnote in Section 6.1.1, since the `name()` method does not take any explicit arguments when invoked on an instance reference, the empty pair of parentheses in the call `$person->name()` can be omitted.

Regarding the syntax for the `age()` method in lines (I) through (L), it is meant to serve a dual purpose. If `age()` is invoked with an argument, as in

```
use Person;
my $person = Person->new( "Trillian", 25 );
$person->age(35);
```

then the `_age` instance variable of the `$person` instance will be changed from its previous value of 25 to its new value 35. However, when this method is invoked without an argument as in

```
use Person;
my $person = Person->new( "Trillian", 25 );
print $person->age();                              # 25
```

the current value of the `_age` instance variable will be retrieved. This dual behavior of the method `age()` is made possible by the conditional assignment in line (K) of the subroutine definition.

The two instance variables of the `Person` class are different in the sense that whereas `_name` is read-only, `_age` is read/write. But what if a client using this class forgets this distinction and tries to make a call as in the second statement below:

```
$person = Person->new( "Zaphod", 114 );
$person->name( "Trillian" );
```

Since `_name` is read-only, a client of the class is not expected to be able to change its value. So, ideally, the second statement above should elicit an error from the class. But, as currently implemented, that is not going to happen. The class will simply ignore the argument, possibly introducing subtle bugs into the client's software using this class.

This sort of an error can be avoided by checking the number of arguments when an accessor method is called, especially if it is meant to be invoked on a class instance without any arguments. Here is a reimplementation of the `name()` method for the `Person` class:

```
sub name {
    die "name() is read-only" unless @_ == 1;
```

[5] As the reader will recall from Section 2.7 of Chapter 2, in Perl all arguments are passed to a function through a special internally defined array variable `@_`. The syntax `$_[0]` therefore gives us access to the first element of the argument array inside the body of the function.

```
        $_[0]->{_name};
    }
```

Now a call such as

```
    $person->name( "Trillian" );
```

would cause the script to terminate after outputting the error message in the argument to `die`. An even better way of writing this subroutine would be

```
    use Carp;

    sub name {
        croak "name() is read-only" unless @_ == 1;
        $_[0]->{_name};
    }
```

The main advantage of using `croak()` from the `Carp` package over the built-in `die` function is that the former reports the location of where the method `name()` is called when `croak()` is invoked. On the other hand, `with die`, Perl will show the location of the `die` statement itself.[6]

While a read-only access method called `name()` for the instance variable `_name` could conceivably be called erroneously with an argument that is meant to be a new name for a `Person` instance, it would be more difficult to make this error if the same method was called `get_name()`. For this reason, the access methods in object-oriented programming are often separated into *get* methods and *set* methods. A `get` method only retrieves the current value of an instance variable and a `set` method changes the value of the variable. Here is a definition of the same `Person` class that we showed earlier but with the `get` and the `set` methods for the instance variables:

```
    package Person;                                                  #(A)

    sub new {                                                        #(B)
        my ($class, $name, $age) = @_;                               #(C)
        bless {                                                      #(D)
            _name => $name,                                          #(E)
            _age  => $age,                                           #(F)
        }, $class;                                                   #(G)
    }                                                                #(H)

    sub get_name { $_[0]->{_name}; }                                 #(I)
```

[6]This benefit of using functions from the `Carp` package was mentioned previously in Section 2.6.2 of Chapter 2. As also mentioned there, for the same reason as for the use of `croak()` shown here, you will also see programmers use `carp()` from the same package as a substitute for the built-in `warn()` function. If the flow of execution hits a call to `carp()`, Perl will report the location of the statement that invoked the function containing the call to `carp()`.

```
sub get_age { $_[0]->{_age}; }                                   #(J)

sub set_age {                                                    #(K)
    my ($self, $age) = @_;                                       #(L)
    $self->{_age} = $age;                                        #(M)
}
```

6.1.4 Packaging a Class into a Module

As mentioned already, a package in Perl is merely a namespace, and it is indeed possible to have multiple packages in the same script file. But when it comes to using a package as a class in the object-oriented sense, it is common to have a single package — and therefore a single class — in a file, thus creating a module file for the class. The suffix for the name of such a file, as for all module files, is `.pm`. Section 2.11 of Chapter 2 discussed in detail how one writes a module in Perl and how Perl searches for a module that is imported into a script.

Shown below is the module file for the `Person` class. It starts with the `Package` declaration in line (A) and ends in the entry 1 in line (O), as required for a module. The code for the constructor in lines (C) through (I) has already been explained, as is also the case with the code for the access methods in lines (J) through (N).

```
package Person;                                                  #(A)

### Person.pm

use strict;                                                      #(B)

sub new {                                                        #(C)
    my ($class, $name, $age) = @_;                               #(D)
    bless {                                                      #(E)
        _name => $name,                                          #(F)
        _age  => $age,                                           #(G)
    }, $class;                                                   #(H)
}                                                                #(I)

sub get_name { $_[0]->{_name}; }                                 #(J)
sub get_age { $_[0]->{_age}; }                                   #(K)
sub set_age {                                                    #(L)
    my ($self, $age) = @_;                                       #(M)
    $self->{_age} = $age;                                        #(N)
}
1                                                                #(O)
```

Next we show how this class can be used in a test script:

```
#!/usr/bin/perl -w

### TestPerson.pl

use strict;                                                          #(A)

use Person;                                                          #(B)

my ($person, $name, $age);                                           #(C)
$person = Person->new( "Zaphod", 114 );                              #(D)
$name = $person->get_name;                                           #(E)
$age = $person->get_age;                                             #(F)
print "name: $name   age: $age\n";      # name: Zaphod   age: 114    #(G)

$person->set_age(214);                                               #(H)
$age = $person->get_age;                                             #(I)
print "name: $name   age: $age\n";      # name: Zaphod   age: 214    #(J)
```

Before ending this subsection, we want to show an even simpler example of a class in Perl:

```
package Simple;
sub new {
    my $class = shift;
    return bless {}, $class;
}
```

The constructor of this class uses an empty hash as the underlying object. You could make an instance of this class by a call such as

```
my $obj1 = Simple->new();
```

6.2 CONSTRUCTORS CAN BE CALLED WITH KEYWORD ARGUMENTS

We stated in Section 2.7.4 of Chapter 2 that when a function takes a large number of arguments, it can be difficult to remember the position of each argument in the argument list of a function call. As shown there, Perl scripts can take advantage of the built-in hash data structure so that functions can be called with keyword arguments.

In addition to the convenience provided by attaching a name with an argument, the keyword-argument pairs can be specified in any order.

The same can be done for a constructor. If a constructor takes a large number of arguments, it is more convenient to supply them in an arbitrary positional order with the help of associated keywords. The next script presents an `Employee` class with six instance variables. The constructor of this class, in lines (A) through (J), expects to be called with keyword arguments, as in the following call

```
my $emp  = Employee->new( name   => "Poly",
                          title  => "boss",
                          dept   => "sales",
                          age    => 28,
                          gender => "female",
                          grade  => "junior");
```

As explained in Chapter 2, the way Perl interprets the big arrow `=>` operator, the above call is equivalent to

```
my $emp = Employee->new("name","Poly","title","boss","dept", \
        "sales","age",28,"gender","female","grade","junior");
```

with the whole argument list in a single logical line of text. Obviously, the alternate entries in the list are the keywords and what follows each keyword is the corresponding argument value. When the constructor in lines (A) through (J) of the `Employee` class sees this argument list, it is used to initialize the local hash `%args` in line (B). The use of a hash locally in the manner shown allows for the order of the name-value pairs in the argument list to the constructor call to be arbitrary. Accessing the hash with the supplied keywords as keys, as shown in lines (D) through (I), allows the constructor to retrieve the actual arguments needed for the instance object.

```
package Employee;

### Employee.pm

use strict;

sub new {                                                       #(A)
    my ($class, %args) = @_;                                    #(B)
    bless {                                                     #(C)
        _name       =>   $args{ name },                         #(D)
        _age        =>   $args{ age },                          #(E)
        _gender     =>   $args{ gender },                       #(F)
        _title      =>   $args{ title },                        #(G)
        _dept       =>   $args{ dept },                         #(H)
        _grade      =>   $args{ grade },                        #(I)
    }, $class;                                                  #(J)
}
```

```
sub get_name { $_[0]->{_name} }                                    #(K)
sub get_age { $_[0]->{_age} }                                      #(L)
sub get_gender { $_[0]->{_gender} }                                #(M)
sub get_title { $_[0]->{_title} }                                  #(N)
sub get_dept { $_[0]->{_dept} }                                    #(O)
sub get_grade { $_[0]->{_grade} }                                  #(P)

sub set_age { $_[0]->{_age} = $_[1] }                              #(Q)
sub set_title { $_[0]->{_title} = $_[1] }                          #(R)
sub set_dept { $_[0]->{_dept} = $_[1] }                            #(S)
sub set_grade { $_[0]->{_grade} = $_[1] }                          #(T)

1
```

Shown below is a script that tests out the Employee class. As shown by the constructor calls in statements that end in lines (A) and (F), the arguments can now be supplied to the constructor in any arbitrary order.

```
#!/usr/bin/perl -w
use strict;

### TestEmployee.pl

use Employee;

my $emp1 = Employee->new( name   => "James",
                          age    => 34,
                          gender => "male",
                          dept   => "sales",
                          title  => "driver",
                          grade  => "junior");                     #(A)
print $emp1->get_name, "\n";             # James                   #(B)
print $emp1->get_age, "\n";              # 34                      #(C)
$emp1->set_age(35);                                                #(D)
print $emp1->get_age, "\n";              # 35                      #(E)

my $emp2 = Employee->new( name   => "Poly",
                          title  => "boss",
                          dept   => "sales",
                          age    => 28,
                          gender => "female",
                          grade  => "junior");                     #(F)
```

```
print $emp2->get_name, "\n";            # Sally          #(G)
print $emp2->get_title, "\n";           # boss           #(H)

$emp2->set_grade("senior");                              #(I)
print $emp2->get_grade, "\n";           # senior         #(J)
```

6.3 DEFAULT VALUES FOR INSTANCE VARIABLES

If desired, it is possible to provide a constructor with default values for one or more of the instance variables defined for the class. When the constructor is meant to be called with the arguments in a specific positional order — as with the constructor for the `Person` class shown previously — the default values can only be specified for what would otherwise be the trailing arguments in a normal constructor call. On the other hand, with a constructor that is meant to be called with keyword arguments, as for the `Employee` class of the previous section, any argument left unspecified in a constructor call can be taken care of by its default value in the body of the constructor.

The next script shows a class, `Flower`, whose constructor specifies default values (or, more precisely speaking, default actions) for each of the three instance variables, `_name`, `_season`, and `_fragrance`, in lines (D), (E), and (F). Using the `||` operator, the default values for the instance variables are provided as disjunctions to the values held by the parameters of the constructor. So if a parameter evaluates to false,[7] it is the alternative on the right of the `||` operator that would be invoked. Of the three defaults for the three instance variables shown in lines (D), (E), and (F), the first calls `croak()` to abort the script if the constructor is called with no name for the `Flower` instance to be constructed. We obviously want a class instance to be formed with at least the name of the flower specified. The default for `_season` invokes the subroutine `_ask_for_season()` of lines (M) through (Q) to elicit the information needed from a human. And the default for `_fragrance` is the string `unknown`.

[7] A parameter such as `$name` would obviously evaluate to false if it does not acquire a value in line (B); that is, if its value is `undef`. But it is critical to realize that a parameter getting set to `undef` is not the only reason for that parameter to evaluate to false in the Boolean test in a line such as (D). A parameter will also evaluate to false if its value is 0, 0.0, or an empty string, in accordance with the truth value semantics used by Perl as described in Section 2.9.2 of Chapter 2. If it is possible for a parameter to legitimately acquire such values and you'd want to then pass on such values to the instance variables, the syntax in lines (D), (E), and (F) would have to be replaced by the following form that uses the `?:` ternary operator:

```
_name    =>    defined($name) ? $name : croak("name required")
```

For previous uses of `defined()` in example code, see Section 2.4 of Chapter 2.

```
package Flower;

### Flower.pm

use strict;
use Carp;

sub new {                                                            #(A)
    my ($class, $name, $season, $frag) = @_;                         #(B)
    bless {                                                          #(C)
        _name       =>   $name    || croak("name required"),         #(D)
        _season     =>   $season  || _ask_for_season($name),         #(E)
        _fragrance  =>   $frag    || 'unknown',                      #(F)
    }, $class;                                                       #(G)
}

sub get_name { $_[0]->{_name}; }                                     #(H)
sub get_season { $_[0]->{_season}; }                                 #(I)
sub get_fragrance { $_[0]->{_fragrance}; }                           #(J)

sub set_season { $_[0]->{season} = $_[1] }                           #(K)
sub set_fragrance { $_[0]->{fragrance} = $_[1] }                     #(L)

sub _ask_for_season {                                                #(M)
    my $flower = shift;                                              #(N)
    print STDOUT "enter the season for $flower: ";                   #(O)
    chomp( my $response = <> );                                      #(P)
    $response;                                                       #(Q)
}

1
```

Shown below is a script for testing out the `Flower` class:

```
#!/usr/bin/perl -w
use strict;

### TestFlower.pl

use Flower;

my $flower1 = Flower->new( "Rose" );                                 #(A)
```

```
        # The user prompted for "season" by line (O) of Flower.pm
        # The user enters 'spring' in response

print $flower1->get_name, "\n";                 # Rose              #(B)
print $flower1->get_season, "\n";               # spring            #(C)
print $flower1->get_fragrance, "\n";            # unknown           #(D)

my $flower2 = Flower->new();                                         #(E)
                        # name required at TestFlower.pl line 17
```

The Flower class suffers from one limitation: It does not make it difficult for a programmer to try to use the subroutine _ask_for_season() directly even though that subroutine is meant for just the internal uses by the class. A client of the Flower class could, for example, make the following invocation:

```
my $flower1 = Flower->new( "Rose" );
$flower1->_ask_for_season();
```

While the result of this external invocation of _ask_for_season() would produce a meaningless result in this case, since the instance object, as opposed to the name of a flower, would be passed as the argument to the subroutine, in general anything could happen, including the injection of a difficult to locate bug in a large script.

Such problems can be fixed by making it impossible to access all subroutines that are intended solely for internal purposes in a class. The following version of the Flower class accomplishes this by first defining an anonymous subroutine in lines (A) through (F) and then assigning a reference to this subroutine to a local variable $ask_for_season:

```
package Flower;

### Flower.pm

use strict;
use Carp;

my $ask_for_season = sub {                                          #(A)
    my $flower = shift;                                             #(B)
    print STDOUT "enter the season for $flower: ";                  #(C)
    my $response = scalar <>;                                       #(D)
    chomp $response;                                                #(E)
    $response;                                                      #(F)
};
```

```
sub new {                                                           #(G)
    my ($class, $name, $season, $frag) = @_;                        #(H)
    bless {                                                         #(I)
        _name       =>  $name    || croak("name required"),         #(J)
        _season     =>  $season  || $ask_for_season->($name),       #(K)
        _fragrance  =>  $frag    || 'unknown',                      #(L)
    }, $class;                                                      #(M)
}

sub get_name { $_[0]->{_name}; }                                    #(N)
sub get_season { $_[0]->{_season}; }                                #(O)
sub get_fragrance { $_[0]->{_fragrance}; }                          #(P)

sub set_season { $_[0]->{season} = $_[1] }                          #(Q)
sub set_fragrance { $_[0]->{fragrance} = $_[1] }                    #(R)

1
```

The mechanism of supplying default values for position-specific arguments can also be applied to the case of keyword arguments. That is, when a constructor is defined to take arguments through name-value pairs, as for the `Employee` class shown in the previous section, any arbitrary instance variable can be provided with a default at the instance construction time. Shown below is a class, `Wine`, whose constructor expects to be supplied with arguments that are paired up with the keywords. Lines (D) through (H) show the defaults for each of the instance variables. Since we want the `_grape` and `_color` instance variables to always be specified for a wine, we make them mandatory through the mechanism of calling on `croak()` to abort the script if either is not provided for in a constructor call. For the other three, we simply specify `unknown` as the default, although we could also have specified subroutine calls — as we did for the `_season` instance variable of the `Flower` class — for fetching a value for the instance variable if it is left unspecified by a client using the class.

```
package Wine;

### Wine.pm

use strict;
use Carp;

sub new {                                                           #(A)
    my ($class, %args) = @_;                                        #(B)
    bless {                                                         #(C)
        _grape          =>  $args{ grape }
                            || croak("grape required"),             #(D)
```

```
        _color          =>  $args{ color }
                            || croak("color required"),          #(E)
        _vintage        =>  $args{ vintage }
                            || 'unknown',                        #(F)
        _growing_region =>  $args{ region }
                            || 'unknown',                        #(G)
        _dryness        =>  $args{ dryness }
                            || 'unknown',                        #(H)
    }, $class;                                                   #(I)
}

sub get_grape { $_[0]->{_grape} }                                #(J)
sub get_color { $_[0]->{_color} }                                #(K)
sub get_vintage { $_[0]->{_vintage} }                            #(L)
sub get_growing_region { $_[0]->{_growning_region} }             #(M)
sub get_dryness { $_[0]->{_dryness} }                            #(N)

sub set_color { $_[0]->{_color} = $_[1] }                        #(O)
sub set_vintage { $_[0]->{_vintage} = $_[1] }                    #(P)
sub set_growing_region { $_[0]->{_growing_region} = $_[1] }      #(Q)
sub set_dryness { $_[0]->{_dryness} = $_[1] }                    #(R)

1
```

6.4 INSTANCE OBJECT DESTRUCTION

Perl comes with automatic garbage collection for reclaiming memory occupied by unreferenced objects.[8] Garbage collection is carried out automatically by the system through the mechanism of reference counting. When you construct a new object, such as an instance from a class, and assign it to a variable, you have a reference count of one for the object. Now suppose you assign the same object to another variable, the reference count for the object goes up to 2, and so on. If one of these variables either goes out of scope or changes its value, the reference count for the object is decremented by one.[9] When the reference count for an object goes down to zero, the memory occupied by the object is reclaimed.

---

[8] See Section 12.1 of Chapter 12 for a brief review of the different approaches to garbage collection.

[9] A more general way to say the same would be: Each time an object is referred to by another object, the reference count of the former is incremented by one. The reference count for an object is decremented by one each time a reference to it is released by some other object.

In the same spirit as a destructor in C++ and the `finalize()` method in Java, Perl allows a programmer to endow a class with a special method named `DESTROY()` that is called automatically for cleanup just before the system reclaims the memory occupied by an instance of the class. This can be important in situations where an instance contains open filehandles, sockets, pipes, database connections, and other system resources. The code to free up these resources can be placed in the `DESTROY()` method. In addition to being invoked when the reference count for an instance object goes down to zero, `DESTROY()` would also be called if the process or the thread in which the Perl interpreter is running is shutting down.

To illustrate the working of the `DESTROY()` method with a simple example, the following script shows a `Function` class whose purpose is to represent function definitions in a C source file.[10] A `Function` instance is characterized by the following four instance variables: (1) `_name` for the name of the function; (2) `_ret_type` for the return type of the function; (3) `_file` for the name of the file in which the function is defined; and (4) `_line_num` for the line number at which the function definition begins in the file. The class `Function` has been provided with `get` and `set` access methods as shown.

In order to demonstrate the role of the `DESTROY()` method in instance object destruction in Perl, the class `Function` has also been provided with this method, as shown in lines (P) through (W). Although our `Function` instances do not appropriate any system resources that would need to be closed or otherwise cleaned up when the instances go out of scope, the `DESTROY()` method shown performs a useful task nevertheless. It writes to a disk file the measured attributes of a function when a `Function` instance is about to go out of scope. That way we retain the information recorded even when the instance holding the information will cease to exist.

```
package Function;

### Function.pm

use strict;
use Carp;

sub new {                                                              #(A)
    my ($class, $name, $ret_type, $file, $line_num) = @_;              #(B)
```

[10]The `Function` class shown is a simple version of a larger class that was used to represent function definitions in a project whose goal was to remodularize legacy source code in C for an old application. This application started out as being well modularized. But, with the passage of time, the code became disorganized as it was extended and modified to meet changing needs. The function objects extracted were used as nodes in a directed function dependency graph, meaning a graph in which an arc from node A to node B means that function A calls function B. The function dependency graph was used as a stepping stone for the derivation of a file dependency graph. Once you have a file dependency graph, you can apply graph clustering algorithms for automated or semiautomated repackaging of source files.

```
    bless {                                                         #(C)
        _name       => $name     || croak("function name required"),#(D)
        _ret_type   => $ret_type || '????',                         #(E)
        _file       => $file     || '????',                         #(F)
        _line_num   => $line_num || '????',
    }, $class;                                                      #(G)
}

sub get_name { $_[0]->{_name} }                                     #(H)
sub get_file { $_[0]->{_file} }                                     #(I)
sub get_ret_type { $_[0]->{_ret_type} }                             #(J)
sub get_line_num { $_[0]->{_line_num} }                             #(K)

sub set_name { $_[0]->{_name} = $_[1] }                             #(L)
sub set_ret_type { $_[0]->{_ret_type} = $_[1] }                     #(M)
sub set_file { $_[0]->{_file} = $_[1] }                             #(N)
sub set_line_num { $_[0]->{_line_num} = $_[1] }                     #(O)

sub DESTROY {                                                       #(P)
    my $record = join ' ', ($_[0]->{_name},                         #(Q)
                            $_[0]->{_file},                         #(R)
                            $_[0]->{_ret_type},                     #(S)
                            $_[0]->{_line_num});                    #(T)
    open FILE, '>> function_archive.txt';                           #(U)
    print FILE "$record\n";                                         #(V)
    close FILE;                                                     #(W)
}
1
```

Shown next is a script that tests out the `Function` class presented above. Line (B) specifies the file that needs to be scanned for the extraction of function objects (although, in practice, you'd need to scan an entire directory tree containing the source code). Line (F) calls on the `extract_functions()` subroutine to extract the function headers from the file and the line numbers containing the function headers. Finally, line (G) associates the name of the file with the function attributes returned in line (F). The function attributes returned in line (F) [even after the file name is appended to them in line (G)] are in the form of a single string, as illustrated by the following two examples:

```
void erase 19 func.c

struct part *find_part 56 func.c
```

where the last substring that terminates in ".c" is the file name, the digit substring before that the line number in the file where the function definition starts, the alphanumeric substring before that the name of the function, and whatever comes before that the return type. So for the first example shown, the return type is just `void`, but for the next example, the return type is `struct part *`. Lines (H) through (K) extract from such strings the four attributes listed previously — the name of the function, the return type, the file name, and the line number in the file — and ship these off to the constructor call shown in line (K). The instances constructed in line (K) are stored away in the `@objects` array. Lines (L) through (O) iterate through this array and print out two of the four instance variables associated with each `Function` instance stored in the array.

```
#!/usr/bin/perl -w
use strict;

### TestFunction.pl

use Function;                                                       #(A)

my $file = "func.c";                                                #(B)
open FILE, $file                                                    #(C)
       or die "unable to open filename: $!";                        #(D)
chomp( my @all_lines = <FILE> );                                    #(E)
my @functions_with_data = extract_functions(@all_lines);            #(F)
@functions_with_data = map { "$_ $file"} @functions_with_data;      #(G)

my @objects = ();                                                   #(H)
foreach (@functions_with_data) {                                    #(I)
    /^(.*\s+\*?)(\w+)\s(\d+)\s(\w+\.\w+)$/;                         #(J)
    push @objects, Function->new( $2, $1, $4, $3 );                 #(K)
}

for my $i (0..$#objects) {                                          #(L)
    print $objects[$i]->get_name() . " " .                          #(M)
          $objects[$i]->get_file() . "\n";                          #(N)
    $i++;                                                           #(O)
}

sub extract_functions {                                             #(P)
    my @all_lines = @_;                                             #(Q)
    my $regex = '^((?:struct\s+)?\w+\s+\*?\s*\w+)\s*\(.*\).*\{';    #(R)
    my @functions = map {/$regex/; $1} @all_lines;                  #(S)
    my $index = 0;                                                  #(T)
    @functions = map {$index++; "$_ $index" if defined $_}
                                                   @functions;      #(U)
    @functions = grep $_, @functions;                               #(V)
    return @functions;                                              #(W)
}
```

When the above script is run on a source code file called `func.c`, the output produced is as shown below:

```
erase func.c
find_part func.c
insert func.c
search func.c
update func.c
print func.c
my_malloc func.c
```

This output is produced by the `for` loop in lines (L) through (O). If you examine the file `function_archive.txt` that is first created and then added to by the `DESTROY()` method of the `Function` module, you will see all of the function attributes stored away in that file.

To briefly explain the code for the `extract_function()` subroutine in lines (P) through (W), the function header itself is extracted by the regex defined in line (R). This regex is based on the assumption that all of the header will be in one line and that the function definition starts at the beginning of a line. In general, this will not be true for complicated functions with long names and with many parameters. However, the definition shown for `extract_functions()` can easily be modified to extract more complicated multiline function headers. The call to `map` in line (U) associates a line number with each extracted function header; this is the line where the function definition starts in a file.

6.4.1 Destructors and the Problem of Circular References

The reference counting approach to garbage collection suffers from one major flaw: If two objects A and B refer to each other, they will not be garbage collected even if no other objects (or variables) are holding references to them. Such circular references create memory leaks that can result in reduced performance by scripts that are involved in solving memory intensive problems.

We will now present an example to demonstrate memory leaks caused by circular references and how care taken in writing a script eliminates such leaks. The example consists of nodes and networks made from nodes. A node will be an instance of the class `Node` shown below, and a network an instance of the class `Network` shown subsequently.

As shown in lines (A) through (F) of the class `Node`, each node is characterized by an integer index, which is the value of the instance variable `_index` in line (D). Each node also holds a reference, via the instance variable `_linked_to` in line (E), to an array of linked nodes. Lines (G) through (c) define for a `Node` instance the methods `get_index()`, `get_links()`, `add_to_links()`, `remove_node_from_links()`, `delete_all_links()` and, finally, `DESTROY()`. The purpose of `DESTROY()` is simply to tell us which node is about to be scooped up by the garbage collection mechanism.

```
package Node;

### Node.pm

use strict;
use Carp;

sub new {                                                           #(A)
    my ($class, $index) = @_;                                       #(B)
    bless {                                                         #(C)
        _index => $index,                                           #(D)
        _linked_to => [],                                           #(E)
    }, $class;                                                      #(F)
}
sub get_index {                                                     #(G)
    my $self = shift;                                               #(H)
    return $self->{ _index };                                       #(I)
}
sub get_links {                                                     #(J)
    my $self = shift;                                               #(K)
    return @{$self->{_linked_to}};                                  #(L)
}
sub add_to_links {                                                  #(M)
    my ($self, $new_node) = @_;                                     #(N)
    push @{$self->{_linked_to}}, $new_node;                         #(O)
}
sub remove_node_from_links {                                        #(P)
    my ($self, $remove_node) = @_;                                  #(Q)
    my @new_links;                                                  #(R)
    for my $node ($self->get_links) {                               #(S)
        if ($node->get_index != $remove_node->get_index) {          #(T)
            push @new_links, $node;                                 #(U)
        }
    }
    $self->{_linked_to} = \@new_links;                              #(V)
}
sub delete_all_links {                                              #(W)
    my $self = shift;                                               #(X)
    $self->{_linked_to} = undef;                                    #(Y)
}
```

```
sub DESTROY {                                                      #(Z)
    my $self = shift;                                              #(a)
    my $index = $self->get_index;                                  #(b)
    print "Node of index $index is about to be destroyed\n";       #(c)
}
1
```

The `Network` class shown next helps us create a network from `Node` instances. We supply the class with a hidden function in lines (A1) through (A7) by using an anonymous subroutine whose reference is held by the `my` variable `$in_net_predicate`. We want this subroutine, used by a number of methods of the `Network` class, to not be accessible outside the class definition. The constructor for the `Network`, shown in lines (B1) through (B5), insists that it be called without any arguments and returns a blessed reference to an array. This array will store the nodes of the network.

As shown by the method `add_new_node()` defined in lines (C1) through (C7) of the script, nodes are inserted into the network one at a time through this method. Lines (C3) through (C6) make sure that the index associated with a new node was not used previously.

That takes us to the two methods `drop_node()` and `delete_node()`. As the names imply, both methods allow a client script to delete a node from the network. Whereas the first, `drop_node()` in lines (D1) through (D7), merely deletes the node from the node array that constitutes an instance of the `Network` class,[11] the second, `delete_node()` in lines (E1) through (E9), also scans the connection lists for all the nodes in the network and makes sure that the deleted node does not appear in those connection lists. This is accomplished by first identifying the `Node` instance corresponding to the integer index of the node to be removed in line (E6) and then removing this node from the connection lists of all other remaining nodes in lines (E7) and (E8). Later in this section we will use the `drop_node()` method to demonstrate the problem of circular references and how they create memory leaks.

The method `show_all_nodes()` in lines (F1) through (F5) prints out a list of all the nodes currently in the network. It prints out the unique integer index associated with each node.

The method `link_nodes()` in lines (G1) through (G9) takes a pair of node indices for its argument list and adds each corresponding node to the link list of the other. It does so after making sure in lines (G3) and (G4) that each node actually exists in the network. The logic of `link_nodes()` creates a symmetric two-way

[11] Note that an instance of the `Network` class is the anonymous array created in line (B4) of the constructor.

connection between the pairs of nodes. If so desired, it should be easy to change the definition of this method so that the links go only one way.

The method `break_link()` in lines (H1) through (H9) allows us to break the connection between a pair of nodes whose integer indices are supplied to the method as arguments. The method first makes sure in lines (H3) and (H4) that the designated nodes are indeed in the network and then locates the `Node` instances corresponding to the integer indices in lines (H6) and (H7). Subsequently, each specified node is deleted from the links list of the other in lines (H8) and (H9).

The method `list_links_for_one_node()` in lines (I1) through (I8) returns the integer indices associated with all the nodes in the connection list of the argument node.

Finally, we have the `DESTROY()` method in lines (J1) through (J4) that first delinks the entire network before an instance of type `Network` goes out of scope. As we will see later, without the delinking operation shown, a script using the `Network` class could easily have memory leaks in it.

```
package Network;

### Network.pm

use strict;
use Carp;

# The predicate tells us whether or not a node specified by
# its integer integer index is currently in the network:
my $in_net_predicate =                                               #(A1)
            sub {                                                    #(A2)
                my ($self, $node_index) = @_;                        #(A3)
                for my $node (@$self) {                              #(A4)
                    my $index = $node->get_index();                  #(A5)
                    return 1 if $node_index == $index;               #(A6)
                }
                croak "node specified not in network;".
                                      " script aborted";             #(A7)
            };

# This is the constructor. Note that a Network instance consists of
# the anonymous array constructed in line (B4):
sub new {                                                            #(B1)
    croak "only no-arg constructor for Network" if @_ > 1;           #(B2)
    my $class = shift;                                               #(B3)
    my $_nodes = [];                                                 #(B4)
    bless $_nodes, $class;                                           #(B5)
}
```

```
# Insert a new node into the network:
sub add_new_node {                                                  #(C1)
    my ($self, $index) = @_;                                        #(C2)
    for my $node (@$self) {                                         #(C3)
        if ($node->get_index == $index) {                           #(C4)
            print "A node with this index already exists.\n";       #(C5)
            return;                                                 #(C6)
        }
    }
    push @$self, Node->new( $index );                               #(C7)
}

# Delete a node specified by its integer index from the network
# by deleting it from the array that constitutes a Network instance:
sub drop_node {                                                     #(D1)
    my ($self, $index) = @_;                                        #(D2)
    for my $node (@$self) {                                         #(D3)
        if ($node->get_index() == $index) {                         #(D4)
            $node = undef;                                          #(D5)
            last;                                                   #(D6)
        }
    }
    @$self = grep $_, @$self;                                       #(D7)
}

# Delete node as in the previous method but also make sure that
# this node is removed from all connection lists:
sub delete_node {                                                   #(E1)
    my ($self, $index) = @_;                                        #(E2)
    my $remove_node;
    my @new_node_list;
    for my $node (@$self) {                                         #(E4)
        push @new_node_list, $node if $node->get_index != $index;   #(E5)
        $remove_node = $node if $node->get_index == $index;         #(E6)
    }
    for my $node (@new_node_list ) {                                #(E7)
        $node->remove_node_from_links( $remove_node );              #(E8)
    }
    @$self = @new_node_list                                         #(E9)
}

sub show_all_nodes {                                                #(F1)
    my $self = shift;                                               #(F2)
    for my $node (@$self) {                                         #(F3)
        my $index = $node->get_index();                             #(F4)
        print "$index " if defined $index;                          #(F5)
    }
    print "\n";
}
```

```
sub link_nodes {                                                   #(G1)
    my ($self, $node1_index, $node2_index) = @_;                   #(G2)
    &$in_net_predicate( $self, $node1_index );                     #(G3)
    &$in_net_predicate( $self, $node2_index );                     #(G4)
    # Get the Node objects for $node1_index and $node2_index
    my ($node1, $node2);
    for my $node (@$self) {                                        #(G5)
        $node1 = $node if $node->get_index() == $node1_index;      #(G6)
        $node2 = $node if $node->get_index() == $node2_index;      #(G7)
    }
    $node1->add_to_links( $node2 );                                #(G8)
    $node2->add_to_links( $node1 );                                #(G9)
}
# Break connection between any two nodes.  This
# has nothing to do with node deletion:
sub break_link {                                                   #(H1)
    my ($self, $node1_index, $node2_index) = @_;                   #(H2)
    &$in_net_predicate( $self, $node1_index );                     #(H3)
    &$in_net_predicate( $self, $node2_index );                     #(H4)
    my @new_links;
    my ($node1, $node2);
    for my $node (@$self) {                                        #(H5)
        # Get hold of the Node objects:
        $node1 = $node if $node->get_index() == $node1_index;      #(H6)
        $node2 = $node if $node->get_index() == $node2_index;      #(H7)
    }
    $node1->remove_node_from_links( $node2 );                      #(H8)
    $node2->remove_node_from_links( $node1 );                      #(H9)
}
# Examine the connection list of the node whose integer index
# is supplied as the explicit argument to this method and
# return the integer indices associated with all the nodes
# in the connection list:
sub list_links_for_one_node {                                      #(I1)
    my ($self, $node_index) = @_;                                  #(I2)
    &$in_net_predicate( $self, $node_index );                      #(I3)
    for my $node (@$self) {                                        #(I4)
        my $index = $node->get_index();                            #(I5)
        if ($index == $node_index) {                               #(I6)
            my @linked_to = $node->get_links;                      #(I7)
            print "Node $node_index linked to: ";
            foreach my $linked_node (@linked_to) {                 #(I8)
                my $linked_node_index = $linked_node->get_index;
                print "$linked_node_index ";
            }
            print "\n";
        }
    }
}
```

```
sub DESTROY {                                                       #(J1)
    my $self = shift;                                               #(J2)
    for my $node (@$self) {                                         #(J3)
        $node->delete_all_links;                                    #(J4)
    }
}
1
```

We will now use the `Node` and `Network` classes to illustrate how memory leaks can be caused by circular references in a script. Lines (C) through (F) of the following script, `TestNetwork1.pl`, construct a network containing three nodes. Line (G) then establishes a connection between the nodes indexed 101 and 102. This causes the node indexed 101 to hold a reference to the node indexed 102 in its connections list and vice versa. Lines (H), (I), and (J) then delete all three nodes from the network by calling `drop_node()`. When we examine the output of this script, we notice that the garbage collection mechanism is able to reclaim the memory occupied by only the node indexed 100. Here is the output of the script:

```
Node of index 100 is about to be destroyed
```

this message being printed out by the `DESTROY` method of the `Node` instance for node 100.

```
#!/usr/bin/perl -w
use strict;

### TestNetwork1.pl

use Network;                                                        #(A)
use Node;                                                           #(B)

my $net = Network->new();                                           #(C)

$net->add_new_node( 100 );                                          #(D)
$net->add_new_node( 101 );                                          #(E)
$net->add_new_node( 102 );                                          #(F)

$net->link_nodes( 101, 102 );                                       #(G)

$net->drop_node( 100 );                                             #(H)
$net->drop_node( 101 );                                             #(I)
$net->drop_node( 102 );                                             #(J)

while (1) {}                                                        #(K)
```

The reason why the other two nodes, 101 and 102, were not destroyed is as follows: While all three nodes may no longer be in the network list of operational nodes because of the invocations of `drop_node()` in lines (H), (I), and (J), we still have the node 101 pointing to 102 and the node 102 pointing to 101. [Recall that the list of operational nodes currently in the network is stored in the anonymous array that constitutes an instance of the `Network` class. This array was created in line (B4) of the constructor.] In other words, we have a classic case of a circular reference between the nodes 101 and 102.

The problem of memory leaks caused by such circular references can be fixed by writing a script more carefully — that is, by paying close attention to the logic of what happens when an object in a script is deleted. In our case, when we delete a node, we also need to delete it from all the connection lists for all the other nodes in the network. *That is exactly what is accomplished by the* `delete_node()` *method of the* `Network` *class.* Shown below is a script, `TestNetwork2.pl`, that is basically the same as `TestNetwork1.pl` except that now we make calls to the `delete_node()` method when we want to get rid of a node, as we show in lines (H), (I), and (J) of the script. As mentioned earlier, this method not only deletes a node from the list of nodes in the `_nodes` instance variable of a network, it also scans all the connection lists of all the nodes and removes the deleted node from each of those lists. This script produces the output:

```
Node of index 100 is about to be destroyed
Node of index 101 is about to be destroyed
Node of index 102 is about to be destroyed
```

Now we see that all three deleted nodes are being properly reclaimed by the garbage collector. Here is the `TestNetwork2.pl` script:

```
#!/usr/bin/perl -w
use strict;

### TestNetwork2.pl

use Network;                                                    #(A)
use Node;                                                       #(B)

my $net = Network->new();                                       #(C)

$net->add_new_node( 100 );                                      #(D)
$net->add_new_node( 101 );                                      #(E)
$net->add_new_node( 102 );                                      #(F)

$net->link_nodes( 101, 102 );                                   #(G)

$net->delete_node( 100 );                                       #(H)
$net->delete_node( 101 );                                       #(I)
```

```
$net->delete_node( 102 );                                                        #(J)

while (1) {}                                                                     #(K)
```

So far we have explained the consequences of circular references through examples in which the network instance was asked to delete each network node individually, as in the lines (H), (I), and (J) of the previous script. But what if we dump the entire network all at once by

```
$net = Network->new();
#   ....
# Code for populating the network instance with nodes goes here
#   ....
$net = undef;
```

Unless care is taken, one would again see that the nodes that are engaged in circular references in the network would not be scoopable by the garbage collection mechanism. The solution here lies in equipping the `Network` class with a `DESTROY()` method that unlinks the entire network when a `Network` instance goes out of scope. By breaking all links in the network, the problem of circular references would become a moot issue. The `Network` class as shown earlier is equipped with such a `DESTROY()` method. The following script, `TestNetwork3.pl`, shows that dumping the whole network all at once in line (H) correctly frees up all the memory despite the circular references introduced by the linking operation in line (G).

```
#!/usr/bin/perl -w
use strict;

### TestNetwork3.pl

use Network;                                                                     #(A)
use Node;                                                                        #(B)

my $net = Network->new();                                                        #(C)

$net->add_new_node( 100 );                                                       #(D)
$net->add_new_node( 101 );                                                       #(E)
$net->add_new_node( 102 );                                                       #(F)

$net->link_nodes( 101, 102 );                                                    #(G)

$net = undef;            # Node of index 102 is about to be destroyed            #(H)
                         # Node of index 101 is about to be destroyed
                         # Node of index 100 is about to be destroyed
while (1) {}                                                                     #(I)
```

We will now show a script, `TestNetwork4.pl`, that more fully tests out the functionality of the `Network` class. We first construct an instance of the `Network` class in line (C) and then populate the network created by the eight nodes in the block of `add_new_node()` statements starting with the one labeled (D). Line (E) invokes `show_all_nodes()` to list the integer indices of all the nodes currently in the network. Starting with line (F), we then use the `link_nodes()` method to connect up pairs of nodes in the network. We can see the connections thus created by calling the `list_links_for_one_node()` method, as we do in the three statements starting with line (G). Lines (K) through (N) show the same functionality as lines (E) through (I) after the deletion of one of the nodes in line (J). Line (O) breaks the connection between the nodes 104 and 107, but without deleting either of these two nodes from the network. We again list the connections for the affected nodes in line (Q) and the next line.

```
#!/usr/bin/perl -w
use strict;

### TestNetwork4.pl

use Network;                                                          #(A)
use Node;                                                             #(B)

my $net = Network->new();                                             #(C)

$net->add_new_node( 100 );                                            #(D)
$net->add_new_node( 101 );
$net->add_new_node( 102 );
$net->add_new_node( 103 );
$net->add_new_node( 104 );
$net->add_new_node( 105 );
$net->add_new_node( 106 );
$net->add_new_node( 107 );

$net->show_all_nodes();                                               #(E)
                          # 100 101 102 103 104 105 106 107
$net->link_nodes( 100, 102 );                                         #(F)
$net->link_nodes( 100, 104 );
$net->link_nodes( 104, 105 );
$net->link_nodes( 104, 106 );
$net->link_nodes( 100, 103 );
$net->link_nodes( 102, 103 );
$net->link_nodes( 104, 107 );

$net->list_links_for_one_node( 100 );                                 #(G)
                          # Node 100 linked to: 102 104 103
$net->list_links_for_one_node( 104 );                                 #(H)
                          # Node 104 linked to: 100 105 106 107
```

```
$net->list_links_for_one_node( 103 );                                  #(I)
                     # Node 103 linked to: 100 102

$net->delete_node(100);                                                #(J)

print "after deleting node 100:\n";                                    #(K)

$net->show_all_nodes();                                                #(L)
                     # 101 102 103 104 105 106 107

#$net->list_links_for_one_node( 100 );                                 #(M)
                     # node specified not in network; script
                     # aborted at TestNetwork.pl line 58

$net->list_links_for_one_node( 104 );                                  #(N)
                     # Node 104 linked to: 105 106 107
$net->list_links_for_one_node( 103 );
                     # Node 103 linked to: 102

$net->break_link(104, 107);                                            #(O)

print "After breaking 104 to 107 link:\n";                             #(P)

$net->list_links_for_one_node( 104 );                                  #(Q)
                     # Node 104 linked to: 105 106
$net->list_links_for_one_node( 103 );
                     # Node 103 linked to: 102

while (1) {}
```

Some readers may be wondering why all our `TestNetwork` scripts ended in the statement

```
while (1) {}
```

It would be difficult to see the consequences of circular references without parking the execution in this infinite loop. You see, as the Perl virtual machine shuts down, it will destroy each of the objects created regardless of the presence of circular references. So transitioning into the do-nothing infinite loop, we can better see what objects are being cleaned up as they go out of scope in the main part of the script.

6.5 CONTROLLING THE INTERACTION BETWEEN DESTROY( ) AND AUTOLOAD( )

Earlier in Section 2.11.4 of Chapter 2 we talked about the role played by the subroutine AUTOLOAD() if a module is supplied with a subroutine of this name. Basically, if a method is invoked on a package name, and if no subroutine of that name exists in the package, Perl ships off the call to AUTOLOAD().

The same would apply to DESTROY(). When Perl searches for an implementation of DESTROY() in a class before actually destroying an instance object, if it does not find such an implementation, the call is farmed out to AUTOLOAD() if it is defined in the package.

In the following script, the class Employee has not been provided with DESTROY() — primarily because it does not really need one since no system resources will be appropriated by Employee instances. However, when the Employee instances constructed in lines (F) and (H) go out of scope, the system will look for a DESTROY() method to invoke on those objects. But not finding such a method, the system will invoke AUTOLOAD() because it is there. In most cases, we would not want AUTOLOAD() to really do anything in such situations. Line (C) of the following example shows how AUTOLOAD(), if needed for a class, can dispose of any implicit calls to DESTROY(). Line (C) uses the fact that the fully qualified name of the subroutine whose invocation causes AUTOLOAD() to be called is stored in the global variable $AUTOLOAD of the package Employee. Therefore, the package qualified name of the variable where the name of the actual method called is stored is $Employee::AUTOLOAD. Line (E) is a stand-in for whatever real purpose there was for including an implementation for AUTOLOAD() in the class definition.

```
#!/usr/bin/perl -w
use strict;

### TestAutoload.pl

#--------------------------- class Employee ---------------------------
package Employee;

# Constructor:
sub new {
    my ( $class, $name, $position ) = @_;
    bless {
        _name =>  $name,
        _position =>  $position
    }, $class;
}
```

```
sub AUTOLOAD {                                                          #(A)
    my $self = shift;                                                   #(B)
    if ( $Employee::AUTOLOAD =~ /::DESTROY/ ) {                         #(C)
        print "Looking for DESTROY but found AUTOLOAD\n";               #(D)
        return;
    }
    print "Employee's AUTOLOAD invoked by $Employee::AUTOLOAD\n";       #(E)
}

#--------------------    Test Code    ------------------------------
package main;

my $emp = Employee->new( "Orpheus", "staff" );                          #(F)

# Will trigger garbage collection of the object of line (F):
$emp = undef;                                                           #(G)

$emp = Employee->new( "Zaphod", "staff" );                              #(H)

# Since get_position() not defined for Employee, the
# following call should go to AUTOLOAD():
$emp->get_position();                                                   #(I)
```

As you would expect, this script produces the following output:

```
Looking for DESTROY but found AUTOLOAD
Employee's AUTOLOAD invoked by Employee::get_position
Looking for DESTROY but found AUTOLOAD
```

The first output line is caused by the `undef` operation in line (G) that discards the instance that was created in line (F). Before reclaiming the memory occupied by this object, Perl seeks out the `DESTROY()` method for the `Employee` class, and, not finding one, invokes `AUTOLOAD()`. The second output line is caused by the call to a nonexistent method in line (I) on the new instance constructed in line (H). This call is also shipped off to `AUTOLOAD()`. The last output line is caused by Perl cleaning up the still existing object of line (H) in the memory before the virtual machine shuts down.

6.6 CLASS DATA AND METHODS

Except for the constructors and a few other functions, the methods shown so far in the class definitions in this chapter have been those that are meant to be invoked on instance objects.[12] A constructor is obviously intended to be invoked directly on a class.

When a method is meant to be invoked directly on a class, it is commonly referred to either as a *class method* or a *static method*.[13] We will now show how one sets up a class method (apart from the constructor) in Perl. We will also show how you can make sure that a class method is not invoked on an instance object.

A class may also contain *class variables*, or *class attributes* or *class data*, all standing for the same thing. Such information is global for the class, meaning global with respect to all the instances of that class. The second script in this section demonstrates how a class can store such information in a global variable — a class variable — and how this information may be retrieved by the clients of the class. The first script, on the other hand, will store the class-level information in a closure over a local variable.

Let's say we have a `Robot` class that allows us to assign a unique serial number to each instance made from the class. Such a class will obviously have to be provided with class-based storage (as opposed to instance-based storage) for keeping track of the serial numbers already assigned so that the next `Robot` instance acquires the next serial number. Such a class may also be provided with a class method for returning the total number of robots already made.

The script shown next defines such a `Robot` class. The class keeps track of the robot serial numbers with the help of a local variable `$_robot_serial_number` initialized in line (B) and an anonymous subroutine whose reference is held by the local variable `$_next_serial` initialized in line (C); this subroutine is a closure over the lexical variable `$_robot_serial_number`.[14] The class includes another anonymous subroutine whose reference is held the local variable `$_total_num` of line (D); this subroutine makes available to the rest of the class the total number of robots already made. Note that this subroutine is also a closure over the variable `$_robot_serial_number`.

The `Robot` class includes a class method `how_many_robots()`, defined in lines (R) through (V), that the clients of this class can invoke directly on the class to ascertain the total number of robots already made. To make sure that the class method of line (R) is invoked only on a class and not on an instance of the class, we build in the protection shown in lines (T) and (U).

Lines (X), (b), and (f) show the construction of three new robots. The outputs returned by the print statements that follow the constructor invocations are shown in

[12]For that reason, those methods are also referred to as *instance methods*. All instance methods expect their implicitly supplied first argument to be an instance.

[13]As we will see in Section 7.7 of Chapter 7, Python makes a distinction between class methods and static methods. But in Perl they mean the same thing.

[14]Closures in Perl were discussed previously in Section 5.10 of Chapter 5.

the commented-out portions just below the print commands. As the reader can see, each successive robot is assigned the next available serial number.

Line (j) invokes the class method `how_many_robots()` directly on the class `Robot`, with the result shown by the output of the print statement in the next line.

```
#!/usr/bin/perl -w
use strict;

### ClassMethod.pl

#------------------------- class Robot ------------------------------
package Robot;                                                        #(A)

my $_robot_serial_num = 0;                                            #(B)
my $_next_serial =    sub { ++$_robot_serial_num };                   #(C)
my $_total_num   =    sub { $_robot_serial_num };                     #(D)

# Constructor:
sub new {                                                             #(E)
    my ( $class, $owner ) = @_;                                       #(F)
    bless {                                                           #(G)
        _owner => $owner,                                             #(H)
        _serial_number => $_next_serial->(),                          #(I)
    }, $class;                                                        #(J)
}

# This instance method can work both as a 'set' and a 'get' method:
sub owner {                                                           #(K)
    my $self = shift;                                                 #(L)
    @_ ? $self->{_owner} = shift                                      #(M)
       : $self->{_owner};                                             #(N)
}

# This is an instance method:
sub get_serial_num {                                                  #(O)
    my $self = shift;                                                 #(P)
    $self->{_serial_number};                                          #(Q)
}

# This is a class method:
sub how_many_robots {                                                 #(R)
    my $class = shift;                                                #(S)
    die "illegal invocation of a static method"                       #(T)
        unless $class eq 'Robot';                                     #(U)
    $_total_num->();                                                  #(V)
}
```

```
#----------------------        Test Code      ------------------------------

package main;

# Construct a robot:
my $bot = Robot->new( "Zaphod" );                                      #(X)
my $name = $bot->owner();                                              #(Y)
my $num = $bot->get_serial_num();                                      #(Z)
print "robot owner: $name   serial number: $num\n";                    #(a)
                       # robot owner: Zaphod   serial number: 1


# Construct a second robot:
$bot = Robot->new( "Trillian" );                                       #(b)
$name = $bot->owner();                                                 #(c)
$num = $bot->get_serial_num();                                         #(d)
print "robot owner: $name   serial number: $num\n";                    #(e)
                       # robot owner: Trillian   serial number: 2


# Construct a third robot:
$bot = Robot->new( "Betelgeuse" );                                     #(f)
$name = $bot->owner();                                                 #(g)
$num = $bot->get_serial_num();                                         #(h)
print "robot owner: $name   serial number: $num\n";                    #(i)
                       # robot owner: Betelgeuse   serial number: 3


# Now invoke the class method:
my $total_production = Robot->how_many_robots();                       #(j)
print "Total number of robots made: $total_production\n";              #(k)
                       # Total number of robots made: 3
```

Shown below is reimplementation of the `Robot` class; we now use the class variable `$robot_serial_nums_used` in line (B) to keep track of the serial numbers already used. Note that the `our` declaration makes `$robot_serial_nums_used` a package variable.[15] We do not show the `get` and `set` methods in this implementation simply to save space. If we had included that portion of the previous implementation, it would remain the same. The behavior of this class is exactly the same as before. Notice that we can access the class variable directly in line (Q).

[15]As explained in Section 2.3.2 of Chapter 2, the `our` declaration is one of three different ways to create package variables in Perl. We could also have employed the `use vars` declaration or the package-qualified naming syntax.

```
#!/usr/bin/perl -w
use strict;

### ClassData.pl

#-------------------------- class Robot ------------------------------
package Robot;                                                     #(A)

# This is a class variable:
our $robot_serial_nums_used = 0;                                   #(B)

# Constructor:
sub new {                                                          #(C)
    my ( $class, $owner ) = @_;                                    #(D)
    bless {                                                        #(E)
        _owner => $owner,                                          #(F)
        _serial_number => $robot_serial_nums_used++,               #(G)
    }, $class;                                                     #(H)
}

# This is a class method:
sub how_many_robots {                                              #(I)
    my $class = shift;                                             #(J)
    die "illegal invocation of a static method"                    #(K)
        unless $class eq 'Robot';                                  #(L)
    $robot_serial_nums_used;                                       #(M)
}

#-----------------------   Test Code    ------------------------------
package main;

my $bot = Robot->new( "Zaphod" );                                  #(N)
$bot = Robot->new( "Trillian" );                                   #(O)

my $total_production = Robot->how_many_robots();                   #(P)
print "Total number of robots made: $total_production\n";
                      # Total number of robots made: 2

# Directly accessing the class variable:
print $Robot::robot_serial_nums_used, "\n";     # 2                #(Q)
```

6.7 REBLESSING OBJECTS

Being typeless (or, said another way, being dynamically typed), it should not come as a surprise to the reader that the type of an instance object can be changed on the fly. This can be done by the simple act of reblessing a previously blessed object into a different class. That is, suppose that a data object was previously blessed into class A, which would endow the object with the behavior programmed into class A through its method definitions. Now suppose we rebless the same object into class B. Subsequently, the object will behave as any instance made directly from class B. So while previously we would call class A's methods on a reference to the object, now we would call class B's methods. The script shown below, `Rebless.pl`, demonstrates this with respect to the `DESTROY()` methods. What happens to a reblessed object with regard to the `DESTROY()` method is particularly interesting. If an object is reblessed into a class different from the one from which it was constructed, at the time of garbage collection it is the `DESTROY()` method of the latest incarnation of the object that will be called.

Lines (A) through (H) define a class `X` with a constructor and a `DESTROY()` method. Lines (I), (J), and (K) show another class, `Y`, that has its own `DESTROY()` method. We construct two instances of type `X` in lines (M) and (N). References to these are held by the variables `x1` and `x2`, respectively. Through the assignment in line (O), the variable `x3` holds a reference to the same instance to which `x1` is pointing. In lines (P), (Q), and (R) we print out the values returned by the built-in `ref()` function for each of the instances created. As expected, the answer is the class name `X` in all three cases.

In line (S), we rebless the object to which `x1` is holding a reference. Lines (T), (U), and (V) demonstrate that `ref()` now returns `Y` for the instances `x1` and `x3`, while originally it returned `X` for the same two instances. As you'd expect, when we invoke `ref()` on `x3` in line (V), we get the same answer as for `x1` in line (T) since the referent objects for both the variables `x1` and `x3` are the same.

Lines (W), (X), and (Y) demonstrate that when the reference count for the instance for which both `x1` and `x3` are holding references goes to zero, it is the `Y`'s destructor that is called, since that is the latest type for the referent object involved. On the other hand, when the instance to which `x2` is holding a reference goes out of scope, it is the `X`'s destructor that is called.

```
#!/usr/bin/perl -w
use strict;

### Rebless.pl

#---------------------------  Class X  ------------------------------
package X;                                                        #(A)
```

```
sub new {                                                            #(B)
    my ($class, $intvalue) = @_;                                     #(C)
    bless { _intvalue => $intvalue }, $class;                        #(D)
}

sub DESTROY {                                                        #(E)
    my $self = shift;                                                #(F)
    my $s = $self->{_intvalue};                                      #(G)
    print "An X instance with int value $s to be destroyed\n";       #(H)
}

#----------------------------  Class Y  ------------------------------
package Y;                                                           #(I)

sub DESTROY {                                                        #(J)
    print "A Y instance is about to be destroyed\n";                 #(K)
}

#----------------------------  Test Code  ----------------------------
package main;                                                        #(L)

my $x1 = X->new(100);                                                #(M)
my $x2 = X->new(200);                                                #(N)
my $x3 = $x1;                                                        #(O)

print ref( $x1 ), "\n";                     # X                      #(P)
print ref( $x2 ), "\n";                     # X                      #(Q)
print ref( $x3 ), "\n";                     # X                      #(R)

bless $x1, "Y";                                                      #(S)

print ref( $x1 ), "\n";                     # Y                      #(T)
print ref( $x2 ), "\n";                     # X                      #(U)
print ref( $x3 ), "\n";                     # Y                      #(V)

$x1 = undef;                                                         #(W)

$x2 = undef;                                                         #(X)
              # An X instance with int value 200 to be destroyed
$x3 = undef;                                                         #(Y)
              # A Y instance is about to be destroyed
```

6.8 OPERATOR OVERLOADING AND CLASS CUSTOMIZATION

Operator overloading gives special meaning to common operators like +, -, *, >, etc., for class type objects. Let's say you have defined a new class and you have overloaded the + operator. Now you would be able to invoke the x+y syntax to "add" two instances constructed from the class. As to what the operator + should mean when its two operands are instance objects depends entirely on the overload definition for the operator. If the class defines a container and each instance of the class stores a sequence of numbers, then the overload definition for + could either mean concatenation of the two operand sequences, or the element-by-element addition of the two sequences, or anything else that seems intuitively plausible and, at the same time, useful from the standpoint of allowing for abbreviated programming syntax.

The overload module that comes bundled with Perl allows you to overload more than 50 operators for a class.[16] To show how this module can be used, the rest of this section will present a class XArray for which we will directly supply overload definitions for the following operators: +, <<, ~, <=>, and cmp. We will also supply XArray with an overload definition for creating a printable string representation of an instance of XArray. All this is accomplished by the following statement in line (B) of the class definition for XArray in the XArray.pm script shown next:

```
use overload '+'   => '_add',
             '""'  => '_str',
             '<<'  => '_left_shift',
             '~'   => '_invert',
             '<=>' => '_compare',
             'cmp' => '_compare',
             'fallback' => 1;
```

First note that this use overload statement comes immediately after the package declaration in line (A) of the script. Note how the use overload statement declares a list of pairs, with the first element of each pair naming the operator to be overloaded and the second naming the method that provides the overload definition. In this manner, the overload module allows any of a very large number of operators to be overloaded. Here is a partial listing:[17]

---

[16]It is interesting to compare the different ways in which Perl and Python support overloading. As discussed in Section 7.11 of Chapter 7, Python comes with certain special method names (most of them with two leading underscores and two trailing underscores) for the purpose of operator overloading. If a class provides a definition for one of these names, that enables a specific operator to be used with the instances constructed from that class.

[17]The reader is referred to the online documentation on the overload module for a full listing of the operators that can be overloaded. The command perldoc -m overload on a Unix/Linux machine will also provide access to this documentation.

```
Conversion Ops:            "", 0+, bool

Arithmetic Ops:            +, +=, -, -=, *, *=, /, /=, %, %=,
                                          **, **=, (and more)

Comparison Ops:            <, <=, >, >=, ==, !=, <=>, lt, le,
                                          gt, ge, eq, ne, comp

Bitwise Logical Ops:       &, |, ^, ~, !

Built-in Functions:        cos, sin, atan2, exp, abs, log,
                                          sqrt, (and more)

Increment,
Decrement Ops:             ++, --  (postfix and prefix versions)

Some Other Ops:            <<, <<=, >>, >>=, x, x=, ., .=
```

The reader should not be misled by how the operators have been grouped together and the names we have used for the categories. For example, let's look at the operators listed under the category "Arithmetic Ops" — there does *not* have to be anything particularly "arithmetic" about what those operators accomplish when overloaded. To illustrate further, consider how the operator `+` is overloaded for the class `XArray`. This class is meant to store a list of items that can either be numbers or strings. For example, as we show in line (T1) of the script `TestXArray.pl` that is presented after the class definition script, an instance `x1` of `XArray` stores the following four items: the number 1, the number 2, the string `hello`, and the number 3:

```
$x1 = XArray->new( [1, 2, "hello", 3] );
```

And, as shown in line (T2) of the same script, another instance `x2` of the same class stores the following four items: the number 7, the number 8, the string `jello`, and the number 9:

```
$x2 = XArray->new( [7, 8, "jello", 9] );
```

The overload definition for `+`, shown in the code for the method `_add()` in lines (F) through (K) of the `XArray.pm` script, carries out an element-by-element addition of the two operand lists stored. But note that while this addition is numeric for the integer elements, it implies concatenation for the string elements. Therefore, if we call

```
print $x1 + $x2;
```

we want the overloading for `+` to return an `XArray` instance that contains the following elements:

```
8   10   hellojello   12
```

That our overloading for + indeed does this is shown by the output printed out in line (T6) of the TestXArray.pl script.[18] About the actual code shown in the definition of _add() in lines (F) through (K) of the XArray.pm script, we first make sure that in a call like $x1 + $x2 the right operand is indeed of type XArray; this is done by calling UNIVERSAL::isa()[19] to verify the actual type of the right operand.[20] About the rest of the code for _add(), the loop in lines (H) through (K) checks the corresponding elements in the two XArray operands. The condition in the statement that ends in line (I) is to check that both the corresponding elements are either numeric or strings. In other words, we want _add() to throw an exception if suppose x1 contains the sequence [23, "hello"] and x2 contains the sequence ["jello", 10]. The statement that ends in line (J) then either adds the two corresponding numbers or concatenates the two corresponding strings, depending on the element type encountered.

Now that we have explained in detail the nature of the class XArray and how we overload the + operator for this class, let's go back to the use overload declaration we showed at the beginning of this section. We will repeat the declaration here for convenience:

```
use overload '+'    => '_add',
             '""'   => '_str',
             '<<'   => '_left_shift',
             '~'    => '_invert',
             '<=>' => '_compare',
             'cmp' => '_compare',
             'fallback' => 1;
```

---

[18]As to why the elements are joined together with underscores will be clear shortly.

[19]Perl's UNIVERSAL class is presented in Chapter 8.

[20]Ordinarily, in object-oriented programming when you overload a binary operator op for a class and you call this operator with the syntax:

```
x op y
```

the system will translate this call into

```
x.op( y )
```

implying that the overload definition as provided for the left-operand object will be invoked and that this definition will be supplied the right-operand object as its explicit argument. So if you have overloaded + and this overload definition allows you to call

```
x + 100
```

then this call will be translated into

```
x.overload_def_for_add( 100 )
```

One very nice feature of the overload module is that it would permit you to make the following call:

```
100 + x
```

and the module would still interpret that as x.overload_def_for_add(100). When the overload module needs to act unconventionally and invoke a method on the right operand, it tells the function invoked about that fact by supplying it with a flag (that is set to 1) as an additional argument.

So what does the second "operator" listed above, `""`, do? You may think of it as the *stringification* operator. The function named to service this operator, `_str()`, creates a string representation of an object. This overload function is shown at line (E) of the next script. The function would be implicitly called if the context wants a string representation of an instance of `XArray`. For example, in the following snippet of code in lines (T1) and (T2) of the `TestXArray.pl` script:

```
$x1 =  XArray->new( [1, 2, "hello", 3] );
print $x1;
```

the overload function `_str()` is used to first create a print representation of the object whose reference is held by `$x1`. The string returned by `_str()` is then supplied to `print()` for displaying the object on the screen. Note the stringification code for `_str()` at line (E) of the script simply uses an underscore to join together the elements held by the `XArray` instance.[21] The single string thus formed is what is returned by `_str()`.[22]

About the third operator shown in the above `use overload` declaration, `<<`, it has traditionally been used as a bitwise left-shift operator. In such traditional usage, the operator may be invoked using syntax like `x<<i` where `x` is an integer; this syntax would typically return an integer whose bit pattern is that of `x` but shifted to the left by `i` positions. Because of these past associations of this operator, an overload definition for `<<` commonly implies shifting to the left some important attribute of the left-operand object. In our case, `XArray`'s overload definition for `<<` at line (L) causes a left *circular* shift of the list held by an `XArray` instance. Therefore, the `$x3 << 2` invocation of this operator in line (T7) of the `TestXArray.pl` script causes `print` in line (T8) to produce the output shown [vis-à-vis what `$x3` looked like in line (T6) of the same script].

That brings us to the fourth operator, `~`, listed in the above `use overload` declaration. Traditionally, this operator, used as a unary operator, has been employed to take a bitwise complement of the bit pattern of an integer operand. That is, traditionally, if `x` is an integer, `~x` would return an integer in which all the `x`'s bits are inverted (meaning, with zeros replaced by ones and ones by zeros). An overload definition for this operator, in our case supplied by the `_invert()` method at line (N) of the next script, inverts in our own sense the contents of the instance to which the operator is applied. As our definition at line (N) shows, the sense of inversion we use is to take the negative of the numeric elements and to reverse the string elements. So if an `XArray` instance is holding the elements 1, 2, `hello`, and 3, the operator `~` applied to this instance would yield an `XArray` instance holding the

[21]Of course, ordinarily, you would just use a blank space to glue together the elements stored in an `XArray` instance in order to create its print representation. We used an underscore to visually highlight the fact that the overload definition for `""` was actually doing some work.

[22]In the same manner that the overload definition supplied for the `""` operator creates a string representation for a class instance, an overload definition supplied for the `0+` operator would create a numeric value for a class instance.

elements -1, -2, `olleh`, and -3. This is illustrated by lines (T9) and (T10) of the `TestXArray.pl` script.

The fifth and the sixth operators listed in the `use overload` declaration, `<=>` and `cmp`, are Perl's three-valued comparison operators, the former for numbers and the latter for strings. Both these operators return -1 when the left operand is less than the right operand, 0 when the two operands are equal, and +1 for the only remaining possibility of the left operand being greater than the right operand. Ordinarily, you would overload `<=>` for a class whose instances are numeric in character, and `cmp` for a class whose instances are string-like in character. Since the `XArray` class does not fall in either category,[23] we overload both, but do so with the same implementation method, `_compare()`, that is defined in lines (P) through (Z) of the script. The `_compare()` method compares the two `XArray` instances element by element. If every element of the left operand is less than the corresponding element of the right operand, `_compare()` returns -1. On the other hand, if every element of the left operand is greater than the corresponding element of the right operand, the function returns +1. If neither of these conditions holds, `_compare()` returns 0. Therefore, according to the comparison logic in `_compare()`, two `XArray` instances are equal if an element-by-element comparison of their contents yields mixed results. Hence, according to `_compare()`, the following instances of `XArray`:

```
$x1  =  XArray->new( [1, 2, "hello"]);
$x2  =  XArray->new( [4, 1, "hello"]);
$x3  =  XArray->new( [0, 1, "yello"]);
```

would all be considered to be equal.[24] About the details of the code in `_compare()`, in line (Q) we refuse to compare two `XArray` instances unless they contain the same number of elements. We then proceed to compare the individual elements in the loop that begins in line (R), while making sure that the corresponding elements are either both numeric or both strings [see line (S)]. The `if-else` block in lines (T) and (U) uses Perl's numeric comparison operators for the number elements and string comparison operators otherwise. The rest of the statements, in lines (V) through (Z), scan through the results obtained for all of the element-by-element comparisons. If they are not all the same, `_compare()` returns 0 for the overall answer. Otherwise, it returns -1 if every one of the element-by-element comparisons is -1, or +1 if every one of the element-by-element comparisons is +1.

That leaves us to explain the `'fallback' => 1` declaration in the `use overload` statement in line (B) of the code. This declaration tells the `overload` module how you want those operators to be treated that you did not list explicitly in the `use overload` statement. You see, using the overload definitions you have supplied, this module has the ability to generate its own overload definitions for some

[23]Or, should we say that it falls in both categories.

[24]You may say they are "equal" because they are not categorically "unequal." That is, since we cannot say definitely that any one of these instances is categorically "less than" or "greater than" any of the other instances, they belong together (in about the same sense as, say, mixed-breed pets form a category unto themselves).

of the other undeclared operators. As a case in point, when you supply an overload definition for the `<=>` operator but not for the other comparison operators, the `overload` module will create its own overload definitions for the other numeric comparison operators `<`, `<=`, `>`, and `>=` provided you have either left the `fallback` keyword unmentioned or set it to 1, as we have done.[25] The difference between setting `fallback` to 1 and leaving it unmentioned is that, in the former case, the `overload` module will try to use Perl's own definition for an operator that cannot be autogenerated from those supplied by the programmer. Whereas, in the latter, `overload` will throw an exception when such operators are encountered in the code. When `fallback` is set explicitly to 0, the `overload` module will *not* try to autogenerate any overload definitions; neither will it use Perl's own operator definitions for those operators you did not include in your `use overload` statement. Therefore, when `fallback` is set to 0, your class should not expect a client to use any operators that are not included explicitly in the `use overload` statement.[26] This explanation should make clear to the reader as to why we are able to use the comparison operators on the `XArray` instances in lines (T11), (T12), and (T13) of the `TestXArray.pl` script even though these operators were not originally included in the statement in line (B) of the script for the `XArray` class.

Shown below is the code for the `XArray` class:

```
package XArray;                                                      #(A)

### XArray.pm

use strict;
use Carp;

# Import 'overload' and declare the operators that will be overloaded
use overload '+'    => '_add',
             '""'   => '_str',
             '<<'   => '_left_shift',
             '~'    => '_invert',
             '<=>' => '_compare',
             'cmp' => '_compare',
             'fallback' => 1;                                        #(B)
```

---

[25]When not explicitly mentioned in a `use overload` statement, `fallback` is by default set to `undef`.

[26]In addition to the autogeneration of the binary-values comparison operators from the three-valued `<=>` and `cmp`, another common autogeneration is for the increment and decrement operators `++` and `--` from the overload definitions for the `+` and `-` operators. Obviously, for the autogeneration of increment and decrement operators, the overload definitions for `+` and `-` would have to accept numeric values for the second argument, which is not the case for our example. Another operator that can be autogenerated from the overload definition for `+` is `+=`, the compound assignment operator. By the same token, a definition for `-=` can be autogenerated from the definition for the `-` operator.

```
# Constructor
sub new {                                                          #(C)
    my ($class, $arr_ref) = @_;
    bless {
        _arr => $arr_ref,
        _size  => scalar( @$arr_ref ),
    }, $class;
}

# Return the number of elements in an instance of XArray:
sub get_size { $_[0]->{_size}; }                                   #(D)

# Allow automatic conversion to a string representation:
sub _str {                                                         #(E)
    my $self = shift;
    return join("_", @{$self->{_arr}});
}

# Gives meaning to the 'x + y' operation:
sub _add {                                                         #(F)
    my ($x1, $x2) = @_;
    croak "Abort: The second arg object is not of type XArray"
            unless UNIVERSAL::isa( $x2, 'XArray');
    my $size1 = $x1->get_size();
    my $size2 = $x2->get_size();
    croak "Aborted: two operands of unequal size in _add"
                    if $size1 != $size2;                           #(G)
    my @result;
    while ($size1--) {                                             #(H)
        my $i = ++$#result;
        croak "Aborted: ummatched element types for '+' operation"
            if $x1->{_arr}[$i] =~ /^\d+$/   !=
               $x2->{_arr}[$i] =~ /^\d+$/;                         #(I)
        $result[$i] =  $x1->{_arr}[$i] =~ /^\d+$/ ?
                           $x1->{_arr}[$i] + $x2->{_arr}[$i] :
                           $x1->{_arr}[$i] . $x2->{_arr}[$i];      #(J)
    }
    return XArray->new( \@result );                                #(K)
}

# Give meaning to the 'x << a' operation:
sub _left_shift {                                                  #(L)
    my ($self, $pos) = @_;
    while ($pos--) {
        _left_shift_by_one( $self );
    }
}
```

```
# Used by the _left_shift() method:
sub _left_shift_by_one {                                              #(M)
    my $self = shift;
    my $first = shift @{$self->{_arr}};
    push @{$self->{_arr}}, $first;
}

# Given meaning to the operation '~x':
sub _invert {                                                         #(N)
    my $self = shift;
    my @result;
    @result = map( {/^\d+/ ? -$_ : join("",reverse(split(//,$_)))}
                        @{$self->{_arr}} );                           #(O)
    return XArray->new( \@result );
}

# For three-valued comparison of XArray objects:
sub _compare {                                                        #(P)
    my ($x1, $x2) = @_;
    croak "Abort: The second arg object is not of type XArray"
            unless UNIVERSAL::isa( $x2, 'XArray');
    my $size1 = $x1->get_size();
    my $size2 = $x2->get_size();
    croak "Aborted: cannot compare two operands of unequal size"
                      if $size1 != $size2;                            #(Q)
    my @compare;
    foreach my $i (0..$size1-1) {                                     #(R)
        croak "Aborted: ummatched element types in the container"
            if $x1->{_arr}[$i] =~ /^\d+$/  !=
               $x2->{_arr}[$i] =~ /^\d+$/;                            #(S)
        if ( $x1->{_arr}[$i] =~ /^\d+$/ ) {                           #(T)
            $compare[$i] = -1 if $x1->{_arr}[$i] < $x2->{_arr}[$i];
            $compare[$i] =  1 if $x1->{_arr}[$i] > $x2->{_arr}[$i];
            $compare[$i] =  0 if $x1->{_arr}[$i] == $x2->{_arr}[$i];
        } else {                                                      #(U)
            $compare[$i] = -1 if $x1->{_arr}[$i] lt $x2->{_arr}[$i];
            $compare[$i] =  1 if $x1->{_arr}[$i] gt $x2->{_arr}[$i];
            $compare[$i] =  0 if $x1->{_arr}[$i] eq $x2->{_arr}[$i];
        }
    }
    if ($compare[0] == -1) {                                          #(V)
        foreach my $i (0..$#compare){
            return 0 if -1 != $compare[$i];
        }
        return -1;                                                    #(W)
    } elsif ($compare[0] == 1) {                                      #(X)
        foreach my $i (0..$#compare){
            return 0 if 1 != $compare[$i];
        }
```

```
        return 1;                                                   #(Y)
    } else {
        return 0;                                                   #(Z)
    }
}

1
```

As should be clear from the explanations that precede the above script, the script shown next is for testing the different operator overloadings for the class `XArray`. Those explanations have already discussed the statements in the lines (T1) through (T14) of the script below. Lines (T15) and (T16) of the script show that a chained invocation of an overloaded operator — the + operator in this case — works as one would expect.

```
#!/usr/bin/perl -w

### TestXArray.pl

use strict;
use XArray;

my $x1 = XArray->new( [1, 2, "hello", 3] );                         #(T1)
print $x1, "\n";                        # 1_2_hello_3               #(T2)

my $x2 = XArray->new( [7, 8, "jello", 9] );                         #(T3)
print $x2, "\n";                        # 7_8_jello_9               #(T4)

my $x3 = $x1 + $x2;                                                 #(T5)
print $x3, "\n";                        # 8_10_hellojello_12        #(T6)

$x3 << 2;                                                           #(T7)
print $x3, "\n";                        # hellojello_12_8_10        #(T8)

my $x4 = ~$x3;                                                      #(T9)
print $x4, "\n";                        # ollejolleh_-12_-8_-10     #(T10)

print "\$x1 is less than \$x2\n"
                    if $x1 < $x2;       # $x1 is less than $x2      #(T11)
print "\$x1 is greater than \$x2\n"
                    if $x1 > $x2;                                   #(T12)
print "\$x1 is 'equal' to \$x2\n"
                    if $x1 == $x2;                                  #(T13)
```

```
$x3 = new XArray( [10, 20, "silly", 30] );                          #(T14)
$x4 = $x1 + $x2 + $x3;                                              #(T15)
print $x4, "\n";                   # 18_30_hellojellosilly_42       #(T16)
```

Before ending this section, we should also point out that one can also supply the implementation subroutines by their references or even as anonymous subroutines in a `use overload` statement. For illustration, the statement in line (B) of the `XArray.pm` script could have been expressed as

```
use overload '+'     => \&_add,
             '""'    => \&_str,
             '<<'    => \&_left_shift,
             '~'     => \&_invert,
             '<=>'   => \&_compare,
             'cmp'   => \&_compare,
             'fallback' => 1;
```

However, it is better to name them as we did in line (B) of the script as it allows the overload definitions to be inherited by the subclasses of a class. More on this topic when we take up the relationship between overloading and inheritance in Chapter 8.

6.9 CREDITS AND SUGGESTIONS FOR FURTHER READING

The reader is referred to the book by Damian Conway [11] for a broader menu of object-oriented concepts in Perl — this was the first book devoted exclusively to Perl OO. The online tutorials that come with Perl documentation, the beginning tutorial `perlboot` by Randal Schwartz and the more advanced tutorial `perltoot` by Tom Christiansen, are also highly recommended.

In Section 6.1.2, we showed the following arrow operator based syntax for constructing an instance of a class:

```
use Person;
my $person = Person->new( .... arg_list .....);
```

where `new()` is a method defined for the class `Person` that returns a reference to an object blessed into the class. Perl also allows the following *indirect object syntax* to be used for making a constructor call:

```
my $person = new Person( .... arg_list .....);
```

The advantage of this syntax is that it looks very much like the constructor syntax in C++ and Java. Perl also allows indirect object syntax to be used for the method calls. For example, the following lines of code

```
use Person;
my $person = Person->new( .... arg_list .....);
my $name = $person->get_name();
```

can be replaced by

```
use Person;
my $person = new Person( .... arg_list .....);
my $name = get_name $person;
```

In the indirect object syntax for method calls, what follows the name of the method is an unparenthesized list that starts with either the class name or the reference to a class instance, followed by the argument to be supplied to the method. See Conway [11] for the pros and cons of using indirect object syntax for constructor and method calls in an object-oriented script.

As mentioned in Section 6.4, the `Function` class shown there was an approximation to a real such class used for the extraction of information related to functions in the analysis of C source code. This is a good place to mention that scripting is used extensively in source-code analysis, especially for the calculation of metrics that measure the overall quality of software. See [54] for some recent work along those lines.

The main source of information regarding the very useful `overload` module discussed in Section 6.8 is the documentation written by the creator of the module, Ilya Zakharevich [71]. This documentation comes with the module. The book by Conway [11] is also a good reference for what you can do with the `overload` module. For online tutorials on the subject of operator overloading in Perl, the reader is referred to the articles by Dave Cross [15] and Hildo Biersma [2].

6.10 HOMEWORK

1. What output does the following script produce before its execution is parked in the infinite loop of line (W)? The script first defines a class `X` in lines (A) through (M). This class is equipped with the `DESTROY()` method in lines (J) through (M). Subsequently, the script defines and populates two different arrays, `@arr` and `@brr`. For the array `@arr`, we first define three scalars, `$x`, `$y`, and `$z`, in lines (N), (O), and (P), respectively, and then push the scalars into the array in line (Q). For the second array, `@brr`, we directly stuff three new instances of `X` into the array in lines (R), (S), and (T).

   After they are populated, both arrays are subsequently `undef`-ed, `@arr` in line (U) and `@brr` in line (V). Now the question is which of the six instances of `X` constructed in the script will be garbage collected before the flow of execution gets into the infinite loop of line (W)?

```
#!/usr/bin/perl -w

### Destroy.pl

use strict;

package X;                                                      #(A)

sub new {                                                       #(B)
    my ($class, $index) = @_;                                   #(C)
    return bless {                                              #(D)
        _index => $index,                                       #(E)
    }, $class;                                                  #(F)
}
sub get_index {                                                 #(G)
    my $self = shift;                                           #(H)
    return $self->{_index};                                     #(I)
}
sub DESTROY {                                                   #(J)
    my $self = shift;                                           #(K)
    my $index = $self->get_index;                               #(L)
    print "X object with index $index being destroyed\n";       #(M)
}

package main;

my $x = X->new(1);                                              #(N)
my $y = X->new(2);                                              #(O)
my $z = X->new(3);                                              #(P)
push my @arr, ($x, $y, $z);                                     #(Q)

my @brr;                                                        #(R)
foreach (4..6) {                                                #(S)
    push @brr, X->new($_);                                      #(T)
}

@arr = undef;                                                   #(U)
@brr = undef;                                                   #(V)

while (1) {}                                                    #(W)
```

2. The `Network` class of Section 6.5.1 hides the `Node` class for the purpose of creating a network of nodes. The user of the `Network` class uses just the integer indices to designate the nodes to use in a network. It is the responsibility of the `Network` class to make the calls to the `Node` constructor for the required nodes.

   Rewrite the earlier `Network` class so that a user of this class will directly "manufacture" the nodes from the `Node` class and supply them to the new `Network` class for the purpose of creating a network. Demonstrate that your implementation will not result in any memory leaks through circular references.

3. Modify the code in the overload definition for the `+` operator in class `XArray` of Section 6.8 so that overload definitions for the increment and decrement operators, `++` and `--`, can be autogenerated by the `overload` module. (Incrementing or decrementing an instance of `XArray` may seem bizarre since each instance is after all a container. For the purpose of this exercise, incrementing could consist of adding one to just the numeric elements in the container. Similarly, decrementing could consist of subtracting one from just the numeric elements.)

4. Using the `overload` module, provide overload definition for the "stringification" operator `""` for the example classes in Sections 6.2 and 6.3 of this chapter.

5. In Section 6.8, we mentioned that the `overload` module allows for the overloaded binary operators to exhibit commutativity (that is, `x op y` will work the same as `y op x`) even when this calls for invoking the overload method definition for the *right* operand. (As mentioned in that section, traditionally it is the method definition for the *left* operand that is used for the operation involved.) Obviously, even when the basic class design permits it, while you may allow commutativity for the `+` operator, you'd want to suppress it for the `-` operator for straightforward reasons. To experiment with these ideas, alter the definition of the `XArray` class in that section so that:

   - It only stores numeric data.
   - Overload the `+` operator so that when called on two instances of `XArray`, it adds the corresponding elements, but, when one of the operands is

a plain number, it adds that number to every element stored in the `XArray` instance.

- Overload the `-` operator so that when called on two instances of `XArray`, it subtracts the elements of the right operand from the corresponding element of the left operand, but, when the right operand is a plain number, it subtracts that number from every element of the left operand.
- The overload definition for `-` should trap the extra flag that will be supplied to it as an extra argument by the `overload` module, indicating that the method was invoked on the right operand. Make sure that your overload definition for `-` throws an exception when this condition is encountered.

6. When you use the `overload` module and supply an overload definition for the `""` operator, that makes it possible for the module to autogenerate the code for the string concatenation operator. Similarly, when you supply a definition for the binary subtraction operator `-`, the module can autogenerate the code for the unary negation operator. Demonstrate these abilities of the `overload` module by experimenting with variants of the `XArray` class of Section 6.8.

7

The Notion of a Class in Python

Since the previous chapter has already introduced the rudiments of the OO vocabulary, in this chapter we can proceed directly to show how the various object-oriented notions at the level of a class are implemented in Python. For a reader skipping through the book, he/she may wish to first review the introductory material in Chapter 6 before proceeding further.

We want to begin this chapter by reminding the reader about the distinction between objects in general, on the one hand, and classes and instances, on the other. This distinction is particularly important in this chapter because practically all entities in Python are objects in the sense of possessing either retrievable data attributes or invocable methods or both using the dot operator that is commonly used in object-oriented programming for such purposes. A user-defined class (for that matter, any class) in Python is an object with certain *system-supplied attributes*. These are not to be confused with the more traditional *programmer-supplied attributes* such as the *class variables* and the *instance variables*, and the *programmer-supplied* methods. By the same token, an instance constructed from a class is an object with certain other *system-supplied attributes* that again are not to be confused with the *programmer-supplied instance variables* associated with an instance and the *programmer-supplied methods* that can be invoked on an instance.

With regard to the OO terminology commonly used in Python, when referring to the data attributes of a class, we will continue to use *instance variables* and *class variables* in the same sense as before. Instance variables of a class will represent the properties of the instances constructed from a class; in general, these would be different for different instances. On the other hand, class variables will represent properties that are global for all the instances constructed from a class. Both the instance variables and class variables are examples of the *attributes* of a class. However, we will now use the word *attribute* in a more general sense as standing for any property, data or method, that can be invoked with the dot operator on either the class or the instances constructed from the class. This usage of "attribute" makes it all encompassing, in the sense that it includes the system-supplied data attributes and methods, the programmer-supplied class and instance variables, and, of course, the programmer-supplied methods.

In the previous chapter, by *method* we meant a function that was part of the implementation code for a class and that was invoked either on the class or on the instances constructed from the class. In the context of object-oriented Python, we will continue to use "method" in the same sense as before. But now we will also use "method" to describe any function, programmer-defined or system-supplied, that can be called using the `obj.method()` syntax where `obj` is an object endowed with functions that are meant to be invoked using the dot operator. Therefore the system-supplied functions that can be invoked with the dot operator on either a class or on the instances constructed from the class will also be referred to as methods.[1]

7.1 DEFINING A CLASS IN PYTHON

We will present the full definition of a Python class in stages. In the subsection that follows, we will start out with a simple example of a class to make the reader familiar with the `__init__()` method whose purpose is to initialize the instance returned by a call to the constructor. This subsection will also focus on the system-supplied data attributes and methods for class objects and instance objects.

7.1.1 Constructors and System-Supplied Attributes

The script shown next demonstrates a simple Python class. Our goal here is to show a class, `Person`, with two instance variables, `name` and `age`, and some code that would permit us to make instances from the class.[2]

---

[1]The system-supplied attributes, both data and methods, employ a special naming convention in Python. Their names typically begin and end with two underscores.

[2]Here is an even more trivial class in Python:

```
class SimpleClass:
    pass
```

An instance of this class may be constructed by invoking its constructor as shown below:

```
x = SimpleClass()
```

As we show in line (A) of the script, a class is defined with the help of the keyword `class`. An instance of a class is constructed by invoking the class name with the function call operator `()`, as in line (E) of the script.[3] The `__init__()` method defined in lines (B), (C), and (D) is automatically invoked for initializing the state of the instance returned by the constructor call `Person()` in line (E). As you would expect, a constructor must allow us to specify values for the instance variables, in this case `name` and `age`, of a class instance. This is done by giving values to `self.name` and `self.age` in lines (C) and (D) in the body of `__init__()`. The first parameter, `self`, of `__init__()` is reserved for the instance created by the memory allocation mechanism that is used under the hood when we make the constructor call `Person()`.[4] The argument for this parameter is supplied implicitly to `__init__()`. The arguments for the rest of the parameters are then taken from the call to the constructor.

```
#!/usr/bin/env python

### ClassSimple.py

#-------------------------        class Person        -------------------------

class Person:                                                                #(A)
    def __init__( self, a_name, an_age ):                                    #(B)
        self.name = a_name                                                   #(C)
        self.age  = an_age                                                   #(D)

#--------------------        end of class definition        --------------------

# Call the constructor:
a_person = Person( 'Zaphod', 114 )                                           #(E)

print a_person.name                         # Zaphod                         #(F)
print a_person.age                          # 114                            #(G)
```

[3]This works because a class name is *callable* in Python, meaning that when it is called like a function with the help of the function-call operator `()`, that results in the execution of some code. In this particular case, the end result is the creation of an instance. What is interesting is that in Python a class instance can also be treated like a *callable* — what that yields depends on whether or not the underlying class implements `__call__()` and what is in that implementation code.

[4]There is nothing special about the parameter name `self`. We could also have defined `__init__()` as:

```
def __init__( arg, a_name, an_age ):
    arg.name = a_name
    arg.age  = an_age
```

Lines (F) and (G) show how we can access the state of an instance by using the dot operator.

Being an object in its own right, every class comes equipped with the following system-supplied attributes:

```
__name__     :   string name of the class

__doc__      :   documentation string for the class

__bases__    :   tuple of parent classes from which the
                 class is derived

__dict__     :   dictionary whose keys are the names of the
                 class data attributes and the methods
                 defined for the class, and whose
                 values are the corresponding bindings

__module__   :   module in which the class is defined
```

And since an instance is also an object in its own right, every instance also comes equipped with its own system-supplied attributes. We are particularly interested in the following two attributes for an instance:

```
__name__     :   string name of the class from which the
                 instance was made

__dict__     :   dictionary whose keys are the names of the
                 instance variables.
```

It is important to realize that the namespace represented by the dictionary `__dict__` for a class object is not the same as the namespace that is represented by the dictionary `__dict__` for an instance object. To illustrate the distinction between the two dictionaries and to also illustrate the values of the above-mentioned system-supplied attributes for the class and instance objects, consider the following variation on the previous script:

```
#!/usr/bin/env python

### ClassSysAttributes.py

#-------------------------    class Person    -------------------------
class Person:                                                       #(A)
    'A very simple class'                                           #(B)
    def __init__( self, a_name, an_age ):                           #(C)
        self.name = a_name                                          #(D)
        self.age  = an_age                                          #(E)
#--------------------    end of class definition    --------------------
```

```
a_person = Person( 'Zaphod', 114 )                                  #(F)
print a_person.name                     # Zaphod                    #(G)
print a_person.age                      # 114                       #(H)

print Person.__name__                   # Person                    #(I)

print Person.__doc__                    # A very simple class       #(J)

print Person.__module__                 # __main__                  #(K)

print Person.__bases__                  # ()                        #(L)

print Person.__dict__                                               #(M)
                       # {'__module__': '__main__',
                       #  '__doc__': 'A very simple class',
                       #  '__init__': <function __init__ at 0x804f5a4>}

print a_person.__class__                # __main__.Person           #(N)

print a_person.__dict__                 # {'age': 114, 'name': 'Zaphod'}  #(O)
```

The class definition in this script is the same as in the previous script, except that we have added a documentation string in line (B). The main difference between the previous script and the one shown here is the addition of lines (I) through (O). In lines (I) through (M) we examine the values of the system-supplied attributes for the class object `Person` and, in lines (N) and (O), we examine the value of two system-supplied attributes for the instance object `a_person` created in line (F) of the script.

As shown in line (I), the value returned for the class attribute `__name__` is the name of the class, `Person`. The value returned for the `__doc__` attribute is the documentation string of line (B). Since the class was defined in a top-level script, the value returned for the `__module__` attribute is `__main__` in line (K). The attribute `__bases__` stores the names of the base classes of a class in an inheritance hierarchy. Since the class `Person` was not derived from any other class, we get back an empty tuple for this attribute in line (L).

Line (M) of the above script yields the namespace dictionary for the class `Person`. When the thread of execution enters a class definition in a Python script, as in line (A) above, Python creates a new namespace that is local to the class. This is the namespace that is printed out when we query the `__dict__` attribute in line (M). *When the thread of execution exits the class definition, the definition of the class is bound to the name of the class in the scope enclosing the class.*

Lines (N) and (O) of the above script show the values returned for the system-supplied attributes of the instance object `a_person`. The `__class__` attribute for this object holds the name of the class from which the instance was created, as shown in line (N). And the attribute `__dict__` holds the instance attributes and their values for the specific instance in question.

7.1.2 Class Definition: The Syntax

Here is a more general definition for a Python class:

```
class MyClass :                                                  #(A)
   'optional documentation string'                               #(B)

   class_var1                                                    #(C)

   class_var2 = val2                                             #(D)

   def __init__( self, val3=default3 ) :                         #(E)
       'optional documentation string'                           #(F)
       instance_var = val                                        #(G)
       rest_of_constructor_suite                                 #(H)

   def some_method( self, some_parameters ) :                    #(I)
       'optional documentation string'                           #(J)
       method_suite                                              #(K)

   ......
   ......
   ......
```

The definition contains an optional documentation string in line (B), followed by the class variables, `class_var1` and `class_var2` in lines (C) and (D). Such variables are global with respect to all the instances constructed from the class; we will discuss such variables in greater detail in Section 7.7. Line (D) shows that a class variable can be given a default value at the time of class definition.

The class definition contains in lines (E) through (H) the method `__init__()` that, as previously mentioned, initializes the memory allocated for the instance created by a call to the constructor. The initialization consists typically of assigning values to the instance variables of the class. For the example shown above, the variable `instance_var` will acquire values on a per-instance basis when instances are constructed from the class. In general, the header of `__init__()` may look like

```
def __init__(self, val1, val2, val3 = default3) :
```

This `__init__()` could be for a class that has three instance variables, with the last default initialized as shown. As mentioned before, the first parameter, typically named `self`, is implicitly set to the instance under construction.

If you do not provide a class with `__init__()`, the system will provide the class with a default version of the same. You override the default definition by providing your own implementation for `__init__()`.

Lines (I) through (K) above show the syntax for a user-defined method for a class. The syntax for such user-defined methods is the same as for stand-alone Python functions (as described in Section 3.8 of Chapter 3), except for the special significance accorded the first parameter, typically named `self`; it is typically meant to be bound to the instance on which the method is invoked. The value for this parameter is supplied implicitly when the method is invoked on a class instance.

Shown next is a Python class `Person` that parallels the Perl's `Person` class in Section 6.1.4 of Chapter 6. Starting in line (A), the class definition includes a documentation string in line (B) and a version string in line (C). The class has two instance variables, `name` and `age`, defined in the body of the instance initializer in lines (F) and (G). The class also comes equipped with two `get` methods, in lines (H) and (J), and one `set` method in line (L).

Line (N) shows a constructor call for creating a new instance of `Person`. As mentioned previously, this call automatically invokes the `__init__()` method whose first parameter, `self`, is set implicitly to the instance under construction. This implicit assignment to the first parameter of a method also takes place when we call the different `get` and `set` methods in lines (O) through (R).

Lines (S) and (T) show the namespace dictionaries associated with the class `Person` and with the instance `person`. Note the addition of the names `get_name`, `get_age`, and `set_age` to the class namespace in line (S).

```
#!/usr/bin/env python

### ClassBasic.py

#---------------------------  class Person  --------------------------
class Person:                                                      #(A)
    'A more detailed Person class'                                 #(B)
    version = 1.0                                                  #(C)

    # Instance initializer:
    def __init__( self, nm, yy ) :                                 #(D)
        'Person instance initializer'                              #(E)
        self.name = nm                                             #(F)
        self.age = yy                                              #(G)
```

```
    def get_name( self ):                                                #(H)
        return self.name                                                 #(I)

    def get_age( self ):                                                 #(J)
        return self.age                                                  #(K)

    def set_age( self, newYY ):                                          #(L)
        self.age = newYY                                                 #(M)
#----------------------- end of class definition --------------------

person = Person( 'Zaphod', 114 )                                         #(N)
print person.get_name()              # Zaphod                            #(O)
print person.get_age()               # 114                               #(P)
person.set_age( 25 )                                                     #(Q)
print person.get_age()               # 25                                #(R)

print Person.__dict__                                                    #(S)
          # {'__module__': '__main__',
          #  'version': 1.0,
          #  '__init__': <function __init__ at 0x804f664>,
          #  'set_age': <function set_age at 0x805a5c4>,
          #  '__doc__': 'My very first Python class',
          #  'get_name': <function get_name at 0x805a554>,
          #  'get_age': <function get_age at 0x805a58c>}

print person.__dict__                                                    #(T)
          # {'age': 25, 'name': 'Zaphod'}
```

7.2 NEW-STYLE VERSUS CLASSIC CLASSES IN PYTHON

Python 2.2 introduced *new-style classes* while retaining the old-style classes for backward compatibility. The old-style classes are now referred to as the *classic classes.* The new-style classes were motivated by the need to subclass the built-in classes. It was not previously possible to extend, say, the string class `str` to create a more customized version of the same. But now you can do that with ease.

All new-style classes are subclassed,[5] either directly or indirectly, from the root class `object`. The `object` class defines a set of methods with default implementations that are inherited by all classes derived from it. A case in point is the `__getattribute__()` method that is automatically invoked whenever any of the

[5] See the introduction to Chapter 6 for what is meant by subclassing and class derivation. These notions will be discussed in much greater detail in Chapters 8 and 9.

other methods defined for the class is called. Its implementation in the `object` class is a do-nothing implementation. However, a class that inherits from `object` can provide an override implementation for `__getattribute__()` if something special needs to be done prior to the execution of the code in the other called methods. The names of the attributes, data and methods, defined for the `object` class can be seen by accessing the namespace dictionary `object.__dict__`. Here are the data and method names stored in this dictionary:

```
__class__        __delattr__    __doc__        __getattribute__
__hash__         __init__       __new__        __reduce__
__reduce_ex__    __repr__       __setattr__    __str__
```

Some of these names should already be familiar to the reader by now. Several of the others we will pick up later in this chapter and in Chapter 9.

Python uses the following two-step procedure for constructing an instance from a new-style class:

1. The call to the constructor creates what may be referred to as a generic instance from the class. The generic instance's memory allocation is customized with the code in the method `__new__()` of the class. The method `__new__()` may either be defined directly for a class or a class may inherit it from one of its parent classes.[6] The method `__new__()` is implicitly considered by Python to be a static method.[7] Its first parameter is meant to be set equal to the name of the class whose instance is desired and it must return the instance created.

2. Then the method `__init__()` of the class is invoked to initialize the instance returned by `__new__()`. If a class does not provide its own `__init__()`, an inherited version of the same is used.

Consider the example shown in the script that follows. We define a class `X` in lines (A) through (F) and provide it with the methods `__new__()` and `__init__()` as shown. Note the syntax of the header of class `X`:

```
class X( object )
```

which declares the system-supplied class `object` to be the base class for `X`. It is this declaration that makes `X` a new-style class, with its instance creation properties as described above. As for the definition we have provided for the class's `__new__()` — especially the need to call the `object`'s `__new__()` in line (D) — that will become clear after the reader has become familiar with the class derivation syntax

[6]If the class does not provide its own implementation for `__new__()`, as to how exactly a search is conducted for this method in the inheritance tree will be explained in Section 9.8 of Chapter 9. The same applies to `__init__()`.

[7]Static methods in Python OO are discussed in Section 7.7. Python is automatically aware of the fact that `__new__()` is static. That is, no special declaration needs to be made in a script for this method to be recognized as static.

in Chapter 9. When we call the constructor in line (G), we get the output shown in the commented-out portion of that line and the next line. This output confirms the fact that both `__new__()` and `__init__()` are pressed into service for instance construction for a new-style class.

```
#!/usr/bin/env python

### NewStyle.py

#---------------------------  class X  --------------------------------
class X( object ):                                                   #(A)

    def __new__( cls ):                                              #(B)
        print "__new__ invoked"                                      #(C)
        return object.__new__( cls )                                 #(D)

    def __init__( self ):                                            #(E)
        print "__init__ invoked"                                     #(F)

#-----------------------------  Test Code  ---------------------------
# Call X's constructor:
xobj = X()                         # __new__ invoked                 #(G)
                                   # __init__ invoked
```

7.3 DEFINING METHODS

As the reader has already seen, a method is defined with the keyword `def`. In that sense, method definitions are the same as the stand-alone functions discussed in Section 3.8 of Chapter 3. However, there is one crucial difference between the parameter structure of a stand-alone function and that of a method: The first parameter of the parameter list of a method must be reserved for the object on which the method is invoked. As already mentioned, this parameter is typically named `self`, but it can be any legal Python identifier.

As the reader already knows from Chapter 3, when Python processes a function definition, it first creates a function object and then binds it to the name of the function. For example, for the following code fragment

```
class X:
    def foo( self , arg1, arg2 ):
        ....implmentation of foo....
```

the name `foo` will be introduced as a key in the namespace dictionary associated with class `X`. The value entered for this key will be the function object corresponding to the body of the function definition. So if you examine the contents of the namespace dictionary for the class by

```
print X.__dict__
```

after the class definition has been digested, you'll see the following sort of an entry in the dictionary:

```
'foo': <function foo at 0x805a5e4>
```

The script `Method.py` shown next defines a class in lines (A) through (G). The definitions for `__init__()`, `foo()`, and `bar()` in the body of class `X` create three function objects that are bound to the names `__init__`, `foo`, and `bar` in the namespace dictionary of class `X`. This fact can be confirmed by examining the namespace dictionary `X.__dict__`.

The `__init__()` in lines (B) and (C) and the method `foo()` in lines (D) and (E) are defined in a straightforward manner. When we invoke the constructor in line (H) using the syntax

```
xobj = X( 10 )
```

the parameter `self` in line (B) is set implicitly to the instance that requires initialization and the parameter `nn` to the value 10. And when we make the method call in line (I)

```
xobj.foo( 20, 30 )
```

the parameter `self` in the definition in line (D) is implicitly set to the instance `xobj`. The parameter `arg1` is set to 20, and the parameter `arg2` to 30.

A method may call any other method of a class, but such a call must always use class-qualified syntax. This is illustrated by the example in lines (F) and (G). Even though the name `foo` is local to the class namespace, when `foo()` is called in line (G), it must be done using the syntax `self.foo()`.

```
#!/usr/bin/env python

### Method.py

#----------------------------  class X  ---------------------------------
class X:                                                              #(A)
    def __init__( self, nn ):                                         #(B)
        self.n = nn                                                   #(C)

    def foo( self, arg1, arg2 ):                                      #(D)
        self.n = arg1 + arg2                                          #(E)
```

```
    def bar( self ):                                                  #(F)
        self.foo( 7, 8 )                                              #(G)
#--------------------   end of class definition  ------------------------

xobj = X( 10 )                                                        #(H)

xobj.foo( 20, 30 )                                                    #(I)
print xobj.n                # 50                                      #(J)

xobj.bar()                                                            #(K)
print xobj.n                # 15                                      #(L)
```

Since all the method names are stored as keys in the namespace dictionary of a class, and since the dictionary keys must all be distinct, this implies that there can exist only one function object for a given method name. Therefore, as a class definition is being digested, if Python sees another definition for the same function name, it will replace the previous function-object binding for the function name with the new one. This is done regardless of the parameter structure of the function.

As a more general case of the above property, a class can have only one attribute of a given name. What that means is that if a class definition contains a data attribute of a given name after a method attribute of the same name has been defined, what will be stored in the class object in the memory is the name as a data attribute. Of course, this also works in reverse. If a class definition contains a data attribute of a given name and then later a method attribute of the same name appears, it is the latter that will be retained.

We should also mention that, unlike Perl, Python strictly enforces the constraint that the number of arguments supplied when a function is called must match exactly the number of parameters in the function definition. When comparing the number of arguments supplied vis-à-vis the number of parameters specified, recall that the first argument is supplied implicitly when a method is invoked on an object.

7.3.1 A Method Can Be Defined Outside a Class

It is not necessary for the body of a method to be enclosed by a class. A function object created outside a class can be assigned to a name inside a class. That name will acquire the binding that will be the function object. Subsequently, that name can be used in a method call as if the method had been defined inside the class. The following example illustrates this.

In the script below, a function `bar()` is defined in lines (A) and (B) outside of any class. By virtue of this definition, the name `bar` acquires a binding that is the function object corresponding to the function definition in lines (A) and (B). Now, in line (D), the name `foo` is a local variable of class `X`. The assignment in line (D) binds `foo` to the function object that was created through the definition in lines (A) and (B). Subsequently, `foo()` will behave as a method for instances of class `X`. The parameter structure of `foo` when called as a method will be the parameter structure of `bar()` in line (A). This is illustrated by the invocation of `foo()` on `xobj` in line (I). This invocation changes the state of the object `xobj`, as can be seen by the output shown in line (J).

```
#!/usr/bin/env python

### MethodOutsideClass.py

def bar( self, arg1, arg2 ):                                          #(A)
    self.n = arg1 + arg2                                              #(B)

#----------------------------  class X  --------------------------------
class X:                                                              #(C)
    foo = bar                                                         #(D)

    def __init__( self, nn ):                                         #(E)
        self.n = nn                                                   #(F)
#--------------------  end of class definition  -----------------------

xobj = X( 10 )                                                        #(G)
print xobj.n                # 10                                      #(H)

xobj.foo( 20, 30 )                                                    #(I)
print xobj.n                # 50                                      #(J)
```

7.3.2 Bound and Unbound Methods

Later in this chapter, we will talk about how to define static and class methods for a Python class. As we will show there, you must use special syntax to tell Python that a method is meant to be used as a static method or as a class method. To appreciate that discussion, it is important to understand what is meant by *bound methods* and *unbound methods* in Python.

In general, when a method is invoked on an instance or on a class, Python creates a *method object* with the following attributes: `im_self`, `im_func`, and `im_class`. The `im_class` attribute is set to the name of the class in which the method is defined and the `im_func` attribute to the function object created from the implementation code for the method. How the `im_self` attribute is set depends on whether the method is called on an instance or on the class. When the method is invoked on an instance, the `im_self` attribute is set to the instance object and the method object is considered to be *bound* to that instance. In this case, the implicitly supplied first argument to the function object stored in `im_func` is the instance object stored in `im_self`. On the other hand, when a method is invoked on a class. the `im_self` attribute is left unbound and, in this case, the method object is considered to be *unbound*. Now there is nothing special as to what is supplied for the first argument to the function object stored in `im_func`. In other words, now all of the arguments in the method call are passed unchanged to the function object.

This we explain with the help of the following script that shows a class `X` with a method `foo()` in lines (A), (B), and (C). In line (D), we create an instance `xobj` of this class. When we output the print representation of the object `X.foo` in line (E), Python tells us that it is an unbound method object.[8] And when we output the print representation of the object `xobj.foo` in line (F), Python tells us that it is a bound method object. Line (G) shows us invoking `foo()` as a bound method. The same method is invoked as an unbound method of class `X` in line (H).

```
#!/usr/bin/env python

### BoundAndUnbound.py

class X:                                                              #(A)
    def foo( self, mm ):                                              #(B)
        print "mm = ", mm                                             #(C)

xobj = X()                                                            #(D)

print X.foo                 # <unbound method X.foo>                  #(E)

print xobj.foo                                                        #(F)
          # <bound method X.foo of <__main__.X instance at 0x403b51cc>>

# Call foo as a bound method:
xobj.foo( 10 )              # mm =  10                                #(G)

# Call foo as an unbound method:
X.foo( xobj, 10 )           # mm =  10                                #(H)
```

[8]Note that calling `X.foo` or `xobj.foo` is not tantamount to making a function call in Python since we are not using the function call operator `()`. These calls merely return function objects.

To fully appreciate the difference between bound and unbound methods, it is best to keep in mind the semantics of the dot operator in the `obj.attribute` construct. The sole duty of the dot operator is to supply us with the attribute named in the right operand for the object named in the left operand. The dot operator in such constructs is merely an *attribute access operator*. However, as to what arguments would be supplied to the function object executed when we use the function-call operator `()` in conjunction with the attribute access operator, as in `obj.attribute()`, that depends on the nature of the left operand to the attribute access operator. When the left operand is an instance object and the right operand the name of a function defined for the class from which the instance was constructed, the construct `obj.attribute` yields a *bound method object*, in the sense the method object exists for a specific instance — that is, the method object is bound to a specific instance. *It is only in this case that the first argument supplied to the function object is set to the instance object that is the left operand of the attribute access operator.* On the other hand, when the left operand to the attribute access operator is a class, in this case the construct yields an *unbound method object*. Now there is nothing special about the first argument that is supplied to the function object. In other words, with an unbound method object, the argument list that would be supplied to the function object corresponds exactly to the parameter list of the method definition.[9]

As we will show in Chapter 9, calling a method as an unbound method, as in line (H) of the script shown above, is particularly useful when a subclass needs to call a base class method.

7.3.3 Using __getattr__() as a Catch-All for Nonexistent Methods

The role played by `AUTOLOAD` in Perl OO is played by the system-supplied method `__getattr__()` for a Python class. If a nonexistent method is invoked on an instance, Python farms out that call to `__getattr__()` provided the underlying class or one of its superclasses implements this method. By a nonexistent method we mean one whose implementation cannot be found either in the class or in the superclasses of the class through search described in Section 9.8 of Chapter 9. For this to work, `__getattr__()` must be defined with two parameters, the first to be bound to the instance on which the method is invoked by the system and the second to be set to the name of the nonexistent method called. Additionally, `__getattr__()` must return a callable object. As mentioned previously in Section 7.1.1, an object is considered

[9]However, an unbound method knows what it must expect for the first argument. So if line (H) of the `BoundAndUnbound.py` script was replaced by the code fragment

```
class Y: pass
yobj = Y()
X.foo( yobj, 10 )
```

you'd get a run-time error with the message that the first argument in the unbound method invocation in the last line above must be an `X` instance.

callable if it can be called with a function-call operation, that is, with the `()` operator, with or without arguments.

The basic use of `__getattr__()` is demonstrated by the following script. Class `X` implements this method in lines (D), (E), and (F). As required by Python, this implementation returns a function object — in this case, the function object bound to the name `undefined_handler`. Lines (G) and (H) provide the function object needed.

In the test code, we first construct an instance `xobj` from class `X` in line (I). When we invoke `foo()` on this instance in line (J), we get the response as dictated by the code in lines (B) and (C). However, when we invoke `bar()` on the same instance — considering that `bar()` is not defined for the class — the call is farmed out to `__getattr__()`. The output shown in the commented-out portions of the lines (K) and (L) is caused by the print statement in line (E) that is executed when `__getattr__()` is invoked and by the print statement in line (H) when the system executes the function object returned in line (F).

Line (M) demonstrates that `__getattr__()` when available for a class is also invoked by default when an attempt is made to access an instance variable that does not exist. In this case, since we did not use the function-call operator `()`, the system does not evaluate the callable object returned by the implementation code for `__getattr__()`. Finally, the commented-out line (N) demonstrates that `__getattr__()` is invoked by the system only when instance attributes, with or without the function-call operator, are accessed. On the other hand, when we invoke a nonexistent attribute directly on a class, Python will raise the `AttributeError` exception and complain that the attribute in question does not exist for the class.

```
#!/usr/bin/env python

### UndefinedMethodHandler.py

#----------------------------  class X  --------------------------------

class X:                                                              #(A)

    def foo( self ):                                                  #(B)
        print "foo called"                                            #(C)

    def __getattr__( self, name ):                                    #(D)
        print "__getattr__() called when %s invoked" % name           #(E)
        return undefined_handler                                      #(F)

#-------------------  end of class definition  ------------------------

def undefined_handler():                                              #(G)
    print "Default handler invoked"                                   #(H)
```

```
#---------------------------- Test Code -------------------------------

xobj = X()                                                         #(I)

xobj.foo()            # foo called                                 #(J)

xobj.bar()            # __getattr__() called when bar invoked      #(K)
                      # Default handler invoked                    #(L)

xobj.baz              # __getattr__() called when baz invoked      #(M)

#X.baz                # ERROR                                      #(N)
```

The previous example showed how a call to any nonexistent method could be handled by an appropriately defined `__getattr__()`. But note that the nonexistent method called in line (K) above did not involve any explicit arguments. What if we wanted to call arbitrary nonexistent methods with explicit arguments and wanted Python to pass on the arguments to a default method handler? In other words, we want Python to now pass on the arguments in the call to a nonexistent method to the callable object returned by `__getattr__()`. The following script shows how this can be done with the help of a function closure. A function closure, as explained in Section 3.8.8 of Chapter 3, is able to trap the values of the variables currently in scope inside the function object returned by the closure.

In the following script[10] when `__getattr__()` is invoked automatically by the system, the parameter `name` in line (D) is set to the name of the (nonexistent) method called by the user. The value of this parameter is supplied to the callable object returned by `__getattr__()`. Execution of the callable object code, in lines (H), (I), and (J), returns through line (J) a function closure that traps from the code-block scope the values for the parameters `*args` and `**kwargs`.[11] The values for these parameters are derived from the argument list in the call to the nonexistent method. In the body of the code associated with the function closure — lines (H) and (I) — the system can now access the name of the nonexistent method called and all the arguments with which it is called.

This should explain the output shown in the commented-out portions of the lines (M) and (N) for the nonexistent method call in line (M), and in the commented-out portions of the lines (O) and (P) for the nonexistent method call in line (O). In each case, the first line of the output is produced by line (E) in the body of

[10]This script is based on an example provided by Mark Andrew.

[11]Sections 3.8.4 and 3.8.5 of Chapter 3 review the use of `*args` and `**kwargs` to capture with the former a tuple of all the position-specific arguments and, with the latter, a dictionary of all the keyword arguments in a function call.

`__getattr__()` and the second line when Python executes the function closure returned by the callable in line (F).

```
#!/usr/bin/env python

### UndefinedMethodWithArgsHandler.py

#--------------------------- class X --------------------------------

class X:                                                               #(A)

    def foo( self ):                                                   #(B)
        print "foo called"                                             #(C)

    def __getattr__( self, name ):                                     #(D)
        print "__getattr__() called when %s invoked" % name            #(E)
        return self.handlerGenerator( name )                           #(F)

    def handlerGenerator( self, name ):                                #(G)
        def undefinedHandler( *args, **kwargs ):                       #(H)
            print name, args, kwargs                                   #(I)
        return undefinedHandler                                        #(J)

#-------------------- end of class definition  -----------------------

xobj = X()                                                             #(K)

xobj.foo()                 # foo called                                #(L)

xobj.bar( 100 )            # __getattr__() called when bar invoked     #(M)
                           # bar (100,) {}                             #(N)

xobj.baz( 100, 200 )       # __getattr__() called when baz invoked     #(O)
                           # baz (100, 200) {}                         #(P)
```

7.3.4 __getattr__() versus __getattribute__()

For new-style classes, Python makes available the `__getattribute__()` method that is called automatically whenever any of the other class methods is invoked. The `__getattribute__()` method is defined for the root class `object` with essentially a do-nothing implementation. It can, however, be overridden in your own class to provide any setup operations before the code in any of the other methods is actually executed.

Probably the most important difference between `__getattr__()`, presented in the previous subsection, and `__getattribute__()` presented here is that whereas the former is called automatically only if a nonexistent method is invoked on an instance, the latter is called automatically every time a method is invoked. The script shown below should make clear this distinction.

Class `X` of the next script implements `__getattr__()` in lines (F), (G), and (H), and overrides `__getattribute__()` in lines (I), (J), and (K). Note that `X` is a new-style class since the syntax in line (A) causes it to be subclassed from the root class `object`.[12] With regard to the implementation of `__getattribute__()`, note especially the statement in line (K); it is the call to the `object`'s `__getattribute__()` that returns the function object associated with the method name that was called originally.

With regard to the test code shown in lines (N) through (Q), the call to `xobj.foo()` in line (O) results in the following output:

```
__getattribute__() called for foo
foo called
```

indicating that the method call was first processed by `__getattribute__()` of line (I) and then subsequently passed on to `foo()` of line (B). For another example involving a method call with arguments, the invocation of `xobj.bar(10)` in line (P) results in the output

```
__getattribute__() called for bar
bar called with mm =  10
```

indicating again that the call was handed over to `__getattribute__()` of the class before being passed on to `bar()` of line (D).

The call in line (Q) is meant to show that if you call a nonexistent method, the default handler `__getattr__()` if available will still be invoked but only after the method call is processed by `__getattribute__()`. Therefore, the call `xobj.baz()` in line (Q) results in the following output:

```
__getattribute__() called for baz
__getattr__() called
Default handler invoked
```

The default handler `__getattr__()` invokes the the global `undefined_handler()` defined in lines (L) and (M).

[12]Chapter 9 goes more deeply into the issues of subclassing a Python class. Also discussed in that chapter is what is meant by a class overriding a method defined for a superclass.

```
#!/usr/bin/env python

### GetAttribute.py

#---------------------------- class X --------------------------------

class X( object ):                                                  #(A)

    def foo( self ):                                                #(B)
        print "foo called"                                          #(C)

    def bar( self, mm ):                                            #(D)
        print "bar called with mm = ", mm                           #(E)

    def __getattr__( self, name ):                                  #(F)
        print "__getattr__() called"                                #(G)
        return undefined_handler                                    #(H)

    def __getattribute__( self, name ):                             #(I)
        print "__getattribute__() called for", name                 #(J)
        return object.__getattribute__(self, name)                  #(K)

#-------------------- end of class definition ------------------------

def undefined_handler():                                            #(L)
    print "Default handler invoked"                                 #(M)

#---------------------------- Test Code ------------------------------

xobj = X()                                                          #(N)

xobj.foo()                      # __getattribute__() called for foo #(O)
                                # foo called

xobj.bar( 10 )                  # __getattribute__() called for bar #(P)
                                # bar called with mm =  10

xobj.baz()                      # __getattribute__ called with  baz #(Q)
                                # __getattr__() called
                                # Default handler invoked
```

7.4 DESTRUCTION OF INSTANCE OBJECTS

Like Perl, Python comes with automatic garbage collection. The basic principle on which garbage collection works in Python is the same as in Perl. Each object created is kept track of through reference counting.[13] Every time an object is assigned to a variable, the reference count associated with the object goes up by one, signifying that there is one more variable holding a reference to the object.[14] And every time a variable holding a reference to some object either goes out of scope or has its referent changed, the reference count associated with the object is decreased by one. When the reference count associated with an object drops down to zero, it becomes a candidate for garbage collection.

In much the same way as `DESTROY()` in Perl, Python provides us with a function `__del__()` whose override definition can be used for cleaning up any acquired system resources, such as memory, stream objects, sockets, etc., before an object is actually destroyed and the memory reclaimed. To illustrate the working of `__del__()`, we will now show a script that parallels the example presented in Section 6.4 of the previous chapter to illustrate Perl's `DESTROY()`.

The next script presents a class `Function` that is an approximation to what you would need for storing information regarding functions if you were scanning source code for its characterization by metrics. As source code — C files in this case — is scanned, you'd look for function headers and store various properties of the detected functions in the instances created from the class `Function`. For the simple example presented here, we are interested in storing the following attributes of each function in a C source file: its name, its return type, the name of the file in which it exists, and the line number in the file where the function definition begins. This should explain the four instance variables in lines (E) through (H) of the `Function` class. For book-keeping purposes, the `__init__()` of the class also stores away the names of the functions in a class variable[15] `funcs_scanned` initialized in line (B). The class also includes a static method in line (O) that can be used to fetch the information stored in the class variable of line (B). The exact syntax used in line (O) will be made clear in Section 7.6.

All of the code for the extraction of function headers (assuming for the simple example here that a function header will always be in one single line) and other information related to a function is extraneous to the class `Function` itself; that code is shown in the test section in lines (W) through (g). The logic that is used for extracting function headers in lines (W) through (g) is the same as for the Perl example in the

[13] A brief review of the different approaches to garbage collection is presented in Chapter 12.

[14] As previously stated in Chapter 6, a more general way to say the same would be: Every time an object is referred to by another object, the reference count of the former is incremented by one. The reference count for an object is decremented by one each time a reference to it is released by some other object.

[15] Section 7.6 explains what is meant by class variables and static and class methods.

previous chapter. We use a regular expression shown in line (Z) to extract the return type and the function name from each function header. This regex must deal with the fact that some return types have multiple "words" in them, as for example in the return type `struct part *`.[16] The utility function `_extract_functions()` returns all four pieces of information regarding a function in the form of a single string. We then break this string for each function into its four parts and, at the same time, construct a `Function` instance in the loop of lines (k) through (q).

The idea behind the `__del__()` method defined in lines (P) through (T) is that when we are done with scanning one or more source files, we want to create a permanent record of the measurements made by writing them out to a disk file. There are obviously various ways of doing this. We could, for example, use the object serialization method that we will present in Chapter 16 to serialize the `Function` instances before writing them out to the disk. However, since our focus here is on illustrating `__del__()`, we will use this method to write out the measurements to the disk. So after you are done processing the source code, if and when a `Function` instance goes out of scope, the implementation of `__del__()` in lines (P) through (T) would write out the measurements made to a disk file. This code basically constructs a single string from the four properties of each function and then archives the string in a disk file.

```
#!/usr/bin/env python

###  Function.py

#----------------------    start class definition    ----------------------
class Function:                                                          #(A)

    # This class variable stores a list of all
    # the extracted functions.  By line (D), only
    # the function names go into this list:
    funcs_scanned = []                                                   #(B)

    # For initializing Function instances.  In line
    # (D), this method also inserts the function name
    # in the static variable of line (B):
    def __init__( self, **args ):                                        #(C)
        Function.funcs_scanned.append(args['name'])                      #(D)
        self._name = args['name']                                        #(E)
        self._ret_type  =  args['ret_type'] or '?????'                   #(F)
        self._file      =  args['file']     or '?????'                   #(G)
        self._line_num  =  args['line_num'] or '?????'                   #(H)
```

[16]Chapter 4 presented the `re` module for regular-expression based string matching in Python.

```
    # Instance get methods:
    def get_name( self ): return self._name                          #(I)
    def get_file( self ): return self._file                          #(J)
    def get_ret_type( self ): return self._ret_type                  #(K)
    def get_line_num( self ): return self._line_num                  #(L)

    # Static method that returns the value stored
    # in the class variable of line (B):
    def get_total_func_count():                                      #(M)
        return len( Function.funcs_scanned )                         #(N)
    get_total_func_count = staticmethod( get_total_func_count )      #(O)

    # Called for dying Function instances:
    def __del__(self):                                               #(P)
        import os                                                    #(Q)
        FILE = os.open( "function_archive.txt", \
                       os.O_RDWR | os.O_CREAT | os.O_APPEND )
        record = ' '.join([self._name, self._file, \
                            self._ret_type, str(self._line_num)])    #(R)
        os.write( FILE, record + "\n" )                              #(S)
        os.close(FILE)                                               #(T)
#----------------------- end of class definition --------------------

if __name__ == "__main__":                                           #(U)

    import re                                                        #(V)

    # Utility subroutine for extracting function
    # return type, function name, file name, and
    # line number in file.  This function returns
    # the four items of information as a single string:
    def _extract_functions( filename ):                              #(W)
        FILE = open( filename )                                      #(X)
        all_lines = FILE.readlines()                                 #(Y)
        regex = re.compile(  \
          r'^((?:struct\s+)?\w+\s+\*?\s*\w+)\s*\(.*\).*\{\s*(\d*)')#(Z)
        all_lines = map( None, all_lines, range( len(all_lines) ) ) #(a)
        all_lines = [ item[0] + str(item[1]) for item in all_lines] #(b)
        functions = map( regex.findall, all_lines )                  #(c)
        functions = filter( None, functions )                        #(d)
        functions = [ list(item[0]) + [filename] \
                      for item in functions]                         #(e)
        functions = [ " ".join( item ) for item in functions ]       #(f)
        return functions                                             #(g)

    # Extract function info from file:
    func_list = _extract_functions( "func.c" )                       #(h)
```

```
# Construct Function instances from the extracted
# information stored in func_list:
func_instances = []                                                    #(i)
regex2 = re.compile( r'^(.*\s+\*?)(\w+)\s(\d+)\s(\w+\.\w+)$' )  #(j)
for header in func_list:                                               #(k)
    m = regex2.search( header )                                        #(l)
    func_instances.append( Function(                                   #(m)
                ret_type   = m.group(1),                               #(n)
                name       = m.group(2),                               #(o)
                line_num   = m.group(3),                               #(p)
                file       = m.group(4) ) )                            #(q)


# Print out the four pieces of information
# extracted for each function:
for func in func_instances:                                            #(r)
    print func.get_name(), func.get_ret_type(), \
          func.get_line_num(), func.get_file()                         #(s)


# Call the static method
print "\n\nTotal number of functions scanned: %d\n\n" % \
                        Function.get_total_func_count()                #(t)
```

The code shown above is in the form of a module file. The first part, in lines (A) through (T), consists of the class definition. The rest of the file, in lines (U) through the end, consists of the ancillary function `_extract_functions()`, the code for processing a source file with this function, and the code for constructing `Function` instances. See Section 3.10 of Chapter 3 on how a module is typically organized in Python.

The output produced by this script is the same as by its Perl version shown in Section 6.4 of the previous chapter, assuming that the C source file used — `func.c` — is the same. As with the Perl version, upon termination this script creates an archive file `function_archive.txt` that contains the function properties deposited there by the dying `Function` instances.

As with any reference counting based approach, garbage collection in Python suffers from the problems that are created by circular references. The memory leaks created by circular references were presented in considerable detail in Section 6.4.1 of the previous chapter. Exactly the same examples could be constructed for Python to demonstrate both the memory leaks and to show how such leaks can be prevented by careful writing of the code. We will leave the construction of Python versions of those examples to the homework section of this chapter.

7.5 ENCAPSULATION ISSUES FOR CLASSES

Python, like Perl, does not provide a mechanism to enforce information hiding that is so central to mainstream OO languages like C++ and Java. Nevertheless, information hiding is necessary for the OO style of code writing for reasons that we outlined at the beginning of Chapter 6. To summarize what was said there, a class can have methods and data attributes that should not be accessed directly outside the class because these methods and attributes are meant to be used in particular ways by other methods of the class. It is for this reason that a class in mainstream OO possesses a public interface consisting of only those data attributes and methods that are allowed to be accessed by other classes. In such languages, when a client of a class is allowed to access a data attribute of the class, it is only through special accessor methods, meaning the `get` and `set` methods. That sort of information hiding cannot be achieved in Perl and Python. In Python, as in Perl, information hiding can only be achieved through programmer cooperation. We can provide a class with special accessor methods for the data attributes and we can then insist that the clients of the class access those attributes only through the accessor methods.

With regard to how open a Python class is from the standpoint of encapsulation, there is yet another issue that a programmer needs to be aware of. As with Perl, a Python class and a Python instance object are so open that they can be modified *after* they are brought into existence at run time.

The following script shows how easy it is to "expand" a class definition after the class is loaded into the current scope. Lines (A) through (E) define a simple class `X` with a single instance variable named `m`. The class also contains one `get` method in lines (D) and (E) for retrieving the value of this instance variable. In line (F), we construct a class instance and set the value of `m` to 10. In line (G), when we retrieve the value of `m` of the class instance, we get 10, as you'd expect.

Line (H) then defines a new function, `foo()`, that, at least at this juncture, has nothing with class `X`. But then in line (I) we assign a value to `X.foo` even though `foo` was not previously an attribute of class `X`. This act of assignment in line (I) *injects* `foo` into class `X`'s namespace and gives this name a binding which is the function definition in line (H). [Note that `foo` on the right-hand side of the assignment in line (I) will evaluate to the function object that corresponds to the definition of the `foo()` function of line (H).] This is confirmed by the output we get in line (K) when we print out the namespace dictionary associated with class `X`. Line (J) demonstrates that we can now invoke `foo()` as a method on an instance of class `X`, in just the same manner that we can invoke the originally defined method `getm()` on an instance of class `X`. In other words, the newly added method `foo()` has the same status vis-à-vis the class `X` as the originally defined method `getm()` for this class.

```
#!/usr/bin/env python

### EncapIssues1.py

#-------------------------   class X  -------------------------------
class X:                                                          #(A)
    def __init__( self, mm ):                                     #(B)
        self.m = mm                                               #(C)
    def getm(self):                                               #(D)
        return self.m                                             #(E)
#-------------------- end of class definition  ----------------------

xobj = X( 10 );                                                   #(F)
print xobj.getm()       # 10                                      #(G)

def foo( self, nn ):                                              #(H)
    print nn

X.foo = foo                                                       #(I)

xobj.foo( 100 )         # 100                                     #(J)

print X.__dict__        # {'__module__': '__main__',              #(K)
                        #  'foo': <function foo at 0x805bf1c>,
                        #  'getm': <function getm at 0x804f5a4>,
                        #  '__init__': <function __init__ at 0x804f664>,
                        #  '__doc__': None}
```

We will now show that it is not only a class that can be modified at run time, a previously constructed instance object can be too. We show a script below to demonstrate this. As before, lines (A) through (E) define a simple class `X` with a single instance variable named `m`. The class also contains one `get` method in lines (D) and (E) for retrieving the value of `m`. In line (F), we construct a class instance and set the value of `m` to 10. In line (G), when we retrieve the value of this instance variable of the instance, we get 10, as you'd expect. The fact that the class instance has only one instance variable of name `m` is confirmed by what is stored in the namespace dictionary `__dict__` associated with the instance `xobj`. This dictionary is shown in line (H). In line (I), we now invoke

```
xobj.n = 100
```

even though `n` is not an instance variable of the class `X`. This statement basically adds an additional instance variable, `n`, to the *instance* object `xobj`. This can be seen in the output we get in line (K) when we print out the namespace dictionary associated with this instance. We repeat the same exercise in lines (L), (M), and (N) where we add yet another instance variable, p, to the instance object xobj. Lines (O), (P), and (Q) demonstrate that all of the modifications we made to the instance xobj in lines (I) and (L) are confined to that instance alone. The new instance constructed in line (O) is in accord with the definition of the class in lines (A) through (E).

```
#!/usr/bin/env python

### EncapIssues2.py

#--------------------------  class X  --------------------------------
class X:                                                          #(A)
    def __init__( self, mm ):                                     #(B)
        self.m = mm                                               #(C)

    def getm(self):                                               #(D)
        return self.m                                             #(E)
#--------------------- end of class definition  -----------------------

xobj = X( 10 );                                                   #(F)
print xobj.getm()             # 10                                #(G)

print xobj.__dict__           # {'m': 10}                         #(H)

xobj.n = 100                                                      #(I)
print xobj.n                  # 100                               #(J)
print xobj.__dict__           # {'m': 10, 'n': 100}               #(K)

xobj.p = 100000                                                   #(L)
print xobj.p                  # 100000                            #(M)
print xobj.__dict__           # {'p': 100000, 'm': 10, 'n': 100}  #(N)

xobj2 = X( 300 )                                                  #(O)
print xobj2.getm()            # 300                               #(P)
print xobj2.__dict__          # {'m': 300}                        #(Q)
```

Next we show a script in which we completely alter the definition of a class — including that of its `__init__()` method — at run time after the class is loaded in. Lines (A) through (E) of the next script define a class X as before and, as before, we construct an instance of X in line (F). In line (G), we invoke the accessor function `getm()` on xobj to retrieve the value of the sole instance variable m. Lines (I), (J), and (K) then define a new three-argument `__init__()` function and line (L) *inducts* it into the namespace of the class. Along the same lines, line (M) defines a new method `getn()` and line (N) inducts that into the namespace of the class.

When we now examine the namespace associated with the class, we get what is shown in the commented-out section in and after line (P). What's interesting here that the `__init__()` in the namespace is not what it was defined to be in lines (B) and (C). The binding for the name `__init__` is now the new definition provided in lines (I), (J), and (K). This can be seen by our failure to construct a class instance in line (Q) when we try to invoke the constructor with a single argument. On the other hand, we have no trouble invoking a two-argument version of the constructor in line (R). Lines (S) and (T) show us using the originally defined `getm()` accessor for retrieving the value of the instance variable `m` and the newly inducted `getn()` for retrieving the value of the new instance variable `n`.

```
#!/usr/bin/env python

### EncapIssues3.py

#--------------------------   class X  --------------------------------
class X:                                                          #(A)
    def __init__( self, mm ):                                     #(B)
        self.m = mm                                               #(C)

    def getm(self):                                               #(D)
        return self.m                                             #(E)
#-------------------- end of class definition  -----------------------

xobj = X( 10 );                                                   #(F)
print xobj.getm()              # 10                               #(G)
print xobj.__dict__            # {'m': 10}                        #(H)

def __init__( self, mm, nn ):                                     #(I)
    self.m = mm                                                   #(J)
    self.n = nn                                                   #(K)

X.__init__ = __init__                                             #(L)

def getn( self ):                                                 #(M)
    return self.n                                                 #(N)

X.getn = getn                                                     #(O)

print X.__dict__       # {'__module__': '__main__',               #(P)
                       #  'getn': <function getn at 0x804f664>,
                       #  'getm': <function getm at 0x805a47c>,
                       #  '__init__': <function __init__ at 0x805bf1c>,
                       #  '__doc__': None}
```

```
#xobj2 = X( 20 )                # ERROR                              #(Q)

xobj3 = X( 100, 200 )                                                #(R)
print xobj3.getm()              # 100                                #(S)
print xobj3.getn()              # 200                                #(T)
```

7.6 DEFINING CLASS VARIABLES, STATIC METHODS, AND CLASS METHODS

The data attributes in most of the Python classes we have shown so far were of the instance-specific kind. But sometimes it is useful to endow a class with data attributes that are global with respect to all the instances constructed from that class. Such attributes are commonly considered to be *static* or *class-based*. We will refer to the global data attributes as the *class variables* of a class; this differentiates such data attributes from the instance variables we have used frequently thus far.

In addition to class variables, we can also have methods that are known as *static methods* and *class methods*. Such methods do not expect their implicitly-supplied first argument to be an instance of the class.[17] While in many other languages, Perl included, static and class methods would be considered to be the same, Python differentiates between the two. A static method in Python receives no implicit arguments when it is invoked. On the other hand, a class method is implicitly supplied with the class object as its first argument.[18]

In this section we will see the usefulness of the class variables and the static and class methods. Whereas a data attribute becomes static, meaning class-based, simply by virtue of its declaration outside of any method in a class definition, for a method to become either static or class-based, you have to use special syntax, as we will illustrate in this section.

First let's see through an example why one would want to define a class with a class variable. Paralleling a similar example in Section 6.6 of the previous chapter, let's say we want a hypothetical factory to turn out robots, each stamped with the name of the owner and, even more importantly, with a serial number. Obviously, there would need to exist some memory location that would store the next available

[17] We can refer to those methods that expect their implicitly-supplied first argument to be an instance of a class as *instance methods*.

[18] Note that although `__new__()` is also supplied with the class object as its first argument, it is a static method. When the system needs to invoke `__new__()` to customize memory allocation for a new instance, the first of the arguments supplied explicitly to the method is the class whose instance is under construction.

serial number for the next robot to roll off the assembly line. In the script below, the class variable `next_serial_number` in line (B) serves this purpose. Being outside the definition of `__init__()`, this class variable will reside in the namespace of the class itself. When a new robot is built by a call to the constructor, as in line (N), the serial number to use is fetched by the per-instance method `get_next_idNum()` of line (F). This method returns the serial number to use for the newly constructed robot and increments `next_serial_number` for the next robot. This is demonstrated by the output shown for the two different robots constructed in lines (O) and (Q).

```
#!/usr/bin/env python

### Static1.py

#-------------------------  class Robot  -----------------------------
class Robot:                                                       #(A)
    next_serial_number = 1                                         #(B)

    def __init__( self, an_owner ):                                #(C)
        self.owner = an_owner                                      #(D)
        self.idNum = self.get_next_idNum()                         #(E)

    def get_next_idNum( self ):                                    #(F)
        new_idNum = Robot.next_serial_number                       #(G)
        Robot.next_serial_number += 1                              #(H)
        return  new_idNum                                          #(I)

    def get_owner( self ):                                         #(J)
        return self.owner                                          #(K)

    def get_idNum( self ):                                         #(L)
        return self.idNum                                          #(M)
#-------------------  end of class definition  -----------------------

robot1 = Robot( "Zaphod" )                                         #(N)
print robot1.get_owner(), robot1.get_idNum()        # Zaphod 1     #(O)

robot2 = Robot( "Trillian" )                                       #(P)
print robot2.get_owner(), robot2.get_idNum()        # Trillian 2   #(Q)
```

Let's now talk about static methods. There are two ways to declare a method to be static. In the older approach (which can still be used), a method is declared static by binding the method name to the callable object returned by `staticmethod()`. In the more modern syntax, the same effect is achieved by using the *method decorator* `@staticmethod`.

In the script shown next, Static2.py, we wish for foo() and bar() to serve as static methods for class X. Note the following older syntax we use in lines (F), (G), and (H):

```
def foo():
    print "foo called"
foo = staticmethod( foo )
```

and following newer syntax used in lines (I), (J), and (K):[19]

```
@staticmethod
def bar():
    print "bar called"
```

The class X in the following script also includes a class variable m initialized in line (B) and an instance variable n initialized in the __init__() method in line (C). Line (D) defines a get method for the class variable m and line (E) a get method for the instance variable n. In addition to the methods foo() and bar(), the class also defines a "method" baz() in lines (L) and (M). As we will show, baz() will turn out to be inaccessible either as an instance method or as a static method.

We construct an instance xobj in line (N) and show the by-now routine retrieval of the instance variable n by invoking getn() on the instance xobj in line (O). Lines (P), (Q), and (R) show us three different ways of accessing the class variable m of line (B).

Lines (S) and (T) demonstrate foo() behaving as a static method of class X. We can call foo() either directly on the class, as we do in line (S), or on an instance of the class, as shown in line (T). When a static method is called on an instance, the instance is *not* passed as an argument to the method — unlike what happens with

---

[19]Under the hood, the two different ways of declaring static methods work the same. That is because

```
@A
def f():
  ...
```

is equivalent to

```
def f():
  ...
f = A(f)
```

Even more generally [66]

```
@A@B@C
def f():
  ...
```

is equivalent to

```
def f():
  ...
f = A(B(C(f)))
```

instance methods. *Instead, the instance on which a static method is called is used merely to find the name of the class corresponding to the instance.* Lines (U) and (V) demonstrate that `bar()` is also a static method of class `X` just like `foo()`. Finally, lines (W) and (X) show that `baz()` of lines (L) and (M) can behave neither as an instance method, nor as a static method for reasons that should be clear by now.

```
#!/usr/bin/env python

### Static2.py

#----------------------------  class X ---------------------------------
class X:                                                          #(A)

    m = 1                                                         #(B)

    def __init__( self, nn ):                                     #(C)
        self.n = nn

    def getm( self ):                                             #(D)
        return X.m

    def getn( self ):                                             #(E)
        return self.n

    # Use the older wrapper-based syntax for
    # defining a static method:
    def foo():                                                    #(F)
        print "foo called"                                        #(G)
    foo = staticmethod( foo )                                     #(H)

    # Use the newer decorator based syntax:
    @staticmethod                                                 #(I)
    def bar():                                                    #(J)
        print "bar called"                                        #(K)

    # This will not serve either as a static method
    # or as a class method or as an instance method:
    def baz():                                                    #(L)
        print "baz called"                                        #(M)

#--------------------  end of class definition  ------------------------

xobj = X( 10 )                                                    #(N)
print xobj.getn()                   # 10                          #(O)

print X.m                           # 1                           #(P)
print xobj.m                        # 1                           #(Q)
```

```
print xobj.getm()              # 1                                  #(R)

# Static method called on class:
X.foo()                        # foo called                         #(S)

# Static method called on instance:
xobj.foo()                     # foo called                         #(T)

# Static method called on class:
X.bar()                        # bar called                         #(U)

# Static method called on instance:
xobj.bar()                     # bar called                         #(V)

#X.baz()                       # Error                              #(W)
#xobj.baz()                    # Error                              #(X)
```

With the basic idea of how to define class variables and static methods out of the way, what follows is a longer script that demonstrates that the same idea works for static methods with arguments and for static methods that need to call other static methods in the same class.

The next script, `Static3.py`, defines a class `X` with a class variable `m` in line (B). The class also contains two other class variables in lines (C) and (D), `p` and `q`, that are bound to lambda functions. The lambda object associated with `q` is made static by redefining the class variable `q` in line (E) by setting its value to the callable returned by `staticmethod()`.

Line (F) then defines the `__init__()` method for the class. This method declares `n` to be an instance variable. The accessor method in lines (G) and (H) is for returning the value of the class variable `m` of line (B). This accessor method can only be invoked on an instance of class `X`. The accessor method in lines (I) and (J) is for returning the value of the instance variable `n`.

Lines (K), (L), and (M) define a no-argument static method `foo()`, and lines (N), (O), and (P) a two-argument static method `bar()`. Lines (Q) through (V) define two static methods, `baz1()` and `baz2()`, with the latter using the former.

In the test code, we construct in line (W) an instance `xobj` from class `X`. Line (X) retrieves the value of the instance data attribute `n`. Lines (Y), (Z), and (a) show the three different ways in which we can retrieve the class variable `m`. In line (b), we invoke the static method `foo()` of line (M) on the class itself, and in line (c) we do the same on the instance. As we should expect, we get the same result from both calls. On the other hand, when we call the instance method bound to `p` of line (C) in the commented-out line (d), we get an error, as we should — since an instance method can only be called on an instance, as shown by the call in line (e). Finally, in lines (f) through (k) we call the other static methods, in each case first on the class and then on the instance, with expected results.

```
#!/usr/bin/env python

### Static3.py

#---------------------------- class X ---------------------------------
class X:                                                            #(A)

    m = 1                                                           #(B)

    p = lambda self, arg1, arg2 = 10: arg1 + arg2                   #(C)

    q = lambda arg1, arg2 = 100: arg1 + arg2                        #(D)
    q = staticmethod( q )                                           #(E)

    def __init__( self, nn ):                                       #(F)
        self.n = nn

    def getm( self ):                                               #(G)
        return X.m                                                  #(H)

    def getn( self ):                                               #(I)
        return self.n                                               #(J)

    def foo():                                                      #(K)
        print "foo called"                                          #(L)
    foo = staticmethod( foo )                                       #(M)

    def bar(arg1, arg2):                                            #(N)
        print arg1 + arg2;                                          #(O)
    bar = staticmethod( bar )                                       #(P)

    def baz1( arg ):                                                #(Q)
        return 2 * arg                                              #(R)
    baz1 = staticmethod( baz1 )                                     #(S)

    def baz2( arg1, arg2 ):                                         #(T)
        return arg1 + 3 * X.baz1( arg2 )                            #(U)
    baz2 = staticmethod( baz2 )                                     #(V)

#----------------------------- Test Code ----------------------------

xobj = X( 10 )                                                      #(W)
print xobj.getn()                # 10                               #(X)
```

```
print X.m                          # 1                                #(Y)
print xobj.m                       # 1                                #(Z)
print xobj.getm()                  # 1                                #(a)

X.foo( )                           # foo called                       #(b)
xobj.foo()                         # foo called                       #(c)

# print X.p(20)                    # Error                            #(d)
print xobj.p(20)                   # 30                               #(e)

print X.q(20)                      # 120                              #(f)
print xobj.q(20)                   # 120                              #(g)

X.bar( 30, 40 )                    # 70                               #(h)
xobj.bar( 30, 40 )                 # 70                               #(i)

print X.baz2( 4, 5 )               # 34                               #(j)
print xobj.baz2( 4, 5 )            # 34                               #(k)
```

As mentioned at the beginning of this section, Python also allows for a method to be declared as a *class method*. Like an instance method, a class method is also provided with an implicit first argument, but now that argument is the class itself. This is illustrated with the help of the following example where we have used the older wrapper-based syntax in lines (B), (C), and (D) and the more modern decorator syntax in lines (E), (F), and (G) to declare two different class methods. Note that in both methods, the parameter `cls` will be set directly to the class corresponding to the object on which the method is invoked. It is because of that reason we are able to access the name of the class in lines (C) and (G).

```
#!/usr/bin/env python

### ClassMethod.py

#----------------------------  class X  ---------------------------------
class X:                                                              #(A)
    def foo(cls):                                                     #(B)
        print "foo() called on object", cls.__name__                  #(C)
    foo = classmethod( foo )                                          #(D)

    @classmethod                                                      #(E)
    def bar(cls):                                                     #(F)
        print "bar() called on object", cls.__name__                  #(G)

#--------------------  end of class definition  ------------------------
```

```
xobj = X()                                                          #(H)

X.foo()                      # foo() called on object X             #(I)
xobj.foo()                   # foo() called on object X             #(J)

X.bar()                      # bar() called on object X             #(K)
xobj.bar()                   # bar() called on object X             #(L)
```

7.6.1 An Instance Variable Hides a Class Variable of the Same Name

The purpose of this subsection is to point out that when `instance.attribute` or `self.attribute` notation is used to access a data attribute of a class, an instance variable of a given name will hide a class variable of the same name. When a class variable gets hidden in this manner, it can still be accessed with the `class.attribute` notation.

Shown below is a script with two class variables `m` and `n` in lines (B) and (C), respectively. In line (E), we also define `m` to be an instance variable. Lines (F) and (H) define two access functions, `getm()` and `getn()`, using identical syntax based on the `self.attribute` notation. Finally, line (J) defines a method `foo()` that uses two different notations to access the attribute name `m`: the `class.attribute` notation and the `self.attribute` notation.

As we can see from the outputs shown in lines (M) and (N), whereas calling `X.m` returns the class-based global value of the variable `m`, calling `xobj.m` returns the instance-specific value. On the other hand, for the class variable `n`, calling both `X.n` and `xobj.n` in lines (Q) and (R) returns the same value — the value assigned in line (C). Line (O) shows that since the `getm()` method uses the `self.attribute` notation in line (G), it returns the instance-specific value associated with the name `m`. Line (P) demonstrates that invoking the `self.attribute` notation inside a class — in this case in the definition of the method `foo` — has the same effect as it does outside; it retrieves the instance-specific value associated with the variable rather than the class-based global value assuming that the same name was used for both.

```
#!/usr/bin/env python

### InstanceVarHidesClassVar.py

#----------------------------  class X  --------------------------------
class X:                                                            #(A)
    m = 10                                                          #(B)
    n = 20                                                          #(C)
```

```
    def __init__( self, mm ):                                         #(D)
        self.m = mm                                                   #(E)

    def getm( self ):                                                 #(F)
        return self.m                                                 #(G)

    def getn( self ):                                                 #(H)
        return self.n                                                 #(I)

    def foo( self ):                                                  #(J)
        return X.m + self.getm();                                     #(K)

#-------------------- end of class definition -----------------------

xobj = X( 100 )                                                       #(L)

print X.m                         # 10                                #(M)
print xobj.m                      # 100                               #(N)
print xobj.getm()                 # 100                               #(O)
print xobj.foo()                  # 110                               #(P)
print X.n                         # 20                                #(Q)
print xobj.n                      # 20                                #(R)
```

7.7 PRIVATE DATA ATTRIBUTES AND METHODS

Python provides a mechanism for endowing a class with private data and methods. This is done through name mangling in such a way that a private name becomes "inaccessible" outside the class. A data attribute name or a method name that has at least two leading underscores and at most one trailing underscore is considered to be private to that class. However, it is important to bear in mind that the "privateness" achieved in this manner still depends a great deal on programmer cooperation. Since the result of name mangling is predictable in advance, the names can still be reached outside the class through their mangled versions.

The class `X` in the next script has:

- A private class variable `__m` in line (B)
- A public class variable `n` in line (C)
- A private instance variable `__p` in line (E)
- A public instance variable `q` in line (F)

In line (G), we construct an instance `xobj` of class `X`. As shown in line (H), we cannot use the usual formula for accessing the instance variable `__p` of `xobj`. However, we have no problem doing the same for the instance variable `q` in line (I).

With regard to the class variables, we are unable to access `__m` using the usual syntax in lines (J) and (K), whereas we have no problem with accessing the class variable `n` in lines (L) and (M).

This brings us to the issue of how Python mangles the private names. A name that has at least two underscores and at most one trailing underscore is renamed by the compiler by attaching to the name an underscore followed by the class name. For example, a name such as

```
__m
```

will be mangled into

```
_X__m
```

if the name of the class is `X`. Obviously, then, it should be possible to access the so-called private names using their new names. This is demonstrated in lines (N), (O), and (P) of the script. Lines (Q) and (R) show that it is the mangled names that the compiler stores in the namespace dictionaries of the class and the class instance.

Lines (S) through (X) demonstrate the fact that a name can be made private only inside a class. Since a data attribute (or a method) can also spring into existence merely by virtue of assignment, one naturally wonders if a private attribute could also be created by assignment outside the class. That this cannot be done is shown by lines (S), (T), and (U) for the case of the class variables, and by lines (V), (W), and (X) for the case of instance variables. When we assign to `X.__m` in line (S), we create a new public class variable `__m` for class `X`, but this is not the same as the private data attribute `__m` of line (B). This can be seen by outputting the class namespace dictionary in line (U). It has an entry for `_X__m`, which corresponds to the `__m` of line (B), and for `__m`, which corresponds to the `__m` of line (S). Line (V) shows us creating a new instance variable `__p` by assignment specifically for the instance `xobj`. But this `__p` is not the same as the `__p` of line (E). When we display the namespace dictionary associated with the instance `xobj` in line (X), we see an entry for `_X__p`, which corresponds to `__p` of line (E), and an entry for `__p`, which corresponds to `__p` of line (V).

```
#!/usr/bin/env python

# Private.py

#------------------------------  class X  ------------------------------
class X:                                                              #(A)
    __m = 10                                                          #(B)
    n = 20                                                            #(C)
```

```
    def __init__( self, pp, qq ):                                   #(D)
        self.__p = pp                                               #(E)
        self.q = qq + self.__p * X.__m + X.n                        #(F)

#------------------------------  Test Code  ------------------------------
xobj = X( 30, 40 )                                                  #(G)

#print xobj.__p        # ERROR                                      #(H)
print xobj.q           # 360                                        #(I)

#print X.__m           # ERROR                                      #(J)
#print xobj.__m        # ERROR                                      #(K)

print X.n              # 20                                         #(L)
print xobj.n           # 20                                         #(M)

print X._X__m          # 10                                         #(N)
print xobj._X__m       # 10                                         #(O)
print xobj._X__p       # 30                                         #(P)

print X.__dict__       # {'__module__': '__main__',                 #(Q)
                       #  '__doc__': None,
                       #  '_X__m': 10,
                       #  '__init__': <function __init__ at 0x804f664>,
                       #  'n': 20}

print xobj.__dict__    # {'_X__p': 30, 'q': 360}                    #(R)

X.__m = 1000           # but this is not the same as __m of line (B) #(S)
print xobj.__m         # 1000                                       #(T)
print X.__dict__       # {'__module__': '__main__',                 #(U)
                       #  '_X__m': 10,
                       #  '__m': 1000,
                       #  '__doc__': None,
                       #  '__init__': <function __init__ at 0x804f664>,
                       #  'n': 20}

xobj.__p = 2000        # but this is not the same as __p of line (E) #(V)

print xobj.__p         # 2000                                       #(W)

print xobj.__dict__    # {'_X__p': 30, 'q': 360, '__p': 2000}       #(X)
```

Our discussion so far has focused on private data attributes of a class. One can also define private methods, as we show in the script below. Obviously, since such a method is not directly accessible outside the class,[20] it can only be used for internal purposes in the other functions of a class.

The following script contains a private method `__bar()` in lines (E) and (F). This method is used in the definition of the method `foo()` in line (H). That `__bar()` cannot be invoked as a regular method on a class instance is shown in line (K). However, when we invoke the method `foo()` in line (L), we have no problems even though the implementation of `foo()` uses `__bar()`.

```
#!/usr/bin/env python

# PrivateFunct.py

#------------------------------  class X  ------------------------------
class X:                                                            #(A)
    __m = 10                                                        #(B)

    def __init__( self, pp ):                                       #(C)
        self.p = pp                                                 #(D)

    def __bar( self ):                                              #(E)
        self.p = self.p * X.__m                                     #(F)

    def foo( self ):                                                #(G)
        self.__bar()                                                #(H)

#-----------------------------  Test Code  ------------------------------
xobj = X( 30 )                                                      #(I)
print xobj.p                # 30                                    #(J)

#xobj.__bar()               # ERROR                                 #(K)

xobj.foo()                                                          #(L)
print xobj.p                # 300                                   #(M)
```

[20] Assuming that a script follows certain naming conventions and does not try to access a method through its mangled name.

7.8 DEFINING A CLASS WITH SLOTS

New-style classes allow the `__slots__` attribute of a class to be used to name a list of instance variables. Subsequently, no additional instance variables can be assigned to instances of such a class. Consider, for example, the class `X` in the following script. It is a new-style class because it is derived from the root class `object`. Line (B) declares the `__slots__` attribute to consist of a list of two instance variables `a` and `b`. Line (C) then creates an instance `xobj` of class `X`. Lines (D) and (E) show that it is okay to assign to the instance variables `a` and `b` of the class. But, as shown in the commented-out line (F), it is not okay to do so for what we wanted to be a new instance variable `c`.

If `X` were to be a classic class — which would be the case if we did *not* subclass `X` from `object` in line (A) — there would be no problem with the assignment in line (F) notwithstanding the `slots` declaration in line (B). For a classic class, the `slots` declaration is a no-op, you could say.

We should also mention that when a class is equipped with the `__slots__` attribute, its instances do not get the namespace `__dict__` attribute. So uncommenting the commented-out line (G) would elicit a run-time error from Python. Line (H) shows the namespace dictionary associated with the class.

```
#!/usr/bin/env python

### ClassWithSlots.py

class X( object ):                                                  #(A)
    __slots__ = ['a', 'b']                                          #(B)

xobj = X()                                                          #(C)

xobj.a = 10              # ok                                       #(D)
xobj.b = 20              # ok                                       #(E)
#xobj.c = 30             # Error                                    #(F)
                         # AttributeError: 'X' object has no attribute 'c'

#print xobj.__dict__ # Error                                        #(G)
          # AttributeError: 'X' object has no attribute '__dict__'

print X.__dict__                                                    #(H)
                         # {'a': <member 'a' of 'X' objects>,
                         #  '__module__': '__main__',
                         #  'b': <member 'b' of 'X' objects>,
                         #  '__slots__': ['a', 'b'],
                         #  '__doc__': None}
```

It should be obvious from the above discussion that if we set the `__slots__` to am empty list for a class by

```
__slots__ = []
```

the instances created from such a class would not be allowed to have any instance variables.

7.9 DESCRIPTOR CLASSES IN PYTHON

A *descriptor class* is a new-style class with an override definition[21] for at least one of the special `__get__()`, `__set__()`, and `__delete__()` methods. When an instance of such a class is used as the value for a class variable in another class, accesses to these values are processed by the `__get__()` and `__set__()` methods of the descriptor class. The class whose class variable values are instances of the descriptor class is known as the *owner class.*

Shown in the next script is a simple descriptor class `DescriptorSimple`, a new-style class obviously since it is subclassed from `object`, that is provided with a single instance variable, `val`, in line (C). The print statements in the override definitions of `__get__()` and `__set__()` in lines (E) and (H) are merely to see these methods getting invoked automatically.[22] Lines (J) through (M) define `UserClass`, again a new-style class, with three class variables, `d1`, `d2`, and `d3`. The first two of these are set to instances of the `DescriptorSimple` class.

We then construct an instance of `UserClass` in line (N). When we try to retrieve the value of the `d1` attribute of the class in line (O), the following message is displayed on the screen:

```
Retrieving with owner instance:  \
                        <__main__.UserClass object at 0x403b5b2c>
and owner type:  <class '__main__.UserClass'>

100
```

where the message in the first two lines is produced by the print statement in line (F). The number shown in the third line is all that is returned by the access `u.d1` in line (O). The same thing happens when Python executes `u.d2` in line (P). Now the following will be displayed on the screen:

---

[21]Chapter 9 explains what it means for a class to override a method of its superclass.

[22]The calls to `__get__()` and `__set__()` of a descriptor class are orchestrated by the `__getattribute__()` method of the owner class. (The owner class will inherit this method from `object`.) If the owner class overrides `__getattribute__()`, the methods `__get__()` and `__set__()` may not be called when accessing instances made from the descriptor class. This also points to why the owner class must also be a new-style class.

```
Retrieving with owner instance:  \
                        <__main__.UserClass object at 0x403b5b2c>
and owner type:  <class '__main__.UserClass'>

200
```

where the value 200 is what is returned by `u.d2` in (P). For comparison, line (Q) shows us accessing the class variable d3 of the class `UserClass`. This straightforwardly results in retrieval of the value of the class variable.

As shown in line (D), `__get__()` is defined with three parameters. The first of these is for the instance of the descriptor class being used by the owner class; the second for the owner-class instance in question; and the third the type of the owner class. If the class variable defined with a descriptor class is invoked directly on the owner class, the second parameter is automatically set to `None`. This is shown by the output produced by the retrieval `UserClass.d1` in line (R):

```
Retrieving with owner instance:  None
and owner type:  <class '__main__.UserClass'>

100
```

To see the `DescriptorSimple`'s `__set__()` in action, we alter the value of the class variables `d1` and `d2` in lines (S) and (T). The assignment in line (S) causes the following output in the terminal window:

```
Setting attribute for owner:  \
             <__main__.UserClass object at 0x403b5b2c>
```

while changing the value stored in the descriptor class instance `d1`. Note from line (G) that `__set__()` is also defined with three parameters, the first for the instance of the descriptor class in question, the second the owner instance, and the third for the new value for the datum stored in the descriptor class instance. This is borne out by the message displayed above. The same message is printed out by the assignment in line (T). Subsequently, when in lines (U) and (V) we retrieve the values for `d1` and `d2`, we see the new values.

We will next point out that `__get__()` and `__set__()` do not behave symmetrically with respect to set accesses if made directly on the owner class, as opposed to on the instances of the owner class. The point being made here is that whereas both `u.d1` and `UserClass.d1` will cause the descriptor class's `__get__()` to be invoked for retrieval, the syntax `u.d1=something` and `UserClass.d1=something` do not behave identically. The former, as you would expect, causes the `__set__()` of the descriptor class to be invoked for changing the datum stored in the descriptor class instance. The latter, however, has a totally different effect — it creates a new entry for the name `d1` in `UserClass`'s namespace dictionary.

In other words, resetting `d1` as shown in line (X) turns `d1` into an *ordinary* class variable and its previous meaning as an instance of a descriptor class is lost. This can be seen by comparing `UserClass`'s namespace dictionaries before and after the assignment in line (X).

```
#!/usr/bin/env python

### DescriptorClass.py

#----------------------  class DescriptorSimple  ----------------------

class DescriptorSimple( object ):                                   #(A)

    def __init__( self, initval=None ):                             #(B)
        self.val = initval                                          #(C)

    def __get__( self, owner_inst, owner_type ):                    #(D)
        print "Retrieving with owner instance: ", owner_inst,     \
                          " and owner type: ", owner_type           #(E)
        return self.val                                             #(F)

    def __set__( self, owner_inst, val ):                           #(G)
        print 'Setting attribute for owner instance: ', owner_inst  #(H)
        self.val = val                                              #(I)

#----------------------  class UserClass  ---------------------------

class UserClass( object ):                                          #(J)
    d1 = DescriptorSimple( 100 )                                    #(K)
    d2 = DescriptorSimple( 200 )                                    #(L)
    d3 = 300                                                        #(M)

#---------------------------  Test Code  ----------------------------

u = UserClass()                                                     #(N)
print u.d1                   # 100                                  #(O)
print u.d2                   # 200                                  #(P)
print u.d3                   # 300                                  #(Q)

print UserClass.d1           # 100                                  #(R)

u.d1 = 400                                                          #(S)
u.d2 = 500                                                          #(T)

print u.d1                   # 400                                  #(U)
print u.d2                   # 500                                  #(V)

print UserClass.__dict__                                            #(W)
    # {'__module__': '__main__', '__doc__': None,
```

```
    #  '__dict__': <attribute '__dict__' of 'UserClass' objects>,
    #  '__weakref__': <attribute '__weakref__' of 'UserClass' objects>,
    #  'd2': <__main__.DescriptorSimple object at 0x403b5b0c>,
    #  'd3': 300,
    #  'd1': <__main__.DescriptorSimple object at 0x403b59ec>}

UserClass.d1 = 600           # Does not do what you might think!!!    #(X)

print UserClass.__dict__                                               #(Y)
    # {'__module__': '__main__', '__doc__': None,
    #  '__dict__': <attribute '__dict__' of 'UserClass' objects>,
    #  '__weakref__': <attribute '__weakref__' of 'UserClass' objects>,
    #  'd2': <__main__.DescriptorSimple object at 0x403b5b0c>,
    #  'd3': 300,
    #  'd1': 600}

print u.__dict__             # {}                                      #(Z)
```

With the basic ideas about descriptor classes out of the way, we will now show an example that illustrates that the use of a descriptor class is not limited to just providing values for the class variables. One can use a descriptor class just as effectively for associating function definitions with class variables.[23] The script that follows uses the same descriptor class we showed in the previous script to create function bindings for the class variables of an owner class. These functions then behave like static methods of the class.

In the following script, the descriptor class, `MyDescriptor`, is the same as used in the previous script, except that now we do not print out the messages that show the invocations of the `__get__()` and the `__set__()` methods. The owner class, `OwnerClass`, in lines (I) through (M) is provided with two class variables, `d1` and `d2`, whose values are set to the two descriptor instances constructed with function-object arguments. The `MyDescriptor` instance assigned to `d1` in line (K) is constructed with the function-object `foo` defined in the global namespace in line (H), and the one assigned to `d2` in line (L) constructed with the function-object `bar` defined in the namespace of the `OwnerClass` class in line (J).

The testing portion of the script begins in line (N) by constructing an instance `x` of the `OwnerClass`. Retrieval of the values of `x.d1` and `x.d2` of this instance in lines (O) and (P) reveals the fact that their values are function objects. When we execute these function objects in lines (T) and (U), the expected happens; invocation of `x.d1()` causes the method definition of `foo()` of line (H) to be executed, and the invocation of `x.d2()` causes the method definition of `bar()` of line (J) to be

---

[23]In fact, this is how the descriptor `staticmethod` works for declaring static methods of a class. See Section 7.6.

executed. Lines (S) and (R) show the namespace dictionaries associated with the class `OwnerClass` and with its instance, respectively.

Line (V) shows that it would be an error to call what is presumably a static method, `bar()`, directly on the instance `x`. This is to be expected since the call in line (V) will invoke `bar()` with one argument that would be supplied implicitly whereas the function is defined to take no arguments. However, the same method can be invoked through the class variable `d2`, as shown in line (U). What this shows is that if we wanted `bar()` to act like a static method of `OwnerClass`, we should be doing so through the class variable `d2`.

Lines (W) and (X) show that we are able to call `d1()` and `d2()` directly on the class `OwnerClass`, as must be the case for all static methods of a class.

In line (Y) we define a new method, `baz()`, and then in line (Z) we assign it to the class variable `d1`. This we do for exercising the `__set__()` method of the descriptor class that is defined in lines (F) and (G). The assignment in line (Z) causes the invocation of the `__set__()` method of the descriptor class to alter the value of the `val` instance variable of the `MyDescriptor` instance held by `d1`. Because the assignment in line (Z) merely causes a modification of the `MyDescriptor` instance already held by `d1`, as opposed to the creation of a new `MyDescriptor` instance, the contents of the namespace dictionary for the `OwnerClass` remain unchanged, as demonstrated by the fact that the namespace dictionaries printed out in lines (S) and (d) are the same.

```
#!/usr/bin/env python

### DescriptorClass2.py

#------------------------  class MyDescriptor  ----------------------

class MyDescriptor( object ):                                     #(A)

    def __init__( self, initval=None ):                           #(B)
        self.val = initval                                        #(C)

    def __get__( self, owner_inst, owner_type ):                  #(D)
        return self.val                                           #(E)

    def __set__( self, owner_inst, val ):                         #(F)
        self.val = val                                            #(G)

#--------------------------  global foo()  --------------------------

def foo():                                                        #(H)
    print "foo called"
```

```
#-------------------------  class OwnerClass  --------------------------

class OwnerClass( object ):                                          #(I)
    def bar():                                                       #(J)
        print "bar called"
    d1 = MyDescriptor( foo )                                         #(K)
    d2 = MyDescriptor( bar )                                         #(L)
    d3 = 300                                                         #(M)

#-----------------------------  Test Code  -----------------------------

x = OwnerClass()                                                     #(N)
print x.d1                   # <function foo at 0x403b225c>          #(O)
print x.d2                   # <function bar at 0x403b2dbc>          #(P)
print x.d3                   # 300                                   #(Q)

print x.__dict__             # {}                                    #(R)

print OwnerClass.__dict__                                            #(S)
    # {'__module__': '__main__', 'bar': <function bar at 0x403b2dbc>,
    #  '__doc__': None,
    #  '__dict__': <attribute '__dict__' of 'OwnerClass' objects>,
    #  '__weakref__': <attribute '__weakref__' of 'OwnerClass' objects>,
    #  'd2': <__main__.MyDescriptor object at 0x403b5a8c>,
    #  'd3': 300,
    #  'd1': <__main__.MyDescriptor object at 0x403b5b0c>}

x.d1()                       # foo called                            #(T)
x.d2()                       # bar called                            #(U)

#x.bar()                     # ERROR                                 #(V)

OwnerClass.d1()              # foo called                            #(W)
OwnerClass.d2()              # bar called                            #(X)

def baz():                                                           #(Y)
    print "baz called"

x.d1 = baz                                                           #(Z)
x.d1()                       # baz called                            #(a)
OwnerClass.d1()              # baz called                            #(b)

print x.__dict__             # {}                                    #(c)

print OwnerClass.__dict__                                            #(d)
    # {'__module__': '__main__', 'bar': <function bar at 0x403b2dbc>,
    #  '__doc__': None,
    #  '__dict__': <attribute '__dict__' of 'OwnerClass' objects>,
    #  '__weakref__': <attribute '__weakref__' of 'OwnerClass' objects>,
```

```
#  'd2': <__main__.MyDescriptor object at 0x403b5a8c>,
#  'd3': 300,
#  'd1': <__main__.MyDescriptor object at 0x403b5b0c>}
```

7.10 OPERATOR OVERLOADING AND CLASS CUSTOMIZATION

One very nice thing about Python is that support for operator overloading and class customization is built into the language itself. In what follows, we will explain this feature of the language with the help of a user-defined container class `XArray`. Our goal is to overload certain operators so that one can write abbreviated and user-friendly syntax for operations that involve instances of this class.

Given a user-defined class `XArray`, let's say that you want to be able to "add" two `XArray` instances by using the `+` operator, as in

```
x1 = XArray(...)
x2 = XArray(...)

x3 = x1 + x2
```

In Python, all you have to do for the `x1 + x2` syntax to work is to provide the class `XArray` with a definition for the `__add__()` method. So your class definition would look something like:

```
class XArray:
    ....
    def __add__( self, xobj ):
        ....
        tell Python what you mean by the addition
        of the objects bound to self and xobj
        ....
```

The "add" example involves giving meaning to the binary operator `+` for a new type. Python also allows you to create your own meaning for unary operations. Consider the very commonly used unary operation of converting an object to its printable string representation. Suppose I want to be able to do the following:

```
x = XArray( ... )
print x
```

When Python sees `print x`, it implicitly calls the method `x.__str__()` for creating a printable string that would represent the instance `x` in some way.

What we have shown so far are only two of a very large number of overloadings that a programmer can supply to customize the behavior of a user-defined class.

Shown below is a longer list of the more commonly used specially named methods for the overloading of various operators. As we explained above, when a programmer supplies definitions for these methods, he/she can subsequently use a more abbreviated syntax for eliciting certain behaviors from the class and the instances made from the class. But note that providing a definition for some of these methods may not make sense for a given class. Depending on the class definition, the programmer must pick and choose the methods that are most appropriate for his/her class.[24] [25]

`__str__(self)` The definition provided for this method is called implicitly by the `str()` constructor to return a printable representation of the object.[26] This definition is also called implicitly by the Python's `print` function.

`__lt__(self, other)` gives meaning to the operation `x<y` where `x` is an instance of the class for which the method definition is supplied and `y` anything that makes sense to the method definition. The parameter `self` would be set to `x` and the parameter `other` to `y`.

`__le__(self, other)` gives meaning to the operation `x<=y` (see the above entry for `__lt__()` for what `x` and `y` stand for).

`__gt__(self, other)` gives meaning to the operation `x>y` (see the above entry for `__lt__()` for what `x` and `y` stand for).

`__ge__(self, other)` gives meaning to the operation `x>=y` (see the above entry for `__lt__()` for what `x` and `y` stand for).

`__eq__(self, other)` gives meaning to the operation `x==y` (see the above entry for `__lt__()` for what `x` and `y` stand for).

`__ne__(self, other)` gives meaning to the operation `x!=y` (see the above entry for `__lt__()` for what `x` and `y` stand for).

`__add__(self, other)` gives meaning to the operation `x+y` (see the above entry for `__lt__()` for what `x` and `y` stand for).

`__div__(self, other)` gives meaning to the operation `x/y` (see the above entry for `__lt__()` for what `x` and `y` stand for).

[24] For an example, the reader may wish to see the author's `BitVector` class [40] for the overloadings and other customizations supplied for that class.

[25] The reader is referred to Section 3.4 of the Python Reference Manual for all of the customizations that are possible for a user-defined class.

[26] A related method is `__repr__()` that is also used to create a string representation of an object. But this string representation must be a valid Python expression that can be used to recreate the object. Since that is not always possible for objects that include other nested objects, `__repr__()` must, in the least, return a printable string of the form `<some_useful_description>`.

`__sub__(self, other)` gives meaning to the operation `x-y` (see the above entry for `__lt__()` for what `x` and `y` stand for). Its meaning in the `operator` module is to subtract the right argument number from the left argument number.

`__mul__(self, other)` gives meaning to the operation `x*y` (see the above entry for `__lt__()` for what `x` and `y` stand for). Its meaning in the `operator` module is to multiply the numbers corresponding to the two operands.

`__pow__(self, a)` gives meaning to the operation `x**y` where `x` is the instance of the class for which the method is defined and `a` whatever makes sense to the definition of the method. Its meaning in the `operator` module is to raise the first argument number to the power of the second argument number.

`__floordiv__(self, other)` gives meaning to the operation `x//y` (see the above entry for `__lt__()` for the meaning of `x` and `y`). Its meaning in the `operator` module is to carry out a "floor division" of the first argument number by the second argument number.[27]

`__neg__(self)` gives meaning to the operation `-x` for returning the "negative" of an instance `x` of the class for which the method is defined (the parameter `self` would be set to `x`). Its meaning in the `operator` module is to negate a number.

`__not__(self)` gives meaning to the operation `not x` where `x` is an instance of the class for which the method is defined (the parameter `self` would be set to `x`). Its meaning in the `operator` module is to take logical negation of Boolean value.

`__abs__(self)` tells Python how to compute the absolute value of an instance (the parameter `self` would be set to the instance). Its meaning in the `operator` module is to return the absolute value of a number.

`__invert__(self)` gives meaning to the operation `~x` for "inverting" the values of the elements stored in an instance `x` of the container class for which the method is defined (the parameter `self` would be set to `x`). Its meaning as defined in the `operator` module is to carry out a bitwise inversion of an integer.

`__lshift__(self, i)` gives meaning to the operation `x<<i` for shifting to the left by `i` positions the elements stored in an instance `x` of a container class for which the method is defined. Its meaning as defined in the `operator` module

[27]As mentioned in Chapter 3, ordinary division for integer operands yields a "floor" integer value. That is, $35/4$ will return 8. On the other hand, $35.0/4$ would yield the floating point value 8.75, as the reader would expect. To force the result to be the floor value even with noninteger operands, the operator // does the job. That is, $35.0//4$ would yield 8.0. Starting with Python 3.0, the / operator will always return the "actual" value of division even for integer arguments [70].

is to return an integer that is obtained by leftward bitwise shift of the left-operand integer, the extent of the shift being the value of the right-operand integer.

`__rshift__(self, i)` gives meaning to the operation `x>>i` for shifting to the right by `i` positions the elements stored in an instance `x` of the container class for which the method is defined. Its meaning as defined in the `operator` module is to return an integer that is obtained by rightward bitwise shift of the left operand integer, the extent of the shift being the value of the right operand integer.

`__mod__(self, a)` gives meaning to the modulo division `x%y`, where `x` is an instance of the class for which the method is defined and `y` whatever makes sense to the definition (the parameter `self` will be set to `x` and the parameter `a` to `y`). Its meaning as defined in the `operator` module is to return a number that is the remainder when the left operand number is divided by the right operand number. The `operator` module does *not* insist that the operands be integers; in other words, floating point numbers are allowed for the operands.

`__and__(self, other)` gives meaning to the `x&y` operation where `x` is an instance of the class for which the method is defined and `y` anything that makes sense to the definition (the parameter `self` will be set to `x` and the parameter `other` to `y`). Its definition in the `operator` module returns the bitwise `and` of the two operands that must both be integers.

`__or__(self, other)` gives meaning to the `x|y` operation (see the above entry for `__and__()` for what `x` and `y` stand for). Its definition in the `operator` module returns the bitwise `or` of two operands that must both be integers.

`__xor__(self, other)` gives meaning to the operation `x^y` (see the above entry for `__or__()` for what `x` and `y` stand for). Its definition in the `operator` module returns the bitwise `exclusive-or` of two operands that must both be integers.

`__contains__(self, other)` gives meaning to the conditional `y in x` where `x` is an instance of the class for which the method is defined and `y` any object that makes sense in the context of that definition. The parameter `self` will be set to `x` and the parameter `other` to `y`.

`__getitem__(self, i)` gives meaning to array-like subscripting for retrieving the value of an element stored in an instance of a container class for which the method is defined. In other words, the method allows for the container to be indexed and for a programmer to use the syntax `x[i]` for fetching an element, where `x` is an instance of the class for which the method is defined and `i` a positional index. The parameter `self` will be set to `x`.

`__setitem__(self, i, val)` gives meaning to array-like subscripting for assigning a new value to an element stored in an instance of a container class for which the method is defined. That is, we can now say `x[i]=val` where `x` is an instance made from the class for which the method is defined, `i` a positional index, and `val` a new value to be stored at the `i`-th position. The parameter `self` will be set to `x`.

`__getslice__(self, i, j)` gives meaning to operations like `x[i:j]` for retrieving a slice of a sequence of objects stored in an instance `x` of a container class for which the method is defined. The parameter `self` will be set to `x`.

`__iter__(self, i, val)` gives meaning to iterative operations that require the loop control variable to acquire successive values stored in an instance of a container class for which the method is defined. More specifically, this method gives meaning to a loop that begins with the incantation `for item in x` where `x` is an instance of the class. This method must return an *iterator object* that must support two methods, one again named `__iter__()` for returning the iterator object itself and the other `next()` for returning the next item.

We now present a class, `XArray`, to illustrate how some of the above methods can be used to customize the behavior of a class, Some of the behavior packed into this class may seem bizarre, but that is intentional. As should be clear from the definition of `__init__()` in line (B) of the script shown next, an instance of the class will store a list of objects. The class design in the script is based on the assumption that the elements stored in an instance of `XArray` will only be numbers and strings.

The rest of the class in the script shows definitions for a handful of the specially named methods we listed above. We start with a definition for `__str__()` in line (C). This will allow Python to implicitly create a string representation of an instance of `XArray`. As a result, when we construct an instance of type `XArray` in line (U) and ask Python to print out this instance in the next line, we get the output shown in the commented-out portion of that line. Note that the string representation of an `XArray` instance consists of joining up all of the elements stored in the instance with the underscore as the glue character.

We next show the definition for `__contains__()` in line (D). As shown in line (W), this allows us to test whether or not an object is in a given instance of `XArray`.

That takes us to the definition of `__getitem__()` in line (E). As mentioned earlier, this allows an instance of type `XArray` to be indexed, implying that any elements stored in the instance can be accessed using array-like subscripting shown in line (Y).

The definition of `__add__()` in line (F) is a bit more involved. That is because we want to use two different rules for "adding" the corresponding elements from two `XArray` instances. One of the rules, in the line below line (G), is for the addition of numeric elements. The other rule, in the line below the test in line (H), is for "adding" two string types. Even though the two rules look the same, Python will carry out numerical addition for the first and string concatenation for the second. This should explain the result we get for the addition of two `XArray` instances in line (Z). Note our calls to `isinstance()` in the body of `__add__()` to make sure that the corresponding elements in the two instances are either both numeric or both strings.

The definition of `__iter__()` in line (J) returns an `X_iterator` object that allows us to use the `for item in container` syntax for the loop in line (a) in the test portion of the script. The `XArray_iterator` class itself is defined in lines (P) through (S). By implementing its own `__iter__()` and `next()`, this class implements the *iterator protocol.* As required by this protocol, the definition of `next()` throws the `StopItertion` exception when there are no more items to be returned.[28]

Lines (K) and (L) define the `__lshift__()` method for class `XArray`. The `_lshift_by_one()` method in line (K) plays an ancillary role in the definition of `__lshift__()` in line (L). As mentioned earlier, the definition for `__lshift__()` allows us to use the syntax shown in line (b) for circularly shifting the elements stored in an `XArray` instance.

Finally, we have the definition for the `__invert__()` method starting in line (M). As stated earlier, this is to allow for the use of the ~ operator for "inverting" the elements stored in an instance of `XArray`, as shown by the call in line (c). Our definition of `__invert__()` negates the numbers and reverses the strings.

```
#!/usr/bin/env python

###  XArray.py

#----------------------------  Class  XArray  -------------------------
class XArray( object ):                                           #(A)

    def __init__( self, arr_arg ):                                #(B)
        self._arr = list(arr_arg)
        self._size = len( arr_arg )


    def __str__( self ):                                          #(C)
        'To create a print representation'
        if self._size == 0:
            return ''
        return '_'.join( map( str, self._arr ) )
```

[28]Chapter 10 goes into exception handling in Python.

```
def __contains__( self, ele ):                                        #(D)
    "To enable 'if a in b' and 'if a not in b' syntax"
    if self._size == 0:
        raise ValueError, "X instance has no elements"
    else:
        if ele in self._arr:
            return True
    return False


def __getitem__( self, i ):                                           #(E)
    "To enable array-like access syntax 'x[i]'"
    return self._arr[i]


def __add__(self, other):                                             #(F)
    "To enable 'x+y' syntax"
    if self._size != other._size:
        raise ValueError("X instances must be of the same size")
    outlist = []
    for i in range( self._size ):
        if isinstance( self[i], (int, long, float) ) and \
                 isinstance( other[i], (int, long, float) ):          #(G)
            outlist.append(self[i] + other[i])
        elif isinstance( self[i], str ) and \
                        isinstance( other[i], str ):                  #(H)
            outlist.append(self[i] + other[i] )
        else:
            raise ValueError("Mismatched elements for '+'")           #(I)
    return XArray( outlist )


def __iter__( self ):                                                 #(J)
    "To enable 'for item in container' syntax for loops"
    return XArray_iterator( self )


def _lshift_by_one( self ):                                           #(K)
    'For in-place left circular shift by 1 position'
    leftmost = self[0]
    self._arr.pop(0)
    self._arr.append( leftmost )


def __lshift__( self, n ):                                            #(L)
    "To enable the syntax 'x<<n' for left-shifting the elements"
    for i in range(n):
        self._lshift_by_one()
```

```
    def __invert__( self ):                                        #(M)
        '''
        To enable inversion with the '~' operator.
        We negate the number elements and reverse the
        string elements
        '''
        import operator   # To demonstrate isNumberType() predicate
        outlist = []
        for i in range( self._size ):
            if operator.isNumberType( self[i] ) == True:           #(N)
                outlist.append( -self[i] )
            else:
                list_of_chars = list( self[i] )                    #(O)
                list_of_chars.reverse()
                reversed = ''.join(list_of_chars)
                outlist.append( reversed )
        return XArray(outlist)

#--------------------- Class X_iterator ----------------------------
class XArray_iterator:                                             #(P)
    def __init__( self, xobj ):                                    #(Q)
        self.items = xobj._arr
        self.index = -1
    def __iter__( self ):                                          #(R)
        return self
    def next( self ):                                              #(S)
        self.index += 1
        if self.index < len( self.items ):
            return self.items[ self.index ]
        else:
            raise StopIteration


#------------------------ Test Code ------------------------------

if __name__ == '__main__':                                         #(T)

    x1 = XArray( (1,2,"hello",3) )                                 #(U)
    print x1                            # 1_2_hello_3

    x2 = XArray( (7,8,"jello",9) )                                 #(V)
    print x2                            # 7_8_jello_9

    print "hello" in x1                 # True                     #(W)

    print x1[2], x2[2]                  # hello jello              #(Y)
```

```
x3 = x1 + x2                                                        #(Z)
print x3                            # 8_10_hellojello_12

for item in x3: print item,         # 8 10 hellojello 12            #(a)
print

x3 << 2                                                             #(b)
print x3                            # hellojello_12_8_10

print ~x3                           # ollejolleh_-12_-8_-10         #(c)
```

7.11 CREDITS AND SUGGESTIONS FOR FURTHER READING

The source document for the information on new-style classes in Python is the essay by the creator of the language, Guido van Rossum [65]. A good tutorial on the subject of description classes is by Raymond Hettinger [27]. With regard to operator overloading and class customization, Section 3 of the Python Reference Manual is a must read. With regard to the definition of static and class methods in Section 7.7, we talked about both the older wrapper-based syntax and the more modern decorator syntax. Decorators, being merely functions, are easy to write for creating any sort of a wrapper for some target function code. See [60] for further details.

7.12 HOMEWORK

1. The following class contains what appears to be a class variable in line (B). This variable, p, is bound to a lambda.

   ```
   class X:                                                         #(A)
       p = lambda self, arg1, arg2 = 10: arg1 + arg2                #(B)

   xobj = X()                                                       #(C)
   print X.p(20)                     # ?????                        #(D)
   ```

   Is it possible to call p directly on the class, as shown in line (D)? In other words, will the lambda of line (B) act like a static method? That is, will the statement in line (D) print out the number 30?

2. Section 7.6 explained how static and class methods are defined in Python. This homework problem should give the reader additional insights of what is achieved by declaring a method static with the help of the `staticmethod()` wrapper. Say you define a class `X` as follows:

```
class X:
    def foo():
        pass
```

and you make the call:

```
X.foo()
```

you would elicit from Python the following error message:

```
TypeError: unbound method foo() must be called with X \
instance as first argument
```

This happens because the method object Python constructs from the `X.foo()` call has its attribute `im_self` set to `None`, causing the method object to be treated as an unbound object. As we mentioned earlier in Section 7.3.2 of this chapter, when Python first creates a method object from a call to a function that is invoked on an object through the dotted notation, it assigns values to the attributes `im_self`, `im_class`, and `im_func` before attempting to execute the method object. If the `im_self` attribute is found to be `None`, the method object is considered to be unbound and the `TypeError` exception raised, as shown above.

We can get around the above problem and make `foo()` behave like a static method if we define a *wrapper class* `Callable` and then supply the function object to be made static as an argument to the wrapper class, as shown in the following script:

```
#!/usr/bin/env python

### Static4.py

#----------------------  class Callable  ------------------------
class Callable:                                                #(A)
    def __init__( self, anycallable ):                         #(B)
        self.__call__ = anycallable                            #(C)

#------------------------  class X  ----------------------------
class X:                                                       #(D)

    def __init__( self, nn ):                                  #(E)
        self.n = nn
    def getn( self ):                                          #(F)
```

```
        return self.n                                              #(G)
    def foo():                                                     #(H)
        print "foo called"                                         #(I)
    foo = Callable( foo )                                          #(J)

#----------------  end of class definition  --------------------

xobj = X( 10 )                                                     #(K)
print xobj.getn()                    # 10                          #(L)

X.foo()                              # foo called                  #(M)
```

Explain why the statement in line (J) is able to "convert" `foo()` into a static method?

Also show a version of the above script in which the method intended to be static takes arguments. Also show cases where one static method calls another static method of a class.

3. Provide Python implementation for a `BitVector` class that stores bit arrays (also called bit strings) by packing them into integers. Bitwise logical operations on the bit arrays may then be carried out by the operators &, |, ^, and . and the bits may be shifted left and right by the operators << and >>. The `BitVector` class should define methods for each of the bitwise logical operations. Here are some other stipulations that the `BitVector` class should meet:

   - You should be able to construct a `BitVector` class from any arbitrary number of bits, odd or even.
   - Provide three different calling modes for the construction of an instance of a `BitVector`: (1) When called with an integer argument N, it should construct a `BitVector` that can hold N bits, all initialized to 0. (2) When called with a list of bits, it should construct a `BitVector` instance that holds only as many bits as in the initialization list, each bit initialized as in the list. And (3) When called with a string, it should consider the string a file name from which to extract the bits for a `BitVector` instance. For the third case, a subsequent method call on the `BitVector` instance should read the required number of bits from the file.

4. Section 7.4 talked about instance destruction in Python. Extend that discussion by writing Python implementations of the `Node` and `Network` classes of Section 6.4.1 of Chapter 6. Thus illustrate that circular references can cause memory leaks in Python scripts in just the same way as they do in Perl scripts.

5. Provide definitions for the `__str__()` method for the example classes in Sections 7.1 and 7.2 so that Python can directly generate printable string representations of the instances made from those classes.

6. As mentioned in Section 6.8 of Chapter 6, Perl's `overload` module allows for the overloaded operators to behave in a commutative fashion even though that implies using the overload method definition for the right operand (See also Problem 5 in the Homework section of Chapter 6.) By contrast, overloading in Python does not allow for such implicit commutativity. That is, even if the right operand object provides a definition for the `__add__()` method, it will not be invoked if you are adding two objects and the left operand is lacking such a method. Demonstrate this fact by experimenting with the class `XArray` we used in Section 7.10 of this chapter. (An implication of this fact is that Python will *not* autogenerate overload definitions for the binary comparison operators from an overload definition supplied for the three-valued `__cmp__()` method.)

8

Inheritance and Polymorphism in Perl

Inheritance is a central feature of object-oriented languages and its most important use is for deriving more specialized classes from existing classes. If a vendor-supplied class is not quite up to the job for a given application, you can derive from it a more specialized subclass and endow it with the required additional behavior. In this chapter, we first briefly review how inheritance is used in mainstream object-oriented languages like C++ and Java. We then talk about how inheritance works in Perl class hierarchies and in what sense it differs from the mainstream OO. The rest of the chapter will address issues such as how a subclass method can call on a superclass method to do part of the work; how a method that is invoked on a subclass instance is searched for in a class hierarchy, assuming that the subclass itself does not provide an implementation for the method; the role played by the `UNIVERSAL` class that every Perl class inherits from; and so on.

8.1 INHERITANCE IN MAINSTREAM OO

Inheritance in mainstream OO languages such as C++ and Java means that a subclass *inherits* the data attributes and the methods of all its parent classes. What the word *inherits* means for such languages is tighter than what would be suggested by a subclass *just acquiring* the data attributes and the methods of its parent classes. In the mainstream OO languages, the memory allocated to an instance of a subclass contains slots for all the instance variables of all the parent classes. So an instance of a subclass has built into it "subinstances" of the parent classes. It is for this reason that a constructor for a subclass must call, explicitly or implicitly, the constructors of its parent classes before it does anything else. The calls to the constructors of the parent classes are needed for the initialization of that portion of the memory of a subclass instance that is meant to hold the parent-class slices.

The fact that a subclass instance in mainstream OO contains inside it "subinstances" of the parent classes does not mean that all of the instance variables of the parent classes are directly *visible* through a subclass instance. Whether or not a parent-class instance variable is visible in a subclass instance depends in mainstream OO entirely on its access qualifier in the parent class. Parent-class instance variables that are tagged *public* and/or *protected* are generally directly visible through a subclass instance.

The inheritance of methods in mainstream OO must be viewed against a background of this tight coupling between a parent class and a subclass. Unless overridden, a subclass inherits all nonprivate methods of all its parent classes. Methods, inherited or directly defined, that can be invoked on an instance of a subclass are allowed to directly refer to all the instance variables, inherited or directly defined, that are visible in the subclass instance. If multiple methods available for invocation on a subclass instance carry the same name, an overload resolution algorithm is employed to ascertain as to which specific method should be invoked for the arguments specified.

Inheritance, along with polymorphism, is also at the heart of one of the basic tenets of object-oriented programming in mainstream OO: *A client of a class hierarchy should program to the most general publicly declared interfaces in the hierarchy.* An interface, usually in the form of an abstract class, declares the methods that are allowed to be invoked on the instances made from the concrete subclasses in the rest of the hierarchy. It is the concrete subclasses that provide implementation code for the methods declared in an interface.

Other uses of inheritance in mainstream OO include the use of abstract classes as *mixin classes* to lend specialized behavior to the classes that are derived from them, incremental development of code through class derivation, and so on.

8.2 INHERITANCE AND POLYMORPHISM IN PERL: COMPARISON WITH MAINSTREAM OO LANGUAGES

Inheritance in Perl (and also Python, as we will see in the next chapter) works very differently compared to how it works in mainstream OO languages such as C++ and Java. Perhaps the biggest difference is caused by the fact that when memory is allocated for a subclass instance in Perl (and in Python also), it does not contain slots for the parent-class instance variables. In other words, a subclass instance in Perl (and in Python also) is a completely separate data object and it does not contain "slices" for the data objects that could be formed from the parent classes. So there is no direct coupling between subclass instances and parent-class instances.

Inheritance in Perl (and also Python) means only that if a method invoked on a subclass instance is not found within the subclass definition itself, it will be searched for in the parent classes. What's interesting is that, even with regard to the determination of which method definition to invoke for a given function call, mainstream OO languages work very differently from Perl (and Python). There is no search for which method definition to use in mainstream OO languages. As mentioned already, mainstream OO languages first make a determination of all the method definitions that are candidates for invocation on an instance of a given type — some of these would be defined directly for the class corresponding to the instance and some inherited from the parent classes. If, for a given function call, there is more than one applicable method in this pool, the mainstream OO languages declare either a compile-time error or throw a run-time exception. Contrast this with what happens in a language like Perl. Here there is an actual search carried out — at least for the first invocation of a method on an instance — for a suitable method definition, first in the pool of the methods defined directly for the class from which the instance was constructed, and then in the parents of that class, and the parents of the immediate parents, and so on up the inheritance tree. This search is carried out in some prespecified manner in all of the ancestor classes, usually in a recursive depth-first left-to-right order with respect to how the parent classes are listed for a subclass. The important thing is that this search stops the moment an applicable definition is found. *Stopping the search in this manner could mean that a more appropriate method that might exist in the unexplored portions of the search space would not be called upon for execution.*

This manner of search for a method in the parent classes (if a definition cannot be found directly in the class that corresponds to the instance on which the method is invoked) automatically allows class instances to behave polymorphically, *albeit with a subtle twist vis-à-vis how polymorphism works in mainstream OO languages.* Polymorphism basically means that an instance of a subclass type can masquerade as an instance of any of the superclass types. So if A and B are superclasses of P, C a superclass of Q, and P and Q superclasses of Z, then an instance of Z should be able to act like an instance of P, Q, A, B, and C, all at the same time. In other words, the type of an instance of Z will not only be Z, but also P, Q, A, B, and C. For the same example in Perl (and also in Python), if you make a method call on an instance of type Z, it will automatically be searched for in class P if the method definition cannot be found in Z itself. If found in P, the instance of type Z will act as if it were of type P. If the method definition is not found in P, the search will continue into class A. If found in A, the instance of type Z will act like an instance of type A. If not found in A, the search will continue in class B. And so on.

The polymorphism that results from Perl's (and Python's) search-based approach to inheritance differs in a subtle way from polymorphism in mainstream OO languages. Whereas a subclass in mainstream OO languages is *equally polymorphic* — if one could use that characterization — with respect to all its parent classes, polymorphic behavior in Perl (and in Python) is weighted more toward the parent classes that appear earlier in the recursive depth-first left-to-right search order through the parent classes of a subclass.

Perl (and Python also) shares with the mainstream OO languages many of the other benefits derived from inheritance. As in the mainstream OO languages, class hierarchies in Perl can be used for incremental development of code. Perl (and Python also) allows for the definition of abstract classes that can be used to declare interfaces to which the users of a class hierarchy can program to, and so on.

8.3 THE ISA ARRAY FOR SPECIFYING THE PARENTS OF A CLASS

The `ISA` array is fundamental to how inheritance works in Perl. Each derived class[1] is provided with a list of parent classes through this array. Shown in the script below is a class `Z` in lines (G), (H), and (I) that is provided with an `ISA` array in line (H). With that declaration, `X` and `Y` become the parent classes of class `Z`. The classes `X` and `Y` themselves are defined in lines (A) through (C), and (D) through (F), respectively. Each class has its own constructor. Class `X` comes equipped with a method called `foo()` in line (C), and class `Y` with a method called `bar()` in line (F).

```
#!/usr/bin/perl -w
use strict;

### InheritanceBasic.pl

#----------------------------  Class X  ------------------------------
package X;                                                       #(A)
sub new { bless {}, $_[0] }                                      #(B)
sub foo { print "X's foo called\n" }                             #(C)

#----------------------------  Class Y  ------------------------------
package Y;                                                       #(D)
sub new { bless {}, $_[0] }                                      #(E)
sub bar { print "Y's bar called\n" }                             #(F)

#----------------------------  Class Z  ------------------------------
package Z;                                                       #(G)
@Z::ISA = qw( X Y );                                             #(H)
sub new { bless {}, $_[0] }                                      #(I)

#----------------------  end of class definitions  --------------------
```

[1]We will use "derived class," "child class," and "subclass" synonymously.

```
package main;                                                    #(J)

print join ' ', keys %Z::, "\n";         # ISA new               #(K)

my $zobj = Z->new();                                             #(L)
$zobj->foo();                            # X's foo called        #(M)
print join ' ', keys %Z::, "\n";         # ISA foo new           #(N)

$zobj->bar();                            # Y's bar called        #(O)
print join ' ', keys %Z::, "\n";         # bar ISA foo new       #(P)
print join ' ', values %Z::, "\n";                               #(Q)
                                         # *Z::bar *Z::ISA *Z::foo *Z::new
```

By virtue of the ISA declaration for class Z in line (H), the three classes together, X, Y, and Z, constitute the inheritance hierarchy shown in Fig. 8.1. So when we invoke a method on an instance of class Z, if that method is not implemented in class Z itself, an implementation is searched for in the parent classes listed in the ISA array defined for class Z. In other words, such a function call is *dispatched up the inheritance tree*.

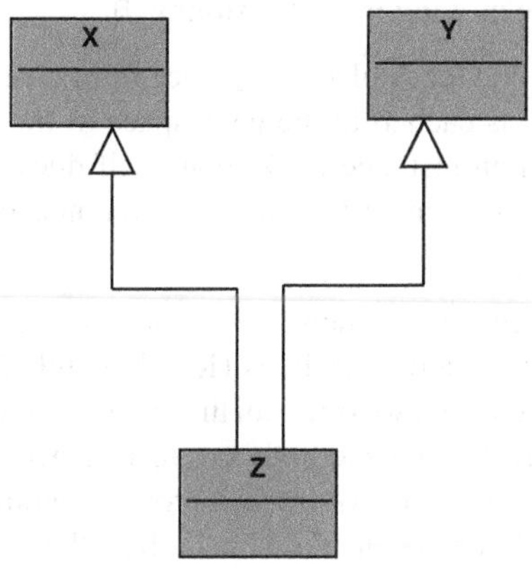

Fig. 8.1

The search for a method implementation in the inheritance tree takes place in a recursive left-to-right depth-first fashion. For a more complete illustration of this search, let's assume for a moment that the inheritance tree looks something like what is shown in Fig.8.2. When a method invoked on an instance of Z is not found within the definition of Z itself, the method name is looked for in the namespace of class

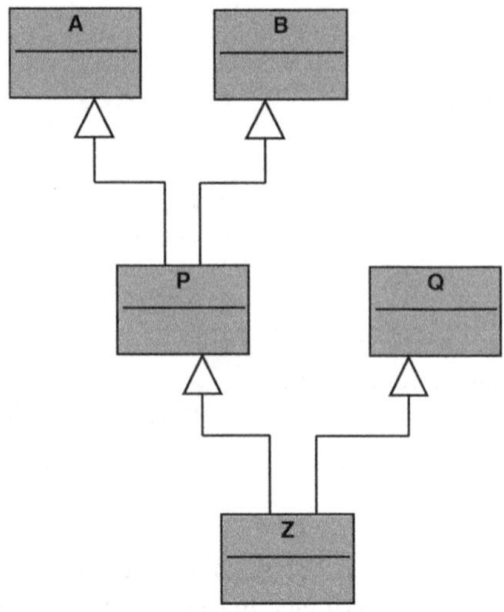

Fig. 8.2

P. If not found there either, the search moves into the namespace of class A. From A it will go to B, before moving into P's sibling Q.

This search for a method takes place only once for a given class. Subsequently, a reference to that method is cached in the namespace of the class itself. To explain, if we invoke `foo()` on an instance of Z that itself does not define `foo()`, after `foo()` is located in one of the ancestors of Z, a reference to this method is included in Z's namespace.

This caching of references to methods defined in the ancestors of a class is demonstrated by the output shown in lines (K), (M) and (P) of the previous script `InheritanceBasic.pl` where we print out the names stored in class Z's namespace dictionary before we invoke any methods on an instance of Z, after we invoke `foo()` belonging to X, and after we invoke `bar()` belonging to Y, respectively. Initially, before any methods are invoked on `zobj`, the namespace dictionary has only two names, `ISA` and `new`, as you'd expect and as you see in the output shown in line (K). But after `foo()` is invoked on `zobj`, the names in the dictionary are as shown in line (N). And, subsequent to invoking `bar()`, the names stored in the dictionary are as shown in line (P). For the curious, we also show the values associated with the names in the dictionary in the output in line (Q). These are the typeglobs associated with the names.[2]

Line (H) of the `InheritanceBasic.pl` script used the package-qualified name for creating the global variable `@ISA` for class Z. In keeping with the discussion in

[2]See Section 2.13 of Chapter 2 for a brief review of typeglobs.

Section 2.3.2 of Chapter 2, we could also have used either of the other two mechanisms for creating this variable: the `our` declaration or the `use vars` declaration. If we had chosen the former, we would replace the syntax

```
@Z::ISA = qw( X Y );
```

in line (H) of the script by the syntax

```
our @ISA = qw( X Y );
```

If, on the other hand, we had chosen to declare `@ISA` with the help of a `use vars` declaration, the statement in line (H) would get replaced by

```
use vars qw(@ISA);
@ISA = qw( X Y );
```

Yet another alternative is to use the `base` pragma. Now you'd replace the statement in line (H) by

```
use base qw( X Y );
```

If the base classes[3] reside in separate files (as is likely to be the case in practice), the base pragma also loads in those modules at compile time before inserting the base-class names in the `@ISA` array for the derived class. The `use base` syntax shown above produces the same effect as

```
BEGIN {
    require X;
    require Y;
    push @ISA, qw( X, Y );
}
```

8.4 AN EXAMPLE OF CLASS DERIVATION IN PERL

Class derivation will now be illustrated more fully with the help of the hierarchy shown in Fig. 8.3 that also incorporates the notion of a mixin class — a specialized parent class that can be used to lend a certain "flavor" to a subclass. A mixin class typically is not provided with a constructor because there is usually no need to construct instances from it. The implementation code for this hierarchy is displayed in the multi-file script shown next.

[3] We will use "base class," "parent class," and "superclass" synonymously.

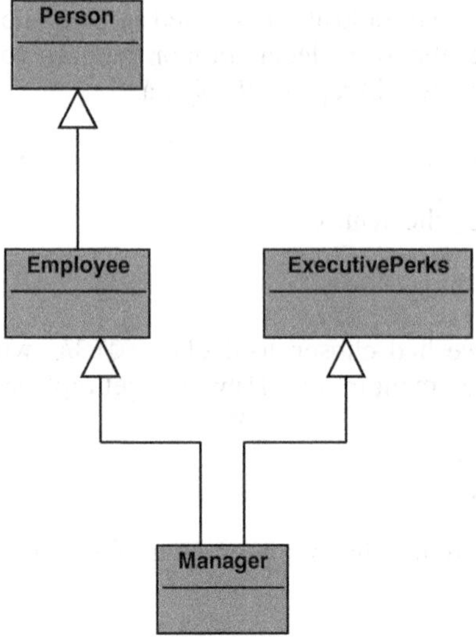

Fig. 8.3

As shown in lines (P1) through (P13) of the code,[4] the root class `Person` is endowed with generic methods `get_name()` and `get_age()` that will be useful for *all* `Persons`. On the other hand, the derived class `Employee` in lines (E1) through (E18) is endowed with the methods `get_position()` and `promote()` that are relevant to all `Employees`, *including* `Managers`, but not `Persons` in general. The further derived class `Manager` in lines (M1) through (M10) includes the method `get_department()` that is applicable only to `Manager` instances. Note how the classes are linked up in parent-child relationships through the declaration of `@ISA` arrays in lines (E2) and (M2). Since a derived class inherits the methods from its parent class, when we invoke, say, `get_name()` on a `Manager` instance, we'd expect Perl to call on the implementation of this method as defined for the class `Person`.

We also supply `Manager` with another parent class, `ExecutivePerks`, defined in lines (X1) through (X6), that contains a class variable `_bonus` and class methods `get_bonus()` and `set_bonus()`. The reason for placing only a class variable and the static get and set methods in `ExecutivePerks` is that we want all `Managers` to have the same bonus. If we change the bonus for one `Manager`, we want that change to be reflected in all `Manager` instances, even those that were constructed before the bonus was changed. You can think of the `ExecutivePerks` class as a mixin class, a class meant for adding a "flavor" to other classes. In this case, the "flavor" added by

[4]Note that the implementation code for each class of the hierarchy is in a separate module file. This is usually the case in production code.

the ExecutivePerks class consists of its static get and set methods for the global bonus information for all the Manager instances. Note that ExecutivePerks has not been provided with a constructor. Ordinarily, it would make no sense to construct an instance of the ExecutivePerks class.

While the implementation for the base-class constructor shown in lines (P2) through (P7) is routine — meaning as explained in Chapter 6 — the implementation for the derived-class constructors in lines (E3) through (E7) for Employee and in lines (M3) through (M7) for Manager is slightly different. Looking at the Employee constructor, we first construct a base-class instance in line (E5) by bundling off the relevant argument to the base-class constructor.[5] We then add the derived-class specific additional information to this object in line (E6). Finally, we rebless the object thus constructed into the derived class so that when we invoke a method on a derived-class instance, the method's implementation would be searched for first in the derived class itself.

Shown below is an implementation of the hierarchy. The implementation shown also includes some test code at the end. A discussion of what is in the test code follows the code shown below.

```
#--------------   Class Person in Person.pm file  --------------------
package Person;                                                  #(P1)

sub new {                                                        #(P2)
    my ( $class, $name, $age ) = @_;                             #(P3)
    my $instance = {                                             #(P4)
        _name => $name,                                          #(P5)
        _age => $age,                                            #(P6)
    };
```

[5]This is being done here purely for programming convenience and is recommended only for very simple hierarchies such as the one shown here. We could have used exactly the same kind of syntax for the subclass constructors as we used in the base class Person. In a general class hierarchy, having a subclass constructor call a parent's constructor for doing part of the instance initialization is safe only when the following two conditions are satisfied: (1) a subclass has only one parent class, or, when multiple parents are involved, only one parent class comes with a constructor; and (2) there are no collisions between the names of the instance variables that a subclass will acquire by executing the parent's constructor code and the names of the additional instance variables introduced directly in the subclass constructor. In an inheritance chain involving more than two classes, this constraint on the instance-variable names may cover multiple classes. For example, if X is a parent of Y and Y is a parent of Z, and that Z's constructor calls Y's constructor for doing a part of the instance creation and Y's constructor calls X's constructor for the same reason, then there must be no collisions between the instance-variable names used in all three classes. A reader not quite sure as to why this constraint exists on the instance variable names has only to reflect on the discussion presented in Section 8.2 where we mentioned that a subclass data object is completely independent of a base-class data object, unlike what happens in systems programming languages like C++ and Java. **Of course, this whole issue concerning instance variable names becomes moot if one engages in defensive scripting and initializes all the subclass instance variables locally in the subclass constructor itself.**

```
    bless $instance, $class;                                        #(P7)
}
sub get_name {                                                      #(P8)
    my $self = shift;                                               #(P9)
    $self->{_name};                                                 #(P10)
}
sub get_age {                                                       #(P11)
    my $self = shift;                                               #(P12)
    $self->{_age};                                                  #(P13)
}
1

#------------  Class Employee in Employee.pm file  ------------------
package Employee;                                                   #(E1)

use Person;
@Employee::ISA = ('Person');                                        #(E2)

sub new {                                                           #(E3)
    my ( $class, $name, $age, $position ) = @_;                     #(E4)
    my $instance = Person->new( $name, $age );                      #(E5)
    $instance->{_position} = $position;                             #(E6)
    bless $instance, $class;                                        #(E7)
}
sub get_position {                                                  #(E8)
    my $self = shift;                                               #(E9)
    $self->{_position};                                             #(E10)
}
my %_promotion_table = (                                            #(E11)
    shop_floor => "staff",                                          #(E12)
    staff => "management",                                          #(E13)
    astt_manager => "manager",                                      #(E14)
    manager => "executive",                                         #(E15)
);
sub promote {                                                       #(E16)
    my $self = shift;                                               #(E17)
    $self->{_position} =
                  $_promotion_table{ $self->{_position} };          #(E18)
}
1

#-------  Class ExecutivePerks in ExecutivePerks.pm file  -----------
package ExecutivePerks;                                             #(X1)

my $_bonus = 0;                                                     #(X2)

sub get_bonus { $_bonus; }                                          #(X3)

sub set_bonus {                                                     #(X4)
```

```
    my ($class, $bonus) = @_;                                       #(X5)
    $_bonus = $bonus;                                               #(X6)
}
1

#-----------------  Class Manager in Manager.pm file  -----------------
package Manager;                                                    #(M1)

use Employee;
use ExecutivePerks;
@Manager::ISA = ("Employee", "ExecutivePerks");                     #(M2)

sub new {                                                           #(M3)
    my ( $class, $name, $age, $position, $department ) = @_;        #(M4)
    my $instance = Employee->new( $name, $age, $position );         #(M5)
    $instance->{_department} = $department;                         #(M6)
    bless $instance, $class;                                        #(M7)
}
sub get_department {                                                #(M8)
    my $self = shift;                                               #(M9)
    $self->{_department};                                          #(M10)
}
1

#--------------------  TestPersonHierarchy.pl file  --------------------
#!/usr/bin/perl -w
use strict;

### TestPersonHierarchy.pl

package main;                                                       #(T1)
use Employee;
use Manager;

my ($name, $age, $position, $dept);                                 #(T2)

my $emp = Employee->new( "Zaphod", 84, "shop_floor" );              #(T3)
print $emp->get_name(), "\n";           # Zaphod                    #(T4)
print $emp->get_age(), "\n";            # 84                        #(T5)
print $emp->get_position(), "\n";       # shop_floor                #(T6)

$emp->promote();                                                    #(T7)
print $emp->get_position(), "\n";       # staff                     #(T8)

my $man = Manager->new( "Trillian", 42, "astt_manager", "sales" );#(T9)
print $man->get_name(), "\n";           # Trillian                 #(T10)
print $man->get_age(), "\n";            # 42                       #(T11)
print $man->get_position(), "\n";       # astt_manager             #(T12)
print $man->get_department(), "\n";     # sales                    #(T13)
```

```
$man->promote();                                                    #(T14)
print $man->get_position(), "\n";        # manager                  #(T15)

$man->set_bonus( 1000 );                                            #(T16)
print $man->get_name(), ": ", $man->get_bonus(),"\n";               #(T17)
                             # Trillian: 1000
my $man2 = Manager->new( "Betelgeuse", 18, "staff", "sales" );      #(T18)
print $man2->get_name(), ": ", $man2->get_bonus(), "\n";            #(T19)
                             # Betelgeuse: 1000
$man2->set_bonus( 5555 );                                           #(T20)
print $man->get_name(), ": ", $man->get_bonus(), "\n";              #(T21)
                             # Trillian: 5555
print $man2->get_name(), ": ", $man2->get_bonus(), "\n";            #(T22)
                             # Betelgeuse: 5555
```

In the test code in lines (T1) through (T22), we first construct an `Employee` instance in line (T3) and invoke `get_name()` and `get_age()` on it in lines (T4) and (T5) even though these methods are not defined for the `Employee` class. Perl uses the `Person` definitions for these methods because `Person` is in the `ISA` array of `Employee`. The invocation `get_position()` in line (T6) works because the instance constructed in line (T3) was blessed into the `Employee` class. Also note the invocation of `promote()` on the `Employee` instance in line (T7). This invocation works for the same reason as that for `get_position()` in line (T6) — because of the `Employee` blessedness of the instance on which the method is invoked.

Now let's look at the `Manager` instance constructed in line (T9). There is no problem with the invocation of `get_name()` and `get_age()` in lines (T10) and (T11) because of the inheritance chain established through the `ISA` arrays for the `Manager` class and for its parent `Employee` class. And when we invoke `Employee`'s `promote()` on the `Manager` instance in line (T14), that also works for the same reason — that `Employee` is in the `ISA` array of `Manager`.

Finally, note from the output shown in lines (T6) through (T22) that we have met the requirement we placed on using `ExecutivePerks` as a second parent for `Manager` — we wanted the bonus to always be the same for all managers and, if we changed it for one manager, we wanted that change reflected for all managers. In line (T16), we set this bonus for `Trillian`. We subsequently construct another `Manager` instance with name `Betelgeuse`. When we check `Betelgeuse`'s bonus in line (T19), we find it to be the same as set previously for `Trillian`. In line (T20), we change `Betelgeuse`'s bonus to a different value. Line (T22) shows that this change is reflected in `Trillian`'s bonus also.

8.5 A SMALL DEMONSTRATION OF POLYMORPHISM IN PERL OO

As mentioned in Section 8.2, polymorphism means that an object can be considered to be of different types simultaneously, and, thus, an object can exhibit different types of behaviors at the same time. Again as mentioned in that subsection, objects acquire an ability to exhibit different types of behaviors simultaneously through the mechanism of inheritance. Consider again the `Person` hierarchy shown in the previous section.[6] In this hierarchy, every `Employee` *is* a `Person` and every `Manager` *is* an `Employee`. Every `Manager` *is also* a `Person`. Therefore, a `Manager` instance should act not only like a `Manager`, but also like an `Employee` and like a `Person`. In other words, a `Manager` instance ought to behave polymorphically.

Polymorphism as described above is indeed exhibited by instance objects in Perl OO. By placing `Person` in the `ISA` array of `Employee` and `Employee` in the `ISA` array of `Manager`, an `Employee` instance inherits the methods of the `Person` class and a `Manager` instance inherits the methods of both the `Person` class and the `Employee` class. This would allow an `Employee` to act like a `Person`. This would also allow a `Manager` to act like an `Employee` and like a `Person`. That is polymorphism in its most basic form.

For strongly typed OO languages like C++ and Java, a particular consequence of polymorphism is the following property: *A derived-class type can be substituted wherever a base-class type is expected.* So if you write a function that needs a base-class argument, by virtue of polymorphism you could call this function with a derived-class instance for the argument. In other words, suppose we write a function in Java:

```
void foo( Person p ) { ... }
```

we can invoke the function in the following manner:

```
Manager man = new Manager( ... );
foo( man );
```

This manifestation of polymorphism in Perl is displayed by the script shown next. Note that the subroutine `foo()` in line (A) of the script expects a `Person` argument because the `get_name()` method that is invoked in the body of the subroutine is defined specifically for the `Person` class. Nonetheless, when the function `foo()` is invoked with an `Employee` argument in line (G) and with a `Manager` argument in line (H), the script behaves like an OO program should — it exhibits polymorphism.

[6] As mentioned at the beginning of Chapter 6, such a hierarchy is referred to as an `IsA` hierarchy.

```
#!/usr/bin/perl -w
use strict;

### Polymorph.pl

use Person;
use Employee;
use Manager;

sub foo {                          #  expects a Person argument      #(A)
    my ($arg) = @_;
    my $nam = $arg->get_name();                                       #(B)
    print "subroutine foo reporting: $nam\n";
}

my $per = Person->new( "Zaphod", 84 );                               #(C)
my $emp = Employee->new( "Orpheus", 84, "shop_floor" );              #(D)
my $man = Manager->new( "Trillion", 42, "astt_manager", "sales" ); #(E)

#foo invoked on a Person:
foo( $per );                           #Zahpod                        #(F)
#foo invoked on an Employee:
foo( $emp );                           #Orpheus                       #(G)
#foo invoked on a Manager:
foo( $man );                           #Trillian                      #(H)
```

8.6 HOW A DERIVED-CLASS METHOD CALLS ON A BASE-CLASS METHOD

The goal of this section is to show how a derived-class method can call a base-class method for doing part of the work and how this is accomplished with the help of the keyword SUPER.

Consider the classes `Worker` and `Foreman`, and the test script `TestSuper.pl` shown next for the two-class hierarchy of Fig. 8.4. Both the `Worker` class and the `Foreman` subclass are provided with the following two methods:

```
promote()
print()
```

but we want the implementations of these methods for the subclass `Foreman` to use the implementations in the base class for part of the work. In other words, we want the `print()` method of `Foreman` to call on the `print()` method of `Worker` for doing part of the work. Along the same lines, we want the `promote()` method of `Foreman` to call on the `promote()` method of `Worker`. The base-class implementations for these methods are shown in lines (W5) and (W6), whereas the derived-class implementations are shown in lines (F3) and (F5).

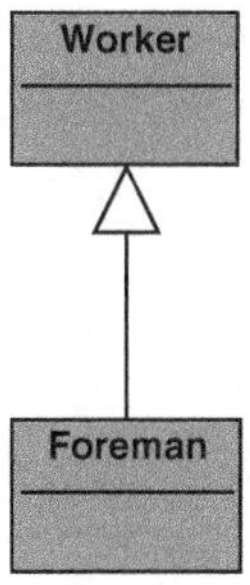

Fig. 8.4

Let's focus on the `print` method first. Whereas its implementation for the base class in line (W6) is routine, note how the derived-class implementation in line (F5) calls on the base-class implementation by using the syntax in line (F6):

```
$instance->SUPER::print();
```

The keyword `SUPER` causes Perl to search for `print()` in the direct and indirect superclasses of `Foreman`. This search proceeds in exactly the same fashion as for any regular method invocation, except that it starts with the direct superclasses. That is, the search is carried out depthwise and applied recursively in a left-to-right order to all the superclasses in the `ISA` array of the derived class.

The keyword `SUPER` is obviously convenient for asking Perl to search for a method in all of the superclasses that converge on a derived class in the inheritance hierarchy. It is also possible to ask Perl to confine its search to a particular superclass (and all the superclasses of that class). This is demonstrated by the implementation of the `promote()` method for the derived-class `Foreman` in line (F3) where we have used the following syntax in line (F4) for invoking the `promote()` of the `Worker` superclass:

```
$instance->Worker::promote();
```

Of course, in this case, the effect achieved by using the syntax `Worker::promote()` is exactly the same as would be achieved by using the syntax `SUPER::promote()`. Later we will illustrate the differences between these two ways of starting the search for a method definition at a higher level in a class hierarchy.

```
#---------------  Class Worker in Worker.pm file  -------------------
package Worker;
sub new {                                                        #(W1)
    my ( $class, $name, $position ) = @_;
    my $instance = {
        _name => $name,
        _position => $position,
    };
    bless $instance, $class;
}
sub get_position {                                               #(W2)
    my $self = shift;
    $self->{_position};
}
sub set_position {                                               #(W3)
    my $self = shift;
    $self->{_position} = shift;
}
my %_promotion_table = (                                         #(W4)
    shop_floor  => "team_leader",
    team_leader => "group_lead",
    group_lead  => "forman",
    foreman     => "manager",
);
sub promote {                                                    #(W5)
    my $self = shift;
    $self->{_position} =
              $_promotion_table{ $self->{_position} };
}
sub print {                                                      #(W6)
    my $self = shift;
    print "$self->{_name}  $self->{_position}  ";
}
1

#---------------  Class Foreman in Foreman.pm file  ------------------
package Foreman;
use Worker;
@Foreman::ISA = ("Worker");

sub new {                                                        #(F1)
    my ( $class, $name, $position, $department ) = @_;
    my $instance = Worker->new( $name, $position );             #(F2)
    $instance->{_department} = $department;
    bless $instance, $class;
}
```

```
sub get_department {
    my $self = shift;
    $self->{_department};
}
sub promote {                                                         #(F3)
    my $self = shift;
    die "A Foreman cannot be promoted beyond 'Manager'"
        if $self->{_position} eq 'manager';
    #call base class's promote by specifying
    #base class name explicitly:
    $self->Worker::promote();                                         #(F4)
}
sub print {                                                           #(F5)
    my $self = shift;
    $self->SUPER::print();                                            #(F6)
    print "$self->{_department}\n";                                   #(F7)
}
1

#--------------------- Test code file:  TestSuper.pl ------------------
#!/usr/bin/perl -w
use strict;

###  TestSuper.pl

package main;
use Worker;
use Foreman;

my ($position, $dept);

my $worker = Worker->new( "Joe", "shop_floor" );                      #(T1)
$worker->promote();                                                   #(T2)
$position = $worker->get_position();
print "$position\n";                 # team_leader

my $forman = Foreman->new( "Amanda", "foreman", "assembly" );        #(T3)
$forman->print();                    # Amanda forman assembly
$forman->promote();                                                   #(T5)
$forman->print();                    # Amanda manager assembly
$forman->promote(); # A foeman cannot be promoted beyond 'Manager'#(T7)
```

It is important to realize that a method call like

```
$self->Class_name::method_name();
```

causes a search for an implementation of `method_name()` to *start* with `Class_name` and, if not found there, to go on to the superclasses of that class. This is demonstrated by the script shown below. Lines (A) through (M) of the script define a class hierarchy consisting of a base class `X`, a derived class `Y`, and a further derived class `Z`. Both `X` and `Z` are provided with a method called `foo()`, the former in line (C) and the latter in line (K). Class `Y` has intentionally not been provided with a method named `foo()`. In line (P), we then construct an instance of type `Z`. Invoking `foo()` on this instance in line (Q) elicits the response we expect — it utilizes the definition of `foo()` in line (K), which in turn, through line (N), causes the ancestor class X's `foo()` defined in line (C) to be invoked. This fact is borne out by the output shown in the commented-out portions of the lines (Q) and (R). However, when we invoke `Y::foo()` on the same instance of class `Z` in line (S), the output corresponds to just the invocation of `foo()` that is defined for class `X`, as evidenced by the output shown in the commented-out portion of that line.[7]

```
#!/usr/bin/perl -w
use strict;

### StartMethodSearchWithNamedClass.pl

#------------------------------ Class X ------------------------------
package X;                                                        #(A)
sub new { bless {}, $_[0] }                                       #(B)
sub foo {                                                         #(C)
    print "X's foo invoked\n";                                    #(D)
}

#------------------------------ Class Y ------------------------------
package Y;                                                        #(E)
@Y::ISA = qw( X );                                                #(F)
sub new { bless {}, $_[0] }                                       #(G)

#------------------------------ Class Z ------------------------------
package Z;                                                        #(H)
@Z::ISA = qw( Y );                                                #(I)
sub new { bless {}, $_[0] }                                       #(J)
sub foo {                                                         #(K)
    my $self = shift;                                             #(L)
    print "Z's foo invoked\n";                                    #(M)
    $self->SUPER::foo();                                          #(N)
}
```

[7] Small examples for explaining various issues related to inheritance and polymorphism will be shown with all the classes in a single file. As the reader would expect, this obviates the need for the "`use` *baseclass*" statement just prior to the declaration of the `@ISA` array in a subclass.

```
#-------------------------- namespace main --------------------------
package main;                                                   #(O)

my $z_obj = Z->new();                                           #(P)

$z_obj->foo();                      # Z's foo invoked           #(Q)
                                    # X's foo invoked           #(R)

$z_obj->Y::foo();                   # X's foo invoked           #(S)
```

As the reader has already seen, the role of the keyword `SUPER` is to ensure that the *search* for a method definition *starts* with the superclass of the class in which `SUPER` is used. Now we want to emphasize that this fact stands *regardless of the object on which* `SUPER` *is invoked.*

This point is made clear with the following script, `SuperNuance.pl`. Lines (A) through (M) of the script define a three-class hierarchy consisting of the classes `X`, `Y`, and `Z`, with `X` as the root class, `Y` as the descendant of `X`, and `Z` as the descendant of `Y`. Both `X` and `Y` have a method `foo()` defined for them. Class `Z` comes with a method `bar()` in line (L) that invokes `SUPER::foo()` on an instance of type `Z`.

Lines (N) through (U) define a two-class hierarchy consisting of the classes `T` and `U`. The base class `T` is provided with its own definition for `foo()` in line (P). The derived class `U` is provided with a method `bar()` in line (S) that, like the `bar()` of class `Z` in line (L), invokes `foo()` on an instance of class `Z` in line (U).

In namespace `main`, we then construct an instance of type `Z` in line (W) and an instance of type `U` in line (Y). On each of these instance objects, we invoke `bar()` in lines (X) and (Z); these invocations produce the outputs shown in the commented-out portions of those lines.

The critical thing to note here is that both the invocations of `SUPER::foo()`, in lines (M) and (U), are on instances of type `Z`. However, the actual `foo()` invoked depends not at all on where `Z` stands in a class hierarchy. It depends entirely on the class in which `SUPER::foo()` is invoked, since only the superclasses of that class will be searched through for a definition of `foo()`.

```
#!/usr/bin/perl -w
use strict;

### SuperNuance.pl

#------------------------ X, Y, Z Class Hierarchy --------------------
package X;                                                      #(A)
sub new { bless {}, $_[0] }                                     #(B)
```

```
sub foo {                                                        #(C)
    print "X's foo invoked\n";
}

package Y;                                                       #(D)
@Y::ISA = qw( X );                                               #(E)
sub new { bless {}, $_[0] }                                      #(F)
sub foo {                                                        #(G)
    my $self = shift;
    print "Y's foo invoked\n";
    $self->SUPER::foo();                                         #(H)
}

package Z;                                                       #(I)
@Z::ISA = qw( Y );                                               #(J)
sub new { bless {}, $_[0] }                                      #(K)
sub bar {                                                        #(L)
    my $self = shift;
    $self->SUPER::foo();                                         #(M)
}

#------------------------- T, U Class Hierarchy ---------------------
package T;                                                       #(N)
sub new { bless {}, $_[0] }                                      #(O)
sub foo {                                                        #(P)
    print "T's foo invoked\n";
}

package U;                                                       #(Q)
@U::ISA = qw( T );                                               #(R)
sub new { bless {}, $_[0] }                                      #(S)
sub bar {                                                        #(T)
    my $z_obj = Z->new();
    $z_obj->SUPER::foo();          # SUPER::foo() called on Z obj   #(U)
}

#--------------------------- package main ----------------------------
package main;                                                    #(V)

my $z_obj = Z->new();                                            #(W)
$z_obj->bar();                     # Y's foo invoked             #(X)
                                   # X's foo invoked
my $u_obj = U->new();                                            #(Y)
$u_obj->bar();                     # T's foo invoked             #(Z)
```

8.7 THE UNIVERSAL CLASS

Every class in Perl inherits implicitly from a class called UNIVERSAL. We can therefore say that UNIVERSAL is implicitly at the root of every class hierarchy in Perl. The UNIVERSAL class plays somewhat the same role in Perl OO that the system-supplied root class object plays for the new-style classes in Python.

Every class implicitly inherits the following methods from UNIVERSAL:

1. isa(class_name)
2. can(method_name)
3. VERSION(need_version)

Of these, the first two can be invoked by a programmer. The third is invoked automatically by the system if a script asks for a particular version number for a Perl library.

The isa() method that every class inherits from UNIVERSAL can be used to test whether a given object is an instance of a particular class. The use of this method is demonstrated by the IsaMethod.pl script below where, in line (A), we import the same Manager class that was defined earlier in Section 8.4. The lines (C), (D), and (E) produce the output yes as shown. On the other hand, line (F) produces the output no because Trillian is not an Executive. Lines (G) and (H) demonstrate that you can invoke isa() directly on a class name.

As shown by the rest of the output in lines (J) through (O), if at run time you dynamically alter the class hierarchy — as we do in line (I) of the script by setting Manager's ISA array to an empty list — the results returned by the isa() method reflect the change.

```
#!/usr/bin/perl -w
use strict;

### IsaMethod.pl

use Manager;                                                           #(A)

#--------------------------  Test Code  -------------------------------
my $man = Manager->new( "Trillian", "manager", "sales" );              #(B)

print $man->isa( 'UNIVERSAL' )  ? "yes\n" : "no\n";      # yes         #(C)
print $man->isa( 'Manager' )    ? "yes\n" : "no\n";      # yes         #(D)
print $man->isa( 'Employee' )   ? "yes\n" : "no\n";      # yes         #(E)
print $man->isa( 'Executive' )  ? "yes\n" : "no\n";      # no          #(F)
print Manager->isa('UNIVERSAL') ? "yes\n" : "no\n";      # yes         #(G)
```

```
print Manager->isa('Employee')  ? "yes\n" : "no\n";        # yes          #(H)

@Manager::ISA = ();                                                       #(I)

print $man->isa( 'UNIVERSAL' )  ? "yes\n" : "no\n";        # yes          #(J)
print $man->isa( 'Manager' )    ? "yes\n" : "no\n";        # yes          #(K)
print $man->isa( 'Employee' )   ? "yes\n" : "no\n";        # no           #(L)
print $man->isa( 'Executive' )  ? "yes\n" : "no\n";        # no           #(M)
print Manager->isa('UNIVERSAL') ? "yes\n" : "no\n";        # yes          #(N)
print Manager->isa('Employee')  ? "yes\n" : "no\n";        # no           #(O)
```

The other programmer-usable method that is inherited from `UNIVERSAL` by every class is `can()`. This method is used to test whether a given class supports a particular method, either directly or through inheritance. A call to `can()` returns a reference to the supported method definition. Its use is demonstrated by the following script, `CanMethod.pl`. Lines (A) through (J) of the script define in a single file a three-class hierarchy in which the classes `X` and `Y` are parents of the class `Z`. Class `X` is equipped with a method `foo()` in line (C), class `Y` with `bar()` in line (F), and class `Z` with `baz()` in line (J). Of course, class `Z` also inherits the methods of the parents `X` and `Y`. Lines (M) and (N) demonstrate the invocation of `can()` on an instance and on a class directly. Lines (O) through (R) demonstrate the fact that `can()` returns a reference to the argument function. This reference may then be subsequently executed, as shown by the call in line (R).

```
#!/usr/bin/perl -w
use strict;

### CanMethod.pl

#---------------------------- Class X ------------------------------
package X;                                                        #(A)
sub new { bless {}, $_[0] }                                       #(B)
sub foo {                                                         #(C)
    print "X's foo invoked\n";
}

#---------------------------- Class Y ------------------------------
package Y;                                                        #(D)
sub new { bless {}, $_[0] }                                       #(E)
sub bar {                                                         #(F)
    print "Y's bar invoked\n";
}

#---------------------------- Class Z ------------------------------
package Z;                                                        #(G)
```

```
@Z::ISA = qw( X Y );                                                #(H)
sub new { bless {}, $_[0] }                                         #(I)
sub baz {                                                           #(J)
    print "Z's baz invoked\n";
}

#------------------------------ main -------------------------------
package main;                                                       #(K)

my $obj = Z->new();                                                 #(L)

print $obj->can( "foo" )   ? "yes\n" : "no\n";  # yes               #(M)
print Z->can( "foo" )      ? "yes\n" : "no\n";  # yes               #(N)
my $which_func = $obj->can( "foo" ) ||                              #(O)
                 $obj->can( "bar" ) ||                              #(P)
                 $obj->can( "baz" );                                #(Q)
&$which_func;                                   # X's foo invoked   #(R)
```

Finally, the third method that is inherited by every class from `UNIVERSAL` is

```
VERSION( need_version )
```

This method is invoked directly by the system when a script asks for a specified version of a package. You can associate a version number with a package by using the sort of statement shown in the second line below:

```
package Manager;
$Manager::VERSION = 5.2;
...
the rest of the Manager.pm code
...
```

Subsequently, when a module is loaded in with the `use` directive, the load request can be customized to a specific version of the module by a statement that looks like

```
use Manager 5.2;
```

This would cause the invocation of the `VERSION` method inherited from `UNIVERSAL` through the following command:

```
Manager->VERSION( 5.2 );
```

which makes sure that the version-number constraint is met by the package that is loaded in.

8.7.1 Adding Functionality to the UNIVERSAL class

As is the case with all data structures in Perl, the `UNIVERSAL` class is open to *post-facto* augmentation by the programmer. Since, implicitly, the `UNIVERSAL` class is at the root of every programmer-defined class hierarchy, any additional methods inserted into `UNIVERSAL` become immediately available to all other classes, including those defined prior to the modification to `UNIVERSAL`.

Shown in lines (A) through (K) of the next script is a three-class hierarchy, with the classes `X` and `Y` serving as the base classes for class `Z`. In the namespace `main`, which starts in line (L), we add in line (M) a programmer-specified method `foo()` to the system-supplied methods for the class `UNIVERSAL`. Note how `UNIVERSAL`'s `foo()` calls a method `boohoo()` in line (P). Only the class `Z` is provided with an implementation for `boohoo()` in line (K).

For the sake of constructing an example in which the additional method defined for `UNIVERSAL` is called by some other method defined for one of the other classes in a hierarchy, we have in line (C) a method `bar()` for class `X`. This method calls `UNIVERSAL`'s `foo()` in line (E). Class `X` is also provided with a method `baz()` in line (Q); this definition is provided in package `main`. This extra method for `X` is provided to point to an interesting property of the system-supplied method `caller()`.

Line (S) constructs a new instance from class `Z`. Because `foo()` is made available through `UNIVERSAL`, the call to `can()` in line (T) returns "yes" to whether or not `Z` supports `foo()`. Line (U) invokes `bar()`, defined originally for class `X`, on the `Z` instance of line (S). Note the output produced by this call to `bar()`; it is repeated below for convenience:

```
X's bar called
UNIVERSAL's foo called by X
Z's boohoo invoked
```

The second line of this output shows that `UNIVERSAL`'s `foo()` was invoked by `bar()` in line (E), as one would expect. The third line of the output indicates invocation of `Z`'s `boohoo()` in line (P) of the definition of `UNIVERSAL`'s `foo()`. This also shows that search for a method, *no matter where it is called*, is carried out in the inheritance tree starting at the class of the instance on which the method is invoked. So when `boohoo()` is invoked on `$self` in line (P), since the variable `$self` will be holding a reference to the `Z` instance of line (S), the search for `boohoo()` starts with class `Z` and moves up the inheritance tree in accordance with the discussion in the next section.

The class name `X` in the second line of the output shown above was produced by the call to the built-in `caller()` in line (N). The output shown correctly points out that `UNIVERSAL`'s `foo()` was invoked inside package `X` — in this case by `X`'s `bar()` in line (E). We now wish to point out that although in most situations in Perl OO, the concept of a *package* is synonymous with the concept of a *class*, the behavior of the built-in `caller()` is one of the exceptions. The package name returned by `caller()` returns the namespace in effect that contains the definition of the calling method *even if that definition injects a method in some other namespace.* So when we call `baz()` in line (V), we get the following output:

```
X's baz called
UNIVERSAL's foo called by main
Z's boohoo invoked
```

Note that the second line now says that `UNIVERSAL`'s `foo()` was called from package `main`. Strictly speaking, that is, of course, true, since `X`'s `baz()` was defined in line (Q) in the namespace `main`. However, if you have gotten accustomed to thinking of packages and classes as synonymous concepts, this behavior of `caller()` comes as a bit of a surprise. One *could* think that line (Q) is injecting a new method into class `X` and that therefore when `UNIVERSAL`'s `foo()` is invoked in line (R), the call to `caller()` in line (N) would return class `X` as the origin of that call, as opposed to the package `main`.

Line (X) shows what happens when `UNIVERSAL`'s `foo()` is invoked on an instance of `X`. As expected and as evidenced by the commented-out message shown in line (X), the call is dispatched to the definition of `foo()` in line (M). However, a run-time exception is thrown by Perl when processing the call to `boohoo()` in line (P). Search for `boohoo()` in this case starts with class `X` and moves up the inheritance tree that converges on `X`. Since no matching definition is found for this call, the script is aborted.

```
#!/usr/bin/perl -w
use strict;

### UniversalAddTo.pl

#--------------------------  Class X  --------------------------------
package X;                                                        #(A)

sub new { bless {}, $_[0] }                                       #(B)

sub bar {                                                         #(C)
    my $self = shift;
    print "X's bar called\n";                                     #(D)
    $self->foo();                                                 #(E)
}

#--------------------------  Class Y  --------------------------------
package Y;                                                        #(F)

sub new { bless {}, $_[0] }                                       #(G)
```

```
#-------------------------  Class Z  --------------------------------
package Z;                                                           #(H)

@Z::ISA = qw( X Y );                                                 #(I)

sub new { bless {}, $_[0] }                                          #(J)

sub boohoo { print "Z's boohoo invoked\n" }                          #(K)

#-------------------------  main  -----------------------------------
package main;                                                        #(L)

sub UNIVERSAL::foo {                                                 #(M)
    my $self = shift;
    my ($package, $filename, $line) = caller;                        #(N)
    print "UNIVERSAL's foo called by $package\n";                    #(O)
    $self->boohoo();                                                 #(P)
}

sub X::baz {                                                         #(Q)
    my $self = shift;
    print "X's baz called\n";
    $self->foo();                                                    #(R)
}

my $obj = Z->new();                                                  #(S)
$obj->can('foo') ? print "yes to foo in Z\n"
                            : print "no to foo in Z\n";              #(T)

$obj->bar();                # X's bar called                         #(U)
                            # UNIVERSAL's foo called by X
                            # Z's boohoo invoked

$obj->baz();                # X's baz called                         #(V)
                            # UNIVERSAL's foo called by main
                            # Z's boohoo invoked

my $obj2 = X->new();                                                 #(W)
$obj2->foo();               # UNIVERSAL's foo called by main         #(X)
                            # >>>>> Runtime exception thown <<<<<
```

8.8 HOW A METHOD IS SEARCHED FOR IN A CLASS HIERARCHY

Section 8.3 of this chapter talked about how a method is searched for in a class hierarchy when it is invoked on a derived-class instance. There our discussion focused on the direct and the indirect superclasses of a derived class that are searched for a given method. The story we told there was not complete since we had not yet introduced the reader to the `UNIVERSAL` class.

Now we will generalize that discussion to include the `UNIVERSAL` class in the search process. We will also address the issue of when exactly a method call is shipped off to the `AUTOLOAD()` of a derived class and the `AUTOLOAD()` of the various direct and the indirect superclasses of a derived class.

Let's say we have

```
package Z;
@Z::ISA = qw( X Y );
```

Now a call like

```
$zobj->foo(..arguments..);
```

where `$zobj` holds a reference to an instance of `Z`, will cause a search to be conducted for the method `foo()` in the following order:

1. Perl first looks for `foo()` in class `Z`. If not found there, the search proceeds to the next stop.

2. Perl looks for `foo()` in the parent class `X`. If not found there, the search proceeds to the next step.

3. Perl looks for `foo()` — and does so recursively in a left-to-right depth-first manner — in the direct and indirect superclasses of `X` but *not* including the system-supplied root class `UNIVERSAL`. If not found in any of those superclasses, the search continues on to the next step.

4. Perl looks for `foo()` in the next base class, `Y`, declared in the `ISA` array of class `Z`. If not found there, the search proceeds to the next step.

5. Perl looks for `foo()` — and does so recursively in a left-to-right depth-first manner — in the direct and indirect superclasses of `Y` but *not* including the system-supplied root class `UNIVERSAL`. If not found there, the search continues on to the next step.

6. After searching through the programmer-specified superclass hierarchy in the manner described above, Perl searches for the method in the root class `UNIVERSAL`. If not found there, the search proceeds to the next step.

7. Perl searches for an implementation of the `AUTOLOAD()` method in exactly the same manner as outlined in the previous six steps. Perl ships off the call `foo()` to the first `AUTOLOAD()` implementation found. If no `AUTOLOAD()` implementation is found, Perl throws a run-time exception.

In the script shown next, `MethodSearch.pl`, we will implement the hierarchy of Fig. 8.5. The classes `X`, `Y`, and `Z` are defined in lines (A), (D), and (I). Class `X` is provided with a method `foo()`, and class `Y` with a method `bar()`. Note that the instances constructed from each class consist of empty arrays.

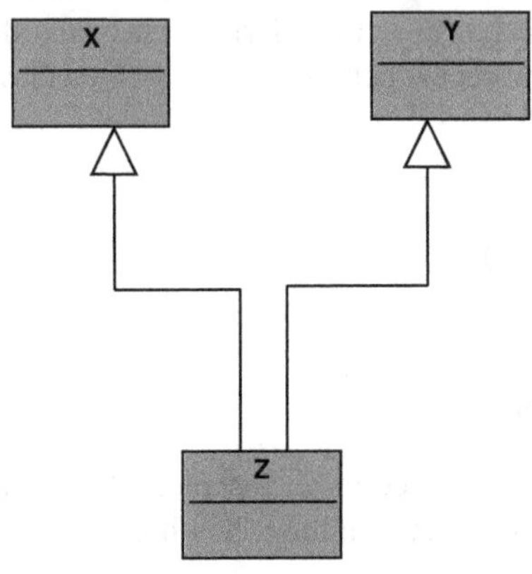

Fig. 8.5

Line (L) constructs a derived-class instance of type `Z`. When line (M) invokes `foo()` on this instance, the search for `foo()` takes place according to the algorithm outlined above, producing the output shown in the commented-out portion of line (M). By the same token, when we invoke `bar()` on the `Z` instance in line (N), it results in the output shown in the commented-out portion of that line.

However, when we invoke `jazz()` on the `Z` instance in line (O), the search for that ends up with the invocation of `AUTOLOAD()` defined for class `Y` in line (G). So the output produced is as shown commented out just below line (O).

Finally, since we have explicitly defined `AUTOLOAD()` for one of the superclasses of `Z`, it will also trap any calls to `DESTROY()` for the `Z` instances. So when the `Z` instance of line (L) goes out of scope, the call to `DESTROY()` for the instance is handled by the `AUTOLOAD()` of class `Y`, producing the output shown in line (Q).

```
#!/usr/bin/perl -w
use strict;

### MethodSearch.pl

#------------------------------ class X ----------------------------
package X;                                                       #(A)

sub new { bless [], shift }                                      #(B)

sub foo { print "foo of class X called\n" }                      #(C)

#----------------------------- class Y -----------------------------
package Y;                                                       #(D)

sub new { bless [], shift }                                      #(E)
sub bar { print "bar of class Y called\n"}                       #(F)
sub AUTOLOAD {                                                   #(G)
    print "AUTOLOAD of class Y invoked by " .                    #(H)
          "function call $Y::AUTOLOAD\n";
}

#----------------------------- class Z -----------------------------
package Z;                                                       #(I)

@Z::ISA = ('X', 'Y');                                            #(J)

sub new { bless [], shift }

#---------------------------- Test Code ----------------------------
package main;                                                    #(K)

my $zobj = Z->new();                                             #(L)

$zobj->foo();         # foo of class X called                    #(M)
$zobj->bar();         # bar of class Y called                    #(N)
$zobj->jazz();                                                   #(O)
         # AUTOLOAD of class Y invoked by function call Z::jazz    #(P)
         # AUTOLOAD of class Y invoked by function call Z::DESTROY #(Q)
```

Note that the search algorithm presented in this section also applies to constructor calls. So if an instance of a derived class is meant to be constructed with a call to new() and if the derived class does not implement this method, Perl will look for it in the direct and indirect superclasses of the derived class in exactly the same manner as outlined in this section.

8.9 INHERITED METHODS BEHAVE AS IF LOCALLY DEFINED

The next script, `InheritedActAsLocal.pl`, defines a base class `X` in lines (A) through (K) and a derived class `Y` in lines (L) through (V). The method `foo()` defined for the base class calls `baz()` in line (G). Both the base class `X` and the derived class `Y` contain separate definitions for `baz()`, the former in lines (H) through (K) and the latter in lines (S) through (V).[8] Class `Y` also contains a method `bar()` in lines (O) through (R). This method calls on `foo()` in line (R). Since this is important to the discussion that follows, we want to remind the reader that `foo()` is only defined for the base class in lines (C) through (G).

So the overall situation with this script is that we have the base-class method `foo()` calling on `baz()` that is defined for both the base class and the derived class. When in line (Z) we invoke `bar()` on a `Y` instance, we get the following output from the script:

```
Y's bar invoked
X's foo invoked
  foo(): instance is of type: Y
Y's baz invoked
  baz(): instance is of type: Y
```

indicating that `Y`'s `bar()` has successfully called `X`'s `foo()`, which in turn has successfully called `Y`'s `baz()` (and *not* `X`'s `baz()`).

What is happening here is that when `Y`'s `bar()` looks for a method definition for the call to `foo()` in line (R), it finds the definition in its parent class `X` in line (C). But this definition is used by `Y` as if it were locally defined within `Y` itself. The first argument supplied to the method `foo()` consists of the `Y` instance. Therefore, when this method definition calls on `baz()`, the search for `baz()` begins with class `Y`.

---

[8]When a method of a base class calls another method of the same class that may however be overridden in a derived class, that introduces a dependency known as the "Fragile Base Class Problem" between the the base class and the derived class. Such a dependency may make it more difficult to maintain and extend the base and the derived classes independently even when their published APIs remain the same. For some recent work on the measurement of the extent of the "fragile base-class problem" in object-oriented software, the reader is referred to [53].

```
#!/usr/bin/perl -w
use strict;

### InheritedActAsLocal.pl

#---------------------------  Class X  -----------------------------
package X;                                                        #(A)

sub new { bless {}, $_[0] }                                       #(B)

sub foo {                                                         #(C)
    my $self = shift;                                             #(D)
    print "X's foo invoked\n";                                    #(E)
    print "  foo(): instance is of type: ", ref( $self ), "\n";   #(F)
    $self->baz();                                                 #(G)
}
sub baz {                                                         #(H)
    my $self = shift;                                             #(I)
    print "X's baz invoked\n";                                    #(J)
    print "  baz(): instance is of type: ", ref( $self ), "\n";   #(K)
}

#---------------------------  Class Y  -----------------------------
package Y;                                                        #(L)

@Y::ISA = qw( X );                                                #(M)

sub new { bless {}, $_[0] }                                       #(N)

sub bar {                                                         #(O)
    my $self = shift;                                             #(P)
    print "Y's bar invoked\n";                                    #(Q)
    $self->foo();                                                 #(R)
}
sub baz {                                                         #(S)
    my $self = shift;                                             #(T)
    print "Y's baz invoked\n";                                    #(U)
    print "  baz(): instance is of type: ", ref( $self ), "\n";   #(V)
}

#--------------------------  Test Code  ------------------------------
package main;                                                     #(W)

my $y_obj = Y->new();                                             #(Y)
$y_obj->bar();                                                    #(Z)
```

8.10 DESTRUCTION OF DERIVED-CLASS INSTANCES

In Chapter 6 we talked about how garbage collection works in Perl and how the `DESTROY()` method of a class — assuming that the class is provided with such a method — is invoked just before the memory occupied by an instance object is reclaimed. We will now show the working of `DESTROY()` in a class hierarchy.

When the reference count associated with a subclass instance goes to zero and it is time to reclaim the memory occupied by the instance, Perl looks for the `DESTROY()` method in the definition of the subclass. If the subclass does not come with such a method, a search for the method is carried out in the direct and the indirect superclasses of the subclass as described in Section 8.8.

The next script, `DestroySubclass.pl`, shows a two-class hierarchy consisting of a base class `Animal` and a derived class `FourLegged`. In the example code shown, only the base class `Animal` is supplied with the `DESTROY()` method, as shown in line (A).

In line (B), we construct a new `Animal` instance and assign it to the variable `$anim`. Subsequently, we `undef` this variable in line (C). This causes the instance constructed in line (B) to become unreferenced. As a result, the `DESTROY()` method of `Animal` is invoked before the memory occupied by the unreferenced instance is reclaimed, as evidenced by the message that is printed out. This message is shown just below line (C).

We then construct a `FourLegged` instance in line (D). The `FourLegged` class was intentionally not provided with a `DESTROY()`. But, on account of inheritance from the base class `Animal`, Perl will seek out and execute `Animal`'s `DESTROY()` before garbage collecting the instance of line (D). `Animal`'s `DESTROY()` in this case will cause the following message to be printed just before the `FourLegged` instance is reclaimed:

```
Memory occupied by the Animal instance named PuttyCat is \
                                         about to be reclaimed
```

At least theoretically, we can't quarrel with the wording of the above message since, by virtue of polymorphism, a `FourLegged` instance is also an `Animal`. The appropriateness of deploying a superclass `DESTROY()` for cleaning up when the memory occupied by a subclass instance is reclaimed depends entirely on what system resources if any are appropriated during the construction of the instance.

```
#!/usr/bin/perl -w
use strict;

### DestroySubclass.pl
```

```
#--------------------------- Class Animal ----------------------------
package Animal;

sub new {
    my ( $class, $name, $weight ) = @_;
    bless {
        _name   => $name,
        _weight => $weight,
    }, $class;
}
sub get_name {
    my $self = shift;
    $self->{_name};
}
sub DESTROY {                                                          #(A)
    my $self = shift;
    my $name = $self->get_name();
    print "Memory occupied by the Animal instance named " .
"$name is about to be reclaimed\n";
}

#----------------------- Class FourLegged ---------------------------
package FourLegged;

@FourLegged::ISA = ("Animal");

sub new {
    my ( $class, $name, $weight, $num_of_teeth ) = @_;
    bless {
        _name    =>  $name,
        _weight =>  $weight,
        _num_of_teetch => $num_of_teeth,
    }, $class;
}

#------------------------ Test Code ---------------------------------
package main;
my $anim = Animal->new( "BigHorn", "300" );                            #(B)
$anim = undef;                                                         #(C)
        # Memory occupied by the Animal instance named BigHorn
        #                    is about to be reclaimed
my $pet = FourLegged->new( "PuttyCat", 15, 16 );                       #(D)
        # Memory occupied by the Animal instance named PuttyCat
        #                    is about to be reclaimed
```

In Section 8.8, we mentioned that a method call invoked on a subclass instance is shipped off to `AUTOLOAD()` if the method cannot be found in the subclass itself and in all of its direct and indirect superclasses. The same thing can be expected to happen for a search for `DESTROY()` if it is not found in the subclass itself and its direct and indirect superclasses. But `AUTOLOAD()` is frequently used to translate method calls into system calls. That is, while being receptive to the other methods calls, we may want `AUTOLOAD()` to ignore a search for `DESTROY()`. This can easily be accomplished by using the same ploy that was shown in Section 6.5 of Chapter 6 for controlling the interaction between `DESTROY()` and `AUTOLOAD()` at the level of a single class.

8.11 DIAMOND INHERITANCE

We have diamond inheritance if a class can inherit from the same ancestor class through two different paths. The simplest possible example of such inheritance is shown in Fig. 8.6 where the class `W` is allowed to inherit from the ancestor class `X` through the two different paths shown, one via class `Y` and the other via class `Z`.

In general, diamond inheritance can create problems in systems programming languages that allow a child class to inherit implementation code from more than one parent class at the same time. A classic example of this is C++. If in C++ the code for class `W` in Fig. 8.6 invokes a method whose implementation code resides in the ancestor class `X`, that could result in a compile-time error (assuming that this `X` method is inherited unaltered by `W` through the two different inheritance paths shown in the figure).

In most cases, diamond inheritance is not be a problem in Perl (and in Python also, as we will see in the next chapter). A Perl class (and a Python class also) does not inherit implementation code from its superclasses in the same sense that a C++ class does. If a child class in Perl does not contain its own implementation for a method, a recursive left-to-right and depth-first search is carried out for a method definition in the direct and indirect superclasses of the child class, as already explained in Section 8.8. The very first method definition found through this search is used for the method call.

While the procedure used to search for a method definition does not care whether there exist multiple inheritance paths between some ancestor class and the child class where the method definition is needed, one does have to watch out for the fact that diamond inheritance in Perl may cause repeated invocation of a method definition in an ancestor class for a single invocation of some method in a child class. In some cases, this could cause a script to behave in a manner that was not intended originally.

Consider the next script, `Diamond.pl`, that implements the `X`, `Y`, `Z`, and `W` diamond hierarchy of Fig. 8.6. Class `X` in lines (A) through (D) comes with a method `foo()`. Class `Y` is provided with a method `bar()` in lines (H) through (J).

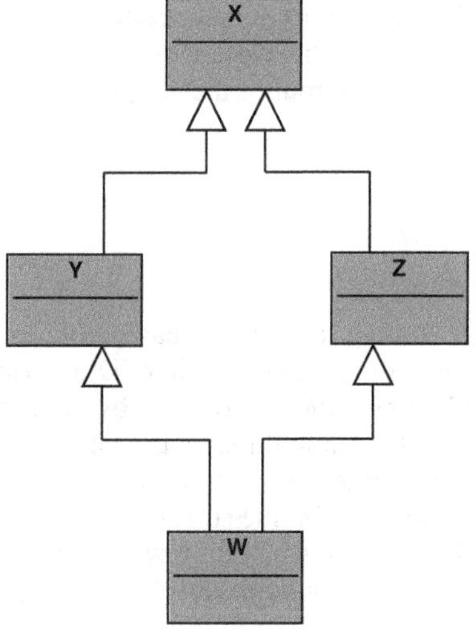

Fig. 8.6

Similarly, class Z comes with a method `baz()` in lines (N) through (P). Finally, class W defined in lines (Q) through (Z) is derived from both Y and Z. This class comes with its own `foo()`, as defined in lines (S) through (Z). In `main`, we first construct an instance of type W in line (b). Subsequently, we invoke `foo()` on this instance in line (c).

Let's now see what happens if we run this script after we have commenting out the following statement in line (D):

```
return if $self->{_foo}{__PACKAGE__}++;
```

Here is the output in this case:

```
W's foo invoked
Y's bar invoked
X's foo invoked
Z's baz invoked
X's foo invoked
```

By tracing backwards the method invocations, we notice that W's `foo()` calls Y's `bar()` and Z's `baz()`. In turn, Y's `bar()` calls X's `foo()` and, more particularly, Z's `baz()` also calls X's `foo()`. So we have a double invocation of the method `foo()` defined for the common ancestor X. Depending on the functionality packed into X's `foo()`, this may or may not be a cause for concern. If X's `foo()` was some kind of a counter, this could indeed be a problem.

To prevent such multiple invocations of an ancestor-class method that is inherited by other classes through different paths, we can use the ploy shown in line (D) of the script. With this line in place, the output of the script is

```
W's foo invoked
Y's bar invoked
X's foo invoked
Z's baz invoked
```

Now X's `foo()` is invoked only once. In this case, when Y's `bar()` invokes X's `foo()`, autovivification causes the statement in line (D) to bring into existence a hash named `_foo` containing the key `__PACKAGE__` that by default will evaluate to false, that in a numerical context is the same thing as the number 0. This allows the flow of execution to proceed beyond line (D) in the implementation code for X's `foo()`. Since the postfix increment operator in line (D) also causes the value associated with the `__PACKAGE__` key to be incremented, any future attempts at accessing the same key would return a positive value, which would cause X's `foo()` to return immediately.

```
#!/usr/bin/perl -w
use strict;

### Diamond.pl

#---------------------------   Class X   -----------------------------
package X;                                                          #(A)

sub new { bless {}, $_[0] }                                         #(B)
sub foo {                                                           #(C)
    my $self = shift;
    return if $self->{_foo}{__PACKAGE__}++;                         #(D)
    print "X's foo invoked\n";
}

#---------------------------   Class Y   -----------------------------
package Y;                                                          #(E)

@Y::ISA = qw( X );                                                  #(F)

sub new { bless {}, $_[0] }                                         #(G)
sub bar {                                                           #(H)
    my $self = shift;
    print "Y's bar invoked\n";                                      #(I)
    $self->SUPER::foo();                                            #(J)
}
```

```
#---------------------------  Class Z  -----------------------------
package Z;                                                      #(K)

@Z::ISA = qw( X );                                              #(L)
sub new { bless {}, $_[0] }                                     #(M)
sub baz {                                                       #(N)
    my $self = shift;
    print "Z's baz invoked\n";                                  #(O)
    $self->SUPER::foo();                                        #(P)
}

#---------------------------  Class W  -----------------------------
package W;                                                      #(Q)

@W::ISA = qw( Y Z );                                            #(R)
sub new { bless {}, $_[0] }                                     #(S)
sub foo {                                                       #(T)
    my $self = shift;
    print "W's foo invoked\n";                                  #(U)
    $self->bar();                                               #(V)
    $self->baz();                                               #(Z)
}

#--------------------------- package main ----------------------------
package main;                                                   #(a)

my $w_obj = W->new();                                           #(b)
$w_obj->foo();                                                  #(c)
```

8.12 ON THE INHERITABILITY OF A CLASS

What would make a class unsuitable for inheritance depends partly on whether it obeys the standard conventions regarding OO syntax and, even when syntactical conventions are not violated, partly on the expectations of the child classes. For example, if the child classes do not provide their own constructors and expect to use a generic constructor supplied by the base class, then, obviously, whether or not the base class provides a constructor would determine if the base class is inheritable. By the same token, if the child classes expect to use through inheritance the base-class method definitions as if the methods were locally defined in the child classes, the base-class methods would have to be written without the base-class name hard-coded in.

Yet another issue that has a bearing on the inheritability of a class is how the `bless()` method is used. This method can be called either with one argument or with two. In all the examples shown so far, we have used the two-argument version of `bless()`. The two-argument version blesses the first argument, which must be a reference, into the class corresponding to the second argument. On the other hand, the one-argument version blesses the argument, which must again be a reference, into the class in which `bless()` is invoked. On the face of it, the two-argument and the one-argument versions do the same thing, but, when inheritance is involved, the latter could lead to unintended consequences.

Consider the script, `Inheritability.pl`, shown below in which the base class is obviously inheritable. The base class includes a constructor in lines (A) through (E) and a method named `foo()` in lines (F) and (G). Hoping to use the base's constructor, the derived class, defined in lines (H) through (M), does not include a constructor of its own. However, it does include an override definition for `foo()` in lines (J) through (M).

As defined, the two classes work together nicely. The package `main` shows us constructing a derived-class instance in line (O). When we invoke `foo()` on this instance in line (P), we see the following output:

```
Derived's foo invoked
Base's foo invoked
```

Now consider the case when we comment out the invocation of the two-argument `bless()` in line (D) and uncomment the commented-out line (E). In other words, we will now use the one-argument `bless()`. Now the same script produces just the following output:

```
Base's foo invoked
```

The reason for this is not hard to see. By default, the one-argument `bless()` blesses the reference into the package in which the function is invoked. Therefore, the call to `new()` in line (O) — even though it is on the class `Derived` — will return an object reference that is actually blessed into the class `Base`. So when we call `foo()` on this reference in line (P), it is the definition of line (F) that is used, and not the definition of line (J).

```
#!/usr/bin/perl -w
use strict;

### Inheritability.pl

package Base;                                                          #(A)

sub new {                                                              #(B)
    my $class = shift;                                                 #(C)
```

```
    bless {}, $class;                                              #(D)
#   bless {};                                                      #(E)
}
sub foo {                                                          #(F)
    print "Base's foo invoked\n";                                  #(G)
}

package Derived;                                                   #(H)

@Derived::ISA = qw( Base );                                        #(I)
sub foo {                                                          #(J)
    my $self = shift;                                              #(K)
    print "Derived's foo invoked\n";                               #(L)
    $self->SUPER::foo();                                           #(M)
}

#---------------------------- package main ----------------------------
package main;                                                      #(N)

my $obj = Derived->new();                                          #(O)
$obj->foo();                   # Derived's foo invoked             #(P)
                               # Base's foo invoked                #(Q)
```

8.13 LOCAL VARIABLES AND SUBROUTINES IN DERIVED CLASSES

Local variables can serve the same useful role in a derived class that they do in a base class. A `my` variable can, for example, be used to hold a reference to an anonymous subroutine that could be a closure over other `my` variables. As with base classes, such variables and subroutines would not be accessible outside the derived class.

It is interesting to see that even when variables and subroutines are defined to be accessible only locally in base classes and in derived classes, one can still establish a "relationship" between the base-class versions and the derived-class versions through the other methods defined for the classes. An example of this is illustrated in the script `DerivedLocalVars.pl` shown next.

The goal of the next script is to maintain a count for the derived-class instances and the base-class instances, but with a twist. Since, by virtue of polymorphism, a derived-class instance is of base-class type also, when we create a derived-class instance, we want the count for the base-class instances to also go up. And when a derived-class instance goes out of scope, we want the counts for both the derived-class instances and the base-class instances to be decremented. On the other hand, when a base-class instance goes out of scope, we want the count for only the base-class instances to go down by one.

This behavior is exhibited by the following script. The counters in both the base and the derived classes are private to each class. The base-class count is held by the private variable in line (B) and the derived-class count by the private variable in line (O). The base-class counter is incremented by the anonymous subroutine in line (C) and the derived-class by a similar subroutine in line (P). The decrementing of the count for the base class is done by the anonymous subroutine in line (D) and for the derived class by the one in line (Q).

The incrementing and the decrementing of the counts in each class is done inside the `new()` and the `DESTROY()` methods, respectively. As shown in line (T), the derived-class constructor calls the base-class constructor. This causes the base-class count to also get incremented when the derived-class count is incremented by the call in line (U). Along the same lines, the derived-class `DESTROY()` calls the base-class `DESTROY()` in line (Z), which causes the base-class count to also get decremented when the derived-class is decremented because a derived-class instance is going out of scope.

Obviously, only the base-class counter will be incremented and decremented when instances that are strictly of the base type are created or destroyed.

The counting behavior of the two classes is illustrated by the test code in lines (d) through (s). As we make instances of the base class in lines (e) and (g), we see the base-class count incremented, as shown by the commented-out output in lines (f) and (h). Line (j) shows the base-class count getting decremented when one of the base-class instances goes out of scope through the action in line (i). Lines (k) and (n) construct two instances of the derived class. Lines (l) and (o) show the resulting count for the derived class, whereas the lines (m) and (p) show how the base-class count is affected by the construction of derived-class instances. Finally, when a derived-class instance goes out of scope in line (q), we see how the base-class and derived-class counts are affected in lines (r) and (s).

```
#!/usr/bin/perl -w
use strict;

### DerivedLocalVars.pl

#-------------------------   class Base  ------------------------------
package Base;                                                      #(A)

my $_count = 0;                                                    #(B)
my $_count_incrementer = sub { $_count++; };                       #(C)
my $_count_decrementer = sub { $_count--; };                       #(D)
```

```
sub new {                                                          #(E)
    my $class = shift;                                             #(F)
    &$_count_incrementer;                                          #(G)
    bless {}, $class;                                              #(H)
}
sub DESTROY {                                                      #(I)
    &$_count_decrementer;                                          #(J)
}
sub get_count {                                                    #(K)
    print "base objects count : $_count\n";                        #(L)
}

#-----------------------   class Derived  ---------------------------
package Derived;                                                   #(M)
@Derived::ISA = qw( Base );                                        #(N)

my $_count = 0;                                                    #(O)
my $_count_incrementer = sub { $_count++; };                       #(P)
my $_count_decrementer = sub { $_count--; };                       #(Q)

sub new {                                                          #(R)
    my $class = shift;                                             #(S)
    my $self = $class->SUPER::new(@_[1..$#_]);                     #(T)
    &$_count_incrementer;                                          #(U)
    bless $self, $class;                                           #(V)
}
sub DESTROY {                                                      #(W)
    my $self = shift;                                              #(X)
    $self->SUPER::DESTROY();                                       #(Z)
    &$_count_decrementer;                                          #(a)
}
sub get_count {                                                    #(b)
    print "derived objects count : $_count\n";                     #(c)
}

#--------------------------   Test Code  -----------------------------

package main;                                                      #(d)

my $base_obj_1 = Base->new();                                      #(e)
$base_obj_1->get_count();             # base objects count: 1      #(f)

my $base_obj_2 = Base->new();                                      #(g)
$base_obj_2->get_count();             # base objects count : 2     #(h)

$base_obj_1 = undef;                                               #(i)
$base_obj_2->get_count();             # base objects count : 1     #(j)

my $derived_obj_1 = Derived->new();                                #(k)
```

```
$derived_obj_1->get_count();          # derived objects count : 1     #(l)
$derived_obj_1->Base::get_count();    # base objects count: 2         #(m)

my $derived_obj_2 = Derived->new();                                    #(n)
$derived_obj_2->get_count();          # derived objects count : 2     #(o)
$derived_obj_2->Base::get_count();    # base objects count : 3        #(p)

$derived_obj_1 = undef;                                                #(q)
$derived_obj_2->get_count();          # derived objects count : 1     #(r)
$derived_obj_2->Base::get_count();    # base objects count : 2        #(s)
```

8.14 OPERATOR OVERLOADING AND INHERITANCE

Section 6.8 of Chapter 6 described in considerable detail how the `overload` module that comes bundled with Perl's standard distribution can be used to overload a large number of operators in a user-defined class. In the context of inheritance, we are now faced with the following questions:

- If an operator is overloaded in the base class, does that overload definition become available in a derived class?
- What if a derived class wants to override the base-class's overload definition for an operator?
- Are there any syntax constraints on the base-class overload definition so that it becomes available in a derived class?

To answer these questions, we will start with the class `XArray` of Section 6.8 of Chapter 6 and extend it into the derived class `MyXArray` shown in the next script.[9]

For our first experiment, let's see what the script does if we uncomment the commented-out line (C). By virtue of the statement in line (C), the derived class also overloads the `""` operator, the overload code being supplied by the `_str()` method at line (H). Recall from Section 6.8 of Chapter 6, in the context of operator overloading in Perl, `""` is called the stringification operator because its implementation code is supposed to return a print representation of the instance object. As you would expect, when we construct an instance of `MyXArray` in line (T1) of the script `TestMyXArray.pl` that is shown after the `MyXArray.pm` script and then ask

[9]Just to make it a bit different, we have gratuitously supplied the derived class `MyXArray` with its own constructor that initializes one more instance variable, `how_many_nums`, in line (F). This instance variable is supposed to keep track of the number of numeric elements in the data stored in an instance of `MyXArray`.

print to print it out in line (T2), the system uses the override definition of _str() in the derived class. For the instance constructed in line (T1) of TestMyXArray.pl, the output is

```
1____2____hello____3
```

Note that _str() as defined in line (H) for the derived class places *four* underscores between the consecutive elements stored in an instance of MyXArray, whereas _str() as defined for the parent class in Section 6.8 of Chapter 6 uses only one underscore.

Let's now see what happens if we leave commented out the use overload declaration in the derived class in line (C) of the script. Now, at least from the outward appearance, class MyXArray does not care to overload the "" operator. However, since the base class overloads this operator, Perl will go ahead and assume that this operator continues to be overloaded for the MyXArray instances also. What's even more interesting is that Perl will seek out the overload definition that is most relevant to the derived class. In our example, Perl will use the override definition of _str() in the derived class itself even though the connection between the "" operator and the method name _str() was established in the base class.[10]

The upshot is that if you overload an operator in a base class, you do not need to overload it again with the use overload declaration in the derived class; the operator will continue to behave in an overloaded fashion in the derived class. Furthermore, if the derived class contains an override definition for the method that implements the operator, it is the override definition that will be used on the instances of the derived class.

The above conclusion is subject to the following caveat: The use overload declaration in the base class must directly name the implementation methods for the operators, as opposed to using references to them (or, even, as opposed to using anonymous subroutines). Suppose you change the use overload statement in line (B) of the script XArray.pm in Section 6.8 of Chapter 6 to

```
use overload '+'    => \&_add,
             '""'   => \&_str,
             '<<'   => \&_left_shift,
             '~'    => \&_invert,
             '<=>' => \&_compare,
             'cmp' => \&_compare,
             'fallback' => 1;
```

where we have used references to all the implementation methods. Now, whereas the script TestXArray.pl of Section 6.8 of Chapter 6 will produce the same results as before, the script TestMyXArray.pl shown here will produce

[10]This is an example of an operator behaving polymorphically in a class hierarchy.

```
1_2_hello_3
```

So now the override definition for `_str()` in the derived class will *not* be used. Obviously, if you uncomment line (C) of the `MyXArray.pm` script, the output of `TestMyXArray.pl` will revert back to what you saw before. That is, if you directly overload an operator for a derived class, its overload definition in the derived class will be used regardless of how the overloading for the same operator is provided for in the base class.

Here is the code for the derived class `MyXArray`. The reader is urged to review the base class `XArray` defined in Section 6.8 of Chapter 6 before examining the code below.

```
package MyXArray;                                                          #(A)

### MyXArray.pm

use strict;
use Carp;
use XArray;    # This is XArray.pm from Section 6.8 of Chapter 6          #(B)

#use overload '""'  => '_str';                                             #(C)

@MyXArray::ISA = ('XArray');                                               #(D)

# Constructor
sub new {                                                                  #(E)
    my ($class, $arr_ref) = @_;
    bless {
        _arr => $arr_ref,
        _size  => scalar( @$arr_ref ),
        _how_many_nums => scalar( grep /^\d+$/, @$arr_ref ),              #(F)
    }, $class;
}

sub get_how_many_nums { $_[0]->{_how_many_nums}; }                        #(G)

sub _str {                                                                 #(H)
    my $self = shift;
    return join("____", @{$self->{_arr}});                                #(I)
}

1
```

Our discussion above concerning the behavior of the `""` operator in the derived class `MyXArray` vis-à-vis its behavior in the base class `XArray` used the following test script:

```
#!/usr/bin/perl -w

### TestMyXArray.pl

use strict;
use MyXArray;

my $arr = MyXArray->new( [1, 2, "hello", 3] );                        #(T1)
print $arr, "\n";                                                      #(T2)
```

For the scripts `MyXArray.pm` and `TestMyXArray.pl` to work as described, the compiler must be able to find the class `XArray` of Section 6.8 of Chapter 6. You could either copy over that class file into the directory where `MyXArray.pm` resides or let Perl know where to find `XArray` by any of the devices discussed in Section 2.11 of Chapter 2.

8.15 CREDITS AND SUGGESTIONS FOR FURTHER READING

We mentioned in Section 8.8 that if you try to construct an instance of a subclass that has not been provided with a constructor, Perl will search for a constructor definition in the direct and indirect superclasses of the subclass in the same manner as for any method whose definition cannot be found in the class. This can sometimes lead to unintended consequences. Conway [11] suggests that the process of instance creation be separated from the process of instance initialization to get around this problem. Regarding operator overloading for a derived class, the authoritative document to read for that is the same as cited earlier in Chapter 6: Ilya Zakharevich's write-up on his `overload` module [71].

8.16 HOMEWORK

1. Extend the following class, `Base`, into the smallest possible derived class. (Your derived class should consist of only one Perl statement.) Test your solution by making an instance of the derived class and invoking `foo()` on it. That is, if your derived class is called `Derived`, you should be able to make the following calls:

```
my $obj = Derived->new();
$obj->foo();                        # Base's foo invoked
```

where the second call should yield the output shown in the commented-out portion of the line. Here is the base class:

```
package Base;
sub new {
    my $class = shift;
    bless {}, $class;
}
sub foo {
    print "Base's foo invoked\n";
}
1
```

2. As mentioned in Section 8.7, every Perl class inherits the `isa()` method from the `UNIVERSAL` class. As shown there, it can be used to check whether a given instance is of a certain type by using the following syntax:

```
$instance = MyClass->new( ..... );
print $instance->isa('SomeClassName') ? "yes\n"  : "no\n";
```

What is the difference between the above call to the inherited `isa()` and the invocation of `isa()` in the following call:

```
$instance = MyClass->new( ..... );
print UNIVERSAL::isa($instance, 'SomeClassName') ? "yes\n"  \
                                                 : "no\n";
```

3. The `Person` hierarchy of Section 8.4 used a promotion table for keeping track of how an employee is promoted through the ranks. This promotion table was stored as an anonymous hash in the `Employee` class. Modify the hierarchy so that the promotion table is stored in a class of its own. Any class that has a need to use this table can inherit from the promotion table class.

4. Section 8.8 talked about how Perl carries out search for a method definition in a class hierarchy. Do you think Perl remembers the location of a method in the search graph so that if the same method were to be called again on the same type of an instance, Perl would go directly to the previously found method (as

opposed to scanning the ancestor classes again)? You could try a script that looks like the following for your experiments:

```
#!/usr/bin/perl -w
use strict;

package X;
sub new { bless {}, $_[0] }
sub foo { print "calling X's foo\n"; }

package Y;
@Y::ISA = ('X');

package main;
my @names = keys( %X::);
print "X's namespace dictionary:   @names\n";
@names = keys( %Y::);
print "Y's namespace dictionary:   @names\n";

my $yobj = Y->new();
$yobj->foo();
@names = keys( %Y::);
print "Y's namespace dictionary after \
              calling X's methods:   @names\n";
```

5. As we discussed in Section 8.10, if you do not provide a derived class with its own `DESTROY()` method, Perl will be happy to use the base class's `DESTROY()` method. But that has the potential of creating entirely unintended effects. Extend the `Node` and the `Network` classes of Section 6.4.1 of Chapter 6 but do not provide the derived classes with their own `DESTROY()` methods. Now show the consequences of the missing derived-class destructors from the standpoint of preventing memory leaks caused by circular references. Your network should consist of the instances made from the derived classes.

6. In Section 8.14, we extended the `XArray` class of Section 6.8 into the `MyXArray` class. While the base class in Chapter 6 was provided with explicit overloadings for a number of operators, only the stringification operator was explicitly overloaded in the derived class in this chapter. Add to the code shown for `TestMyXArray.pl` in Section 8.14 to demonstrate that all the operators that were explicitly overloaded for the base class remain overloaded in the derived class. Show that this applies also to the base-class operators whose overloadings are autogenerated by the `overload` module.

7. Section 8.14 talked about the base-class operators behaving polymorphically with respect to the derived-class overload definitions. We demonstrated this property for only the stringification operator. Show that this property applies to all the other operators, those that are directly overloaded for the base class and those whose overloadings are autogenerated by the `overload` module.

8. This question deals with operator overloadings for a class that is derived from multiple ancestors. By constructing simple examples, show that the set of overloaded operators for a derived class is the union of overloaded operators for all its ancestor classes. What happens to the overloading in a derived class when the same operator is overloaded differently in different ancestor classes? (Recall from Section 6.8 of Chapter 6 that the autogeneration of operator overloadings is controlled by the value given to the `fallback` key in the `use overload` declaration. A derived class inherits the value for this key from the first overloaded ancestor class in a left-to-right depth-first scan of all the ancestor classes [71].)

9

Inheritance and Polymorphism in Python

This chapter addresses issues related to subclassing in Python OO. We talk about the code required for instance creation in a subclass if part of the work must be carried out by the code in a superclass; how Python searches for a method that is not directly defined for a subclass but is available from one or more superclasses; how a method defined for a subclass can get part of the work done through a call to a superclass method; and so on. With regard to subclass instance creation for new-style classes, this chapter goes into the different roles played by `__new__()` and `__init__()` as they are directly defined in a subclass and as they are inherited from the superclasses. How the subclass and superclass definitions of these methods must work together will be explained with a couple of examples that extend built-in classes into more specialized classes. With regard to how Python searches for a method in the class hierarchy, this chapter first goes into some shortcomings of the left-to-right depth-first algorithm that is used by the classic classes of Python (and that, as mentioned in the previous chapter, is also used by Perl) and then presents the desirable properties that should be possessed by a good search algorithm. Subsequently, we present the new search algorithm used for the new-style classes of Python that has the desirable properties. The chapter ends on a discussion of operating overloading for a derived class vis-à-vis the overload definitions in a base class.

The terminology used in this chapter is the same as in the previous chapter. We will use "subclass," "child class," "derived class," and "extended class" synonymously. So extending a class, deriving a class from another class, and subclassing from a base class mean the same thing. We will also use "superclass," "parent class," and "base class" synonymously.

Before proceeding to the next section, the reader should note that the discussion we presented in Sections 8.1 and 8.2 of the previous chapter is equally relevant here. (This should be obvious from our references to Python in that discussion.) The points we made there in comparing inheritance and polymorphism in Perl to the same in the systems programming languages like C++ and Java apply equally well to Python. As stated there, inheritance and polymorphism work in similar ways in Perl and Python. To a reader skipping though the book, it is highly recommended that he/she review those two sections of the previous chapter before proceeding further.

9.1 EXTENDING A CLASS IN PYTHON

Paralleling the discussion in Section 8.4 of Chapter 8, we will use the class hierarchy of Fig. 9.1 to demonstrate the class derivation syntax in Python. As with the Perl example, the base class `Person` will be endowed with generic methods such as `get_name()`, `get_age()`, etc., and the derived class `Employee` will be equipped with a special method called `promote()`. The further derived class `Manager` will also inherit some of its behavior from a mixin class `ExecutivePerks` that will only contain a class variable, `_bonus`, and class methods for retrieving and modifying the value of this variable. Our goal again is that the bonus awarded to all `Manager` instances be the same and that if the bonus is changed for one `Manager`, that change be reflected in the bonus values for all other `Manager` instances, even those that were constructed prior to the change in bonus. Each derived class inherits the methods from its parent class(es). So when we invoke, say, `get_name()` on a `Manager` instance, we'd expect Python to use the implementation of this method as defined for the class `Person`.

In Python, a class is derived from other classes by placing the names of the parent classes in the header of the subclass, as in

```
class child_class( parent_class_1,  parent_class_2,  ... ) :
```

In the multifile script shown next, this is the syntax used to derive `Employee` from `Person` in line (E1), and `Manager` from `Employee` and `ExecutivePerks` in line (M1). Note that the instance initializer for the `Employee` class calls on the instance initializer of the `Person` class in line (E6) for doing part of the work. This is purely for convenience as it results in more compact code for instance initialization in a derived class.[1] For our example here, this would cause the execution of the

[1]But note that, in general, this is **not** a safe way to write the instance initializer code. Having a subclass `__init__()` call the parent's `__init__()` for doing part of the initialization (using the syntax shown in the example code) is safe only if the following two conditions hold: (1) The subclass has a single parent, or, if multiple parents are involved, only one parent is provided with its own `__init__()`; and (2) there are no collisions between the names of the instance variables that a subclass will acquire by executing the parent's `__init__()` code and the names of the additional instance variables introduced

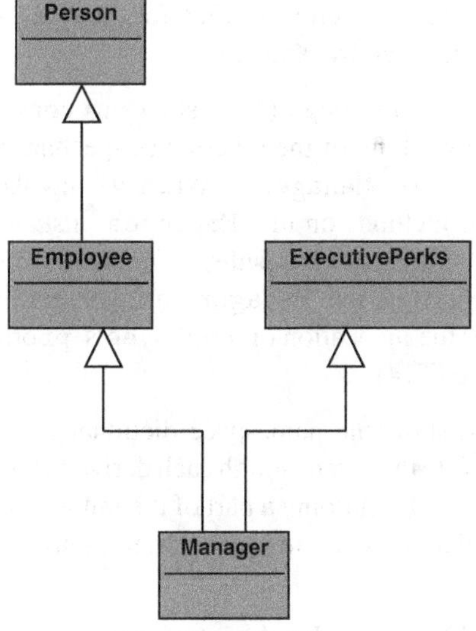

Fig. 9.1

statements in lines (P6) and (P7) when the statement in line (E6) is called. For a more verbose depiction of `Employee`'s `__init__()`, we could have directly replaced the statement in line (E6) by the statements in lines (P6) and (P7). Along the same lines, the instance initializer for `Manager` in line (M4) calls on the instance initializer of the `Employee` to do part of the work.

Note also the class variable `_promotion_table` in line (E10) of the `Employee` class; it points to a dictionary that tells the system how an individual in one rank is supposed to be promoted to another rank. `Employee` also comes with an instance method, `promote()`, in lines (E14) and (E15) that carries out a promotion in accordance with the `_promotion_table` dictionary. Both the class variable `_promotion_table` and the instance method `promote()`, in addition to the rest

---

directly in the subclass's `__init__()`. In a single-inheritance chain involving more than two classes, this constraint on the instance-variable names may cover multiple classes. For example, if `X` is the parent of `Y` and `Y` is the parent of `Z`, and that the `__init__()` of `Z` calls the `__init__()` of `Y` for doing a part of the initialization and the `__init__()` of `Y` calls the `__init__()` of `X` for the same reason, then there must be no collisions between the instance-variable names used in all three classes. **This issue of name collisions becomes moot if one initializes all the subclass instance variables locally in the subclass's `__init__()`.** As to why this constraint exists on the names of the instance variables when a subclass's `__init__()` calls a base class's `__init__()`, the reader should reflect on the fact that a subclass instance is a data object that is independent of any base classes, unlike what happens in systems programming languages like C++ and Java (as we previously mentioned in Sections 8.1 and 8.2 of the previous chapter). So when a subclass's `__init__()` calls its parent's `__init__()`, the result is the execution of the statements of the latter within the former for the initialization of the instance variables named in the parent class but now acquired by the subclass, as opposed to the creation of a base-class slice within a subclass object.

of the contents of Employee, directly specified for the class itself or inherited from its parent Person, are inherited by Manager.

The test code in lines (T1) through (T24) shows us constructing different class instances and testing the working of the inheritance mechanism from the base class Person to the derived class Manager. When we invoke the inherited or the directly-defined accessor methods on the Employee instance emp in lines (T2), (T3), and (T4), we get the expected results. The same thing happens when we invoke the accessor methods on the Manager instance man in lines (T9) through (T12). Note in particular the invocation of Employee's promote() method on the Manager instance in line (T14).

Lines (T5) and (T13) show the namespace dictionaries associated with the instances emp and man. Note that even though each derived class's __init__() used the base class's __init__() for doing a part of the initialization that was needed in the derived class, all of derived-class instance variables are in the namespace of the emp and man instances.

Lines (T16) through (T22) show that the interface that Manager inherits from its mixin parent class ExecutivePerks works as expected. When we set the managers' bonus through the Trillian instance in line (T16), we get the same value for Betelgeuse's bonus in line (T19). And when we change Betelgeuse's bonus in line (T20), we see that change through the Trillian instance in line (T22). Recall that our goal is for all Manager instances to have the same bonus. That was the reason for making _bonus a class variable for ExecutivePerks.

The test code also shows in lines (T23) and (T24) the __bases__ attribute of the Manager class and the namespace dictionary __dict__ associated with the same class. Note that the Manager class's namespace dictionary shows the methods that are defined directly for the class, in addition to the module name and the doc string.

```
#-----------------   Class Person in file Person.py   ------------------
class Person:                                                      #(P1)
    'The Person root class'                                        #(P2)
    version = 1.0                                                  #(P3)

    def __init__( self, nm, yy ) :                                 #(P4)
        'Person constructor'                                       #(P5)
        self._name = nm                                            #(P6)
        self._age = yy                                             #(P7)
    def get_name( self ):                                          #(P8)
        return self._name                                          #(P9)
    def get_age( self ):                                           #(P10)
        return self._age                                           #(P11)
    def set_age( self, newYY ):                                    #(P12)
        self._age = newYY                                          #(P13)
```

```
#---------------  Class Employee in file Employee.py   ----------------
from Person import Person

class Employee( Person ):                                            #(E1)
    'Employee class is derived from Person class'                    #(E2)
    version = 1.0                                                    #(E3)

    def __init__( self, nm, yy, pos ) :                              #(E4)
        'Employee constructor'                                       #(E5)
        Person.__init__(self, nm, yy)                                #(E6)
        self._position = pos                                         #(E7)

    def get_position( self ):                                        #(E8)
        return self._position                                        #(E9)

    _promotion_table = { 'shop_floor' : 'staff',                     #(E10)
                         'staff'        : 'management',              #(E11)
                         'astt_manager' : 'manager',                 #(E12)
                         'manager'      : 'executive',               #(E13)
                       }

    def promote( self ):                                             #(E14)
        self._position = self._promotion_table[ self._position ]     #(E15)

#---------  Class ExecutivePerks in file ExecutivePerks.py   ----------
class ExecutivePerks:                                                #(X1)

    _bonus = 0                                                       #(X2)

    def get_bonus(): return ExecutivePerks._bonus                    #(X3)
    get_bonus = staticmethod( get_bonus )                            #(X4)

    def set_bonus(bonus): ExecutivePerks._bonus = bonus              #(X5)
    set_bonus = staticmethod( set_bonus )                            #(X6)

#--------------  Class Manager in file Manager.py   --------------------
from Employee import Employee
from ExecutivePerks import ExecutivePerks

class Manager( Employee, ExecutivePerks ) :                          #(M1)
    'Manager is derived from Employee and ExecutivePerks'            #(M2)

    def __init__( self, nm, yy, pos, dept ):                         #(M3)
        Employee.__init__(self, nm, yy, pos )                        #(M4)
        self._department = dept                                      #(M5)

    def get_department( self ):                                      #(M6)
        return self._department                                      #(M7)
```

```
#----------   Test Code in file TestPersonHierarchy.py   -------------
#!/usr/bin/env python

from Person import *
from Employee import *
from ExecutivePerks import *
from Manager import *

# Construct an Employee instance:
emp = Employee( "Zaphod", 84, "shop_floor" )                         #(T1)
print emp.get_name()              # Zaphod                           #(T2)
print emp.get_age()               # 84                               #(T3)
print emp.get_position()          # shop_floor                       #(T4)
print emp.__dict__                                                   #(T5)
#         {'_age': 84, '_position': 'shop_floor', '_name': 'Zaphod'}

# Check if promote() works for Employee instances:
emp.promote()                                                        #(T6)
print emp.get_position()          # staff                            #(T7)

# Construct a Manager instance:
man = Manager( "Trillian", 42, "astt_manager", "sales" )             #(T8)
print man.get_name()              # Trillian                         #(T9)
print man.get_age()               # 42                              #(T10)
print man.get_position()          # astt_manager                    #(T11)
print man.get_department()        # sales                           #(T12)
print man.__dict__                                                  #(T13)
#          {'_age': 42, '_position': 'astt_manager',
#           '_department': 'sales', '_name': 'Trillian'}

# Check if inherited promote() works for Manager instances:
man.promote()                                                       #(T14)
print man.get_position()          # manager                         #(T15)

# Test the interface inherited by Manager from ExecutivePerks:
man.set_bonus( 1000 )                                               #(T16)
print "bonus for ", man.get_name(), ": ", man.get_bonus()           #(T17)
                         #  bonus for  Trillion :  1000
man2 = Manager( "Betelgeuse", 18, "staff", "sales" )                #(T18)
print "bonus for ", man2.get_name(), ": ", man2.get_bonus()         #(T19)
                         #  bonus for  Betelgeuse :  1000

man2.set_bonus( 5555 )                                              #(T20)
print "bonus for ", man.get_name(), ": ", man.get_bonus()           #(T21)
                         # bonus for  Trillion :  5555
print "bonus for ", man2.get_name(), ": ", man2.get_bonus()         #(T22)
                         # bonus for  Betelgeuse :  5555
```

```
# Check some system-supplied attributes for Manager class:
print Manager.__bases__                                       #(T23)
          # (<class Employee.Employee at 0xb7e95e9c>,
          #  <class ExecutivePerks.ExecutivePerks at 0xb7e95ecc>)
print Manager.__dict__                                        #(T24)
          # {'__module__': 'Manager',
          #  '__doc__': 'Manager is derived from Employee and Execu.',
          #  '__init__': <function __init__ at 0xb7ea5224>,
          #  'get_department': <function get_department at 0xb7ea525c>}
```

9.2 EXTENDING A BASE-CLASS METHOD IN A SINGLE-INHERITANCE CHAIN

As mentioned previously in Chapter 8, sometimes it is useful for a derived-class method to get a part of its work done by a base-class method.[2] When a derived-class method makes a call to a base-class method, we say that the derived-class is extending the base-class method. The syntax for doing this is straightforward in a single-inheritance chain, that is, when every derived class in a class hierarchy has just one parent superclass. We will address later the issue of how the same can be done for the case of multiple inheritance, that is, when a subclass is derived from multiple parents. Extending base-class methods when multiple inheritance is involved becomes a nontrivial issue in the presence of *diamond inheritance*, that is, when multiple parents of a subclass may themselves be subclassed from a common ancestor class.

The multifile script shown next illustrates the notion of method extension for the case of the single-inheritance chain of Fig. 9.2. The derived-class method `promote()` of line (F4) calls in line (F5) the base-class method of the same name[3] as defined in line (W6). Along the same lines, the derived-class method `myprint()` of line (F6) calls in line (F7) the base-class method of the same name as defined in line (W7).

For the derived-class definitions for both `promote()` and `myprint()`, note the special syntax used for calling the base-class method:

[2]For Python, the reader has already seen an example of this in the previous section in the implementation code for the `Person` class hierarchy. The `__init__()` of each subclass called its parent's `__init__()` for doing a part of the instance initialization. So this section is merely a reiteration of that idea for the case of general methods.

[3]When extending a method, it is not necessary for the derived-class method name to be the same as the base-class method name. Likewise in Perl.

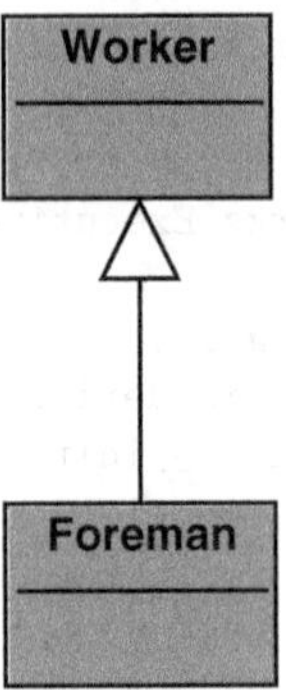

Fig. 9.2

```
base_class_name.method_name( self, arguments_if_any )
```

where the first parameter, `self`, must be the same as the first parameter in the header of the derived-class method.

```
#----------------  Class Worker in file Worker.py  --------------------
class Worker:                                                      #(W1)

    def __init__( self, a_name, a_position ):                      #(W2)
        self.name = a_name
        self.position = a_position

    def get_position( self ):                                      #(W3)
        return self.position

    def set_position( self, new_position ):                        #(W4)
        self.position = new_position

    promotion_table = {                                            #(W5)
        'shop_floor'  : 'team_leader',
        'team_leader' : 'group_lead',
        'group_lead'  : 'foreman',
        'foreman'     : 'manager'
    }

    def promote( self ):                                           #(W6)
        self.position = Worker.promotion_table[ self.position ]

    def myprint( self ):                                           #(W7)
        print "Name:", self.name, " Position:", self.position,
```

```
#---------------- Class Foreman in file Forman.py --------------------
from Worker import Worker

class Foreman( Worker ):                                            #(F1)
    def __init__( self, a_name, a_position, a_department ):         #(F2)
        Worker.__init__( self, a_name, a_position )
        self.department = a_department

    def get_department( self ):                                     #(F3)
        return self.department

    def promote( self ):                                            #(F4)
        if ( self.position == 'manager' ):
            print "A Foreman cannot be promoted beyond 'Manager'"
            return
        Worker.promote( self )                                      #(F5)

    def myprint( self ):                                            #(F6)
        Worker.myprint( self )                                      #(F7)
        print "Dept:", self.department                              #(F8)


#----------- Test Code in TestDerivedCallingBase.py ------------------
#!/usr/bin/env python
from Worker import Worker
from Foreman import Foreman

emp = Worker( "Joe", "shop_floor" )                                 #(T1)
emp.promote()                                                       #(T2)
position = emp.get_position()                                       #(T3)
print "position:",  position      # position: team_leader           #(T4)

man = Foreman( "Amanda", "foreman", "assembly" )                    #(T5)
man.myprint()   # Name: Amanda  Position: foreman  Dept: assembly   #(T6)
man.promote()                                                       #(T8)
man.myprint()   # Name: Amanda  Position: manager  Dept: assembly   #(T9)
man.promote()   # A Foreman cannot be promoted beyond 'Manager'    #(T10)
```

9.3 A SIMPLE DEMONSTRATION OF POLYMORPHISM IN PYTHON OO

All of the comments we made in Sections 8.2 and 8.5 of Chapter 8 regarding what polymorphism means generally and how it is exhibited by Perl OO apply here also. As stated there, polymorphism means that an object can be considered to be of different types simultaneously, or, stated equivalently, an object can exhibit different types of behaviors at the same time. In the context of programming, by behavior we mean the methods that a programmer is allowed to invoke on an object. As with Perl, the inheritance mechanism of Python automatically ensures that an instance constructed from a class will behave polymorphically vis-à-vis the superclasses of that class.

For example, in the `Person` hierarchy of Section 9.1, an `Employee` can be expected to also behave as a `Person`. That is, if a `Person` method is invoked on an `Employee` instance, the system will be able to find the method in the class hierarchy and execute it. By the same token, a `Manager` will be able to act as an `Employee` and also as a `Person`. So we can say that an `Employee` instance will behave polymorphically vis-à-vis the `Person` class and a `Manager` instance will behave polymorphically vis-à-vis both the `Employee` class and the `Person` class.

The script shown next illustrates that Python also exhibits the second manifestation of polymorphism mentioned in Section 8.5 of Chapter 8. This relates to writing a function that although expecting a base-class argument is just as happy to work with a derived-class argument. The function `foo()` in line (A) of the script expects a `Person` argument because the `get_name()` method that is invoked in the body of the function is defined specifically for the `Person` class. Nonetheless, when the function `foo()` is invoked with an `Employee` argument in line (G) and with a `Manager` argument in line (H), the script behaves like an OO program should — it exhibits polymorphism.

```
#!/usr/bin/env python

### Polymorph.py

from Person import Person
from Employee import Employee
from Manager import Manager

def foo( arg ):                    #  expects a Person argument        #(A)
    nam = arg.get_name()                                               #(B)
    print "foo called with name: %s" % nam

per = Person( "Zaphod", 84 )                                           #(C)
emp = Employee( "Orpheus", 84, "shop_floor" )                          #(D)
man = Manager( "Trillion", 42, "astt_manager", "sales" )               #(E)
```

```
# foo invoked on a Person:
foo( per )                          #Zahpod                   #(F)
# foo invoked on an Employee:
foo( emp )                          #Orpheus                  #(G)
#foo invoked on a Manager:
foo( man )                          #Trillian                 #(H)
```

9.4 DESTRUCTION OF DERIVED-CLASS INSTANCES IN SINGLE-INHERITANCE CHAINS

Earlier, in Section 7.4 of Chapter 7, we talked about the destruction of instance objects in Python. We mentioned there that a programmer-supplied definition for the function `__del__()` will be invoked just before an instance object is scooped up by the garbage collection mechanism (which happens when the reference count for the instance object goes to zero).

One can also provide a separate `__del__()` function for a derived class if an instance constructed from the class acquires system resources such as filehandles, sockets, and so on, that would need to be freed up just before the memory occupied by the instance object is reclaimed. The manner in which `__del__()` works for a derived-class instance is the same as that for a base-class instance.

In this section, we want to show what happens when only the base class is provided with a definition for `__del__()` and the derived class is not. In the following script, the base class `Animal` has a `__del__()` defined in lines (D) through (E). The derived class `FourLegged` of line (F) does not have its own `__del__()`. In lines (G), (I), and (J), we construct two `Animal` instances and one `FourLegged` instance.

When the variables holding references to these instances go out of scope, the system invokes the corresponding `__del__()` methods if they are available. So when the reference count for the `anim` instance of line (G) goes to zero on account of the statement in line (H), `Animal`'s destructor is invoked. This is clear from the message that is printed out, as shown in the commented-out lines just below line (G).

By the same token, when the next `Animal` instance of line (I) and the `FourLegged` instance of line (J) go out of scope because of program termination, Python invokes their `__del__()` methods. The `__del__()` method that is invoked for the derived-class instance of line (J) is the one that is defined for the base class in line (D), as should be clear from the last message that is printed out. Even though the message that is printed out for the derived-class instance mentions the name of the base class in it, strictly speaking we cannot quarrel with it since, by polymorphism, a derived-class instance is also of the base-class type.

```
#!/usr/bin/env python

### DestroyDerived.py

#--------------------------  class Animal  ----------------------------
class Animal:                                                       #(A)

    def __init__(self, a_name, wght ):                              #(B)
        self._name = a_name
        self._weight = wght
    def get_name( self ):                                           #(C)
        return self._name
    def __del__( self ):                                            #(D)
        nam = self.get_name()
        print "Memory occupied by the Animal instance named " +\
              nam + " is about to be reclaimed"

#----------------------  class FourLegged  ---------------------------
class FourLegged( Animal ):                                         #(F)
    def __init__( self, a_name, wght, num_of_teeth ):
        Animal.__init__( self, a_name, wght )
        self._num_of_teetch = num_of_teeth

#------------------------  Test Code  --------------------------------
anim = Animal( "BigHorn", 300 )                                     #(G)
anim = None                                                         #(H)
    # Memory occupied by the Animal instance named BigHorn is \
    # about to be reclaimed
anim = Animal( "SabreTooth", 400 )                                  #(I)
pet = FourLegged( "PuttyCat", 15, 16 )                              #(J)
    # Memory occupied by the Animal instance named SabreTooth is \
    #  about to be reclaimed
    # Memory occupied by the Animal instance named PuttyCat is \
    #  about to be reclaimed
```

9.5 THE ROOT CLASS object

Earlier in Chapter 7, we mentioned that Python supports two different kinds of classes, classic classes and new-style classes. A new-style class is subclassed from the system-supplied `object` class or from a child class of the `object` class. As mentioned already in the Python review in Chapter 3, all built-in classes such as lists, tuples, dictionaries, and so on, are new-style classes. This allows them to be subclassed for defining more specialized utility classes.

Here are some details to remember concerning the role played by the root class `object` for the new-style classes in Python:

- The memory allocated for an instance of a new-style class is customized[4] by the static method `__new__()`. If a user-defined class is not provided with an implementation for this method, its inherited definition from one of the superclasses is used. Since `object` is at the root of the inheritance graph of all new-style classes, in the absence of any other class making available a `__new__()`, the system-supplied definition for `object`'s `__new__()` is used.

- An instance returned by `__new__()` is automatically initialized by a class's `__init__()` method. If a class does not directly provide a definition for this method, an inherited definition is used. If a definition is not available from one of the user-defined superclasses, `object`'s `__init__()` is used.

- For new-style classes, an instance `xobj`'s class can be ascertained by calling `xobj.__class__`. For classic classes, the same is accomplished by calling `type(xobj)`. Calling `type(xobj)` works for new-style classes also.

- To ascertain whether an instance `xobj` is of a certain specific type in a class hierarchy, we can use the function `isinstance()`, as, for example, in the call `isinstance(xobj,class_name)`.

- When a list of instance variables is assigned to the `__slots__` attribute of a new-style class, an instance of that class cannot be assigned any additional instance variables. This was illustrated with the help of `ClassWithSlots.py` and `ClassWithSlots2.py` scripts of Section 7.8 of Chapter 7. This constraint is not enforced for a classic class. An instance of a new-style class with the `__slots__` attribute does not get the `__dict__` attribute.

- A new-style class comes equipped with the `__getattribute__()` method that is inherited from `object`. A class is free to provide an override definition for this method. This method is accessed whenever any class method is accessed. Earlier, in Section 7.3.4 of Chapter 7 we showed the difference between the `__getattr__()` and the `__getattribute__()` methods.

- When multiple inheritance in involved, a subclass derived from a mixture of classic and new-style classes is treated as a new-style class.

- The root class `object` is the base for *all* built-in types.

[4]The generic memory allocation is carried out by the constructor, meaning the class name called with the function-call operator `()`.

- You cannot multiply inherit from the different built-in types. For example, you cannot construct a class that inherits from both the built-in `dict` and the built-in `list`.

- When the constructor of a built-in type is called without any arguments, it results in an instance with an appropriate default state. For example, `str()` returns an empty string, and `int()` returns the integer 0.

- The built-in types `staticmethod`, `super`, `classmethod`, and `property` have special roles in Python OO. Calls to the constructors for these classes return function objects. For example, when `staticmethod()` is called with a class method as its argument, the function object returned by the call can then behave like a static method of the class, as already demonstrated in Section 7.6 of Chapter 7.

9.6 SUBCLASSING FROM THE BUILT-IN TYPES

Since all the built-in types are the new-style classes, let's first review how an instance of a built-in type is created. As mentioned in Section 7.2 of Chapter 7, there are two separate steps involved: the static method `__new__()` is deployed to return an uninitialized instance and then the instance method `__init__()` is used to initialize the object returned by `__new__()`. This orchestration of instance creation and initialization is carried out by the class constructor, which is the class name acting as a callable. Whereas `__new__()` returns a new instance, `__init__()` does not return anything. That is, the job of `__init__()` is only to initialize the state of the object returned by `__new__()`.

A more accurate way of stating the respective responsibilities of `__new__()` and `__init__()` would be that it is the former's responsibility to return a new instance, and that it is the latter's responsibility to add a mutable state to the object returned by the former. Since the immutable built-in types — `int`, `long`, `float`, `complex`, `str`, `unicode`, and `tuple` — are defined by classes that give rise to immutable instances, they have do-nothing `__init__()` methods, since there is no need to add a mutable state to such instances. By the same token, the main work involved in constructing instances of the built-in mutable types — `list`, `dict`, `file`, `staticmethod`, `classmethod`, `super`, and `property` — is carried out by the instance initializer `__init__()`. For mutable types, `__new__()` is therefore a do-nothing method.[5]

[5]The constructor, meaning the class name called with the function-call operator `()`, will do the memory allocation for the instance created for the mutable types before `__init__()` gets to work on it for adding the mutable state.

The relative responsibilities of `__new__()` and `__init__()` as stated above have important bearing on how the mutable types and the immutable types are subclassed. Obviously, if you want to subclass an immutable type, you should extend the base class's `__new__()` and let the derived class make do with the inherited `__init__()`, unless, of course, you want the derived class to possess a mutable state. By the same token, if you want to subclass a mutable type, you should extend the base class's `__init__()` and leave alone the base-class's `__new__()`.

Section 3.6 of Chapter 3 has already shown how we can extend the built-in `int` and `str` classes to create more specialized integer and string classes.[6] In what follows, we will show how one can extend the built-in container classes `dict`, `list`, and `tuple`.

9.6.1 Subclassing the Built-In dict

The goal of this section is to show a simple example of how the built-in `dict` class can be subclassed to create a more specialized dictionary class. As stated earlier, a dictionary is defined with the `{}` operator, as in

```
d = { 'a': 1, 'b' : 2, 'c' : 3 }
```

A dictionary may also be created by any of the following direct calls to the constructor of the `dict` class:

```
d = dict( { 'a': 1, 'b' : 2, 'c' : 3 } )                  #(A)
d = dict( [ ['a', 1], ['b', 2], ['c', 3] ] )              #(B)
d = dict( a = 1, b = 2, c = 3 )                           #(C)
```

An empty dictionary can be created by either of the following calls:

```
d = {}
d = dict()
```

As the reader can see, when a dictionary is created with a call to the constructor, the call may have no arguments, in which case an empty dictionary is returned, or one argument, as in lines (A) and (B) above, or a tuple of keyword arguments, as in line (C).

Let's say that we want to extend the system-supplied `dict` class — let's call the extended class `MyDict` — that takes two arguments for its constructor, the first a tuple of keys and the second a tuple of values, as in

```
d = MyDict( ('a', 'b', 'c'), (1, 2, 3) )
```

---

[6]This would be a good time to review Section 3.6 of Chapter 3 if the reader skipped over that material at his/her first pass through that chapter.

and that then returns the dictionary `{ 'a':1, 'b':2, 'c':3 }`, the exact order of the key-value pairs not being important. In all other respects, we want `MyDict` to behave exactly like the built-in `dict`.

The script shown next, `SubclassingDict.py`, could be thought of as a first cut at implementing `MyDict`. Since `dict` is a mutable type, we alter the behavior of `dict`'s constructor by extending its `__init__()` method in lines (B) through (T). Lines (C) and (D) of this override definition are meant to take care of the `dict` style calls to the `MyDict` constructor:

```
MyDict( { 'a' : 1, 'b' : 2, 'c' : 3 } )

MyDict( [ ['a', 1], ['b', 2] ] )

MyDict()
```

In all these cases, `MyDict` is called with a single argument, which will be a tuple of the argument shown in the above calls. We extract the argument from the tuple with the syntax `args[0]` in line (D) and ship it to `dict`'s `__init__()` as shown in that line.

Lines (E) through (R) are there to give the `MyDict` class the desired functionality — that is, we want to be able to construct a dictionary from two separate tuples, one for just the keys and the other for just the values. The `if` statements in lines (F) and (H) ensure that we are indeed dealing with the case when the arguments are tuples, and the `if` statement in line (J) makes sure that the two tuples supplied as arguments contain the same number of elements. The `while` loop in lines (N) through (Q) then extracts the elements from each of these two tuples and synthesizes a single argument from all the data, which is then fed to the base-class `dict`'s `__init__()` in line (R).

Finally, lines (S) and (T) take care of the case when we make a keyword argument call to `MyDict`, as in

```
MyDict( a=1, b=2, c=3 )
```

In this case, we let the base class's `__init__()` handle the call directly in line (T).

Lines (U) through (g) demonstrate that, except for the additional behavior programmed into it, `MyDict` behaves in exactly the same manner as the built-in `dict`. We start by constructing a new dictionary from the two tuples shown in the call to `MyDict()` in line (U). Lines (V), (W), and (X) show that the resulting dictionary object is considered to be an instance of `MyDict`, `dict`, and `object`, all at the same time, as we would expect it to be. Lines (Y) through (g) show that the `MyDict` instance constructed in line (U) responds to the same operations as the built-in `dict`.

Lines (h) through (p) show that `MyDict`'s `__init__()` correctly handles the arguments that one would normally use for invoking `dict`'s constructor. Of course, `MyDict`'s `__init__()` calls on `dict`'s `__init__()` to do the job, as it should.

```
#!/usr/bin/env python

### SubclassingDict.py

#--------------------------  class MyDict  ---------------------------
class MyDict( dict ):                                              #(A)
    def __init__( self, *args, **keyargs ):                        #(B)
        if ( len( args ) == 1 ):                                   #(C)
            dict.__init__( self, args[0] )                         #(D)
            return
        if ( len( args ) == 2 ):                                   #(E)
            if (not isinstance( args[0], tuple )):                 #(F)
                raise Exception( "wrong data type for first arg" ) #(G)
            if (not isinstance( args[1], tuple )):                 #(H)
                raise Exception( "wrong data type for second arg" ) #(I)
            if ( len( args[0] ) != len( args[1] ) ):               #(J)
                raise Exception( "two args of unequal length" )    #(K)
            newarg = {}                                            #(L)
            i = 0                                                  #(M)
            while ( i < len( args[0] ) ):                          #(N)
                d = { args[0][i] : args[1][i] }                    #(O)
                newarg.update( d )                                 #(P)
                i = i + 1                                          #(Q)
            dict.__init__( self, newarg )                          #(R)
            return
        if ( keyargs ):                                            #(S)
            dict.__init__( self, keyargs )                         #(T)

#----------------------------  Test Code  ------------------------------
if __name__ == '__main__':

    d1 = MyDict( ('a', 'b', 'c'), (1, 2, 3) )                      #(U)

    print isinstance( d1, MyDict )    # True                       #(V)
    print isinstance( d1, dict )      # True                       #(W)
    print isinstance( d1, object )    # True                       #(X)

    print d1                    # {'a': 1, 'c': 3, 'b': 2}         #(Y)
    print d1.keys()             # ['a', 'c', 'b']                  #(Z)
    print d1.values()           # [1, 3, 2]                        #(a)
    print d1.items()            # [('a', 1), ('c', 3), ('b', 2)]   #(b)
    print d1.has_key( 'a' )     # True                             #(c)
    print len(d1)               # 3                                #(d)

    d2 = dict( [ ['c', 0], ['d', 4] ] )                            #(e)
    d1.update( d2 )                                                #(f)
    print d1                    #{'a': 1, 'c': 0, 'b': 2, 'd': 4}  #(g)
```

```
d3 = MyDict( a=1, b=2, c=3 )                                        #(h)
print d3                     # {'a': 1, 'c': 3, 'b': 2}             #(i)

d4 = MyDict( { 'a' : 1, 'b' : 2, 'c' : 3 } )                        #(j)
print d4                     # {'a': 1, 'c': 3, 'b': 2}             #(k)

d5 = MyDict( [ ['a', 1], ['b', 2] ] )                               #(l)
print d5                     # {'a': 1, 'b': 2}                     #(m)

d6 = MyDict()                                                       #(n)
d6.update( { 'a' : 1 } )                                            #(o)
print d6                     # {'a': 1}                             #(p)
```

9.6.2 Subclassing the Built-In list

We will now show another example of how one might subclass a built-in mutable type — in this case the type `list`. This example parallels and then builds on the example of the previous subsection. Like the `MyDict` dictionary subclass, the `MyList` subclass here allows us to construct a `list` object from an "unbundled" sequence of items. The `MyList` class also comes with additional functionality, over and above what is provided by its parent `list` class. We will supply `MyList` with a method that returns a histogram of the items in the list. More specifically, here is how `MyList` extends the built-in type `list`:

- The `MyList` constructor returns a list instance from the following call that shows the items to be placed in the list in the form of multiple arguments to the constructor:

  ```
  li =  MyList( 'a', 'b', 1, 2 )
  ```

  Note that the built-in `list` constructor insists that the number of arguments supplied in a call to the constructor not exceed one. So if we want to construct a list from the items that are shown on the right-hand side above, the call to the list constructor will have to look something like this:

  ```
  li =  list( ['a', 'b', 1, 2] )
  ```

  Of course, we could also have bundled all the items together in the form of a single tuple.

- We want `MyList` to have a method, `hist()`, that returns a histogram of all the items in the list. The histogram, in the form of a dictionary, will show the frequency of occurrence of each item in the list.

The script shown next, SubclassingList.py, is an implementation of MyList as derived from the built-in list. Since list is a mutable type, MyList extends its parent's __init__() in lines (B) through (G). As was mentioned earlier, the built-in mutable types possess a do-nothing implementation for the __new__() and all of the work of initializing the state of the instance created by the constructor is done by the __init__() method. So it is this method that needs to be overridden by MyList if it wants to provide a new way of constructing a list instance. Lines (C), (D), and (E) of the __init__() shown below are simply for handing off the constructor call to the parent's __init__(). It is the code in line (G) that allows the MyList constructor to be called with "unbundled" arguments.

The histogramming capability of the MyList class is implemented in lines (H) through (N) of the script below. This code basically scans the list and, for each item, increments the histogram count of the item for its every repeat occurrence in the list.

In the test code shown in the rest of the script, we start out by constructing an instance of MyList in line (O). Lines (P), (Q), and (R) inform us that the instance created is simultaneously of type MyList, list, and object. Line (S) prints out the list of items in the container instance created in line (O). Lines (T) and (U) show that the histogram method of lines (H) through (N) is working as expected. Lines (V) and (W) show that the histogramming function does its job even on a MyList instance that was created with the help of the list's __init__().

Lines (X) through (d) should establish that one can use the same operations[7] on a MyList instance as on a list instance. The statement in line (X) first extracts a slice from the MyList instance and then appends to it another list with the + operator. Lines (Y) and (Z) show us constructing an empty MyList, which is basically an empty list. Lines (a) through (e) show that we can construct MyList instances with single-argument calls to the constructor — as one does with the list constructor. Obviously, as mentioned already, this works because the MyList's __init__() passes on such calls to the list's __init__() in line (D) of the script.

[7]Since we did not overload any of the operators for MyList, the object returned by an operator would be of type list, as opposed to MyList. For the simple example we present here, that does not pose a problem since our only reason for extending list is to enable one more mode of construction and to allow for histogramming. However, note that Python makes it extremely easy to overload operators. See Section 7.10 of Chapter 7 and Section 9.11 of this chapter for operator overloading in Python.

```
#!/usr/bin/env python

### SubclassingList.py

#---------------------------  class MyList  ----------------------------

class MyList( list ):                                                 #(A)

    def __init__( self, *args ):                                      #(B)
        if ( len(args) == 1 ):                                        #(C)
            list.__init__( self, args[0] )                            #(D)
            return                                                    #(E)
        else:                                                         #(F)
            list.__init__( self, args )                               #(G)

    def hist( self ):                                                 #(H)
        histogram = {}                                                #(I)
        for item in self:                                             #(J)
            if ( histogram.has_key( item ) ):                         #(K)
                histogram[item] += 1                                  #(L)
            else: histogram[item] = 1                                 #(M)
        return histogram                                              #(N)

#----------------------------  Test Code  ------------------------------
if __name__ == '__main__':

    list1 = MyList( 'a', 'b', 't', 'd', 'a', 't' )                    #(O)

    print isinstance( list1, MyList )   # True                        #(P)
    print isinstance( list1, list )     # True                        #(Q)
    print isinstance( list1, object )   # True                        #(R)

    print list1                 # ['a', 'b', 't', 'd', 'a', 't']      #(S)
    his = list1.hist()                                                #(T)
    print his                   # {'a': 2, 'b': 1, 't': 2, 'd': 1}    #(U)

    list2 = MyList( ['hello', 'jello', 'hello'] )                     #(V)
    print list2.hist()          # {'jello': 1, 'hello': 2}            #(W)

    print list1[2:4] + ['c','d'] # ['t', 'd', 'c', 'd']               #(X)

    list3 = MyList()                                                  #(Y)
    print list3                 # []                                  #(Z)

    list4 = MyList( ['a', 'b', 'c'] )                                 #(a)
    print list4                 # ['a', 'b', 'c']                     #(b)
```

```
list5 = MyList( ('a', 'b', 'c') )                              #(c)
print list5                   # ['a', 'b', 'c']                #(d)

print MyList({'a':1, 'b':2}) # ['a', 'b']                      #(e)
```

9.6.3 Subclassing the Built-In tuple

As should be clear from the discussion at the beginning of Section 9.5, there is a big difference between how you extend a built-in mutable type and how you extend a built-in immutable type. For built-in mutable types, all of the work that goes into bringing into existence the mutable state of an instance is done by the `__init__()` method of the class. For such types, the instance that is initially created by the constructor is automatically handed over to the `__init__()` for the addition of the state, implying that `__new__()` is a do-nothing method for such types. On the other hand, all of the initialization work for the built-in immutable types is done by the `__new__()` static method of the class. Since there is no mutable state to be added to the instance in such cases, `__init__()` is a do-nothing method for such types.

It therefore follows that if we wish to subclass an immutable type, what must remain immutable in the instances made from the subclass must go into the extension of the `__new__()` method. And if the subclass is to also have a mutable state, the code for specifying that must be placed in the `__init__()` of the subclass.

This is demonstrated by the following script in which we subclass the immutable type `tuple`. We provide the subclass with override definitions for both `__new__()` and `__init__()`, the former because we want to be able to construct a tuple from an "unbundled" sequence of items,[8] and the latter because we want to endow the subclass with two new instance variables, one for the number of numeric elements stored in a tuple and the other for the "owner" of the tuple.[9] The two instance variables will constitute the mutable state of an instance of the subclass. In keeping with the names given to the extensions of the built-in classes shown previously in this section, we will call the subclass `MyTuple`.

Lines (B) through (F) of the next script show `MyTuple`'s override definition for `__new__()`. If the constructor is called with a single argument, we simply pass on that argument to the parent class's `__new__()` in line (F). On the other hand, when called with unbundled items that we want to see placed in a tuple, we ship off the argument tuple containing these items to the parent class's `__new__()` in line (D).

---

[8]The constructor for the built-in `tuple` accepts only one argument.

[9]Whether or not it makes sense for a container to have an owner is besides the point.

Lines (G) through (N) show the implementation of MyTuple's override for the `__init__()` of the parent class. As mentioned earlier, the purpose of MyTuple's `__init__()` is to provide a tuple instance with two instance variables, one for keeping track of how many numeric types are stored in a MyTuple instance and the other for the owner of the instance. The respective instance variables are named num_numeric and owner. The former we set within `__init__()` itself in line (N) and the latter through the set_owner() method in line (P). Lines (I) and (J) take care of the situation when the MyTuple constructor is called in the same way as a tuple constructor, that is, with a single "bundled" argument containing the items to be placed in the tuple. If this bundled form is a tuple, a list, or a dictionary, we extract the form by the args[0] call and then count the number of the numeric types in it in lines (K), (L), and (M). On the other hand, if the MyTuple constructor is called with "unbundled" items to be placed in the tuple, we directly pass the flow of control to the counting of the numeric elements in lines (K), (L), and (M).

In the test code shown in lines (Q) through (c), we first construct a MyTuple instance in line (Q). Line (S) shows that we can access its data attribute num_numeric to determine the number of numeric elements in the tuple. Lines (T) and (U) are meant to show that a MyTuple container responds to the same operations[10] as a regular tuple. In the operations shown there, we first extract a slice of the MyTuple instance and then replicate it twice.

Lines (V) and (Y) show that MyTuple instances can be constructed with the same kind of constructor calls as for regular tuple instances — which is not surprising because MyTuple hands over all single-argument calls to the `__new__()` of its parent tuple. That the MyTuple instances are indeed mutable is illustrated by the assignment in line (b).

```
#!/usr/bin/env python

### SubclassingTuple.py

#--------------------------  class MyTuple  ----------------------------

class MyTuple( tuple ):                                              #(A)

    def __new__( cls, *args ):                                       #(B)
        if ( len(args) > 1 ):                                        #(C)
            return tuple.__new__( cls, args )                        #(D)
        else:                                                        #(E)
            return tuple.__new__( cls, args[0] )                     #(F)
```

[10]Since we did not overload any operators for MyTuple, the object returned by an operator will be of type tuple, as opposed to MyTuple. Operator overloading is easy in Python, as mentioned in the footnote in the previous subsection.

```
    def __init__( self, *args ):                                         #(G)
        num_numbers = 0                                                  #(H)
        if ( len(args) == 1 and \
             isinstance( args[0], (tuple, list, dict) ) ):              #(I)
            args = args[0]                                               #(J)
        for item in args:                                                #(K)
            if (isinstance(item, (int, long, float))):                   #(L)
                num_numbers = num_numbers + 1                            #(M)
        self.num_numeric = num_numbers                                   #(N)

    def set_owner( self, aname ):                                        #(O)
        self.owner = aname                                               #(P)

#---------------------------  Test Code  ----------------------------
if __name__ == '__main__':

    t1 = MyTuple( 'a', 'b', 'c', 4, 5.25 )                               #(Q)
    print t1                        # ('a', 'b', 'c', 4, 5.25)           #(R)
    print t1.num_numeric            # 2                                  #(S)

    t2 = t1[1:3] * 2                                                     #(T)
    print t2                        # ('b', 'c', 'b', 'c')               #(U)

    t3 = MyTuple( [ 'a', 3, 'c' ] )                                      #(V)
    print t3                        # ('a', 3, 'c')                      #(W)
    print t3.num_numeric            # 1                                  #(X)

    t4 = MyTuple( { 'a' : 1, 'b' : 2 } )                                 #(Y)
    print t4                        # ('a', 'b')                         #(Z)
    print t4.num_numeric            # 0                                  #(a)

    # MyTuple is mutable:
    t4.set_owner( "Trillian" )                                           #(b)
    print t4.owner                  # Trillian                           #(c)
```

9.7 ON OVERRIDING __new__() AND __init__()

The goal of this section is to summarize Guido van Rossum's recommendations on how to use `__new__()` and `__init__()` when extending classes [65]. The reader has already seen us use and discuss several of these recommendations in the class derivation examples presented in Section 3.6 of Chapter 3 and in the previous section of this chapter. What follows in this section are these recommendations stated more succinctly, along with some others:

- As mentioned already, `__new__()` is a static method. The examples we presented in Section 3.6 of Chapter 3 and in the previous section for extending the built-in classes show that there is no need to invoke the `staticmethod()` constructor to get `__new__()` to behave as a static method. That is because `__new__()` is special cased to be static.

- The first parameter of `__new__()` must be reserved for the class whose instance is to be returned by `__new__()`. This parameter will be set explicitly to the class object by its constructor.

- Extension of `__new__()` in a subclass must return an instance. Typically, the last executed statement in your code for `__new__()` will be the instance returned by a call to the parent class's `__new__()`.

- When calling a parent class's `__new__()`, the first argument must be the subclass whose instance is supposed to be returned by the call.

- If a subclass derived from a built-in immutable type is supposed to have a mutable state, the place to define the mutable state is in the `__init__()` of the subclass. Note that `__init__()` is not supposed to return anything; it carries out its responsibilities by side effect.

- A class's `__init__()` is automatically called after its `__new__()`.

- The `__init__()` for the immutable built-in types is a do-nothing method; for such types an instance is completely initialized by `__new__()`. By the same token, the `__new__()` for the mutable built-in types is a do-nothing method.

- If `__new__()` and `__init__()` are not directly defined for a subclass, the inherited definitions for these two methods are used.

Lest we leave the reader with the impression that `__new__()` is only to be used for the customization of the immutable part of the state and `__init__()` for the initialization of the mutable part, we will now present Guido van Rossum's recommended approach to the implementation of the singleton design pattern. This example will illustrate that any special logic needed for creating a new instance may also need to be placed in `__new__()`. A class that implements the singleton design pattern does not allow for more than one instance to be constructed from the class. If a repeat attempt is made to construct another instance, it is the same previously constructed instance that is returned. As we will show in the next script, the code for ensuring that only one instance of a singleton class is ever made is placed in the `__new__()` method of the class. Let's now see how exactly this is done.

The script shown next, MySingleton.py, contains van Rossum's definition for a singleton class in lines (A) through (J). When the Singleton constructor is called for the first time, the call in line (C):

```
cls.__dict__.get( "__it__" )
```

returns None because Singleton's namespace dictionary __dict__ does not yet contain an entry for the key __it__. As a result, the statements in lines (F), (G), and (H) are executed. The statement in line (F) will create a new generic instance of Singleton. This instance is next initialized in line (G) by the invocation of the user-defined init() method. Since a generic instance of Singleton is not supposed to contain any state — the idea is that a more useful class with state would be subclassed from the Singleton class — the initializer init() in lines (I) and (J) is a no-op. It is needed nonetheless since Singleton *could* be subclassed without the subclass providing its own init(). Note that line (F) causes the instance returned by the call to object's __new__() to become the value of a class variable __it__. This class variable would subsequently become available through the namespace dictionary of the class in line (C) upon a future attempt at creating another instance of Singleton.

Now the interesting question is why van Rossum did not use __init__() for carrying out the initialization that is supposedly now the responsibility of init() in lines (G) and (H), or the responsibility of the extensions of this method in any subclasses of Singleton. The reason has to do with the fact that the invocation of __init__() is orchestrated by the system; the class constructor automatically calls an applicable __init__() *after* __new__() has finished constructing an instance. In the current case, we want to invoke the initializer inside the code for Singleton's __new__(). So we use a user-named and user-specified method init(). Note the system will still call __init__() after __new__() has finished its work. For lack of an override definition, the system will use the no-op __init__() of object in the current case.

As mentioned, van Rossum recommends that a singleton class that actually does something useful be subclassed from Singleton. Lines (K), (L), and (M) show an example of singleton class with state. Note that the state is being specified in the extension of the init() method — as opposed to the more common case of specifying state in the override of the __init__() method. This makes sense in light of the comments made previously about the responsibility of the init() method as called in line (G) and as default defined in lines (I) and (J).

When we call the constructor for MySingleton in line (N), eventually that results in the call to init() in line (G). But note that this invocation of init() is on an instance of type MySingleton. So, in order to execute that call, Python first seeks out an init() method defined directly for MySingleton. In our case, MySingleton indeed provides its own init(). So that code is executed and thus a state is added to the MySingleton instance.

Subsequently, when we make another call to the `MySingleton` constructor in line (P), it is the same `MySingleton` instance that was previously constructed in line (N) that is returned — despite the argument given to the constructor being different from the argument supplied in line (N). This is borne out by the statements in lines (Q), (R), and (S).[11]

```
#!/usr/bin/env python

### MySingleton.py

#------------------------  class Singleton  ------------------------
class Singleton( object ):                                        #(A)
    def __new__( cls, *args, **kwds ):                            #(B)
        it = cls.__dict__.get( "__it__" )                         #(C)
        if it is not None:                                        #(D)
            return it                                             #(E)
        cls.__it__ = it = object.__new__( cls )                   #(F)
        it.init( *args, **kwds )                                  #(G)
        return it                                                 #(H)

    def init( self, *args, **kwds ):                              #(I)
        pass                                                      #(J)

#-----------------------  class MYSingleton  -----------------------
class MySingleton( Singleton ):                                   #(K)
    def init( self, mm ):                                         #(L)
        print "init of MySingleton called"
        self.m = mm                                               #(M)

#---------------------------  Test Code  ---------------------------
x = MySingleton( 10 )                                             #(N)

print x.__class__               # <class '__main__.MySingleton'>  #(O)

y = MySingleton( 20 )                                             #(P)
print x is y                    # true                            #(Q)
print x.m                       # 10                              #(R)
print y.m                       # 10                              #(S)
```

[11] As mentioned previously in Chapter 3, the call to `get()` in line (C) of the script is tantamount to a combination of a call to `has_key()` and keyword-indexed access using the `[]` operator. In other words, line (C) works the same as

```
it = None
if (cls.__dict__.has_key("__it__")):
    it = cls.__dict__["__it__"]
```

9.8 MULTIPLE INHERITANCE

Like Perl, Python allows a class to be derived from multiple base classes. As mentioned previously, the header of such a derived class would look like

```
class derived_class( base1, base2, base3, .... ):
    ....body of the derived class....
```

Now the following question arises: Suppose we invoke a method on a derived-class instance and the method is not defined directly in the derived class, in what order will the base classes be searched for an implementation of the method? The order in which the class and its bases are searched for the implementation code is commonly referred to as the *Method Resolution Order* (MRO) in Python. Different MRO algorithms are used for for the classic classes and for the new-style classes.

In what follows, we will first discuss the MRO for classic classes in Python — it is the same as in Perl.[12] Next, we will present the MRO for the new-style classes.

9.8.1 Method Resolution Order for Classic Classes

Consider the example of multiple inheritance shown in Fig. 9.3 for classic classes:

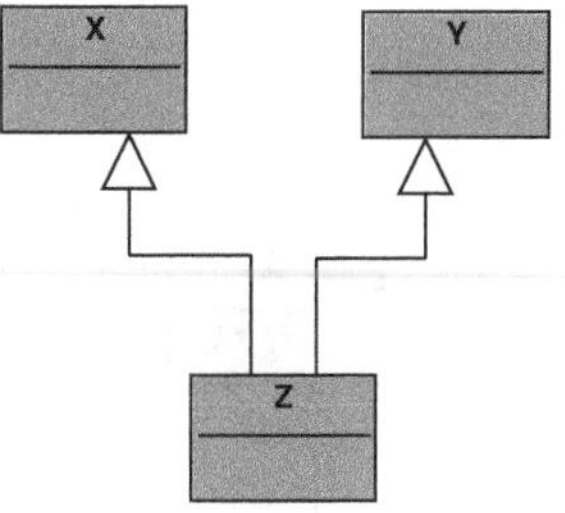

Fig. 9.3

Since class Z is derived from the base classes X and Y, the header of class Z will look like

```
class Z( X, Y):
    ....body of class Z....
```

Let's now construct an instance of Z and invoke a method on it:

```
zobj = Z( ...arguments... )
```

[12]The algorithm presented in Section 8.8 of Chapter 8 constitutes Perl's MRO.

```
zobj.foo()
```

If `Z` does not implement `foo()`, Python would need to search through the base classes in some order for an implementation of this method. In the MRO for classic classes, the direct and the indirect superclasses are searched in a left-to-right depth-first fashion. In our example, that means that Python will first search in class `X` and then in class `Y`. As to what is meant by depth-first, assume that `X` is also a derived class. Now, after searching through `X`, `X`'s bases will be searched for an implementation of `foo()`, again in a left-to-right order, and so on with respect to `X`'s other ancestors if it should have additional ancestors.

With multiple inheritance, it is obviously possible to create diamond inheritance loops of the sort shown in Fig.9.4. As mentioned in the previous chapter, this happens when a class is derived from two or more bases that are themselves derived from a common ancestor class. Since in Python, as in Perl, inheritance merely means a "linking" of the namespace dictionary of a subclass with that of a superclass, inheritance loops of the sort shown in Fig.9.4 do not create the same issues that they do in languages such as C++ that also allow multiple inheritance of implementation code. Nonetheless, as mentioned in Section 8.11 of the previous chapter, you still have to be careful when subclass methods call the methods of their superclasses; we will see later in this chapter how one deals with the situation of subclasses calling superclass methods in class hierarchies with loops. In what follows, we will show a simple example of multiple inheritance to demonstrate in action the MRO for classic classes. The example is simple because the subclasses do not call any methods of the superclasses.

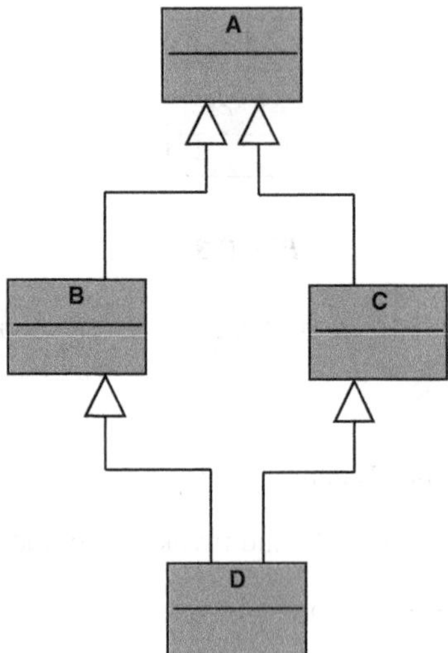

Fig. 9.4

The class A of line (A) of the script serves as a base for the classes B and C of lines (C) and (E). Finally, class D sits at the bottom of the hierarchy, being derived from both B and C. Each of the classes A, B, and C has its own version of `foo()`. So, at least theoretically speaking, class D inherits `foo()` from both inheritance paths, from and through B, and from and through C. In reality, that is not the case. The left-to-right depth-first search order used by the MRO algorithm for classic classes guarantees that class D will see only B's version of `foo()`. This is borne out by the output shown in the commented-out portion of the line (I). Of course, if desired, we can force Python to choose a particular version of `foo()` by using the more specialized syntax shown in lines (J) and (K). The general form of this syntax is:

```
superclass.method_name( derived_class_instance,  other_args )
```

This is the same syntax we used earlier in Section 9.2 when a subclass method needed to call a particular superclass method. We will have more to say about this syntax later in Section 9.9.

```
#!/usr/bin/env python

### MultiWithDiamond.py

#----------------------------  class A  -----------------------------
class A:                                                          #(A)
    def foo( self ):                                              #(B)
        print "A's foo() invoked"

#----------------------------  class B  -----------------------------
class B(A):                                                       #(C)
    def foo( self ):                                              #(D)
        print "B's foo() invoked"

#----------------------------  class C  -----------------------------
class C(A):                                                       #(E)
    def foo( self ):                                              #(F)
        print "C's foo() invoked"

#----------------------------  class D  -----------------------------
class D(B, C):                                                    #(G)
    pass

#---------------------------  Test Code  ----------------------------
d_obj = D()                                                       #(H)
d_obj.foo()                  # B's foo() invoked                  #(I)
C.foo( d_obj )               # C's foo() invoked                  #(J)
A.foo( d_obj )               # A's foo() invoked                  #(K)
```

The MRO algorithm for classic classes is described by the following recursive function taken from [65]:

```
def classic_lookup( cls, name ):
    "Look up name in cls and its base classes"
    if cls.__dict__.has_key(name):
        return cls.__dict__[name]
    for base in cls.__bases__:
        try:
            return classic_lookup( base, name )
        except AttributeError:
            pass
    raise AttributeError, name
```

9.8.2 Desirable Properties of Name Lookup in Class Hierarchies

The previous subsection presented the left-to-right depth-first MRO that is used to search for a method (actually the name of any attribute) in a hierarchy of classic classes. We will refer to this lookup algorithm as the LRDF algorithm for obvious reasons. Straightforward though it is, it has some serious shortcomings for complex class hierarchies, especially hierarchies with inheritance loops, as in Fig. 9.4.[13]

Let's say that both A and C in the class hierarchy of Fig. 9.4 provide separate implementations for a method named foo().[14] When we call foo() on a C instance, obviously it will be C's foo() that will be invoked. Now let's also say that B and D do not implement foo(). If we call foo() on a D instance, the LRDF rule will invoke A's foo() and not C's foo() even though C is closer to D than A with regard to inheritance. This is counterintuitive[15] and can be a source of errors. If only A and C are provided with foo(), a programmer would expect that when foo() is called on a D instance, it will be C's foo() that will be invoked, as opposed to A's.

This limitation of the LRDF-based MRO can be formalized by saying that it lacks *monotonicity*. For a more precise definition of monotonicity in name lookup in inheritance graphs, we need to introduce the notion of *superclass linearization*.[16] In general, a superclass linearization of a class C is the list of all the classes, starting

[13]The shortcomings we present here for the LRDF algorithm apply to Perl also since, as presented in Section 8.6 of the previous chapter, Perl uses the same approach to name lookup in a class hierarchy.

[14]For the discussion in this subsection, ignore the implementation of the hierarchy of Fig. 9.4 shown in the previous script.

[15]It is counterintuitive in the sense that after you get accustomed to C exhibiting its foo() behavior, you'd expect D — since it is derived from C — to exhibit the same behavior. If suddenly B's insertion in the superclass list of D — knowing fully well that B does not possess foo() — causes D to acquire its foo() behavior from a different class, in this case A, you'd be perplexed indeed.

[16]The *linearization* for a given class C is also known as the *class precedence list* of C.

with C, that should be searched sequentially from left to right for a name. The superclass linearization for a class C will be denoted L[C].

Here are the superclass linearizations of the different classes in the hierarchy of Fig.9.4 as produced by the LRDF-based MRO:

```
L[A] = A
L[B] = B A
L[C] = C A
L[D] = D B A C A
```

When we examine L[C], C's methods would get priority over A's methods. However, when we examine L[D], it is exactly the opposite — A's methods would get priority over C's methods.

For an MRO algorithm to be monotonic, if P precedes Q in the linearization of R, then P must precede Q in the linearization of every subclass that is derived from R. In the above example, C precedes A in the linearization of C, yet A precedes C in the linearization of D, which is a subclass of C. Therefore, as mentioned already, the LRDF-based MRO for name lookup is not monotonic.

A good MRO algorithm for superclass linearization must be monotonic. A good MRO algorithm must also preserve *local precedence ordering*. What that means is that the order in which the immediate base classes of a given class R make their appearance in the linearization of R or any of its subclasses must not violate the base class order for R. In other words, if P comes before Q in the immediate bases of R, then P must come before Q in the linearization of R and in the linearizations of the direct and indirect subclasses that are derived from R.

So whereas monotonicity refers to the priority to be accorded to the names in a class vis-à-vis the names in a superclass, local precedence order deals with the priority to be accorded to the names in one base class vis-à-vis the names in another base class at the same level of inheritance.

It can be shown rather trivially that some class hierarchies simply do not allow for superclass linearizations that are monotonic and that preserve the local precedence order. This happens particularly if two individual classes in a hierarchy inherit from two separate bases, but in opposite order. Consider the following hierarchy:

```
class A: pass
class B( A ): pass
class C( A ): pass
class D( B, C ): pass
class E( C, B ): pass
class F( D, E ): pass
```

for which we can draw the class diagram that is shown in Fig.9.5.

Note that the inheritance arc from E to B is not drawn as directly as the inheritance arc from D to C. This is intentional as the left-to-right order of the arcs emanating

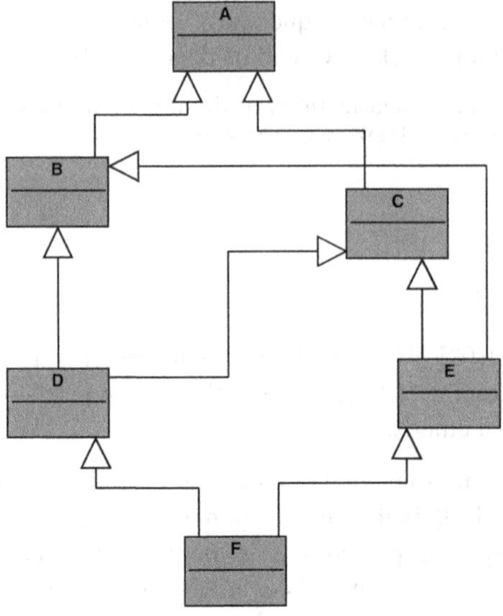

Fig. 9.5

from a class indicates the order of appearance of the bases in its base-class list. The base-class list for `D` is `(B,C)`; on the other hand, it is `(C,B)` for `E`. It would be impossible to construct good superclass linearizations for this hierarchy since `B` must come before `C` in the linearizations for `D` and all its subclasses, and `C` must come before `B` in the linearizations `E` and all its subclasses. That is clearly impossible to satisfy for class `F`. It is instructive to see the linearizations produced by the LRDF MRO algorithm for this class hierarchy:

```
L[A] = A
L[B] = B A
L[C] = C A
L[D] = D B A C A
L[E] = E C A B A
L[F] = D B A C A E C A B A
```

9.8.3 The C3 Algorithm for MRO for New-Style Classes

Python uses Dylan's C3 algorithm [1] to derive superclass linearizations in multiple inheritance hierarchies consisting of new-style classes. The MRO for each class is stored in the `__mro__` attribute of the class. The goal of this section is to explain the C3 algorithm. The explanation that follows is based on Simionato's presentation of the C3 algorithm [59]. First a bit of notation is in order.

Suppose the superclass linearization of a class `C` consists of the following classes:

```
(P, Q, R, S, ....)
```

We will talk about the `head` and the `tail` of a linearization as consisting of the first element and the rest of the list, respectively. Therefore, we can write:

```
L[C]            =    (P, Q, R, S, ....)
head( L[C] )    =    P
tail( L[C] )    =    (Q, R, S, ..... )
```

We will use the operator `+` to denote a *joining* of a class `P` with a list `(Q R S ...)`, as in

```
P + (Q, R, S, ....)   =   (P, Q, R, S, .....)
```

and to denote *joining of two linearizations*:

```
(P, Q, R) + (S, T, U, ....)   =   (P, Q, R, S, T, U .....)
```

The C3 algorithm states that the linearization of a class `C` consists of `C` followed by a merging of all the linearizations for each of the bases of `C` and the list consisting of the bases. Therefore, if class `C` is defined as

```
class C( P, Q, R, ....) : pass
```

then

```
L[C] = C + merge( L[P], L[Q], L[R], ...., bases( C ) )
```

or, equivalently, as

```
L[C] = C + merge( L[P], L[Q], L[R], ...., ( P, Q, R, ... ) )
```

Obviously, how the `merge` step is carried out is critical to the operation of the algorithm. This is how merge is carried out in C3:

1. Start with the head of the first list.

2. If the selected head is not in the tail of every other list (including lists that occur before the list from which the head was chosen), then

   - place the head in the output of merge.
   - remove this element from all the lists in the argument to merge (including lists that occur before the list from which the head was selected).
   - go back to step 1.

3. Otherwise, skip over the list from which the head was selected and pick the head of the next list.

4. Go back to step 2 with the new selected head.

5. If you reach a state where the argument lists to `merge()` are all emptied out, you are done; accept the output list as the result of merge.

6. Otherwise, declare failure in merge.

Let's apply this algorithm to the following multiple inheritance hierarchy:

```
class O: pass
class A( O ): pass
class B( O ): pass
class C( O ): pass
class D( A, B ): pass
class E( B, C ): pass
class Z( D, E ): pass
```

that corresponds to the class diagram shown in Fig. 9.6. Starting at the top of the

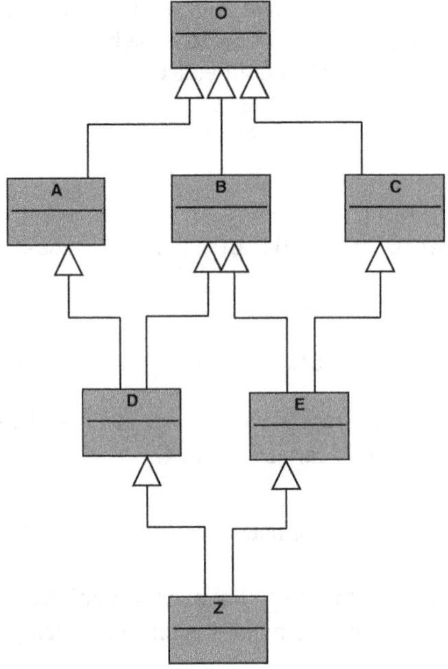

Fig. 9.6

hierarchy, it is trivial to write down the C3 linearizations for the class at the root and at the level below:

```
L[O]    =   (O)
L[A]    =   A + merge( L[O], (O) )    =  A + (O)   =   (A, O)
L[B]    =   B + merge( L[O], (O) )    =  B + (O)   =   (B, O)
L[C]    =   C + merge( L[O], (O) )    =  C + (O)   =   (C, O)
```

Let's now apply the steps of the algorithm, especially the merge steps, to derive the linearization for class D:

```
L[D]   =   D + merge( L[A], L[B], (A, B) )
```

where the third argument to `merge()` is the list of bases of D, as required by C3. Substituting for `L[A]` and `L[B]`, we can write

```
L[D]   =   D + merge( (A, O), (B, O), (A, B) )
```

To invoke the merge steps, we choose the head of the first list, A, in the arguments to `merge()` and ascertain whether it is in the tails of any of the other lists. Since A is not in the tails of any of other lists, we choose A as the output of `merge()` at this time. At the same time, we remove A from all the lists given to `merge()`. So we get the following for a reduced form of the linearization equation:

```
L[D]   =   D + (A) + merge( (O), (B, O), (B) )
```

The next item in the first list is O. However, since O is in the tail of the second list, we skip over to the second list and choose its head, the element B. Since B is not in the tail of any of the lists given to `merge()` in this call, we choose B for the output of merge at this time, while removing it from all the lists given to `merge()`. As a result, the above linearization equation reduces to

```
L[D]   =   (D, A) + B + merge( (O), (O) )
```

which trivially leads to

```
L[D]   =   (D, A, B, O)
```

The linearization of class E follows a very similar derivation, with the result as follows:

```
L[E] = E + merge( L[B], L[C], (B, C) )
```

which after substitution for `L[B]` and `L[C]` becomes

```
L[E] = E + merge( (B, O), (C, O), (B, C) )
```

Applying the merge steps, we get the result

```
L[E] = (E, B, C, O)
```

That brings us to the linearization of class Z at the bottom of the hierarchy. By definition

```
L[Z] =  Z + merge( L[D], L[E], (D, E) )
```

Substituting for `L[D]` and `L[E]`, we can write

```
L[Z] =  Z + merge( (D, A, B, O), (E, B, C, O), (D, E) )
```

Invoking the merge steps, we get the following derivation:

```
L[Z]  =  Z + merge( (D, A, B, O), (E, B, C, O), (D, E) )
      =  Z + (D) + merge( (A, B, O), (E, B, C, O), (E) )
      =  (Z, D) + A + merge( (B, O), (E, B, C, O), (E) )
      =  (Z, D, A)  +  E + merge( (B, O), (B, C, O) )
      =  (Z, D, A, E) +  B  + merge( (O), (C, O) )
      =  (Z, D, A, E, B) + C + merge( (O), (O) )
      =  (Z, D, A, E, B, C, O)
```

As mentioned earlier, when Python sees a new-style class in a script, it uses the C3 algorithm to determine the method resolution order for the class and stores the MRO thus found in the `__mro__` attribute of the class. The script shown next, `ShowMRO.py`, demonstrates this for the same multiple inheritance hierarchy that we analyzed in the above example (Fig.9.6).

About the `ShowMRO.py` script, note that the classes defined in lines (C) through (I) are the new-style classes despite the fact that they do not descend explicitly from the built-in root class `object`. That is because of the object assigned to the global variable `__metaclass__` in line (A).[17] We assign to this global variable a class object that is a subclass of the built-in `type`. As the reader can see, the main purpose of the class created in lines (A) and (B) is to override the method `__repr__()`. We will soon provide the reason for this override. But first let's state why the statements in lines (C) through (I) of the script constitute new-style classes.

As we will explain in Section 9.10 of this chapter, Python creates a new class object by first scanning through its programmer-supplied definition and then executing the following statement at the end:

```
M( name, bases, dict )
```

where `name` is the name of the programmer-defined class, `bases` the tuple of bases supplied in the class header, and `dict` the namespace dictionary created for the class that was created when Python scanned through the class definition. `M` is the name of the metaclass to use for the purpose of creating a new class object from the class definition. Ordinarily, if a programmer-defined class is subclassed from `object`, it is the `object`'s metaclass `type` that is used for the purpose, and that fact turns the programmer-defined class into a new-style class. However, the same can be accomplished by a programmer-defined metaclass that is the value of the global `__metaclass__` and that is subclassed from `type`, as we have done in line (A) of the script.

---

[17]By the syntax used in lines (A) and (B) of the script, `__metaclass__` is evidently the name of a class. This name is bound to the class object that corresponds to the class definition in those two lines. The class named `__metaclass__` is evidently a subclass of `type`.

The main reason for the override of `__repr__()` in line (B) is that we want the class names to be printed out more compactly.[18] This is accomplished by changing the default meaning of `__repr__()`, which, as mentioned in Section 7.10 of Chapter 7, is ordinarily used by Python to determine the string representation of an object from which the object can be recreated if desired. Our override definition for `__repr__()` says that the string representation of a class object is just its programmer-defined class name. To illustrate what is accomplished by this override, if we replace line (B) with the keyword `pass`, the output of the print statement in line (Q) will look like:

```
(<class '__main__.A'>, <class '__main__.O'>, <type 'object'>)
```

as opposed to the less cluttered

```
(A, O, <type 'object'>)
```

The commented-out portions of lines (O) through (V) show the MROs for each of the classes in the multiple inheritance hierarchy of lines (C) through (I). The MROs shown are the same as in the worked-out example earlier, except for the appearance of

```
<type 'object'>
```

as the last item in each MRO tuple. This corresponds to the root class `object` that was not explicitly taken into account in the hand-worked example earlier in this section.[19] Lines (K) through (N) establish that each class defined in lines (C) through (I) is of the type `__metaclass__` defined in line (A). But note that since the programmer-defined `__metaclass__` is of type `type`, it would be correct to say that all of the classes defined in the hierarchy are also of type `type`. Therefore, an invocation such as `isinstance(A,type)` would return `True`.[20] As mentioned earlier, `type` is the metaclass for the root class `object`. It is interesting to note that the call `isinstance(A,object)` also returns `True`, and that is the case for all the classes in the hierarchy of the example.

[18]The override definition uses a lambda expression. Python's lambda expressions were reviewed in Section 3.8.6 of Chapter 3.

[19]This is a good place to mention that if a name cannot be found in any of the classes in the MRO class list, the search is continued into the metaclass from which the individual classes were made.

[20]A class is an "instance" of a metaclass in the same sense that we construct an instance object from a class. In other words, a metaclass is to a class what a class is to an instance. We will have more to say about metaclasses in Python in Section 9.10.

```
#!/usr/bin/env python

### ShowMRO.py

class __metaclass__(type):                                              #(A)
    __repr__ = lambda cls: cls.__name__                                 #(B)

class O: pass                                                           #(C)
class A( O ): pass                                                      #(D)
class B( O ): pass                                                      #(E)
class C( O ): pass                                                      #(F)
class D( A, B ): pass                                                   #(G)
class E( B, C ): pass                                                   #(H)
class Z( D, E ): pass                                                   #(I)

print type( object )        # <type 'type'>                             #(J)
print type( O )             # <class '__main__.__metaclass__'>          #(K)
print type( A )             # <class '__main__.__metaclass__'>          #(L)
print type( B )             # <class '__main__.__metaclass__'>          #(M)
print type( Z )             # <class '__main__.__metaclass__'>          #(N)

print object.__mro__        # (<type 'object'>,)                        #(O)
print O.__mro__             # (O, <type 'object'>)                      #(P)
print A.__mro__             # (A, O, <type 'object'>)                   #(Q)
print B.__mro__             # (B, O, <type 'object'>)                   #(R)
print C.__mro__             # (C, O, <type 'object'>)                   #(S)
print D.__mro__             # (D, A, B, O, <type 'object'>)             #(T)
print E.__mro__             # (E, B, C, O, <type 'object'>)             #(U)
print Z.__mro__             # (Z, D, A, E, B, C, O, <type 'object'>) #(V)
```

9.8.4 On Designing Multiple-Inheritance Hierarchies

A given multiple-inheritance hierarchy may reflect poor design even if the superclass linearizations for all its classes are monotonic and preserve local precedence order. To illustrate this point, consider again the class hierarchy of Fig. 9.6. The previous subsection showed the following linearization for class `Z` at the bottom of the hierarchy:

```
L[Z] =  (Z, D, A, E, B, C, O)
```

This linearization says that the methods of class `A` would win over the methods of class `E` despite the fact that the latter is obviously closer to `Z` as far as inheritance goes. So if it is indeed the case that both `A` and `E` have to offer the same or similar attributes and methods to Z, then it becomes incumbent upon us to place E before D in the declaration of the base classes for Z. Note that issues such as this would also arise with the classic classes. The LRDF algorithm would also place A before E in the MRO for class Z.

A basic problem with both C3 and LRDF algorithms is that the recency of class derivation is not explicitly taken into account in order to figure out what to inherit from where in a given inheritance structure. To take into account the recency of class derivation, a derived class could examine all of the methods and other attributes made available to it by all the superclasses, and, if the derived class were to inherit two or more definitions for the same name, it could apply an overload resolution algorithm (which could factor in the recency of derivation) to choose one.

Problem 1 in the Homework section of this chapter presents a specific example of the issues created when the recency of derivation in an inheritance graph is not taken into account when determining the MRO for a class.

9.9 USING super( ) TO CALL A BASE-CLASS METHOD

Earlier in Sections 9.2 and 9.8.1 , we mentioned that a derived-class method needing to call a particular superclass method must use the following syntax:

```
superclass.method_name( self, arguments_if_any )
```

where `superclass` is the particular superclass whose method `method_name` the derived class is interested in. The parameter `self` would be bound to the instance, presumably of the derived class, on which we wish to invoke the superclass method. The example in Section 9.2 involved a single-inheritance chain, and the one in Section 9.8.1 the case of multiple inheritance.

We will now talk about a different kind of a call from a subclass method to a base-class method. We want a method call made in a subclass to be dispatched to its base classes without the subclass explicitly naming the base classes for that method call or the order in which the base classes should be searched for the method call. In response to the method call received, the recipient base class may do all of the work itself — and that would be the end of the story — or, it may do only part of the work itself and then dispatch up the call again to its own bases for the rest of the work. So a method call may propagate up an inheritance path by similar calls at each inheritance level in the class hierarchy. If an inheritance loop is encountered in this upward propagation of method calls, we may want the propagation to take place through all branches of the loop. That is, in a hierarchy of the sort shown in Fig. 9.7, if Z's `foo()` calls on `foo()` in its base classes (without naming the bases explicitly), we want that to automatically translate into calls to B's `foo()` and C's `foo()` since they provide implementations for `foo()`. And if the `foo()` methods in both B and C call `foo()` in their own bases, we want A's `foo()` to be invoked

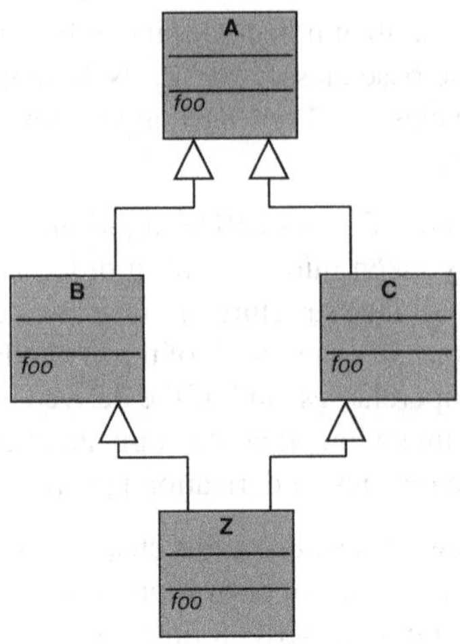

Fig. 9.7

— with the stipulation that `A`'s `foo()` is invoked only once despite the fact that both children of `A` will be making separate calls to `A`'s `foo()`.

For a practical application of method calls propagating upwards through an inheritance graph, let's say that the mission of each `foo()` is to write to the disk the state information stored in the class variables of the class whose `foo()` is invoked. So our goal would be to call `foo()` on a derived class (or its instance) and to then see the propagation of the `foo()` calls upward along an inheritance path that makes sense. (The inheritance path could, for example, be the one that corresponds to the MRO for the derived class, since that would after all be the source of the superclass resources for the derived class). For each execution of `foo()` we would want the information stored in the respective class variables to be written out to the disk. For the hierarchy shown in Fig.9.7, we would want `Z`'s `foo()` to output the state stored in the class variables of `Z` and to then call `foo()` belonging to the parent classes. So we would want the `foo()` calls to be dispatched to the classes `B` and `C`. We would want the invocations of `foo()` belonging to `B` and `C` to output the state information in their respective class variables and to then call the same method in the common superclass `A`. But when both `B` and `C` call `A`'s `foo()`, we do not want there to be a double invocation of that method from class `A` *since we would not want the information stored in the class variables of* `A` *to be written out twice.*

A call to a base-class method that can propagate upward in an inheritance graph in the manner described above is the job of the keyword `super` in Python. Before we explain how `super` does its work, we will show it in action in the next script, `Super.py`, that implements the class hierarchy of Fig. 9.8. As shown in lines (A), (B), and (C), and in lines (L), (M), and (N) of the script, the method `foo()` is defined originally for the base classes `A` and `D`. However, note the definition of the same

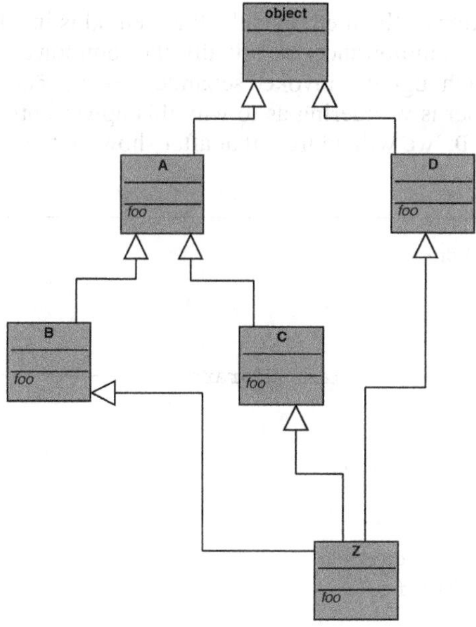

Fig. 9.8

method in the derived classes `B` and `C` in lines (D) through (K). In particular, note the syntax used for the calls to `super()` in lines (G) and (K) in the two derived-class implementations of `foo()`:

```
super(B, self).foo()        in the definition of foo() for class B

super(C, self).foo()        in the definition of foo() for class C
```

This syntax is special and must be adhered to strictly for `super()` to work correctly. It is important that the first argument to `super()` be the name of the class in which `super()` is invoked and the second argument the instance on which the calling function is invoked. Therefore, the parameter for the second argument will be the same as the first parameter of the calling function — typically `self`. The name of the base-class method called — this is what comes after the dot in the above syntax — does not have to be the same as the name of the subclass calling method.

Finally, lines (O) through (R) present `Z` that is subclassed from `B`, `C`, and `D`. As seen in line (R), the method `foo()` of this class also makes a call to `super()` using the same syntax as explained above.

In the test code, we construct a `Z` instance and then invoke `foo()` on it in lines (S) and (T), which yields the output shown in the commented-out section below line (T). So the call to `foo()` on a `Z` instance propagates upwards through the superclasses to the highest level possible in the inheritance hierarchy, with `foo()` from each class encountered being called along the way. When an inheritance loop is encountered in this upward propagation of the method calls, the method is invoked in both arms of the loop leading to the common ancestor. Finally, the common ancestor A's foo() is called only once even though it is invoked separately by the foo() methods in both B and C. If the reader is wondering as to why this upward propagation of method calls did not include D, we will address that after showing the code below.

```
#!/usr/bin/env python

### Super.py

#------------------------  Class Hierarchy  --------------------------
class A( object ):                                                #(A)
    def foo(self):                                                #(B)
        print "A's foo called"                                    #(C)
class B( A ):                                                     #(D)
    def foo(self):                                                #(E)
        print "B's foo called"                                    #(F)
        super(B, self).foo()                                      #(G)
class C( A ):                                                     #(H)
    def foo(self):                                                #(I)
        print "C's foo called"                                    #(J)
        super(C, self).foo()                                      #(K)
class D( object ):                                                #(L)
    def foo(self):                                                #(M)
        print "D's foo called"                                    #(N)
class Z( B, C, D ):                                               #(O)
    def foo(self):                                                #(P)
        print "Z's foo called"                                    #(Q)
        super(Z, self).foo()                                      #(R)

#-------------------------  Test Code  ------------------------------
z = Z()                                                           #(S)
z.foo()                                                           #(T)
                    # Z's foo called
                    # B's foo called
                    # C's foo called
                    # A's foo called
print Z.__mro__                                                   #(U)
                      # (<class '__main__.Z'>, <class '__main__.B'>,
                      # <class '__main__.C'>, <class '__main__.A'>,
                      # <class '__main__.D'>, <type 'object'>)
```

It is interesting to note that if we change the order of the base classes in line (O) of the above script from (B,C,D) to (D,B,C), the output produced by the call in line (T) becomes:

```
Z's foo called
D's foo called
```

In this case, the call to `super()` in line (R) of class `Z` is completely "absorbed" by the parent class `D`.

So how is it that when the base-class list of `Z` starts with `B` and `C`, Python is able to propagate the method call `foo()` to both these classes? It seems that Python is somehow able to anticipate that since both `B` and `C` descend from a common ancestor `A`, the call to `foo()` should propagate over to both `B` and `C`, and then eventually `A`. But that `D`, being on a separate inheritance path, should play no role in how `Z`'s `foo()` is executed.

Python is able to show this seemingly magical behavior by simply propagating the `super()` call sequentially to all the classes in the MRO of the class where `super()` is first invoked. The MRO for class `Z` in the script above, as produced by the C3 algorithm, is

```
(Z, B, C, A, D, object)
```

as shown by the output of the statement in line (U) of the script. Therefore, `Z`'s invocation of `super()` would go to `B`, `B`'s invocation of `super` would go to `C`, `C`'s to `A`, `A`'s to `D`, and `D`'s to `object`. This would be the case as long as `self` in each call to `super()` is an instance of type `Z`. That is because it is through the type of the instance bound to `self` that `super()` figures out as to which MRO to use. For the example at hand, the `super()` does not extend to `D` despite its presence in the MRO of `Z` because `foo()` of `A` does not call `super()`.

Obviously, then, if we reverse the order of bases of class `Z` — that is, if the bases are listed as `(D,B,C)` as opposed to `(B,C,D)` — the MRO of class `Z` would change to

```
(Z, D, B, C, A, object)
```

Now `Z`'s call to `super()` would invoke `foo()` of `D`. But since `D`'s `foo()` does *not* call `super()`, there would be no further propagation of `super()`.

9.10 METACLASSES IN PYTHON

A metaclass is a template for constructing a class object from a class definition. To quote Guido van Rossum [65]: "... a metaclass is simply 'the class of a class.' Any class whose instances are themselves classes is a metaclass." Metaclasses can be used to give classes made from them some enduring characteristics, such as those of mutability or immutability.

Python needs a metaclass to form a class object from a class definition. Let's say we have a class definition:

```
class MyClass:
    ... code ...
```

When Python gets to the end of the class definition, it executes the following statement for creating a class object that will be the "value" associated with the name `MyClass`:

```
some_metaclass( MyClass, base_tuple, dict )                    #(A)
```

where the `base_tuple` is a tuple of bases for the class, and `dict` the namespace dictionary created during the scan of the class definition. The metaclass used in the call in line (A), `some_metaclass`, is chosen on the basis of the following considerations:

- If `dict['__metaclass__']` exists, it is used. The namespace dictionary here, `dict`, is the same as the third argument in the metaclass constructor call in line (A) above. Frequently, the metaclass for a class is supplied by the programmer by giving a value to the variable `__metaclass__` inside the class definition. This creates an entry for `dict['__metaclass__']` in the namespace dictionary for the class.
- Otherwise, if `base_tuple` is not empty, the metaclass corresponding to a base class is used.
- Otherwise, if there exists a global variable named `__metaclass__`, the object that is the value of this variable is used. This is the strategy we used in the script `ShowMRO.py` in Section 9.8.3. We needed to use a customized metaclass there in order to abbreviate the print representation of a class.
- Otherwise, the classic metaclass `types.ClassType` is used.

Since all new-style classes are subclassed from the special class `object` and since `type` is `object`'s metaclass, unless otherwise specified a new-style class will by default acquire the metaclass `type` also. The metaclass for classic classes is typically `types.ClassType`.

The metaclasses supplied by Python, such as `type`, can be subclassed to form hierarchies of their own. The metaclasses in such a hierarchy can be used to create different sorts of classes. It is also possible to create entirely new metaclasses of your own in a script.

Recall the system-supplied `__class__` attribute that was introduced in Chapter 7. As mentioned there, this attribute returns the class name when invoked on an instance. The same attribute returns the name of the metaclass when invoked on a new-style class. One can also use the built-in one-argument `type()` function for the same. For classic classes, while one can retrieve the class name for an instance through the `__class__` attribute, as the reader saw in Chapter 7, the attribute is not defined for the classes themselves. So to retrieve the metaclass of a classic class, you have to invoke the one-argument `type()` function.

9.10.1 Using a Metaclass

The next script, `UsingMetaclass.py`, shows a simple example of a metaclass that is used to contribute some class-wide behavior to all the class objects constructed with its help.

The script presents a metaclass named `MyMetaclass` in lines (A) through (M). There are three things that this metaclass contributes to each class: (1) The class method[21] `bar()` defined in line (B); (2) the class variable `datum` defined in line (H); and (3) the instance method defined in line (K) by the assignment of the function object created in line (I). The reason why the second contribution results in a class variable and the third contribution in an instance method is because the statements in lines (H) and (K) directly modify the namespace dictionary of the class under construction. As was mentioned earlier, a class object is created by Python when, after it has finished scanning a class definition, it invokes a metaclass constructor with three arguments. These three arguments become the values of the parameters `cls`, `tuple_bases`, and `dict` in line (C). The first of these, `cls`, is set to the name of the class under construction,[22] the second, `tuple_bases`, to a tuple of base classes for the class under construction, and the last, `dict`, to the namespace dictionary of the class compiled during a scan of the class definition. So by directly entering information into this dictionary in lines (H) and (K) we achieve the same effect as if the class object under construction had a class variable named `datum` and an instance method named `foo`. Recall from Chapter 7 that the names of the class variables and the instance methods along with their bindings are stored in the namespace dictionary of a class.

Lines (N) through (W) show code for a class named `X` that asks for `MyMetaclass` to be used as a metaclass for the creation of class objects from the class definition. Note how in line (O) we set the class variable `__metaclass__` to the metaclass object created earlier. So when Python searches for a metaclass at the end of scanning the definition for class `X`, it uses the metaclass of line (A). This is in accord with the rules we listed at the beginning of Section 9.10 for how Python chooses a metaclass that it needs for constructing a class object from a class definition.

To help the reader see how a metaclass is used in the construction of a class object, our definition of the metaclass prints out in lines (D) through (G) all the arguments with which the metaclass constructor is called. We have also placed certain print statements in the definition of `__init__()` of class `X` to see how an instance of `X` is initialized.

[21] See Section 7.6 of Chapter 7 for class methods and class variables in Python.

[22] It is important to note that the `cls` parameter is set to just the *name* of the class under construction and *not* to a class object. Since the class object is still undergoing construction when the metaclass constructor is called, it does not exist yet.

The reader will also notice the presence of commented-out small strings that look like `#1#`, `#2#`, `#3#`, etc., toward the end of each print statement in both the metaclass's `__new__()` and class `X`'s `__init__()`. These are there to indicate to the reader the order in which the various print statements of the metaclass code and the instance initializer for the class were executed during the construction of the class object at the end of the class definition and during the creation of an instance from the class object in line (Y). As far as this order is concerned, nothing is output until Python has finished scanning the definition of class `X`, that is, until Python has digested first the lines (A) through (M) for the metaclass definition and then the lines (N) through (W) for the definition of class `X`. In order to make a class object from the definition in lines (N) through (W), Python makes the following call:

```
MyMetaClass( 'X', (object,), dict )
```

where the third argument, `dict`, is the namespace dictionary constructed for class `X`. This constructor call is custom allocated by the call to the metaclass's `__new__()` in lines (C) through (M). The print statements inside this `__new__()` will therefore be the first ones to produce any output. The commented-out portions of the lines (D) through (F) and the commented-out block below line (G) display the arguments with which the metaclass's `__new__()` is invoked.

After the `__new__()` of the metaclass has finished execution, we have a class object for `X`. At this time, the flow of execution is just past the end of the definition of class `X`, meaning just past the end of line (W). Next comes the executable statement in line (X). Notice that its output order is shown as `#6#` since this output is displayed after the output produced by the statement in line (L).

Next comes the construction of the instance `xobj` of `X` in line (Y). This triggers the invocation of `X`'s instance initializer `__init__()` in lines (P) through (U). That should explain the output order shown for the print statements in this segment of the script.

After the instance `xobj` is all constructed, we get to the execution of the code in lines (Z) through (f). The statements in lines (a) and (b) show that `datum`, "injected" into class `X` by the metaclass in line (H), working as a class variable of `X`. Line (d) shows the method `foo()`, injected into class `X` by the metaclass in line (K), working as an instance method. We get an error when we try to invoke `foo()` as a class method in line (c).

Line (e) demonstrates the metaclass's `bar()`, defined in line (B), acting as a class method of `X`. That is so because the class is passed as the first argument — in this case the only argument — to the method. This should be evident by the output shown in the commented-out portion of line (e). Finally, line (f) shows the namespace dictionary for the instance `xobj`.

```
#!/usr/bin/python

### UsingMetaclass.py

#----------------------- MyMetaClass --------------------------------
class MyMetaClass( type ):                                          #(A)

    def bar( cls ): print "snackbar from class ", cls.__name__      #(B)

    def __new__( meta_cls, cls, tuple_bases, dict ):                #(C)
        print meta_cls       # <class '__main__.MyMetaClass'>   #1#  #(D)
        print cls            # X                                #2#  #(E)
        print tuple_bases    # (<type 'object'>,)               #3#  #(F)
        print dict                                              #4#  #(G)
                # {'__module__': '__main__',
                #  '__metaclass__': <class '__main__.MyMetaClass'>,
                #  'getn': <function getn at 0x403b2df4>,
                #  '__init__': <function __init__ at 0x403b2dbc>}
        dict[ 'datum' ] = 1000                                      #(H)
        def metameth( arg ):                                        #(I)
            print "metameth called with arg:", arg                  #(J)
        dict[ 'foo' ] = metameth                                    #(K)
        print meta_cls.__dict__                                 #5#  #(L)
                # {'__module__': '__main__',
                #  'bar': <function bar at 0x403b2d4c>,
                #  '__new__': <staticmethod object at 0x4036835c>,
                #  '__doc__': None}
        return super( MyMetaClass, meta_cls ).__new__( meta_cls,
                                 cls, tuple_bases, dict )           #(M)

#--------------------------- class X --------------------------------
class X( object ):                                                  #(N)

    __metaclass__ = MyMetaClass                                     #(O)

    def __init__( self, nn ):                                       #(P)
        print self.__class__    # <class '__main__.X'>          #7#  #(Q)
        print self.__class__.__class__                          #8#  #(R)
                                # <class '__main__.MyMetaClass'>
        print self.__class__.__dict__                           #9#  #(S)
            # {'__module__': '__main__',
            #  '__metaclass__': <class '__main__.MyMetaClass'>,
            #  'getn': <function getn at 0x403b2e2c>,
            #  '__dict__': <attribute '__dict__' of 'X' objects>,
            #  '__weakref__': <attribute '__weakref__' of 'X' objects>,
            #  'foo': <function metameth at 0x403b202c>,
            #  'datum': 1000, '__doc__': None,
```

```
        #  '__init__': <function __init__ at 0x403b2df4>}
        self.n = nn                                                     #(T)
        print self.__dict__      # {'n': 10}                     #10#  #(U)

    def getn( self ):                                                   #(V)
        return self.n                                                   #(W)

#----------------------------- Test Code ---------------------------
print "start testing"       # start testing                     #6#   #(X)

xobj = X( 10 )                                                        #(Y)

print xobj.getn()           # 10                                #11#  #(Z)
print xobj.datum            # 1000                              #12#  #(a)
print X.datum               # 1000                              #13#  #(b)
#X.foo()                    # Error                                   #(c)
xobj.foo()           # metameth called with arg:
                     #     <__main__.X object at 0x403b5bac>    #14#  #(d)
X.bar()                     # snackbar from class  X            #15#  #(e)
print xobj.__dict__         # {'n': 10}                         #16#  #(f)
```

9.10.2 Using setattr( ) and delattr( ) in a Metaclass

Now that the reader has a basic understanding of how a metaclass is used for creating a class object from a class definition, this subsection will show an example in which a metaclass uses the built-in `setattr()` and `delattr()` functions, respectively, to either provide a class under construction with a new attribute or to delete an existing attribute. We will also use the example in this section to illustrate a metaclass that contains overrides for both `__new__()` and `__init__()`.

Lines (A) through (M) of the script shown next define a metaclass `MyMeta` and lines (N) through (T) a class `X` that specifies via its class variable `__metaclass__` that `MyMeta` be used as a metaclass for creating class objects from the class definition. The `__new__()` of the metaclass basically invokes `type`'s `__new__()` to carry out the allocation, as shown in line (G). As shown in the commented-out portions of the lines (E) and (F), when the metaclass constructor is called at the end of the definition of class `X`, the first argument to the metaclass's `__new__()` is set to the metaclass object, and the second to the *name* of the class object under construction. Although their values are not displayed, the third argument is set to the bases of the class object under construction, and the last to its namespace dictionary.

As one would expect and as confirmed by the outputs shown in lines (I) and (J), the first argument to the metaclass's `__init__()` is the class object that is returned by the metaclass's `__new__()` and the second argument remains the same as in the call to `__new__()`, that is, it is the name of the class under construction. The third and the last arguments to the metaclass's `__init__()` also remain the same as for the call to the metaclass's `__new__()`.

With regard to the code in the `__init__()` of the metaclass, note how after the class object is initialized by the `super()` call in line (K), we invoke `setattr()` in line (L) to add an additional attribute to the class object under construction and `delattr()` in line (M) to delete an existing attribute of the class object. The call to `setattr()` adds a new class method `foo()` to the class object under construction, and the call to `delattr()` in line (M) deletes the existing attribute `bar` from the definition of the class. Recall, the metaclass code is executed for creating a class object from a class definition. Therefore, the `__init__()` of the metaclass knows through its `dict` argument what attributes are currently defined for the class object.

The successful addition of the attribute `foo` and the deletion of the attribute `bar` of line (T) are illustrated by the test code in lines (U) through (X). As we see in lines (V) and (W), we are able to invoke `foo()` of lines (B) and (C) on both an instance of `X` and on `X` itself. We also see that the argument passed to this method is the class object in both cases — which is what is supposed to happen with a class method. Line (X) also shows the namespace dictionary for class `X`. As can be seen from the output shown, while the dictionary contains an entry for `foo`, it does not contain an entry for `bar`.

```
#!/usr/bin/env python

### MetaWithSetDel.py

#-------------------------  MyMeta metaclass  --------------------------
class MyMeta( type ):                                                #(A)

    def foo( cls ):                                                  #(B)
        print "foo called with arg: ", cls                           #(C)

    def __new__( meta, classname, bases, dict ):                     #(D)
        print meta               # <class '__main__.MyMeta'>         #(E)
        print classname          # X                                 #(F)
        return super(MyMeta, meta).__new__(meta,
                                    classname, bases, dict)          #(G)

    def __init__( cls, classname, bases, dict ):                     #(H)
        print cls                # <class '__main__.X'>              #(I)
        print classname          # X                                 #(J)
        super( MyMeta, cls ).__init__(cls, classname, bases, dict)   #(K)
        setattr( cls, 'foo', cls.foo )                               #(L)
        delattr( cls, 'bar' )                                        #(M)
```

```
#----------------------------  class X  ---------------------------------
class X( object ):                                                  #(N)
    __metaclass__ = MyMeta                                          #(O)

    def __init__( self, nn ):                                       #(P)
        self.n = nn                                                 #(Q)

    def getn( self ):                                               #(R)
        return self.n                                               #(S)

    def bar( self ): pass                                           #(T)

#------------------------------  Test Code  ---------------------------
xobj = X(10)                                                        #(U)

xobj.foo()         # foo called with arg:  <class '__main__.X'>    #(V)

X.foo()            # foo called with arg:  <class '__main__.X'>    #(W)

print X.__dict__                                                    #(X)
           # {'__module__': '__main__',
           #  '__metaclass__': <class '__main__.MyMeta'>,
           #  'getn': <function getn at 0x403b2df4>,
           #  '__dict__': <attribute '__dict__' of 'X' objects>,
           #  'foo': <bound method MyMeta.foo of <class '__main__.X'>>,
           #  '__weakref__': <attribute '__weakref__' of 'X' objects>,
           #  '__doc__': None,
           #  '__init__': <function __init__ at 0x403b2dbc>}
```

9.11 OPERATOR OVERLOADING AND INHERITANCE

Section 7.10 of Chapter 7 presented in some detail how the many built-in operators of Python can be overloaded for a new user-defined class. So that the derived-class operator overloading in Python can be compared with the same in Perl, let's now raise the same questions that we did for Perl in Section 8.14 of Chapter 8:

- If an operator is overloaded in the base class, does that overload definition become available in a derived class also?
- What if the derived class wanted to override the base-class's overload definition for an operator?
- Are there any syntax constraints on the base-class overload definition so that it becomes available in a derived class?

To answer these questions in a manner similar to our Perl discussion, we will start with the class `XArray` of Section 7.10 of Chapter 7 and extend it into the derived class `MyXArray` shown in the next script. Just to make the derived class a bit different from the base class, we gratuitously supply the derived class `MyXArray` with its own `__init__()` that initializes one more instance variable, `_how_many_nums`, in line (C). This instance variable is supposed to keep track of the number of integer elements stored in an instance of `MyXArray`. Note that the derived-class definition of `__str__()` at line (E) uses four underscores as the glue between the successive elements of the container, as opposed to a single underscore that was used in the base-class definition of the same method.

If you run the script as shown, it prints out the outputs shown in lines (H) and (J), the first for an instance of the base class `XArray` and the second for an instance of the derived class `MyXArray`. This is to be expected. When you specifically ask for a derived-class instance to be stringified, the system must use the stringification function for the derived class (if one is available, which is indeed the case in our example).

Next if you run the script by commenting out the definition of `__str__()` at line (E), the two outputs produced by the `print` statements in lines (H) and (J) would be the same. In this case, when Python is trying to stringify the derived-class instance in line (J), it will use the base-class definition of `__str__()` as provided in the code shown in Section 7.10 of Chapter 7.

The derived-class behavior regarding the stringification operation achieved with `__str__()` is exhibited by all other specially named methods listed in Section 7.10 of Chapter 7 for providing overload definitions for the various commonly used operators in Python.

The upshot is that if your derived class overrides the base-class overload definition for an operator, Python will use the derived-class definition for a derived-class instance. But should there be no derived-class overload definition, Python will use the base-class definition. With regard to the third question posed at the beginning of this section, there are no syntax constraints on a base-class overload definition for it to become available in a derived class.

```
#!/usr/bin/env python

### MyXArray.py

from XArray import XArray
```

```
#--------------------------- Class MyXArray --------------------------
class MyXArray( XArray ):                                           #(A)

    def __init__( self, arr_arg ):                                  #(B)
        self._arr = list(arr_arg)
        self._size = len( arr_arg )
        self._how_many_nums = \
            len( filter( lambda x: isinstance(x, int), arr_arg ) )  #(C)

    def get_how_many_nums( self ):                                  #(D)
        return self._how_many_nums

    def __str__( self ):                                            #(E)
        'To create a print representation'
        if self._size == 0:
            return ''
        return '____'.join( map( str, self._arr ) )


#------------------------   Test Code   ------------------------------

if __name__ == '__main__':                                          #(F)

    x_base = XArray( (1,2,"hello",3) )                              #(G)
    print x_base                          # 1_2_hello_3             #(H)

    x_derived = MyXArray( (1,2,"hello",3) )                         #(I)
    print x_derived                       # 1____2____hello____3    #(J)
```

9.12 CREDITS AND SUGGESTIONS FOR FURTHER READING

The discussion in this chapter on all issues related to multiple inheritance in Python has drawn significantly from the original explanations supplied by Guido van Rossum [65]. The presentation of the C3 algorithm in Section 9.8.3 for figuring out the method resolution order for Python's new-style classes is based on Michele Simionato's tutorial [59]. The reader will also find useful the on-line tutorial on metaclass programming by David Mertz and Michele Simionato [50]. With regard to operator overloading issues, the reader is referred to same material as listed in the "Credits and Suggestions" section of Chapter 7 — Section 3 of the Python Reference Manual.

9.13 HOMEWORK

1. As mentioned in Section 9.8.4, both LRDF and C3 algorithms for finding the MRO of a class do not take into account the recency of class derivation in an inheritance graph. Use the two class diagrams of Fig. 9.9 to show what problems this can create. For both these class diagrams, assume that some

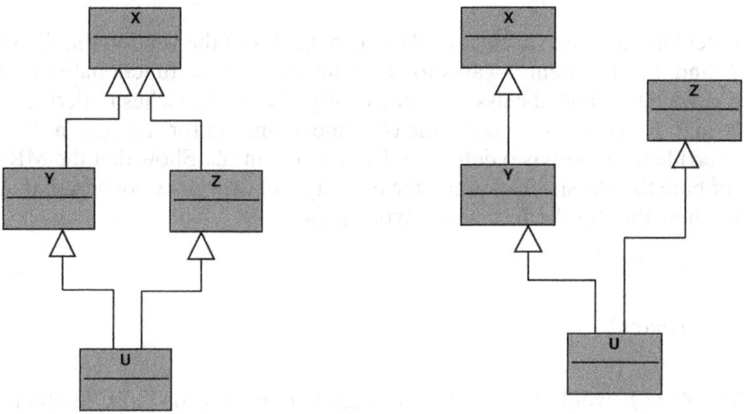

Fig. 9.9

vendor has supplied a client with the classes X, Y and Z, with either both Y and Z as subclassed from X, as shown on the left, or with just Y subclassed from X and with Z as a stand-alone class, as shown on the right. Also assume that class X comes with default definitions for two methods `foo()` and `bar()`:

```
class X:
    def foo(): pass
    def bar(): pass
```

Further assume that the classes Y and Z provide override definitions for the methods `foo()` and `bar()`, but separately:

```
class Y(X):
    def foo():
        ... some specialized code  for foo() ...

class Z(X):
    def bar():
        ... some specialized code for bar() ...
```

This corresponds to the class diagram on the left where we have a case of diamond inheritance. For the diagram on the right, assume we have

```
class Y(X):
    def foo():
        ... some specialized code  for foo() ...

class Z:
    def bar():
        ... some specialized code for bar() ...
```

After having gotten accustomed to the behavior of the vendor-supplied classes Y and Z, the client[23] wants to combine some of the functionality of both in a new client-created class U. Specifically, the client wishes to derive U from Y and Z so that U can use the override definition for foo() in Y and the override (or otherwise) definition for bar() in Z. Show that the MRO used for both the classic classes and the new-style classes does not permit that. That is, show that for the following invocations:

```
u = U()
u.foo()
u.bar()
```

Y's foo() would be called as desired, but not Z's bar(). In other words, U will have to make do with the default definition of bar() in the root class X. [However, if method inheritance explicitly took into account the recency of class derivations — as it does for some systems programming languages — u.foo() would invoke Y's foo() and u.bar() would invoke Z's bar().]

2. Section 9.8 talked about how Python carries out the search for a method definition in a class hierarchy. Do you think Python remembers the location of a method in the search graph so that if the same method were to be called again on the same type of an instance, Python would go directly to the previously found method (as opposed to scanning the ancestor classes again)? You could try the following sort of a script for your experiments:

```
#!/usr/bin/env python

class X:
    def foo(self):
        print "calling X's foo"
class Y(X):
    pass
```

[23] Assume the client does not have the freedom to alter the vendor-supplied code and that the client's understanding of the vendor code is limited to its published API.

```
print "X's namespace dictionary:    ", X.__dict__
xobj = X()
print xobj.__dict__

print "Y's namespace before calling X's methods:    ", Y.__dict__
yobj = Y()
yobj.foo()
print "Y's namespace after calling X's methods:    ", Y.__dict__
```

3. How many times do you believe `X's __del__()` would be called when you run the following script? If you have convinced yourself that X's `__del__()` would be called at all, why?

```
#!/usr/bin/env python

class X:
    def __del__(self):
        print "X's destructor called"

class Y(X): pass

class Z:
    def __init__(self, xobj):
        self.x = xobj

y = Y()
z1 = Z( y )
z2 = Z( y )
z3 = Z( y )
```

4. In Section 9.11, we extended the `XArray` class of Chapter 7 into the `MyXArray` class. While the base class in Chapter 7 was provided with explicit overloadings for a number of Python's built-in operators, only the stringification operation was explicitly overloaded in the derived class. Add to the code shown for `MyXArray.py` in Section 9.11 to demonstrate the derived-class operator overloadings achieved by virtue of the override definitions in the derived class for some of the other commonly used operators.

5. This question deals with operator overloadings for a class that is derived from multiple ancestors. By constructing simple examples, show that the set of overloaded operators for a derived class is the union of the overloaded operators for all its ancestor classes. What happens to the overloading in the derived class when the same operator is overloaded differently in different ancestor classes? Compare the classic and the new-style classes with respect to this issue.

10

Handling Exceptions

There can be two different kinds of errors associated with a script: (1) the errors of syntax, which will be caught during the compilation phase when the script is checked for its syntactic correctness; and (2) run-time errors, which can be caused by any of a large number of conditions, such as a variable acquiring a value that a script is not designed to handle,[1] wrong kind of data in a file or a database, invalid or otherwise unrecognizable information supplied by a human user in response to a query from a script, nonexistent files, excessively long network delays, etc.

The first kind of errors — also known as compilation errors — are commonly dealt with during the program development phase. Therefore, a properly written script should not show such errors during its useful lifetime, as long as the underlying language platform and the execution environment remain the same. However, even a properly written script can fall prey to the second kind of errors — the run-time errors. If not handled appropriately, the usual consequence of a run-time error is that the script would be aborted and the flow of control handed back to the operating system. *Exception handling* deals with the language-supplied mechanisms for trapping run-time errors and, if desired, initiating remedial measures for dealing with such error conditions. These run-time errors may either be generated internally by the execution environment, as in division by zero, or they may be forced by a programmer when a certain unacceptable condition is recognized in a script.

[1] For example, a script could have been written under the assumption that a variable, used as a divisor, would not acquire a zero value. What if run-time conditions cause the value of this variable to become zero?

When a run-time error is forced by the programmer, it is referred to as either *throwing an exception* or *raising an exception*. The data object that is either *thrown* or *raised* is referred to as the *exception object*. Typically, a script or a function inside a script will call another function that has the potential of throwing an exception under certain conditions. The calling function must make provision for *catching* the exception object. If for some reason an exception is uncaught, the execution of the script is brought to an immediate halt.

This chapter first reviews Perl's `die` operator that is used ordinarily to immediately halt the execution of a script should certain conditions be detected. But, as our review will mention, when `die` is called inside an `eval` block, it only causes an immediate exit from the block. This forms the basis for exception handling in Perl using the `eval` operator. We will show how invoking `die` inside an `eval` block is tantamount to throwing an exception, with the special global variable `$@` catching the thrown exception outside the `eval` block. Next we present a more object-oriented approach to exception handling in Perl using the `Exception` module available from `www.cpan.org`. The object-oriented mechanism is essentially a wrapper around the `eval` based approach. We will also briefly mention two other popular Perl modules for object-oriented exception handling: `Exception::Class` and `Error`, each with its special features. One of the big advantages of the object-oriented approaches to exception handling is that you can create different exception classes for different kinds of errors. So when you trap an exception, you know readily as to the nature of the run-time error that was the cause of the exception.

The rest of the chapter will focus on the exception handling support provided by Python. As we will see, all exception handling in Python is intrinsically object-oriented. All exception classes in Python are derived from the root class `Exception` that is defined in the `exceptions` module. This module also includes a large number of Python's more specialized classes that are derived from `Exception`. These more specialized classes can be used for raising specific exceptions in response to particular circumstances detected at run time. For example, in keeping with our previous comment about the advantages of object-oriented exception handling, if a script makes an attempt to access a nonexistent attribute for an object, Python will throw the `AttributeError` exception. So catching this exception (or seeing this exception in the error report displayed on the terminal if a script is aborted) would tell us right away as to what went wrong. This chapter includes a review of the more commonly used exception classes of Python.

10.1 REVIEW OF die FOR PROGRAM EXIT IN PERL

While C uses the `exit()` function for immediate program exit,[2] the same is accomplished in Perl with the `die` operator. Unless called inside an `eval` block, the main job of `die` is to terminate the currently running script with a nonzero exit status. When called inside an `eval` block, `die` causes immediate exit from the `eval` block and the flow of control shifts to the statement immediately following the block.

The `die` operator is used in the following four different ways in Perl:

1. When making a system request, such as opening a file, changing the current directory, etc., a failure of the request is used to trigger the execution of a `die` statement that causes immediate exit from the script. In such cases, the cause of the failure is frequently available through the special variable `$!`. Since `die` also causes its string argument to be printed out, including the variable `$!` in this argument can tell a programmer what caused the failure of the system call. Here is an example of an attempt to open a file in the append mode:[3]

```
open OUT, ">> record.txt"
    or die "Unable to open record.txt: $!";
print OUT "hello world";
```

   Suppose the write permission for the file `record.txt` is off when the `open` statement is executed, Perl will not be able to open the file for writing into. In this case, `open` will return `undef` indicating failure. Since `undef` is construed as false, the operand on the right-hand side of the `or` operator — the `die` statement — will be executed. Note the string argument supplied to `die` ends in the special scalar variable `$!` and there does not exist a newline terminator at the end. This structure of the argument to `die` will cause the following sort of error message to be displayed on the terminal screen should the call to `open` fail:

```
Unable to open record.txt: Permission denied at Test.pl line 7.
```

   assuming that the previously shown fragment of code was in a script file named `Test.pl`. Note the information that Perl adds to the programmer-specified

---

[2] C's `exit()` takes one integer argument that represents the *exit status* of the program should this statement be executed. It is the exit status that is handed by the process in which the program is running to the operating system. If immediate program termination is desired with no intimation of an error condition to the operating system, `exit()` is called with argument 0. The value of 0 returned by a program to the operating system means that the program executed successfully. A nonzero argument supplied to `exit()` implies that an error occurred during the execution of the program. What error condition is meant by a nonzero exit status is implementation dependent. Commonly, exit status of 1 indicates a syntax error in the command-line arguments, exit status of 2 means an error condition encountered during processing, exit status of 3 means a missing configuration file, and so on.

[3] Perl's file I/O syntax was reviewed in Section 2.6.2 of Chapter 2.

error message in the string argument to `die`. This additional information consists of the cause of the failure — in this case "`Permission denied`" — and the name of the script, along with the line number in the script where the failure occurred.

2. The same as above — meaning that we are again talking about using `die` for script termination should a system request end in failure — except that we now terminate the string argument to `die` in a newline, as in the example below:

```
open OUT, ">> record.txt"
    or die "Unable to open record.txt: $!\n";
print OUT "hello world";
```

   Should `open` fail, the `die` statement will be executed as before. However, the presence of the newline terminator in the string argument to `die` suppresses the file name and the line number in the error message that is printed out. Therefore, in this case, `die` will cause the following sort of message to be printed out upon the failure of the system request in the left operand of `or`:

```
Unable to open record.txt: Permission denied
```

3. An unacceptable data condition in a script can be made to trigger a call to `die`. Consider, for example, the following script that asks a user to enter a volume, a length, and a width in lines (B), (C), and (D), respectively. The script calculates and returns the value of height in line (G). In lines (E) and (F), the script makes sure that the data entered by the user is non-negative for the volume and positive for the length and the width dimensions. If these conditions on the data entered by the user are not satisfied, line (F) invokes `die` to terminate the script immediately. Since this use of `die` is triggered by data conditions within the script, it would be erroneous to include the special variable `$!` inside the string argument to `die`. Recall, that this variable stores a textual description of the cause of failure of a system request.

```
#!/usr/bin/perl -w
use strict;

### DieForExit.pl

while (1) {                                                          #(A)

    print "What is the volume: "; chomp( my $vol = <STDIN> );       #(B)
    print "What is the length: "; chomp( my $len = <STDIN> );       #(C)
    print "What is the width: "; chomp( my $wid = <STDIN> );        #(D)
```

```
    if ( $vol < 0 or $len <= 0 or $wid <= 0 ) {                  #(E)
        die "Illegal data entry by user.  Stopped";              #(F)
    }

    print "The height is: ", $vol / ( $len * $wid ), "\n";       #(G)
}
```

Since the string argument to `die` in line (F) does not include the line terminator, if the user should enter an illegal value, this call to `die` will cause immediate termination of the script and the display of the following message in the terminal window:

```
Illegal data entry by user. Stopped at DieForExit.pl line 12.
```

Note the additions made — the file name and the line number — to the argument supplied to `die` in line (F).

4. The same as in the previous case — meaning that we are again talking about using `die` for terminating the execution of a script because of unacceptable data conditions in the script as opposed to the failure of a system request — but now we want to suppress from the output message the file name and the line number that corresponds to the `die` statement. This we accomplish by terminating the string argument to `die` in the newline character, as in the following variation of what is in line (F) of the above script:

   ```
   die "Illegal data entry by user.  Stopped.\n";
   ```

   Should the user make an illegal entry for any of the three requested numbers, this `die` statement will cause immediate exit from the script and the following message will be printed out:

   ```
   Illegal data entry by user.  Stopped.
   ```

10.2 eval FOR EXCEPTION HANDLING IN PERL

The most commonly used mechanism for exception handling in Perl is based on the `eval` operator. An exception thrown inside an `eval` block causes immediate exit from the block to the statement that follows the block. The error information related to the exception is deposited in the special variable `$@`. Therefore, if a `die` statement is executed inside an `eval` block either because of the failure of a system call or because of unacceptable data or program conditions, the error condition can be examined outside the `eval` block and, if desired, remedial action taken.

This suggests the following syntax for trapping run-time errors and possibly taking remedial action should there be an error. You place the code that you want to "protect" inside an `eval` block. Immediately outside the block, you test the special variable `$@` to see if it contains anything. If this test evaluates to true, you then proceed to take whatever action is warranted. This syntax can be displayed in the following manner:[4]

```
eval {
    ... code ...
};
if ( $@ ) {
  ....error handling code ...
}
```

We will now use the above syntax to write a different version of our height calculator script. Recall that in `DieForExit.pl` the `die` statement caused immediate program termination. That program did not give the user a chance to correct the error condition caused by the entry of incorrect data. On the other hand, the script shown next, `EvalForExceptions1.pl`, puts the user-interaction part of the code of the earlier script inside an `eval` block. Now when one or more of the user entries is discovered to be inappropriate and the `die` statement executed in line (F), the flow of control immediately switches to line (I). Since the string argument to `die` in line (G) is deposited in the special variable `$@`, the conditional in line (I) would evaluate to true in this case and the message in line (J) would be printed out. This message would look like

```
Error report from eval: Illegal data entry by user.  Try again.
```

After the message is printed out, the flow of control would go back to line (B) for the next iteration of the `while` loop.

---

[4]Note that some programmer do not like to use this syntax to trap run-time errors. They say that there is always the theoretical possibility that the global variable `$@` might get reset between the time it is set in the `eval` block and the time it is tested in the conditional of the `if` statement that follows the block. So, conceivably, even if the code inside the `eval` ran without problems, the conditional of the `if` might still evaluate to true — resulting in buggy behavior from the script. These programmers prefer the following syntax:

```
eval {
    ... code ...
    1;
} or do {
  .... error handling using $@ ....
};
```

In this alternative syntax, when the code in the `eval` block runs to completion, it will always return true since we explicitly included the always true statement "`1;`" at the end of the block. In this case, contrary to the previous syntax, we can be absolutely certain that the error handling block would not be run. But should the code in the `eval` block throw an exception, it will not return true. This would cause the error handling code to be executed.

```
#!/usr/bin/perl -w
use strict;

# EvalForExceptions1.pl

while (1) {                                                              #(A)
    eval {                                                               #(B)
        print "What is the volume: "; chomp( my $vol = <STDIN> );        #(C)
        print "What is the length: "; chomp( my $len = <STDIN> );        #(D)
        print "What is the width: "; chomp( my $wid = <STDIN> );         #(E)

        if ( ($vol < 0) || ($len <= 0) || ($wid <= 0) ) {                #(F)
            die "Illegal data entry by user.  Try again.\n";             #(G)
        }

        print "The height is: ", $vol / ( $len * $wid ), "\n";           #(H)
    };
    if ( $@ ) {                                                          #(I)
        print "Error report from eval: $@";                              #(J)
    }
}
```

We will now show that the information that is deposited in `$@` does not have to be a string; it can be any scalar, including a reference to another object.[5] In the following version of the above script, the scalar `$x` in line (A) is a reference to a string object. The call to `die` in line (H) will deposit this reference in the special variable `$@`. Subsequently, when the flow of control shifts to line (J), the string reference deposited in `$@` is dereferenced in line (K) and printed out. As a result, if any of the quantities requested from a human in lines (D), (E), and (F) turns out to be inappropriate, the error message of line (A) will be displayed in the terminal window.

```
#!/usr/bin/perl -w
#use strict;

# EvalForExceptions2.pl

my $x = \"You entered an illegal value. A reference to this \
          error message is the argument to die. Try again.\n";      #(A)
```

[5]Chapter 5 presented the notion of a reference in Perl.

```
while (1) {                                                              #(B)
    eval {                                                               #(C)
        print "What is the volume: "; chomp( my $vol = <STDIN> );        #(D)
        print "What is the length: "; chomp( my $len = <STDIN> );        #(E)
        print "What is the width: "; chomp( my $wid = <STDIN> );         #(F)

        if ( ($vol < 0) || ($len <= 0) || ($wid <= 0) ) {                #(G)
            die $x;                                                      #(H)
        }

        print "The height is: ", $vol / ( $len * $wid ), "\n";           #(I)
    };
    if ( $@ ) {                                                          #(J)
        print ${$@};                                                     #(K)
    }
}
```

The fact that `die`, when invoked inside an `eval` block, can deposit any scalar, including a reference to an object, in the special variable `$@` allows us to designate class type objects for exception handling. In the following variation on the height-calculator scripts shown previously we want `die` to deposit in `$@` a different exception object for each of the three different possible errors. As the reader will recall, the user has to supply three numbers to the script, one for the volume, one for the length, and one for the width. The previous two scripts carried out a single test for detecting errors in all three and, if an error was found, a single string or a reference to the string was deposited by `die` in the variable `$@`. But now we want to test each user input separately and, if an error is detected, we want `die` to deposit a reference to a different exception object in `$@`.[6]

To meet these requirements, the next script first defines a root class `Exception` in lines (A) through (F). This class is provided with a constructor, `new()`, defined in lines (B) through (D). This constructor will be inherited by the three subclasses of the root class we define next. Note that since our class definitions do not include any instance variables, we use an empty hash as the underlying data structure, as should be evident from line (D). Lines (E), (I), and (L) then define the three exception classes — `VolumeNegativeException`, `LengthNegativeException`, and `WidthNegativeException` — we need for the three kinds of errors. All these classes are derived from the root class `Exception`, the subclass to parent-class connections established through the `ISA` statements such as the one shown in line

---

[6]This is a common feature of the object-oriented approach to exception handling. A separate exception class is defined for each different kind of error. As we will show in the example presented here, these separate classes are all usually derived from the same root exception class.

(F). Lines (N), (O), and (P) construct the three exception objects that will be thrown for each of the three possible errors.

Let's now examine the main part of the script in lines (Q) through (X) — this is the part that is supposed to be the replacement for the height calculation scripts shown earlier. These lines show basically the same flow of control as in the earlier scripts, except that now we check for the correctness of each user input separately. For example, when we get the user input for the volume in line (S), should it happen to be negative, we ask `die` in line (T) to deposit in `$@` the exception object whose reference is held by the variable `$errVol`. Similarly, if the user-supplied value for the length in line (U) should prove to be not positive, we ask `die` in the next line to deposit the reference held by `$errLength` in the variable `$@`. We do the same with the width value supplied by the user in line (V). Each of the three conditions will immediately transfer the program execution to the `if`-conditional statement in line (X), which in turn will invoke the `toString()` method on the object reference held by `$@`. So if the length value entered by the human was not positive, the message output by the print statement in line (X) would be

```
Length must be a positive number. Start over.
```

```
#!/usr/bin/perl -w
#use strict;

# EvalForExceptions3.pl

#------------------------  base class Exception  ----------------------
package Exception;                                                #(A)
sub new {                                                         #(B)
    my ( $class ) = @_;                                           #(C)
    bless {}, $class;                                             #(D)
}

#---------------  derived class VolumeNegativeException  -------------
package VolumeNegativeException;                                  #(E)
@VolumeNegativeException::ISA = ('Exception');                    #(F)
sub toString {                                                    #(G)
    "Negative volume is not allowed. Start over.\n";              #(H)
}

#---------------  derived class LengthNegativeException  -------------
package LengthNegativeException;                                  #(I)
@LengthNegativeException::ISA = ('Exception');                    #(J)
sub toString {                                                    #(K)
    "Length must be a positive number. Start over.\n";
}
```

```
#---------------- derived class WidthNegativeException --------------
package WidthNegativeException;                                   #(L)
@WidthNegativeException::ISA = ('Exception');
sub toString {
    "Width must be a positive number. Start over.\n";
}

#-------------------- class HeightCalculator ----------------------
package HeightCalculator;                                          #(M)

my $errVol    = VolumeNegativeException->new();                   #(N)
my $errLength = LengthNegativeException->new();                   #(O)
my $errWidth  = WidthNegativeException->new();                    #(P)

while (1) {                                                        #(Q)
    eval {                                                         #(R)
        print "What is the volume: "; chomp( my $vol = <STDIN> );  #(S)
        die $errVol if $vol < 0;                                   #(T)

        print "What is the length: "; chomp(my $length = <STDIN>); #(U)
        die $errLength if $length <= 0;

        print "What is the width: "; chomp( my $width = <STDIN> ); #(V)
        die $errWidth if $width <= 0;

        print "The height is: ", $vol / ($length * $width), "\n";  #(W)
    };
    print $@->toString() if $@;                                    #(X)
}
```

10.3 USING THE Exception MODULE FOR EXCEPTION HANDLING IN PERL

As we demonstrated in the previous section, you can establish your own classes for an object-oriented approach to exception handling in Perl. What we showed there was fairly rudimentary, as the classes were provided with bare minimum functionality — just sufficient to demonstrate how the `eval-die` combination can be used for an object-oriented approach to the throwing and catching of exceptions in Perl.[7]

[7] The exception classes in object-oriented software systems are fairly simple anyway. They often need only one or two instance variables for storing the nature of the error and one or two accessor functions so that this information can be extracted by the exception handlers.

For a programmer wishing to use the object-oriented approach to exception handling in Perl production code, it is more convenient to use the `Exception` module[8] that is easily downloadable from `www.cpan.org`. This module provides the following methods for the class `Exception`:

`new()`: For constructing a new instance of the `Exception` class. Unless overridden, this method can also be used for constructing instances from the programmer-defined subclasses of `Exception`. This method can be called with a string argument indicating the cause of the exception.

`raise()`: For throwing an exception object. By providing `raise()` with a string argument, the exception object can be supplied with additional text that augments the text supplied to the constructor `new()`. This additional text can carry information about the execution environment at the instant the exception is thrown.

`confess()`: For catching an exception object and displaying the text message packed with the object.

`croak()`: For catching an exception object, displaying the text message packed with the object, and terminating the script immediately.

The code in which you want to trap the exceptions thrown at run time is placed inside a `try` block, which is followed by exception handling code in one or more `except` blocks.[9] An `except` block can be made to be responsive to either all possible exceptions thrown by the code inside the `try` block or to just a subset of them. When at run-time an exception is thrown by a statement in the `try` block, the rest of the `try` block is skipped and the control shifts to the first matching `except` block. If it is not possible to use any of the `except` blocks for handling the exception, the execution of the script terminates immediately. An exception can be thrown inside a `try` block either by calling `raise()`, as we will show below, or by just calling `die`. An exception thrown by `die` is converted into a class-type exception object by the `Exception` module.

The use of the `Exception` package for exception handling is illustrated in the `BankAccount` example in the next script, `ExceptionOO.pl`, that uses two different types of exception objects for dealing with two different cases: (1) when the amount to be withdrawn exceeds the limit on a one-time withdrawal; and (2) when it exceeds

---

[8] As mentioned in the introduction to this chapter, other popular modules for object-oriented exception handling in Perl include the `Exception::Class` module that makes it easy to create exception class hierarchies and the `Error` module that allows for the more modern `try-catch` syntax for exception handling. Both of these are readily downloadable from `www.cpan.org`.

[9] The code placed inside the `try` block is sometimes referred to as the *protected code* since — depending on how the exceptions generated by this code are handled — this code can be guaranteed to not cause run-time crashes.

the balance remaining in the account. The exception object for the first case is of type `AmountExceededException` and, for the second, of type `OverdraftException`.

Line (A) of the script uses the argument `:all` to call on the module loader to import all exportable names from the module. Lines (B) through (E) then define the two subclasses of the class `Exception`, `AmountExceededException` and `OverdraftException`. Since these subclasses do not override any of the methods made available by the root class, all those methods can be accessed through the subclass instances. Lines (I) and (J) construct two instances that can be thrown as exception objects, the first an instance of `AmountExceededException` and the second an instance of `OverdraftException`. The constructor calls in lines (I) and (J) both take two arguments, the first a symbolic name for the exception object and the second a text message that would be common to all uses of that exception object. So the symbolic name of the first exception object is `amount_exceeded` and of the second `overdrafted`.

Lines (K) through (R) define a `withdraw_money()` function. In line (M) this function checks whether the amount to be withdrawn exceeds the limit on single-transaction withdrawal; if the limit is violated, it throws an exception in line (N) by calling `raise` on the exception object `err1`. Similarly, in line (O) a check is made on whether the amount to be withdrawn exceeds the balance in the account; if the balance is exceeded, an exception is thrown by calling `raise()` on the exception object `err2`. In each case, in lines (N) and (P), we supply a string argument to `raise()` that is added to the text message already stored in the exception objects at the time the instances were constructed in lines (I) and (J), respectively.

The user interaction with the bank account takes place in the `while` loop in lines (S) through (Z). We invoke the `withdraw_money()` function in line (V) inside a `try` block, which allows any exceptions thrown to be caught by the `when-except` constructs of lines (W) and (Y). What follows the `when` keyword and comes before the `except` keyword acts like the argument to `catch` in C++ and Java, in the sense that the `except` block is invoked only when a certain attribute of the exception object matches the entry that immediately follows `when`.[10] A missing `when` clause makes the subsequent `except` block a wildcard exception handler, meaning that the `except` block becomes the exception handler for all exceptions thrown inside the `try` block.

---

[10]An `except` block can be made to handle multiple exceptions by placing all the desired exception objects in an anonymous array following the `when` keyword. This array is also allowed to contain symbolic names for the exception objects, and regexes that can match the text messages carried by the exception objects. For example, if we wanted a single `except` block to serve as the sole exception handler for the exceptions thrown by the code in the try block, we could write the following redundant form for the `when` clause:

```
when [$err1, 'amount_exceeded', $err2, 'overdrafted'], except {
    ... exception handling code ...
}
```

In a `when` clause, an exception object may be matched by naming the variable that holds a reference to the object, such as the variable `$err1` in line (W); or through the symbolic name given to the exception object via the first argument to the constructor, as in lines (I) and (J); or through a regex that will match the text message carried by the exception object. Just for variety, we have used the second approach in the `when` clause of line (Y).

Also note in the following script that we take two different actions in response to the catching of the two different exception objects. Line (X) invokes the `confess()` method that merely displays the text message held by the exception object, but does not otherwise terminate the script. In other words, when `confess()` is invoked in line (X), after the message is printed out, the next iteration of the `while` loop of line (S) would be started. On the other hand, line (Z) invokes `croak()`, which causes the script to terminate immediately.

```
#!/usr/bin/perl -w
use strict;

# ExceptionOO.pl

use Exception qw(:all);                                                  #(A)

#--------------------  class AmountExceededException  ----------------
package AmountExceededException;                                         #(B)

@AmountExceededException::ISA = ('Exception');                           #(C)

#----------------------  class OverdraftException  --------------------
package OverdraftException;                                              #(D)

@OverdraftException::ISA = ('Exception');                                #(E)

#------------------------  class BankAccount  ------------------------
package BankAccount;                                                     #(F)

use Exception qw(:all);                                                  #(G)

my $balance = 1000;                                                      #(H)

my $err1 = AmountExceededException->new( 'amount_exceeded',              #(I)
                  'You have exceeded the limit on a '.
                  'single withdrawal by requesting' );
my $err2 = OverdraftException->new( 'overdrafted',                       #(J)
                  'There is insufficient balance in '.
                  'your account. You wanted to withdraw');
```

```
sub withdraw_money {                                              #(K)
    my $amount = shift;                                           #(L)
    if ( $amount > 200 and $amount < $balance ) {                 #(M)
        $err1->raise( "an amount of $amount." );                  #(N)
    } elsif ( $amount > $balance ) {                              #(O)
        $err2->raise( "an amount of $amount." );                  #(P)
    }
    $balance = $balance - $amount;                                #(Q)
    print "New balance is $balance\n";                            #(R)
}

while (1) {                                                       #(S)
    try {                                                         #(T)
        print "How much do you need? "; chomp(my $amount = <STDIN>);#(U)
        withdraw_money( $amount );                                #(V)
    } when $err1, except {                                        #(W)
        shift->confess;                                           #(X)
    } when 'overdrafted', except {                                #(Y)
        shift->croak;                                             #(Z)
    }
};
```

10.3.1 Polymorphic Behavior in OO Exception Handling

An important question related to the object-oriented approach to exception handling is whether the exception handlers behave polymorphically. Let's say an exception class `ExcepB` is derived from the exception class `ExcepA`. Suppose a `try` block is followed by a handler for `ExcepA`, but the actual exception thrown is an object of type `ExcepB`. If the exception handling system meets the modern expectations of object-oriented programming, the handler for `ExcepA` should trap the exception since, after all, an instance of type `ExcepB` is also an instance of type `ExcepA`.

The object-oriented exception handling framework provided by the `Exception` module[11] does not behave polymorphically in the sense described above. That is because it is not possible to specify the *type* of exception objects that a handler is supposed to trap. Exception handlers can only be triggered either by references to specific instances of exception classes, or by symbolic id's assigned to these instances, or by the matching of regexes with the messages carried by the instances.

[11] If the reader chooses to experiment with the other two popular modules for Perl exception handling, the `Exception::Class` module and the `Error` module, he/she wish to test them also for polymorphic behavior.

The next script is perhaps the closest we can come to demonstrating that exception handling with the `Exception` module is not polymorphic. We define a new exception class `Error` in line (B), ostensibly for a new Perl module specialized for some application, and make it a subclass of the root exception class `Exception`. Line (D) defines an exception class `SpecialError_1`, derived from `Error`, and line (E) defines a further derived class `SpecialError_2` derived from `SpecialError_1`. Lines (J) and (K) create two exception objects from the two classes `SpecialError_1` and `SpecialError_2`, respectively.

Line (N) throws the second exception object, `$err2`. In a polymorphic exception handling framework, you'd expect that a handler written for exceptions of type `SpecialError_1` would trap this exception. But if you run this script, you'll notice that the exception `$err2` does not at all get trapped by the handler of lines (O), (P), and (Q). Instead, it gets trapped by the handler in lines (R), (S), and (T), which is the handler written expressly for `$err2`.

```
#!/usr/bin/perl -w
use strict;

### ExceptionOOPolymorph.pl

use Exception qw(:all);                                              #(A)

#-------------------  base exception class Error  ---------------------
package Error;                                                       #(B)
@Error::ISA = ('Exception');                                         #(C)

#------------------  derived class SpecialError_1  --------------------
package SpecialError_1;                                              #(D)
@SpecialError_1::ISA = ('Error');                                    #(E)

#--------------  further derived class SpecialError_2  ----------------
package SpecialError_2;                                              #(F)
@SpecialError_2::ISA = ('SpecialError_1');                           #(G)

#---------------------------  Test Code  ----------------------------

package MyWork;                                                      #(H)

use Exception qw(:all);                                              #(I)

my $err1 = new SpecialError_1 'e1', 'throwing e1 exception';         #(J)

my $err2 = new SpecialError_2 'e2', 'throwing e2 exception';         #(K)

try {                                                                #(L)
#    $err1->raise( "exception object's id is e1" );                  #(M)
```

```
    $err2->raise( "exception object's id is e2" );              #(N)
} when $err1, except {                                          #(O)
    print "this is a handler for err1\n";                       #(P)
    shift->confess;                                             #(Q)
} when $err2, except {                                          #(R)
    print "this is a handler for err2\n";                       #(S)
    shift->confess;                                             #(T)
}
```

10.4 EXCEPTION HANDLING IN PYTHON

All run-time errors in Python result in the throwing of instances of exception classes that may either be built-in or programmer-defined. In that sense, all exception handling in Python is object-oriented. All exception classes in Python, whether built-in or user-defined, are derived from the class `Exception` that is defined in the module `exceptions`.[12] This module is imported automatically into a script.

To trap any exceptions thrown by one or more statements, the statements must be placed inside the `try` clause of a `try-except` statement. The `except` clauses are the handlers for the exceptions thrown by the code protected by the `try` clause. One can have any number of `except` clauses, each designed for one or a small number of specific exceptions.

The `try-except` construct allows for two optional clauses: `else` and `finally`. The `else` clause if used must follow all `except` clauses; it is meant for code that must be executed if the `try` block does *not* raise an exception. The `finally` clause if used must also be placed at the end of the `try-except` construct; it can be used for cleanup operations whether or not an exception was actually thrown.

So the organization of the code for exception handling looks like:

```
try:                                                            #(A)
    ... protected code ...                                      #(B)
except NameOfException_1, e:                                    #(C)
    ... exception handling code ...                             #(D)
except NameOfException_2, e:                                    #(E)
    ... exception handling code ...                             #(F)
except:                                                         #(G)
    ... wildcard exception handler ...                          #(H)
```

---

[12]The requirement that a user-defined exception class be derived from `Exception` was not being enforced at the time of writing of this book. Nonetheless, in order to be future-compatible, it is recommended that programmers derive their exception classes, directly or indirectly, from `Exception`.

```
else:                                                        #(I)
    ....
finally:                                                     #(J)
    ... clean-up code ...                                    #(K)
```

By `NameOfException_1` and `NameOfException_2` in lines (C) and (E) we mean the name of the exception class whose instance will be trapped by the handler. Obviously, we can have any number of such clauses that are meant to trap exceptions of specific types. The variable `e` in the same lines is bound to the specific exception instance that is trapped by that exception handler. Lines (I) through (K) illustrate the placement of the `else` and `finally` clauses.

To illustrate the use of the `try-except` syntax, suppose you run the following script:

```
#!/usr/bin/env python
x = 1.0/0.0
print x
print "done with the script"
```

The operating system will come back with the following error report:

```
Traceback (most recent call last):
  File "test.py", line 2, in <module>
    1.0/0.0
  ZeroDivisionError: float division
```

indicating that the division by zero in the statement `1.0/0.0` in line 2 of the script caused the `ZeroDivisionError` exception to be raised, which, in the absence of any programmer-defined handler, resulted in the script being aborted. But now let's carry out the division by zero inside a `try` clause as in

```
#!/usr/bin/env python
try:                                                         #(B)
    x = 1.0/0.0                                              #(C)
    print x                                                  #(D)
except ZeroDivisionError:                                    #(E)
    pass                                                     #(F)
print "done with the script"                                 #(G)
```

Now there is no problem with the script running to completion.[13] The exception thrown by the division by zero in line (C) will be trapped by the exception handler in line (E). Since we have a do-nothing exception handler here, the exception will simply be absorbed and the flow of control will pass to line (G), which will print out

[13]Note that the except clause does not include in line (E) an identifier that would be bound to the exception object actually caught. That is because in this example we have no interest in extracting any information from the exception object.

the message shown there. Since the root class for exception classes is `Exception`, the above script could also have been written as:

```
#!/usr/bin/env python
try:
    x = 1.0/0.0
    print x
except Exception:
    pass
print "done with the script"
```

This demonstrates that a Python exception handler behaves polymorphically. An exception handler will accept all exceptions that correspond to the classes named after the `except` identifier, *or any of the subclasses thereof.*

Another way to write the above script is to use the wildcard form of the exception handler. This is, the handler that does not name an exception class in the `except` clause, as in:[14]

```
#!/usr/bin/env python
try:
    x = 1.0/0.0
    print x
except:
    pass
print "done with the script"
```

If no exception is thrown by any of the statements in a `try` clause, all `except` clauses associated with the `try` clause are skipped over and that is the end of the execution of the `try` clause. However, when an exception is thrown by any statement in the `try` clause, the rest of the statements in the `try` clause are skipped over and search is immediately initiated for a matching `except` clause for handling the exception. If no handler is found, the processing of the script is immediately terminated.

Python has the concept of a *value* associated with an instance of an exception class. This is the value of the `args` instance variable that is defined for the root class `Exception` and that is inherited by all classes derived from `Exception`. The value that is assigned to the instance variable `args` can be either a single string or a tuple containing several items of information. For built-in exception classes, any arguments to the constructor are directly assigned to `args`. If a constructor is invoked with a single string argument, the value of `args` becomes a tuple containing just that string. And if a constructor is invoked with multiple arguments, a tuple of

[14]This syntax comes in handy for fast debugging of small scripts in situations when you are less concerned about the precise nature of the exception thrown and more about the rest of the program flow. With this syntax, any exception whatsoever thrown by the protected code inside the `try` clause will be absorbed by the wildcard `except` clause.

those arguments becomes the value of `args`. The method `__str__()` defined for `Exception` returns a printable string representation for whatever is stored in `args`.[15]

The following script illustrates the role of the `args` instance variable — and, at the same time, demonstrates the use of the `raise()` method for raising an exception. Line (B) invokes the constructor for the `TypeError` exception[16] with the string argument "`a TypeError instance thrown`". The exception object thus constructed is then supplied as the argument to `raise()` for throwing the exception. A singleton tuple containing just the string argument provided to the constructor becomes the value of the instance variable `args` for the `TypeError` instance constructed. Subsequently, after the exception is caught in line (D), when we print out the value of this instance variable in line (E), we get what is shown in the commented-out portion of that line. The string representation of an exception object is the string value of what is stored in the `args` instance variable. This is illustrated by the output shown in the commented-out portion of line (F). This string representation is constructed implicitly by the `__str__()` method of the exception class, which is in keeping with the role of the `__str__()` method as explained in Section 7.10 of Chapter 7.

```
#!/usr/bin/env python

### ExceptionTypeError.py

try:                                                                    #(A)
    raise TypeError( "a TypeError instance thrown" )                    #(B)
#    raise TypeError, "a TypeError instance thrown"                     #(C)
except TypeError, e:                                                    #(D)
    print e.args              # ('a TypeError instance thrown',)       #(E)
    print e                   # a TypeError instance thrown             #(F)
```

When the constructor invocation supplied to `raise()` contains only one argument, as it did in line (B) of the above script, `raise()` can also be invoked in the manner shown in the commented-out line (C).

[15] As mentioned earlier in Section 7.10 of Chapter 7, when a class implements the `__str__()` method, it overloads the "stringification" operation. That is, it tells Python how to create a printable string representation for an instance of that class.

[16] This is the exception that would be thrown if you tried to supply inappropriate operands to an operator; for example, if you tried to do `"hello" + 1234`.

10.5 PYTHON'S BUILT-IN EXCEPTION CLASSES

The module `exceptions` also defines a large number of built-in exception classes. Apart from the classes `StopIteration` and `SystemExit`, all the other built-in exception classes are derived from the base class `StandardError`, which itself is a subclass of the root class `Exception`.[17]

Here is a sampling of the built-in exception classes in Python:

AssertionError:

This exception is thrown when an assertion fails. An *assertion* is an expression that is supplied as either the only argument or the first of the two arguments to `assert`. This expression is evaluated for its truth value. The expression must evaluate to true for the thread of execution to proceed beyond the call to `assert`. If the expression evaluates to false, an `AssertionError` exception is thrown. An optional second argument to `assert` is supplied to the exception object that is thrown should the assertion fail.[18]

The following script shows a working example that traps exceptions of type `AssertionError`. The script defines a `User` class with the instance variables `name` and `age` in lines (B) through (P). The class is provided with a `change_name()` method that takes an optional second argument for a new name. Since invoking `change_name()` without a new name makes no sense, we call on `assert` in line (J) to tell us whether or not a new name has been provided. If the first argument to `assert` checks out to be true, no exception will be thrown and the thread of execution will shift to line (P). However, if `change_name()` is invoked without a new name, the first argument to `assert` in line (J) will evaluate to false. In this case, an `AssertionError` exception is thrown and the second argument to `assert` is passed on to the constructor of the exception instance. When this exception is trapped in line (K), the variable e is given a reference to the exception. As a consequence, line (L) prints out the message

```
Enter new name:
```

[17]Both the built-in classes `StopIteration` and `SystemExit` are derived directly from `Exception`. A call to `sys.exit()` implicitly throws an exception of type `SystemExit`. If this exception is not caught, the execution of the script terminates immediately.

[18]A call to `assert` is translated internally into the code

```
if __debug__:
    if not first_arg_to_assert:
        raise AssertionError, second_arg_to_assert
```

where `__debug__` is set by default to 1. It is set to 0 when Python is run in the optimized mode by its being invoked with the `-o` option. What that implies is that the `assert` statement would not really be executed in optimized runs of Python. In that sense, `assert` is useful only during the debugging phase of a script.

The name supplied by the user becomes the value of the variable `new_name`. Line (M) makes sure that the user did not just hit the Enter key on the keyboard without supplying a name. If the user did not supply a name, the function `sys.exit()` is invoked with exit code 1 to signify error to the operating system. This, as mentioned before, throws the exception `SystemExit`. Since the script does not provide a handler for this exception, the script is terminated.

```
#!/usr/bin/env python

### AssertionError.py

import sys                                                              #(A)

#--------------------------  class User  -----------------------------
class User:                                                             #(B)
    def __init__( self, a_name, an_age = 140 ):                         #(C)
        self.name = a_name                                              #(D)
        self.age = an_age                                               #(E)
    def get_name( self ):                                               #(F)
        return self.name                                                #(G)
    def change_name( self, new_name = None ):                           #(H)
        try:                                                            #(I)
            assert new_name, "Enter new name: "                         #(J)
        except AssertionError, e:                                       #(K)
            new_name = raw_input( e )                                   #(L)
            if len( new_name ) == 0:                                    #(M)
                print "nothing entered --- script aborted"              #(N)
                sys.exit( 1 )                                           #(O)
        self.name = new_name                                            #(P)

#---------------------------  Test Code  ----------------------------
user = User( "Zaphod" )                                                 #(Q)
user.change_name()                                                      #(R)
print user.get_name()                                                   #(S)
```

AttributeError:

This exception is thrown when an attribute named for an object cannot be found. For example, the following script defines an empty class `X` in lines (A) and (B). If we uncomment line (C) and try to retrieve the value of the nonexistent attribute `m` of class `X`, Python will throw an `AttributeError` exception.

The code in lines (D) through (H) illustrates the trapping of the `AttributeError` exception. Line (E) does the same thing as line (C), but inside a `try` clause. So the exception raised in line (E) does not cause a run-time abort. Instead, it is trapped by the exception handler of lines (F) and (G). Line (G) creates by assignment an attribute `m` for class `X` and gives it a value of 100. This is what is returned when we subsequently retrieve the value of this attribute in line (H).

```
#!/usr/bin/env python

### AttributeError.py

class X:                                                              #(A)
    pass                                                              #(B)

#print X.m                # will throw AttributeError                 #(C)

try:                                                                  #(D)
    print X.m                                                         #(E)
except AttributeError:                                                #(F)
    X.m = 100                                                         #(G)

print X.m                 # 100                                       #(H)
```

EOFError:

This exception is thrown when a built-in reader function like `raw_input()` or `fileinput.input()` is made to read beyond the end-of-file condition on either the standard input or file input. To illustrate, suppose a script contains the following line of code:

```
x = raw_input( "Enter your name: " )
```

and the user, instead of entering his/her name, "tries" to terminate the session by hitting Ctrl-D, which is generally translated by the operating system into the end-of-file (EOF) condition. When that happens, `raw_input()` will throw an `EOFError` exception.

Shown below is a script that does not quit until the user enters what could pass for a name. By trapping the `EOFError` exception in line (G), the script sends the control back to the beginning of the `while` loop in line (A). The user is then asked again for his/her name. In line (D), the script checks that the user indeed entered something and that the first character of what the user entered is an alphabetic character. If these conditions are violated, the user is informed of the illegal entry in line (E) and asked to enter the name again. If the user should enter Ctrl-D, that exception is trapped in line (G) and the user informed of the unacceptable entry in line (H).

The script can, of course, be terminated without supplying a valid name by entering Ctrl-C that generates a keyboard interrupt exception that the script does not handle.

```
#!/usr/bin/env python

### EOFError.py

while True:                                                           #(A)
    try:                                                              #(B)
        name = raw_input( "enter your name: " )                      #(C)

        if ( (name == "") or (not name[0].isalpha()) ):              #(D)
            print "\nThat was an illegal entry. ",                    #(E)
        else: break                                                   #(F)
    except EOFError:                                                  #(G)
        print "\nThat was an illegal entry. ",                        #(H)

print "you entered your name as: ", name                              #(I)
```

It is important to bear in mind that whereas the built-in input functions like `raw_input()` and `fileinput.input()` raise the `EOFError` exception upon encountering the end-of-file condition unexpectedly, input functions such as `read()`, `readline()`, and `readlines()` that are defined for file objects[19] simply return an empty string if forced to read the end-of-file condition and beyond. Consider the case when we have a text file `hello.txt` that contains just the string `hello` and nothing else, not even newlines or blank spaces. Let's now try to read this five-character text file with 10 iterations of the read loop shown in lines (B), (C), and (D) of the following script.

```
#!/usr/bin/env python

### EOFErrorNot.py

file = open( "hello.txt" )                                            #(A)
for i in range(10):                                                   #(B)
    char = file.read(1)                                               #(C)
    print "character at position ", i, ": ", char                     #(D)
file.close()                                                          #(E)
```

Line (D) of the script produces the following output:

[19] See Section 3.7.2 of Chapter 3 for a review of file objects and the methods supported by them.

```
character at position  0 :  h
character at position  1 :  e
character at position  2 :  l
character at position  3 :  l
character at position  4 :  o
character at position  5 :
character at position  6 :
character at position  7 :
character at position  8 :
character at position  9 :
```

As the reader can see, no exception is thrown when `read()` hits the end-of-file condition after reading the character `o`. For each attempt at reading after that, `read()` merely returns an empty string. Similar behavior would be exhibited by `readline()` and `readlines()` if they encounter the end-of-file condition. The above script used `read(1)` for reading one byte at a time. As mentioned in Section 3.7.2 of Chapter 3, this function can be invoked with an arbitrary integer argument `N` for reading `N` bytes at a time. If the end-of-file condition is encountered during those `N` bytes, `read()` will return as many bytes as it can read up to the end-of-file condition.

Here is another example of where an input function does not throw an `EOFError` exception:

```
#!/usr/bin/env python

### EOFErrorNot2.py

import fileinput                                                          #(A)
for line in fileinput.input():                                            #(B)
    print fileinput.filename(), fileinput.filelineno(), ': ', line        #(C)
```

The call `input()` on the module `fileinput` in line (B) allows a read loop to be written for extracting information from a bunch of text files at the same time. The following syntax in line (B) of the script:

```
for line in fileinput.input():
```

reads from all the files whose names are supplied as command-line arguments to the script. The methods `filename()`, `filelineno()`, etc., defined in the `fileinput` module keep track of which file is being read and the number of the most recent line read from the file. Let's say we call the above script with the invocation

```
EOFErrorNot2.py  hello.txt  empty.txt  jello.txt
```

where the text file `hello.txt` contains just the string `hello`, the file `empty.txt` nothing at all, and the text file `jello.txt` just the string `jello`. With this invocation, the script produces the following output:

```
hello.txt 1 :  hello
jello.txt 1 :  jello
```

The fact that the middle file, `empty.txt`, was empty and immediately presented the input function with the end-of-file condition does not cause any exceptions to be thrown. An empty file is closed as soon as it is opened.

IOError:

The `IOError` exception is thrown by I/O functions that must interact with the system environment. For example, in the following code fragment

```
filehandle = open( "nonexistent.txt" )
line = filehandle.readline()
```

if the file `nonexistent.txt` does not exist, the call to `open()` will throw an `IOError` exception. Similar other reasons that would also cause this exception to be thrown include the disk being full, what was expected to be a text file turning out not to be so, reading from a file opened specifically for writing or the other way around, and so on.

The system interaction errors of the kind that result in the `IOError` exception to be thrown are often characterized by an error code, usually a small integer, and a brief error message that describes the nature of this error.[20] The error code and the error message from a caught `IOError` exception object can be retrieved from its attributes named `errno` and `strerror`. These two values are also stored as a tuple in the `args` attribute of the exception object. So in the following code fragment, if the file `nonexistent.txt` does not really exist, the three print statements would produce the outputs shown in the commented-out portions of the lines.

[20]In C, the error code associated with the failure of such system calls is available through the variable `errno` defined in the `errno.h` header file. The value of this variable at the start of program execution is zero. So if we call a library function that signals error by depositing a nonzero value in `errno`, a subsequent test for whether or not `errno` is nonzero tells us immediately if the function was executed successfully. Since a previous function call may have changed the value of `errno`, it is important to clear its value *before* calling a function that uses `errno` to signal error. In a C program, the error message corresponding to an error code can be obtained by passing the value of `errno` as the argument to the `strerror` library function in the `string.h` header file of the C standard library, or even more directly to the `perror()` function defined in the `stdio.h` header file.

```
try:
    filehandle = open( "nonexistent.txt" )
    line = filehandle.readline()
except IOError, e:
    print e.args                  # (2, 'No such file or directory')
    print e.errno                 # 2
    print e.strerror              # No such file or directory
```

A shorter way to write the same code would be

```
try:
    filehandle = open( "nonexistent.txt" )
    line = filehandle.readline()
except IOError, (error_num, error_message):
    print "I/O error code: %s   Error message: %s" % \
                                 (error_num, error_message )
```

since what follows the name of the exception in the except clause would be matched to the value of the args attribute of the exception object. For a nonexistent file, this code fragment would produce the formatted output:

```
I/O error code: 2  Error message: No such file or directory
```

ImportError:

This exception is raised when the import statement fails because the named module cannot be located. This exception is also raised when an attempt is made to import a specific name with the from..import.. syntax and it fails.

Let's say we have a module named test_module whose contents are as follows:[21]

```
#!/usr/bin/env python
constant_1 = 1000
constant_2 = 2000
```

The module merely defines two constants constant_1 and constant_2 as shown. Let's now say that we use the syntax

```
import test_module.py
```

as in the commented-out line (A) of the next script, to import this module into the script, forgetting that we are not supposed to include the suffix .py in the name of the module. If we uncomment line (A) of the script and comment out line (B), the

[21] Note that test_module.py will be the name of the file containing the module code.

`import` command will throw the `ImportError` exception. The error message that will show up in the terminal window will be

```
ImportError: No module named .py
```

That is because, for Python, the dotted notation in the argument to `import` corresponds to the directory structure housing the modules. So `import test_module.py` would cause Python to search for a file named either `py.py` or `py.pyc` in a *directory* called `test_module`. Obviously, the correct syntax for the `import` statement is as shown in line (B).

Line (H) shows another `import` statement that if uncommented will cause the `ImportError` exception to be thrown. Since our `test_module` does not contain the name `constant_3`, the following error message will appear in the terminal:

```
ImportError: cannot import name constant_3
```

```
#!/usr/bin/env python

### ImportError.py

#import test_module.py                  # ImportError:                #(A)
                                        #    No module named .py
import test_module                                                    #(B)
print test_module.constant_1            # 1000                        #(C)
print test_module.constant_2            # 2000                        #(D)

from test_module import constant_1, constant_2                        #(E)
print constant_1                        # 1000                        #(F)
print constant_2                        # 2000                        #(G)

#from test_module import constant_3     # ImportError: cannot         #(H)
                                        # import name constant_3
```

IndexError:

This exception is thrown if a script tries to access a sequence element at an illegal integer index. For example, the following script defines a tuple of three elements in line (A). So if we uncomment line (E) and try to access the fourth element of the tuple, we'll get the error message:

```
IndexError: tuple index out of range
```

```
#!/usr/bin/env python

### IndexError.py

t = ('zero', 'one', 'two')                                          #(A)

print t[0]              # 'zero'                                    #(B)
print t[1]              # 'one'                                     #(C)
print t[2]              # 'two'                                     #(D)

# print t[3]            # IndexError: tuple index out of range      #(E)
```

KeyError:

This exception is thrown when a named key cannot be found in the keys currently in a dictionary. In the following script, line (A) creates a dictionary with just the keys a and b and their corresponding values. Line (D) nonetheless tries to access a nonexistent key, c, which causes the exception KeyError to be thrown. The error message that this results in is shown in the commented-out portion of that line.

```
#!/usr/bin/env python

### KeyError.py

x = {'a' : 1, 'b' : 2}                                              #(A)

print x['a']              # 1                                       #(B)
print x['b']              # 2                                       #(C)

print x['c']              # KeyError: 'c'                           #(D)
```

NameError:

This exception is thrown upon the failure of name lookup for global and local names that are meant to be reached without module qualifications.[22] Let's say that your

[22] Section 3.10 of Chapter 3 talks about the module qualified naming syntax for accessing variables that are imported from other modules.

script has a statement like `print x` and the variable `x` was not mentioned previously in the script, Python will throw the `NameError` exception.

NotImplementedError:

See Chapter 11 for how this exception is used to define an abstract class in Python.

Other Exception Classes:

The exception classes we have described so far represent only a small sampling of all such classes made available by Python. Fig. 10.1 displays the entire class hierarchy of the built-in exception classes. The purpose of many of the classes not explained previously should be evident from the class names.

What the figure does not show are the seven subclasses of the `Warning` class. These are: `UserWarning`, `DeprecatedWarning`, `PendingDeprecationWarning`, `SyntaxWarning`, `RuntimeWarning`, and `FutureWarning`.

10.6 CREDITS AND SUGGESTIONS FOR FURTHER READING

For exception handling in Perl, two highly recommended modules, besides the `Exception` module by Pete Jordan that we used in our example scripts in Section 10.3, are the `Exception::Class` module by Dave Rolsky and the `Error` module originally by Graham Barr and now maintained by Shlomi Fish. As mentioned in Section 10.3, the first, `Exception::Class`, makes it easy to create a hierarchy of exception classes for a given application, and the second, `Error`, has the convenience of allowing for the modern `try-catch` syntax for exception handling. With regard to exception handling in Python, the reader is referred to Section 8 of the Python tutorial by Guido van Rossum [66] for additional reading on how Python deals with errors and exceptions.

10.7 HOMEWORK

1. Rework the two Perl scripts of Section 10.3 using the `Exception::Class` and the `Error` exception handling modules that you can easily download from `www.cpan.org`.

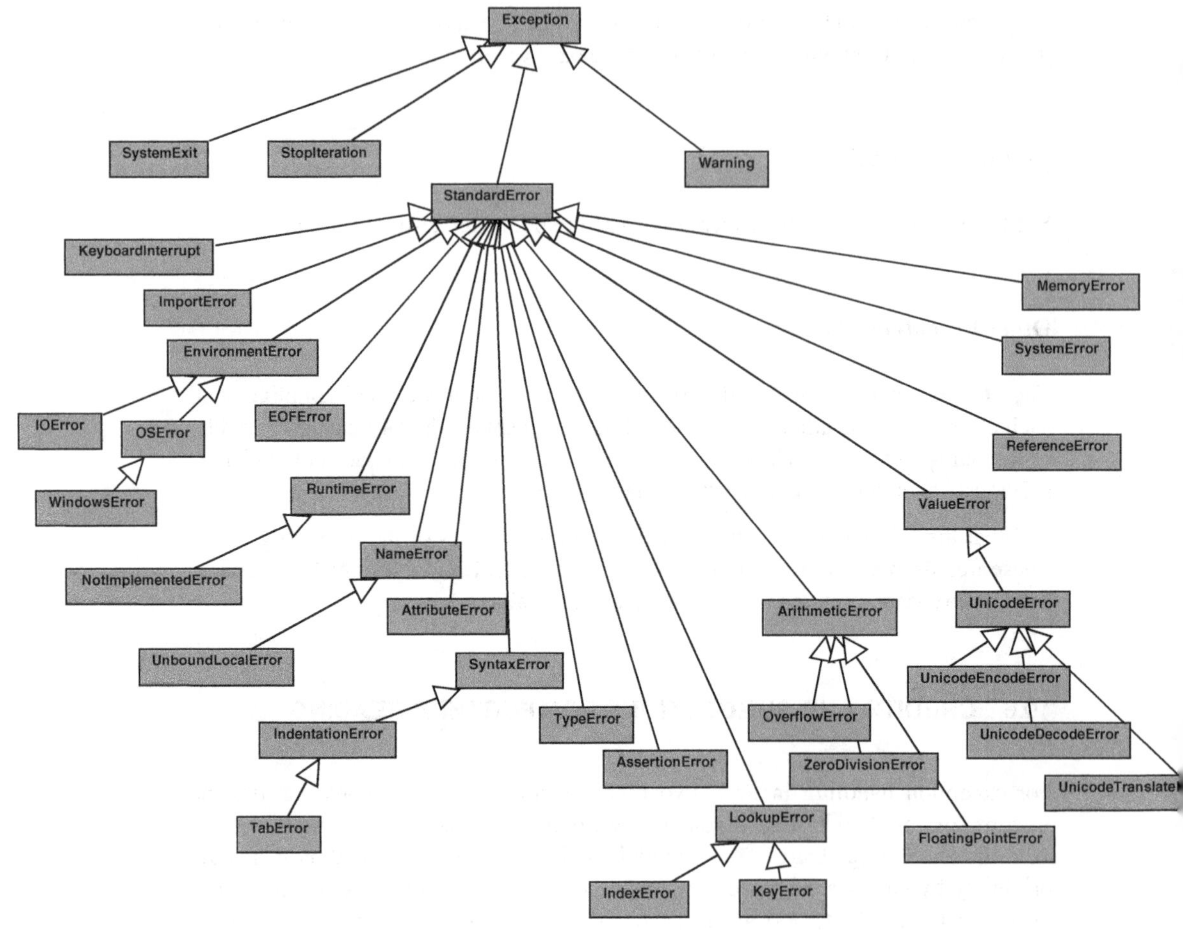
Exception
SystemExit
StopIteration
Warning
StandardError
KeyboardInterrupt
ImportError
EnvironmentError
IOError
OSError
WindowsError
EOFError
RuntimeError
NotImplementedError
NameError
UnboundLocalError
AttributeError
SyntaxError
IndentationError
TabError
TypeError
AssertionError
LookupError
IndexError
KeyError
ArithmeticError
OverflowError
ZeroDivisionError
FloatingPointError
MemoryError
SystemError
ReferenceError
ValueError
UnicodeError
UnicodeEncodeError
UnicodeDecodeError
UnicodeTranslate

Fig. 10.1

2. Write a Python script that prompts a user for an integer within a specific range. Your script should raise the `ValueError` exception if the user violates the range constraint.

3. Write a Perl script to do the same as what is described in the previous homework problem. Use the `die` operator inside an `eval` block to throw an exception.

4. In the following Python script named `Puzzling.py`

```
#!/usr/bin/env python
try: import mod3
except: import mod2 as mod1
mod1.foo()
```

assume that the module `mod3` does *not* exist. Also assume that the module file for `mod1` contains just the following statement

```
def foo(): print "foo of module mod1 called"
```

and the module file for `mod2` contains just the following statement:

```
def foo(): print "foo of module mod2 called"
```

When we execute the script `Puzzling.py`, we get the following output:

```
foo of module mod2 called.
```

implying that `foo()` in the module file for `mod2` was called. But the call to `foo()` in the script is on module `mod1`. Explain this behavior of `Puzzling.py`.

5. In Section 10.3.1, we used the Perl script `ExceptionOOPolymorph.pl` to demonstrate that the object-oriented exception handling made possible by the `Exception` module does *not* behave polymorphically. Construct a similar example in Python to demonstrate that exception handling in Python is *always* polymorphic with respect to the exception classes that are in parent-child relationships.

6. For this Python homework, write your own IO exception class `MyIOError` by extending the system-supplied `IOError` class. Your `MyIOError` class should log all error messages into an appropriately named log file. In order to demonstrate the workings of your `MyIOError` class, write a class called `FileIO` and provide it with read and write methods for reading just one string or just one integer from a disk file. The methods should *not* assume that the string or the integer to be read is in a line by itself or that it begins at the very beginning of the file. In other words, if the file contains the following entries:

```
****1234********76********
908*******3334
```

where each star denotes a space, then calling a method such as `readOneInt()` on a stream object connected to this file should return just the number 1234 at the first attempt, the number 76 at the second attempt, and so on. Make sure that your IO methods throw exceptions of type `MyIOError` to take care of conditions such as a missing file, the file being empty, the file containing wrong kind of data, etc.

Suggestion: Your `MyIOError` class may look something like

```
class MyIOError( IOError ):
    def __init__(self, value):
        handle = open( "log.txt", 'w' )
        handle.write( value )
        handle.close
        self.value = value
    def __str__(self):
        return repr(self.value)
```

And the `FileIO` class could be something like

```
class FileIO( object ):
    def __init__(self, name ):
        self.filename = name
    def readOneInt( self ):
        try:
            ..code for reading just one int..
        except IOError, arg:
            raise MyIOError( str(arg) )
    def readOneWord( self ):
        ..code..
    def readOneFloat( self):
        ..code..
```

11

Abstract Classes and Methods

Abstract classes play an important role in object-oriented programming in general. An abstract class can lend organization to the other classes in a class hierarchy. It can also represent some specialized behavior that can be mixed with other classes. Abstract classes are also useful for building an implementation incrementally.

An abstract class can help with knowledge organization by serving as the root of a hierarchy of other concrete classes. It can thus pull together what might otherwise be disparate bits of knowledge encapsulated in the subclasses. A classic and frequently used example of this is the `Shape` hierarchy of classes shown in Fig. 11.1. Obviously,

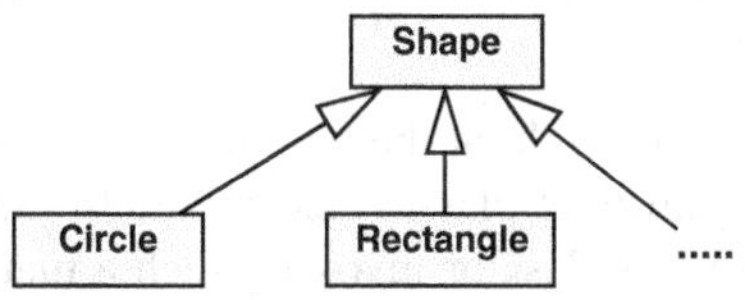

Fig. 11.1

while we can construct objects of type `Circle`, `Rectangle`, and so on, it would make no sense to construct an object of type `Shape`. Shape is an abstract notion and a class used to represent this notion will not be the usual sort of a class, since such a class would probably not need a constructor (as making a concrete instance out of an abstract class sounds like a contradiction in terms). Yet the class `Shape`, formulated as an *abstract class*, serves a critical role, because it pulls together all the other classes into a single hierarchy. As to what we mean by pulling together other classes, this question is deeper than it appears at first sight.

What we mean by the `Shape` class pulling together the other classes has to do with inheritance and polymorphism. Taking advantage of inheritance, we could place in the `Shape` class all of the code that is common between its various subclasses, making our code more efficient. And, given a list of `Shape` objects, some of which may actually be `Circle` objects, some `Rectangle` objects, and so on, we could invoke a function such as `area()` on the entire list. Polymorphism would then automatically invoke object-specific `area()` on each `Shape` in the list. This assumes that we have at least declared `area()` as one of the functions for the root class `Shape` and that we have provided implementation code for `area()` in each of the subclasses. When a function is only declared in a root class for such polymorphic effects vis-à-vis the subclasses, the root-class declaration of the function is referred to as an *abstract function* or an *abstract method.*

In the rest of this chapter, we will show how we can define abstract classes and methods in Perl and Python. Both these scripting languages do not provide direct support for abstract classes and methods. However, one can "kluge up" classes that behave like abstract classes and endow them with methods that act like abstract methods.

11.1 ABSTRACT CLASSES AND METHODS IN PERL

This section presents the first of the two approaches one can take in Perl to make classes and methods abstract — by having the constructors and the methods throw exceptions should they be called. By having a constructor throw an exception, we obviously make it impossible to construct instances from that class. And by having a method definition throw an exception right off the top, we make it impossible to call that method on an instance of a subclass *unless the subclass provides an override definition for the method.*

However, we must mention right at the beginning a fundamental shortcoming of this approach to defining abstract classes and methods: an inadvertent attempt at creating an instance of such a class or invoking such a method on an instance of a concrete subclass could result in a *run-time error,* which is contrary to the principles of good software design. The next subsection presents a different approach that consists of compile-time checking for whether all the methods of an abstract class are defined in a concrete subclass. But this approach suffers from its own shortcomings, as we will see.

The next Perl script, `ShapeHierarchy.pl`, shows how one can implement a shape hierarchy with an abstract class at the root of the hierarchy. Note the definition for the abstract class `Shape` in lines (A) through (F) of the script. All that the constructor for this class does and all that its methods do is to throw an exception immediately. Obviously, it is not possible to make instances from this class. And since no instances of this class can be created, it is out of the question that any of the methods listed for the class — even if the methods did not throw exceptions — can be invoked on a Shape instance constructed directly from the definition of the class. Nonetheless, we provide exception-throwing definitions for these methods so that they are not invoked on subclass instances unless those subclasses provide override definitions for the methods.

Subclasses Circle and Rectangle are shown in lines (G) through (P) of the script. As shown, they provide implementations for the abstract methods area() and circumference() inherited from the parent class Shape. However, just to make a point about abstract methods, neither class provides an override definition for the abstract method some_property() of Shape. In that sense, the method some_property() remains abstract in the subclasses.

Lines (Q) through (Y) show the code used for testing the Shape hierarchy. As shown in lines (Q) and (U), we can construct instances from the subclasses Circle and Rectangle. And, as shown in lines (R) and (S) for the case of Circle and in lines (V) and (W) for the case of Rectangle, we can invoke the methods area() and circumference() on these instances. But, as shown in lines (T) and (X), invoking the inherited some_property() on these Circle and Rectangle instances will elicit a run-time error since this method is not overridden in the derived classes. Finally, line (Y) shows that trying to create an instance of the Shape class will also elicit a run-time error on account of the exception thrown by the constructor in line (C).

```
#!/usr/bin/perl -w
use strict;

### ShapeHierarchy.pl

#-------------------  Abstract Base Class Shape  -----------------------
package Shape;                                                       #(A)
use Carp;                                                            #(B)

sub new {                                                            #(C)
    croak "Shape is an abstract class.  No instances allowed:";
}

sub area { croak "No implementation provided. Illegal call:"; }      #(D)

sub circumference {                                                  #(E)
    croak "No implementation provided. Illegal call:";
}

sub some_property {                                                  #(F)
    croak "No implementation provided. Illegal call:";
}
```

```
#---------------------  Derived Class Circle  -------------------------
package Circle;                                                   #(G)
use Carp;

@Circle::ISA = qw(Shape);                                         #(H)

sub new {                                                         #(I)
    my ($class, $rad) = @_;
    my $r_circle = {
        radius => $rad,
    };
    bless $r_circle, $class;
    $r_circle;
}
sub area {                                                        #(J)
    my $circle = shift;
    my $radius = $circle->{radius};
    3.14159 * $radius * $radius;
}
sub circumference {                                               #(K)
    my $circle = shift;
    my $radius = $circle->{radius};
    2* 3.14159 * $radius;
}

#------------------  Derived Class Rectangle  ------------------------
package Rectangle;                                                #(L)
use Carp;

@Circle::ISA = qw(Shape);                                         #(M)

sub new {                                                         #(N)
    my ($class, $height, $width) = @_;
    my $r_rect = {
        height => $height,
        width  => $width,
    };
    bless $r_rect, $class;
    $r_rect;
}
sub area {                                                        #(O)
    my $rect = shift;
    my $w = $rect->{width};
    my $h = $rect->{height};
    $w * $h;
}
```

```
sub circumference {                                                  #(P)
    my $rect = shift;
    my $w = $rect->{width};
    my $h = $rect->{height};
    2 * ( $w + $h );
}

#--------------------------- Test Code ------------------------------
package Test;

my $shape1 = Circle->new( 2.5 );                                     #(Q)
print $shape1->area(), "\n";                                         #(R)
print $shape1->circumference(), "\n";                                #(S)
#$shape1->some_property();                    # ERROR                #(T)

my $shape2 = Rectangle->new(3, 4 );                                  #(U)
print $shape2->area(), "\n";                                         #(V)
print $shape2->circumference(), "\n";                                #(W)
#$shape2->some_property();                    # ERROR                #(X)

#my $shape = Shape->new();                    # ERROR                #(Y)
```

11.1.1 Compile-Time Checking of Method Implementation

As mentioned already, a major disadvantage of the previous approach for defining abstract classes and methods is that a violation of the contract of such classes and methods is not noticed until run-time. That is, should one inadvertently try to make an instance of what is presumably an abstract class or should one try to invoke an abstract method on a derived-class object, an exception will be thrown at run-time.

We will now present a different approach that makes sure at compile time that all of the methods are implemented in what is supposed to be a concrete subclass of an abstract superclass. The key to this approach is the `import()` static method[1] that a class can be endowed with, as we explain in what follows.

Recall from Section 2.11.2 of Chapter 2 that when you make the following sort of a call in a script

```
use Some_Module;
```

that call is translated by the compiler into

[1]Perl's static methods are reviewed in Section 6.6 of Chapter 6. A static method can be called directly on the class.

```
BEGIN {
    require Some_Module;
    Some_Module->import();
}
```

where `BEGIN` causes the *compile-time execution* of the block that comes next. Assuming that the module was not loaded previously, the `require` directive pulls in the source code associated with the designated module from the disk into the memory and then executes it to create namespace bindings for the subroutine names and global variables in that module. The `import()` statement that comes next decides which of the names of the module file just pulled in can be accessed directly (that is, without package qualification) in the current namespace. It is important to realize that the definition used for the `import()` method is as made available by the code just pulled in by `require()`.

We will now show how the traditional role of `import()` in a module file can be modified so that there is compile-time checking of whether the abstract methods of a parent class are implemented in a subclass. But we should mention at the outset that each class has to be in its own file for this approach to work.

In the multifile script presented next, shown in lines (S1) through (S6) is the implementation of `import()` for the `Shape` abstract class. The basic logic embedded here is provided by the `foreach` loop in lines (S4) through (S6). This loop checks for each method name supplied in the argument list in line (S4) and makes sure that a method of this name is implemented in the package bound to the variable `$pkg`. So if `$pkg` is bound to the name of a subclass that is supposed to be concrete and if that subclass has not provided implementations for the methods `area()` and `circumference()`, the loop of lines (S4) through (S6) will result in a compile-time error. The `can()` method used in line (S5) succeeds if the package to the left of the arrow has an implementation for the method name supplied as the argument to `can()`.

We will now explain how exactly `import()` of lines (S1) through (S6) is invoked so that the variable `$pkg` would be bound to a subclass that is expected to provide implementations for the methods listed in line (S4). Shown in lines (C1) through (C17) is the subclass `Circle` that resides in a separate module file named `Circle.pm`. And, shown in lines (R1) through (R20) is the subclass `Rectangle` that resides in the module file `Rectangle.pm`. Let's now focus on line (T1) in the test code in the script file named `TestAbstractClass.pl`. This line says

```
use Circle;
```

which is interpreted as

```
BEGIN {
    require Circle;
    Circle->import();
}
```

The `require` command pulls the `Circle.pm` file into the memory. The compiler begins to execute this file, and immediately encounters another `use` directive in line (C1). This again gets interpreted as

```
BEGIN {
    require Shape;
    Shape->import();
}
```

The compiler now pulls the file `Shape.pm` into the memory, executes the file, and invokes `Shape`'s `import()`. Since the command being executed at this time is `Shape`'s `import()`, the binding for the variable `$pkg` in line (S2) is `Shape`. And since the definition being used for `import()` resides in the `Shape` package, the binding of the variable `__PACKAGE__` would also be `Shape`. This would result in the invocation of the `return` statement in line (S3), causing immediate return from `import()`.

With the loading of `Shape` completed, the compiler now scans the rest of the `Circle.pm` file and through line (C2) becomes aware of the fact that `Circle` is a subclass of `Shape`. After the file `Circle.pm` is loaded in and executed, the compiler invokes `Circle`'s `import()` — which is the same as `Shape`'s `import()` — to take care of the `import()` part of the `use` directive of line (T1). This creates the binding `Circle` for the variable `$pkg`. However, since the `import()` method being used belongs to the package `Shape`, the binding for `__PACKAGE__` would remain `Shape`. So now the `import()` can use its `foreach` loop in lines (S4) through (S6) to ascertain whether `Circle` provides implementations for the methods `area()` and `circumference()`. The process also takes place vis-à-vis the loading of the `Rectangle` module in line (T3).

```
#-----------------------  Module file: Shape.pm  -----------------------
### Shape.pm

package Shape;
use Carp;

sub import {                                                          #(S1)
    my $pkg = shift;                                                  #(S2)
    return if $pkg eq __PACKAGE__;                                    #(S3)
    foreach my $meth ( qw( area circumference ) ) {                   #(S4)
        $pkg->can($meth)                                              #(S5)
            or croak("Class $pkg does not implement $meth");          #(S6)
    }
}

1;
```

```
#----------------------  Module file: Circle.pm  ----------------------
package Circle;

### Circle.pm

use Shape;                                                         #(C1)

@ISA = qw(Shape);                                                  #(C2)

sub new {                                                          #(C3)
    my ($class, $rad) = @_;                                        #(C4)
    my $r_circle = {                                               #(C5)
        radius => $rad,                                            #(C6)
    };
    bless $r_circle, $class;                                       #(C7)
    $r_circle;                                                     #(C8)
}
sub area {                                                         #(C9)
    my $circle = shift;                                            #(C10)
    my $radius = $circle->{radius};                                #(C11)
    3.14159 * $radius * $radius;                                   #(C12)
}
sub circumference {                                                #(C13)
    my $circle = shift;                                            #(C14)
    my $radius = $circle->{radius};                                #(C15)
    2* 3.14159 * $radius;                                          #(C16)
}
1;                                                                 #(C17)

#--------------------  Module file: Rectangle.pm  --------------------
package Rectangle;

### Rectangle.pm

use Shape;                                                         #(R1)

@ISA = qw(Shape);                                                  #(R2)

sub new {                                                          #(R3)
    my ($class, $h, $w) = @_;                                      #(R4)
    my $r_rect = {                                                 #(R5)
        height => $h,                                              #(R6)
        width  => $w,                                              #(R7)
    };
    bless $r_rect, $class;                                         #(R8)
    $r_rect;                                                       #(R9)
}
```

```
sub area {                                                      #(R10)
    my $rect = shift;                                           #(R11)
    my $w = $rect->{width};                                     #(R12)
    my $h = $rect->{height};                                    #(R13)
    $w * $h;                                                    #(R14)
}
sub circumference {                                             #(R15)
    my $rect = shift;                                           #(R16)
    my $w = $rect->{width};                                     #(R17)
    my $h = $rect->{height};                                    #(R18)
    2 * ( $w + $h );                                            #(R19)
}
1;                                                              #(R20)

#-----------------  Test file: TestAbstractClass.pl  ------------------
#!/usr/bin/perl -w

### TestAbstractClass.pl

use strict;

use Circle;                                                     #(T1)
use Rectangle;                                                  #(T2)

my $shape1 = Circle->new( 2.5 );                                #(T3)
print $shape1->area(), "\n";              # 19.6349375          #(T4)
print $shape1->circumference(), "\n";     # 15.70795            #(T5)
#$shape1->some_property();                # ERROR               #(T6)

my $shape2 = Rectangle->new(3, 4 );                             #(T7)
print $shape2->area(), "\n";              # 12                  #(T8)
print $shape2->circumference(), "\n";     # 14                  #(T9)
#$shape2->some_property();                # ERROR               #(T10)

#my $shape = Shape->new();                # ERROR               #(T11)
```

Our explanation of the working of `Shape`'s `import()` can probably be made easier to understand if the reader uses the following version of the `Shape.pm` file. The implementation of `import()` in this version includes additional lines (A), (B), (C), and (D) that print out the values of the variables `$pkg` and `__PACKAGE__`, and additionally the value returned by the function `caller()` in line (A).

```
### Shape.pm

package Shape;
use Carp;

sub import {
    my $pkg = shift;

    my $caller = caller;                                                    #(A)
    print "The caller is $caller\n";                                        #(B)
    print "The variable \$pkg is $pkg\n";                                   #(C)
    print "The variable __PACKAGE__ is ", __PACKAGE__, "\n\n";              #(D)

    return if $pkg eq __PACKAGE__;
    foreach my $meth ( qw( area circumference ) ) {
        $pkg->can($meth)
            or croak("Class $pkg does not implement $meth");
    }
}
1;
```

With this version of the `Shape.pm` file, the following output is produced by running the `TestAbstractClass.pl` script:

```
The caller is Circle
The variable $pkg is Shape
The variable __PACKAGE__ is Shape

The caller is main
The variable $pkg is Circle
The variable __PACKAGE__ is Shape

The caller is Rectangle
The variable $pkg is Shape
The variable __PACKAGE__ is Shape

The caller is main
The variable $pkg is Rectangle
The variable __PACKAGE__ is Shape

19.6349375
15.70795
12
14
```

The function `caller()` in line (A) of the new version of `Shape.pm` returns the name of the package that called `import()`.

The first three lines of the output shown above were produced by the compiler processing the `use Shape` call in line (C1) during the loading of the `Circle` module as required by line (T1). As mentioned before, this call gets decomposed into a `require Shape` command, which pulls into the memory and executes the `Shape.pm` file, and a call to `Shape`'s `import()` method. Since this call to `import()` is on the `Shape` package, the binding given to `$pkg` is the string `Shape`. And, since the call to `import()` was made in the context of the execution of the `Circle` module code, the caller as returned by the `caller()` method is `Circle`. Finally, since the `import()` method being executed belongs to the `Shape` package, the value of `__PACKAGE__` is `Shape`. That explains the first three lines of the output shown above.

The above explanation referred to the `require Circle` part of the `use Circle` directive of line (T1). Next comes the call to `Circle`'s `import()` as the second part of the same directive. The context for this invocation of `import()` is obviously the `main` of `TestAbstractClass.pl`. Therefore, the invocation of `caller()` in line (A) returns `main`. Since this call to `import()` will be on the `Circle` package, the variable `$pkg` inside `import()` will be bound to `Circle`. But since the implementation code for `import()` will still be coming from the `Shape` package, the binding for `__PACKAGE__` will remain `Shape`. This therefore explains the second group of three lines in the output.

The third and the fourth groups of three-line outputs can be explained in the same manner vis-à-vis the `Rectangle` module.

11.1.2 Compile-Time Enforcement for Multilevel Class Hierarchies

The example of the previous subsection had a two-level class hierarchy. We had the abstract `Shape` class at the root and the concrete subclasses `Circle` and `Rectangle` as derived from `Shape`. The `import()` we defined for the `Shape` class unfortunately falls short for multilevel class hierarchies where a concrete class may be built up incrementally from multiple abstract classes along an inheritance path. What we need is an `import()` method that will recursively "climb up" an inheritance path and ascertain whether or not a given module being imported into a working script has implemented all of the abstract methods in all of the parents of a module. Such an `import()` will be presented in this subsection.

Consider the `Foo-Bar-Baz` example of Fig. 11.2 in which `Bar` is derived from `Foo` and `Baz` from `Bar`.[2] Through the argument list provided at line (F8) of the multifile script shown next, the `import()` of the class `Foo` insists that a concrete

[2]This example was taken from the material posted at `www.perlmonks.thepen.com`.

subclass derived from `Foo` had better possess an implementation for the method `foo()`. The class `Bar` itself does not implement the method `foo()` mentioned in line (F8) of class `Foo`. Instead, `Bar's` `import()` insists in line (B10) that a concrete subclass derived from `Bar` had better implement the method `bar()`. In effect, the base class `Foo` is declaring `foo()` as its abstract method, and the subclass `Bar` is declaring its own abstract method `bar()`. The class `Baz` at the bottom of the hierarchy is supposed to provide implementations for all of the abstract methods of `Foo` and `Bar`. The class `Baz` shown in lines (Z1) through (Z10) of the

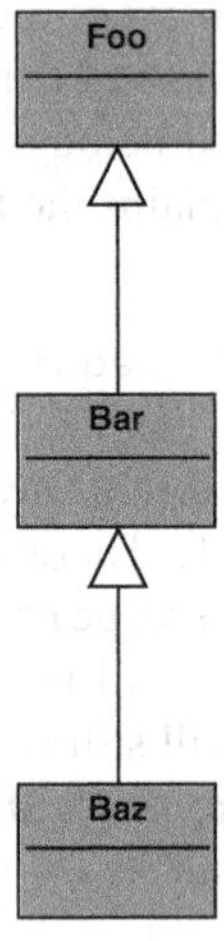

Fig. 11.2

script constitutes an acceptable derivation from the parent classes `Foo` and `Bar` on account of the method implementations provided in lines (Z8) and (Z9). If we were to comment out one or both of these implementations, an attempt to run the script `Test.pl` in lines (T1) through (T4) would result in a compile-time error.

Let's now see how the `import()` method defined separately for each of the abstract classes `Foo` and `Bar` works in this example. In both implementations for `import()` — in lines (F1) through (F11) for class `Foo` and in lines (B3) through (B13) for the case of `Bar` — we have included the statements that tell us who the caller was and the values for the variables `$pkg` and `__PACKAGE__`. For `Foo`, these are in lines (F4), (F5), and (F6), and for `Bar` in lines (B6), (B7), and (B8).

When comparing the `import()` in the script shown below with the `import()` of the previous subsection, the only meaningful difference is the recursive call represented by the statement in line (F11) for `Foo` and in line (B13) for the case of `Bar`.

```
#---------------------- Module File:  Foo.pm -------------------------
package Foo;
use Carp;

sub import {                                                      #(F1)
    my $pkg = shift;                                              #(F2)

    my $caller = caller;                                          #(F3)
    print"Foo: The caller is $caller\n";                          #(F4)
    print"Foo: The variable \$pkg is $pkg\n";                     #(F5)
    print"Foo: The variable __PACKAGE__ is ", __PACKAGE__, "\n\n"; #(F6)

    return if $pkg eq __PACKAGE__;                                #(F7)
    foreach my $meth ( qw( foo ) ) {                              #(F8)
        $pkg->can( $meth ) or                                     #(F9)
            croak("Class $pkg does not implement $meth");        #(F10)
    }
    $pkg->SUPER::import( @_ );                                   #(F11)
}

1;                                                               #(F12)

#---------------------- Module File:  Bar.pm -------------------------
package Bar;
use Carp;
use Foo;                                                          #(B1)
@ISA = qw( Foo );                                                 #(B2)

sub import {                                                      #(B3)
    my $pkg = shift;                                              #(B4)

    my $caller = caller;                                          #(B5)
    print"Bar: The caller is $caller\n";                          #(B6)
    print"Bar: The variable \$pkg is $pkg\n";                     #(B7)
    print"Bar: The variable __PACKAGE__ is ", __PACKAGE__, "\n\n"; #(B8)

    return if $pkg eq __PACKAGE__;                                #(B9)
    foreach my $meth ( qw( bar ) ) {                             #(B10)
        $pkg->can( $meth )                                       #(B11)
            or croak("Class $pkg does not implement $meth");     #(B12)
    }
    $pkg->SUPER::import( @_ );                                   #(B13)
}

1;                                                               #(B14)
```

```
#---------------------- Module File:  Baz.pm ------------------------
package Baz;

use Bar;                                                       #(Z1)
@ISA = qw( Bar );                                              #(Z2)

sub new {                                                      #(Z3)
    my ($class) = @_;                                          #(Z4)
    my $ref = {};                                              #(Z5)
    bless $ref, $class;                                        #(Z6)
    $ref;                                                      #(Z7)
}

sub foo { print "This is method foo\n"; }                      #(Z8)
sub bar { print "This is method bar\n"; }                      #(Z9)

1;                                                             #(Z10)

#--------------------- Test Script:  Test.pl ------------------------
#!/usr/bin/perl -w
use strict;

use Baz;                                                       #(T1)

my $bz = Baz->new();                                           #(T2)
$bz->foo();                                                    #(T3)
$bz->bar();                                                    #(T4)
```

When we run the script `Test.pl` shown above, we get the following output:

```
Foo: The caller is Bar
Foo: The variable $pkg is Foo
Foo: The variable __PACKAGE__ is Foo

Bar: The caller is Baz
Bar: The variable $pkg is Bar
Bar: The variable __PACKAGE__ is Bar

Bar: The caller is main
Bar: The variable $pkg is Baz
Bar: The variable __PACKAGE__ is Bar

Foo: The caller is Bar
Foo: The variable $pkg is Baz
Foo: The variable __PACKAGE__ is Foo
```

```
This is method foo
This is method bar
```

To explain this output, note that when we run `Test.pl`, which is in a file all by itself, at the beginning the compiler knows nothing about the classes `Foo` and `Bar` and about the relationship between them. When the compiler gets to line (T1), it will translate the `use` directive there into

```
BEGIN { require Baz; Baz->import(); }
```

The `require` directive immediately pulls in the module file `Baz.pm` into the memory. As Python begins to scan `Baz.pm` for compilation and execution, it encounters at the beginning the `use` directive in line (Z1). So the compiler now pulls `Bar.pm` into the memory and starts scanning that file. At the beginning of that file is another `use` directive in line (B2). So the compiler pulls `Foo.pm` into the memory. After `Foo.pm` has been executed, the compiler calls the `import()` method on that module. Since the loading of `Foo` was called for by `Bar`, the caller as returned by the method `caller()` in line (F2) is `Bar`. And since `import()` is being invoked on the module `Foo`, the binding of the variable `$pkg` is `Foo`. Additionally, since the method `import()` that is being executed belongs to the package `Foo`, the binding of the variable `__PACKAGE__` is also `Foo`. That explains the first three lines in the program output shown above. That completes the loading of the `Foo` module as called for by the `use` directive of line (B2) that was encountered during the loading of the `Bar` module.

To explain the second group of three lines in the output, the compiler now proceeds to scan the rest of the `Bar.pm` file that is in the memory for compilation and execution. Execution of `Bar.pm` code completes the job of the `require Bar` part of the `use Bar` directive of line (Z1). The compiler must now invoke `import()` on the package `Bar` as the second part of the same directive. This causes the string `Bar` to be assigned to the variable `$pkg` in line (B4). Since this call to `import()` was in the context of the loading of `Baz`, the caller as returned by `caller()` is `Baz`. Finally, since it is the definition of `import` in `Bar` that is invoked, the value of `__PACKAGE__` is `Bar`. Since the values of `$pkg` and `__PACKAGE__` are identical, line (B9) of `Bar`'s `import()` will be executed for an immediate return from the method.

That completes the loading of `Bar` into `Baz` as called for by line (Z1) of `Baz.pm`. The compiler now scans the rest of `Baz` to complete the mandate of the `require Baz` part of the `use Baz` directive of line (T1). To execute the `import()` on the `Baz` package, Python must use parent class `Bar`'s `import()`. As a result, the variable `$pkg` in line (B4) will be set to `Baz`, but the value of `__PACKAGE__` will be `Bar`. This explains the other two output lines in the third three-line grouping.

The fourth three-line grouping in the output is produced when the thread of execution in the above-mentioned invocation of `Bar`'s `import()` reaches the following recursive call to the `import()` of `Bar`'s parent `Foo`:

```
$pkg->SUPER::import( @_ );
```

This call is in line (B13) of `Bar.pm`. This would be the call to `Foo`'s `import()`.[3] Since this call to `Foo`'s `import()` emanated from `Bar`'s `import()`, the caller as returned by `caller()` in line (F3) will be `Bar`. And since the call to `import()` is on `Baz`, the variable `$pkg` in line (F2) will be bound to `Baz`. Finally, since it is `Foo`'s `import()` that is being invoked, the value of `__PACKAGE__` will be `Foo`. That explains the fourth three-line grouping in the output.

The last two lines of the output are produced by lines (T3) and (T4) of `Test.pl`.

11.2 ABSTRACT CLASSES IN PYTHON

As for Perl, a Python class is abstract if it is not possible to construct instances from that class and if the class nevertheless declares a certain functionality that may be implemented by its more concrete subclasses. And, in general, a method in a class is abstract if the method itself cannot be invoked but if its override implementations in the subclasses can be invoked on the instances constructed from the subclasses.

A Python class can be made abstract by having its `__init__()` raise the exception `NotImplementedError`.[4] And a method in a class can be made abstract by having its implementation raise the same exception. When a method is made abstract in this manner, there is the expectation that full implementation code for the method would be supplied in a subclass.

Shown below is a `Shape` hierarchy in Python. The root class `Shape` in lines (A) through (F) is abstract because its instance initializer in lines (B) and (C) forbids instance creation by raising the `NotImplementedError` exception. The methods `area()` and `circumference()` defined for the `Shape` class in lines (D) and (F) are abstract for the same reason — they both raise the `NotImplementedError` exception.

The class `Circle` of lines (H) through (K) is derived from `Shape` and provides implementations for the inherited methods `area()` and `circumference()`. This class also possesses a valid constructor, meaning a constructor that will actually create instances from the class definition. The derived class `Rectangle` of lines (L) through (O) also possesses a valid constructor and valid implementations for the methods `area()` and `circumference()`.

---

[3]It is through these recursive calls to `import()` that every abstract class along an inheritance path in a multilevel hierarchy can make sure that the concrete class being loaded into the `main` of a script has implementations for all of the abstract methods.

[4]Recall from Chapter 7 that the constructor of a class automatically (and always) calls the class's `__init__()` method for instance initialization.

Lines (P) through (S) define a global function `get_shape_properties()` that works only if the argument is a `Shape` instance. This is ensured by the following `assert` statement in line (Q):

```
assert isinstance( x, Shape )
```

What's important here is to realize that this assertion will succeed for any `x` that is an instance of any class belonging to the `Shape` hierarchy. In our example, this means that the method `get_shape_properties()` can be invoked for either `Circle` instances or `Rectangle` instances, but it will not work for any argument object outside of the `Shape` hierarchy.

Line (T) of the test code shows that it is illegal to construct an instance from the `Shape` class directly. If we uncomment that line, line (C) of the script will throw the exception `NotImplementedError`. Now suppose we comment out the lines (B) and (C) and allowed for the construction of an instance of `Shape` via the default constructor that Python supplies for a class in the absence of a programmer-defined constructor. Now it will be safe to uncomment the call in line (T). But, as shown in lines (U) and (V), invoking the methods `area()` and `circumference()` on a `Shape` instance would still elicit an error from the script because those methods are abstract for the `Shape` class. Lines (W) through (Z) show us constructing instances from the two concrete subclasses in the `Shape` hierarchy and computing the area and the circumference properties of the instances.

```
#!/usr/bin/env python

### Shape.py

#---------------------------  class Shape  ----------------------------
class Shape:                                                          #(A)
    def __init__( self ):                                             #(B)
        raise NotImplementedError("abstract class - no constructor")#(C)
    def area(self):                                                   #(D)
        raise NotImplementedError( "abstract root class" )            #(E)
    def circumference(self):                                          #(F)
        raise NotImplementedError( "abstract root class" )            #(G)

#--------------------------  class Circle  ----------------------------
class Circle( Shape ):                                                #(H)
    def __init__( self, rad ):                                        #(I)
        self.radius = rad
    def area(self):                                                   #(J)
        return 3.14159 * self.radius * self.radius
    def circumference(self):                                          #(K)
        return 2 * 3.14159 * self.radius
```

```
#--------------------------  class Rectangle  ---------------------------
class Rectangle( Shape ):                                              #(L)
    def __init__( self, len, wid ):                                    #(M)
        self.length = len
        self.width = wid
    def area(self):                                                    #(N)
        return self.length * self.width
    def circumference(self):                                           #(O)
        return 2 * (self.length + self.width)

#------------------------------------------------------------------------
#                global function get_shape_properties()
#------------------------------------------------------------------------
def get_shape_properties( x ):                                         #(P)
    assert isinstance( x, Shape )                                      #(Q)
    print x.area()                                                     #(R)
    print x.circumference()                                            #(S)

#------------------------------------------------------------------------
#                              Test code
#------------------------------------------------------------------------
#shape1 = Shape()                       # ERROR                        #(T)
#print shape1.area()                    # ERROR                        #(U)
#print shape1.circumference()           # ERROR                        #(V)

shape2 = Circle( 4 );                                                  #(W)
get_shape_properties( shape2 )          # 50.26   25.13                #(X)

shape3 = Rectangle( 4, 5 )                                             #(Y)
get_shape_properties( shape3 )          # 20   18                      #(Z)
```

11.3 CREDITS AND SUGGESTIONS FOR FURTHER READING

Readers interested in constructing abstract base classes in Perl should also look up the `Class::Virtual` and `Abstract` modules downloadable from `www.cpan.org`. Regarding abstract classes and methods in Python, the reader is referred to a posting by Ivo Timmermans [64].

11.4 HOMEWORK

1. In the Perl multifile scripts of Section 11.1, replace all directives such as

```
use Some_Module;
```

with the following pieces of code

```
BEGIN {
    require Some_Module;
    Some_Module->import();
}
```

and show that you get the same result as before. Additionally, explain why the following replacement syntax also does the same job (although it does not make explicit the fact that `import()` is being invoked on the same module that `require` just pulled in):

```
BEGIN {
    require Some_Module;
    import Some_Module;
}
```

Recall that `import()` is implemented as a static method of a class.

2. Section 9.1 presented an example of a class hierarchy to illustrate the concepts of inheritance and polymorphism in Python OO. Change the design of this hierarchy by making the `ExecutivePerks` an abstract class. As an abstract class, `ExecutivePerks` will serve as a mixin class and it will become incumbent upon the `Manager` class to implement the methods declared in the `ExecutivePerks` class.

3. Do the same as what is called for in the previous problem but for the Perl class hierarchy of Sections 8.4 and 8.5 of Chapter 8.

12

Weak References for Memory Management

As mentioned previously in our discussion related to object destruction in Chapters 6 and 7, both Perl and Python come with automatic garbage collection. To recap, if some previously allocated memory is no longer in use, it will automatically be deallocated by the garbage collection mechanism. When an object is allocated memory on the heap, a variable will typically hold a reference to such an object. If the variable is subsequently assigned some other value, the previously created object becomes unreferenced. If there exist no other variables (or other objects such as containers) holding references to such an object, the object is considered to be *unreachable*. It is the job of the garbage collection mechanism to free up the memory occupied by such unreachable objects.

Any approach to garbage collection must take into account the possibility that there can exist multiple variables (and multiple other objects) holding references to the same object in the memory. For example, when a reference to an object is passed as an argument to a function, the corresponding parameter in the body of the function will also hold a reference to the same object.[1] This would cause the reference count for the object to become 2. As another example, consider the case when a previously created object is stored in a container. Once again you will have two different entities holding references to the same object: the variable to which the object was assigned when it was first created and the container element that also points to the same object.

[1]An alternative is to pass the object itself as an argument to a function, but for large objects that would be inefficient for obvious reasons.

12.1 A BRIEF REVIEW OF MEMORY MANAGEMENT

There are basically three different ways to allocate memory in a computer program: *static allocation* for objects that must persist for the entire run of the program, *stack allocation* for storing nonstatic local variables and function parameters, and *heap allocation* for storing objects that are created during program execution.[2] Since there are virtually no run-time costs associated with static and stack allocations, we won't talk about them further. As for heap allocation, the run-time cost depends on how the memory management system keeps track of the memory that is still free, the memory that was assigned previously to the objects, and the memory that is reclaimed from the expired objects.

Perhaps the simplest approach to keeping track of the previously allocated memory on the heap is by maintaining a list of all of the currently available memory blocks. This can be in the form of a linked list of pointers to the memory blocks. In this scheme, the first few bytes of each block are used to indicate the size of the block and whether or not the block is indeed free; it may not be free if it just got allocated. (Note that the size information translates directly into a pointer to the next block.) If we need to allocate for a new object, the memory management system can traverse the linked list of pointers until it finds a block that is at least as large as what is needed for the allocation. If a free block is larger than what is needed, the system can divide up the block, use what is needed, and declare the remaining to be a free block by placing an appropriate header at the beginning of the block. At the time of deallocation, the system would, as you'd expect, change the allocation bit in the

[2]Since both Perl and Python sit on top of C, it is useful to briefly review these three modes of allocation in C. In a C program, a statement such as

```
static int data[100];
```

will call for static allocation for an array of 100 `ints`. This memory will be allocated from a segment of memory set aside permanently for static variables. There is no run-time cost associated with such allocations. On the other hand, a statement such as the following inside a code block

```
int data[100];
```

will allocate memory on the stack for the local array variable `data`. When the array variable goes out of scope, this memory will be deallocated. Allocating and deallocating this memory is cheap at run time. Allocation merely requires that we add to the memory address stored in the stack pointer for the top of the stack. Deallocation merely requires that we subtract from the memory address stored in the stack pointer. Finally, a C declaration such as

```
int* ptr = malloc( 100 * sizeof(int) );
```

inside a code block calls for heap allocation of memory at run time. It is this dynamic allocation that is the focus of memory management and garbage collection. A programmer uses this type of allocation for objects that are large or that need to persist longer than a single function call but shorter than the entire program. Depending on how the free memory is kept track of and the manner in which the memory from expired objects is reclaimed, heap allocation and deallocation may extract significant run-time costs for certain applications.

header of that block and make it free again. The deallocation step could also include coalescing the freed up memory with the next block if it is also found to be free.[3]

No matter how one keeps track of the available memory, it is clear that memory allocation and deallocation can involve significant overhead at run time. Also, when a memory management system intersperses free space with occupied blocks of memory, it may run into the problem of *memory fragmentation*. Fragmentation means that the deallocations during program execution may create a large number of free "holes" in the memory map, but none may be sufficiently large to accommodate the next object that needs to be allocated. So even though your memory manager says that a large amount of memory is still available, it may nonetheless fail to carry out the next allocation. Another problem related to memory management is known as the *memory locality problem* or the *problem of poor locality of reference*. If two objects that need to refer to each other are far separated in the address space, an operating system using virtual memory may be able to keep only one of them in its active memory at any time. This could extract a performance penalty at run time if both objects are being used simultaneously and one or the other object needs to be paged in constantly.[4]

An important component of any modern memory management system is automatic garbage collection. A garbage collection system is supposed to figure out what objects are no longer needed by a program and to then free up the memory occupied by such objects. Several basic strategies for garbage collection include:

Reference Counting: This is probably the simplest approach and also the one most frequently used with scripting languages like Perl and Python. In reference-counting-based garbage collection, every time a new variable acquires a reference to an object, the reference count associated with the object goes up by one. And every time a variable loses a previously held reference to an object (say, because the variable went out of scope), the reference count associated with the object decreases by one. When the reference count associated with an object goes to zero, the object is deallocated. Reference-counting-based garbage collection becomes transparent to the user if the compiler supports it. If the compiler generates the code needed for incrementing and decrementing the reference counts, the garbage collection process becomes smoothly integrated with the run-time execution of the script. What that implies is that,

[3]Variations on this theme include maintaining a linked list of free blocks in size order, as opposed to address order; maintaining multiple linked lists of pointers, each specialized to certain sized memory blocks; maintaining a bidirectional linked list to make it faster to scan the list in both directions; etc.

[4]The performance penalty extracted when paging is involved can be gauged from the fact that whereas it takes around 100 clock cycles to access a piece of information in the main random-access memory, it may take anywhere from 1,000 to 10,000 clock cycles to access information that a virtual memory system has stored away on the hard disk. By the way, for even faster access compared to what is provided by the main memory, the objects would need to be stored in a CPU cache (around 5 clock cycles), or, if they are small enough, in the CPU registers where things happen instantaneously.

at run time, the execution of the script does not have to be paused to clean up the memory. The main shortcoming of the reference-count-based garbage collection is the problem caused by circular references, as demonstrated by the example in Section 6.4.1 of Chapter 6. We will revisit this problem later in this chapter.

Tracing: Tracing garbage collectors are based on the notion of tracing the reachability links of all the objects previously allocated, this action being triggered whenever the remaining available memory is considered to be too low. An object is considered to be reachable if it is referenced by another reachable object or by an object currently in the call stack. (You could say that the objects currently in the call stack constitute the root set of a reachability graph whose nonroot nodes are all the other objects.) All unreachable objects become candidates for deallocation. One of the main problems with tracing-based garbage collection is that, to the user, a memory-intensive program appears to freeze up when the garbage collection kicks in. *The suspension of the main program during the garbage collection cycle is made necessary by the fact that we do not want the reachability status of an object to change during garbage collection.* Another disadvantage of this approach is that all of the previously allocated objects must be scanned twice, once to figure out which objects are reachable from the root set, and then again to delete the unreachable objects. Depending on how exactly they are implemented, tracing-based garbage collectors can be further categorized as follows:

Mark and Sweep: This is the most basic implementation of a tracing garbage collector. Starting from the objects on the call stack, the marking phase traces out the reference tree, setting a reachability bit in the header of each memory block visited. Subsequently, all the blocks in the heap are visited and those that are occupied but not otherwise marked are freed. It is this need to sweep the entire heap at each garbage collection cycle that is a major disadvantage of the mark-sweep method. In at least the simplest implementations of this method, the main program remains suspended during both the marking and the sweep phases.

Copy and Compact: In a copying garbage collector, the heap is divided into two equal parts. At any given time, only one of the two halves is used during program execution. A garbage collection cycle consists of tracing out the reference tree as before and copying the objects encountered into the other half of the heap. After all the live objects have been copied over in this manner, the active memory for program execution switches to the half of the heap that just acquired all the objects. Vis-à-vis the mark-sweep approach, the main advantage of the copying approach is that the heap need not be swept for the unreachable objects, which results in zero deallocation cost. Another advantage of a copying garbage collector is that the copied live objects can be "compacted" into the bottom of the heap. This can greatly improve the memory locality of the objects (see the earlier comment about the problem of memory locality). Compaction also causes the allocation cost to become practically zero, since the allocation of N bytes for a new object can now be as simple as incrementing the top-of-the-heap pointer by N. That is, there would now be no need for a best-fit or first-fit algorithm to search for a free block of memory for the new N-byte object that requires allocation. All of these benefits can be had but at the cost of having to copy all live objects from one half of the memory to the other half.

Mark and Compact: This approach combines the mark-sweep and the copy-compact approaches. Garbage collection consists of two phases: In the mark phase, the reference tree is traced out as in mark-and-sweep. In the second phase, instead of sweeping the entire heap to look for the unreachable objects, the live objects marked in the first phase are all copied to the bottom of the heap. The rest of the heap is then considered to be free.

Generational: Generation here refers to the age of an object. Generational garbage collectors are based on the notion that the more recent an object, the more likely that it will be found unreachable in the current garbage collection cycle. So it makes sense to divide the heap into multiple sections, each for a different generation of objects. Each heap section can then be processed with a different algorithm for garbage collection. For example, the section of the heap devoted to young objects may be garbage-collected with the copy-compact method. Since the live objects of recent vintage are likely to be few in number, the copy-compact method should work efficiently for young objects. On the other hand, for the heap space devoted to the near-permanent objects, such as class objects that once created are likely to persist for the entire duration of the program, mark-compact would probably be more suitable. Each cycle of garbage collection would also have to include moving surviving objects from one section of the heap to another section that is reserved for higher-longevity objects.

Except for the reference-counting-based methods, all of the garbage collection approaches we have presented above require the application program to pause while garbage collection is taking place. This can create serious problems for applications that require near real-time behavior, as when a large number of client-based transactions must be carried out without interruption.[5] Of the various nonreference-counting-based methods presented, the generational-based method when implemented on a multiprocessor machine with multiple garbage collection threads, one for each generation of objects, comes closet to giving pause-free performance.[28]

---

[5] Garbage collectors that require the main application program to pause during each garbage collection cycle are also known as the `Stop-the-World` garbage collectors.

12.2 GARBAGE COLLECTION FOR MEMORY-INTENSIVE APPLICATIONS

A key notion in all the garbage collection methods we have described so far is that as long an object is in use, it ought not be deallocated. On the face of it, this notion sounds like something that should never be violated by a computing platform. It sounds like a principle of good software design.

But further thinking leads one to realize that this may not be a good strategy for certain memory-intensive applications, such as when you download images, sound files, or video clips through a web browser. If a running program had to choose between having to delete a large video clip (that could subsequently be reloaded if it is needed again) and having to throw an out-of-memory run-time exception that would shut down the program, the former would be the thing to do.

Smart memory management therefore calls for allowing a system to not treat all created objects the same. There should be a way to differentiate between objects so that some are considered more disposable than others. One can imagine that the systems of the future would execute automated tools in a background thread that would constantly assess the relative importance of the different objects currently in the fast memory with regard to ongoing computations so that the less important objects could be moved to slower memory. Such objects could be fetched back into the fast memory when needed again. But such automated tools are not yet available.

However, as a step in that direction, many modern programming languages allow for what are known as *weak references*. When an object resident in the memory can only be accessed through a weak reference, it becomes a candidate for deallocation when memory starts running short. This can then be used for smart memory management and caching in applications that create large but recreatable-when-needed data objects.

12.3 THE CIRCULAR REFERENCE PROBLEM

Recall that both Perl and Python use reference counting based garbage collection. All reference-counting-based garbage collection schemes suffer from the circular reference problem. We illustrated this problem with a network example in Section 6.4.1 of Chapter 6. As mentioned there, when two objects refer to each other, you have a circular reference. To continue the earlier discussion with another example, think of creating a `Corporation` instance in an object-oriented script that points to `Employee` instances. Let's assume that each `Employee` instance has an attribute that points back to the corporation that hired the employee. When you originally create a `Corporation` instance, its reference count is set to 1. This count is incremented as the `Corporation` attribute of each employee is set to the same corporation. Now when you dissolve the corporation, its reference count would be decremented, but it will not become zero since one or more employees would be holding references to the corporation. As a result, the memory allocated to the corporation would not be reclaimed as long as any of the employees is holding a reference to the corporation. It is not only the corporation that may exhibit this indestructibility property under such circumstances — the various employees may also prove to be indestructible because their reference counts would not go to zero as long as the indestructible corporation is holding references to them.

Weak references are useful for solving the circular reference problem that besets reference-counting-based garbage collection methods. Later in this chapter we will show how the notion of weakening a reference can be used to get rid of this problem in Perl and Python.

12.4 WEAK VERSUS STRONG REFERENCES

Both Perl and Python allow for weak references. In order to distinguish between weak references and the traditional references, it is common to refer to the latter as *strong references*. The objects pointed to by the strong references are reference counted. When you obtain a weak reference to an object, the reference count associated with the object is not incremented. When you *weaken* what was previously a strong reference, you decrement by 1 the reference count associated with the object.

12.5 WEAK REFERENCES IN PERL

The goal of this section is to illustrate how the circular reference problem in Perl can be dealt with through the mechanism of *reference weakening* as provided by the `weaken()` method of the `Scalar::Util` module. This module comes with the standard Perl distribution.

The script shown next, `CircularRef1.pl`, defines two classes `X` and `Y`. We have provided class `X` with two instance variables, `id`, specified directly by the constructor in line (X5), and `yobj`, specified by the `setYfield()` method in line (X8). The class `Y` also has two instance variables, the first, `id`, is specified by the constructor in line (Y5), and the second, `xobj`, by the `setXfield()` method in line (Y8).

The classes `X` and `Y` have also been endowed with the `DESTROY()` method. Before an instance of type `X` or `Y` is garbage collected, its `DESTROY()` will be invoked, as discussed in Section 6.4 of Chapter 6. As should be clear from the syntax in lines (X11) and (Y11), the `DESTROY()` methods will help us figure out which specific instance is about to be scooped up by the garbage collection mechanism.

Lines (T1) and (T2) of the test code construct two instance objects, one from class X and the other from class Y. By calling on the two `set` methods, as shown in lines (T3) and (T4), we set the X instance's `yobj` data attribute to the Y instance and the Y instance's `xobj` data attribute to the X instance. This creates a circular reference between the two instance objects.

Now consider the following two cases[6] for executing this script:

1. When the statement in line (T6) is commented out, meaning when we do *not* weaken the reference to the Y instance stored in the `yobj` field of the X instance.
2. When the script is executed as shown, meaning that we do not comment out line (T6).

The output produced by the script when we comment out line (T6) is

```
Creating X object: id = 1
Creating Y object: id = 1
```

It is interesting to see that, in this case, Perl is not able to destroy the instance objects constructed in lines (T1) and (T2) even after we `undef` in lines (T8) and (T9) the variables holding references to the instances. As explained before, this is because Perl's garbage collection is based on reference counting — when the reference count associated with an object goes to zero, it is deallocated. In our example, the X and the Y instances both will have a reference count of 2 associated with them. For the X instance, one of these two counts is for the reference held by the variable `$x` and the other for the reference held by the `xobj` data attribute of the Y instance. Similarly, for the reference count of 2 for the Y instance of line (T2). So even after we `undef` the variables in lines (T8) and (T9), the reference counts for the X and the Y instances do not go to zero. Hence they are not deallocated.

However, when we execute the script as shown, that is, with line (T6) not commented out, the output becomes

```
Creating X object: id = 1
Creating Y object: id = 1
Y obj will be destroyed: id = 1
X obj will be destroyed: id = 1
```

The call to `weaken()` in line (T6) decrements the reference count for the Y instance. Now when we `undef` the variables in lines (T8) and (T9), the reference count for the Y instance will go to zero. This would cause the Y instance to be marked for garbage collection. The destruction of the Y instance would cause the reference count for the X instance to also be decremented to zero, causing its eventual destruction also.

[6] Ignore for a moment the commented-out lines (T5) and (T7). They will remain commented-out for the two cases.

In case the reader is wondering, we use the infinite `while` loop in line (T10) to "park" the flow of execution there in order to prevent the destruction of the objects because of the imminent shutdown of the virtual machine executing the Perl bytecode.[7] When the virtual machine shuts down, all objects will obviously be destroyed willy-nilly and, when possible, Perl will invoke their `DESTROY()` methods regardless of the presence of any circular references between them. We are not interested in that sort of object destruction. Our interest is more in the memory leakage caused by circular references while the virtual machine is running.

To see that the weakening of a reference is not tantamount to a "nulling" of the reference, the reader can uncomment the two print statements in lines (T5) and (T7). The output of the script with the two print statements uncommented is

```
Creating X object: id = 1
Creating Y object: id = 1
before weakening: Y=HASH(0x804b424)
after weakening: Y=HASH(0x804b424)
Y obj will be destroyed: id = 1
X obj will be destroyed: id = 1
```

As the reader can see, the reference to the `Y` instance held by the `X` instance remains unaltered after we invoke `weaken()` on this reference.

Finally, the reader should note that we need to weaken either the `Y` reference held by the `X` instance or the `X` reference held by the `Y` instance in order to get rid of the circular reference problem in this example. Weakening, say, the reference held by `$y` would not work for fixing the memory leakage caused by the circular reference.

```
#!/usr/bin/perl -w

### CircularRef1.pl

use strict;
use Scalar::Util qw( weaken );                                          #(A)

#---------------------------  class X  --------------------------------
package X;                                                              #(X1)

sub new {                                                               #(X2)
    my ($class, $id) = @_;                                              #(X3)
    print "Creating X object: id = " . $id . "\n";                      #(X4)
    return bless { id => $id }, $class;                                 #(X5)
}
```

[7] We used the same ploy in Section 6.4.1 of Chapter 6 to illustrate the problems caused by circular references.

```
sub setYfield {                                                       #(X6)
    my ($ref, $yobj) = @_;                                            #(X7)
    $ref->{ yobj } = $yobj;                                           #(X8)
}
sub DESTROY {                                                         #(X9)
    my $ref = shift;                                                  #(X10)
    print "X obj will be destroyed: id = " . $ref->{id} . "\n";       #(X11)
}

#---------------------------  class Y  --------------------------------
package Y;                                                            #(Y1)

sub new {                                                             #(Y2)
    my ($class, $id, $xobj) = @_;                                     #(Y3)
    print "Creating Y object: id = " . $id . "\n";                    #(Y4)
    return bless { id => $id, xob => $xobj }, $class;                 #(Y5)
}
sub setXfield {                                                       #(Y6)
    my ($ref, $xobj) = @_;                                            #(Y7)
    $ref->{ xobj } = $xobj;                                           #(Y8)
}
sub DESTROY {                                                         #(Y9)
    my $ref = shift;                                                  #(Y10)
    print "Y obj will be destroyed: id = " . $ref->{id} . "\n";       #(Y11)
}

#-------------------------  Test Code  --------------------------------
package main;

my $x = X->new(1);                                                    #(T1)
my $y = Y->new(1);                                                    #(T2)
$x->setYfield( $y );                                                  #(T3)
$y->setXfield( $x );                                                  #(T4)

#print "before weakening: ", $x->{yobj}, "\n";                        #(T5)
weaken( $x->{yobj} );                                                 #(T6)
#print "after weakening: ", $x->{yobj}, "\n";                         #(T7)

$x = undef;                                                           #(T8)
$y = undef;                                                           #(T9)

while(1) {}                                                           #(T10)
```

The next script, `CircularRef2.pl`, is a variation of the above script in that we now create a very large number of circular references in a `while` loop, as shown in lines (T3) through (T10) of the script. The classes `X` and `Y` in this script are the same as before. At the end of each iteration, when the flow of control hits the right brace of the `while` block, the variables `$x` and `$y` will go out of scope. So the referents of these variables, meaning the instance objects constructed in lines (T4) and (T5), should get destroyed when the flow of execution hits the right brace in line (T10). But if you run the script after you have commented out the call to `weaken()` in line (T8), you will see an output like the following:[8]

```
Creating X object: id = 0
Creating Y object: id = 0
Creating X object: id = 1
Creating Y object: id = 1
Creating X object: id = 2
Creating Y object: id = 2
....
DONE WITH THE WHILE LOOP
....
Y obj will be destroyed: id = 2
X obj will be destroyed: id = 2
Y obj will be destroyed: id = 1
X obj will be destroyed: id = 1
X obj will be destroyed: id = 0
Y obj will be destroyed: id = 0
```

This output demonstrates that the instance objects constructed in lines (T4) and (T5) are not getting destroyed even after the local variables that hold references to these instances go out of scope in line (T10). Instance destruction takes place only after all of the iterations of the while loop have been gone through and only because the Perl virtual machine is about to shut down. *This demonstrates a huge memory leak in the script.*

But now consider the following output obtained when you run the script as shown — meaning with the call to `weaken()` in line (T8) included:

```
Creating X object: id = 0
Creating Y object: id = 0
Y obj will be destroyed: id = 0
X obj will be destroyed: id = 0
Creating X object: id = 1
Creating Y object: id = 1
Y obj will be destroyed: id = 1
X obj will be destroyed: id = 1
Creating X object: id = 2
Creating Y object: id = 2
Y obj will be destroyed: id = 2
```

[8]Both the outputs shown for the script `CircularRef2.pl` were produced by running only three iterations of the `while` loop, that is, by uncommenting the statement in line (T2) and commenting out line (T3). The reasons for that should be obvious.

```
    X obj will be destroyed: id = 2
    ....
    DONE WITH THE WHILE LOOP
```

Now the object destruction is taking place as you would expect it and there is no memory leak in the script.

```
#!/usr/bin/perl -w

### CircularRef2.pl

use strict;

use Scalar::Util qw( weaken );

#---------------------------  class X  ---------------------------------
package X;                                                             #(X1)

sub new {                                                              #(X2)
    my ($class, $id) = @_;                                             #(X3)
    print "Creating X object: id = " . $id . "\n";                    #(X4)
    return bless { id => $id }, $class;                               #(X5)
}
sub setYfield {                                                        #(X6)
    my ($ref, $yobj) = @_;                                             #(X7)
    $ref->{ yobj } = $yobj;                                            #(X8)
}
sub DESTROY {                                                          #(X9)
    my $ref = shift;                                                   #(X10)
    print "X obj will be destroyed: id = " . $ref->{id} . "\n";       #(X11)
}

#---------------------------  class Y  ---------------------------------
package Y;                                                             #(Y1)

sub new {                                                              #(Y2)
    my ($class, $id, $xobj) = @_;                                      #(Y3)
    print "Creating Y object: id = " . $id . "\n";                    #(Y4)
    return bless { id => $id, xob => $xobj }, $class;                 #(Y5)
}
sub setXfield {                                                        #(Y6)
    my ($ref, $xobj) = @_;                                             #(Y7)
    $ref->{ xobj } = $xobj;                                            #(Y8)
}
```

```
sub DESTROY {                                                      #(Y9)
    my $ref = shift;                                               #(Y10)
    print "Y obj will be destroyed: id = " . $ref->{id} . "\n";    #(Y11)
}

#-------------------------- Test Code --------------------------------
package main;

my $i = 0;                                                         #(T1)
#while ($i < 3) {                                                  #(T2)
while ($i < 100000) {                                              #(T3)
    my $x = X->new($i);                                            #(T4)
    my $y = Y->new($i);                                            #(T5)
    $x->setYfield( $y );                                           #(T6)
    $y->setXfield( $x );                                           #(T7)
    weaken( $x->{yobj} );                                          #(T8)
    $i++;                                                          #(T9)
}                                                                  #(T10)

print "\n\nDONE WITH THE WHILE LOOP\n\n";                          #(T11)
```

12.5.1 Can Perl's Reference Weakening Be Used for In-Memory Caching?

Some languages, like Java, provide memory weakening mechanisms that can be used for in-memory caching of large multimedia objects. By using weak references for such objects, the memory occupied by them can be reclaimed, if necessary, and the destroyed objects reloaded from the web if needed again. This approach obviously has merit over letting the Java virtual machine throw the `OutOfMemoryError` exception that would otherwise shut down an application. So an interesting question is whether the reference weakening provided by `Scalar::Util::weaken()` can be used for in-memory caching in Perl in the same sense.

In this subsection we will show that the reference weakening made possible by `Scalar::Util::weaken()` cannot be used for caching. It is not because there is any problem with the implementation of the `Scalar::Util::weaken()` subroutine itself; it is because of the way garbage collection is carried out in Perl.

Since a Perl object is deallocated as soon as its reference count goes to zero, an object whose reference has been weakened will be immediately reclaimed if no other variables are holding strong references to the object — *even when there is no pressure on the memory.*

If a reference-weakening mechanism is to be useful for caching, the garbage collector must let an object live as long as there is no pressing need to reclaim the memory occupied by the object. Only if the memory is running short, should an object that has only weakened references (and no strong references) get reclaimed.

In the rest of this section, we will first show a script, `MemoryTest.pl`, that pushes memory utilization to the limit by constructing larger and larger objects. In the script that comes after that, `MemoryTestWithWeakRef.pl`, we will then show the same code again, except that the references to these objects will be weakened. The output produced by the second script will be used to demonstrate that the reference-counting-based garbage collection in Perl simply does not allow for in-memory caching with the reference-weakening mechanism.

Shown below is the first script that pushes the memory used to its limits. The script defines a class `MemoryBlock` starting in line (A) and provides the class with two methods, `get_print_representation()` in line (K) and `DESTROY()` in line (L). There is only one reason for creating a `MemoryBlock` instance — to create an object that acquires a designated amount of memory. A `MemoryBlock` instance holds a reference to an array, as shown in line (I). The size of the array is set in line (E); that is where memory is allocated for the array, the size of the memory as specified by the parameter `$size` of the constructor in line (C). Each `MemoryObject` instance has an ID associated with it, as specified by the value of the parameter `$id` of the constructor in line (C). Whenever a new `MemoryBlock` instance is constructed, the call to `print` in line (J) prints out the instance ID and its size.

```
#!/usr/bin/perl -w

### MemoryTest.pl

use strict;

#------------------------   class MemoryBlock   --------------------------
package MemoryBlock;                                                    #(A)

sub new {                                                               #(B)
    my ( $class, $id, $size ) = @_;                                     #(C)
    my @arr = ();                                                       #(D)
    $#arr = $size - 1;                                                  #(E)
    my $block_ref = {                                                   #(F)
        id => $id,                                                      #(G)
        size => $size,                                                  #(H)
        array_ref => \@arr,                                             #(I)
        };
    bless $block_ref, $class;
    print "MemoryBlock created: " . "{id=" . $block_ref->{id} .        #(J)
        ", size=" . $block_ref->{size} . "}" . "\n";
    $block_ref;
}
```

```
sub get_print_representation {                                        #(K)
    my $block_ref = shift;
    return "{id=" . $block_ref->{id} .
        ", size=" . $block_ref->{size} . "}";
}
sub DESTROY {                                                         #(L)
    my $block_ref = shift;
    print "MemoryBlock about to be destroyed: {id=" .
        $block_ref->{id} .
        ", size=" . $block_ref->{size} . "}" . "\n";
}

#----------------------------  Test Code  -----------------------------
package main;

my @blocks = ();                                                      #(M)
my $size = 262144;                                                    #(N)

my $i = 0;
while (1) {                                                           #(O)
    $blocks[$i] = MemoryBlock->new( $i, $size );                      #(P)
    print_blocks(\@blocks);                                           #(Q)
    $size *= 2;                                                       #(R)
    $i++;                                                             #(S)
}
sub print_blocks {                                                    #(T)
    my $ref_all_blocks = shift;
    print "All blocks: ";
    foreach ( @$ref_all_blocks ) {                                    #(U)
        print $_->get_print_representation;                           #(V)
    }
    print "\n\n";
}
```

Let's now focus on the test code in the above script. Through the `while` loop in lines (P) through (S), the test code constructs larger and larger `MemoryBlock` instances and stores the references to these instances in the array `@blocks`. Each new `MemoryBlock` instance is twice as large as the previous one on account of the size multiplication in line (R). Obviously, at some point, there will be no more free memory left for constructing the next instance in the `while` loop. When that happens, Perl shuts down, but only after running the `DESTROY()` methods for all the instance objects resident in the memory. This is demonstrated by the output produced shown below. Each iteration through the `while` loop produces one "`MemoryBlock created`" statement and one "`All blocks`" statement in the output. The "`MemoryBlock created`" statement is for the new `MemoryBlock` instance created in that iteration and the "All blocks" statement is for the total contents of the @blocks array up to that point.[9]

```
MemoryBlock created: {id=0, size=262144}
All blocks: {id=0, size=262144}

MemoryBlock created: {id=1, size=524288}
All blocks: {id=0, size=262144}{id=1, size=524288}

MemoryBlock created: {id=2, size=1048576}
All blocks: {id=0, size=262144}{id=1, size=524288}
            {id=2, size=1048576}

MemoryBlock created: {id=3, size=2097152}
All blocks: {id=0, size=262144}{id=1, size=524288}
            {id=2, size=1048576}{id=3, size=2097152}

MemoryBlock created: {id=4, size=4194304}
All blocks: {id=0, size=262144}{id=1, size=524288}
            {id=2, size=1048576}{id=3, size=2097152}
            {id=4, size=4194304}

MemoryBlock created: {id=5, size=8388608}
All blocks: {id=0, size=262144}{id=1, size=524288}
            {id=2, size=1048576}{id=3, size=2097152}
            {id=4, size=4194304}{id=5, size=8388608}

MemoryBlock created: {id=6, size=16777216}
All blocks: {id=0, size=262144}{id=1, size=524288}
            {id=2, size=1048576}{id=3, size=2097152}
            {id=4, size=4194304}{id=5, size=8388608}
            {id=6, size=16777216}

MemoryBlock created: {id=7, size=33554432}
All blocks: {id=0, size=262144}{id=1, size=524288}
            {id=2, size=1048576}{id=3, size=2097152}
            {id=4, size=4194304}{id=5, size=8388608}
            {id=6, size=16777216}{id=7, size=33554432}

MemoryBlock created: {id=8, size=67108864}
All blocks: {id=0, size=262144}{id=1, size=524288}
            {id=2, size=1048576}{id=3, size=2097152}
            {id=4, size=4194304}{id=5, size=8388608}
            {id=6, size=16777216}{id=7, size=33554432}
            {id=8, size=67108864}
```

[9] The output was slightly reformatted for the presentation here. For example, all the "All blocks" entries are supposed to be in a single line, but we have placed them in successive lines for better readability.

```
MemoryBlock created: {id=9, size=134217728}
All blocks: {id=0, size=262144}{id=1, size=524288}
            {id=2, size=1048576}{id=3, size=2097152}
            {id=4, size=4194304}{id=5, size=8388608}
            {id=6, size=16777216}{id=7, size=33554432}
            {id=8, size=67108864}{id=9, size=134217728}

OUT OF MEMORY!

MemoryBlock about to be destroyed: {id=9, size=134217728}
MemoryBlock about to be destroyed: {id=8, size=67108864}
MemoryBlock about to be destroyed: {id=7, size=33554432}
MemoryBlock about to be destroyed: {id=6, size=16777216}
MemoryBlock about to be destroyed: {id=5, size=8388608}
MemoryBlock about to be destroyed: {id=4, size=4194304}
MemoryBlock about to be destroyed: {id=3, size=2097152}
MemoryBlock about to be destroyed: {id=2, size=1048576}
MemoryBlock about to be destroyed: {id=1, size=524288}
MemoryBlock about to be destroyed: {id=0, size=262144}
```

We will now introduce reference-weakening in the previous script to see if we can do in-memory caching of the `MemoryBlock` instances. The answer will be that we cannot because of how garbage collection is carried out in Perl.

Shown below is essentially the same script as above except that now in line (S) we weaken the references to the newly created `MemoryBlock` instances. The other changes we had to make in the following script include the incorporation of the `defined` test in line (X) of the `print_blocks()` subroutine. This was made necessary for the same reason that makes it impossible to do caching with weakened references in Perl — as the reader will see shortly from the explanation that follows the script.

```
#!/usr/bin/perl -w

### MemoryTestWithWeakRef.pl

use strict;
use Scalar::Util qw(weaken);

#-------------------------  class MemoryBlock  --------------------------
package MemoryBlock;                                                #(A)

sub new {                                                           #(B)
    my ( $class, $id, $size ) = @_;                                 #(C)
    my @arr = ();                                                   #(D)
```

```
    $#arr = $size - 1;                                                    #(E)
    my $block_ref = {                                                     #(F)
        id => $id,                                                        #(G)
        size => $size,                                                    #(H)
        array_ref => \@arr,                                               #(I)
        };
    bless $block_ref, $class;
    print "\nMemoryBlock created: " .                                     #(J)
        "{id=" . $block_ref->{id} .
        ", size=" . $block_ref->{size} . "}" . "\n";
    $block_ref;
}
sub get_print_representation {                                            #(K)
    my $block_ref = shift;
    return "{id=" . $block_ref->{id} .
        ", size=" . $block_ref->{size} . "}";
}
sub DESTROY {                                                             #(L)
    my $block_ref = shift;
    print "MemoryBlock about to be destroyed: {id=" .
        $block_ref->{id} .
        ", size=" . $block_ref->{size} . "}" . "\n";
}

#---------------------------  Test Code  ------------------------------
package main;                                                             #(M)

my @blocks = ();                                                          #(N)
my $size = 262144;                                                        #(O)

my $i = 0;
while (1) {                                                               #(P)
    $blocks[$i] = MemoryBlock->new( $i, $size );                          #(Q)
    print_blocks(\@blocks);                                               #(R)
    weaken $blocks[$i];                                                   #(S)
    $size *= 2;                                                           #(T)
    $i++;                                                                 #(U)
}
sub print_blocks {                                                        #(V)
    my $ref_all_blocks = shift;
    print "All blocks: ";
    foreach ( @$ref_all_blocks ) {                                        #(W)
        print $_->get_print_representation if defined;                    #(X)
    }
    print "\n";
}
```

When we run this script, the output looks like

```
MemoryBlock created: {id=0, size=262144}
All blocks: {id=0, size=262144}
MemoryBlock about to be destroyed: {id=0, size=262144}

MemoryBlock created: {id=1, size=524288}
All blocks: {id=1, size=524288}
MemoryBlock about to be destroyed: {id=1, size=524288}

MemoryBlock created: {id=2, size=1048576}
All blocks: {id=2, size=1048576}
MemoryBlock about to be destroyed: {id=2, size=1048576}

MemoryBlock created: {id=3, size=2097152}
All blocks: {id=3, size=2097152}
MemoryBlock about to be destroyed: {id=3, size=2097152}
....
....
```

As the reader can see, each `MemoryBlock` instance is destroyed soon after its reference, created in line (Q), is weakened in line (S). That is not surprising because the weakening decrements to zero the reference count associated with the instance and so it is immediately deallocated. As a consequence, the `@blocks` array, to which we keep on adding references to the new `MemoryBlock` instances in line (Q), actually holds only the latest `MemoryBlock` instance.[10]

Since the `MemoryBlock` instances whose references are weakened are immediately destroyed, we conclude that reference weakening cannot be used for in-memory caching in Perl.

Before ending this section, we want to point out quickly that the actual memory occupied by the `MemoryBlock` instances created in line (P) of the `MemoryTest.pl` script and line (Q) of the `MemoryTestWithWeakRef.pl` script is much larger than what would be indicated by the number of array elements specified. Unlike arrays in systems programming languages, there is considerable memory overhead associated with a Perl array.[11]

---

[10]This should also make clear as to why we had to include the `defined` test in line (X). Since reference weakening in line (S) causes the `MemoryBlock` instances to be destroyed, we would be trying to access *nulled* elements for all the array indices except for the last in line (X).

[11]A Perl array holds pointers of type `SV*` to scalars. What you store as an array element is held inside an `SV` data structure. Declaring and preallocating memory for an array through statements like

```
my @arr = ();
$#arr = 99;
```

would, of course, create an empty array of size 100 elements. Assuming 4 bytes for a pointer, the memory occupied by the contiguous elements of the array itself would be only 400 bytes. But to determine the total memory occupied by the structure created, you'd have to include the memory occupied by the instances of

Shown below is a script that uses the `size()` and the `total_size()` functions from the `Devel::Size` module to print out the actual sizes of the `MemoryBlock` instances created. Note the incorporation of the module `Devel::Size` in lines (B) and (P) and the invocation of the `size()` function in line (M) and the `total_size()` function in line (V). The `size()` function reports the memory occupied by the top level of a hierarchical data structure. This suffices to find the actual memory occupied by the array in line (M). The function `total_size()`, on the other hand, descends down a hierarchical data structure and returns the size of the total memory occupied by all of the contents of the data structure.

```
#!/usr/bin/perl -w

### MemoryTestWithActualSize.pl

use strict;

#------------------------  class MemoryBlock  -------------------------
package MemoryBlock;                                               #(A)

use Devel::Size qw(size);                                          #(B)

sub new {                                                          #(C)
    my ( $class, $id, $size ) = @_;                                #(D)
    my @arr = ();                                                  #(E)
    $#arr = $size - 1;                                             #(F)
    my $block_ref = {                                              #(G)
        id => $id,                                                 #(H)
        size => $size,                                             #(I)
        array_ref => \@arr,                                        #(J)
        };
    bless $block_ref, $class;
    print "MemoryBlock created: " . "{id=" . $block_ref->{id} .    #(K)
        ", array size=" . $block_ref->{size} . "}" .               #(L)
        ", actual size=" . size( \@arr ) . "\n";                   #(M)
    $block_ref;
}
sub get_print_representation {                                     #(N)
    my $block_ref = shift;
    return "{id=" . $block_ref->{id} .
        ", size=" . $block_ref->{size} . "}";
}
```

the SV data structure to which each array element would be pointing. As we mention in the text that follows, the actual size of the structure can be found by invoking `size()` and `total_size()` functions from the module `Devel::Size` and the function `report_size()` from the module `Devel::Size::Report`.

```
sub DESTROY {                                                        #(O)
    my $block_ref = shift;
    print "MemoryBlock about to be destroyed: {id=" .
        $block_ref->{id} .
        ", size=" . $block_ref->{size} . "}" . "\n";
}

#---------------------------- Test Code -----------------------------
package main;

use Devel::Size qw(total_size);                                      #(P)

my @blocks = ();                                                     #(Q)
my $size = 262144;                                                   #(R)

my $i = 0;
while ( $i < 2 ) {                                                   #(S)
    $blocks[$i] = MemoryBlock->new( $i, $size );                     #(T)
    print "The actual size of the MemoryBlock $i is: " .             #(U)
                total_size( $blocks[$i] ). "\n";                     #(V)
    print_blocks(\@blocks);                                          #(W)
    $size *= 2;
    $i++;
}
sub print_blocks {                                                   #(X)
    my $ref_all_blocks = shift;
    print "All blocks: ";
    foreach ( @$ref_all_blocks ) {
        print $_->get_print_representation;
    }
    print "\n\n";
}
```

The output of this script is shown below. Note that the actual size of a `MemoryBlock` instance is roughly four to five times what would be directly indicated by the number of elements in the array contained in each such object.

```
MemoryBlock created: {id=0, array size=262144}, actual size=1048716
The actual size of the MemoryBlock 0 is: 1049047
All blocks: {id=0, size=262144}

MemoryBlock created: {id=1, array size=524288}, actual size=2097292
The actual size of the MemoryBlock 1 is: 2097623
All blocks: {id=0, size=262144}{id=1, size=524288}

MemoryBlock about to be destroyed: {id=1, size=524288}
MemoryBlock about to be destroyed: {id=0, size=262144}
```

12.6 WEAK REFERENCES IN PYTHON

To parallel our discussion of Section 12.5, we will now present an example of circular references in Python. We will then show that what was accomplished by the `Scalar::Util::weaken()` reference-weakening method in Perl is achieved by the `weakref.ref()` method in Python.

In the same manner as the Perl script `CircularRef1.pl`, the Python script presented next, `CircularRef1.py`, defines two classes `X` and `Y`. Class `X` comes with two instance variables: `id` for giving an ID number to each instance of class `X` and `yobj` for holding a reference to an instance of type `Y`. Class `Y` also comes with two instance variables: `id` for holding an identity number and `xobj` for holding a reference to an instance of type `X`. The data attribute `yobj` of an `X` instance is set by `setYfield()` of line (X5) and the data attribute `xobj` of a `Y` instance by `setXfield()` of line (Y5). Each class is also provided with a destructor that would be invoked just prior to garbage collection of the instances of the two classes.[12]

In the test code, we first construct two instance objects, one of type `X` in line (T1) and the other of type `Y` in line (T2). The ID number for both instances is set to 1. Line (T3) sets the `yobj` data attribute of the `X` instance to the `Y` instance. But note that line (T5) sets the data attribute `xobj` of the `Y` instance to a *weak reference* to the `X` instance. This is done by invoking the method

```
weakref.ref()
```

on the `X` instance of line (T1). The data attribute `xobj` of the `Y` instance then stores the weak reference returned by this method. Calling `weakref.ref()` in this manner ensures that the reference count associated with the argument object, the one to which the variable `x` points, is not incremented. So whereas the assignment in line (T3) increments the reference count associated with the `Y` instance, the assignment in line (T5) leaves unaltered the reference count associated with the `X` instance.

The fact that the data attribute `yobj` of the `X` instance is holding a reference to a `Y` instance and that the data attribute `xobj` of the `Y` instance is holding a *weak* reference to the `X` instance is confirmed by the print statements in lines (T6) and (T7). Line (T8) demonstrates that when you *evaluate* a weak reference through a function call, as we do by calling `xobj()` in `print y.xobj()`, what we get back is the actual object for which a weak reference was created by a call to `weakref.ref()`.

---

[12]Python gives users some control over the actual freeing up of the memory occupied by the *deallocated* objects. (Obviously, after an object is deallocated, you will not be able to access it even if the memory occupied by the object has not yet been reclaimed.) This is done through the gc module; you can invoke the garbage collector by calling `gc.collect()`. Python has its own special way of dealing with container objects. Such objects are placed in an internal list when first allocated and taken off this list when deallocated (because the reference count associated with them goes to zero). Getting deallocated in this manner does not mean that the memory associated with them is immediately freed up. The garbage collector is called upon to free up the memory associated with such objects when the number of allocations exceeds the number of deallocations by a certain user-selectable threshold.

Unlike what was the case with the weak references in Perl, if you want to access the attributes of the original referent of a weak reference in Python, you must first evaluate the weak reference to gain access to that object.[13] This is demonstrated by the statements in lines (T9) through (T13). Retrieving the `id` attribute of the `X` and `Y` instances in lines (T9) and (T10) yields what you would expect. However, when you try to retrieve the same attribute through the references held by the data attributes `xobj` and `yobj` in line (T11) and the commented-out line (T12), it works for the strong reference held by the former, but not for the weak reference held by the latter. Python throws an exception if you uncomment the commented-out statement in line (T12). That is because the actual referent of `yobj` is an object of type `weakref` and this class does not possess an instance variable named `id`. In order to retrieve the attributes of the original object whose reference was weakened by calling `weakref.ref()`, you must evaluate the weak reference, as we do in the successful call in line (T13).

```
#!/usr/bin/env python

### CircularRef1.py

import weakref                                                          #(A)

#--------------------------  class X  -------------------------------
class X:                                                                #(X1)
    def __init__( self, id ):                                           #(X2)
        print "Creating X object: id = " + str(id)                      #(X3)
        self.id = id                                                    #(X4)
    def setYfield( self, yobj ):                                        #(X5)
        self.yobj = yobj                                                #(X6)
    def __del__( self ):                                                #(X7)
        print "X obj will be destroyed: id = " + str(self.id)           #(X8)

#--------------------------  class Y  -------------------------------
class Y:                                                                #(Y1)
    def __init__( self, id ):                                           #(Y2)
        print "Creating Y object: id = " + str(id)                      #(Y3)
        self.id = id                                                    #(Y4)
    def setXfield( self, xobj ):                                        #(Y5)
        self.xobj = xobj                                                #(Y6)
    def __del__( self ):                                                #(Y7)
        print "Y obj will be destroyed: id = " + str(self.id)           #(Y8)
```

[13]The reader has probably already suspected that this would be the case from the difference in what is returned by the calls `y.xobj` and `y.xobj()` in lines (T7) and (T8).

```
#--------------------------  Test Code  --------------------------------
x = X(1)                   # Creating X object: id = 1             #(T1)
y = Y(1)                   # Creating Y object: id = 1             #(T2)
x.setYfield( y )                                                   #(T3)
#y.setXfield( x  )                                                 #(T4)
y.setXfield( weakref.ref( x ) )                                    #(T5)

print x.yobj               # <__main__.Y instance at 0x401f9d6c>   #(T6)
print y.xobj                                                       #(T7)
                   # <weakref at 0x401f0c0c; to 'instance' at 0x401f16ec>
print y.xobj()             # <__main__.X instance at 0x401f16ec>   #(T8)

print x.id                 # 1                                     #(T9)
print y.id                 # 1                                    #(T10)
print  x.yobj.id           # 1                                    #(T11)
#print y.xobj.id           # ERROR                                #(T12)
print y.xobj().id          # 1                                    #(T13)

x = None                                                          #(T14)
y = None                                                          #(T15)

while(1): pass                                                    #(T16)
```

When we execute the above script, the output is

```
Creating X object: id = 1
Creating Y object: id = 1
 <__main__.Y instance at 0x401f3d4c>
 <weakref at 0x401f0c0c; to 'instance' at 0x401f16ec>
 <__main__.X instance at 0x401f16ec>
 1
 1
 1
 1
 X obj will be destroyed: id = 1
 Y obj will be destroyed: id = 1
```

Except for the last two lines above, we have already explained what produces this output. Focusing now on the last two lines of the output, these show that both the X and the Y instances of lines (T1) and (T2) are being deallocated when we null the references held by the variables x and y in lines (T14) and (T15). So the script as shown does *not* suffer from the circular reference problem.

If we wanted to, we could create the circular reference problem in the above script by commenting out line (T5) and using instead the statement in line (T4). But now we must also comment out line (T13) and use instead the statement in line (T12). In addition, we must also comment out line (T8). With these three changes, the output of the script is

```
Creating X object: id = 1
Creating Y object: id = 1
<__main__.Y instance at 0x401f3d4c>
<__main__.X instance at 0x401f16ec>
1
1
1
1
```

Since the destructors for the instance objects of lines (T1) and (T2) are never called despite the fact that we null the references held by the variables `x` and `y` in lines (T14) and (T15), it is clear that we have a memory leak in the script.

The script shown next, `CircularRef2.py`, is the Python version of the Perl script `CircularRef2.pl`. This script creates a large number of circular references to demonstrate memory leaks at a larger level. The classes `X` and `Y` used in the script are the same as in the previous Python script. However, the test code now constructs inside a `while` loop in lines (T3) through (T9) a large number of instance pairs that circularly refer to each other. Through line (T6), the `X` instance created during that iteration holds a strong reference to the `Y` instance created in the same iteration. However, through line (T7), the `Y` instance holds only a weak reference to the `X` instance. At the end of the `while` block, both the `X` and the `Y` instances go out of scope. The output produced by the test code is

```
Creating X object: id = 0
Creating Y object: id = 0
Creating X object: id = 1
X obj will be destroyed: id = 0
Creating Y object: id = 1
Y obj will be destroyed: id = 0
Creating X object: id = 2
X obj will be destroyed: id = 1
Creating Y object: id = 2
Y obj will be destroyed: id = 1
....
DONE WITH THE WHILE LOOP
....
X obj will be destroyed: id = 2
Y obj will be destroyed: id = 2
```

However, if we were to use the strong reference in the commented-out line (T7) instead of the weak reference in line (T8), the output produced would be

```
Creating X object: id = 0
Creating Y object: id = 0
Creating X object: id = 1
Creating Y object: id = 1
Creating X object: id = 2
Creating Y object: id = 2
....

DONE WITH THE WHILE LOOP
```

which shows there is no object destruction taking place despite the fact the two constructed instance objects inside the `while` loop of lines (T3) through (T9) are going out of scope at the end of each iteration.

In order to keep the output produced to a manageable size (and to not have to wait for all of the iterations to end), the two outputs shown above were produced by going through only three iterations of the `while` loop of lines (T3) through (T9).

```
#!/usr/local/bin/python

### CircularRef2.py

import weakref                                                          #(A)

#-------------------------  class X  ------------------------------
class X:                                                                #(X1)
    def __init__( self, id ):                                           #(X2)
        print "Creating X object: id = " + str(id)                     #(X3)
        self.id = id                                                    #(X4)
    def setYfield( self, yobj ):                                        #(X5)
        self.yobj = yobj                                                #(X6)
    def __del__( self ):                                                #(X7)
        print "X obj will be destroyed: id = " + str(self.id)          #(X8)

#-------------------------  class Y  ------------------------------
class Y:                                                                #(Y1)
    def __init__( self, id ):                                           #(Y2)
        print "Creating Y object: id = " + str(id)                     #(Y3)
        self.id = id                                                    #(Y4)
    def setXfield( self, xobj ):                                        #(Y5)
        self.xobj = xobj                                                #(Y6)
    def __del__( self ):                                                #(Y7)
        print "Y obj will be destroyed: id = " + str(self.id)          #(Y8)
```

```
#-------------------------- Test Code --------------------------------
i = 0;                                                        #(T1)
#while (i < 3):                                               #(T2)
while (i < 100000):                                           #(T3)
    x = X(i)                                                  #(T4)
    y = Y(i)                                                  #(T5)
    x.setYfield( y )                                          #(T6)
#     y.setXfield( x )                                        #(T7)
    y.setXfield( weakref.ref( x ) )                           #(T8)
    i = i+1                                                   #(T9)

print "\n\nDONE WITH THE WHILE LOOP\n\n";                     #(T10)
```

12.6.1 Can Python's Weak References Be Used for In-Memory Caching?

We will now show that because the basic mechanism for garbage collection in Python is the same as in Perl — reference counting — it is not possible to use Python's weak references for in-memory caching, just as was the case with Perl. To remind the reader, a cooperative garbage collector will let an object pointed to by a weak reference live as long as there is no pressure on the memory. But when the main criterion for memory deallocation is the reference count going down to zero, it is difficult to exploit weak references for in-memory caching.

As we did with Perl, we will give this demonstration with the help of the following two scripts. In the first script, `MemoryTest.py`, all we will do is to construct ever larger objects until hitting the memory limits of the system.[14] Subsequently, in a second script, `MemoryTestWithWeakRef.py`, we will only store the weak references to the larger and larger objects. But, since a weak reference does not add to the reference count of the referent, the objects constructed will be immediately deallocated. Thus caching of such objects would not be possible.

Shown below is the first of the two scripts. Lines (A) through (J) define a class `MemoryBlock`. The sole reason for this class is that its instances can be made to occupy large amounts of memory. This is accomplished with the help of the instance variable `arr` whose value is set in line (E) as follows:

```
self.arr = [None] * size
```

[14]As with Perl, these memory constraints are imposed by the underlying operating system. If the operating system permits the use of virtual memory, the sizes of the objects constructed could exceed the size of the fast memory available to the process in which the script is being executed. If the system has to resort to virtual memory, its run-time performance for very large objects will take a big hit due to page swapping.

where the operator `*` returns a list containing `size` number of elements, each element being the null object `None`.[15] We endow the `MemoryBlock` class with a `get_print_representation()` method in line (G) so that we can identify an instance of this type in the memory, and with a `__del__()` method in line (I) that would be automatically invoked just before the memory occupied by a `MemoryBlock` instance is deallocated.

In the test code, in lines (R) through (V) of the `while` loop, we insert references to increasingly larger `MemoryBlock` instances into the continuously expanding list `blocks`.

```
#!/usr/bin/env python

### MemoryTest.py

#------------------------  class MemoryBlock  -------------------------
class MemoryBlock:                                                  #(A)
    def __init__( self, id, size ):                                 #(B)
        self.id = id                                                #(C)
        self.size = size                                            #(D)
        self.arr = [None] * size                                    #(E)

        print "MemoryBlock created: " + "{id=" + str(self.id) + \
                     ", size=" + str(self.size) + "}"               #(F)

    def get_print_representation( self ):                           #(G)
        return "{id=" + str(self.id)  + ", size=" + str(self.size) + "}"
                                                                    #(H)
    def __del__( self ):                                            #(I)
        print "MemoryBlock about to be destroyed: {id=" + \
            str(self.id) + ", size=" + str(self.size) + "}"         #(J)

#---------------------------  Test Code  ------------------------------
blocks = []                                                         #(K)
size = 262144                                                       #(L)

def print_blocks( all_blocks ):                                     #(M)
    print "All blocks: ";                                           #(N)
    for block in all_blocks:                                        #(O)
        print block.get_print_representation()                      #(P)
    print "\n"
```

[15]As mentioned in Chapter 3, this is a convenient way to preallocate memory for a list if you know the size of the list in advance. See the Homework section of that chapter for a debatable comparison of time efficiencies of preallocation vis-à-vis letting a list grow dynamically on an as-needed basis.

```
i = 0                                                              #(Q)
while ( 1 ):                                                       #(R)
    blocks.insert(i, MemoryBlock( i, size ))                       #(S)
    print_blocks(blocks)                                           #(T)
    size *= 2                                                      #(U)
    i = i + 1                                                      #(V)
```

If you run this script, the output will be along the following lines:

```
MemoryBlock created: {id=0, size=262144}
All blocks:
{id=0, size=262144}

MemoryBlock created: {id=1, size=524288}
All blocks:
{id=0, size=262144}
{id=1, size=524288}

MemoryBlock created: {id=2, size=1048576}
All blocks:
{id=0, size=262144}
{id=1, size=524288}
{id=2, size=1048576}

MemoryBlock created: {id=3, size=2097152}
All blocks:
{id=0, size=262144}
{id=1, size=524288}
{id=2, size=1048576}
{id=3, size=2097152}

....
```

We have shown the output only partially. The script will continue to construct larger and larger objects until the memory limit set by the operating-system is reached.

Now let's consider the following version of the above script. It is the same script as before, except that now in line (U) we store weak references in the list `blocks`.

```
#!/usr/bin/env python

### MemoryTestWithWeakRef.py

import weakref                                                     #(A)
```

```
#------------------------  class MemoryBlock  -------------------------
class MemoryBlock:                                                  #(B)
    def __init__( self, id, size ):                                 #(C)
        self.id = id                                                #(D)
        self.size = size                                            #(E)
        self.arr = [None] * size                                    #(F)

        print "MemoryBlock created: " + "{id=" + str(self.id) + \
                    ", size=" + str(self.size) + "}"                #(G)

    def get_print_representation( self ):                           #(H)
        return "{id=" + str(self.id)  + ", size=" + str(self.size) + "}"
                                                                    #(I)
    def __del__( self ):                                            #(J)
        print "MemoryBlock about to be destroyed: {id=" + \
            str(self.id) + ", size=" + str(self.size) + "}"         #(K)

#----------------------------  Test Code  -----------------------------
blocks = []                                                         #(L)
size = 262144                                                       #(M)

def print_blocks( all_blocks ):                                     #(N)
    print "All blocks: ";                                           #(O)
    for block in all_blocks:                                        #(P)
        if ( block() != None ):                                     #(Q)
            print block().get_print_representation()                #(R)
    print "\n"

i = 0                                                               #(S)
while ( 1 ):                                                        #(T)
    new_block = weakref.ref(MemoryBlock( i, size ))                 #(U)
    blocks.insert(i, new_block )                                    #(V)
    print_blocks(blocks)                                            #(W)
    size *= 2                                                       #(X)
    i = i + 1                                                       #(Y)
```

The output of this script is shown below. It is clear that the new `MemoryBlock` instance constructed in line (U) is immediately deallocated as soon as it goes out of scope at the end of the `while` block. That is because the `new_block` variable inside the `while` block only has a weak reference to the new instance. The reference count associated with the instance stays at zero, ensuring its immediate deallocation at the end of the block.

```
MemoryBlock created: {id=0, size=262144}
MemoryBlock about to be destroyed: {id=0, size=262144}
All blocks:
```

```
MemoryBlock created: {id=1, size=524288}
MemoryBlock about to be destroyed: {id=1, size=524288}
All blocks:

MemoryBlock created: {id=2, size=1048576}
MemoryBlock about to be destroyed: {id=2, size=1048576}
All blocks:

MemoryBlock created: {id=3, size=2097152}
MemoryBlock about to be destroyed: {id=3, size=2097152}
All blocks:

MemoryBlock created: {id=4, size=4194304}
MemoryBlock about to be destroyed: {id=4, size=4194304}
All blocks:

MemoryBlock created: {id=5, size=8388608}
MemoryBlock about to be destroyed: {id=5, size=8388608}
All blocks:

....
```

12.7 CREDITS AND SUGGESTIONS FOR FURTHER READING

For a comprehensive book on automatic memory management, the reader is referred to the work by Richard Jones and Rafael Lins [39]. Richard Jones also maintains a web page devoted to garbage collection issues [38], including a page with links to practically everything that has ever been published on memory management issues [37]. For a quick read on some of the modern trends in garbage collection, the reader is referred to the articles by Goetz [24], Gottry [25], Holling [28], and Gillam [22]. Goetz in particular lists eight criteria for evaluating a garbage collector. The brief overview on memory management and garbage collection presented in Section 12.1 is based on these articles. About the material presented in the rest of this chapter, the `MemoryBlock` class and the `MemoryTest` scripts shown are patterned after code examples provided by Alexandre Pereira Calsavara at `Builder.com` for a couple of studies on how to use Java's `WeakReference` and `SoftReference` classes for in-memory caching.

12.8 HOMEWORK

1. In the network example presented in Section 6.4.1 of Chapter 6, we had to take special care to eliminate memory leakage that could potentially be caused by circular references when the nodes of the network refer to one another. Rework that code using weak references to keep the circular reference problem from rearing its ugly head.

2. Problem 4 in the Homework section of Chapter 7 called for creating a Python implementation of the network code shown in Section 6.4.1 of Chapter 6. Rework your Python implementation using weak references to eliminate the problem of circular references.

13

Scripting for Graphical User Interfaces

Tk is a commonly used toolkit for creating graphical user interfaces (GUI) with Perl and Python. It was originally developed by Ousterhout to be driven by the *Tool Command Language* (Tcl). However, over the years, Perl and Python wrappers have been written for Tk. More precisely, the commonly used Perl wrapper is written for pTk, a portable version of Tk.[1] The combination of the Perl wrapper and the pTk toolkit is referred to as Perl/Tk. With regard to Python, the standard wrapper for Tk is known as Tkinter, an abbreviation of *Tk interface*. Tkinter, which comes with the language distribution, uses the original Tk framework directly and does not rely on pTk. The Perl module file for Perl/Tk is `Tk.pm`. The Python module file that provides the same functionality is `Tkinter.py`. This chapter provides an introduction to these modules.

13.1 THE WIDGET LIBRARIES

A widget is usually a graphical component, such as a button or a scrollbar. As with all GUI toolkits, the widget libraries of Perl/Tk and Python's Tkinter can be categorized in the following fashion:

[1] The original version of Tk came with some embedded Tcl. To make a direct connection between a scripting language like Perl and the Tk toolkit, Nick Ing-Simmons got rid of the embedded Tcl to create pTk.

Top-Level Containers: When you create a new graphical application, the top-level window for the application is one of these container widgets. A top-level container widget holds intermediate-level container widgets or atomic widgets. Perl/Tk's top-level container widgets are `MainWindow` and `Toplevel`. Both `MainWindow` and `Toplevel` create visible windows on a terminal screen.[2]

In Python, Tkinter's top-level widget is `Toplevel`. As with Perl/Tk, a Tkinter application is allowed to display multiple GUI windows simultaneously on a terminal screen, each corresponding to a different `Toplevel`.

A widget containing other widgets gives rise to the notion of a *containment hierarchy*. In a containment hierarchy, a widget is allowed to have multiple children, but at most a single parent. A Perl/Tk containment hierarchy is rooted at a `MainWindow` widget. A script is allowed to create multiple `MainWindow` widgets, each serving as the root of its own containment hierarchy. A `Toplevel`, if used, resides in the containment hierarchy of a `MainWindow`. If a `MainWindow` contains multiple `Toplevels`, each can be manipulated independently.[3]

On the other hand, in Python, a containment hierarchy is rooted at a `Toplevel` widget. Python does not directly support a widget called `MainWindow`. But that does not take anything away from Tkinter because whatever can be accomplished with a `MainWindow` in Perl/Tk is accomplished with a `Toplevel` in Tkinter. If your GUI displays multiple `Toplevel` windows in Python, it is possible to manipulate each of them independently.

Intermediate-Level Containers: Intermediate-level containers are often not directly visible but are nonetheless useful for organizing the visual layout of graphical objects they hold, especially in relation to the graphical objects in the same containment hierarchy. The intermediate-level container in both Perl/Tk and Tkinter is `Frame`.

Atomic Widgets: These self-contained graphical components are held by top-level and intermediate-level widgets. Examples of these are: `Button`, `Checkbutton`, `Listbox`, and so on.

---

[2]The `MainWindow` widget is identical to the `Toplevel` widget in all but one respect: It is the containment hierarchy rooted at a `MainWindow` that is made visible by running the event processing loop, `MainLoop`. Obviously, if the containment hierarchy contains one or more `Toplevels`, those too will become visible. However, a `Toplevel` may be manipulated independently of other `Toplevels` or the `MainWindows` in a script. For example, you can independently close a `Toplevel` (by clicking on the system-supplied button labeled "X" that is usually at the upper right-hand corner of an application window) without affecting the other `Toplevel` or the `MainWindow` widgets. A `Dialog` window will usually be a `Toplevel` widget within the same `MainWindow` widget.

[3]By manipulation we mean subjecting a graphical component to various forms of user interaction. The user may, for example, close the component or move it on the screen.

Utilities: Both Perl/Tk and Tkinter provide utility classes for handling such important matters as providing control over the physical layout of a GUI, for controlling the look and feel, for specifying fonts and colors, and so on.

13.2 MINIMALIST GUI SCRIPTS

We will now show some elementary scripts in Perl and Python for constructing GUI windows on a terminal screen. The goal here is to present some of the most basic method calls that go into writing GUI scripts.

13.2.1 Some Minimalist Perl/Tk Scripts

The following simple example shows the three essential things that must hold true in any nontrivial Perl/Tk script: First, you must create a top-level window, a `MainWindow`, to house the atomic and intermediate widgets of the GUI. Next, you must place one or more atomic and/or intermediate widgets in the top-level window. Finally, you must park the flow of control in the event processing loop. As we will explain later, the event processing loop waits for the user to interact with the GUI and, in response to each input from the user, invokes a *callback function*. In the script shown next, `FirstWindow.pl`, the needed top-level window is created in line (B). The statement in lines (G) through (K) creates a new widget that is then placed in the top-level window by the statement in lines (L) through (N). Finally, the event processing loop is started by calling `MainLoop` in line (O).

To explain the script in greater detail, line (A) imports `Tk`, the main Perl/Tk module. Line (B) is a call to `MainWindow`'s constructor. Line (C) sets the title of the main window; this title will show up in the upper border of the window. If you don't set the title as in line (C), Perl/Tk will set it by default to the name of the file containing the GUI code. In line (D), we set the size of the top-level window and its position relative to the upper left-hand corner of the screen. Note the syntax used for the argument to the `geometry()` method:[4]

```
"200x150+50+100"
```

---

[4]The argument supplied to the `geometry()` is referred to as the *geometry string*. It must conform to the following regular expression:

```
^=?(\d+x\d+)?([+-]\d+[+-]\d+)?$
```

where the first `\d+` corresponds to the width and the second `\d+` to the height, both in pixels by default, but in grid units for gridded windows. The third `\d+` is for the x-coordinate of the upper left corner of the GUI window and the last for the y-coordinate, both in pixels. The negative choices for the positional coordinates create displacements with respect to the bottom right corner of the screen. Note that the size specification is optional, as is the location specification.

The first two numbers that are separated by x, 200 and 150, are the width and height of the window in pixels. Next comes the separator symbol + followed by two more numbers, also separated by +. These last two numbers, 50 and 100, are the horizontal and the vertical offsets for the upper left-hand corner of the window in relation to the upper left-hand corner of the screen. Lines (E) and (F) prescribe the maximum and the minimum limits on the window size should the user try to resize it manually by dragging one of its corners with the mouse cursor.

Lines (G) through (K) create a `Label` object. A `Label` is for displaying a piece of textual information that can occupy multiple lines of text. A label can also display a bitmap. The call to the `Label` constructor shown is presented with only a very small number of all the allowable options for this widget. The `text` option sets the textual information that will be displayed in the label. The `anchor` option sets the position of the text within the label. The value `s` for this option stands for `south`; it will cause the displayed text to stick to the bottom edge of the label. The default for this option is to display the text in the center of the label. The `relief` option controls how the label will appear vis-à-vis its background; the visual effect is achieved by shading the boundary pixels. The various choices here are `flat`, `groove`, `raised`, `ridge`, and `sunken`. The options `width` and `height` in lines (J) and (K) control the size of the label; we want the label to be 10 characters wide and 3 lines high.

In line (L) we then invoke the `pack()` *geometry manager*. A geometry manager's job is to position a widget inside the enclosing widget — in this case, to position the label inside the main window. As will be explained in greater detail in Section 13.3, the `pack()` geometry manager recognizes four positions inside the container widget: `left`, `right`, `top`, and `bottom`. The `side` option in line (L) will cause the label to stick to the top edge of the main window.[5] The options in lines (M) and (N) tell the pack geometry manager how to position the label within the space allocated to it. The pack geometry manager assigns an *allocation rectangle* to each widget it needs to place in the container. Subsequently, it uses a set of parameters to position the widget itself in its allocated space. The options `padx` and `pady` determine the amount of spacing between edges of the allocation rectangle and the actual widget itself. So with `pady` set to 5 pixels, as in line (N), there will have to exist a vertical spacing of at least 5 pixels between the top of the label widget and the edge of the top-level window.[6]

The last line of the script, line (O), calls `MainLoop`. This first causes the GUI to be drawn on the screen and it then initiates the event processing loop. Any Perl code after that statement will not be executed as long as any of the `MainWindow` widgets is still visible on the screen. It is only after all the `MainWindow` widgets are closed, either by the user clicking on the system-supplied window closing button or

[5] Actually, the `side` option controls the position of the *allocation rectangle* inside the containing widget.

[6] As mentioned earlier, the x-coordinate is oriented horizontally from left to right and the y-coordinate vertically from top to bottom, the origin being at the upper left-hand corner of the screen. So `padx` expresses the buffer spacing in the horizontal direction and `pady` in the vertical direction.

programmatically by a call to `destroy()`, that the flow of execution can go past the call to `MainLoop`. Therefore, if there is a need to carry out any cleanup operations with regard to the system resources appropriated earlier in the script, you would want to place them after the call to `MainLoop`.

```
#!/usr/bin/perl -w

### FirstWindow.pl

use strict;
use Tk;                                                                       #(A)

my $mw = MainWindow->new();                                                   #(B)
$mw->title( "My First Window" );                                              #(C)
$mw->geometry( "200x150+50+100" );                                            #(D)
$mw->maxsize( 400, 500 );                                                     #(E)
$mw->minsize( 100, 200 );                                                     #(F)

my $label = $mw->Label( -text     =>    'hello',                              #(G)
                        -anchor   =>    's',                                  #(H)
                        -relief   =>    'groove',                             #(I)
                        -width    =>    10,                                   #(J)
                        -height   =>    3,                                    #(K)
                      );
$label->pack( -side => 'top',                                                 #(L)
              -padx => 10,                                                    #(M)
              -pady => 5 );                                                   #(N)

MainLoop();                                                                   #(O)
```

The GUI produced by this script is shown in Fig. 13.1.

That it is possible to have multiple `MainWindow` widgets in a GUI is illustrated by the following script. This script creates two main windows, the first in lines (A) and (B), and the second in lines (C) and (D). They are both of the same size, but are positioned at two different locations on the screen. This script also shows us using the `Button` widget. As far as the options are concerned, the `Button` widget is very similar to the `Label` widget, except for the additional `command` option shown in lines

Fig. 13.1

(G) and (K). This option points to a function — referred to as a *callback* — that will be invoked automatically by the system when the user clicks on the button.[7] [8]

```
#!/usr/bin/perl -w
use strict;

### TwoMainWindows.pl

use Tk;

my $mw1 = MainWindow->new( -title => "First Window" );                #(A)
$mw1->geometry( "200x150+50+100" );                                    #(B)

my $mw2 = MainWindow->new( -title => "Second Window" );               #(C)
$mw2->geometry( "200x150+300+150" );                                   #(D)
```

[7]Such a function is known as a *callback* because its invocation is not a part of the normal flow of execution for a computer program. The invocation of such a function is directly controlled by the operating system, usually in response to the interrupts generated by a user interacting with the GUI. For example, a user clicking on a mouse button produces an interrupt that eventually gets translated into a signal to the operating system. An operating system is provided with default handlers for all signals, but your script is allowed to supply override definitions for the handlers in the form of callbacks.

[8]We should also mention that, by default, the button behavior specified through the `command` option applies only to what is referred to as *button 1* on a multibuttoned mouse. More specifically, the behavior is meant for the *release* of button 1, as opposed to the *pressing* or the *clicking* of this button. As an alternative to the `command` option, one can also specify a callback directly by defining a binding between the button action and the callback using the syntax:

```
$button->bind( '<ButtonRelease-1>' => name_of_the_callback );
```

Obviously, using the `command` option in the button constructor makes for more convenient syntax.

```
$mw1->Button(                                                    #(E)
             text => 'Click Here',                               #(F)
             command => sub {print "Hello From First Window\n";}  #(G)
            )->pack();                                           #(H)

$mw2->Button(                                                    #(I)
             text => 'Click Here Also',                          #(J)
             command => sub {print "Hello From Second Window\n";} #(K)
            )->pack();                                           #(L)

MainLoop();                                                      #(M)
```

The GUI produced by this script consists of two windows, each like the one shown in Fig. 13.1. When you click on the buttons in the respective windows, you will see the messages of lines (G) and (K) printed out in the terminal window in which the script `TwoMainWindows.pl` is executed. If you close one of the main windows by clicking on the system-supplied close button, the other window will continue to function.

The reader will notice in lines (H) and (L) that we call `pack()` directly on the `Button` objects returned by the constructor calls in lines (E) and (I). This makes it unnecessary to declare variables with names like `$button1` and `$button2` that we would have needed otherwise. Recall how we used the variable `$label` in the script `FirstWindow.pl`. This variable stored a reference to the `Label` object that was created in line (G) of that script; subsequently we invoked the geometry manager `pack()` on the reference in line (L) of that script.

We will now show that a GUI identical to the above can be constructed with one `MainWindow` widget and one `Toplevel` widget. The `TwoMainWindows.pl` script created two containment hierarchies, each rooted in a separate `MainWindow` widget. The script shown next, `MainAndToplevel.pl`, creates a single containment hierarchy that is rooted in the single `MainWindow` created in the script in line (A). In line (C), we construct another top-level window, but this time using the constructor for `Toplevel`. As far as the look and feel is concerned, this `Toplevel` widget is same as the second `MainWindow` widget of `TwoMainWindows.pl`, but this time it is subservient to the `MainWindow` widget of line (A). This fact can be demonstrated by clicking on the system-supplied "close" button for the `MainWindow` widget and seeing the entire GUI disappear from the screen. By comparison, closing either of the two main windows created by `TwoMainWindows.pl` does not affect the other.

```
#!/usr/bin/perl -w
use strict;

### MainAndToplevel.pl

use Tk;

my $mw = MainWindow->new( -title => "First Window" );                #(A)
$mw->geometry( "200x150+50+100" );                                   #(B)

my $top = $mw->Toplevel( -title => "Second Window" );                #(C)
$top->geometry( "200x150+300+150" );                                 #(D)

$mw->Button(                                                         #(E)
            text => 'Click Here',                                    #(F)
            command => sub {print "Hello From First Window\n";}      #(G)
          )->pack();                                                 #(H)

$top->Button(                                                        #(I)
             text => 'Click Here Also',                              #(J)
             command => sub {print "Hello From Second Window\n";}    #(K)
           )->pack();                                                #(L)

MainLoop();                                                          #(M)
```

13.2.2 Some Minimalist Tkinter Scripts

Using Tkinter, we will now present Python's versions of the scripts shown in the previous subsection. We start with the script FirstWindow.py shown next. In line (A), we import all the names that are exported by the Tkinter module. Line (B) constructs a Toplevel window; this will be the *root window* for this GUI. Lines (C) through (F) set the various attributes of the top-level window using syntax that is essentially identical to what we used in lines (C) through (F) of the Perl script FirstWindow.pl. See the explanation there for the size and location syntax used in line (D).

Lines (G) through (L) create a Label object. The main difference between the Python syntax here and the Perl syntax in FirstWindow.pl is how the parent-child containment relationship is expressed in the two cases. In Tkinter, the top-level window is the parent for the Label widget because the former is the first argument to the latter's constructor. The rest of the syntax shown for the Label constructor, for anchoring the text inside the label, for setting width and the height of the label, and so on, is similar to what we showed earlier for Perl/Tk. Recall from the Perl/Tk case that the `relief` option specifies how the label will appear vis-à-vis its background, the effect achieved by appropriately shading the boundary pixels.

In exactly the same manner as the Perl/Tk example shown earlier, in line (M) we then invoke the `pack()` geometry manager. As the reader already knows, a geometry manager's job is to position a widget inside the enclosing widget — in this case, position the label inside the main window. The options shown work in exactly the same manner as explained earlier. The last line of the script, line (P), calls `mainloop()`. As with Perl/Tk, this first causes the GUI to be drawn on the screen and then initiates the event processing loop. The flow of control stays parked in this loop as long as any of the windows created by the GUI program is still on the screen. When all the windows are closed, the flow of control can go past the call to `mainloop()`.

```
#!/usr/bin/env python

###  FirstWindow.py

from Tkinter import *                                              #(A)

mw = Tk()                                                          #(B)
mw.title( "My First Window" )                                      #(C)
mw.geometry( "200x150+50+100" );                                   #(D)
mw.maxsize(400, 500)                                               #(E)
mw.minsize(100, 200)                                               #(F)

label = Label( mw,                                                 #(G)
               text="hello",                                       #(H)
               anchor  = 's',                                      #(I)
               relief  = 'groove',                                 #(J)
               width  = 10,                                        #(K)
               height = 3  )                                       #(L)

label.pack( side = 'top',                                          #(M)
            padx = 10,                                             #(N)
            pady = 5 )                                             #(O)

mainloop()                                                         #(P)
```

The next script, `TwoMainWindows.py`, demonstrates that one can create multiple `Toplevel` windows in the same script. The two top-level windows created in the script serve as the root objects for the two *independent* containment hierarchies in the GUI, as was the case with the two `MainWidget` windows for the Perl/Tk example in `TwoMainWindows.pl`. That the two containment hierarchies are independent can be demonstrated by closing either GUI window (by, say, clicking on the system-supplied "X" button at the upper right hand corner of one of the windows) and noticing that the other continues to operate as before. Each top-level window contains a Button widget. Each button has its own callback function, as supplied through the command option in lines (L) and (P). The callbacks are defined in lines (H) and (I). As mentioned in the previous subsection, the applicable callback is invoked automatically by the operating system when a user clicks the GUI button in either of the windows.

Also note that unlike the previous Python script, we now invoke the layout manager pack() directly on the Button object returned by the constructor calls in lines (J) and (N). This makes it unnecessary to declare separate variables for each of the buttons. As was the case with the label widget in the previous example, each button is placed in its container widget through the first argument supplied to the constructor.

```
#!/usr/bin/env python

###  TwoMainWindows.py

from Tkinter import *                                                  #(A)

mw1 = Tk()                                                             #(B)
mw1.title( "First Window" )                                            #(C)
mw1.geometry( "200x150+50+100" );                                      #(D)

mw2 = Tk()                                                             #(E)
mw2.title( "First Window" )                                            #(F)
mw2.geometry( "200x150+300+150" );                                     #(G)

def but1print(): print "hello from button 1"                           #(H)
def but2print(): print "hello from button 2"                           #(I)

Button( mw1,                                                           #(J)
        text = 'Click Here',                                           #(K)
        command = but1print                                            #(L)
      ).pack()                                                         #(M)

Button( mw2,                                                           #(N)
        text = 'Click Here',                                           #(O)
        command = but2print                                            #(P)
      ).pack()                                                         #(Q)

mainloop()                                                             #(R)
```

13.3 GEOMETRY MANAGERS FOR AUTOMATIC LAYOUT

All modern GUI systems allow a programmer to specify where to place a widget generally[9] in the GUI window. It then becomes the job of the GUI geometry manager to carry out the needed geometric calculations and to place the widgets accordingly. This is the most efficient way to program up a GUI if the number of widgets is small and if there is some easily describable symmetry to the placement of the widgets. This approach also ensures that the GUI will retain its overall look and feel as the user changes the size of the top-level window to suit his/her convenience. In addition to the geometry managers, the GUI systems also provide functions for placing the widgets at specific coordinates in relation to a reference point in the top-level window. In this section, we will look at Tk's geometry managers `pack()` and `grid()` that are made available by both Perl/Tk and Tkinter for automatic placement of widgets in a container.

The scripts of this section will also be used to point to some interesting differences between Perl/Tk and Python's Tkinter that are not about layout control. For example, the preferred way to construct a scrollable widget in Perl/Tk is by calling the `Scrolled` constructor with its first argument set to the name of the widget that needs to be equipped with a scrollbar. On the other hand, the preferred way to construct a scrollable widget in Python is to treat a scrollbar as an independent component that is placed alongside the widget that needs to be scrolled in a `Frame`. Another important difference relates to how text is inserted at initialization into an `Entry` widget that is used for displaying one-liners and for eliciting one-line responses from a user. Perl/Tk uses the `textvariable` option for the initial text to be displayed. On the other hand, Python's Tkinter calls on the `insert()` method for the job.

13.3.1 Automatic Layout in Perl/Tk

Perl/Tk comes with four geometry managers, also known as layout managers, for automatically controlling the layout of the widgets in a containment hierarchy. These are `pack`, `grid`, `form`, and `place`. Of these `pack` and `grid` are the most frequently used; both these will be demonstrated in this section with examples. Of the remaining two, the `place` geometry manager is useful for fine-grained manual control over the positioning of the widgets at specific coordinates. The `form` geometry manager works like a combination of `pack` and `place`.

[9] An example of a general placement would be a programmer telling the GUI framework to place a button at the bottom of the GUI. It then becomes the job of the GUI framework to figure out what the "bottom of the GUI" means. Note that "bottom of the GUI" is not necessarily a single fixed point on the terminal screen, especially if you allow the user to resize the window at his/her will and the programmer wants the button to always show up at the same place in relation to the rest of the GUI.

As mentioned earlier, the pack geometry manager recognizes the following four positions in the container widget: top, bottom, left, and right. For example, when pack() is called on a widget with the side option set to top, the widget is assigned an allocation rectangle against the top edge of the container. The exact position of the widget within its allocation area is then controlled by the various options used in the call to pack().

The script shown next, PackGeom.pl, places a different widget against each of the four sides of the main GUI window. Lines (E) through (I) create a Button widget and line (J) asks the pack geometry manager to place the allocation rectangle for the button against the top side of the main window. Line (K) defines the subroutine that serves as a callback in line (I) for the button widget.

Lines (M), (N), and (O) create an Entry widget and, at the same time, request the pack geometry manager to place it against the bottom edge of the main window.[10] The textvariable option in line (M) serves two purposes simultaneously: It can be used to place some initial information in the Entry widget and it can also be used to fetch the text string entered there by the user. The value given to the textvariable option in line (M) places in the Entry widget the information string that is on the right side of the assignment in line (L). The fresh information entered in the widget by the user is fetched by the get() method in line (R). Line (R) is actually a part of the binding we define in lines (P) through (T) for the event that corresponds to the user hitting the Enter key on the keyboard. The binding is to the callback in lines (Q) through (T). So whenever the user hits the return key while entering information in the Entry widget, the callback is executed. The callback first fetches in line (R) the text entered in the Entry widget, then it clears the widget in line (S), and, finally, it displays in the terminal window the text string that was entered by the user.

Lines (U) through (Y) create a Label widget and line (Z) asks the pack geometry manager to place it against the left side of the main window. Since we have previously explained this widget, the syntax used for the constructor and for the call to pack() should hold no surprises.

Lines (a) through (f) create a Listbox for the right side of the main window.[11] Instead of calling the Listbox constructor directly, which we could have done, we call the Scrolled() method for the main window in line (a) and supply to it the string Listbox as its first argument.[12] Using w for the scrollbars option in line

[10]An Entry widget is used to elicit from the user a single line of text. For example, your GUI could be a form that employs Entry widgets to request from a user his/her first name, last name, age, and so on. It is always a good idea to check that the information supplied by the user through an Entry widget is valid.

[11]A Listbox is commonly used to display a vertically arranged list of text strings. A user can select an item by clicking on it. If you want the user to be able to select multiple items at the same time, that can be achieved by setting the selection mode to either extended or multiple.

[12]This is the preferred way to create widgets with attached scrollbars. The other way would be to call the Listbox constructor with its yscrollcommand option set to a Scrollbar widget constructed

(b) says that we want the scrollbar at the "west" side of the Listbox.[13] Line (c) specifies that only one item is to be selected at one time. Lines (d) and (e) of the call to the Scrolled() method specify that we want the Listbox to be 10 characters wide and for it to display 3 items in three separate lines. We provided the Listbox with a vertical scrollbar since we intend to place more than 3 items in the widget. Line (f) is a call to the pack geometry manager to place the Listbox widget against the right side of the main window. Line (g) inserts a list of 5 color names into the Listbox. The first argument to the insert() method specifies the insertion point for the entry of the rest of the arguments; end means to start inserting at the end of what is currently in the Listbox. Finally, lines (h) and (i) establish a callback for the mouse click on the item selected in the Listbox. The callback calls on the configure() method to change the background color to the name selected by pressing the left button.

```
#!/usr/bin/perl -w

###  PackGeom.pl

use strict;
use Tk;

my $mw = MainWindow->new( -title => "Pack Layout" );                        #(A)
$mw->geometry( "400x200+50+100" );                                          #(B)
$mw->maxsize( 400, 500 );                                                   #(C)
$mw->minsize( 100, 200 );                                                   #(D)

# Widget for the top side of the main window:

$mw->Button(                                                                #(E)
             -text => 'Click Here for a Greeting',                          #(F)
             -anchor  => 'c',                                               #(G)
             -relief  => 'raised',                                          #(H)
             -command =>  \&print_message,                                  #(I)
           )->pack( -side => 'top', -padx => 10, -pady => 5 );              #(J)

sub print_message { print "Good Morning to you!\n"; }                       #(K)
```

---

separately. The advantage of the latter approach is that you can associate the same scrollbar with multiple widgets. This would allow a user to scroll multiple widgets simultaneously with the same scrollbar.

[13]One can choose from n, s, e, and w for the scrollbars option. If a scrollbar is meant to be optional, use the choices on, os, oe, and ow, where the letter o stands for *optional*.

```
# Widget for the bottom side of the main window:

my $entry_var ="Hit <CR> and then enter text here followed by <CR>";#(L)
my $entry_widget = $mw->Entry( -textvariable => \$entry_var,        #(M)
                               -width => 42,                         #(N)
                             )->pack( -side => 'bottom' );          #(O)

$entry_widget->bind( '<Return>' =>                                  #(P)
    sub {                                                            #(Q)
        my $input = $entry_widget->get . "\n";                      #(R)
        $entry_widget->delete( 0, 'end' );                          #(S)
        print "User entered in entry widget: $input\n";              #(T)
    }
);


# Widget for the left side of the main window:

$mw->Label( -text  => 'hello',                                      #(U)
            -anchor => 'c',                                          #(V)
            -relief => 'groove',                                     #(W)
            -width => 10,                                            #(X)
            -height => 2,                                            #(Y)
          )->pack( -side => 'left', -padx => 10, -pady => 5 );      #(Z)


# Widget for the right side of the main window:

my $listbox = $mw->Scrolled( "Listbox",                             #(a)
                             -scrollbars => 'w',                     #(b)
                             -selectmode => 'single',                #(c)
                             -width => 10,                           #(d)
                             -height => 3,                           #(e)
                           )->pack( -side => 'right' );             #(f)
$listbox->insert('end', 'red', 'green', 'blue', 'magenta', 'pink'); #(g)
$listbox->bind( '<Button-1>', sub { $listbox->configure(            #(h)
    -background => $listbox->get( $listbox->curselection() ) ) } ); #(i)

MainLoop();                                                          #(j)
```

Fig.13.2 shows the GUI created by `PackGeom.pl`. The button at the top when clicked prints out a greeting in the terminal window in which you run this script. The label on the left is just informational. The list box on the right displays a scrollable list of colors. When you press the left button of the mouse on a color name, the background color in the list box changes to that color. The text entry widget at the bottom is there for the user to enter a line of text. When the user hits the Enter key to end the entry of text in this widget, a message that includes the text just entered is displayed in the terminal window.

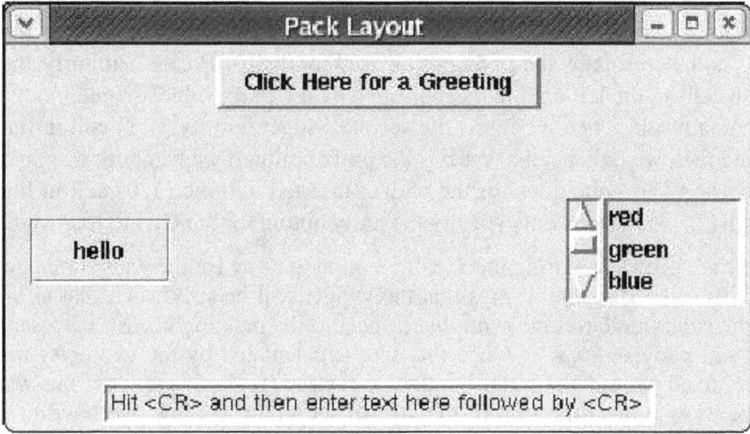

Fig. 13.2

The GUI we show in Fig. 13.2 has the four widgets placed symmetrically against each of the four sides of the enclosing main window. In general, with the `pack` geometry manager, whether or not you achieve this symmetry depends on the packing order of the widgets. We achieved symmetry because we first packed in the top and the bottom widgets, and then the left and the right widgets. If we had first invoked `pack()` on the left widget and then, say, the top widget, we would not see the symmetry of Fig. 13.2. Calling `pack()` on the left widget first would appropriate a part of the left side of the main window for this widget; this space would not be available for layout for the widgets to follow. The layout reasoning used by the `pack` geometry manager is sequential with respect to the widgets to be inserted into a container and is not designed to yield a globally optimal result. What that means is that when `pack()` is invoked on a new widget, space is allocated to the widget on the basis of whatever space remains in the container after the previous calls to `pack()` are taken care of. We should also mention that `pack()` tries to ensure that the widgets being placed in a container do not overlap.

We will now briefly explain the working of the other commonly used layout manager in Perl/Tk — the `grid` geometry manager. The next script, `GridGeom.pl`, places in the GUI window the same four widgets as used in `PackGeom.pl` — `Button`, `Label`, `Entry`, and `Listbox` — but this time in the cells of a 2×2 grid. For the placement of the first widget in the call to `grid()` in lines (G) through (J), we specify its cell by using the `row` and `column` options. The `padx` and `pady` options control the extent of padding between the widget and the cell boundaries. In this case, we are asking for a padding of 60 pixels horizontally and 40 pixels vertically for the button in the cell $(0, 0)$.[14] The actual width of the $(0, 0)$ cell is determined by the largest horizontal extent required for any of the cells in the 0th column of the grid. By the same token, the actual height of the $(0, 0)$ cell is determined by the largest vertical extent needed for any of the cells in the topmost row of the grid. In our example, the height of both cells in the top row is controlled by the vertical extent of the $(0, 0)$ cell — and therefore by the pady option used for the $(0, 0)$ cell. Similarly, the width of both cells in the left column is controlled by the padx value assigned to the $(0, 0)$ cell. As a result, when we insert the second widget into its $(0, 1)$ cell in lines (K), (L), and (M), we only need to specify the padx option if we want our display to look symmetric. The same goes for the widget inserted into the $(1, 0)$ cell in lines (W) through (Z) — we need only specify the pady option for the GUI to look symmetric.

Line (Z) shows us setting the `sticky` option to `nsew` for the widget that goes into the $(1, 0)$ cell. This option says that the widget will be sized such that all its sides abut the cell boundaries but with due respect to the padding needs expressed by the padx and pady options.[15] Once this size is calculated by the geometry manager, it stays fixed even if the main window is resized.[16] [17] If we want the widget to change its size in proportion to the size of the main window, we have to use the `gridColumnconfigure()` and `gridRowconfigure()` methods. For example, if we wanted the label widget in cell $(1, 0)$ to change in size automatically in accordance with any size changes of the main window, we would need to insert the following two statements just after line (i) of the script:

```
$mw->gridRowconfigure(1, -weight => 1);
$mw->gridColumnconfigure(0, -weight => 1);
```

The call to `gridRowconfigure()` will allow the widgets in the designated row to become taller or shorter (provided their corresponding `sticky` option is set) as the main window is resized. And the call to `gridColumnconfigure()` will cause the widgets in the named column to become wider or narrower as the main window is resized (again provided their corresponding `sticky` option is set). The `weight` option is factored in on a relative basis, the default `weight` being zero for all rows and columns. The widgets in columns and rows of weight 0 do not get resized at all as the main window is resized. A column or row of weight 2 will be enlarged or shrunk, as the case may be, at twice the rate compared to a column or row of weight 1.

---

[14] With regard to cell indexing, the first index increases to the right, along the x-axis of the screen coordinates, and the second index increases downwards, along the y-axis of the screen coordinates.

[15] In general, the values for the `sticky` option are `n`, `s`, `e`, and `w`. These, as you would expect, stand for "north", "south", "east", and "west." They can be combined in any order depending on which sides of the widget are supposed to follow the `sticky` constraint.

[16] If we had not used the `sticky` option, the widget would have been sized to its natural dimensions, meaning its size would be set to whatever was needed to hold the information in the label.

[17] The notion of an "allocation rectangle" does not apply to the `grid` geometry manager. The role that the allocation rectangle plays in `pack`'s layout reasoning is played by the cell rectangle in the layout reasoning carried out by the `grid` geometry manager.

```
#!/usr/bin/perl -w

### GridGeom.pl

use strict;
use Tk;

my $mw = MainWindow->new( -title => "Grid Layout" );                    #(A)

# Widget for cell (0,0):
my $button = $mw->Button(                                               #(B)
                  -text => 'Click Here for a Greeting',                 #(C)
                  -relief  =>    'raised',                              #(D)
                  -command =>  sub {                                    #(E)
                                 print "Good Morning to you!\n";        #(F)
                               }
                  )->grid( -row => 0,                                   #(G)
                           -column => 0,                                #(H)
                           -padx => 60,                                 #(I)
                           -pady => 40 );                               #(J)


# Widget for cell (0,1):
my $entry_widget = $mw->Entry->grid( -row => 0,                         #(K)
                                     -column => 1,                      #(L)
                                     -padx => 60 );                     #(M)
$entry_widget->bind( '<Return>' => sub {                                #(N)
           my $input = $entry_widget->get . "\n";                       #(O)
           $entry_widget->delete( 0, 'end' );                           #(P)
           print "User entered in entry widget: $input\n";              #(Q)
       } );


# Widget for cell (1,0):
my $label = $mw->Label( text    =>    'hello',                          #(R)
                        anchor  =>    'c',                              #(S)
                        relief  =>    'groove',                         #(T)
                        width   =>    10,                               #(U)
                        height  =>    2,                                #(V)
                      )->grid( -row => 1,                               #(W)
                               -column => 0,                            #(X)
                               -pady => 40,                             #(Y)
                               -sticky => "nsew",                       #(Z)
                             );
```

```
# Widget for cell (1,1):
my $listbox = $mw->Scrolled( "Listbox",                                  #(a)
                              -scrollbars => 'w',                        #(b)
                              -selectmode => 'single',                   #(c)
                              -width => 10,                              #(d)
                              -height => 3,                              #(e)
                   )->grid( -row => 1, -column => 1 );                   #(f)
$listbox->insert('end', 'red', 'green', 'blue', 'magenta', 'pink'); #(g)
$listbox->bind( '<Button-1>', sub { $listbox->configure(                 #(h)
    -background => $listbox->get( $listbox->curselection() ) ) } ); #(i)

MainLoop();                                                              #(j)
```

The GUI produced by this script is shown in Fig. 13.3. The user can interact with this GUI in the same manner as with the one shown in Fig. 13.2.

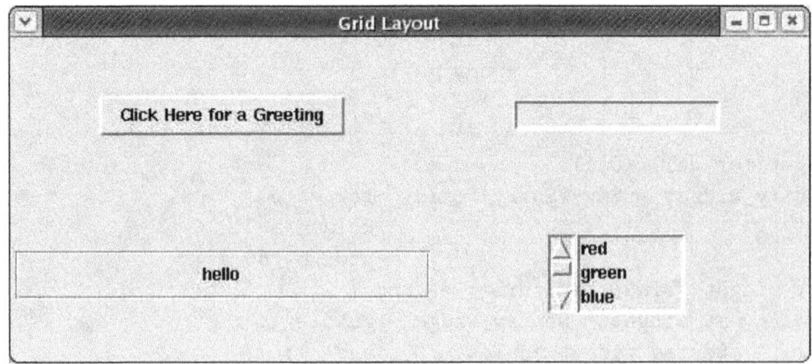

Fig. 13.3

13.3.2 Automatic Layout in Python's Tkinter

We will now show Tkinter scripts that parallel the Perl/Tk scripts of the previous subsection. The next script, `PackGeom.py`, does exactly the same thing as the Perl script `PackGeom.pl` shown earlier and produces the GUI of Fig. 13.2. Lines (A) through (E) establish the size and location of the top-level window for the GUI. In the rest of the script, we construct the widgets for each of the four sides of the top-level window. For the `Button` widget in lines (G) through (L) that attaches itself to the top side, the basic syntax for the constructor and for packing remains the same as in the Perl/Tk script `PackGeom.pl`. There are more significant differences in the syntax for the `Entry` widget in lines (M) through (V) that is displayed at the bottom of the main window. Whereas the Perl/Tk example used the `textvariable` option of the

Entry constructor for supplying the initial string shown in line (M) here, now we call on the insert() method in line (P) to do the job.

As for the Label widget that goes on the left side of the top-level window, the code shown in lines (W) through (c) uses basically the same syntax as for the Perl/Tk script. But there are significant differences for the case of the Listbox widget in lines (d) through (r). The Perl/Tk code shown for PackGeom.pl called the Scrolled constructor with the string "Listbox" as its first argument to give us a scrollable list box. But now we pack a Scrollbar and a Listbox into a Frame container and then place the Frame where it needs to go in the top-level window. The calls to pack() in lines (l) and (m) are with respect to the Frame, since they follow the call to the Frame constructor in line (d). However, the call to frame.pack() in line (n) is for the placement of the Frame widget in the top-level window.

```
#!/usr/bin/env python

### PackGeom.py

from Tkinter import *

mw = Tk()                                                             #(A)
mw.title( "Pack Layout" )                                             #(B)
mw.geometry( "400x200+50+100" )                                       #(C)
mw.maxsize( 400, 500 )                                                #(D)
mw.minsize( 100, 200 )                                                #(E)

#----------   Widget for the top side of the main window   -------------

def buttprint(): print "Good Morning to you!\n"                       #(F)

Button( mw,                                                           #(G)
        text = 'Click Here for a Greeting',                           #(H)
        anchor  = 'c',                                                #(I)
        relief  = 'raised',                                           #(J)
        command =  buttprint                                          #(K)
      ).pack( side = 'top', padx = 10, pady = 5 )                     #(L)


#---------   Widget for the bottom side of the main window   -----------

entry_var = "Hit <CR> and then enter text here followed by <CR>"      #(M)

entry_widget = Entry( mw,                                             #(N)
                      width = 42,                                     #(O)
                    )
entry_widget.insert(0, entry_var)                                     #(P)
entry_widget.pack( side = 'bottom' )                                  #(Q)
```

```
def entryAction( event ):                                               #(R)
    input = entry_widget.get() + "\n"                                   #(S)
    entry_widget.delete( 0, 'end' )                                     #(T)
    print "User entered in entry widget: %s\n" % input                  #(U)

entry_widget.bind( "<Return>", entryAction )                            #(V)


#----------   Widget for the left side of the main window   ------------

Label( mw,                                                              #(W)
       text    = 'hello',                                               #(X)
       anchor  = 'c',                                                   #(Y)
       relief  = 'groove',                                              #(Z)
       width   = 10,                                                    #(a)
       height  = 2,                                                     #(b)
      ).pack( side = 'left', padx = 10, pady = 5 )                      #(c)


#----------   Widget for the right side of the main window   -----------

frame = Frame( mw )                                                     #(d)
scrollbar = Scrollbar( frame, orient = 'vertical' )                     #(e)
listbox = Listbox( frame,                                               #(f)
                   yscrollcommand = scrollbar.set,                      #(g)
                   selectmode = 'single',                               #(h)
                   width = 10,                                          #(i)
                   height = 3,                                          #(j)
                 )
scrollbar.config( command = listbox.yview )                             #(k)
scrollbar.pack( side = 'left', fill = 'y' )                             #(l)
listbox.pack( side = 'right', fill = 'both', expand = 1 )               #(m)
frame.pack( side = 'right' )                                            #(n)
listbox.insert( 'end', 'red', 'green', 'blue', 'magenta', 'pink' )  #(o)

def listBoxAction(event):                                               #(p)
    listbox.configure(background=listbox.get(listbox.curselection()))
                                                                        #(q)

listbox.bind( '<Double-Button-1>', listBoxAction )                      #(r)

mainloop()                                                              #(s)
```

All of the comments we made in the previous subsection regarding how the placement achieved with `pack()` depends strongly on the order in which the widgets are inserted in a container also apply to Tkinter.

Our next script, `GridGeom.py`, illustrates the other commonly used layout manager, the `grid` geometry manager. This script is Python's implementation of the Perl/Tk grid packing example we showed earlier in `GridGeom.pl`.

The syntax used for placing a widget in a cell, as illustrated in lines (I) through (L) for the first of the four widgets, is the same as for the Perl/Tk case earlier, except, of course, for the basic language differences. The comments we made earlier about using `row` and `column` options to specify the cell position of a widget and how the options padx and pady can be used to set the padding between the widget and the cell boundaries also apply here, as one would expect since the underlying toolkit is the same. As with Perl/Tk, the width of each column is determined by the widest component in any of the rows of that column. By the same token, the height of each row is determined by the height needed for the tallest component in any of the columns of that row. The geometric reasoning for determining the cell sizes takes into account the padding specified by the padx and pady options. This should explain why we have not specified the pady option in lines (Q), (R), and (S) for the component that goes into the second column of the top row. We want the height of the first row of the grid to be controlled by the leftmost cell, that is, by the padx option in line (K). All of the comments we made earlier about the `sticky` option in line (h) and how it affects the resizing of the widget in the cell as the main window is resized by the user also hold here.

With regard to the syntax used for creating the individual widgets, it is the same as in the previous Python script. The GUI produced by this script is the same as shown earlier in Fig. 13.3.

```
#!/usr/bin/env python

###  GridGeom.py

from Tkinter import *

mw = Tk()                                                           #(A)
mw.title( "Grid Layout" )                                           #(B)

#--------------------    Widget for cell (0,0)   ----------------------

def buttprint(): print "Good Morning to you!\n"                     #(C)
```

```
Button( mw,                                                              #(D)
        text = 'Click Here for a Greeting',                              #(E)
        anchor  = 'c',                                                   #(F)
        relief  = 'raised',                                              #(G)
        command =  buttprint                                             #(H)
      ).grid( row = 0,                                                   #(I)
              column = 0,                                                #(J)
              padx = 60,                                                 #(K)
              pady = 40 )                                                #(L)


#--------------------   Widget for cell (0,1)   ----------------------

entry_var = "Hit <CR> and then enter text here followed by <CR>"        #(M)

entry_widget = Entry( mw,                                                #(N)
                      width = 42,                                        #(O)
                    )
entry_widget.insert(0, entry_var)                                        #(P)
entry_widget.grid( row = 0,                                              #(Q)
                   column = 1,                                           #(R)
                   padx = 60 )                                           #(S)

def entryAction( event ):                                                #(T)
    input = entry_widget.get() + "\n"                                    #(U)
    entry_widget.delete( 0, 'end' )                                      #(V)
    print "User entered in entry widget: %s\n" % input                   #(W)

entry_widget.bind( "<Return>", entryAction )                             #(X)


#--------------------   Widget for cell (1,0)   ----------------------

Label( mw,                                                               #(Y)
       text    = 'hello',                                                #(Z)
       anchor  = 'c',                                                    #(a)
       relief  = 'groove',                                               #(b)
       width   = 10,                                                     #(c)
       height  = 2,                                                      #(d)
      ).grid( row = 1,                                                   #(e)
        column = 0,                                                      #(f)
        pady = 40,                                                       #(g)
        sticky = "nsew",                                                 #(h)
      )


#--------------------   Widget for cell (1,1)   ----------------------

frame = Frame( mw )                                                      #(i)
```

```
scrollbar = Scrollbar( frame, orient = 'vertical' )                      #(j)
listbox = Listbox( frame,                                                #(k)
                   yscrollcommand = scrollbar.set,                       #(l)
                   selectmode = 'single',                                #(m)
                   width = 10,                                           #(n)
                   height = 3,                                           #(o)
                 )
scrollbar.config( command = listbox.yview )                              #(p)
scrollbar.pack( side = 'left', fill = 'y' )                              #(q)
listbox.pack( side = 'right', fill = 'both', expand = 1 )                #(r)
frame.grid( row = 1, column = 1 )                                        #(s)
listbox.insert( 'end', 'red', 'green', 'blue', 'magenta', 'pink' )       #(t)

def listBoxAction(event):                                                #(u)
    listbox.configure(background=listbox.get(listbox.curselection()))
                                                                         #(v)

listbox.bind( '<Double-Button-1>', listBoxAction )                       #(w)

mainloop()                                                               #(x)
```

13.4 EVENT PROCESSING

The events[18] produced by a user interacting with a GUI are placed by the machine's *window manager* in the *event queue* of the GUI. The window manager keeps track of the stacking order of the windows on a terminal screen and ascertains as to which window generated the event. For example, when a user clicks on a GUI button, the window manager can determine from the coordinates of the mouse pointer the identity of the window to which the event belongs. The window manager then simply places the event in the event queue of the corresponding GUI. A GUI application runs an *event processing loop* for reacting to these events on a continuous basis.

For each event received, the event processing loop determines the identity of the widget that is responsible for the event. If the event was caused by a user clicking a mouse button when the mouse pointer was on top of a GUI button, the event would be associated with that specific GUI button. Once this widget–event association is established, we can loosely say that the GUI widget in question *emitted* the event and refer to the widget as the *source* of the event.

[18]Those new to GUI programming and scripting should find useful an introduction to the topics of events and event processing in Section 17.13 of Chapter 17 of [41].

13.4.1 Callbacks and Event Descriptors

After the source of the event has been identified, one or more functions may need to be invoked in response to that event. These functions, known as *callbacks*, must be registered with the widgets. As mentioned earlier in Section 13.2.1, these functions are called callbacks because they are not invoked directly in a script. All that you as a programmer can do in a script is to set up an association between the event types that can be emitted by a widget and the callbacks that are to be executed in response to those event types. It is the underlying operating system that hands the flow of control to a callback registered for a widget when an event specific to that widget is emitted.

As the reader has already seen, a callback may be registered with the source of an event with either the `command` option to the constructor of the source widget or by calling the `bind()` method on the widget. With the `command` option, a button could, for example, be constructed by the syntax:

```
Perl/Tk:      $mw->Button( -command =>  \&buttprint );

Tkinter:      Button( mw, command = buttprint )
```

where `buttprint` is the name of the callback to be executed when the button is pressed. The same can also be accomplished with a call to `bind()`:[19]

```
Perl/TK:      $button = $mw->Button();
              $button->bind( '<ButtonRelease-1>' => \&buttprint );

Tkinter:      button = Button( mw )
              button.bind( '<ButtonRelease-1>' = buttprint )
```

In the call to `bind()`, the syntax `<ButtonRelease-1>` is known as the *event descriptor*, which, in this case, consists of the *event type* `ButtonRelease` followed by the *event detail* 1. This event detail refers to button-1 of the mouse. In general, an event descriptor is written in the following angle-bracket-delimited form:

```
<modifiers-event_type-event_detail>
```

where the string inside the angle brackets consists of three dash-separated components: `modifiers`, `event_type`, and `event_detail`. The `event_type` may be one of `ButtonPress`, `ButtonRelease`, `KeyPress`, `KeyRelease`, `Enter`, `Leave`, `Motion`, and a host of others. The modifiers in the event descriptor syntax are supposed to represent any additional inputs a user may supply at the same time as the input corresponding to the event type. For example, pressing the control key

[19]We could also have used the following syntax in the call to `bind()`:

```
$button->bind( '<ButtonRelease>' => \&print_message );
```

which by dropping the button number leaves out the event detail. But now a press of any of the buttons on the mouse would trigger the callback.

would serve as a modifier for the event type Button. Pressing both the control and the escape keys would be two modifiers acting simultaneously on an event type like Button. When multiple modifiers are present, they must be dash separated. The commonly used modifier keywords are Control, Alt, Meta, Shift, Double, Triple, etc.

So far we have talked about the event modifiers and the event types. What about the event detail? For mouse-based interactions with a GUI, the event detail consists of the button number, as we showed in some previous calls to bind(). For key type events corresponding to the alphanumeric keys, the event detail is simply the name of the key, meaning the character printed on top of the key. This character is usually referred to as the *keysym* — for key symbol.

Here are some examples of event descriptors for mouse buttons and alphanumeric keys:

```
<ButtonRelease-1>        for trapping button release for button-1

<Double-Button-1>        for trapping a double click of button-1

<Control-Key-c>          for trapping Control-c

<Key-k>                  for trapping keypress for lowercase 'k'

<Key-K>                  for trapping keypress for uppercase 'K'
```

In event descriptors, the event *type* Button is considered to be synonymous with ButtonPress and the event type Key to be synonymous with KeyPress.

13.4.2 The Event Object Handed to the Callbacks

Often when a callback is invoked in response to some user interaction with a GUI, the implementation code for the callback must somehow become aware of the various attributes of the user interaction. Did the user click the mouse button, or merely press the button without releasing it? Which button was pressed if a mouse has multiple buttons, as is most commonly the case? Did the user press some combination of keys on the keyboard? If so, which keys? For a callback to take such information into account, the operating system automatically hands it, directly or indirectly, an *event object*.[20] In the rest of this section, we will show the syntax used in Perl/Tk and Tkinter for getting hold of this object inside a callback.

13.4.2.1 Passing the Event Object to a Callback in Perl/Tk

When a callback is invoked by the system, at the least it is handed a reference to the source widget that emitted the event triggering the callback. This reference is stored in the variable `$Tk::widget`. The system also makes available to the callback an event object that contains information relevant to the event. This event object is available through the variable `$Tk::event`. The following script demonstrates using the event object to figure out the *keysym* associated with a given key on the keyboard and also its associated decimal integer.[21] Line (B) of the script creates a binding between the event descriptor `<KeyPress>` and the callback `get_key_info` that is defined in lines (C) through (H). Since the event descriptor does not include event detail, the event would be triggered by a user pressing *any* key on the keyboard. In the callback, the event object is accessed in line (F). The methods `K()` and `N()` when invoked on the event object in line (G) return the keysym associated with the pressed key and the corresponding integer encoding.

```
#!/usr/bin/perl -w

### GetKeySym.pl

use strict;
use Tk;

my $mw = MainWindow->new( -title => "Testing Callback" );                #(A)

$mw->bind( '<KeyPress>' => \&get_key_info );                             #(B)
```

[20]For a given event, only the most "specific" callbacks are invoked, while allowing for multiple callbacks to be invoked if they are all at equal level of specificity. To understand what we mean by specificity, let's say we have defined callbacks for both the general `<KeyPress>` event that is associated with the pressing of *any* key on the keyboard of a machine and for the more specific `<Return>` event associated with the pressing of just the `Return` (or the `Enter`) key. When a user hits the `Return` (or the `Enter`) key, only the callback associated with the `<Return>` event will be invoked.

[21]The system associates two attributes with each key: a symbolic name referred to as the *keysym* and a decimal integer. For alphanumeric keys, the keysym is just the name of the character on the key. For example, for the key marked J, when used in the lowercase mode, the keysym is j, and when used in the uppercase mode, the keysym is J. The corresponding decimal integers are 106 and 74, these being the ASCII encodings of the characters j and J, respectively. To get the system to interpret the J key as the uppercase, you also have to press the Shift key, which obviously will amount to a separate key press. While we are on the subject of keysyms, note that it is not so straightforward to figure out the keysyms of the nonalphanumeric keys on your keyboard. For example, one of the keys on the keyboard of the laptop the author uses is labeled PgUp for "page up." However, its keysym is `Prior`, as can be verified by running the `GetKeySym.pl` script and pressing the PgUp key.

```
sub get_key_info {                                                   #(C)
#     my $w = $Tk::widget;                                           #(D)
#     my $e = $w->XEvent;                                            #(E)
    my $e = $Tk::event;                                              #(F)
    my ($key_sym_name, $key_num ) = ($e->K, $e->N);                  #(G)
    print "keysym=$key_sym_name, numeric=$key_num\n";                #(H)
}

MainLoop;                                                            #(I)
```

The commented-out lines in the above script, lines (D) and (E), show an alternative way to access the event object in a callback. We can first access the source widget that is passed to the callback through the `$Tk::widget` variable and then call the method `XEvent` on the source widget.

The output produced by the above script when you press the A key on the keyboard is

```
keysym=a, numeric=97
```

On the other hand, when you enter the uppercase A by first pressing the Shift key and, while keeping Shift pressed, also pressing the A key, the output produced is

```
keysym=Shift_L, numeric=65505
keysym=A, numeric=65
```

assuming that the Shift key pressed is the one on the left side of the keyboard. As the reader will recall, the number 97 is the ASCII value in decimal for the lowercase a and 65 the ASCII value in decimal for the uppercase A.

The event object that is passed to a callback has other methods besides the `K()` and the `N()` methods shown above. As the reader would expect, not all of the methods are applicable for a given event. For example, the event object handed over to a callback defined for a key-press event for a text widget will not contain the x- and y-coordinates of the mouse pointer.

The next script, `EventMethods.pl`, shows some of these other methods defined for an event object. In lines (A), (B), and (C), the script creates a GUI that has a button and a canvas inside the main window.[22] In lines (D), (E), and (F), the script associates the same callback with all three widgets of the GUI.[23] Line (I) prints out

[22]A `Canvas` widget can be used for rendering shapes, strings, and even images. By trapping mouse events that capture the position of the mouse pointer on the screen and its motion, you can also create interactive drawing programs and image manipulation programs with a `Canvas` widget.

the reference to the event object. Line (J) shows us retrieving the reference to the widget that gave rise to the event. As mentioned earlier, the event object passed to the callback can also be retrieved by accessing the source widget and then invoking the `XEvent` method on the source widget, as we do in line (K). Therefore, the print output of both the lines (I) and (K) should be the same. In line (L), we invoke the `A()` method to retrieve the keysym associated with the event object — assuming that a keypress/release is relevant to the event. In our example, since we are trapping the keypress events associated with the main window in line (D), the method call `A()` of line (L) should return the keysym associated with the key pressed, provided the key pressed has an ASCII code associated with it.[24] The method `K()` in line (M) would be invoked for all keypress events.

Lines (N) and (O) display the `(x,y)` coordinates for all events that have such coordinates associated with them. For example, clicking a mouse button at any point in the canvas widget would give rise to an event that carries the coordinate information related to where exactly the mouse button was clicked. A keypress for any location of the mouse pointer in the GUI also generates an event with the `(x,y)` coordinates of the mouse pointer. Whereas line (N) returns the coordinates relative to the upper left corner of your terminal screen, line (O) returns the coordinates relative to the upper left corner of the widget that generates the event.

```
#!/usr/bin/perl -w

### EventMethods.pl

use strict;
use Tk;

my $mw = MainWindow->new( -title => "Testing Callback" );                 #(A)
my $b = $mw->Button( -text => "click here" )->pack( -side => 'top');#(B)
my $c = $mw->Canvas()->pack( -side => 'bottom' );                         #(C)

$mw->bind( '<KeyPress>' => \&testEventMethods );                          #(D)
$b->bind( '<Button>' => \&testEventMethods );                             #(E)
$c->CanvasBind( '<Button>' => \&testEventMethods );                       #(F)

sub testEventMethods {                                                    #(G)
    my $e = $Tk::event;                                                   #(H)
    print "\n\nEvent object: $e\n";                                       #(I)
    print "Source widget: ", $e->W, "\n";                                 #(J)
```

[23]Note that the Canvas widget has its own bind method, `CanvasBind()`, for binding callbacks with the events that can be produced by this widget. We will have more to say about `CanvasBind()` in Section 13.4.5.

[24]The conditional returns in lines (L) and (M) allow for the fact that an event produced by the click of a mouse button does not carry any keysym information.

```
    print "Event object: ", $e->W->XEvent, "\n";                    #(K)
    print "Key (ASCII only): ", ($e->A ? $e->A : ''), "\n";         #(L)
    print "Key (any): ", ($e->K ? $e->K : ''), "\n";                #(M)
    print "(x,y) coord relative to laptop screen: ",
                              $e->X, ", ", $e->Y, "\n";             #(N)
    print "(x,y) coord relative to widget: ",
                              $e->x, ", ", $e->y, "\n";             #(O)
}
MainLoop;                                                           #(P)
```

Shown below are the output messages printed out by the script when a user interacts with the GUI by first clicking the mouse on the GUI button, then clicking the mouse at the center of the canvas widget, and, finally, pressing the Z key while the mouse pointer is at the lower right hand corner of the GUI:

```
Event object: XEvent=SCALAR(0x81bf514)
Source widget: Tk::Button=HASH(0x8276170)
Event object: XEvent=SCALAR(0x81bf514)
Key (ASCII only):
Key (any):
(x,y) coord relative to laptop screen: 873, 38
(x,y) coord relative to widget: 44, 12


Event object: XEvent=SCALAR(0x82b1e08)
Source widget: Tk::Canvas=HASH(0x82632e8)
Event object: XEvent=SCALAR(0x82b1e08)
Key (ASCII only):
Key (any):
(x,y) coord relative to laptop screen: 870, 156
(x,y) coord relative to widget: 148, 102


Event object: XEvent=SCALAR(0x81bf4d8)
Source widget: MainWindow=HASH(0x8069124)
Event object: XEvent=SCALAR(0x81bf4d8)
Key (ASCII only): z
Key (any): z
(x,y) coord relative to laptop screen: 1014, 257
(x,y) coord relative to widget: 292, 231
```

As the reader can see, in each case the source widget is different. When the GUI button is clicked, the source widget shown in the first grouping of output messages is the GUI button. Then, when the mouse is clicked in the middle of the canvas, the source widget is the canvas in the second grouping of the output messages. Finally, when the Z key is pressed, the source widget is the main window itself. The event objects for all three cases are different, as they should be.

13.4.2.2 Passing the Event Object to a Callback in Tkinter

The following Python script does the same thing as the Perl/Tk script `GetKeySym.pl` shown earlier. It traps the keyboard action by a user and prints out in a terminal window the key names and their corresponding ASCII values. The callback is defined in lines (D), (E), and (F). The callback is bound to the event descriptor `<KeyPress>` in line (C). When the callback is invoked, it is handed an event object, which is an instance of class `Event`. As shown in line (E), the attributes `keysym` and `keysym_num` of the event object contain the information we need to extract from the object. Since the event descriptor in line (C) does not include event detail, the callback will be triggered by pressing *any* key on the keyboard. The GUI produced by the script behaves in the same manner as the Perl/Tk script shown earlier — for any keypress it prints out a pair of values: the symbolic name of the key and its associated numeric value.

```
#!/usr/bin/env python

### GetKeySym.py

from Tkinter import *

mw = Tk()                                                               #(A)
mw.title( "Testing Callback" )                                          #(B)
mw.bind( '<KeyPress>', lambda e: get_key_info(e) )                      #(C)

def get_key_info(event):                                                #(D)
    (key_sym_name, key_num ) = (event.keysym, event.keysym_num)         #(E)
    print "keysym=%s, numeric=%s\n" % (key_sym_name, key_num)           #(F)

mainloop()                                                              #(G)
```

Our next script, `EventMethods.py`, parallels the Perl/Tk script of the same name (except, of course, for the suffix) and illustrates some of the other methods associated with the event object that is handed to a callback. In lines (I), (J), and (K), this script registers the same callback, `testEventMethods()`, with the key-press events in the root window, with the mouse clicks on the button widget, and with the mouse clicks in the canvas widget.

Line (N) of the script shows that when you invoke the `widget` attribute on an event object, you get the widget that caused the event. For example, if you clicked the mouse on a GUI button, the call in line (N) will return the identity of the GUI button. To make sense of the value returned by the `widget` attribute, you need to know how Tkinter keeps track of all the widgets in a GUI.[25] Tkinter gives internally generated names to widget instances, widget classes, the application level, and so on. These names are called *tags*. The tag for the root widget of a GUI is represented by a dot, that is, by the `.` symbol. Any child widget of the root widget is represented by a string `.n` for some unique positive integer n. When a child widget under the root contains its own child widget, that gets represented by the `.n.m` string, and so on.[26] The `widget` attribute of an event object, as in the call in line (N), returns the full dot-delimited name of the widget that gave rise to the event. So the call in line (N) will, in general, return a string like

$$.n_1.n_2.n_3 \cdots .n_p$$

assuming that the widget is at the pth level in the containment hierarchy descending from the root window. If you only need to know the tag assigned to a widget relative to its parent, you need to invoke the `winfo_name()` method on the event-causing widget returned by the attribute `widget`, as shown by the syntax in line (O). So the same widget that returns the above string will return only n_p through the `winfo_name()` method in line (O).

We have already talked about the `keysym` and `keysym_num` attributes of the event object. When the event consists of a user pressing a key on the keyboard, the attribute `keysym` in line (S) will return the symbolic name of the key, and the attribute `keysym_num` in line (P) the ASCII code associated with the key. If the callback is triggered by something other than a keyboard interaction, we obviously do not expect the attributes `keysym` and `keysym_num` to contain any meaningful values. Tkinter stores the string `??` in these attributes in such cases.

Lines (V) and (W) illustrate the methods that return the x- and the y-coordinates of the mouse pointer. If you want to know the coordinates of the pointer relative to the upper left-hand corner of the terminal screen, you must query the attributes `x_root` and `y_root` of the event object, as shown by line (V). On the other hand, if you want to know the coordinates of the mouse pointer relative to the upper left-hand corner of the widget in which the mouse pointer currently resides, that information is stored in the attributes `x` and `y` of the event object, as shown in line (W).

```
#!/usr/bin/env python

### EventMethods.py

from Tkinter import *                                                  #(A)
```

[25] Tkinter's naming convention for the widgets is the same as Tk's.

[26] The resulting names are very similar to directory pathnames except for the fact that the role played by the forward slash (or backslash) in directory pathnames is played here by the dot.

```
mw = Tk()                                                              #(B)
mw.title( "Testing Callback" )                                         #(C)
mw.bind( '<KeyPress>', lambda e: testEventMethods() )                  #(D)
b = Button( mw, text = "click here"  )                                 #(E)
b.pack( side = 'top' )                                                 #(F)
c = Canvas( mw )                                                       #(G)
c.pack( side = 'bottom' )                                              #(H)

mw.bind( '<KeyPress>', lambda e: testEventMethods( e ) )               #(I)
b.bind( '<Button>', lambda e: testEventMethods( e ) )                  #(J)
c.bind( '<Button>', lambda e: testEventMethods( e ) )                  #(K)

def testEventMethods( e ):                                             #(L)
    print "\n\nEvent object: %s" % e                                   #(M)
    print "Source widget (returned by e.widget): %s" % \
                                e.widget                               #(N)
    print "Source widget (returned by e.widget.winfo_name): %s" % \
                                e.widget.winfo_name()                  #(O)
    if e.keysym_num != '??':                                           #(P)
        print "Key (ASCII only): %s" % e.keysym_num                    #(Q)
    else: print "Key (ASCII only):  "                                  #(R)
    if e.keysym != '??':                                               #(S)
        print "Key (any): %s" % e.keysym                               #(T)
    else: print "Key (any): "                                          #(U)
    print "(x,y) coord relative to laptop screen: %s, %s" % \
                              (e.x_root, e.y_root)                     #(V)
    print "(x,y) coord relative to widget: %s, %s\n" %  (e.x, e.y)     #(W)

mainloop()                                                             #(X)
```

Shown below are the messages printed out by the above script when a user interacts with the GUI by first clicking on the GUI button, followed by clicking the mouse at the center of the canvas widget, and, finally, followed by pressing the Z key while the mouse pointer is near the lower right-hand corner of the GUI:

```
Event object: <Tkinter.Event instance at 0x402f5b6c>
Source widget (returned by e.widget): .1076661932
Source widget (returned by e.widget.winfo_name): 1076661932
Key (ASCII only):
Key (any):
(x,y) coord relative to laptop screen: 146, 41
(x,y) coord relative to widget: 34, 15


Event object: <Tkinter.Event instance at 0x402f5b6c>
```

```
Source widget (returned by e.widget): .1076661676
Source widget (returned by e.widget.winfo_name): 1076661676
Key (ASCII only):
Key (any):
(x,y) coord relative to laptop screen: 151, 148
(x,y) coord relative to widget: 146, 94


Event object: <Tkinter.Event instance at 0x402f5b6c>
Source widget (returned by e.widget): .
Source widget (returned by e.widget.winfo_name): tk
Key (ASCII only): 122
Key (any): z
(x,y) coord relative to laptop screen: 297, 255
(x,y) coord relative to widget: 292, 229
```

13.4.3 Instance, Class, and Application-Level Event Descriptors for Callback Bindings

The event descriptors available for a given widget instance (and the associated callbacks if they are defined) can come from three sources: (i) they may be defined directly for the widget instance; (ii) they may be defined for the class of which the widget is an instance; and (iii) they may be defined for the entire application. It is common to define an event descriptor (and its associated callback) for a widget class. Subsequently, the event descriptor (and its associated callback) become available for all the instances of that class. Obviously, if a specific widget acquires an event descriptor (and its associated callback) from the class definition, in most cases the implementation code for the callback will have to identify the actual source widget for the triggering event.

In addition to the three sources listed above, a widget instance also acquires[27] the event descriptors (and their associated callbacks) from its parents in the containment hierarchy to which the widget instance belongs. We will explain this point further at the end of this section.

To see all the event descriptors that are defined at the class level and that are available for a specific widget, we make the following invocation in Perl/Tk:

```
$widget->bind( class_name_for_the_widget )
```

and the following in Tkinter:

[27] We intentionally did not use the word "inherits" here since a containment hierarchy in a GUI script must not be confused with a class hierarchy in object-oriented programming and scripting.

```
widget.bind_class( class_name_for_the_widget )
```

For example, to see all the event descriptors supplied by the Button class for the individual GUI buttons, you make the following call in Perl/Tk:

```
$widget->bind( Tk::Button )
```

and the following in Tkinter:

```
b = Button()
b.bind_class( 'Button' )
```

These calls return the event descriptors:

```
<Key-Return>
<Key-space>
<ButtonRelease-1>
<Button-1>
<Leave>
<Enter>
```

where `<Key-Return>` is the event descriptor for the event generated when you hit the return key on the keyboard with the mouse pointer on the button. When you hit the space bar under similar circumstances, the event generated corresponds to the descriptor `<Key-space>`. The reader has already seen the event descriptors `<ButtonRelease-1>` and `<Button>`, the latter being a shorthand for the descriptor `<ButtonPress>`. As the reader will recall, the event detail 1 that follows the event type Button refers to the leftmost button on the mouse. The event descriptors `<Leave>` and `<Enter>` describe the events for when the mouse pointer enters and leaves a GUI button.

In addition to the system-supplied class-level event descriptors, you are at freedom to declare additional event descriptors that can be at the application level, at the class level, or for specific widget instances. In the next couple of scripts, one in Perl/Tk and the other in Tkinter, we will demonstrate how we can complement the system-supplied event descriptors with user-defined ones at both the class level and the instance level.

13.4.3.1 Designating Additional Event Descriptors in Perl/Tk

As the reader should expect, line (C) of the Perl/Tk script GetEventDescriptors.pl shown next will output the system-supplied event descriptors for the callback bindings for the Button class.[28] Lines (D) and (E) use the three-argument version of

[28]Recall from Chapter 5 that the ref operator returns the class name of the referent. In our case, ref would return Tk::Button in line (C) of the script.

`bind()` to create two additional bindings for the `Button` class; these are for the press and release of button-2 of the physical mouse. These would be included in the output produced in line (F). Subsequently, a button constructed from the `Button` class would have available to it these additional event descriptors and the associated callbacks.

As already mentioned, it is also possible to supply additional callback bindings for just a single instance of a widget. This we demonstrate in lines (G) through (L). For the specific GUI button to which the variable `$b` holds a reference, these lines declare button press event descriptors and their associated callbacks for the press and release of button-3, button-4, and button-5 of the physical mouse.[29]

```
#!/usr/bin/perl -w

### GetEventDescriptors.pl

use strict;
use Tk;

my $mw = MainWindow->new();                                              #(A)
my $b = $mw->Button();                                                   #(B)

print "All system-supplied event descriptors for \
the Button class:\n\n";
print join( "\n", $b->bind( ref $b ) ), "\n\n";                          #(C)

# Declare additional event descriptors for the Button class:
$b->bind( 'Tk::Button', '<Button-2>', sub { $mw->foo2 } );               #(D)
$b->bind( 'Tk::Button', '<ButtonRelease-2>', sub { $mw->foo2 } );        #(E)

print "All event descriptors defined for Button class \
including the new ones:\n\n";
print join( "\n", $b->bind( ref $b ) ), "\n";                            #(F)

# Declare event descriptors for a specific button instance:
$b->bind( '<Button-3>', sub { $mw->foo3 } );                             #(G)
$b->bind( '<Button-4>', sub { $mw->foo4 } );                             #(H)
$b->bind( '<Button-5>', sub { $mw->foo5 } );                             #(I)
$b->bind( '<ButtonRelease-3>', sub { $mw->bar3 } );                      #(J)
$b->bind( '<ButtonRelease-4>', sub { $mw->bar4 } );                      #(K)
$b->bind( '<ButtonRelease-5>', sub { $mw->bar5 } );                      #(L)

print "\nAll user-defined event descriptors for \
```

---

[29] We are obviously thinking of a hypothetical mouse with five buttons. Tk allows the event detail integer for buttons to go up to 5.

```
a specific button:\n\n";
print join( "\n", $b->bind ), "\n";                                    #(M)
```

Shown below is the output of this script. We have already explained the first batch of output lines, as produced by line (C) of the script. The second batch is produced by line (F) of the script after we add in lines (D) and (E) two more callback bindings at the class level for two additional event descriptors. The final batch of output lines is produced by the statement in line (M). These output lines show the event descriptors for the additional user-defined callback bindings for a specific button.

```
All system-supplied event descriptors for
the Button class:

<Key-Return>
<Key-space>
<ButtonRelease-1>
<Button-1>
<Leave>
<Enter>


All event descriptors defined for Button class
including the new ones:

<ButtonRelease-2>
<Button-2>
<Key-Return>
<Key-space>
<ButtonRelease-1>
<Button-1>
<Leave>
<Enter>

All user-defined event descriptors for
a specific button:

<ButtonRelease-5>
<ButtonRelease-4>
<ButtonRelease-3>
<Button-5>
<Button-4>
<Button-3>
```

When the same event descriptor for a widget possess both a class-level callback binding and an instance-level callback binding, both callbacks are invoked, first at the class level and then at the instance level.

13.4.3.2 Designating Additional Event Descriptors in Tkinter

In accordance with the explanation provided earlier, line (D) of the following script shows how to get a listing of all the class-level event descriptors for the `Button` class. Lines (E) and (F) show us adding two more event descriptors to this class. All of the event descriptors, including the new ones we just supplied, will be printed out by the statement in line (G). Lines (H) through (M) show us providing the specific button instance of line (C) with six additional event descriptors (under the assumption that we are dealing with a hypothetical five-button mouse).

```
#!/usr/bin/env python

### GetEventDescriptors.py

from Tkinter import *                                                    #(A)

mw = Tk()                                                                #(B)
b = Button( mw )                                                         #(C)

print "All system-supplied event descriptors for\n" +  \
"the Button class:\n"
print "\n".join( b.bind_class( b.winfo_class() ) ) + "\n\n"              #(D)

def foo(): pass

# Declare additional event descriptors for the Button class:
b.bind_class( 'Button', '<Button-2>', foo )                              #(E)
b.bind_class( 'Button', '<ButtonRelease-2>', foo )                       #(F)
print "All event descriptors defined for Button class\n" + \
"including the new ones:\n"
print "\n".join( b.bind_class( b.winfo_class() ) ) + "\n\n"              #(G)

# Declare event descriptors for a specific button instance:
b.bind( '<Button-3>', foo)                                               #(H)
b.bind( '<Button-4>', foo )                                              #(I)
b.bind( '<Button-5>', foo )                                              #(J)
b.bind( '<ButtonRelease-3>', foo )                                       #(K)
b.bind( '<ButtonRelease-4>', foo )                                       #(L)
b.bind( '<ButtonRelease-5>', foo )                                       #(M)
```

```
print "\nAll user-defined event descriptors\n" +    \
"for this specific button:\n"
print "\n".join( b.bind() ) + "\n\n"                               #(N)
```

The output of this script is the same as shown for the earlier Perl/Tk script `GetEventDescriptors.pl`

13.4.3.3 Callback Search Order in Perl/Tk

Tk associates a list of tags called *binding tags* with each widget in a GUI in order to search for the applicable callbacks when an event related to a widget takes place. The tags in the list can be the names of specific widgets, the names of widget classes, or the keyword `all` that stands for the application level. The search order is expressed using Tk's naming convention for tags: the dot `.` stands for the root widget; a name like `.foo` for an immediate successor of the root widget in the containment hierarchy; a name like `.foo.bar` for a widget that is at the next level below the widget named `.foo`; and so on.

The binding tags associated with a widget can be obtained by invoking the method `bindtags()` on the widget. For example, when this function is called on a specific button, what is returned is an array like:

```
Tk::Button   .button   .   all
```

This list starts with a tag that is the class of the widget on which `bindtags()` was invoked, followed by the widget instance itself, followed by the root widget, and, finally, followed by `all` for the application level. The call `$b->bindtags` in line (D) on the script shown next returns the array of tags shown above. This list represents the search order in which the system will look for a callback binding for an event descriptor.

The rest of the script shown below loops through the list returned in line (D) to construct the set of all the event descriptors that apply to a button widget. It is convenient to use a set container for this since a set automatically eliminates any duplications in the event descriptors associated with the different tags returned by `bindtags()`. However, since a set is not native to Perl, the statements in lines (E) and (F) of the script are meant to simulate the behavior of a set container. We take advantage of the fact that all the keys in a Perl hash must be distinct. So we convert the array returned by `$b->bind( tag )` in line (E) into a hash by associating an arbitrarily specified value of 1 with every key that corresponds to an element of the array. Line (F) carries out a union of the two sets, one corresponding to the previously accumulated hash `%event_descriptors` and the other to the new `%event`. About line (E), note that when `bind()` is called with a single argument that is a tag — in the sense of the tags returned by `bindtags()` — it returns the event descriptors associated directly with that tag.

```
#!/usr/bin/perl -w

### GetAllEventDescriptors.pl

use strict;
use Tk;

my $mw = MainWindow->new();                                             #(A)
my $b = $mw->Button()->pack();                                          #(B)

my %event_descriptors;                                                  #(C)

foreach my $tag ( $b->bindtags ) {                                      #(D)
    my %events = map { $_ => 1 } $b->bind( $tag );                      #(E)
    %event_descriptors =
          map { $_ => 1 } keys %event_descriptors, keys %events;        #(F)
}

print join "\n", keys %event_descriptors;                               #(G)
```

When you run this script, the output will look like

```
<Enter>
<ButtonRelease-1>
<<LeftTab>>
<Alt-Key>
<Key-space>
<Key-Return>
<Key-Tab>
<Key-F10>
<Button-1>
<Leave>
```

As mentioned above, the list returned by `bindtags()` indicates the order in which the current widget, its class, the root widget, and the application level will be searched for a callback for a given event descriptor. If all of these contain callbacks for an event descriptor, an occurrence of that event will cause *all* of those callbacks to be invoked. This is illustrated by the next script in which a button instance, the `Button` class, the root widget, and the application level have all been provided with callback bindings for the `<Button>` event, which is the event of pressing any of the buttons on the physical mouse. As shown in the next script, Perl/Tk uses `bind()` for binding a callback to a widget instance, a widget class, and to the application. When `bind()` is called with just two explicit arguments, as in lines (D) and (H), you create a callback binding for the widget instance on which the method is invoked. On the other hand, when you call `bind()` with three explicit arguments and the first one is the name of a class, as in line (F), you create a class-level binding. If the first argument in a call to bind() with three explicit arguments is the keyword `all`, as in line (J), you create an application-level binding.

```
#!/usr/bin/perl -w

### CallbackSearchOrder.pl

use strict;
use Tk;

my $mw = MainWindow->new();                                              #(A)

my $b = $mw->Button()->pack();                                           #(B)

sub foo_tops { print "callback for Toplevel instance invoked\n" }        #(C)
$mw->bind( '<Button>', \&foo_tops);                                      #(D)

sub foo_Butt { print "callback for Button class invoked\n" }             #(E)
$b->bind( 'Tk::Button', '<Button-1>', \&foo_Butt );                      #(F)

sub foo_butt { print "callback for Button instance invoked\n" }          #(G)
$b->bind( '<Button>', \&foo_butt);                                       #(H)

sub foo_App { print "callback for Application level invoked\n" }         #(I)
$b->bind( 'all', '<Button>', \&foo_App);                                 #(J)

MainLoop;                                                                #(K)
```

If you run this script and press once the left button on the physical mouse while the screen mouse pointer is on the GUI button, you will see the following messages displayed on the screen:

```
callback for Button class invoked
callback for Button instance invoked
callback for Toplevel instance invoked
callback for Application level invoked
```

This is in keeping with the observation made earlier that Perl/Tk first looks for class-level callbacks before looking for instance-level callbacks. We can change this search order and make it identical to the search order we will show in the next subsection for Tkinter by inserting the following two lines of code between, say, the lines (J) and (K) of the above script:[30]

```
my @tags = $b->bindtags;
$b->bindtags( [@tags[1, 0, 2, 3]] );
```

Now Perl/Tk will look for instance-level callbacks before class-level callbacks since the argument supplied to `bindtags()` in the second statement above will switch the order of the first two elements in the `@tags` array constructed in the first statement.

We even have the freedom to break the search for the applicable callbacks anywhere we wish as the list of tags returned by `bindtags()` is scanned. The break can be affected by invoking the method `break` on the tag where the search is supposed to stop. For example, if in the new search order as brought about by the above two statements, we do not want the search to go beyond the button instance, we would need to change the callback definition in line (G) of the script as follows:

```
sub foo_butt {
    my $tag = shift;
    print "callback for Button instance invoked\n";
    $tag->break;
}
```

With regard to `bindtags()`, when this method is called with a single argument that is `undef`, it removes all callback bindings associated with the tag on which the method is called.

13.4.3.4 Callback Search Order in Tkinter

From the previous subsection, the reader already knows that Tk associates a list of *binding tags* with each widget in a GUI in order to search for the applicable callbacks when an event related to a widget takes place. Again as mentioned earlier, the tags in the list can be the names of specific widgets, the names of widget classes, or the keyword `all` that stands for the application level. The naming convention for the widgets in the tag list is the same as mentioned in the previous subsection (and as also explained for the case of Tkinter in Section 13.4.2.2): the dot `.` stands for the root widget; a name like `.foo` for an immediate successor of the root widget in the containment hierarchy; a name like `.foo.bar` for a widget that is at the next level below the widget named `.foo`; and so on.

As in the previous subsection, the binding tags associated with a widget can be obtained by invoking the method `bindtags()` on the widget. For example, the Tkinter call

---

[30]This code snippet is from Steve Lidie's tutorial article "Perl/Tk: Binding Basics" at `http://www.foo.docs/tpj/issues/vol2_3/tpj0203-0006.html`.

```
button.bindtags()
```

on a specific button could return the tuple[31]

```
('.1076660716', 'Button', '.', 'all')
```

This tuple starts with a tag that is the name of the button on which `bindtags()` was invoked, followed by the class of the widget, followed by the root widget, and, finally, followed by `all` for the application level. This tuple represents the search order in which the system will look for a callback binding for an event descriptor. Every widget inherits the `bindtags()` method from the class `Misc`.

The next script, `GetAllEventDescriptors.py`, shows us using `bindtags()` to obtain a list of all the event descriptors that would be applicable to the button constructed in line (B). The call to `bindtags()` in line (D) returns a tuple such as the one shown above. We then loop through the tuple in lines (D) and (E) and construct the set of all the event descriptors for the button widget. It is convenient to use the `set` container for `event_descriptors` because it automatically ensures the elimination of any duplicate event descriptors from the different tags returned by `bindtags()`. The statement in line (E) constructs a union of the set constructed so far and the new set corresponding to the tag being processed.

```
#!/usr/bin/env python

### GetAllEventDescriptors.py

from Tkinter import *

mw = Tk()                                                          #(A)
b = Button( mw )                                                   #(B)

event_descriptors = set()                                          #(C)

for tag in b.bindtags():                                           #(D)
    event_descriptors |= set( b.bind_class( tag ) )                #(E)

print "\n".join( event_descriptors )                               #(F)
```

Here is an example of the output produced by the above script:

[31]Notice that the order of the first two elements in the tuple returned by `bindtags()` for Tkinter here is opposite to what we saw in the previous subsection for Perl/Tk. Here the widget tag name comes before the class for the button instance. So, by default, Tkinter will first invoke instance-level callbacks, if they exist, before class-level callbacks, if they are defined.

```
<Leave>
<<PrevWindow>>
<Key-F10>
<ButtonRelease-1>
<Key-space>
<Alt-Key>
<Button-1>
<Enter>
<Key-Tab>
```

As mentioned above, the tuple returned by `bindtags()` indicates the order in which the current widget, its class, the root widget, and the application level will be searched for a callback for a given event descriptor. If all of these contain callbacks for an event descriptor, an occurrence of that event will cause *all* of those callbacks to be invoked. This is illustrated by the next script in which a button instance, the `Button` class, the root widget, and the application level have all been provided with callback bindings for the `<Button>` event, which is the event of pressing any of the buttons on the physical mouse. The call to `bind()` in line (D) binds the callback `foo_tops()` of line (H) to the root window of the GUI. Line (E) binds the callback `foo_butt()` of line (I) to the specific button instance created in line (B). The call to `bind_class()` in line (F) binds the callback `foo_Butt()` of line (J) to the `Button` class. And, finally, the call to `bind_all()` in line (G) binds the callback `foo_App()` of line (K) to the application level.

```
#!/usr/bin/env python

### CallbackSearchOrder.py

from Tkinter import *

mw = Tk()                                                              #(A)
b = Button( mw )                                                       #(B)
b.pack()                                                               #(C)

mw.bind( '<Button>', lambda e: foo_tops() )                            #(D)
b.bind( '<Button>', lambda e: foo_butt() )                             #(E)
b.bind_class( 'Button', '<Button-1>', lambda e: foo_Butt() )           #(F)
b.bind_all( '<Button>', lambda e: foo_App() )                          #(G)

def foo_tops():  print "callback for Toplevel instance invoked"        #(H)
def foo_butt(): print "callback for Button instance invoked"           #(I)
def foo_Butt(): print "callback for Button class invoked"              #(J)
def foo_App(): print "callback for Application level invoked"          #(K)

mainloop()                                                             #(L)
```

When you run the above script and press just once (or click once) the left button of the physical mouse while the mouse pointer is over the GUI button, the following messages would be printed out:

```
callback for Button instance invoked
callback for Button class invoked
callback for Toplevel instance invoked
callback for Application level invoked
```

Note the order in which the callbacks are invoked. When the physical mouse button is pressed over the GUI button, first the callback registered with that specific GUI button is invoked. This is followed by the callback registered with the class `Button`. That is followed by the callback for the root window. And, finally, the application-level callback is invoked. It would obviously be the case that if you press the mouse button outside the area occupied by the GUI button (but still within the GUI window), only the callbacks for the root window and for the application will be invoked. If this chaining of the callbacks creates undesirable effects, the chain can be broken by having a callback that should be the last in the chain return the string `"break"`. To illustrate this point, let's say that in the above script we replace the callback definition in line (I) by the definition shown below:

```
def foo_butt(e):
    print "callback for Button instance invoked"
    return "break"
```

Now if you press the left button of the physical mouse while the mouse pointer is on the GUI button, only the first of the four messages shown above will appear on the screen. That is because only the instance-level callback will be invoked in this case.[32]

13.4.4 Passing Arguments to Callbacks

Ordinarily, the system invokes a callback with just one argument — the `Event` object corresponding to the user interaction. But what if we want additional information to be passed to the callback? For example, we may want a click on a GUI button to print out a message whose content becomes available only at run time. In this section, we will see how arguments can be passed to callbacks that are designated with the `command` option and through the `bind()` method.

[32] We have only talked about how to add callback bindings to a widget tag. It is also possible to remove any previously declared callback bindings by calling unbind versions of the bind calls. For example, to remove any instance-level bindings created by `bind()`, we can call `unbind()`. This method takes for its last argument a function ID that is returned by the call to `bind()`. Similarly, `bind_class()` has the corresponding `unbind_class()` to remove class-level bindings and `bind_all()` the corresponding `unbind_all()` to remove application-level bindings.

13.4.4.1 Passing Arguments to Callbacks in Perl/Tk

Let's start by summarizing how we have specified the callbacks thus far. When we specified a callback with the `command` option and the callback was an anonymous subroutine, we used the following syntax:

```
-command =>  sub { callback code }
```

in either the widget constructor or in a call to `configure()` invoked on the widget. The `command` option was set in the following manner when it used a named subroutine for a callback:

```
-command =>  \&name_of_callback
```

When, instead of using the `command` option, we invoked `bind()` to specify a callback, we used the syntax

```
$widget->bind( event_descriptor, sub { ...callback code...} )
```

when we needed to specify an anonymous subroutine for the callback and the syntax

```
$widget->bind( event_descriptor, \&callback_name )

sub callback_name { ...callback code... }
```

when we needed to use a named subroutine for the callback. In all these cases there was no need for any explicit arguments to be passed to the callbacks.

When arguments need to be passed to a callback that is specified with the `command` option, it is done by setting the option to an array reference. The first element of this array is a reference to the callback and the rest of the elements the arguments to be passed to the callback. Therefore, with the `command` option, we now use the following syntax in either the widget constructor or in the `configure()` function:

```
-command =>  [\&name_of_callback, arg1, arg2, ...]
```

or

```
-command =>  [ sub { ...callback_code... }, arg1, arg2, ...]
```

Except for one very important difference, the same holds true when a callback is specified with the `bind()` method. The important difference is that the first argument that the operating system supplies to the callback is not what it appears in the bind declaration. The first argument that is actually supplied to the callback is a reference to the source widget itself. The rest of the arguments passed to the callback are as listed in the array whose reference is supplied as the second argument to `bind()`. Confusion can stem from the fact that the first element of this array in the call to bind is actually the name of the callback. This is illustrated by the example shown below. The second argument to `bind()` is a reference to an anonymous array, the first element of which is a reference to the callback and the rest of the elements the arguments to be supplied to the callback. In order to get to the two explicit arguments, arg1 and arg2, listed in line (A), the callback must first shift out the reference to the source widget, as it does in line (B). Line (C) then yields the arguments mentioned in line (A).

```
$widget->bind(event_descriptor, [\&callback_name, arg1, arg2]) #(A)

sub callback_name {                                              #(B)
    my $widget = shift;                                          #(C)
    my ($arg1, $arg2) = @_;                                      #(D)
}
```

This difference between how the callbacks retrieve their arguments for the case when they are registered by the command option and when they are registered by a call to bind() is illustrated by the callback code for the buttons b5, b6, b7, and b8 in the script PassArgsToCallbacks.pl shown next. The script also includes examples, for the buttons b1, b2, b3, and b4, of callbacks that do not expect any arguments.

To explain the script in greater detail, lines (B) through (I) create the eight buttons we need to show the eight different examples of callbacks. The first four buttons, b1 through b4, are for callbacks that will not expect any arguments, and the last four, buttons b5 through b8, are for cases where the callbacks expect the two arguments listed in lines (N) and (O).

The callbacks expecting no arguments are shown in lines (J) through (M). For the first two buttons, b1 and b2, we register the callbacks with the command option supplied to the configure() method. The callback for b1 is defined in the same line, line (J), in which it is registered with b1. On the other hand, the callback for b2 is supplied in the form of a reference to a named subroutine.

The callback registrations in lines (L) and (M) for buttons b3 and b4 are carried out by the bind() method. For b3, the callback definition in line (L) is supplied in the same line as the call to bind(). Whereas, for b4, the second argument to bind() in line (M) consists of a reference to a named subroutine.

That brings us to the four examples of callback registrations in lines (R) through (o) where the callbacks are expecting the two arguments of lines (P) and (Q). Lines (R) and (S) show us using the command option for registering the callbacks for buttons b5 and b6. Note how the command option in the configure() method is now set to an array reference in both cases. In line (R), for button b5, the first element of the array is a reference to a named subroutine, saysomething_1() of lines (q) through (u). On the other hand, for button b6 in lines (S) through (c), the first element in the array is an anonymous subroutine. Both the named subroutine saysomething_1() of lines (q) through (u) and the anonymous subroutine of lines (T) through (Y) extract the two arguments from the function call straightforwardly, the former in line (r) and the latter in line (U). Note also in both cases that we use the global variable Tk::widget in lines (V) and (s) to retrieve the widget which triggered the callbacks. Subsequently, we used the following syntax to retrieve the button label inside a callback:

```
my $butt_lbl = $widget->cget( '-text' );
```

The method `cget()`, which stands for *configuration get*, queries the various option fields of a widget and retrieves the value of the option that is supplied to it as the argument. You can think of `cget()` as the opposite of `configure()`; the former is generally used to fetch the value of a particular option and the latter is generally used to set the value of one or more options. These two methods work for all widgets and images in Perl/Tk.

Now compare the callback syntax for the buttons `b5` and `b6`, on the one hand, with callback syntax for the buttons `b7` and `b8` on the other. For `b7` and `b8`, we register the callbacks with the `bind()` method. Now the callbacks, in lines (e) through (j) for `b7` and in lines (v) through (y) for `b8`, include an extra shift out of the argument array `@_`. That is because now when the callbacks are invoked, the first argument supplied will be a reference to the widget that triggered the callback. As a result, there is no need now to call `Tk::widget` to retrieve the identity of the widget producing the event.

```
#!/usr/bin/perl -w

### PassArgsToCallbacks.pl

use strict;
use Tk;

my $mw = MainWindow->new();                                          #(A)
my $b1 = $mw->Button(-text => "b1")->grid(-row => 0, -column => 0); #(B)
my $b2 = $mw->Button(-text => "b2")->grid(-row => 0, -column => 1); #(C)
my $b3 = $mw->Button(-text => "b3")->grid(-row => 1, -column => 0); #(D)
my $b4 = $mw->Button(-text => "b4")->grid(-row => 1, -column => 1); #(E)
my $b5 = $mw->Button(-text => "b5")->grid(-row => 2, -column => 0); #(F)
my $b6 = $mw->Button(-text => "b6")->grid(-row => 2, -column => 1); #(G)
my $b7 = $mw->Button(-text => "b7")->grid(-row => 3, -column => 0); #(H)
my $b8 = $mw->Button(-text => "b8")->grid(-row => 3, -column => 1); #(I)

# For the buttons b1 through b4, the
# callbacks need no arguments:

$b1->configure( -command => sub { print "b1 says hello to me\n" } );#(J)
$b2->configure( -command => \&says_b2 );                             #(K)
$b3->bind( '<Button-1>', sub { print "b3 says hello to me\n" } );   #(L)
$b4->bind( '<Button-1>', \&says_b4 );                                #(M)

sub says_b2 { print "b2 says hello to me\n" }                        #(N)
sub says_b4 { print "b4 says hello to me\n" }                        #(O)


# The callbacks for b5, b6, b7, and b8
```

```
# need the following two as arguments:

my $arg1 = "hello";                                                   #(P)
my $arg2 = "to me";                                                   #(Q)

$b5->configure( -command => [ \&saysomething_1, $arg1, $arg2 ] );     #(R)

$b6->configure( -command => [                                         #(S)
                              sub {                                   #(T)
                                my ($p, $q) = @_;                     #(U)
                                my $butt = $Tk::widget;               #(V)
                                my $butt_lbl = $butt->cget('-text');#(W)
                                print "$butt_lbl says $p $q\n";       #(X)
                              },                                      #(Y)
                              $arg1,                                  #(Z)
                              $arg2                                   #(a)
                            ]                                         #(b)
              );                                                      #(c)

$b7->bind( '<Button-1>', [                                            #(d)
                           sub {                                      #(e)
                             my $butt = shift;                        #(f)
                             my $butt_lbl = $butt->cget( '-text' ); #(g)
                             my ($p, $q) = @_;                        #(h)
                             print "$butt_lbl says $p $q\n";          #(i)
                           },                                         #(j)
                           $arg1,                                     #(k)
                           $arg2                                      #(l)
                         ]                                            #(m)
           );                                                         #(n)

$b8->bind( '<Button-1>', [ \&saysomething_2, $arg1, $arg2 ] );        #(o)

MainLoop;                                                             #(p)

sub saysomething_1 {                                                  #(q)
    my ($p, $q) = @_;                                                 #(r)
    my $widget = $Tk::widget;                                         #(s)
    my $butt_lbl = $widget->cget( '-text' );                          #(t)
    print "$butt_lbl says $p $q\n";                                   #(u)
}

sub saysomething_2 {                                                  #(v)
    my ($widget, $p, $q) = @_;                                        #(w)
    my $butt_lbl = $widget->cget( '-text' );                          #(x)
    print "$butt_lbl says $p $q\n";                                   #(y)
}
```

The GUI produced by the above script is shown in Fig. 13.4. If you click the mouse button on the GUI buttons `b1` through `b8` in order, you will see the following lines of output in the terminal window in which the GUI is invoked:

```
b1 says hello to me
b2 says hello to me
b3 says hello to me
b4 says hello to me
b5 says hello to me
b6 says hello to me
b7 says hello to me
b8 says hello to me
```

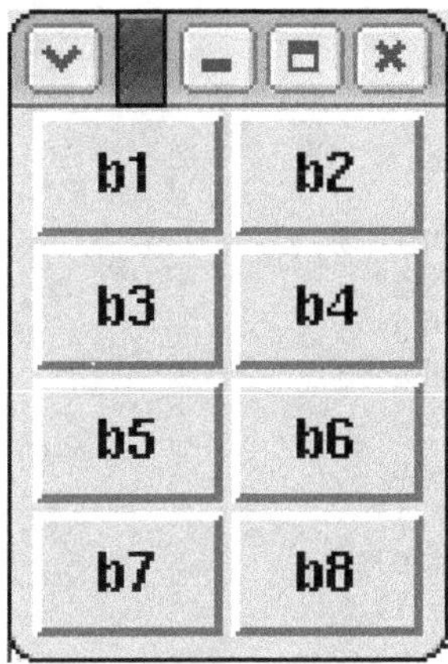

Fig. 13.4

13.4.4.2 Passing Arguments to Callbacks in Tkinter

We will now illustrate how explicit arguments can be passed to a callback in Tkinter. In the following script, the callbacks associated with the first two buttons, `b1` and `b2`, do not need any arguments. These callbacks are defined in lines (I) and (J). For button `b1`, the callback is registered with the `command` option in line (K). And, for button `b2`, the callback is registered with the `bind()` function in line (L).

The callbacks associated with the buttons `b3` and `b4`, on the other hand, do require the two arguments shown in lines (M) and (N). The callback for `b3` is defined in lines (Q), (R), and (S), and the callback for `b4` in lines (T), (U), and (V). The callback of lines (Q), (R), and (S) expects its first argument to be a widget, whereas the callback of lines (T), (U), and (V) expects its first argument to be an `Event` object. The former callback is meant to be registered with its widget with the `command` option, as shown in line (O), whereas the latter callback is meant to be registered with a call to the `bind()` method, as shown in line (P).

Note that difference in the syntax of the `lambda` functions in lines (O) and (P). The difference is accounted for by the fact that a callback registered with `bind()` is handed exactly one argument object — the `Event` object corresponding to the user interaction. On the other hand, a callback registered with the `command` option is not handed any argument objects at all. In either case, both `lambda`'s return callable objects that are closures over all the arguments in line (O) and over the last two arguments in line (P).

```
#!/usr/bin/env python

### PassArgsToCallbacks.py

from Tkinter import *

mw = Tk()

b1 = Button( mw, text = "b1" )                                              #(A)
b2 = Button( mw, text = "b2" )                                              #(B)
b3 = Button( mw, text = "b3" )                                              #(C)
b4 = Button( mw, text = "b4" )                                              #(D)

b1.grid(row = 0, column = 0)                                                #(E)
b2.grid(row = 0, column = 1)                                                #(F)
b3.grid(row = 1, column = 0)                                                #(G)
b4.grid(row = 1, column = 1)                                                #(H)

# For the buttons b1 through b2, the callbacks need no arguments:
def says_b1(): print "b1 says hello to me\n"                               #(I)
def says_b2( e ): print "b2 says hello to me\n"                            #(J)
b1.configure( command =  says_b1 )                                         #(K)
b2.bind( '<Button-1>', says_b2 )                                            #(L)

# The callbacks for b3 and b4 need the following two as arguments:
arg1 = "hello"                                                              #(M)
arg2 = "to me"                                                              #(N)

# Register the callbacks:
b3.configure( command = lambda: saysomething_1( b3, arg1, arg2 ) )  #(O)
b4.bind( '<Button-1>', lambda e: saysomething_2( e, arg1, arg2 ) )  #(P)

def saysomething_1( wdg, p, q ):                                            #(Q)
    butt_lbl = wdg.cget( 'text' )                                           #(R)
    print "%s says %s %s\n" % (butt_lbl, p, q)                              #(S)
```

```
def saysomething_2( evt, p, q ):                                          #(T)
    butt_lbl = evt.widget.cget( 'text' )                                  #(U)
    print "%s says %s %s\n" % (butt_lbl, p, q)                            #(V)

mainloop()                                                                #(W)
```

13.4.5 Supplying Event Attributes to Callbacks Through Ev( ) in Perl/Tk

As mentioned previously, a callback may need access to the various attributes of the event that triggered the callback. For example, when you click a mouse button for some location of the mouse pointer, you may need to know the coordinates of the mouse pointer. (This would be important for drawing applications.) Previously we stated that, when a callback is invoked by the system, the system supplies to the callback an event object through the variable `Tk::event`. The callback can then retrieve various attributes of the event by invoking methods on the event object.

We will now show a feature of Perl/Tk that permits the event attributes to be supplied directly as arguments to a callback. This is accomplished with the help of a special method `Ev()`. If a callback argument is in the form of `Ev()`, with `Ev()`'s argument set to a special letter, the callback will be supplied with the event attribute corresponding to that letter. To illustrate how `Ev()` is used, consider the events produced by pressing a mouse button inside a canvas widget. A canvas widget is meant for drawing shapes, rendering images, and so on. So when you press a mouse button inside a canvas, the canvas widget would want to know the `(x,y)` coordinates of the mouse pointer at that instant and would want to supply these coordinates to a callback. This can be done with the help of the following call to a special variant of `bind()`:[33]

```
$canvas->CanvasBind( "<Button-1>",
                        [\&name_of_callback, Ev('x'), Ev('y')] );
```

Therefore, if we just wanted to print out the `(x,y)` coordinates of the mouse pointer on the canvas each time the left button of the mouse is pressed, we could use

```
$canvas->CanvasBind( "<Button-1>",
                        [\&printxy, Ev('x'), Ev('y')] );
```

[33]The regular `bind()` for a canvas is for registering callbacks with the individual items of shapes and images you may place on the canvas. (Each item on a canvas, such as a shape, an image, and so on, is given a unique ID number, which is a positive integer. A canvas item can be manipulated through its item ID.) So if you want to associate a callback with the canvas itself, you have to call `CanvasBind()` instead.

```
sub printxy {
    my ($canvas, $x, $y) = @_;
    print "x: $x  y: $y\n";
}
```

We may think of Ev() as a "nested callback"' because it is invoked inside the primary programmer-defined callback for trapping the button-press events in the example shown above.

The one-letter arguments that can be specified for Ev() are the same as the one-letter methods that can be invoked on a Tk::event object inside a callback.[34] The script shown below illustrates us registering a callback named getEventProps() for the button-press event on a canvas object. This we do with the help of the previously mentioned CanvasBind() method in lines (C) through (K). Notice the construction of the second argument to CanvasBind(): It consists of an array all of whose elements after the first are calls to Ev() with various one-letter arguments. What each one-letter argument gets us is mentioned in the commented-out portions of lines (E) through (I). Inside the body of the callback, in lines (M) through (X), we first fetch these arguments and then print them out.[35]

```
#!/usr/bin/perl -w

### EventAttributesAsCallbackArgs.pl

use strict;
use Tk;

my $mw = MainWindow->new();                                            #(A)
my $canvas = $mw->Canvas( -cursor => 'crosshair' )->pack;              #(B)

$canvas->CanvasBind( '<Button>',                                       #(C)
                   [ \&getEventProps,                                  #(D)
                     Ev('x'),          # for x-coord of mouse pointer  #(E)
                     Ev('y'),          # for y-coord of mouse pointer  #(F)
```

[34]Section 13.4.2.1 showed some examples of these one-letter methods called on a Tk::event object inside a callback.

[35]The example uses the following syntax for the construction of the canvas widget in line (B):

```
my $canvas = $mw->Canvas( -cursor => 'crosshair' )->pack;
```

Since we don't really want to place anything on the canvas, we are content with the default values for the other options for the Canvas constructor. Nonetheless, since we do want to press the mouse button inside the canvas, it seems to be the right place to show the frequently used value for the cursor option that can be supplied to the constructor. As you'd expect, setting this option as shown makes the mouse pointer look like a crosshair. On Linux, a list of all the values that can be used for the cursor option can usually be found in the file cursorfont.h in the /usr/X11R6/include/X11/ directory.

```
                 Ev('b'),            # for button identity              #(G)
                 Ev('t'),            # for the time of the event        #(H)
                 Ev('W')             # for the source widget            #(I)
               ]                                                        #(J)
        );                                                              #(K)

sub getEventProps {                                                     #(L)
    my $widget = shift;                                                 #(M)
    my $x = shift;                                                      #(N)
    my $y = shift;                                                      #(O)
    my $button = shift;                                                 #(P)
    my $time = shift;                                                   #(Q)
    my $win = shift;                                                    #(R)
    print "widget: $widget\n" .                                         #(S)
          "mouse-pointer position x: $x\n" .                            #(T)
          "mouse-pointer position y: $y\n" .                            #(U)
          "button: $button\n" .                                         #(V)
          "time: $time\n" .                                             #(W)
          "widget: $win\n\n";                                           #(X)
}

MainLoop;
```

If you press, say, the right button of a three-button mouse when the mouse pointer is inside the canvas, you will see the following sort of output produced by the above script:

```
widget: Tk::Canvas=HASH(0x829ad28)
mouse-pointer position x: 105
mouse-pointer position y: 92
button: 3
time: 203576040
widget: Tk::Canvas=HASH(0x829ad28)
```

Note that the output produced by line (S) of the script is the same as the output produced by line (X). That makes sense because the first argument passed to the callback is a reference to the event-producing widget. The same widget reference is yielded by `Ev('W')` in line (I).

13.4.6 Turning Callbacks On and Off

The next two scripts, one in Perl/Tk and the other in Tkinter, demonstrate how one can turn a callback on and off at run time. The GUI produced by the script can be used to make "art nouveau" drawings by rapidly moving the mouse pointer over the canvas in a random fashion. An example is shown in Fig. 13.5. The drawing process is enabled and disabled by pressing and releasing the left mouse button as the mouse is in motion. The GUI consists of a canvas widget with a couple of GUI buttons at the bottom, one for saving the canvas drawing in a postscript file and the other for terminating the script.

13.4.6.1 Turning Callbacks On and Off in Perl/Tk

The script shown next, `DrawArt.pl`, constructs a canvas widget in lines (F) through (I) and two GUI buttons that go below the canvas in lines (K) through (P). The callbacks for the two GUI buttons are both registered with the `command` option in lines (K) through (P), the callbacks consisting of anonymous subroutines in lines (L) and (O). Note particularly in line (L) the convenience of the syntax for saving a drawing to a postscript file:

```
$canvas->postscript( -file => "picture.ps")
```

The script uses the variable `$drawEnable`, first defined in line (R), to keep track of the state of the drawing process. Its value is 1 when the motion of the mouse is supposed to result in arc-like artifacts on the canvas and 0 when the mouse motion is meant to be ignored. The value of `$drawEnable` is toggled by the statement in line (U) of the `drawingControl()` callback. The call to `CanvasBind()` in line (Q) binds this callback to the pressing of the left button of the physical mouse. So on every alternate press of the left button of the physical mouse, the variable `$drawEnable` changes from 0 to 1 and from 1 back to 0. The callback registration in line (Q) also supplies the mouse pointer coordinates to the callback code using the `Ev()` method discussed in Section 13.4.5.

The arc-like artifacts that are drawn on the canvas are produced by the callback `draw()` that is defined in lines (c) through (f). This callback is bound to the event `<Motion>` of the mouse by

```
$canvas->CanvasBind("<Motion>", [\&draw, Ev('x'), Ev('y')]);
```

in line (b) of the script, but only when the `$drawEnable` is set to 1. When `$drawEnable` is zero, we use the syntax

```
$canvas->CanvasBind( "<Motion>", "" );
```

in line (W) to turn off the callback previously bound to `<Motion>`. It is generally true in Tk that when the second argument supplied to an event binding function is an empty string, the previously bound callback for the same event gets turned off.

The global variables `$startX` and `$startY` of line (S) are initialized for each arc-like artifact with a press of the left mouse button in lines (Z). When drawing is permitted by `$drawEnable`, these two variables are continually updated in line (f) as the mouse pointer is moved over the canvas. The drawing itself is carried out by calling the `createArc()` method of the `Canvas` widget in line (e). Unless otherwise directed by the `style` option, this method draws a shape that looks like a pie slice from an oval defined by two pairs of `(x,y)` coordinates corresponding to the two opposite corners of the bounding rectangle.[36] The region is filled with the color that is specified by the `fill` option. By default, the boundary pixels of the region are shown in black. In line (e), the two corners of the bounding rectangle are supplied by `(startX, startY)` and the position `(x,y)` for the current position of the mouse pointer, all measured in pixel offsets from the upper left-hand corner of the canvas widget. Since `(startX, startY)` are continually updated with the current position, if you move the mouse very slowly, the two corners of the bounding rectangle will be very close to one another. The resulting pie shape will simply appear something like a dot on the canvas. However, if you move the mouse pointer fairly rapidly over the canvas, you will see a sequence of small pie slices being drawn on the canvas.

```
#!/usr/bin/perl -w

### DrawArt.pl

use strict;
use Tk;

my $mw = MainWindow->new;                                            #(A)
$mw->configure( -title => "Art Nouveau",                             #(B)
                -height => 650,                                      #(C)
                -width => 600 );                                     #(D)
$mw->resizable( 0, 0 );                                              #(E)

my $canvas = $mw->Canvas( -height => 600,                            #(F)
                          -width => 600,                             #(G)
                          -cursor => "crosshair"                     #(H)
                        )->pack( -side => 'top' );                   #(I)

my $frame = $mw->Frame->pack( 'side' => 'bottom' );                  #(J)
$frame->Button( -text => 'Save',                                     #(K)
                -command =>
                  sub {$canvas->postscript( -file => "picture.ps")}#(L)
              )->pack( -side => 'left' );                            #(M)
$frame->Button( -text => 'Exit',                                     #(N)
                -command => sub { exit }                             #(O)
              )->pack( -side => 'right' );                           #(P)

$canvas->CanvasBind( "<Button-1>",
                        [\&drawingControl, Ev('x'), Ev('y')] );      #(Q)
```

---

[36]By default, the angular extent of the pie is 90 degrees. However, that can be changed by setting the `extent` option. For further information on the `style`, `extent`, and `fill` options mentioned here (and many others not mentioned) for `createArc()`, see the Perl/Tk documentation.

```
my $drawEnable;                                                        #(R)
my ($startX, $startY);                                                 #(S)

# Turn drawing on and off with consecutive clicks of the
# left button of the mouse
sub drawingControl {                                                   #(T)
    $drawEnable = ++$drawEnable % 2;                                   #(U)
    unless ($drawEnable) {                                             #(V)
        $canvas->CanvasBind( "<Motion>", "" );                         #(W)
    } else {                                                           #(X)
        my $canv = shift;                                              #(Y)
        ($startX, $startY) = @_;                                       #(Z)
        print "Button pressed at: x=$startX  y=$startY\n";             #(a)
        $canv->CanvasBind("<Motion>", [\&draw, Ev('x'), Ev('y')]);  #(b)
    }
}

sub draw {                                                             #(c)
    my ($canv, $x, $y) = @_;                                           #(d)
    $canv->createArc( $startX, $startY, $x, $y,
                              -width => 4, -fill => 'red' );           #(e)
    ($startX, $startY) = ($x, $y);                                     #(f)
}

MainLoop;                                                              #(g)
```

The GUI produced by this script is shown in Fig. 13.5. The figure also illustrates what sort of a drawing you can create with this GUI.

13.4.6.2 Turning Callbacks On and Off in Tkinter

The following script, `DrawArt.py`, is the Python version of `DrawArt.pl`. As before, the GUI consists of a canvas object where a user can create "art nouveau" by dragging the mouse pointer on the canvas in random rapid strokes. The bottom of the GUI has two buttons, one for terminating the script and the other for saving the artwork to a postscript file. The canvas is created in lines (E) through (I) and the two buttons in lines (J) through (S). The two buttons are first grouped together inside a frame and the frame placed at the bottom of the GUI.

The main callback in the script is `drawControl()` in lines (X) through (g). With consecutive presses of the left button of the physical mouse, the drawing action is either enabled or disabled. This is done by toggling the value of the global variable `drawEnabled` in line (Z). Note the syntax in line (b) for disabling the drawing action:

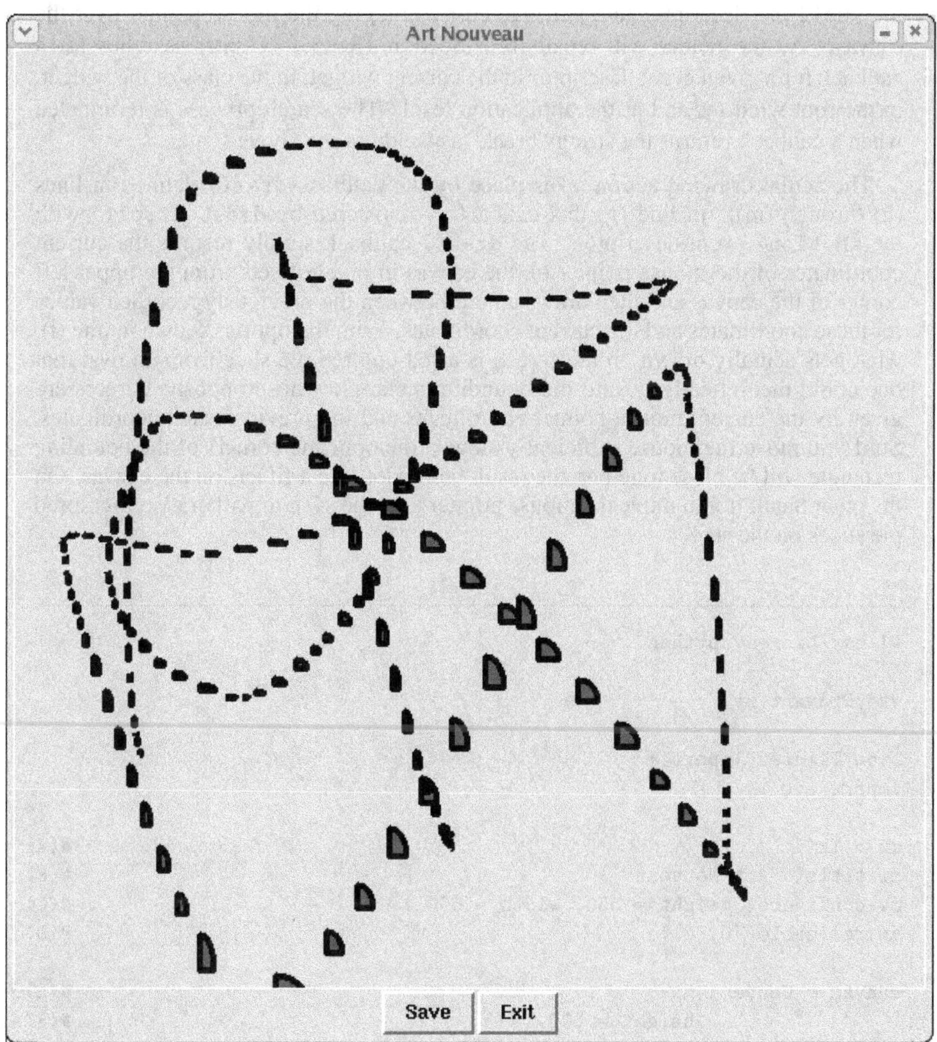

Fig. 13.5

```
canvas.bind( "<Motion>", lambda e: "break" )
```

This not only disables the callback that may have been registered by the statement in line (g), but also wards off any "higher-level" callbacks (either user-defined or provided by default by some future version of Tkinter) that may be associated with the `<Motion>` descriptor that is triggered by dragging the mouse pointer over the canvas. As the reader will recall from Section 13.4.3.3, Tkinter searches for a callback for a given event descriptor in the current widget, in the class of the widget, in the root window, and at the application level. The search process is terminated when a callback returns the string "break" as we do in the above syntax.

The actual drawing action takes place by the callback `draw()` defined in lines (h) through (m). In line (g) this callback is registered by `drawControl()` with the `<Motion>` event descriptor. The `draw()` callback simply records the current coordinates of the mouse pointer on the canvas in pixel offsets from the upper left corner of the canvas and then draws an arc between the previously recorded values for these coordinates and the current coordinates. With the options shown in line (l), what gets actually drawn on the screen is a red-colored pie slice from an oval that one could theoretically fit into the bounding rectangle whose opposite corners are given by the current mouse-pointer coordinates and the previous such coordinates. So if you move the mouse sufficiently slowly, the opposite corners of the bounding rectangle will be close together, the result being dot-like artifacts on the canvas. On the other hand, if you move the mouse pointer fast, the system will draw red-colored pie slices on the screen.

```
#!/usr/bin/env python

### DrawArt.py

from Tkinter import *
import sys

mw = Tk()                                                        #(A)
mw.title( "Art Nouveau" )                                        #(B)
mw.configure( height = 650, width = 600 )                        #(C)
mw.resizable( 0, 0 )                                             #(D)

canvas = Canvas( mw,                                             #(E)
                 height = 600,                                   #(F)
                 width = 600,                                    #(G)
                 cursor = "crosshair" )                          #(H)
canvas.pack( side = 'top' )                                      #(I)
```

```
frame = Frame(mw)                                                    #(J)
frame.pack( side = 'bottom' )                                        #(K)
Button( frame,                                                       #(L)
        text = 'Save',                                               #(M)
        command = lambda: canvas.postscript( file = "picture.ps")    #(N)
      ).pack( side = 'left' )                                        #(O)
Button( frame,                                                       #(P)
        text = 'Exit',                                               #(Q)
        command = lambda: sys.exit(0),                               #(R)
      ).pack( side = 'right' )                                       #(S)

drawEnable = 0                                                       #(T)
startX = None                                                        #(U)
startY = None                                                        #(V)

canvas.bind( "<Button-1>", lambda e: drawingControl( e ) )           #(W)

# Turn drawing on and off with consecutive clicks of the
# left button of the mouse
def drawingControl( evt ):                                           #(X)
    global drawEnable, startX, startY                                #(Y)
    drawEnable = (drawEnable + 1) % 2                                #(Z)
    if not drawEnable:                                               #(a)
        canvas.bind( "<Motion>", lambda e: "break" )                 #(b)
    else:                                                            #(c)
        canv = evt.widget                                            #(d)
        startX, startY = evt.x, evt.y                                #(e)
        print "Button pressed at: x=%s  y=%s\n" % (startX, startY)  #(f)
        canv.bind( "<Motion>", lambda e: draw( e ) )                 #(g)

def draw( evt ):                                                     #(h)
    global startX, startY                                            #(i)
    canv, x, y = evt.widget, evt.x, evt.y                            #(j)
    canv.create_arc( startX, startY, x, y,                           #(k)
                            width = 4, fill = 'red' )                #(l)
    startX, startY = x, y                                            #(m)

mainloop()                                                           #(n)
```

This script gives us the same GUI as shown earlier in Fig. 13.5. The pictures that you can draw on the GUI are also of the same type as illustrated in that figure.

13.5 WIDGETS INVOKING CALLBACKS ON OTHER WIDGETS

We will now show a simple example, patterned after the `CrazyWindow` examples presented in [41], that shows how the events occurring in one widget can cause changes to take place in another widget. More specifically, words entered in a text widget will cause shapes to pop up in a canvas widget. The GUI produced by the following two scripts, shown in Fig. 13.6, consists of a text widget on the left and a canvas widget on the right. The user enters a "story" on the left. In the particular example shown here, when a word entered is the name of a color, a tile corresponding to that color pops up at a random location on the canvas widget. The particular state of the GUI shown in Fig. 13.6 corresponds to the user having entered the following words in the text widget:

```
A blue fish jumped over a red fox and became green with brown envy
```

and the tiles shown on the canvas widget correspond to the colors blue, red, green, and brown.[37]

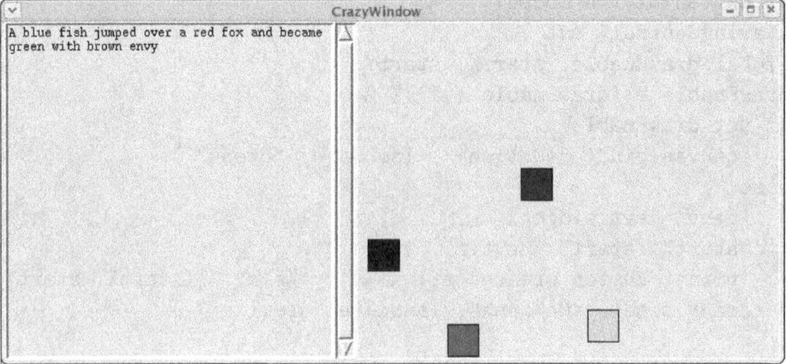

Fig. 13.6

13.5.1 Widgets Invoking Callbacks on Other Widgets in Perl/Tk

To explain the next script, lines (A) through (I) set up the GUI with its main window and with a text area on the left in the main window and the canvas area on the right. Line (J) gives the keyboard focus to the text widget. This allows the user to start entering the text right away when the GUI first comes up on the screen. Without the statement in line (J), the user will first have to position the mouse cursor explicitly in the text area and click on the left mouse button so that the text widget acquires the keyboard focus. In line (K) we bind the key press events to the `word_accumulator()`

[37] The reader will obviously not be able to see these colors in the black-and-white book reproduction of the figure.

callback. The purpose of this callback, defined in lines (M) through (W), is to form individual words from the characters entered by the user. The conditional in line (P) says that a series of characters entered successively forms a word when the user presses either the space bar or the return key. How the `keysym` value of a key pressed by the user is obtained by the statements in lines (N) and (O) should be clear to the reader from our earlier discussions in Sections 13.4.2.1. In the rest of the code in the callback, we first form two random `x` and `y` coordinates in line (S).[38] Subsequently, we compare the words formed from the user-entered characters against the names of some of the colors. When a match is found, we invoke the `createRectangle()` method on the canvas widget to draw a 30 pixel by 30 pixel tile of the matching color on the canvas object at the previously calculated random coordinates, as shown by the code in lines (T) and (U) for the case of matches with the name `red`.[39]

```
#!/usr/bin/perl -w

###  CrazyWindow.pl

use strict;
use Tk;

my $mw = MainWindow->new( -title => "CrazyWindow" );                   #(A)

my $textWindow = $mw->Scrolled( 'Text',                                #(B)
                                -width => 45,                          #(C)
                                -scrollbars => 'e',                    #(D)
                                -setgrid => 'true',                    #(E)
                              )
                     ->pack( -side => 'left' );                        #(F)

my $drawWindow = $mw->Canvas()                                         #(G)
                   ->pack( -side => 'right',                           #(H)
                           -fill => 'y', -expand => 1 );               #(I)

$textWindow->focus;                                                    #(J)
```

[38] As mentioned earlier in Chapter 2, `int(rand(N))` returns a random number between 0 and `N-1`, both inclusive.

[39] When symbolic names, such as `red`, `green`, etc., are used for naming colors, they must correspond to the list of names in the `/usr/X11R6/lib/X11/rgb.txt` for X server based invocations of the `CrazyWindow` script. Although not appropriate for the `CrazyWindow`, in general a color may also be named by its R, G, and B component values expressed in the form of a hex string. The hex string could be formed by using `sprintf()` as in the following example:

```
my ($red, $green, $blue) = (100, 128, 200);
my $color = sprintf( "#%02x%02x%02x", $red, $green, $blue );
print "$color\n";                   # #6480c8
```

where the component color values are non-negative decimal integers between 0 and 255.

```
$textWindow->bind( '<KeyPress>' => \&word_accumulator);                    #(K)

my $word = '';                                                             #(L)

sub word_accumulator {                                                     #(M)
    my $e = $Tk::event;                                                    #(N)
    my ($keysym_text, $keysym_decimal ) = ($e->K, $e->N);                  #(O)
    if ( $keysym_text ne 'space' and $keysym_text ne 'Return' ) {          #(P)
        $word .= $keysym_text;                                             #(Q)
    } else {                                                               #(R)
        my ($x, $y) = (int(rand(280)), int(rand(300)));                    #(S)
        if ( $word eq 'red' ) {                                            #(T)
            $drawWindow->createRectangle( $x, $y, $x+30, $y+30,
                                  -fill => 'red' );                        #(U)
        } elsif ( $word eq 'blue' ) {                                      #(V)
            $drawWindow->createRectangle( $x, $y, $x+30, $y+30,
                                  -fill => 'blue' );
        } elsif ( $word eq 'brown' ) {
            $drawWindow->createRectangle( $x, $y, $x+30, $y+30,
                                  -fill => 'brown' );
        } elsif ( $word eq 'green' ) {
            $drawWindow->createRectangle( $x, $y, $x+30, $y+30,
                                  -fill => 'green' );
        } elsif ( $word eq 'black' ) {
            $drawWindow->createRectangle( $x, $y, $x+30, $y+30,
                                  -fill => 'black' );
        } elsif ( $word eq 'orange' ) {
            $drawWindow->createRectangle( $x, $y, $x+30, $y+30,
                                  -fill => 'orange' );
        } elsif ( $word eq 'yellow' ) {
            $drawWindow->createRectangle( $x, $y, $x+30, $y+30,
                                  -fill => 'yellow' );
        }
        $word = '';                                                        #(W)
    }
}

MainLoop;                                                                  #(X)
```

13.5.2 Widgets Invoking Callbacks on Other Widgets in Tkinter

The next script, `CrazyWindow.py`, does the same thing as its Perl/Tk version shown above. Lines (A) through (O) construct the top-level GUI with a scrollbar-equipped text window on the left and a canvas on the right. As mentioned before, the user enters a story in the text window. As the user is entering text, for certain chosen words entered by the user (that are the names of colors), a colored tile pops up at a random location in the canvas on the right. The callback word_accumulator(), registered with the text widget in line (R), is triggered by all keyboard entries by the user. The callback, shown in lines (S) through (n), extracts each character entered by the user in the text window while being mindful of the common word boundaries. It joins the characters into whole words, as should be evident from the syntax used in lines (V) and (W). When a word is recognized as being the name of one of the colors listed in lines (Z) through (m), the callback create_rectangle() is invoked on the canvas widget on the right side of the GUI.

```
#!/usr/bin/env python

### CrazyWindow.py

import random
from Tkinter import *

mw = Tk()                                                              #(A)
mw.title( "CrazyWindow" )                                              #(B)
scrollbar = Scrollbar( mw, orient = 'vertical' )                       #(C)
textWindow = Text( mw,                                                 #(D)
                   width = 45,                                         #(E)
                   setgrid = 'true',                                   #(F)
                   yscrollcommand = scrollbar.set,                     #(G)
                )
scrollbar.config( command = textWindow.yview )                         #(H)
scrollbar.pack( side = 'left', fill = 'y' )                            #(I)
textWindow.focus()                                                     #(J)
textWindow.pack( side = 'left' )                                       #(K)

drawWindow = Canvas( mw )                                              #(L)
drawWindow.pack( side = 'right',                                       #(M)
                 fill = 'y',                                           #(N)
                 expand = 1 )                                          #(O)

word = ''                                                              #(P)
ran = random.Random()                                                  #(Q)

textWindow.bind( '<KeyPress>', lambda e: word_accumulator( e ) )       #(R)

def word_accumulator( evt ):                                           #(S)
    global word, ran                                                   #(T)
    keysym_text, keysym_decimal = evt.keysym, evt.keysym_num           #(U)
    if ( keysym_text != 'space' and keysym_text != 'Return' ):         #(V)
        word += keysym_text                                            #(W)
    else:                                                              #(X)
        x, y = ran.randint(0,280), ran.randint(0,300)                  #(Y)
```

```
        if word == 'red' :                                                    #(Z)
            drawWindow.create_rectangle( x, y, x+30, y+30,
                                             fill = 'red' )                  #(a)
        elif word == 'blue' :                                                 #(b)
            drawWindow.create_rectangle( x, y, x+30, y+30,
                                             fill = 'blue' )                 #(c)
        elif word == 'brown':                                                 #(d)
            drawWindow.create_rectangle( x, y, x+30, y+30,
                                             fill = 'brown' )                #(e)
        elif word == 'green':                                                 #(f)
            drawWindow.create_rectangle( x, y, x+30, y+30,
                                             fill = 'green' )                #(g)
        elif word == 'black':                                                 #(h)
            drawWindow.create_rectangle( x, y, x+30, y+30,
                                             fill = 'black' )                #(i)
        elif word == 'orange':                                                #(j)
            drawWindow.create_rectangle( x, y, x+30, y+30,
                                             fill = 'orange' )               #(k)
        elif word == 'yellow':                                                #(l)
            drawWindow.create_rectangle( x, y, x+30, y+30,
                                             fill = 'yellow' )               #(m)
        word = ''                                                             #(n)

mainloop()                                                                    #(o)
```

13.6 MENUS

Menus are indispensable to much programming required for graphical user interfaces. Menus allow a user-driven display of alternatives with regard to a mode of interaction with a GUI. For example, if a user wants to interact with a file, the various choices for this interaction are usually presented to the user in the form of a drop-down menu under the File label at the top of the GUI.

To endow a GUI with a menu, one typically first constructs a *menubar* that is commonly displayed at the top of a top-level window. A menubar is constructed by calling the `Menu()` method on an instance of a top-level widget. The menubar is populated with *menubuttons* that are most commonly shown as a horizontal array of items in the menubar. Clicking on a menubutton results typically in a drop-down display of a menu, an action that is referred to as the *posting* of a menu. The menu items in a drop-down list may be grouped for visual convenience with the help of *separators*, usually horizontal lines. The top-most item of visual display in a drop-down menu may also be a line-like feature that acts as a *tearoff* device. If you click on a tearoff at the top of a menu, it causes the menu to get separated; the menu could then be moved and parked at a more convenient location on the screen.

13.6.1 Menus in Perl/Tk

The next script, `CascadingMenu.pl`, shows a simple example of a cascading menu — a menu whose items when clicked cause submenus to get posted on the screen. In line (A), we construct the main window of the GUI and in line (B) we place a text area in the main window. Line (C) constructs a menubar by invoking `Menu()`[40] on `$mw` and line (D) endows the main window with the menubar. Lines (E) and (H) call on the `cascade()` method to create two menubuttons that will be placed horizontally in the menubar.[41] The label for one of the menubuttons is `Help`, as provided by the `label` option in line (E), and the label for the other menubutton is `Level_0`, as provided by the same option in line (H). Setting the `underline` option to an integer value n causes the nth character of the label to be underlined for designating a keyboard shortcut for a menu item.[42] The `tearoff` option specifies that the submenu attached with the menubutton can be torn off by clicking on the tearoff line that is made visible when this option is set to 1.

Lines (K) through (e) then specify the menus to be associated with the menubuttons `Level_0` and `Help` in the menubar. Since we invoke `command()` in line (K), as opposed to `cascade()`, that says that the drop-down menu posted by clicking on `Help` in the menubar will contain the label `About` and that this label will accept a callback, the callback supplied by the `command` option in line (L).

The drop-down menu associated with the menubutton `Level_0` of the menubar is defined by the calls in lines (N) and (P). We therefore have two items in this drop-down menu, the command item `Exit` of line (N) and the cascade item `Level_1`of line (P). When selected, we obviously want the label `Level_1` to post a submenu. This submenu consists of a cascade of submenus, as defined by the calls to `cascade()` in lines (S) through (a). The menu item at the tail end of this cascade, `Level_4` created in line (Y), also has associated with it a submenu, since it is brought into existence through the `cascade()` function. The submenu associated with `Level_4` is the command item `Click Here` created in line (b) with an associated callback.

---

[40]A call to `Menu()` just returns a menu widget. This widget becomes the menubar for a top-level window because we supply it as the value for the `menu` option to the `configure()` method invoked on the top-level window [see line (D) of the script]. As we show later, the widget returned by `Menu()` can also be used as a menu item.

[41]We could also have invoked `command()` directly on `$mbar` to create a menubutton that when clicked would result in the invocation of a callback. Whereas the `cascade()` method creates a menu item that when clicked will cause a submenu to be posted to the right, the `command()` method creates a menu item that accepts a callback. So we may refer to a menu item as a *cascade* item or as a *command* item, depending on whether it was created by a call to `cascade()` or a call to `command()`.

[42]Pressing the key corresponding to the underlined character while you are also pressing the Alt key will cause that menu item to be selected. You can ignore the case of the underlined character. Character position indexing is zero-based for supplying a value to the `underline` option.

```
#!/usr/bin/perl -w

### CascadingMenu.pl

use Tk;

my $mw = new MainWindow;                                                  #(A)
my $txt = $mw->Scrolled( 'Text', -width => 50, -scrollbars => 'e' )
             ->pack();                                                    #(B)
my $mbar = $mw->Menu();                                                   #(C)
$mw->configure( -menu => $mbar );                                         #(D)

# Two menubuttons for the menubar:

my $help = $mbar->cascade( -label => "Help",                              #(E)
                           -underline => 0,                               #(F)
                           -tearoff => 0 );                               #(G)

my $level_0 = $mbar->cascade( -label => "Level_0",                        #(H)
                              -underline => 0,                            #(I)
                              -tearoff => 1, );                           #(J)

# The menu for the 'Help' menubutton in the menubar:

$help->command( -label => "About",                                        #(K)
                -command => sub { $txt->insert( 'end',                    #(L)
      "Click on the Level_0 button to see a cascading menu" ) } );        #(M)

# The menu for the 'Level_0' menubutton in the menubar:

$level_0->command( -label => "Exit",                                      #(N)
                   -command => sub { exit } );                            #(O)

my $level_1 = $level_0->cascade( -label => "Level_1",                     #(P)
                                 -underline => 1,                         #(Q)
                                 -tearoff => 1 );                         #(R)

my $level_2 = $level_1->cascade( -label => "Level_2",                     #(S)
                                 -underline => 2,                         #(T)
                                 -tearoff => 1 );                         #(U)

my $level_3 = $level_2->cascade( -label => "Level_3",                     #(V)
                                 -underline => 3,                         #(W)
                                 -tearoff => 1 );                         #(X)

my $level_4 = $level_3->cascade( -label => "Level_4",                     #(Y)
                                 -underline => 4,                         #(Z)
```

```
                        -tearoff => 1 );                              #(a)

$level_4->command( -label => "click here",                            #(b)
                -command => sub { $txt->insert( 'end',                 #(c)
               "hello from the tail end of a cascaded menu\n") });#(d)
MainLoop;                                                              #(e)
```

The GUI produced by the above script is shown in Fig. 13.7. The state of the GUI shown corresponds to the user first selecting the Level_0 menubutton from the menubar and then selecting the Level_1 cascade menu item from the drop-down menu.[43]

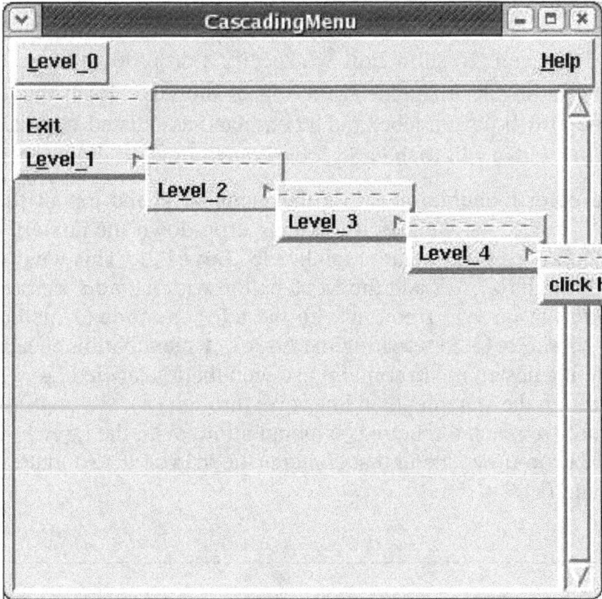

Fig. 13.7

[43]If it is desired to create a menu that would pop up through button-like action anywhere in a window, the method to use is `Menubutton()`. By supplying an appropriate value for the `direction` option, the menu constructed with `Menubutton()` can be made to pop up in any of the cardinal directions.

13.6.2 Menus in Tkinter

The next script, `CascadingMenu.py`, shows a cascading menu in Tkinter. The GUI produced by this script is the same as by the previous Perl/Tk script. Line (D) first constructs an instance of a menubar by calling on the `Menu()` constructor and supplying to it as the argument the widget that is to be adorned with the menubar. The menubar is placed in the widget with the `configure()` call in line (E).

Lines (F) through (M) construct two menubuttons for the menubar. The first menubutton is given the label `Level_0` and the second the label `Help`. The first menubutton is created by the code in lines (G), (H), and (I), and the drop-down menu associated with this menubutton by the call to the `Menu()` constructor in line (F). Similarly, the second menubutton is constructed in lines (K), (L), and (M), and the drop-down menu associated with this menubutton by the call to the `Menu()` constructor in line (J). Notice the call to the `add_cascade()` method for creating the menubuttons in lines (G) and (K).

Lines (N), (O), and (P) show how we specify a drop-down menu to go with the `Help` menubutton in the menubar at the top of the GUI. Each menubutton in the drop-down menu will have a label and a command associated with it. So we create this menubutton with a call to the `add_command()` method in line (N).

About the other menubutton inside the menubar at the top of the GUI — the one labeled `Level_0` — we specify that its drop-down menu start with an `Exit` menubutton, followed by a menubutton labeled `Level_1`. This we do with the help of lines (Q) through (V). We add the `Exit` button with the `add_command()` method in line (Q) and the `Level_1` button with the `add_cascade()` method in line (T). We use `add_cascade()` for creating the `Level_1` menubutton because we want to associate with it a nested menu containing a menubutton labeled `Level_2`. We bring that about through the statements in lines (W) through (Z). We continue this process of nesting, until we reach the `Level_4` menubutton. With the `Level_4` menubutton, we associate a drop-down menu that contains the `click here` button, as shown in lines (i), (j), and (k).

```
#!/usr/bin/env python

### CascadingMenu.py

from Tkinter import *

mw = Tk()                                                            #(A)
text = Text( mw, width = 50 )                                        #(B)
text.pack()                                                          #(C)

mbar = Menu( mw )                                                    #(D)
mw.configure( menu = mbar )                                          #(E)
```

```
# Two menu buttons for the menubar:
level_0_menu = Menu( mbar, tearoff = 1 )                              #(F)
mbar.add_cascade( label = "Level_0",                                  #(G)
                  menu = level_0_menu,                                #(H)
                  underline = 1)                                      #(I)
helpmenu = Menu( mbar, tearoff = 0 )                                  #(J)
mbar.add_cascade( label = "Help",                                     #(K)
                  menu = helpmenu,                                    #(L)
                  underline = 0)                                      #(M)

# The menu for the 'Help' menubutton in the menubar:
helpmenu.add_command( label = "About",                                #(N)
                      command = lambda: text.insert('end',            #(O)
             "Click on the Level_0 button to see a cascading menu"))#(P)

# The menu for the 'Level_0' menubutton in the menubar:
level_0_menu.add_command( label = "Exit",                             #(Q)
                          command = mw.quit );                        #(R)

level_1_menu = Menu( mbar, tearoff = 1 )                              #(S)
level_0_menu.add_cascade( label = "Level_1",                          #(T)
                          underline = 1,                              #(U)
                          menu = level_1_menu )                       #(V)

level_2_menu =  Menu( mbar, tearoff = 1 )                             #(W)
level_1_menu.add_cascade( label = "Level_2",                          #(X)
                          underline = 2,                              #(Y)
                          menu = level_2_menu )                       #(Z)

level_3_menu =  Menu( mbar, tearoff = 1 )                             #(a)
level_2_menu.add_cascade( label = "Level_3",                          #(b)
                          underline = 3,                              #(c)
                          menu = level_3_menu )                       #(d)

level_4_menu =  Menu( mbar, tearoff = 1 )                             #(e)
level_3_menu.add_cascade( label = "Level_4",                          #(f)
                          underline = 4,                              #(g)
                          menu = level_4_menu )                       #(h)
level_4_menu.add_command( label = "click here",                       #(i)
                          command = lambda: text.insert( 'end',       #(j)
                 "hello from the tail end of a cascaded menu\n" ) ) #(k)
mainloop()                                                            #(l)
```

13.6.3 Radiobutton, Checkbutton, and Option Menus

While the previous script showed the most commonly used drop-down or pop-up menus, there are also available other kinds of menus that can be useful for eliciting a user's selection from a small set of choices. These other kinds of menus are radiobutton menus, checkbutton menus, and option menus. All of these menus accept a `variable` option for declaring a variable that acquires a value depending on the selection made by the user. A radiobutton menu is best for selecting one from a list of choices. When an alternative selection is made with a radiobutton menu, any previous selection gets automatically deselected. A checkbutton is best when multiple selections are desired simultaneously from a list of choices. With checkbuttons, each item must be toggled independently for selection or deselection. Like a radiobutton menu, an option menu is also good for selecting one item from the different choices available. An option menu displays the item selected in the label field at the head of the menu. These three types of menus will now be explained with the next two scripts.

13.6.3.1 Radiobutton, Checkbutton, and Option Menus in Perl/Tk

The script `MenuRadOptCheck.pl` creates a GUI consisting of a menubar with two menu buttons, `Choose_Color` and `Choose_Numbers`, the former a radiobutton menu and the latter a checkbutton menu. The main part of the GUI is a text area for displaying the values acquired by the relevant variables when a user makes selections from the different menus. The bottom of the GUI contains an option menu button. The two sides of the option menu button consist of the unclaimed portions of the main window background. We use this visible background area for coloration when a user chooses a color from the option menu. The GUI is shown in Fig. 13.8. The GUI shown corresponds to the state when the user has not yet clicked on any of the radiobuttons, but has clicked on two of the checkbuttons. Both the radiobutton menu attached to the `Choose_Color` menu and the checkbutton menu attached to the `Choose_Numbers` menu are shown in their tearoff forms to make them simultaneously visible.[44] The GUI shown also corresponds to the selection of the `cyan` option from the option menu at the bottom. If this GUI were to be shown in color, the area surrounding the button at the bottom would appear cyan. The options made available by the options menu are shown separately in Fig. 13.9 below the main GUI.

To explain the script, lines (A) through (D) set up the main window with a menubar at the top and with a text area that is 50 characters wide. Line (E) creates a `Choose_Color` menubutton for the menubar. The radiobutton menu associated with this menubutton is created by lines (G) through (M). Note the `variable` option supplied to each radiobutton of this menu. The value given to the `value` option

[44]Obviously, clicking on one of the radiobuttons, say the one labeled `green`, would make the entire text area green.

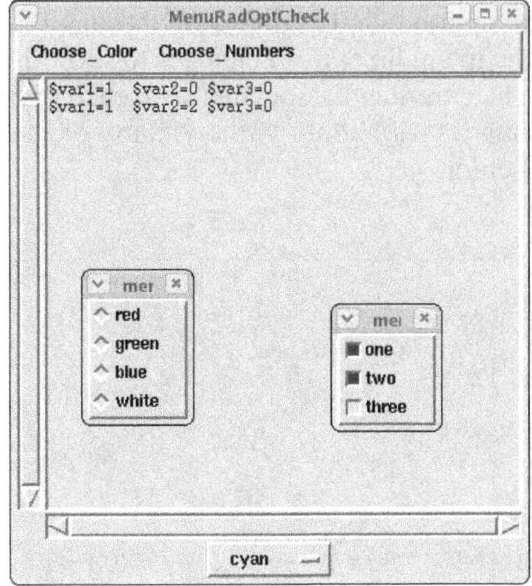

Fig. 13.8

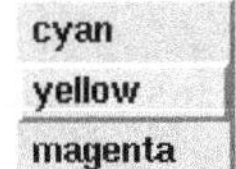

Fig. 13.9

gets assigned to the `variable` when the user selects that radiobutton from the menu. All other radiobuttons that have the same `variable` option get deselected when a user selects a particular radiobutton. The command associated with each radiobutton executes the subroutine `radio_set_bg()` defined in lines (d), (e), and (f). This subroutine changes the color of the text area accordingly.

A second menubutton, `Choose_Numbers`, for the menubar is created in line (O). In lines (P) through (V), we create a checkbutton menu consisting of three items for associating with this menubutton. Each checkbutton of this menu can be toggled independently so as to set the value of the variable supplied with the `variable` option to either an *onvalue* or an *offvalue*.[45] Note that we chose different onvalues for the three checkbuttons, but have the same offvalue of 0 for all three. As with the radiobuttons, associated with each checkbutton is a variable that is supplied with the `variable` option. But note that the variables supplied for the three checkbuttons are different, unlike the case for the different radiobuttons when we used the same variable. Also associated with each check button is a command that prints out the values of all the checkbutton variables.

[45]The default onvalue is 1 and the default offvalue 0.

Finally, we have the option menu in lines (W) through (b). As mentioned earlier, with an option menu the menu label itself changes to show the selection made by the user from the menu. The command associated with each option selection causes the main window background, visible only in the vicinity of the option menubutton, to change to the selected color.

```
#!/usr/bin/perl -w

### MenuRadOptCheck.pl

use Tk;

my $mw = new MainWindow;                                                    #(A)
my $txt = $mw->Scrolled( 'Text', -width => 50 )->pack();                    #(B)
my $mbar = $mw->Menu();                                                     #(C)
$mw->configure( -menu => $mbar );                                           #(D)

# A menu consisting of radio buttons:

my $radio_select = $mbar->cascade( -label => "Choose_Color" );              #(E)
my $var;                                                                    #(F)
$radio_select->radiobutton( -label => 'red',                                #(G)
                            -value => 'red',                                #(H)
                            -variable => \$var,                             #(I)
                            -command => \&radio_set_bg,                     #(J)
                          );
$radio_select->radiobutton( -label => 'green',                              #(K)
                            -value => 'green',
                            -variable => \$var,
                            -command => \&radio_set_bg,
                          );
$radio_select->radiobutton( -label => 'blue',                               #(L)
                            -value => 'blue',
                            -variable => \$var,
                            -command => \&radio_set_bg,
                          );
$radio_select->radiobutton( -label => 'white',                              #(M)
                            -value => 'white',
                            -variable => \$var,
                            -command => \&radio_set_bg,
                          );

# A menu consisting of check buttons:

my ($var1, $var2, $var3) = (0, 0, 0);                                       #(N)
my $check_select = $mbar->cascade( -label => "Choose_Numbers" );            #(O)
$check_select->checkbutton( -label => 'one',                                #(P)
```

```
                              -onvalue => 1,                     #(Q)
                              -offvalue => 0,                    #(R)
                              -variable => \$var1,               #(S)
                              -command => \&print_nums,          #(T)
                            );
$check_select->checkbutton( -label => 'two',                    #(U)
                              -onvalue => 2,
                              -offvalue => 0,
                              -variable => \$var2,
                              -command => \&print_nums,
                            );
$check_select->checkbutton( -label => 'three',                  #(V)
                              -onvalue => 3,
                              -offvalue => 0,
                              -variable => \$var3,
                              -command => \&print_nums,
                            );

# An option menu:

my $color_option;                                               #(W)
$mw->Optionmenu( -variable => \$color_option,                   #(X)
                 -options => ['cyan', 'yellow', 'magenta'],     #(Y)
                 -command =>                                    #(Z)
                 sub {$mw->configure(-background => $color_option)} #(a)
               )->pack();                                       #(b)

MainLoop;                                                       #(c)

sub radio_set_bg {                                              #(d)
    $txt->configure( -background => $var );                     #(e)
    $txt->insert('end', "value of \$var: $var\n");              #(f)
}

sub print_nums {                                                #(g)
    $txt->insert( 'end', "\$var1=$var1  \$var2=$var2 \$var3=$var3\n");
}
```

13.6.3.2 Radiobutton, Checkbutton, and Option Menus in Tkinter

The following Tkinter script produces exactly the same GUI as the previous Perl/Tk script. The GUI consists mainly of a text widget that is adorned at the top with two menubuttons labeled `Choose_Color` and `Choose_Numbers`, the former associated with a drop-down radiobutton menu and the latter with a drop-down checkbutton menu. When you select the Choose_Color menubutton, you see a drop-down menu consisting of a sequence of radiobuttons, all associated with a single variable. Selecting the Choose_Numbers menubutton results in a drop-down menu consisting of a sequence of checkbuttons, each checkbutton associated with a previously designated variable. Finally, clicking on the option menu at the bottom of the GUI reveals a list of options. When you select an option, the label at the head of the option list changes accordingly.

The reader will notice more than the usual differences between Tkinter and Perl/Tk for creating radiobutton, checkbutton, and option menus. Perhaps the most significant difference between the previous Perl/Tk script and the Python script shown next is with regard to the variables associated with the menus. Whereas we could use ordinary variables in Perl/Tk script for the job, in Tkinter the variables must be instances made from the Tkinter classes StringVar or IntVar. The instances made from these classes are commonly known as *control variables*. What makes a control variable particularly useful is that it remembers all the widget instances that depend on it for signaling the values selected by a user. The two methods that are most commonly invoked on a control variable are set() and get(), the former for initializing its value and the latter for retrieving its current value. When the value of a control variable is initialized by a call to set(), if the value chosen is one of the previously acceptable values for a widget that uses the variable, the displayed state of the widget will correspond to that of the variable. For example, if a sequence of radiobuttons use the same control variable that is initialized to a value represented by one of the radiobuttons, that will cause the corresponding radiobutton to look selected (meaning that it looks "sunken" as opposed to "raised") when the GUI is first brought up.[46]

The menu construction in the script begins in line (D) with the construction of a menubar for the main window and with its placement in line (E) at the top of the main window of the GUI. This menubar houses the top-level menubuttons of the GUI. The menubuttons and the associated drop-down menus are constructed in lines (F) through (h). In each case, we first construct the drop-down menu and then bind it to a menubutton of the menubar. The radiobutton menu is constructed in lines (F) through (P). We first create in line (F) a control variable that will be shared by all the radiobuttons and then initialize it in line (G). Since this initialization corresponds to a value for one of the radiobuttons, that radiobutton will appear sunken when the GUI is first brought up. The radiobutton menu itself is an instance of the Menu class, as shown by the call in line (H). Lines (I) through (Q) place three radiobuttons in the menu by calling add(), each time with its first argument set to the keyword

---

[46]It is also possible to directly associate a callback with a control variable. A callback binding for a control variable is created by calling the trace_variable() on the control variable. For example, instead of using the command option in line (g) to designate the callback for the option menu, we could use the following syntax to accomplish the same:

```
color_option.trace_variable('rw', lambda e1,e2,e3: option_changed())
```

radiobutton. All the radiobuttons trigger the callback radio_set_bg() defined in lines (l) through (o). This callback changes the background color in the text widget to the color selected by the radiobutton. Finally, we call on add_cascade() in lines (Q) and (R) to create a menubutton for the menubar and to associate the radiobutton menu just created with that menubutton.

The checkbutton menu is constructed in the same manner in lines (S) through (d). Line (S) starts out by designating the variables needed for each of the checkbuttons. The onvalue and the offvalue for each variable are specified when the individual checkbuttons are constructed, as illustrated by the code in lines (U) through (Z) for the first checkbutton. As with the radiobutton menu, lines (c) and (d) call on call_cascade() to create a menubar menubutton for the checkbutton menu. We associate the same callback with all the checkbuttons; the callback is defined in lines (p), (q), and (r).

Finally, in lines (e) through (h), we endow the GUI with an option menu widget at the bottom. As stated earlier, an option menu accomplishes the same thing as a group of radiobuttons — they are both interaction mechanisms for implementing a one-of-many selection. With an option menu, the item selected is displayed in the label at the head of the menu. The control variable associated with the menu is declared in line (e) and it is initialized in line (f) to the value cyan. Note the syntax for the OptionMenu constructor call in line (g). It is different from the other menu constructor calls, in the sense that the OptionMenu constructor takes a comma-separated list of options starting with the third argument. Keyword arguments, such as the command option in line (g), can be supplied after the end of the options list. The second argument to the constructor is the control variable to be used for the widget. And, the first argument is the parent widget for the menu. The callback for the option menu is defined in lines (i), (j), and (k). The user's interaction with the option menu changes the background color at only the bottom of the GUI where the option menu is located. That is because line (k) calls for changing the background color for the main widget which can peek through only at the bottom. The rest of the GUI window is occupied by the menubar at the top and the text widget below that.

```
#!/usr/bin/env python

### MenuRadOptCheck.py

from Tkinter import *

mw = Tk()                                                        #(A)

text = Text( mw, width = 50 )                                    #(B)
text.pack()                                                      #(C)

menubar = Menu( mw )                                             #(D)
mw.configure( menu = menubar )                                   #(E)
```

```
#----------------------  A Radiobutton Menu  -------------------------
# Build a drop-down menu consisting of radio buttons under
# the label "Choose_Color":

var = StringVar()                                                  #(F)
var.set( 'white' )                                                 #(G)
radiobutton_menu = Menu( menubar, tearoff = 0 )                    #(H)
radiobutton_menu.add( 'radiobutton',                               #(I)
                      label = 'red',                               #(J)
                      value = 'red',                               #(K)
                      variable = var,                              #(L)
                      command = lambda: radio_set_bg(),            #(M)
                    )
radiobutton_menu.add( 'radiobutton',                               #(N)
                      label = 'blue',
                      value = 'blue',
                      variable = var,
                      command = lambda: radio_set_bg(),
                    )
radiobutton_menu.add( 'radiobutton',                               #(O)
                      label = 'green',
                      value = 'green',
                      variable = var,
                      command = lambda: radio_set_bg(),
                    )
radiobutton_menu.add( 'radiobutton',                               #(P)
                      label = 'white',
                      value = 'white',
                      variable = var,
                      command = lambda: radio_set_bg(),
                    )

menubar.add_cascade( label = "Choose_Color",                       #(Q)
                     menu = radiobutton_menu,                      #(R)
                   )

#----------------------  A Checkbutton Menu  -------------------------
# A menu consisting of check buttons:

var1, var2, var3 = IntVar(), IntVar(), IntVar()                    #(S)

checkbutton_menu = Menu( menubar, tearoff = 0 )                    #(T)
checkbutton_menu.add( 'checkbutton',                               #(U)
                      label = 'one',                               #(V)
                      onvalue = 1,                                 #(W)
                      offvalue = 0,                                #(X)
                      variable = var1,                             #(Y)
                      command = lambda: print_nums(),              #(Z)
                    )
```

```
checkbutton_menu.add( 'checkbutton',                                   #(a)
                      label = 'two',
                      onvalue = 2,
                      offvalue = 0,
                      variable = var2,
                      command = lambda: print_nums(),
                    )
checkbutton_menu.add( 'checkbutton',                                   #(b)
                      label = 'three',
                      onvalue = 3,
                      offvalue = 0,
                      variable = var3,
                      command = lambda: print_nums(),
                    )
menubar.add_cascade( label = "Choose_Numbers",                         #(c)
                     menu = checkbutton_menu,                          #(d)
                   )

#-----------------  An Optionmenu at the bottom  ---------------------

# Set up an option menu at the bottom of the GUI:

color_option = StringVar()                                             #(e)
color_option.set( 'cyan' )                                             #(f)
option_menu = OptionMenu(mw, color_option, 'cyan','yellow','magenta',
                         command = lambda e: option_changed() )        #(g)
option_menu.pack()                                                     #(h)


#-------------------------  callbacks  --------------------------------

def option_changed():                                                  #(i)
    global color_option                                                #(j)
    mw.configure( background = color_option.get() )                    #(k)

def radio_set_bg():                                                    #(l)
    global text, var                                                   #(m)
    text.configure( background = var.get() )                           #(n)
    text.insert('end', "value of %s: %s\n" % ("var", var.get()) )      #(o)

def print_nums():                                                      #(p)
    global text, var1, var2, var3                                      #(q)
    text.insert( 'end', "var1=%d  var2=%d var3=%d\n"
                        % (var1.get(), var2.get(), var3.get() ) )      #(r)

mainloop()                                                             #(s)
```

13.7 A PHOTO ALBUM VIEWER

We will now present a small GUI that can be used as a photo album viewer. The main purpose of the album viewer is to be able to see the individual GIFs in a slide show whose speed of presentation is under the control of the user. We want the user to be able to pause the slide show, skip to an earlier photo, resume a paused slide show, and so on. The user should also be able to view the photos individually or all at once as thumbnails. Additionally, we want the application to permit the user to convert any JPEGs into GIFs either individually or all at the same time.

Figs. 13.10 and 13.11 display the GUI for this application. Fig. 13.10 is the main window of the application that comes equipped with a menubar and a text area for displaying information regarding the current activity of the application. To make them visible simultaneously, we have shown all the menus in their tearoff form. The left-to-right order of the torn-off menus corresponds to the left-to-right order of the corresponding menu items in the menubar at the top of the GUI. There are currently five GIFs in the directory; these are listed under the `Photos` menu at the left. For reasons that will be clear shortly, the `Convert` menu is currently empty. The `Slideshow` menu shows the two buttons for starting and stopping the slide show. Finally, the `Misc` menu shows the four commands listed for it; these will be explained shortly.

The other top-level window of the GUI, titled as the `Slideshow Controller` in Fig. 13.11, is for providing the user with a slider for controlling the speed of the slide presentation and various other buttons for starting the slide show, for pausing the slide show, for skipping back, resuming, etc. The `Slideshow Controller` window also contains a button for clearing the text area of the main window.

The `Photos` menu lists all the GIFs in the directory in which the script is run. Clicking on any of these displays the photo on the screen. The `Convert` menu lists all the JPEGs in the directory. Clicking on any of these converts that JPEG into a GIF. When that happens, the new GIF is appended to the list of GIFs that shows up under the `Photos` menu.[47] The `Slideshow` menu, as mentioned already, contains two buttons for starting and stopping the slideshow. The `Misc` menu contains buttons for showing in the form of a visual directory all the GIFs and all the JPEGs in the directory in which the script is run. This menu also contains a button for converting all the JPEGs all at once into their GIF versions.

In what follows we will show a Perl/Tk implementation for the photo album viewer. We will leave its Tkinter implementation as an exercise for the reader. The translation of the Perl/Tk implementation into Tkinter should be relatively straightforward in light of all the comparative code examples we have shown so far for Perl/Tk and Tkinter.

---

[47] This is an example of a menu that changes dynamically as the user interacts with the GUI.

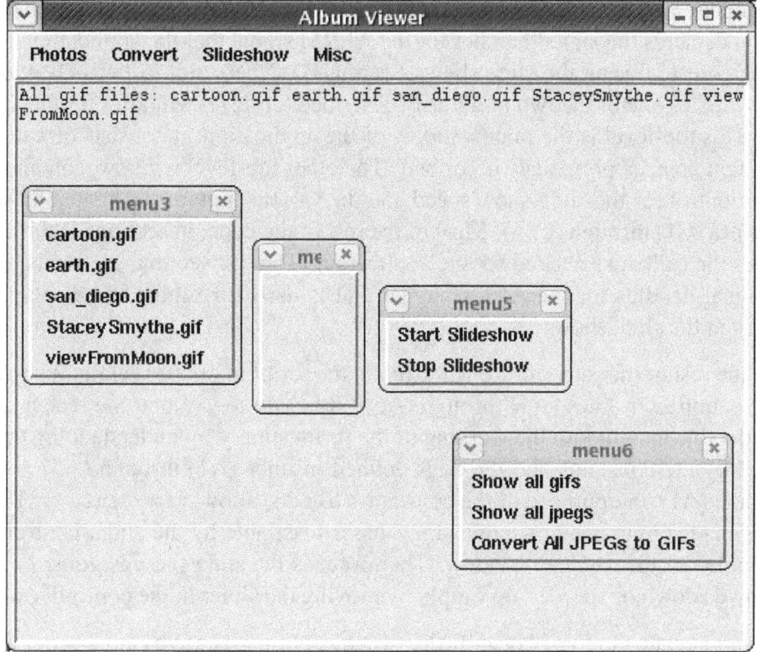

Fig. 13.10

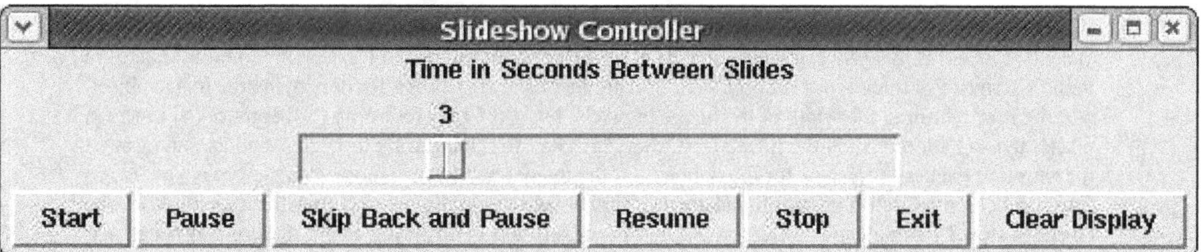

Fig. 13.11

The PhotoAlbumViewer.pl script shown next is divided into "sections" A through N. The sections are indicated by the scheme used for numbering the lines of the script. Section A of the script, consisting of lines (A1) through (A6), is meant for defining the various constants and the flags needed by the script; the last line of this section declares the signal handler for the ALRM signal that the application uses for timing control during the slide show. Section B of the script in lines (B1) through (B43) creates one of the two previously described top-level windows for the application. This top-level is the main window of the application; it consists of a menubar and a text area, as previously described. The other top-level window, containing the slider control for the slide show speed and the various buttons, is created by section C in lines (C1) through (C34). Most of the rest of the code, in sections D through M, defines the callbacks needed for the application. The last section, section N, defines the signal handler for the ALRM signal that is used for timing the display of the images in the slide show.

In the rest of this section, we will explain the script in greater detail. We will start with section A in lines (A1) through (A6). It is safe to say that the reader can get considerable insight into the working of the script simply by understanding the roles played by the constants and the flags defined in lines (A1) through (A5). Starting with line (A1), the purpose of the constant $slide_show_time_interval in this line is made obvious by its name. Its value is resettable by the slider control of the Slideshow Controller window. Therefore, as the slide show is going on, it can be slowed down or speeded up simply by moving the slider in the controller window.

To appreciate the role played by the variable $user_destroyed_image_window of line (A2), you have to understand how the album viewer displays the images. As described by the code for the callback display_image() in lines (D1) through (D35), first a Photo instance is constructed in lines (D11) and (D12) from the GIF image that needs to be displayed.[48] This new Photo instance is displayed in the canvas of a new top-level window constructed in lines (D25) and (D27). This allows the application to display images of varying sizes. But constructing a new top-level window for each fresh image means that this window must be destroyed before the

---

[48]Photo is one of the three *image types* supported by Perl/Tk, the other two being Bitmap and Pixmap. What that means is that you can create objects of type Photo, Bitmap, and Pixmap to represent images in Perl/Tk scripts. All three types support the following methods: delete() for destroying the image object, width() for returning the width of the image in pixels, height() for returning the height of the image in pixels, type() for returning the image type, configure() for configuring a specific option, and cget() for returning the current values for the options. Of the three, Photo is the most versatile type. The Photo type has been provided with additional methods for image manipulation and transformation. A Photo object is stored internally in full color (32 bits per pixel) and is displayed using dithering if necessary. Objects of type Photo are typically constructed from images in GIF, PPM/PGM, and BMP formats. However, with appropriate modules downloaded from CPAN, a Photo object can also be constructed from an image in JPEG, PNG, and TIFF formats. The Bitmap type is meant specifically for the bitmaps in the XBM format and the Pixmap type for the pixmaps in the XPM format. We should also mention that BMP designates the Win32 bitmap, XBM the Unix bitmap, PPM the Unix Portable Pixmap, XPM the X pixmap, GIF the Graphic Interchange Format, and TIFF the Tagged Image Format File. The XBM bitmaps and XPM pixmaps are character files, as opposed to binary data.

next image is displayed in its own new top-level window. This destruction of the previously displayed top-level is carried out in line (D3). There is an important reason for why this destruction is carried out subject to the two conditions being true in line (D2). You see, it can happen that the user may choose to himself/herself destroy the image-display top-level window by clicking on the system-supplied button at the top of the window. (This is more likely to happen when the slide show is run at a very slow speed.) If the user exercised that option, then there would be nothing left to destroy in line (D3) and invoking `destroy()` on a nonexistent window would elicit a run-time exception from the application. To ward off such situations, we define the variable `$user_destroyed_image_window` in line (A2). By setting this variable to 1 in the callback associated with the `<Destroy>` event in line (D34), we can detect in line (D2) whether or not the user destroyed the display window before proceeding to invoke `destroy()` in line (A3).

The variable `$slideshow_timer_flag` of line (A3) is needed for controlling the process of displaying the images in a slide show at time intervals set by the `$slide_show_time_interval` variable of line (A1). The variable of line (A3), `$slideshow_timer_flag`, is set to 1 by the signal handler for the ALRM signal defined in lines (N1) through (N4). [Line (A5) makes the declaration that `alarm_handler` is the handler for the ALRM signal.] The alarm is set by calling `alarm()` in line (K8) inside the `slideshow()` subroutine. After displaying an image in line (K6), the `slideshow()` function calls `alarm()` in line (K8) and then patiently waits for the operating system to issue the ALRM signal inside the `while` loop of line (K9). As the reader can see, this is done with the help of the `$slideshow_timer_flag` variable.

The variable `$slideshow_on_off_flag` is used for pausing and resuming the slide show. As indicated in lines (G2), (H3), (I2), and (J3), this flag is turned off or on depending on the currently desired state of the application. The slide show is run by the `foreach` loop in lines (K3) through (K9). Before the loop is started, the value of the flag `$slideshow_on_off_flag` is set to 1 in either the line (I2) or the line (J3). But if the value of the flag gets set to 0 by either the `pause()` callback in line (G2) or the `skip_back_and_pause()` callback in line (H3), the `foreach` loop of line (K3) gets terminated.

The variable `$slide_index` of line (A5) keeps track of the currently displayed image during the slide show. As the slide show is progressing, this variable is incremented in line (K7). When the slide show is paused by either the `pause()` callback of line (G1) or the `skip_back_and_pause()` callback of line (H1), `$slide_index` retains the index of the latest image shown. Subsequently, when the slide show is resumed by the `restart_slideshow()` callback of line (J1), the fact that the `foreach` loop of line (K3) starts with the index pointed to by `$slide_index` causes the slide show to resume at the right place.

The rest of the code should be fairly self-explanatory. Note in particular the use of the `ImageMagick` package for converting JPEGs into GIFs in the `image_convert()` callback in lines (E1) through (E15) and in the `convert_all_jpegs()` callback in lines (F1) through (F15). The conversion is carried by making a system call to `convert()` of this package in lines (E6) and (F8). Also note how we add the name of the new GIF file to the `Photos` menu in lines (E7) and (E8), and how we delete the name of the same GIF file from the `Convert` menu in line (E9). Also note how we delete the name of the just converted JPEG file from the array `@unique_jpegs` in lines (E11) through (E14). The array `@unique_jpegs` is meant to contain the names of only those JPEG files that have not yet been converted into GIFs.

Another feature of note in the script is the use of the `xdpyinfo` utility in line (D15) to figure out the size of the terminal screen. The purpose of the code in lines (D15) through (D24) is to ensure that the entire image will fit inside the terminal screen. Digital cameras these days, even the inexpensive ones, are capable of producing images that contain more pixels than can be accommodated in any regular-sized terminal screen. So when a large image is encountered, we copy the original `Photo` instance into a new `Photo` instance by subsampling the original and then choose the new `Photo` instance for display.

```
#!/usr/bin/perl -w

### PhotoAlbumViewer.pl

use strict;
use Tk;

# Constants, flags, alarm handler
my $slide_show_time_interval = 3;    # in seconds                       #(A1)
my $user_destroyed_image_window = 0;                                    #(A2)
my $slideshow_timer_flag;                                               #(A3)
my $slideshow_on_off_flag = 1;                                          #(A4)
my $slide_index;                                                        #(A5)
$SIG{ALRM} = \&alarm_handler;                                           #(A6)

# Set up the GUI and its menubar at the top:
my $mw = MainWindow->new( -title => "Album Viewer" );                   #(B1)
$mw->geometry( "80x50+0+0" );                                           #(B2)
my $top;                                                                #(B3)
my $menubar = $mw->Menu;                                                #(B4)
$mw->configure( -menu =>  $menubar );                                   #(B5)
my $file_menu = $menubar->cascade( -label => 'Photos' );                #(B6)
my $format_conversion_menu = $mw->Menu;                                 #(B7)
$menubar->cascade( -label => 'Convert',                                 #(B8)
                   -menu => $format_conversion_menu );                  #(B9)
my $slideshow_menu = $menubar->cascade( -label => 'Slideshow' );       #(B10)
my $misc_menu = $menubar->cascade( -label => 'Misc' );                 #(B11)

# The text area of the GUI for displaying the status reports:
my $textWindow = $mw->Scrolled( 'Text',                                #(B12)
```

```
                                -scrollbars => 'ow',              #(B13)
                                -setgrid => 'true',               #(B14)
                             )->pack( -side => 'bottom',          #(B15)
                                   -expand => 1,                  #(B16)
                                   -fill => 'both'                #(B17)
                                 );
# Set up the menus for the menubar:
my @gif_files = glob "*.gif";                                     #(B18)
$textWindow->insert( 'end', "All gif files: @gif_files\n");       #(B19)
# Register 'display_image' callback with the buttons
# of the 'Photo' menu:
foreach my $i (0 .. $#gif_files) {                                #(B20)
    my $menu_item =                                               #(B21)
       $file_menu->command( -label =>  "$gif_files[$i]",          #(B22)
             -command => [\&display_image, $gif_files[$i] ] );    #(B23)
    $menu_item->configure( -columnbreak => 1 ) unless $i % 30;    #(B24)
}

# Get all JPEG files for which there are no current
# GIF versions for the 'Convert' menu:
my @jpeg_files = glob "*.jpg";                                    #(B25)
my %gif_files = map { $_ => 1 } @gif_files;                       #(B26)
my @unique_jpegs =                                                #(B27)
    grep { ! exists_jpeg_in_gifs( $_, %gif_files ) } @jpeg_files; #(B28)
# For each not yet converted JPEG image, register the
# 'image_convert' callback with each button of the 'Convert' menu:
if ($#unique_jpegs >= 0) {                                        #(B29)
    foreach my $i (0 .. $#unique_jpegs) {                         #(B30)
        $format_conversion_menu->command(                         #(B31)
                 -label => "convert $unique_jpegs[$i] to gif",    #(B32)
                 -command => [\&image_convert, $unique_jpegs[$i] ]#(B33)
        );
    }
}
# Two items for the Slideshow menu:
$slideshow_menu->command( -label => "Start Slideshow",            #(B34)
                          -command => \&start_slideshow );        #(B35)
$slideshow_menu->command( -label => "Stop Slideshow",             #(B36)
                          -command => \&stop_slideshow );         #(B37)
# Items for the Misc menu:
$misc_menu->command( -label => "Show all gifs",                   #(B38)
             -command => sub { system "display \'vid:\*.gif\'" });#(B39)
$misc_menu->command( -label => "Show all jpegs",                  #(B40)
             -command => sub { system "display \'vid:\*.jpg\'" });#(B41)
$misc_menu->command( -label => "Convert All JPEGs to GIFs",       #(B42)
             -command => \&convert_all_jpegs );                   #(B43)

# Setup for the slideshow controller window:
my $controller = $mw->Toplevel( -title => "Slideshow Controller" );#(C1)
```

```
$controller->geometry( "+0-40" );                                   #(C2)
$controller->Label( -text =>  "Time in Seconds Between Slides" )
           ->pack( -side => 'top' );                                 #(C3)
$controller->Scale(  -length => 300,                                 #(C4)
                     -sliderlength => 20,                            #(C5)
                     -variable => \$slide_show_time_interval,        #(C6)
                     -from => 1,                                     #(C7)
                     -to => 10,                                      #(C8)
                     -orient => 'horizontal'                         #(C9)
                   )->pack();                                        #(C10)
my $frame = $controller->Frame->pack();                              #(C11)
$frame->Button( -text => "Start",                                    #(C12)
                -command => \&start_slideshow,                       #(C13)
              )->pack( -side => 'left' );                            #(C14)
$frame->Button( -text => "Clear Display",                            #(C15)
                -command =>
                    sub { $textWindow->delete( '1.0', 'end') },      #(C16)
              )->pack( -side => 'right' );                           #(C17)
$frame->Button( -text => "Exit",                                     #(C18)
                -command => sub { exit },                            #(C19)
              )->pack( -side => 'right' );                           #(C20)
$frame->Button( -text => "Stop",                                     #(C21)
                -command => \&stop_slideshow,                        #(C22)
              )->pack( -side => 'right' );                           #(C23)
$frame->Button( -text => "Resume",                                   #(C24)
                -command => \&restart_slideshow,                     #(C25)
              )->pack( -side => 'right' );                           #(C26)
$frame->Button( -text => "Skip Back and Pause",                      #(C27)
                -command => \&skip_back_and_pause,                   #(C28)
              )->pack( -side => 'right' );                           #(C29)
$frame->Button( -text => "Pause",                                    #(C30)
                -command => \&pause_slideshow,                       #(C31)
              )->pack( -side => 'right');                            #(C32)

$controller->raise( $mw );                                           #(C33)
$frame->focus;                                                       #(C34)

MainLoop;                                                            #(C35)

#-------------------------- The Callbacks ----------------------------

# The following callback is registered with the buttons
# of the 'File' menu.  This subroutine is also called by
# the 'slideshow()' callback, and the 'skip_back_and_pause()'
# callback:
sub display_image {                                                  #(D1)
    if (defined $top and $user_destroyed_image_window == 0) {        #(D2)
        $top->destroy;                                               #(D3)
    }
```

```
$user_destroyed_image_window = 0
                if $user_destroyed_image_window;                   #(D4)
my $image_scaled_predicate = 0;                                    #(D5)
my $filename = shift;                                              #(D6)
if (!$filename) {                                                  #(D7)
    $textWindow->insert( 'end',
                 "display_image called without filename\n" );  #(D8)
    return;                                                        #(D9)
}
$textWindow->insert( 'end', "\nDisplaying $filename\n" );         #(D10)

# Construct a Photo object for the image:
my $photo = $mw->Photo('image', -height => 0, -width => 0 );      #(D11)
$photo->read( $filename );                                         #(D12)
my ($image_width, $image_height) =
                ( $photo->width, $photo->height );                #(D13)
$textWindow->insert( 'end',
  "image width: $image_width  image height: $image_height\n");#(D14)

my ($screen_width, $screen_height) =
    `xdpyinfo | grep dimensions` =~ /(\d+)x(\d+)/;                #(D15)
my $newphoto =
        $mw->Photo('newimage', -height => 0, -width => 0 );       #(D16)
if ( $image_width > $screen_width
              or $image_height > $screen_height ) {               #(D17)
    $image_scaled_predicate = 1;                                   #(D18)
    my $x = int($image_width / $screen_width + 1);                 #(D19)
    my $y = int($image_height / $screen_height + 1);               #(D20)
    if ( $x > $y ) {                                               #(D21)
        $newphoto->copy( $photo, -subsample => $x );               #(D22)
    } else {                                                       #(D23)
        $newphoto->copy( $photo, -subsample => $y );               #(D24)
    }
}

# Construct a new window for displaying the image:
$top = $mw->Toplevel;                                              #(D25)
$top->geometry("-0+0");                                            #(D26)
my $canvas = $top->Canvas()->pack( -side => 'top' );               #(D27)

if (  $image_scaled_predicate ) {                                  #(D28)
    my $label =$canvas->Label(-image=>$newphoto,-anchor=>'nw')#(D29)
                        ->pack( -side => 'top');                   #(D30)
} else {                                                           #(D31)
    my $label = $canvas->Label(-image=>$photo,-anchor=>'nw')  #(D32)
                        ->pack( -side => 'top');                   #(D33)
}
```

```
    $canvas->CanvasBind( '<Destroy>',
                         sub { $user_destroyed_image_window = 1 });#(D34)
    $canvas->update;                                                 #(D35)
}

# Used as a callback for the items of the 'Convert' menu:
sub image_convert {                                                  #(E1)
    my $filename = shift;                                            #(E2)
    my $gif_filename = $filename;                                    #(E3)
    $gif_filename =~ s/\.jpg$/\.gif/;                                #(E4)
    $textWindow->insert('end',"\n\nConverting $filename to gif\n");#(E5)
    system "convert $filename $gif_filename";                        #(E6)
    $file_menu->command( -label =>  "$gif_filename",                 #(E7)
               -command => [\&display_image, $gif_filename ] );#(E8)
    $format_conversion_menu->delete( "convert $filename to gif" ); #(E9)
    my $i = 0;                                                       #(E10)
    # find index of converted jpeg in @unique_jpegs
    my @where = map {$i++; ($_ =~ /$filename/) ? $i : undef}
                                                  @unique_jpegs; #(E11)
    @where = grep {defined $_} @where;                               #(E12)
    my $where = $where[0] - 1;                                       #(E13)
    splice @unique_jpegs, $where, 1;                                 #(E14)
    $textWindow->insert('end',
            "\n\nFinished converting $filename to gif\n");      #(E15)
}

# This callback registered with the "Convert All JPEGs to GIFs"
# button of the 'Misc' menu:
sub convert_all_jpegs {                                              #(F1)
    $textWindow->insert('end', "\nConverting all jpegs to gifs\n");#(F2)
    if ( $#unique_jpegs >= 0 ) {                                     #(F3)
        foreach my $i (0 .. $#unique_jpegs) {                        #(F4)
            $textWindow->insert( 'end',
                "Converting  $unique_jpegs[$i] to GIF format\n");  #(F5)
            my $gif_filename = $unique_jpegs[$i];                    #(F6)
            $gif_filename =~ s/\.jpg$/\.gif/;                        #(F7)
            system "convert $unique_jpegs[$i] $gif_filename";        #(F8)
            $file_menu->command( -label =>  "$gif_filename",         #(F9)
                   -command => [\&display_image, $gif_filename ]);#(F10)
            $format_conversion_menu->delete(
                             "convert $unique_jpegs[$i] to gif" );#(F11)
        }
        @unique_jpegs = ();                                          #(F12)
        $textWindow->insert('end',
                      "Finished converting all jpegs to gifs\n");#(F13)
    } else {                                                         #(F14)
        $textWindow->insert('end',"\nNo jpegs left to convert\n");#(F15)
    }
}
```

```
# This callback is registered with the "Pause" button of the
# slideshow controller window:
sub pause_slideshow {                                                  #(G1)
    $slideshow_on_off_flag = 0;                                        #(G2)
    $textWindow->insert( 'end', "\n\nSLIDESHOW PAUSED\n\n" );          #(G3)
}

# This callback is registered with the "Skip Back and Pause"
# button of the slideshow controller window:
sub skip_back_and_pause {                                              #(H1)
    return if $slide_index == 0;                                       #(H2)
    $slideshow_on_off_flag = 0;                                        #(H3)
    my @slide_files = glob "*.gif";                                    #(H4)
    $slide_index = $slide_index - 2;                                   #(H5)
    $textWindow->insert( 'end',
           "\n\nDisplay previous: $slide_files[$slide_index]\n" ); #(H6)
    display_image( $slide_files[$slide_index] );                       #(H7)
    $textWindow->insert( 'end', "\n\nSLIDESHOW PAUSED\n\n" );          #(H8)
}

# This callback registered with the "Start Slideshow" button
# of the 'Slideshow' menu and the "Start" button of the
# slideshow controller window:
sub start_slideshow {                                                  #(I1)
    $textWindow->insert( 'end', "\n\nSTARTING SLIDESHOW\n\n" );        #(I2)
    $slideshow_on_off_flag = 1;                                        #(I2)
    $slide_index = 0;                                                  #(I4)
    slideshow();                                                       #(I5)
}

# This callback is registered with the "Resume" button of
# the slideshow controller window:
sub restart_slideshow {                                                #(J1)
    $textWindow->insert( 'end', "\n\nRESTARTING SLIDESHOW\n\n" );  #(J2)
    $slideshow_on_off_flag = 1;                                        #(J3)
    slideshow();                                                       #(J4)
}

# This subroutine is called by the start_slideshow() and the
# restart_slideshow() callbacks:
sub slideshow {                                                        #(K1)
    my @slide_files = glob "*.gif";                                    #(K2)
    foreach my $i ($slide_index .. $#slide_files) {                    #(K3)
        return if $slideshow_on_off_flag == 0;                         #(K4)
        $slideshow_timer_flag = 0;                                     #(K5)
        display_image( $slide_files[$i] );                             #(K6)
        $slide_index++;                                                #(K7)
        alarm( $slide_show_time_interval );                            #(K8)
```

```
        while (1) { last if $slideshow_timer_flag; }                  #(K9)
    }
    $textWindow->insert( 'end', "\n\nSLIDESHOW FINISHED\n" );         #(K10)
}

# This callback registered with the "Stop Slideshow" button
# of the 'Slideshow' menu and the "Stop" button of the
# slideshow controller window:
sub stop_slideshow {                                                  #(L1)
    $textWindow->insert( 'end', "\n\nSTOPPING SLIDESHOW\n" );         #(L2)
    $slideshow_on_off_flag = 0;                                       #(L3)
}

# Used in line (A32) as a predicate for checking if a GIF
# version of a JPEG file is available:
sub exists_jpeg_in_gifs {                                             #(M1)
    my $jpeg_file = shift;                                            #(M2)
    my %gif_set = @_;                                                 #(M3)
    $jpeg_file =~ s/\.jpg//;                                          #(M4)
    my %gif_stems = map {s/\.gif//;$_} %gif_set;                      #(M5)
    return 1 if exists $gif_stems{$jpeg_file};                        #(M6)
    return 0;                                                         #(M7)
}

# For the alarm handler defined in line (A5):
sub alarm_handler {                                                   #(N1)
    my ($now) = (localtime =~ /(..:..:..)/);                          #(N2)
    $textWindow->insert('end',"\nalarm handler invoked at $now\n");#(N3)
    $slideshow_timer_flag = 1;                                        #(N4)
}
```

13.8 CREDITS AND SUGGESTIONS FOR FURTHER READING

The book by Lidie and Walsh [44] is highly recommended for those wishing to gain a deeper understanding of Perl/Tk. For online documentation, look up the Tk module in the "ActivePerl" User's Guide [32]. For Tkinter, the most frequently used reference manual is by Lundh [46]. The reader will also find useful the reference manual for Tkinter by Shipman [58] and the book by Grayson [26]. Python also comes preloaded with the Tix module that is an extension to the widget set provided by Tkinter. Other extensions of Tkinter that do not come preloaded with Python are the megawidgets toolkit and the pure-Python Tkinter 3000 Widget Construction Kit (WCK).

Both Perl and Python provide wrappers for many other GUI toolkits besides the Tk we have described in this chapter. Although these other wrappers do not come preloaded with the standard distribution of the languages, they are easily available from the Internet. Some of these include the Python wrapper wxPython for the C++ based wxWindows toolkit; PyGTK for the GTK widget set; PyQt for the C++ based Qt toolkit; PyKDE for the KDE desktop environment (based on the Qt class library) that is commonly used on Linux platforms; JPython (also known as Jython) for accessing Java's AWT/Swing classes; win32all.exe for accessing Microsoft Foundation Classes from Python on Windows machines; and so on. Of these, the wxPython module is a particularly recommended alternative to Tkinter for designing production quality GUI interfaces because of the former's much richer widget set and its powerful HTML and image viewers.

The reader may also want to explore graphical GUI builder tools. The one for Tkinter is called SpecTix.

13.9 HOMEWORK

1. Using the `Tk::LCD` module that you can download from `www.cpan.org`, write a Perl script for a countdown timer. Use a slider widget (see Section 13 for an example of a slider in Perl/Tk) to control the length of time the timer is set for. The LCD display should show how much time is left. When the timer is started, the start and reset buttons should be disabled and the stop button enabled. When the timer expires or is stopped, the stop button should be disabled and the start and reset buttons enabled.

2. Write a Python version of the `PhotoAlbumViewer` of Section 13.7.

3. Modify the `PhotoAlbumViewer` script of Section 13.7 (and also the Python script that you write as a solution to the previous problem) to transform the images silently into the format best for displaying them. In other words, the user should not have to bother with the transformation details.

4. Write a color-mixer GUI in Perl and Python whose upper half consists of a canvas widget that shows the result of mixing red, green, and blue color components. The lower half of the GUI should consist of three minidisplays,

each showing the color selected in a small canvas-based display. Attach a slider with each minidisplay to allow the user to smoothly control the color value selected.

14

Multithreaded Scripting

Concurrency achieved through multithreading and multiprocessing has become central to the design of systems that must remain responsive to user interaction over large variations in computational load. For example, a database server on a network becomes more responsive if it assigns a separate process or a separate thread to each incoming request. In this way the main database server process can immediately detect incoming requests, while the other processes and/or threads cater to the requests received previously. As another example, consider the case of a modern multimedia GUI that must allow for the downloading and playback of sound files, video clips, and so on. By assigning potentially long-duration and sometimes compute-intensive tasks to different processes or threads, the GUI can stay responsive to further user interaction. So, as a long video clip is being downloaded in one thread, its playback can start in another thread. If the user does not like what he/she sees, a button click can immediately kill all the threads associated with the video download and playback.

Although the above paragraph refers to multiprocessing and multithreading as if they are the same, the two are quite different. A thread of execution takes place within a process. While a process typically requires its own address space, multiple threads of execution share the address space of the process in which they reside. This permits multiple threads to more easily access the same data in the memory. Also, the time it takes to switch between threads is shorter than the time it takes to switch between processes. Additionally, interthread communication is faster than interprocess communication.

Any performance enhancement obtained with multithreading depends critically on the degree of thread support provided by the operating system. It is possible for a language to provide thread support without the operating system doing the same. Threads supplied by a language are commonly referred to as *user-mode threads* and the threads supplied by the operating system as *kernel threads*. When the operating system provides no thread support of its own, one can still achieve a modicum of concurrency bit it will be limited by the poor quality of thread cooperation. Thread cooperation is usually achieved by putting long running threads to sleep for short durations every so often. With user-mode threads without any underlying kernel support, putting a single thread to sleep may cause all the threads to fall sleep at the same time. On the other hand, when the operating system provides kernel threads, the user-mode threads may now be mapped to kernel threads to achieve superior concurrency.

In modern multithreading, the processor is assigned to each thread for a fixed interval of time, called the *quantum*. Assigning quanta of time to the different threads is referred to as *timeslicing*. How the timesliced threads are scheduled for execution depends usually on the priority levels that can be assigned to the different threads. Most commonly, timesliced threads of equal priority are scheduled for execution in a round-robin fashion. This is referred to as *preemptive scheduling*.

Thread support in Perl is provided by the `threads` package. With this package, you can launch what are referred to as the *interpreter threads*, or *ithreads* for short. Each thread of execution runs its own Perl interpreter. When a thread is launched in a Perl script, a *copy* of each of the data objects defined up to that point is supplied to the interpreter running in the thread. The resulting data isolation between the threads makes for safer multithreaded scripting. But many applications require data objects to be shared between different threads. In Perl multithreading, the shared data objects must be explicitly declared as such with the help of the `shared` feature, as we will show later in this chapter.

Thread support in Python is provided by the `thread` and the `threading` modules, the latter an extension of the former. Whereas the `thread` module provides all of the basic multithreading functionality, the `threading` module presents a more modern interface. The interface for the `threading` module is designed roughly along the lines of Java's `Thread` class. All of the code that needs to be executed in a separate thread is placed in the `run()` method of an instance of the `threading` class.

There is an interesting difference between Perl and Python with regard to how an object is shared with a newly created thread. As mentioned earlier, Perl directly makes copies of all the current objects for a new thread (unless explicitly forbidden to do so). That is understandable in Perl because the language gives you direct access to objects. That is, if you define an array `@arr` in Perl, then you can think of `@arr` as the array itself. On the other hand, in Python all variables hold references to objects and there is no such thing as direct access to an object. So, in Python, when you set a variable `arr` to a list, `arr` by itself is not a list; it is a variable that holds a reference (think pointers) to a list structure. So when Python makes copies of all the variables currently in scope for a newly created thread, the new thread get copies of the references, but those copied references will point to the same objects as before.

14.1 BASIC MULTITHREADING IN PERL

As mentioned, thread support in Perl is provided by the `threads` package. A new thread is created and launched by calling `create()`, or its synonym `new()`. The code that needs to run in a thread is supplied as a subroutine reference to this function. Let's say we want the following subroutine to be executed in a separate thread:

```
sub print_message {
    print "Hello!";
}
```

We supply a reference to the subroutine to the method `create()` of the `threads` package:

```
use threads;
threads->create( \&print_message );
```

Arguments can be passed to the subroutine that is meant to be executed in a separate thread by simply adding them on to the argument list of `create()`:

```
use threads;
threads->create( \&print_message, arg1, arg2, ... );
```

Basically, that is all there is to launching a thread in Perl — at least for the simple case when there are no thread coordination issues to resolve and there are no data objects shared by the threads. In what follows, we will first address the issue of simple thread coordination with the help of the `join()` function.

The next script, `ThreadsBasic.pl`, creates (and launches) three threads in lines (A), (B), and (C). The process in which the script is running then tries to print out the word `you!` in line (D). Note how each thread is supplied with a reference to the same subroutine but with a different argument in lines (A), (B), and (C). We obviously want the script to output the message

```
Good Morning to you!
```

with the first three words supplied by the three separate threads and the last by the process that launches the threads. But the script as written carries no guarantees that the words will be written out in the correct order. That is because there exists a *race condition* between the threads among themselves and between the threads and the process in which the threads are running. It is entirely possible that, after launching the threads, the process may race to the end before the threads have had a chance to do their jobs, in which case all you will see on the terminal would be the word `you!`. If this were to happen, the threads would be destroyed when the process terminates. The race phenomenon can be accentuated by uncommenting the statements in lines

(H) and (I). By making each thread a little bit longer to execute, you increase the probability that the main process will finish up before all of the threads have printed out their messages. If you run the script with the lines (H) and (I) uncommented, the output you see may be just `you!` or `Good you!` or, occasionally, the entire string `Good Morning to you!`.

```
#!/usr/bin/perl -w

### ThreadsBasic.pl

use strict;
use threads;

my $t1 = threads->create(\&print_message, "Good");                #(A)
my $t2 = threads->create(\&print_message, "Morning");             #(B)
my $t3 = threads->create(\&print_message, "to");                  #(C)

print "you!\n";                                                   #(D)

sub print_message {                                               #(E)
    my $message = shift;                                          #(F)
    print "$message ";                                            #(G)
#     my $i = 0;                                                  #(H)
#     while ( $i++ < 100000 ) {}                                  #(I)
}
```

A simple way to regulate the race condition between the threads (or between a process and the threads contained therein) is by using `join()`. When a process or a thread A invokes `join()` on a thread B, A suspends itself and waits for B to finish up before resuming further execution. In the following version of the above script, the process that is executing the script invokes `join()` on each of the threads in lines (D), (E), and (F). This would cause the process to halt its own execution until those threads are through with the tasks assigned to them.

```
#!/usr/bin/perl -w

### ThreadsBasicWithJoin.pl

use strict;
use threads;

my $t1 = threads->create(\&print_message, "Good");                #(A)
my $t2 = threads->create(\&print_message, "Morning");             #(B)
```

```
my $t3 = threads->create(\&print_message, "to");                  #(C)

$t1->join;                                                         #(D)
$t2->join;                                                         #(E)
$t3->join;                                                         #(F)

print "you!\n";                                                    #(G)

sub print_message {                                                #(E)
    my $message = shift;                                           #(F)
    print "$message ";                                             #(G)
#     my $i = 0;                                                   #(H)
#     while ( $i++ < 100000 ) {}                                   #(I)
}
```

The above script is still imperfect. With regard to thread coordination, the only guarantee it gives us is that `you!` will be printed out after the words `Good`, `Morning`, and `to`, but there are no guarantees as to the order in which those first three words might be printed out. The guarantee regarding `you!` holds even if we uncomment the loop in lines (H) and (I). But what about getting the other three words to be printed out in the correct order? *That would be an inappropriate expectation from any multithreaded program.* You see, the example we used in the previous two scripts, although convenient for quickly explaining how thread coordination is achieved with `join()`, is really not appropriate for any sort of concurrent processing. The degree of serial control that would be needed for all the words to come out in the correct order runs antithetical to the spirit of concurrent processing. Concurrent programming with either multithreading or multiprocessing is good for solving only those problems that lend themselves to a measure of independent processing, as when downloading video clips from the web while keeping the GUI responsive to a user's interactions. Or, as when assigning a separate thread to each chat room participant in a client-server chatroom program. Many such applications require some thread coordination and even some sharing of the data objects, but by and large much processing takes place independently in each thread of execution.

The function `join()` is also useful for capturing in the main thread (or the main process) the data returned by the different threads. This is demonstrated by the script `ThreadsReturnData.pl` shown next where each of the three threads launched in lines (C), (D), and (E) is called upon to shuffle the elements of the same array, the array of line (A). Invoking `join()` on the threads in lines (F), (G), and (H) not only gives the threads a chance to finish execution before the main process runs to termination, it also captures from each thread the array reference returned by `shuffle()` in line (V). Subsequently, when we print out the shuffled arrays, we get the outputs shown in the commented-out portions of the lines (I), (J), and (K).

```
#!/usr/bin/perl -w

### ThreadsReturningData.pl

use strict;
use threads;

my @arr = 0..10;                                                        #(A)
print "@arr\n";                      # 0 1 2 3 4 5 6 7 8 9 10           #(B)

my $t1 = threads->create(\&shuffle, \@arr);                             #(C)
my $t2 = threads->create(\&shuffle, \@arr);                             #(D)
my $t3 = threads->create(\&shuffle, \@arr);                             #(E)

my $shuffled_1 = $t1->join;                                             #(F)
my $shuffled_2 = $t2->join;                                             #(G)
my $shuffled_3 = $t3->join;                                             #(H)

print "@$shuffled_1\n";              # 9 3 2 8 1 6 4 7 10 0 5           #(I)
print "@$shuffled_2\n";              # 4 2 1 5 6 10 9 0 8 3 7           #(J)
print "@$shuffled_3\n";              # 4 9 1 10 3 8 6 7 0 5 2           #(K)

print "@arr\n";                      # 0 1 2 3 4 5 6 7 8 9 10           #(L)
shuffle( \@arr );                                                       #(M)
print "@arr\n";                      # 7 6 1 5 3 2 8 4 0 10 9           #(N)

# Fisher-Yates shuffle:
sub shuffle {                                                           #(O)
    my $arr_ref = shift;                                                #(P)
    my $i = @$arr_ref;                                                  #(Q)
    while (  $i-- ) {                                                   #(R)
        my $j = int rand( $i + 1 );                                     #(S)
        @$arr_ref[ $i, $j ] = @$arr_ref[ $j, $i ];                      #(T)
    }                                                                   #(U)
    return $arr_ref;                                                    #(V)
}
```

The above script also points to a very important feature of Perl multithreading: *Each thread makes a local copy of the argument objects supplied to it.* The Fisher-Yates shuffle routine we have shown in lines (O) through (V) carries out an in-place randomization of the array. We used this randomization algorithm intentionally to illustrate the fact that the structural changes made to the array inside each thread are not visible in the main process in which the script is running. When we print out the value of `@arr` in line (L) after having supplied the same array to the three threads, we see its elements unchanged from their initialization in line (A). The modifications that `shuffle()` makes to `@arr` are actually made to the local copies of the array in each thread.[1] The fact that `shuffle()` does carry out an in-place randomization of the array is shown by calling the function directly on the array, as we do in line (M) and printing out its elements, as shown in line (N).

14.2 BASIC MULTITHREADING IN PYTHON

As mentioned already, multithreading in Python is provided by the `thread` and the `threading` modules. Although the `thread` module provides all of the basic multithreading functionality, you are more likely to use the `threading` module (that is derived from the `thread` module) for Python multithreading since it provides a more modern interface. In what follows, we will first show a basic multithreaded script using the `thread` module, followed by the same script using the `threading` module. All of our subsequent examples are based on the `threading` module.

The following script uses the `thread` module to create and launch three threads in lines (E), (F), and (G). The process in which the script is executing then tries to print out the message fragment `you!` in the terminal window in line (I). Each of the threads created in lines (E), (F), (G) is asked to execute the same function, `print_message()`, but with a different argument.

```
#!/usr/bin/env python

###  ThreadsBasic1.py

import thread                                                         #(A)

def print_message( arg ):                                             #(B)
#   for i in range(1000000): pass                                     #(C)
    print arg,                                                        #(D)

thread.start_new_thread( print_message, ("Good",) )                   #(E)
thread.start_new_thread( print_message, ("Morning",) )                #(F)
```

[1] An alternative to the Fisher-Yates method is the `shuffle()` function from the `List::Util` module. But this function *returns* a shuffled array, as opposed to carrying out an in-place randomization of the array elements. That is, if we say

```
use List::Util 'shuffle';
my @shuffled_arr = shuffle( @arr );
```

the returned array `@shuffled_arr` is a shuffled version of the argument array `@arr`. The argument array `@arr` itself will be left unmodified.

```
thread.start_new_thread( print_message, ("to",) )                  #(G)

#for i in range(1000000): pass                                     #(H)

print "you!\n"                                                     #(I)
```

We would obviously like this script to output the message `Good Morning to you!`. But, as was the case with the Perl script `ThreadsBasic.pl`, because of the race condition that exists among the threads, on the one hand, and between the threads and the main process executing the Python script, on the other, there is no guarantee that the words `Good`, `Morning`, and `to` will be output in the correct order and before the final word `you!`. In fact, chances are that the main process will reach the statement in line (I) before the threads execute their respective calls to the `print_message()` function. If that were to happen, what fate would befall the three threads is implementation dependent. The threads could finish execution and print out their respective words in some nondeterministic order, or the threads may simply die when the main process reaches termination after printing out just `you!`.

As the above script illustrates in lines (E), (F), and (G), with the `thread` module, the code that you want to see executed in a separate thread must be supplied as a function call argument to the `start_new_thread()` method. A call to this method creates a thread and makes it available to the scheduler for processor assignment. This syntax for creating and launching new threads is similar to the syntax we showed for the Perl scripts in Section 14.1.

If you run the script as shown, depending on the implementation, most likely you'll see just the following output on your terminal screen:

```
you!
```

If you uncomment line (H), the output *may* become

```
Good Morning to you!
```

Now, because of the computations we introduce in the main process, the three threads may get a chance to run to completion. But it is important to note that we still have no guarantee that the first three words of the message would be output in the correct order. The order in which the first three words will make their appearance in the output depends on how the thread scheduler assigns the processor to the individual threads.

With line (H) uncommented, if you also uncomment line (C), you are likely to see a more jumbled up version of the above output as that would increase the number of times each thread is timesliced and scheduled.[2]

The next script is another implementation of the previous script; this time we use the `threading` module. Multithreaded scripting with this module can be carried out using the same style of programming as in Java (see Chapter 18 of [41]). For example, a common approach to multithreaded programming in Java consists of extending the `Thread` class and placing all the code that needs to be executed in a separate thread in the override definition of the `run()` method of this class. Subsequently, a thread is considered to be born when an instance is created from this new class. The thread is made *runnable* by calling `start()` on the instance. What that means is that the thread instance is now available for scheduling for time on the processor.

This style of multithreading is shown in the next script. In lines (A) through (H), we first create a class `HelloThread` by extending the class `Thread` from the `threading` module. In the `__init__()` of the class in lines (C) through (E), we first specify an instance variable, `message`, in line (D) and then call on the parent class's `__init__()` in line (E) for the rest of the initialization of a thread instance. The code that we want to run in a separate thread is placed in the `run()` method in lines (F) and (H). In our case, all we want to do is to print out the content of the instance variable `message`.

Lines (I), (J), and (K) then create three separate threads. In line (L), we invoke `start()` on the threads. Now the three threads are available to the thread scheduler for time on the processor. In line (M), we ask the main process in which the script is running to print out the last word of the message.

```
#!/usr/bin/env python

###  ThreadsBasic2.py

import threading                                                    #(A)

class HelloThread( threading.Thread ):                              #(B)

    def __init__( self, message ):                                  #(C)
        self.message = message                                      #(D)
        threading.Thread.__init__(self)                             #(E)
```

[2]In keeping with our earlier Perl discussion, note that the words of the message `Good Morning to you!` being printed out in the correct order is *not* the real goal of our script here. As with the Perl example, we are using this simple script merely to illustrate some of the basic concepts of multithreading. To reiterate our earlier observation for emphasis, the sort of serial control you need to get the words to be printed out in the correct order runs counter to the spirit of what is meant to be accomplished by multithreading.

```
    def run( self ):                                                #(F)
#       for i in range(1000000): pass                              #(G)
        print self.message,                                         #(H)

t1 = HelloThread( "Good" )                                          #(I)
t2 = HelloThread( "Morning" )                                       #(J)
t3 = HelloThread( "to" )                                            #(K)

map( lambda x: x.start(), (t1, t2, t3) )                            #(L)

print "you!\n"                                                      #(M)
```

Depending on the implementation, the output of this script may look like

```
you!

Good Morning to
```

which shows that, for one particular implementation of the Python threads, all the threads created by this script ran to completion despite the race condition between the main process and the threads. There is, of course, also the race condition among the threads. The effects of this race condition can be made more evident by making each thread longer to compute (thereby increasing the probability of the thread getting timesliced). The can be accomplished by uncommenting the statement in line (G). If you do so, the output of the script with the same implementation that produced the previous output may look like

```
you!

to Morning Good
```

or some variation thereof with regard to the order of the last three words.

A certain measure of thread coordination (and thus a certain measure of control over the competition between the threads for time on the processor) can be achieved by one thread (or process) invoking `join()` on another thread. When a thread invokes `join()` on another thread, the calling thread *blocks* until the thread on which `join()` was invoked has finished its execution. In the script shown below, the process in which the script is executed invokes `join()` in line (M) on the three threads created previously in lines (I), (J), (K). Apart from this change, this script is the same as the one shown earlier. When this script is run, we can be sure that the first three words of our good-morning message will always be printed out *before* the last part `you!`.

```
#!/usr/bin/env python

###  ThreadsBasicWithJoin.py

import threading                                                    #(A)

class HelloThread( threading.Thread ):                              #(B)

    def __init__( self, message ):                                  #(C)
        self.message = message                                      #(D)
        threading.Thread.__init__(self)                             #(E)

    def run( self ):                                                #(F)
#       for i in range(1000000): pass                               #(G)
        print self.message,                                         #(H)

t1 = HelloThread( "Good" )                                          #(I)
t2 = HelloThread( "Morning" )                                       #(J)
t3 = HelloThread( "to" )                                            #(K)

map( lambda x: x.start(), (t1, t2, t3) )                            #(L)
map( lambda x: x.join(), (t1, t2, t3) )                             #(M)
print "you!\n"                                                      #(N)
```

If you run this script, you *may* see the following output:

```
Good Morning to you!
```

But note that there is no guarantee that the first three words of the message will be printed out in the correct order. The invocation of `join()` in the above script resolves the competition between the main process in which the script runs and the three threads but does not address the race condition among the threads. So the first three words of the message could be printed out in any order. To increase the odds of the first three words to be output in some jumbled order, you can uncomment line (G); that will increase the length of execution time for each thread and thus increase the number of times each thread will be subject to timeslicing and scheduling. With line (G) uncommented, you may see the following for the output produced by the script:

```
to Morning Good you!
```

The next script does the same thing as the Perl script `ThreadsReturningData.pl` of Section 14.1. There the purpose was to show that, for the case of Perl, `join()` could be used for both thread coordination and for capturing the data returned by the threads. It is not possible to use `join()` in the same manner in

Python. That is, in Python `join()` can only be used for thread coordination, as the reader just saw in the previous script. In Python, the retrieval of data privy to a thread can be accomplished by using one or more instance variables, as we show in the script below. As was the case with the Perl script, the script shown below creates multiple threads. Each thread is supplied with the same 10-element array of integers and asked to shuffle the array randomly. The array supplied to each thread is stored in the `arr` instance variable of the thread. After a thread has finished execution, the shuffled array is retrieved from the same instance variable, as shown in lines (S), (T), and (U). Note that the call to `randint()` in line (L) returns a random integer from a range that is bounded by and *inclusive* of both arguments supplied to the method.

```
#!/usr/bin/env python

### ThreadedShuffle.py

import threading                                                         #(A)

import random                                                            #(B)
ran = random.Random()                                                    #(C)

class ThreadedShuffle( threading.Thread ):                               #(D)
    def __init__( self, alist ):                                         #(E)
        self.arr = alist                                                 #(F)
        threading.Thread.__init__(self)                                  #(G)

    def run( self ):                                                     #(H)
        self._shuffle()                                                  #(I)

    # Fisher-Yates shuffle:
    def _shuffle(self):                                                  #(J)
        for i in range( len(self.arr) - 1, -1, -1 ):                     #(K)
            j = ran.randint( 0, i )                                      #(L)
            self.arr[i], self.arr[j] = self.arr[j], self.arr[i]          #(M)

t1 = ThreadedShuffle( range(10) )                                        #(N)
t2 = ThreadedShuffle( range(10) )                                        #(O)
t3 = ThreadedShuffle( range(10) )                                        #(P)

map( lambda x: x.start(), (t1, t2, t3) )                                 #(Q)
map( lambda x: x.join(), (t1, t2, t3) )                                  #(R)

print t1.arr            # [9, 4, 3, 5, 2, 7, 8, 1, 6, 0]                 #(S)
print t2.arr            # [8, 4, 2, 7, 9, 6, 5, 3, 0, 1]                 #(T)
print t3.arr            # [0, 7, 3, 6, 8, 9, 1, 4, 2, 5]                 #(U)
```

14.3 THREAD COOPERATION WITH sleep( )

When the computational load is significantly different in different threads, it is a good idea for the more burdened threads to put themselves to sleep every once in a while so that the other threads will have greater access to the CPU. The same would be the case when some threads are engaged in relatively less urgent but longer lasting computations; such threads should also put themselves to sleep every once in a while to increase the CPU time for the other threads. We present a small example of this in the next two scripts, one in Perl and the other in Python, where only some of the threads are put to sleep in the middle of their computations. This allows the other threads to finish up sooner.[3]

14.3.1 Using sleep( ) for Thread Cooperation in Perl

The next script, `ThreadCooperationWithSleep.pl`, creates 10 threads in lines (B), (C), and (D). Each thread is asked to execute the subroutine `do_it()` of lines (K) through (Q). To randomize the execution times for the threads, we call the subroutine `keepBusy()` with a random argument. The call to `int(rand(5))` in the argument to `keepBusy()` in line (L) returns a pseudorandom integer between 0 and 4, both inclusive, with a uniform distribution over this range. This integer becomes the number of seconds that we want `keepBusy()` to run its `while` loop for in line (J).

Note the calls to the static method `self()` and to the instance method `tid()` in line (L). During threaded execution, a call to

```
threads->self
```

returns the current thread. Each thread that is created by Perl is given a unique integer ID that is returned by invoking `tid()` on the thread. This integer is incremented for each new thread. So our call

[3]Putting threads to sleep for enhanced thread cooperation works only if there exists operating-system kernel support for multithreading. In the absence of such support, as we mentioned in the introduction to this chapter, you have merely what are known as *user-level threads*, and the operating system knows nothing about the threads in your program. In the absence of kernel support, putting a single thread to sleep may cause the entire process in which all the threads reside to go to sleep, in effect causing all the threads to be put to sleep at the same time. Actually, if the operating system does not directly support multithreading by providing *kernel threads*, any blocking action in any of the threads is likely to cause all the threads to block at the same time. In addition to sleep, blocking activities also include most system calls and most I/O. The `perlthrtut` tutorial that comes with the Perl core documentation states: "The main difference between user-mode threads and kernel threads is with respect to blocking. *With kernel threads, things that block a single thread don't block other threads.* This is not the case with user-mode threads, where the kernel blocks at the process level and not the thread level." Note that even with kernel threads, there is only one thread being executed at any time in a process, regardless of the number of processors available to the system. To allow for concurrency in execution that exploits the parallelism made possible by multiple processors, the operating system must provide what are known as *multiprocessor kernel threads*.

```
my $threadID = threads->self->tid();
```

returns the integer ID of the current thread. Perl assigns the ID of 0 to the main thread, meaning the Perl process that is spawning the threads. The first thread created is given the ID of 1, the next the ID of 2, and so on.[4]

In line (N) of the script, we put all the threads with even-numbered IDs to sleep for 10 seconds. A combination of the random amount of time for which we keep each thread busy through `keepBusy()` and the 10 seconds for which we keep just the even ID threads asleep causes the script to produce the following output from the statement in line (Q):

```
do_it executed by thread 5 at time 16
do_it executed by thread 1 at time 16
do_it executed by thread 3 at time 17
do_it executed by thread 9 at time 19
do_it executed by thread 7 at time 19
do_it executed by thread 2 at time 25
do_it executed by thread 10 at time 28
do_it executed by thread 4 at time 28
do_it executed by thread 8 at time 29
do_it executed by thread 6 at time 29
```

By looking at the time at which each thread finished executing the `do_it` routine, you can see the 10-second sleep time that each even-numbered thread is subject to. You can also see that the finish times for all the odd-numbered threads are within a 4 second spread. The same is the case for the spread of the finish times for all the even-numbered threads. Recall that 4 is the largest value for the argument to `keepBusy()` in line (M). Here is the script:

```
#!/usr/bin/perl -w

###  ThreadCooperationWithSleep.pl

use strict;
use threads;                                                    #(A)

my @threads;                                                    #(B)
foreach my $i (1 .. 10) {                                       #(C)
    $threads[$i] = threads->new( \&do_it );                     #(D)
}
```

[4]We should also mention that two threads can be compared for equality, meaning for answering the question whether or not they are the same thread object, by supplying them as arguments to `equal()` or by using the overloaded == operator.

```
foreach my $i (1 .. 10) {                                          #(E)
    $threads[$i]->join;                                            #(F)
}

sub keepBusy {                                                     #(G)
    my $how_many_seconds = shift;                                  #(H)
    my $curr = time;                                               #(I)
    while ( time < $curr + $how_many_seconds ) {}                  #(J)
}

sub do_it {                                                        #(K)
    my $threadID = threads->self->tid();                           #(L)
    keepBusy( int(rand(5)) );                                      #(M)
    # Threads with even ID's to sleep for 10 seconds:
    sleep( 10 ) unless $threadID % 2;                              #(N)
    my $curr = time;                                               #(O)
    # Get just the last two digits of the
    # current time in seconds:
    my ($seconds) = $curr =~ /(\d\d)$/;                            #(P)
    print "do_it executed by thread $threadID at time $seconds\n"; #(Q)
}
```

14.3.2 Using sleep( ) for Thread Cooperation in Python

The next script is a Python version of the previous example of how threads should be put to sleep every once in a while so that the other threads will have greater access to the processor. Following the earlier examples of Python multithreading based on using the `threading` module, we first define a multithreadable class `DoitThread` by deriving it from the `threading.Thread` class in lines (E) through (T). Note that this time we use a keyword argument in the header of the class's `__init__()` in line (F). The argument supplied is for the parameter `name`. A value supplied for this parameter is appended to the string `Thread-` and the resulting string becomes the name of the thread. So if the `name` parameter in line (F) were to be set to `foo`, the name of the `DoitThread` instance would be `Thread-foo`.[5] The name of a thread can subsequently be retrieved by invoking the `getName()` method, as we show in line (N).

As mentioned earlier, all of the code that we want to see executed in a separate thread must be placed in the override definition of the `run()` method of our multithreadable class. Since our goal here is to parallel the previous Perl exam-

[5]The name of a thread can also be set by calling the `setName()` method of the `threading.Thread` class.

ple, our implementation code for `run()`, shown in lines (H) and (I), calls the `_do_it()` method that is defined in lines (M) through (T). The `_do_it()` first extracts in lines (N), (O), and (P) the integer id that we use to name each thread. In line (Q), it then invokes the `keepBusy()` method of lines (J), (K), and (L) to keep the thread busy in a do-nothing loop for a random interval of time not exceeding 4 seconds. [Recall from Chapter 3 that `randint()` invoked on an instance of the class `Random` that is defined in the module `random` returns a random integer bounded by and inclusive of the two arguments supplied to the method.] Subsequently, in line (R) only those threads with even integer id are put to sleep for 10 seconds.

```
#!/usr/bin/env python

### ThreadCooperationWithSleep.py

import threading                                                    #(A)
import time                                                         #(B)
import random                                                       #(C)
ran = random.Random()                                               #(D)

class DoitThread( threading.Thread ):                               #(E)

    def __init__( self, name = id ):                                #(F)
        threading.Thread.__init__(self)                             #(G)

    def run( self ):                                                #(H)
        self._do_it()                                               #(I)

    def keepBusy( self, howmany_secs ):                             #(J)
        curr = int( time.time() )                                   #(K)
        while ( int(time.time()) < curr + howmany_secs ): pass      #(L)

    def _do_it(self):                                               #(M)
        threadName = self.getName()                # Thread-N       #(N)
        hyphenIndex = threadName.index( '-' )                       #(O)
        threadID = threadName[hyphenIndex+1:]                       #(P)
        self.keepBusy( ran.randint( 0, 4 ) )                        #(Q)
        # Threads with even ID's to sleep for 10 seconds:
        if int(threadID) % 2 == 0: time.sleep( 10 )                 #(R)
        # Get just the last two digits of the
        # current time in seconds:
        curr = int( time.time() ) % 60                              #(S)
        print "do_it executed by thread %s at time %d" % \
                                         (threadID, curr)           #(T)

threads = [ DoitThread(i) for i in range(1,11) ]                    #(U)
map( lambda x: x.start(), threads )                                 #(V)
```

The output produced by this script is the same as for the previous Perl script:

```
do_it executed by thread 7 at time 12
do_it executed by thread 5 at time 13
do_it executed by thread 9 at time 14
do_it executed by thread 1 at time 15
do_it executed by thread 3 at time 16
do_it executed by thread 8 at time 23
do_it executed by thread 6 at time 23
do_it executed by thread 4 at time 23
do_it executed by thread 2 at time 24
do_it executed by thread 10 at time 25
```

where the last integer in each line is the seconds part of the current clock time. These times show that the five even-numbered threads were subject to a sleep delay of 10 seconds, as called for by the statement in line (R). You can also see that the finish times for all the odd-numbered threads are within a spread of 4 seconds, and that the same is the case for the finish times for all the even-numbered threads. The 4-second spread is accounted for by the upper bound on the duration of the do-nothing interval introduced by the call to `keepBusy()` in line (Q).

14.4 DATA SHARING BETWEEN THREADS AND THREAD INTERFERENCE

Multithreaded scripting, as multithreaded programming in general, is simplest when the different threads can operate independently, that is, when they share no data objects during their execution. When the threads are given the ability to access and modify the same data object, there is always a potential for a script to exhibit incorrect behavior. In the next subsection, we will show how one designates in Perl the objects that are meant to be shared between the different threads. The same subsection will illustrate how easy it is for a multithreaded Perl script to exhibit incorrect behavior in the presence of such objects. The subsection after that will do the same for Python.

14.4.1 Object Sharing and Thread Interference in Perl

As mentioned previously, by default a thread makes local copies of all the variables and data of the parent thread or process. Therefore, any arguments supplied to the subroutine named in the thread constructor are copies of the objects as they existed in the parent thread or process. Any changes made by a thread to these local copies would obviously not be visible outside the thread. But there exist many situations when multiple threads must have access to the same data object. For example, in an inventory management system, multiple clients would need to be given access to the same database objects. Perl gives us a special module, `threads::shared`, to permit data sharing by the threads. When this module is imported, setting the `shared` attribute of an object causes that object to be shared by the threads launched subsequently. Therefore,

```
use threads;
use threads::shared;
my $p = 5;
my $q:shared = 5;
my $t1 = threads->create(sub {... so domething to $p and $q ...});
my $t2 = threads->create(sub {... so domething to $p and $q ...});
```

will cause the variable `$q` to be shared between the process executing Perl and the threads `$t1` and `$t2`. Any changes to the value of this variable made by either of these threads (or by the process executing the Perl script) would be immediately visible in all the threads and the process. This is demonstrated with the next script, `SharedData.pl`. The variable `$p` of line (C) is unshared. So each thread will possess a local copy of this variable. On the other hand, the variable `$q` of line (D) is shared by the thread of line (E) and the process executing the script. The code executed by the thread causes both `$p` and `$q` to be incremented, as is seen by the commented-out output shown in line (F) produced by the print statement in line (E). But outside the thread, in line (G), the change in `$p` made by the thread is not visible since `$p` continues to have the value given to it in line (C). However, the value of the shared `$q`, as seen in line (G), reflects the change made to this variable by the thread in line (E).

```
#!/usr/bin/perl -w

### SharedData.pl

use strict;
use threads;                                                              #(A)
use threads::shared;                                                      #(B)

my $p = 5;                                                                #(C)
my $q:shared = 5;                                                         #(D)

threads->create( sub { print ++$p, "  ",  ++$q, "\n" } )->join;          #(E)

                                # output:   6  6                          #(F)

print "$p  $q\n";               # output:   5  6                          #(G)
```

Shared data objects must be handled with care in a multithreaded application. It is all too easy for the threads to interfere with one another when they share objects, causing incorrect program behavior. The next script demonstrates how easy it is for an implementation to return erroneous results when multiple threads are allowed simultaneous access to the same data object. The three threads in the script share the array

```
my @dataObj : shared = (50, 50);
```

defined in line (C) of the script. When an array is declared to be a shared object, its elements also become shared automatically, as long as an object known to be nonshared is not used as an array element.[6] Each of the three threads launched in lines (D), (E), (F) seeks to make a large number of equal and opposite changes to the two elements of `@dataObj`. The changes are carried out by the `repeatedSwaps()` subroutine, defined in lines (U) through (Y), that is assigned to each thread. The actual addition and subtraction operations on the two elements of `@dataObj` are the responsibility of the `itemSwap()` subroutine of lines (J) through (N). The call to `rand(10)` in line (K) returns a uniformly distributed pseudorandom number that is greater than or equal to 0 and less than 10. Basically, the right-hand side in line (K) returns a small integer between -5 and +4. The `itemSwap()` function adds this integer to the first element of the array in line (L) and then subtracts the same integer from the second element of the array in line (N).

Note the call to `keepBusy()` inside `itemSwap()` in line (M). This call merely tries to keep the processor busy for a little while between the two equal and opposite swapping actions. This is to increase the probability of thread interference so that we can see the erroneous output without having to go through too many iterations of `itemSwap()`. As mentioned previously, most modern operating systems use preemptive scheduling for selecting the next thread for execution on the processor. In preemptive scheduling, equal priority threads (that are not currently blocked) are timesliced and scheduled for execution in a round-robin fashion. So the longer it takes a function to complete its task, the greater the chance that it will be timesliced somewhere in the middle.

Also note that the `repeatedSwaps()` function of lines (V) through (a) invokes `test()` every 100th iteration in line (Y) for printing out the sum of the two elements of `@dataObj`.

```
#!/usr/bin/perl -w

### ThreadInterference.pl

use strict;
use threads;                                                    #(A)
```

[6]The same is true for hashes. When a hash is declared to be a shared object, all its keys and values become shared implicitly, as long as a previously declared nonshared object is not used in either of the two roles.

```
use threads::shared;                                              #(B)

my @dataObj : shared = (50, 50);                                  #(C)

my $t1 = threads->create( \&repeatedSwaps );                      #(D)
my $t2 = threads->create( \&repeatedSwaps );                      #(E)
my $t3 = threads->create( \&repeatedSwaps );                      #(F)

$t1->join;                                                        #(G)
$t2->join;                                                        #(H)
$t3->join;                                                        #(I)

sub itemSwap {                                                    #(J)
    my $x = int ( -4.999999 + rand(10 ) );                        #(K)
    $dataObj[0] += $x;                                            #(L)
    keepBusy();                                                   #(M)
    $dataObj[1] -= $x;                                            #(N)
}

sub keepBusy {                                                    #(O)
    my $i = 0;                                                    #(P)
    while ( $i++ < 10000 ) {}                                     #(Q)
}

sub test {                                                        #(R)
    my $sum = $dataObj[0] + $dataObj[1];                          #(S)
    print "Sum: $sum\n";                                          #(T)
}

sub repeatedSwaps {                                               #(U)
    my $j = 0;                                                    #(V)
    while ( $j++ < 500 ) {                                        #(W)
        itemSwap();                                               #(X)
        test() unless $j % 100;                                   #(Y)
    }
}
```

The output of the above script is shown below. As the reader can see, something is seriously wrong. Considering that `itemSwap()` makes equal and opposite changes to the two elements of `@dataObj`, you would expect `test()` to yield the value of

100 for the sum of the two elements of this array.[7] So it must be the case that the threads are interfering with one another.

```
Sum: 98
Sum: 102
Sum: 103
Sum: 97
Sum: 103
Sum: 105
Sum: 96
Sum: 96
Sum: 102
Sum: 101
Sum: 107
Sum: 112
Sum: 106
Sum: 107
Sum: 104
```

As to the source of thread interference in `ThreadInterference.pl`, the suspects are the statements of the `itemSwap()` and the `test()` subroutines. On the face of it, it would seem that the add and the subtract operations in lines (L) and (N) should not result in any problems because even if some thread A was taken off the processor after completing the add operation in line (L), and a thread B next on the processor executed one or both of the operations in lines (L) and (N), eventually thread A would get to the opposite operation in line (N) to negate the change made earlier. If threads could only be interrupted at the level of the statements shown in `itemSwap()`, this would indeed be the case and probably you would not see thread interference. But thread interruption takes place at a much lower level of execution. Each statement of `itemSwap()` is compiled into multiple atomic operations that will typically be at the level of loading data into registers, performing operations on the data contained in the registers, transferring register data to memory, etc. It is at this level that the threads will be interrupted with preemptive scheduling. Imagine a thread being interrupted after the addition called for in line (L) to the first element of the `@dataObj` array that was just transferred to a register for the sake of this arithmetic operation. Let's say that this interruption takes place before the new value is transferred back to where the first element is stored in the memory. Assuming that the next thread is able to complete all of the operations of `itemSwap()` within its allocated time, when the first thread gets back to transferring the register content to the location designated for

[7] We should mention that when an object is declared to be shared in the manner shown, we have the guarantee that the act of multiple threads trying to change the state of the object will not corrupt the object. In other words, the process of reading from and writing into the memory locations assigned to a shared object does not lead to data corruption even when multiple threads are trying to carry out these operations concurrently. Nonetheless, a multithreaded implementation with shared objects can still produce erroneous results as we show here.

the first element of the `@dataObj` array, what is actually transferred will reflect the change made by the second thread.

It is interesting to note that even if `itemSwap()` was not vulnerable to thread interference, we still have the possibility of seeing an erroneous output because of thread interference in the code for `test()` in lines (R), (S), and (T). If a thread were to get interrupted in the middle of adding up the two elements of the shared array in line (S), what it will eventually report for the output in line (T) will be wrong.

14.4.2 Object Sharing and Thread Interference in Python

Of the two Perl scripts shown in the previous subsection, it is neither possible nor necessary to show a Python version of the Perl script `SharedData.pl`. That is because of two reasons: (1) With the interface provided by Python's `threading.Thread` class, you create threads by instantiating the `threading.Thread` class — that is, by making calls to the constructor of this class. And (2) all variables in Python, as mentioned in Chapter 3, actually hold references to the objects that are assigned to them. So when you pass a data object as an argument to the constructor of a multithreadable class in Python, what you actually pass to the constructor is a reference to the data object, the referent — meaning the data object — itself is not copied for what is supplied to the constructor. In other words, the original data object will be directly available inside the constructor through the reference supplied to it. This implies that objects can be shared between the threads simply by supplying them as arguments to the constructor of a multithreadable class.

But, as with all multithreaded implementations, object sharing between the threads in Python, while necessary for many applications, carries computational risks in the form of thread interference. The script shown next, `ThreadInterference.py`, illustrates both how objects can be shared between the threads and the problems caused by thread interference by the presence of such objects.

The script starts out by defining a `DataObject` class in lines (A) through (N). An instance made from this class is meant to be shared by the different threads that we create later in the script. The `DataObject` class is endowed with two instance variables, `dataItem1` and `dataItem2`, as shown in lines (C) and (D), both initially set to 50. This class is also supplied with the method `itemSwap()` in lines (E) through (I). This method adds and subtracts a small randomly selected integer from the two instance variables. At the end of these operations, we should expect the sum of the two instance variables to add up to 100 — provided nothing goes wrong by way of thread interference. The method `test()` in lines (J), (K), and (L) is for printing out the sum of the two instance variables. And the method `keepBusy()`, defined in lines (M) and (N) and invoked in line (H), is meant to increase the length of time it takes to carry out the add and subtract operations in `itemSwap()`. As the reader will recall from our Perl discussion in the previous subsection, this increases the probability of thread interference without having to go through too many iterations of `itemSwap()`.

Our multithreadable class in this example is defined in lines (O) through (W). Its `__init__()` is supplied with a `DataObject` instance as its argument. The `run()` method of the multithreadable class calls the `itemSwap()` method of the `DataObject` instance repeatedly and, every 100th iteration, calls on the `test()` method of the `DataObject` instance to check on the sum of the two integer values stored in the data object.

The last part of the script first constructs a `DataObject` instance in line (X). This object is then supplied as the argument in the three calls to the thread constructor in lines (Y), (Z), and (a). The three threads created in this manner will have access to the same `DataObject` instance.

```
#!/usr/bin/env python

### ThreadInterference.py

import threading
import time

import random
ran = random.Random()

#------------------------   class DataObject   ------------------------
class DataObject( object ):                                          #(A)

    def __init__( self ):                                            #(B)
        self.dataItem1 = 50                                          #(C)
        self.dataItem2 = 50                                          #(D)

    def itemSwap(self):                                              #(E)
        x = -5 + ran.randint(0,10)                                   #(F)
        self.dataItem1 -= x                                          #(G)
        self.keepBusy()                                              #(H)
        self.dataItem2 += x                                          #(I)

    def test(self):                                                  #(J)
        sum = self.dataItem1 + self.dataItem2                        #(K)
        print "Sum: %d" % sum                                        #(L)

    def keepBusy( self ):                                            #(M)
        for i in range(100000): pass                                 #(N)
```

```
#---------------------   class RepeatedSwaps   ------------------------
class RepeatedSwaps( threading.Thread ):                          #(O)

    def __init__( self, dataObject ):                             #(P)
        self.dataObject = dataObject                              #(Q)
        threading.Thread.__init__(self)                           #(R)

    def run( self ):                                              #(S)
        for i in range (500):                                     #(T)
            self.dataObject.itemSwap()                            #(U)
            if i % 100 == 0:                                      #(V)
                self.dataObject.test()                            #(W)

#--------------------------   launch threads ------------------------

d = DataObject()                                                  #(X)

t1 = RepeatedSwaps(d)                                             #(Y)
t2 = RepeatedSwaps(d)                                             #(Z)
t3 = RepeatedSwaps(d)                                             #(a)

map( lambda x: x.start(), (t1, t2, t3) )                          #(b)
```

A given run of the script may produce an output that looks like

```
Sum: 100
Sum: 104
Sum: 103
Sum: 98
Sum: 100
Sum: 106
Sum: 105
Sum: 106
Sum: 101
Sum: 102
Sum: 100
Sum: 104
Sum: 94
Sum: 104
Sum: 101
```

As with the Perl script of the previous subsection, we are obviously seeing the effects of thread interference. The values stored in the two instance variables `dataItem1` and `dataItem2` in lines (C) and (D) are getting corrupted. Each thread is adding and subtracting the same random number from these two data items in lines (G) and (I). So even if the threads are timesliced in the middle of these two operations [the likelihood of which we have increased by juxtaposing `keepBusy()` between the two operations in line (I)], we nevertheless expect the sum of the values stored in `dataItem1` and `dataItem2` to always add up to 100 at the end of the day, as they say. But that obviously is not the case. As we mentioned in our Perl discussion, if the thread interaction vis-à-vis the shared object took place at the high-level of program description depicted in the script, we would not see any data corruption of the sort shown above. But, as stated earlier, each high level statement of the script is compiled into multiple atomic operations that consist typically of loading data into the registers, performing operations on the data, transferring the contents of the registers back to the memory, etc. When multiple threads interfere at this level, we see the kind of data corruption effects shown above.[8]

14.5 SUPPRESSING THREAD INTERFERENCE WITH LOCKS

Multithreading languages in general provide the following three mechanisms — usually referred to as *synchronization primitives* — for suppressing thread interference and for thread coordination when, in order to proceed forward, one thread needs another thread to bring about certain changes to shared data objects: (1) locks, (2) semaphores, and (3) condition variables. All three are available with Perl's `ithreads` and with Python's `threading` module. The rest of this section focuses on the use of locks for the suppression of thread interference in Perl and Python. Subsequently, Section 14.6 will explain how the same can be accomplished with the help of semaphores that are more general than the locking primitives of the next two subsections. Finally, in Section 14.7 we will explain how the condition variables can be used for thread coordination in Perl and Python.

14.5.1 Using lock( ) for Thread Synchronization in Perl

In Perl, a thread can call `lock()` to acquire a lock on a shared object that is vulnerable to thread interference. When a thread acquires a lock on a shared data object by supplying it as an argument to `lock()`, that object becomes unavailable to any other thread until the thread that acquired the lock relinquishes it. If another thread seeks to acquire a lock on a previously locked object, the thread blocks until that object is freed. *A thread gives up its lock implicitly when it exits the outermost code block that called for the locking operation.*

[8]As was the case with the Perl script of the previous subsection, an additional source of thread interference in the above script is the `test()` method in lines (J), (K), and (L). The threads could step on each other's toes in the middle of the addition operation in line (K).

The following script illustrates how we can use `lock()` to eliminate thread interference in the `ThreadInterference.pl` script shown previously in Section 14.4.1. The executing thread is now asked to place a lock on the shared object in lines (I) and (R). Any other thread that gets to either of these lines will block until the thread that acquired the lock relinquishes it. The unlocking action takes place automatically when the execution exits the outermost block with the `lock()` statement in it. What we get from this locking and unlocking action is that only one of the three threads is allowed to execute the code in lines (J) through (M) and in lines (S) and (T). The thread executing these pieces of code cannot be interrupted, thus eliminating thread interference.

```
#!/usr/bin/perl -w

### NoThreadInterference.pl

use strict;
use threads;
use threads::shared;

my @dataObj : shared = (50, 50);                                    #(A)

my $t1 = threads->create( \&repeatedSwaps );                        #(B)
my $t2 = threads->create( \&repeatedSwaps );                        #(C)
my $t3 = threads->create( \&repeatedSwaps );                        #(D)

$t1->join;                                                          #(E)
$t2->join;                                                          #(F)
$t3->join;                                                          #(G)

sub itemSwap {                                                      #(H)
    lock( @dataObj );                                               #(I)
    my $x = int ( -4.999999 + rand(10 ) );                          #(J)
    $dataObj[0] -= $x;                                              #(K)
    keepBusy();                                                     #(L)
    $dataObj[1] += $x;                                              #(M)
}

sub keepBusy {                                                      #(N)
    my $i = 0;                                                      #(O)
    while ( $i++ < 10000 ) {}                                       #(P)
}

sub test {                                                          #(Q)
    lock( @dataObj );                                               #(R)
    my $sum = $dataObj[0] + $dataObj[1];                            #(S)
    print "Sum: $sum\n";                                            #(T)
}
```

```
sub repeatedSwaps {                                                   #(U)
    my $j = 0;                                                        #(V)
    while ( $j++ < 500 ) {                                            #(W)
        itemSwap();                                                   #(X)
        test() unless $j % 100;                                       #(Y)
    }
}
```

The output of the above script is shown below. As is obvious, we have gotten rid of the interference problem with the earlier version of this script.

```
Sum: 100
Sum: 100
Sum: 100
Sum: 100
Sum: 100
Sum: 100
Sum: 100
Sum: 100
Sum: 100
Sum: 100
Sum: 100
Sum: 100
Sum: 100
Sum: 100
Sum: 100
```

It is interesting to reflect on the fact that it is not necessary to lock the shared object `@dataObj` in line (I) of `NoInterference.pl` for the elimination of interference. A lock on any previously defined shared variable[9] would have achieved the same effect. That is, if we had declared somewhere in the beginning section of the script a variable

```
my $z:shared;
```

and then written the code for the `itemSwap()` function in the following manner:

```
sub itemSwap {
    lock ($z);
    my $x = int ( -4.999999 + rand(10) );
    $dataObj[0] -= $x;
    keepBusy();
    $dataObj[1] += $x;
}
```

---

[9]Only shared variables can be locked.

where we now invoke `lock($z)` instead of `lock(@dataObj)` in the first statement of the subroutine, we would have achieved the same interference-free results. The reason for this has to do with the fact that basically what we want is an interruption-free execution of the code in `itemSwap()`. Locking any object whatsoever in the first statement of the subroutine achieves that effect. After a thread has obtained a lock by calling `lock($z)` in our example, this statement will block every other thread that reaches this point in its execution. These other threads will stay blocked until the lock has been relinquished at the exit point of the subroutine.[10] [11]

When a multithreaded application uses complex data structures, just locking a high-level object may not suffice for error-free execution of the code if some other threads in another part of the application have unfettered access to the lower-level elements of the data structures. We illustrate this with the help of the following example in which the array `@dataObj` of line (C) is a shared object whose two elements are subject to repeated modifications by the `itemSwapSynchronized()` and the `itemSwap()` subroutines invoked by the threads launched in lines (D) through (G). The elements of the array `@dataObj` are references to the scalars `$p` and `$q`, both shared objects. While the changes made by the threads in lines (D) and (E) to the two elements of the array `@dataObj` take place after the object is locked in line (J), the threads in lines (F) and (G) make direct changes to the variables `$p` and `$q` without first putting locks on these variables in lines (O) through (U). Note that the changes made by `itemSwapSynchronized()` and `itemSwap()` are equal and opposite to the two elements of the array `@dataObj`. Therefore, in the absence of thread interference, the sum of the integers stored at the two elements of the array `@dataObj` should always be 100.[12]

[10] As to which thread from all the blocked threads will be selected next for acquiring the lock depends on the nature of the thread scheduling algorithm. If preemptive scheduling is in effect, all the blocked threads get their turn at acquiring the lock in a round-robin fashion.

[11] What this demonstrates is that `lock()`, in addition to being useful for locking specific objects, is also useful for locking sections of code. When used to merely lock a section of code, the variable supplied to `lock()` does not have to hold any useful data. Used in this manner, the argument to `lock()` behaves very much like a *mutex* in POSIX threads. The name *mutex*, an abbreviation of *mutual exclusion*, is one of the two thread synchronization primitives provided by POSIX, the other being the *condition variable*. See Chapter 18 of [41] for further information regarding mutex locks for multithreaded programming with C and C++.

[12] Line (H) of this script also shows the use of

```
threads->list
```

to return a list of all the threads that are currently running and not detached. A thread becomes detached by calling `detach()` on it. A detached thread continues to run even after the main thread that spawned it has died. Daemon threads are created in this manner.

```
#!/usr/bin/perl -w

### InterferenceAnyway.pl

use strict;
use threads;
use threads::shared;

my $p : shared = 50;                                            #(A)
my $q : shared = 50;                                            #(B)

my @dataObj : shared = (\$p, \$q);                              #(C)

threads->create( \&repeatedSynchronizedSwaps );                 #(D)
threads->create( \&repeatedSynchronizedSwaps );                 #(E)
threads->create( \&repeatedSwaps );                             #(F)
threads->create( \&repeatedSwaps );                             #(G)

foreach (threads->list) { $_->join; }                           #(H)

sub itemSwapSynchronized {                                      #(I)
    lock( @dataObj );                                           #(J)
    my $x = int ( -4.999999 + rand(10 ) );                      #(K)
    ${$dataObj[0]} += $x;                                       #(L)
    keepBusy();                                                 #(M)
    ${$dataObj[1]} -= $x;                                       #(N)
}
sub itemSwap {                                                  #(O)
#    lock($p);                                                  #(P)
#    lock($q);                                                  #(Q)
    my $x = int ( -4.999999 + rand(10 ) );                      #(R)
    $p += $x;                                                   #(S)
    keepBusy();                                                 #(T)
    $q -= $x;                                                   #(U)
}
sub keepBusy {                                                  #(V)
    my $i = 0;                                                  #(W)
    while ( $i++ < 10000 ) {}                                   #(X)
}
sub test {                                                      #(Y)
    lock( @dataObj );                                           #(Z)
    lock($p);                                                   #(a)
    lock($q);                                                   #(b)
    my $sum = ${$dataObj[0]} + ${$dataObj[1]};                  #(c)
    print "Sum: $sum\n";                                        #(d)
}
```

```
sub repeatedSynchronizedSwaps {                                    #(e)
    my $j = 0;                                                     #(f)
    while ( $j++ < 500 ) {                                         #(g)
        itemSwapSynchronized();                                    #(h)
        test() unless $j % 100;                                    #(i)
    }
}
sub repeatedSwaps {                                                #(j)
    my $j = 0;                                                     #(k)
    while ( $j++ < 500 ) {                                         #(l)
        itemSwap();                                                #(m)
        test() unless $j % 100;                                    #(n)
    }
}
```

The output of this script is shown below. We again see corrupted output despite the fact that both `itemSwap()` and `itemSwapSynchronized()` make equal and opposite changes to the two elements of `@dataObj` array. For obvious reasons, that is not surprising since the changes brought about by `itemSwap()` take place under unlocked conditions.

```
Sum: 102
Sum: 100
Sum: 100
Sum: 100
Sum: 100
Sum: 100
Sum: 96
Sum: 92
Sum: 97
Sum: 96
Sum: 100
Sum: 99
Sum: 102
Sum: 102
Sum: 100
Sum: 99
Sum: 98
Sum: 98
Sum: 98
Sum: 100
```

If we were to uncomment the two statements in lines (P) and (Q), we would again see interference-free behavior from this script.

Different threads trying to lock different objects concurrently can cause the threads to deadlock. Let's say a thread wants to acquire a lock on a resource that is already locked by another thread. But, in order to release the lock, this other thread may be waiting for the first thread to do something, causing both threads to get simultaneously blocked. This is illustrated by the following example that is a small variation on an example in the `perlthrtut` tutorial that comes with the Perl core documentation. After the first thread is launched in line (C), it immediately goes on to acquire a lock on the shared variable `$a` in line (G). In the meantime, a second thread is also launched in line (D). This thread immediately goes on to acquire a lock on the shared variable `$b` in line (M). Especially because both threads engage in some busy work in lines (H) and (N) after their respective locking operations of lines (G) and (M), it is highly likely that by the end of the busy work of lines (H) and (N), they are both simultaneously holding locks, the first thread to `$a` and the second thread to `$b`. Therefore, the locking operation of line (I) would fail for the first thread, and the same would be the case for the locking operation of line (O) for the second thread. As a consequence, we have a deadlock between the two threads. Neither thread would be able to proceed forward and the program would hang.

```
#!/usr/bin/perl -w

### Deadlock.pl

use strict;
use threads;
use threads::shared;

my $a : shared = 0;                                                  #(A)
my $b : shared = 0;                                                  #(B)

threads->new( \&sub1 );                                              #(C)
threads->new( \&sub2 );                                              #(D)
foreach (threads->list) { $_->join }                                 #(E)

sub sub1 {                                                           #(F)
    lock( $a );                                                      #(G)
    keepBusy( 1 );                                                   #(H)
    lock( $b );                                                      #(I)
    $b++;                                                            #(J)
    print "sub1:    \$a = $a    \$b = $b\n";                         #(K)
}

sub sub2 {                                                           #(L)
    lock( $b );                                                      #(M)
    keepBusy( 1 );                                                   #(N)
    lock( $a );                                                      #(O)
    $a++;                                                            #(P)
    print "sub2:    \$a = $a    \$b = $b\n";                         #(Q)
}
```

```
sub keepBusy {                                                          #(R)
    my $how_many_seconds = shift;                                       #(S)
    my $curr = time;                                                    #(T)
    while ( time < $curr + $how_many_seconds ) {}                       #(U)
}
```

14.5.2 Locks for Thread Synchronization in Python

Python's `threading` module includes a class called `Lock` whose instances can be used to acquire locks on shared data objects. The locking and unlocking mechanism works the same as already explained for the case of Perl. A thread acquires a lock at the beginning of the code segment that must run free of thread interference by invoking `acquire()` on a `Lock` instance. All of the subsequent code statements, until the statement where the thread releases the lock by invoking `release()` on the same `Lock` instance, can only be executed by the thread that has the lock. If thread B wants to execute a protected section of the code while thread A has a lock on it, thread B will block until the lock is released by thread A. If multiple threads are waiting to enter a protected section of the code, one of them is chosen at random after the lock is released.

The following script is an interference-free version of `ThreadInterference.py` of Section 14.4.2. We construct an instance of `threading.Lock` in line (A). This object will be used to lock segments of code, as we will show. The `DataObject` class in lines (B) through (S) is the same as in `ThreadInterference.py` except for the calls to `lock.acquire()` in lines (G) and (N) and the calls to `lock.release()` in lines (L) and (P). Now only one thread at a time will be allowed to execute the statements in lines (H) through (K) and in line (O). This should eliminate the thread interference problem we saw earlier.

```
#!/usr/bin/env python

### NoThreadInterference.py

import threading

import random
ran = random.Random()

lock = threading.Lock()                                                 #(A)
```

```
#------------------------    class DataObject   -----------------------
class DataObject( object ):                                           #(B)

    def __init__( self ):                                             #(C)
        self.dataItem1 = 50                                           #(D)
        self.dataItem2 = 50                                           #(E)

    def itemSwap(self):                                               #(F)
        lock.acquire()                                                #(G)
        x = -5 + ran.randint(0,10)                                    #(H)
        self.dataItem1 -= x                                           #(I)
        self.keepBusy()                                               #(J)
        self.dataItem2 += x                                           #(K)
        lock.release()                                                #(L)

    def test(self):                                                   #(M)
        lock.acquire()                                                #(N)
        sum = self.dataItem1 + self.dataItem2                         #(O)
        lock.release()                                                #(P)
        print "Sum: %d" % sum                                         #(Q)

    def keepBusy( self ):                                             #(R)
        for i in range(100000): pass                                  #(S)

#--------------------    class RepeatedSwaps    -----------------------
class RepeatedSwaps( threading.Thread ):                              #(T)

    def __init__( self, dataObject ):                                 #(U)
        self.dataObject = dataObject                                  #(V)
        threading.Thread.__init__(self)                               #(W)

    def run( self ):                                                  #(X)
        for i in range (500):                                         #(Y)
            self.dataObject.itemSwap()                                #(Z)
            if i % 100 == 0:                                          #(a)
                self.dataObject.test()                                #(b)

#--------------------------    launch threads -----------------------

d = DataObject()                                                      #(c)

t1 = RepeatedSwaps(d)                                                 #(d)
t2 = RepeatedSwaps(d)                                                 #(e)
t3 = RepeatedSwaps(d)                                                 #(f)

map( lambda x: x.start(), (t1, t2, t3) )                              #(g)
```

As you'd expect, the output of this script is:

```
Sum: 100
Sum: 100
Sum: 100
Sum: 100
Sum: 100
Sum: 100
Sum: 100
Sum: 100
Sum: 100
Sum: 100
Sum: 100
Sum: 100
Sum: 100
Sum: 100
Sum: 100
```

This output confirms that by placing locks on sections of the code vulnerable to thread interference we stopped the shared data objects from getting corrupted.

We will *not* show a Python version of the Perl script `InterferenceAnyway.pl` that demonstrated that it may not suffice to lock high-level objects in a script if their lower level constituents are directly accessible and open to possible thread interference. In Perl, it was possible to lock a high-level object and at the same time declare its low-level components directly accessible to all threads. With the object-oriented style of multithreading made possible by Python's `threading` module, the data components of a high-level object are much more tightly encapsulated. Additionally, in Python you always lock sections of code. (In Perl, you may lock objects or you may lock sections of code.) So as long as all sections of code vulnerable to thread interference are protected by locks, the overall script will be thread-safe regardless of whether a thread is trying to access a high-level object or its constituents.

The `threading` module also contains the class `RLock` that allows one to construct a *reentrant lock*. A reentrant lock can be acquired multiple times by the same thread — something likely to happen in recursive function calls containing protected sections of code. On the other hand, a nonreentrant lock, such as the one constructed from the class `Lock`, once locked, cannot be locked again by any thread, including the thread that locked it in the first place. The method calls for locking and unlocking a reentrant lock are the same as for a regular lock.

Using the `RLock` class, we will now present a variation on the Perl thread deadlock example `Deadlock.pl` of the previous subsection. Our goal here is to demonstrate how easy it is for a thread to monopolize the CPU. The multithreadable class in the script contains two methods `_foo()` and `_bar()` that call each other recursively through protected sections of the code. Since the calls are recursive, for protection we construct a lock of type `RLock` in line (A).[13] For protection,[14] we place the implementation code for `_foo()` and `_bar()` within calls to `lock.acquire()` and `lock.release()`, as shown in the script.

```
#!/usr/bin/env python

### ShuttingOutThreadsDemo.py

import threading

lock = threading.RLock()                                          #(A)

#--------------------  class DeadlockDemoThread  ----------------------

class ShuttingOutThreadsDemo( threading.Thread ):                 #(B)

    def __init__( self, opt ):                                    #(C)
        self.option = opt                                         #(D)
        threading.Thread.__init__(self)                           #(E)

    def run( self ):                                              #(F)
        if self.option == 'optionA':                              #(G)
            self._foo( 5 )                                        #(H)
        else:                                                     #(I)
            self._bar( 5 )                                        #(J)

    def _foo( self, i ):                                          #(K)
        lock.acquire()                                            #(L)
        print "_foo called by %s with i=%d" % (self.getName(), i) #(M)
        if i == 0:                                                #(N)
            lock.release()                                        #(O)
            return                                                #(P)
        self.keepBusy()                                           #(Q)
        self._bar( i - 1 )                                        #(R)
        lock.release()                                            #(S)
```

---

[13]If you used a nonreentrant lock of type `Lock` in line (A), the script would hang immediately. Here is the reason for that: Let's say Thread-1 has invoked `_foo()`. Thread-1 will now acquire the lock in line (L). (Now this thread would not be timesliced until this lock is released at a later time.) Thread-1 will next call `_bar()` in line (R). Now Thread-1 will want to reacquire the same lock in line (U). Since a nonreentrant lock cannot be reacquired by the *same* thread, the thread would block indefinitely, causing the application to hang.

[14]Pretend for a moment that `keepBusy()` is actually engaged in something that we want to be thread-safe.

```
    def _bar( self, i ):                                                   #(T)
        lock.acquire()                                                     #(U)
        print "_bar called by %s with i=%d" % (self.getName(), i)         #(V)
        if i == 0:                                                         #(W)
            lock.release()                                                 #(X)
            return                                                         #(Y)
        self.keepBusy()                                                    #(Z)
        self._foo( i-1 )                                                   #(a)
        lock.release()                                                     #(b)

    def keepBusy( self ):                                                  #(c)
        for i in range(1000000): pass                                      #(d)

#------------------------  launch threads  ----------------------------

t1 = ShuttingOutThreadsDemo( 'optionA' )                                   #(e)
t2 = ShuttingOutThreadsDemo( 'optionB' )                                   #(f)

map( lambda x: x.start(), (t1, t2) )                                       #(g)
```

If you comment out the calls to `lock.acquire()` and `lock.release()` in lines (L), (O), (S), (U), (X), and (b), you will see the following output:

```
_foo called by Thread-1 with i=5
_bar called by Thread-2 with i=5
_foo called by Thread-2 with i=4
_bar called by Thread-1 with i=4
_foo called by Thread-1 with i=3
_bar called by Thread-1 with i=2
_bar called by Thread-2 with i=3
_foo called by Thread-1 with i=1
_foo called by Thread-2 with i=2
_bar called by Thread-1 with i=0
_bar called by Thread-2 with i=1
_foo called by Thread-2 with i=0
```

This shows the two threads being executed cooperatively. It is likely that while Thread-1 is in the middle of its do-nothing loop of `keepBusy()`, it is timesliced and the processor is handed over to Thread-2, and so on. However, if you run the script as shown above, you get the following output:

```
_foo called by Thread-1 with i=5
_bar called by Thread-1 with i=4
_foo called by Thread-1 with i=3
_bar called by Thread-1 with i=2
_foo called by Thread-1 with i=1
_bar called by Thread-1 with i=0
```

```
_bar called by Thread-2 with i=5
_foo called by Thread-2 with i=4
_bar called by Thread-2 with i=3
_foo called by Thread-2 with i=2
_bar called by Thread-2 with i=1
_foo called by Thread-2 with i=0
```

This shows that Thread-1 completely shuts out Thread-2 until its own termination, *negating the whole point of concurrent processing through multithreading*. This happens because when Thread-1 first invokes `_foo()`, it immediately acquires the lock in line (L). Now this thread will not be timesliced until this particular acquisition of the lock is relinquished by a call to `release()`. [That is, the recursion level for `release()` must match the recursion level at which `acquire()` was invoked.] Thread-1 next calls `_bar()` in line (R), causing the thread of execution to move into that function without the release of the lock acquired in line (L). Thread-1 now acquires the same lock again (but with the recursion level incremented). Subsequently, Thread-1 calls `_foo()` again without this newly acquired lock getting released. In this manner, Thread-1 continues its interruption-free execution through recursive invocations of `_foo()` and `_bar()` until the boundary condition of either line (N) or line (W) is met. The unwinding of the recursion then causes all the acquired locks to be released. It is only after that that Thread-2 can get time on the processor.

14.6 USING SEMAPHORES FOR ELIMINATING THREAD INTERFERENCE

Multithreading in Perl and Python also includes support for semaphores for regulating the entry of threads into designated sections of the code. As with locks, semaphores can be used to provide exclusive access to one thread at a time to a section of the code. But, being more general, semaphores can grant access to more than one thread at a time if that is desired.

A semaphore is equipped with a private counter for keeping track of how many threads have been allowed entry into the protected section of the code and a private queue for holding the threads that are currently denied entry. A semaphore supports two methods that are called `down()` and `up()` in `ithreads` for the case of Perl and `acquire()` and `release()` in the `threading` module for the case of Python. The first, `down()` in Perl and `acquire()` in Python, is usually invoked at the beginning of a protected section of the code and the second, `up()` in Perl and `release()` in Python, at the exit from the protected section of the code. A thread can get past `down()` or `acquire()` only if the current value stored in the counter exceeds zero. When a thread is allowed permission into the protected code, the counter is decremented. The value of the counter is not allowed to become negative. If the value stored in the counter is already zero when a thread gets to the `down()` or the `acquire()` statement, the thread is blocked and stored away in the semaphore's queue. When a thread executes `up()` or `release()` at the exit point of the protected code, the value stored in the counter is incremented, which causes one of the waiting threads to be allowed entry into the protected code by executing `down()` or `acquire()`. The important point to remember is that `down()` in Perl and `acquire()` in Python always decrement the counter, but never to a value below zero, and `up()` in Perl and `release()` in Python always increment the counter. If `down()` or `acquire()` encounters a thread that is trying to decrement its value that is currently 0, the thread is suspended temporarily.

Obviously then, a binary semaphore, that is, a semaphore in which the counter is initialized to 1, can be used as a lock in the same sense as explained in the previous section. But, equally obviously, by initializing the counter to a value larger than 1, a semaphore can be used to give multiple but a specified number of threads permission to enter the protected code. Also, an application can be started with the counter set to zero for a certain section of the code that should not be accessed by the threads as the application is being initialized. Subsequently, after the initialization of the application is completed, the value of the counter can be set to a number that reflects however many threads can be allowed to simultaneously execute the protected code concurrently. *Also note that whereas a lock is owned by the thread or the process that acquired the lock, a semaphore is not owned by anyone.* Ordinarily, an acquired lock (especially if it is of the reentrant kind) can only be released by the thread or the process that acquired the lock. On the other hand, the `down()` and `up()` functions in Perl and the `acquire()` and `release()` functions in Python can be executed independently by any thread or process whatsoever.[15]

14.6.1 Semaphores in Perl

We will now show a semaphore version of the `NoThreadInterferene.pl` script presented previously. Lines (A) and (B) of the next script create two semaphores, `$semaphore1` and `$semaphore2`. Line (C) declares a shared array for the three threads created in lines (D), (E), and (F), the same that we had for the `NoThreadInterference.pl` script. The rest of the code is also the same as for `NoThreadInterference.pl` except that we now use semaphores in the `itemSwap()` and `test()` functions. Note the calls to `down()` and `up()` in lines (I) and (N) of `itemSwap()` and in lines (S) and (W) of `test()`.

[15]Taking advantage of all of these features of semaphores is highly nontrivial for complex systems. When different threads or processes are allowed to carry out the incrementing and the decrementing operations on a semaphore counter, the only way to be certain that the semaphores are working correctly is by constructing a formal proof of concurrency.

```
#!/usr/bin/perl -w

### NoInterferenceWithSemaphores.pl

use strict;
use threads;
use threads::shared;
use Thread::Semaphore;

my $semaphore1 = Thread::Semaphore->new();                                      #(A)
my $semaphore2 = Thread::Semaphore->new();                                      #(B)

my @dataObj : shared = (50, 50);                                                #(C)

threads->create( \&repeatedSwaps );                                             #(D)
threads->create( \&repeatedSwaps );                                             #(E)
threads->create( \&repeatedSwaps );                                             #(F)

foreach (threads->list) { $_->join; }                                           #(G)

sub itemSwap {                                                                  #(H)
    $semaphore1->down;                                                          #(I)
    my $x = int ( -4.999999 + rand(10 ) );                                      #(J)
    $dataObj[0] -= $x;                                                          #(K)
    keepBusy();                                                                 #(L)
    $dataObj[1] += $x;                                                          #(M)
    $semaphore1->up;                                                            #(N)
}
sub keepBusy {                                                                  #(O)
    my $i = 0;                                                                  #(P)
    while ( $i++ < 10000 ) {}                                                   #(Q)
}
sub test {                                                                      #(R)
    $semaphore2->down;                                                          #(S)
    my $thread_id = threads->self->tid();                                       #(T)
    my $sum = $dataObj[0] + $dataObj[1];                                        #(U)
    print "Thread $thread_id   Sum: $sum\n";                                    #(V)
    $semaphore2->up;                                                            #(W)
}
sub repeatedSwaps {                                                             #(X)
    my $j = 0;                                                                  #(Y)
    while ( $j++ < 500 ) {                                                      #(Z)
        itemSwap();                                                             #(a)
        test() unless $j % 100;                                                 #(b)
    }
}
```

The output of a given run of this script is shown below:

```
Thread 3    Sum: 100
Thread 1    Sum: 100
Thread 2    Sum: 100
Thread 2    Sum: 100
Thread 3    Sum: 100
Thread 1    Sum: 100
Thread 3    Sum: 100
Thread 1    Sum: 100
Thread 2    Sum: 100
Thread 3    Sum: 100
Thread 2    Sum: 100
Thread 3    Sum: 100
Thread 1    Sum: 100
Thread 1    Sum: 100
Thread 2    Sum: 100
```

As each thread reaches the `down()` statement, either in line (I) or line (S) of the script, the decision as to whether to let the thread proceed into the protected code or suspend it is made solely on the basis of the value in the semaphore's counter that by default is initialized to 1. So the very first thread will get through, but only after the value stored in the counter is decremented to 0. As long as the counter value stays 0, all subsequent threads reaching the same `down()` statement get suspended and put away in the semaphore's internal queue. A thread exiting the protected code executes `up()` to bump up the counter. This allows one of the suspended threads to be considered for entry into the protected code; and so on.

If we were to run the same script as shown above, but with the call to `down()` in line (I) commented out, we would get the following sort of output that so clearly shows the effect of thread interference.

```
Thread 1    Sum: 104
Thread 2    Sum: 99
Thread 3    Sum: 96
Thread 1    Sum: 101
Thread 2    Sum: 100
Thread 3    Sum: 99
Thread 1    Sum: 100
Thread 2    Sum: 102
Thread 3    Sum: 97
Thread 1    Sum: 100
Thread 2    Sum: 105
Thread 3    Sum: 106
Thread 1    Sum: 96
Thread 2    Sum: 102
Thread 3    Sum: 100
```

If it is desired to create a semaphore with its counter set to, say, 10, that can be done with the following constructor call:

```
my $semaphore = Thread::Semaphore->new( 10 );
```

And if it is desired to call `down()` and `up()` with arguments, as opposed to assuming a default of 1 for the arguments, we can make calls like

```
$semaphore->down( 5 );
....
....
$semaphore->up( 5 );
```

When the semaphore counter is decremented by calling `down()` with a specified argument, the value of the counter is reduced by *at least* 1 regardless of the argument supplied to `down()`. Therefore, `down(0)` and `down(1)` both cause the counter to be decremented by 1.

14.6.2 Semaphores in Python

The next script is the Python version of the semaphore-based thread-safe script `NoThreadInterferenceWithSemaphores.pl` shown in the previous subsection. The `threading` module in Python comes with a class named `Semaphore` whose instance can be used as a semaphore. As mentioned already at the beginning of this section, what `down()` does for decrementing the internal counter of a semaphore in Perl is achieved by calling `acquire()` in Python, and what `up()` does for incrementing the counter in Perl is done by `release()` in Python. Line (A) of the script constructs a semaphore by calling the constructor of the class `threading.Semaphore`. We then designate the protected sections of the code by calling `acquire()` and `release()` on the semaphore in lines (G) and (L) and in lines (N) and (P).

```
#!/usr/bin/env python

### NoThreadInterferenceWithSemaphores.py

import threading

import random
ran = random.Random()

semaphore = threading.Semaphore()                                    #(A)
```

```
#------------------------   class DataObject  ------------------------
class DataObject( object ):                                        #(B)

    def __init__( self ):                                          #(C)
        self.dataItem1 = 50                                        #(D)
        self.dataItem2 = 50                                        #(E)

    def itemSwap(self):                                            #(F)
        semaphore.acquire()                                        #(G)
        x = -5 + ran.randint(0,10)                                 #(H)
        self.dataItem1 -= x                                        #(I)
        self.keepBusy()                                            #(J)
        self.dataItem2 += x                                        #(K)
        semaphore.release()                                        #(L)

    def test(self, caller):                                        #(M)
        semaphore.acquire()                                        #(N)
        sum = self.dataItem1 + self.dataItem2                      #(O)
        semaphore.release()                                        #(P)
        print "%s   Sum: %d" % (caller.getName(), sum)             #(Q)

    def keepBusy( self ):                                          #(R)
        for i in range(100000): pass                               #(S)

#--------------------   class RepeatedSwaps   -----------------------
class RepeatedSwaps( threading.Thread ):                           #(T)

    def __init__( self, dataObject ):                              #(U)
        self.dataObject = dataObject                               #(V)
        threading.Thread.__init__(self)                            #(W)

    def run( self ):                                               #(X)
        for i in range (500):                                      #(Y)
            self.dataObject.itemSwap()                             #(Z)
            if i % 100 == 0:                                       #(a)
                self.dataObject.test(self)                         #(b)

#-------------------------   launch threads ------------------------

d = DataObject()                                                   #(c)

t1 = RepeatedSwaps(d)                                              #(d)
t2 = RepeatedSwaps(d)                                              #(e)
t3 = RepeatedSwaps(d)                                              #(f)

map( lambda x: x.start(), (t1, t2, t3) )                           #(g)
```

The output of this script is the same as for the Perl semaphore script shown earlier. This output has no thread interference.

14.7 USING CONDITION VARIABLES FOR AVOIDING DEADLOCK

We showed previously that when different threads share a data object, one must always be wary of thread interference. In those examples, all of the different threads were trying to make the same kind of a change to a shared data object. Now let's consider a situation where the different threads try to make different changes to a shared object. If the changes are predicated on the current state of the data object, the threads may deadlock. Threads may also potentially deadlock if different threads make different but coupled changes to different shared objects. By coupled changes we mean that the change made to a shared object would be predicated on the current state of the other shared objects.

Consider, for example, the case of a bank account that is shared by multiple customers. Some customers may deposit money into the account, whereas other customers may withdraw. Obviously, a withdrawing customer would not be able to accomplish the task if the current balance in the account is less than the amount needed to be withdrawn. The withdrawing customer would need to wait until the depositors placed sufficient funds into the account. While such a scenario would not necessarily result in a true deadlock, since all that a withdrawing customer has to do is to wait, variations on the scenario can indeed result in a true deadlock. Consider, for example, a single agent controlling two bank accounts. Let's say all that the agent is allowed to do is to shift random amounts between the accounts. If a thread represents the activities of depositing and withdrawing funds from each account, the two threads representing the two accounts could easily deadlock. If the amount needed to be withdrawn from each account exceeded the current balance in the account, each account would wait indefinitely for a deposit before allowing the withdrawal to take place. This kind of a deadlock is obviously irresolvable.

14.7.1 Condition Variables for Avoiding Deadlock with Perl Threads

We next show a Perl script that mirrors the former situation described above — a shared multicustomer account with some depositor threads and some withdrawer threads. The script illustrates how a potential deadlock in this case can be avoided by thread synchronization using a condition variable and the `cond_wait()` and `cond_signal()` functions. The script creates three depositor threads in lines (C) and (D) and three withdrawer threads in lines (E) and (F). Each thread carries out its assigned duty indefinitely, the depositor threads in the `while` loop of lines (V) through (b) and the withdrawer threads in the `while` loop of lines (f) through (l). The actual deposit action in the depositor threads takes place by calling `deposit()` defined in lines (H) through (L), and the actual withdraw action in the withdrawer threads by calling `withdraw()` in lines (M) through (Q).

At the very outset, the script defines in line (B) a variable `$cv` to serve as a *condition variable*. This variable is used as a signalling object by the `cond_signal()` and `cond_wait()` functions that are called in lines (L) and (Q), respectively. When a withdrawer thread is unable to proceed because of insufficient funds in the shared account, the thread calls `cond_wait()` in line (Q) to relinquish any locks held by the thread and to suspend itself from further execution. The argument supplied to `cond_wait()` designates the condition variable through which the suspended thread would want to be notified of any changes in the balance held by the account. Subsequently, when a depositor thread makes a change to those data objects, it calls `cond_signal()`, with the same condition variable as its argument, to notify the suspended withdrawer threads that a change was made to the account. This signalling action by a depositor thread will cause one of the withdrawer threads to reacquire the lock it previously relinquished. However, if the new balance in the account is still not sufficient for the amount to be withdrawn, the thread would again be suspended and another suspended thread given a chance. All this is orchestrated by the following `while` loop of lines (P) and (Q):

```
while ( $account_balance < $draw ) {
    cond_wait( $cv );
}
```

For the withdrawer thread selected by the thread scheduler after the condition variable is signaled, the flow of execution in the thread, with its reacquired lock, will shift back to the conditional of the `while` loop. If the conditional evaluates to true, the execution of `cond_wait($cv)` would cause the lock to be relinquished once again. This would go on for each selected withdrawer thread for every signalling of the condition variable by the depositor threads.

```
#!/usr/bin/perl -w

### MultiCustomerAccount.pl

use strict;
use threads;
use threads::shared;

my $account_balance : shared = 0;                                    #(A)
my $cv : shared;                                                     #(B)

foreach (1 .. 3) {                                                   #(C)
    threads->new( \&multiple_deposits );                             #(D)
}
foreach (1 .. 3) {                                                   #(E)
    threads->new( \&multiple_withdrawals );                          #(F)
}
```

```
foreach (threads->list) { $_->join }                                #(G)

sub deposit {                                                       #(H)
    my $dep = shift;                                                #(I)
    lock( $cv );                                                    #(J)
    $account_balance += $dep;                                       #(K)
    cond_signal( $cv );                                             #(L)
}
sub withdraw {                                                      #(M)
    my $draw = shift;                                               #(N)
    lock( $cv );                                                    #(O)
    while ( $account_balance < $draw ) {                            #(P)
        cond_wait( $cv );                                           #(Q)
    }
    $account_balance -= $draw;                                      #(R)
}
sub multiple_deposits {                                             #(S)
    my $i = 0;                                                      #(T)
    my $x;                                                          #(U)
    while ( 1 ) {                                                   #(V)
        $x = rand( 10 );                                            #(W)
        deposit( $x );                                              #(X)
        if ( $i++ % 10 == 0 ) {                                     #(Y)
            my $threadid = threads->self->tid;                      #(Z)
            printf(
              "balance after $i deposits by thread $threadid: \t\t%d\n",
                                  $account_balance );               #(a)
        }
        keepBusy( 1 );                                              #(b)
    }
}
sub multiple_withdrawals {                                          #(c)
    my $i = 0;                                                      #(d)
    my $x;                                                          #(e)
    while ( 1 ) {                                                   #(f)
        $x = rand( 10 );                                            #(g)
        withdraw( $x );                                             #(h)

        if ( $i++ % 10 == 0 )  {                                    #(i)
            my $threadid = threads->self->tid;                      #(j)
            printf(
            "balance after $i withdrawals by thread $threadid: \t%d\n",
                                      $account_balance );           #(k)
        }

        keepBusy( 1 );                                              #(l)
    }
}
```

```
sub keepBusy {                                                    #(m)
    my $how_many_seconds = shift;                                 #(n)
    my $curr = time;                                              #(o)
    while ( time < $curr + $how_many_seconds ) {}                 #(p)
}
```

Here is a portion of the output produced by this script. As the reader can see, thread synchronization achieved through `cond_wait()` and `cond_signal()` prevents the account from going negative.

```
balance after 1 deposits by thread 1:          1
balance after 1 deposits by thread 2:          5
balance after 1 deposits by thread 3:          6
balance after 1 withdrawals by thread 4:       10
balance after 1 withdrawals by thread 5:       2
balance after 1 withdrawals by thread 6:       4
balance after 11 deposits by thread 1:         20
balance after 11 deposits by thread 2:         25
balance after 11 deposits by thread 3:         30
balance after 11 withdrawals by thread 6:      15
balance after 11 withdrawals by thread 4:      7
balance after 11 withdrawals by thread 5:      4
balance after 21 deposits by thread 3:         62
balance after 21 deposits by thread 1:         43
balance after 21 deposits by thread 2:         51
balance after 21 withdrawals by thread 5:      42
balance after 21 withdrawals by thread 6:      44
balance after 21 withdrawals by thread 4:      37
....
....
```

The benefit of thread synchronization achieved through the signaling of the condition variable becomes all the more apparent if you run the script after commenting out the call to `cond_signal()` in line (L).[16] Now the action of a depositor thread would not trigger an attempt to schedule a suspended withdrawer thread for time on the processor.[17] Now, depending on the peculiarities of the thread scheduler, the withdrawer threads are less likely to be scheduled than the depositor threads for time on the processor. Here is a portion of the output when line (L) is commented out. As the reader can see, the bank account is now growing continuously despite the fact

[16] It obviously makes no sense to comment out the `while` loop containing the `cond_wait()` statement in lines (P) and (Q), since that would cause the account to go negative.

[17] In some multithreaded systems, when using condition variables, a blocked withdrawer thread would not be able to come off its suspended state as long as the condition variable is not signalled.

that the depositor threads and the withdrawer threads use similar random numbers for the deposit and withdraw actions.

```
balance after 1 deposits by thread 1:          7
balance after 1 deposits by thread 2:          10
balance after 1 deposits by thread 3:          16
balance after 1 withdrawals by thread 4:       18
balance after 1 withdrawals by thread 5:       14
balance after 1 withdrawals by thread 6:       5
balance after 11 deposits by thread 2:         72
balance after 11 deposits by thread 3:         80
balance after 11 deposits by thread 1:         82
balance after 11 withdrawals by thread 4:      83
balance after 11 withdrawals by thread 5:      81
balance after 21 deposits by thread 1:         120
balance after 21 deposits by thread 2:         129
balance after 21 deposits by thread 3:         130
balance after 21 withdrawals by thread 5:      115
balance after 21 withdrawals by thread 4:      132
....
....
```

14.7.2 Condition Variables for Avoiding Deadlock with Python Threads

The following script does the same thing in Python that our previous script did in Perl: It demonstrates how a condition variable and its signalling can be used to prevent an avoidable deadlock between the threads. As before we have a multicustomer bank account. There exist three depositors and three withdrawers, each in the form of a separate thread, operating on the same bank account.

We first create a lock in line (A) and a condition variable for the lock in line (B). We define the `Account` class in lines (C) through (P). Since we want the deposit and withdraw acts to be thread-safe, we protect the code for these actions with the lock, as shown in (F) through (J) for `deposit()` and in lines (K) through (P) for `withdraw()`. Note particularly how we use condition variable signalling in lines (I) and (N). If the amount to be withdrawn by a withdrawer thread exceeds the balance in the account, we call `wait()` on the condition variable. This causes the thread to release its lock. Such a thread will be put back in contention for the CPU time only after receiving the `notifyAll()` signal that is issued by a depositor thread in line (I). Obviously, as long as the condition of the `while` clause in line (N) is not satisfied, the withdrawer thread will keep on being shoved into the wait status.

The multithreadable objects in this script are constructed from the class `Depositor` in lines (Q) through (c) and the class `Withdrawer` in lines (d) through (p). In lines (q), (r), and (s), the instances made from these classes are handed the account they are supposed to operate on as a constructor argument. A `Depositor` instance invokes the account's `deposit()` method in line (Y); the method is asked to deposit a small random amount `x` into the account. Similarly, a `Withdrawer` instance invokes the account's `withdraw()` method in line (l); the method is asked to withdraw a small random amount `x` from the account. In both the `Depositor` and the `Withdrawer` threads, we print out the balance in the account after every 10 deposit/withdraw actions. For the depositor threads, this is done in line (b) and for the withdrawer threads in line (o). Finally, we launch the threads in line (t).

```
#!/usr/bin/env python

### MultiCustomerAccount.py

import threading
import time

import random
ran = random.Random()

lock = threading.RLock()                                                  #(A)
cv = threading.Condition(lock)                                            #(B)

#--------------------  utility class Account  ---------------------
class Account( object ):                                                  #(C)

    def __init__( self ):                                                 #(D)
        self.balance = 0                                                  #(E)

    def deposit( self, dep ):                                             #(F)
        lock.acquire()                                                    #(G)
        self.balance += dep                                               #(H)
        cv.notifyAll()                                                    #(I)
        lock.release()                                                    #(J)

    def withdraw( self, draw ):                                           #(K)
        lock.acquire()                                                    #(L)
        while ( self.balance < draw ):                                    #(M)
            cv.wait()                                                     #(N)
        self.balance -= draw                                              #(O)
        lock.release()                                                    #(P)

#---------------  multithreadable class Depositor  -----------------
class Depositor( threading.Thread ):                                      #(Q)

    def __init__( self, acnt ):                                           #(R)
        self.account = acnt                                               #(S)
        threading.Thread.__init__(self)                                   #(T)
```

```
    def run(self):                                                     #(U)
        i = 0                                                          #(V)
        while 1:                                                       #(W)
            x = ran.randint(0,10)                                      #(X)
            self.account.deposit( x )                                  #(Y)
            i += 1                                                     #(Z)
            if i % 10 == 0:                                            #(a)
                print "balance after deposits %d" % \
                                              self.account.balance     #(b)
            time.sleep( 1 )                                            #(c)

#----------------  multithreadable class Withdrawer  -----------------
class Withdrawer( threading.Thread ):                                  #(d)

    def __init__( self, acnt ):                                        #(e)
        self.account = acnt                                            #(f)
        threading.Thread.__init__(self)                                #(g)

    def run(self):                                                     #(h)
        i = 0                                                          #(i)
        while 1:                                                       #(j)
            x = ran.randint(0,10)                                      #(k)
            self.account.withdraw( x )                                 #(l)
            i += 1                                                     #(m)
            if i % 10 == 0:                                            #(n)
                print "balance after withdrawals %d" % \
                                             self.account.balance      #(o)
            time.sleep( 1 )                                            #(p)

#-------------------------  launch threads  -------------------------

acct = Account()                                                       #(q)

depositors = [ Depositor(acct) for i in range(3) ]                     #(r)
withdrawers = [ Withdrawer(acct) for i in range(3) ]                   #(s)

map( lambda x: x.start(), depositors + withdrawers )                   #(t)
```

If you run this script after commenting out the condition variable signalling in line (I) and in lines (M) and (N), you may see an output like this:

```
balance after deposits -52
balance after deposits -46
balance after deposits -36
balance after deposits -31
```

```
balance after deposits -23
balance after withdrawals -23
balance after withdrawals -23
balance after withdrawals -33
....
....
```

You can see that there is no protection against the balance going negative. In this case, a withdrawer thread goes ahead with the withdrawal even when sufficient funds do not exist in the account to cover the withdrawal. This results in negative account balances. However, if you run the script as shown above, you will see an output like the following. Now we have a guarantee that a withdrawer thread will be made to wait until there exists a sufficient balance in the account to cover the amount of the withdrawal.

```
balance after deposits 18
balance after deposits 20
balance after deposits 27
balance after withdrawals 25
balance after withdrawals 17
balance after withdrawals 17
balance after deposits 26
balance after deposits 26
balance after deposits 26
balance after withdrawals 23
balance after withdrawals 17
balance after withdrawals 7
balance after deposits 12
....
....
```

14.8 CREDITS AND SUGGESTIONS FOR FURTHER READING

For an introduction to the basic vocabulary of multithreading in object-oriented systems, see Chapter 18 of [41]. The "perlthrtut — Tutorial on Threads in Perl" by Dan Sugalski that comes with the core Perl documentation is an excellent source of information on ithreads in Perl. As already acknowledged in the main body of the chapter, the Perl script `Deadlock.pl` in Section 14.5.1 is only a small variation on an example in that tutorial. Chapter 17 of the "source book" on Perl [68] contains many useful pointers and caveats regarding multithreading in Perl. For further reading on multithreading in Python, Sections 15.2 and 15.3 of the Python Library Reference contain information on the `thread` and the `threading` modules.

14.9 HOMEWORK

1. The goal of this script is to use the `Time::HiRes` module to carry out the following comparative performance study. The script calculates 1000 square-roots of a large number in each thread. Each thread performs this calculation a certain number of times controlled by the value of `$iterations`. We refer to each iteration involving 1000 square-root calculations as one transaction.

   The basic purpose of the homework is to figure out whether using locks slows down the execution time on a per-transaction basis or speeds it up. We also wish to compare the performance to the case when we use a multiprocessing script as opposed to a multithreaded script. You are supplied with a multithreaded script here, but you must create your own multiprocessing version of this script.

   The script shown below has two parts, one in lines (F) through (W) is to go through `$iterations` number of transactions in each thread, each transaction consisting of 1000 square-root calculations. The second part, in lines (Y) through (q) is for the calculation of the min, the max, the mean, the median, the standard-deviation, and the histogram of the per-transaction elapsed time. This is done with the help of the `Statistics::Descriptive` module that we import in line (B).

   Run the script as shown and examine the various statistics of the transaction processing time. Note in particular the mean, the min, the max, and the median times. Now comment out the locking statement in line (P) and see what happens. Depending on your particular system (depending especially on the properties of the threads supplied by the operating system to which the threads created by `ithreads` will be mapped to), you may be surprised. You may see a much larger variation between the max time, the min time, and the mean when you run the script without the lock in line (P). This presumably happens because a transaction running without a lock can be interrupted midstream.

```
#!/usr/bin/perl -w

### PerformanceWithThreads.pl

use Time::HiRes qw( gettimeofday tv_interval );                    #(A)
use Statistics::Descriptive;                                       #(B)
use File::Temp ("tempfile");                                       #(C)
use threads;                                                       #(D)
use strict;                                                        #(E)

my $threads = 2;                                                   #(F)
my $iterations = 100;                                              #(G)
#my $iterations = 5;
my (undef, $statfile) = tempfile();                                #(H)
open( FH, ">>$statfile" );                                         #(I)
my $lock;
```

```
for (1 .. $threads) {                                              #(J)
    threads->create( \&do_it );                                    #(K)
}
foreach (threads->list) {                                          #(L)
    $_->join;                                                      #(M)
}
sub do_it {                                                        #(N)
    for (1 .. $iterations ) {                                      #(O)
        lock( $lock );                                             #(P)
        my $t0 = [gettimeofday()];                                 #(Q)
        # start transaction
        for (1 .. 1000) {                                          #(R)
            my $res = sqrt( 123456789012345 );                     #(S)
        }
        # end transaction
        my $elapsed = tv_interval( $t0 );                          #(T)
        print FH $elapsed . "\n";                                  #(U)
#        print "$elapsed  ";                                       #(V)
    }
}
close FH;                                                          #(W)
sleep( 5 );                                                        #(X)
analyzeStats();                                                    #(Y)
sub analyzeStats {                                                 #(Z)
    print "\n\nAnalysing stats from data in $statfile: \n";        #(a)
    open( FH, "$statfile" );                                       #(b)
    chomp( my @data = <FH> );                                      #(c)
    if (@data) {                                                   #(d)
        my $stat = Statistics::Descriptive::Full->new();           #(e)
        $stat->add_data( @data );                                  #(f)
        print "Count:     ", $stat->count() . "\n";                #(g)
        print "Mean:      ", $stat->mean() . " secs\n";            #(h)
        print "StdDev:    ", $stat->standard_deviation()." secs\n";
                                                                   #(i)
        print "Median:    ", $stat->median() . " secs\n";          #(j)
        print "Minimum:   ", $stat->min() . " secs\n";             #(k)
        print "Maximum:   ", $stat->max() . " secs\n\n\n";         #(l)
        my %hist = $stat->frequency_distribution( 20 );            #(m)
        for (sort {$a <=> $b} keys %hist) {                        #(n)
            print "bin = $_, count = $hist{$_}\n";                 #(o)
        }
    } else {                                                       #(p)
        print "There appears to be no data.\n";                    #(q)
    }
}
```

2. Write a Python script that can serve as a poor man's multithreaded web search engine. Your script should accept a list of root URLs for creating the search database consisting of a dictionary whose keys are the URLs and whose values are the corresponding web page contents. Your search engine should have the following features:

   (a) Your search engine should expand its search recursively starting from the list of root URLs supplied initially. Terminate the script when a certain prespecified depth of search is reached. Note that, in general, the number of URLs visited will grow exponentially with the depth of search.

   (b) *Fetch each web page in a separate thread.* If no response is received within a certain prespecified time (let's call this time `HTTP_TIMEOUT`), place the entry `TIMEOUT` against the URL key in the search database. [A relatively easy way to implement this feature is to make the thread a daemon thread and to then have the parent thread invoke `join()` on the daemon thread with timeout equal to `HTTP_TIMEOUT`.]

   (c) If a connection cannot be established with a URL, place the entry `FAILED` against that URL in the search database.

   (d) Note that when your search engine visits a URL, the web server in charge of that URL may actually redirect the query to a different URL. (This happens more commonly than you might think.) Make sure that your search database stores only the actual URLs, that is, the URLs visited via redirection. That way if redirection caused multiple URLs to be mapped to the same target URL, your search database would only store the target URL and its contents.

   (e) You may wish to use the `HTMLParser` module to extract all the URLs referenced in a web page and to also extract its actual data content. The parsing action carried out by the `HTMLParser` class is event based, meaning that it automatically invokes handler methods in response to certain "events" during a document scan. For example, if a starting HTML tag is encountered during a document scan, the method `handle_starttag()` is invoked automatically. Extend the system-supplied `HTMLParser` class so that it is your override definitions for the handlers that are used.

   (f) You may wish to use the `urllib` module to actually read the contents of a web page. The `urllib.urlopen()` method returns a stream object whose various methods, such as `read()`, can be used to fetch the contents of a web page.

15

Scripting for Network Programming

There is no disputing the fact that networked operations of computers have become central to the world enterprise.[1] Much of this networking is based on the client-server model of communications.

Central to the client-server model is the notion of a port and communicating by means of a socket through that port. A port is typically assigned a 16-bit address, giving it an integer value between 1 and 65,535. A server, such as a web server, monitors a designated port for incoming requests from clients. A client wishing to communicate with a server sends the server its socket number that is a combination of the client's IP address and the port number at which the client expects to hear from the server. The server acknowledges the client's request for a connection by sending its own socket number to the client. It is important to note that the client and the server roles apply to individual communication links and not necessarily to individual machines. One machine can be a client with respect to another's role as a server on one communication link, and, at the same time, act like a server with respect to the other machine's role as a client on another communication link.

Of the 65,535 port numbers that are possible, the first 1024 are reserved by ICANN (the Internet Corporation for Assigned Names and Numbers) for well-known services such as HTTP, FTP, Echo, SSH, Telnet, POP3, and so on. Port numbers over 1024

[1] Networking has always been central to all human enterprises. Life itself seems to acquire a certain meaninglessness if imagined devoid of human interconnections. With the passage of time, each wave of technological progress has brought us new ways of interacting with others, ways that are more economical, easier to use, and that allow the participants to reach each other in ways not possible before.

are generally available for use by user-defined programs. But note that various high-numbered ports also have designated applications of general interest associated with them. For example, the ports 7007 through 7011 are marked for certain specific services offered by Sun Microsystems. On Unix and Linux machines, the system file `/etc/services` contains a listing of the port numbers already registered in a network for the various services offered.

There are two fundamentally different types of communication links one can establish through a port. The first type is a one-to-one connection that uses handshaking, sequencing, and flow control to ensure that all the data packets sent from one end of a communication link are received at the other. The second is a simpler and faster one-shot messaging link — that may also be operated in one-to-many or many-to-many modes — that does *not* use handshaking and flow control and therefore carries no guarantee that the data packets sent are actually received at the destination. The first type of a link is governed by the Transmission Control Protocol (TCP) and the second type by the User Datagram Protocol (UDP). Because handshaking, sequencing, and flow control are built into TCP, we may also refer to it as a *reliable connection-based stream protocol*. TCP gives us an open connection between a server and a client for transferring an arbitrary number of bytes between the two on a continuous and ongoing basis. On the other hand, what UDP gives us is less a connection and more a way of sending a short message to a destination without requiring verification that the message was actually received. Being one-shot messages, UDP packets are by necessity self-delimiting. That is, each UDP datagram indicates exactly where it begins and ends.

Despite the fact that UDP does not guarantee that a receiver will receive all the packets sent by a sender, it plays an extremely vital role in the Internet communications.[2] While you'd of course want a TCP link for downloading web documents, transporting email, etc., a UDP link is ideal for video and audio telecasts where the speed of packet transfer carries a higher value and occasional loss of a packet can be easily tolerated. The reliability of TCP gained through flow control (and retransmissions when necessary) extracts, as one would expect, a speed penalty. Even the setup of a TCP connection with all its handshaking takes much longer than is the case with UDP.[3]

---

[2]To underscore its vital role in the operation of the Internet, UDP is used by the Internet's domain name service (DNS) that translates host names into their IP addresses and vice versa. If a machine's request for a name lookup fails to get a response from a DNS server, the machine simply resends the request to the server. So, except for occasional delay, there is no real penalty on account of missed communication with a DNS server.

[3]As reported in Stevens [63], on the average it takes eight times as long to set up and take down a TCP connection as it does to transmit a single byte under UDP.

15.1 SOCKETS

As mentioned earlier, when machine A sends its packets to machine B, the packets are sent to a specific port on machine B.[4] The actual endpoints of this communication link are *sockets*. It is the socket on machine A that knows about the Internet address of the destination machine, the port to use on the destination machine, and the protocol to use when communicating with that machine. As the reader would expect, one can construct either a TCP socket or a UDP socket. There is also a third category of sockets, the Unix-domain sockets, that are used for interprocess communications on the same machine.

In general, a socket has the following three attributes:

Socket's Domain: The domain specifies what address family will be recognized by the socket. Different address families use different formats for constructing the addresses of other processes or other nodes in a network. The two most commonly used specifications for a socket's domain are `AF_INET` and `AF_UNIX`. When a socket's domain is chosen to be `AF_INET`, the socket will recognize the address family corresponding to the TCP/IP protocol.[5] The prefix `AF` in `AF_INET` stands for "address family" and the rest, `INET`, can be thought of as standing for the Internet.[6] The `AF_INET` sockets, informally referred to as the *Internet-domain sockets*, need the IP addresses and the port numbers to define communication endpoints. On the other hand, when a socket's domain is set to `AF_UNIX`, the socket recognizes the address family for interprocess communications within the same machine. The `AF_UNIX` sockets, informally referred to as the *Unix-domain sockets*, use file pathnames as addresses to processes for interprocess communications on the same machine.[7] In addition

---

[4]The same applies when a machine wants to receive incoming packets from another machine in a network. The incoming traffic must be received at a particular port through an appropriately configured socket.

[5]Under version 4 (IPv4) of the TCP/IP protocol, those addresses are of the form `128.46.144.10:80`, where we have the IP address in its *dotted-quad* notation followed by a port number, the two separated by a colon. Under IPv4, an IP address is a 32-bit object that for human readability is considered to be divided into four 8-bit fields, with each field an integer between 0 and 255. The IP addresses are thus usually shown as these four integers separated by the decimal dot. Under version IPv6 of TCP/IP, an IP address is a 128-bit object. At this time the IPv6 addresses are used only for the Internet backbones. With the advent of dynamic host addressing made possible by DHCP (Dynamic Host Configuration Protocol) and network address translation, it is believed that the use of IPv6 addresses is unlikely to proliferate in the near future beyond their current use.

[6]In addition to the `AF` series of symbolic constants for naming a socket domain, one also has the `PF` series, as in `PF_INET`, `PF_UNIX`, etc. The `AF` and the `PF` symbolic constants evaluate to the same integer values. The distinction between the two is a historical artifact [62].

[7]It is not uncommon to use the Internet-domain sockets for interprocess communications also on the same machine, but an interprocess communication link on the same machine would probably be more efficient with a Unix-domain socket. By the way, despite their name, it is not uncommon to see the Unix-domain sockets implemented on non-Unix platforms. The POSIX name for `AF_UNIX` is `AF_LOCAL`.

to AF_INET and AF_UNIX, other possible specifications for a socket's domain include AF_INET6 for the TCP/IP version 6 protocol, AF_APPLETALK, AF_IPX, AF_X25, etc.

Socket type: The *type* of a socket determines some basic properties of the communication that the socket will undertake. There are three different socket types; these are represented by the symbolic constants SOCK_STREAM, SOCK_DGRAM, and SOCK_RAW. A socket of type SOCK_STREAM provides an endpoint for a two-way one-to-one connection for a reliable transport of bytes that carries the guarantee that all the bytes that were sent will be received in the order in which they were sent. A socket of type SOCK_DGRAM transmits and receives messages called *datagrams* of a fixed maximum length without any error detection as to whether a sent datagram was actually received, much less received in a specific sequence. In other words, in a communication endpoint of type SOCK_DGRAM, there is no acknowledgment of the received bytes, no repeat transmission in case a packet gets lost, no ordering, etc. A socket of type SOCK_RAW provides access, but only when authorized by the TCP/IP virtual machine, to the packet creation protocols for manual creation of packets with externally specified packet headers.

Socket's protocol: This attribute specifies the protocol that will be used; it must agree with the socket domain attribute. The protocol chosen must also agree with the socket type attribute. The different possible values for the protocol attribute are: tcp, udp, icmp, and raw.

The three socket attributes described above are not independent. Obviously, the reliable connection-oriented communications represented by the SOCK_STREAM socket type can only be carried out with a tcp-like protocol. Similarly, the message-oriented communication represented by the SOCK_DGRAM socket type requires a udp-like protocol. For both of these cases, the address families would most commonly be those represented by AF_INET. With regard to the Unix-domain sockets, when the address family is represented by AF_UNIX, we can specify either a one-to-one bidirectional communication link by setting the type to SOCK_STREAM, or a one-to-many (or many-to-many) message-oriented link by setting the socket type to SOCK_DGRAM. For Unix-domain sockets, the protocol attribute is left unspecified.

In Perl, both the Internet-domain and the Unix-domain sockets can be constructed using the socket() method from the Socket module that comes with the standard Perl distribution. Just as a call to open() makes its first argument a filehandle, a call to socket() makes its first argument a socket handle. Here is how you could construct a socket handle, called SOCK for convenience, for an Internet-domain client that wishes to establish a reliable connection-oriented communication link with a server:

```
use Socket;
socket(SOCK, AF_INET, SOCK_STREAM, 'tcp')
```

And, here is how you'd construct a socket handle for a Unix-domain client:

```
use Socket;
socket(SOCK, AF_UNIX, SOCK_STREAM, 0)
```

After obtaining a socket handle in this manner, you'd connect it to a destination address by a call to Perl's built-in function `connect()`. Subsequently, you can treat the socket handle as a read/write handle and read from it or write to it just as you can with a filehandle in Perl. The low-level `Socket` module allows the three attributes of a socket to be specified more or less independently. But, obviously, as mentioned previously, they cannot be completely independent since the socket domain, the socket type, and the protocol have to mutually agree.

In Python, the `socket` module that comes with the standard distribution of the libraries provides support for socket programming. One typically constructs a socket object by invoking `socket()`. This constructor call takes three arguments, all with defaults. The arguments stand for the socket address family, the socket type, and the protocol number. If you want to use the default values for the arguments, a call such as

```
from socket import *
sock = socket()
```

returns a `socket` instance for the address family `AF_INET` and for the socket type `SOCK_STREAM`. This is the socket you'd need for a reliable connection-oriented communication link in a Python script. Of course, if we wanted to make explicit, say, the first two arguments, we could also use the syntax

```
sock = socket( AF_INET, SOCK_STREAM )
```

The other choices for the first argument are `AF_INET6` for IPv6 sockets and `AF_UNIX` for Unix-domain sockets. The other choices for the second argument are `SOCK_DGRAM` for a UDP socket, and `SOCK_RAW` for manual creation of packets.

Going back to Perl, its standard distribution also comes with a higher level socket module, `IO::Socket`, that is simpler to use because it is aware of the mutual dependence between the socket attributes. The module file for `IO::Socket` also contains its two subclasses, `IO::Socket::INET` and `IO::Socket::UNIX`, the former meant for the Internet sockets and the latter for the Unix sockets.[8] Instead of first constructing a socket handle and then connecting it to the remote destination, a single invocation of the constructor for `IO::Socket::INET` yields a connected socket handle, as demonstrated by the following snippet of code that seeks to connect

---

[8]We should also mention that `IO::Socket` itself is derived from `IO::Handle`, the base class for object-oriented I/O in Perl. The `IO::Handle` class is equipped with all of the I/O functions like `print()`, `printf()`, `close()`, `stat()`, `sysread()`, `syswrite()`, etc. All of these methods are inherited by the `IO::Socket::INET` class. In addition, the `IO::Socket::INET` class makes available the socket-oriented methods such as `accept()`, `connect()`, `bind()`, and `sockopt()`. In addition to `IO::Socket`, the other subclasses of `IO::Handle` are `IO::File` and `IO::Pipe`, the former for object-oriented file I/O, as you'd expect, and the latter for object-oriented interprocess communication with pipes.

with port 13 of the "time-of-day" server maintained by the National Institute of Standards and Technology in Boulder, Colorado.

```
use IO::Socket;

my $sock = IO::Socket::INET->new(
                        Proto    => "tcp",
                        PeerAddr => "time-A.timefreq.bldrdoc.gov",
                        PeerPort => "13",
           )
           or die "cannot make a connection: $!";

while ( <$sock> ) { print }
```

Note the use of the `Proto`, `PeerAddr`, and `PeerPort` options for specifying the protocol, the host address, and the port, respectively. The argument supplied with the `PeerAddr` option can also be in the dotted-quad notation like `132.163.4.101`.

15.2 CLIENT-SIDE SOCKETS FOR FETCHING DOCUMENTS

A simple example of client-side scripting consists of fetching documents from web servers. Web servers typically listen on port 80 for incoming requests for documents. The request received from a client must adhere to certain rules of syntax in order to be meaningful to the server. These rules of syntax are laid out in the Hypertext Transfer Protocols (HTTP). Under HTTP 1.0 and 1.1, a client can ask a server for a named document by sending a `GET` request to the server. In general, a `GET` request from a client to a server consists of multiple lines that look like

```
GET pathname_to_resource HTTP 1.x
header1 : value1
header2 : value2
....
blank_line
```

HTTP 1.0 defines 16 headers, all optional. HTTP 1.1 defines 46 headers, with just the `Host` header mandatory. Each line of a `GET` request must end in the *Internet line terminator*. The HTTP standard requires the Internet line terminator to consist of the two-character sequence `\r\n`.[9] The `Host` header will, of course, be the

[9]In documentation, this pair of character is also commonly shown as <CR><LF> or just `CRLF`. CR, an acronym for "Carriage Return," and LF, an acronym for "Line Feed," are the official names for two of the characters in the ASCII table, the former with octal value 015 and the latter with octal value 012. The character escape representation of CR is `\r` and the numeric escape representation of the same in octal form `\015`. The character escape representation for LF is `\n` and the numeric escape representation of the same in octal form `\012`. Although the HTTP standard requires `\r\n` as the line terminator, most HTTP servers will also accept just `\n`.

URL (Uniform Resource Locator) of the web server. As to why the server needs to know its own URL in a request received from a client, it is because HTTP/1.1 allows for multiple URLs to be mapped to the same IP address. A GET request is transmitted over the Internet using the IP address. Thus there is no confusion about the destination of a GET request even if multiple URLs correspond to that address. However, the response of the server can be made to be different for each different URL corresponding to that IP address. This is supposed to permit conservation of IP addresses and to allow for "vanity" URLs. Note also in the above syntax that a GET request must end in a blank line. This is to allow for the line terminators to be used for marking the end of the headers in a GET request.

15.2.1 Fetching Documents in Perl

The script shown next, `ClientSocket.pl`, is based on an example in the `perlipc` documentation page that comes with the standard Perl distribution.[10] The script is meant to be called in the following manner for pulling in the main web page (that is commonly named `Index.html`, `index.html`, `index.shtml`, etc.) for a given URL:

```
ClientSocketFetchDocs.pl  www.scriptingwithobjects.com  /
```

where the second argument, meaning the / symbol, stands for the document root for a given URL. To fetch any other document made available by the same HTTP server, we just need to use the pathname to that document for the second argument, as in

```
ClientSocketFetchDocs.pl  www.scriptingwithobjects.com  /errata.html
```

The script can also be called with a list of document pathnames and it will fetch them one after another. With these calls, line (B) of the script will be set to the URL of the web site.

Line (C) declares the variable `$EOL` to be the Internet line terminator. Line (D) declares the variable `$BLANK`, which stands for a blank line, as consisting of two repeats of the line terminator. As mentioned already, according to the HTTP standard, a blank line is needed at the end of a typical GET request under the HTTP 1.0 and HTTP 1.1 protocols. For each requested document in the command line, the `foreach` loop in line (E) makes a separate connection with the HTTP server in line (F). The call to `IO::Socket::INET->new()` in line (F) constructs a new socket and tries to connect it to the remote server named in line (G) at the port named in line (H). In the event a socket cannot be constructed or a connection cannot be established with the server, the system error is stored in the global variable `$!`. A more verbose

[10] The documentation page `perlipc` can be viewed with the command `man perlipc` on Unix and Linux machines and via the `Core Documentation` menu item of ActivePerl User Guide on Windows platforms. This documentation page deals with all aspects of Perl's interprocess communications.

description of the error is available through the global variable `$@`. Note the three options specified in lines (F), (G), and (H). The options are the same as shown earlier in the snippet of code at the end of Section 15.1. We have specified the port 80 in line (H).[11] Although this is typically the port monitored by HTTP servers, some servers meant for specialized services prefer the ports 1080, 8080, etc. It is also possible to call `IO::Socket::INET` with a single argument that consists of the address of the remote machine followed by the port number, the two separated by a colon. The address of the remote machine can be either in its symbolic host-name form or in the dotted-decimal form.

Note the invocation of `autoflush()` in line (J). By default the autoflush property of a newly created socket is on. We have included the statement here anyway merely to emphasize the important role played by this property of the socket. If for some reason the autoflush property is off, the system will most likely buffer the outgoing `GET` request formed in lines (K), (L), and (M). Such buffering could cause the client to believe that the server was not responding immediately to its requests. Since we want a `GET` request to be transmitted immediately to the server, we want to make sure that the `autoflush` feature is turned on.

About the two headers that are incorporated in the `GET` request to the HTTP server in lines (L) and (M), we have already stated that the one in line (L) is mandatory in HTTP 1.1 and given the reasons for why this header is required. About the optional header shown in line (M), HTTP/1.1 stipulates that a connection initiated by a client be persistent, subject to certain timeouts, of course. The earlier protocol, HTTP/1.0, basically operated on the basis of the server receiving a one-line request from a client, transmitting the requested resource to the client in response, and immediately shutting down the connection. This used to create a slow interaction between a client and a server. Just imagine a client requesting a web page with inlined documents, meaning documents that are only referenced in the main web page by their names embedded in special HTML tags. A browser making an HTTP/1.0 request for such a web page would need to make a separate connection for each such inlined document. To help make pages with inlined documents quicker to download, HTTP/1.1 defines a *persistent connection* where a number of documents can be requested over a single connection, one at a time. Persistent connections are the default in HTTP/1.1. The optional request header in line (M) changes the default behavior of the HTTP server.[12]

Finally, the loop in line (N) fetches the document from the HTTP server one line at a time and prints it out at the standard output. Although we have used the line

---

[11] The port number can be either just the number, or, for standard services, just the name of the service, or a combination of the two, as shown in line (H).

[12] Other features of HTTP 1.1 that do not exist in HTTP 1.0 deal with (a) content negotiation between a client and the HTTP server; (b) chunked transfers; (c) byte ranges; (d) proxies and caches; (e) more status codes; (f) new request methods; (g) digest authentication; (h) various new headers such as Retry-After, Max-Forwards, etc.; (i) definition of media types; etc.

input operator <> for reading from the socket in line (H), the `IO::Socket::INET` also supports two other functions for this purpose: `read()` and `sysread()`.

```
#!/usr/bin/perl -w

### ClientSocket.pl

use IO::Socket;
use strict;

die "usage: $0 host_document ..." unless @ARGV > 1;                #(A)

my $host = shift(@ARGV);                                           #(B)

my $EOL = "\r\n";                                                  #(C)

my $BLANK = $EOL x 2;                                              #(D)

foreach my $document ( @ARGV ) {                                   #(E)
        my $sock = IO::Socket::INET->new( Proto     => "tcp",      #(F)
                                          PeerAddr  => $host,      #(G)
                                          PeerPort  => "http(80)", #(H)
                                        )
                   or die $@;                                      #(I)
        $sock->autoflush(1);    #turned on by default anyway       #(J)
        print $sock    "GET $document HTTP/1.1" . $EOL .           #(K)
                       "Host: $host". $EOL .                       #(L)
                       "Connection: closed" . $BLANK;              #(M)
        while ( <$sock> ) { print }                                #(N)
        close $sock;                                               #(O)
}
```

15.2.2 Fetching Documents in Python

The next script, `ClientSocketFetchDocs.py`, is a Python version of the previous Perl script for fetching a document from a web server. As was the case with the Perl script, the call syntax for fetching the main web page at a given URL is exemplified by

```
ClientSocketFetchDocs.py  www.scriptingwithobjects.com  /
```

And, as before, we can also place in the command line a list of documents to fetch after the URL provided we have listed the pathnames to the documents relative to the document root (as represented by the / symbol).

In line (A), we import the `socket` module. As mentioned earlier in this chapter, this is the main module in Python for socket programming. Line (C) defines the Internet line terminator that is in accord with the explanation we gave earlier regarding how each line in a GET request is supposed to be terminated. Line (D) defines what is meant by a blank line that is needed to end a GET request for a document. Line (E) extracts the URL of the web server as the first command-line argument.

In the rest of the script, we make a separate connection with the host for each document that needs to be fetched. As mentioned already, HTTP/1.1 connections are persistent by default. So a more efficient way to write our script for fetching multiple documents at the same document root would be to construct a socket object only once, connect it to port 80 of the server, and then loop through the GET requests for the different documents. But there are many servers out there that do not support persistent connections; these servers immediately shut down a connection after responding to a single GET request.[13] The script as shown will work for such servers also. For each connection, we construct a TCP/IP socket in line (G) and connect it to the remote web server on its port 80 in line (H). Lines (I) through (M) take care of the eventuality that our attempt to establish an HTTP connection with the server may not succeed. Lines (N) through (Q) synthesize the GET request for each document. How this string must be composed was previously explained for the Perl case. Finally, we read the response from the server in the `while` loop in lines (R) through (U).

```
#!/usr/bin/env python

### ClientSocketFetchDocs.py

import sys
import socket                                                            #(A)

if len(sys.argv) < 3:                                                    #(B)
    sys.exit( "Need at least two command line arguments " +
              "the first naming the host and the second " +
              "naming the document at the host" )
EOL = "\r\n"                                                             #(C)
BLANK = EOL * 2                                                          #(D)

host = sys.argv[1]                                                       #(E)
```

[13]To write a client script that would work with both the servers that allow persistent connections and those that do not, the client would need to check if the server was responding to the requests after the first. If not, the client would then switch to establishing a new connection separately for each document requested.

```
for doc in sys.argv[2:]:                                              #(F)
    try:
        sock = socket.socket( socket.AF_INET, socket.SOCK_STREAM )   #(G)
        sock.connect( (host, 80) )                                    #(H)
    except socket.error, (value, message):                           #(I)
        if sock:                                                      #(J)
            sock.close()                                              #(K)
        print "Could not establish a client socket: " + message      #(L)
        sys.exit(1)                                                   #(M)

    sock.send( str( "GET %s HTTP/1.1 %s" +                            #(N)
                    "Host: %s%s" +                                    #(O)
                    "Connection: closed %s" )                         #(P)
                        % (doc, EOL, host, EOL, BLANK) )              #(Q)
    while 1:                                                          #(R)
        data = sock.recv(1024)                                        #(S)
        if data == '': break                                          #(T)
        print data                                                    #(U)
```

15.3 CLIENT-SIDE SCRIPTING FOR INTERACTIVE SESSION WITH A SERVER

The client-side scripts we have shown so far are meant for situations where a client wants to fetch a single document or a specific set of documents from a server. In those scripts, the client sent a specially formatted request (or sometimes a sequence of specially formatted requests under HTTP 1.1) to the server and expected the server to yield the requested document(s). We will now show how a client script can be written if the client wants to engage in an interactive session with a server. A remote login session or a chatroom session are examples of such continuous interactive sessions with a server.

One of the primary things to watch out for when writing a client-side script for a continuous interactive session with a server is that the client should not expect every individual transmission received from the server to end in a line terminator. The client therefore should not use a line-based input operator (such as <> in Perl) for reading the transmissions from the server. Not using the line-based input operators for reading the server transmissions opens up another issue — the issue related to the buffering of the server transmissions at the client end. Ordinarily, in a character-based interaction, whatever is received from the server will be placed in a buffer associated with the output stream, which could be STDOUT if all that the client wants to do is to display in the terminal window the strings received from the server. Ordinarily, this stream is flushed with the receipt of a line terminator. But if the server is allowed to send a string without a line terminator, you'd need to override this default behavior of the output stream. In the scripts to follow in this section, we will show how that can be done in Perl and Python.

These scripts will also demonstrate a client forking off a child process to read the messages received from the server and to display the same on the client's terminal, while the parent process takes care of writing to the server the information entered by the client through its keyboard.

15.3.1 Maintaining an Interactive Session with a Server in Perl

As we mentioned above, a client must not use a line-input-based operator for reading the messages received from the server and, if the server messages are meant to be displayed on the client terminal as soon as they are received, the client must also override the default flushing behavior of the output buffer associated with STDOUT. By default, the output buffer is flushed only when a line terminator is received. The following statement in line (M) of the script shown next would cause each transmission received from the server to be displayed on the client's terminal immediately:[14]

```
STDOUT->autoflush(1);
```

The script we show next, a small modification of a similar example in the perlipc Perl documentation page, uses two separate processes for reading from the server and for writing to the server. While the parent process takes care of writing to the server the information entered on the keyboard of the client, a child process takes care of reading the server's messages and displaying those on the client's terminal. The following statement in line (J) of the script:

```
my $pid =  fork();
```

creates a child process. This function, as explained in Section 2.17.4 of Chapter 2, returns in the parent process the process ID (PID) of the child process if the child process was created successfully; the value returned by the above call in the child process is 0. Otherwise, it returns undef. After this statement is executed successfully, there will be two processes running concurrently for executing the remaining script. Assuming that a child process was created successfully, lines (L) through (Q) of the script will only be executed in the parent process. Note the provision made in line (Q) for terminating the child process if the socket connection is closed by the server. This works because the call to sysread() in line (O) is

[14] Another way to achieve the same effect is to make nonzero the value of the $| global variable. By making its value nonzero, the currently selected output filehandle or socket handle is automatically autoflushed. Note that the default value for this variable is 0. Also note that, by default, the standard output stream STDOUT is line-buffered if the output is a terminal (it is block buffered otherwise). By making the value of $| nonzero, the output is written out as it becomes available. The value of $| has no effect on input buffering.

a blocking read, meaning that the thread of execution will just wait for `sysread()` to return.[15] When used as a blocking read, `sysread()` returns 0 only when it sees the end-of-file condition. Otherwise, it either blocks (that is, it waits indefinitely for the server to send something) or returns the number of bytes read from the input buffer, which will be 1 when the third argument supplied to it is 1, as is the case in the implementation shown.[16] If the server were to terminate the connection, `sysread()` will return 0 in the conditional of the `while` loop, causing the execution of the `kill()` statement to terminate the child process. The function `kill()` is for sending a signal to another process.[17] In this case, the parent process is sending the signal `SIGTERM` to the process whose process id is `$pid`, which is the child process.

The section of the code in lines (R) through (U) of the script will only be executed in the child process. This section takes care of sending the client's messages to the server.

Note that line (H) of the script associates a signal handler with the `SIGINT` signal that would result from a keyboard-generated interrupt if the user on the client side were to press Ctrl-C for terminating the client script. Ordinarily, the client-side script will always be on unless the server shuts down the connection from its side. As already mentioned, when the server shuts down the connection, the statement in line (Q) will also terminate the client-side script. Here is the script:

```
#!/usr/bin/perl -w
use strict;

###  ClientSocketInteractive.pl

use IO::Socket;                                                    #(A)

die "usage: $0 host port" unless @ARGV == 2;                       #(B)

my ($host, $port) = @ARGV;                                         #(C)
```

---

[15] See Section 2.6.2 of Chapter 2 for further information regarding `sysread()`.

[16] A socket handle can be made to carry out nonblocking reads by calling `fcntl()`. But note that it is more complicated to fetch data from a nonblocking read than from a blocking read. With nonblocking reads, you have to be able to make a distinction between the input buffer being just momentarily empty (because the sender at the other end of the communication link is just being slow) and the end of input caused by the server closing the connection. In the nonblocking mode, the function `sysread()` returns `undef` when the input buffer is momentarily empty and 0 when the end-of-file condition is encountered. In the former case, the error variable `$!` is set to `EAGAIN`. The value of this error variable can be used to invoke `sysread()` repeatedly until there is input to be read again.

[17] See Section 2.18 of Chapter 2 discusses how to send and trap signals in Perl.

```
my $socket = IO::Socket::INET->new(PeerAddr   => $host,          #(D)
                                   PeerPort   => $port,          #(E)
                                   Proto      => "tcp",          #(F)
                                  )
    or die "can't connect to port $port on $host: $!";           #(G)

$SIG{INT} = sub { $socket->close; exit 0; };                     #(H)

print STDERR "[Connected to $host:$port]\n";                     #(I)

# create a child process
my $pid =  fork();                                               #(J)
die "can't fork: $!" unless defined $pid;                        #(K)

# Parent process: receive information from the remote site:
if ($pid) {                                                      #(L)
    STDOUT->autoflush(1);                                        #(M)
    my $byte;                                                    #(N)
    while ( sysread($socket, $byte, 1) == 1 ) {                  #(O)
        print STDOUT $byte;                                      #(P)
    }
    kill("TERM", $pid);                                          #(Q)
} else {                                                         #(R)
    # Child process: send information to the remote site:
    my $line;                                                    #(S)
    while (defined ($line = <STDIN>)) {                          #(T)
        print $socket $line;                                     #(U)
    }
}
```

This client script can be exercised by calling a server (to be presented in Section 15.4) by a command line like:

```
ClientSocketInteractive.pl  RVL4.ecn.purdue.edu  9000
```

where 9000 is the port number monitored by the server on a machine whose host name is `RVL4.ecn.purdue.edu`.

15.3.2 Maintaining an Interactive Session with a Server in Python

The next script, `ClientSocketInteractive.py`, is a Python client that can maintain a continuous interactive session with a server. To mirror the Perl script, we fork off a child process that takes care of the sending part of the communication link, while the parent process takes care of the receiving part. As previously presented in Section 3.15.3 of Chapter 3, in Python you create a child process by calling `os.fork()`. The script makes this call in line (S). Since the client-side script will always be on (provided the server has not shut down its side of the connection), we need to be able to take down the client by a keyboard-generated interrupt (as generated by pressing Ctrl-C). This can be done by associating an appropriate signal handler with the `SIGINT` signal. As previously presented in Section 3.16 of Chapter 3, signal handlers in Python are specified by the `signal()` method of the `signal` module. Line (R) of the script associates the signal handler of lines (N) through (Q) with the `SIGINT` signal. Finally, we want the client to shut down gracefully should the server terminate the connection. This is accomplished in line (d) of the script by using the `os.kill()` function to send the `SIGTERM` signal to the child process.

After the command-line arguments for the name of the remote server and the port used by the server are fetched in line (F), lines (G) and (H) of the script set up a TCP/IP socket connection with the server. Lines (I) through (M) take care of the possibility that something might go awry while requesting a connection with the server. (For example, the server may not be up and running, we may have used an incorrect port number, etc.) As mentioned earlier, line (S) forks off a child process. From this point on, the rest of the script is executed in two separate processes, with the difference that the value of `child_pid` in the child process is 0, whereas it is the process ID (PID) of the child process in the parent process. As a result, the block of statements in lines (U), (V), and (W) will only be executed in the child process, and the rest of the script in lines (X) through (d) only in the parent process. The child process code uses a line-based read function to read each line of text entered by the user on the client side. As each line is read from the keyboard buffer in line (V), it is shipped off to the server in line (W). Since we use a blocking read function, `readline()` in line (V), it waits until the user enters anything at all on the keyboard.

The parent process, also uses a blocking read in line (V), but this time only one byte at a time is read from the message received from the server. Each byte that is read in line (Z) is immediately flushed out in line (b) to the standard output of the client, meaning the terminal used for the interactive session with the server.

```
#!/usr/bin/env python

### ClientSocketInteractive.py

import sys                                                          #(A)
import socket                                                       #(B)
import os                                                           #(C)
import signal                                                       #(D)

if len(sys.argv) < 3:                                               #(E)
    sys.exit( "Need at least two command line arguments, the " +
              "first naming the host and the second the port" )
```

```
host, port = sys.argv[1], int(sys.argv[2])                          #(F)

try:
    sock = socket.socket( socket.AF_INET, socket.SOCK_STREAM )      #(G)
    sock.connect( (host, port) )                                    #(H)
except socket.error, (value, message):                              #(I)
    if sock:                                                        #(J)
        sock.close()                                                #(K)
    print "Could not establish a client socket: " + message         #(L)
    sys.exit(1)                                                     #(M)

def sock_close( signum, frame ):                                    #(N)
    global sock                                                     #(O)
    sock.close                                                      #(P)
    sys.exit(0)                                                     #(Q)

signal.signal( signal.SIGINT, sock_close )                          #(R)

# create a child process
child_pid =  os.fork();                                             #(S)

if child_pid == 0:                                                  #(T)
    # Child process: send information to the remote site:
    while 1:                                                        #(U)
        line = sys.stdin.readline()                                 #(V)
        sock.send( line )                                           #(W)
else:                                                               #(X)
    # Parent process: receive information from the remote site:
    while 1:                                                        #(Y)
        byte = sock.recv(1)                                         #(Z)
        if byte == '': break                                        #(a)
        sys.stdout.write( byte )                                    #(b)
        sys.stdout.flush()                                          #(c)
    os.kill( child_pid, signal.SIGKILL )                            #(d)
```

As with the Perl client, you can start up a session on the client side with a command line like

```
ClientSocketInteractive.py  RVL4.ecn.purdue.edu  9000
```

assuming that a server running on `RVL4.ecn.purdue.edu` is monitoring port 9000 for connection requests from clients. The next section shows examples of such servers in Perl and Python.

15.4 SERVER SOCKETS

A server application uses a special kind of a socket, called a *server socket*, that does nothing but listen at a designated port for incoming client requests for socket connections. The server socket comes with an important method — `accept()` — that when invoked causes the server to monitor the designated port for an incoming client request for a connection. When a request is received, the `accept()` method spits out a socket handle for communicating with that client. Just as easily as one can read from a file and write to it with a filehandle, one can read client messages with the socket handle returned by `accept()` and send messages to the client by writing to the socket handle.

15.4.1 Server Sockets in Perl

As mentioned, a server socket's main duty is to monitor a designated port for client requests for connections and, when a client request is received, to spit out a socket handle that can subsequently be used for bidirectional communications with the client. In Perl, one can use the same `IO::Socket::INET` class that we used in the client script of the previous section for constructing a server socket provided its constructor is supplied with certain specific arguments. When you want a call to `IO::Socket::INET->new()` to return a server socket, at the least you must supply the constructor with values for the `LocalPort`, `Listen`, and `Proto` options, as we do in the following example:

```
$server_sock = IO::Socket::INET->new(LocalPort => 9000,
                                     Listen => 5,
                                     Proto => 'tcp',
                                    );
```

The value supplied for `LocalPort` causes the server application to monitor port 9000 for incoming client requests for connections.[18] Another way of saying the same thing is that port 9000 is *registered* for the server application, or, speaking more specifically, port 9000 is assigned to a particular instance of `IO::Socket::INET`.

[18] You'd obviously not be able to use a port for your server script if it is already registered for some other application or, even if not registered, it is currently being used by some other application. On Linux and Unix machines, you can see what ports have already been registered for many standard applications by looking at the services translation file `/etc/services`. To see all the ports currently in use, registered or not, you can use the `netstat` command with either the `-a` or the `-l` flags, the former for all the sockets and the latter for just the listening sockets. The `netstat` command on both Unix/Linux and Windows machines prints out a report on the current status of the network interfaces and services. When called without flags, it returns a table of all currently open sockets. When supplied with different flags, it can return the status of the network interfaces, kernel routing tables, etc. Before selecting port 9000, the author tested its availability by using the command

```
netstat -a | grep 9000
```

Also note that ports under 1024 can only be used with superuser privileges.

Yet another way of saying the same thing is that by supplying a value for `LocalPort`, we *bind* the instance of `IO::Socket::INET` to that port. In the above constructor call, we could also have set the `LocalHost` option, `LocalAddr` being its synonym, as in the following example:

```
$server_sock = IO::Socket::INET->new(LocalHost => '192.168.1.131',
                                     LocalPort => 9000,
                                     Listen => 5,
                                     Proto => 'tcp',
                                    );
```

Now the instance of `IO::Socket::INET` will be bound to the specified combination of the host IP address and the port number.[19] For machines equipped with multiple network interfaces, the different interfaces would in general correspond to different IP addresses. Not setting the `LocalHost` option in the constructor call allows `IO::Socket::INET` to accept connections from all of the interfaces of the server machine on the designated numeric port number. The same would be the case if the `LocalHost` option is set to the host name of the machine in its symbolic form. But now, of course, a client must use that specific host name for the server when requesting a connection. When the `LocalHost` option is set to an IP address in the dotted-quad form, as in the above example, then client connections are accepted only through the network interface that corresponds to that IP address.[20] We should also mention that the value supplied for `LocalHost` can also be in the form of what is known as a *packed IP address*, that is, a 32-bit binary string whose each byte corresponds to a number in the dotted-quad notation.[21]

---

[19] We could also have set the `LocalHost` option to the symbolic host name.

[20] Note that if you set the `LocalHost` option to the string `localhost`, you'll only be able to connect to the server from client processes running on the same machine. On the other hand, if the `LocalHost` option is set to a symbolic host name (that is not `localhost`) or an IP address (that is not `127.0.0.1`), client processes from both the local machine (meaning the server machine) and remote machines would be able to talk to the server application. But the client processes running on the server machine must use that host name or the IP address when requesting a connection with the server application even though both the client and the server applications are running on the same machine. In other words, now the client processes running on the server machine will *not* be able to use the following sort of syntax:

```
ClientScript localhost 9000
```

[21] Perl makes it easy to convert back and forth between the dotted-quad notation and the packed binary strings for the IP addresses, as demonstrated below:

```
# split the dotted-quad form into the individual integers:
($a, $b, $c, $d) = split /\./, '192.168.1.131';
# pack the four integers into a binary string:
$packed_ip_address = pack 'C4', $a, $b, $c, $d;
# retrieve the four integers from a packed binary string:
($a, $b, $c, $d) =  unpack 'C4', $packed_IP_address;
# form the dotted-quad string from the four integers:
$dotted_quad_IP_address = join '.', $a, $b, $c, $d;
```

As mentioned previously in Section 2.6.2 of Chapter 2, the letter `C` in the first argument to `pack()` and `unpack()` means that each of the subsequent items is to be considered to be an `unsigned char`, and the

Let's now revisit the `LocalPort` option in the two previous examples of the calls to `IO::Socket::INET->new()`. For standard services, the argument supplied for this option can also be specified as the name of the service or the name of the service followed by the numeric value of the port in parentheses. It is also possible to fire up a server without setting the `LocalPort` option provided the numeric port number is supplied as a colon-separated trailing part of the argument associated with the `LocalHost` option, as in the following form:

```
$server_sock = IO::Socket::INET->new(LocalHost => '192.168.1.131:9000',
                                     Listen => 5,
                                     Proto => 'tcp',
                                    );
```

You may also be able to construct a server application without explicitly mentioning the port number if you are willing to accept a system-supplied port number. For example, a particular run of the server script we show next in which we did not mention the port number to monitor in any form caused the system to assign the high-numbered port 32823 to the server socket. That fact was established by looking at the output of the network analysis tool `netstat` when invoked with the `-a` flag.

We also used the options `Listen` and `Proto` in the examples we have shown so far for constructing a server socket. The `Listen` option designates the number of incoming client connection requests that can be queued to wait for processing. Basically, this number sets the limit on how many clients can hookup with the server concurrently. Specifying this option is mandatory for creating a *listening socket*, which is the same thing as a server socket. The `Listen` option causes the built-in function `listen()` to be called under the hood, which informs the operating system that this socket will be a listening socket for incoming client requests for connections. Without `listen()` being invoked on a socket, `accept()` will not work in a script. As we will see shortly, it is the `accept()` that, as you'd expect, accepts a request-for-connection call from a client. The `Proto` option specifies the communication protocol to be used by the socket.

We said at the beginning of this section that when a server socket receives a request for a connection from a client, it should construct a separate socket object for a bidirectional communication link with the client so that the server socket can go back to its main job of monitoring the port that is assigned to it. This is accomplished by a method that is most commonly called `accept()`. When `accept()` receives a request for a connection from a client, it returns a new socket connected to the client. The rest of the server script can use this connected socket attached to the client for communicating with the client. When called inside a loop, the `accept()` method can go back to waiting for the next request-for-connection by a client. We illustrate

---

number 4 that follows the letter `C` means that `pack()` should expect four items and that `unpack()` should produce four items.

this with the help of the next script, `ServerSocketSingleClient.pl`, that is only a slight variation on an example that comes with the `perlipc` documentation page.

Lines (C) through (F) of the script create a server socket using the syntax explained already, except for the use of the special symbol `SOMAXCONN` in line (D). This symbol, defined in one of the low-level socket libraries used by the high-level module `IO::Socket`, stands for the system-dictated maximum number of client connections that the server socket can wait on at any given time.[22] The call to the constructor in lines (C) through (F) also sets `Reuse` option to 1. This is useful during debugging since it allows immediate reuse of the port that is supposed to be monitored by the server after the server process is killed and then started again in quick succession. If you don't set the `Reuse` option as shown, a restart of the server process will not succeed as long as the various buffers assigned to the server process during its previous run are not cleared out.

In the rest of the server script, line (I) invokes `accept()` in an infinite loop, which causes the server to wait indefinitely for the incoming client requests for connecting with the server. A client request causes `accept()` to spit out a socket handle that becomes the value of the variable `$client_soc`. The server can now read the client messages through this socket handle and send information to the client through the same socket handle. The first thing the server does is to send the client a welcome message in line (J) where the variable `$0` will be bound to the name of the server script. Next the server tries to find the URL of the client by the statement in line (K):[23]

```
my $hostinfo = gethostbyaddr($client_soc->peeraddr);
```

The argument `$client_soc->peeraddr` returns the client's IP address in the dotted-quad notation. The call to `gethostbyaddr()` does a reverse DNS lookup and returns an array reference; the first element of this array is the client URL. The URL can be retrieved either by accessing directly the first element of this array or by invoking

```
$hostinfo->name
```

as we do in line (L), where `$hostinfo` is the record returned by `gethostbyaddr()` in line (K). To allow for the possibility that a reverse DNS lookup may not work for a particular IP (since not all IP addresses are registered), we also provide the following alternative in line (L):[24]

---

[22]The value of this special constant was 128 for the Linux machine on which the author ran the server script shown.

[23]The one argument invocation of `gethostbyaddr()` shown works only when you import the `Net::hostent` module, as we have done in line (B). The built-in `gethostbyaddr()` requires an additional argument that represents the socket's domain. For the example shown, that would be `AF_INET`.

[24]Note that in line (L) we first check that `$hostinfo` is defined before proceeding to execute `$hostinfo->name`. Failure to do so will elicit a run-time exception should `gethostbyaddr()` fail in the reverse DNS lookup. The exception will be thrown because you'd be trying to invoke `name()` on an undefined object.

```
$client_soc->peerhost
```

which may be able to fetch either the client's host name or its IP address from one of the optional headers supplied by the client at the time of the initial request.

Before we explain the rest of the script, we must state its overall purpose. We want to use the script to display a sequence of commands to the client and have the client select one of the commands by entering its name in the terminal window on the client side. We want this command to be executed on the server side and, finally, we want the result (if any) of that operation to be sent back to the client. We want this interaction between the server and the client to take place in a loop until the client enters `exit` or `quit`. The server script `ServerSocketSingleClient.pl` makes the following commands available to the client for execution on the server side:

date : The server returns to the client the output of the `localtime()` function.

time : The same as above.

ls : The server executes the Unix command `ls -al` on the server side and "reveals" to the client the various items (files and subdirectories) that are in the same directory as the server script.

pwd : The server executes the Unix command `pwd` and sends back to the client the full pathname to the current working directory on the server side.

user : The server executes the Unix command `whoami` that, in this case, would return to the client the login identity of the user running the server script.

rmtilde : The server executes the Unix command `rm *~` to delete all server-side files whose names end in tilde.[25]

The interaction with the client is controlled by the inner `while-continue` loop in lines (N) through (Z). The line input operator applied to the socket handle in the conditional of the `while` block in line (N) returns `undef` should the connection with the client terminate either because the client closed the connection or due to some network problem. Until then, the conditional carries out a blocking read of the socket handle, meaning that the operator `<>` waits patiently until a string of characters is received from the client. Detection of a newline character at the end of a character string received from the client causes the line input operator `<>` to return the string. At that point, the control shifts to line (O) in the body of the inner `while` loop.

The inner `while` loop in lines (N) through (Z) receives the entries made by a user on the client side in response to the prompt `command:` that is displayed on the

[25] *One of the reasons for showing this server script is to impress upon the reader the ease with which a malicious intruder could wreak havoc on the server side if the intruder surreptitiously installed a harmful script on the server and then proceeded to interact with it in the manner shown here.*

client screen during the time the server-client connection is alive. The user on the client side is supposed to enter one of the following in response to the prompt:

```
quit  exit  date  time  ls  pwd  user  rmtilde
```

As the reader can tell from line (P), when the client-side user enters either `quit` or `exit`, that causes the flow of control to exit the inner `while` loop. On the other hand, when the user enters either `date` or `time`, the statement in line (Q) causes the output of Perl's built-in `localtime()` function to be sent to the client. If the user enters `ls` on the client side, that causes the server to execute the command `ls -al` in line (R) and to send its output to the client. Similarly, when the user types `pwd`, that entry is captured in line (S) and the output of the locally executed command `pwd` is sent to the client (which allows the client to figure out the pathname to the directory in which the server script is executed). Along the same lines, an entry of `user` by the client is processed by line (T) of the server script, causing the output of the command `whoami` to be sent to the client (which reveals to the client the name of the account under which the server script is run). Finally, if the user on the client side enters `rmtilde`, the entry is processed by line (U), which causes the deletion of all server-side files whose names end in the ~ character.

Note that as the client is engaged in an interaction with the server through the inner `while` loop that starts in line (N), we want each iteration of the loop to start by printing out the prompt `Command:` on the client screen. Line (M) takes care of the first time appearance of this prompt. For subsequent interactions, it is the print statement in line (Y) in the `continue` block that takes care of sending the prompt to the client. As was mentioned in Chapter 2, when a `while` block is followed by a `continue` block, the code in the latter block is executed before the evaluation of the conditional of the `while` block for each pass through the `while` block after the first.

```
#!/usr/bin/perl -w
use strict;

### ServerSocketSingleClient.pl

use IO::Socket;                                                        #(A)
use Net::hostent;                                                      #(B)

my $server_soc = IO::Socket::INET->new( LocalPort => 9000,             #(C)
                                        Listen    => SOMAXCONN,        #(D)
                                        Proto     => 'tcp',            #(E)
                                        Reuse     => 1);               #(F)
die "No Server Socket" unless $server_soc;                             #(G)

print "[Server $0 accepting clients]\n";                               #(H)
while (my $client_soc = $server_soc->accept()) {                       #(I)
    print $client_soc "Welcome to $0; Enter 'help' to see commands.\n";
```

```
                                                                    #(J)
    my $hostinfo = gethostbyaddr($client_soc->peeraddr);            #(K)
    printf "[Connect from %s]\n",
             $hostinfo ? $hostinfo->name : $client_soc->peerhost;   #(L)
    print $client_soc "Command? ";                                  #(M)
    while ( <$client_soc> ) {                                       #(N)
        next unless /\S/;                                           #(O)
        if    (/quit|exit/i) { last; }                              #(P)
        elsif (/date|time/i) { printf $client_soc "%s\n",
                                              scalar localtime;}    #(Q)
        elsif (/ls/i )        { print  $client_soc `ls -al 2>&1`; } #(R)
        elsif (/pwd/i )       { print  $client_soc `pwd 2>&1`;}     #(S)
        elsif (/user/i)       { print  $client_soc `whoami 2>&1`; } #(T)
        elsif (/rmtilde/i)    { system "rm *~"; }                   #(U)
        else {                                                      #(V)
          print $client_soc
             "Commands: quit exit date ls pwd user rmtilde\n";      #(W)
        }
    } continue {                                                    #(X)
        print $client_soc "Command? ";                              #(Y)
    }                                                               #(Z)
    close $client_soc;                                              #(a)
}
```

The shell redirection `2>&1` used in lines (R), (S), and (T) of the script merges the error stream with the output stream. This would cause the client to see any error messages generated by the execution of the commands on the server side.

You can run this server by invoking in a command line:

```
ServerSocketSingleClient.pl
```

as long as port 9000 is free to use. Earlier we mentioned how you can determine whether or not any particular port is available for a server application.

15.4.2 Server Sockets in Python

We now show a Python version of the previous server script. Besides showing how one constructs a server socket in Python, the overall goal of the next script is the same as in the previous Perl script: We want the server to make available to a client the following menu of "dangerous" and "not so dangerous" commands:

- date
- time

- ls
- pwd
- user
- rmtilde

When a client selects one of these commands, we want the server script to execute the command on the server machine and send back to the client any results obtained by the execution of the command.[26]

About the script that is presented next, the module `sys` imported in line (A) is needed for terminating the script with a call to `sys.exit(1)` in line (N) should something go wrong while trying to create a server socket, and for gaining access to the name of the server by calling `sys.argv[0]` in the messages composed in lines (O) and (R). The module `socket` imported in line (B) is needed for constructing a server socket in line (G). The modules `time`, `os`, and `commands` imported in lines (C), (D), and (E) are required for the execution of the various commands made available by the server to a remote client. As shown in line (F), the server script monitors the same port as the previous Perl script, that is, port 9000.

To create a server socket, we start out by constructing a regular socket instance in line (G), using the same syntax as for a client socket. In line (H), we then bind it to the host on which the server script will be run.[27] We turn the socket object constructed in lines (G) and (H) into a server socket by calling `listen()` on the object. The argument given to this method designates the number of incoming client connection requests that can be queued to wait for processing. The code in lines (K) through (N) takes care of the situation should there be problems with the creation of the server socket.

The forever `while` block in lines (P) through (u) parks the flow of control in an infinite loop where, in line (Q), the server socket waits patiently for incoming requests for connection from prospective clients. When a client checks in, the `accept()` method in line (Q) returns a tuple consisting of two elements, a regular socket — which we will refer to as a client socket for convenience — for establishing a two-way communication link with the client and the *socket number* of the client,

---

[26] A reader skipping through the book may wish to look through the previous subsection for what exactly is executed on the server side by these commands and why some of them are potentially "dangerous."

[27] A more general form of this call is `bind((socket.gethostname(), port))`. But note that this call will fail unless the symbolic name of the server machine can be resolved by DNS lookup. For local testing of the script, line (H) can also be replaced by

```
server_sock.bind( ('localhost', port) )
```

Now a client script running on the same machine must call on the server script by using the following sort of a command line:

```
name_of_the_client_script  localhost  9000
```

which itself is a tuple consisting of two elements, first the IP address of the client and the second the port used by the client at its own end for communicating with the server. If we had wanted to, we could have printed out this tuple by inserting the following statement between the lines (Q) and (R):

```
print address
```

Line (R) then uses the client socket to send a welcome message to the client. Line (S) invokes `getpeername()` on the client socket; this call returns a tuple consisting of two elements, the first the IP address of the client and the second the port being used by the client. The tuple returned by this call is the same as what was returned earlier as the second item of the two objects by the call to `accept()` in line (Q).

The nested `while` loop in lines (V) through (u), again a forever loop, is for engaging the client in an interactive session that can be as long as the client wants it to be. The code in lines (X) through (c) gives us a line-based reader for the messages sent by the client. We string together the individual characters sent by the client until a newline character is seen. The rest of the code is for comparing the string entered by the client with a menu of commands made available by the server for amusing the client. Whereas a string such as `date` or `time` entered by the client invokes the Python function `time.ctime()` for the response string, a client-entered string such as `ls` or `user` or `pwd` requires the script to launch a system command whose output would then be sent back to the client. In Perl, we used the backticks to execute system commands whose output we wanted to capture in the form of a string that could then be sent back to the client. In Python the same is accomplished by supplying a system command as a string argument to either the

```
commands.getstatusoutput()
```

method or the

```
commands.getoutput()
```

method.[28] Line (l) shows how to use the former. A call to the former method returns a tuple of two elements, the first the exit status of the system command executed and the second the output produced by the system command. The system command is executed by combining the error stream with the output stream so that any error reports will also show up in the output. On the other hand, a call to `commands.getoutput()` returns just the output; that is, the exit status of the system command is not returned. It is for this reason that we explicitly access the second element of the tuple returned by `commands.getstatusoutput()` in line (l) for the output of the `ls -al` command.

We use `commands.getoutput()` to capture the output for the next two system commands, `pwd` and `whoami`, in lines (n) and (o). We have explicitly specified the shell redirection `2>&1` for both these commands, although that is unnecessary

---

[28]The `commands` module provides wrapper functions for `os.popen()`.

since `commands.getoutput()`, like `commands.getstatusoutput()`, does that for us anyway. We just wanted to show that it is not an error if you include this redirection out of habit in the argument to `getoutput()`. As stated earlier, this redirection merges the error stream with the output stream for the execution of the system command. For the last command option given to the client, `rmtilde`, the statement in line (q) makes do by supplying it as the argument to `os.system()`. As the reader knows from Section 3.15.1 of Chapter 3, `os.system()` is used to launch a system command in a child process in Python.

```
#!/usr/bin/env python

###  ServerSocketSingleClient.py

import sys                                                                #(A)
import socket                                                             #(B)
import time                                                               #(C)
import os                                                                 #(D)
import commands                                                           #(E)

port = 9000                                                               #(F)
try:
    server_sock = socket.socket(socket.AF_INET, socket.SOCK_STREAM) #(G)
    server_sock.bind( ('', port) )                                        #(H)
    server_sock.listen(5)                                                 #(I)
except socket.error, (value, message):                                    #(J)
    if server_sock:                                                       #(K)
        server_sock.close()                                               #(L)
    print "Could not establish server socket: " + message                 #(M)
    sys.exit(1)                                                           #(N)
print "[Server %s accepting clients]" % sys.argv[0]                       #(O)

while 1:                                                                  #(P)
    (client_sock, address) = server_sock.accept()                         #(Q)
    client_sock.send( "Welcome to %s; type help for command list." \
                      % sys.argv[0] )                                     #(R)
    client_name, client_port = client_sock.getpeername()                  #(S)
    print "Client %s connected using port %s " % \
                              (client_name, client_port)                  #(T)
    client_sock.send( "\nCommand? " )                                     #(U)
    while 1:                                                              #(V)
        client_line = ''                                                  #(W)
        while 1:                                                          #(X)
            client_byte = client_sock.recv(1)                             #(Y)
            if client_byte == '\n' or client_byte == '\r':                #(Z)
                break                                                     #(a)
            else:                                                         #(b)
                client_line += client_byte                                #(c)
        if client_line.isspace() or client_line == '':                    #(d)
```

```
            client_sock.send( '\nCommand? ' )                     #(e)
        elif  client_line == 'quit' or client_line == 'exit':       #(f)
            break                                                 #(g)
        elif client_line == 'date' or client_line == 'time':        #(h)
            client_sock.send( time.ctime() )                      #(i)
            client_sock.send( '\nCommand? ' )                     #(j)
        elif 'ls' in client_line:                                 #(k)
#           client_sock.send( commands.getoutput( "ls -al" ) )
            client_sock.send(commands.getstatusoutput("ls -al")[1]) #(l)
            client_sock.send('\nCommand? ')
        elif 'pwd' in client_line:                                #(m)
            client_sock.send( commands.getoutput( "pwd 2>&1" ) )    #(n)
            client_sock.send('\nCommand? ')
        elif 'user' in client_line:                               #(n)
            client_sock.send( commands.getoutput( "whoami 2>&1" ) ) #(o)
            client_sock.send('\nCommand? ')
        elif 'rmtilde' in client_line:                            #(p)
            os.system( "rm *~" )                                  #(q)
            client_sock.send('\nCommand? ')
        else:                                                     #(r)
            client_sock.send(                                     #(s)
               "Commands: quit exit date ls pwd user rmtilde" )     #(t)
            client_sock.send("\nCommand? ")
    client_sock.close()                                           #(u)
```

You can run this server by invoking in the command line

```
ServerSocketSingleClient.py
```

as long as the port 9000 is free to use. All of the comments we made in our Perl discussion on how to determine whether a specific port is available for a server also apply here.

15.5 ACCEPT-AND-FORK SERVERS

The Perl and Python server scripts of Section 15.4 suffer from a very serious shortcoming: While a client is interacting with the server, the server is not available to monitor the port assigned to it. The two scripts we show next eliminate this shortcoming by creating a separate child process for each client. The socket handle returned for a client by `accept()` is shipped off to a separate child process. The parent process goes back to monitoring the server port. As these server scripts call `fork()` to create child processes, we may also refer to them as *forking servers*. To keep the example code from becoming too long, the scripts we show next, while clearly demonstrating the principles underlying a forking server, engage a client in a simple interactive session: All that these scripts do is to echo back to the client the information received from the client after it is prepended with the name provided by the client. Being forking servers, the servers are able to handle multiple clients simultaneously (unlike the servers in the previous two scripts). Accept-and-fork servers are also known as *multiprocessing servers*.

15.5.1 An Accept-and-Fork Server in Perl

To explain how an accept-and-fork server can be programmed in Perl, let's start with the infinite loop that begins in line (N) of the script `AcceptAndForkServer.pl` shown next. The explanation for the lines that come before that will be supplied as we go through the statements of the infinite loop.

The infinite loop starts out by invoking `accept()` in line (O) to monitor the port that is registered for the server by the constructor call `IO::Socket::INET->new()` in line (I). As described in Section 15.4.1, when a request for a connection from a client is received, `accept()` returns a socket handle connected to the client. As was explained in Section 2.17.4 of Chapter 2, the call to `fork()` in line (Q) creates a child process that, at the instant it is created, is identical to the parent process, in the sense that it possesses *copies* of all the data objects defined up to the point where `fork()` was called. The call to `fork()` returns a processor ID (PID) of 0 in the child process and the actual PID assigned to the child process in the parent process. Although all of the code after line (Q) is executed in both the parent and the child processes, the statements in lines (S) through (j) will only be executed in the child processes on account of the conditional in line (S).

In the block of code that is only executed by a child process, the child process starts out by closing its copy of the server socket in line (T). This reflects the fact that the job of monitoring the server port is assigned to the parent process only. The child process then tries to ascertain the IP address of the client so that the server can maintain a record of the clients signing in. As mentioned in the explanation of our previous Perl server script in Section 15.4.1, the argument `$client_soc->peeraddr` in line (U) returns the client's IP address in the dotted-quad notation. The call to `gethostbyaddr()` does a reverse DNS lookup and returns an array reference; the first element of this array is the host address of the client in symbolic form. If the reverse DNS lookup succeeds, this host address can be retrieved either by accessing directly the first element of the array or by invoking `$hostname->name`, as we do in line (V). In the event the reverse DNS operation failed, we can try to retrieve the IP address of the client from the client socket address by calling `client_sock->peerhost`; this alternative is included in line (V).[29] Line (W) then

[29]As mentioned previously, when a client first requests a connection with a server, it sends to the server its *socket number* that is a combination of the client's IP address and the port number on which it expects

formats a message containing the network name or the IP address of the client. This message is subsequently printed on the server screen in line (X).[30] Line (Y) sends a welcome message to the client in which the name of the server script and the host name of the server machine are identified. Line (Z) asks the client user what name he/she wishes to use while interacting with the server. The child process then sends a hello message to the client in line (c).

The `while` loop of lines (d) and (e) then takes care of engaging the client in a continuous echo-back interaction. In line (e), the server simply echos back the message received from the client after prefixing the string with the name of the client as elicited in lines (a) and (b). As mentioned in our previous Perl server in Section 15.4.1, the read from the socket handle in line (d) is blocking. The line input operator in the conditional in line (d) simply waits until a newline-terminated string appears from the client, at which time it outputs that string. When the connection with the client breaks, the line input operator returns `undef`, which causes exit from the `while` loop of line (d). Because each client is handled by a separate child process, it is obviously possible for the server to interact with multiple clients simultaneously.

When the child process terminates by executing `exit(0)` in line (j), the signal `SIGCHLD`, sometimes also called `SIGCLD`, is sent to the parent process by the operating system. As mentioned in Section 2.17.4 of Chapter 2, upon receipt of this signal, the parent can immediately check on the exit status of the child process by invoking either `wait()` or `waitpid()`. This is usually accomplished by providing a handler that traps the `SIGCHLD` signal and then invokes either `wait()` or `waitpid()`. Such a signal handler is defined in line (H) of the script. The call to `wait()`, ordinarily blocking, returns immediately in our case with the PID of the

---

to hear back from the server. When needed, you can yourself construct a socket number for an Internet socket in a Perl script by calling the built-in function `sockaddr_in()` where "in" in the name of the function refers to Internet. This function takes two arguments, the numerical value of the port number and the host address in its binary representation. The binary representation can be constructed from its dotted-quad form or the symbolic host name form by calling the built-in function `inet_aton()`.

[30]We call on the built-in function `warn()` to display the client's request-for-connection message on the server screen. Ordinarily this function sends its argument to the standard error stream `STDERR`, which unless redirected would be the terminal window in which the server script is called. However, this default behavior of `warn()` is overridden if a signal handler for what is known as the *pseudo-signal* `__WARN__` is provided by the user. It is then the signal handler, in the form of a subroutine binding for `SIG{__WARN__}`, that is invoked to process the argument provided to `warn()`. Our server script provides such a signal handler in line (F). This signal handler calls on the `prefix()` subroutine of lines (C) through (E) to prepend to the argument provided to `warn()` the date/time string and the PID of the process in which `warn()` was invoked. As a result, the call to `warn()` in line (X) will display the following sort of a message on the server terminal:

```
[Fri Dec  21 15:29:48 2007] [26576] [Connection request from 192.168.1.12]
```

where the first pair of brackets contain the time stamp, the next pair the process ID, and the third the argument string supplied to `warn()` in line (X) of the script. Supplying a signal handler for `__WARN__` is referred to as a *warn hook*. A warn hook cannot be called from inside one. Therefore, the call to `warn()` in line (F) does not result in an endless loop. Also note that `warn()`, when not handled by a warn hook, attaches a line terminator to the end of its string argument. Finally, the role of the pseudo-signal `__DIE__` vis-à-vis `die` is the same as that of `__WARN__` vis-à-vis `warn`.

terminated child process. Failure to call `wait()` in the `SIGCHLD` signal handler will leave behind a zombie version of the terminated child process, as explained in Section 2.17.4 of Chapter 2.

For the rest of the code shown below, the purpose of the `prefix()` function in lines (C), (D), and (E) was explained in a footnote in this section. The same footnote also goes into the role played by signal handlers defined in lines (F) and (G) for the *pseudo-signals* `__WARN__` and `__DIE__`.

```
#!/usr/bin/perl -w
use strict;

### AcceptAndForkServer.pl

use IO::Socket;        # for IO::Socket::INET                          #(A)
use Net::hostent;      # for 1-arg version of gethostbyaddr            #(B)

sub prefix {                                                           #(C)
    my $now = localtime;                                               #(D)
    "[$now] [$$]" . shift( @_ );                                       #(E)
}

$SIG{__WARN__} = sub { warn prefix shift };                            #(F)
$SIG{__DIE__} = sub { die prefix shift };                              #(G)
$SIG{CLD} = $SIG{CHLD} = sub { wait; };                                #(H)

my $server_sock = IO::Socket::INET->new(LocalPort => 9000,             #(I)
                                        Listen => 5,                   #(J)
                                        Reuse => 1,                    #(K)
                                        Proto => 'tcp',                #(L)
                                        );
die "No Server Socket: $@\n" unless $server_sock;                      #(M)

while (1) {                                                            #(N)
    my $client_sock = $server_sock->accept();                          #(O)
    next unless defined $client_sock;                                  #(P)
    my $pid = fork();                                                  #(Q)
    die "Cannot fork: $!" unless defined( $pid );                      #(R)
    # child process:
    if ($pid == 0) {                                                   #(S)
        $server_sock->close;                                           #(T)
        my $hostinfo = gethostbyaddr($client_sock->peeraddr);          #(U)
        my $hostname = $hostinfo ?
                           $hostinfo->name : $client_sock->peerhost;#(V)
        my $msg =
            sprintf "[Request for connection from %s]\n", $hostname; #(W)
        warn "$msg";                                                   #(X)
```

```
        print $client_sock "Welcome to server script $0 " .
                              "running at $ENV{HOSTNAME}\n\n";          #(Y)
        print $client_sock "Enter your cyberspace name:";               #(Z)
        my $client_name = <$client_sock>;                               #(a)
        $client_name =~ s/^\s*(\S.*\S)\s*\n?$/$1/;                      #(b)
        print $client_sock "Hello $client_name\n\n";                    #(c)
        while ( defined( my $mesg = <$client_sock> ) ) {                #(d)
            print $client_sock "$client_name: $mesg\n";                 #(e)
        }                                                               #(f)
        $client_sock->close or warn $@;                                 #(g)
        $msg = sprintf "[Connection closed by %s from %s]\n",
                       $client_name, $hostname;                         #(h)
        warn "$msg";                                                    #(i)
        exit( 0 );                                                      #(j)
    }
}
close $server_sock;                                                     #(k)
```

This server script can be run as a background process by the command line

```
AcceptAndForkServer.pl &
```

A client may use a command line like the following to initiate interaction with the server:

```
client_script  128.46.144.10  9000
```

where `client_script` could be either the Perl script or the Python script shown in Section 15.3 and where the IP address shown belongs to the host on which the server is running.[31] Obviously, you are also allowed to use the symbolic host name for the server machine in the above command line. For running the client script on the same host on which the server is running, the client could also use the following incantation:

```
client_script  localhost  9000
```

15.5.2 An Accept-and-Fork Server in Python

The next script is an accept-and-fork server in Python. We will begin our explanation of the script with the creation of a server socket in lines (K) through (T). This part

[31]Obviously, whereas the server script can be run as a background process, the client script must be run as a foreground process since otherwise the client-user will not be able to interact with the server.

of the code is the same as in the earlier Python server in Section 15.4.2. After we have a server socket, we park the flow of control in the `accept()` method in line (X). When a new client request for a communication link comes in, `accept()` spits out a socket handle that we will refer to as a "client socket" for convenience. The client socket is supplied to the child process created in line (a). This way each client gets its own child process for communicating with the server for an arbitrary length of time and the server is free to always be available for fresh client requests.

Within the child server process devoted to communicating with a specific client, we first get in line (f) the IP address of the client machine and the port used on the client machine for communicating with the server. (As mentioned earlier, the combination of the two constitutes the client's *socket number*.) Lines (g) and (h) then print out on the server console a message indicating the arrival of the new client. At the same time, in line (i) the server sends a welcome message back to the client. Line (j) requests the client to enter his/her name to be used in the server-client conversation. Line (k) calls on the `get_client_line()` function, whose definition starts in line (J), to fetch the entry made by the client. Note how the newline terminator is dropped from the value returned by this function. In line (l), the child server process sends to the client a hello message that mentions the client by his/her name. The forever loop in lines (m) through (v) is to allow a client to engage in an arbitrarily long conversation with the server. Basically, the loop retrieves each line of text sent by the client and echos it back after the text is prepended with the name of the client. The `if` clause in line (o) is for detecting when the client has terminated the connection from his/her end. This works because we use a blocking read function, `recv()` in `get_client_line()`. The read function waits indefinitely for the client to send something. However, when the client breaks off a connection, the call to `recv()` returns with an empty string. When a client terminates a session, we print out a status message on the server console in lines (p) and (q) and shut down the client socket in line (r).

The rest of the code in the script consists of the utility method `prefix()` in lines (B), (C), and (D), and the signal handlers in lines (E) and (F). The `prefix()` function is to generate the time stamp and the process ID for the status reports posted on the server console. Displaying the process ID facilitates seeing the creation and destruction of child server processes as the clients check in and check out. The signal handler `sigchld_sig_handler()` in line (E) is for trapping the `SIGCHLD` signal that the operating system issues to the parent process when a child process terminates. By executing `wait()`, the parent process can immediately check on the exit status of what remains of the terminated child process (the zombie, as explained in Section 2.17.4 of Chapter 2). That is necessary for the zombies to get cleaned up. The signal handler `interrupt_sig_handler()` in line (F) is to cleanly kill the parent process should there be a keyboard interrupt in the form of a Ctrl-C entry on the server side.

```
#!/usr/bin/env python

###  AcceptAndForkServer.py

import sys, socket, time, os, signal                                    #(A)

def prefix( message ):                                                  #(B)
    now = time.ctime()                                                  #(C)
    return "[%s] [%s] %s" % (now, os.getpid(), message)                 #(D)
def sigchld_sig_handler( signum, frame ):                               #(E)
    os.wait()
def interrupt_sig_handler( signum, frame ):                             #(F)
    os.kill( os.getpid(), signal.SIGKILL )

signal.signal( signal.SIGINT,  interrupt_sig_handler )                  #(G)
signal.signal( signal.SIGCHLD, sigchld_sig_handler )                    #(H)

client_sock = client_name = client_hostname = None                      #(I)

# Read a line of text from the client side.  Return an empty
# string when EOF is detected.
def get_client_line(client_sock):                                       #(J)
    client_line = ''
    while 1:
        client_byte = client_sock.recv(1)
        if not client_byte:
            client_line = ''
            break
        elif client_byte == '\n' or client_byte == '\r':
            client_line += client_byte
            break
        else:
            client_line += client_byte
    return client_line

port = 9000                                                             #(K)

try:                                                                    #(L)
    server_sock = socket.socket(socket.AF_INET, socket.SOCK_STREAM) #(M)
    server_sock.bind( ('', port) )                                      #(N)
    server_sock.listen(5)                                               #(O)
except socket.error, (value, message):                                  #(P)
    if server_sock:                                                     #(Q)
        server_sock.close()                                             #(R)
    print "No server socket: %s" % prefix(message)                      #(S)
    sys.exit(1)                                                         #(T)
```

```
print "[Server %s accepting clients]" % sys.argv[0]                   #(U)

while 1:                                                              #(V)
    client_sock = None
    try:                                                              #(W)
        client_sock, address = server_sock.accept()                   #(X)
    except socket.error, (value, message): pass                       #(Y)
    if not client_sock: continue                                      #(Z)
    child_pid = os.fork()                                             #(a)
    if child_pid == 0:                                                #(b)
        if not client_sock:                                           #(c)
            os.kill( os.getpid(), signal.SIGKILL )                    #(d)
            continue                                                  #(e)
        client_hostname,client_side_port = client_sock.getpeername()#(f)
        message = "[Request for connection from %s]\n" \
                                          % client_hostname           #(g)
        print prefix( message )                                       #(h)
        client_sock.send(
          "Welcome to server script %s running at %s" \
                     % (sys.argv[0], os.environ['HOST']) )            #(i)
        client_sock.send( "\nEnter your cyberspace name: " )          #(j)
        # get client name and get rid of the newline terminator:
        client_name = get_client_line( client_sock )[0:-1]            #(k)
        client_sock.send( "Hello %s\n\n" % client_name )              #(l)
        while 1:                                                      #(m)
            message = get_client_line( client_sock )                  #(n)
            if not message:                                           #(o)
                closing_msg = "[Connection closed by %s from %s]\n" \
                          % (client_name, client_hostname)            #(p)
                print prefix(closing_msg)                             #(q)
                client_sock.close()                                   #(r)
                break                                                 #(s)
            else:                                                     #(t)
                # get rid of the newline terminator
                message = message[0:-1]                               #(u)
                client_sock.send("%s: %s\n" % (client_name,message))#(v)
        os.kill( os.getpid(), signal.SIGKILL )                        #(w)

server_sock.close()                                                   #(x)
```

This server can be run as a background process by the command line

```
AcceptAndForkServer.py &
```

As with the Perl server shown in the previous subsection, a client may use a command line like the following to initiate interaction with the Python server:

```
client_script  128.46.144.10  9000
```

where `client_script` could be either the Perl script or the Python script shown in Section 15.3 and where the IP address (which can also be the symbolic host name) shown belongs to the host on which the server is running. For testing purposes, you may want to run the client script on the same machine as the server. This can be done with a command line like

```
client_script  localhost  9000
```

15.6 PREFORKING SERVERS

The accept-and-fork servers we presented in the previous section, while allowing for simultaneous communication links with multiple clients, can become bogged down if the requests for connection from prospective clients are received in rapid succession. As the reader will recall, the main server process in that approach spends a majority of its time staying blocked in the call to `accept()` that waits for a new request for connection from a client. When such a request is received, `accept()` returns a socket handle that is shipped off to a child process for the actual job of communicating with the client. Therefore, in an accept-and-fork server, each client request entails the overhead of starting a new child process. If too many requests show up bunched up in time, this overhead can extract a significant performance penalty.

We will now present an alternative server design that uses preforking. The new approach presents to the world a certain fixed number of child server processes ready to go. These server processes are forked off from a master server process. When a request for a connection is received from a client, one of the previously spawned[32] child server processes immediately springs to action, first with its own `accept()` to handle the client call and then by establishing a two-way communication link with the client via the socket handle returned by `accept()`. If another request for a connection is received in the meantime, a second waiting child server process with its own `accept()` springs to action for handling that client, and so on for the other incoming client requests.

After forking off the child server processes, the master server process invokes `wait()` *to wait on these child processes to terminate.*[33] A child server process terminates when the two-way communication link with the client (handled by that process) comes to an end. When `wait()` returns because a child server process died, we have, obviously, one less child server process. So the master server process

[32] As we are being colloquial here, "spawning" is being used in the same sense as "forking." However, strictly speaking, as stated previously in Chapters 2 and 3, the two do not mean the same with regard to process creation.

[33] It is obviously the case that the master server process blocks in `wait()`.

proceeds to fork off another in order to keep constant the total number of available child server processes.

It is interesting to reflect on the fact that whereas an accept-and-fork server spends almost all its time staying blocked in `accept()`, *in a preforking server the master server process spends practically all its time blocked in* `wait()`. From the standpoint of the quality of service perceived by the clients, staying blocked in `wait()` is preferable to staying blocked in `accept()`. By staying blocked in `wait()`, the master server spits out a new child server as soon as one of the currently running child servers dies. On the other hand, by staying blocked in `accept()`, an accept-and-fork server must fork off a new child process instantaneously when a new client checks in. *So, for a preforking server, new server processes are spawned without the imperative of having to respond immediately to a client, since other previously spawned child servers are available for that purpose.*

Unless properly handled, a difficulty that arises with preforking is that you could have all the *child* servers blocking concurrently on `accept()`. If you were to allow[34] for such concurrent blocking, an incoming request-for-connection from a client would cause the operating system to possibly wake up all the server processes to compete for the client. This can put a strain on the system resources available to the operating system, especially if the number of preforked server processes is large and they all have to be woken up to deal with a new client checking in. Fortunately, it is relatively easy to take care of this problem and to ensure that even when you have multiple previously forked server processes ready to go, only one of them will be able to use its `accept()` to trap the incoming request-for-connection from a new client.

The solution consists of engaging all the child server processes in a low-level competition in which there is only one winner, the winner getting to use its `accept()` to monitor the port assigned to the server. This competition typically consists of obtaining a lock on some file designated for this purpose.[35] For example, with `flock()`, which stands for *file lock*, only one process is allowed to obtain a lock on a file if the lock is designated to be an *exclusive lock*. If multiple processes invoke `flock()` concurrently on the same file, the operating system will grant an exclusive lock to only one of them in some manner that is best thought of as arbitrary. The process acquiring the lock qualifies to call `accept()`. This process would, of course, block until a request-for-connection is received from a client. When such a request is received, that would cause `accept()` to return a socket handle to the process. The process would subsequently release its lock on the file, which would allow the operating system to assign the lock to one of the other waiting server processes.

---

[34] Some operating systems, such as Solaris, forbid multiple processes calling `accept()` on the same server socket [62].

[35] Such a file can be empty since its contents serve no purpose.

15.6.1 Perl Implementation of a Preforking Server

We will now explain the Perl script shown next, `PreForkingServer.pl`, for a preforking server.[36] The script is divided primarily into two sections, the main section consisting of the lines labeled (A1) through (A21), and the rest of the script consisting of the supporting subroutines. The main section constructs a master server socket in lines (A14) through (A17). The loop in lines (A19) and (A20) calls on the `fork_a_slave()` function to fork off child server sockets from the master server socket. The number of these child server sockets is set by the constant `$SLAVE_COUNT` defined in line (A11). The `fork_a_slave()` function, shown in lines (B1) through (B6), calls `fork()` in line (B4) to spawn off a child process that is a duplicate of the master server socket process. The statement in line (B5), executed only in the child process, gets a copy of the master server socket of line (A14) bound to the variable `$master_server_socket`. The main Perl process in which the master server socket was originally created exits at line (B6) after returning the PID of the child process created.

Note that, in addition to creating the needed preforked child processes, the loop in lines (A19) and (A20) stores the PIDs of the child processes in the hash `%kids`. The keys of the hash entries are the PIDs of the child processes and the values the string `slave`.

As soon as the main server process has finished forking off the child processes in the loop of lines (A19) and (A20), the thread of execution in the main process moves to line (A21) with a call to `dead_process_cleanup_and_replacement()`. This function, defined in lines (C1) through (C9), causes the main process to block indefinitely in line (C3) with a call to `wait()`. The main process is able to return from `wait()` only if it receives from the operating system the `SIGCHLD` signal indicating that some process has terminated. Lines (C6) through (C9) then ascertain whether the dead process was one of the child processes whose PID was stored in the `%kids` hash. If the dead process was indeed one of the previously forked-off child processes, we call on `fork_a_slave()` again in line (C9) to fork off a replacement for the dead child process. That keeps the total number of available child server-socket processes at the same number. Since the `wait()` in line (C3) is called inside an infinite loop, it is in this `while` loop that the main Perl process, which is also the master server process, spends the rest of its lifetime. All it does is to wait for the child server processes to die and to create replacements for them as and when they do die.

Let's now focus on the specifics of what the child server processes do. As mentioned earlier, the main Perl process forks off a child server process in line (B4). A copy of the master server socket is then shipped off to the child server socket in line (B5) where it is supplied as the argument to the function `child_server()` that

[36]This implementation is based on and many of its constructs drawn directly from Randal Schwartz's Anonymizing Proxy Server [55].

is defined in lines (D1) through (D21). The child server process first constructs a new `IO::File` object in line (D3) from the lock file named originally in line (A4).[37] Next, in line (D6) the child server process tries to acquire an *exclusive lock* on the lock file.[38] As was mentioned earlier, this is a simple but effective way to impose sequential control that ensures that only one of the child server processes will be blocked in the call to `accept()` at any given time. The child server process that

---

[37]The `IO::File` provides an object-oriented interface for Perl's filehandles. So whereas with the built-in function `open()` you'd use the following syntax to attach a filehandle with a disk file and to then, say, read from it:

```
open( FILEHANDLE, $filename )
my $str = <FILEHANDLE>
```

with the `IO::File` module, you can use the following object-oriented syntax for doing the same:

```
use IO::File;
my $filehandle = IO::File->new( $filename, 'r' );
my $str = <$filehandle>
```

One can also use the POSIX file control flags `O_XXXX` in this syntax:

```
use IO::File;
my $filehandle = IO::File->new( $filename, O_RDONLY );
my $str = <$filehandle>
```

This works because `IO::File` automatically exports the following constants from the `Fcntl` module: `O_RDONLY` for read only; `O_WRONLY` for write only; `O_RDWR` for simultaneous read and write; `O_CREAT` for creating the file if it doesn't exist; `O_EXCL` for failing if the file already exists; `O_APPEND` for appending to the file; `O_TRUNC` for truncating the file; and `O_NONBLOCK` for nonblocking access. The `Fcntl` module is the Perl interface to C's `fcntl.h` header file that contains the POSIX file control definitions.

[38]Here are some important things to bear in mind about the Perl's built-in resource locking function `flock()` invoked in line (D6):

- `flock()` waits indefinitely until the lock is granted, unless the second argument is the integer 4, in which case `flock()` returns immediately and you must check its return value to make sure that a lock was acquired.
- `flock()` returns 1 on success and 0 on failure.
- If one process has an *exclusive lock* on a resource, no other process can access that resource during the duration of the lock. When `flock()` succeeds with the `LOCK_EX` flag, we have an exclusive lock.
- The locking achieved with `flock()` is *advisory*. Advisory locking is a mechanism by which cooperating processes can signal to each other their usage of a resource and whether or not that usage is critical. (What that means is that it is not a mechanism to protect against intruding processes that do not cooperate in locking.)

As shown in line (D6), `flock()` is called with two arguments, the first a filehandle and the second an integer that specifies the nature of the lock desired on the system resource attached to the filehandle. When the second argument is 1, we have a shared lock. As implied by its name, multiple processes are allowed to hold a lock on a system resource at the same time. On the other hand, if the second argument is the integer 2, a process acquires an exclusive lock, a lock that can only be held by one process at a time. To unlock a previously locked resource, the second argument must be 8. As was mentioned earlier, a call to `flock()` will block ordinarily until the lock is acquired. A nonblocking invocation of this function is obtained by using the integer 4 for the second argument. When the integer 8 is bitwise-or'ed with either the integer 1 or the integer 2, we obtain nonblocking versions of those locks. Frequently, the POSIX symbolic constants `LOCK_SH`, `LOCK_EX`, `LOCK_UN`, and `LOCK_NB` are used in place of the integers 1, 2, 8, and 4, respectively. These constants can be made available in a Perl script provided you import the module `Fcntl` with the `:fcntl` tag, as we do in line (A2).

acquires the lock gets to invoke its `accept()` in line (D8). *This then becomes the chosen server process to wait for the next request for connection from a client.* When a client request is received, `accept()` returns with a socket handle to the client. Subsequently, the child server process releases its lock on the lock file in line (D11). The socket handle returned by `accept()` is handed over to the function `handle_io_with_client()` in line (D15). The thread of execution returns from `handle_io_with_client()` when the client-server connection terminates. At that point, the child server process executes the code in lines (D16) and (D20). This part of the script is simply to measure the various times associated with the client-server interaction for each client. These various times are acquired by calling

```
my @start_times = (times, time);
```

in line (D12) before starting the interaction with a client and by calling

```
my @finish_times = (times, time);
```

in line (D17) after the connection with the client has come to a close. Subtracting the two time arrays `@start_times` and `@finish_times` returns the timing information we need.[39] Finally, the child process self-destructs in line (D21).

---

[39]The function `times()` in these calls returns a four-element list giving the user and system times in seconds for this process and the children of this process. For example, the following call will set the values of the variables shown on the left to their respective times:

```
($user, $system, $cuser, $csystem) = times;
```

The first two variables shown on the left, `$user` and `$system`, are the user and the system times for the process in which `times()` is invoked. The variables `$cuser` and `$csystem` are the user and the system times for the children of the process in which `times()` is invoked. Both the user and the system times are in seconds from the start of the process in which the script is being executed. By *user time* is meant the CPU usage time for executing loops, function calls, etc. And by *system time* is meant the CPU usage time expended in low-level system calls for opening files, starting processes, etc. To explain further the distinction between the user time and the system time, consider the case of a Perl script whose job is to open a text file and test each line of the text for a pattern. The act of opening the file is a system call and is measured by the system time. The more compute-intensive act of pattern matching is measured by the user time. The rest of this footnote provides a rationale for calling both `times()` and `time()` in the script. You see, in addition to the user time and the system time, there is a third time associated with program execution, the time expended in waiting for, say, access to shared resources. For example, if multiple processes are competing for CPU time, each process will have to wait for its turn on the processor. Similarly, if a program involves interaction with resources on the Internet, a program may have to enter wait states depending on the network traffic, etc. There does not exist a direct way to measure the third time — the time spent waiting for things to happen. Yet, since it is a critical element of the overall performance of a script, it may need to be recorded to assess the overall computational efficiencies. This time can be measured by measuring the *total elapsed time* from the start of a script. By subtracting the sum of the user time and the system time from the total elapsed time, one can ascertain the time spent waiting. In Perl, the elapsed time can be measured by invoking the function `time()` at the beginning of a program and at the point where the function `times()` is invoked. The function `time()` returns the total time in seconds from an epoch, usually January 1, 1970. By subtracting the value returned by `time()` at the beginning of a program from the value returned at the moment we invoke `times()`, we can measure the elapsed time between the two. This should explain the calls to both `times()` and `time()` in the script.

With regard to the rest of the script, we have already explained the purpose of the function `prefix()` of lines (A6) through (A8) in a footnote in Section 15.5.1. That same section also talks about the role played by the signal handlers for the pseudo-signals `__WARN__` and `__DIE__` in lines (A9) and (A10).

With regard to the function `setup_signals()` called in line (A11) and defined in lines (F1) through (F7), this function is needed only if you want the user-initiated death (such as with a keyboard interrupt or with a `kill` command invoked on a specific PID) of any single server process, the master or any of its children, to result in the death of all the processes. If you don't call this function and you kill one of the child server processes with, say, the `kill` command in a terminal window, a new child server process would be automatically created by the code in lines (C1) through (C9) of the script. On the other hand, with the help of the function call in line (A11), deliberately killing any of the server processes will kill them all. So it is important to understand the working of this function. Basically, `setup_signals()` ensures that if the operating system sends a terminating signal to any of the processes in a process group, it is broadcast to all the processes in the group, but in such a way that we do not get into an infinite loop of signal-handler invocations.

To explain the implementation of `setup_signals()`, let's start with the call to the built-in function `setpgrp()` in line (F2). Ordinarily, this function can take two arguments, as in the following call:

```
setpgrp(PID, PGRP)
```

This sets the process *group* ID to `PGRP` of a process whose process ID is `PID`. This function can therefore be used to move the process corresponding to the first argument from one process group to another.[40] If the first argument, `PID`, is 0, `setgrp()` uses the process ID of the current process, meaning the process that calls `setpgrp()`, for its first argument. If the second argument, `PGRP`, is 0, the process ID of the process specified by the first argument is used for `PGRP`. When the two arguments are equal either by specification or because the second argument is 0, the process whose process ID is the first argument becomes a process group leader. In this manner, the group leader role can be bestowed on the process specified by the first argument. The call in (F2) is equivalent to

```
setpgrp(0, 0)
```

which sets the process group ID of the current process, the process that calls `setpgrp()`, equal to its process ID. That makes the current process a process group leader and also a session leader. The advantage of doing this is that if a signal is sent to the current process, by virtue of its also being the group leader, the signal will be broadcast to all the processes in the group.

---

[40]The beginning material in Section 2.17 of Chapter 2 reviews the notions of process group, process group ID (PGID), process group leader, session leader, etc.

That brings us to the block of code in lines (F3) through (F7). This block of code uses the same anonymous subroutine to define signal handlers for three different signals, `SIGHUP`, `SIGINT`, and `SIGTERM`.[41] To understand the anonymous subroutine, note that, being a signal handler, the subroutine code is executed only when the operating system has sent to a process one of the three signals mentioned in line (F3). Furthermore, when the subroutine is called for execution, it is called with one argument that is the name of the signal. Therefore, in the anonymous subroutine, the argument assigned to the variable `$sig` will be `HUP` if the signal received by a process is `SIGHUP`, `INT` if the signal received is `SIGINT`, and `TERM` if the signal received is `SIGTERM`. Line (F5) changes on the fly the signal handler for the signal for which the handler is invoked to `IGNORE`, *but only for the process in which* `setup_signals()` *is being executed.*[42] By using zero as the second argument to the built-in function `kill()`, line (F6) broadcasts the signal bound to `$sig` to all the other processes in the process group. As the reader will recall from Chapter 2, ordinarily the second argument to `kill` is the PID of the intended destination of the signal named in the first argument. Finally, line (F7) will cause the process that received the one of the signals of line (F3) to self-destruct.

Our child server processes do not fork off processes of their own. But if they did, the same signal setup function we have shown in lines (F1) through (F7) would work. That is because the signal handlers for a parent process are inherited by all its child processes.

```
#!/usr/bin/perl -w
use strict;

### PreForkingServer.pl

#--------------------------  main  ----------------------------------
use IO::Socket;                                                  #(A1)
use Fcntl ':flock';                                              #(A2)
use IO::File;                                                    #(A3)
```

---

[41]The signals mentioned in the code in lines (F3) through (F7) are described in Section 2.18 of Chapter 2. For the case of Unix-like platforms, the signal `SIGHUP` (whose Perl name is `HUP`) for "hang up" is sent by the operating system to all the processes connected to a modem or an Xterm should the modem get disconnected or should the Xterm be closed. The default action by the operating system, unless overridden as we do in lines (F3) through (F7), is to terminate the processes receiving this signal. We also mentioned in Chapter 2 that the Unix signal `SIGINT` (Perl name: `INT`) is sent to all processes connected to the terminal when a user enters Ctrl-C in the terminal window. And the signal `SIGTERM` (Perl name: `TERM`) is the software termination signal. When the operating system sends this signal to a process, the process is terminated unless a signal handler for this signal does otherwise.

[42]Note that resetting the signal handler to `IGNORE` in line (F5) may be important on some platforms. Commenting out line (F5) and forcing the main process to terminate by, say, the keyboard entry of Ctrl-C may cause the machine to get trapped in an infinite loop of the invocations of the signal handler. When that happens, the only way to regain control over the machine could be by shutting off the power and then rebooting it.

```
use constant PIDFILE      =>   "/tmp/prefork.pid";                       #(A4)

my $LOG = 1;                                                              #(A5)

sub prefix {                                                              #(A6)
    my $now = localtime;                                                  #(A7)
    "[$now] [$$] " . shift;                                               #(A8)
}

$SIG{__WARN__} = sub { warn prefix shift };                               #(A9)
$SIG{__DIE__} = sub { die prefix shift };                                #(A10)
setup_signals();                                                         #(A11)

my $SLAVE_COUNT = 3;                                                     #(A12)

my %kids;                                                                #(A13)
my $master_server_socket =IO::Socket::INET->new(LocalPort => 9000,#(A14)
                                                Listen => 1,      #(A15)
                                                Reuse => 1,       #(A16)
                                                Proto => 'tcp',   #(A17)
                                              )
or die "Cannot create master server socket: $!";                         #(A18)

for ( 1..$SLAVE_COUNT ) {                                                #(A19)
    $kids{ fork_a_slave( $master_server_socket ) } = "slave";            #(A20)
}

dead_process_cleanup_and_replacement();                                  #(A21)


#----------------------  support functions  --------------------------
sub fork_a_slave {                                                        #(B1)
    my $master_server_socket = shift;                                     #(B2)
    my $pid;                                                              #(B3)
    defined ($pid = fork) or die "Cannot fork: $!";                       #(B4)
    # The child receives a copy of the master server socket
    child_server($master_server_socket) unless $pid;                      #(B5)
    $pid;                                                                 #(B6)
}
sub dead_process_cleanup_and_replacement {                                #(C1)
    while (1) {                                                           #(C2)
        my $pid = wait;                                                   #(C3)
        my $was = delete ($kids{$pid}) || "?unknown?";                    #(C4)
        warn("child $pid ($was) terminated status $?") if $LOG;           #(C5)
        if ($was eq "slave") {                                            #(C6)
            sleep 1;                                                      #(C7)
            warn "replacing a terminated process with a new one";         #(C8)
            $kids{ fork_a_slave($master_server_socket) } = "slave";#(C9)
        }
```

```
    }
}
sub child_server {                                                       #(D1)
    my $copy_of_master_server_socket = shift;                            #(D2)
    my $fh = IO::File->new(PIDFILE, O_RDWR | O_CREAT )                   #(D3)
            or die "cant open lock file: $!";                            #(D4)
    warn "child started" if $LOG;                                        #(D5)
    flock $fh, LOCK_EX;                                                  #(D6)
    warn("child has lock") if $LOG;                                      #(D7)
    my $client_soc = $copy_of_master_server_socket->accept               #(D8)
                                   or die "accept: $!";                  #(D9)
    warn "child releasing lock" if $LOG;                                 #(D10)
    flock $fh, LOCK_UN;                                                  #(D11)
    my @start_times = (times, time);                                     #(D12)
    $client_soc->autoflush(1);                                           #(D13)
    warn("connect from ", $client_soc->peerhost) if $LOG;                #(D14)
    handle_io_with_client( $client_soc );                                #(D15)
    if ($LOG) {                                                          #(D16)
        my @finish_times = (times, time);                                #(D17)
        for (@finish_times) {                                            #(D18)
            $_ -= shift @start_times;
        }
        warn(sprintf "TIMES: %.2f %.2f %.2f %.2f %d\n",
                                   @finish_times);                       #(D19)
    }
    warn("child terminating") if $LOG;                                   #(D20)
    exit 0;                                                              #(D21)
}
sub handle_io_with_client {                                              #(E1)
    my $client_sock = shift;                                             #(E2)
    print $client_sock "Enter your cyberspace name:";                    #(E3)
    my $client_name = <$client_sock>;                                    #(E4)
    $client_name =~ s/^\s*(\S.*\S)\s*\n?$/$1/;                           #(E5)
    print $client_sock "Hello $client_name\n";                           #(E6)
    while ( defined( my $mesg = <$client_sock> ) ) {                     #(E7)
        print $client_sock "$client_name: $mesg\n";                      #(E8)
    }
    $client_sock->close or warn $@;                                      #(E9)
}
sub setup_signals {                                                      #(F1)
    setpgrp;                                                             #(F2)
    $SIG{HUP} = $SIG{INT} = $SIG{TERM} = sub {                           #(F3)
        my $sig = shift;                                                 #(F4)
        $SIG{$sig} = 'IGNORE';                                           #(F5)
        kill $sig, 0;                                                    #(F6)
        die "killed by $sig";                                            #(F7)
    };
}
```

This server can be run by calling in the command line

```
PreForkingServer.pl
```

As with the interactive servers shown previously in this chapter, a client may use a command line like the following to initiate interaction with the Python server:

```
client_script  128.46.144.10  9000
```

where `client_script` could be either the Perl script or the Python script shown in Section 15.3 and where the IP address (which can also be the symbolic host name) shown belongs to the host on which the server is running. You can replace the IP address above with the string `localhost` for testing with a client running on the same machine as the server. With the server running on a local machine, the reader may wish to run multiple clients in different terminal windows of the same machine to see the server processes being created and destroyed as the clients make and break connections with the server.

15.6.2 Python Implementation of a Preforking Server

Shown next is a Python implementation of the preforking server. The scripts starts out by declaring the three main constants used:

- The constant `PIDFILE` in line (B1) for naming the empty lock file that is used for selecting the winner of a competition among the child server processes to earn the right to use `accept()` for trapping the next client.
- The constant `LOG` in line (B2) that when set will print out various status messages on the console of the machine running the master server process. These messages show the new child server processes being created and then destroyed as new clients check in and check out.
- The constant `SLAVE_COUNT` in line (B3) that controls how many preforked child server processes will always be available for servicing the clients. This number needs to be chosen carefully in a production server since when the total number of clients being serviced simultaneously equals `SLAVE_COUNT`, all of the preforked servers would be occupied and none would be available to field its `accept()` for the next incoming client request for a connection. When that happens, a new client will simply hang until one of the child servers has terminated, which, as the reader knows from our earlier discussion in Section 15.6, would cause a new child server process to come into existence for servicing the waiting client.

As mentioned in the introductory portion of Section 15.6, we do not want multiple child servers to vie simultaneously for the next client. In other words, we do not want multiple child server processes to simultaneously field their `accept()` methods for the next request for connection from a new client. Our strategy is for the child servers to engage in a low-level competition, with only the winner allowed to field its `accept()` method to wait for the next client. For Python, the low-level competition consists of having the child server processes invoke `fcntl.flock()` to acquire an exclusive lock on the lock file named by the `PIDFILE` constant. As mentioned in a long footnote in the previous subsection, only one process is allowed to acquire such a lock. The other processes block until the lock is released, and then they can again participate in the next competition.

The script uses the following signals: `SIGINT`, `SIGTERM`, `SIGKILL`, `SIGHUP`, and `SIGCHLD`. As mentioned previously in Section 3.16 of Chapter 3, the default action taken when a process receives any of the first four signals is to terminate any further execution. As the reader has seen previously, this default reaction to a signal can be overridden for `SIGINT`, `SIGTERM`, and `SIGHUP` by providing user-defined signal handlers. (Since the `SIGKILL` signal cannot be trapped in a script, it causes immediate termination of the process without any possible cleanup of the program environment, such as the flushing of IO buffers, closing of open files, etc.)

As was the case with the Perl implementation in the previous subsection, the process termination signals `SIGINT`, `SIGTERM`, and `SIGHUP` need to be handled with care if we want a user-initiated termination of either the main server process or any of the child server processes to kill all the server processes. If you depend on the default behavior of the processes to these signals, overall the server will appear to be Hydra-headed because any manual killing of a server process (by, say, issuing in the command line the `kill` command on the PID of a server process) will only cause regeneration of another child server process. As with the Perl implementation, the function `setup_signals()` in lines (C5) through (C9) and the signal-handler code in lines (C1) through (C4) is supposed to help us deal with this problem. On the basis of the same logic as presented for the Perl case, the call to `os.setpgrp()` in line (C6) allows the process in which this method is being executed to act as the process group leader. This would obviously be the main server process since it is that process which calls `os.setpgrp()` in line (J2). The calls in lines (C7), (C8), and (C9) then establish the signal handlers for the trio of signals `SIGINT`, `SIGTERM`, and `SIGHUP` using the function definition in lines (C1) through (C4).[43] When this definition is called for execution, line (C2) first resets the signal handler for the signal that was received by the process to `SIG_IGN`, which stands for `IGNORE` used in the Perl script, but only for the process that received the signal whose receipt is causing the execution of the signal handler code. As mentioned for the Perl case, this resetting is important to prevent the signal handling mechanism from getting trapped in an infinite loop. Next, line (C4) broadcasts the untrappable signal `SIGKILL` to all the processes in the process group of which the current process is the group leader. That

---

[43]To appreciate this signal-handler code, note that it would only be executed for a process that has received any of the three signals, `SIGINT`, `SIGTERM`, and `SIGHUP`.

obviously includes the current process. As a result, all of the server processes would be destroyed.

With regard to the signals, also note the extremely important role played by the signal `SIGCHLD` even though no signal handler is designated explicitly for it. The master server process stays blocked in the call to `wait()` in line (H3). When a child server process terminates, the operating system sends the `SIGCHLD` signal to the master server process. This causes `wait()` to check on the exit status of the terminated process and to return this value in line (H3). Subsequently, the master server process forks off another child server process to replace the dead child server process in line (H13). After that, the master server process goes back to waiting for a child process to die in line (H3).

Continuing with the description of the script, we have two utility functions in lines (D1) through (D16). The first of these, `get_client_line()` in lines (D1) through (D13), gives us a line-based facility for reading the messages sent by a client. The second, `prefix()` in lines (D14), (D15), and (D16), attaches useful diagnostic information (the time stamp and the current process ID) to the argument string. This is to permit us to examine the creation and destruction of the child server processes as new clients check in and then check out. We used both these functions in our previous Python script in Section 15.5.2 also.

The rest of the script is best explained by going backwards from the section titled `main` in lines (J1) through (J16). The `main` first constructs the master server socket in lines (J5), (J6), and (J7). Subsequently, it creates three child server sockets in the loop in lines (J14) and (J15). The PIDs of these child server sockets are stored in a dictionary called `kids`. Each entry in this dictionary is a key-value pair, with the child server PID as the key and the string `slave` as the value.[44] In line (J15), the child server processes are created by calling the function `fork_a_slave()` defined in lines (G1) through (G4). Finally, the master server process calls in line (J16) the function `dead_process_cleanup_and_replacement()` of lines (H1) through (H13), where the process stays blocked in the call to `wait()` in line (H3) in a forever loop. The master server is allowed to return from `wait()` in line (H3) only when it receives the `SIGCHLD` signal from the operating system that signifies that a child server process has terminated. In that event, the master server process proceeds to create a new child server process by calling `fork_a_slave()` in line (H13). The PID of the replacement child server process is again stored in the `kids` dictionary.

Let's now focus on child server processes created by calls to `fork()` in line (G2) of `fork_a_slave()`. Through the conditional in line (G3), a child server process executes the function `child_server()` defined in lines (F1) through (F27). Note that a child server is supplied with a copy of the master server socket in the call to

[44]As the reader will see shortly, when a child server process dies, it is removed from the dictionary `kids` and replaced by a new child server process. If we had wanted to, for logging and record keeping, we could keep the PIDs of the dead child server processes in the `kids` dictionary after changing the corresponding values from `slave` to, say, `dead`.

child_server() in line (G3). The very first thing that a child server process does is to try to obtain a lock on the empty lock file pointed to by PIDFILE. As mentioned earlier, this is for the purpose of ensuring that only one child process gets to use its accept() to monitor the server port at any one time. The call to fcntl.flock()[45] in line (F6) blocks until an exclusive lock can be successfully acquired on the named file through the file object created in line (F5). When such a lock is acquired, the call to flock() returns 1. The child server acquiring the lock gets to use its accept() in line (F13) to wait for the next connection request from a client.

As soon as a new client checks in, accept() in line (F13) returns a client socket for a two-way communication link between the child server and the client. Upon the construction of the client socket, the child server relinquishes the lock on the PIDFILE in line (F19) so that one of the other waiting child servers can get a turn to use its accept() method for monitoring the port assigned to the server. The child server process then hands the flow of control to handle_io_with_client() in line (F21) for a two-way communication session between the server and the client. The function handle_io_with_client(), defined in lines (E1) through (E20), sends a greeting message to the client in line (E7), requests the client's name in line (E8), and then in a forever loop in lines (E11) through (E20) reads each line sent by the client and echos it back to the client after prepending the line with the name supplied by the client.

A client terminates the conversation with the server by closing the socket at its end. On the server side, this condition is tested by the value returned by the recv() method in line (D4) and subsequently by the emptiness of the string received in line (E13). When the flow of control returns back to child_server() in line (F22), the child server process prints out the status messages and calculates the processor and other times associated with the interaction with the client in lines (F23) and (F24). The call to os.times() returns a 5-tuple of floating-point numbers indicating the accumulated times in seconds for (1) the user time, (2) the system time, (3) children's user time, (4) children's system time, (5) and elapsed real time since the epoch. For an explanation of these times, see the discussion on the Perl version of this script.

```
#!/usr/bin/env python

###  PreForkingServer.py

import sys, socket, time, os, signal, fcntl                          #(A)

#----------------------  define constants  ---------------------------
PIDFILE = "/tmp/prefork.pid"                                        #(B1)
LOG = 1                                                             #(B2)
SLAVE_COUNT = 3                                                     #(B3)
```

[45] A footnote in the previous subsection explains the syntax used for calling flock(), especially the constants used for its second argument.

```
#---------------------- set up signal handlers -----------------------
def signal_handler( signum, frame ):                                  #(C1)
    signal.signal( signum,  signal.SIG_IGN )                          #(C2)
    if LOG: print "killed %s by %s" % (os.getpid(), signum)           #(C3)
    os.kill( 0, signal.SIGKILL )                                      #(C4)

def setup_signals():                                                  #(C5)
    os.setpgrp()                                                      #(C6)
    signal.signal( signal.SIGINT,  signal_handler )                   #(C7)
    signal.signal( signal.SIGTERM,  signal_handler )                  #(C8)
    signal.signal( signal.SIGHUP,  signal_handler )                   #(C9)

#---------------------- utility functions  --------------------------
# Read a line of text from the client side.  Return an empty
# string when EOF is detected.
def get_client_line( client_sock ):                                   #(D1)
    client_line = ''                                                  #(D2)
    while 1:                                                          #(D3)
        client_byte = client_sock.recv(1)                             #(D4)
        if not client_byte:                                           #(D5)
            client_line = ''                                          #(D6)
            break                                                     #(D7)
        elif client_byte == '\n' or client_byte == '\r':              #(D8)
            client_line += client_byte                                #(D9)
            break                                                    #(D10)
        else:                                                        #(D11)
            client_line += client_byte                               #(D12)
    return client_line                                               #(D13)


def prefix( message ):                                               #(D14)
    now = time.ctime()                                               #(D15)
    return "[%s] [%s] %s" % (now, os.getpid(), message)              #(D16)

#---------------- slave server process I/O function -----------------
# The following function is called by child_server():
def handle_io_with_client( client_sock ):                             #(E1)
    client_hostname, client_side_port = client_sock.getpeername()     #(E2)
    if LOG:                                                           #(E3)
        message = "[Request for connection from %s]" \
                                        % client_hostname             #(E4)
        print prefix( message )                                       #(E5)
    client_sock.send(                                                 #(E6)
      "Welcome to server script %s running at %s" \
                % (sys.argv[0], os.environ['HOST']) )                 #(E7)
    client_sock.send( "\nEnter your cyberspace name: " )              #(E8)
    # get client name and get rid of the newline terminator:
    client_name = get_client_line( client_sock )[0:-1]                #(E9)
```

```
    client_sock.send( "Hello %s\n\n" % client_name )                    #(E10)
    while 1:                                                            #(E11)
        message = get_client_line( client_sock )                        #(E12)
        if not message:                                                 #(E13)
            closing_msg = "[Connection closed by %s from %s]" \
                      % (client_name, client_hostname)                  #(E14)
            print prefix(closing_msg)                                   #(E15)
            client_sock.close()                                         #(E16)
            break                                                       #(E17)
        else:                                                           #(E18)
            # get rid of the newline terminator
            message = message[0:-1]                                     #(E19)
            client_sock.send("%s: %s\n" % (client_name, message)) #(E20)

#----------------------  child server process  -----------------------
# The following function is called by the function fork_a_slave()
def child_server( copy_of_master_server_socket ):                       #(F1)
    if LOG:                                                             #(F2)
        message = "Child server process %s started" % os.getpid()  #(F3)
        print prefix( message )                                         #(F4)
    fd = os.open( PIDFILE, os.O_RDWR | os.O_CREAT )                     #(F5)
    fcntl.flock( fd, fcntl.LOCK_EX )                                    #(F6)
    if LOG:                                                             #(F7)
        message = "Child server process %s has lock" % os.getpid() #(F8)
        print prefix( message )                                         #(F9)
    client_sock = None                                                  #(F10)
    while not client_sock:                                              #(F11)
        try:                                                            #(F12)
            client_sock,address =  \
                       copy_of_master_server_socket.accept()  #(F13)
        except socket.error, (value, message): pass                     #(F14)
        if client_sock: break                                           #(F15)
    if LOG:                                                             #(F16)
        message = \
            "Child server process %s releasing lock" % os.getpid()#(F17)
        print prefix( message )                                         #(F18)
    fcntl.flock( fd, fcntl.LOCK_UN )                                    #(F19)
    start_times = os.times()                                            #(F20)
    handle_io_with_client( client_sock )                                #(F21)
    if LOG:                                                             #(F22)
        finish_times = os.times()                                       #(F23)
        processor_times = [ finish_times[i] - start_times[i] \
                                     for i in range(5) ]       #(F24)
        print "Processor Times for Client Session: ", \
                                         processor_times      #(F25)
    if LOG: print "Child server process %s terminating" \
                                            % os.getpid()     #(F26)
    os.kill( os.getpid(), signal.SIGKILL )                              #(F27)
```

```
#---------  function for forking off child server processes   ----------
def fork_a_slave( master_server_socket ):                            #(G1)
    slave_pid = os.fork()                                            #(G2)
    # The child is actually receiving a copy
    # of the master server socket:
    if slave_pid == 0: child_server( master_server_socket )          #(G3)
    return slave_pid                                                 #(G4)

#------------  dead server process cleanup and replacement  ------------
def dead_process_cleanup_and_replacement( master_server_socket ):  #(H1)
    while 1:                                                         #(H2)
        pid, exit_status = os.wait()                                 #(H3)
        if LOG:                                                      #(H4)
            message =   \
              "Child server process %s terminated with status %s" \
                      % (pid, exit_status)                           #(H5)
            print prefix( message )                                  #(H6)
        was = kids.pop(pid)                                          #(H7)
        if was == "slave":                                           #(H8)
            time.sleep(1)                                            #(H9)
            if LOG:                                                  #(H10)
                messge = \
            "Replacing a terminated server process with a new one"#(H11)
                print prefix( message )                              #(H12)
            kids[ fork_a_slave(master_server_socket) ] = "slave"   #(H13)

#-------------------------   main   -----------------------------------
client_sock = client_name = client_hostname = None                   #(J1)
setup_signals()                                                      #(J2)
port = 9000                                                          #(J3)
try:                                                                 #(J4)
    master_server_sock =         \
                  socket.socket(socket.AF_INET, socket.SOCK_STREAM)#(J5)
#   master_server_sock.bind( (socket.gethostname(), port) )
#   master_server_sock.bind( ('localhost', port) )
    master_server_sock.bind( ('', port) )                            #(J6)
    master_server_sock.listen(1)                                     #(J7)
except socket.error, (value, message):                               #(J8)
    if master_server_sock:                                           #(J9)
        master_server_sock.close()                                   #(J10)
    print "No master server socket: %s" % prefix(message)           #(J11)
    sys.exit(1)                                                      #(J12)
kids = {}                                                            #(J13)
for i in range(3):                                                   #(J14)
    kids[ fork_a_slave( master_server_sock ) ] = "slave"            #(J15)
# Park the master server process here waiting for
# a child server process to die:
dead_process_cleanup_and_replacement( master_server_sock )          #(J16)
```

The comments we made immediately after the Perl preforking server apply here also with regard to the running of the server and how a client script may make a connection with the server.

15.7 MULTIPLEXED CLIENTS AND SERVERS

The rate at which information can be transferred machine-to-machine in a typical network is often an order of magnitude slower than the rate at which CPUs operate in modern machines. This allows for the use of another approach to concurrent I/O in client and server scripts: *multiplexing*. Multiplexed clients and servers create a pool of sockets in a single process that are then cyclically polled to see if they are ready to be read from or written to. Perl provides the `IO::Select` module[46] and Python the `select` module that have the smarts built into them for polling a pool of stream objects (handles in Perl and file objects in Python) in general[47] and for returning a subset thereof, all the returned stream objects ready for their intended operations. All you have to do is to call `select()`, a static method of the respective modules, on a pool of stream objects. When invoked in an infinite loop, a call to `select()` at each iteration returns all the stream objects that are ready for either reading or writing.

Multiplexing is obviously an alternative to forking for achieving concurrency in client–server operations.[48] So if a particular operating system does not support forking (or multithreading), you may still be able to achieve concurrency with multiplexing.

15.7.1 Socket Multiplexing in Perl

The script shown next, `MultiplexedClient.pl`, is a multiplexed version of the client script `ClientSocketInteractive.pl` presented earlier in Section 15.3.1. The script uses multiplexing only with regard to the sockets meant for reading from. Note the construction of a new instance of `IO::Select` in line (I).[49] This instance will serve as a container for the sockets in our script. Lines (J) and (K) then insert two sockets into this container, one of these being the socket for communicating with the server and the other for fetching information from the client's keyboard. Subsequently, the infinite loop in lines (M) through (Z) calls `select()` on the socket pool in line (N). The call to `select()` blocks until there is a socket that is

---

[46]Perl's built-in `select()` does the same thing as the `select()` method of the `IO::Select` class.

[47]We are using the terms *handle* for Perl and *file objects* for Python here generically to stand for stream objects in general. These could be filehandles, sockets, pipes, etc.

[48]Multiplexing is also an alternative to the use of multithreading for achieving concurrency.

[49]A call to `IO::Select->new()` can also be with arguments that designate the streams you want monitored. The stream objects when supplied as arguments to `new()` [or, for that matter, to the `add()` and `remove()` methods] can be in the form of filehandles, sockets, glob references to streams, etc.

ready to either read from or write to. The argument structure of a general call to `select()` is made clear by the following:

```
IO::Select->select( monitord_read_handles,
                    monitored_write_handles,
                    sockets_monitored_for_exceptions,
                    timeout )
```

where the first three arguments are objects of type `IO::Select`. The first argument contains the handles meant for reading from, the second the handles meant for writing to, and the third the sockets that we want monitored for exceptions.[50] If the last argument is not provided, a call to `select()` blocks until at least one of the handles in the `IO::Select` container is ready for its intended purpose. If a value in seconds is provided for the last argument, the blocking action ends at the termination of that time interval. A handle is considered ready for reading if there is at least one byte of data in the handle's input/receive buffer.[51] And a handle is considered ready for writing if the output/send buffer will accommodate at least one more byte of data.

A call to `select()` returns an array of three elements, the first a reference to an array of all handles ready to read from, the second a reference to an array of all handles ready to write to, and the last a reference to an array of sockets that have exceptions. In our case, since only the reading operations are multiplexed, we extract the first element of the array returned by `select()` in line (N). Therefore, when the thread of execution gets to line (O), there must exist at least one of the two sockets placed in the `$socket_container` object that is ready for reading. The `for` loop in lines (O) through (Z) checks each ready socket/handle against the items placed in the `$socket_container` object and then uses `sysread()` to extract the information from the ready socket.

As shown by the script, all its I/O is carried out by the low-level functions `sysread()` and `syswrite()`. Both these functions do not use the standard I/O buffering used by functions such as `read()`, `print()`, etc.[52]

---

[50]The third argument does not work for filehandles in general; it only works for sockets.

[51]A handle is also considered ready for reading if it is in the end-of-file state.

[52]It is interesting to note that both `read()` and `sysread()` take similar argument structure. For example, the second and the third statements shown below constitute valid calls to these functions:

```
my $buffer = 1024;
my $num_bytes = read( STDIN, $buffer, 100 );
my $num_bytes = sysread( STDIN, $buffer, 100 );
```

But since `read()` uses the standard I/O buffering, a call to this function does not return until it can fetch the exact number of bytes requested by the third argument (unless the input stream is in the end-of-file condition). By contrast, `sysread()`, since it does not use the standard I/O buffering, returns even if it cannot fetch the number of bytes specified by its third argument. Note that in both cases, the functions return the actual number of bytes read. Let's now see what is meant by the statement that `sysread()` and `syswrite()` do not use *standard buffering*, considering especially that all I/O operations must be subject to buffering of some kind in order to deal with the mismatch between the usually high computational speed of a CPU and the usually low I/O speed of a physical device or the network. What happens is that

The reader is probably wondering about the argument in the call to `add()` in line (K):

```
$socket_container->add( \*STDIN );
```

What this call shows is the safe way to pass a filehandle to a subroutine — as a reference to the typeglob associated with the filehandle. While a filehandle can be passed as an ordinary string argument to a subroutine in the same package, that does not work if the subroutine is in another package. A filehandle loses its source package affiliation when passed as a string argument in a subroutine call.

```
#!/usr/bin/perl -w
use strict;

### MultiplexedClient.pl

use IO::Socket;                                                           #(A)
use IO::Select;                                                           #(B)
use constant BUFSIZE => 1024;                                             #(C)

die "usage: $0 host port" unless @ARGV == 2;                              #(D)

my ($host, $port) = @ARGV;                                                #(E)

my $socket = IO::Socket::INET->new(PeerAddr  => $host,                    #(F)
                                   PeerPort  => $port,
                                   Proto     => "tcp",
                                  )
    or die "can't connect to port $port on $host: $!";
```

---

the high-level I/O operations — such as those called for in a script — may be subject to several layers of buffering, ranging all the way from the very low-level buffer embedded in the disk hardware, to the buffer associated with the disk driver, to the buffer maintained by the operating system, and, finally, to the buffer used by the software platform underlying the scripting language. For the I/O operations specified in a script in Perl or Python, this last buffer will be the one associated with the standard I/O library of C; this buffer is usually referred to as the *stdio* buffer. For example, when you invoke `print()` in Perl, the information is first written into the output stdio buffer. Similarly, when you invoke the line-input operator `<>` or the function `read()` in Perl, the information will be read from the input stdio buffer. By default, the stdio buffers do not allow their contents to be flushed before the buffer is full. This can create problems in network applications in which a client engaged in an interactive session with a server wants to send a small amount of information to the server and wait for the server's response before sending additional information. If the information sent stays in the output stdio buffer on the client side, the server will never see it and, in the absence of a response from the server, the client will be unable to proceed further, causing the client-server interaction to deadlock. The solution is to turn off stdio buffering by turning on the *autoflush* mode for the filehandle or the socket handle, as the case may be. When using object-oriented syntax, the autoflush mode can be turned off by invoking the `autoflush()` method on the filehandle. The same effect is achieved by setting to true the value of the special variable `$|`. *The other way to avoid stdio buffering is to use the lower level* `sysread()` *and* `syswrite()` *functions for I/O.*

```
$SIG{INT} = sub { $socket->close; exit 0; };                          #(G)
print STDERR "[Connected to $host:$port]\n";                          #(H)

my $socket_container = IO::Select->new();                             #(I)
$socket_container->add( $socket );                                    #(J)
$socket_container->add( \*STDIN );                                    #(K)

my $buffer;                                                           #(L)
while ( 1 ) {                                                         #(M)
    ( my $readable_handles ) = IO::Select->select( $socket_container,
                                              undef, undef, 0 );#(N)

    #  When the control gets to this point, there is at least one
    #  socket handle to read from or written to.  For the moment,
    #  worry only about the read side.
    for my $sock ( @$readable_handles ) {                             #(O)
        if ( $sock eq $socket ) {                                     #(P)
            if ( sysread( $socket, $buffer, BUFSIZE ) > 0 ) {         #(Q)
                syswrite( STDOUT, $buffer );                          #(R)
            } else {                                                  #(S)
                warn "Connection closed by server";                   #(T)
                exit 0;                                               #(U)
            }
        }
        if ( $sock eq \*STDIN ) {                                     #(V)
            if ( sysread( STDIN, $buffer, BUFSIZE ) > 0 ) {           #(W)
                syswrite( $socket, $buffer );                         #(X)
            } else {                                                  #(Y)
                $socket->close;                                       #(Z)
            }
        }
    }
}
```

To test this client, you could fire up the server `AcceptAndFork.pl` of Section 15.5.1 and then use the above script to connect with the server with a call like

```
MultiplexedClient.pl  ip_address_or_hostname_of_server  port_number
```

Another way to test the above client script would be to use the server we present next.

The next script, `MultiplexedServer.pl`, is a server that uses multiplexing to talk to several clients concurrently. Any of the clients we have shown previously would be able to interact with this server. The script constructs a TCP server socket in line (D). Subsequently, in line (F), the script constructs an instance of `IO::Select` to serve as a container for the sockets that will be multiplexed. The first item we add to this container is the server socket itself in line (G).

Using the hash `%clientnames` in line (H) points to an important difference between multiprocessing servers on the one hand and multiplexed servers on the other. In a multiprocessing server, each client is handled by a separate process and all matters pertaining to that client can be kept track of by the child process created for the client. For example, for an accept-and-fork server, if a client wishes to be known by a particular name, that name can be assigned to a variable in the child process for the client. But in a multiplexing server, there is only one process shared by all clients. Therefore, any information specific to a client cannot be kept track of in the same manner. To get around this problem, the hash `%clientnames` stores the one piece of client-specific information that we want to keep track of for each client — the name that the client wishes to use — as the value associated with each client socket that is created by `accept()`. The client sockets are stored as the keys in this hash.[53]

Next we call `IO::Select->select()` in line (J) inside the `while` loop of lines (I) through (Z) to return a list of sockets that are ready to be read.[54] These are all stored in an array whose reference is held by the variable `$readable_handles` in line (J).[55] The `for` loop in lines (K) through (Z) then processes each of the ready sockets. If the server socket is ready to go, we first invoke `accept()` on it in line (M) to construct a new client socket. Subsequently, lines (O) through (S) first send a welcome message to the client and then elicit from the client the name he/she wishes to use in the exchange with the server. The last part of this introductory exchange with the client consists of sending a hello greeting to the client in line (S). We next add the newly created client socket to the `IO::Select` socket container in line (T) and, in line (U), make a key-value entry in the `%clientnames` hash with the key consisting of the newly created client socket and the value consisting of the name that the client wishes to use in the exchanges with the server.

If, on the other hand, the socket that is ready to go is a client socket, we first retrieve the name of the client associated with that socket in line (W). Lines (Y) and (Z) then read from the client socket the information sent by the client and echo it back to the client after prepending the echo-back with the name of the client. Note that the `sysread()` called in line (Y) can only read a maximum of `BUFSIZE` bytes at one time, this constant having been specified previously in line (C). If the client

[53]If we wanted to store multiple pieces of client-specific information in such a hash, we could create an array for what needs to be stored and store references to such arrays as the values associated with the keys.

[54]The server socket will be returned by the call in line (J) at every cycle of the `while` loop because it is always ready for the `accept()` method to be invoked on it.

[55]For more information about the syntax to use when calling `IO::Select->select()`, see the discussion about this function in connection with the multiplexed client script shown earlier in this section.

sends in more information than this, they will be read by the server in separate cycles of the call to `sysread()`.[56]

```
#!/usr/bin/perl -w
use strict;

### MultiplexedServer.pl

use IO::Socket;                                                     #(A)
use IO::Select;                                                     #(B)
use constant BUFSIZE => 1024;                                       #(C)

my $server_sock = IO::Socket::INET->new(LocalPort => 9000,          #(D)
                                        Listen => 5,
                                        Reuse => 1,
                                        Proto => 'tcp',
                                        );
die "No Server Socket: $@\n" unless $server_sock;                   #(E)

my $socket_container = IO::Select->new();                           #(F)
$socket_container->add( $server_sock );                             #(G)

my %clientnames;                                                    #(H)

while (1) {                                                         #(I)
    ( my $readable_handles ) = IO::Select->select( $socket_container,
                                          undef, undef, 0 );#(J)
    for my $sock ( @$readable_handles ) {                           #(K)
        if ( $sock eq $server_sock ) {                              #(L)
            my $client_sock = $server_sock->accept();               #(M)
            next unless defined $client_sock;                       #(N)
            syswrite($client_sock, "Welcome to server script $0 " .
                          "running at $ENV{HOSTNAME}\n\n");         #(O)
            syswrite($client_sock, "Enter your cyberspace name:");  #(P)
            my $client_name = <$client_sock>;                       #(Q)
            $client_name =~ s/^\s*(\S.*\S)\s*\n?$/$1/;              #(R)
            syswrite($client_sock, "Hello $client_name\n\n");       #(S)
            $socket_container->add( $client_sock );                 #(T)
            $clientnames{$client_sock} = $client_name;              #(U)
        } else {
            next unless exists $clientnames{ $sock };               #(V)
            my $theclient = $clientnames{ $sock };                  #(W)
```

[56] See [62] for how to get around this and other limitations of the script shown here.

```
            my $buffer;                                              #(X)
            if ( sysread( $sock, $buffer, BUFSIZE ) > 0 ) {          #(Y)
                syswrite($sock, "$theclient: $buffer\n");            #(Z)
            }
        }
    }
}
close $server_sock;
```

15.7.2 Socket Multiplexing in Python

As mentioned in the introduction to Section 15.7, multiplexing of the `file` objects in Python is achieved with the `socket` module. The `select()` method from this module serves the same purpose as the method of the same name in the Perl `IO::Select` module.

The script that comes next, `MultiplexedClient.py`, is a multiplexed version of the client script `ClientSocketInteractive.py` shown earlier in Section 15.3.2. As with the multiplexed Perl client of the previous subsection, the Python script uses multiplexing only with regard to the sockets meant for reading from. The beginning part of the script, between lines (A) and (Q), creates a client socket and sets up a signal handler for keyboard interrupts. This part is the same as for our earlier Python clients. What is new now is in lines (R) through (l). We first declare a container, a list in this case, for the sockets that will be supplied to the `select.select()` method. Note in particular that, unlike Perl, now we do not need a special container for the file objects that we want multiplexed. Lines (S) and (T) then insert the two file objects into the container, the client socket created earlier in lines (F) through (L) and the standard input stream for reading the information entered by the user in a terminal window of the client machine. The rest of the script, in lines (U) through (l), spins for ever through the sockets in the socket container with the caveat that the call to `select.select()` in line (V) blocks until at least one of the file objects is ready for reading, which happens when the input/receive buffer associated with the file object contains at least one byte of data (or is in the end-of-file state).

The argument structure of a general call to `select.select()` in line (V) is the same as for the Perl case. This call returns a list of the file objects that are ready for their intended purpose. As in the Perl case, we set the last argument of `select()`, the timeout argument, to zero, which means that the call to `select()` will block indefinitely until at least one of the file objects is ready for reading from or writing to or has encountered an exception. After the call to `select.select()` returns, we then loop through each file object to first identify it and to then take the corresponding action. If the file object is the client socket, we invoke `recv()` on it in line (Y). This call will read a maximum of `BUFSIZE` bytes from the input/receive buffer associated with the socket. If the client socket is in the end-of-file condition, the otherwise blocking call to `recv()` in line (Y) will return an empty string. Since under normal conditions this can only happen when the server has closed the connection on its side, we proceed to terminate the client session in line (e). On the other hand, if the file object returned by `select.select()` is the input stream attached to the keyboard, we make the blocking call `readline()` to fetch the line entered by the user. Subsequently, we ship off this line to the server in line (j).

```
#!/usr/bin/env python

### MultiplexedClient.py

import sys, socket, select, signal                                     #(A)

if len(sys.argv) != 3:                                                 #(B)
    sys.exit( "Need exactly two command line arguments, the " +
              "first naming the host and the second the port" )        #(C)

BUFSIZE = 1024                                                         #(D)

host, port = sys.argv[1], int(sys.argv[2])                             #(E)

try:
    sock = socket.socket( socket.AF_INET, socket.SOCK_STREAM )         #(F)
    sock.connect( (host, port) )                                       #(G)
except socket.error, (value, message):                                 #(H)
    if sock:                                                           #(I)
        sock.close()                                                   #(J)
    print "Could not establish a client socket: " + message            #(K)
    sys.exit(1)                                                        #(L)

def sock_close( signum, frame ):                                       #(M)
    global sock                                                        #(N)
    sock.close()                                                       #(O)
    sys.exit(0)                                                        #(P)

signal.signal( signal.SIGINT, sock_close )                             #(Q)

socket_container = []                                                  #(R)
socket_container.append( sock )                                        #(S)
socket_container.append( sys.stdin )                                   #(T)
```

```
while 1:                                                               #(U)
    readable_handles =          \
              select.select( socket_container, [], [], 0 )[0]          #(V)
    for file_object in readable_handles:                               #(W)
        if file_object == sock:                                        #(X)
            bytes_read = sock.recv( BUFSIZE )                          #(Y)
            if len(bytes_read) > 0:                                    #(Z)
                sys.stdout.write( bytes_read )                         #(a)
                sys.stdout.flush()                                     #(b)
            else:                                                      #(c)
                print "Connection closed by server"                    #(d)
                sys.exit(0)                                            #(e)
        if file_object == sys.stdin:                                   #(f)
            bytes_read = sys.stdin.readline(BUFSIZE )                  #(g)
            sys.stdin.flush()                                          #(h)
            if len(bytes_read) > 0:                                    #(i)
                sock.send( bytes_read )                                #(j)
            else:                                                      #(k)
                sock.close()                                           #(l)
```

As with all the other client scripts for interacting with a server that we have shown so far, to use this client you would make a call like

```
MultiplexedClient.py  ip_address_or_hostname_of_server  port_number
```

where `port_number` is the port monitored by the server for incoming client connections.

We next show a server script, `MultiplexedServer.py`, that also uses multiplexing for all file objects meant for reading. In this case, the number of sockets that will be multiplexed is controlled primarily by the argument to `listen()` in line (O) since that argument sets the maximum number of clients that are allowed to talk to the server at the same time. Of course, the socket container will always include the server socket, but then it will also contain one client socket for each client checking in. The server socket is placed in the socket container in line (W) and the individual client sockets, as they are formed, in the main `while` loop in line (l).

The script consists of two parts. In the first part, in lines (A) through (U), we set up the utilities and create a server socket as for our previous Python servers. The second part consists of a forever loop that starts with calling `select.select()` on the socket container in line (Z), extracting all the currently readable sockets and doing what is necessary for each readable socket in the rest of the `while` block.

The dictionary `clientnames` declared in line (X) is used for storing key-value pairs in which the keys are the client sockets spit out by the call to `accept()` in line (e) and the values the names that the clients wish to use when conversing with the server. So when `select()` subsequently identifies that a client socket is ready to go, we can retrieve the corresponding client name from the dictionary and prepend the name to the echo-back. Retrieval of the client name takes place in line (p), reading of the client message in line (q), and the echo back to the client in line (x). Since the reading of the client message in line (q) is through a blocking call to `recv()` in the `get_client_line()` method, if `recv()` returns with an empty string, that under normal conditions means that the client has terminated the connection. We check for this condition in line (r). If the connection with the client is indeed broken, we call `del()` in line (u) to delete from the `clientnames` dictionary the key-value pair corresponding to the client socket.

```
#!/usr/bin/env python

### MultiplexedServer.py

import sys, socket, time, os, signal, select                             #(A)

def prefix( message ):                                                   #(B)
    now = time.ctime()                                                   #(C)
    return "[%s] [%s] %s" % (now, os.getpid(), message)                  #(D)

def interrupt_sig_handler( signum, frame ):                              #(E)
    os.kill( os.getpid(), signal.SIGKILL )                               #(F)
signal.signal( signal.SIGINT,  interrupt_sig_handler )                   #(G)

client_sock = None                                                       #(H)

# Read one line from client.  Return empty string when EOF detected
def get_client_line(client_sock):                                        #(I)
    client_line = ''
    while 1:
        client_byte = client_sock.recv(1)
        if not client_byte:
            client_line = ''
            break
        elif client_byte == '\n' or client_byte == '\r':
            client_line += client_byte
            break
        else:
            client_line += client_byte
    return client_line                                                   #(J)

port = 9000                                                              #(K)

try:                                                                     #(L)
    server_sock = socket.socket(socket.AF_INET, socket.SOCK_STREAM) #(M)
    server_sock.bind( ('', port) )                                       #(N)
    server_sock.listen(5)                                                #(O)
except socket.error, (value, message):                                   #(P)
```

```
    if server_sock:                                                  #(Q)
        server_sock.close()                                          #(R)
    print "No server socket: %s" % prefix(message)                   #(S)
    sys.exit(1)                                                      #(T)

print "[Server %s accepting clients]" % sys.argv[0]                  #(U)

socket_container = []                                                #(V)
socket_container.append( server_sock )                               #(W)

clientnames = {}                                                     #(X)

while 1:                                                             #(Y)
    readable_sockets = \
              select.select( socket_container, [], [], 0 )[0]        #(Z)
    for file_object in readable_sockets:                             #(a)
        if file_object == server_sock:                               #(b)
            client_sock = None                                       #(c)
            while not client_sock:                                   #(d)
                client_sock, address = server_sock.accept()          #(e)
            message = \
              "[Request for connection from %s at client port %s]\n"\
                                                   % address         #(f)
            print prefix( message )                                  #(g)
            client_sock.send(
              "Welcome to server script %s running at %s" \
                          % (sys.argv[0], os.environ['HOST']) )      #(h)
            client_sock.send( "\nEnter your cyberspace name: " )     #(i)
            # get client name and get rid of the newline terminator:
            client_name = get_client_line( client_sock )[0:-1]       #(j)
            client_sock.send( "Hello %s\n\n" % client_name )         #(k)
            socket_container.append( client_sock )                   #(l)
            clientnames[client_sock] = client_name                   #(m)
        else:                                                        #(n)
            if not clientnames.has_key(file_object): continue        #(o)
            client_name = clientnames[ file_object ]                 #(p)
            client_line = get_client_line( file_object )             #(q)
            if not client_line:                                      #(r)
                closing_msg = "[Connection closed by %s from %s]\n" \
                          % (client_name, address[0])                #(s)
                print prefix(closing_msg)                            #(t)
                del( clientnames[file_object] )                      #(u)
            else:                                                    #(v)
                client_line = client_line[0:-1]                      #(w)
                file_object.send("%s: %s\n" % (client_name,  \
                                                 client_line))       #(x)

server_sock.close()                                                  #(y)
```

15.8 UDP SERVERS AND CLIENTS

We will now present the other approach for networking — the UDP-based approach. Using UDP requires a change in the mind-set you bring to bear on the problems related to the exchange of information in a network. As mentioned in the introduction to this chapter, TCP gives you the guarantee that the information transmitted will be received correctly and entirely if it is received at all. With UDP there are no such guarantees. A UDP-based communication link is more like a conversation among people who must always be thought of as imperfect listeners. You may ask a question, but you may not get a response if the listener is not paying attention or if the listener did not get the question because of excessive noise in the background. Nevertheless, what is surprising is that a simple, fast, and genuinely useful communication model can be built on top of such imperfect communications. After all, if you ask a question and you do not get a response, you can always ask the question again. Additionally, if you are giving a speech, you may consider it to be successful even if not all of the audience is paying attention, particularly if you have the expectation that those who got it will eventually propagate the word to those who did not. Along the same lines, for what is just one of the many applications of UDP, machines use the UDP-based approach to query domain-name servers for the IP addresses associated with the symbolic host names. When a query does not yield an answer within a certain time interval, the query is repeated. For the same application, UDP-based communication is also used for disseminating the mappings between the symbolic hostnames and the IP addresses from the central repositories of such mappings to other servers closer to the end users.

At the implementation level, perhaps the most significant difference between a TCP connection and a UDP communication link is that the latter has no need for a server-side listening socket. In a TCP connection, the continuously running listening socket on the server side monitors through a method usually called `accept()` a designated port for incoming client requests for connection. When a client checks in, it is the `accept()` method of the listening socket that spits out a regular socket for a two-way TCP-based communication link between the server and the client. Such server-side listening is not germane to the UDP communication model. With UDP, the sockets on the server side and the client side are completely symmetrical. If there is any difference at all between the two, it is that the server-side UDP socket must be on at all times so that it can respond to UDP clients.

Since the servers and clients have no guarantee that either's message will be received by the other, it would be easy for a UDP communication link to get stuck in a deadlock, unless of course precautions are taken to the contrary. Let's say that a client has sent a UDP request to a server. Now if the client carries out a blocking read for the server's response, the client may have to wait forever if the client's message failed to reach the server or the server's response got lost on its way to the client. This would be a deadlock for the client since, being stuck in a blocking read, it would not be able to repeat its request to the server. The solution, as you might guess, lies in subjecting the calls to blocking read functions to timeouts, as we will see in the scripts to follow.

15.8.1 UDP Sockets in Perl

A UDP socket in Perl can be established using the same `IO::Socket::INET` class as before. Here is the syntax for creating a UDP socket for a UDP server:

```
my $sock = IO::Socket::INET->new( LocalPort => 9000,              #(a)
                                  Reuse => 1,
                                  Proto => 'udp',
                                );
```

What is important here is that the `Proto` option sets the protocol as `udp`. But what really distinguishes this invocation of the `IO::Socket::INET` constructor for the case of a UDP socket from a similar invocation for the case of a TCP socket is that now we do not set the `Listen` option. A TCP server needs a listening socket that can spit out a regular socket for communicating with a client upon receiving a request-for-connection from the client. On the other hand, a UDP server socket is a regular socket unto itself — it does not need to create other sockets. In fact there is no difference between a server-side UDP socket and a client-side UDP socket. They both engage in very symmetrical send-a-message/receive-a-message communication pattern, except for the fact that the server-side socket must operate inside an infinite loop waiting for a datagram to be received, to which it can later respond.[57] Shown below is the basic control loop of a UDP server where the variable `$sock` is set by calling the `IO::Socket::INET` constructor as shown in line (a) above:

```
my ($mesg_in, $mesg_out);
while (1) {
    next unless $sock->recv( $mesg_in, MAX_MSG_LEN );              #(b)
    $mesg_out = .........                                          #(c)
    $sock->send( $mesg_out ) or die "send(): $!\n";                #(d)
}
```

The function of this UDP server is to receive a datagram through the call to `recv()` in line (b), store the datagram in the local variable `mesg_in`, constitute a response

[57] A *datagram* refers to a particular format for the data packets that are exchanged between the two end-points of a communication link. The first five or six 32-bit words of a datagram are called the *header*. The header contains all the information about the origin and the destination of the datagram. A datagram is fragmented into smaller units if its size exceeds what is known as the *maximum transmission unit* (MTU) for a network — typical value for MTU being 1500 bytes. When a UDP datagram is fragmented, the pieces are transmitted independently; the operating system at the receiving end tries to reassemble them back into what the datagram looked like at the sending end. If any of the pieces is missing, the entire datagram is discarded. Unlike TCP, no attempt is made at a retransmission of the datagram under such circumstances. This is one of the reasons why UDP communication works best when the messages are kept short, preferably shorter than the MTU. The MTU of a network can be found by using a command like `ifconfig` or `netstat`.

and store it in the variable mesg_out in line (c), and, finally, send the response back to the client by calling send() in line (d). The constant MAX_MSG_LEN specifies the maximum size of a datagram that the socket is willing to accept from a client. Should the datagram be longer, it is truncated to this maximum size.

To bring out the symmetry between the send-and-receive operations on the server side and the same operations on the client side, here is how the code for communicating through a UDP socket on the client side *could* look like:[58]

```
my $sock = IO::Socket::INET->new( Proto      => "udp",                  #(e)
                                  PeerAddr   => $host,
                                  PeerPort   => $port,
                                ) or die  $@;
my ($mesg_in, $mesg_out);
$mesg_out =  ...........
$sock->send( $mesg_out ) or die "send(): $!\n";                          #(f)
$sock->recv( $mesg_in, MAX_MSG_LEN ) or die "recv(): $!\n";              #(g)
print "$mesg_in\n";                                                       #(h)
```

So the basic socket usage syntax is identical between the server side and the client side. Of course, as mentioned previously, the receive call (and the send call also in most cases) on the server side must be made inside a while loop to wait for a client's datagram. Additionally, for obvious reasons, the server first invokes recv() and then responds with send(). On the other hand, a client first invokes send() to transmit a datagram to the server and then invokes recv() to receive the server's response.

Going back to the server-side calls in lines (b), (c), and (d) above, there does not appear to be an explicit mention of the client's address anywhere. So how does the server know in line (d) where to send the response that the client is expecting? The client's address is part of the datagram received by the server when recv() is called in line (b). In fact, while the actual text message from the client is stored away in the local variable $mesg_in in line (b), the function recv() itself returns the IP address of the client in packed binary form.[59] In simple applications of UDP sockets, the value returned by recv() in line (b) can be discarded because this value is implicitly stored away in some of the attributes of the instance of the

[58]In principle, a UDP socket can always be constructed without specifying a numeric value for the local port number to use, as shown in line (e) here. (Recall, the local port to use is specified with the LocalPort option. On the other hand, the port to use at the destination is specified with the PeerPort option.) But doing so only makes sense on the client side. When a client-side UDP socket is constructed without specifying a local port number, the system assigns to the client an *ephemeral port*; these are high-numbered ports reserved by the operating system for outgoing calls when the user does not mention a port number. Regarding UDP sockets on the server side, you'd want to specify a numeric value for the local port to use with the LocalPort option, as we did in line (a) at the beginning of this subsection, because that is a part of the server address the client needs to know. What is specified with the LocalPort option for a server socket becomes the port set with the PeerPort option for a client socket.

[59]Unless, of course, there was an error during the execution of recv(), in which case the function returns undef, with the error code stored in the special variable $!.

`IO::Socket::INET` class created in line (a). For example, the port used by the client can be retrieved by calling `$sock->peerport` and the symbolic host name of the client by calling `$sock->peerhost`. If the client's host name is not directly available, the IP address of the client can be retrieved by calling `$sock->peeraddr`. So the upshot is that in the server code fragment shown in lines (b), (c), and (d) above, the server implicitly knows where to send the response in line (d).

While the basic functioning of UDP server and client sockets is symmetric with respect to the send and receive calls, in practice a UDP client must also guard against conditions that might cause it to deadlock in the manner we mentioned earlier in the introduction to Section 15.8. To explain this deadlock condition with the code fragment shown in lines (f), (g), and (h) above, let's say the client first sends some message data to the server in line (f). This call will almost always succeed because all that `send()` does is to ask the operating system to queue up the message in its send buffer for onward transmission.[60] The call to `send()` returns the number of bytes actually queued up. Next, in line (g), the client invokes `recv()` for the response back from the receiver. *A most notable aspect of* `recv()` *is that it blocks until a datagram is received from the server.* So, should the client's datagram to the server or the server's response get lost for some reason, the client will continue to stay blocked for ever — a deadlock situation for the client. Therefore, it is best to set a timeout on this call. That way if a datagram is not received from the server within a specified time, the client can repeat the request to the server. The timeout on the `recv()` function call can be established with the help of Perl's built-in `alarm()` function.[61] When invoked with an argument set to a timeout period in seconds, a call to `alarm()` causes the operating system to issue the `SIGALRM` signal to the script at the end of the timeout period. For example, calling `alarm(10)` will cause the operating system to issue the `SIGALRM` signal to the script after exactly 10 seconds have elapsed. The call `alarm(0)` cancels any previous calls to `alarm()`.

We will next show two scripts, one for a UDP server and the other for a UDP client. Starting with the server script `UDPServer.pl` shown next, note that the lines (C), (I), and (O) of this script correspond to the statements shown in lines (a), (b), and (d) of the explanation above. We first construct a UDP server socket in line (C) and specify 9000 for the local port to use. Then we invoke `recv()` and `send()` inside an infinite loop in lines (I) and (O). When a message from a client is received, we retrieve the client's address and the port used by the client in lines (J) through (L). This is done purely in order to display this information in the terminal window on the server machine in line (M). We next synthesize a response to the client in line (N). This response is then shipped off to the client in line (O). The server and client scripts are based on the assumption that a client will send to the server messages like

```
N: What's my lucky number today?
```

[60] A successful return from a call to `send()`, therefore, carries no guarantee whatsoever that the message was placed on the network wire, much less delivered to its destination.

[61] The `alarm()` function was used previously in Section 13.7 of Chapter 13 to control the time interval between the presentation of the successive images in a slideshow controller script.

where N is set to 1 when the request is made for the first time. But should the client not hear back from the server within a certain timeout interval, the client resends the message with N set to 2. Each repeat transmission bumps up the value of N by one. (As we will show when we present the client-side script, the client gives up when N exceeds a preset bound.) The response from the server takes the form

```
(Request: M)(Client Send Sequence Num: N)  Your lucky number: XXX
```

where the value of N is the same as the integer at the beginning of the message received from the client. The server also keeps track of all of the messages it has received from all the clients out there; the value assigned to M is this number. It is this response that is put together in the different pieces of the statement that ends in line (N).

As to the reasons why we have chosen to index the repeat requests from a client and the number of requests processed by the server, we will explain that after presenting the client-side script. For now, here is the server:

```
#!/usr/bin/perl -w
use strict;

### UDPServer.pl

use IO::Socket;                                                      #(A)
use constant MAX_MSG_LEN => 2048;                                    #(B)

my $server_sock = IO::Socket::INET->new( LocalPort => 9000,          #(C)
                                         Reuse => 1,                 #(D)
                                         Proto => 'udp',             #(E)
                                       );
die "No UDP Server Socket: $@\n" unless $server_sock;                #(F)

my ($mesg_in, $mesg_out);                                            #(G)
my $i = 0;
while (1) {                                                          #(H)
    next unless $server_sock->recv( $mesg_in, MAX_MSG_LEN );         #(I)
    $i++;
    my $peerhost = gethostbyaddr( $server_sock->peeraddr, AF_INET )
        || $server_sock->peerhost;                                   #(J)
    my $peerport = $server_sock->peerport;                           #(K)
    my $length = length( $mesg_in );                                 #(L)
    my $client_send_sequence = $mesg_in =~ /^(\d+):/;
    warn "Received $length bytes from [$peerhost, $peerport]\n";     #(M)
    my $lucky_num = int rand 1000;
    $mesg_out = "(Request: $i)" .
                "(Client Send Sequence Num: $client_send_sequence)" .
                " Your lucky number: $lucky_num";                    #(N)
```

```
    $server_sock->send( $mesg_out ) or die "send(): $!\n";             #(O)
}
$server_sock->close;                                                    #(P)
```

We next present a UDP client to go with the UDPServer.pl server shown above. In relation to the server, the design of the client UDPClientWithTimeout.pl shown next is made slightly complex by the need to set a timeout on the call to recv() to deal with potential deadlocks that may be caused by delayed or lost datagrams, as explained previously. The client script first constructs a UDP socket in lines (F), (G), and (H). Note that we do not set the LocalPort option in the call to the constructor; it is unnecessary to do so on the client side for simple two-way client-server communications, as we explained earlier in a footnote in this section. As far as the server address is concerned, the socket is informed of those through the PeerAddr and PeerPort options. The client sends a message to the server by calling send() in line (M) and then waits for the server's response through the call to recv() in line (Q).

The most noteworthy aspect of the client is how it deals with the fact that recv() blocks until it receives a message from the server. To prevent this blocking property from creating the deadlock we mentioned earlier in this section, we associate a timeout with the call to recv(). This is accomplished with the help of a combination of Perl's alarm() function and the fact that, as explained in Section 10.2 of Chapter 10, we can use eval to trap a run-time exception, with the text message associated with the exception stored in the special variable $@.

The first thing we do inside eval in lines (N) through (V) is to define a signal handler for the SIGALRM signal. As was mentioned earlier in this section, the operating system will issue the SIGALRM signal to the client at the termination of the timeout interval supplied to the alarm() function in line (P). You can say that the call in line (P) sets the alarm and the alarm goes off at the end of TIMEOUT by raising the SIGALRM signal. Next, we invoke recv() in line (Q). If this call returns within TIMEOUT seconds, we turn off the alarm by calling alarm(0) in line (R). But if a datagram is not received within the timeout interval, the operating system will raise the SIGALRM signal and place the eval execution in an error state. The signal will be trapped by the signal handler of line (O). The signal handler will increment the $retries variable and, through the invocation of die, will cause immediate exit from the eval code block, while at the same time setting the global variable $@ to the error message put out by die.[62] In our case, the error message will be exactly the string that is supplied as the argument to die. Subsequently, the flow of execution will shift to the if block of line (T). This will cause a message to be printed out on

[62] It is important that the string argument supplied to die in line (O) terminates in the newline character \n. As explained in Section 10.1 of Chapter 10, without this newline terminator, the error message output by the call to die will include the name of the script file and the line number of the statement that invoked die.

the client console and initiate another iteration of the `while` loop that starts in line (L).

```
#!/usr/bin/perl -w
use strict;

### UDPClientWithTimeout.pl

use IO::Socket;                                                          #(A)
use constant MAX_MSG_LEN => 2048;                                        #(B)
use constant TIMEOUT => 5;
use constant MAX_RETRIES => 10;

die "usage: $0 host port" unless @ARGV == 2;                             #(C)

my $host = shift @ARGV;                                                  #(D)
my $port = shift @ARGV;                                                  #(E)

my $sock = IO::Socket::INET->new( Proto      => "udp",                   #(F)
                                  PeerAddr   => $host,                   #(G)
                                  PeerPort   => $port,                   #(H)
                                )
                 or die $@;                                              #(I)
my $mesg_in;                                                             #(J)
my $retries = 1;                                                         #(K)

my $send_sequence_num = 1;
while ($retries < MAX_RETRIES ) {                                        #(L)
    $sock->send("$send_sequence_num: What's my lucky number today?")
                 or die "send() failed: $!";                             #(M)
    ++$send_sequence_num;
    eval {                                                               #(N)
        local $SIG{ALRM} = sub { ++$retries and die "timeout\n" };       #(O)
        alarm(TIMEOUT);                                                  #(P)
        $sock->recv( $mesg_in, MAX_MSG_LEN )
                          or die "recv() failed: $!";                    #(Q)
        alarm(0);                                                        #(R)
        print "$mesg_in\n";                                              #(S)
    };
    if ( $@ eq "timeout\n" ) {                                           #(T)
        print "recv() timed out. Trying send() again " .
                 "with send sequence num: $send_sequence_num\n";         #(U)
    } else { last }                                                      #(V)
}
```

We now present the reasons why we chose to include an integer index in each client-to-server message and two integer indices in the replies sent by the server. Recall that a `UDPClientWithTimeout.pl` client sends messages of the following form to the server:

```
N: What's my lucky number today?
```

where `N` is the integer index that is incremented in a new request to the server if no response is received to the previous request within a timeout period. Also recall that the server `UDPServer.pl` responds back with a message of the following form:

```
(Request: M)(Client Send Sequence Num: N)  Your lucky number: XXX
```

where the integer index `N` has the same value as in the client message to which the server is responding and where the second integer index `M` is for keeping track of the total number of client requests (from all clients) the server has responded to so far.

Obviously, we could have written the server and the client scripts without prefixing the messages with the labels in the manner shown. Using the labels allows one to see the consequences of delayed or missing datagrams and also points to how by attaching identification labels with the messages, one might deal with UDPs lack of reliability guarantee. Experimenting with reliability problems caused by network delays is particularly easy when the server is running on a Unix-like platform. All you have to do is to fire up the server as a foreground process and then suspend its execution by entering Ctrl-Z on the keyboard. When a client sends its messages to the server in its suspended state, the operating system on the server side will queue up the client requests. So the console on the client side will display a status message for each repeated request to the server. These status messages will look like

```
recv() timed out. Trying send() again with send sequence num: 2
recv() timed out. Trying send() again with send sequence num: 3
recv() timed out. Trying send() again with send sequence num: 4
recv() timed out. Trying send() again with send sequence num: 5
recv() timed out. Trying send() again with send sequence num: 6
```

Subsequently, when you resume the server process, the server will respond to all queued-up requests. Its response back to the client for the first queued-up request will be seen by the client as the following message:

```
(Request: 1)(Client Send Sequence Num: 1) Your lucky number: 704
```

which assumes that all the client datagrams reached the server and that the client datagrams were queued up on the server side in the same order in which they were sent by the client. This would ordinarily be the case in small local networks. But, obviously, in a large network there would be no guarantee that the client messages would arrive at the server in any particular order and some of them may never arrive at all. The client will see messages similar to the above for at least some of the other queued-up requests at the server end. By examining the two integer indices in the responses received by the client, one can get some sense of the reliability of a particular server-client communication link.

15.8.2 UDP Sockets in Python

As mentioned in the introduction to Section 15.8, you do not need a listening socket on the server side with UDP. Besides the lack of listening sockets in UDP, the additional significant difference between the TCP and the UDP sockets is that whereas with the former you make repeated calls to the send and the receive methods until all the data is transferred, with the latter you make a single call to the send method to transmit the entire datagram and a single call to the receive method to receive the same.

We also stated in the introduction to Section 15.8 that the server and the client sockets under UDP are identical. However, as explained earlier, the order in which the send and the receive methods are invoked on them on the client side is opposite of the order in which the same methods are invoked on the server side. On the server side, the server stays blocked in a call to the receive method. When a client datagram is received, the receive method returns with the message and the client's socket number. Subsequently, the server sends to the client, using the received socket number as the destination address, its response to the client query. The client, on the other hand, first invokes its send method to transmit a query to the server and then stays blocked in its receive method to wait for the server's response.

Shown below is a Python UDP server that, upon receiving a request for a lucky number from a client, sends back a random number to the client. We construct a UDP socket in lines (I) and (J). Note the second argument to the socket constructor, the constant `socket.SOCK_DGRAM`, that tells the system that this will be a UDP socket. The forever loop in lines (Q) through (e) then waits in the blocking call to `recvfrom()` in line (R) for clients to send their datagrams. When a client datagram is received, `recvfrom()` returns a tuple whose first element is the datagram payload (that is, the actual message sent by the client) and the second element the client's socket number. Line (U) extracts from the client socket number the IP address of the client and the port used by the client at its own end.

To make sense of the rest of the server script, note that (as with the Perl UDP server) this UDP server is based on the assumption that the client will send to the server a query string that looks like

```
N: What's my lucky number today?
```

where `N` is set to 1 for the first request from the client. This number is incremented for each subsequent request if the client does not hear back from the server within a certain timeout interval. Lines (W) through (a) of the script extract this number from the beginning of a client request. This number and the number that the server uses to keep track of all received client requests (the number stored in the variable `i`) are used to synthesize a response string in line (d). This response string sent back to the client looks like

```
(Request: M)(Client Send Sequence Num: N)  Your lucky number: XXX
```

where the integer index N has the same value as in the client message to which the server is responding and where the second integer index M is for keeping track of the total number of client requests (from all clients) the server has responded to so far.[63] This response string is sent back to the client in line (e). Note the two-argument invocation of sendto() in line (e). It is the second argument to this method that informs the socket about the destination address for the message in the first argument.

```
#!/usr/bin/env python

### UDPServer.py

import sys, socket, os, signal, re, random                           #(A)

def interrupt_sig_handler( signum, frame ):                          #(B)
    os.kill( os.getpid(), signal.SIGKILL )                           #(C)
signal.signal( signal.SIGINT,  interrupt_sig_handler )               #(D)

ran = random.Random()                                                #(E)

port = 9000                                                          #(F)
MAX_MSG_LEN = 2048                                                   #(G)

try:                                                                 #(H)
    server_sock = socket.socket(socket.AF_INET, socket.SOCK_DGRAM)   #(I)
    server_sock.bind( ('', port) )                                   #(J)
except socket.error, (value, message):                               #(K)
    if server_sock:                                                  #(L)
        server_sock.close()                                          #(M)
    print "No server socket: %s" % message                           #(N)
    sys.exit(1)                                                      #(O)

i = 0;                                                               #(P)
while 1:                                                             #(Q)
    mesg_in, client = server_sock.recvfrom( MAX_MSG_LEN )            #(R)
    if not mesg_in: continue                                         #(S)
    i += 1                                                           #(T)
    peerhost, peerport = client                                      #(U)
    length = len( mesg_in )                                          #(V)
    m = re.search( r'^(\d+):', mesg_in )                             #(W)
```

[63]For a reader skipping through the book, see the discussion at the end of the previous subsection for why we chose to include the two integer indices in the server's response to a client.

```
    if m != None:                                                    #(X)
        client_send_sequence = m.group(1)                            #(Y)
    else:                                                            #(Z)
        client_send_sequence = ''                                    #(a)
    print "Received %s bytes from [%s, %s]" \
                                  % (length, peerhost, peerport)     #(b)
    lucky_num = ran.randint( 0, 1000 )                               #(c)
    mesg_out = "[Request: %s] " % i + \
               "[Client Send Sequence Num: %s] " \
                                  % client_send_sequence + \
               " Your lucky number: %s" % lucky_num                  #(d)
    server_sock.sendto( mesg_out, client )                           #(e)

server_sock.close()                                                  #(f)
```

The script shown next, `UDPClient.py`, is a UDP client that goes with the server shown above. The socket itself is created using essentially the same syntax in lines (E) and (F) as we used for the server in the script above, the main difference being that the call to `bind()` on the server side is replaced by the call to `connect()` on the client side.[64] After the socket is established, the interaction with the server is carried out with the call to `send()` and `recv()` in lines (L) and (M). Note in particular that we could also have used the following syntax for the statement in line (M):

```
    message, address = sock.recvfrom( MAX_MSG_LEN )
```

This is identical to the receive syntax used on the server side. As indicated earlier, this method returns a pair of items consisting of the message followed by the socket number of the sender.

```
#!/usr/bin/env python

### UDPClient.py

import sys, socket, select, signal                                   #(A)

if len(sys.argv) != 3:                                               #(B)
    sys.exit( "Need exactly two command line arguments, the " +
              "first naming the host and the second the port" )
```

[64]Actually the call to `connect()` in line (F) is not necessary here if we replace the call to `send()` in line (L) by a call to `sendto()` as shown below

```
    sock.sendto( "What's the lucky number today?", (host, port) )
```

Note that now the send method has two arguments, with the second argument, a tuple, representing the socket number of the server.

```
MAX_MSG_LEN = 2048                                                  #(C)

host, port = sys.argv[1], int(sys.argv[2])                          #(D)

try:
    sock = socket.socket( socket.AF_INET, socket.SOCK_DGRAM )       #(E)
    sock.connect( (host, port) )                                    #(F)
except socket.error, (value, message):                              #(G)
    if sock:                                                        #(H)
        sock.close()                                                #(I)
    print "Could not establish a client socket: " + message         #(J)
    sys.exit(1)                                                     #(K)

sock.send( "What's the lucky number today?" )                       #(L)

message = sock.recv( MAX_MSG_LEN )                                  #(M)
print message                                                       #(N)
```

The client script shown above suffers from a serious shortcoming. For reasons stated in the introduction to Section 15.8, this UDP client has the potential of getting deadlocked if the client's query fails to reach the server or the server's response fails to reach the client. In either case, the client will stay blocked indefinitely in the call to the receive method in line (M) of the above script.

We can get around this problem by subjecting the receive call to a timeout, as in the script `UDPClientWithTimeout.py` shown next. With the `socket` module, the timeout attribute of a socket can be set by calling `settimeout()` with its argument set to the timeout interval in seconds, as we show in line (M) of the next script. As a consequence, when the server's response in not received within `TIMEOUT` seconds, the call to `recv()` in line (T) throws the `socket.timeout` exception, which we trap in line (U). Trapping of the `timeout` exception causes the message of line (V) to be printed out on the client's terminal and the call to `continue` in line (W) sends the thread of execution back to the conditional of the `for` loop in line (O).

As with the Perl version of this script, to see the client repeatedly query the server (up to a maximum of `MAX_RETRIES` times) if the server's answer is not received within `TIMEOUT` seconds of each transmission to the server, fire up as a foreground process either the Perl or the Python version of the UDP server shown earlier. Now enter Ctrl-Z in the server terminal to suspend the server temporarily. Next invoke the client script on some other machine with a command line like

```
UDPClientWithTimeout.py  hostname_or_ip_address_of_server  port_num
```

When a UDP client sends a message to the server in its suspended state, the operating system on the server side queues up the requests. If you keep the server suspended for more than 5 seconds, the client-side socket will timeout repeatedly through multiple iterations of the loop in lines (O) through (Y) of the script below. The client will send a fresh query to the server after each timeout, with the variable `send_sequence_num` incremented for each fresh request. If you revive the server before the end of the `MAX_RETRIES` number of iterations of the `for` loop in the script below, the server will respond to each of the queued up requests on its side. As the script is written below, only the first of these to arrive back at the client side is accepted by the client (since the client script terminates after the receipt of the first response). As the server sends back to the client the value of the integer stored in `send_sequence_num`, we can tell by the response printed out in line (X) as to which of the queued up requests on the server side was processed first by the server.

```
#!/usr/bin/env python

###  UDPClientWithTimeout.py

import sys, socket, select, signal                                      #(A)

MAX_MSG_LEN = 2048                                                      #(B)
TIMEOUT = 5                                                             #(C)
MAX_RETRIES = 10                                                        #(D)

if len(sys.argv) != 3:
    sys.exit( "Need exactly two command line arguments, the " +
              "first naming the host and the second the port" )

host, port = sys.argv[1], int(sys.argv[2])                              #(E)

try:
    sock = socket.socket( socket.AF_INET, socket.SOCK_DGRAM )           #(F)
    sock.connect( (host, port) )                                        #(G)
except socket.error, (value, message):                                  #(H)
    if sock:                                                            #(I)
        sock.close()                                                    #(J)
    print "Could not establish a client socket: " + message             #(K)
    sys.exit(1)                                                         #(L)

sock.settimeout( TIMEOUT )                                              #(M)
send_sequence_num = 1                                                   #(N)

for retry in range( 1, MAX_RETRIES ):                                   #(O)
    sock.send("%s: What's my lucky number today?"%send_sequence_num)#(P)
    send_sequence_num += 1                                              #(Q)
    mesg_in = None                                                      #(R)
    try:                                                                #(S)
        mesg_in = sock.recv( MAX_MSG_LEN )                              #(T)
    except socket.timeout, message:                                     #(U)
```

```
        print "recv() timed out. Trying send() again " + \
                    "with send sequence num: %s" % send_sequence_num#(V)
        continue                                                    #(W)
    print mesg_in                                                   #(X)
    break                                                           #(Y)
```

15.9 BROADCASTING WITH UDP

Broadcasting in Internet communications means to send information to the *broadcast address* of a subnetwork. A subnetwork — also called *subnet* for short — is defined by its network address, which as explained below, is the common stem of the IP addresses of all the machines in a portion of the network that is connected to the same router. The information sent to the broadcast address will, in general, be seen by all the machines in the subnet. Such information is not allowed to leave the boundaries of the subnet.[65]

As mentioned at the beginning of this chapter, every machine connected to a network has an IP (Internet Protocol) address, which under the IP version 4 (IPv4) protocol is a 32-bit address and under IP version 6 (IPv6) a 128-bit address.[66] An IP address consists of two parts: the *network part* and the *host part.* To illustrate with an IPv4 example, a typical machine in the author's laboratory has an IP address that looks like `128.46.144.10`. The network portion of this address is `128.46.144` and the host portion just 10. The separation of an IP address into its network and host portions is carried out with the help of what is known as the *subnet mask.* In its binary representation, the subnet mask for a network has 1's in all the positions that correspond to the network address and 0's in the rest of the positions. So for the network that resides in the author's laboratory, the subnet mask would be `255.255.255.0`.[67]

---

[65] Another way of saying the same thing would be that broadcasting is limited to a local subnet. That is, the packets that are broadcast cannot cross subnet boundaries because the routers are prohibited from passing on such packets to other routers.

[66] A more precise way of saying this is that every *network interface* must have a distinct IP address. A network interface may come in the form of a separate *network interface card* (NIC) or a *wireless adapter card* or in the form of a software module that performs similar functions. The basic role of a network interface is to prepare the data for placing it on the network "wire" and to control the flow of data between the computer and the rest of the network. (For low-level communications, an interface is also characterized with a unique address called the MAC address. MAC stands for Media Access Control.) A machine may contain multiple interfaces if it is simultaneously connected to multiple networks or if it serves as a gateway between two or more networks. Such a machine would obviously possess multiple IP addresses, one for each of its interfaces.

[67] It may seem as if the subnet mask is a redundant piece of information. One might think that a router should be able to locate a machine from its IP address and the network address, without also

The *broadcast address* of a subnet is the IP address of any of the machines in that subnet but with all the host bits set to 1. So the broadcast address for the subnet that resides in the author's laboratory is 128.46.144.255. If we were to further divide the lab network into two subnets by using the subnet mask 255.255.255.128, the broadcast addresses of the two newly created subnets would be 128.46.144.127 and 128.46.144.255.

When a machine sends information to the broadcast address of a subnet, that information is seen by all the broadcast-capable network interfaces in the subnet. It is true that, at least in ethernet-based networks, all of the packets in a given network are seen by all the network interfaces anyway. But, in such networks, a network interface accepts only those unicast[68] packets that are intended specifically for it. On the other hand, a broadcast-capable network interface does not apply any such filtering to the broadcast packets. The interface passes on such packets without filtering to the operating system of the machine to which the interface is attached.[69]

15.9.1 UDP Broadcasting in Perl

We now present a broadcast server and a broadcast client in Perl. The broadcast server script, BroadcastServer.pl, presented next calls on the IO::Socket::INET's constructor in line (B) to return a UDP socket. Unlike a typical TCP/IP or UDP

---

needing the subnet mask. But not really. Whereas the network address 128.46.144 would get the packets into the author's laboratory, but what if we decided to carve out two subnets from the lab network, which we could do by deciding to use a subnet mask of 255.255.255.128 in a router in the lab? The subnet mask 255.255.255.128 would help the local router figure out that there are two subnets operating in the lab and the router will forward the packets accordingly. Similarly, a subnet mask of 255.255.255.192 would tell the router that the lab network has been divided into four subnets. *Note that routers, critical to the hierarchical organization of the Internet, only recognize network addresses and not the individual computer addresses.* In a hierarchical resolution of the IP addresses, the routers recognize the network portions of the addresses with the help of the subnet masks. The router to which your computer is connected only talks to other routers; it does not talk to the remote computers directly. A router works at the *network layer* of the TCP/IP stack of the Internet protocols.

[68] *Unicasting* implies the transmission of information from a specific sender to a specific receiver. For example, a TCP/IP or a UDP based connection between a server and a client amounts to unicasting. Broadcasting, on the other hand, assumes that the sender has no single recipient in mind. A broadcasting sender will go ahead and send out the information to whomsoever wishes to receive it in the network.

[69] In comparing unicasting with broadcasting, we should also mention that unicasting is inefficient and wasteful of network capacity when the same information needs to be sent to a large number of machines in the same subnet. With unicasting, the sender will use some kind of a loop to send the same file to the different IP addresses. As a result, for the case of, say, distributing video in a local network, with unicasting you could end up with the same video frames coursing through the subnet over and over. This duplication is avoided with broadcasting. When a video is broadcast in a local network, each frame will traverse the network only once and all the parties interested in picking up the information will do so. An additional advantage of broadcasting is that it gives a measure of anonymity to the receivers of the information. Broadcasting is also useful for the resource discovery that is needed by a machine that wants to use DHCP (Dynamic Host Configuration Protocol) to obtain an IP address, the subnet mask, the default gateway, etc. from a DHCP server.

server, we do *not* set the `LocalPort` option for the socket. In the simple example shown here, no particular benefit would be derived by asking the server to use a specific local port. After all, the clients interested in catching the broadcasts are *not* going to be making connections with the server. So we are happy with whatever port is assigned to the server by the system — usually a high-numbered ephemeral port[70] — for use locally to send out the broadcasts. To convert the UDP socket just constructed into a broadcast socket, line (D) sets the `SO_BROADCAST()` option of the socket to true by calling the `sockopt()` method.

Although we do not care what port the server uses locally for the outgoing broadcasts, we do want the server to send the broadcasts to a specific port on the destination machines. That port number, 9000 in the example script, is specified in line (E). As was mentioned in a footnote in Section 15.5.1, the call to `inet_aton()` in line (E) converts the address in its dotted-quad form into the binary representation. The call to `sockaddr_in()` in the same line then yields the broadcast socket number that combines the destination port number with the broadcast IP address. The broadcast socket number thus constructed is then supplied to the `send()` function through the `$dest` variable in line (K).

As can be seen in line (E), we used for broadcast address the special all-one's address `255.255.255.255` as opposed to a more typical broadcast address like `128.46.144.255`. The all-one's address is supposed to act like a broadcast address. As with the true broadcast address, the packets sent to the all-one's address are seen by all the broadcast-capable interfaces in a subnet and such packets are not forwarded by a router to other routers.[71] It is obviously more convenient to use the all-one's as the broadcast address because it eliminates the need to know what part of the IP addresses in a given subnet corresponds to the network address of the subnet.

About the rest of the script shown below, note that unlike the UDP servers presented previously, the broadcast server does not wait for a client question before responding with an answer. In the `while` loop in lines (H) through (M), the server simply broadcasts the following announcement every 5 seconds:

```
[N]  Hark! The king hath arrived!\n";
```

where the integer `N` is incremented with each fresh broadcast of the message. Including this integer in the outgoing messages allows one to see whether or not all of the broadcasts are received by a client.

---

[70] We talked about ephemeral ports earlier in a footnote in Section 15.8.1 of this chapter.

[71] Using the all-one's address for broadcast may have unforeseen effects if the broadcasting machine is *multi-homed*, meaning that if such a machine has multiple network interfaces, each belonging to a different subnet. Such a machine may broadcast to all the subnets or to just one that is designated as the default choice for broadcasts.

```
#!/usr/bin/perl -w
use strict;

### BroadcastServer.pl

use IO::Socket;                                                    #(A)

my $sock = IO::Socket::INET->new( Proto => 'udp' );                #(B)
die "No UDP Server Socket: $@\n" unless $sock;                     #(C)
$sock->sockopt( SO_BROADCAST() => 1 ) or die "sockopt: $!";        #(D)

my $dest = sockaddr_in( 9000, inet_aton( '255.255.255.255' ) );    #(E)
my $msg_broadcast;                                                 #(F)
my $msg_id = 1;                                                    #(G)
while (1) {                                                        #(H)
    $msg_broadcast = "[$msg_id]  Hark! The king hath arrived!\n";  #(I)
    print "broadcasting message of id: $msg_id\n";                 #(J)
    send( $sock, $msg_broadcast, 0, $dest ) or die "send(): $!";   #(K)
    sleep( 5 );                                                    #(L)
    $msg_id++;                                                     #(M)
}
$sock->close;                                                      #(N)
```

If the all-one's as the broadcast address in line (E) does not work for your network, you might try replacing that line with something like:

```
my $dest = sockaddr_in( 9000, inet_aton( '128.46.144.255' ) );
```

where we have used the actual network address followed by all-one's for just the local portion.

We will next show a client to go with the above server. The most notable thing about the client shown next, `BroadcastClient.pl`, is that the socket constructor uses the `LocalPort` option, as opposed to the `PeerPort` option. We want the client to listen on this port for the incoming *broadcasts*.

```
#!/usr/bin/perl -w
use strict;

### BroadcastClient.pl

use IO::Socket;                                                    #(A)
use constant MAX_MSG_LEN => 1024;                                  #(B)
```

```
my $sock = IO::Socket::INET->new( LocalPort  => '9000',                #(C)
                                  Proto      => "udp",                 #(D)
                                )
                     or die $@;                                         #(E)
my $mesg_in;                                                            #(F)
while (1) {                                                             #(G)
    $sock->recv( $mesg_in, MAX_MSG_LEN ) or die "recv(): $!";           #(H)
    print "$mesg_in\n";                                                 #(I)
}
```

To experiment with the server and client scripts, all you have to do is to fire up the server by calling

```
BroadcastServer.pl
```

The clients can now be fired up *on other computers* in the local network with the command line

```
BroadcastClient.pl
```

15.9.2 UDP Broadcasting in Python

The broadcast server in Python we show next is based on the same logic as the previously shown Perl broadcast server. We want the server socket to broadcast a message in the local subnet every 5 seconds. The server socket is happy to use any port that is assigned to it by the operating system for the outgoing messages. However, we do want the server to target the messages to a specific port on the client machines; in our case it is port 9000.

We first construct a UDP socket in line (C). Since it is the `bind()` method that tells a server which port to use for outgoing messages, the call `bind(('',0))` in line (D), with its port argument set to 0, gives the server the freedom to use any free port for broadcasting. The constructed socket is declared to be a broadcast socket by the call to `setsockopt()` in line (J). The first argument to `setsockopt()` specifies the level at which the option listed in the second argument is to be applied. In our case, we want to apply the option at the socket level itself (as opposed to, say, the protocol level). This is done by setting the first argument to `SOL_SOCKET`. The second argument names the option that is to be set or unset. Since we want to turn the socket into a broadcast socket, we name the option as `SO_BROADCAST` in the second argument. The third argument then sets the option of the second argument to `True`.

To take care of the requirement that we want the broadcasts to land at port 9000 of the subnet machines, we construct the destination address as shown in line (K). Note especially the angle-bracket delimited keyword <broadcast> in this construction.

The destination address constructed in line (K), which in effect is the broadcast socket number, is then supplied to the `sendto()` method in line (P).

As with the Perl broadcast server, we want the periodically repeated outgoing messages to carry an integer prefix indicating the transmission number. This is done so that a client can tell which specific broadcasts it is receiving. The message integer prefix in the script below is stored in the variable `mesg_id` and inserted into the outgoing messages in line (N).

```
#!/usr/bin/env python

### BroadcastServer.py

import sys, socket, time                                                #(A)

try:                                                                    #(B)
    server_sock = socket.socket(socket.AF_INET, socket.SOCK_DGRAM)    #(C)
    server_sock.bind( ('', 0) )                                         #(D)
except socket.error, (value, message):                                  #(E)
    if server_sock:                                                     #(F)
        server_sock.close()                                             #(G)
    print "No UDP server socket: %s" % message                          #(H)
    sys.exit(1)                                                         #(I)

server_sock.setsockopt(socket.SOL_SOCKET, socket.SO_BROADCAST, True)#(J)

dest = '<broadcast>', 9000                                              #(K)

msg_id = 1                                                              #(L)

while 1:                                                                #(M)
    msg_broadcast = "[%s]  Hark! The king hath arrived!\n" % msg_id #(N)
    print "broadcasting message of id: %s" % msg_id                     #(O)
    server_sock.sendto( msg_broadcast, dest )                           #(P)
    time.sleep( 5 )                                                     #(Q)
    msg_id += 1                                                         #(R)
```

Shown below is a Python client for the broadcast server. The call to `bind()` in line (D) ensures that the client will listen on port 9000 for incoming messages. The blocking call to `recv()` in line (F) retrieves a message whenever it shows up at that port.

```
#!/usr/bin/env python

###  BroadcastClient.py

import socket                                                       #(A)

MAX_MSG_LEN = 1024                                                  #(B)

sock = socket.socket(socket.AF_INET, socket.SOCK_DGRAM)             #(C)
sock.bind( ('', 9000) )                                             #(D)

while 1:                                                            #(E)
    mesg_in = sock.recv( MAX_MSG_LEN )                              #(F)
    print mesg_in                                                   #(G)
```

15.10 MULTICASTING WITH UDP

Examined from a user's perspective, a multicast transport service works very much like television or radio. At least in theory, you should be able to set up a multicasting server at any point in the Internet, and any machine anywhere else in the network should be able to receive the transmitted information merely by the act of joining the multicast group associated with the server. In analogy with television and radio, the sender of the information does not care to know who the recipients are.[72] A multicast group is not limited to a local area network. At least in principle, any one from anywhere should be able to join a multicast group and participate in intragroup many-to-many communications. This sets multicasting apart from Internet broadcasting that we presented in the previous section. As we mentioned there, routers are prohibited from forwarding broadcast packets outside of their network boundaries, which limits broadcasting to specific network boundaries.[73]

Multicasting uses the network bandwidth much more efficiently because a packet meant for multiple recipients is sent out as a single packet. If you are multicasting a

[72]Because of there being no need for a sender to know the recipients' identities, multicast datagrams are sent using UDP.

[73]If the routers are multicast-capable, one can, of course, use multicasting in a local area network, meaning a network of computers with the same network address. (See the previous section for what is meant by the network portion of an Internet address.) The multicast information in a local area network will be sent by the router to only those machines that have subscribed to the service. As the reader will recall from the previous section, the broadcast information on a local area network, on the other hand, is seen by *all* the machines in the local area network.

video stream to, say, 1000 subscribers, the routers — if they are multicast-capable — will figure out the best routing so that no more than one stream is traveling through any segment of the network that contains one or more subscribers, and no packets at all are sent to those segments of the network that do not contain any subscribers. Compare this to the case of unicasting a video stream to 1000 IP addresses. Now for each destination IP address, there will be a separate video stream coursing its way through the network. That could cause a 1000-fold increase in the network bandwidth requirement on some of the physical links (especially those that are immediate to the source node) for maintaining the same real-time quality of service as when only a single stream is sent from the source.[74] With multicasting, on the other hand, network traffic is not duplicated to the maximum extent possible. If the 1000 subscribers all happen to be in the same network at the receiving end of the transmission, the video stream will not be duplicated until it reaches the destination routers.

To work as intended, multicasting obviously depends on the ability of the routers to keep track of the subscribers and, working collectively, to map out the optimum multicast routing topologies.[75] When a new subscriber joins a multicast group, the subscriber's machine sends an IGMP (Internet Group Management Protocol) membership message to a multicast-capable router to which the machine is connected. From that point on, it is that router's responsibility to locate the incoming multicast packets for the subscriber (and for all other local subscribers with membership in the same group).[76]

The routers engaged in delivering multicast traffic must execute a multicast routing protocol. Working in concert with a group management protocol (such as IGMP for IPv4), a multicast routing protocol enables a router to establish with the other routers a tree topology for the delivery of a sender's datagrams to the members of a multicast group. The best known of these protocols are DVMRP (Distance Vector Multicast Routing Protocol), PIM (Protocol Independent Multicasting), and MOSPF (Multicast Open Shortest Path First). The oldest of these protocols, DVMRP, associates a time-to-live (TTL) field with a multicast packet. The value of the TTL field determines how many routers a multicast packet is allowed to cross. Each transmission through a router decrements the TTL by one; the packets with TTL values of zero are ignored.[77] Under the DVMRP protocol, a source-based delivery tree is constructed by the root

---

[74] Imagine the consequences of such large-scale duplication in network traffic on costly transcontinental physical links.

[75] Since multicast addressing is built into the IPv6 protocol, any router that recognizes IPv6 will be automatically enabled for multicasting. However, with regard to IPv4, multicast addressing was added on to the protocol after it was already in widespread use. As a result, many IPv4 routers even today are not enabled for multicasting. And some IPv4 routers may only be able to send multicast IP packets, but not receive them. Routers with no multicasting support simply discard all multicast traffic.

[76] IGMP is for IPv4 only. The corresponding group management protocol for IPv6 is MLD (Multicast Listener Discovery).

[77] This also implies that a packet originating from a host with a TTL of 0 stays confined to that host. A TTL of one, which by the way is the default, for a new multicast packet means that the packet will be restricted to the same subnet in which the packet originates.

router (the router whose subnet contains the multicast source) *flooding* all destination routers with an outbound multicast packet. Starting with the "leaf" routers, the destination routers that do not contain any subscribers in their subnets return *prune messages* back toward the root router. During this backward propagation of the prune messages, when a prune message is received from a router, the subnet connected to that router is pruned away from the delivery tree. The DVMRP approach works well when there are only a small number of routers and a small number of multicast groups. The fact that each router must remember how it relates to its neighboring routers for each multicast source — referred to as having *to maintain state* for each sender — simply does not scale up to arbitrarily large and complex networks with an arbitrarily large number of multicast groups and an arbitrarily large number of senders within those groups. The other protocols, PIM and MOSPF, attempt to eliminate some of these shortcomings of DVMRP.

A multicast IP address signifies a group. These addresses, each 32 bits long under IPv4, range from `224.0.0.0` to `239.255.255.255`. These are also known as the class D addresses. A class D address is identified by the first 4 bits of the address being `1110`. The rest of a class D address — 28 bits — is referred to as the group ID of the multicast group that the address represents.[78] The 255 addresses in the range `224.0.0.1` and `224.0.0.255` are reserved mostly for administrative tasks. A multicast message sent to most of these 255 addresses will not cross subnet boundaries. Of these, `224.0.0.1` is known as the "all-hosts" group. A message sent to this address is forwarded by the router to all the hosts in the same subnet in which the source resides. In that sense, multicasting to the address `224.0.0.1` amounts to broadcasting as described in the previous section.

Since, in general, a multicast IP address signifies a group, a class designed specifically for multicast socket programming must provide methods for joining a group and departing from it. In addition, such a class must also allow one to set the TTL field of the outgoing packets. Obviously, if we wanted a multicast to stay confined to the local area network, we would use a value of 1 for the TTL. If, on the other hand, we want a multicast to cross local area subnet boundaries but stay confined to, say, a corporate network, we would use a larger value of TTL, the exact number depending on the "depth" of the network when viewed as a hierarchy of nodes in which the leaf nodes are the hosts and the interior nodes the routers.

---

[78]These multicast addresses are for IPv4. Under IPv6, the 128 bits of a multicast address are divided into four fields. The first field is 8 bits long; it must be all 1's for an IPv6 address to be recognized as a multicast address. The second field, 4 bits long, signifies the degree of permanency of the address. The third field, also 4 bits long, declares the scope of the address. The remaining 112 bits contain the group ID of a multicast group. Unlike the unicast IP addresses, a multicast IP address cannot be separated into a network portion and a host portion.

15.10.1 Multicasting in Perl

We will next show two scripts by Lincoln Stein [62], one for a multicast server and the other for a multicast client. These are based on Stein's `IO::Socket::Multicast` class that is derived from the `IO::Socket::INET` class that we used in several of the scripts shown so far. The `IO::Socket::Multicast` class makes it easy to join a multicast group, to drop one's group membership, to set the TTL of the outgoing messages, to choose the interface to use for outgoing multicast datagrams for multihomed machines, etc. By default, a socket constructed with `IO::Socket::Multicast` is based on the UDP protocol.

In the multicast server script shown below, we construct a UDP socket in lines (C) and (D) and set its `PeerAddr` option to the multicast destination address shown in line (B). Therefore, the multicast datagrams sent out will be available to the subscribers on their port 2000 — these are the subscribers who join the multicast group `226.1.1.2`. The TTL of the multicast is set in line (E). We obviously want this multicast to be received outside of the subnet in which the server resides. Whether or not that actually happens would depend on the capabilities of the routers. The server itself just sends out the time-date information every 10 seconds. Each outgoing message carries an integer ID that is stored in the `$mesg_id` variable.

```
#!/usr/bin/perl -w
use strict;

### MulticastServer.pl

use IO::Socket::Multicast;                                           #(A)

use constant DESTINATION => '226.1.1.2:2000';                        #(B)

my $sock = IO::Socket::Multicast->new( Proto => 'udp',               #(C)
                                       PeerAddr => DESTINATION,      #(D)
                                     );
$sock->mcast_ttl( 255 );                                             #(E)

my $mesg_id = 1;                                                     #(F)
while (1) {
    my $message = localtime;                                         #(G)
    $message .= "     [$mesg_id]\n";                                 #(H)
    print "multicasting $mesg_id\n";                                 #(I)
    $sock->send( $message ) || die "Couldn't send: $!";              #(J)
    sleep 10;                                                        #(K)
    ++$mesg_id;                                                      #(L)
}
```

The client shown next also uses a UDP socket that is constructed in lines (D) and (E). But note that we now set its `LocalPort` option to 2000, the port to which the server multicasts are directed. For the client to receive a multicast, it must join the multicast group to which the server messages are directed. This is accomplished in line (F). The loop in lines (G) through (J) repeatedly invokes the `recv()` function to scoop up the incoming multicast datagrams.

```
#!/usr/bin/perl -w
use strict;

###  MulticastClient.pl

use IO::Socket::Multicast;                                              #(A)

use constant GROUP => '226.1.1.2';                                      #(B)
use constant PORT => '2000';                                            #(C)

my $sock = IO::Socket::Multicast->new( Proto => 'udp',                  #(D)
                                       LocalPort => PORT,               #(E)
                                     );

$sock->mcast_add( GROUP ) || die "Couldn't set group: $!\n";            #(F)

while (1) {                                                             #(G)
    my $data;                                                           #(H)
    next unless $sock->recv( $data, 1024 );                             #(I)
    print $data;                                                        #(J)
}
```

15.10.2 Multicasting in Python

Shown next is a multicast server in Python, `MulticastServer.py`. It is a UDP socket whose time-to-live attribute is set to 8 via the `IP_MULTICAST_TTL` option in line (E).[79] The first argument to the `setsockopt()` method in that line accounts for the fact that this option needs to be specified at the protocol level, that is, at the `IPPROTO_IP` level (as opposed to at, say, the socket level). Line (B) specifies the IP address for the multicast group and line (C) the port number on the subscriber machines to which the multicast messages will be directed. Multicast messages are sent by the usual `sendto()` method in line (L) with its second argument set to the

[79]As mentioned earlier, setting TTL to 1 will confine the multicast messages to the local subnet. Commenting out line (E) will set the TTL to 1 by default.

socket number constructed from the group IP address in line (B) and the port number in line (C). The multicasts that are put on the wire every 5 seconds consist of the time-date information returned by the call to `time.ctime()` in line (I).

```
#!/usr/bin/env python

### MulticastServer.py

import socket, time                                                    #(A)

DESTI_GROUP = '226.1.1.2'                                              #(B)
DESTI_PORT  = 2000                                                     #(C)

sock = socket.socket( socket.AF_INET, socket.SOCK_DGRAM )              #(D)

sock.setsockopt( socket.IPPROTO_IP, socket.IP_MULTICAST_TTL, '8' )     #(E)

dest = DESTI_GROUP, DESTI_PORT                                         #(F)

msg_id = 1                                                             #(G)
while 1:                                                               #(H)
    message = repr( time.ctime() )                                     #(I)
    message = "%s  [%s]" % (message, msg_id)                           #(J)
    print "multicasting %s" % msg_id                                   #(K)
    sock.sendto( message, dest )                                       #(L)
    time.sleep( 5 )                                                    #(M)
    msg_id += 1                                                        #(N)
```

The next script shown, `MulticastClient.py`, is a multicast client in Python. Note the syntax used in line (H) for joining a multicast group. The group membership information, provided by calling `setsockopt()`, is at the IP layer of the TCP/IP protocol stack; this fact is established by the first argument to `setsockopt()`. The specifics of the group that the client wishes to join are supplied trough the `mreq` argument to `setsockopt()` that is put together in line (G). The special constant `IP_ADD_MEMBERSHIP` for the second argument to `setsockopt()` means that the client wishes to join the group.[80] The `struct` module[81] used in line (G) is for creating a packed binary representation from the values that are provided to its `pack()` method starting with its second argument. The first argument, `4sl`, referred to as the format string, says to pack the first four bytes of the information

[80]The option `IP_DROP_MEMBERSHIP` drops membership from a multicast group. Membership in a group also terminates automatically when a client socket enabled for multicasting is closed.

[81]We will have more to say about the `struct` module of Python and its `pack()` and `unpack()` methods in the next chapter.

contained in the rest of the arguments into a 4-byte string, followed by an integer whose size is also 4 bytes. The call to `inet_aton()` in line (G) returns a 32-bit packed binary form of the dotted-quad string representation of the IP address in line (C). The third argument in line (G), `INADDR_ANY` means that if the machine has multiple interfaces, the socket would be able to receive multicast packets from any of its interfaces.

```
#!/usr/bin/env python

### MulticastClient.py

import socket, struct                                                    #(A)

MAX_MSG_LEN = 1024                                                       #(B)
GROUP = '226.1.1.2'                                                      #(C)
PORT = 2000                                                              #(D)

sock = socket.socket(socket.AF_INET, socket.SOCK_DGRAM)                  #(E)
sock.bind( ('', 2000) )                                                  #(F)

mreq = struct.pack( '4sl', \
                    socket.inet_aton( GROUP ), socket.INADDR_ANY )       #(G)
sock.setsockopt( socket.IPPROTO_IP, socket.IP_ADD_MEMBERSHIP, mreq )#(H)

while 1:                                                                 #(I)
    mesg_in = sock.recv( MAX_MSG_LEN )                                   #(J)
    print mesg_in                                                        #(K)
```

15.11 CREDITS AND SUGGESTIONS FOR FURTHER READING

Many of the idioms used in the example scripts in Perl shown in this chapter were borrowed from two sources: the `perlipc` documentation page by Tom Christiansen and the book by Lincoln Stein [62]. As already acknowledged in the body of the chapter, the scripts `ClientSocket.pl`, `ClientSocketInteractive.pl`, and `ServerSocketSingleClient.pl`, are only small variations on the examples shown in the `perlipc` documentation page. In this book, Stein [62] has also shown how UDP broadcasts can be used for resource discovery and how broadcast-capable interfaces can be discovered at run-time by invoking `ioctl()`. The multiplexed client `MultiplexedClient.pl` of Section 15.7.1 is only a small variation on

Lincoln Stein's script. And, as already mentioned, the multicast server and client scripts of Section 15.10 are taken directly from [62].

The preforking servers presented in Section 15.6 are based on Randal Schwartz's Anonymizing Proxy Server [55]. Several of the constructs used in the Perl version of the preforking server are drawn directly from Randal Schwartz's implementation. For the constructs that were borrowed, the names of the variables and the functions have been intentionally left unchanged so that the reader can go directly from the implementation shown here to Schwartz's implementation that serves a larger purpose.

Our discussion on multicasting focused exclusively on what is also known as IP multicasting — multicasting that is provided by the IP layer in the TCP/IP stack. Another approach to multicasting is known as the *end system multicasting* [8] that seeks to use host machines themselves — as opposed to the routers — for determining the delivery tree for the multicast packets and for group management. While the advantage of this approach is that it can be achieved with simpler routers, the disadvantage is the introduction of redundancies in some of the physical links.

For socket programming in Python, the example scripts in the `Demo/sockets` directory of the Python source tree are very educational. Another recommended source that contains a comprehensive treatment of networking with Python is the book by John Goerzen [23]. We should also draw the reader's attention to the Twisted framework [31] for event-driven network programming with Python.

15.12 HOMEWORK

1. When you check your email with your laptop, your laptop is most likely serving as a POP3 client[82] to fetch email from a machine that is acting as a maildrop for your account. For this to work, the maildrop machine must be running a POP3 server. (If your maildrop machine is a Unix machine, it is likely that all your incoming email is stored in a file whose pathname is `/var/mail/user_account_name`. A POP3 server on such a machine can dole out the messages stored at this pathname to a remote POP3 client.) Write a Perl script based on the POP3 protocol (you may

[82] POP stands for *Post Office Protocol* and POP3 is version 3 of this protocol. This protocol is described in the following standards: RFC 1939 (Post Office Protocol — Version 3), RFC 2195 (IMAP/POP AUTHorize Extension for Simple Challenge/Response), and RFC 2449 (POP3 Extension Mechanism). The protocol addresses the retrieval of email from a remote server over a TCP/IP connection. A more modern protocol, but one that is not yet as widely supported by email servers, is the IMAP protocol. IMAP allows multiple clients to access the same mailbox on a server. While one may have a choice of using either POP3 or IMAP for retrieving email from a server, in order to send email outbound through an email server one must use the SMTP (Simple Mail Transfer Protocol) protocol.

use the `Mail::POP3Client` module for the POP3 functionality) that retrieves your email via an encrypted TCP/IP communication link. Use the `IO::Socket::SSL` module for server authentication and for encryption.[83] Note that port 995 is reserved for POP3 over SSL. Your POP3 client should possess the following functionality:

- It should require no graphics interface. In other words, it should be possible to use the client with a simple command-line interface from a terminal window.
- It should be possible to retrieve email from a server with a command line like

  ```
  POP3Client.pl  user_name@hostname.purdue.edu
  ```

  assuming that the client script is named `POP3Client.pl`. The script should prompt the user for the password to the account from which email is to be retrieved.
- The command shown above should display in the terminal window a message list that is simply a display of a sequence of integers, starting with 1 for the oldest message and ending at the integer index associated with the most recent image.
- The client should then display a text-based "whatnow" menu that looks like

  ```
  What would you like to do next? Here are the options:
       delete M - N
       delete N
       show headers for N
       show message body for N
       show message list again
       quit or exit
  ```

  where a command like "`delete 3 - 13`" should cause the deletion of the messages numbered 3 through 13, and "`delete 3`" should cause just that message to be deleted. The other commands speak for themselves.

[83]The Perl `IO::Socket::SSL` module does the same thing through encrypted and authenticated network links that `IO::Socket::INET` does but without security. The `IO::Socket:SSL` module is a front end to the `Net::SSLeay` module, that in turn is an interface to the `OpenSSL` libraries. `OpenSSL` is an implementation of the SSL (Secure Sockets Layer) and the TLS (Transport Layer Security) protocols. (SSL was developed originally by Netscape to provide secure and authenticated connections between browsers and servers in 1995. IETF made SSL version 3 an open standard in 1999 and called it TLS version 1.) SSL/TLS allows for either server-only authentication or server-client authentication. In server-only authentication, the client receives the server's certificate. (A certificate binds a name to a public key and includes other pertinent information such as the valid dates, the name of the Certificate Authority, etc.) The client verifies the server's certificate and generates a secret key that it then encrypts with the server's public key. The client sends the encrypted secret key to the server; the server decrypts it with its own private key and subsequently uses the client-generated secret key to encrypt the messages meant for the client. In the server-client authentication, in addition to the secret key, the client also sends to the server its certificate that the server uses for authenticating the client.

2. The Perl implementation shown for the preforking server in Section 15.6.1 used a hash, `%kids`, to keep track of the the child server processes. The keys in this hash are the PIDs of the child servers and the values the string `slave`. When a child server died (because a client closed the connection), the corresponding key-value pair for the child server catering to that client was removed from the hash and replaced by the entry for a new child-server process. Modify that implementation so that key-value pairs for the dying child-server processes are retained in the `%kids` hash for logging and record keeping purposes. In the hash, change the value associated with a dying child server process to a string formed from the clock time when the client terminates the connection. Next write a utility function that examines the contents of the hash and prints out various statistics regarding the usage of the server.

3. The Python implementation shown for the preforking server in Section 15.6.2 used a dictionary, `kids`, for accomplishing the same thing as was achieved by the hash `%kids` for the Perl implementation we refer to in the previous problem. Modify the Python code related to the use of this dictionary in order to achieve the same goal as stated in the previous homework problem.

4. Write Perl and Python scripts for a chat server. Create a `ChatServer` class that forks off a new child process for each incoming client. This child process should construct an instance of a `ClientHandler` class for handling all the communication chores with regard to that client. The main server process will obviously hand over to the `ClientHandler` instance the client socket returned by the `accept()` method. The `ClientHandler` instance can then use this socket for bidirectional communication with the remote client. On first contact, a new `ClientHandler` instance must welcome the client and print in the client's terminal all of the chat that has occurred up to that point in time. Subsequently, the `ClientHandler` instance for each client must broadcast the messages emanating from the client to all the other chatroom participants.[84]

5. Following the discussion in Section 15.6 of this chapter, create Perl and Python preforked versions of the chat server scripts of the previous problem.

---

[84]Chapter 19 of [41] shows C++ and Java implementations of such a chat server.

16

Interacting with Databases

The simplest form of a database is a table. Consider, for example, a table representation of a small personal library consisting of a couple of hundred books. The various columns of this table could correspond to items of information such as the title of a book, its author, its publisher, its publication date, and so on. In the memory of a computer, a table such as this could be represented by a *flat file* in which each line contains either comma-separated or tab-separated variable-length items of information on each book.[1] Another way to create a flat-file representation for the table would be by using fixed-sized records for the rows of the table and, within each record, fixed-sized fields[2] for the different column entries.

Although easy to implement and easy to interact with, flat files can only be used for small databases. The main shortcoming of flat files is that the length of time it takes to reach an item of information can be linearly proportional to the size of the database. For example, if in a simplistic flat-file database of books you wanted

[1] If the database is small and read-only, then comma-separated or tab-separated entries in flat files can work very well. However, if the users are allowed to modify such a database and if a replacement entry is longer than the old entry, accommodating the replacement would require that all the downstream entries be shifted in the memory in order to create room for the new entry. This can significantly degrade the performance of a database. Flat-file databases with comma- or tab-separated entries work best when, at run time, you can read the entire database file from the disk into the fast memory, interact with the database — even modify the database if necessary — and then, when you are done interacting with the database, write out the flat file back to the disk.

[2] At least for the fields, fixed size does not mean that all fields have to be of the same size.

to retrieve the year of publication for a book titled *Zazen*, you may have to walk through practically the entire database before you hit the correct entry.

Faster databases, still intended for only small applications, consist of disk-based hash tables. For such a database, a hash function is used to assign a unique code to each row of the database table on the basis of one or more column entries. The hash codes are subsequently mapped to unique memory addresses. In this manner, for a small library database, each row of the table would be stored at a unique memory address on the basis of, say, the book title. When unique memory addresses can be successfully assigned to the different rows of a table, each row of the table can be retrieved in constant time, meaning in time that is independent of the size of the table. However, when this ideal condition cannot be satisfied,[3] two or more rows of the table may be mapped to the same hash code. When that happens, only one table row is assigned the memory address corresponding to that hash code. Stored along with the chosen table row are pointers to the other table rows that were assigned the same hash code.[4]

The database systems that are needed for large commercial applications are of the relational variety. A relational database stores information in the form of multiple tables so that any duplications within each table are kept to a minimum. Consider again a database of books, but this time for a large library. Let's say that for each book we also want to store the publisher's name, address, and phone number, and the publisher's regional representative's name, address, and phone number. If we assume that all the books in the library are published by a small number of publishers, it is easy to see that if we store all the books in a single table, there will be a large degree of redundancy in the table, since the publisher-related information for all the books put out by the same publisher will be the same. A relational database for the same example would consist of three separate tables: one for the books, one for the publishers, and one for the publishers' regional representatives. Each row of the book

[3]This could happen either because of the limitations of the hashing function used or because, with respect to the data that is hashed, there exist identical entries in the different rows of the database table, such as when hashing is carried out with respect to book titles and there exist multiple books with the same title but with different authors.

[4]While a hash-table-based database *can* give constant-time data access, it is not guaranteed. The retrieval efficiency in actual practice depends on the hash function used vis-à-vis the statistical peculiarities of the keys used for generating the hash codes. Another commonly used approach for disk-based databases consists of storing the rows of the table in a key-sorted order, usually in the form of a height-balanced binary tree (called the red-black tree), where the keys consist of entries in a designated column of the table. Although not as efficient as the hash-table-based approach when the hashing function is effective in dispersing the keys uniformly over the buckets of the hash table, the tree-based approach carries an $O(\log N)$ performance guarantee for information retrieval, where N is the number of rows in the table. Another reason for using a tree-based approach in some applications is that it lends itself efficiently to retrieval for range queries, that is, a query where you want to access information within a range for the keys, such as when you want to retrieve all the books from a library database whose titles' first letters are in the range, say, a through k. Hash-based representations are inefficient for range queries because they disperse the rows in a random fashion. Some systems, while storing information in disk-based hash tables, allow you to quickly construct their sorted tree-based representations at run time; that obviously lends efficiencies to sorted retrieval.

table would contain an identification tag for the publisher of that book and another identification tag for the publisher's representative. The publisher table would then show the association between the publisher identification tags and all the relevant publisher information. The same goes for the table that stores information on the publishers' regional representatives.

This chapter will consider each of the three different database types separately. We will first show scripts that interact with simple databases stored as flat files. Next, we will discuss how one interacts with databases stored as disk-based hash tables. Our treatment of disk-based hash tables includes the Perl's tie mechanism that translates ordinary access to a variable into a method call on a class-type object; this allows for the creation of *persistent objects* in a script. Also included in the same general discussion is the subject of the *serialization* of complex data structures that enables their storage in a disk file; when the file is read back into the main memory, the complex data structure can be recreated by *deserialization*. Finally, we will show scripts that interact with a full-featured relational database management system such as the MySQL database manager.

16.1 FLAT-FILE DATABASES: WORKING WITH CSV FILES

In this section we will show Perl and Python implementations for a flat-file database system that keeps its records in the form of comma-separated values (CSV).[5] The implementations are based on the assumption that the database information is stored in a disk file in the following format:

```
row index,last name,first name,major,university,city,phone
1,kak,avi,engineering,purdue univ,west lafayette,765 123-4567
2,smythe,stacey,art history,purdue univ,lafayette,123-3472
3,beeblecrox,zaphod,travel,school of cosmology,tatooine,987-9988
4,skywalker,luke,aeronautics,hoth college,tatooine,4ZV 398 9999
....
....
```

where we will refer to each line as a *record* and to each comma-separated position in each record as a *field*. The first line shown above is special because it describes the *schema* of the database; it tells us what meaning to associate with each comma-separated value in all other records of the database. The schema shown tells us that

[5]Obviously, there is nothing sacrosanct about the use of a comma to separate the different items of information in a record. Any other character that does not appear in the various items of information stored in the database could also be used as a separator. Tabs are also frequently used for this purpose.

the first value stored in a record is its row index,[6] the second the last name of an individual, the third the first name, and so on.

Let's say that we expect the following command-line functionality from a database such as the one described above:

- We want to be able to read the disk-based database file into a script and then write back to the disk an updated version of the file after the user has changed the database by interacting with the script.
- We want to be able to view all of the items in a given column of the database table.
- We want to be able to view a database record on the basis of a chosen last name.
- We want to be able to enter into an interactive mode in which a user is prompted for the action to be taken vis-à-vis the database.
- And so on.

In the subsection that follows, we will show a Perl script that possesses such functionality. The subsection that comes after that will then demonstrate a Python script with the same functionality.

16.1.1 A Perl Script for Working with a CSV File

In the script shown below, we have defined a class `CSV` whose various methods permit the kind of functionality listed above. When the database disk file is read into the script, it is stored as an anonymous array of references to arrays. Each array reference contained in the top-level array is for a separate record in the disk file. A reference to the top-level array is stored as the value of the `_db` instance variable, as shown in line (C5) of the constructor code. The instance variable `_dbfile` shown in line (C4) stores the name of the disk file that contains the database table. The constructor for the `CSV` class, defined in lines (C1) through (C6), returns a blessed reference to the hash whose keys are the two instance variables.

The method `populate_database_from_disk_file()` in lines (D1) through (D8) reads the individual records from the disk file and then calls on the method `enter_record_from_file()` defined in lines (G1), (G2), and (G3) to actually insert a reference to the array representation of each record into the top-level array pointed to by the `_db` instance variable. It is also possible to directly enter

[6] Even when a database is stored as shown, it is convenient to think of it as a table, with each record as a row and each comma-separated value as a column entry.

a new record into the database from the command line by invoking the method enter_new_record_from_terminal() defined in lines (H1) through (H6).

The class has also been provided with additional methods like show_schema() in lines (F1) through (F5) for displaying the entries in the first record where the schema is stored. As the reader will recall from what we said at the beginning of Section 16.1, we refer to the first record as the schema because it tells us what meaning to associate with each field of a record in the rest of the disk file. The method retrieve_column() in lines (J1) through (J4) and the method retrieve_row() in lines (K1) through (K3), as the names indicate, retrieve a single column and a single row, respectively. Each takes an integer argument that specifies the zero-based index of the column or the row. Another retrieval method provided for the class is show_row_for_last_name() in lines (L1) through (L7), which retrieves the row for a given last name. This row is displayed in the following format:

```
  row index:  5
  last name:  anna
 first name:  polly
      major:  home economics
 university:  sunshine university
       city:  perfectville
      phone:  X74 987 0909
```

where the entries at the left are taken from the database schema in the first record of the database and the entries on the right from the database table row whose integer index is supplied to show_row_for_last_name(). Note that this method returns the integer index associated with that row.

The CSV class also includes a method called interactive() in lines (M1) through (M26) that allows a user to examine and modify the database in a continuous interactive mode. When in this mode, the user is first shown a list of all the last names in the database; this is accomplished by the statements in lines (M6) and (M7). Subsequently, through the statements in lines (M8) through (M13), the user is shown the record of the individual he/she wishes to view and possibly change. If the user does want to modify a record, lines (M14) through (M25) then prompt the user for the old item of information that needs to be changed and its replacement. When the user has terminated his/her interaction with the database, the modified version of the database is written back to the disk.

Finally, note the method write_database_to_file() in lines (E1) through (E7) for writing out the memory-stored database back to the disk file.

The script that comes after the one we show next demonstrates the CSV class in action.

```
package CSV;                                                    #(A)

### CSV.pm

use strict;                                                     #(B)

sub new {                                                       #(C1)
    my ($class, $db_file) = @_;                                 #(C2)
    bless {                                                     #(C3)
        _dbfile  => $db_file,                                   #(C4)
        _db => [],                                              #(C5)
    }, $class;                                                  #(C6)
}
sub populate_database_from_disk_file {                          #(D1)
    my $self = shift;                                           #(D2)
    open FILE, $self->{_dbfile}
           or die "unable to open file: $!";                    #(D3)
    while (<FILE>) {                                            #(D4)
        chomp;                                                  #(D5)
        my @record = split /\,/, $_;                            #(D6)
        $self->enter_record_from_file( @record );               #(D7)
    }
    close FILE;                                                 #(D8)
}
sub write_database_to_file {                                    #(E1)
    my $self = shift;                                           #(E2)
    my $file = $self->{_dbfile};
    open FILE, ">$file"
            or die "unable to open file: $!";                   #(E3)
    for my $i (0..@{$self->{_db}}-1) {                          #(E4)
        my $csv_string = join ',', @{$self->{_db}[$i]};         #(E5)
        print FILE "$csv_string\n";                             #(E6)
    }
    close FILE;                                                 #(E7)
}
sub show_schema {                                               #(F1)
    my $self = shift;                                           #(F2)
    my @schema = @{$self->{_db}[0]};                            #(F3)
    my $print_string = join "    ", @schema;                    #(F4)
    print "$print_string\n";                                    #(F5)
}
sub enter_record_from_file {                                    #(G1)
    my ($self, @entries) = @_;                                  #(G2)
    push @{$self->{_db}}, \@entries;                            #(G3)
}
```

```
sub enter_new_record_from_terminal {                                  #(H1)
    my ($self, @entries) = @_;                                        #(H2)
    my $last_row_index = @{$self->{_db}} - 1;                         #(H3)
    unshift @entries, $last_row_index + 1;                            #(H4)
    push @{$self->{_db}}, \@entries;                                  #(H5)
    $self->write_database_to_file;                                    #(H6)
}
sub retrieve_column {                                                 #(J1)
    my ($self, $column_index) = @_;                                   #(J2)
    for my $i (1..@{$self->{_db}}-1) {                                #(J3)
        print "$self->{_db}[$i][$column_index]\n";                    #(J4)
    }
    print "\n";
}
sub retrieve_row {                                                    #(K1)
    my ($self, $row_index) = @_;                                      #(K2)
    print "@{$self->{_db}[$row_index]}\n";                            #(K3)
}
sub show_row_for_last_name {                                          #(L1)
    my ($self, $value) = @_;                                          #(L2)
    for my $i (1..@{$self->{_db}}-1) {                                #(L3)
        if ( $self->{_db}->[$i][1] eq $value ) {                      #(L4)
            for my $j (0..@{$self->{_db}[0]}-1) {                     #(L5)
                printf "%15s:  %s\n", $self->{_db}->[0][$j],
                                      $self->{_db}->[$i][$j];         #(L6)
            }
            print "\n"; return $i;                                    #(L7)
        }
    }
}
sub interactive {                                                     #(M1)
    my $self = shift;                                                 #(M2)
    while (1) {                                                       #(M3)
        print "\nDo you wish to have an interactive session " .
              "with the database?" .  "\nEnter yes or no:  ";         #(M4)
        if ( <STDIN> =~ /y(es)?/i ) {                                 #(M5)
            print "\nLast names stored in the database:\n\n";         #(M6)
            $self->retrieve_column(1);                                #(M7)
            print "Whose record do you wish to view/change? ";        #(M8)
            my $last_name = <STDIN>;                                  #(M9)
            chomp $last_name;                                        #(M10)
            print "\nHere is the record for this last name:\n\n"; #(M11)
            my $row_index =
                     $self->show_row_for_last_name( $last_name ); #(M12)
            print "Do you wish to change this record?\n" .
                                "Enter yes or no: ";                 #(M13)
```

```
            if ( <STDIN> =~ /y(es)?/i ) {                      #(M14)
                print "Old entry: ";                           #(M15)
                my $old_entry = <STDIN>;                       #(M16)
                chomp $old_entry;                              #(M17)
                print "New entry: ";                           #(M18)
                my $new_entry = <STDIN>;                       #(M19)
                chomp $new_entry;                              #(M20)
                for my $j (1..@{$self->{_db}[$row_index]}-1){  #(M21)
                    if ($self->{_db}[$row_index][$j]
                                            eq $old_entry){#(M22)
                        $self->{_db}[$row_index][$j] = $new_entry;#(M23)
                    }
                }
            } else { next; }                                   #(M24)
        } else { last; }                                       #(M25)
    }
    $self->write_database_to_file;                             #(M26)
}
1
```

Shown below is a test script for exercising the CSV class. The test script is invoked with a command line like

```
TestCSV.pl data.db
```

where `data.db` is the name of the file that contains the database in the form shown at the beginning of Section 16.1. The last command executed by the test script in line (K) is to call the `interactive()` method for initiating the continuous interaction mode between the user and the database. In this mode, the user is prompted for various actions that are stated in lines (M4), (M8), (M13), (M15), and (M19) in the code for `interaction()` in the CSV class.

```
#!/usr/bin/perl -w
use strict;

### TestCSV.pl

die "needs one command line arg, the name of the database file"
    unless @ARGV == 1;                                         #(A)

use CSV;                                                       #(B)

my $db = CSV->new( $ARGV[0] );                                #(C)
$db->populate_database_from_disk_file;                         #(D)
$db->show_schema;                                              #(E)
```

```
$db->retrieve_column( 2 );                                              #(F)
$db->show_row_for_last_name( "smythe" );                                #(G)
$db->retrieve_row( 2 );                                                 #(H)
$db->enter_new_record_from_terminal( "anna","polly",
                          "home economics","sunshine university",
                          "perfectville","X74 987 0909");               #(I)
$db->retrieve_row( 5 );                                                 #(J)
$db->interactive;                                                       #(K)
```

What we have shown above is merely a rudimentary version of a script for working with a CSV database. It would be easy to create a faster version of this script by also storing on the disk an association list that shows how the last names are mapped to the row indexes. The code shown in the `interactive()` method of the `CSV` class can also be made more user-friendly and provided with many more modes of interaction. We will leave such modifications to the `CSV` class to one of the problems in the Homework section of this chapter.

16.1.2 A Python Script for Working with a CSV File

The Python script shown next, `CSV.py`, provides a user with the same database functionality as the Perl script `CSV.pl` of the previous subsection. The script defines a class, `CSV`, whose `__init__()` in lines (C1) through (C3) specifies the instance variable `_db` for holding a reference to a list of lists, one for each record read from the disk file. The name of the disk file containing the database is stored in the instance variable `_dbfile`. The `populate_database_from_disk_file()` method in lines (D1) through (D10) uses the same logic as the Perl method of the same name, except for the fact that since `file` objects in Python support the iterator protocol, it is possible to use the syntax shown in line (D7) for reading one line at a time from the disk file.[7] After a database is read into the script by the `populate_database_from_disk_file()` method and modified through, say, the `interactive()` method shown later in lines (M1) through (M19), the database can be written back to the disk file by the method `write_database_to_file()` defined in lines (E1) through (E10).

When a database file is read into the script, each record is converted into a Python list by the call to `split()` in line (D8). Subsequently, the call to the method `enter_record_from_file()` in line (D9) appends the list created for a new record to list of lists held by the instance variable `_db`. What `enter_record_from_file()`, defined in lines (G1) and (G2), does for a record acquired from a disk file, the method `enter_new_record_from_terminal()`, defined in lines (H1) through (H6), does

[7] Section 3.7.2 of Chapter 3 talks about using a `file` object as an iterator.

for a record entered directly from the terminal, except for the fact that the latter must also calculate the total number of records currently in the database in order to figure out the row number to prepend to the new record.

The `show_schema()` method in lines (F1) through (F4) displays in the terminal window the database schema, that is, the first record in the database. This row consists of the labels for each of the columns of the table.

The methods `retrieve_column()` and `retrieve_row()` do the obvious when supplied with the column index and the row index, respectively. The method `show_row_for_last_name()` shows in a nicely formatted manner all of the database entries for a given last name. (This formatting is displayed in the explanation that precedes the Perl version of the class.) As with the Perl method of the same name, note how the formatting is carried out by embedding the appropriate conversion specifiers in the first argument to `print()` in line (L5).

Finally, there is the `interactive()` method in lines (M1) through (M19) that is structured along the same lines as the method of the same name for the Perl version of the code. As for the differences between the two versions, lines (M4) and (M11) use the string method `find()` to determine whether the answer supplied by the user is in the affirmative. For the Perl case, we had used regex matching for the same.

Lines (T1) through (T10) serve to test the `CSV` class in the same manner that `TestCSV.pl` did for the Perl version of the class.

```
#!/usr/bin/env python

### CSV.py

import re                                                            #(A)

class CSV( object ):                                                 #(B)

    def __init__( self, db_file ):                                   #(C1)
        self._dbfile =  db_file                                      #(C2)
        self._db     =  []                                           #(C3)

    def populate_database_from_disk_file( self ):                    #(D1)
        FILE = None                                                  #(D2)
        try:                                                         #(D3)
            FILE = open( self._dbfile )                              #(D4)
        except IOError:                                              #(D5)
            print "unable to open %s" % self._dbfile                 #(D6)
        for line in FILE:                                            #(D7)
            record = re.split( r',', line[0:-1] )                    #(D8)
            self.enter_record_from_file( record )                    #(D9)
        FILE.close()                                                 #(D10)
```

```
def write_database_to_file( self ):                                #(E1)
    FILE = None                                                    #(E2)
    try:                                                           #(E3)
        FILE = open( self._dbfile, 'w' )                           #(E4)
    except IOError:                                                #(E5)
        print "unable to open %s" % self._dbfile                   #(E6)
    csv_strings = [  ','.join(item) for item in self._db ]         #(E7)
    all_csv_strings = '\n'.join( csv_strings )                     #(E8)
    FILE.write( all_csv_strings )                                  #(E9)
    FILE.close()                                                  #(E10)

def show_schema( self ):                                           #(F1)
    schema = self._db[0]                                           #(F2)
    print_string = "    ".join( schema )                           #(F3)
    print print_string                                             #(F4)

def enter_record_from_file( self, record ):                        #(G1)
    self._db.append( record )                                      #(G2)

def enter_new_record_from_terminal( self, *entries ):              #(H1)
    num_rows_in_db = len( self._db )                               #(H2)
    new_record = list( entries )                                   #(H3)
    new_record.insert(0, repr(num_rows_in_db) )                    #(H4)
    self._db.append( new_record )                                  #(H5)
    self.write_database_to_file()                                  #(H6)

def retrieve_column( self, column_index ):                         #(J1)
    for i in range( 1, len(self._db) ):                            #(J2)
        print self._db[i][column_index]                            #(J3)

def retrieve_row( self, row_index ):                               #(K1)
    print self._db[row_index]                                      #(K2)

def show_row_for_last_name( self, lname):                          #(L1)
    for i in range(1, len( self._db ) ):                           #(L2)
        if self._db[i][1] == lname:                                #(L3)
            for j in range( len( self._db[0] ) ):                  #(L4)
                print "%15s:  %s\n" % (self._db[0][j], \
                                            self._db[i][j])        #(L5)
            return i                                               #(L6)

def interactive( self ):                                           #(M1)
    while 1:                                                       #(M2)
        answer = raw_input("\nDo you wish to have an " +
                           "interactive session with the " +
                           "database? \nEnter yes or no:  ")       #(M3)
```

```
        if answer.find( 'y' ) is not -1:                        #(M4)
            print "\nLast names stored in the database:\n"     #(M5)
            self.retrieve_column(1)                             #(M6)
            last_name = raw_input("Whose record do you wish " +
                                  "to view/change? ")           #(M7)
            print "\nHere is the record for this last name:\n" #(M8)
            row_index = self.show_row_for_last_name(last_name) #(M9)
            answer=raw_input("Do you wish to change this record?\n"+
                             "Enter yes or no: " )              #(M10)
            if answer.find( 'y' ) is not -1:                    #(M11)
                old_entry= raw_input( "Old entry: " )           #(M12)
                new_entry = raw_input( "New entry: " )          #(M13)
                for j in range(1, len(self._db[row_index])):   #(M14)
                    if self._db[row_index] [j] == old_entry:    #(M15)
                        self._db[row_index] [j] = new_entry     #(M16)
            else: continue                                      #(M17)
        else: break                                             #(M18)
    self.write_database_to_file()                               #(M19)


if __name__ == '__main__':                                      #(T1)

    db = CSV( "data.db" )                                       #(T2)
    db.populate_database_from_disk_file()                       #(T3)
    db.show_schema()                                            #(T4)
    db.retrieve_column(2)                                       #(T5)
    db.show_row_for_last_name( 'smythe' )                       #(T6)
    db.retrieve_row(2)                                          #(T7)
    db.enter_new_record_from_terminal("annaz","pollyz", \
              "home economicsz", "sunshine universityz", \
              "perfectvillez","X74 987 0909z")                  #(T8)
    db.retrieve_row(5)                                          #(T9)
    db.interactive()                                            #(T10)
```

16.2 FLAT-FILE DATABASES: WORKING WITH FIXED-LENGTH RECORDS

Compared to what was shown in the previous section, it is possible to construct a more efficient flat-file database by using fixed-length records and, within each record, fixed-length fields for the different items of information. When fixed-length records (and fixed-length fields within the records) are used, one knows in advance where exactly each record begins and ends and the precise division of the memory allocated for a record among the different fields. Perl's built-in functions `pack()`

and unpack() that we introduced in Section 2.1.2 of Chapter 2 and methods of the same names from Python's struct module make it convenient to construct such databases. To illustrate how these functions are used, let's say we want to store in a database a sequence of records like the ones shown below:

```
adam,john,765-123-4567
smythe,stacey,765-444-6666
....
....
```

where the line breaks and the commas shown are merely to help the reader visually separate the individual records (one record per line) and the different fields in a record; they are not needed for the storage scheme that we present in this section. As the reader can see, each record here consists of three fields, one for the last name, one for the first name, and one for the phone number. Let's now assign a fixed length to each field that is sufficiently large to accommodate the longest possible value in that field:

```
last_name   first_name     phone
<---10-->   <---10--->   <---12---->
```

Obviously, if a value is longer than the space reserved for a field, it will have to be truncated. This allocation will result in 32-character records. As previously explained in Chapter 2, the following call to pack() will return a 32-character string, with the padding character set to null. That is, if the value specified for a field does not fill up the space allocated to it, the rest of the positions will have the null character (ASCII value 0) in them.[8]

```
my $str = pack( "a10 a10 a12","kak","avi","765-123-4567" );
```

The same thing can be accomplished in Python by

```
import struct
str = struct.pack( "10s 10s 12s","kak","avi","765-123-4567" )
```

If the string returned by these calls to pack() is now supplied to unpack(), we can recover the different fields packed into the string. That is, for the case of Perl, we can recover the three fields by

---

[8]If you try to print out the string returned by this call to pack() in Perl or struct.pack() in Python, you'll see something like

```
kakavi765-123-4567
```

where all the values are juxtaposed together and with seemingly no sense of the specified widths associated with the different item of information. This happens because the null characters that are in the unused positions in each field are unprintable. So the string returned by pack() is indeed 32 characters long, but print() will only output the printable characters. For the case of Perl, if the template character is changed from a to A in the first argument to pack(), the space character is used for padding as opposed to the null character. Now if you print out the string returned by pack(), you can actually see a 32-character string.

```
my ($lname, $fname, $phone) = unpack( "a10 a10 a12", $str );
```

For Python, the same is accomplished by

```
lname, fname, phone = struct.unpack( "10s 10s 12s", str )
```

A function that comes in handy when navigating through a database that stores its information in the form of fixed sized records in a disk file is the built-in `seek()` in Perl and the `file` class's method of the same name for Python. Here is the argument structure for a call to `seek()` in Perl:

```
seek( FILEHANDLE, POSITION, WHENCE )
```

For Python, a call to `seek()` takes the following form:

```
FILEHANDLE.seek( POSITION, WHENCE )
```

where the meanings of `POSITION` and `WHENCE` are the same as before. To recall our discussion in Chapters 2 and 3, a call to `seek()` causes the file pointer to be positioned at `POSITION` in the file associated with the stream `FILEHANDLE`. If `WHENCE` is 0, the file pointer is positioned with respect to the beginning of the file; if 1, then with respect to the current position; and if 2, with respect to the end of the file. Because the records are of fixed size and because the field widths inside the records stay constant, a call to `seek()` can take the file pointer to exactly the position where we carry out either a read or a write operation. For the case of Perl, while the write operations can be carried out by calling the usual `print()` function, the read operations are best carried out by calling the built-in

```
read( FILEHANDLE, SCALAR, LENGTH )
```

where the number of bytes is controlled by the third argument, `LENGTH`. The bytes that are read from the disk are stored in the scalar variable that is the second argument. For the case of Python, we invoke the `write()` method of the `file` class to write out a string at the location set by an earlier call to `seek()`. The read operations from the file, starting at the location set by an earlier call to `seek()`, can be carried out by

```
record = FILEHANDLE.read( LENGTH )
```

if we want to read off `LENGTH` number of bytes.

16.2.1 A Perl Script for Working with Fixed-Length Records

Shown below is a simple script that first creates in lines (B) through (G) a database consisting of fixed-sized records with the help of `pack()` and then provides an interactive facility in lines (H) through (h) for browsing the database and/or changing it. The interactive facility starts by scanning the database file in lines (J) through (O) and constructing a hash whose keys are the last names as stored in the first field of each record and whose values are the "row indices" implicitly associated with the records. For example, the last name in the first record in the database entered in line (C) is `kak`, so we store a key-value pair with the key set to `kak` and the value set to 0 in the hash `%names` in line (O). The last name in the next record is `smythe`; this results in the storage of a key-value pair with the key set to `smythe` and the value set to 1 in the same hash in line (O); and so on. The advantage of using the `%names` hash in this manner is that it immediately gives us the "row index" associated with a record on the basis of the last name.

In the interactive mode, line (R) of the script first shows all the last names to the user. The user is then asked whose record he/she wishes to see; this is done in line (S). The last name entered by the user is used to retrieve the row number of the corresponding record in line (V). The call to `seek()` in line (W) is then used to position the file pointer at the beginning of that record. Subsequently, the call to `read()` in line (X) retrieves that record. This record is first unscrambled in line (Y) and then shown to the user in line (Z). Lines (a) through (f) first prompt the user for the old value in the record that needs to be changed and then ask the user for its new value; subsequently, the record is modified to reflect the new value. Finally, in line (h), the modified record is packed into a database string and the packed string written out to the disk file at the location that belongs to this record.

```
#!/usr/bin/perl -w
use strict;

### FixedSizedRecords.pl

use constant RECORD_LEN => 32;                                          #(A)

# Create a small database of fixed-sized records:
open(FILE, ">data2.db");    # die stuff                                 #(B)
print FILE pack("a10 a10 a12","kak","avi","765-123-4567");              #(C)
print FILE pack("a10 a10 a12","smythe","stacey","765-234-6666");        #(D)
print FILE pack("a10 a10 a12","beeblecrox","zaphod","111-987-9988");#(E)
print FILE pack("a10 a10 a12","skywalker","luke","4ZV 398 9999");     #(F)
close FILE;                                                             #(G)

# Open the database for user interaction:
open(FILE, "+< data2.db") or die "unable to open file: $!";             #(H)
my ($buff, %names);                                                     #(I)

# Make a hash with last names as keys and record positions as values:
for (my $i=0;;$i++) {                                                   #(J)
    my $file_pointer = $i * RECORD_LEN;                                 #(K)
    seek(FILE, $file_pointer, 0);                                       #(L)
    last unless read(FILE, $buff, 10);                                  #(M)
    $buff =~ s/\0*$//;                                                  #(N)
    $names{$buff} = $i;                                                 #(O)
}
```

```
# User interaction:
while (1) {                                                          #(P)
    print "Last names of the individuals in the database:\n\n";      #(Q)
    print map "$_\n", sort keys %names;                              #(R)
    print "\nWhose record would you like to see? Enter last name: ";#(S)
    chomp( my $response = <STDIN> );                                 #(T)
    last unless exists $names{$response};                            #(U)
    my $row_index = $names{$response};                               #(V)
    seek(FILE, $row_index * RECORD_LEN, 0);                          #(W)
    read(FILE, $buff, 32);                                           #(X)
    my ($lname, $fname, $phone) = unpack( "a10 a10 a12", $buff );    #(Y)
    printf "\nHere it is:    %s\t%s\t%s\n", $lname, $fname, $phone; #(Z)
    printf "\nEnter the old value you'd like to change: ";           #(a)
    chomp( my $old = <STDIN> );                                      #(b)
    printf "\nNow enter the new value: ";                            #(c)
    chomp( my $new = <STDIN> );                                      #(d)
    foreach ($lname, $fname, $phone) {                               #(e)
        last if s/$old/$new/;                                        #(f)
    }
    seek(FILE, $row_index * RECORD_LEN, 0);                          #(g)
    print FILE pack( "a10 a10 a12", $lname, $fname, $phone );        #(h)
}
```

16.2.2 A Python Script for Working with Fixed-Length Records

Shown below is a Python script for working with fixed-length records. As with the Perl version, we first create a small database consisting of fixed-length records in lines (D) through (I). Note the calls to `struct.pack()` for this purpose; these calls return a packed string representation of the last three arguments to the method. The format string `"10s 10s 12s"` in the first argument reserves the first 10 bytes of the output string for the first item to be packed, the next 10 bytes for the second item to be packed, and the last 12 bytes for the last item to be packed. Each call to `struct.pack()` returns a 32-byte string.

Lines (J) through (S) of the script then scan the database file and create a dictionary whose keys are the last names and whose corresponding values the "row indices" associated with each of the records. This dictionary is useful for the user interaction we establish in lines (T) through (k) of the script. For example, the database is introduced to the user in lines (U) and (V) as a list of the last names and then the user is asked if he/she would like to change the information associated with one of them. When a user enters a particular last name in line (W), the script queries the dictionary in line (Y) to figure out which record of the database to retrieve and unpack in lines (Z) through (c). In line (d), the user is subsequently asked to enter the value that needs to be changed in the record just retrieved. Line (l) then writes out the updated record back to the disk file at its appropriate location. Before we write the modified record back to the file, we check whether the user attempted to alter the first field — the field reserved for the last name — in lines (h), (i), and (j). Since we use the last names for the keys in the interaction dictionary established in lines (K) through (S), we obviously do not want the users to alter this field.

```
#!/usr/bin/env python

### FixedSizedRecords.py

import struct, sys                                                   #(A)

RECORD_LEN = 32                                                      #(B)
FILE = None                                                          #(C)

# Create a small database of fixed-sized records:
try:
    FILE = open("data2.db", "w")                                     #(D)
    FILE.write( struct.pack("10s 10s 12s","kak",\
                                      "avi","765-123-4567"))         #(E)
    FILE.write(struct.pack("10s 10s 12s","smythe",\
                                      "stacey","765-234-6666"))      #(F)
    FILE.write(struct.pack("10s 10s 12s","beeblecrox",\
                                      "zaphod","111-987-9988"))      #(G)
    FILE.write(struct.pack("10s 10s 12s","skywalker",\
                                      "luke","4ZV 398 9999"))        #(H)
except IOError, inst:
    print "Error in file IO: ", inst
if FILE: FILE.close()                                                #(I)

# Open the database for user interaction:
names = {}                                                           #(J)
try:                                                                 #(K)
    # Open the file in read/write mode:
    FILE = open("data2.db", "r+")                                    #(L)
    i = 0
    while 1:                                                         #(M)
        file_pointer = i * RECORD_LEN                                #(N)
        FILE.seek( file_pointer, 0 )                                 #(O)
        last_name = FILE.read( 10 )                                  #(P)
        if not last_name: break                                      #(Q)
        last_name = last_name.strip("\x00")                          #(R)
        names[last_name] = i                                         #(S)
        i += 1
except IOError, inst:
    print "Error in creating a name-row_index dictionary: ", inst
```

```
while 1:                                                                #(T)
    print "\nLast names of the individuals in the database:\n"          #(U)
    for item in sorted( names.keys() ): print item                      #(V)
    response = raw_input(\
        "\nWhose record would you like to see? Enter last name: " ) #(W)
    if not names.has_key( response ): break                             #(X)
    row_index = names[ response ]                                       #(Y)
    FILE.seek( row_index * RECORD_LEN, 0 )                              #(Z)
    buff = ''
    try:
        buff = FILE.read( 32 )                                          #(a)
    except IOError, inst:
        print "read error: ", inst
        sys.exit(1)
    record = list( struct.unpack( "10s 10s 12s", buff ) )              #(b)
    print "\nHere it is:    %s\t%s\t%s" % \
                        (record[0], record[1], record[2])               #(c)
    old = raw_input("\nEnter the old value you'd like to change: ") #(d)
    new = raw_input( "\nNow enter the new value: " )                    #(e)
    for i in range( len(record) ):                                      #(f)
        if record[i].strip("\x00") == old: record[i] = new; break       #(g)
    if i == 0:                                                          #(h)
        print( "illegal change: changing last name not allowed" )       #(i)
        continue                                                        #(j)
    try:
        FILE.seek( row_index * RECORD_LEN, 0 )                          #(k)
        FILE.write( struct.pack( "10s 10s 12s", \
                        record[0], record[1], record[2] ) )             #(l)
    except IOError, inst:
        print "write error: ", inst
        sys.exit(1)

if FILE: FILE.close()                                                   #(m)
```

16.3 DATABASES STORED AS DISK-BASED HASH TABLES

After flat files, we have disk-based hash tables as the next more sophisticated form of a database for storing information consisting of key-value pairs. Such databases are frequently used in Unix application programs for storing away information that requires persistence. An application may, for example, need to store away the user-specified values for various configuration parameters so that the application can be restarted in the same mode each time. Or an application may need to store its current run-time state, as specified by certain state parameters and their associated values, so that it can be restarted in that state should it be brought to a halt by the user or by some other factor in the environment. Another common example of system-level use of such databases is for the storage of user authentication information where the key-value pairs consist of user names and the associated encrypted passwords.

In Unix-like systems, data persistence for information that consists of key-value pairs is provided by various kinds of libraries that are commonly referred to as DBM libraries. These libraries store the key-value pairs on a disk either in hash tables or in sorted and balanced binary trees. As one would expect, database lookups can be extremely fast with DBM even for large databases. When a DBM is based on a hash, the hashing function directly translates a key into the location of the corresponding value in the storage. And when a DBM is based on a sorted binary tree, a small number of key comparisons, the number being logarithmic in the size of the database, leads to the location of the sought value. Depending on the DBM system, the hashing function for the case of storage based on hash tables and the comparison criterion for the case of tree-based storage may be stored along with the data on the disk.[9] [10]

Over the years, the following variations on the basic DBM have become available:

NDBM, for New DBM, is available through the Perl module `NDBM_File` and the Python module `dbm`. This was the successor to the original DBM. NDBM removed one of the main limitations of DBM which was that it did not allow for more than one database to be open at one time.

SDBM, for Simple DBM or Substitute DBM, is available through the Perl module `SDBM_File`. Faster than NDBM, it is optimized for speed for hash tables when the values associated with the keys are small in size.

GDBM, for GNU DBM, is available through the Perl module `GDBM_File` and the Python module `gdbm`. It is an efficient and versatile database system that at the same time is easy to use. GDBM contains support for concurrency, something

---

[9]Older versions of DBM store the indexing and the data in two separate files. The file with the `.dir` suffix stores the indexing information and the one with the `.pag` suffix the data. For backward compatibility, NDBM and SDBM also create two disk files, but all the information, indexing and data, is stored together in both files — the two files created are identical. SDBM also creates a `.dir` file and a `.pag` file, but the former is empty and the latter (usually much smaller than the files created with other DBM systems) contains all the information. GDBM creates a single file, whose name is the same as specified in the call to `dbmopen()` without any suffixes; this file contains all the indexing information and the data. DB also stores all its information in a single file whose name is the same as specified in the call to `dbmopen()`. Of the DBMs listed here, the old DBM and NDBM do not allow locking and hence are unsafe for concurrent updating by multiple users/processes. Additionally, some of the DBMs impose restrictions on the sizes of the keys and the values stored in the database.

[10]For binary-tree-based storage, the default comparison criterion is usually lexicographic. However, a user is given the option to override the default.

that was lacking in the original DBM. As a result, multiple users/processes can use a GDBM database simultaneously.

DB, provides a choice between hash-based storage, storage based on height-balanced and sorted binary trees, and storage based on flat files. Its Perl interface is provided by the module `DB_File` and the Python interface by the module `bsddb`. Python's `dbhash` provides higher level wrappers for the `bsddb` module.

Note that the database files produced by these different versions of DBM are not interchangeable. Of the versions listed here, only the GDBM and the DB packages are open source. As previously mentioned, a significant shortcoming of the original DBM was that it did not allow for more than one database to be open at any one time. This limitation was removed in NDBM that was the first successor to the old DBM. The other versions of DBM also do not suffer from this limitation.

As we will see in the rest of this section, Perl and Python make it extremely easy to interact with a DBM database.

16.3.1 Perl's dbmopen( ) for Interacting with a Disk-Based Hash Table

In Perl, you can call the built-in function `dbmopen()` to directly bind a DBM database to a named hash.[11] As shown in line (A) of the next script, the basic syntax of a call to `dbmopen()` looks like:

```
dbmopen my %hist, "mydb", 0644
```

As shown, a call to `dbmopen()` takes three arguments: the name of what is commonly referred to as a *disk-based hash* whose key-value pairs are stored on the disk, the stem to be used for naming one or more files that the disk-based hash will be bound to,[12] and the permissions that apply to the database. The third argument is a decimal integer in either the decimal, or the hex, or the octal representation. Obviously, when the third argument begins with a 0, as is the case here, the decimal integer is being specified in octal form. As should be familiar to the Unix users, with the permissions set to 0644, the owner of the database has read/write permissions, the group to which the owner belongs just the read permission, and all others also just the read permission.

---

[11]The more modern way to interact with a disk-based hash in Perl is with the `tie` mechanism that we present in Section 16.4 of this chapter.

[12]The declaration shown will, in general, create two disk files, `mydb.dir` for storing the index and `mydb.pag` for storing the data. But, as we mentioned earlier, the newer DBMs place all of the information in a single `.pag` file even when they create a `.dir` file for backward compatibility.

After establishing a binding between a hash and the disk file(s) in the manner shown above, the hash can be treated in exactly the same manner as a regular Perl hash. So if we subsequently say

```
$hist{ abracadabra } = 2000;
```

a key-value pair with the key set to the string `abracadabra` and the value set to 2000 will be written out to the database on the disk. And if we say

```
print $hist{ abracadabra };
```

the value associated with the key `abracadabra` as stored on the disk will be written out to the standard output.

To further demonstrate `dbmopen()` in a working script, let's say that we want to construct a histogram of all the words in a text file and we want to store the histogram in a DBM database file. A histogram is a natural candidate for a hash because it consists of word-count pairs. So the individual words can serve as the keys in a hash and the associated counts as the values. The script shown below creates such a disk-based database. In line (C), we initialize the database to an empty hash. Line (D) opens the text file for which we want to construct the word-count database. The loop in lines (E) through (H) then scans the text file that is read one line at a time in line (E), splits the line into words using white space as a separator in line (G), cleans the words of any punctuation marks sticking to them also in line (G), and, finally, creates a histogram for the lowercase version of all the words in line (H).

```
#!/usr/bin/perl -w
use strict;

### DBM.pl

dbmopen my %hist, "mydb", 0644                                      #(A)
    or die "Can't create DBM files: $!";                            #(B)
%hist = ();                                                         #(C)

open FILE, "story.txt";                                             #(D)

while (<FILE>) {                                                    #(E)
    chomp;                                                          #(F)
    my @clean_words = map { /([a-z0-9_]+)/i;$1 } split;             #(G)
    map { $hist{ "\L$_" }++ } @clean_words;                         #(H)
}

foreach ( sort keys %hist ) {                                       #(I)
    printf( "%s\t%d\n", $_, $hist{$_} );                            #(J)
}
```

By default, a Perl script uses the NDBM library. However, it is straightforward to use any of the other DBMs by importing the corresponding Perl interface module. For example, if you wanted to use SDBM for the script above, you'd insert the statement

```
use SDBM_File;
```

before the call to `dbmopen()` in line (B). By the same token, you'd import `GDBM_File` or `DB_File` if you wanted the script to use the GDBM or the DB database system.

The print loop shown in lines (I) and (J) of the script shown above creates a sorted display of the histogram stored in the database.

16.3.2 Python for Interacting with Disk-Based Hash Tables

Python's DBM interfaces are provided by the following modules: `dbm`, which is a wrapper for the Unix `ndbm` library; `gdbm`, which is the wrapper for the Unix library of the same name; and `dbhash`, which is a wrapper for the lower-level Python module `bsddb` that serves as a front-end for the BSD's (Berkeley Software Distribution) database library `db`.

Python also provides a module called `anydbm` that uses the `whichdb` module to figure out the type of the DBM database stored on the disk and then automatically invokes the correct DBM module for communicating with the database. If `anydbm` is used to create a new database, it searches through a list consisting of `dbhash`, `gdbm`, and `dbm` modules and uses the first module it can find. If none of the three is available, `anydbm` defaults to the slower pure-Python module `dumbdbm`.[13]

---

[13]Except for the pure-Python but slower `dumbdbm` module, all other DBM modules are in the optional part of a Python installation and may not be available on all platforms. As mentioned earlier in the footnote in the introduction to Section 16.3, also note that the different DBM modules store the database information differently. For the case of Python, when you create a database with the `dbm` module and designate a name for the database, there is only one file created on the disk and the name of this file is what you specified followed by the `.db` suffix. Suppose you named the database as `mydb`, the `dbm` module will store all of the information in a single disk file called `mydb.db`. When you query the type of the database created by calling `whichdb.whichdb('mydb')`, the answer you get back is `dbm`, as you would expect. However, if you make the call `whichdb.whichdb('mydb.db')`, the answer you get back is `dbhash`. When you create a database with the `dbhash` module, again only a single file is deposited on the disk. If you named the database `mydb` in your Python script, the name of the file created is the same. In this case, `whichdb.whichdb('mydb')` reports, as you'd expect, that the database type is `dbhash`. If you use the pure-Python `dumbdbm` module for creating the database, what is actually deposited on the disk are three separate files. If you named the database as `mydb` in the script, the disk files created now are `mydb.dir`, a text file that contains the index; `mydb.bak`, another text file that may be used as a backup for storing the index; and `mydb.dat`, a binary file for storing the data. If you invoke `whichdb.whichdb('mydb')`, it reports back `dumbdbm` for the type of the database, as you would expect. Finally, if you create your database with the `anydbm` module, for the Python installation used by the author, the system selects the `dbhash` for the job. Now, as already mentioned for the case of `dbhash`, only a single file named `mydb` is deposited on the disk.

Shown next is a script, `DBM.py`, whose goal is the same as for the Perl script `DBM.pl` shown previously, which is to construct a disk-based histogram for the words in a text file. As stated previously, a convenient way to store a word histogram is as a dictionary, with the words serving as the keys and the word counts as the corresponding values. In our case, we want the dictionary to be stored in the form of a DBM database.

In lines (A) and (B), the script says that it would like to use the `dbm` module as its first choice for persistent storage.[14] But if `dbm`, an optional module for Python installations, is not available, the script would make do with the slower pure-Python module `dumbdbm`. Line (D) calls on `dbm.open()` — which could actually turn out to be a call to `dumbdbm.open()` — for a database handle to the database named `mydb`. This will cause the system to look for a disk file named `mydb.db`. The second argument to the `dbm.open()` command in line (D) is an optional flag that when used must be one of the following: `r` for a read-only access to the database; `w` for read/write access; `c` for read/write and create if (and only if) the database did not exist previously; and `n` for always creating a new empty database that is open for reading and writing. If left unspecified, the second argument defaults to `r`. The third argument, also optional, expresses the permissions allowed for the database. This argument is used only when the database is first created. With the octal 0644 that we used earlier in the previous subsection, the creator of the database has read/write permissions, but others read only. The default for the third argument is the octal 0666.

Lines (I) and (J) read the entire contents of the named text file into a single string called `allwords`. Line (N) calls on the `split()` method of the `str` class to split the `allwords` string into words. Since `split()` is called without any arguments, the partitioning of `allwords` is carried out on the basis of the white-space characters (spaces, tabs, newlines, returns, and formfeeds). An arbitrary number of adjoining white-space characters is treated as a single delimiter for the purpose of breaking up `allwords`. Subsequently, line (O) calls on the `strip()` method of the `str` class to drop any punctuation marks that may be sticking to the words, and on the `lower()` to convert the word into all lowercase.

To understand lines (P) and (Q), note that the Python DBM modules enforce the requirement of the underlying Unix DBM libraries that the keys and the values stored in the database be all strings. This means that the integer word counts for our word histogram will have to be stored as strings. In line (Q), to update the histogram with a new word, we must first check whether or not the histogram already has an entry for it. If the word was never seen before, we must first create a key-value pair entry in the hash table for the new word and initialize its count to 1. To accomplish this, we first call

```
hist_db.get(word, 0)
```

[14]The syntax in lines (A) and (B) of the script `DBM.py` is of the same form as used earlier in Problem 4 in the Homework section of Chapter 10.

in line (Q). This call returns the string value associated with `word` if `word` is already a key in the dictionary. However, if such a key does not exist, `get(word,0)` creates a new key-value entry in the dictionary, sets the value equal to 0, and returns 0. In either case, we convert the value returned by `get()` to an integer by calling `int()`, increment the integer value, and then reconvert the result into a string for storage in the database, as shown in line (Q).

Lines (U) and (V) of the script show how we can call on the `whichdb` module to determine the type of a DBM database stored on the disk.

```
#!/usr/bin/env python

### DBM.py

import sys

try: import dbm                                                        #(A)
except: import dumbdbm as dbm                                          #(B)

try:                                                                   #(C)
    hist_db = dbm.open( "mydb", 'n', 0644 )                            #(D)
except dbm.error, err:                                                 #(E)
    print "unable to open the database: ", err                         #(F)
    sys.exit(1)                                                        #(G)

try:                                                                   #(H)
   FILE = open( "story.txt", 'r' )                                     #(I)
   allwords = FILE.read()                                              #(J)
except IOError, inst:                                                  #(K)
    print "IO Error: ", inst                                           #(L)
    sys.exit(1)                                                        #(M)

word_list = allwords.split()                                           #(N)
word_list = [word.strip(',.!?').lower() for word in word_list]         #(O)

for word in word_list:                                                 #(P)
    hist_db[word] = str( 1 + int( hist_db.get(word, 0) ) )             #(Q)

for word in sorted( hist_db.keys() ):                                  #(R)
    print( "%s\t%s" % (word, hist_db[word]) )                          #(S)

hist_db.close()                                                        #(T)

import whichdb                                                         #(U)
print whichdb.whichdb( "mydb" )             # dbm                      #(V)
```

As mentioned previously, the DBM modules enforce the requirement that both the keys and the values in the database be strings. This constraint is relaxed by the `shelve` module that only requires that the keys be strings. With the `shelve` module, a value for a key can be any arbitrary Python object provided it can be serialized by the `pickle` module. Internally, the `shelve` module calls on the `anydbm` module to set up the DBM database. So the calls to `shelve.open()` for communicating with the database are internally translated into the calls to `anydbm.open()`.[15]

Shown next is an extended version of the previous script that cannot use — at least as straightforwardly as we will show below — any of the DBM modules for the persistent word-histogram it constructs. This script constructs a histogram that not only shows how many times a word appears in a text file, but also all of the positions at which the word appears in `word_list`, the list of all the words read from the text file. Therefore, we now want the key-value database stored on the disk to look like:

```
a       [1, [34]]
are     [2, [2, 5]]
city    [2, [36, 39]]
flying  [1, [6]]
good    [3, [14, 23, 27]]
great   [2, [35, 49]]
city    [4, [7, 16, 43]]
...
...
...
```

This database says that there is only one occurrence of the word "a" and it is at the position index 34. Similarly, there are two occurrences of the word "are" at positions 2 and 5, and so on. Therefore, whereas each key is still a string in the new histogram, the value we want to store for each key is now a list that consists of an integer item and an embedded list. As shown in the next script, we can easily construct this sort of a persistent database with the `shelve` module.

Except for the call to `shelve.open()` in line (D), everything in this script is the same up to line (I) as in the previous script. What happens after line (I) is important for understanding a significant "restriction" on the use of the `shelve` module. You see, if `hist_db` was an ordinary fast-memory-based dictionary (the usual kind of a dictionary), the loop in lines (J) through (R) could be replaced by the more straightforward loop:

[15] A call to `shelve.open()` also takes on an argument for a parameter that is named `writeback`. By default `writeback` is `False`. When set to `True`, any new entries for the database or any modifications to the database are not written out to the disk until the database is closed or until `sync()` is called to flush the changes to the disk.

```
for i in range(len(word_list)):
    word = word_list[i]
    if word not in hist_db:
        hist_db[word] = [1, [i]]
    else:
        hist_db[word][0] = 1 + hist_db[word][0]
        hist_db[word][1].append(i)
```

which simply says that if a word is not already a key in the database, we need to create a key-value pair entry for it where the key is the word and the value the list `[1,[i]]` with `i` being the position of the word in the input list. But if the word is already serving as a key in the database, we want to increment the count associated with the word and append the position index of the word to the embedded list in the value associated with that key.

The above loop is obviously straightforward, but it cannot be used as it is in the `Shelve.py` script shown below. That is because the value stored in the persistent medium (the disk file) by `shelve` for a given key is the serialized (that is, pickled in Python-speak) version of the object. That makes the value object not directly accessible for modification. The value object must be pulled back into the fast memory (which causes its deserialization) and then manipulated for any changes before it is put back into persistent storage. Compare the loop shown above with the actual loop implemented in the script in lines (J) through (R). The beginning part of the loop, in lines (J) through (M), stays unchanged. That is because the database access in line (M) is a simple assignment, meaning that it is a straightforward write to the disk (it does not require reaching inside an object stored on the disk). The part of the loop that is very different is in lines (O) through (R). We now wish to increment the number stored in the first element of the list and, at the same time, append a new entry at the back of the embedded list. In line (O), we therefore retrieve the object from the persistent storage; this causes its deserialization. We are now free to modify the object, which is what we do in lines (P) and (Q). Subsequently, we write the mutated object back into the persistent storage through the assignment in line (R).

```
#!/usr/bin/env python

### Shelve.py

import sys                                                              #(A)
import shelve                                                           #(B)

try:                                                                    #(C)
    hist_db = shelve.open( "mydb", 'n' )                                #(D)
except shelve.error, err:                                               #(E)
    print "unable to open the database: ", err
    sys.exit(1)
```

```
try:
   FILE = open( "story.txt", 'r' )                                  #(F)
   allwords = FILE.read()                                           #(G)
except IOError, inst:
    print "IO Error: ", inst
    sys.exit(1)

word_list = allwords.split()                                        #(H)
word_list = [word.strip(',.!?').lower() for word in word_list]      #(I)

for i in range(len(word_list)):                                     #(J)
    word = word_list[i]                                             #(K)
    if word not in hist_db:                                         #(L)
        hist_db[word] = [1, [i]]                                    #(M)
    else:                                                           #(N)
        temp = hist_db[word]                                        #(O)
        temp[0] += 1                                                #(P)
        temp[1].append(i)                                           #(Q)
        hist_db[word] = temp                                        #(R)

for word in sorted( hist_db.keys() ):                               #(S)
    print( "%s\t%s" % (word, hist_db[word]) )                       #(T)

hist_db.close()                                                     #(U)
```

16.4 USING DBMS THROUGH THE TIE MECHANISM IN PERL

Perl gives us a neat facility for binding a variable to a class-type object so that any subsequent accesses to the variable are translated automatically into method calls on the object. When you assign a new value to such a variable, the simple assignment syntax implicitly invokes a method that can write out the new value of the variable to a DBM database for achieving data persistence. When a variable is bound to an object so that the usual operations on the variable result *implicitly* in calls to the various methods defined for the object, we say the variable has been *tied* to the object.

The syntax for tying a variable to an object is

```
tie( var,  class_name,  list_of_args )                              #(A)
```

where the first argument, `var`, is the variable that needs to be bound to an instance of the class named in the second argument, `class_name`. The third argument, `list_of_args`, is then supplied to a specially named function that actually creates the binding between the first-argument variable and an instance of the class named in the second argument. As to which function is used for creating this binding depends on whether the variable in the first argument in line (A) is a scalar, an array, or a hash. When the variable is a scalar, the call to `tie()` shown in line (A) above uses the `TIESCALAR()` method of the class named in the second argument. For this to work, the class named in the second argument must implement a static method named `TIESCALAR()`. On the other hand, when the variable named in the first argument to `tie()` is of type array, the call to `tie()` uses the method `TIEARRAY()` of the class named in the second argument. By the same token, when the variable named in the first argument is of type hash, `tie()` calls on the method `TIEHASH()` of the second-argument class for creating the binding needed. In all three cases, `list_of_args` supplied through the last argument in line (A) is passed on to the function creating the binding. Also, in all three cases, the call to `tie()` returns whatever is returned by the function creating the binding. This will usually be a blessed reference, as we will see shortly with an example.[16]

In addition to one or more of the three methods named above — `TIESCALAR()`, `TIEARRAY`, and `TIEHASH()` — a class whose instance is to be tied to a variable must also provide implementations for certain other named methods so that the variable can act as expected. If the class is meant for tying to scalar variables, then for the variables to act like Perl's regular scalar variables, the class must provide implementations for `STORE()`, `FETCH()`, `DESTROY()` and, possibly, `UNTIE()`. The code in the `STORE()` method would be executed when the variable is assigned a new value. This code could do to the new value whatever the programmer's heart desires. For example, one could write out the new value to the disk, if data persistence is the goal (although, as the reader will see shortly, using a hash variable is the preferred way to do that). Similarly, the programmer-supplied code in `FETCH()` would return the latest value of the variable from wherever it was placed by `STORE()`. The purpose of the code provided for `DESTROY()` would be to carry out cleanup operations should the variable go out of scope or be intentionally destroyed at run time. And, finally, the purpose of the code written for `UNTIE()` is to again carry out any cleanup operations needed before the binding between the variable and its associated object is removed.[17] [18]

To further illustrate the idea of tying a variable to an object, let's consider the case when the variable is a scalar and let's say that the job of the object is to "secretly"

---

[16]The three methods, `TIESCALAR()`, `TIEARRAY`, and `TIEHASH()`, are all constructors since their main job is to return a blessed reference to an object that can be thought of as an instance of the class for which these methods are defined.

[17]The `STORE()`, `FETCH()`, `DESTROY()`, and `UNTIE()` methods named here are for scalar variables. For array variables, the programmer may need to provide implementation code for some or all of the following methods: `FETCH()`, `STORE()`, `FETCHSIZE()`, `STORESIZE()`, `CLEAR()`, `PUSH()`, `POP()`, `SHIFT()`, `UNSHIFT()`, `SPLICE()`, `LIST()`, `EXTEND()`, `DESTROY()`, and `UNTIE()`. And for a tied hash variable to act like Perl's regular hash variables, the relevant methods are `FETCH()`, `STORE()`, `DELETE()`, `CLEAR()`, `EXISTS()`, `FIRSTKEY()`, `NEXTKEY()`, `DESTROY()`, and `UNTIE()`.

[18]As mentioned previously in Chapter 2, Perl uses the convention that the methods whose names are all uppercase are meant to be called implicitly by the system.

add a bias to whatever value is assigned to the variable. We will store the value of the bias in `bias` and the true value of the variable in `true_val`, both instance variables of a class named `X`. How we can do this is illustrated in the next script, `TieScalar.pl`. The script first defines a class `X` in lines (A) through (W). The class provides implementations for the methods `TIESCALAR()`, `FETCH()`, `STORE()`, and `DESTROY()`. The `TIESCALAR()` method in lines (B) through (F) returns a blessed reference to a hash.[19] As shown in lines (D) and (E), an instance of `X` returned by `TIESCALAR()` comes with two data attributes, `bias` and `true_val`.[20] Initially, when an instance of `X` is created for tying to a variable, it is through the following call to `tie()`:

```
tie my $x, 'X', (500);
```

The items in the list that is the third argument to `tie()` are supplied as explicit arguments to `TIESCALAR()`, the name of the class being the first implicit argument (as is always the case with constructor calls). So the above call will assign the value of 500 to the data attribute `$bias` in line (C) of the script. This would cause the attributes `bias` and `true_val` of the instance returned to be both set to 500. The method `FETCH()` in lines (N), (O), and (P) returns the true value stored for the variable to which the instance constructed is tied; this is the value that will be returned if we try to just read the value of the variable. The method `STORE()` takes in the value assigned to the variable, adds the bias to this value, and stores the result as the true value of the variable. The method `DESTROY()` in lines (T) through (W) prints out a brief message before the variable is garbage collected. The methods `true_value()` and `get_bias()`, with their lowercase names, are meant to be called explicitly. The former returns the value stored in the `true_val` attribute when the method is called without an explicit argument, and the latter simply returns the value of the bias.

It is the code in the main section of the script, in lines (X) through (x) that should give the reader some deeper insights into the workings of tied variables. Line (Y) ties the variable `$x` to an instance of class `X`. Although one commonly discards the value returned by `tie()` [even when it returns a value; recall that `tie()` returns whatever is returned by `TIESCALAR()`], we have chosen to assign the returned value to the variable `$xobj`. This value will be a blessed reference to the instance of `X` constructed for tying to the variable `$x`. After the call to `tie()` in line (Y), assignments to `$x` in lines (Z) and (b) and attempts to read its value in lines (a) and (c) implicitly invoke the `STORE()` and `FETCH()` methods of class `X`, as confirmed by the outputs shown in lines (a) and (c).

---

[19] It is not necessary for `TIESCALAR()` to return anything. But, as previously mentioned, whatever is returned by `TIESCALAR()` will be returned by the call to `tie()`. If `TIESCALAR()` is programmed to return nothing, a reference to the object that is tied to the variable can still be obtained by calling the built-in function `tied()` with the tie variable as its argument, as we will show later in this example.

[20] What we have frequently called "instance variables" in the past will be referred to as "data attributes" in this section. This is to avoid confusion between the "variable" to which an instance of a class is tied and the "variables" that represent the state of such an instance.

Line (d) ties another variable, `$y`, to an instance of `X`. In line (e), we initialize a new variable `$z` by adding the two tied variables `$x` and `$y`. But, as one would expect, `$z` is an ordinary scalar, devoid of the magic associated with `$x` and `$y`. This fact is confirmed by line (i) which if uncommented will result in an error since there is no object tied to `$z`. On the other hand, when we invoke `tied()` on the variables `$x` and `$y` in lines (g) and (h), we can retrieve the references to the objects that are bound to those variables.

Line (j) shows that whereas the variable `$x` is tied to an instance of class `X`, as a data type `$x` continues to remain just a scalar. So uncommenting line (j) will result in an error since `$x` does not hold a reference to anything. But, of course, if, as shown in line (k), we invoke the function `ref()` on the reference returned by the call to `tie()` in line (Y), we find out that `tie()` constructed an object of type `X`.

The purpose of lines (l), (m), and (n) is to demonstrate that there are two ways to get hold of the object to which a variable is tied to: You can do it either by trapping the value returned by `tie()` or by calling `tied()` on the variable to which the object is tied.[21] So we get the same results in lines (m) and (n) even though in line (m) we invoke `get_bias()` on the reference returned by `tied()`, and in line (n) we invoke the same method on the reference returned by `tie()` in line (Y).

The rest of the script in lines (o) through (x) demonstrates the fact that a reference to the object constructed for tying is held by the system and that this object will not be garbage collected until you untie the variable from its object. So even when we `undef` the variable `$xobj` in line (o) that holds the reference returned by `tie()` in line (Y), the variable `$x` continues to be magical, as demonstrated by lines (p) and (q). However, after we untie the variable in line (r), the tie object is destroyed as evidenced by the output message produced that is shown just below line (r).

After a tied variable is untied, as we do in line (r), it continues to hold its last value, as shown by the output produced by line (s). However, if we assign a new value to it, as we do in line (t), that value will not have the bias added to it. So the output produced in line (u) is the same as the value assigned to the variable in line (t).

Lines (v), (w), and (x) show that we are allowed to use the `TIESCALAR()` method as a regular constructor that returns a blessed reference to an instance of the class. We can invoke on the returned reference any of the methods defined for the class. However, as the reader would expect, the object constructed in this manner bears no relation to the instance constructed by a call to `tie()` even though that call also uses `TIESCALAR()` for instance construction.

---

[21] This obviously assumes that `TIESCALAR()` is programmed to return a blessed reference to the object constructed. If that is not the case, then the only way to get hold of the object tied to a variable is by calling `tied()` as shown.

```
#!/usr/bin/perl -w
use strict;

### TieScalar.pl

#-------------------------  class X  -------------------------------
package X;                                                       #(A)

sub TIESCALAR {                                                  #(B)
    my ( $class, $bias ) = @_;                                   #(C)
    bless { bias => $bias,                                       #(D)
            true_val => $bias                                    #(E)
          }, $class;                                             #(F)
}
sub true_value {                                                 #(G)
    my $ref = shift;                                             #(H)
    @_ ? $ref->{true_val} = shift                                #(I)
       : $ref->{true_val};                                       #(J)
}
sub get_bias {                                                   #(K)
    my $ref = shift;                                             #(L)
    $ref->{bias};                                                #(M)
}
sub FETCH {                                                      #(N)
    my $ref = shift;                                             #(O)
    return $ref->{true_val};                                     #(P)
}
sub STORE {                                                      #(Q)
    my $ref = shift;                                             #(R)
    $ref->{true_val} = $ref->{bias} + shift;                     #(S)
}
sub DESTROY {                                                    #(T)
    my $ref = shift;                                             #(U)
    my $true_val = $ref->true_value();                           #(V)
    print "An X object of datum $true_val " .
                            "about to be destroyed\n";           #(W)
}

#---------------------------  main  ---------------------------------

package main;                                                    #(X)

my $xobj = tie my $x, 'X', (500);                                #(Y)

$x = 100;                                                        #(Z)
print "$x\n";                     # 600                          #(a)
$x = 200;                                                        #(b)
```

```
print "$x\n";                     # 700                               #(c)

tie my $y, 'X', (1000);                                               #(d)
my $z = $x + $y;                  # but $z has no magic               #(e)
print "$z\n";                     # 1700                              #(f)

print tied( $x ), "\n";           # X=HASH(0x804ccf4)                 #(g)
print tied( $y ), "\n";           # X=HASH(0x806d248)                 #(h)
#print tied( $z ), "\n";          # ERROR                             #(i)

#print ref( $x );                 # ERROR                             #(j)
print ref( $xobj ), "\n";         # X                                 #(k)

my $ref = tied( $x );                                                 #(l)
print $ref->get_bias, "\n";       # 500                               #(m)
print $xobj->get_bias, "\n";      # 500                               #(n)

$xobj = undef;                    # X's destructor NOT called         #(o)
$x = 300;                         # $x still has magic                #(p)
print "$x\n";                     # 800                               #(q)
untie $x;                         # X's destructor called             #(r)
    # output: "An X object of datum 800 is about to be destroyed"
print "$x\n";                     # 800                               #(s)
$x = 300;                         # $x no longer has magic            #(t)
print "$x\n";                     # 300                               #(u)

$xobj = X->TIESCALAR(500);                                            #(v)
print ref( $xobj ), "\n";         # X                                 #(w)
print $xobj->get_bias, "\n";      # 500                               #(x)
```

Now that the reader understands the concept of tying a variable to an object, we are ready to explain how this concept can be used for data persistence. Tying a variable for data persistence involves tying a hash variable to an instance of a class whose methods are designed to interact with a disk-based DBM database. This causes the hash to reside on the disk, as opposed to in the fast memory of the computer. So when you enter a new key-value pair into the hash, the information is silently written out to the disk. And when you try to retrieve the value associated with a key using the syntax one commonly uses for hashes, the value is fetched from the database on the disk. As far as the user is concerned, the script looks very much like any other script that uses a hash for storing the key-value pairs, but now the actual storage is on the disk. When a hash is used in this manner, it is also referred to as a *disk-based hash*.

The basic syntax for tying a hash variable to a disk-based database file is the same as the syntax shown earlier for tying a scalar variable:

```
tie( hash_name,  class_name,  list_of_args );
```

This is the syntax used in line (C) of the script shown next. However, unlike the scalar example shown earlier, this time we do not ourselves have to define a class for implementing the behavior we want from the tied hash. That is because we can now use a predefined class such as `SDBM_File` in a module of the same name that comes with the standard Perl distribution. That should explain the first and the second arguments in line (C) of the script. By virtue of the syntax shown above, the other three arguments in line (C), that is

```
'my_database',  O_RDWR|O_CREAT,  0640
```

are supplied as arguments to the constructor `TIEHASH()` of the class `SDBM_File`. The first of these, `my_database`, will be the name of the SDBM database on the disk; it is in this database that the disk-based hash `%h` will be stored. The second argument, `O_RDWR|O_CREAT`, is a bitwise or'ed combination of the two flags `O_RDWR` and `O_CREAT` that are defined in the `Fcntl` module, with `O_RDWR` causing the database files to be opened in read/write mode and `O_CREAT` causing those files to be created if they do not already exist.[22] The last argument specifies the permissions on the database in the form of an octal number. In this case, the database files will be readable and writable by the owner of the database, but only readable to the other members of the group to which the owner of the database may belong.

With the hash `%h` tied to the DBM database by the statement in line (C), all of the usual hash operations on `%h` will be with respect to the database on the disk. So the key-value pairs created in lines (E), (F), and (G) will actually be written out to the disk and stored in the `my_database` database. And when we access these key-value pairs in line (H) for the purpose of printing them out, we will be retrieving them from the disk file. The output produced is shown in the commented-out section just below line (I). In line (J), we untie the hash `%h`, which should cause the destruction of the `SDBM_File` instance created in line (C) for binding with the variable `%h`.

In the rest of the script, in lines (K) through (O), we first tie another hash, `%g`, to the same database. In this case, the goal is merely to read the database through `%g`. So, in line (K), we specify the flag `O_RDONLY` for read-only. The output produced by the loop in lines (H) and (I) is shown in the commented-out section just below line (N).

---

[22]As mentioned previously in Chapter 15, the `Fcntl` module is a wrapper for the C header file `fcntl.h` that declares the POSIX functions: `open()` that opens a file for I/O and returns a file-descriptor to the file for that purpose; `close()` for closing a file descriptor; the functions `read()` and `write()` for file I/O using the descriptors; the `fcntl()` function for changing the properties of the file-descriptors; etc. This header file also declares various macros that are used for specifying the I/O properties of the file-descriptors. The name `fcntl` stands for "file control." The importance of the `Fcntl` Perl module (and of the `fcntl.h` header file in C) lies in the fact that all I/O in Unix-like systems amounts to I/O with a file. For example, to access one of the two serial ports `S0` and `S1` made available by Linux, you open the device files `/dev/ttyS0` and `/dev/ttyS1`, respectively, by calling the POSIX function `open()` defined in the `fcntl.h` header file.

```
#!/usr/bin/perl -w
use strict;

### TieHash.pl

use Fcntl;                                                              #(A)
use SDBM_File;                                                          #(B)

tie my %h, 'SDBM_File', 'my_database', O_RDWR|O_CREAT, 0640             #(C)
    or die "Cannot connect with the database: $!";                      #(D)

$h{ a } = 10;                                                           #(E)
$h{ b } = 20;                                                           #(F)
$h{ c } = 30;                                                           #(G)

while ( my ($key, $value) = each %h ) {                                 #(H)
    print "$key ===>>> $value\n";                                       #(I)
}
                                #     a ===>>> 10
                                #     b ===>>> 20
                                #     c ===>>> 30
untie %h;                                                               #(J)

#  Test reading from the disk file named 'my_database'
tie my %g, 'SDBM_File', 'my_database', O_RDONLY, 0640                   #(K)
    or die "Cannot connect with the database: $!";                      #(L)

while ( my ($key, $value) = each %g ) {                                 #(M)
    print "$key --->>> $value\n";                                       #(N)
}
                                #     a --->>> 10
                                #     b --->>> 20
                                #     c --->>> 30
untie %g;                                                               #(O)
```

In the example above, we had a system-supplied class SDBM_File that we used to tie to a hash. What if you want to define your own class for tying to a hash? If you want to define your own class, it must provide all the functionality that is needed for a Perl hash. As mentioned previously, this functionality consists of the class providing implementation code for the following methods: STORE(), FETCH(), DELETE(), EXISTS(), FIRSTKEY(), NEXTKEY(), CLEAR(), UNTIE(), and DESTROY(). As implied by the names of these functions, the method STORE() would be implicitly invoked by assignment statements such as $h{a}=1, assuming that the name of the tied hash is %h. On the other hand, the method FETCH() would be implicitly invoked when we attempt to retrieve the value associated with a key. The method `DELETE()` would provide the implementation needed for executing statements like `delete $h{a}` and the method `EXISTS()` for statements like `exists $h(a)`. The methods `FIRSTKEY()` and `NEXTKEY()` would allow us to walk through the hash one key-pair at a time. The method `CLEAR()` would be the implementation for executing statements like `%h=()`.

16.5 SERIALIZATION OF COMPLEX DATA STRUCTURES FOR PERSISTENCE

As already demonstrated in Sections 16.3 and 16.4, a regular hash, one consisting of key-value pairs in which both the keys and the values are strings, can easily be stored in a persistent manner though the use of a disk-based hash in the form of a DBM file. However, a more complex data structure — say a hash in which the values are references to anonymous hashes or anonymous arrays — cannot be stored directly in a DBM file since the references have meaning only when the information is still in the fast memory.[23]

To store a complex data structure, you must first serialize it. *Serialization* means that a nested hierarchical structure will be expressed as a linear structure consisting of strings in such a way that the original structure can be restored by a *deserialization* step. The linear structure produced by serialization can be stored away on a disk as a text file and brought back into the fast memory at a later time to reestablish the original complex data structure. The three commonly used Perl modules for serialization are `FreezeThaw`, `Data::Dumper`, and `Storable`. With regard to Python, the most commonly used module for serialization is `pickle`.

In the rest of this section, we will first demonstrate serialization/deserialization in Perl using the `Storable` module. We will follow that with a similar Python example using the `pickle` module.

In the Perl script shown next, lines (B) through (E) create a mixture of simple and complex data structures. In line (B), we have a reference to an anonymous array. The right-hand side in line (C) returns a reference to a nested hash; the values associated with the top-level keys in the hash are themselves references to anonymous hashes.[24] And then we have two ordinary scalars in lines (D) and (E). Line (G) then calls the `store()` function of the `Storable` module for the serialization of these four data structures and, at the same time, for the storage of the serialized representation in a text file called `test.txt`. Note that the first argument supplied to `store()` is the reference returned by Perl's anonymous array constructor `[]`; this array contains the

---

[23]Note that the script `Shelve.py` of Section 16.3.2, where we stored a nested data structure in a DBM file, used the `pickle` module under the hood for the serialization of the data structure.

[24]Anonymous arrays and hashes were presented in Chapter 5.

four top-level scalars on the left-hand sides of the assignments in lines (B) through (E). In general, the `store()` function creates a serialized representation of the object whose reference is supplied as the first argument and then writes it out to the disk file whose name is supplied as the second argument.

The retrieval from a disk file containing a serialized representation is carried out by the `retrieve()` function with the name of the text file supplied as the argument to the function, as shown in line (J).

The `retrieve()` function returns a reference to the object that was stored away by the `store()` function. In our case, we supplied the `store()` function with a reference to an anonymous array. The `retrieve()` function therefore returns a reference to the anonymous array it creates in the fast memory using the information pulled from the database disk file. Lines (L), (N), (R), and (S) then recover from this array its individual elements. The first element, retrieved in line (L), is a reference to an anonymous array of pets. Line (M) retrieves this array and prints out its contents. Line (N) retrieves the reference to the anonymous hash. Line (P) extracts the keys of the hash and line (Q) prints them out. In line (R) we recover the first of the two scalars stored in the top-level array, and so on.[25]

```
#!/usr/bin/perl -w
use strict;

###  Serialization.pl

use Storable;                                                              #(A)

my $pets = ["poodle", "chihuahua", "huskie"];                              #(B)
my $fruit = { banana  =>  { color =>  'yellow',                            #(C)
                            price =>  0.35 },
              orange  =>  { color => 'orange',
                            price =>  0.28 } };
my $current_year = 2008;                                                   #(D)
my $name = "Beeblecrox";                                                   #(E)

eval {                                                                     #(F)
    store( [$pets, $fruit, $current_year, $name], 'test.txt' );            #(G)
};
if ($@) {                                                                  #(H)
    print "Error in eval: $@";                                             #(I)
}
```

[25]We intentionally chose different symbolic names for the top-level scalars at the storage time and at the retrieval time. This was simply to point out that it is not necessary for those names to be the same. The same is true of the `FreezeThaw` approach to serialization.

```
#------------------------------------------------------------------------
# Retrieving data from the disk file:

my $recover = retrieve( 'test.txt' );                                #(J)

print $recover, "\n";              # ARRAY(0x805191c)               #(K)
my $beasts = $recover->[0];                                          #(L)
print "@$beasts\n";                # poodle chihuahua huskie        #(M)

my $froot = $recover->[1];                                           #(N)
print "$froot\n";                  # HASH(0x808b798)                #(O)
my @allkeys = keys( %$froot );                                       #(P)
print "@allkeys\n";                # orange banana                  #(Q)

print "$recover->[2]\n";           # 2008                           #(R)

print "$recover->[3]\n";           # Beeblecrox                     #(S)
```

As mentioned, serialization in Python is carried out with the `pickle` module (or with the faster but not subclassable `cPickle` module). Shown next is a Python version of the previous Perl script. After creating the data items in lines (B) through (H), the script calls on `pickle.dumps()` in line (I) for serializing a tuple of all the data objects. The call to `pickle.dumps()` returns a serialized string that can be deserialized by calling `pickle.loads()`, as we do in line (J). Lines (K) through (N) demonstrate that the deserialized structure recovered from the serialization contains all of the data object we asked `pickle` to serialize. Whereas `pickle.dumps()` returns a serialized string, `pickle.dump()` writes out the serialization directly to a text file, as we show in line (O). The output file thus produced can be deserialized by calling `pickle.load()`, as we do on line (P).

```
#!/usr/bin/env python

###  Serialization.py

import pickle                                                        #(A)

pets  = ("poodle", "chihuahua", "huskie")                            #(B)
fruit = { "banana" : { "color" : 'yellow',                           #(C)
                       "price" :  0.35 },                            #(D)
          "orange" : { "color" : 'orange',                           #(E)
                       "price" :  0.28 } }                           #(F)
current_year = 2008                                                  #(G)
name = "Beeblecrox"                                                  #(H)
```

```
# Serialize the above objects into a single byte stream:
serialized_output = pickle.dumps((pets, fruit, current_year, name)) #(I)

# Recover the individual objects from the serialized stream:
recover = pickle.loads( serialized_output )                       #(J)

print recover[0]    # ('poodle', 'chihuahua', 'huskie')            #(K)

print recover[1]    # {'orange': {'color': 'orange',               #(L)
                    #             'price': 0.28000000000000003},
                    #  'banana': {'color': 'yellow',
                    #                      'price': 0.34999999999999998}}
print recover[2]    # 2008                                         #(M)

print recover[3]    # Beeblecrox                                   #(N)

#---------------------------------------------------------------------
# Directly write out the serialization to a file:
pickle.dump((pets, fruit, current_year, name),open('backup.p', 'w'))#(O)

#---------------------------------------------------------------------
# Restore the objects from the disk file:
restored = pickle.load( open( 'backup.p' ) )                       #(P)

print restored      # exactly the same as for the 'recover' string  #(Q)
```

16.6 RELATIONAL DATABASES

That brings us to what are currently the most sophisticated databases — the *relational databases*. These databases are sophisticated in the sense that they store interlinked multi-tabular information of arbitrary complexity in fast and efficient data structures, and they require a database server to be installed and configured for a user to be able to interact with them. These databases also allow for a user's privileges to be controlled selectively at the level of individual operations on the database tables.[26]

[26]For example, a user may only be allowed to insert new rows into a specified set of tables of a database. Or a user could be given permissions for inserting new rows and/or for their deletion, but again for a specified set of tables, etc. In MySQL all of the user-related information is kept in a database called `mysql` that ordinarily can only be accessed by someone with root privileges to the database system. As to what specific permissions are allowed for each user, that information is stored in a table called `db` in the `mysql` database. A display of the column headings of this table obtained by the `describe db` command in the `mysql` monitor shows that, in general, a user can be given privileges selectively for the following

A relational database, in general, consists of a collection of tables, each table optimally representing some aspect of the information. Consider, for example, a database for storing information on all the books in a library. Let's say that we want to store the following information on each book:

```
Title
Author
Year
ISBN
NumberOfCopies
Publisher
PublisherLocation
PublisherURL
PublisherRep
PublisherRepPhone
PublisherRepEmail
```

Let's assume that the library has 100,000 books that are published by, say, 100 publishers. For the sake of making a point, let's also assume that each publisher is represented equally well in the library. If we stored all of this book-related information in a single "flat" table with 11 columns, one for each of the items listed above, the information in at least 3 of the columns — those under the column headings `Publisher`, `PublisherLocation`, and `PublisherURL` — would be the same for the 1000 rows corresponding to each publisher. That obviously is not an efficient way to store the information. There would be too much "redundancy" in the table. Since it goes without saying that the larger the number of entries that need to be made to create a table, the greater the probability of an error creeping into one or more of the entries, our table would be at an increased risk of containing erroneous information. The table with the column headings as shown above will also have redundancies with regard to the "PublisherRep" information.

Now consider an alternative design consisting of three tables, one containing information generic to each book, the other containing information generic to each publisher, and the third containing information generic to each publisher rep:

```
BookTable:
    Title
    Author
    Year
    ISBN
    PublisherID
    PublisherRepID

PublisherTable:
    PublisherID
```

SQL operations: `SELECT`, `INSERT`, `UPDATE`, `DELETE`, `CREATE`, `DROP`, `GRANT`, `REFERENCES`, `INDEX`, `ALTER`, `CREATE_TMP_TABLE`, and `LOCK_TABLES` operations.

```
        PublisherName
        PublisherLocation
        PublisherURL

    PublisherRepTable:
        PublisherRepID
        RepName
        RepPhone
        RepEmail
```

We now associate unique identifiers, possibly numerical in nature, in the form of `PublisherID` and `PublisherRepID` to "link" the main book table, `BookTable`, with the other two tables, `PublisherTable` and `PublisherRepTable`.

These three tables together would constitute a typical modern relational database. Given this database, we may now query the database for information that for simple queries can be extracted from a single table, but that for more complex queries may require simultaneous access to multiple tables. Here are examples of simple queries that can be fulfilled from just a single table:

- Retrieve all book titles published in a given year
- Retrieve all book titles published by a given author
- Retrieve all publishers located in France
- Retrieve all publisher rep names
- etc.

and here are examples of queries that require simultaneous access to more than one table in the database:

- Retrieve all book titles along with the name of the publisher for each book
- Retrieve all books for which the designated publisher rep is given
- Retrieve all book titles published last year along with the name of the publisher for each and the name of the publisher's rep
- etc.

Other possible interactions with the database could consist of updating the database as the library acquires additional books, modifying the entries, and so on.

Over the years, a command language called SQL, for *Structured Query Language*, has come into widespread use for interacting with relational databases, especially the server-based databases.[27] A relational database system typically comes with what is known as a *database driver* that, on the one hand, understands the SQL statements fed to it by a user and, on the other, the internal representations used for the rows and the columns of the database tables. This allows the database driver to execute the SQL commands for either fetching information from the database or for modifying the database entries.[28]

16.7 PERL FOR INTERACTING WITH RELATIONAL DATABASES

The previous section provided a brief overview of the basic multi-table structure of a relational database. Now we will show how one can write Perl scripts to interact with such a database. When we need to show database specific examples, we will use the open-source MySQL database system for that purpose.

In Perl, the work of translating SQL commands into operations on database tables is carried out by a combination of the DBI module and a database-specific driver module. DBI, which stands for *database independent interface*, defines a standard interface that a Perl script can use to communicate with any of a large number of commercial and open-source database systems. DBI achieves its database independence by delegating database-specific duties to drivers particular to the database systems. By convention, the database-specific driver modules are named `DBD::xyz`, where `xyz` stands for the specific database. For example, the driver module for the MySQL relational database system is called `DBD::mysql`, the driver for the Oracle database system `DBD::Oracle`, the one for the Sybase `DBD::Sybase`, the one for text files (that contain comma-separated fields in each record) `DBD::CSV`, and so on. Obviously, the acronym DBD in these names stands for *database driver*. In addition to dispatching the method invocations that call for interacting with the actual database to the appropriate DBD module, the DBI module also carries out error checking and handling, dynamic loading of driver modules, etc.

The DBI module's functionality is used through a set of handles that work very much like the filehandles and the socket handles that we talked about in Chapters 2 and 15. DBI defines the following handles: the *driver handle*, the *database handle*, and the *statement handle*. The following three subsections provide a brief introduction to each of these handles. Included in this discussion are the conventions one typically follows in naming the variables that hold the handles. Subsequently,

---

[27] The desktop-based databases are usually accessed through graphical user interfaces. But even here the graphical input supplied by a user may be converted into an SQL statement that then is used to interact with the database.

[28] Chapter 20 of [41] provides a quick review of the SQL commands we have used in this section. This is done there through the medium of two interactive sessions with a MySQL database through the `mysql` monitor.

we will quickly review some of the other conventions used in DBI. Finally, we will present a couple of scripts that use DBI.

16.7.1 DBI: Database Driver Handle

This handle, used to talk directly to the database driver, is useful for such administrative tasks as creating a new database, deleting an existing database, shutting down the database server, and so on. By convention, the variable that stores a reference to the instance of the driver module being used is named `$drh`. Here is a typical call that constructs a driver handle for a MySQL database server:

```
$drh = DBI->install_driver( 'mysql' );
```

Subsequently, methods may be invoked on `$drh`, as in the following example where we are trying to create a new MySQL database:

```
$rc = $drh->func("createdb", $dbname, [host,user,password,], 'admin');
```

where the first, the second, and the last arguments are mandatory.[29] The last argument, `admin`, means that you are trying to execute one of the `mysqladmin` commands for database administration. Administrative operations, and therefore the `admin`-type calls to `func`, are meant for creating and dropping databases, changing

---

[29]Of course, it is more likely to be the case that you'll create a new database by logging directly into the database server as an administrator. For example, with MySQL you could first gain access to the monitor for the database server by

```
mysql -u root -p mysql
```

Subsequently, you could create a new database by

```
mysql> create database database_name;
```

where `mysql>` is the monitor prompt. Usually, after you have created a new database, you'd need to create an "admin" account with certain specific administrative privileges for the database. The admin account can be created by

```
mysql> grant all privileges on database_name.* to admin_name \
                                   identified by 'password';
```

where the password must be within single quotes. If you wanted to give this account certain other privileges outside of those concerning the new database just created, say like the FILE privileges, you would say

```
mysql> grant file on *.* to admin_name;
```

You would now set up new user accounts for this new database by something like

```
mysql> grant select,insert,update,delete on database_name.* \
                 to a_new_user_name identified by 'password';
```

After you are done creating all the admin and user accounts, you'd activate them by

```
mysql> flush privileges;
```

Finally, you can quit the monitor by

```
mysql> quit
```

passwords, reloading grant tables, flushing tables to disk, flushing log files, and so on.[30]

16.7.2 DBI: Database Handle

A database handle is a child of the applicable driver handle.[31] It is through a database handle that a Perl script connects with a database. In that sense, a database handle is your script's gateway to the database. One of the primary functions of this handle is to convey SQL statements to the database server.

By convention, the variable that stores a reference to an instance of the database handle is named `$dbh`. A database handle is typically created by a `connect()` call as shown in the second statement below:

```
$dsn = "DBI:mysql:database=database_name; host=localhost";
$dbh = DBI->connect( $dsn, $user, $password,
                     { RaiseError => 1, AutoCommit => 1 } );
```

where the first statement names the data source. Note the special syntax for naming the data source; note especially its colon delimited substrings. The prefix `DBI` must come before the first colon and the name of the driver must be between the two colons. What comes after the second colon is passed verbatim to the `connect()` method of the database driver in the second statement above. This additional text that comes after the second colon is specific to each different type of a database. Some database systems require the name of the database, the name of the host, the name of the port, etc., whereas others may require only a single word identifier that points to a more complex string stored away in some configuration file.

Getting back to the second statement above that returns a database handle, note that the final argument in the call to `connect()` is optional. When supplied, this argument consists of an anonymous hash that is used to set values for the various attributes of the database handle. The two most commonly set handle attributes are `RaiseError` and `AutoCommit`. By default the `RaiseError` attribute is off

---

[30] Instead of creating a database through the `mysql` terminal monitor, as we showed in the previous footnote, we could also do the same with the following `mysqladmin` command line:

```
mysqladmin -u root -p create new_database_name
```

Here is an example of a call to `mysqladmin` that drops a database:

```
mysqladmin -u root -p drop new_database_name
```

Another useful invocation of the `mysqladmin` command is

```
mysqladmin -u root -p version
```

that displays on the terminal some useful information related to licensing and some statistics concerning the operation of the server since it was last brought up. In all of the `mysqladmin` calls shown, the `-p` option causes you to be prompted for a password.

[31] That obviously implies that all of the driver handle methods can be invoked on a database handle.

(meaning set to 0). Turning on this attribute, as we have done in the call shown above, causes the DBI module to provide automatic error handling that consists of outputting an error message and invoking `die()` to terminate the script should anything go wrong.[32] If the `RaiseError` attribute is turned off (as it is by default), one must perform error checking manually. Such would be the case with the following version of the `connect()` call for constructing a database handle:

```
$dbh = DBI->connect( $dsn, $user, $password )
             or die "Can't connect to database: $DBI->errstr\n";
```

Note that the message that will be printed out should the connection fail will contain a database-specific reason for failure as supplied by the variable `$DBI::errstr`. When performing manual error checking for methods invoked on a database handle, the database-specific reason for failure can be retrieved from `$dbh->errstr` as opposed to the variable `$DBI->errstr` shown above.

With regard to the `AutoCommit` attribute, although on (meaning set to 1) by default, it is recommended that the setting of this attribute be shown explicitly. When `AutoCommit` is on, each SQL statement communicated to the database makes its changes to the database immediately. On the other hand, when this attribute is off, the changes called for are not actually reflected in the database until a subsequent call to `$dbh->commit()`. Before `commit()` is called, the changes can be undone by calling `$dbh->rollback()`. Setting `AutoCommit` to off is important for transaction processing. A single transaction may call for making changes to multiple tables of a database. You would either want all of the changes to take place or none. That is exactly what is accomplished with the autocommit feature turned off. Consider a case when a transaction calls for inserting a new row into the employee table (because a new employee joined the organization) and also inserting a new row in the department table reflecting the addition of the new employee. Should it happen that we are unable to make the second insertion for whatever reason after the first insertion is carried out successfully, we will have an inconsistent database. With `AutoCommit` turned off, this will not happen, because now you will call `commit()` after the two insert statements to make the two changes simultaneously.

[32]Obviously, the behavior of `die()` to terminate a script can be overridden by defining one's own `$SIG{__DIE__}` signal handler. We should also mention that there is another useful handle attribute for error handling: `PrintError`. It is on by default. When on, it causes warning messages to be handled by Perl's built-in `warn()` function, which unless overridden by `$SIG{__WARN__}` causes the warning messages to be printed out on the screen. See Section 15.5.1 of Chapter 15 for further information regarding the roles played by the pseudo-signals `__DIE__` and `__WARN__` vis-à-vis the built-in `die()` and `warn()`.

16.7.3 DBI: Statement Handle

A statement handle is created from a database handle and is a child of the latter.[33] A statement handle can be used for a variety of purposes, initially for preparing an SQL statement for later execution and, after the SQL statement is executed, as a means to extract the information returned by the database in response to the SQL statement. By convention, a statement handle is represented by `$sth`. A statement handle is constructed from a database handle by invoking `prepare()` on the latter, as in

```
$sth   =   $dbh->prepare( $statement );
```

where `$statement` is an SQL statement. Once you have a statement handle, it can eventually be executed by the call syntax `$sth->execute`. The usefulness of preparing a statement first and executing it later should be obvious from the following example that uses a *placeholder* "?" whose value is supplied later when `execute()` is called on the statement handle:[34]

```
$sth = $dbh->prepare( 'SELECT * FROM BookTable
                                WHERE author_lastname = ?' );
print "Enter author's last name: ";
while ( $author_lastname = <STDIN> ) {
    chomp $author_lastname;
    $sth->execute( $author_lastname )
}
```

When performing manual error checking for methods invoked on a statement handle, the database-specific reason for failure can be retrieved from the variable `$sth->errstr`.

16.7.4 DBI: Some Other Naming Conventions Used in Scripts

We have already mentioned that by convention, and to the extent feasible, one uses the following variables to hold the references to the three handles defined by DBI: `$drh` for the driver handle, `$dbh` for the database handle, and `$sth` for the statement handle. We will now describe some of the other DBI conventions for naming variables. For starters, it is permissible to use the variable `$h` for any of the three handles discussed so far if for some reason the recommended names `$drh`, `$dbh`, and `$sth` cannot be used.

The variable `$rc` stands for *return code*. If the value returned by a method call is Boolean, we refer to the value as a return code. For example, invoking `commit()` on a database handle, as in

---

[33] That obviously implies that all of the database handle methods can be invoked on a statement handle.

[34] Not all drivers support placeholders.

```
$rc  = $dbh->commit;
```

returns true if it succeeded; otherwise it returns false. When a method call returns a more general integer value, the *return value* is represented by a variable named `$rv`, as in

```
$rv  = $sth->rows;
```

where the right-hand side returns the number of rows affected by the SQL in the statement held by `$sh`. To elaborate on this particular call, if the number of rows is not known or is not available, `$rv` is set to -1. For example, if the SQL statement in `$sth` is

```
UPDATE BookTable SET NumCopies = NumCopies + 1 WHERE Year > 1996;
```

and then if we call the method `row()` as shown above, the value returned would be the number of rows in `BookTable` in which the entry in the `Year` field is greater than the number 1996.[35]

Another naming convention in the scripts using DBI is that the variable `$ary_ref` is used to hold a reference to a row of the *result table* returned by a `SELECT` query. Successive invocations of `fetchrow_arrayref()` on the statement handle return a reference to each row of the result table. To illustrate, shown below is a scriplet whose purpose is to fetch the list of the names and the associated phone numbers from a table called `Friends`. This table presumably contains other information also on each of the friends, information such as the email address, postal address, fax number, etc. But we want the `SELECT` query in line (A) to only retrieve the name and the phone number from each row of the `Friends` table. After the query is executed in line (B), the number of fields in the returned information can be obtained by checking the value of the `NUM_OF_FIELDS` attribute of the statement handle, as we do in line (C). In this case, the value of this attribute would be 2 for the two fields `Name` and `Phone`. Lines (D), (E), and (F) show how a `while` loop can be set up to successively obtain references to each of the rows of the result table returned by `SELECT`. Each row is returned as an array; a reference to this array is stored in the variable `$ary_ref`. So by dereferencing the array reference and indexing the resulting array, as we do in line (F), we can retrieve each entry in each row.[36] [37]

---

[35]This is how `rows()` can be expected to behave on non-SELECT SQL statements. For `SELECT`, `rows()` will return the total number of rows affected only after all the rows have been fetched from the database.

[36]Note that if the value of a field in the database table from which `SELECT` is retrieving information is `NULL`, that value will show up as `undef` in line (F). Also note that when there are no more rows to be fetched from the result table, `fetchrow_arrayref()` returns `undef` in line (D). Since an error condition may also cause `fetchrow_arrayref()` to return `undef`, defensive scripting requires that (if your database handle does not have its `RaiseError` attribute set) you also check the value returned by `$sth->err` afterwords to make sure you indeed retrieved all the rows of the result table.

[37]In case the reader is puzzled by the syntax in line (F), it is simply to produce a comma-separated output for the field values in each row. A comma is prepended to every field value except when `$i` is zero. For obvious reasons, we do not prepend a comma to the very first value in a row.

```
$sth =
  $dbh->prepare("SELECT Friends.Name,
                               Friends.Phone FROM Friends");          #(A)
$sth->execute;                                                        #(B)
$numFields = $sth->{ 'NUM_OF_FIELDS' };                               #(C)
while ( my $ary_ref = $sth->fetchrow_arrayref ) {                     #(D)
    for ( my $i = 0; $i < $numFields; $i++ ) {                        #(E)
        printf( "%s%s", $i ? "," : "", $$ary_ref[$i] );               #(F)
    }
    print "\n";
}
```

Just as `$ary_ref` by convention holds a reference to the array corresponding to a row of the result table returned by the `SELECT` statement, again by convention `@ary` directly holds the list of field values. Here is a different way of writing the above scriplet; it uses the array variable `@ary`. Instead of invoking `fetchrow_arrayref()`, we now invoke `fetchrow_array()` on the statement handle to retrieve the list of field values in a single row of the result table.

```
$sth =
  $dbh->prepare("SELECT Friends.Name, Friends.Phone FROM Friends");
$sth->execute;
while ( my @ary = $sth->fetchrow_array ) {
    for ( my $i = 0; $i < @ary; $i++ ) {
        printf( "%s%s", $i ? "," : "", $ary[$i] );
    }
    print "\n";
}
```

Other naming conventions that are used in scripts based on DBI include `$rows` to designate the number of rows already processed. If this information is not available, the value of `$rows` should be set to -1. Also included in the naming conventions is using the variable `$fh` for filehandles.

16.7.5 An Example

We will now show a simple example to further illustrate how one uses the DBI module for creating a MySQL database and then how one might retrieve information from the database. The example consists of two scripts, one for creating a database and the other for retrieving information from the database created by the first script.

The first script, CreateMyFriendsDB.pl, creates a MySQL database named MyFriends. This script, shown next, invokes in line (G) the install_driver() static method of the DBI module to install the driver for the MySQL database system.[38] Just to show how one can do so, we then check the version number of the driver in line (H). This information is stored in the VERSION static attribute of the DBD::mysql module. In line (I) we erase the MyFriends database if it was already there from a previous run of the script.[39]

Note the use of the func() method in lines (I) and (K). DBI specifies that this function be reserved for calling methods that are supposed to be private to the driver module. (As already shown, this method can also be invoked on a database handle. That works because a database handle is the child of a driver handle.) The func() methods returns 1 or 0 depending on whether the database operation specified by its first argument succeeded or failed. So if the database MyFriends had not been created previously, the call to func() in line (I) would return 0. We intentionally do not trap this error condition because we want to ignore it for an obvious reason: We want the database to be dropped *if* it is there, otherwise we do not care. However, when we use the same func() in line (J) to create the database, we trap the error by calling die() in line (K). We next connect with the newly created database in line (M). We set the handle attributes RaiseError and AutoCommit both to 1 for reasons explained previously.

Now we are ready to populate the new database with tables. The code in lines (N) and (R) creates two tables, Friends and Rovers, the latter presumably the name of a club. The CREATE TABLE command in line (N) declares that the Friends table is to have three columns, with the labels Name, Phone, and Email, the first being the PRIMARY KEY. A field can be designated as a PRIMARY KEY if it can uniquely

---

[38] An alternative approach that is frequently used consists of calling DBI->connect() method directly without first installing the database driver. This you can do even when you must first carry out some administrative chores before interacting with the database. For illustration, the following code snippet calls connect() to first connect with the mysql database that MySQL uses to store user and privileges information. The database handle thus returned is then used to create a new database called MyFriends. When connect() is called before loading the driver explicitly, the DBI module figures out automatically as to which driver to install from the name of the data source that is in the first argument to connect().

```
my $dbh = DBI->connect( 'DBI:mysql:database=mysql', 'root',
            $password, { RaiseError => 1, AutoCommit => 1 } );
$dbh->func('createdb', 'MyFriends', $host, 'root', $password, 'admin');
$dbh->disconnect;
my $dsn = "DBI:mysql:database=MyFriends; host=localhost";
$dbh = DBI->connect( $dsn, 'kak', $password_for_kak,
                      { RaiseError => 1, AutoCommit => 1 } );
```

[39] A less drastic action would be to only delete the tables of the database for every fresh run of the script, as opposed to deleting the database directory itself. Tables can be deleted by the SQL statement DROP TABLE. Yet another alternative is to keep the tables also for each run of the script but only delete the contents of the tables by using the SQL statement DELETE FROM.

identify a row, that is if no two rows will have the same value for that field.[40] As stated in line (N), the three fields for the `Friends` table are of type `CHAR(30)`, `INT`, and `CHAR(30)`, respectively.[41] The `Rovers` table declared in line (R) has just two fields called `Name`, of type `CHAR(30)`, and `RovingTime` of type `CHAR(10)`. The rest of the code consists of making row entries into the two tables.

We have used the `DBI` method `do()` to execute the SQL statements for creating tables and for inserting information into the tables. In general, non-SELECT-type SQL statements are communicated to the database by calling `do()` as shown. On the other hand, `SELECT` statements are communicated through a combination of `prepare()` and `execute()`, as mentioned previously in Section 16.7.3 and as we will demonstrate further in the next script. It is important to note that `do()` does *not* return a statement handle; it is programmed to return the number of rows affected. As a consequence even non-SELECT statements that are expected to return some database information, besides the number of rows affected, need to be executed by the `prepare()-execute()` combination.

```
#!/usr/bin/perl -w

### CreateMyFriendsDB.pl

use strict;
use DBI;                                                                 #(A)

my $driver = 'mysql';                                                    #(B)
my $user = 'kak';                                                        #(C)
my $database = 'MyFriends';                                              #(D)
my $host = 'localhost';                                                  #(E)
my $password = "xxxxxx";                                                 #(F)

my $drh = DBI->install_driver( $driver );                                #(G)
print "Version of DBD mysql module:    ", $DBD::mysql::VERSION, "\n";#(H)

$drh->func('dropdb', $database, $host, $user, $password, 'admin');  #(I)

$drh->func('createdb', $database, $host, $user, $password, 'admin') #(J)
    or die "Cannot create new database: $DBI::errstr\n";                #(K)
```

[40] Characterization of a key as `PRIMARY` is supposed to distinguish it from its declaration as a `FOREIGN KEY`. When a field is declared to be a foreign key in a table, it informs the table that the key in question is a primary key in another table.

[41] `CHAR(n)` is one of the character string data types supported by SQL. Some of the others being `CHAR`, `VARCHAR(n)`, and so on. The difference between `CHAR(n)` and `VARCHAR(n)` is that for the former the system will pad the string with blanks if the number of characters in the string is fewer than `n`. No padding is used for the latter. `INT` is one of the data types for representing numerical information in SQL, the others being `SMALLINT`, `NUMERIC`, `DECIMAL`, `REAL`, `DOUBLE PRECISION`, `FLOAT`, and so on.

```
my $dsn = "DBI:mysql:database=MyFriends; host=localhost";            #(L)

my $dbh = DBI->connect( $dsn, $user, $password,
                        { RaiseError => 1, AutoCommit => 1 } );      #(M)

$dbh->do( "CREATE TABLE Friends ( Name CHAR(30) PRIMARY KEY, " .
                           "Phone INT, Email CHAR(30) )" );          #(N)
$dbh->do( "INSERT INTO Friends VALUES ( 'Ziggy Zaphod', " .
                           "4569876, 'ziggy\@sirius' )" );           #(O)
$dbh->do( "INSERT INTO Friends VALUES ( 'Yo Yo Ma', " .
                           "3472828, 'yoyo\@yippy' )" );             #(P)
$dbh->do( "INSERT INTO Friends VALUES ( 'Gogo Gaga', " .
                           "27278927, 'gogo\@garish' )" );           #(Q)

$dbh->do( "CREATE TABLE Rovers ( Name CHAR(30) NOT NULL, " .
                           "RovingTime CHAR(10) )" );                #(R)
$dbh->do( "INSERT INTO Rovers VALUES ( 'Dusty Dodo', '2 pm' )" );    #(S)
$dbh->do( "INSERT INTO Rovers VALUES ( 'Yo Yo Ma', '8 pm' )" );      #(T)
$dbh->do( "INSERT INTO Rovers VALUES ( 'Bebe Beaut', '6 pm' )" );    #(U)

$dbh->disconnect;                                                    #(V)
```

The next script, `RetrieveFromMyFriendsDB.pl`, shows the use of the DBI module for retrieving information from the MySQL database that was constructed by the previous script. The main purpose of the script is to find out from the `MyFriends` database whether any of the friends (these are individuals listed in the `Friends` table of the database) are also in the `Rovers` club, and, if there happen to be any such friends, to also find out what their roving time is. We also use this script to illustrate a couple of additional features of the `DBI` module.

Lines (B) and (C) connect with the `MyFriends` database. As explained previously, the correct database driver module is loaded automatically before the connection is established, the identity of the driver inferred from the name of the data source. Lines (D) and (E) show a simple example of using the `prepare()`–`execute()` combination to communicate an SQL command to the database. Because we expect the database to return the names of the tables, we could not have used the `$dbj->do()` call to execute the SQL statement `SHOW TABLES`. As mentioned previously, the `$dbh->do()` invocation only returns the number of rows affected. On the other hand, `$dbh->prepare()` returns a statement handle that after the call to `$sth->execute()` can be put to use for retrieving the information returned by the database, as we show in lines (F) and (G). Note the call to `$sth->fetchall_arrayref()` for retrieving at once all of the information returned by the database. What this method returns *from a prepared and executed statement* is a reference to an array of references. DBI returns the output of the SQL command `SHOW TABLE` in the form of a reference to an array whose each element is a reference to the name of a table. This should explain the syntax in lines (H), (I), and (J). Calling `$sth->finish()` in line (K) turns off the `Active` attribute of the statement handle constructed in line (D).[42]

Lines (L) through (P) illustrate how one makes a `SELECT` query to retrieve a portion of a database table. In this case, we want to retrieve just the names and the associated phone numbers from the `Friends` table. In line (L), `SELECT` and `FROM` are SQL keywords. Note the use of the Perl quoting operator `qq{}` that has the same effect as double quoting a string. Although not needed in this case, a `qq{}` string would permit the `$` and `@` variables to be interpolated into the string. Perl also provides the operator `q{}` that single-quotes a string. As one would expect, `q{}` does not permit interpolations. Using the `qq{}` and `q{}` operators frees up the single and double quotes for use inside SQL statements.[43]

Finally, in lines (Q) through (Z), we get to the main purpose of this script, which is to find the friends (from the `Friends` table) who are also members of the `Rovers` club, and, further, to find the roving time of such friends. The `SELECT` query for answering these questions is formed in line (Q). In line (S), we obtain a reference to the array that contains the column headings for the result table returned by the `SELECT` query. Line (T) gives us the number of columns in the result table. The loop in lines (U) and (V) then prints out the column headings for the result table. The result table itself is fetched one row at a time in line (W). The fields in each row are printed out by the loop in lines (X) and (Y).

```
#!/usr/bin/perl -w

### RetrieveFromMyFriendsDB.pl

use strict;
use DBI;                                                                #(A)

my $dsn = "DBI:mysql:database=MyFriends;host=localhost";                #(B)
my $dbh = DBI->connect( $dsn, 'kak', 'avikak',
                    { RaiseError => 1, AutoCommit => 1 } );             #(C)
print "succesfully connected \n";

my $sth = $dbh->prepare( "SHOW TABLES" );                               #(D)
$sth->execute;                                                          #(E)
my $tables_ref = $sth->fetchall_arrayref();                             #(F)
```

[42] All handles, database and statement, possess an attribute called `Active`. A database handle is active as long as it is connected to the database. A statement handle is active as long as it has some more information to fetch from the database. Ordinarily, when all the data is fetched via a statement handle, the driver automatically calls `$sth->finish()` on the handle. So, strictly speaking, we really do not need it in line (K) of the script. That line is included just so we could talk about this method.

[43] DBI also provides a method `$dbj->quote(arg)` that can be used to provide automatic escaping of any special characters, including quote marks, inside an argument string.

```
print "\nNumber of tables: " . @$tables_ref . "\n";                     #(G)
my @tabarr = @$tables_ref;                                              #(H)
print "First table: ", @{$tabarr[0]}, "\n";                             #(I)
print "Second table: ", @{$tabarr[1]}, "\n";                            #(J)
$sth->finish;                                                           #(K)

$sth = $dbh->prepare( qq{SELECT Friends.Name, Friends.Phone
                                             FROM Friends} );           #(L)
$sth->execute;                                                          #(M)
print "\nNames and phone numbers from the Friends table:\n";
while ( my @ary = $sth->fetchrow_array ) {                              #(N)
    for ( my $i = 0; $i < @ary; $i++ ) {                                #(O)
        printf( "%s%s", $i ? "\t" : "        ", $ary[$i] );             #(P)
    }
    print "\n";
}
print "\n\n";

$sth = $dbh->prepare( q{SELECT Friends.Name, Rovers.RovingTime
          FROM Friends, Rovers WHERE Friends.Name = Rovers.Name} ); #(Q)
$sth->execute;                                                          #(R)
print "Friends who are also in the Rovers club:\n";
my $names = $sth->{ 'NAME' };                                           #(S)
my $numFields = $sth->{ 'NUM_OF_FIELDS' };                              #(T)
for ( my $i = 0; $i < $numFields; $i++ ) {                              #(U)
    printf( "%s%s", $i ? "\t\t" : "", $$names[$i] );                    #(V)
}
print "\n";
while ( my $ref = $sth->fetchrow_arrayref ) {                           #(W)
    for ( my $i = 0; $i < $numFields; $i++ ) {                          #(X)
        printf( "%s%s", $i ? "\t" : "", $$ref[$i] );                    #(Y)
    }
    print "\n";
}
$dbh->disconnect;                                                       #(Z)
```

Here is the output produced by the above script:

```
succesfully connected

Number of tables: 2
First table: Friends
Second table: Rovers

Names and phone numbers from the Friends table:
        Ziggy Zaphod    4569876
```

```
        Yo Yo Ma          3472828
        Gogo Gaga         27278927

    Friends who are also in the Rovers club:
    Name            RovingTime
    Yo Yo Ma        8 pm
```

16.8 PYTHON FOR INTERACTING WITH RELATIONAL DATABASES

Whereas in Perl you interact with a relational database through the API of a database-independent module (that in turn talks to a given database through a driver module specific to that database), the approach taken in Python is different. Python specifies a database-independent API, *which is an interface specification only*, for interacting with relational databases. The module writers are then expected to create drivers for interacting with relational databases compliant with this API. The latest version of Python's database-independent API is DB-API v2.0. And the compliant open-source driver module for interacting with MySQL databases is `MySQLdb`.

As far as the APIs go, perhaps the most significant difference between the Perl's DBI module and the Python's DB-API interface is that the functionality of the latter is based primarily on the notion of cursors. A database cursor is an object that keeps track of the current context of a user's interaction with the database. You can think of a cursor as an object that keeps track of the current row that the user has just accessed, or of a group of rows accessed at the same time, or of the row-column entries fetched by a query in the form of a virtual table, etc. The DB-API specification says that you should first call a driver module's `connect()` method in order to get hold of a connection object and then call `cursor()` on the connection object to obtain a cursor object. You can then communicate SQL commands to the database through the `execute()` method of the cursor object. It is the cursor object's responsibility to keep track of the user's current position as he/she is navigating through the database and to buffer any information sent back by the database to the user. In the user's Python script, a common way to retrieve the information sent back by the database is by calling methods such as `fetchone()`, `fetchall()`, etc., on the cursor object.

The next script shows some of the more commonly used features of the open-source `MySQLdb` module that implements Python's DB-API V2.0. The overall goal of the script is the same as that of the first Perl script in Section 16.7.5 — to create a small relational database named `MyFriends` that consists of two tables, `Friends` and `Rovers`, the latter being the name of a club. The second script in this section will then show how one can interact with this database with a query that cannot be answered without accessing both tables of the database.

We start by constructing a connection object by invoking `connect()` directly on `MySQLdb` in the statement that ends in line (D). The `connect()` method takes a large number of keyword arguments; of these, four are shown in the statement that ends in line (D). The keyword `db` is for supplying the name of the MySQL database that the user wants to interact with.[44]

About the exception handling in lines (E), (F), and (G), and also in lines (f) through (j) at the end of the script, note that DB-API v2.0 defines a set of exception classes that can be used in user scripts to trap different kinds of errors. The most general of these exception classes is `MySQLdb.Error` that we have used in lines (E) and (h).[45] However, there are many specialized classes derived from the `MySQLdb.Error` class that are designed to trap different kinds of errors that are likely to arise in a Python script when using `MySQLdb`. For example, as shown in lines (f) and (g), the subclass `MySQLdb.ProgrammingError` can be used to trap errors in the SQL syntax used in a script. The subclass `MySQLdb.DataError` can be used to trap errors, such as division by zero, occurring during numerical processing of the database data; and so on.

Line (H) of the script shows what you have to do to turn on the autocommit feature of the database driver. As was mentioned earlier, leaving this feature off may be important for transaction-oriented interactions with a database. Transactions usually involve multiple interrelated changes to a database that must take place on an all-or-none basis. With the autocommit feature off, all the changes made to a database are buffered until a function usually named `commit()` is called to affect those changes simultaneously. The alternative is to call another function usually called `rollback()` to undo all the changes that are still in the buffer. According to DB-API v2.0, the `commit()` and `rollback()` methods must be included in the suite of methods made available by a connection object. The other two methods that a connection object must make available are `close()` and `cursor()`. The former we have used in line (k) of the script and the latter we take up for discussion in what follows.

As already mentioned, according to DB-API v2.0, much of a user's interaction with a database takes place through a cursor object that is constructed by calling `cursor()` on a connection object, as we have done in line (J). Subsequently, a user interacts with the database by communicating SQL commands to the database through the `cursor.execute()` method. If any results are expected back from the database, they would be stored in the cursor object that communicated the SQL command to the database. The result object can be retrieved from the cursor object by invoking either `cursor.fetchone()` or `cursor.fetchall()` on the cursor

---

[44] At the least, `MySQLdb.connect()` must be called with `host`, `user`, and `passwd` options. The `db` option can be specified later by sending the SQL command `USE database_name` to the database through a statement like:

```
cursor.execute( 'USE MyFriends' )
```

where `MyFriends` is the name of the database and `cursor` is the object returned by invoking `cursor()` on the connection object.

[45] The `try-except` syntax of Python for exception handling is explained in Chapter 10.

object, the former for fetching the result object one row at a time and the latter for fetching all the rows simultaneously. Since each row of the result object is represented by a tuple, `cursor.fetchone()` returns a single tuple and `cursor.fetchall()` a tuple of tuples.

Lines (K) through (R) of the script demonstrate that you are allowed to carry out administrative operations on the database through a cursor object, provided, of course, the connection you opened earlier is authorized for those operations. Administrative operations include determining the version number of the MySQL database manager used, dropping existing databases, creating new databases, etc. Lines (K), (L), and (M) show us sending the SQL command `SELECT VERSION()` to the database. The database then returns the version number as a single row in the form of a tuple. We retrieve this tuple in line (L) by invoking `fetchone()` on the cursor object and print out the value in line (M). We show two more administrative operations in lines (N), (O), and (P). We drop the entire `MyFriends` database in line (N). If you are experimenting with a script such as the one shown here, you would obviously not want to insert the same rows into the database tables with each run of the script. So either you must drop the database as created by the previous run of the script and start with a clean slate, or you must delete the previously constructed tables and then start afresh by populating these tables again. Lines (N), (O), and (P) represent the first approach. If you comment out lines (N), (O), and (P) and uncomment the commented-out lines (Q) and (R), you will be using the second approach.

To understand the rest of the script, recall its purpose as stated earlier in this section. We want to create a database named `MyFriends` consisting of two tables, `Friends` and `Rovers`. As indicated by the `CREATE TABLE` statement in line (S), the `Friends` table has three columns: `Name`, `Phone`, and `Email`. The `Rovers` table, as shown in line (W), has two columns: `Name` and `RovingTime`. The data types for the columns are the same as for the Perl example shown earlier.

Lines (a) through (d) show us sending the `DESCRIBE table_name` query to the database. For the `DESCRIBE Friends` query shown, the database sends back the following tuple of tuples:

```
(('Name', 'char(30)', '', 'PRI', '', ''),
 ('Phone', 'int(11)', 'YES', '', None, ''),
 ('Email', 'char(30)', 'YES', '', None, ''))
```

where the first two entries in each tuple consist of the name of the column field and its SQL data type. The third entry, if set to `YES` means that the value for this field is allowed to be `NULL`. The fourth entry, when it is `PRI`, means that this field is allowed to serve as a primary key for the database, meaning that the values for this field can be used to uniquely identify each row of the table. The next entry is for any default value associated with this field. The final entry is for any additional attribute that the user may wish to associate with this column. We extract the tuple of tuples by invoking `fetchall()` on the cursor object, as shown in line (b). Lines (c) and (d) then extract the first two items from each tuple. The output produced by the loop in these two lines is:

```
Name:   char(30)
Phone:  int(11)
Email:  char(30)
```

Finally, we close the cursor object in line (e) and the database connection in line (k).

```
#!/usr/bin/env python

### CreateMyFriendsDB.py

import sys                                                              #(A)
import MySQLdb                                                          #(B)

try:                                                                    #(C)
    conn = MySQLdb.connect( host='localhost',
                            user='kak',
                            passwd='xxxxxx',
                            db='MyFriends')                             #(D)
except MySQLdb.Error, e:                                                #(E)
    print "Unable to connect to database. Error %d: %s" % \
                                  (e.args[0], e.args[1])                #(F)
    sys.exit(1)                                                         #(G)

conn.commit()                                                           #(H)

try:                                                                    #(I)
    cursor = conn.cursor()                                              #(J)

    cursor.execute( "SELECT VERSION()" )                                #(K)
    row = cursor.fetchone()                                             #(L)
    print row[0]                   # 4.1.10a-standard                   #(M)

    cursor.execute( 'DROP DATABASE IF EXISTS MyFriends' )               #(N)
    cursor.execute( 'CREATE DATABASE MyFriends' )                       #(O)
    cursor.execute( 'USE MyFriends' )                                   #(P)
#   cursor.execute('DROP TABLE IF EXISTS Friends')                      #(Q)
#   cursor.execute('DROP TABLE IF EXISTS Rovers')                       #(R)

    # Create a new table called Friends and insert rows into it:
    cursor.execute( "CREATE TABLE Friends (Name CHAR(30) PRIMARY KEY, "+
                              "Phone INT, Email CHAR(30) )" )           #(S)
    cursor.execute( "INSERT INTO Friends VALUES ( 'Ziggy Zaphod', " +
                              "4569876, 'ziggy\@sirius' )" )            #(T)
    cursor.execute( "INSERT INTO Friends VALUES ( 'Yo Yo Ma', " +
                              "3472828, 'yoyo\@yippy' )" )              #(U)
    cursor.execute( "INSERT INTO Friends VALUES ( 'Gogo Gaga', " +
                              "27278927, 'gogo\@garish' )" )            #(V)
```

```
    # Create a new table called Rovers and insert rows into it:
    cursor.execute( "CREATE TABLE Rovers ( Name CHAR(30) NOT NULL, " +
                          "RovingTime CHAR(10) )" )                    #(W)
    cursor.execute( "INSERT INTO Rovers VALUES ('Dusty Dodo'," +
                                       " '2 pm')" )                    #(X)
    cursor.execute( "INSERT INTO Rovers VALUES ('Yo Yo Ma'," +
                                       " '8 pm')" )                    #(Y)
    cursor.execute( "INSERT INTO Rovers VALUES ('Bebe Beaut'," +
                                       " '6 pm')" )                    #(Z)

    cursor.execute( "DESCRIBE Friends" )                               #(a)
    result = cursor.fetchall()                                         #(b)
    for record in result:                                              #(c)
        print "%s:\t%s" % (record[0], record[1])                       #(d)

    cursor.close()                                                     #(e)

except MySQLdb.ProgrammingError, e:                                    #(f)
    print "Possible SQL Syntax Error %d: %s" % (e.args[0],e.args[1])#(g)
except MySQLdb.Error, e:                                               #(h)
    print "Error %d: %s" % (e.args[0], e.args[1])                      #(i)
    sys.exit(1)                                                        #(j)

conn.close()                                                           #(k)
```

Shown next is a Python script, `RetrieveFromMyFriendsDB.py`, that mimics the Perl database retrieval script shown earlier in Section 16.7.5. As with that earlier script, our main goal is to query the `MyFriends` database created by the previous Python script (or, for that matter, by the first Perl script of Section 16.7.5) and find out which of our friends in the `Friends` table are also rovers, as listed in the `Rovers` table.

We first connect with the `MyFriends` database by calling `MySQLdb.connect()` in the statement that ends in line (D). In line (K), we execute the SQL command `SHOW TABLES` to see all the tables in the database. Next, in lines (O) and (P), we retrieve from the `Friends` table two of its columns, `name` and `Phone`, for each of our friends. These are then displayed on the terminal by the loop in lines (Q) and (R).

Line (S) then makes the main SQL query, which is to find out which of our friends are also in the rover club and what their roving time is. Lines (T), (U), and (V) extract the retrieved information from the cursor object and display the result.

```
#!/usr/bin/env python

### RetrieveFromMyFriendsDB.py

import sys                                                          #(A)
import MySQLdb                                                      #(B)

try:                                                                #(C)
    conn = MySQLdb.connect( host='localhost', user='kak',
                            passwd='xxxxxx',  db='MyFriends')       #(D)
except MySQLdb.Error, e:                                            #(E)
    print "Unable to connect to database. Error %d: %s" % \
                                  (e.args[0], e.args[1])            #(F)
    sys.exit(1)                                                     #(G)

try:                                                                #(I)
    cursor = conn.cursor()                                          #(J)

    cursor.execute( "SHOW TABLES" )         # Friends               #(K)
                                            # Rovers
    result = cursor.fetchall()                                      #(L)
    for record in result:                                           #(M)
        print "%s" % record[0]                                      #(N)

    cursor.execute("SELECT Friends.Name,Friends.Phone FROM Friends")#(O)
    result = cursor.fetchall()                                      #(P)
    for record in result:                                           #(Q)
        print "%s\t%s" % (record[0], record[1])                     #(R)
                                            # Ziggy Zaphod    4569876
                                            # Yo Yo Ma        3472828
                                            # Gogo Gaga       27278927

    cursor.execute("SELECT Friends.Name, Rovers.RovingTime \
           FROM Friends, Rovers WHERE Friends.Name = Rovers.Name" ) #(S)
    result = cursor.fetchall()                                      #(T)
    for record in result:                                           #(U)
        print "%s\t%s" % (record[0], record[1])                     #(V)
                                            # Yo Yo Ma      8 pm
    cursor.close()                                                  #(W)

except MySQLdb.ProgrammingError, e:                                 #(X)
    print "Possible SQL Syntax Error %d: %s" % (e.args[0],e.args[1])#(Y)
except MySQLdb.Error, e:                                            #(Z)
    print "Error %d: %s" % (e.args[0], e.args[1])                   #(a)
    sys.exit(1)                                                     #(b)

conn.close()                                                        #(c)
```

As the reader would expect, the results produced by the above script are identical to those shown at the end of Section 16.7.5 for the case of the Perl retrieval script.

The two Python scripts we have shown do not present all of the functionality of the DB-API, especially with regard to all of the methods that can be invoked on cursor objects. We have only shown examples of `execute()`, `fetchone()`, and `fetchall()` methods. The additional methods supported by the cursor objects are `fetchmany()`, `nextset()`, `setinputsize()`, and `setoutputsize()`. Whereas `fetchone()` fetches from the cursor object a single row of the result object returned by an SQL query and `fetchall()` fetches back all of the rows, `fetchmany()` brings back a set of rows, the size of the set specified by the argument to the method.[46] The `setinputsizes()` method can be used to specify memory sizes for the different parameters in the next call to `execute()`. Similarly, the `setoutputsizes()` method can be used to specify memory sizes for the next fetch operation.

16.9 CREDITS AND SUGGESTIONS FOR FURTHER READING

Of the various DBMs we mentioned in Section 16.3, NDBM uses Ken Thompson's hashing algorithm whereas SDBM uses Larson's dynamic hashing algorithm [42, 43]. Dynamic hashing refers to changing the hashing function as the size of a hash table grows. For more recent work on dynamic hashing, see [18]. Some variations on dynamic hashing include linear hashing [45], extendable hashing [19], and spiral storage [48]. Our treatment of DBI barely scratches the surface of this and the related driver modules.

A reader interested in writing Perl scripts for relational databases is urged to check out the book by Descartes and Bunce [17]. For Python, the official home of the DB-API v2.0 is the PEP (Python Enhancement Proposal) 249. All Pythons PEPs are available at `http://www.python.org/dev/peps/`.

Homework Problems 4 and 5 listed below are the Perl and Python versions of a similar problem in the "Database Programming" chapter of [41].

16.10 HOMEWORK

1. Write more efficient Perl and Python implementations for the `CSV` classes presented in Sections 16.1.1 and 16.1.2. You can make this class more efficient by also storing on the disk an association list (using a hash in Perl and a

[46] The number of rows to fetch by `fetchmany()` can also be specified by the `arraysize` attribute of the cursor object.

dictionary in Python) that shows how the last names of the individuals are mapped to the row numbers of the database table. Assuming that no two last names are the same, such an association list would allow you to fetch a record, using the last name as the key, from the database table in time that is independent of the size of the database.

2. In light of the discussion regarding garbage collection in Chapter 10, explain why the tied object is not garbage collected in the script `TieScalar.pl` of Section 16.4 when in line (o) we `undef` the variable `$xobj` that holds the blessed reference returned by the call to `tie()` in line (Y) of the script.

3. Write a lazy version of a typical DBM module. By lazy we mean that the module keeps the key-value pairs in a cache until a method — such methods are typically named `sync()` — is called that would write out the contents of the cache to the disk. By lazy we also mean that an item fetched from the disk would also be kept in the cache in case it is needed again. In addition to the disk-based storage and a cache, you may also want to create a storage that you could call "flash." Any new key-value pairs or any modified key-value pairs would go into the flash memory. That way, the `sync()` method would only have to write out the contents of "flash" back to the disk.[47] [48]

4. Using the `DBI` and the `DBD::mysql` modules, write a Perl script that can serve as a front end server to a MySQL database. Your script should perform the following tasks:

   (a) Establish a password-protected connection between a client and the database. The client must specify his/her username, password, and the database name.

   (b) Report back any error messages to the client if there is any error while connecting with the MySQL database and allow the client to try to reconnect repeatedly until the client enters "exit" as the username.

---

[47]Therefore, if you accessed a key-value pair from the disk with a large object for the value, it would stay in the cache if you do not modify the object. Your lazy implementation would be all the more efficient if this large object needs to be accessed frequently but there is no need to modify it.

[48]A lazy DBM implementation has been posted as a recipe by Alec Thomas at `http://aspn.activestate.com/ASPN/Cookbook/`. You may wish to create your own implementation before looking at the posted solution.

(c) Execute each SQL statement received from the client and display the retrieved results to the client as necessary.

(d) Display on the client's terminal an error message if the SQL command is invalid.

(e) Continue receiving SQL statements from the client until "exit" is entered by the user.

5. Use the `MySQLdb` module to create a Python version of the database frontend server of the previous problem.

17

Processing XML with Perl and Python

As the technologies for the dissemination of information have become varied, a need has arisen for representing and maintaining information in a manner that is independent of the output devices for displaying the information.

Consider a medical doctor making rounds. The doctor may carry a handheld wireless device that provides him/her with the latest patient information. He/she may wish to follow up on the interaction with a patient by examining the patient record on a regular desk-top monitor. For reasons having to do with human cognition and perception, the format used for displaying the information on a full-sized desktop monitor may not be appropriate for the small screen of the wireless handheld device. Should it be necessary to use different formats for the two different display devices, we have the option of creating two separate documents, one for each format. But just imagine the extra workload entailed in ensuring that the two documents, which differ only in the formatting of information, remain consistent every time the patient record is updated.

XML eliminates the problem of having to maintain a separate document for each different output format. We can specify a content document — an XML document — that remains the same for different presentation formats. Different stylesheets can then be used to transform the presentation of the XML document to suit a particular device. Now any content changes would only need to be made to a single document, the XML document.

The acronym XML stands for *eXtensible Markup Language*. In contrast to the *Hyper Text Markup Language* (HTML), XML is extensible in that you are allowed to define your own tags to mark up the different portions of a document. An XML tag denotes a meaning for a distinctly demarcated portion of a document, whereas an HTML tag merely controls how a portion of a document is displayed. Consider the case when a certain portion of a document stands for an individual's home address. With XML, one could place the address between the `<ADDRESS>` and `</ADDRESS>` tags. Subsequently, a stylesheet, usually in the form of an XSL file, would convert the address block into a formatted display whose layout would be controlled by what is put in the XSL file. XSL stands for *eXtensible Style Language*. The program that converts an XML document into a displayable HTML document using an XSL stylesheet is usually written in XSLT (*eXtensible Stylesheet Language Transform*). Therefore, we can say that whereas XML specifies the *semantic structure* of a document, XSL specifies the rules for its *presentation*.[1]

Another reason for the growing importance of XML is that it has become the *lingua franca* for the interoperability needed for the rapidly emerging business of *web services*. In the context of web services, interoperability means a client should be able to make a *remote procedure call* (RPC) on a web server. This is the same as saying that a client should be able to call a function whose implementation resides on a remote web server. The called function usually represents a service provided by the server, a service presumably desired by many clients.

Note that a client clicking on a URL in a web browser, a commonplace activity by now, is also an example of interoperability, albeit in its simplest form. In practically all cases, this interaction works fine regardless of the differences between the platforms used by the client and the server. The client sends a specific string to a specific port on the server. The string contains a mutually agreed-upon encoding of the client's request as well as an encoding of such client-side information as its IP address and the port at which the client will be waiting for the answer. The server interprets the string, separates out the request, and responds with the document requested. Web services generalize this human-computer interaction to a computer-computer interaction in which a client machine invokes a function on a server machine. In other words, for web services interaction, a client needs to make a remote procedure call on the server.

Compared to a local procedure call, a remote procedure call is inherently more complex, especially when the function to be invoked on the remote machine requires certain argument objects that must also be supplied by the client. If the result of this remote procedure call is a complex data structure that needs to be sent back to the client, that adds to the overall complexity. Other complicating factors in remote procedure calls include: (1) the error handling needed on the client side

---

[1] Although XML burst on the scene as recently as 1996, it owes its genesis to GML (Generalized Markup Language) whose development was begun in the 1960s at IBM and continued there by Charles Goldfarb, Ed Mosher, and Ray Lorie over a span of 20 years. GML, originally intended for searching through computer files of legal records, was adopted by ISO (International Standards Office) as SGML (Standard Generalized Markup Language). Unfortunately, SGML has proved to be too complex for most applications. So now there exist two offshoots of SGML: HTML, created by Tim Berners-Lee in 1989, and, more recently, XML.

when a problem occurs on the server side or in the network; (2) issues related to the incorporation of client-side global variables in the RPCs issued by a client; (3) a client's ability, or lack thereof, to invoke a function for its side effects, as opposed to just its return value; (4) need for authentication in order to ensure on the server side that the requests made by a client are legitimate and that, on the client side, the answers received from the server are legitimate; and so on.[2]

These interoperability problems related to remote procedure calls have been addressed to varying degrees in the past in well-known protocols like: CORBA (Common Object Request Broker Architecture) from OMG (the Object Management Group); COM+ from Microsoft; ONC RPC (Open Network Computing RPC) developed under the stewardship of Sun Microsystems; Java's RMI (Remote Method Invocation); and others. All of these protocols for RPC have been found to be useful in different applications. However, none has acquired the universality that people believe will be achieved by the flavor of RPC incorporated in *World Wide Web Consortium*'s (W3C) formulation of web services.

Service Component	*Suggested Framework/Protocol/Language*
Discovery Service (Registry, Indexing, Peer-to-Peer)	UDDI (Universal Description, Discovery, and Integration Framework)
Web Service Description	WSDL (Web Services Description Language)
Transaction Messaging	SOAP (Simple Object Access Protocol)

Table 17.1

According to W3C's specifications [34], a web service consists typically of an implementation of the "architecture stack" shown in Table 17.1.[3] The top layer of

[2]RPC implementations do not concern themselves with the reliability of the client-server communication links. If an application using RPC sits on top of a reliable transport layer such as TCP, reliability of the client-server information exchange will be guaranteed by TCP itself. If, on the other hand, RPC is supposed to use an unreliable transport such as UDP, then the application must also implement its own time-out, retransmission, and duplicate detection policies.

[3]Since the client and the server operate in different processing environments, they must communicate over a network through hardware/software protocol stacks. The stack shown in Table 17.1, adapted from a figure in [34], can be thought of as sitting on top of the stack that corresponds to the transport chosen for a web service. As mentioned in [34], having to go through a protocol stack necessarily implies that

the protocol stack shown in Table 17.1 is intended for the discovery of a web service by those wanting to use it. The provided discovery mechanisms can be as simple as making a URL to a web service available through a search engine, and as sophisticated as posting the name and a brief description of the service at some centralized registry based on the *Universal Description, Discovery, and Integration Framework* (UDDI). The second layer of the stack in Table 17.1 is for providing a complete formal description of the web service, preferably in the *Web Services Description Language* (WSDL). A WSDL-based description, itself an XML document, contains all of the information on the web service that a client would need, such as the names of the server-based functions that a client is allowed to call, the argument objects needed by the functions (to be supplied by the client), the types of the objects returned by the server to the client, etc. The last layer of the protocol stack in Table 17.1 tells us how the messaging needed for RPC is to be carried out between a client and a server. The recommended protocol for this is the XML-based *Simple Object Access Protocol* (SOAP). SOAP specifies how the arguments needed for a remote function call and the returned results from a server must be serialized[4] and represented as XML documents. SOAP also specifies the mechanisms for handling server and network errors, etc. Although not mandated, W3C's preferred transport for SOAP is as provided by the *Hyper Text Transport Protocol* (HTTP).

So it is easy to see the very large role that has been assigned to XML for the implementation of web services.

In the rest of this chapter, we will first see how XML can be used to specify content for a document in a manner that is independent of its presentation. We then present Perl and Python scripts for extracting information from such documents. As we show, for simple XML documents, it is easy to devise a regex that takes us straight to the part of the document that you want to extract. However, for more complex documents, especially when the document structure is variable, one must use scripts that call on parsers to break the document into its constituent parts. We then take up the subject of XML for web services. We show how some publicly available Perl and Python modules can be used to construct web-services servers and clients, first with XML-RPC and then with SOAP. XML-RPC is a simpler cousin of SOAP. Finally, we present simple examples of stylesheets written in XSLT for converting an XML document into an HTML document.

---

remote procedure calls would be slower compared to direct invocations of functions in the same processing environment.

[4]Serialization of argument objects before they can be transported to a server for an RPC is also known as *marshalling*. Recovering an object from its serialized form is called *deserialization*, as the reader already knows from Chapter 16, or *unmarshalling*.

17.1 CREATING AN XML DOCUMENT

Shown below is a very elementary XML document that contains the `Hello World` message. The document resides in a file named `HelloWorld.xml`.[5]

```
<?xml version="1.0"?>                                        <!-- A -->

<!-- HelloWorld.xml -->                                      <!-- B -->

<GREETING>                                                   <!-- C -->
<SALUTATION>Hello</SALUTATION>                               <!-- D -->
<TARGET>World</TARGET>                                       <!-- E -->
</GREETING>                                                  <!-- F -->
```

As shown above, the very first line of an XML document must declare the nature of the document and the version of XML to which it conforms.[6] The comments in an XML document are indicated in the same manner as in the more familiar HTML documents, with the `<!--comment-->` notation.[7] Line (B) of the document shows a comment line where we have placed the name of the file containing the document.

The actual XML content of the file starts in line (C). It consists of the *root element* `GREETING`. The root element contains two *subelements*, `SALUTATION` and `TARGET`. Our XML document says that the salutation consists of the word `Hello` and the intended target is `World`. An XML document designer is free to choose any names whatever for the elements. The goal is to choose names that convey the meaning associated with the information content of the element. The name `GREETING` for the root element is justified because the purpose of the information contained in this element is after all to convey a greeting. Similarly, the name `SALUTATION` for the first subelement is justified because that describes the information it holds. The name of the second subelement, `TARGET`, is justified for a similar reason.

---

[5]In case the reader is wondering, here is the smallest possible XML document:

```
<?xml version="1.0"?><a/>
```

This document contains only one empty element named `a`. The definition of an empty element is presented later in this section.

[6]No white space is allowed before this declaration.

[7]It is important to realize that the comment delimiters in this notation consist of two separate parts: the opening `<!` and the closing `>` parts, and the opening and closing double-dashes. The delimiters `<!` and `>` are meant to place the document in an SGML context in which a comment is denoted by enclosing it within a pair of double dashes. What that implies is that any additional double dashes inside a comment could confuse the parser.

Here is a list of things to remember when creating an XML document:

1. Although you can give whatever names you wish to the elements in an XML document, you have to bear in mind that XML is case-sensitive. So an element named `SALUTATION` is not the same as an element named `Salutation`.

2. Unless empty, an XML element is defined by a *start tag*, followed by what is referred to as the *element content*, followed by an *end tag*, as in

```
<TAG>some_content</TAG>
```

   where the start tag is `<TAG>`, the end tag `</TAG>`, and the element content `some_content`. The element content itself may consist of nested elements or data.

3. The identifier that follows the opening angle bracket of a start tag is referred to as the *name of the element*. Therefore, the name of the following element is `SALUTATION`:[8]

```
<SALUTATION> Hello </SALUTATION>
```

4. In general, a start tag consists of the element name followed by an arbitrary number of *attribute-value pairs* in the form `attribute="value"`, as in

```
<BOOK PUBLISHER="John Wiley" ISBN="047-017-9236">
    Scripting With Objects
</BOOK>
```

   This element is named `BOOK` and it has two *attributes* named `PUBLISHER` and `ISBN`. The *values* associated with these attributes are as shown. The value for an attribute *must* be single or double quoted. The same attribute name cannot appear more than once in a start tag.

5. Every element that begins with a start tag must end in an end tag that contains the same element name as in the start tag, as illustrated by the end tag `</TARGET>` below:

```
<TARGET> World </TARGET>
```

6. An element is allowed to be empty, meaning that an element may contain a start tag and an end tag, but no content:

```
<BOOK PUBLISHER="John Wiley" TITLE="SwO" ISBN="0470179236"></BOOK>
```

7. Another commonly used syntax for an empty element is

---

[8]Strictly speaking, the name of an element is meant to be its *type*.

```
<BOOK PUBLISHER="John Wiley" TITLE="SwO" ISBN="047-017-9236" />
```

where we have only one tag that is *self-closing*. In this case, the ending delimiter for the tag is />.

8. There can exist only one root element in an XML document. But a root element may contain any number of subelements, those subelements may contain any number of their own subelements, and so on. (A subelement is also commonly referred to as a *child element*.) Additionally, any number of siblings can have the same element name, as in the following example:

```
<?xml version="1.0"?>
<LIBRARY>
    <BOOK PUBLISHER="John Wiley" ISBN="047-017-9236">
        Scripting with Objects
    </BOOK>
    <BOOK PUBLISHER="Addison-Wesley" ISBN="020-163-3612">
        Design Patterns
    </BOOK>
</LIBRARY>
```

where the root element LIBRARY contains two BOOK elements as subelements.

9. Ignoring for a moment what is known as CDATA, the content of a nonempty and non-nested element — that is, the material you place between the start tag and the end tag — is referred to as the *character data*. The rest of an XML document is the *markup*. The markup includes all of the information that is placed between the tag delimiters < and >.[9]

10. If either the ampersand character & or the left-angle-bracket character < is needed inside an element's character data, it must be replaced by its corresponding *numeric character reference*. Alternatively, these characters can be replaced by their *symbolic character references*. For example, the & character can be replaced by the symbolic reference & and the < character by the symbolic reference < inside an element's character data. Note that the terminating semicolon is a part of the symbolic reference in each case. Section 17.5.3 provides further information on representing symbols by their numeric and symbolic character references.

11. Another way to deal with characters in element content that would otherwise be construed as markup is to incorporate them in a CDATA section. A CDATA section begins with the <![CDATA[string and ends in the]]> string.

[9]In general, markup takes the form of *start tags*, *end tags*, *empty elements*, *entity references*, *character references*, *comments*, *CDATA section delimiters*, *document type declarations*, *processing instructions*, *XML declarations*, and any white space that is at the top level of the document entity (that is, outside the document element and not inside any other markup) [33].

Within a CDATA section, the ampersand and the left angle bracket *must* occur in their literal form. So in the following element

```
<booktitle>
<![CDATA[<strong>Scripting with Objects</strong>]]>
</booktitle>
```

the strings `<strong>` and `</strong>` are not considered to be markup. Instead, they are both recognized as the character-data content of the `booktitle` element. As mentioned in the footnote that goes with the item 9 above, the special delimiters used for CDATA sections are included in the markup.

12. Any constraints on the markup in an XML document can be specified with the help of *document type declarations* that must appear before the root element of the document. A *document type declaration* (DTD) declares (or points to an external entity containing this material) the markup allowed and the constraints on the markup in the rest of the XML document. These constraints are usually referred to as *document type definitions*. Section 17.5 provides further information on DTDs.

13. A more up-to-date approach to specifying the constraints on the structure of a document is through XML Schemas. Section 17.6 presents a quick review of XML schemas.

14. An XML element delimited by the 2-character sequences `<?` and `?>` is known as a *processing instruction*. What we showed in the very first line of the XML document at the beginning of this section is an example of a processing instruction.

17.2 EXTRACTING INFORMATION FROM SIMPLE XML DOCUMENTS

Ordinary pattern matching suffices for extracting information from simple XML documents, especially if their logical structure is known precisely in advance. To illustrate this, let's say we are given the following XML document:

```
<?xml version="1.0"?>

<!-- The name of this XML document is: Phonebook.xml -->

<phonebook>
    <listing>
        <first>John</first>
        <middle>C.</middle>
        <last>Hancock</last>
```

```
        <phone type="home">1-800-123-4567</phone>
      </listing>
    <listing>
        <first>Susan</first>
        <last>Anthony</last>
        <phone type="work">1-800-234-5678</phone>
    </listing>
    <listing>
        <first>Zaphod</first>
        <middle> Doubleheaded</middle>
        <last>Beeblecrox</last>
        <phone type="cell">9-000-666-1234</phone>
    </listing>
    <listing>
        <first>Trillian</first>
        <last>Earthling</last>
        <phone type="work">9-000-222-2345</phone>
    </listing>
    <listing>
        <first>Miss</first>
        <last>Importante</last>
        <phone type="cell">0-111-234-8888</phone>
    </listing>
</phonebook>
```

Let's further say that our goal is to construct an associative list of key-value pairs whose keys are the names of the individuals and whose values the corresponding phone numbers. Our further goal is to print out the names and the phone numbers, sorted by the last names, in the following format:

```
Anthony, Susan            1-800-234-5678
Beeblecrox, Zaphod        9-000-666-1234
Earthling, Trillian       9-000-222-2345
Hancock, John             1-800-123-4567
Importante, Miss          0-111-234-8888
```

Both of these goals are easily accomplished by the two scripts, `ExtractEleInfo.pl` in Perl and `ExtractEleInfo.py` in Python, presented next.

Presenting first the Perl script, it is meant to be called with the following command line:

```
ExtractEleInfo.pl  Phonebook.xml
```

The script slurps in the entire file `Phonebook.xml` into the string `$the_whole_file` in line (E). The pattern match, evaluated with the `//g` modifier in line (F), returns a list of contents of each of the `listing` elements of `Phonebook.xml`. If we were to print out the array `@listings` produced in line (F), we would see the following where each three- or four-line grouping constitutes one element of the array:

```
<first>John</first>
<middle>C.</middle>
<last>Hancock</last>
<phone type="home">1-800-123-4567</phone>

<first>Susan</first>
<last>Anthony</last>
<phone type="work">1-800-234-5678</phone>

<first>Zaphod</first>
<middle> Doubleheaded</middle>
<last>Beeblecrox</last>
<phone type="cell">9-000-666-1234</phone>

<first>Trillian</first>
<last>Earthling</last>
<phone type="work">9-000-222-2345</phone>

<first>Miss</first>
<last>Importante</last>
<phone type="cell">0-111-234-8888</phone>
```

Lines (H) through (K) then extract the name and the phone number from each element of the `@listings` array and deposit this information in the hash `%phonebook`. Note the `//sx` modifier shown in line (K) for the pattern match operation. As mentioned in Section 4.11.4 of Chapter 4, the `//s` modifier allows the character class `.` to match newline characters, and the `//x` modifier allows us to express a regular expression in multiple lines and for the comments to be embedded in a regular expression, as we do in lines (H) through (K).

Finally, line (L) defines a template for formatting the output. As explained earlier in Section 2.10 of Chapter 2, the function `formline()` called in line (N) uses its first-argument template to deposit a formatted string constructed from the rest of its arguments into the global variable `$^A` whose corresponding name in the `English` package is `$ACCUMULATOR`.

```
#!/usr/bin/perl -w

### ExtractEleInfo.pl

use strict;                                                          #(A)
use English;                                                         #(B)
```

```
die "needs one command line arg, the name of the XML file"
    unless @ARGV == 1;                                                  #(C)

$INPUT_RECORD_SEPARATOR = undef;                                        #(D)

my $the_whole_file = <>;                                                #(E)

my @listings = $the_whole_file =~ /<listing>(.*?)<\/listing>/sg;       #(F)

my %phonelist;                                                          #(G)

map {m/<first>(.*)<\/first>.*?                  # get first name       #(H)
       <last>(.*)<\/last>.*?                     # get last name        #(I)
       <phone.*>(.*)<\/phone>                    # get phone num        #(J)
      /sx; $phonelist{"$2, $1"} = $3 } @listings;                       #(K)

my $template = "@<<<<<<<<<<<<<<<<<<<<      @>>>>>>>>>>>>>>>";           #(L)
foreach (sort keys %phonelist) {                                        #(M)
    formline( $template, $_, $phonelist{$_} );                          #(N)
    print $ACCUMULATOR, "\n";                                           #(O)
    $ACCUMULATOR = "";                                                  #(P)
}
```

Python version of the above script is shown next. The match modifiers for the multiline regex in lines (M), (N), and (O) are now supplied as the flags `re.DOTALL` and `re.VERBOSE` to the `re.compile()` method that returns a regular expression object. As mentioned in Section 4.11.4 of Chapter 4, the flag `re.VERBOSE` causes all white space in a regex to be ignored (unless the white space is inside a character class or is backslashed). Also, in each line of a multiline regex, the flag `re.VERBOSE` causes the first `#` character and all the characters that follow that `#` until the end of the line to be ignored (unless `#` appears inside a character class or is backslashed). The `re.DOTALL` flag allows the character class `.` to match any character, including the newline characters. Recall that the default behavior of `.` is to match any character except the newline character.

Another noteworthy feature used in the regex in lines (M), (N), (O) is that it employs named groups through the `(?P<name>...)` syntax. As mentioned in Section 4.11.4 of Chapter 4, this causes the name `first` to be associated with the substring that is consumed by the match with the capturing group shown in line (M). By the same token, the names `last` and `ph` become associated with the substrings consumed by the capturing parentheses in lines (N) and (O). Subsequently, we retrieve those substrings in line (U) through their respective names.

```
#!/usr/bin/env python

### ExtractEleInfo.py

import sys                                                              #(A)
import re                                                               #(B)

if len(sys.argv) is not 2:                                              #(C)
    sys.exit( "Name the XML file in the command line")                  #(D)

try:                                                                    #(E)
    FILE = open( sys.argv[1], 'r' )                                     #(F)
except IOError, e:                                                      #(G)
    print "Cannot open file: ", e                                       #(H)
    sys.exit(1)                                                         #(I)

the_whole_file = FILE.read()                                            #(J)

regex = r'<listing>(.*?)<\/listing>'                                    #(K)
matches = re.findall( regex, the_whole_file, re.DOTALL )                #(L)

regex =  re.compile( r'''<first>(?P<first>.*)<\/first>.*?  # first   #(M)
                         <last>(?P<last>.*)<\/last>.*?     # last    #(N)
                         <phone.*>(?P<ph>.*)<\/phone>''',  # phone   #(O)
                     re.DOTALL | re.VERBOSE )                           #(P)
phonelist = {}                                                          #(Q)
for listing in matches:                                                 #(R)
    m = re.search( regex, listing )                                     #(S)
    if m is not None:                                                   #(T)
        phonelist["%s, %s" % (m.group('first'), m.group('last'))] = \
                         m.group('ph')                                  #(U)

for item in sorted( phonelist.items() ):                               #(V)
    print "      %-20s\t%15s" % item                                    #(W)
```

17.3 XML NAMESPACES

XML namespaces prevent name collisions between element and attribute names in the same XML document. They allow the same local name for an element or an attribute to stand for different things. Different usages of the same name can be encapsulated in different namespaces.

Every namespace has a name that is frequently referred to as its *namespace URI*. That is because the name of a namespace must be expressed in the form of a URI.[10] However, it often looks like a URL. Except for the *default namespace*, every namespace also has a convenient *prefix* associated with its name. The name of a namespace and its associated prefix must be declared in the start tag of an element, as in

```
<NS:MyElement  xmlns:NS="http://www.mywebsite.com/NSnames/">
    .....
    .....
</NS:MyElement>
```

where `xmlns` is a reserved symbol (see footnote this page). The namespace declaration in the start tag of the element `MyElement` says that this element and all its subelements should be aware of the namespace whose name is

```
http://www.mywebsite.com/NSnames/
```

and that this namespace will be referred to by the `NS:` prefix. So all the element and attribute names, which appear in the element `MyElement` (and all its subelements), that are prefixed with `NS:` belong to the `http://www.mywebsite.com/NSnames/` namespace. We can also say that the prefix `NS:` maps the name that follows to the namespace associated with the prefix.

In addition to the namespaces that have prefixes associated with them, an XML document may also use a prefix-free *default namespace*. Subsequent to the declaration of a default namespace in the start tag of an element, all unprefixed element names used in the element and its subelements are considered to belong to the default namespace. A default namespace is declared by directly assigning a namespace URI to the reserved attribute `xmlns`, as in

```
<MyElement  xmlns="http://www.mywebsite.com/NSnames/">
    .....
</MyElement>
```

[10]A URI, *Uniform Resource Identifier*, is used to label a category of names, features, resources, properties, and so on, so that they can be differentiated from other such names, features, resources, properties, and so on. The more familiar URL, *Uniform Resource Locator*, is a type of URI. In general, a URI begins with a *scheme* that, in most cases, is a designator for a communication protocol like `ftp` or `http`, but can also be something like `file`. The scheme is followed by a colon, and then followed by a string of characters. When a namespace URI looks like a URL, it does not necessarily mean that a web browser would be able to find anything at that address. Even when a namespace URI (especially when it looks likes a regular URL) does not point to an actual web site, it nevertheless carries a special meaning for the XML processor for deciding how to process a particular element or attribute name that belongs to the namespace represented by that URI. Having said that, it is generally true that many namespace URIs, particularly when they look like regular URLs, point to a document at that address. For example, the reserved prefix `xmlns:` is associated with the following namespace URI:

```
http://www.w3.org/2000/xmlns/
```

If you point your browser to this URL, it displays a message announcing that this namespace URI stands hereby assigned and that the reserved prefix `xmlns:` is to be associated with this namespace.

A default namespace can be "undeclared" by assigning an empty string to the attribute `xmlns`, as in

```
<MyElement xmlns="">
    .....
</MyElement>
```

Now any unprefixed names in the element `MyElement` and its subelements will be considered to belong to no namespace.

A namespace with a prefix has *scope*. Through its prefix, the scope of a namespace extends from the element in whose start tag the prefix is defined to include all its subelements — unless that prefix is mapped to a different namespace in a subelement.

A default namespace also has scope in exactly the same manner as a namespace with a prefix. Previously we mentioned that an unprefixed element name is considered to belong to a default namespace. Now we qualify that statement by saying that an unprefixed name belongs to a default namespace provided the default namespace is in scope. However, this only applies to unprefixed element names. *Unprefixed attribute names are always considered to belong to no namespace even if the default namespace is in scope.* Note that attributes of the same name in two different elements are considered to be distinct. When a default namespace is not in scope, an unprefixed element name belongs to no namespace.

Shown below is an example of an XML document that declares two namespaces that have prefixes associated with them and one default namespace. Since all three declarations are made in the root element of the document, their scope extends to the entire XML document.

```
<?xml version="1.0" encoding="iso-8859-1"?>
<NS1:A xmlns:NS1="http://www.mywebsite.com/NS1names/"
     xmlns:NS2="http://www.mywebsite.com/NS2names/"
     xmlns="http://www.mywebsite.com/NS3names/"
>
    <NS1:B NS1:x="hello" y="jello" NS2:z="mello">hellomello</NS1:B>
    <C w="cello"/>
    <D xmlns="">
        <E e="pqr"></E>
    </D>
</NS1:A>
```

In this document, the element names `A` and `B`, and the attribute name `x` are mapped by the prefix `NS1:` to the

```
http://www.mywebsite.com/NS1names/
```

namespace. The attribute name `z` is mapped by the prefix `NS2:` to the

```
http://www.mywebsite.com/NS2names/
```

namespace. The unprefixed element name `C` belongs to the default namespace

```
http://www.mywebsite.com/NS3names/
```

On the other hand, the element names `D` and `E` and the attribute names `y`, `w`, and `e`, all unprefixed, do not belong to any namespace at all. Note that in element `D` we change the default namespace to point to an empty name. So the default namespace created originally in the root element ceases to be in scope starting with element `D`.

An element or attribute name that carries a prefix is called a *qualified name*. What comes before the colon and including the colon is called the *namespace prefix*. What follows the colon is called the *local name*. A namespace declaration *maps* a namespace prefix to a URI reference. A qualified name is allowed to contain only one colon. You can think of a namespace prefix serving as a convenient proxy for the string that is the namespace URI, convenient in the sense that the latter can contain characters that are not normally allowed in the element and attribute names.

17.4 PARTITIONING AN XML DOCUMENT INTO ITS CONSTITUENT PARTS

The goal in this section is to introduce the reader to Robert Cameron's [5] single regular expression that can be used to partition an XML document into its markup and character data components.[11] While it is indeed instructive to realize that a single regex can do the job of extracting all of the different components of an XML document, what is even more educational is to see how Cameron goes about deriving this regex. By the different components of an XML document, we mean the start and the end tags for each of the elements, the attributes associated with the start tags, the comments, the processing instructions, the character data strings contained in the elements, any DTD declarations, and so on. Cameron's regex partitions a correct XML document into a list of strings corresponding to these components in such a way that the original document can be recovered by simply concatenating the component strings. For an incorrect XML document, the original document can still be recovered from the extracted components, but now the component strings would carry evidence of why the document was incorrect. Cameron refers to such partitioning as an *ordered partition* that obeys *the input partitioning property*. This

[11] Cameron refers to such partitioning as *shallow parsing*, the characterization *shallow* accounting for the fact that, without additional processing, the extracted components themselves do not reveal the deep structure of the markup. By deep structure we mean relationships such as the sibling and the parent-child relationships between the elements.

property states that every input character must appear exactly once in some partition and that the order in which the characters appear must be preserved.[12]

Cameron's regex returns three kinds of strings for an XML document:

- Markup strings that include their starting and ending angle-bracket delimiters. Cameron's regex treats everything that is delimited by the opening and closing angle brackets as markup. Therefore, element start tags, element end tags, comments, CDATA sections,[13] processing instructions, and DTD declarations are all examples of markup. If there are any attributes in the start tag of an element, all of that information stays intact in the markup string extracted for the start tag. By the same token, a DTD declaration even if it includes nested markup such as a processing instruction is extracted as a single markup string.

- Maximal length character strings found between markup items in the document source. The character strings preserve white space and line boundaries. Maximal length property means that there cannot be two consecutive such items in the partition. Note that such strings cannot contain a left angle bracket at any position since that character marks beginning of markup.

- Error strings that start with a left angle bracket but do not terminate in a closing right angle bracket. Consider the following flawed XML input:

  ```
  <A>hello<B jello</B></A>
  ```

---

[12]To fully conform to W3C specifications, XML processing should ideally include support for the 16-bit Unicode character set (ISO 10646). While the 16 bits give Unicode the power to represent practically all the characters used in the different languages of the world, the 2-byte character representation of Unicode makes for inefficient storage and transmission of text that is in English and other closely related languages (whose characters can be well represented by the 7-bit ASCII code). To get around this problem, a multioctet (octet means 8 bits, the same thing as a byte for all practical purposes these days) code named UTF-8 was invented that retains a single byte representation for the characters in the ASCII set, but has multibyte representations for the other character sets. The 1-byte characters of UTF-8, which are the same as the ASCII characters, all start with the high-order bit set to 0. The high-order bit of all the bytes used for multioctet representations is always 1. The different bytes in a multioctet character are distinguished by the number of leading 1's. This allows ASCII-based applications to not choke up when presented with UTF-8 input; such applications can either ignore or simply pass through the octets that start with leading 1's. (Also note that, in addition to the character-by-character coding, a UTF-8 representation of a string must use its first 2 bytes to state the total number of bytes needed for all the characters in the string.) So whereas XML processing requires Unicode support, at least using the multioctet UTF-8 encoding of Unicode, most regex packages are based on the 8-bit extended ASCII (also known as ISO-8859-1 or more commonly as ISO-Latin-1). Cameron has pointed out that it is possible to use 8-bit regular expression packages to process UTF-8 encoding of Unicode for XML provided some care is taken in the treatment of non-ASCII characters. The DFA (Deterministic Finite Automaton) underlying a regular expression package that can process ISI-8859-1 characters typically transitions into a super-ASCII acceptance state when it sees a non-ASCII character, meaning a character whose octet has its high-order bit set to 1. If the super-ASCII acceptance state has a super-ASCII self transition, then it becomes rather straightforward to use the same DFA for accepting UTF-8 characters. See Cameron [5] for details.

[13]Strictly speaking, only the starting and the ending delimiters of a CDATA section are considered to be part of the markup, as was stated earlier in Section 17.1.

The start tag of the `B` element is missing the right angle bracket. When this input is processed by Cameron's regex, we get the following partition:

```
Item 0:   <A>
Item 1:   hello
Item 2:   <B
Item 3:   jello
Item 4:   </B>
Item 5:   </A>
```

The partitioning process itself is silent about the missing right angle bracket error that is in item 2. Recognition of such error strings in the output is left to a secondary process that would check each item of the output for its legitimacy. It is important to realize that just because an item looks illegal, it does not mean that the syntax error is confined to just that portion of the XML document. An alternative correct version of the above XML input would have `jello` as an attribute name for the `B` element, and the error would consist of a missing assignment operator after `jello`, followed by a missing value, and followed by a missing right angle bracket.

If an XML document contains entity references,[14] these are not partitioned out by Cameron's regex. Recognizing the entity references and making the called for substitutions entails a two-step process, which goes against the spirit of what is meant to be accomplished with a regex-based partitioning of a document — extraction of all the components in a *single* pass through the document. Obviously, after a document is partitioned, one could try to recognize the entity references and carry out whatever changes are called for to the information extracted from the document.

In the rest of this section, we will first explain the different parts of Cameron's regex with the help of the Perl script `TestREX.pl` that is shown next. After that, we will show a Python version of the same script.

Using Cameron's notation, `$XML_SPE`, for this regex,[15] the idea is to scan a document source with the regex to yield the desired non-overlapping partition. In Perl, that can be achieved with the global modifier `//g` as shown below:

```
@parition = $XML_document =~ /$XML_SPE/g;
```

where we have assumed that the entire source file is read into a single string `$XML_document`. We will now show how Cameron goes about deriving a regular expression for `$XML_SPE`.

The basic idea that goes into deriving a regex for `$XML_SPE` is as follows: As explained in Section 4.11.2 of Chapter 4, in regular expression matching in a list

[14] See Section 17.5.3 for what is meant by an *entity reference*.

[15] `XML_SPE` stands for XML Shallow Parsing Expression.

context, if the regex consists of alternations and if the global option `//g` is set, the entire input string will be scanned with the regex and, at each position of the regex vis-à-vis the input string, whatever portion of the input string is consumed by the regex match will be output as a separate substring. This is illustrated by the following example:

```
my $regex  =  "he|je|me|ye|lo";
my $input_string  =  "hello jello mello yello";
my @arr  =  $input_string  =~  /$regex/g;
print "@arr\n";                                   # he lo je lo me lo ye lo
```

Getting back to `$XML_SPE`, as the `//g` option causes the document source to be scanned with this regex, if either a character data string or a markup string is identified at each position of the regex vis-à-vis the document source, we want that string to be output as a separate item. We therefore want `$XML_SPE` to consist of the following alternation:

```
$XML_SPE = "$TextSE|$MarkupSPE";
```

where `$TextSE`, which stands for *Text Scanning Expression*, is for the extraction of character data, and `$MarkupSPE`, which stands for *Markup Shallow Parsing Expression*, is for the extraction of markup. The order in which the two alternation choices show up is immaterial. We will now use the constraint that a character data string, meaning a nonmarkup string, is not allowed to contain the left angle bracket. We can therefore write

```
$TextSE = "[^<]+";
```

The portion of the regex that corresponds to `$MarkupSPE` must first enforce the constraint that the string consumed by it must begin with the `<` character. The structure of the rest of the regex depends on the syntax of the specific markup that needs to be matched with `$MarkupSPE`. To express this fact, Cameron uses the following four different alternation choices for `$MarkupSPE`:

```
$MarkupSPE  =  "<(?:!(?:$DeclCE)?|\\?(?:$PI_CE)?|" .
                    "/(?:$EndTagCE)?|(?:$ElemTagCE)?)";       #(A)
```

where each `CE` stands for a *completion expression*. After starting with the `<` character, note the use of the nonextracting grouping[16] parentheses `(?: )` for grouping together all four alternation choices. The first completion expression, represented by `$DeclCE`, is meant for extracting all declaration-type markup, such as comments, DTD declarations, and CDATA sections. The opening delimiter for all such markup is the `<!` string. The second completion expression, `$PI_CE`, is for extracting processing instructions; the opening delimiter for a processing instruction is the `<?` string. The third completion expression, `$EndTagCE`, is for extracting the element end tags; the opening delimiter for such tags is the `</` string. The last

[16]See Section 4.8 of Chapter 4 for nonextracting versus extracting groupings.

completion expression above, `$ElemTagCE`, is for extracting the rest of the start tag of an element, including the attributes if there are any. This completion expression will also extract self-closing element tags. The reader will notice the following about all four alternation choices in the statement in line (A) above:[17]

- Nonextracting grouping parentheses `(?: )` enclose each completion expression. Nonextracting grouping parentheses also surround all of the alternation choices taken together.
- Each completion expression is optional.

The most fundamental reason for using the nonextracting grouping parentheses as opposed to the extracting kind is that the latter alter what the `//g` match modifier returns in a list context in the presence of alternations in a regex. For example, with the regex and the input string set as:

```
$regex = 'lo|h\w*';                                              #(B)
$input_string = "hello jello mello yello";                       #(C)
```

the regex match in line (D) below produces the output shown in line (E):

```
@arr  =  $input_string  =~  /$regex/g;                           #(D)
print "@arr\n";                      # hello lo lo lo            #(E)
```

But when the regex of line (B) includes grouping parentheses of the extracting kind as shown below:

```
$regex = '(lo)|h\w*';                                            #(F)
```

the regex match operation produces a different output, as shown in line (H):

```
@arr  =  $input_string  =~  /$regex/g;                           #(G)
print "@arr\n";                      #  lo lo lo                 #(H)
```

However, if we now use nonextracting grouping parentheses in the regex as shown below:

```
$regex = '(?:lo)|h\w*';                                          #(I)
```

the same matching operation reproduces the result of line (E), as shown in line (K) below:

---

[17]The need for two backslashes at the beginning of the second alternation choice has to do with the default meaning of a backslash in a *double-quoted* string in Perl. As explained in Section 2.1.2 of Chapter 2, by default a backslash in a double-quoted string in Perl is the beginning of an escape sequence. So if we replaced `\\?` by `\?` in the regex construction in line (A) above, Perl will think of the latter as a character escape — but that is not what we want. So we escape the needed backslash with an additional backslash. Therefore, in the regex produced, what looks like `\\?` in line (A) will only be the `\?` string — which is what we want. Note that our goal is to use the `?` character as an ordinary character in the regex. So we must suppress its metacharacter role.

```
@arr  =  $input_string  =~  /$regex/g;                                    #(J)
print "@arr\n";                          #  hello lo lo lo                #(K)
```

As to why the individual completion expressions in line (A) above should be within grouping parentheses at all, that is because we want to make sure that no matter what regex gets substituted for the variable representing a completion expression, all of it will be considered to be optional. As to why a completion expression should be optional, that has to do with making the partitioning process fault-tolerant. We want the partitioning to always succeed even in the presence of syntax errors in the source document. Let's say that, for a given position of the regex vis-à-vis the source document, the regex shown in line (A) above is able to consume the string `<!` but that there is not a match with the completion expression represented by `$DeclCE`. That would imply a syntax error in the source document. If that is indeed the case, we want the partitioning process to return at least the string `<!` for this position of the regex in the document source.

We have yet to show the regexes for the completion expressions on the right-hand side of the assignment in line (A) above. These are defined as follows:

```
$DeclCE    =    "--(?:$CommentCE)?|\\[CDATA\\[(?:$CDATA_CE)?|" .
                                 "DOCTYPE(?:$DocTypeCE)?";               #(L)

$PI_CE    =   "$Name(?:$PI_Tail)?";                                      #(M)

$EndTagCE    =    "$Name(?:$S)?>?";                                      #(N)

$ElemTagCE    =    "$Name(?:$S$Name(?:$S)?=(?:$S)?" .
                                 "(?:$AttValSE))*(?:$S)?/?>?";           #(O)
```

where `$CommentCE`, `$CDATA_CE`, and `$DocTypeCE` in line (L) are, respectively, the completion expressions for extracting the comment blocks, the CDATA section, and the DTD declarations. Note that these completion expressions come after additional syntax constraints on these markup types. The comment block completion expression `$CommentCE` follows the mandatory double dashes that must appear after the starting `<!` string. Similarly, the CDATA completion expression `$CDATA_CE` follows the mandatory `[CDATA[` that must follow the opening `<!` string.[18] By the same token, the DTD completion expression `$DocTypeCE` follows the mandatory `DOCTYPE` that must come after the opening string `<!` in a DTD declaration.

[18] In case the reader is wondering about the two backslash escapes for each appearance of the `[` character in line (L), the reason is the same as for the two backslashes that precede the first appearance of the `?` character in the second alternation choice in line (A). As explained in the previous footnote in this section, in a regex defined with a double-quoted string, you need two backslashes where you would use only one in a definition that uses a single-quoted string. So what appears as the `\\[` string in the regex construction in line (L) will only be `\[` in the actual regex, which is what we want in order to suppress the usual meaning of the `[` character. Recall that ordinarily `[` is a metacharacter in a regex since its role is to denote the beginning of a character class, as explained in Chapter 4.

In both the end tag completion expression in line (N) and the element tag completion expression in line (O), the scalar variable `$S` stands for an arbitrary amount of white space as defined by

```
$S = "[ \\n\\t\\r]+";
```

where the reason for using two backslashes for the white-space characters is the same as for using two backslashes in lines (A) and (L) above. The element tag completion expression in line (O) above allows for the extraction of an arbitrary number of attribute name-value pairs through the following regex fragment:

```
(?:$S$Name(?:$S)?=(?:$S)?(?:$AttValSE))*
```

which includes an arbitrary amount of white space before the attribute name, between the attribute name and the assignment operator, an arbitrary amount of white space after that, and, finally, a scanning expression for the corresponding attribute value.

The next step would obviously be to provide definitions for the scalar variables on the right-hand side of the assignments in the lines labeled (L), (M), (N), and (O) in the preceding explanation. The reasoning that goes into developing those definitions is along the same lines as what the reader has already seen. We will therefore go ahead and simply show all of the derivational steps together in the following script named `TestREX.pl`. All of Cameron's derivational steps are in lines (A) through (Y) of the script.[19]

```
#!/usr/bin/perl -w

### TestREX.pl

use strict;

# All of the regular expressions shown below that lead up to
# the definition of the XML shallow parsing expression that
# is assigned to $XML_SPE are by Robert Cameron

# Define the shallow parsing exression:

my $TextSE = "[^<]+";                                           #(A)
my $UntilHyphen = "[^-]*-";                                     #(B)
my $Until2Hyphens = "$UntilHyphen(?:[^-]$UntilHyphen)*-";       #(C)
my $CommentCE = "$Until2Hyphens>?";                             #(D)
my $UntilRSBs = "[^\\]]*](?:[^\\]]+])*]+";                      #(E)
my $CDATA_CE = "$UntilRSBs(?:[^\\]>]$UntilRSBs)*>";             #(F)
my $S = "[ \\n\\t\\r]+";                                        #(G)
my $NameStrt = "[A-Za-z_:]|[^\\x00-\\x7F]";                     #(H)
```

[19] Robert Cameron refers to his shallow parser as REX.

```
my $NameChar = "[A-Za-z0-9_:.-]|[^\\x00-\\x7F]";                        #(I)
my $Name = "(?:$NameStrt)(?:$NameChar)*";                               #(J)
my $QuoteSE = "\"[^\"]*\"|'[^']*'";                                     #(K)
my $DT_IdentSE = "$S$Name(?:$S(?:$Name|$QuoteSE))*";                    #(L)
my $MarkupDeclCE = "(?:[^\\]\"'><]+|$QuoteSE)*>";                       #(M)
my $S1 = "[\\n\\r\\t ]";                                                #(N)
my $UntilQMs = "[^?]*\\?+";                                             #(O)
my $PI_Tail = "\\?>|$S1$UntilQMs(?:[^>?]$UntilQMs)*>";                  #(P)
my $DT_ItemSE = "<(?:!(?:--$Until2Hyphens>|[^-]$MarkupDeclCE)|" .
                        "\\?$Name(?:$PI_Tail))|%$Name;|$S";             #(Q)
my $DocTypeCE =
        "$DT_IdentSE(?:$S)?(?:\\[(?:$DT_ItemSE)*](?:$S)?)?>?";           #(R)
my $DeclCE = "--(?:$CommentCE)?|\\[CDATA\\[(?:$CDATA_CE)?|".
                          "DOCTYPE(?:$DocTypeCE)?";                     #(S)
my $PI_CE = "$Name(?:$PI_Tail)?";                                       #(T)
my $EndTagCE = "$Name(?:$S)?>?";                                        #(U)
my $AttValSE = "\"[^<\"]*\"|'[^<']*'";                                  #(V)
my $ElemTagCE = "$Name(?:$S$Name(?:$S)?=(?:$S)?" .
                          "(?:$AttValSE))*(?:$S)?/?>?";                 #(W)
my $MarkupSPE = "<(?:!(?:$DeclCE)?|\\?(?:$PI_CE)?|" .
                        "/(?:$EndTagCE)?|(?:$ElemTagCE)?)";             #(X)
my $XML_SPE = "$TextSE|$MarkupSPE";                                     #(Y)


# This function invoked in a list context will partition
# an XML document into its markup and character data components:
sub ShallowParse {                                                      #(a)
  my($XML_document) = @_;                                               #(b)
  return $XML_document =~ /$XML_SPE/g;                                  #(c)
}

# Read the XML source document:
$/ = undef;                                                             #(d)
my $string = <>;                                                        #(e)

my @parse_result = ShallowParse( $string );                             #(f)
my $num_tokens = @parse_result;                                         #(g)
print "Number of tokens extracted: $num_tokens\n\n";                    #(h)

my $i = 0;
foreach (@parse_result) {                                               #(i)
    print "Item $i:      $_\n" if  $_ !~ /^\s*$/;                       #(j)
    $i++;
}
```

We will invoke the above script on the following XML document named `test.xml`. Note that this document is intentionally "malformed," with white space and line breaks thrown in here and there, to see how it would be partitioned by `TestREX.pl`. Here is the document:

```
<?xml version="1.0"?>

<!--
          The name of this <document> is test.xml
-->

<list_of_entries xmlns="http://www.w3.org/1999/xhtml">

  <entry>
<eg> <![CDATA[ <?xml version="1.0"?>
<!DOCTYPE greeting SYSTEM "hello.dtd">
<greeting>Hello, world!</greeting>
]]></eg>
      <name type="singsong">wonwon</name>
      <phone>  32323-38373 </phone>
  </entry>
  <self_enclosed/>
    </list_of_entries>
```

Invoking `TestREX.pl` on the above document produces the output shown below. In the output shown, we have filtered out the tokens that consist of white-space characters only for the sake of conserving space. This is accomplished by the conditional of the `if` clause in line (`j`) of the `TestREX.pl` script. If we did not use this filter, in the output shown below you would see "Item 2:" after the "Item 1:" line that is shown. The second item would consist of the two line breaks that exist between the first line of the XML document and the comment block that comes after that. The same is true for the other missing items in the list shown below — all the missing items consist of some sequence of blank spaces and line breaks. Here is the output:

```
Number of tokens extracted: 27

Item 1:       <?xml version="1.0"?>
Item 3:       <!--
          The name of this <document> is test.xml
-->
Item 5:       <list_of_entries xmlns="http://www.w3.org/1999/xhtml">
Item 7:       <entry>
Item 9:       <eg>
Item 11:       <![CDATA[ <?xml version="1.0"?>
```

```
<!DOCTYPE greeting SYSTEM "hello.dtd">
<greeting>Hello, world!</greeting>
]]>
Item 12:        </eg>
Item 14:        <name type="singsong">
Item 15:        wonwon
Item 16:        </name>
Item 18:        <phone>
Item 19:          32323-38373
Item 20:        </phone>
Item 22:        </entry>
Item 24:        <self_enclosed/>
Item 26:        </list_of_entries>
```

Shown below is a Python version of the REX shallow parser. The shallow parsing regex and all of its individual components are the same as before. The main coding differences are owing to the use of string interpolation for combining components for the Perl case and string concatenation for the case of Python. Another way of writing the Python version would be to interpolate the lower level components into format strings for the higher level components. The XML partitioning produced by the following script is exactly the same as by the previous Perl script, as the reader would of course expect.

```
#!/usr/bin/env python

### TestREX.py

### Python version of Robert Cameron's REX XML shallow parser
### as posted by David Niergarth

import re                                                                  #(A)

TextSE = "[^<]+"                                                           #(B)
UntilHyphen = "[^-]*-"                                                     #(C)
Until2Hyphens = UntilHyphen + "(?:[^-]" + UntilHyphen + ")*-"              #(D)
CommentCE = Until2Hyphens + ">?"                                           #(E)
UntilRSBs = "[^\\]]*](?:[^\\]]+])*]+"                                      #(F)
CDATA_CE = UntilRSBs + "(?:[^\\]>]" + UntilRSBs + ")*>"                    #(G)
S = "[ \\n\\t\\r]+"                                                        #(H)
NameStrt = "[A-Za-z_:]|[^\\x00-\\x7F]"                                     #(I)
NameChar = "[A-Za-z0-9_:.-]|[^\\x00-\\x7F]"                                #(J)
Name = "(?:" + NameStrt + ")(?:" + NameChar + ")*"                         #(K)
QuoteSE = "\"[^\"]*\"|'[^']*'"                                             #(L)
DT_IdentSE= S+Name+ "(?:" + S + "(?:" + Name + "|" + QuoteSE + "))*"#(M)
MarkupDeclCE = "(?:[^\\]\"'><]+|" + QuoteSE + ")*>"                        #(N)
```

```
S1 = "[\\n\\r\\t ]"                                                      #(O)
UntilQMs = "[^?]*\\?+"                                                   #(P)
PI_Tail = "\\?>|" + S1 + UntilQMs + "(?:[^>?]" + UntilQMs + ")*>"        #(Q)
DT_ItemSE = "<(?:!(?:--" + Until2Hyphens + ">|[^-]" + MarkupDeclCE + \
        ")|\\?" + Name + "(?:" + PI_Tail + "))|%" + Name + ";|" + S #(R)
DocTypeCE = DT_IdentSE + "(?:" + S + ")?(?:\\[(?:" + DT_ItemSE + \
                                ")*](?:" + S + ")?)?>?"                  #(S)
DeclCE = "--(?:" + CommentCE + ")?|\\[CDATA\\[(?:" + CDATA_CE + \
                                ")?|DOCTYPE(?:" + DocTypeCE + ")?"       #(T)
PI_CE = Name + "(?:" + PI_Tail + ")?"                                    #(U)
EndTagCE = Name + "(?:" + S + ")?>?"                                     #(V)
AttValSE = "\"[^<\"]*\"|'[^<']*'"                                        #(W)
ElemTagCE = Name + "(?:" + S + Name + "(?:" + S + ")?=(?:" + S + \
                                ")?(?:" + AttValSE + "))*(?:" + S + ")?/?>?"  #(X)
MarkupSPE = "<(?:!(?:" + DeclCE + ")?|\\?(?:" + PI_CE + ")?|/(?:" + \
                                EndTagCE + ")?|(?:" + ElemTagCE + ")?)"  #(Y)
XML_SPE = TextSE + "|" + MarkupSPE                                       #(Z)

# Parsing function:
def ShallowParse(XML_document):                                          #(a)
return re.findall(XML_SPE, XML_document)                         #(b)

if __name__ == '__main__':                                               #(c)
    import sys                                                           #(d)
    # Read the XML source document:
    FILE = open( sys.argv[1] )                                           #(e)
    doc_str = FILE.read()                                                #(f)
    parse_result = ShallowParse( doc_str )                               #(g)
    num_tokens = len(parse_result)                                       #(h)
    print "Number of tokens extracted: ",  num_tokens                    #(i)
    for i in range(len(parse_result)):                                   #(j)
        if parse_result[i]:                                              #(k)
            print "Item %s:  %s" % (i, parse_result[i])                  #(l)
        else: print "item %s: " % i                                      #(m)
```

17.5 DOCUMENT TYPE DEFINITIONS FOR XML DOCUMENTS

As mentioned earlier, ordinarily an XML document is not required to obey any particular constraints regarding its structure. One can name the root element whatever one wants, give it any number of subelements, name them whatever one wants, and so on. One is also free to use any attributes in the start tags of the elements and use any character data for the element content. Of course, for a document to be called an XML document it must be well-formed, meaning that it must obey all of the well-formedness constraints listed earlier in Section 17.1.

As long as an XML document is used only for "local" applications — meaning applications used by a small number of individuals with a shared understanding of the structure of the XML document — it is sufficient for the document to be just well-formed. However, when XML documents are used to exchange information in networked applications that are potentially open-ended as to who may use those applications, the documents must conform to some additional conventions. To illustrate, if we created an XML-based phonebook of the following sort:

```
<?xml version="1.0"?>
<phonebook>
    <listing>
        <first>Zaphod</first>
        <middle>D.</middle>
        <last>Beeblecrox</last>
        <phone type="home">1-800-123-4567</phone>
     </listing>
     ....
     ....
```

it would not be of much use to a client whose document analyzer is expecting the following sort of a phonebook:

```
<?xml version="1.0"?>
<Phonebook>
    <Entry>
        <Name>Zaphod D. Beeblecrox</Name>
        <Type>home</Type>
        <Phone>1-800-123-4567</Phone>
    </Entry>
     ....
     ....
```

Besides the matter of case difference in how the root element is named, the two phonebook styles also differ with respect to the naming of the element that holds each entry in the phonebook, the content of this element, etc.

These sorts of problems can be avoided by incorporating a *document type declaration* at the beginning of an XML document. A document type declaration tells the XML processor that the structure of the root element must conform to the document type definition (DTD) to which either the XML document is linked or which is provided directly at the beginning of the document.

Here is an example of an XML document with a document type declaration that links the document to an external DTD:

```
<?xml version="1.0"?>
<!DOCTYPE phonebook SYSTEM "phonebook.dtd">

<!-- The name of this XML document is: PhonebookWithExtDtd.xml -->

<phonebook>
    <listing>
        <first>John</first>
        <middle>C.</middle>
        <last>Hancock</last>
        <phone type="home">1-800-123-4567</phone>
      </listing>
    <listing>
        <first>Susan</first>
        <last>Anthony</last>
        <phone type="work">1-800-234-5678</phone>
    </listing>
    <listing>
        <first>Zaphod</first>
        <middle> Doubleheaded</middle>
        <last>Beeblecrox</last>
        <phone type="cell">9-000-666-1234</phone>
    </listing>
    <listing>
        <first>Trillian</first>
        <last>Earthling</last>
        <phone type="work">9-000-222-2345</phone>
    </listing>
    <listing>
        <first>Miss</first>
        <last>Importante</last>
        <phone type="cell">0-111-234-8888</phone>
    </listing>
</phonebook>
```

Note the document type declaration in the second line of the document:

```
<!DOCTYPE phonebook SYSTEM "phonebook.dtd">
```

This declaration says that the structure of this XML document is specified by a DTD in an external file called `phonebook.dtd`. The DTD may declare the element types used in the document, how the elements relate to one another, what sort of values they may contain, and so on. As shown above, a document type declaration is delimited by `<!` and `>` and it always begins with the keyword `DOCTYPE`. The next identifier in the declaration is the name of the root element whose *content model* is specified by the designated DTD. The third identifier is either SYSTEM or PUBLIC. What follows SYSTEM is, in general, meant to be a URL if the DTD is to be found at an external source. What follows SYSTEM is also referred to as a *system identifier*. When the resource pointed to by a system identifier is on the local machine, it can just be a pathname to the resource. When the third identifier in the document type declaration is PUBLIC, that gives the XML processor a greater latitude in searching for the resource named in the next identifier. Said another way, the resource named by a system identifier must be found at exactly the location named in the identifier. On the other hand, the processor can use its own discretion to locate the resource named with a public identifier.

Shown below are the contents of the DTD file phonebook.dtd:

```
<?xml version="1.0" encoding="UTF-8"?>

<!--
 File: phonebook.dtd
 This is a DTD file for the phonebook root element.
-->

<!ELEMENT phonebook (listing*)>
<!ELEMENT listing (first, middle*, last, phone+)>
<!ELEMENT first (#PCDATA)>
<!ELEMENT middle (#PCDATA)>
<!ELEMENT last (#PCDATA)>
<!ELEMENT phone (#PCDATA)>
<!ATTLIST phone type CDATA #REQUIRED>
```

The declarations in this file are delimited by either <!ELEMENT and >, or by <!ATTLIST and >. An <!ELEMENT declaration is considered to be a *content model* for the XML element that is named immediately after the keyword ELEMENT. The content model tells us what can go inside that element and in what order. The above DTD file contains six such declarations. On the other hand, an <!ATTLIST declaration tells us what attributes are allowed inside the target XML element. This declaration may also include an additional keyword indicating whether or not a given attribute is optional or required.

The next three subsections present in greater detail the structure of DTD declarations.

17.5.1 Declaring the Content Model for an Element in a DTD

A content model DTD declaration, meaning a declaration that starts with <!ELEMENT, can take one of the following forms:

1. The element content model may designate an empty element by a declaration like

   ```
   <!ELEMENT myElement EMPTY>
   ```

   Such an element may serve as a marker in a document, as, for example, the empty HTML element <BR/> for line breaks. An empty element can also carry information through its attributes.

2. If there are no constraints on the contents of an element, that fact can be declared in a DTD with the help of the keyword ALL, as in

   ```
   <!ELEMENT myElement ALL>
   ```

3. The element content model may specify that the element cannot contain any other nested elements, but only character data devoid of any embedded markup. This can be accomplished with the following sort of a declaration:

   ```
   <!ELEMENT phone (#PCDATA)>
   ```

   The keyword #PCDATA stands for *parsed-character data*. This means that the XML parser that checks the document for its validity as specified by the DTD will scan the content of the phone element to identify any entity references contained therein. If the parser finds an entity reference, it will substitute the replacement text for the entity before continuing with the parse.[20] In general, an entity is capable of pulling into an XML document both markup and character data. But when an entity is used in the content of an element whose DTD declaration declares the content to be #PCDATA, the entity is not allowed to include markup.

4. The element content model may specify that the element contains nested elements only. How the nested elements may appear is dictated by a formula that uses the symbols

   ```
   , ? + * | ( )
   ```

   in very much the same manner as the metacharacters in regular expressions.[21] Here is the meaning to be ascribed to each of these symbols:

---

[20]Entities in XML documents are discussed in Section 17.5.3.

[21]An exception to this observation being the comma symbol which serves as an AND operator in a DTD declaration.

- The comma symbol means sequencing; the element on the left must come before the element on right.
- The symbol ? implies optional, that is, at most one of the elements of the type that is postfixed with this symbol.
- The symbol + means at least one.
- The symbol * means an arbitrary number, including zero.
- The symbol | means alternation.

To show some examples of this type of declaration, the declaration

```
<!ELEMENT phonebook (listing*)>
```

says that a `phonebook` can be composed of any number, including zero, of `listing` elements. The declaration

```
<!ELEMENT listing (first, middle*, last, phone+)>
```

says that the content of a `listing` element must start with an element of type `first`. Subsequently, any number, possibly zero, of elements of type `middle` are allowed, followed by exactly one element of type `last`. After that must come at least one element of type `phone`. The following declaration

```
<!ELEMENT A (B?, (C | D)*) >
```

says that an element of type `A` must optionally contain an element of type `B`, followed by an arbitrarily long sequence of `C` and `D` elements. So any of the following sequences of elements would be legal for the content of element `A`:

```
BCCDD
BCDCDCD
BDDDDD
CCCC
B
CDDC
```

5. An element content model may include character data *along with other nested elements* provided the formula used for expressing this content model looks like

```
<!ELEMENT paragraph (#PCDATA | <italics> | <footnote> )*>
```

which says that the content of a `paragraph` element is either parsed character data or an element of type `italics` or an element of type `footnote`, with an arbitrary number of repetitions of any of these allowed. Such element declarations are particularly convenient for embedding tags in running text for the purpose of highlighting, marking, etc. The above element declaration would, for example, serve as a content model for the following `paragraph` element of an XML document:

<paragraph>Large object-oriented programs are no different. <italics>The idea is to think of large software (sometimes running into millions of lines of code) as consisting of a society of objects</italics>: objects that possess sufficient intelligence<footnote>In ways that parallel human intelligence</footnote> to interpret messages received from other objects and to then respond with appropriate behavior; objects that <italics>inherit properties and behaviors</italics> from higher-level objects and permit lower-level object to inherit properties and behaviors from them; and so on.<footnote>This paragraph was taken from the book "Programming with Objects".</footnote></paragraph>

17.5.2 Declaring Attributes in a DTD

A DTD declaration that starts with `<!ATTLIST` constitutes an *attribute list declaration* for an element, the name of the element being the next identifier, as in the following example:

```
<!ATTLIST phone type CDATA #REQUIRED>
```

This says that the `phone` element has one attribute, `type`, whose value must be of type `CDATA` and that the inclusion of this attribute is mandatory for the `phone` element.

The general syntax for declaring attributes for an element is

```
<!ATTLIST element_type
    attribute_1    value_type    qualifier
    attribute_2    value_type    qualifier
    attribute_3    value_type    qualifier
>
```

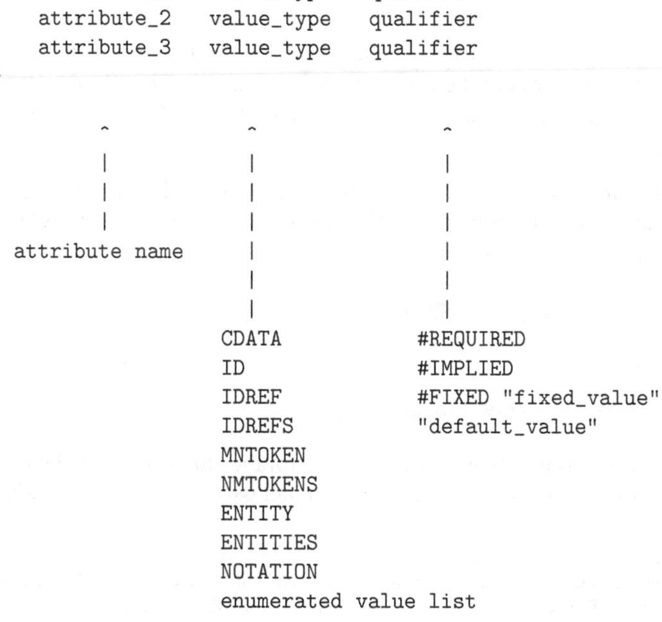

Note the large number of choices available for expressing the data type of the value of an attribute. Of these, CDATA, which stands for *character data*, is the most accommodating, since a value that is CDATA can be any quoted string of characters or character entity references; it can also include internal general entity references as long as they point to replacement strings that look like CDATA and do not include markup. Entity references are discussed in the next subsection.

The data type ID, which stands for *unique identifier*, for an attribute value is special, in the sense that no two attribute names can have the same ID value associated with them. If, per chance, we have two separate attribute names whose values are of type ID and they are both assigned the same value for this attribute, the XML parser will declare an error. The value of such an attribute is a string of characters that must begin with a letter and can contain numbers, letters, and certain punctuations.

The data type IDREF, standing for *identifier reference*, is meant to be a value that refers to the ID value of another element. Its plural version, IDREFS, which stands for *identifier reference list*, is a space-separated list of IDREFs.

The data type NMTOKEN, which stands for *name token*, can be any quoted string of characters that begins with a letter and that contains letters, numbers, and certain punctuations. Any white space between the quotes is removed by the XML processor. Its plural version, NMTOKENS, is a sequence of NMTOKENs separated by spaces. If multiple white space characters are found between successive NMTOKENs, all but one are eliminated by the XML processor. Any leading and trailing white space is also removed.

When the data type of an attribute value is ENTITY, an entity name for any of the general entities declared in the DTD can be used as the value for the attribute.[22] Its plural version, ENTITIES, means that the value of the attribute is a list of entity names separated by spaces.

When the declared data type for an attribute is NOTATION, the value of the attribute can be one of the notation labels in the DTD used. Notation labels are declared with the following syntax in a DTD:

```
<!NOTATION label_name identifier>
```

as, for example, in

```
<!NOTATION jpeg SYSTEM "image/jpeg">
```

Regarding the data type *enumerated value list* for the attribute value, the following syntax demonstrates an attribute list declaration that uses an enumerated value list:

[22]Note that the attribute value in this case is the *name* of an entity inside single or double quotes, and not an entity reference. The next subsection talks about entities in XML documents.

```
<!ATTLIST phone type (home | work | cell | secretary) #REQUIRED>
```

where the parenthesized list that follows the attribute name `type` is a list of alternative values for the attribute. With this declaration, an XML document will now be allowed to have the following sort of a `phone` element:

```
<phone type="cell">
```

As mentioned below, with the qualifier `#REQUIRED` included in the attribute list declaration shown above, the user *must* supply the attribute in question.

That brings us to the qualifiers, the ending portion of an attribute list declaration. As shown previously, it must be one of

```
#REQUIRED
#IMPLIED
#FIXED "fixed_value"
"default_value"
```

As already mentioned, when the qualifier is `#REQUIRED`, the attribute must be supplied. On the other hand, when the qualifier is `#IMPLIED`, the attribute becomes optional. When the qualifier is `#FIXED`, the value for the attribute must be what is specified in the DTD and cannot be altered subsequently. An example of such a declaration is

```
<!ATTLIST phone type #FIXED "home">
```

where the identifier that follows the symbol `#FIXED` is the fixed value for the attribute named `type`. With this declaration in a DTD, the beginning tag of a `phone` element must look like

```
<phone type="home">
```

The last of the qualifiers consists of supplying a default value for an attribute using syntax that looks like

```
<!ATTLIST phone type (home | work | cell | secretary) "cell">
```

where the default value, `cell`, is shown at the end of the declaration. What that means is that if the user did not supply the `type` attribute of the phone element, as in

```
<phone>1-234-567-8910</phone>
```

the XML parser will assume the following:

```
<phone type="cell">1-234-567-8910</phone>
```

17.5.3 Declaring Entities in a DTD

An entity in an XML document is a place-holder for either a single character, or some character data (with possibly embedded markup), or some object that the XML processor is expected to leave alone by not parsing it. What the XML processor substitutes for an entity may come from a local definition in a DTD, or from an external source, such as another file in the same machine, or from a file that resides elsewhere in the network. As a simple illustration of the use of an entity, the DTD for an XML document may contain the following entity declaration:

```
<!ENTITY booktitle "Scripting With Objects">
```

Subsequently, wherever the following *entity reference* shows up:

```
&booktitle;
```

it will be replaced by the string `Scripting With Objects`. This makes entities useful as abbreviations for recurring text in a document. In general, nothing prevents us from including markup in the replacement value for an entity, as in the following declaration:

```
<!ENTITY booktitle
  <maintitle>"Scripting With Objects"</maintitle>
  <subtitle>"A Comparative Presentation of Object-Oriented
                         Scripting with Perl and Python"</subtitle>
>
```

Now wherever the entity reference `&booktitle;` appears, it will be replaced by all of the text shown for the entity `booktitle`, including the embedded markup. Obviously, using such an entity reference in some contexts — such as in the value for an attribute — would be illegal since it includes markup.

As the above example demonstrates, after you have declared an entity in a DTD, it is used in an XML document through an *entity reference* that consists of the name of the entity prefixed with the ampersand symbol and postfixed with a semicolon; that is, through the notation

```
&entity_name;
```

Such entities are called *general entities.* There is also another category of entities, called *parameter entities*, that are used only inside a DTD. These are referenced through the notation

```
%entity_name;
```

A general entity can be of the following three types, with the types broken into subtypes:

1. character entities
   (a) predefined character entities
   (b) number character entities
   (c) named character entities
2. mixed-content entities
   (a) internal entities
   (b) external entities
3. unparsed entities

A reference to a character entity results in the replacement text being composed of a single character. On the other hand, a reference to a mixed-content entity can fetch into an XML document any amount of text and markup. When either of these entities is encountered, the XML processor momentarily halts the parsing action to fetch the replacement character data; the replacement character data is then substituted for the entity and the parsing action resumed from the beginning of the replacement material. If for some reason you do not want the replacement material to be parsed — because, say, it is a non-XML object such as an image — then you'd want to use an unparsed entity. We will later show the syntax to use for declaring such entities.

Going back to character entities, because the five characters

```
&   '   "   >   <
```

are crucial to XML markup, they obviously cannot be used directly in the text strings that are meant to be either element content or attribute values. If needed in roles other than for expressing markup, these characters can be incorporated in an XML document through the following entities:

```
amp    apos    quot    gt    lt
```

An entity reference to `amp`, through the `&` notation, fetches the ampersand character into the XML document. By the same token, the entity reference `'` fetches the single quote mark, the entity reference `"` fetches the double quote mark, the entity reference `>` fetches the `>` character, and the entity reference `<` fetches the `<` character into an XML document. The five character entities shown above are the *predefined character entities*. They are predefined in the sense that they are provide by the XML processor and that you do not need to declare them in a DTD.

The *number character entities* are for importing Unicode characters into an XML document. A Unicode character has a 16-bit representation and each character is assigned a decimal integer index ranging from 0 to 65,535. The entity name of each character is the symbol `#` followed by the decimal integer index for the character. For example, the integer index for the uppercase `A` of English is 65, the same as its ASCII code in decimal. Its entity name is therefore `#65`. This entity can be referenced in an XML document through the `A` notation. Similarly, the integer index associated with the registered-trademark symbol (circle with the letter R in it) is 174. Its entity name is therefore `#174` and it can be referenced in an XML document through the `®` notation. The integer index associated with a Unicode character may also be expressed using the hexadecimal notation that consists of the letter `x` followed by the hex digits for the integer index. The hex representation for the uppercase `A` is the `x41` string. Its entity name in hex would therefore be `#x41` and the corresponding entity reference the `A` string.

XML allows a mnemonic name to be associated with the integer index of a Unicode character. However, these names are not directly provided by the XML processor. In other words, you have to also specify the definition source for the names before you can use them. When Unicode characters are used through their mnemonic names, we refer to them as *named character entities*. A named character entity is referenced in the same manner as the other character entities, that is, with the ampersand prefix and a semicolon postfix. Say if `reg` is the name of the registered-trademark character, it can be referenced in an XML document with the `®` notation.

That brings us to the subject of *mixed-content entities*. When the replacement text is provided in the DTD directly, we have a mixed-content entity of the *internal* kind. On the other hand, a mixed-content entity of the *external* kind pulls in text and markup from a named external source. The DTD declaration for an external entity must include either the keyword `SYSTEM` or the keyword `PUBLIC`, as illustrated by the syntax:

```
<!ENTITY section1 SYSTEM "section1.xml" >
```

The last identifier in the declaration is, in general, meant to be a URI to a source of character data and markup. The URI may be the name of a local file or a URL to a file someplace else in the network.[23] As with the use of these flags in document type declarations, the keyword `SYSTEM` is for informing the XML processor that the resource named is to be found exactly where indicated.[24] Subsequently, when the above-mentioned entity is referenced in an XML document through

```
&section1;
```

the entire contents of the file `section1.xml` will be pulled into the XML document. If this operation took place during the parsing of the document, the parsing action would resume after the import of the `section1.xml` file from the point where this file was inserted into the document. External mixed-content entities can thus serve to link an XML document with external sources of text and markup. In this manner, one can create a large XML document from smaller parts.

---

[23] A footnote in Section 17.3 explains the difference between URIs and URLs.

[24] On the other hand, the keyword `PUBLIC` given the XML processor greater freedom in locating the named resource.

With regard to the last category of general entities — *unparsed entities* — as mentioned earlier, they are needed if you wish to embed a non-XML data object, such as an image, in an XML document. You would obviously not want such imported content to be subject to XML parsing. To keep such objects out of the purview of the parser, the DTD declaration for a nonparsed entity must include the keyword NDATA in addition to either SYSTEM or PUBLIC, as in the following example:

```
<!ENTITY image1 SYSTEM "photo1.jpg" NDATA JPEG>
```

Subsequently, an XML document can refer to the entity by using the &image1; notation.

17.6 XML SCHEMAS

Specifying the structure of an XML document with DTDs predates namespaces. Since namespaces have become so central to many important applications of XML, there needed to be another approach for doing the job of DTDs. The other approach that is namespace-aware is referred to as *XML schemas*. XML schemas have two other advantages over DTDs: Unlike a DTD document, an XML schema itself is written in XML. Additionally, an XML schema allows for customization of the data types used in an XML document.[25] Whereas DTDs support only 10 data types, XML schemas support practically all the data types used in databases — over 44 of them. What's more, XML schemas allow us to create new data types by deriving from the existing data types.

An XML schema document uses the namespace

```
http://www.w3.org/2001/XMLSchema
```

to specify the vocabulary you need for describing your XML documents. An XML schema will also insist that the new vocabulary you create be within a namespace of your choosing. This namespace is named with the targetNamespace attribute of the top-level xsd:schema element that contains your schema definitions, as we will see shortly. Here is what the beginning portion of the start tag of the xsd:schema element in a schema file looks like:

```
<xsd:schema xmlns:xsd="http://www.w3.org/2001/XMLSchema"
        targetNamespace="...name_of_new_namespace..."
        ...
        ...
>
```

[25] By customization is meant subjecting a data type to certain constraints that could relate to its range, the precision, and so on. For example, requiring an integer value of an attribute to be between 1 and 100 would be a constraint that can be expressed easily in XML schema but not in DTD.

The start tag starts out by saying the name of the element, `schema`, belongs to the namespace pointed to by the namespace prefix `xsd`.[26] Next, it names the namespace that goes with the `xsd` prefix. Subsequently, it provides a value for the `targetNamespace` attribute for naming the namespace for the element and attribute names in your XML documents.[27] [28]

17.6.1 Declaring Elements and Attributes in a Schema

An important job of a schema is to declare the elements that are allowed to be used in an XML document. An XML element may be declared in a schema to be either of type complex or of type simple. A *complex element* is allowed to contain subelements and can possess attributes. On the other hand, a *simple element* cannot contain subelements and also cannot possess any attributes.

When a complex element is needed in an instance document,[29] it is declared in the schema as being of type `complexType`. For example, let's say that we want the schema to describe the following XML source document element

```
<AAA xx="pp">
    <BBB>qq</BBB>
</AAA>
```

The following schema file, named `AAASchema.xsd`, would do the job:

```
<?xml version="1.0"?>
<xsd:schema xmlns:xsd="http://www.w3.org/2001/XMLSchema"
      targetNamespace="http://AAAnamespace"
      elementFormDefault="qualified">                       <!-- A -->
    <xsd:element name="AAA">                                 <!-- B -->
        <xsd:complexType>                                    <!-- C -->
            <xsd:sequence>                                   <!-- D -->
                <xsd:element name="BBB" type="xsd:string" /> <!-- E -->
            </xsd:sequence>                                  <!-- F -->
```

[26]The prefix `xsd` stands for XML Schema Definition. It is used by convention to denote the namespace in which the schema itself is defined, although in practice any prefix could be used for that purpose, as long as the namespace associated with the prefix is what is shown in the start tag of the `xsd:schema` element here.

[27]An instance document is validated with a schema document. But what about the validation of a schema document, which itself is an XML document? An XML schema document is implicitly validated by a parser with the schema described in `XMLSchema.xsd`. You can think of the contents of `XMLSchema.xsd` as a schema for schemas.

[28]It is interesting to note that since DTD processing and XML schema processing are completely independent, they can be combined. If combined, DTD validation is carried out before schema validation to allow for the entities to be resolved.

[29]In the same sense that a class in object-oriented programming is a template for the instances constructed from that class, a schema is a template for the conforming XML documents. We refer to each XML document that conforms to a schema as *an instance document* corresponding to that schema.

```
            <xsd:attribute name="xx" type="xsd:decimal" />    <!-- G -->
        </xsd:complexType>                                    <!-- H -->
    </xsd:element>                                            <!-- I -->
</xsd:schema>
```

Note that the schema definitions are contained in the root `xsd:schema` element, as previously explained. Again as explained earlier, the namespace prefix `xsd` points to the `http://www.w3.org/2001/XmLSchema` namespace. In addition to naming the target namespace with the `targetNamespace` attribute, in line (A) the schema says that only qualified names will be allowed in the instance documents, meaning that the names outside of any namespace will not be permitted in the instance documents. (Recall that the target namespace is the namespace in which the schema will place all the new names declared in the schema — the names intended for the instance documents described by the schema.) The declaration of the element `AAA` begins in line (B). As stated in line (C), this element will be of type `complexType`, implying that it will be allowed to contain subelements and possess attributes. The subelements of `AAA` are declared with the help of the `xsd:sequence` element in line (D). As a subelement of `AAA`, line (E) says that `BBB` is an element of simple type and that its content is of type `xsd:string`. After closing the `xsd:element` in line (F), we then declare the sole attribute `xx` for the element `AAA` in line (G), which also mentions that the value of the attribute is of type `xsd:decimal`.

The following instance document shows how the above schema can be called inside a document to constrain its contents. The schema declared in the file `AAASchema.xsd` shown above is introduced into the document with the help of the `xsi:schemaLocation` attribute where the prefix `xsi` points to the `http://www.w3.org/2001/XMLSchema-instance` namespace. Note that the value of this attribute consists of a pair of strings, the first naming the target namespace defined with the `targetNamespace` attribute in the schema file and the second naming the file that contains the schema.[30]

```
<?xml version="1.0"?>
<AAA xmlns="http://AAAnamespace"
     xmlns:xsi="http://www.w3.org/2001/XMLSchema-instance"
     xsi:schemaLocation="http://AAAnamespace  AAASchema.xsd"
     xx="234.00">
    <BBB>qq</BBB>
</AAA>
```

---

[30]The elements in an instance document can also be placed in a *null namespace* by using the attribute `xsi:noNamespaceSchemaLocation` instead of `xsi:schemaLocation`. The value of the `xsi:noNamespaceSchemaLocation` attribute will contain a single string (as opposed to the two shown for `xsi:schemaLocation`) that is the name of the schema file. The attribute `targetNamespace` will, of course, be missing in the `schema` element of a schema file that declares elements in the null namespace.

Let's say that the name of the above instance document is `TestAAA.xml`. We can validate the document with respect to the schema of `AAASchema.xsd` by calling on, say, the Xerces parser by[31]

```
PParse -n -s -f TestAAA.xml
```

where the flag `-n` enables namespace processing, the flag `-s` enables schema processing, and the flag `-f` enables full constraint checking. When using the parsing function `PParse`, the default is off with respect to all three.

17.6.2 Specifying Constraints on Subelement Relationships

The schema specification gives us three elements, `xsd:sequence`, `xsd:choice`, and `xsd:all`, for stating the conditions that must be satisfied by the child elements of a given element with regard to how they relate to their parent element:

`sequence:` All the elements declared in an `xsd:sequence` must occur in the parent element and must do so in the order listed.

`choice:` It is sufficient for at least one of the elements supplied through `xsd:choice` to occur in a parent element.

`all:` The elements named in `xsd:all` are allowed to occur in any order in a parent element.

Consider the following example: We want a set of XML documents to contain a root element `AAA` with a required attribute `xx`. This root element must contain the following child elements in the following order: `BBB`, `CCC`, and `DDD`. For its content, the element `DDD` must contain at least one of the following elements: `EEE`, `FFF`, and `GGG`. Additionally, the element `GGG` must contain, *in arbitrary order*, the following three elements `HHH`, `III`, and `JJJ`.

These conditions are stated by the schema document `SubEleRelSchema.xsd` shown next. Lines (B) through (I) declare the root element `AAA`. The element `xsd:sequence` in line (D) will insist that `BBB` of line (E), `CCC` of line (F), and `DDD` of line (G) be the direct child elements of `AAA` and that they appear in the order shown inside an `AAA` element. While we have directly defined in the respective lines the data types that can be used for the contents of `BBB` and `CCC`, for `DDD` we have taken a different approach. For this element, all we have done in line (G) is to provide a reference to the declaration for the `DDD` element elsewhere in the schema. This is the main purpose served by the `ref` attribute in that line.[32]

---

[31] Xerces is an open source XML parser from the Apache XML project. If not already installed, it can be downloaded from `xerces.apache.org`. XML parsing is presented in Section 17.7.

[32] In general, the value of the `ref` attribute must reference a global element declaration. An element declaration in a schema is *global* if it occurs as a direct descendant of the `xsd:schema` element. Attribute declarations can also be made global in this manner.

In order to indicate that the DDD element can contain any of the EEE, FFF, and GGG subelements, note the use of `xsd:choice` in line (K). And that GGG can contain HHH, III, and JJJ in any arbitrary order is indicated with the help of `xsd:all` in line (Q).

```
<?xml version="1.0"?>
<xsd:schema xmlns:xsd="http://www.w3.org/2001/XMLSchema"
      targetNamespace="http://AAAnamespace"
      xmlns:aaa="http://AAAnamespace"
      elementFormDefault="qualified">                              <!-- A -->
    <xsd:element name="AAA">                                        <!-- B -->
        <xsd:complexType>                                           <!-- C -->
            <xsd:sequence>                                          <!-- D -->
                <xsd:element name="BBB" type="xsd:string" />        <!-- E -->
                <xsd:element name="CCC"
                            type="xsd:normalizedString" /><!-- F -->
                <xsd:element ref="aaa:DDD" />                       <!-- G -->
            </xsd:sequence>
            <xsd:attribute name="xx"
                      type="xsd:nonNegativeInteger" />              <!-- H -->
        </xsd:complexType>                                          <!-- I -->
    </xsd:element>
    <xsd:element name="DDD">                                        <!-- J -->
        <xsd:complexType>
            <xsd:choice>                                            <!-- K -->
                <xsd:element name="EEE" type="xsd:anyURI" />        <!-- L -->
                <xsd:element name="FFF" type="xsd:date" />          <!-- M -->
                <xsd:element ref="aaa:GGG" />
            </xsd:choice>                                           <!-- N -->
            <xsd:attribute name="xx" use="optional"
                                      type="xsd:byte" />            <!-- O -->
        </xsd:complexType>
    </xsd:element>
    <xsd:element name="GGG">                                        <!-- P -->
        <xsd:complexType>
            <xsd:all>                                               <!-- Q -->
                <xsd:element name="HHH" />                          <!-- R -->
                <xsd:element name="III" />                          <!-- S -->
                <xsd:element name="JJJ" />                          <!-- T -->
            </xsd:all>
        </xsd:complexType>
    </xsd:element>
</xsd:schema>
```

The schema file shown above also illustrates some of the built-in simple types of XML schema for specifying element content. While the content of the BBB element is of type xsd:string in line (E), that of CCC is xsd:normalizedString in line (F).[33] For the child elements of DDD, we declare the content of EEE to be of type xsd:anyURI in line (L) and of FFF to be of type xsd:date in line (M).[34] For the elements HHH, III, and JJJ, we declare the content to be default type, which is xsd:anyType. When the type of a value for an element or an attribute is xsd:anyType, we can use any legal XML construct for the value.

What follows is an instance document named TestSchema2.xml that conforms to the schema shown above. The order of appearance of the child elements of the root element AAA corresponds exactly to how it was prescribed in the schema. In this document, we also exercised the choice that was available for the child elements of DDD — we chose GGG. Further, we also exercised the choice that was available with regard to the order of appearance of the child elements of GGG.

```
<?xml version="1.0"?>
<AAA xmlns="http://AAAnamespace"
     xmlns:xsi="http://www.w3.org/2001/XMLSchema-instance"
     xsi:schemaLocation="http://AAAnamespace  SubEleRelSchema.xsd"
     xx="45">
    <BBB>qq</BBB>
    <CCC>12</CCC>
    <DDD>
        <GGG>
            <JJJ />
            <HHH />
            <III />
        </GGG>
    </DDD>
</AAA>
```

Validation of the above document vis-à-vis the schema in SubEleRelSchema.xsd can be carried out with the Xerces parser by the same command line invocation as shown previously:

```
PParse -n -s -f TestSchema2.xml
```

Which and how many of the declared child elements appear in a parent element in an instance document can be further controlled by specifying *occurrence constraints*.

---

[33]For a string that is intended to be a normalized string, any white-space characters corresponding to carriage returns, line feeds, and tabs are converted into blank spaces.

[34]A date is expressed in the form yyyy-mm-dd, as in 2008-01-24.

The schema shown below states that the root element AAA contain at most three BBB elements, or at most a single CCC element, or at most a single DDD element, or none of any of these at all. The fact that AAA is allowed to be empty is owing to the zero value of the minOccurs attribute in lines (E), (F), and (G). If AAA chooses BBB as its child element, it is allowed to have a maximum of three of these. On other hand, if AAA chooses either CCC or DDD, it can only have a maximum of one of those. The fact that AAA can have a maximum of three of BBB is a consequence of the value given to the maxOccurs attribute. And the fact that at most one of CCC or DDD can be had by AAA results from default value for maxOccurs when it is not assigned a value by the schema designer.

```
<?xml version="1.0"?>
<xsd:schema xmlns:xsd="http://www.w3.org/2001/XMLSchema"
      targetNamespace="http://AAAnamespace"
      elementFormDefault="qualified">                          <!-- A -->
   <xsd:element name="AAA">                                    <!-- B -->
       <xsd:complexType>                                       <!-- C -->
           <xsd:choice>                                        <!-- D -->
               <xsd:element name="BBB"
                         minOccurs="0" maxOccurs="3" />        <!-- E -->
               <xsd:element name="CCC" minOccurs="0" />        <!-- F -->
               <xsd:element name="DDD" minOccurs="0" />        <!-- G -->
           </xsd:choice>
       </xsd:complexType>
   </xsd:element>
</xsd:schema>
```

The following instant document is legal according to the above schema:

```
<?xml version="1.0"?>
<AAA xmlns="http://AAAnamespace"
     xmlns:xsi="http://www.w3.org/2001/XMLSchema-instance"
     xsi:schemaLocation="http://AAAnamespace ChoiceZero.xsd">
    <BBB />
    <BBB />
    <BBB />
</AAA>
```

In all the schema examples we have shown so far, the parent element could contain only other elements. But what about the case when a parent element must be allowed to contain character data in addition to any child elements? By using a `complexType` element and declaring the `mixed` attribute of the element to be true, the element will be allowed to contain plain character data. In the example shown below, the root element `AAA` is of type `complexType` and its `mixed` attribute is set to `true` in line (B). Now the `AAA` element will be allowed to contain plain character data in addition to the required child elements BBB, CCC, and DDD.

```
<?xml version="1.0"?>

<!--  file: MixedContent.xsd -->

<xsd:schema xmlns:xsd="http://www.w3.org/2001/XMLSchema"
      targetNamespace="http://AAAnamespace"
      elementFormDefault="qualified">
    <xsd:element name="AAA">                                  <!-- A -->
        <xsd:complexType mixed="true">                        <!-- B -->
            <xsd:sequence>                                    <!-- C -->
                <xsd:element name="BBB" />                    <!-- D -->
                <xsd:element name="CCC" />                    <!-- E -->
                <xsd:element name="DDD" />                    <!-- F -->
            </xsd:sequence>
        </xsd:complexType>
    </xsd:element>
</xsd:schema>
```

The following instance document, named `TestSchema4.xml`, agrees with the schema shown above:

```
<?xml version="1.0"?>
<AAA xmlns="http://AAAnamespace"
     xmlns:xsi="http://www.w3.org/2001/XMLSchema-instance"
     xsi:schemaLocation="http://AAAnamespace MixedContent.xsd">
    "testing mixed content schema"
    <BBB />
    "testing mixed content schema again"
    <CCC />
    "testing mixed content schema and yet again"
    <DDD />
</AAA>
```

If the goal is to specify an element that only takes character data for its content, there is another way to do that — with the help of a `simpleContent` element shown in the schema below. The schema, in a file named CharacterContentOnly.xsd, prescribes with the help of xsd:simpleContent in line (C) and xsd:extension in line (D) that the element AAA in an instance document can only contain character data. Just for variety, the schema also specifies an optional attribute with a default value for the AAA element in line (E).

```
<?xml version="1.0"?>

<!--  file: CharacterContentOnly.xsd -->

<xsd:schema xmlns:xsd="http://www.w3.org/2001/XMLSchema"
      targetNamespace="http://AAAnamespace"
      elementFormDefault="qualified">
    <xsd:element name="AAA">                                    <!-- A -->
        <xsd:complexType>                                       <!-- B -->
            <xsd:simpleContent>                                 <!-- C -->
                <xsd:extension base="xsd:string">               <!-- D -->
                    <xsd:attribute name="xx"
                         type="xsd:string"
                         use="optional" default="pp" />         <!-- E -->
                </xsd:extension>
            </xsd:simpleContent>
        </xsd:complexType>
    </xsd:element>
</xsd:schema>
```

The following document, TestSchema5.xml, is legal according to the above schema:

```
<?xml version="1.0"?>

<!-- file: TestSchema5.xml -->

<AAA xmlns="http://AAAnamespace"
     xmlns:xsi="http://www.w3.org/2001/XMLSchema-instance"
     xsi:schemaLocation="http://AAAnamespace CharacterContentOnly.xsd">

        "testing character content only schema"
        "here is a second line"

</AAA>
```

17.6.3 Deriving New Data Types

A very useful feature of XML schemas is that they allow you to derive new data types from existing data types. When you derive a new data type from a simple built-in type, you can express the modifications in your new data type by assigning values to what are known as the *facets* of the built-in types. We will now show an example in which we will derive a restricted string type from the built-in `string` type by placing constraints on the length of the string and on the characters allowed in the string. This we will do with the help of the following three facets defined for the built-in `string` type: `minLength`, `maxLength`, and `pattern`.[35]

Ordinarily, there can be an arbitrary number of characters in a string. But let's say that we want to extend the built-in string into a data type `myString` with the following restrictions: we want the number of characters in a `myString` to be between 5 and 7, with the first five as being the letters between a and z and the additional one or two consisting of the decimal digits between 0 and 9. This seemingly tall order can be fulfilled with the declaration of `myString` shown in lines (F) through (J) of the following schema. Line (G) says that `myString` is being derived from `xsd:string` by *restriction*. Lines (H), (I), and (J) then assign values to the facets `minLength`, `maxLength`, and `xsd:pattern`. Note in particular the value assigned to the facet `xsd:pattern` — it is a regular expression.[36]

```
<?xml version="1.0"?>

<!-- file: DerivedDataType.xsd -->

<xsd:schema xmlns:xsd="http://www.w3.org/2001/XMLSchema"
      targetNamespace="http://AAAnamespace"
      elementFormDefault="qualified">

   <xsd:element name="AAA">                                         <!-- A -->
       <xsd:complexType mixed="true">                               <!-- B -->
           <xsd:sequence>                                           <!-- C -->
               <xsd:element name="BBB" type="xsd:string" />  <!-- D -->
               <xsd:element name="CCC" type="myString" />    <!-- E -->
           </xsd:sequence>
       </xsd:complexType>
   </xsd:element>
```

[35]The other facets defined for the built-in `string` type are `length`, `enumeration`, and `whiteSpace`.

[36]The regular expressions that are used in assigning a value to the `pattern` facet are similar to Perl's regular expressions, except mostly for the fact that the anchor metacharacters `^` and `$` of Perl regexes are not used in XML schemas because the pattern specified is matched against the entire sequence of characters in the corresponding string in an instance document.

```
    <xsd:simpleType name="myString">                          <!-- F -->
        <xsd:restriction base="xsd:string">                   <!-- G -->
            <xsd:minLength value="5" fixed="true" />          <!-- H -->
            <xsd:maxLength value="7" fixed="false" />         <!-- I -->
            <xsd:pattern value="[a-z]{5}[0-9]*" />            <!-- J -->
        </xsd:restriction>
    </xsd:simpleType>

</xsd:schema>
```

Shown below is an instant document that will be validated by the schema shown above. Note that the content of the BBB element in line (A) is a regular string. On the other hand, the content of the CCC element in line (B) is a string of type `myString` as defined in the schema.

```
<?xml version="1.0"?>

<!-- file: TestSchema6.xml -->

<AAA xmlns="http://AAAnamespace"
     xmlns:xsi="http://www.w3.org/2001/XMLSchema-instance"
     xsi:schemaLocation="http://AAAnamespace DerivedDataType.xsd">
    <BBB> hello I am here </BBB>                               <!-- A -->
    <CCC>zabcz6</CCC>                                          <!-- B -->
</AAA>
```

That brings to an end our discussion on XML schemas. There is a lot more to this topic than what was presented here. For additional information, the reader is referred to the books devoted to the subject and/or the specification documents. Section 17.10 also points to some online tutorial presentations that the reader will find helpful.

17.7 PARSING XML DOCUMENTS

An XML document may be checked either for just its *well-formedness* or for its *validity*. An XML document is *well-formed* if its markup and text obey all the constraints listed in Section 17.1 (except those that mention document type definitions and schemas). For an XML document to be *valid*, it must, of course, first be well-formed; the document must in addition conform to the *grammar* laid out through DTDs or through schemas. When a document is checked for only its well-formedness, that is also referred to as a *nonvalidating parse* of the document. On the other hand, a *validating parse* consists of checking the XML document against a DTD or against a schema or against both. A document that is only well-formed but not necessarily valid is allowed to have any element, an element may possess any attributes, and an element may be empty or may contain anything at all in terms of other elements and text.

There are two kinds of parsers for XML documents, *event-driven* (also referred to as *event-based*) parsers,[37] and *tree-building parsers*. A typical event-driven parser scans an XML document character by character and emits events based on what character it is seeing at the current time instant and what characters it has seen previously. For example, when the parser sees the > character, it recognizes that as the end of a tag. Based on what it has seen previously, the parser knows whether it is seeing the end of a start-tag for an element, the end of an end-tag, the end of a comment, and so on. Depending on the type of the tag recognized, the parser emits an appropriate event.

Event-driven parsers expect the user of a parser to supply handlers for the events. These handlers act like *callbacks* in GUI programming, meaning that a chosen handler is automatically invoked when an event is signalled by the parser.

A noteworthy advantage of event-driven parsers is that your script can engage in parse-based analysis of a document on the fly as the document is being digested by the parser. What that implies is that as soon as, say, the character data content of an element has been recognized, it can immediately be shipped off to the character-data handler that you registered with the parser. The important thing to note is that this could happen long before the parser has finished scanning the entire document. As different segments of a document are recognized in an event-based parse, you also have the option of storing these away in lightweight data structures.

The tree-building parsers, on the other hand, carry out a more conventional parse of an XML document. Such parsers scan through the entire document and construct its parse tree. This tree can then be used as a *document object model* (DOM) for the document. The node at the root of a DOM tree represents the root element of the document. The children of the root node in a DOM must obviously correspond to the immediate subelements of the root element, and so on.

With tree-building DOM parsers, a tree-based document representation is available in its entirety in the memory of the computer. Subsequently, this representation can be manipulated for any of a variety of reasons, such as content search, document transformation, and so on. This representation of the document, with or without any modifications, can also be streamed to the output either as an XML document or a document in some other style, such as an HTML document. An additional advantage of DOM parsers is that they are much simpler to program than the event-based parsers.

---

[37]Event-driven parsers are also commonly referred to as *stream-oriented* parsers.

Common implementations of DOM parsers suffer from the shortcoming that they can run into memory limitations for very large documents. Imagine a large book manuscript that uses XML for its formatting markup. In a pure DOM-based XML editor, you'd need to store the DOM tree for the entire manuscript in the memory of the computer before you can make changes to the contents of any of its elements. This would obviously be inefficient compared to the more common editors that allow you to make changes to one chapter (or, to one section) at a time.[38] Event-driven parsers do not suffer from this limitation because such parsers do not have to create an internal representation for the entire document. However, there is a price to pay for this memory efficiency of event-driven parsers — lack of ability to carry out in-memory manipulation of a large document. With a pure event-driven parser, you could not, for example, reorder the elements in an XML document or resolve cross references between the elements. You'd also not be able to validate an XML document against a DTD or a schema file with a pure event-driven parser.

It is important to mention that the worlds of event-driven parsing and tree-based parsing are not as disjoint as the above discussion would imply. It is indeed possible to create a DOM tree from the output of an event-driven parser. As the event handlers detect different types of tags and character data in a document, the objects thus found can, for example, engage in stack operations, as is commonly done in traditional parsing, to yield a DOM tree at the end of document scanning.

Since an XML parser may be event-driven and yet produce the DOM tree, the overall parser behavior is more easily characterized by its API (Application Programming Interface), meaning by the published functions and attributes that the parser makes available to the outside world for extracting various properties of an XML document and/or for manipulating the document. A commercial-grade XML parser will typically conform to either the SAX API or the W3C DOM API,[39] or both. The acronym SAX stands for *Simple API for XML.* The SAX API, its current version being called SAX 2.0 API, is the culmination of the efforts in the open-source community to standardize the APIs for event-driven parsing of XML documents.[40] The DOM API was produced by W3C as a part of its XML-related standardization efforts.[41]

---

[38]This shortcoming of DOM parsers is expected to be fixed in PDOM (persistent DOM) parsers that are currently in development.

[39]The DOM API, still evolving, comes in three different *levels* at this time. The simplest, Level 1, does not include namespaces. Support for namespaces was incorporated in Level 2. The last, Level 3, is still in draft form.

[40]The original SAX API had support for only the elements, the attributes, and the processing instructions. It did not, for example, provide support for namespaces, CDATA sections, and so on. All of these and much more are included in the SAX 2.0 API (also commonly referred to as SAX2 API).

[41]The DOM API does not mandate that the entire parse tree for an XML document reside in the fast memory of a computer. It only mandates that the parser present the prescribed interface to the outside world for interacting with the internal representation of a document.

Getting back to the subject with which this section started — validating versus nonvalidating parsers — it is obviously easy to make a DOM parser validating. The DOM tree captures the deep structure of a document that can be checked against the constraints that must be satisfied by the various components of an XML document. To make an event-driven parser validating is more challenging, since, *ordinarily*, it will not create an internal representation for the entire document. Without a representation that shows all of the relationships between the different elements would obviously make it more difficult to test a document against any nonlocal constraints expressed in DTD or schema files.

Before ending this section, we also want to mention that there are many Perl and Python modules available now that can be used for parsing XML documents. The oldest Perl module that gained high prominence when it first came out is the `XML::Parser` module by Larry Wall and Clark Cooper. This module acts as a wrapper for James Clark's C-based stream-oriented XML parser called `expat`. More recently, the Perl community has created parsing modules that conform to the SAX2 API. These include the modules `XML::SAX::Expat` and `XML::SAX::ExpatXS`, both sitting on top of the `expat` C library; `XML::LibXML::SAX`, which sits on top of the `libxml2` C library developed for the Gnome project; `XML::Xerces`, which sits on top of the Xerces XML parser (written in C++ and Java); `XML::SAX::PurePerl` that is purely Perl; and a few more. The main roots of `XML::SAX::Expat` and `XML::SAX::ExpatXS` go to the `XML::Parser` module (and therefore to the C-based `expat` library). Python's support for the SAX2 API is provided by the `xml.sax` module, and for the DOM API by the `xml.dom`, and `xml.dom.minidom` modules. The `xml.dom.minidom` module conforms to the W3C's DOM Level 1 specification; in addition, it includes the namespaces feature of DOM Level 2. The `xml.dom` module conforms to the DOM Level 2 specification.

17.7.1 An Example of a Lightweight DOM Parser in Perl

We will now show some of the basic processing steps you'd need to implement in Perl for a simple nonvalidating lightweight DOM parser. Let's say that for a small-scale application, we want to write our own nonvalidating lightweight parser that has the following features:

1. The parser should construct a tree data structure whose root node corresponds to the root element of the XML document.

2. Each node of the tree should correspond to an XML element of the document.

3. A node corresponding to an element should point to all the child nodes that correspond to the subelements of the element.

4. A node should store a hash that contains all the attribute-value pairs for the XML element if the element has any attributes at all. A node should also store the text value of the element, if the element has a text value.

5. The parser should blank out any comments even when they occupy multiple lines in the document and even when they contain embedded markup.

6. Since the parser is supposed to be nonvalidating, it may ignore all internal DTD declarations and any references to external DTDs.

7. For the sake of simplicity, the parser is allowed to ignore all entity references.[42]

8. The parser should accept the *qualified name syntax* for the element and the attribute names, but the parser is not required to carry out namespace-based processing of the document. Therefore, when an element or an attribute name consists of two parts, a namespace prefix and a local name, separated by a colon, the entire string can be considered to be a local name.

The next script, `SimpleElement.pm`, defines a Perl utility class `SimpleElement`; we will use instances of this class as nodes in a parse tree. As indicated in lines (E4) through (E7) of the script, a node in a parse tree is characterized by the instance variables `_tagname`, `_text`, `_attributes`, and `_childElements`. The instance variable `_tagname` holds the name of the XML element that corresponds to the node. Although not explicitly enforced in the class definition, the process of node construction by the parser will ensure that a node always has a value for `_tagname`. All other instance variables are shown with default values. These default values, shown in lines (E5), (E6), and (E7), are changed by the parser depending on specifics of the corresponding element in the XML document. If an XML element contains text between the start tag and the end tag, the text string is stored away in the instance variable `_text` of line (E5). If an XML element has one or more attributes in the start tag, the instance variable `_attributes` is set to a reference to a hash holding those attribute-value pairs. And if an element contains child elements, references to the nodes corresponding to the child elements are stored in an anonymous array whose reference is held by the instance variable `_childElements`.

The methods defined in lines (E9) through (E17) are for getting and setting the different instance variables. For the element attributes, we provide in line (E13) a get method for retrieving the value associated with a specific attribute, and in line (E14) another get method for retrieving a reference to the hash containing all the attribute-value pairs. The get and set methods for the other two instance variables, `_text` and `_childElements` are straightforward.

[42] It would be easy to account for entity references in the parser code shown.

```
package SimpleElement;

### SimpleElement.pm

sub new {                                                               #(E1)
    my ($class, $tagname) = @_;                                         #(E2)
    bless {                                                             #(E3)
        _tagname => $tagname,                                           #(E4)
        _text => "",                                                    #(E5)
        _attributes => {},                                              #(E6)
        _childElements => [],                                           #(E7)
    }, $class;                                                          #(E8)
}
sub getTagName {                                                        #(E9)
    my $self = shift;
    $self->{_tagname};
}
sub setTagName {                                                        #(E10)
    my ($self, $tagname) = @_;
    $self->{_tagname} = $tagname;
}
sub getText {                                                           #(E11)
    my $self = shift;
    $self->{_text};
}
sub setText {                                                           #(E12)
    my ($self, $text) = @_;
    $self->{_text} .= " $text";
}
sub getAttribute {                                                      #(E13)
    my ($self, $attribute_name) = @_;
    $self->{_attributes}{$attribute_name};
}
sub getAttributeHash {                                                  #(E14)
    my $self = shift;
    $self->{_attributes};
}
sub setAttribute {                                                      #(E15)
    my ($self, $attribute_name, $value) = @_;
    $self->{_attributes}{$attribute_name} = $value;
}
sub addChildElement {                                                   #(E16)
    my ($self, $newSimpleElement) = @_;
    push @{$self->{_childElements}}, $newSimpleElement;
}
```

```
sub getChildElements {                                        #(E17)
    my $self = shift;
    $self->{_childElements};
}
1
```

Shown next is an implementation of a Perl class `SimpleDOMParser` that we will subsequently use as a tree-based parser whose behavior conforms to the specifications listed at the beginning of this subsection. As shown in line (P1), the parser uses the `SimpleElement` class defined above. As already mentioned, instances created from the `SimpleElement` class will serve as the nodes of the parse tree.

The constructor of the parser class, in lines (P2) through (P8), uses the instance variables `_documentName` and `_rootDOMTree` to hold, respectively, the name of the XML document being parsed and the root of the parse tree. The parser also uses the instance variable `_all_elements` to store all the elements in a flat list in the form of an array. This is simply to facilitate searching through the elements for element content. A user can interact with the parser with the help of the methods defined in lines (P9), (P10), and (P11). If a document is not too large, the names of all the elements in the document can be displayed by invoking the method `showAllElements()` of line (P9). If only a total count of the elements in the document is needed, that can be obtained by calling the method `countElements()` of line (P10). And, finally, if it is desired to find all the elements whose text values contain a given string, we can use the method `searchElementsForString()` of line (P11). It would be easy to write other methods along the same lines to manipulate and/or transform the document in various ways.

The actual job of parsing a document is carried out by the method `parse()` in lines (P12) though (P61). To parse a document, this method is called as shown in the second line below:

```
my $parser = SimpleDOMParser->new();
$parser->parse( "xml_document_name.xml" );
```

Once a document is parsed, it can be displayed for testing purposes (assuming, of course, that the document is small enough to not overwhelm the output device) by the following call:

```
$parser->displayDOMTree();
```

As for the processing carried out in `parse()`, it is done in two parts. The first part, in lines (P15) through (P27) accomplishes the following:

- First, all of the document is read into a single string is the slurp mode in line (P17).[43]

- In line (P18), all of the newline characters in the single-string representation of the document are replaced by blank spaces.

- Line (P19) gets rid of any internal DTD declaration blocks. Remember, our simple parser is supposed to be only nonvalidating. So we have no use for these blocks. For the same reason, line (P20) gets rid of references to external DTDs.

- Line (P21) gets rid of any comment blocks.

- Line (P22) is meant to take care of the following problem: Sometimes it is necessary for the element content or an attribute value to contain embedded angle-bracket-enclosed markup that is not really a part of the XML markup. The left and the right angle-brackets for such non-XML markup are supposed to be replaced, respectively, by the entity references < and > so that there is no confusion with the legitimate XML markup. Nevertheless, some writers of XML documents only replace the left angle bracket with the entity reference < without bothering to also use the replacement entity reference for the right angle bracket. Changing > to the entity reference > in such cases, as we do in line (P22), makes it easier to carry out the parse.

- What we have done so far may be referred to as the conditioning of the XML document for the removal of "irrelevant" parts and potentially troublesome characters. Now we are ready to split the document into its constituent parts with the help of the statement in lines (P23) through (P26), repeated below for convenience:

```
my @tokens =
    $document =~ /(<.+?>)?                      # extract tags
                  ([^<>]*)?                     # extract text
                  (<!\[CDATA\[.*?\]\]>)?/gx;    # extract CDATA
```

  The left-hand side of the assignment, meaning the array @tokens, provides a list context for the regex match on the right-hand side of the assignment. Note that the regex consists of the following three parts, all optional,

```
(<.+?>)?
([^<>]*)?
(<!\[CDATA\[.*?\]\]>)?
```

[43]The author has parsed documents as large as 5 megabytes in this manner. As a case in point, the parser being presented was tested on the document big.xml of size 5,052,472 bytes. This is one of the six documents used originally by Clark Cooper in his second benchmarking study of six stream-oriented XML parsers [12].

that we are able to place in three separate lines with the help of the `//x` modifier shown in line (P26). As indicated in the commented out portion of line (P23), the first part of the regex is for extracting the tags. It uses the nongreedy version of the quantifier metacharacter `+` to see the very next occurrence of `>` after a `<` as the end of the tag. The second portion of the regex is for extracting the text from element content. The last part of the regex is for extracting the `CDATA` character strings. Note that each part of the overall regex is inside grouping parentheses. As the reader knows from Chapter 4, when grouping parentheses are used in a regex match in a list context, the regex engine returns a list of all the substrings extracted by each of the groupings in the regex.

- The above operation of splitting the document string into its basic constituents is capable of producing empty tokens. This happens because of the greedy metacharacter `*` in the second portion of the three-line regex shown in the previous step. It allows for text strings of zero length. The statement in line (P27) eliminates such zero content array elements in `@tokens`.

- The operations on the document listed so far are capable of generating just white-space tokens in the `@tokens` array. This is particularly the case if there is white space between consecutive XML elements in the document. The operation in line (P28) eliminates such array elements from `@tokens`.

- Other types of white space that in most cases can be safely ignored includes the leading and the trailing white space in the text tokens stored in `@tokens`. The statement in line (P29) gets rid of such white space.

- Finally, we get rid of any processing instructions in the XML document in line (P30). As mentioned in Section 17.1, these XML elements, delimited by the two-character sequences `<?` and `?>`, are commonly used as containers for the information useful for or needed by specific XML processors. The name that follows immediately after the opening `<?` is presumably the recipient of the information conveyed by the processing instruction.

The commented-out block between the lines (P30) and (P31) is useful for troubleshooting the parser, especially when the parser encounters something unanticipated in a large XML document. Often in such cases, an exception will be thrown by the `die` statement in line (P42). As shown, the message carried by this exception prints out the integer index of the `@tokens` array element whose processing led to the parsing error. The `for` loop in the commented-out block between lines (P30) and (P31) can then be used to print out some array elements from `@tokens` that come before and some that come after the exception-triggering element. The two other commented-out statements in the block between (P30) and (P31) are also useful for troubleshooting with small XML documents.

This brings us to the logic used for parsing in lines (P31) through (P68). We will accomplish parsing using the same stack operations as implemented by Yang [69] in his `SimpleDOMParsers`:

```
    -- get new token (P34)
    -- if the token is an end-tag (P36)
        -- compare name of the end-tag with the name of
               the start-tag at the top of tag stack (P39)
            -- if the two names are the same, pop the tag-stack (P40)
            -- else declare parse failure (P42)
    -- if no root yet and the token is a start-tag (P47)
        -- assign attributes to root element  (P52)
        -- push the tag as root into the tag stack (P54)
    -- else if the token is a start-tag (P55)
        -- assign attributes to a new element  (P60)
        -- add the new element to the subelement list of the
                element currently at the top of the stack (P61)
        -- push the start-tag into the tag stack (P63)
    -- else assign text value or CDATA to the element whose
                start-tag is at the top of the tag stack (P66)
    -- if no more input tokens and if tag stack not empty,
                           declare parse failure (P67)
```

Each parsing action statement presented above includes at its end the corresponding line number in the `SimpleDOMParser.pm` script below.

```
package SimpleDOMParser;

### SimpleDOMParser.pm

use SimpleElement;                                                    #(P1)

# The root of the DOM tree is of type SimpleElement as defined in the
# the module of the same name.  This root becomes the value of the
# _rootDOMTree instance variable.  As elements are discovered, they
# are all stored away in the array whose reference is held by the
# instance variable _all_elements.
sub new {                                                             #(P2)
    my $class = shift;                                                #(P3)
    bless {                                                           #(P4)
        _documentName => undef,                                       #(P5)
        _rootDOMTree => undef,                                        #(P6)
        _all_elements => [],                                          #(P7)
    }, $class;                                                        #(P8)
}
sub showAllElements {                                                 #(P9)
    my $self = shift;
    my @ele_names = map $_->getTagName, @{$self->{_all_elements}};
    print "\nELEMENT TYPES:  @ele_names\n";
}
```

```
sub countElements {                                                 #(P10)
    my $self = shift;
    @{$self->{_all_elements}};
}
sub searchElementsForString {                                       #(P11)
    my ($self, $str) = @_;
    my @eles = grep {$_->getText =~ /$str/} @{$self->{_all_elements}};
    my @ele_names = map $_->getTagName, @eles;
    if (@ele_names) {
       print "\nThe string \"$str\" found in the " .
             "following elements:  @ele_names\n";
   } else {
       print "\nThe string \"$str\" not found in any element\n";
   }
}
sub parse {                                                         #(P12)
    my ($self, $filename) = @_;                                     #(P13)
    $self->{_documentName} = $filename;                             #(P14)
    local $/ = undef;                                               #(P15)
    open FILEIN, $self->{_documentName};                            #(P16)
    my $document = <FILEIN>;                                        #(P17)
    # Get rid of newlines:
    $document =~ s/[\n\r]/ /g;                                      #(P18)
    # Get rid of any internal DTD declaration blocks:
    $document =~ s/<!DOCTYPE\s+\w+[^\]]*?\]>/ /g;                   #(P19)
    # Get rid of any DTD references:
    $document =~ s/<!DOCTYPE[^<>]+?>/ /g;                           #(P20)
    # Get rid of any comment blocks:
    $document =~ s/<!--.*?-->/ /g;                                  #(P21)
    # Replace '&lt; ... >, by  '&lt; .... &gt;'
    $document =~ s/(\&lt;[^<> ]*?)>/$1\&gt;/g;                      #(P22)
    # Break the document into tags and text:
    my @tokens =                                                    #(P23)
        $document =~ /(<.+?>)?                     # extract tags   #(P24)
                      ([^<>]*)?                    # extract text   #(P25)
                      (<!\[CDATA\[.*?\]\]>)?/gx;   # extract CDATA  #(P26)
    #Get rid of empty array elements produced by the previous operation:
    @tokens = grep $_, @tokens;                                     #(P27)
    # Get rid of any just whitespace array elements produced by
    # the previous operations:
    @tokens = grep !/^\s*$/, @tokens;                               #(P28)
    # Get rid of any white space before and/or
    # after the text elements:
    @tokens = map {/^\s*(.*?)\s*$/; $1} @tokens;                    #(P29)
    # Get rid of any XML processing instructions:
    @tokens = grep !/^<\?/, @tokens;                                #(P30)
```

```
# The following commented out block is useful for troubleshooting:
#   for (my $i = 407; $i < 427; $i++) {
#     print "$i>>  $tokens[$i]\n";
#   }
#   print "@tokens\n";
#   foreach (@tokens) { print "$_\n"; }

my $root = undef;                                              #(P31)
my @tag_stack;                                                 #(P32)
my $element_index = 0;                                         #(P33)
foreach my $token (@tokens) {                                  #(P34)
    $element_index++;                                          #(P35)
    # Are we looking at an end tag?
    if ($token =~ /^<\//) {                                    #(P36)
        # get name of the end tag:
        $token =~ /^<\/([\w:-]*)/;                             #(P37)
        my $tagname = $1;                                      #(P38)
        if ($tagname eq $tag_stack[0]->getTagName) {           #(P39)
            shift @tag_stack;                                  #(P40)
        } else {                                               #(P41)
            die "Parse error: invalid tag " .                  #(P42)
                "nesting with tagname \'$tagname\' at " .
                "element index $element_index\n";
        }
        next;                                                  #(P43)
    # Are we looking at a start tag?
    } elsif ($token =~ /^<[^!]/) {                             #(P44)
        # get tag name
        # the //g option is for \G anchor in (P49) and (P54)
        $token =~ /^<([\w:-]*)/g;                              #(P45)
        my $tagname = $1;                                      #(P46)
        # Establish root if this is the first start tag:
        unless (defined $root) {                               #(P47)
            $root = SimpleElement->new( $tagname );            #(P48)
            # Extract the attributes part of the root element:
            $token =~ /\G(.*)>$/;                              #(P49)
            # If attributes are found:
            if ($1) {                                          #(P50)
                # Construct attribute name-value pairs:
                my @att_val_pairs =                            #(P51)
                         $1 =~ /([\w:-]+)\s*=\s*"(\S+)"/g;
                while (@att_val_pairs) {                       #(P52)
                    $root->setAttribute(shift @att_val_pairs,
                                        shift @att_val_pairs);
                }
            }
            # Push root into the elements unless it is a
            # self-closing element, in which case this is the
            # only node in the document:
```

```
                push @{$self->{_all_elements}}, $root;              #(P53)
                unshift @tag_stack, $root unless $token =~ /\/>$/;#(P54)
            } else {                                                #(P55)
                die "Parse error: Found element outside root element\n"
                    unless @tag_stack;                              #(P56)
                my $ele = SimpleElement->new( $tagname );           #(P57)
                # Extract the attribute portion of the start tag:
                $token =~ /\G(.*)>$/;                               #(P58)
                # If attributes are found:
                if ($1) {
                    # Attribute names can contain ':' and
                    # attribute values can contain all characters
                    # permissible in a URL:
                    my @att_val_pairs =                             #(P59)
                            $1 =~ /([\w:-]+)\s*=\s*"(\S+)"/g;
                    while (@att_val_pairs) {                        #(P60)
                        $ele->setAttribute( shift @att_val_pairs,
                                            shift @att_val_pairs);
                    }
                }
                $tag_stack[0]->addChildElement( $ele );             #(P61)
                push @{$self->{_all_elements}}, $ele;               #(P62)
                # Push the new element into the elements
                unshift @tag_stack, $ele unless $token =~ /\/>$/; #(P63)
            }
            next;                                                   #(P64)
        } else {                                                    #(P65)
            $tag_stack[0]->setText( $token );                       #(P66)
        }
    }
    die "Parse error: Probably some end tag missing\n"              #(P67)
            if @tag_stack;
    $self->{_rootDOMTree} = $root;                                  #(P68)
}

# The actual work of displaying the DOM tree is done by the
# the local function _display_element shown next:
sub displayDOMTree {                                                #(P69)
    my $self = shift;
    print "\nThe parse tree:\n\n";
    _display_element( $self->{_rootDOMTree}, "" );
}
sub _display_element {                                              #(P70)
    my ($ele, $display_offset) = @_;
    if (!$display_offset) {
        print $ele->getTagName;
    } else {
        print $display_offset, $ele->getTagName;
    }
```

```
    my $ele_attributes = $ele->getAttributeHash;
    if ( %$ele_attributes ) {
        print " (attributes:  ";
        while ( my ($key, $value) = each %$ele_attributes ) {
            print " $key = $value";
        }
        print ") ";
    }
    my $text = $ele->getText;
    print " (Text: $text)" if $text =~ /\S/;
    print "\n";
    my $children = $ele->getChildElements;
    $display_offset .= "     ";
    foreach my $child (@$children) {
        _display_element( $child, $display_offset );
    }
}
1
```

The SimpleDOMParser class also includes a method, displayDOMTree(), in line (P69) that is convenient for displaying small DOM trees in a terminal window. This is particularly useful when trying the parser on hitherto untested XML constructs. The actual work of displaying the tree is carried out by a local function, _display_element(), of line (P70) that calls itself recursively as it descends down the parse tree.

Shown below is a small test script, TestDOMParser.pl, for checking out the workings of SimpleDOMParser:

```
#!/usr/bin/perl -w

### TestDOMParser.pl

use SimpleDOMParser;                                                  #(T1)

my $docname = shift;                                                  #(T2)
die "Can't find \"$docname\"" unless -f $docname;                     #(T3)

my $parser = SimpleDOMParser->new();                                  #(T4)
$parser->parse($docname);                                             #(T5)
$parser->showAllElements();                                           #(T6)
my $n = $parser->countElements();                                     #(T7)
print "\nNumber of elements: $n\n";                                   #(T8)
$parser->displayDOMTree();                                            #(T9)
$parser->searchElementsForString( "hello" );                          #(T10)
```

When we call `TestDOMParser.pl` on an XML file that contains just the following:

```
<?xml version="1.0"?>
<phonebook xmlns="http://www.w3.org/1999/xhtml" />
```

we get the following output:

```
ELEMENT TYPES:  phonebook
Number of elements: 1
The parse tree:
phonebook (attributes:   xmlns = http://www.w3.org/1999/xhtml)

The string ``hello'' not found in any element
```

Recall that the last statement of `TestDOMParser.pl` searches for the string `hello` in all the elements in the XML source document. This explains the last part of the output shown above.

When we call `TestDOMParser.pl` on the following visually confusing but well-formed XML document:

```
<?xml version="1.0"?>

<!--
The name of this <document>
is test.xml
-->

<list_of_entries xmlns="http://www.w3.org/1999/xhtml">

  <entry>
<eg><![CDATA[<?xml version="1.0"?>
<!DOCTYPE greeting SYSTEM "hello.dtd">
<greeting>Hello, world!</greeting>
]]></eg>
      <name>wonwon</name>
      <phone>  32323-38373 </phone>

  </entry>

  <self_enclosed_element />
<entry>
  <entry>
      hello how are you
      <name>tintin jinjin kinkin </name>
      junjun dundun kunkun
      <phone
```

```
type = "home"   payment_mode="cash">  000-999-88 </phone>
      koot soot doot

  </entry>
</entry>

</list_of_entries>
```

we get the following parse information displayed in the terminal:

```
ELEMENT TYPES:  list_of_entries entry eg name phone \
                    self_enclosed_element entry entry name phone

Number of elements: 10

The parse tree:

list_of_entries (attributes:   xmlns = http://www.w3.org/1999/xhtml)
    entry
        eg (Text:  <![CDATA[<?xml version=''1.0''?>
                    <greeting>Hello, world!</greeting> ]]>)
        name (Text:  wonwon)
        phone (Text:  32323-38373)
    self_enclosed_element
    entry
        entry (Text:  hello how are you junjun dundun
                                    kunkun koot soot doot)
            name (Text:  tintin jinjin kinkin)
            phone (attributes:   payment_mode = cash
                                type = home)  (Text:  000-999-88)

The string ''hello'' found in the following elements:  entry
```

The first output line lists all of the element names found in the document that was parsed. The next line lists the number of these elements — in this case 10. The parse is displayed starting in the fourth line. The indentations in the successive lines in the parse represent the parent-child relationships between the elements in the document. The first line of the parse says that the root element is named `list_of_entries` and it shows its attribute-value pair. The next indented line says that the root element has a subelement named `entry`, that in turn, as displayed in the next few lines, has three subelements: `eg`, `name`, and `phone`. The parser displays the content of each of these subelements of the entry element in the respective lines. The just-described eg element is followed by its sibling element self_enclosed_element. Next comes another entry element as a child of the root element. The parser correctly tells us that this entry element has a subelement of the same name, and so on. Note that some of the output lines are split into two in order to not overflow the width of this page.

17.7.2 A Lightweight DOM Parser in Python

We will now describe a Python implementation of the simple nonvalidating DOM parser. This parser has the same eight features as listed at the beginning of the previous subsection. The parser constructs a tree data structure whose root node corresponds to the root element of the XML document. Each node of the parse tree corresponds to an XML element of the document and the children of the node to the subelements. Each node stores a dictionary that contains the attribute-value pairs in the start tag of the corresponding XML element when the element possesses attributes. Each node also stores the text value of an element when it has any such value. As before, our parser will blank out all comments even when they occupy multiple lines and even when they contain embedded markup. Since the parser is meant to be nonvalidating, it also ignores all internal DTD declarations and any references to external DTDs. The parser also ignores all entity references. However, the parser does accept the qualified naming syntax for the element and the attribute names, but does not carry out namespace-based processing of the document.

Shown next is the Python version of the SimpleElement Perl class of the previous subsection; each node of the parse tree will be an instance of SimpleElement. As seen in lines (E3) though (E6), each such instance stores the tag name of the corresponding XML element, the attribute-value pairs in the start tag of the element, the text value of the element, and a list of the child nodes corresponding to the subelements of the element. Lines (E3) through (E6) also show the default values for the instance variables. The rest of the code for SimpleElement, in lines (E7) through (E15), defines the various methods needed for getting and setting the instance variables. Note in particular that the method setText() in line (E10); it returns the SimpleElement instance on which the method is invoked. This is to permit the following sort of a chained invocation for adding a child node to a parent element:

```
ele.addChildElement( SimpleElement('first').setText('John') )
```

The test code starting in line (E17) creates by hand a parse tree for the element shown in the commented-out block between the lines (E16) and (E17).

```
#!/usr/bin/env python

### SimpleElement.py

class SimpleElement:                                              #(E1)
    def __init__(self, tagname):                                  #(E2)
        self._tagname = tagname                                   #(E3)
        self._text = ""                                           #(E4)
        self._attributes = {}                                     #(E5)
        self._childElements = []                                  #(E6)

    def getTagName(self):                                         #(E7)
        return self._tagname

    def setTagName(self,tagname):                                 #(E8)
        self._tagname = tagname

    def getText(self):                                            #(E9)
        return self._text

    def setText(self, text):                                      #(E10)
        self._text += " " + text
        return self

    def getAttribute(self, attribute_name):                       #(E11)
        return self._attributes[attribute_name]

    def getAttributeDict(self):                                   #(E12)
        return self._attributes

    def setAttribute(self, attribute_name, value):                #(E13)
        self._attributes[attribute_name] = value

    def addChildElement(self, newSimpleElement):                  #(E14)
        self._childElements.append( newSimpleElement )

    def getChildElements(self):                                   #(E15)
        return self._childElements

if __name__ == '__main__':                                        #(E16)

    # The test code shown below creates by hand a tree structure that
    # described the following element:
    #
    #<famous>
    #    <listing>
    #        <first>John</first>
```

```
#         <middle>C.</middle>
#         <last>Hancock</last>
#       </listing>
#     <listing>
#         <first>Susan</first>
#         <last>Anthony</last>
#     </listing>
#</famous>

root = SimpleElement( 'famous' )                                #(E17)
ele = SimpleElement( 'listing' )
root.addChildElement( ele )
ele.addChildElement( SimpleElement( 'first ' ).setText( 'John' ) )
ele.addChildElement( SimpleElement( 'last ' ).setText( 'Hancock' ) )
ele = SimpleElement( 'listing' )
root.addChildElement( ele )
ele.addChildElement( SimpleElement( 'first ' ).setText( 'Susan' ) )
ele.addChildElement( SimpleElement( 'last' ).setText( 'Anthony' ) )

for ele1 in root.getChildElements():                            #(E18)
    for ele2 in ele1.getChildElements():
        print ele2.getText()
```

Shown next is the Python implementation for the `SimpleDOMParser` Perl class of the previous subsection. The implementation starts by defining the utility function `_display_element()` in line (P5). This function, initially supplied with the root node of the parse tree, calls itself recursively on the children of the argument node. For each call to a node of the parse tree, it prints out the element tag name associated with the node, the list of the attribute-value pairs in the start tag of the XML element corresponding to that node, the text value of the XML element, and then, with a horizontal offset, does the same for each child node.

The definition of the `SimpleDOMParser` class, in lines (P6) through (P73), parallels the definition of the Perl version of the class in the previous subsection. As for any noticeable differences between the parsing method `parser()` in lines (P21) through (P70) and its Perl version shown earlier, note that we no longer have to backslash the forward slash in lines where we look for an XML end tag, such as the tag `</phonebook>`. This is the case in line (P41) where we test whether we are looking at an end tag, and in line (P42) where we extract the tag name in the end tag. We do not need to escape the forward slash because it does not carry a special meaning in Python regular expressions.

As for the other differences of note between the Python version shown next and the Perl version shown earlier, note how in line (P25) we use the `translate()` method of the string class to get rid of the newline characters from the string that the document file is read into. The second argument to translate() is a "delete list" of characters; if a character in the delete list appears in the string on which translate() is invoked, it must be deleted. The first argument to translate() is referred to as the *translation table*. It is a permutation of the 256 characters that can be represented by a single byte, the permutation reflecting the desired mapping function. If the goal is to only delete certain characters from the string on which translate() is invoked (and not to also map them), then obviously we do not need any permutation. The permutation table for such a case can be generated by calling string.maketrans('',''), as we have done in line (P25).

In the parsing function that begins in line (P21), we first get rid of the newline characters, any DTD declarations, DTD references, and SGML comments (even when they span multiple lines of the source document) in lines (P25) through (P28). We are able to delete multiline comment blocks from the source document because the entire document is read into a single string in line (P24). Line (P29) takes care of the problem caused by the presence of angle brackets in the element content and attribute values.[44]

After all the "cleanup" in lines (P21) through (P29), we finally partition the document into its XML tokens in line (P30). At this point, the tokens consist of the tags, the strings that contain the attribute-value pairs for the tags, the element content strings, and the CDATA character strings. In the statement that ends in line (P30), note how we construct our regex — we construct a compiled version of the regex with the re.VERBOSE option. As previously explained in Chapter 4, this option allows us to express the regex in multiple lines for better readability. This option also allows us to embed comments inside a regex, as shown. The call to re.findall() in the statement that ends in line (P30) returns a list of tuples, with each tuple consisting of the individual substrings matched by all the capturing groups in the regex.[45] Line (P33) then creates a flat list from the list of tokens, at the same time getting rid of any empty tokens (that is, tokens consisting of empty strings or strings of just the white-space characters). In line (P34), we then get rid of the tokens that consist of XML processing instructions, since they are not relevant to our simple nonvalidating parser.

With the list of tokens output by line (P34), we are now ready to construct a DOM tree. As with most tree-building parsers, the parsing action in lines (P39) through (P70) consists of two basic stack operations: (1) When a token is recognized to be a start tag, it is pushed into the stack [see lines (P49) through (P67)]. And (2) When a token is recognized to be an end tag, its tag name is compared with the tag name of the token currently at the top of the stack; if they match, the stack is popped [see lines (P41) through (P48)]. If not, a parse failure is declared. If the stack is nonempty and

[44]As mentioned in the previous subsection, any angle-bracket delimiters for non-XML markup in element content and attribute values should be replaced by their entity references < and >. But some otherwise valid XML documents may only replace the left angle bracket by its entity reference. The statement in line (P29) takes care of this problem.

[45]See Section 4.9 of Chapter 4 for a further explanation of the list of tuples returned by re.findall().

a token is recognized to be a start tag, it is declared to be a child of the token currently at the top of the stack and then pushed into the stack [see lines (P62) through (P66)]. If a token is neither a start tag nor an end tag, it is declared to be an element value [line (P69)]. Note that a token corresponding to a self-closing element is not pushed into the stack, although it is declared to be a child of the token currently at the top of the stack; this is ensured by the conditional of the `if` statement in line (P65). Also note that we are using a list as a stack. Its `append()` method pushes tokens into the stack and its `pop()` method pops the stack.

```
#!/usr/bin/env python

### SimpleDOMParser.py

import string                                                        #(P1)
import re                                                            #(P2)
import sys                                                           #(P3)
import SimpleElement                                                 #(P4)

#-------------------------  Utility routine  -------------------------

def _display_element( ele, display_offset ):                         #(P5)

    if not display_offset:
        print ele.getTagName(),
    else:
        print display_offset, ele.getTagName(),

    ele_attributes = ele.getAttributeDict()
    if ele_attributes:
        print " (attributes:  ",
        for item in ele_attributes.items():
            print item[0] + " = " + item[1],
        print ") ",

    text = ele.getText()
    if text: print "(Text: %s)" % text,
    print

    children = ele.getChildElements()
    display_offset += "    "
    for child in children:
        _display_element( child, display_offset )
```

```
#------------------------ Class SimpleDOMParser ---------------------

# The root of the DOM tree is of type SimpleElement as defined in the
# the module of the same name.  This root becomes the value of the
# _rootDOMTree instance variable.  All elements regardless of their
# level are stored in the list _all_elements.  This is to facilitate
# search for text values of the leaf nodes

class SimpleDOMParser:                                              #(P6)
    def __init__(self):                                             #(P7)
        self._documentName = None                                   #(P8)
        self._rootDOMTree = None                                    #(P9)
        self._all_elements = []                                     #(P10)

    def showAllElements(self):                                      #(P11)
        ele_names =map(lambda node:node.getTagName(),self._all_elements)
        print "\nELEMENT TYPES:  ", ele_names

    def countElements(self):                                        #(P12)
        return len(self._all_elements)

    def searchElementsForString(self, str):                         #(P13)
        eles = filter( lambda node: re.search( str, node.getText() ), \
                       self._all_elements)                          #(P14)
        ele_names = map(lambda node:node.getTagName(), eles)        #(p15)
        if ele_names:                                               #(P16)
            print "\nThe string %s found in the following elements: " \
                  % str,                                            #(P17)
            for ele in ele_names: print "%s " % ele,                #(P18)
        else:                                                       #(P19)
            print "\nThe string %s not found in any element" % str#(P20)

    # The workhorse:
    def parse(self, filename):                                      #(P21)
        self._documentName = filename                               #(P22)
        FILEIN = open(self._documentName)                           #(P23)

        # Read the whole document into a single string:
        document = FILEIN.read()                                    #(P24)

        # Get rid of newlines:
        document=document.translate(string.maketrans('',''),'\n\r')
                                                                    #(P25)
        # Get rid of any internal DTD declaration blocks:
        document = re.sub( r'<!DOCTYPE\s+\w+[^\]]*?\]>', ' ', \
                           document)                                #(P26)
        # Get rid of any DTD references:
        document = re.sub( r'<!DOCTYPE[^<>]+>', ' ', document )    #(P27)
```

```
# Get rid of any comment blocks:
document = re.sub( r'<!--.*?-->', ' ', document )          #(P28)

# Replace '&lt; ... >, by  '&lt; .... &gt;'
document = re.sub(r'(\&lt;[^<> ]*?)>',r'\1\&gt', document)#(P29)

# Break the document into tags and text:
token_tuples = re.findall( \
    re.compile( r'''(<.+?>)?                      # extract tags
                    ([^<>]*)                      # extract text
                    (<!\[CDATA\[.*?\]\]>)?''',    # extract CDATA
                re.VERBOSE ), document )                   #(P30)
tokens = []                                                #(P31)
for tupl in token_tuples: tokens += tupl                   #(P32)

# Get rid of empty tokens or tokens with just white space:
tokens = [token.rstrip().lstrip() for token in tokens \
        if token.rstrip().lstrip() is not '']              #(P33)

# Get rid of any XML processing instructions:
tokens = filter(lambda x: not re.match( r'<\?', x),tokens)#(P34)

#The following commented out line is useful for troubleshooting:
#for i in range(400,427): print tokens[i]                  #(P35)
#print "All tokens: ", tokens                              #(P36)

tag_stack = []                                             #(P37)
element_index = 0                                          #(P38)
for token in tokens:                                       #(P39)
    element_index += 1                                     #(P40)
    if re.match( r'</', token ):                           #(P41)
        # We are looking at an end tag like </phonebook>
        # get name of the end tag:
        m = re.search( r'^</([\w:-]*)', token )            #(P42)
        tagname = m.group(1)                               #(P43)
        if tagname == \
               tag_stack[len(tag_stack)-1].getTagName():  #(P44)
            tag_stack.pop()                                #(P45)
        else:                                              #(P46)
            raise Exception("Parse error: invalid tag " + \
                "nesting with tagname " + tagname +  \
                " at element index " + str(element_index))#(P47)
        continue                                           #(P48)
    elif re.match( r'<[^!]', token ):                      #(P49)
        # We are looking at a start tag like <phonebook>
        m = re.search( r'^<([\w:-]*)', token )             #(P50)
        tagname = m.group(1)                               #(P51)
        ele = SimpleElement.SimpleElement( tagname )       #(P52)
```

```
                # Extract the attributes part of the new element:
                m = re.search( r'(.*)>$', token[m.end():] )          #(P53)
                rest_of_token = m.group(1)                           #(P54)
                if rest_of_token:                                    #(P55)
                    # Construct attribute name-value pairs:
                    att_val_pairs = \
                       re.findall(r'([\w:-]+)\s*=\s*"(\S+)"', \
                                  rest_of_token)                     #(P56)
                    for tupl in att_val_pairs:                       #(P57)
                        ele.setAttribute(tupl[0], tupl[1])           #(P58)
                self._all_elements.append( ele )                     #(P59)
                # Establish root if this is the first start tag:
                if not self._rootDOMTree:                            #(P60)
                    self._rootDOMTree = ele                          #(P61)
                else:                                                #(P62)
                    if len(tag_stack) == 0:                          #(P63)
                        raise Exception("Parse Error: Found element"
                                     "outside the root element\n")#(P64)
                    tag_stack[len(tag_stack)-1].addChildElement(ele)
                if not token.endswith( r'/>' ):                      #(P65)
                    tag_stack.append( ele )                          #(P66)
                continue                                             #(P67)
            else:                                                    #(P68)
                tag_stack[len(tag_stack)-1].setText( token )         #(P69)
        if len(tag_stack) > 0:                                       #(P70)
            raise Exception("Parse error: Probably some tag missing\n")

    def displayDOMTree( self ):                                      #(P71)
        print "The parse tree:\n"                                    #(P72)
        _display_element( self._rootDOMTree, "" )                    #(P73)


if __name__ == '__main__':                                           #(P74)
    parser = SimpleDOMParser()                                       #(P75)
    parser.parse( sys.argv[1] )                                      #(P76)
    parser.showAllElements()                                         #(P77)
    N = parser.countElements()                                       #(P78)
    print "\nNumber of Elements: %d\n" % N                           #(P79)
    parser.displayDOMTree()                                          #(P80)
    parser.searchElementsForString( "hello" )                        #(P81)
```

This parser produces the same output as its Perl version in the previous subsection. The reader is urged to invoke the parser on the same sample XML documents as shown at the end of the previous subsection.

17.7.3 An Example of a Lightweight Event-Driven Parser in Perl

We will now present a lightweight event-driven parser based on Robert Cameron's REX regular expression. As shown earlier in Section 17.4, scanning an XML document with REX results in the partitioning of the document into its markup and character data components. To create an event-driven parser, all you have to do is to attach what are known as *code evaluation expressions* with the corresponding component extractors in REX's shallow-parsing regex.[46] By receiving a backreference to the part of the document consumed by a certain portion of the regex, a code evaluation expression can respond appropriately to the detection of a specfic pattern in the document. For example, when the start tag of an XML element is recognized, a subsequent code evaluation expression in the regex can call a user-supplied function to process that tag.

In what follows, we will first make small modifications to REX by embedding code evaluation expressions in it.[47] As an XML document is scanned for matches with the shallow-parsing regex of REX, the code evaluation expressions will be invoked automatically when certain components are recognized in the document.

To see how we can associate a code evaluation expression with a component extractor in REX, let's revisit the top-level syntax for this regex as shown in line (Y) of `TestREX.pl` in Section 17.4:

```
my $XML_SPE = "$TextSE|$MarkupSPE";
```

As the reader will recall from Section 17.4, scanning a source document with `$XML_SPE` and spitting out the consumed strings at each position in the scanning process partitions the document into its components. The expression shown for `$XML_SPE` says that the two highest-level components of an XML document are the character-data components and the markup components. In order to get a signal that a character-data component was recognized by `$TextSE`, we rewrite the above expression in the following form in line (P37) of the script shown next:

```
my $XML_SPE = "($TextSE)(?{_char_handler(\$^N)})|$MarkupSPE";
```

where we first place `$TextSE` inside the grouping parentheses `()` and then follow that up with the following code evaluation expression:

[46] As mentioned in Chapter 4, a code evaluation expression that is placed between the delimiters `(?{` and `})` is a piece of Perl executable code that you can embed in a regular expression. Code evaluation expressions are zero-width assertions, meaning that in and of themselves they do not consume any characters from the input string. In that sense, they are like the word-boundary metacharacter `\b`.

[47] The module `EventBasedParserUsingRex` presented in this section was inspired by Paul Kulchenko's `XML::Parser::Lite` module available for download at `www.cpan.org`. If the reader merely wants to use an event-driven XML parser that is built on top of Cameron's REX, the time-tested `XML::Parser::Lite` parser is the way to go. The goal of the `EventBasedParserUsingRex` module shown here is to illustrate *how* we can modify a regular-expression-based tokenizer to turn it into an event-driven parser.

```
_char_handler(\$^N)
```

inside the delimiters `(?{` and `})`. This code evaluation expression is a call to the function `_char_handler()` with the argument `$^N`. The argument is a backreference to the substring consumed by the most recent grouping parentheses `()`.[48] The backslash that precedes the argument is to suppress the usual meaning of `$` in a double-quoted string, which is to carry out variable interpolation. In this manner, we make the function `_char_handler()` behave as the *event handler* for character data.

Next we will discuss how we should modify the `$MarkupSPE` part of `$XML_SPE` in order to react to certain specified markup events encountered during the scanning of an XML document. Reproduced below is the regex for `$MarkupSPE` from line (X) of `TestREX.pl` in Section 17.4:

```
my $MarkupSPE = "<(?:!(?:$DeclCE)?|\\?(?:$PI_CE)?|" .
                          "/(?:$EndTagCE)?|(?:$ElemTagCE)?)";
```

Since we want our next script to trap element start-tag and end-tag events, we rewrite the above `$MarkupSPE` in the form shown in line (P36) of the next script. This modified form for `$MarkupSPE` is reproduced below for convenience:[49]

```
my $MarkupSPE = "<(?:!(?:$DeclCE)?|\\?(?:$PI_CE)?|" .
                "/(?:($EndTagCE)(?{_end_tag_handler('<'.\$^N)}))?|".
                "(?:($ElemTagCE)(?{_start_tag_handler('<'.\$^N)}))?)";
```

As we did with `$TextSE` earlier, we will now associate code evaluation expressions with the extractor `$EndTagCE` for the end tags and with the extractor `$ElemTagCE` for the start tags. So what was previously just `(?:$EndTagCE)?` now becomes

```
(?:($EndTagCE)(?{_end_tag_handler('<'.\$^N)}))?
```

where the code evaluation expression calls the function `_end_tag_handler()` with an argument that is a concatenation of `<` and `$^N`. As explained previously, the variable `$^N` will be set to the string extracted by the most recent grouping parentheses. In our case, those are the parentheses that surround `$EndTagCE` in the above expression. We prepend the symbol `<` to the string assigned to `$^N` simply

---

[48]We would get the same result if we replace the code evaluation expression in `$XML_SPE` by

```
_char_handler(\$1)
```

since `($TextSE)` is the first extracting grouping in `$XML_SPE`. If there are multiple extracting groupings in a long regular expression and you wish to get hold of the string extracted by the most recent grouping, it is more convenient to use the `$^N` syntax — especially if you are building up a regular expression incrementally, as is indeed the case with REX. The usefulness of `$^N` will become clearer when we show the code evaluation expressions for other groupings extracted by `$XML_SPE`.

[49]The forward slash that is at the end of the first of the three double-quoted strings in line (P36) of the next script is at the beginning of the second double-quoted string here. This is to make it easier to compare the extended form of `$MarkupSPE` with its original form.

to provide all the tag characters to the `_end_tag_handler()` function. Note that `<` is the first character of the expression that defines `$MarkupSPE`. That means the character `<` would already have been consumed by the time the scanner gets to the string consumed by `$EndTagCe`. Note also that we place the grouped `($EndTagCE)` and its associated code evaluation expression inside the nonextracting grouping parentheses `(?: )` for the purpose of making the entire expression optional. Recall from Section 17.4 that `$EndTagCE` is supposed to be optional in REX.

The regex shown above for `$MarkupSPE` also includes a code evaluation expression that goes with the start tag extractor `$ElemTagCE`. This code evaluation expression calls the handler `_start_tag_handler()` as shown. As should be clear from the makeup of `$ElemTagCE` as shown in line (P35) of the next script, `$ElemTagCE` is also capable of extracting self-closing start tags from an XML document.

The `$MarkupSPE` does not include code evaluation expressions for `$DeclCE` and `$PI_CE` simply because we have chosen not to do so. If we wanted to include *callbacks* for, say, the comment blocks, DTD declarations, processing instructions, etc., we would have associated code evaluation expressions with those parts of `$MarkupSPE` also.[50]

The rest of what is in the module below deals with the packaging of the parser as a class and endowing the class with a constructor and with other methods. As can be seen from the constructor, shown in lines (C1) through (C9), the parser is provided with instance variables `_documentName`, `_startTagHandler`, `_endTagHandler`, `_selfClosingTagHandler`, and `_charHandler`. The first of these instance variables, `_documentName`, is for holding the name of the XML file to be parsed. The other instance variables are for holding the names of the handler subroutines provided by the user of the parser. The parser itself calls the internally defined event handlers defined in lines (H1) through (H14). If any additional processing of the events is desired by the user of the parser, these event handlers then call the user-supplied event handlers that are bound to the instance variables in lines (C5) through (C8). The user-supplied subroutines are bound to the instance variables by the `setHandlers()` method in lines (S1) through (S8) of the parser module.

In case the reader is wondering, the class variable `$parser_instance` is for holding the instance of the parser returned by the constructor. This ploy is needed because of the syntax constraints on the executable code in the code evaluation expressions in a regex. The callbacks in the parser can only call class methods. But these class methods must subsequently be able to invoke the handler methods bound to the instance variables in lines (C4) through (C8). In the implementation shown

[50] This is a good time to mention that we can refer to the code-evaluation-expression functions `_char_handler()`, `_end_tag_handler()`, and `_start_tag_handler()` as callbacks. These functions will be called automatically during a scan of the source document as certain events are recognized.

below, this is accomplished through the calls on `$parser_instance` as shown in lines (H4), (H6), (H10), and (H14).

Finally, the pragma declaration `use re 'eval'` in line (A) is needed for the following reason: By default, Perl does not allow for the construction of regular expressions by interpolation if the strings to be interpolated contain code evaluation expressions. The reason for this is not difficult to understand. As mentioned in the Perl documentation, it would be all too easy to call, say, `system('rm -rf *')` in a code evaluation expression to wipe out an entire directory tree.[51] The declaration `use re 'eval'` bypasses this security restriction.

```
### EventBasedParserUsingRex.pm

package EventBasedParserUsingRex;

use strict;
use re 'eval';                                                              #(A)

my $parser_instance;                                                        #(B)

# Constructor:
sub new {                                                                   #(C1)
    my $class = shift;                                                      #(C2)
    $parser_instance = bless {                                              #(C3)
        _documentName => undef,                                             #(C4)
        _startTagHandler => undef,                                          #(C5)
        _endTagHandler => undef,                                            #(C6)
        _selfClosingTagHandler => undef,                                    #(C7)
        _charHandler => undef,                                              #(C8)
    }, $class;                                                              #(C9)
}
sub setHandlers {                                                           #(S1)
    my $self = shift;                                                       #(S2)
    my %handlers = @_;                                                      #(S3)
    $self->{_startTagHandler} = $handlers{StartTag};                        #(S4)
    $self->{_endTagHandler} = $handlers{EndTag};                            #(S5)
    $self->{_selfClosingTagHandler} = $handlers{SelfClosingTag};            #(S6)
    $self->{_charHandler} = $handlers{CharData};                            #(S7)
    $parser_instance = $self;                                               #(S8)
}

# The main parsing function.  Call syntax
#    $parser = EventBasedParserUsingRex->new();
#    $parser->parse( $document_name );
```

[51] A regular expression that is constructed by interpolation is considered to be potentially *tainted* in Perl.

```
sub parse {                                                         #(P1)
    my ($self, $filename) = @_;                                     #(P2)
    $self->{_documentName} = $filename;                             #(P3)
    local $/ = undef;                                               #(P4)
    open FILEIN, $self->{_documentName};                            #(P5)
    my $document = <FILEIN>;                                        #(P6)
    my $XML_SPE = $self->makeParseRegex();                          #(P7)
    my @tokens = $document =~ /$XML_SPE/g;                          #(P8)
    return @tokens;                                                 #(P9)
}

# All of the regular expressions shown below are from the REX shallow
# parser for XML by Robert Cameron:
sub makeParseRegex {                                                #(P10)
    my $self = shift;                                               #(P12)
    my $TextSE = "[^<]+";                                           #(P13)
    my $UntilHyphen = "[^-]*-";                                     #(P14)
    my $Until2Hyphens = "$UntilHyphen(?:[^-]$UntilHyphen)*-";       #(P15)
    my $CommentCE = "$Until2Hyphens>?";                             #(P16)
    my $UntilRSBs = "[^\\]]*](?:[^\\]]+])*]+";                      #(P17)
    my $CDATA_CE = "$UntilRSBs(?:[^\\]>]$UntilRSBs)*>";             #(P18)
    my $S = "[ \\n\\t\\r]+";                                        #(P19)
    my $NameStrt = "[A-Za-z_:]|[^\\x00-\\x7F]";                     #(P20)
    my $NameChar = "[A-Za-z0-9_:.-]|[^\\x00-\\x7F]";                #(P21)
    my $Name = "(?:$NameStrt)(?:$NameChar)*";                       #(P22)
    my $QuoteSE = "\"[^\"]*\"|'[^']*'";                             #(P23)
    my $DT_IdentSE = "$S$Name(?:$S(?:$Name|$QuoteSE))*";            #(P24)
    my $MarkupDeclCE = "(?:[^\\]\"'><]+|$QuoteSE)*>";               #(P25)
    my $S1 = "[\\n\\r\\t ]";                                        #(P26)
    my $UntilQMs = "[^?]*\\?+";                                     #(P27)
    my $PI_Tail = "\\?>|$S1$UntilQMs(?:[^>?]$UntilQMs)*>";          #(P28)
    my $DT_ItemSE = "<(?:!(?:--$Until2Hyphens>|[^-]$MarkupDeclCE)|".
                        "\\?$Name(?:$PI_Tail))|%$Name;|$S";         #(P29)
    my $DocTypeCE =
          "$DT_IdentSE(?:$S)?(?:\\[(?:$DT_ItemSE)*](?:$S)?)?>?";#(P30)
    my $DeclCE = "--(?:$CommentCE)?|\\[CDATA\\[(?:$CDATA_CE)?|" .
                              "DOCTYPE(?:$DocTypeCE)?";             #(P31)
    my $PI_CE = "$Name(?:$PI_Tail)?";                               #(P32)
    my $EndTagCE = "$Name(?:$S)?>?";                                #(P33)
    my $AttValSE = "\"([^<\"]*)\"|'[^<']*'";                        #(P34)
    my $ElemTagCE = "$Name(?:$S($Name)(?:$S)?=(?:$S)?" .
                          "(?:$AttValSE))*(?:$S)?/?>?";             #(P35)
    my $MarkupSPE = "<(?:!(?:$DeclCE)?|\\?(?:$PI_CE)?|/" .
                  "(?:($EndTagCE)(?{_end_tag_handler('<'.\$^N)}))?|".
                  "(?:($ElemTagCE)(?{_start_tag_handler('<'.\$^N)}))?)";
                                                                    #(P36)
    my $XML_SPE = "($TextSE)(?{_char_handler(\$^N)})|$MarkupSPE";  #(P37)
    return $XML_SPE;                                                #(P38)
}
```

```
# Handler code:

sub _start_tag_handler {                                              #(H1)
    my $tagname_and_attributes = shift @_;                            #(H2)
    if ( (index($tagname_and_attributes,'/>') > 0)  and
         $parser_instance->{_selfClosingTagHandler} ) {               #(H3)
        $parser_instance->
              {_selfClosingTagHandler}->($tagname_and_attributes);    #(H4)
    } elsif ($parser_instance->{_startTagHandler}) {                  #(H5)
        $parser_instance->
              {_startTagHandler}->($tagname_and_attributes);          #(H6)
    }
}
sub _end_tag_handler {                                                #(H7)
    my $tagname = shift @_;                                           #(H8)
    if ( $parser_instance->{_endTagHandler} ) {                       #(H9)
        $parser_instance->{_endTagHandler}->($tagname);              #(H10)
    }
}
sub _char_handler {                                                  #(H11)
    my $string = shift;                                              #(H12)
    if ( $parser_instance->{_charHandler} ) {                        #(H13)
        $parser_instance->{_charHandler}->($string);                 #(H14)
    }
}
1
```

The script that follows, `TestEventBasedParserUsingRex.pl`, uses the event-based parser of the previous script to parse an XML document. It first constructs an instance of the parser in line (T4) and then sets up the user-supplied event handlers in lines (T5) through (T8). The handlers themselves are defined in lines (T9) through (T12). It finally calls the `parse()` method of the parser on the document to be parsed.

```
#!/usr/bin/perl -w

### TestEventBasedParserUsingRex.pl

use EventBasedParserUsingRex;                                         #(T1)

my $docname = shift;                                                  #(T2)
die "Can't find \"$docname\"" unless -f $docname;                     #(T3)

my $parser = EventBasedParserUsingRex->new();                         #(T4)
```

```
$parser->setHandlers( StartTag => \&startTagHandler,                #(T5)
                      EndTag   => \&endTagHandler,                  #(T6)
                      SelfClosingTag => \&selfClosingTagHandler,    #(T7)
                      CharData => \&charHandler,                    #(T8)
                    );
sub endTagHandler {                                                 #(T9)
    my $tag_name = shift;
    print "end of element '$tag_name'\n";
}
sub startTagHandler {                                              #(T10)
    my $tagname_and_attributes = shift;
    print "start of element '$tagname_and_attributes'\n";
}
sub selfClosingTagHandler {                                        #(T11)
    my $tagname_and_attributes = shift;
    print "self-closing element '$tagname_and_attributes'\n";
}
sub charHandler {                                                  #(T12)
    my $string = shift;
    return if $string eq "\n";
    print "character data:  $string\n";
}
$parser->parse($docname);                                          #(T13)
```

When `TestEventBasedParserUsingRex.pl` is invoked on the following visually confusing but well-formed XML document:

```
<?xml version="1.0"?>

<!--
        The name of this <document> is test.xml
-->

<list_of_entries xmlns="http://www.w3.org/1999/xhtml">

  <entry>
<eg> <![CDATA[ <?xml version="1.0"?>
<!DOCTYPE greeting SYSTEM "hello.dtd">
<greeting>Hello, world!</greeting>
]]></eg>
      <name type="singsong">wonwon</name>
      <phone>  32323-38373 </phone>
  </entry>
  <self_enclosed/>
</list_of_entries>
```

we get the following output:

```
character data:

character data:

start of element '<list_of_entries xmlns=''http://www.w3.org/1999/xhtml''>'
character data:

start of element '<entry>'
start of element '<eg>'
character data:
end of element '<eg>'
character data:

start of element '<name type=''singsong''>'
character data:  wonwon
end of element '<name>'
character data:

start of element '<phone>'
character data:    32323-38373
end of element '<phone>'
character data:

end of element '<entry>'
character data:

self-closing element '<self_enclosed/>'
end of element '<list_of_entries>'
```

The first two invocations of the character data handler, evidenced by the two appearances of `character data:` at the top of the output, are caused by the presence of two consecutive newline characters immediately at the end of the first line in the source document. That line itself is a processing instruction. Since the parser does not contain a callback for processing instructions, that line itself is ignored. However, the two consecutive newline characters after that are passed on to the character data handler. The rest of the output is self-explanatory.

17.7.4 Using the Perl Module XML::Parser for Event-Driven XML Parsing

XML::Parser is one of the best known early modules for event-driven parsing of XML documents. As mentioned in our brief library survey at the end of the introduction to Section 17.7, this module sits on top of the XML::Parser::Expat module that is a lower-level interface to James Clark's event-driven expat library in C.[52]

The next script, UsingXmlParser.pl, shows how one can use the XML::Parser. As we show in line (E) of the script, you first construct an XML::Parser::Expat object. This call to the constructor can take a number of options of which we have only used the ErrorContext option in line (E). When this option is set to an integer value, such as 2, many lines before and after the line in which a parsing error occurs will be shown in the output. Other options that can be specified in the constructor call include Style, ProtocolHandling, Namespaces, etc. When set to true, the Namespaces option causes namespace processing to be carried out during the parse. What that means is that the parser separately recognizes the namespace prefix and the local name when a name has a colon in it and then keeps track of the names taking into account their namespaces.

After you have constructed an instance of XML::Parser::Expat, as in line (E) of the script, you can invoke any of a large number of methods defined for the class XML::Parser::Expat to set up the various attributes of the parser. For example, line (F) calls the setHandlers() method to register the shown event handlers with the parser. In the keyword-argument pairs supplied to setHandlers(), the keywords Start and End are for supplying the handler subroutines for the start-tag and end-tag events. Similarly, the keyword Char is for supplying the handler for the character data. The keywords CdataStart and CdataEnd designate the handlers to be used for the events corresponding to the beginning and the end of a CDATA section. The keyword Comment is for supplying the handler to be used when the parser finds a comment in the document. In all, XML::Parser::Expat allows for 18 event handlers to be specified in this manner. Except for the events triggered by start tags and end tags, the parser will call the default handler, specified by the keyword Default in the call in line (F), for all those events for which a handler is not listed.[53]

In the handler code in lines (I) through (O), note how we invoke methods on the XML::Parser::Expat instance to obtain different bits of information about what the parser saw in the document when the corresponding event was triggered. For example, the current_line() method returns the number of the line where the event-producing item was seen in the document. When event-producing items span multiple

[52]To add to the library "survey" at the end of the introduction to Section 17.7, the Perl modules XML::Parser and XML::Parser::Expat, originally written by Larry Wall, are now maintained by Matt Sergeant and Clark Cooper, respectively.

[53]If no handlers are specified, the parser will only check an XML document for its well-formedness.

lines — as, for example, with a multiline comment block, `current_line()` returns the number for the starting line of the block. The method `current_element()` returns the name of the element that is currently open when the event-producing item is recognized. So when the start tag of a new element is seen, `current_element()` returns the parent element of the new element, if there is a parent element. Otherwise, it returns `undef`. For the character data in the content section of an element, `current_element()` returns the name of the element whose content is being viewed. The method `depth()` returns the nesting depth of the currently open element. In all there are over 30 methods that can be called on an `XML::Parser::Expat` instance to retrieve various properties of the document environment at the point where an event was triggered.

Also note that not all the handlers receive the same number of explicit arguments. Obviously, every handler receives the implicitly supplied argument that is the `XML::Parser::Expat` instance constructed in line (E). As for the arguments supplied explicitly, the start-tag handler, for example, is passed a list that consists alternately of attribute names and attribute values. The end-tag handler receives only one explicit argument, the name of the element whose end tag triggered the event. The comment handler also gets only one explicit argument — the comment block, as you would expect.

```
#!/usr/bin/perl -w

### UsingXmlParser.pl

my $file = shift;                                                      #(A)
die "Can't find file \"$file\"" unless -f $file;                       #(B)

use strict;                                                            #(C)
use XML::Parser;                                                       #(D)

# The call to 'new' returns an object
# of type XML::Parse::Expat
my $parser = new XML::Parser( ErrorContext => 2 );                     #(E)

$parser->setHandlers( Start        =>     \&start_tag_handler,         #(F)
                      End          =>     \&end_tag_handler,
                      Char         =>     \&char_handler,
                      CdataStart   =>     \&cdata_start_handler,
                      CdataEnd     =>     \&cdata_end_handler,
                      Comment      =>     \&comment_handler,
                      Default      =>     \&default_handler,
                    );
```

```
eval {                                                           #(G)
    $parser->parsefile( $file );
};
if ($@) {                                                        #(H)
    print "error in the source file: $@\n";
} else {
    print "document well formed\n";
}

# Handlers:
sub start_tag_handler {                                          #(I)
    my ($p, @data) = @_;
    my $ele = shift @data;
    my $line = $p->current_line;
    my $parent_ele = $p->current_element;
    my $depth = $p->depth;
    print "Line $line: start tag of the element '$ele' with \n" .
      "              the attribute data '@data' (start_tag_handler)\n";
    print "          Parent Element: $parent_ele  " if $parent_ele;
    print "   Element Nesting Depth: $depth\n" if $depth > 0;
}
sub end_tag_handler {                                            #(J)
    my ($p, $ele) = @_;
    my $line = $p->current_line;
    print "Line $line: end tag of '$ele' element (end_tag_handler)\n";
}
sub char_handler {                                               #(K)
    my ($p, $data) = @_;
    my $line = $p->current_line;
    if ($data eq "\n") {
        print "Line $line: only '\\n' found (char handler)\n";
        return;
    }
    my $open_ele = $p->current_element;
    my $depth = $p->depth;
    $data =~ s/\s/\\s/g;
    print "Line $line: trapped '$data' (char handler)\n";
    print "            Open Element: '$open_ele' ".
          "    Element Nesting Depth: $depth\n";
}
# The CDATA content itself is not passed to this handler.  The
# CDATA content triggers char events.
sub cdata_start_handler {                                        #(L)
    my $p = shift;
    my $line = $p->current_line;
    my $open_ele = $p->current_element;
    print "Line $line: CDATA section begins, Open Element: $open_ele ".
          "(cdata_start_handler)\n";
}
```

```
sub cdata_end_handler {                                              #(M)
    my $p = shift;
    my $line = $p->current_line;
    print "Line $line: end of CDATA section (cdata_end_handler)\n";
}
# Note that an entire comment will be delivered with a single
# call to the handler:
sub comment_handler {                                                #(N)
    my ($p, $comment) = @_;
    my $line = $p->current_line;
    print "Line $line: comment block starts (comment handler)\n";
    print "            The comment is: $comment";
}
sub default_handler {                                                #(O)
    my ($p, $data) = @_;
    $data =~ s/[ ]/\\s/g;
    $data =~ s/\n/\\n/sg;
    my $line = $p->current_line;
    print "Line $line: default handler invoked for: $data\n";
}
```

We will demonstrate the working of the above script on the XML document shown below. The line numbers shown on the left are not in the original document; they make it easier to understand the output produced by the `UsingXmlParser.pl` script.

```
1.    <?xml version="1.0"?>
2.
3.    <!--
4.              The name of this <document> is test.xml
5.    -->
6.
7.    <list_of_entries xmlns="http://www.w3.org/1999/xhtml">
8.
9.      <entry>
10.   <eg><![CDATA[ <?xml version="1.0"?>
11.   <!DOCTYPE greeting SYSTEM "hello.dtd">
12.   <greeting>Hello, world!</greeting>
13.   ]]></eg>
14.         <name type="singsong">wonwon</name>
15.         <phone>  32323-38373 </phone>
16.     </entry>
17.     <self_enclosed/>
18.   </list_of_entries>
19.
```

When `UsingXmlParser.pl` is invoked on the above XML document, we get the output shown below. The line number label that starts each item of the output corresponds to the line of the input document that the parser was scanning for the output produced. As to why there should be some consecutive output items with the same starting line number — for example, we have two output items for Line 1 of the source document — will be clear from the explanation that follows the output.

```
Line 1: default handler invoked for: <?xml\sversion="1.0"?>
Line 1: default handler invoked for: \n\n
Line 3: comment block starts (comment handler)
          The comment is:
          The name of this <document> is test.xml
Line 5: default handler invoked for: \n\n
Line 7: start tag of the element 'list_of_entries' with
             the attribute data
               'xmlns http://www.w3.org/1999/xhtml' (start_tag_handler)
Line 7: only '\n' found (char handler)
Line 8: only '\n' found (char handler)
Line 9: trapped '\s\s' (char handler)
          Open Element: 'list_of_entries'     Element Nesting Depth: 1
Line 9: start tag of the element 'entry' with
             the attribute data '' (start_tag_handler)
         Parent Element: list_of_entries     Element Nesting Depth: 1
Line 9: only '\n' found (char handler)
Line 10: start tag of the element 'eg' with
             the attribute data '' (start_tag_handler)
         Parent Element: entry     Element Nesting Depth: 2
Line 10: CDATA section begins, Open Element: eg (cdata_start_handler)
Line 10: trapped '\s<?xml\sversion="1.0"?>' (char handler)
          Open Element: 'eg'     Element Nesting Depth: 3
Line 10: only '\n' found (char handler)
Line 11: trapped '<!DOCTYPE\sgreeting\sSYSTEM\s"hello.dtd">' (char handler)
          Open Element: 'eg'     Element Nesting Depth: 3
Line 11: only '\n' found (char handler)
Line 12: trapped '<greeting>Hello,\sworld!</greeting>' (char handler)
          Open Element: 'eg'     Element Nesting Depth: 3
Line 12: only '\n' found (char handler)
Line 13: end of CDATA section (cdata_end_handler)
Line 13: end tag of 'eg' element (end_tag_handler)
Line 13: only '\n' found (char handler)
Line 14: trapped '\s\s\s\s\s\s' (char handler)
          Open Element: 'entry'     Element Nesting Depth: 2
Line 14: start tag of the element 'name' with
             the attribute data 'type singsong' (start_tag_handler)
         Parent Element: entry     Element Nesting Depth: 2
Line 14: trapped 'wonwon' (char handler)
          Open Element: 'name'     Element Nesting Depth: 3
```

```
Line 14: end tag of 'name' element (end_tag_handler)
Line 14: only '\n' found (char handler)
Line 15: trapped '\s\s\s\s\s\s' (char handler)
          Open Element: 'entry'     Element Nesting Depth: 2
Line 15: start tag of the element 'phone' with
             the attribute data '' (start_tag_handler)
         Parent Element: entry     Element Nesting Depth: 2
Line 15: trapped '\s\s32323-38373\s' (char handler)
          Open Element: 'phone'     Element Nesting Depth: 3
Line 15: end tag of 'phone' element (end_tag_handler)
Line 15: only '\n' found (char handler)
Line 16: trapped '\s\s' (char handler)
          Open Element: 'entry'     Element Nesting Depth: 2
Line 16: end tag of 'entry' element (end_tag_handler)
Line 16: only '\n' found (char handler)
Line 17: trapped '\s\s' (char handler)
          Open Element: 'list_of_entries'     Element Nesting Depth: 1
Line 17: start tag of the element 'self_enclosed' with
             the attribute data '' (start_tag_handler)
         Parent Element: list_of_entries     Element Nesting Depth: 1
Line 17: end tag of 'self_enclosed' element (end_tag_handler)
Line 17: only '\n' found (char handler)
Line 18: end tag of 'list_of_entries' element (end_tag_handler)
Line 18: default handler invoked for: \n
document well formed
```

Note that line 1 of the document triggers an event that is handled by the default handler. Under the hood, the parser recognizes line 1 of the document as consisting of a processing instruction. If we had wanted to, we could have specified a separate handler for this with the keyword `Proc` in the call in line (F) of the `UsingXmlParler.pl` script. Since that handler does not exist, the parser instead uses the default handler that is provided.

Line 1 of the XML document ends in the newline character, followed immediately by another newline character in line 2. Both of these characters are perceived by the parser as such and both together again trigger the default event handler. These characters do not constitute a character-data event for the `char_handler()` because the character data for that handler must be between a start tag and an end tag.

The parser then finds a comment block starting in line 3 of the document. The corresponding event causes the `comment_handler()` method to be invoked, which produces the output shown. After the end of the comment in line 5, we have a newline character, followed by another newline character. Both these characters together again trigger the default handler for the same reason as already mentioned.

In line 7 of the input document, the parser finds the start tag for the element `list_of_entries`. This triggers a call to `start_tag_handler()`. The handler is supplied with a list of the attribute-value pairs found in the start tag — in our case, there is only one pair. The start-tag handler prints it out, as shown in the output for line 7. The newline character at the end of line 7 triggers the character data handler `char_handler()` because the character is between the start tag and the end tag of an element. For the same reason, the only character found in line 8 — a newline — also triggers a call to `char_handler()`. Again for the same reason, the first two blank spaces together at the beginning of line 9 also trigger `char_handler()`.

After the beginning two blank spaces in line 9, the parser finds the start tag of the `entry` element, which causes the invocation of `start_tag_handler()`. Note that this start tag does not contain any attributes.

In line 10, the parser first detects a start tag for the element `eg` and then detects a CDATA section; the former causes the invocation of `start_tag_handler()` and the latter the invocation of `cdata_start_handler()`. What is in the rest of line 10 and what follows in lines 11 and 12 causes multiple invocations of the character data handler `char_handler()`. Finally, in line 13, the parser detects the end of the `CDATA` section, triggering the invocation of `cdata_end_handler()`. In the same line, the parser also finds the end tag for the `eg` element, as evidenced by the invocation of `end_tag_handler()`.

Line 14 starts with six blank spaces. Because these appear inside the `entry` element, the six spaces together are shipped off to the character data handler. In the same line, the parser next finds the start tag of a new element, `name`. And so on.

17.7.5 Using the Perl SAX Parser Modules

As mentioned earlier in the introduction to Section 17.7, many newer Perl modules for parsing XML documents conform to the SAX2 interface, or, more precisely, to the Perl SAX 2.0 interface [30, 57]. The API for Perl SAX 2.0 says that all of the event handler methods will be bundled into a class and an instance of this class will be supplied to the parser constructor through syntax that looks like:

```
my $parser = Some_Perl_SAX_Parser->new(
                     Handler => MySAXEventHandler->new() );        #(A)
```

where `Handler` is a keyword that the parser constructor recognizes. Although supplying an event handler in this fashion suffices for a majority of applications, the SAX2 API also allows for handler instances to be specified separately for different classes of events. Shown below is a list of the keywords that can be used in the manner of the `Handler` keyword above for supplying more focused handler instances:

`ContentHandler`: A handler instance supplied through this keyword receives all document content events. For the most part, these are the same events that would ordinarily be supplied to the handler that is specified with the `Handler` keyword. The additional events that can be specified through the `ContentHandler` interface include those related to the start and the end of namespace scopes, etc.

`DTDHandler`: A handler instance supplied through this keyword receives all DTD events.

`EntityResolver`: If the parser is supplied with an entity resolver through this keyword, it is used for resolving all external entities references. If an entity resolver is not supplied, the parser performs its own default entity resolution. This is useful in applications that build XML documents from databases and other specialized input sources. (Section 17.5.3 talked about entities in XML documents.)

`ErrorHandler`: A handler instance supplied through this keyword is notified of all error events encountered during the parsing operation. If an error handler is not registered with the parser, any error events encountered during parsing may be ignored. But, depending on the implementation, it is also possible that further parsing would be suspended. The parsing operation must come to a halt if a well-formedness or a validation error is detected.

If any of the handler instances corresponding to the four keywords listed above is absent in the call to the parser constructor, SAX 2.0 API requires that the parser use the default handler specified through the `Handler` keyword for those classes of events.[54]

The call in line (A) above constructs an instance of the parser and, at the same time, registers a handler instance with it. After a parser instance is constructed in this manner, it may be called upon to parse an XML source with any of the API methods `parse_file()`, `parse_string()`, and `parse_uri()`, as in the following calls:[55]

```
$parser->parse_file( some_xml_file );

$parser->parse_string( an_xml_string );

$parser->parse_uri( some_uri );
```

An event handler class whose instance is supplied to the parser constructor is expected to provide handler methods — usually referred to as *callbacks* for reasons previously mentioned — for those events that are important to an application. If a

---

[54]SAX 2.0 also allows for a separate declaration handler to be specified for the XML reader. This handler, incorporated in the parser as a `http://xml.org/sax/handlers/DeclHandler` feature, provides information about the DTD declarations in an XML document. But note that data-related DTD declarations are already reported through the `DTDHandler` interface.

[55]In all cases, the call to the actual parsing function returns whatever is returned by the `end_document()` handler function.

callback is not provided for a certain type of event, that event is ignored by the parser. For most routine applications, an event handler class meant for processing content events provides definitions for some or all of the following methods:

`start_document()`: This callback receives notification when the parser starts processing the document. No explicit arguments are supplied to this callback.

`end_document()`: This callback receives notification when the parser is finished with the document. No explicit arguments are supplied to this callback. This method is also called if parsing is abandoned because of a fatal error.

`start_element()`: This callback is notified as soon as the parser has recognized an element start tag. The callback is called with one explicit argument that consists of a reference to an anonymous hash with the following structure:[56]

```
key:    Name
value:  name of the tag

key:    LocalName
value:  local name value

key:    Prefix
value:  the prefix

key:    NamespaceURI
value:  the URI for the namespace

key:    Attributes
value:  a reference to a hash with the following structure:

        key: name of an attribute (in JClark notation)
        value: a reference to a hash with the following structure

            key:    LocalName
            value:  local name of the attribute

            key:    Prefix
            value:  the prefix string

            key:    Value
            value:  value of the attribute

            key:    Name
            value:  namespace qualified name of the attribute
```

[56]Ordinarily, the namespace-related information is supplied in the argument to the `start_element()` callback only when the namespaces feature is on (which it is by default).

```
            key:    NamespaceURI
            value:  the name of the namespace

        key:    name of another attribute (in JClark notation}
        value:  a reference to a hash with the following structure

            key:    LocalName
            value:  local name of the attribute

            key:    Prefix
            value:  the prefix string

            key:    Value
            value:  value of the attribute

            key:    Name
            value:  namespace qualified name of the attribute

            key:    NamespaceURI
            value:  the name of the namespace

      .....
      .....
```

The JClark notation mentioned above means that if an attribute name is in a particular namespace, then the name of the attribute in the above data structure is `{namespace_name}attribute_name`. For names that are not in any specific namespace, the JClark notation for an attribute name is `{}attribute_name`. Note that this callback is also notified when an empty element is encountered. In fact, for an empty element, a notification to this callback is immediately followed by a notification to the `end_element()` callback we show next.

`end_element()`: This callback is notified when the parser sees the end tag for an element. The callback is provided with one explicit argument, a reference to an anonymous hash that contains the following information:

```
key:    Name
value:  name of the tag

key:    LocalName
value:  local name value

key:    Prefix
value:  the prefix

key:    NamespaceURI
value:  the URI for the namespace
```

`characters()`: This callback is notified when the parser recognizes chunks of character data that may be contained in an element or in a CDATA section. The callback is invoked with one explicit argument, a string consisting of the character data recognized as a single chunk. It is possible that all of the character data that exists between the start tag and the end tag of an element (or in a CDATA section) may result in more than one call to this callback. How the contiguous character data gets fragmented into several chunks is controlled by the `join-character-data` feature of the parser.

`comment()`: This callback is notified when a comment block is recognized. The callback is invoked with one explicit argument, which is a reference to an anonymous hash that contains a single key-value pair, with key being `Data` and the value the string of characters constituting the comment.

`processing_instruction()`: This callback is notified when a processing instruction is encountered in an XML document. The callback is notified with a reference to an anonymous hash containing two key-value pairs. The two keys are `Target` and `Data`. The value associated with the first key, `Target`, is the string that comes right after the opening delimiter `<?` of a processing instruction. The value associated with the other key, `Data`, is the rest of the processing instruction before the closing delimiter.

`start_cdata()`: This callback is notified at the beginning of a CDATA section. It is called with no explicit arguments. The contents of the CDATA section trigger the `characters()` callback and can therefore be retrieved through that callback.

`end_cdata()`: This callback is notified at the end of a CDATA section. As with the `start_cdata()` callback, it is called with no explicit arguments.

The Perl SAX 2.0 API supports many other callbacks for a detailed parse of an XML document. These callbacks can be employed to capture DTD events, for intercepting external entities, for signalling various other types of lexical events, etc.

A useful top-level SAX module for XML processing with Perl is `XML::SAX`. It can keep track of the SAX parsers available in your system and make them available as needed. More particularly, its submodule `XML::SAX::ParserFactory` can look at all the installed SAX parsers and make one available with the desired *features*.[57] The name of a feature must be a URI, although frequently it is a

[57] Parser *features* and *properties* defined in Java SAX2 have been lumped together in Perl SAX 2.0 under *features*. In Java SAX2, a feature can only take a Boolean value, whereas a property is allowed to take an arbitrary object as its value. A common example of a feature is *validation*; it is either true or false. If it is false, the parser will not validate an XML document against a schema or a DTD. Another common example of a feature is *namespaces*; again it is either true or false. If it is true, that means that the parser can extract unprefixed local names and the namespace URIs for the element and attribute names. An example of a property is one that tells the parser where to find the schema to validate the document

URL.[58] The URIs that are allowed for naming a feature frequently have the prefix `http://xml.org/sax/features/` followed by an identifier specific to the feature. Perl SAX parsers may also use the prefix `http://xmlns.perl.org/sax`, followed again by an identifier specific to the feature. In general, every SAX 2.0 compliant parser must support at least the following two features:

```
http://xml.org/sax/features/namespaces

http://xml.org/sax/features/namespace-prefix
```

When the `namespaces` feature is turned on,[59] meaning when its value is set to 1, the parser will make available the raw tag names through the `Name` keyword in the `start_element()` callback and the various constituents of a namespace-qualified element name through the `NamespaceURI`, `LocalName`, and `Prefix` keywords. This makes redundant what would otherwise be accomplished by the `namespace-prefixes` feature. For this reason, Perl SAX 2.0 parsers ignore the `namespace-prefix` feature. Some other features of the Perl SAX 2.0 parsers are

```
http://xml.org/sax/features/xmlns-uris

http://xmlns.perl.org/sax/version-2.1

http://xmlns.perl.org/sax/join-character-data

http://xmlns.perl.org/sax/ns-attributes

http://xmlns.perl.org/sax/locator

http://xml.org/sax/features/validation
```

Setting the `xmlns-uris` feature to 1 places the namespace declaration attributes in the `http://www.w3.org/2000/xmlns/` namespace. The read-only feature `version-2.1`, when set to 1, indicates that the parser conforms to the version 2.1 of Perl SAX. The `join-character-data` feature, set by default to 1, controls the behavior of the parser with regard to character data fragmentation. The `ns-attributes` feature, set by default to 1, causes the namespace attributes to be reported as common attributes. The `locator` feature, set by default to 1, indicates that the parser is able to supply the location of the last character of a SAX event. Locations are measured in terms of row and column positions in a document. The first line is 1, as is the first column of each line. The last feature mentioned above, `validation`, when set to 1, implies that the parser supports validation of an XML document via a DTD.

against. This distinction between features and properties is not important in Perl SAX 2.0 where a feature is allowed to take any value.

[58] A footnote in Section 17.3 addresses the distinction between URIs and URLs.

[59] This feature is on by default.

Getting back to the top-level XML::SAX module, this module supports the following methods for managing the SAX parsers: parsers(), add_parser(), remove_parser(), and save_parsers(). The script below shows how you can call the parsers() method to determine which SAX parsers are currently installed in your system. This method returns a reference to a hash with two keys, Name and Features. The value associated with the Name key is the name of the parser and the value associated with the Features key is a reference to an anonymous hash whose keys are the feature names and whose values the corresponding feature values. The loop in lines (D) through (K) goes through each key-value pair of the hash returned by the call to parsers() in line (B) and prints out the information after ascertaining whether the value is a scalar, as it would be for the Name key, or a hash reference, as it would be for the Features key. For the latter case, the loop in lines (J) and (K) prints out all the feature names and their associated values.

```
#!/usr/bin/perl -w

### XmlSax.pl

use strict;
use XML::SAX;                                                    #(A)

my $parsers = XML::SAX->parsers();                               #(B)

my @parsers = @$parsers;                                         #(C)

foreach (@parsers) {                                             #(D)
    while ( my( $key, $val ) = each %$_ ) {                      #(E)
        if ( ref( $val ) eq "" ) {                               #(F)
            print "$key  =>   $val \n";                          #(G)
        } elsif ( ref( $val ) eq "HASH" ) {                      #(H)
            print "$key:  => \n";                                #(I)
            while ( my ($k, $v) = each %$val ) {                 #(J)
                print "          $k => $v\n";                    #(K)
            }
        }
    }
    print "\n\n=================\n\n";
}
```

The output of this script would obviously depend on what SAX parsers are installed on your machine. Here is the output on the author's machine:

```
Features:  =>
        http://xml.org/sax/features/namespaces => 1
Name  =>   XML::SAX::PurePerl

=================

Features:  =>
        http://xml.org/sax/features/namespaces => 1
Name  =>   XML::LibXML::SAX::Parser

=================

Features:  =>
        http://xml.org/sax/features/namespaces => 1
Name  =>   XML::LibXML::SAX

=================

Features:  =>
        http://xml.org/sax/features/namespaces => 1
        http://xml.org/sax/features/external-general-entities => 1
        http://xml.org/sax/features/external-parameter-entities => 1
Name  =>   XML::SAX::Expat

=================

Features:  =>
        http://xml.org/sax/features/namespaces => 1
        http://xml.org/sax/features/external-general-entities => 1
        http://xmlns.perl.org/sax/version-2.1 => 1
        http://xmlns.perl.org/sax/locator => 1
        http://xml.org/sax/features/xmlns-uris => 1
        http://xmlns.perl.org/sax/join-character-data => 1
        http://xmlns.perl.org/sax/ns-attributes => 1
Name  =>   XML::SAX::ExpatXS
```

This output demonstrates that all the installed SAX parsers support the `namespaces` feature, as they are required to.

We will now show in the next script an example of a Perl SAX parser in action. Our example will use the `XML::LibXML::SAX` parser module.[60] But — and that

[60]The Perl module `XML::LibXML::SAX`, by Matt Sergeant and Christian Glahn, is an interface to the Gnome projects' C library `libxml2` for both SAX and DOM parsing of XML.

speaks to the fact that all SAX 2.0 parsers must conform to the same API — we could have used the other SAX 2.0 parsers also with only minimal changes in the next script in order to achieve the same results.

To use a SAX processor, you need to first define an event handler class of your own and that is best done by subclassing it from the `XML::SAX:Base` class.[61] Although you are, of course, free to write an event handler class from scratch, using the `XML::SAX::Base` class makes for a much safer script as the base class provides the needed default implementations for all the event handlers. The base class also automatically hands over the events to the default handler associated with the keyword `Handler` if, say, no handler is provided through the `ContentHandler` keyword. Note the call to the `use base` pragma in line (H2) for declaring `XML::SAX::Base` as the base of the `MySAXEventHandler` class defined in the script. As explained in Section 8.3 of Chapter 8, this pragma first invokes `require` on the base class and then pushes it into the `@ISA` array.

The rest of the `MySAXEventHandler` class in the next script defines overrides for various event handlers in lines (H3) through (H43). With regard to what arguments are received by each handler and what sort of information can be extracted from the arguments, the definitions shown conform to the presentation of these handlers earlier in this section. As mentioned earlier, the most elaborate of the data structures received as an argument is by the `start_element()` event handler. In lines (H8) through (H11), we first extract the raw name of the element through the `Name` key, then just the local name through the `LocalName` key, the namespace prefix associated with the name through the `Prefix` key, and, finally, the namespace URI to which the prefix is mapped through the `NamespaceURI` key. In line (H12), we check if there is a nonempty hash associated with the `Attributes` key. If there is, we then extract all the attribute name-value pairs in lines (H14) through (H18). The inner loop in lines (H16) and (H17) retrieves all the different portions of the attribute name — its local name, its namespace prefix, the applicable namespace URI, etc.

Lines (T2) through (T9) first show how we can pass an instance of our own event handler class to an instance of the parser constructed from the `XML::LibXML::SAX`

---

[61] This is also the base class to use for creating your own XML-to-XML, XML-to-HTML, or, for that matter, XML-to-anything filter for document transformation. However, when writing an event handler for a filter, each callback must call the corresponding callback of `XML::SAX::Base`. For example, the last executable statement of the `start_element` of a filter callback would be as shown below:

```
sub start_element {
    my ($self, $element) = @_;
    ....
    ....
    $self->SUPER::start_element($element);
}
```

This also applies to the callbacks defined for SAX drivers. In the context of XML processing, a *driver* is a program that can extract information from a non-XML source, such as a database, and stream it to the output where it can be recognized as a stream of events and thus processed by a stream-based event-driven parser.

class and then how we can parse an XML document. In line (T5) we construct an instance of `XML::LibXML::SAX` and supply it an instance of `MySAXEventHandler` as the argument. In lines (T6) through (T8) we read an XML file into a single string `$doc`, which is then fed to the parser in line (T9).

```
#!/usr/bin/perl -w

### LibXmlSaxParser.pl

use strict;

#-------------------- MySAXEventHandler Class -----------------------

package MySAXEventHandler;                                           #(H1)

use base qw(XML::SAX::Base);                                         #(H2)

sub start_document {                                                 #(H3)
    my $self = shift;                                                #(H4)
    print "parsing started\n";                                       #(H5)
}
sub start_element {                                                  #(H6)
    my ($self, $element) = @_;                                       #(H7)
    print "start tag recognized for element: '$element->{Name}'\n";#(H8)
    print "    LocalName: '$element->{LocalName}'\n";                #(H9)
    print "    Prefix:  '$element->{Prefix}'\n";                    #(H10)
    print "    NamespaceURI:  '$element->{NamespaceURI}'\n";        #(H11)
    if (%{$element->{Attributes}}) {                                #(H12)
        print "    Attributes:\n";                                  #(H13)
        while (my ($key, $val) = each %{$element->{Attributes}}){ #(H14)
            print "        $key: \n";                               #(H15)
            while ( my ($k, $v)  = each %$val ) {                   #(H16)
                print "            $k  =   $v\n";                   #(H17)
            }
            print "\n";
        }
        print "\n";
    }                                                               #(H18)
}
sub characters {                                                    #(H19)
    my ($self, $characters) = @_;                                   #(H20)
    print "character handler invoked " .
          "for string: '$characters->{Data}'\n";                    #(H21)
}
```

```
sub end_element {                                                      #(H22)
    my ($self, $element) = @_;                                         #(H23)
    print "end tag recognized for element: '$element->{Name}'\n"; #(H24)
    print "    LocalName: '$element->{LocalName}'\n";                  #(H25)
    print "    Prefix:  '$element->{Prefix}'\n";                       #(H26)
    print "    NamespaceURI:  '$element->{NamespaceURI}'\n";           #(H27)
}
sub end_document {                                                     #(H28)
    my $self = shift;                                                  #(H29)
    print "parsing ended\n";                                           #(H30)
}
sub processing_instruction {                                           #(H31)
    my ($self, $pi) = @_;                                              #(H32)
    print "processing instruction recognized " .
          "for target '$pi->{Target}'\n";                              #(H33)
    print "    processing instruction data: '$pi->{Data}'\n";          #(H34)
}
sub comment {                                                          #(H35)
    my ($self, $comment) = @_;                                         #(H36)
    print "comment block recognized: '$comment->{Data}'\n";            #(H37)
}
sub start_cdata {                                                      #(H38)
    my $self = shift;                                                  #(H39)
    print "start of CDATA section detected\n";                         #(H40)
}
sub end_cdata {                                                        #(H41)
    my $self = shift;                                                  #(H42)
    print "end of CDATA section detected\n";                           #(H43)
}

#------------------------ using the parser --------------------------
package main;                                                          #(T1)

my $docname = shift;                                                   #(T2)
die "Can't find \"$docname\"" unless -f $docname;                      #(T3)

use XML::LibXML::SAX;                                                  #(T4)

my $parser = XML::LibXML::SAX->new(
               Handler => MySAXEventHandler->new() );                  #(T5)
local $/ = undef;                                                      #(T6)
open( FILEIN, $docname );                                              #(T7)
my $doc = <FILEIN>;                                                    #(T8)
$parser->parse_string( $doc );                                         #(T9)
```

When we invoke the above script on the following XML document named `test8.xml`

```
<?xml version="1.0" encoding="iso-8859-1"?>
<NS1:A xmlns:NS1="http://www.mywebsite.com/NS1names/"
     xmlns:NS2="http://www.mywebsite.com/NS2names/"
     xmlns="http://www.mywebsite.com/NS3names/"
>
    <NS1:B NS1:x="hello" y="jello" NS2:z="mello">hellojellomello</NS1:B>
    <C w="cello"/>
</NS1:A>
```

we get the following output:

```
parsing started
start tag recognized for element: 'NS1:A'
    LocalName: 'A'
    Prefix:  'NS1'
    NamespaceURI:  'http://www.mywebsite.com/NS1names/'
    Attributes:
        {http://www.w3.org/2000/xmlns/}NS1:
            LocalName  =   NS1
            Prefix  =   xmlns
            Value  =   http://www.mywebsite.com/NS1names/
            Name  =   xmlns:NS1
            NamespaceURI  =   http://www.w3.org/2000/xmlns/

        {}xmlns:
            LocalName  =   xmlns
            Prefix  =
            Value  =   http://www.mywebsite.com/NS3names/
            Name  =   xmlns
            NamespaceURI  =

        {http://www.w3.org/2000/xmlns/}NS2:
            LocalName  =   NS2
            Prefix  =   xmlns
            Value  =   http://www.mywebsite.com/NS2names/
            Name  =   xmlns:NS2
            NamespaceURI  =   http://www.w3.org/2000/xmlns/

character handler invoked for string: '
    '
```

```
start tag recognized for element: 'NS1:B'
    LocalName: 'B'
    Prefix:  'NS1'
    NamespaceURI:  'http://www.mywebsite.com/NS1names/'
    Attributes:
        {}y:
            LocalName  =   y
            Prefix  =
            Value  =   jello
            Name  =   y
            NamespaceURI  =

        {http://www.mywebsite.com/NS1names/}x:
            LocalName  =   x
            Prefix  =   NS1
            Value  =   hello
            Name  =   NS1:x
            NamespaceURI  =   http://www.mywebsite.com/NS1names/

        {http://www.mywebsite.com/NS2names/}z:
            LocalName  =   z
            Prefix  =   NS2
            Value  =   mello
            Name  =   NS2:z
            NamespaceURI  =   http://www.mywebsite.com/NS2names/

character handler invoked for string: 'hellojellomello'
end tag recognized for element: 'NS1:B'
    LocalName: 'B'
    Prefix:  'NS1'
    NamespaceURI:  'http://www.mywebsite.com/NS1names/'
character handler invoked for string: '
    '
start tag recognized for element: 'C'
    LocalName: 'C'
    Prefix:  ''
    NamespaceURI:  'http://www.mywebsite.com/NS3names/'
    Attributes:
        {}w:
            LocalName  =   w
            Prefix  =
            Value  =   cello
            Name  =   w
            NamespaceURI  =

end tag recognized for element: 'C'
    LocalName: 'C'
    Prefix:  ''
    NamespaceURI:  'http://www.mywebsite.com/NS3names/'
```

```
character handler invoked for string: '
'
end tag recognized for element: 'NS1:A'
    LocalName: 'A'
    Prefix:   'NS1'
    NamespaceURI:   'http://www.mywebsite.com/NS1names/'
parsing ended
```

As mentioned already, it would be easy to "plug" in some other SAX 2.0 parser into the script we just presented. For example, if we wanted to use the `XML::SAX::Expat` module, all we have to do is to replace lines (T4) and (T5) by

```
use XML::SAX::Expat;
my $parser = XML::SAX::Expat->new(
                  Handler => MySAXEventHandler->new() );
```

Earlier we talked about the features that are associated with the different parsing modules. After we construct a parser instance, as above, we can set its features by calling the `set_feature()` method:

```
$parser->set_feature('http://xml.org/sax/features/namespaces', 0);
```

which should turn off the namespace processing by the parser.

The example we showed above called the `parse_string()` method to carry out the job of parsing. Earlier in this section, we listed the different parsing methods that are made available by the SAX 2.0 parsers. We could have, for example, called `parse_uri()` directly on a file name, as in

```
$parser->parse_uri( "filename.xml" );
```

17.7.6 Event-Driven XML Parsing with xml.sax in Python

Python's support for the SAX2 API is provided by the `xml.sax` module. The `make_parser()` method of this module returns an XML parser; this will usually be the first of the SAX parsers found installed on a system.[62] More precisely, `make_parser()` returns an `XMLReader` object whose `parse()` method can then be used to process an input source for the production of SAX events.

---

[62]It is also possible to call `make_parser()` with a second argument that is a list of strings naming specific SAX parsers. In this case, `make_parser()` returns an instance of the first parser from the list that is found installed in the system.

The `xml.sax` module also makes available the following handler classes, all derived from the base class `xml.sax.handler`, for the actions to be taken in response to the different types of events encountered as an XML document is scanned:

```
class ContentHandler

class DTDHandler

class EntityResolver

class ErrorHandler
```

These classes provide default implementation for the methods whose override definitions provided by a user result in the desired parser behavior. A user extends these classes, usually just the `ContentHandler` class for the simplest of the parsers, and then registers them with the reader object returned by the `xml.sax.make_parser()` method by calling the `set...handler` methods of the `XMLReader` class.

The next script, `XmlSaxParser.py`, does the same thing in Python that was accomplished by the `LibXmlSaxParser.pl` Perl script shown in the previous subsection. The script first defines a class `MyHandlers` by extending the `ContentHandler` class in lines (B) through (V). The `MyHandlers` class provides override definitions for the methods shown. These methods would be invoked automatically for the same events that are associated with the methods of similar names in the earlier Perl SAX discussion in Section 17.7.4. One major difference between the Perl SAX script shown earlier and the script here is that for Perl SAX the handler methods are supplied with an event object; the various attributes associated with the event are then extracted from the event object. For example, the explicit argument supplied to the `start_element()` method in the `LibXmlSaxParser.pl` script is an event object that can subsequently be queried with keywords such as `Name`, `LocalName`, `Prefix`, etc., to extract the various attributes of a start tag. For the Python case, the `startMethod()` is supplied explicitly with the name and the attributes associated with a start tag. If it is desired to extract separately the name prefix and the local name, the code for that must be supplied in the override definition for `startMethod()`.

Lines (Y) and (Z) of the script first construct a reader object and then set its content handler to a `MyHandlers` instance. In line (f) then we invoke the `parse()` method of the `XMLReader` class to process the XML file whose name is stored in the variable `xmldoc`. In addition to an XML file, `parse()`'s argument can also be a URL for an XML source, a `file` object, or an `xml.sax.InputSource` instance.

A handler class can also be used to set the various parser features and properties we mentioned earlier in Section 17.7.5. These features and properties are defined as symbolic constants for the base class `xml.sax.handler`. Line (a) shows how we can list all the features supported by the parser in use.[63] As we mentioned in Section 17.7.5, the two mandatory features for every compliant SAX parser are

```
http://xml.org/sax/features/namespaces
```

and

```
http://xml.org/sax/features/namespace-prefix
```

When the first of these is set to `True` (the default is `False`), the parser carries out namespace processing. And when the second is set to `True` (the default is again `False`), the parser can report the original prefixed names and attributes used for namespace declarations. To demonstrate that the features and properties are stored as symbolic constants in the `xml.sax.handler` class, line (b) shows us querying the symbolic constant `feature_namespaces`. It returns the feature shown in the commented-out line below line (b).

SAX parsers accessible through the `xml.sax` API report their errors through the `SAXParseException` class. This class is derived from the base class `SAXException` that provides the methods `getMessage()` and `getException()`, the former yielding a human-readable message describing the error and the latter an exception object. These two methods, along with some other methods that can be invoked on the exception object trapped, are shown in lines (f) through (k). The `getLineNumber()`, `getColumnNumber()`, `getPublicId()`, and `getSystemId()` are defined for the `xml.sax.Locator` class. The last of these, `getSystemId()`, will usually return the name of the XML source that is being parsed. The method `getPublicId()` returns the public identifier for the current event if it has one.

```
#!/usr/bin/env python

### XmlSaxParser.py

import xml.sax                                                          #(A)

#------------------------  class MyHandlers  ------------------------
class MyHandlers( xml.sax.ContentHandler ):                             #(B)
    def startElement( self, name, attributes ):                         #(C)
        print "start tag recognized for element: " + name               #(D)
        if attributes:                                                  #(E)
            print "    Attributes:"                                     #(F)
            for item in attributes.items():                             #(G)
                print "        ", item[0], " = ", item[1]               #(H)
            print                                                       #(I)
```

[63] In our Perl SAX discussion in Section 17.7.5, we mentioned the convention that must be followed for the names of the SAX parser features and properties. Such names must begin with the prefix `http://xml.org/sax/features/` that is then followed by an identifier that is specific to a feature. It is a list of such names that is returned by the call in line (a).

```
    def characters( self, content ):                                 #(J)
        content = content.lstrip().rstrip()                          #(K)
        if content:                                                  #(L)
            print "character handler invoked for string: ", content #(M)

    def endElement( self, name ):                                    #(N)
        print "end tag recognized for element: " + name             #(O)

    def startDocument( self ):                                       #(P)
        print "document parse started"                               #(Q)

    def endDocument( self ):                                         #(R)
        print "end of document reached --- parse ended"              #(S)

    def processingInstruction( self, target, data ):                 #(T)
        print "processing instruction recognized for target ",target#(U)
        print "    processing instruction data: " + data             #(V)

#---------------------- end of MyHandlers class --------------------

if __name__ == '__main__':                                           #(W)

    import sys
    if len( sys.argv ) is not 2:
        sys.exit( "need an xml file" )
    xmldoc = sys.argv[1]                                             #(X)

    # make_parser() returns a xml.sax.XMLReader object:
    reader = xml.sax.make_parser()                                   #(Y)
    reader.setContentHandler( MyHandlers() )                         #(Z)

    print xml.sax.handler.all_features                               #(a)
    print xml.sax.handler.feature_namespaces                         #(b)
                          # http://xml.org/sax/features/namespaces

    try:                                                             #(c)
        reader.parse( xmldoc )                                       #(d)
    except xml.sax.SAXParseException, e:                             #(e)
        print "  parsing error:     ", e.getMessage()                #(f)
        print "  in line:           ", e.getLineNumber()             #(g)
        print "  at location:       ", e.getColumnNumber()           #(h)
        print "  exception raised: ", e.getException()               #(i)
        print "  for event ID:      ", e.getPublicId()               #(j)
        print "  for system ID:     ", e.getSystemId()               #(k)
        sys.exit(1)                                                  #(l)
```

When invoked on the XML document `test8.xml` shown near the end of Section 17.7.5, the above script produces the output shown below. What is shown does not include the output produced by lines (a) and (b).

```
document parse started
start tag recognized for element: NS1:A
    Attributes:
       xmlns:NS2  =  http://www.mywebsite.com/NS2names/
       xmlns:NS1  =  http://www.mywebsite.com/NS1names/
       xmlns  =  http://www.mywebsite.com/NS3names/

start tag recognized for element: NS1:B
    Attributes:
       y  =  jello
       NS1:x  =  hello
       NS2:z  =  mello

character handler invoked for string:  hellojellomello
end tag recognized for element: NS1:B
start tag recognized for element: C
    Attributes:
       w  =  cello

end tag recognized for element: C
end tag recognized for element: NS1:A
end of document reached --- parse ended
```

Note that, unlike the case for the Perl script `LibXmlSaxParser.pl`, this output does not include the invocation of the `characters()` method for white-space characters like blank spaces and newline characters. That is because line (K) of the script filters those invocations out.

17.7.7 DOM Parsing in Python with xml.dom.minidom

We will now show two examples that illustrate how Python's `xml.dom.minidom` module can be used to construct a DOM parse tree and how information about the parsed XML document can be plucked from the tree. The module `xml.dom.minidom` is a lightweight implementation of the still evolving full-blown DOM interface.[64]

[64] As mentioned at the end of the introduction to Section 17.7, the `xml.dom.minidom` module largely conforms to DOM Level 1 specification. However, it also includes the namespace feature of DOM Level

As should be clear by now, a DOM parser constructs a tree of nodes that reflects the hierarchical organization of the elements in an XML document. The goal of our first script in this section, `MinidomParse.py`, is to give the reader a sense of how one can descend down a DOM tree and examine the various attributes associated with the nodes. The script itself can be invoked on any XML document. For the purpose of our explanation, we will invoke it on the following XML document. We will refer to this document as `test9.xml`.

```
<?xml version="1.0" encoding="iso-8859-1"?>
<NS1:A xmlns:NS1="http://www.mywebsite.com/NS1names/"
      xmlns:NS2="http://www.mywebsite.com/NS2names/"
      xmlns="http://www.mywebsite.com/NS3names/"
>
    <NS1:B NS1:x="hello" y="jello" NS2:z="mello">hellojellomello</NS1:B>
    <C w="cello"/>
    <AAA> aaa </AAA>
    abc123xyz
    <BBB> bbb </BBB>
    <CCC> <![CDATA[ <?xml version="1.0"?>
           <!DOCTYPE greeting SYSTEM "hello.dtd">
           <greeting>Hello, world!</greeting>
           ]]>
    </CCC>
</NS1:A>
```

The root node of the DOM tree for the above document should correspond to the root element whose name is `NS1:A`, with the prefix `NS1:` standing for the `http://www.mywebsite.com/NS1names/` namespace. The root node should point to six child nodes corresponding to the subelements `NS1:B`, `C`, `AAA`, a pure character-data node, `BBB`, and `CCC`. Note that the subelement named `C` is self-closing. Also note that the names of the last five subelements are in the default namespace `http://www.mywebsite.com/NS3names/`. The rest of the structure of `test9.xml` should also be obvious by inspection.

Line (A) of the script shown next calls `xml.dom.minidom.parse()` to construct a DOM for the document shown above. The call to `parse()` returns a `Document` instance. The parse tree itself is obtained by querying the `documentElement` attribute of this instance, which is what we do in line (B).[65] The object we get hold of in line

2. The following DOM objects have not been implemented in `xml.dom.minidom`: `CharacterData`, `CDATASection`, `Notation`, `Entity`, `EntityReference`, and `DocumentFragment`.

[65] If you were to examine all of the contents of the `Document` instance returned by `parse()` for the `test9.xml` document, the first node would correspond to the mandatory processing instruction in the very first line of the document. It is the second node that corresponds to the root of the parse tree. The

(B) — which, precisely speaking, is the root node of the DOM tree — is of type `Node`; this is the base class for all the components in an XML document.

We then define the function `print_node_info()` in lines (E) through (c) of the script. This function is called on the root node in line (d); subsequently the function calls itself recursively in line (c) on the child nodes.[66]

The class `Node` that is used to represent each node of the DOM tree defines a large number of methods for retrieving all of the information stored at the nodes. This information can range from the name of the node if the node is an element, its type, the child nodes, if any, etc. In the script below, we extract different things at a node depending on its type. A node can be of the following types in the DOM API:

```
ELEMENT_NODE
ATTRIBUTE_NODE
TEXT_NODE
CDATA_SECTION_NODE
ENTITY_NODE
PROCESSING_INSTRUCTION_NODE
COMMENT_NODE
DOCUMENT_NODE
DOCUMENT_TYPE_NODE
NOTATION_NODE
```

The script shown below looks for only three types of nodes: the type `ELEMENT_NODE` in lines (H) through (S), the type `TEXT_NODE` in lines (T) through (V), and the type `CDATA_SECTION_NODE` in lines (W), (X), and (Y). The type of a node in the DOM tree is determined from its `nodeType` attribute, as shown in lines (H), (T), and (W). For the nodes that represent elements, we extract the various name-related properties in lines (I) through (L). Lines (M), (N), and (O) take care of the fact that for a majority of XML documents an XML element at the bottom of the parse tree contains character data.[67] In the DOM tree itself, this text will appear as a child node of type `TEXT_NODE`. In lines (M) through (O) we extract this string data by querying the `data` attribute of the first child of the element under consideration. We also check in line (P) whether an element type node has any attributes associated with it. In lines (Q), (R), and (S), we then process the attribute-value pairs. In lines (T) through (Y) we extract the character data stored in nodes of types `TEXT_NODE` and `CDATA_SECTION_NODE`. Note that we store all of the nodes that we have already examined in a set declared

---

DOM API requires that the root node of the parse tree be stored in the `documentElement` attribute of the `Document` instance returned by `parse()`.

[66]The `Document` type in the DOM API supports many useful methods such as `getElementsByTagName()`, `getElementsByTagNameNS()`, `createElement()`, `createElementNS()`, `createAttribute()`, etc. When a method name ends in `NS`, that means that the method can carry out a namespace-based operation.

[67]The DOM API requires all the character data to be stored in Unicode. This fact becomes especially important when comparing string values. Let's say that we have deposited a string value retrieved from the DOM tree in a variable `x` and we want to know if it equals `trillian`, we would need to execute the conditional `x == u"trillian"`. Note the `u` prefix for the string literal.

in line (D). Before a node is examined, we make sure in line (F) that it is not one of the previously opened nodes. This is just for convenience in the execution flow in the script, necessitated by the fact that a child node is accessed at different locations: first in lines (M) through (O) if the child is a text node and then again through the recursive call in lines (Z) through (c).

```
#!/usr/bin/env python

### MinidomParse.py

import xml.dom.minidom
import sys

if len( sys.argv ) is not 2:
    sys.exit( "need an xml file to parse" )
xmldoc = sys.argv[1]

dom = xml.dom.minidom.parse( xmldoc )                                #(A)
rootNode = dom.documentElement                                       #(B)
print rootNode                 #<DOM Element: NS1:A at 0x4035b56c>   #(C)

nodeset = set([])                                                    #(D)

def print_node_info( node, offset ):                                 #(E)
    print
    if node not in nodeset:                                          #(F)
        nodeset.add( node )                                          #(G)
        if node.nodeType == node.ELEMENT_NODE:                       #(H)
            print offset, "node name: ", node.nodeName               #(I)
            print offset, "node local name: ", node.localName        #(J)
            print offset, "node name prefix: ", node.prefix          #(K)
            print offset, "namespace URI: ", node.namespaceURI       #(L)
            try:
                if node.firstChild.data:                             #(M)
                    nodeset.add( node.firstChild )                   #(N)
                    print offset, "node data: ",node.firstChild.data#(O)
            except: pass
            if node.hasAttributes():                                 #(P)
                print offset, "Attributes: "                         #(Q)
                for item in node.attributes.items():                 #(R)
                    print offset, "  ", item[0], "  ", item[1]       #(S)
        elif node.nodeType == node.TEXT_NODE:                        #(T)
            if node.data.lstrip().rstrip():                          #(U)
                print offset, "purely text node: ", \
                      node.data.lstrip().rstrip()                    #(V)
                print
```

```
        elif node.nodeType == node.CDATA_SECTION_NODE:                   #(W)
            print offset, "CDATA Section Node: "                         #(X)
            print offset, node.data                                      #(Y)
        if node.hasChildNodes():                                         #(Z)
            offset += "    "                                             #(a)
            for node in node.childNodes:                                 #(b)
                print_node_info( node, offset )                          #(c)

print_node_info( rootNode, "" )                                          #(d)
```

The output produced by this script on the `test9.xml` document shown earlier is as follows:

```
<DOM Element: NS1:A at 0x4035b56c>

 node name:  NS1:A
 node local name:  A
 node name prefix:  NS1
 namespace URI:  http://www.mywebsite.com/NS1names/
 node data:

 Attributes:
    xmlns:NS2     http://www.mywebsite.com/NS2names/
    xmlns:NS1     http://www.mywebsite.com/NS1names/
    xmlns    http://www.mywebsite.com/NS3names/

    node name:  NS1:B
    node local name:  B
    node name prefix:  NS1
    namespace URI:  http://www.mywebsite.com/NS1names/
    node data:  hellojellomello
    Attributes:
       y    jello
       NS1:x    hello
       NS2:z    mello

    node name:  C
    node local name:  C
    node name prefix:  None
    namespace URI:  http://www.mywebsite.com/NS3names/
    Attributes:
       w    cello

    node name:  AAA
    node local name:  AAA
```

```
node name prefix:  None
namespace URI:  http://www.mywebsite.com/NS3names/
node data:   aaa

purely text node:  abc123xyz

node name:  BBB
node local name:  BBB
node name prefix:  None
namespace URI:  http://www.mywebsite.com/NS3names/
node data:   bbb

node name:  CCC
node local name:  CCC
node name prefix:  None
namespace URI:  http://www.mywebsite.com/NS3names/
node data:

   CDATA Section Node:
    <?xml version=''1.0''?>
      <!DOCTYPE greeting SYSTEM ''hello.dtd''>
      <greeting>Hello, world!</greeting>
```

Our next script shows a more common use of DOM parsing. Let's say that we construct a DOM parse tree of the `Phonebook.xml` document shown earlier in Section 17.2. We now want to construct from the DOM tree a telephone directory with the more usual "flat-file" display in which each line starts with the last name that is followed by the first name and followed, finally, by the phone number. The following script does the job; it produces the phonebook display shown immediately after the `Phonebook.xml` document in Section 17.2. The script invokes the `getElementsByTagName()` in line (C) to construct a list of all the `listing` nodes in the document. It then loops through this list as shown in line (D). For each `listing` node, we first retrieve the `last` element that stores the last name as its data. Then we retrieve the first name, and, finally, the phone number using the same syntax.

```
#!/usr/bin/env python

### PhonebookDomParser.py

import xml.dom.minidom

dom = xml.dom.minidom.parse( 'Phonebook.xml' )                          #(A)
rootNode = dom.documentElement                                          #(B)
```

```
listings = rootNode.getElementsByTagName( 'listing' )                #(C)

for listing in listings:                                             #(D)
  lastName = listing.getElementsByTagName('last')[0].childNodes[0].data
  firstName =listing.getElementsByTagName('first')[0].childNodes[0].data
  phone = listing.getElementsByTagName('phone')[0].childNodes[0].data
  print "      %-10s %-10s\t%15s" % (lastName, firstName, phone)
```

17.8 XML FOR WEB SERVICES

As mentioned at the beginning of this chapter, web services are based on the notion that one machine can call a procedure implemented in another machine in a network and receive the results of the procedure call. We will refer to the former machine as a *client* and the latter machine as a *service provider*. Perhaps the most straightforward example of such a remote procedure call (RPC) would be a client asking the service provider to execute a function and to then send the results back. However, a remote procedure call (RPC) could also consist of a client querying a specific cell in a database table accessible to the service provider, launching a script on the service provider's machine, etc.

The concept of a web service requires that a remote procedure call work regardless of what operating systems and languages are used on the client's machine and the service provider's machine. For such interoperability to work over disparate platforms, you need a *lingua franca* for messaging and a set of conventions for the naming of the procedures that can be called, for supplying the arguments to the procedures, for declaring the data types in the arguments, and so on.[68] As we now know, the *lingua franca* today is XML. As for the conventions, we have two protocols, the SOAP protocol and its simpler cousin, the XML-RPC protocol. We will explore both of these protocols in the several subsections that follow.

17.8.1 XML-RPC for Remote Procedure Calls

XML-RPC is a protocol for:

- Translating a procedure call and its arguments into an XML message
- Packaging the XML message into an HTTP/1.0 POST request

[68] And, of course, you need a transport — HTTP in most cases — for carrying the messages.

- Unpackaging the received response to retrieve the result of the remote procedure call

As we mentioned in the introduction to this chapter, translating a procedure call and its arguments into an XML message is referred to as *serialization* or *marshalling* of the procedure call. And the unpackaging of the received response to retrieve the results as *deserialization* or *unmarshalling* of the response.

XML-RPC uses the root element `methodCall` and, within the root element, the element `methodName`, for the XML representation of the remote procedure call. To see the roles played by these two elements, let's say a server in a network provides a service that consists of a client being able to call the following function at the server and the server then sending back the results from this function call:

```
sub sumAndDifference {
    my ($x, $y) = @_;
    return {'sum' => $x + $y, 'difference' => $x - $y};
}
```

A call to this function if made locally in the server machine would look like

```
sumAndDifferent(5, 3);
```

This call, consisting of the name of the function, followed by its two arguments, 5 and 3, would be encapsulated under XML-RPC into a root element of type `methodCall`:

```
<methodCall>
    <methodName>sumAndDifference</methodName>
    <params>
        <param><value><i4>5</i4></value></param>
        <param><value><i4>3</i4></value></param>
    </params>
</methodCall>
```

Note that the name of the function is contained in the `methodName` element[69] and all the arguments are supplied through the `params` element. Note particularly the syntax for marshalling one argument:

```
<param><value><i4>5</i4></value></param>
```

The actual value of the argument is contained in the `value` element but is enclosed by the element type `i4` in this case. The tag `i4` stands for a 4-byte integer. In general, a `value` element can contain as a subelement any value-type tag shown in the first column of Table 17.2. As indicated by the last row of the table, it is possible for a

[69]The characters in the name of the remote procedure in the `methodName` element can only be the letters A through Z and a through z, the digits 0 through 9, the underscore, the dot, the colon, and the forward slash. This allows a procedure name to start with a directory pathname. This choice of characters also permits a remote procedure call to be a request to fetch the contents of a cell from a database table.

value element to directly contain a value without enclosing it in a nested value-type subelement. When that is done, the value type is considered to be string.[70]

Tagname for Declaring Value Type	*Description*	*Example of Actual Value*
i4 or int	a four-byte signed integer	-2345
double	signed double-precision floating point number	-234.678
boolean	0 for false 1 for true	1
string	sequence of characters	hello world
dateTime.iso8601	date and/or time	20050504T13:24:28
base64	a base64 encoded object	Aasbe763wRWswlsd==
struct	a structure containing name-value pairs	see text
array	a sequence of values	see text
no declaration	string	

Table 17.2

As indicated by Table 17.2, XML-RPC allows for hierarchical data structures to be specified for the arguments in remote procedure calls. For example, if the value for an argument is best described as a structure of name-value pairs, then what you need in the value element is a struct subelement like the one in the following example:[71]

[70] A string can contain any character except for the following two: < and &. However, these two may be represented by their entity references < and &. Additionally, for a double, only the decimal point notation is allowed.

[71] The order in which the name-value pairs show up in a struct is not important. In other words, two structs if they contain the same name-value pairs regardless of the order are equivalent.

```
<struct>
    <member>
        <name>speed</name>
        <value><i4>22</i4></value>
    </member>
    <member>
        <name>accelaration</name>
        <value><double>3.8</double></value>
    </member>
</struct>
```

For representing a linear array-like sequence of data items, a `value` element can also contain an `array` subelement like the following:

```
<array>
    <data>
        <value><string>hello</string></value>
        <value>jello></value>
        <value><int>1234</int></value>
        <value><boolean>0</boolean></value>
    </data>
</array>
```

Note that all of the individual items of the array are contained in a single subelement, `data`. The value of each array item is contained in a `value` subelement of the `data` element. The array itself has no name.

To illustrate an example of an array in an XML-RPC encoding of a function call, the encoding we showed earlier for the call to `sumAndDifference()` could also be expressed in the following form that uses an array:

```
<methodCall>
    <methodName>sumAndDifference</methodName>
    <params>
        <param>
            <value>
                <array>
                    <data>
                        <value><i4>5</i4></value>
                        <value><i4>3</i4></value>
                    </data>
                </array>
            </value>
        </param>
    </params>
</methodCall>
```

Now the arguments 5 and 3 needed by the `sumAndDifference()` function would be sent to the remote server in the form of a single array consisting of two items. Of course, for this to work, you'd need to slightly alter the implementation code for the `sumAndDifference()` function at the web service provider:

```
sub sumAndDifference {
    my $arrayref = shift;
    my ($x, $y) = @$arrayref;
    return {'sum' => $x + $y, 'difference' => $x - $y};
}
```

Note that the array will be received by the `sumAndDifference()` function at the server in the form of a reference.

17.8.2 XML-RPC in Perl

The next script, `XmlRpcProtoLevelClient.pl`, is a working example of an XML-RPC client making a remote procedure call to the function `sumAndDifference()` at a service provider elsewhere in the network. This script uses `LWP::UserAgent`[72] and its associated Perl modules for providing HTTP transport for the messages between the client and the server. We will refer to this client as *a protocol-level encoded client*, since the client makes explicit the XML-RPC encoding of the function call. This encoding will be carried out manually. In other words, we will manually synthesize an XML-RPC payload for the HTTP request object. (Subsequently, we will show a much easier way to carry out both steps.)

In line (B) of the script, we manually construct the XML-RPC encoding for the function call by using the "here doc" facility of Perl that was explained in Section 2.10 of Chapter 2. Line (E) of the script then constructs an `HTTP::Request` object for a `POST` request.[73] Line (F) sets the mandatory header `content_type` of

---

[72]The module namespace prefix `LWP` stands for the Perl *Library for World Wide Web Programming*. To see if you already have the `LWP` modules installed, enter the following in a command line:

```
perl -MLWP -le "print( LWP->VERSION)"
```

If not already there, you can install the `libwww-perl` distribution from `www.cpan.org`. In addition to the main three modules, `LWP::UserAgent`, `HTTP::Request`, and `HTTP::Response`, this distribution contains roughly 100 other modules, most of them needed for doing behind-the-scenes work as your LWP-based script interacts with the web. (See the LWP manual or Appendix A of [4] for a listing of these modules.) The main job of managing an Internet connection is the responsibility of the `LWP::UserAgent` module that acts like a *virtual browser* vis-à-vis an HTTP server. This module brings together the following three important classes: `HTTP::Request`, `HTTP::Response`, and `LWP::Protocol`. The basic notion in using the `LWP::UserAgent` class is that you supply one of its `request()` methods with an `HTTP::Request` object that is configured appropriately with regard to the *method* to be used in the request (whether GET, or POST, or HEAD, etc.), the URL of the web server, the various mandatory and optional request headers, and so on. The `UserAgent` instance dispatches the request using the relevant protocol. If the web server returns a reply, the call to `UserAgent's request()` returns an `HTTP::Response` object. Subsequently, one can extract from the `HTTP::Response` object the actual reply sent by the server.

[73]Of the several "methods" defined by the HTTP standard to characterize the various forms of request that a client can make on a server, the most common are `GET` and `POST`. The difference between the two is

the request object. In line (G), we insert our XML-RPC message payload into the request. The `LWP::UserAgent` instance constructed in line (H) with default settings dispatches the request to the web service provider. The call in line (H) returns an `HTTP::Response` object, whose payload we extract and print out in line (I). The XML-RPC payload of the response is always encapsulated in a `methodResponse` root element. For the example being presented, the response payload is

```
<?xml version=''1.0''?>
<methodResponse>
 <params>
  <param>
   <value>
    <struct>
     <member><name>difference</name><value><i4>2</i4></value></member>
     <member><name>sum</name><value><i4>8</i4></value></member>
    </struct>
   </value>
  </param>
 </params>
</methodResponse>
```

Note that the structure of the `methodResponse` root element is identical to the `methodCall` root element of the XML-RPC request except for the missing `methodName` element. Also note the use of the XML-RPC data type `struct` for the key-value pairs returned by the RPC call. The syntax of the `struct` element is as explained before.

Lines (J), (K), and (L) of the client script are useful for the case when the web service provider sends back an error response.[74] In case of error, the XML-RPC server returns a `methodResponse` root element that consists of a `fault` subelement.[75] The actual error response consists of a `struct` with two name-value members, one for the `errorcode` name and the other for the `faultString` name. Here is an example of the response received when the `methodName` element's content is

---

that, with the former, any information in the form of `key=value` pairs is encoded within the URL itself, whereas with the latter, each `key=value` pair occupies a separate line in the body of the HTTP request. To clarify, recall that in general, an an HTTP or an FTP type of URL has the following syntax:

```
scheme://username@serverAddress:port/pathToFile?queryString
```

where the first part, `scheme`, would be either HTTP or FTP. In a GET request, all the `key=value` pairs needed to be sent to the server are encoded within the `queryString` by substituting `+` for each blank space, by inserting a `&` between the successive `key=value` pairs, and by subsequently URL encoding the query string (see Homework section of Chapter 4 for what is meant by URL encoding). On the other hand, the `key=value` pairs of a `POST` request are placed in separate lines in the body of the HTTP request.

[74]An HTTP *response* falls into one of the following four categories: *informational*, *successful*, *redirection*, and *error*.

[75]A `methodResponse` element *must* contain either a `params` subelement or a `fault` subelement as its immediate descendant, the former if the call was successful and the latter if not.

"erroneously" entered as `sumAndDiff` as opposed to `sumAndDifference` in the outgoing RPC request:

```
<?xml version=''1.0''?>
<methodResponse>
 <fault>
  <value>
   <struct>
    <member>
     <name>faultString</name>
     <value><string>no such method 'sumAndDiff'</string></value>
    </member>
    <member>
     <name>faultCode</name>
     <value><i4>3</i4></value>
    </member>
   </struct>
  </value>
 </fault>
</methodResponse>
```

As the reader can see, the `faultString` element contains a helpful message as to the reason for the error response. Pattern matching in line (J) of the script looks for this element and its contents so that the error message can be printed out. Note the `//s` match modifier in line (J). This is to enable the extraction of the fault string even when it is in multiple lines. As explained in Chapter 4, this match modifier allows the dot metacharacter in a regex to also eat up any newline characters in the content of the `faultString` element.

When a call to the server is successful, the pattern match with the multiline regex in lines (M) through (R) extracts the answer from the XML object returned by the server.[76] The regex shown contains two extracting parentheses and two nonextracting parentheses. The two extracting parentheses extract the name of a parameter and the corresponding value, and the global `//g` modifier in line (R) extracts all such name-value pairs from the XML response. For the example shown, the response extracted in this manner is

```
difference 2 sum 8
```

this being printed out by line (S) of the script.

---

[76]As mentioned in Chapter 4, the `//x` modifier shown in line (R) allows a regex to be written in multiple lines and with comments to be placed in each line.

```
#!/usr/bin/perl -w

### XmlRpcProtoLevelClient.pl

use strict;
use LWP::UserAgent;                                                    #(A)

# The payload:
my $msg =<< "EOT";                                                     #(B)
<?xml version="1.0"?>
<methodCall>
    <methodName>sumAndDifference</methodName>
    <params>
        <param><value><i4>5</i4></value></param>
        <param><value><i4>3</i4></value></param>
    </params>
</methodCall>
EOT

my $uri = 'http://128.46.144.238:8080/RPC2';                           #(C)
#my $uri = "http://localhost:8080/RPC2";                               #(D)
my $request = HTTP::Request->new( POST => $uri );                      #(E)
$request->content_type( "text/xml" );                                  #(F)
$request->content( $msg );                                             #(G)

# The $response object below is of type HTTP::Response
my $response = LWP::UserAgent->new->request( $request );               #(H)
print $response->content . "\n";                                       #(I)

if ($response->content =~ /<faultstring.*>(.*)<\/faultstring>/s) {     #(J)
    print $1;                                                          #(K)
    die;                                                               #(L)
}

my @result = $response->content =~ /<name>(.*?)<\/name>                #(M)
                                    <value>                            #(N)
                                    (?:<.*?>)?                         #(O)
                                    ([^<>]*?)                          #(P)
                                    (?:<.*?>)?                         #(Q)
                                    <\/value>/xsg;                     #(R)
print "@result\n";                                                     #(S)
```

The purpose of the XML-RPC client we showed in the above script was to demonstrate the basic features of how a client makes a remote procedure call on an XML-RPC web-service provider. But, obviously, having to directly encode a method call with many arguments into an XML-RPC payload for an HTTP request would be much too burdensome. So, for actual work with XML-RPC, it is much more efficient to use a module that does the payload packaging work you. Shown next is a script[77] that uses the `Frontier::Client` module for setting up an XML-RPC client. After you construct an instance of the client, as in line (D) of the next script, calling a procedure on a remote server is as simple as what is shown in line (K). When the arguments to be supplied for the remote procedure call are simple and straightforward — meaning that when what looks like an integer is actually an integer and not a string and so on — the syntax in line (K) can be further simplified to

```
my $result = $client->call( 'sumAndDifference', 5, 3 );
```

However, if you want to enforce the XML-RPC data types on the arguments, it is best to first call the appropriately named `Frontier::Client` methods — methods with names like `int()`, `base64()`, and so on — for packaging the arguments, as we have done in lines (H) and (J) of the script. When XML-RPC encoding is enforced, as in lines (H) and (J) of the script, what gets supplied to the `call()` method in line (K) are the references to `Frontier::RPC2` objects.[78] This is demonstrated in line (I) by displaying the `Frontier::Client`'s construction of the first argument.[79]

The result of function execution on the remote machine can be obtained through key-indexed accesses into the response hash returned by the RPC call in line (K). Lines (L), (M), and (N) show us retrieving and then displaying the `sum` and the `difference` portions of the returned answer.

```
#!/usr/bin/perl -w

### XmlRpcDaemonServerClient.pl

use Frontier::Client;                                                  #(A)
use strict;                                                            #(B)

my $server_url = 'http://128.46.144.238:8080/RPC2';                    #(C)
#my $server_url = 'http://localhost:8080/RPC2';
```

---

[77]The name of the script, `XmlRpcDaemonServerClient.pl`, is supposed to convey the fact that this client is meant for a *daemon server*, as opposed to, say, a CGI-based server. Section 17.8.4 presents CGI-based clients and servers for XML-RPC. By the way, the previous client script, `XmlRpcProtoLevelClient.pl` is also meant for a daemon server. We will show a daemon server at the end of this section.

[78]`Frontier::Client` uses the `Frontier::RPC2` class for coding and decoding XML-RPC calls.

[79]The call to the `Frontier::Client` constructor in line (D) constructs a generic `LWP::UserAgent` instance. Invoking `call()` in line (K) then supplies the instance with its payload — an appropriately configured `HTTP::Request` object. Upon receiving the payload, the `LWP::UserAgent` instance dispatches the request to the HTTP server.

```
my $client = Frontier::Client->new(                                    #(D)
                                   url => $server_url,                 #(E)
#                                  debug => 1                          #(F)
                                  );                                   #(G)
my $arg1 = $client->int(5);                                            #(H)
print "$arg1\n";      # Frontier::RPC2::Integer=SCALAR(0x817480c)      #(I)
my $arg2 = $client->int(3);                                            #(J)
my $result = $client->call( 'sumAndDifference', $arg1, $arg2 );        #(K)

my $sum = $result->{'sum'};                                            #(L)
my $difference = $result->{'difference'};                              #(M)
print "Sum: $sum, Difference: $difference\n";                          #(N)

my $arg = $client->string( "Trillian" );                               #(O)
print "$arg\n";       # Frontier::RPC2::String=SCALAR(0x82805ec)       #(P)
$result = $client->call( 'sayHello', $arg );                           #(Q)
print "$result\n";                                                     #(R)
```

The above script also shows a call to a second method, `sayHello()`, on the remote server. For this call, we first construct an XML-RPC string object in line (O) and then feed it to the RPC call in line (Q). The server's definition of the `sayHello()` method is

```
sub sayHello {
    my $sender = shift;
    return "Hello to $sender from an XML-RPC daemon server\n";
}
```

We used the following `Frontier::Daemon` server[80] for both the client examples shown in this subsection. `Frontier::Daemon` is derived from `HTTP::Daemon` and that makes it an HTTP/1.1 server. To program the web services procedures into the HTTP server, we first construct an anonymous hash in line (F). The keys in this hash are the function names that can be used by RPC clients for remote procedure calls and their values the references to the implementation code. Subsequently, we supply this hash as a value for the `methods` parameter to the `Frontier::Daemon` constructor in line (G).[81]

[80]The XML-RPC server shown is a *daemon* server, in the sense that it is a stand-alone server, as opposed to a server that rides piggyback on, say, the Apache web server.

[81]In keeping with the XML-RPC specifications, `Frontier::Daemon` only accepts `POST` requests and insists that the pathname portion of a request URL must terminate in the `POST` request handler `/RPC2`. If these conditions are not fulfilled, the `Frontier::Daemon` sends back a 403 error response (which corresponds to "access forbidden").

```
#!/usr/bin/perl

### XmlRpcDaemonServer.pl

use Frontier::Daemon;                                                       #(A)

sub sumAndDifference {                                                      #(B)
    my ($x, $y) = @_;                                                       #(C)
    return {'sum' => $x + $y, 'difference' => $x - $y};                     #(D)
}

sub sayHello {                                                              #(E)
    my $sender = shift;
    return "Hello to $sender from an XML-RPC daemon server\n";
}

$methods = {'sumAndDifference' => \&sumAndDifference,
            'sayHello'         => \&sayHello,
           };                                                               #(F)

# From local host, call me at http://localhost:8080/RPC2
# From a remote host, call me at http://128.46.144.238:8080/RPC2
Frontier::Daemon->new( LocalPort => 8080,
                       methods => $methods,
                     )
    or die "Couldn't start HTTP server: $!";                                #(G)
```

17.8.3 XML-RPC in Python

Our first Python implementation, `XmlRpcProtoLevelClient.py`, will parallel the first Perl client script for XML-RPC. Like its Perl counterpart, the Python script, shown next, is a protocol-level encoding of a client, since it makes explicit at the protocol level the XML-RPC encoding of the function calls. As with the Perl script, we will manually synthesize the XML-RPC payload for the HTTP request object. Line (D) of the script puts together the XML-RPC payload for the invocation of `sumAndDifference()` at the server.

The client side HTTP transport services in Python are provided by the `httplib` module imported in line (A). This module consists of two classes, `HTTPConnection` and `HTTPResponse`. In line (G), we set the debug level to 1 for the `HTTPConnection` class. This allows the HTTP message sent to the server and its various headers to be displayed on the client's terminal, which can be useful when debugging HTTP-related syntax in the code. Line (H) constructs an HTTP connection object in the `idle` state. The call to `putRequest()` in line (I) causes the connection object to transition to the `request-started` state, meaning that the HTTP client has commenced sending the request to the server. Lines (J) through (M) send the various headers to the HTTP server in accordance with the HTTP 1.1 protocol. The end of the headers is marked with the call to `endheaders()` in line (N), which sends a blank line to the server. Subsequently, the XML-RPC payload synthesized earlier in line (D) is sent to the server in line (O) as the body of the HTTP request. At this point, the connection object is in the `unread-response` state.

Line (P) fetches the response in the form of an `HTTPResponse` object. After we get hold of the response object, the first thing we check for is the HTTP status code of the received response. For example, if the handler named in line (F) is no longer available at the server, the server will send back a response with the status code of 403, which stands for a client trying to access a "forbidden" resource at the server. A status code of 200 means that the request was successfully processed by the HTTP server. But note that the status code of 200 does not necessarily mean that the remote procedure call worked successfully. To illustrate, suppose the client makes an error in the XML encapsulation of the remote procedure call, the XML-RPC server will return an error message that will be forwarded by the HTTP server to the client with a status code of 200. As far as the HTTP server is concerned, that is a successful request-response interaction, although it is not successful from the standpoint of getting the desired result from the XML-RPC server.

Next comes the task of figuring out if the response sent back by the web service provider contains an error message, indicating that the remote procedure call was not successful. The regular expression we devise in line (T) is meant to extract the `fault` element if it is present in the response. If such an element is found, then in the statement that ends in line (Y) we devise a more elaborate regex to extract the values associated with the `faultString` and the `faultCode` elements of the `struct` element of the response.[82] Lines (a) through (d) then print out these values.

In the absence of an XML-RPC error report, the XML-RPC call was successful. The regex we devise in lines (f) through (l) pulls out the different parts of the response. The nature of this regex obviously depends on us knowing the structure of the response for successful invocations of the remote method.

[82]See the XML packaging of the XML-RPC error response in the Perl discussion in the previous subsection.

```
#!/usr/bin/env python

### XmlRpcProtoLevelClient.py

import httplib                                                          #(A)
import re                                                               #(B)
import sys                                                              #(C)

msg = """\
<?xml version="1.0"?>
<methodCall>
    <methodName>sumAndDifference1</methodName>
    <params>
        <param><value><i4>5</i4></value></param>
        <param><value><i4>3</i4></value></param>
    </params>
</methodCall>
"""                                                                     #(D)
host = "128.46.144.238:8080"                                            #(E)
handler = "/RPC2"                                                       #(F)

#httplib.HTTPConnection.debuglevel = 1                                  #(G)

# send request:
conn = httplib.HTTPConnection( host )                                   #(H)
conn.putrequest( "POST", handler )                                      #(I)
conn.putheader( "User-Agent", "element-xmlrpc" )                        #(J)
conn.putheader( "Host", host )                                          #(K)
conn.putheader( "Content-Type", "text/xml" )                            #(L)
conn.putheader( "Content-Length", str( len(msg) ) )                     #(M)
conn.endheaders()    # send a blank line to signify end of headers     #(N)
conn.send(msg)       # send body of message, end with two blank lines#(O)

# get response:
# getresponse() returns an HTTPResponse object:
response = conn.getresponse()                                           #(P)
if response.status != 200:                                              #(Q)
    raise Exception(response.reason, response.status)

# get resonse body:
response_content =  response.read()                                     #(R)
#print response_content                                                 #(S)

# check if the respose contains a fault report:
regex1 = re.compile( r'<fault>(.*)<\/fault>', \
                     re.MULTILINE | re.DOTALL )                         #(T)
m = regex1.search( response_content )                                   #(U)
```

```
if m is not None:                                                    #(V)
    regex2 = re.compile( r'''faultCode.*<value><.*?>
                             ([^<>]*)            # get fault string #(W)
                             <.*></value>.*
                             faultString.*<value><.*?>
                             ([^<>]*)            # get fault code   #(X)
                             <.*></value>.*''',
                           re.VERBOSE | re.DOTALL )                  #(Y)
    m_fault = regex2.search( m.group(1) )                            #(Z)
    if m_fault is not None:                                          #(a)
        faultCode = m_fault.group(1).rstrip()                        #(b)
        faultString = m_fault.group(2).rstrip()                      #(c)
        print "XML-RPC request failed: %s; faultCode: %s" % \
              (faultString, faultCode)                               #(d)
    sys.exit(1)                                                      #(e)

# extract the results:
regex3 = re.compile( r'''<name>(.*?)<\/name>                        #(f)
                         <value>                                     #(g)
                         (?:<.*?>)?                                  #(h)
                         ([^<>]*?)                                   #(i)
                         (?:<.*?>)?                                  #(j)
                         <\/value>''',                               #(k)
                     re.VERBOSE | re.DOTALL )                        #(l)

result = regex3.findall( response_content.replace('\n', '' ) )       #(m)
print result              # [('sum', '8'), ('difference', '2')]      #(n)
```

As was the case with the first Perl XML-RPC script of the previous subsection, the above script is obviously not the way to go if you are making remote procedure calls that require many arguments. It would be much too onerous to hand-craft the XML-RPC payloads for those cases. The next script[83] leaves all of that work to the `xmlrpclib` module that comes with the standard Python distribution. This module provides a class, `ServerProxy`, whose instance can serve as a local proxy for the remote XML-RPC server. Each function provided by the server for remote invocation becomes an attribute of the proxy server object on the client side. This is demonstrated by lines (C) through (H) in the next script. In our case, the server provides the function `sumAndDifference()` for remote invocation; so calling `sumAndDifference` on the proxy server in line (H) returns a local stub for this

[83]The name of the script, `XmlRpcDaemonServerClient.py`, is meant to convey the fact that this client is meant for a daemon server, as opposed to, say, a CGI-based server. We will show a daemon server in Python at the end of this section. The CGI-based XML-RPC clients and servers in Python are presented in Section 17.8.5. By the way, the previous client, `XmlRpcProtoLevelClient.py`, is also meant for a daemon server.

remote function. We can then call this stub with arguments as shown in line (I). We can also use the syntax shown in line (K) that creates a convenient illusion that the remote function is being called directly with the arguments (as if we were making a local function call). The call in line (K) works because, as the reader will see later, the remote server for the example being presented also supports the function `sayHello()` for remote invocation.[84]

When a remote procedure call succeeds, `xmlrpclib` also unmarshals the returned result object for us. This makes it possible to directly print out the results, as shown in line (J) and the commented-out line just below line (K). When a remote procedure call fails, it may either be because of problems with the HTTP transport or because the XML-RPC server did not like what it received. As already mentioned, transport-level failures can be detected by examining the HTTP status code of the response object. In our script, this is accomplished by the statements in lines (L) and (M) where we refer to such errors as the protocol-related errors. An example of such an error would be if we named the handler something other than `/RPC2` in line (C). That would result in the HTTP server returning a status code of 403 that stands for forbidden. Receipt of this status code would cause `ServerProxy` to throw the `ProtocolError` exception that we trap in line (L). Assuming that there are no protocol-related errors (that is, the HTTP status code returned by the server is 200), the next possible source of problems is with the processing of the XML-RPC request by the XML-RPC server. If the XML-RPC server does not like the remote procedure invocation, it will return a fault string and a fault code. When these are seen by the proxy server on the client side, it raises the `Fault` exception that we trap in line (N). In our case, this will happen if suppose we enter `SumDiff` for the name of the remote function on the right-hand side in line (H). We trap all other errors by the `except` clause in line (P). This is where the error would be trapped if, say, the client were to try to reach the server on a nonexistent port.

```
#!/usr/bin/env python

### XmlRpcDaemonServerClient.py

import xmlrpclib                                                     #(A)

try:                                                                 #(B)
    server_url = 'http://128.46.144.238:8080/RPC2'                   #(C)
    server = xmlrpclib.ServerProxy( server_url )                     #(D)
    print server                                                     #(E)

#   print server.system.listMethods()                                #(F)
#   print server.system.methodSignature( 'sumAndDifference' )        #(G)
```

[84]By default, the proxy server instance constructed in line (D) uses UTF-8 encoding for outgoing requests. However, that can be changed by supplying the encoding used as an argument to the `ServerProxy` constructor in line (D).

```
    sumAndDiff = server.sumAndDifference                                   #(H)
    result = sumAndDiff( 5, 3 )                                            #(I)
    print result                  # {'sum': 8, 'difference': 2}           #(J)

    print server.sayHello( "Trillian" )                                    #(K)
                # Hello to Trillian from an XML-RPC daemon server

except xmlrpclib.ProtocolError, e:                                         #(L)
    print "Protocol Error: ", e                                            #(M)
except xmlrpclib.Fault, e:                                                 #(N)
    print "XML-RPC Fault: ", e                                             #(O)
except Exception, e:                                                       #(P)
    print "Error: ", e                                                     #(Q)
```

The above script also includes two commented-out statements that would work with those XML-RPC servers that support the XML Introspection API. This API allows the following methods to be invoked by a client: `system.listMethods()` that returns a list of function names available for remote invocation at the XML-RPC server; `system.methodSignature(name)` that returns an array whose first element is the return type from the function named in the argument and whose other elements are the parameter types for the function call; and `system.methodHelp(name)` that returns the documentation string associated with the remote function named in the argument.

The two Python XML-RPC client scripts we have shown so far in this section can be used with the Perl XML-RPC daemon server presented at the end of Section 17.8.2. If you also wanted the server to be in Python, the next script would do the job. This script uses the `SimpleXMLRPCServer` module for a stand-alone XML-RPC daemon server whose transport capability is provided by the `SocketServer.TCPServer` class. By default, all HTTP requests received by the daemon server are handled by an instance of `SimpleXMLRPCRequestHandler` that is automatically created when an instance of `SimpleXMLRPCServer` is constructed.

The script creates an instance of the daemon server in line (F). In lines (G) and (H), we call on the `register_function()` method of the server to register the two methods defined in lines (B) and (D) for remote invocation. The call to `register_introspection_functions()` in line (I) registers with the server the introspection functions mentioned earlier: `system.listMethods()`, `system.methodSignature(name)`, and `system.methodHelp(name)`. Finally, the call to `server_forever()` in line (J) places the call to the request handler in an infinite loop so that the server can act as a daemon server.[85]

[85]The class `SimpleXMLRPCServer` also provides a method called `register_instance()` for registering an instance object with the server. A remote client can then call methods on the registered instance.

```
#!/usr/bin/env python

### XmlRpcDaemonServer.py

import SimpleXMLRPCServer                                           #(A)

def sumAndDifference( arg1, arg2 ):                                 #(B)
    return { 'sum' : arg1 + arg2, 'difference' : arg1 - arg2 }      #(C)

def sayHello( sender ):                                             #(D)
    return "Hello to %s from an XML-RPC daemon server" % sender     #(E)

server = SimpleXMLRPCServer.SimpleXMLRPCServer(('localhost', 8080)) #(F)

server.register_function( sumAndDifference )                        #(G)
server.register_function( sayHello )                                #(H)
server.register_introspection_functions()                           #(I)

server.serve_forever()                                              #(J)
```

17.8.4 CGI-Based XML-RPC Servers and Clients in Perl

We will now present a CGI-based XML-RPC server. Unlike a daemon server, a CGI-based server does not have to be up and running all the time. The "up and running all the time" portion of the work is now done by the web server that hosts the CGI-based XML-RPC server.

The CGI-based server shown next serves out the `SumAndDifference()` and `hello()` methods of the `ACMEWebService` package defined in lines (A) through (H).[86] What specific methods the server doles out is controlled by the anonymous hash supplied to the `process_cgi_call()` function in line (K). That function, defined in lines (L) through (X), first makes sure in lines (N) through (S) that the client request is legal, reads the body of the incoming request in line (U), constructs an instance of the `Frontier::RPC2` class in line (W), invokes the `serve()` method of this class to process the incoming RPC, and then finally asks the `send_xml()` function defined in lines (c) through (g) to send the answer back to the client.

[86] Since the server does not construct an instance of this class, the constructor `new()` we have shown in lines (B) through (E) is superfluous. It is included just to make the served-out class the same as for our SOAP examples to be shown later.

```
#!/usr/bin/perl -Tw
use strict;
$!++;                       # disable buffers associated with std output

### XMLRPC_CGIServerInPerl.cgi

#--------------------------- class ACMEWebService ----------------------
package ACMEWebService;                                           #(A)

sub new {                                                          #(B)
    my $self = shift;                                              #(C)
    my $class = ref($self) || $self;                               #(D)
    bless { _acemwebservice => shift } => $class;                  #(E)
}
sub hello {                                                        #(F)
    return "hello world from the XML-RPC CGI server in Perl";
}
sub bye {                                                          #(G)
    return "goodbye world from the XML-RPC CGI server in Perl";
}
sub sumAndDifference {                                             #(H)
    my ($self, $x, $y) = @_;
    return { "sum" => $x + $y, "difference" => $x - $y };
}

#------------------------------  main  --------------------------------
package main;                                                      #(I)
use Frontier::RPC2;                                                #(J)

process_cgi_call(
      {'ACMEWebService.sumAndDifference' =>
                 \&ACMEWebService::sumAndDifference,
       'ACMEWebService.hello' =>
                 \&ACMEWebService::hello} );                       #(K)

sub process_cgi_call {                                             #(L)
    my ($served_funcs) = @_;                                       #(M)

    my $method = $ENV{ 'REQUEST_METHOD' };                         #(N)
    http_error(405, "Method Not Allowed") unless $method eq "POST"; #(O)

    my $type = $ENV{ 'CONTENT_TYPE' };                             #(P)
    http_error( 400, "Bad Request" ) unless $type eq "text/xml";   #(Q)

    my $length = $ENV{ 'CONTENT_LENGTH' };                         #(R)
    http_error( 411, "Length Required" ) unless $length > 0;       #(S)
```

```
    # Fetch our body
    my $body;                                                    #(T)
    my $count = read STDIN, $body, $length;                      #(U)
    http_error( 400, "Bad Request" ) unless $count == $length;   #(V)

    my $coder = Frontier::RPC2->new;                             #(W)
    send_xml( $coder->serve( $body, $served_funcs ) );           #(X)
}

# Send an HTTP error and exit
sub http_error( $$ ) {                                           #(Y)
    my ($code, $message) = @_;                                   #(Z)
    print << "EOD";                                              #(a)
status: $code $message
Content-type: text/html
<title>$code $message</title>
<h1>$code $message</h1>
<p>Unexpected error processing XML-RPC request.</p>
EOD
    exit 0;                                                      #(b)
}

# Send an XML document (but don't exit)
sub send_xml() {                                                 #(c)
    my ($xml_string) = @_;                                       #(d)
    my $length = length( $xml_string );                          #(e)
    print << "EOD";                                              #(f)
Status: 200 OK
Content-type: text/html
Content-length: $length

EOD
    # We want precise control over whitespace here
    print $xml_string;                                           #(g)
}
```

A CGI-based server is typically placed in the `cgi-bin` directory of a web server. Obviously, the server would only be accessible if a web server providing the HTTP backbone is running continuously on the machine.[87]

Shown below is a `Frontier::Client` that make a call to the server shown above.

[87] If you are using the Apache web server, we should also mention that it is extremely useful to check the `logs/error_log` file if the CGI script is not behaving as expected.

```
#!/usr/bin/perl -w

### XMLRPC_ClientForCGIServer.pl

use Frontier::Client;
use strict;

my $server_url = 'http://localhost/cgi-bin/XMLRPC_CGIServerInPerl.cgi';
                                                                      #(A)
my $server = Frontier::Client->new( url => $server_url );             #(B)
my $result = $server->call('ACMEWebService.sumAndDifference', 5, 3);#(C)
my $sum = $result->{'sum'};                                           #(D)
my $difference = $result->{'difference'};                             #(E)
print "Sum: $sum, Difference: $difference\n";                         #(F)
                                   # Sum: 3, Difference: 3
$result = $server->call('ACMEWebService.hello');                      #(G)
print "$result\n";                                                    #(H)
           # hello world from the XML-RPC CGI server in Perl
```

17.8.5 CGI-Based XML-RPC Servers and Clients in Python

The next script is a CGI-based XML-RPC server in Python. As shown in line (B), we now use the `CGIXMLRPCRequestHandler` class of the `SimpleXMLRPCServer` module to handle the incoming XML-RPC requests. In order to parallel the Perl example of the previous subsection, we again define the methods to be doled out inside a class called `ACMEWebService` in lines (C) through (I). We register an instance of this class with the server in line (J) and do the same for the introspection functions in line (K).[88] As with the Perl CGI server, you'd need to place this script in the `cgi-bin` directory if you are using the Apache HTTP server.

```
#!/usr/bin/env python

### XMLRPC_CGIServerInPython.cgi

import SimpleXMLRPCServer                                             #(A)

handler = SimpleXMLRPCServer.CGIXMLRPCRequestHandler()                #(B)
```

[88] We talked about the XML Introspection API in Section 17.8.3.

```
class ACMEWebService:                                                 #(C)
    def sayHello(self):                                               #(D)
        return "hello world from the Python CGI XML-RPC server"       #(E)
    def bye(self):                                                    #(F)
        return "goodbye world from the Python CGI XML-RPC server"     #(G)
    def sumAndDifference(self, arg1, arg2 ):                          #(H)
        return { 'sum' : arg1 + arg2, 'difference' : arg1 - arg2 }   #(I)

handler.register_instance( ACMEWebService() )                         #(J)
handler.register_introspection_functions()                            #(K)

handler.handle_request()                                              #(L)
```

Shown below is an XML-RPC client that works with the server shown above. Note that although we defined the server methods for remote invocation inside the ACMEWebService, we call them directly on the proxy server instance in lines (C), (D), and (E).[89]

```
#!/usr/bin/env python

### XMLRPC_ClientForCGIServer.py

import xmlrpclib

server_url = 'http://localhost/cgi-bin/XMLRPC_CGIServerInPython.cgi'#(A)
server = xmlrpclib.ServerProxy( server_url )                          #(B)


print server.sumAndDifference( 5, 3 )                                 #(C)
                              # {'sum': 8, 'difference': 2}
print server.sayHello()                                               #(D)
               # hello world from the Python CGI XML-RPC server
print server.bye()                                                    #(E)
               # goodbye world from the Python CGI XML-RPC server
```

[89]If you used this client script with the Perl CGI server XMLRPC_CGIServerInPerl.cgi of the previous subsection, you'd need to modify the statements in lines (C), (D), and (E) by making package-qualified calls to the methods involved. For example, you'd need to replace line (C) by

```
print server.ACMEWebService.sumAndDifference(5, 3)
```

17.8.6 SOAP for Remote Procedure Calls

The simplicity and brevity of XML-RPC are obviously important selling points in its favor. But as an XML-based packaging protocol for RPC, it lacks some important features that are now incorporated in SOAP (Simple Object Access Protocol),[90] the XML-based packaging protocol standardized by W3C. For example, XML-RPC does not allow for named `structs` and named `arrays`. XML-RPC also does not permit namespaces to be used for qualifying the elements and their attributes. SOAP also permits new data types to be defined for information exchange between clients and servers. Additional features of SOAP (that are absent in XML-RPC) include the ability to specify the recipient of a message and ways to include message-specific processing instructions.[91]

The SOAP packaging of a remote procedure call consists of an *envelope root element* containing a *body element*, with the latter encapsulating the payload — meaning the information needed for invoking a remote procedure. Let's say a client wishes to make the remote procedure call

```
SumAndDifference( 5000, 8000 )
```

and that it is known to the client that the function `SumAndDifference()` is defined in a class `ACMEWebService` at the remote server. The SOAP message that the client would need to send to the server would be as follows at its simplest:

```
<SOAP-ENV:Envelope
  xmlns:SOAP-ENV="http://schemas.xmlsoap.org/soap/envelope/"
  xmlns:xsi="http://www.w3.org/1999/XMLSchema-instance"
  xmlns:xsd="http://www.w3.org/1999/XMLSchema">
>
  <SOAP-ENV:Body>
    <service:SumAndDifference xmlns:service="urn:ACMEWebService">
        <arg1 xsi:type="xsd:int">5000</arg1>
        <arg2 xsi:type="xsd:int">8000</arg2>
    </service:SumAndDifference>
  </SOAP-ENV:Body>
</SOAP-ENV:Envelope>
```

[90]SOAP is also sometimes expanded into *Service Oriented Access Protocol.*

[91]Our discussion here related to SOAP focuses solely on its use in RPC (Remote Procedure Call). However, another large application of SOAP is in EDI (Electronic Data Interchange). Some applications of EDI include electronic transmissions of invoices, purchase orders, etc. When SOAP is used for EDI, it is also referred to as "document-style" SOAP, as opposed to the "RPC-style" SOAP we present in this chapter.

Note in particular the start tag of the Envelope element. The name of the element, Envelope, is obviously namespace qualified. The prefix, SOAP-ENV:,[92] must point to one of the following two URIs:[93] [94]

```
http://schemas.xmlsoap.org/soap/envelope/        for SOAP 1.1

http://www.w3.org/2001/06/soap-envelope          for SOAP 1.2
```

The start tag of the Envelope element maps the prefix SOAP-ENV: to the namespace reserved for SOAP 1.1. Also note in the start tag the namespace bindings for the prefixes xsi: and xsd:.[95] These prefixes allows us to declare in the payload (meaning the body) of the SOAP message the data types for the arguments for a remote procedure. For example, the body of the SOAP message shown for invoking SumAndDifference() on a remote server includes the following element:

```
<arg1 xsi:type="xsd:int">5000</arg1>
```

Through this element, a client tells the SOAP server that an argument is being supplied for a procedure hosted by the server and that the type of this argument is an integer as defined in the namespace associated with the prefix xsd:.

Let's now examine more fully the payload of the client-to-server SOAP request for invoking the function SumAndDifference() on the remote server:

```
<SOAP-ENV:Body>
    <service:SumAndDifference xmlns:service="urn:ACMEWebService">
        <arg1 xsi:type="xsd:int">5000</arg1>
        <arg2 xsi:type="xsd:int">8000</arg2>
    </service:SumAndDifference>
</SOAP-ENV:Body>
```

The child subelement of the Body element names the procedure the client wants to invoke at the server. Note that this subelement maps the prefix service: to the namespace in which the server has placed the particular service requested. For the example shown, SumAndDifference() is a method that presumably belongs to the class ACMEWebService at the SOAP server.

---

[92]The prefix SOAP-ENV: is a convenient abbreviation of "SOAP Envelope." One can use any prefix one wants, as long as it points to the correct namespace.

[93]Recall from the discussion in Section 17.3 that URIs (Uniform Resource Indicator) used for namespaces are *not* meant to be resolved in the same sense that the more common URLs are always resolved. A namespace URI merely tells the XML processor how a particular name is to be understood. URNs (Uniform Resource Name) and URLs (Uniform Resource Locator) are subsets of URIs. In other words, a URL is a URI, as is a URN.

[94]The two versions of SOAP, 1.1 and 1.2, are largely the same. Nonetheless, a version 1.1 SOAP processor may have difficulty understanding a version 1.2 SOAP message. By examining the SOAP namespace specified, the recipient of a SOAP message can detect version mismatch.

[95]The namespace prefix xsd: was introduced in the introduction to Section 17.6 and the prefix xsi: in Section 17.6.1.

In general, a SOAP message must consist of exactly one root element that serves as the envelope for the message. It can contain only one body element that contains the payload to be delivered to the RPC server. The body element can consist of any valid XML syntax. A SOAP message is also allowed to contain an optional header element between the start tag of the `Envelope` element and before the `Body` element. Although, in general, the header element can contain any well-formed XML, typically it will consist of an arbitrary number of *header blocks*. Shown below is a header element with a single header block that sets to true the value of the special attribute `mustUnderstand`:

```
<SOAP-ENV:Header>
    <header:transaction xmlns:header="soap-transaction"
                        SOAP-ENV:mustUnderstand="true">
        <transactionID>1234</transactionID>
    </header:transaction>
</SOAP-ENV:Header>
```

When the `mustUnderstand` attribute is set to true in the manner shown, the recipient of the SOAP message must be able to make sense of that header block. If unable to understand the header block, the recipient must reject the entire SOAP message and send an error notification to the sender. When this attribute is absent or when it is set to false, the recipient will simply ignore an incomprehensible header. Header blocks are useful for supplying bookkeeping information relevant to a SOAP message (such as an identification number), authentication credentials, message routing information, etc.[96]

17.8.7 SOAP Servers and Clients in Perl

To illustrate in action the SOAP protocol introduced in the previous subsection, the next Perl script, `SOAPClientProto.pl`, is a SOAP client that makes an RPC call for the `SumAndDifference()` method provided by a web service. This is a *protocol-level encoded client* because it makes explicit at the protocol level the SOAP encoding of what the client expects from the server.

The client in `SOAPClientProto.pl` uses the `LWP::UserAgent` module for the HTTP transport needed for shipping off the request to the server. (The same `LWP::UserAgent` module was used earlier in Section 17.8.2. See the footnote there regarding the `libwww-perl` library that contains this module. As mentioned there, the main three modules in the library are `LWP::UserAgent`, `HTTP::Request`, and `HTTP::Response`.) In the first part of the script, we synthesize in line (B) the outgoing SOAP message whose syntax was explained in the previous subsection.

[96]The last — message routing information — is particularly important in transaction processing that requires that the SOAP message be first authenticated by a designated third party before it is accepted by the recipient. Such third parties are specified by the `actor` attribute in SOAP headers.

An alternative form of the outgoing message, shown in line (A), has been rendered inoperational with the `=` and `=cut` tokens we mentioned earlier in a footnote at the beginning of Chapter 3 when comparing Perl and Python's approaches for rendering sections of code inoperational during the debugging phase of code development. The inoperational version of the message in line (A) contains optional headers that we will soon explain.

Lines (D) through (G) then construct an HTTP request object and supply it with the mandatory headers.[97] Line (H) inserts the SOAP message into the HTTP request object. Line (I) calls on an instance of `LSW::UserAgent` to ship off the request to its destination, to wait for the response, and to then return an HTTP response object. The commented-out print statement in line (I) comes in handy for troubleshooting. If we uncomment this statement, we can see the following XML message returned by the server:

```
<?xml version=''1.0'' encoding=''UTF-8''?>
<SOAP-ENV:Envelope
    xmlns:xsi="http://www.w3.org/1999/XMLSchema-instance"
    xmlns:SOAP-ENC="http://schemas.xmlsoap.org/soap/encoding/"
    xmlns:SOAP-ENV="http://schemas.xmlsoap.org/soap/envelope/"
    xmlns:xsd="http://www.w3.org/1999/XMLSchema"
    SOAP-ENV:encodingStyle="http://schemas.xmlsoap.org/soap/encoding/"
>
    <SOAP-ENV:Body>
        <namesp12:SumAndDifferenceResponse
                        xmlns:namesp12="urn:ACMEWebService">
            <s-gensym52>
                <difference xsi:type="xsd:int">-3</difference>
                <sum xsi:type="xsd:int">13</sum>
            </s-gensym52>
        </namesp12:SumAndDifferenceResponse>
    </SOAP-ENV:Body>
</SOAP-ENV:Envelope>
```

As with the client's SOAP request, the SOAP response received back from the server consists of the `Envelope` root element, with the actual result of the remote method call in the `Body` subelement. Note that, compared to the start tag of the `Envelope` element in the outgoing request shown in the synthesized message in line (B), the start tag of the same element in the received response has the following two additional attribute-value pairs:

```
    xmlns:SOAP-ENC="http://schemas.xmlsoap.org/soap/encoding/"
    SOAP-ENV:encodingStyle="http://schemas.xmlsoap.org/soap/encoding/"
```

[97]Note in particular the `SOAPAction` header being supplied in line (G) for the HTTP request object. Some web services like to see the `SOAPAction` header so that the SOAP handler needed can be called up without parsing the SOAP XML in the received request.

These additional attribute-value pairs are also in the version of the outgoing message shown in line (A) that was rendered inoperational with the `=` and `=cut` tokens. In both these attribute-value pairs, the URIs on the right of the assignment operator are the same. The first maps the prefix `SOAP-ENC:` to the namespace that is also the value of the attribute `encodingStyle` shown in the second line above. The `encodingStyle` attribute indicates the encoding rules used by the sender of the SOAP message for the serialization of a part of the message. The particular value shown for this attribute is usually referred to as the *SOAP encoding* or sometimes as the *Section 5 encoding* since it is described in Section 5 of the SOAP 1.1 specification.[98] The `encodingStyle` attribute can be placed anywhere in a SOAP message and applies to the element in whose start tag it is placed and all its subelements. The SOAP data types are declared in the namespace pointed to by the prefix `SOAP-ENC:`. Later we will have more to say about the SOAP data types.

Let's now look at the body of the SOAP response received from the server:

```
<SOAP-ENV:Body>
    <namesp12:SumAndDifferenceResponse
                      xmlns:namesp12="urn:ACMEWebService">
        <s-gensym52>
            <difference xsi:type="xsd:int">-3</difference>
            <sum xsi:type="xsd:int">13</sum>
        </s-gensym52>
    </namesp12:SumAndDifferenceResponse>
</SOAP-ENV:Body>
```

The important thing to note here is the name of the element that contains the response to the invocation of the `SumAndDifference()` method by the client: `SumAndDifferenceResponse`. That is, the server simply appends the string `Response` to the name of the method called by the client; this the server does for encapsulating the result of that method call.

In the rest of the script `SOAPClientProto.pl` shown below, we first check in lines (K) through (W) whether the server returned an error by seeking out the `faultstring` element in line (K). Note the `//s` modifier supplied to the match operator. As explained in Section 4.11.3 of Chapter 4, this will take care of the possibility that any error response received may span multiple lines. Subsequently, in the regex match in lines (L) through (Q) we extract the meaningful part of the response received from the server — the part that contains the actual parameters and values. Lines (S) through (V) then help us separate out the parameter names and their corresponding values.

---

[98]This encoding style is relevant only when SOAP is used for RPC, as opposed to document exchange.

```
#!/usr/bin/perl -w

### SOAPClientProto.pl

use strict;

my ($arg1, $arg2) = (5, 8);

=description
my $msg =<< "EOT";                                                    #(A)
<SOAP-ENV:Envelope
    xmlns:SOAP-ENC="http://schemas.xmlsoap.org/soap/encoding/"
    SOAP-ENV:encodingStyle="http://schemas.xmlsoap.org/soap/encoding/"
    xmlns:xsi="http://www.w3.org/1999/XMLSchema-instance"
    xmlns:SOAP-ENV="http://schemas.xmlsoap.org/soap/envelope/"
    xmlns:xsd="http://www.w3.org/1999/XMLSchema">
<SOAP-ENV:Body>
    <m:SumAndDifference xmlns:m="urn:Demo">
        <arg1 xsi:type="xsd:int">$arg1</arg1>
        <arg2 xsi:type="xsd:int">$arg2</arg2>
    </m:SumAndDifference>
</SOAP-ENV:Body>
</SOAP-ENV:Envelope>
EOT
=cut

my $msg =<< "EOT";                                                    #(B)
<SOAP-ENV:Envelope
    xmlns:SOAP-ENV="http://schemas.xmlsoap.org/soap/envelope/"
    xmlns:xsi="http://www.w3.org/1999/XMLSchema-instance"
    xmlns:xsd="http://www.w3.org/1999/XMLSchema">
>
<SOAP-ENV:Body>
    <service:SumAndDifference xmlns:service="urn:ACMEWebService">
        <arg1 xsi:type="xsd:int">$arg1</arg1>
        <arg2 xsi:type="xsd:int">$arg2</arg2>
    </service:SumAndDifference>
</SOAP-ENV:Body>
</SOAP-ENV:Envelope>
EOT

require LWP::UserAgent;                                               #(C)

my $uri = "http://localhost:8080";                                    #(D)
my $request = HTTP::Request->new( POST => $uri );                     #(E)
$request->content_type( "text/xml" );                                 #(F)
```

```
$request->header( SOAPAction =>
                      "urn:ACMEWebService#SumAndDifference" );      #(G)
$request->content( $msg );                                          #(H)
my $response = LWP::UserAgent->new->request( $request );            #(I)
#print $response->content . "\n";                                   #(J)

# In case of fault, the returned fault message may be in multiple lines.
# We want the 'dot' metacharacter in the regex below to also eat up any
# newline characters in the contents of the 'faultstring' element:
if ($response->content =~ /<faultstring.*>(.*)<\/faultstring>/s) {  #(K)
    print $1;
    die;
}

my $result = "";
my @result_items = ();
if ($response->content =~ /<.*?SumAndDifferenceResponse.*?>         #(L)
                           <[^<>]*>                                  #(M)
                           (.*)                                      #(N)
                           <[^<>]*>                                  #(O)
                           <\/.*?SumAndDifferenceResponse>           #(P)
                          /x) {                                      #(Q)
    $result = $1;                                                    #(R)
    @result_items = $result =~ /<([^<>\s]*)[^<>]*>                   #(S)
                                ([^<>]*)                             #(T)
                                <\/[^<>]*>                           #(U)
                               /gx;                                  #(V)
}

print "Result:  @result_items\n";                                    #(W)
```

The purpose of showing the SOAP client `SOAPClientProto.pl` was to explain how XML is used in a SOAP request and in a server's response to that request. But, for obvious reasons, it would be much too difficult to use XML directly for complex requests that require customized data objects as arguments for remote procedures. In such cases, it is much more convenient to use a library-based approach in which the interface provided by the library allows a client to call a remote procedure using essentially the same syntax as for a local function call. It becomes the job of the library to translate the remote procedure calls into the XML messages as required by the SOAP protocol.

A popular Perl library (meaning a collection of modules) that fulfills this need is `SOAP::Lite`. This library can be used for SOAP clients, as shown in the next script, as well as for SOAP servers, as we will show later.[99] The next script, `SOAPClientSOAPLite.pl`, presents a `SOAP::Lite` client that does the same work as the `SOAPClientProto.pl` client shown earlier. The client-side code in the next script consists of using the method `proxy()`, as shown in line (C), for designating the *end-point* of the SOAP call — meaning the URL of the SOAP server — and the method `uri()` to designate the namespace whose method will be invoked by the client.[100] For object-oriented servers, the `uri()` method specifies a URI that is a concatenation of the URL of the server and the name of the class whose method the client will be calling, as shown in line (D) of the script.

After the call in lines (C) and (D), we have a client instance that is aware of the end-point for the remote method call and of the namespace URI at the server to be used. If we were to print out the variable `$client` after line (D), we would see something like

```
SOAP::Lite=HASH(0x80e6844)
```

The statement in lines (E) and (F) causes the client to connect with the server and invoke the `new()` method of the class whose URI was supplied through the `uri()` method on the client side. The call in line (E) returns a stub reference to an instance of the server class `ACMEWebService`. The stub serves as a proxy for an instance of the server class whose methods the client will be calling. A method called on the stub reference gets translated into a SOAP-encoded remote procedure call. If we were to print out the variable `$stub` after lines (E) and (F), we would see something like

```
ACMEWebService=HASH(0x854aa2c)
```

which shows that `$stub` holds a blessed reference to an instance of the class `ACMEWebService`.[101] In lines (G), (H), and (I), we ask the client object to call the `SumAndDifference()` method using the syntax shown. Finally, in lines (J) and (K) we iterate through the key-value pairs of the hash object returned by the RPC call. For the example shown, the output of lines (J) and (K) is

```
difference => -3000
sum => 13000
```

[99]The `SOAP::Lite` library consists of six separate module files: `SOAP::Lite.pm`, `SOAP::Transport::HTTP.pm`, `SOAP::Transport::POP3.pm`, `SOAP::Transport::MAILTO.pm`, `SOAP::Transport::LOCAL.pm`, and `SOAP::Transport::TCP.pm`. The first two of these are the main module files. The module file `SOAP::Lite.pm` contains the following 14 different classes: `SOAP::Lite`, `SOAP::Transport`, `SOAP::Data`, `SOAP::Header`, `SOAP::Parser`, `SOAP::Serializer`, `SOAP::Deserializer`, `SOAP::SOM`, `SOAP::Constants`, `SOAP::Trace`, `SOAP::Schema`, `SOAP::Schema::WSDL`, `SOAP::Server`, and `SOAP::Server::Object`. The module file `SOAP::Transport::HTTP.pm` contains the classes `SOAP::Transport::HTTP::Client`, `SOAP::Transport::Server`, `SOAP::Transport::HTTP::Server`, `SOAP::Transport::HTTP::CGI`, `SOAP::Transport::HTTP::Daemon`, and `SOAP::Transport::HTTP::Apache`.

[100]This call to `proxy()` will also automatically import the required transport module for dispatching SOAP calls. If the URL argument to `proxy()` specifically mentions the `http` scheme, then the transport module `SOAP::Transport::HTTP` will be imported into the script.

[101]Calling the built-in function `ref()` with `$stub` as its argument will return `ACMEWebService`.

```
#!/usr/bin/perl -w

### SOAPClientSOAPLite.pl

use SOAP::Lite;                                                   #(A)

my $client = SOAP::Lite->new;                                     #(B)

$client->proxy( 'http://localhost:8080' )                         #(C)
       ->uri("http://localhost/ACMEWebService" );                 #(D)

my $stub = $client->call( 'new' )                                 #(E)
                  ->result;                                       #(F)

#print "$client\n";
#print "$stub\n";
#print ref($stub), "\n";

my $answer = $client                                              #(G)
             ->SumAndDifference( $stub, 5000, 8000 )              #(H)
             ->result;                                            #(I)

while ( my ($key, $value ) = each %$answer) {                     #(J)
    print "$key => $value\n";                                     #(K)
}
```

What is actually returned in lines (G) and (H) of the above script is a `SOAP::SOM` instance. The class `SOAP::SOM` is defined in the module file for `SOAP::Lite.pm`. So the call in line (I) invokes `result()` on a `SOAP::SOM` instance, which simply returns whatever was returned on the server side by the method execution — but only if that execution resulted in the return of just one item. For example, if the function executed on the server returns a reference to an anonymous hash, then `result()` in line (I) will return that reference. However, if the execution of the requested function on the server side returns a list of items, the call to `result()` will only return the first item of the list. The method `result()` is only one of the various methods one can call on a `SOAP::SOM` object to get at the answer. Other possibilities are `paramsout()`, `paramsall()`, `valueof()`, etc. These can be used to gain access to any or all of the parameters returned by the server. Other methods supported by `SOAP::SOM` include `envelope()` for retrieving the `Envelope` element of the response received from the server, `body()` for retrieving the `Body` subelement from the response, `fault()` for retrieving the `Fault` subelement, etc.

The next script, `SOAPDaemonServer.pl`, presents the `SOAP::Lite` server that was used for testing both the clients shown so far.[102] This is a daemon server, meaning that it is a stand-alone server (as opposed to riding piggyback on, say, the Apache web server). In line (B), we first import the `SOAP::Transport::HTTP` module. As mentioned previously in a footnote in this section, the ".pm" file for this module contains six different classes for the six different applications of HTTP logic in a SOAP application: Client, Server, CGI, Daemon, Apache, and FCGI (for Fast CGI). Each class contains the high-level logic pertinent to the use of HTTP for SOAP, and, except for the `Daemon` class, employs the functionality of some other agent for the actual job of transporting the SOAP messages. For example, the `SOAP::Transport::HTTP::Client` class calls on the `LWP::UserAgent` class for the task of acting as a virtual browser vis-à-vis an HTTP-based SOAP server. Of all the classes, the `SOAP::Transport::HTTP::Daemon` class — used in the script in line (D) — is intended to be used as a daemon server. This class is subclassed from the `SOAP::Transport::Server` class that encodes in the high-level HTTP-based server logic. The `SOAP::Transport::Server` class is itself derived from the root class `SOAP::Server` where the basic interface of a SOAP server is defined.[103]

The actual daemon server is constructed in lines (D), (E), and (F) through the following call:

```
my $daemon = SOAP::Transport::HTTP::Daemon
                -> new( LocalAddr => 'localhost', LocalPort => 8080 )
                -> dispatch_to( 'ACMEWebService' );
```

The call to `new()`[104] constructs an instance of the `Daemon` server and the call to `dispatch_to()` routes the request to the package `ACMEWebService`. In this server example, the class that this server dishes out is included in the server code in lines (I) through (P). Actually, this class can correspond to any module that can be located via the `@INC` global variable on the server side. In other words, we could have placed the `ACMEWebService` package in a separate file called `ACMEWebService.pm` and included a pathname to that module in `@INC`. In the use of `dispatch_to()` shown here, we have named a single package as its argument. One is also allowed to call this method with a directory pathname, in which case all the modules located at that pathname become available to clients. Another alternative is to supply `dispatch_to()` with a specific package-qualified method name, in which case only that particular method will be accessible to the clients. Finally, the call to `handle()` in line (H) places the daemon server just constructed in an infinite

---

[102] Note that you have to have root privileges to run the server script.

[103] A server constructed from `SOAP::Transport::HTTP::Server` would need access to a more specific protocol-based HTTP server for carrying out the typical server duties of monitoring a port and responding to client requests.

[104] The constructor, meaning `new()`, can be called with no arguments, in which case the default port is 8080. If the `LocalAddr` option is not specified in the constructor call, the server can be called with any hostname/IP-address applicable to the machine. However, when the `LocalAddr` option is specified, the server must be called with that name.

loop in which it monitors the designated server port for incoming client requests and dispatches each request to the appropriate method.[105]

Note also the commented-out line (A) in the script. If uncommented, it will turn on the trace feature of `SOAP::Lite` for debugging purposes. It is possible to make this command more specific by using the following syntax:

```
use SOAP::Lite +trace =>
    qw(method fault);
```

This will output the parameter values for all SOAP messages that contain the `faultstring` element.

```
#!/usr/bin/perl -w

### SOAPDaemonServer.pl

use strict;
#use SOAP::Lite +trace;                                                   #(A)
use SOAP::Transport::HTTP;                                                #(B)

# Don't want to die on 'Broken pipe' or Ctrl-C
$SIG{PIPE} = $SIG{INT} = 'IGNORE';                                        #(C)

my $daemon = SOAP::Transport::HTTP::Daemon                                #(D)
              -> new( LocalAddr => 'localhost', LocalPort => 8080 ) #(E)
              -> dispatch_to( 'ACMEWebService' );                         #(F)

print "SOAP server started at ", $daemon->url, "\n";                      #(G)
$daemon->handle;                                                          #(H)

#--------  SOAP clients can call on the ACMEWebService class  ---------

package ACMEWebService;                                                   #(I)

sub new {                                                                 #(J)
    my $self = shift;                                                     #(K)
    my $class = ref($self) || $self;                                      #(L)
    bless { _acemwebservice => shift } => $class;                         #(M)
}
```

[105] Line (C) of the script disables the signal handlers for any interrupts that may be caused by broken pipes, etc. That also means that the server program cannot be terminated by entering Ctrl-C on the keyboard in the same terminal window in which you launched the server. To kill the server, you have to explicitly call `kill` on the PID of the server.

```
sub hello {                                                    #(N)
    return "hello world from the soap daemon server";
}
sub bye {                                                      #(O)
    return "goodbye, world from the soap daemon server";
}
sub SumAndDifference {                                         #(P)
    my ($self, $x, $y) = @_;
    return { "sum" => $x + $y, "difference" => $x - $y };
}
```

17.8.8 Perl Clients for SOAP Servers with WSDL Descriptions

Writing client code is particularly trivial for a web service whose description is available in the form of a WSDL document. As mentioned in the introduction to this chapter,[106] WSDL (Web Services Description Language) is an XML-based language for describing a web service. A WSDL document consists of the following XML elements:

`definitions`: This is the root element of all WSDL documents. The `name` attribute in its start tag declares the name of the web service. The other attributes in the start tag declare all the namespaces used in the rest of the document.

`types`: This optional element declares all the data types used in the SOAP messages exchanged between a client and the server. If a web service uses only the basic data types such as integers, strings, etc., the `types` element need not be declared in a WSDL. In such cases, the default source for the data types is taken to be the W3C XML Schema specification.[107] However, note that the XML Schema specification allows for new data types to be defined for SOAP-based services. If a web service uses some custom data type, it must be declared in the `types` element.

`message`: There can be an arbitrary number of these elements. Each such element describes a single one-way message, its name, and, through the `part` subelements, the parameters to be used in the message. A `part` subelement has a

[106] A reader skipping through this book is urged to review the introduction to this chapter — especially Table 17.1 shown there — where we presented the role of WSDL in the web services "architecture stack."

[107] You do not need to declare the `types` element in a WSDL document if a web service uses the following basic types declared in the W3C XML Schema specification: `string`, `boolean`, `float`, `double`, `decimal`, `binary`, `integer`, `positiveInteger`, `negativeInteger`, `long`, `int`, `short`, `byte`, `nonPositiveInteger`, `nonNegativeInteger`, `unsignedLong`, `unsignedInt`, `unsignedShort`, `unsignedByte`, `date`, and `time`.

type attribute that allows us to specify the data type of a parameter. The value of this attribute must be specified as an XML Schema QName — meaning that it must be namespace qualified. For example, if a parameter is meant to be a string, the value of the type attribute would usually be xsd::string where the prefix xsd: would point to the W3C XML Schema specification in the start tag of the definitions root element.

portType: A portType element defines what constitutes a complete client-server operation. This definition is in terms of some or all of the message elements declared previously. We can think of a web service as a collection of *ports*, or, to be more specific in terms of the WSDL terminology, as a collection of portType elements. Each portType element must have a name, which is the value of the name attribute of the start tag of the corresponding portType element. The name of a portType is *not* the name of the web service as declared in the start tag of the definitions root element. The name of a portType is simply the name of a possible complete operation, which is often a two-way operation, between a client and the server.

binding: This element declares how a complete operation, as represented by its portType element, is to be transmitted over the wire. Most commonly, this element declares the "SOAP over HTTP" as the transport mechanism for the operation corresponding to a portType.

service: This element declares the URL to be used for each complete web-service operation as declared by its portType element and the associated transport as declared in the binding element.

WSDL specification allows two additional elements: documentation and import. While the reason for the first is obvious, the second, import, allows other WSDL documents and XML schemas to be incorporated. The import element permits WSDL documents to be be designed in a modular fashion.

To make the above description of WSDL more comprehensible, displayed below is a WSDL document for the ACMEWebService we used in the SOAP server near the end of Section 17.8.7. This WSDL document exposes only the hello() method of that web service. Since WSDL documents can easily become extremely long and unwieldy, we have shown the document for just one of the three methods supported by ACMEWebService. The explanations already provided for the different elements of a WSDL document, along with the comments shown below, should make the syntax used clear.

```
<?xml version="1.0" ?>

<!-- definitions is the root element of a WSDL document.  Its
     'name' attribute declares the name of the web service.
     Its other attributes declare all the namespaces used
     in the rest of the document. Note that the attribute
     'targetNamespace' is an XML Schema convenion that allows
     a WSDL document to refer to itself.   -->
<definitions name="ACMEWebService"
    targetNamespace="urn:ACMEWebService"
    xmlns:tns="urn:ACMEWebService"
    xmlns:xsd="http://www.w3.org/2001/XMLSchema"
    xmlns:soap="http://schemas.xmlsoap.org/wsdl/soap/"
    xmlns="http://schemas.xmlsoap.org/wsdl/">
    xmlns:wsdl="http://schemas.xmlsoap.org/wsdl/"
    xmlns:soapenc="http://schemas.xmlsoap.org/soap/encoding/"
>

    <!-- Section for declaring all message elements: -->
    <!-- Note that the unprefixed names 'message' and
         part belong to the default namespace declared
         previously.  -->
    <message name="helloRequest">
    </message>
    <message name="helloResponse">
        <part type="xsd:string" />
    </message>

    <!-- Group message elements into a complete two-way transaction: -->
    <portType name="ACMEWebServicePortType">
        <operation name="hello">
            <input message="tns:helloRequest" />
            <output message="tns:helloResponse" />
        </operation>
    </portType>

    <!-- Describe how a complete transaction, as described by its
         portType element, will be transmitted over the wire:  -->
    <binding name="ACMEWebServiceBinding"
                     type="tns:ACMEWebServicePortType">
        <soap:binding style="rpc"
              transport="http://schemas.xmlsoap.org/soap/http" />
        <operation name="hello">
            <soap:operation soapAction="" />
            <input>
                <soap:body use="encoded"
                    namespace="urn:ACMEWebService"
```

```
                encodingStyle=
                    "http://schemas.xmlsoap.org/soap/encoding/" />
            </input>
            <output>
                <soap:body use="encoded"
                    namespace="urn:ACMEWebService"
                    encodingStyle=
                        "http://schemas.xmlsoap.org/soap/encoding/" />
            </output>
        </operation>
    </binding>

    <!-- For each client-server transaction, as described by its
         portType and the associated transport as declared in the
         binding element, declare the URL for invoking the service: -->
    <service name="ACMEWebService">
        <documentation>This is the famous ACME Web Service</documentation>
        <port name="ACMEWebServicePort"
                        binding="tns:ACMEWebServiceBinding">
            <soap:address location="http://localhost:8080" />
        </port>
    </service>

</definitions>
```

Using the WSDL document above, notice how simple the code becomes for a client in the following implementation. In line (B), the `service()` method of the `SOAP::Lite` module parses the WSDL file to return a stub for the server class made available through the web service and to initialize the communication substrate needed for the interaction with the server. As shown in line (C), the client can subsequently call the remote methods directly on the stub.

```
#!/usr/bin/perl -w

### SOAPClientUsingWSDL.pl

use SOAP::Lite;                                                         #(A)

my $stub = SOAP::Lite->service( "file:ACMEWebService.wsdl");           #(B)
my $result = $stub->hello();                                            #(C)
print "$result\n";                                                      #(D)
```

We next show a SOAP client for searching the web. As with the client shown above, the client presented next also uses a WSDL document, `GoogleSearch.wsdl`, provided by Google, and the `service()` method of `SOAP::Lite` to generate a local stub of the web service.[108] The `GoogleSearch.wsdl` document, also known as the Google API, says that the web service provided by Google supports the following client-invocable procedures:

```
doGoogleSearch

doGetCachedPage

doSpellingSuggestion
```

Of these, the `doGoogleSearch` procedure returns what you see in a browser when you Google a string of characters. As for the arguments that you must supply to `doGoogleSearch`, here is the relevant snippet from `GoogleSearch.wsdl`:

```
<message name="doGoogleSearch">
    <part name="key"              type="xsd:string"/>
    <part name="q"                type="xsd:string"/>
    <part name="start"            type="xsd:int"/>
    <part name="maxResults"       type="xsd:int"/>
    <part name="filter"           type="xsd:boolean"/>
    <part name="restrict"         type="xsd:string"/>
    <part name="safeSearch"       type="xsd:boolean"/>
    <part name="lr"               type="xsd:string"/>
    <part name="ie"               type="xsd:string"/>
    <part name="oe"               type="xsd:string"/>
</message>
```

What the various parameters stand for is displayed in the commented-out portions of the lines (G) through (P) of the script `GoogleSearch.pl` shown next. Note that before you can use this script you have to first establish an account with Google and acquire from the organization a license key.[109] We assign the license key to the variable `$key` in line (B); it subsequently becomes the first argument to `doGoogleSearch()` in line (G). About some of the other arguments supplied to `doGoogleSearch()`, the value assigned to `$query` can be any string that you would normally enter in a browser for Google search.[110]

---

[108]Such clients can be useful in applications that want to monitor the web electronically for emerging/changing information on a topic.

[109]Google uses the key for authentication and for limiting the total number of queries from any one account to 1000 per day.

[110]All nonalphanumeric characters except

```
+   -   "   &
```

in a query string are treated as word boundaries unless they exist within double-quoted strings. Outside a double quoted string, the special character + can be used to force the search to include a word that Google might otherwise ignore. Unless otherwise directed by, say, the + marker, Google ignores common words

The third argument is the start index and the fourth the maximum number of items to be fetched as long as the maximum does not exceed 10. So by stepping the third argument in multiples of 10, one can conceivably retrieve all the items Google is aware of, provided you do not make more than 1000 queries in a single day. The automatic search result filtering, activated (or deactivated) by the Boolean value supplied for the fifth argument in line (K), is for filtering out near-duplicate returns. The sixth argument, supplied in line (L), specifies no country restriction. The "safe search" feature activated in line (M) is for controlling adult content. The next argument, in line (N), can be used to place restrictions on the language of the documents that the search should be confined to. The last two arguments, in lines (O) and (P), are currently ignored because they have been deprecated. Originally, they were meant for specifying the encoding to be used for outgoing query strings and for incoming search results. Now, by default, the query strings and the returned responses are encoded in UTF-8.

That brings us to the rest of the script in lines (Q) through (b) whose purpose is to extract the textual information from the data object contained in the response received from Google. To understand the logic used in this part of the script, you have to examine the data type of the Google response. It is described by the following subelement in the `types` element of `GoogleSearch.wsdl`:

```
<xsd:complexType name="GoogleSearchResult">
  <xsd:all>
    <xsd:element name="searchTime"           type="xsd:double"/>
    <xsd:element name="documentFiltering"    type="xsd:boolean"/>
    <xsd:element name="searchComments"       type="xsd:string"/>
    <xsd:element name="estimateIsExact"      type="xsd:boolean"/>
    <xsd:element name="searchQuery"          type="xsd:string"/>
    <xsd:element name="startIndex"           type="xsd:int"/>
    <xsd:element name="endIndex"             type="xsd:int"/>
    <xsd:element name="searchTips"           type="xsd:string"/>
    <xsd:element name="estimatedTotalResultsCount"
                                   type="xsd:int"/>
    <xsd:element name="directoryCategories"
                                   type="typens:DirectoryCategoryArray"/>
    <xsd:element name="resultElements"
                                   type="typens:ResultElementArray"/>
  </xsd:all>
</xsd:complexType>
```

What this says is that the response object is a collection of name-value pairs. Most of the parameter names shown above should already be familiar to a user of Google. For example, `searchTime` is a text string that shows the total

---

such as "where" and "how," and single digits and characters. The special character `-` can be used to exclude a word. The character `&` is treated like an alphanumeric character. The query string is also allowed to contain special search-control words such as `OR`, `site:`, `daterange:`, etc., that can profoundly affect what is returned by the search engine.

server time in seconds it takes Google to return the search results. The parameter `estimatedTotalResultsCount` is the estimated total number of entries available in the database for the query string. The value of the Boolean variable `estimateIsExact` tells whether or not the estimated total count for the database entries is exact. The value associated with `searchComments` can be a message that indicates what if any modifications (such a deletion of common words) were made to the query string. The parameter `searchTips` may point to a message as to how the user should modify the query string for a better result the next time. For some queries, the parameter `directoryCategories` points to a list of Google directories that are related to the query string. The actual search results that you see in the browser window are returned via the `resultElements` parameter that points to a data object of type `resultElementArray`. The WSDL file defines this type to be

```
<xsd:complexType name="ResultElementArray">
  <xsd:complexContent>
    <xsd:restriction base="soapenc:Array">
      <xsd:attribute ref="soapenc:arrayType"
                          wsdl:arrayType="typens:ResultElement[]"/>
    </xsd:restriction>
  </xsd:complexContent>
</xsd:complexType>
```

This is essentially saying that a data object of type `resultElementArray` is an array of data objects of type `ResultElement`. The type `ResultElement` is defined as

```
<xsd:complexType name="ResultElement">
  <xsd:all>
    <xsd:element name="title"          type="xsd:string"/>
    <xsd:element name="URL"            type="xsd:string"/>
    <xsd:element name="summary"        type="xsd:string"/>
    <xsd:element name="snippet"        type="xsd:string"/>
    <xsd:element name="cachedSize"     type="xsd:string"/>
    <xsd:element name="hostName"       type="xsd:string"/>
    <xsd:element name="directoryTitle" type="xsd:string"/>
    <xsd:element name="relatedInformationPresent"
                              type="xsd:boolean"/>
    <xsd:element name="directoryCategory"
                              type="typens:DirectoryCategory"/>
  </xsd:all>
</xsd:complexType>
```

Thus we know that a `ResultElement` is a collection of name-value pairs. The URL of each search item returned is associated with the parameter `URL` in a `ResultElement`. What is associated with `snippet` is a text excerpt from the web page to which the URL points. The value associated with the parameter `title` is the title of the web page pointed to by the URL; and so on.

For the query string "programming with objects," the loop in lines (R), (S), and (T) of the script returned the following output on a given run of the script:

```
GoogleSearchResult=HASH(0x85ffcc0)
searchTime    =>   0.491856
endIndex    =>   10
searchComments    =>
documentFiltering    =>   0
searchTips    =>
estimatedTotalResultsCount    =>   2490000
searchQuery    =>   programming with objects
startIndex    =>   1
resultElements    =>   ARRAY(0x86078d0)
directoryCategories    =>   ARRAY(0x8606d24)
estimateIsExact    =>   0
```

As mentioned, the actual search results are stored in the array that is accessible through the `resultElements` parameter. When we print out this array in line (U), we get something like the following:

```
ResultElement=HASH(0x8608e60) ResultElement=HASH(0x860b1fc) .......
.......
.......
```

This is to be expected since each element of the `resultElements` array is a reference to an array of type `ResultElement`. The loop in lines (W) through (b) scans the `resultElements` array and prints out three of the values stored in each `ResultElement` subarray. The output produced in a given run of the script is shown below partially: like

```
Concurrent <b>Programming</b> in Java: Tutorials and design patterns
http://g.oswego.edu/dl/pats/aopintro.html
Concurrent <b>Programming</b> in Java. This page once contained
drafts of material that was<br>  <b>...</b> Concurrent
<b>Programming</b> in Java: Design Principles and
Patterns <b>...</b>

<b>Programming</b> With <b>Objects</b>
http://programmingwithobjects.com/
<b>...</b> <b>Programming</b> with <b>Objects</b>: A
Comparative Presentation of <b>Object</b>-Oriented <b>...</b>
<br>  approach for the teaching and learning of <b>object</b>
-oriented <b>programming</b> in the <b>...</b>

........
........
```

Here is the source code for `GoogleSearch.pl`:

```
#!/usr/bin/perl -w

### GoogleSearch.pl

use SOAP::Lite;                                                          #(A)

my $key = 'xxxxxxxxxxxxxxxxxxxxxxxxxxxxxxxx';                            #(B)

my $query = join ' ', @ARGV;                                             #(C)
die "need something to search for\n" unless $query;                      #(D)

my $googleSearch = SOAP::Lite->service( "file:GoogleSearch.wsdl");  #(E)

my $result = $googleSearch->doGoogleSearch(                              #(F)
              $key,            # key supplied by Google                  #(G)
              $query,          # the query string                        #(H)
              0,               # start index for retrieved items         #(I)
              10,              # max num (< 10) of items                 #(J)
              "false",         # deactivate filtering of duplicates      #(K)
              "",              # no country restriction                  #(L)
              "true",          # activate 'safe search'                  #(M)
              "",              # no language restriction                 #(N)
              "",              # input encoding  (ignored)               #(O)
              "");             # output encoding (ignored)               #(P)

print "$result\n";                                                       #(Q)

if (%$result) {                                                          #(R)
    while ( my ($key, $val) = each %$result ) {                          #(S)
        print "$key    =>    $val\n";                                    #(T)
    }
    my @resultArray = @{$result->{resultElements}};                      #(U)
    print "@resultArray\n\n";                                            #(V)

    foreach my $result ( @resultArray ) {                                #(W)
        print                                                            #(X)
          join "\n",                                                     #(Y)
            $result->{title} || "no title",                              #(Z)
            $result->{URL},                                              #(a)
            $result->{snippet} || "no snippet",                          #(b)
            "\n";
    }
}
```

17.8.9 SOAP Servers and Clients in Python

What `SOAP::Lite` does in Perl can be accomplished in Python by the `SOAPpy` module that can be downloaded from the `sourceforge` web site. Paralleling the `SOAP::Lite` server we presented near the end of Section 17.8.7, what follows next is a `SOAPpy` server in Python. This web service provides four methods for remote invocation. Three of these — `hello()`, `bye()`, and `SumAndDifference()` — are packaged in the class `ACMEWebService` in lines (C) through (H) of the script, and the fourth, `sayHelloWorld()`, is provided as a stand-alone function in lines (I) and (J). Line (K) then makes the server available on port 8080. That line also says that all the names made available for remote invocation will be in the namespace `ACMEWebService`.[111] Line (L) registers an instance of the `ACMEWebService` class with the server and line (M) does the same for the stand-alone function `sayHelloWorld()`. Finally, we place the server in a forever loop in line (N).

```
#!/usr/bin/env python

### SOAPDaemonServer.py

import SOAPpy                                                        #(A)

class ACMEWebService:                                                #(B)
    def hello(self):                                                 #(C)
       return "hello world from ACMEWebService " + \
                 "of the stand-alone SOAP daemon server"             #(D)
    def bye(self):                                                   #(E)
        return "goodbye, world from the soap daemon server"          #(F)
    def SumAndDifference(self, arg1, arg2 ):                         #(G)
        return { "sum" : arg1 + arg2, "difference" : arg1 - arg2 }   #(H)

def sayHelloWorld():                                                 #(I)
    return "Hello World from a stand-alone SOAP Daemon Server"       #(J)

server = SOAPpy.SOAPServer(("localhost", 8080), \
                           namespace="urn:ACMEWebService")           #(K)

server.registerObject(ACMEWebService())                              #(L)
server.registerFunction(sayHelloWorld)                               #(M)
server.serve_forever()                                               #(N)
```

[111] The name of the namespace does not have to match the name of the class used for packaging the methods on the server side. Of course, you have to register an instance of the class with the server.

Shown below is a `SOAP` client in Python. The client makes a local proxy of the remote server in lines (B), (C), and (D). Turning on the debug option, as we have done in line (E), causes all of the outgoing and incoming messages to be printed out. Each message is divided into two parts: the HTTP headers and the SOAP content. The client calls the various methods made available by the server in lines (H), (I), and (J).

```
#!/usr/bin/env python

### SOAPClientProto.py

import SOAPpy                                                          #(A)

#proxy_server = SOAPpy.SOAPProxy("http://localhost:8080/")

proxy_server = SOAPpy.SOAPProxy("http://localhost:8080/",              #(B)
                 namespace="urn:ACMEWebService",                       #(C)
                 soapaction="urn:ACMEWebService#SumAndDifference")     #(D)

SOAPpy.Config.debug = 1                                                #(E)

print proxy_server.sayHelloWorld()                                     #(F)
print proxy_server.hello()                                             #(G)
response = proxy_server.SumAndDifference( 5000, 6000 )                 #(H)
print response.sum                # 11000                              #(I)
print response.difference         # -1000                              #(J)
```

17.8.10 Python Clients for SOAP Servers with WSDL Descriptions

Of course, as already demonstrated with Perl in Section 17.8.8, writing a SOAP client becomes extremely easy if you have access to a WSDL description of the web service. The WSDL file we showed in Section 17.8.8 exposed the `hello()` method of `ACMEWebService` we have used in our various web services examples. The following client-side script uses the same WSDL file to construct a local proxy for the remote server in line (B). We can then straightforwardly call a remote method on the proxy server, as shown in line (C).

```
#!/usr/bin/env python

### SOAPClientUsingWSDL.py

import SOAPpy                                                          #(A)

proxy_server = SOAPpy.WSDL.Proxy( 'ACMEWebService.wsdl' )              #(B)
result = proxy_server.hello()                                          #(C)
print result                                                           #(D)
```

We next show a Python client that uses Google's SOAP API for retrieving the search results. As was the case with the Perl script for doing the same in Section 17.8.8, the next script uses in line (H) the WSDL document `GoogleSearch.wsdl` provided by Google to create a local proxy for the remote document search facility. Our presentation in Section 17.8.8 has already explained the structure of this document, especially what it says about the different arguments needed by the main search function `doGoogleSearch()` that we invoke in lines (P) through (Z). That discussion also explained the structure of the response object returned by the Google web service. That should explain the syntax we use in lines (a) through (i) to extract the various attributes in the result object and the syntax used in lines (j) through (q) to actually print out the search results. Note that we prefer to print out the search results inside a `try–except` block to ward against the possibility that the search item may contain Unicode characters that cannot be locally decoded.

As for the code shown in lines (I) through (O), that is to illustrate how one can extract the names of the different methods made available by the remote service, the types of arguments that the methods take, and the return types. All of this information is, of course, in the WSDL document. But the syntax shown in lines (I) through (O) makes it easier to see the information if it is needed. The call in line (I) to `methods.keys()` on the local proxy for the remote server returns the names of all the methods that can be invoked remotely. The returned strings are shown in the commented-out line below line (I). The invocation of `inparams` as shown in line (L) returns the arguments needed by a remote method. The name and the type of each argument can be ascertained as shown in line (M). Similarly, calling `outparams` as shown in line (N) returns the type of the object returned by the method. The following output is produced by the code in lines (J) through (O):

```
doGoogleSearch
            key string
              q string
          start int
     maxResults int
         filter boolean
       restrict string
```

```
        safeSearch boolean
                lr string
                ie string
                oe string
            return GoogleSearchResult

    doGetCachedPage
               key string
               url string
            return base64Binary

    doSpellingSuggestion
               key string
            phrase string
            return string
```

that shows that the `doGoogleSearch()` method takes 10 named arguments, the types of these being as shown under the method name above. It returns an object of type `GoogleSearchResult`.[112] The other two remote methods, `doGetCachedPage()` and `doSpellingSuggestion()`, take three arguments each as shown.

```
#!/usr/bin/env python

### GoogleSearch.py

import SOAPpy                                                              #(A)
import sys                                                                 #(B)

key = r'xxxxxxxxxxxxxxxxxxxxxxxxxxxxxxxxx'                                 #(C)
query = ' '.join( sys.argv[1:] )                                           #(D)
if not query.lstrip().rstrip():                                            #(E)
    print "exiting --- nothing to search for"                              #(F)
    sys.exit(0)                                                            #(G)

googleSearch = SOAPpy.WSDL.Proxy( "file:GoogleSearch.wsdl" )               #(H)

print googleSearch.methods.keys()                                          #(I)
      # [u'doGoogleSearch', u'doGetCachedPage', u'doSpellingSuggestion']

for method in googleSearch.methods.keys():                                 #(J)
    print method                                                           #(K)
    for item in googleSearch.methods[ method ].inparams:                   #(L)
        print "%15s\t%s" %  (item.name, item.type[1])                      #(M)
```

[112] The precise definition of what is meant by the different data types and the namespace in which these data types are defined is as explained earlier in Section 17.8.8.

```
    for item in googleSearch.methods[ method ].outparams:           #(N)
        print "%15s\t%s" %  (item.name, item.type[1])               #(O)

result = googleSearch.doGoogleSearch(                               #(P)
              key,             # key supplied by Google             #(Q)
              query,           # the query string                   #(R)
              0,               # start index for retrieved items    #(S)
              10,              # max num (< 10) of items            #(T)
              False,           # deactivate filtering of duplicates #(U)
              "",              # no country restriction             #(V)
              False,           # deactivate 'safe search'           #(W)
              "",              # no language restriction            #(X)
              "",              # input encoding  (ignored)          #(Y)
              "")              # output encoding (ignored)          #(Z)

print
print "searchQuery: ", result.searchQuery                           #(a)
print "startIndex: ", result.startIndex                             #(b)
print "estimatedtotalResultsCount: ",  \
                          result.estimatedTotalResultsCount         #(c)
print "endIndex: ", result.endIndex                                 #(d)
print "searchTime: ", result.searchTime                             #(e)
print "searchComments: ", result.searchComments                     #(f)
print "documentFiltering: ", result.documentFiltering               #(g)
print "searchTips: ", result.searchTips                             #(h)
print "directoryCategories: ", result.directoryCategories           #(i)
print

if result.resultElements:                                           #(j)
    for item in result.resultElements:                              #(k)
        try:                                                        #(l)
            print item.title or "no title"                          #(m)
            print item.URL                                          #(n)
            print item.snippet or "no snippet"                      #(o)
            print                                                   #(p)
        except UnicodeEncodeError: pass                             #(q)
```

As the reader would expect, the search output produced by this script is the same as for the Perl Google client in Section 17.8.8.

17.8.11 CGI-Based SOAP Servers and Clients in Perl

As we showed with XML-RPC in Sections 17.8.4 and 17.8.5, it is sometimes more convenient to set up a CGI-based server. As with all CGI-based material on the web, such servers remain dormant until called through a web server on a machine. CGI servers are placed typically in the `cgi-bin` directory of the web server on a machine.

Using the `SOAP::Lite` library, a CGI-based server is typically constructed by supplying the class you want to serve out as an argument to the `dispatch_to()` method of the `SOAP::Transport::HTTP::CGI` class, as in

```
SOAP::Transport::HTTP::CGI
    ->  dispatch_to( 'ACMEWebService')
    ->  handle;
```

The method `handle()` serves the same purpose as for a daemon server — its job is to service a client request and provide a response when appropriate. The above syntax essentially creates a SOAP wrapper around the `ACMEWebService` class.[113] The class supplied as the argument to `dispatch_to()` can correspond to any module that can be located via the `@INC` global variable on the server side.[114]

Shown below is the code for a CGI server `SOAPCGIServer.cgi` that works the same as the daemon server `SOAPDaemonServer.pl` shown earlier near the end of Section 17.8.7.

```
#!/usr/bin/perl -Tw
use strict;
$!++;                       # disable buffers associated with std. output

### SOAPCGIServer.cgi

use SOAP::Transport::HTTP;                                           #(A)

SOAP::Transport::HTTP::CGI                                           #(B)
    ->  dispatch_to( 'ACMEWebService')                               #(C)
    ->  handle;                                                      #(D)
```

[113]By supplying additional comma-separated class names as arguments to `dispatch_to()`, a server can be made to serve out multiple classes at the same time.

[114]When the class to which the client calls are dispatched is in the same file as the SOAP wrapper, we have what is referred to as *static dispatch internal*. On the other hand, if the class to be served out is elsewhere but can be located via the pathnames in the global `@INC` variable, we have *static dispatch external*. If neither of these two situations holds, we are allowed to simply supply a directory pathname as the argument to `dispatch_to()`. In this case, all the classes available at that pathname become candidates for serving out via the SOAP wrapper. Since the exact class needed would only be known at run time in this case, we now have what is referred to as *dynamic dispatch*. Dynamic dispatch can be a useful alternative because a SOAP server is not allowed to change the value of `@INC` for security reasons.

```
#-------------------------- class ACMEWebService -----------------------
package ACMEWebService;                                              #(E)

sub new {                                                            #(F)
    my $self = shift;                                                #(G)
    my $class = ref($self) || $self;                                 #(H)
    bless { _acemwebservice => shift } => $class;                    #(I)
}
sub hello {                                                          #(J)
    return "hello world from the soap daemon server";
}
sub bye {                                                            #(K)
    return "goodbye, world from the soap daemon server";
}
sub SumAndDifference {                                               #(L)
    my ($self, $x, $y) = @_;
    return { "sum" => $x + $y, "difference" => $x - $y };
}
```

Shown below is a client for this CGI server. Except for the argument to `proxy()` in line (D), this client works the same as the client `SOAPClientSOAPLite.pl` shown earlier in Section 17.8.7. The argument to proxy here is based on the assumption that the above CGI server is placed in the `cgi-bin` directory of the Apache web server.

```
#!/usr/bin/perl -w

### SOAPClientForCGIServer.pl

use SOAP::Lite;                                                      #(A)

my $proxy =
    SOAP::Lite                                                       #(B)
        -> uri("http://192.168.1.131/ACMEWebService" )               #(C)
        -> proxy('http://192.168.1.131/cgi-bin/SOAPCGIServer.cgi'); #(D)

print $proxy                                                         #(E)
          -> hello()                                                 #(F)
          -> result;                                                 #(G)
print "\n";

my $answer =  $proxy                                                 #(H)
                  -> SumAndDifference( 5000, 8000 )                  #(I)
                  -> result;                                         #(J)
while ( my ($key, $value ) = each %$answer) {                        #(K)
    print "$key => $value\n";                                        #(L)
}
```

17.9 XSL FOR TRANSFORMING XML

As was stated earlier, XML is used primarily to specify the meaning of the different parts of a document and that the presentation of a document is not the main concern of XML. The idea is to embed XML tags in a document, the tags specifying what meaning to ascribe to the different portions of the document. Subsequently, the document content can be transformed on the fly into different presentation formats depending on the end consumer of the content. For example, we may wish to transform the same XML content into HTML, WAP, TXT, and so on, for different presentation styles and formats.

Content transformation of an XML document, whether for the purpose of presentation or for creating a different XML document, is carried out with the help of an XSL file that serves as a *stylesheet* for the XML document. As mentioned in the introduction to this chapter, XSL stands for eXtensible Style Language. In particular, one uses XSLT (for eXtensible Stylesheet Language Transform), a subset of XSL, for specifying the rules for transforming an XML document.[115] Note that since an XSL document is also an XML document, its structure can be specified with a DTD file or with an XML schema file.

At the least, every XSL file must contain the `stylesheet` element that declares the version of the XSL specification and that places this element name in the namespace shown below as pointed to by the `xsl:` namespace prefix. Therefore, the following constitutes the shortest possible XSL file:

```
<?xml version="1.0" ?>
<xsl:stylesheet version="1.0"
        xmlns:xsl="http://www.w3.org/1999/XSL/Transform">
</xsl:stylesheet>
```

where the first element is necessitated by the fact that every XSL document is also an XML document.

A stylesheet consists of template matching rules, each encapsulated with the following delimiting syntax in an XSL file:

```
<xsl:template match=".....">
....
</xsl:template>
```

Template matching always starts, implicitly or explicitly, with the root node of the XML document. In an XSL file, this node is represented by the `/` symbol. So if we wanted a template rule to be applied to the root node of a source document, its syntax would look like

[115]Xalan is a popular XSLT engine for processing stylesheets. Xalan, written in C++, uses the Xerces XML parser. As mentioned previously, Xerces, written in C++ or Java, has Perl and Python bindings.

```
<xsl:template match="/">
....
</xsl:template>
```

The fact that template matching that begins with the root node[116] is to be applied to all the child nodes can be made explicit in an XSL file by:

```
<xsl:template match="/">
    <xsl:apply-templates />
</xsl:template>
```

The application of template matching to the child nodes can be made selective by supplying the `apply-templates` element with a `select` attribute, as in[117]

```
<xsl:template match="/">
    <xsl:apply-templates select="//....." />
    <xsl:apply-templates select="//....." />
    <xsl:apply-templates select="//....." />
    .....
</xsl:template>
```

Now only those child nodes whose names match with the `select` arguments will be subject to further template matching rules. Without such a selection mechanism in place, all child nodes (and their descendant nodes) that do not match with the provided templates are subject to default processing. This is illustrated with the two-file example shown below. The template matching rule in lines (A), (B), and (C) says that only the `OilPalette` subelement of the root element in the source document needs to be processed further, implying that the rest of the subelements of the root element are to be ignored. As to the transformation that is to be applied to the `OilPalette` element, that is stated by the transformation rule in lines (G), (H), and (I).

[116]The "node" in this section means the same thing as an "element" in an XML document and a "child node" the same as a "subelement." Obviously, there is a one-to-one correspondence between the elements of an XML document and the nodes in the document's DOM, as explained in Section 17.7.

[117]The operator `//` is an XPath operator that stands for the current and the child nodes. Strictly speaking, `//` is a shorthand for *descendant-or-self* axis. The XPath standard defines 13 *axes* for accessing the different portions of an XML document from any given location. If the path to a node begins with a single forward slash `/`, that represents an absolute path with respect to the root of the document — just as in directory pathnames. One can select all of the child nodes of a given node by using the XPath operator `*` as in directory pathnames. Additionally, if multiple child nodes carry the same name, they can each be accessed with the subscript operator, that is, with `[i]` for the i-*th* child node. In general, the XPath operator `[]` takes a predicate expression as its argument whose evaluation returns a node set. One of the 13 axes for reaching into an XML document is the *attribute* axis that contains the value of a named attribute of a node; the named attribute is specified with the `@` XPath operator. A child node with a specific value for a given attribute can be reached with the `[@attribute_name]` operator that follows the name of the parent node. Additional XPath operators that are frequently used are `.` for accessing the self axis (meaning the current node) and `..` for accessing the parent axis (meaning the parent node), etc.

```
................ file: TemplateMatchSelect.xsl .......................

<?xml version="1.0"?>
<xsl:stylesheet version="1.0"
         xmlns:xsl="http://www.w3.org/1999/XSL/Transform">
<xsl:output method="text" />

<xsl:template match="/">                                     <!-- A -->
    <xsl:apply-templates select="//OilPalette" />            <!-- B -->
</xsl:template>                                              <!-- C -->

<xsl:template match="WaterColorsPalette">                    <!-- D -->
    <xsl:text>WaterColorsPalette Selected</xsl:text>         <!-- E -->
</xsl:template>                                              <!-- F -->

<xsl:template match="OilPalette">                            <!-- G -->
    <xsl:text>OilPalette Selected</xsl:text>                 <!-- H -->
</xsl:template>                                              <!-- I -->

</xsl:stylesheet>

................ file: TemplateMatchSelect.xml .......................

<?xml version="1.0"?>
<Palettes>
    <WaterColorsPalette>                                     <!-- J -->
        <colors>
            <color>red</color>
            <color>blue</color>
        </colors>
    </WaterColorsPalette>
    <OilPalette>                                             <!-- K -->
        <colors>
            <color>magenta</color>
            <color>black</color>
        </colors>
    </OilPalette>
    <WaterColorsPalette>                                     <!-- L -->
        <colors>
            <color>green</color>
            <color>yellow</color>
        </colors>
    </WaterColorsPalette>
</Palettes>
```

We can use the Xalan XSLT engine to transform the XML document shown above with the stylesheet also shown above using the following command line:

```
xalan -out out.txt -in TemplateMatchSelect.xml        \
                              -xsl TemplateMatchSelect.xsl
```

This command line works for Xalan version 1.10.0 using the Xerces XML parser version 2.7.0 on a Ubuntu Linux platform. The `out.txt` file produced contains the message

```
OilPalette Selected
```

which is in accordance with line (H) of the stylesheet. Note that the transformation rule for the `WaterColorsPalette` element in lines (D), (E), and (F) of the stylesheet file is simply ignored because of the matching constraints stated in lines (A), (B), and (C).

In general, the `xsl:apply-templates` instruction, when used without the `select` attribute, causes the processing of all of the child nodes of the current node from the source document. Also, in general, the value of the `select` attribute, when used, is an expression that must return a node set. The selected set of nodes is processed in document order unless a sorting specification is present.[118] This can sometimes have unintended consequences. Consider the example shown next. The matching with the root node in line (A) of the stylesheet shown below will cause the template of lines (D), (E), and (F) to be applied to *all* the `BBB` nodes of the XML source document, which is what you'd expect. [As to what precisely is accomplished by the template of lines (G), (H), and (I) is explained in the next subsection. As explained there, the `xsl:value-of` element returns the text content of an element.] And for each `BBB` node, the call to match in line (E) will cause the template of lines (G), (H), and (I) to be applied to *all* the `CCC` elements of the source document, *which you may or may not expect.* One might think that the transformation called in line (E) would only be applied to those CCC elements that are contained within the current BBB element. But that is not the case, as evidenced by the following output of the transformation for the XML source document shown:[119]

```
111  333  444  111  333  444  111  333  444
```

Note that the middle `111 333 444` in the output correspond to the `BBB` element of line (N) which does not even contain its own `CCC` element. This happens because

---

[118]When the `select` attribute is used, the standard also allows us to use another optional attribute `mode`. If an `xsl:apply-template` element contains a value for the `mode` attribute, then only the template with the same mode value will be used.

[119]The problem is caused by the fact that a node expression like `//CCC` in line (E) returns `all` the CCC nodes in the source document regardless of the level of nesting at which they exist. On the other hand, a node expression like `CCC` would only return the child `CCC` nodes. Nonetheless, it would not be uncommon for a beginning XSL programmer to have written the stylesheet of lines (A) through (I) hoping that the output for the XML document of lines (J) through (S) would be just

```
111  333
```

every BBB element calls for matches with all CCC elements regardless of where they happen to be in the source document — on account of the node expression //CCC in line (E).

```
........................ file: Test2.xsl ..............................

<?xml version="1.0"?>
<xsl:stylesheet xmlns:xsl =
          "http://www.w3.org/1999/XSL/Transform" version = "1.0" >
<xsl:output method = "text" indent = "yes" />

<xsl:template match = "/" >                                   <!-- A -->
    <xsl:apply-templates select = "//BBB" />                  <!-- B -->
</xsl:template>                                               <!-- C -->

<xsl:template match = "BBB" >                                 <!-- D -->
    <xsl:apply-templates select = "//CCC" />                  <!-- E -->
</xsl:template>                                               <!-- F -->

<xsl:template match = "CCC" >                                 <!-- G -->
    <xsl:value-of select = "." />                             <!-- H -->
</xsl:template>                                               <!-- I -->

</xsl:stylesheet>


........................ file: Test.xml ..............................

<?xml version="1.0"?>
<AAA >                                                        <!-- J -->
    <BBB>                                                     <!-- K -->
        <CCC> 111 </CCC>                                      <!-- L -->
    </BBB>                                                    <!-- M -->
    <BBB> 222 </BBB>                                          <!-- N -->
    <BBB>                                                     <!-- O -->
        <CCC> 333 </CCC>                                      <!-- P -->
    </BBB>                                                    <!-- Q -->
    <CCC> 444 </CCC>                                          <!-- R -->
</AAA>                                                        <!-- S -->
```

The problem with the stylesheet shown above can be fixed by changing the syntax in line (E) to read

```
<xsl:apply-templates select = "CCC" />
```

Now the output produced by the stylesheet for the same source document looks like

```
111 333
```

Let's now go to the following minimalist stylesheet shown at the beginning of this section:

```
<?xml version="1.0" ?>
<xsl:stylesheet version="1.0"
       xmlns:xsl="http://www.w3.org/1999/XSL/Transform">
</xsl:stylesheet>
```

Since no transformation rules are included in this stylesheet, it results in default processing for all the nodes of the XML document, which consists of sending to the output the character content of each element in the source document. To illustrate, suppose we place the stylesheet shown in a file called `Default.xsl` and suppose we use it to transform an XML file called `Ex1.xml` whose contents are

```
<?xml version="1.0"?>
<A>
  hello
  <B>
    mello
    <C>
      yello
    </C>
  </B>
</A>
```

Now if we invoke the XALAN engine to transform the source document by

```
xalan -out out.txt -in Ex1.xml -xsl Default.xsl
```

we will see the following in the `out.txt` file:[120]

```
<?xml version=''1.0'' encoding=''UTF-8''?>
  hello

    mello

      yello
```

[120]Here we have not shown all of the white space, especially the vertical white space, in the output. If we wanted to, the white space sent to the output can be controlled for each element by an instruction like

```
<xsl:strip-space elements="A B C" />
```

and

```
<xsl:preserve-space elements="A B C" />
```

where the value supplied to the `elements` attribute is a white-space separated list of element names.

The default output for each node of the source document is produced by simply dropping the markup in that element and retaining only the character data that constitutes the element content. This can be confirmed by changing the contents of the source file to look like:

```
<?xml version="1.0"?>
<A> hello <B> mello <C> yello </C> </B> </A>
```

Now the content of the output file for the same XSL file would look like

```
<?xml version=''1.0'' encoding=''UTF-8''?> hello  mello  yello
```

The default output produced by the rule-less XSL file shown previously "tries" to produce an XML output, as one might infer by the first line of the output. However, the two outputs shown are not valid XML. As the reader will recall, an XML document must contain a root element in order to be valid.[121] If we wished just straight text for the output and did not desire to see that first line shown in the two outputs above, we need to insert the following element in the XSL file:

```
<xsl:output method="text"/>
```

Now the XSL file would look like

```
<?xml version="1.0"?>
<xsl:stylesheet version="1.0"
    xmlns:xsl="http://www.w3.org/1999/XSL/Transform">
<xsl:output method="text" />
</xsl:stylesheet>
```

With this stylesheet, the output file for the first XML document shown above becomes

```

hello

  mello

    yello

```

and for the second

```
  hello  mello  yello
```

[121]The root element for the output document must be specified in the stylesheet for an XML-to-XML transformation.

In general, the `method` attribute of the self-closing element `xsl:output` would vary depending on what is needed for the output document. For example, if we want to transform an XML document into an HTML document, this element would be

```
<xsl:output method="html" />
```

In the rest of this section, we will be concerned solely with XML-to-HTML transformations. We will present of the other more commonly used XSL elements in the context of that transformation.

17.9.1 Generating Output Text with xsl:value-of

A commonly used XSL element is `xsl:value-of` that is used to create some text for the output. What text is returned depends on what value is supplied to the `select` attribute of the node. For example, the syntax

```
<xsl:value-of select="//element_name" />
```

produces for the output the text content of the named element. The following syntax, a variation on the above,

```
<xsl:value-of select="." />
```

produces for the output the text content of the current node being processed. The value supplied for `select` can also be a function such as `position()`, `name()`, etc.

Another application of `xsl:value-of` is shown in the next two-file example where it grabs for the output the value of an attribute. Note that the `@` prefix for what is assigned to `select` in line (C). As explained in the XPath-related footnote in Section 17.9, this would cause the value of the attribute `country`, if it exists, to be sent to the output. If such an attribute does not exist for a `WaterColorPalette` element, that element will be ignored for the purpose of the transformation.

```
................. file: TemplateMatchValueSelectAtt.xsl ..............

<?xml version="1.0"?>
<xsl:stylesheet version="1.0"
          xmlns:xsl="http://www.w3.org/1999/XSL/Transform">
<xsl:output method="text" />                                   <!-- A -->
<xsl:template match="WaterColorsPalette">                      <!-- B -->
   <xsl:value-of select="@country" />                          <!-- C -->
</xsl:template>
</xsl:stylesheet>
```

```
.................. file: TemplateMatchValueSelectAtt.xml ..............

<?xml version="1.0"?>
<Palettes>
    <WaterColorsPalette country="french">                  <!-- D -->
        <colors>                                           <!-- E -->
            <color>red</color>                             <!-- F -->
            <color>blue</color>                            <!-- G -->
        </colors>                                          <!-- H -->
    </WaterColorsPalette>
    <OilPalette>                                           <!-- I -->
        <colors>                                           <!-- J -->
            <color>magenta</color>                         <!-- K -->
            <color>black</color>                           <!-- L -->
        </colors>                                          <!-- M -->
    </OilPalette>
    <WaterColorsPalette>                                   <!-- N -->
        <colors>                                           <!-- O -->
            <color>green</color>                           <!-- P -->
            <color>yellow</color>                          <!-- Q -->
        </colors>                                          <!-- R -->
    </WaterColorsPalette>                                  <!-- S -->
</Palettes>
```

This example produces the output:

```
    french


            magenta
            black
```

Note how the stylesheet ignored the second `WaterColorsPalette` element in lines (N) through (S) of the source XML file — nothing is output for this element. Also note again that the element `OilPalette` is subject to default processing.

17.9.2 Transforming XML into HTML

We will now introduce some of the other XSL elements through a specific example of transforming an XML document into an HTML document. We will use the following XML document, named `Library.xml`, for this purpose:

```
<?xml version="1.0"?>
<LIBRARY>
    <BOOK YEAR="1935" LANGUAGE="English" CATEGORY="history">
        <TITLE>Noxious Fumes</TITLE>
        <AUTHOR>
            <LASTNAME>Phuric</LASTNAME>
            <RESTOFNAME>Sul</RESTOFNAME>
        </AUTHOR>
        <ISBN>3636-7737-10</ISBN>
        <PUBLISHER>WordMasters</PUBLISHER>
    </BOOK>
    <CD GENRE="Stationary Rock">
        <TITLE>Jailhouse Frock</TITLE>
        <ARTIST>
            <NAME>Lil' Somethin</NAME>
        </ARTIST>
        <TRACKS>6</TRACKS>
        <PUBLISHER>Cosmic Music</PUBLISHER>
    </CD>
    <BOOK YEAR="1998" LANGUAGE="French" CATEGORY="fiction">
        <TITLE>Nozy Noztrils</TITLE>
        <AUTHOR>
            <LASTNAME>Hairs</LASTNAME>
            <RESTOFNAME>Lus</RESTOFNAME>
        </AUTHOR>
        <ISBN>3687-9944-10</ISBN>
        <PUBLISHER>Wordsmiths</PUBLISHER>
    </BOOK>
    <CD GENRE="Neo Classical">
        <TITLE>Eternation of Life</TITLE>
        <ARTIST>
            <NAME>Johannes Munificent</NAME>
        </ARTIST>
        <TRACKS>1</TRACKS>
        <PUBLISHER>Music of the Nether World</PUBLISHER>
    </CD>
</LIBRARY>
```

Let's say we want to display the above document in an HTML browser in the form of a table that lists only the book titles along with their authors. In other words, we want the output tabular presentation to ignore the CDs in the XML file. This is accomplished by the stylesheet `LibraryBooks.xsl` shown next. This stylesheet is our introduction to the frequently used `xsl:for-each` element to iterate over a set of nodes.

To explain the stylesheet, note first of all the value supplied to the `method` attribute of the `xsl:output` element in line (A). We now specifically ask the XSLT transformer to produce HTML output. As for the transformation itself, obviously one of the first things we need to do is to output the usual tags and the associated information that goes at the beginning of any HTML file. This is accomplished by the template lines that immediately follow the match with the root node in line (B). A part of this output, starting in line (C), is for the creation of a table in the browser window. After outputting the column headers, in line (D) we set up an iteration loop that goes over each `BOOK` node returned by the expression `//BOOK` supplied to `select`. Each such `BOOK` node is subject to template processing as defined by the syntax between line (E) and (J). This syntax calls for the creation of a new row of the table for each book and for the insertion of the title in the first column and the name of the author in the second column.

```
<?xml version="1.0"?>
<xsl:stylesheet version="1.0"
          xmlns:xsl="http://www.w3.org/1999/XSL/Transform">
<xsl:output method="html" />                                  <!-- A -->

<xsl:template match="/">                                      <!-- B -->
<HTML>
<HEAD>
<TITLE>My Library of Books and CDs</TITLE>
</HEAD>
<BODY BGCOLOR="white">
<PRE>
</PRE>
<TABLE BORDER="5" CELLPADDING="4" CELLSPACING="2">            <!-- C -->
<TR>
<TD>Title</TD><TD>Author or Artist Name</TD>
</TR>                                                         <!-- D -->
<xsl:for-each select="//BOOK" >                               <!-- E -->
<TR>
<TD>
    <xsl:value-of select="TITLE" />                           <!-- F -->
    </TD>
    <TD>
        <xsl:value-of select="AUTHOR/FIRSTNAME" />            <!-- G -->
        <xsl:text> </xsl:text>                                <!-- H -->
        <xsl:value-of select="AUTHOR/LASTNAME" />             <!-- I -->
    </TD>
    </TR>
</xsl:for-each>                                               <!-- J -->
</TABLE>
</BODY>
</HTML>
</xsl:template>
</xsl:stylesheet>
```

If we use the following command line on the two files shown above

```
xalan -out out.html -in Library.xml -xsl LibraryBooks.xsl
```

the output file `out.html` produced as a result contains the information shown below:

```
<HTML>
<HEAD>
<META http-equiv=''Content-Type'' content=''text/html; charset=UTF-8''>
<TITLE>My Library of Books and CDs</TITLE>
</HEAD>
<BODY BGCOLOR=''white''>
<PRE></PRE>
<TABLE BORDER=''5'' CELLPADDING=''4'' CELLSPACING=''2''>
<TR>
<TD>Title</TD><TD>Author or Artist Name</TD>
</TR>
<TR>
<TD>Noxious Fumes</TD><TD>Sul Phuric</TD>
</TR>
<TR>
<TD>Nozy Noztrils</TD><TD>Lus Hairs</TD>
</TR>
<TR>
<TD>Attila the Hun</TD><TD>Wus Nofun</TD>
</TR>
</TABLE>
</BODY>
</HTML>
```

The `xsl:for-each` control element in line (E) of the stylesheet processes the nodes returned by the `select` attribute in the document order, meaning the order in which they show up in the source document. But what if you wanted to output the book information in some sorted order? A sorted output can be produced by inserting the element

```
<xsl:sort />
```

immediately after line (E) in the `LibraryBooks.xsl` stylefile. This will cause the `BOOK` nodes to be sorted according to the text content of each node. In our case, the text content of each `BOOK` node is what would be returned by applying `xsl:value-of` to the node, which is the book title followed by the first and the last names of the author, followed by the ISBN number, followed by the name of the publisher. In order to sort the books on a specific item, say the last name of the author, the call to `xsl:sort` can be replaced by[122]

```
<xsl:sort select="AUTHOR/LASTNAME" />
```

Another element that comes in handy in selective application of transformation rules is `xsl:if`. For example, we may use the following construct in an XML-to-XML transformation. Using a Boolean test inside the start tag of an `xsl:if` element, we first check if the `TYPE` attribute of a `BOOK` element in the source document is `comedy`. If so, we output the same attribute for the output XML document. We then repeat the same with the other possible attribute values in each `BOOK` element of the source document.[123]

```
<xsl:template match="BOOK">
    <BOOK>
    <xsl:if test="boolean(@TYPE='comedy')">
        <xsl:attribute name="TYPE">
            <xsl:text>comedy</xsl:text>
        </xsl:attribute>
    </xsl:if>
    <xsl:if test="boolean(@TYPE='history')">
        <xsl:attribute name="TYPE">
            <xsl:text>history</xsl:text>
        </xsl:attribute>
    </xsl:if>
    <xsl:if test="boolean(@TYPE='computer science')">
        <xsl:attribute name="TYPE">
            <xsl:text>computer science</xsl:text>
        </xsl:attribute>
    </xsl:if>
    <xsl:apply-templates />
    </BOOK>
</xsl:template>
```

17.10 CREDITS AND SUGGESTIONS FOR FURTHER READING

Early notable work on the development of event-driven parsers for XML consisted, on the one hand, of the development of Java SAX parsers, and, on the other, of the C-based `expat` parser by James Clark, both nonvalidating. Expat stands for EX*tensible*

---

[122]Our explanation talked about `xsl:sort` as applied to the nodes serviced by the `xsl:for-each` element. `xsl:sort` can also be used to sort the nodes serviced by the `xsl:apply-templates` element. See the standard for further details.

[123]The goal of such a transformation rule could be to selectively output only some of the attributes from the source-document elements to the corresponding output-document elements.

markup language Parser Toolkit. The SAX "movement" is an open-source effort, led by Jon Bosak, the founder of XML, David Megginson, Tim Bray, and others. See `www.saxproject.org` for a history of SAX and its current status.

An excellent tutorial for XML Schemas is by Robert Costello [14]. Part 0 of the XML Schema standard [35] at `www.w3.org` also makes for great reading. Another wonderful online tutorial for XML Schemas is at `www.zvon.org`.

For further information on how to use the Perl's `XML::Parser` module, see the tutorial article by Clark Cooper [13].

Petr Cimprich [10] has compared the performance of the following Perl SAX 2.0 parsers: `XML::SAX::Expat`, `XML::SAX::ExpatXS`, `XML::LibXML::SAX`, `XML::LibXML::SAX::Parser`, and `XML::Xerces`. He has shown that module performance depends on markup density.

The implementation of the DOM parser in Section 17.7.1 was inspired by Guang Yang's lightweight XML parsers in Java, C#, and VisualBasic [69].

As mentioned already, in the context of XML processing, a *driver* is a program that can extract information from a non-XML source, such as a database, and stream it to the output where it can be processed by an XML parser. A SAX driver converts the information extracted from a non-XML source into SAX events. An example of a SAX driver program is `XML::SAXDriver::Excel` that converts Microsoft Excel spreadsheet entries into SAX events. Examples of these SAX events are the start of a new row of the spreadsheet, start of a cell in a new column in a row, the end of a cell, the end of a row, etc. Such events would be handed over to the `start_element` and `end_element` callbacks. The data in each cell of the spreadsheet would trigger events for the `characters` callback. An XML *filter* is a program that converts one XML document into another XML document by modifying the structural relationship between the elements, the properties of the elements, or the content of the elements. An XML SAX filter typically modifies a stream of events generated by either a driver or a some SAX parser.

Our SOAP examples were simple and used the `SOAP::Lite` Perl module to illustrate a SOAP-based interaction between a client and web-service provider. For more complex applications, where you may have to tie together multiple web services in some sort of a *work flow*, a more appropriate tool is `Axis`, the SOAP implementation from Apache.

See Paul Kulchenko's example implementations of servers and clients in the `examples` subdirectory of the `SOAP::Lite` source code directory.

An excellent tutorial for XSLT is at `www.zvon.org`. This site actually carries an excellent array of online tutorials and references on practically everything that has anything to do with XML.

The attributions and credits mentioned above are in addition to many others in the main body of the chapter.

17.11 HOMEWORK

1. Extend the scripts `ExtractEleInfo.pl` and `ExtractEleInfo.py` of Section 17.2 to include the type of phone in the output table. That is, your output should now have another column, possibly to the right of the name column, that indicates whether the phone is a cell phone, a work phone, etc.

2. As you saw in Chapter 4, Python allows for the capturing groups in a regex to be named. In general, this is a very convenient feature for large multiline regular expressions with multiple embedded groups. With named groups, you can use the name tags (as opposed to integer indices) to access the matching substrings. As you also saw, the regex for the REX shallow parser for XML is extremely complex. (Try printing out the entire regex bound to the `XML_SPE` variable in the `TestREX.py` script in Section 17.4.) As shown, the regex uses nonextracting groups. If we could use the named groups, we could then extract the different components of a source document corresponding to the different components of the regex shown in `TestREX.py`. Is it possible to do so? Explain your answer.

3. We showed the XML document `Library.xml` in Section 17.9.2. That section also showed an XSL file for transformation this XML source document into an HTML document that could be displayed in a web browser. But that transformation only showed the books in the library. For this homework:

   (a) Extend the XSL file of Section 17.9.2 so that the HTML file contains two separate tables, one for the books and the other for the CDs.

   (b) Write an HTML document that gives the user the option to see either just the book table or just the CD table or both and calls on some Javascript code to apply the needed XSL transformation to the XML source document.

   (c) Further extend the XSL file to also give the user the option of configuring their own tables for either the books or the CDs or both. For example, some users may not like to see the ISBN column for either table. And some users may like to see just the titles of the books and the CDs.

4. Do the previous homework problem with the output shown sorted for each case, the sorting to be accomplished using the author's or artist's last name as the sort key.

References

1. K. Barrett, B. Cassels, P. Haahr, D. A. Moon, K. Playford, and P. T. Withington. A monotonic superclass linearization for dylan. *OOPSLA*, 1996.

2. Hildo Biersma. *Operator Overloading in Perl.* `http://www.foo.be/docs/tpj/issues/vol4\_3/tpj0403-0012.html`, 1999.

3. Barry W. Boehm. *Software Engineering Economics.* Prentice-Hall, 1981.

4. Sean M. Burke. *Perl and LWP.* O'Reilly, 2002.

5. Robert Cameron. *REX: XML Shallow Parsing with Regular Expressions.* `http://fas.sfu.ca/pub/cs/TR/1998/CMPT1998-17.html`, 1998.

6. Brett Cannon. *Design of the CPython Compiler.* `http://www.python.org/dev/peps/pep-0339/`, 2005.

7. Tom Christiansen and Nathan Torkington. *Perl Cookbook.* O'Reilly Media, Inc., Second Edition, 2003.

8. Y. Chu, S. G. Rao, S. Seshan, and H. Zhang. A Case for End System Multicast. *IEEE Journal on Selected Areas in Communications, Special Issue on Networking Support for Multicasting*, 20, 2002.

9. Wesley J. Chun. *Core Python Programming (2nd Edition).* Prentice Hall PTR, 2006.

Scripting with Objects. By Avinash C. Kak

10. Petr Cimprich. *Perl Parser Performance.* http://www.xml.com/pub/a/2004/09/15//pl-perf.html, 2004.

11. Damian Conway. *Object Oriented Perl: A Comprehensive Guide to Concepts and Programming Techniques.* Manning Publications, 2000.

12. Clark Cooper. *Benchmarking XML Parsers.* http://www.xml.com/pub/a/Benchmark/article.html.

13. Clark Cooper. *Using the Perl XML::Parser Module.* http://www.xml.com/lpt/a/98/09/xml-perl.html, 1998.

14. Robert Costello. *XML Schemas.* http://www.xfront.com/xml-schema.html.

15. Dave Cross. *What is Overloading?* http://perl.com/lpt/a/754, 2003.

16. Martin D. Davis, Ron Sigel, and Elaine J. Weyuker. *Computability, Complexity, and Languages.* Morgan Kaufman, Second Edition, 1994.

17. Alligator Descartes and Tim Bunce. *Programming the Perl DBI, Database Programming with Perl.* O'Reilly & Associates, 2000.

18. R. J. Enbody and H. C. Du. Dynamic hashing schemes. *ACM Computing Surveys*, 20 (2):85–113, 1998.

19. Ronald Fagin, Jurg Nievergelt, Nicholas Pippenger, and H. Raymond Strong. Extendible hashing — a fast access method for dynamic files. *ACM Transactions on Database Systems*, 4 (3):315–344, September 1979.

20. Stephen Ferg. *Debugging in Python.* http://www.ferg.org/papers/debugging_in_python.html, 2003.

21. Jeffrey Friedl. *Mastering Regular Expressions, Third Edition.* O'Reilly Media, 2006.

22. Richard Gillam. *An Introduction to Garbage Collection.* http://www.concentric.net/~rtgillam/pubs/Garbage1.html, 2004.

23. John Goerzen. *Foundations of Python Network Programming.* Apress, 2005.

24. Brian Goetz. *Java Theory and Practice: A Brief History of Garbage Collection.* http://www.ibm.com/developerworks/java/library/j-jtp10283/, 2003.

25. Ken Gottry. *Pick Up Performance with Generational Garbage Collection.* http://www.javaworld.com/javaworld/jw-01-2002/jw-0111-hotspotgc.html, 2002.

26. John Grayson. *Python and Tkinter Programmming.* Manning Publications, 2000.

27. Raymond Hettinger. *How-To Guide for Descriptors.* `http://users.rcn.com/python/download/Descriptor.htm`, 2004.

28. Greg Holling. *J2SE 1.4.1 Boosts Garbage Collection.* `http://www.javaworld.com/javaworld/jw-03-2003/jw-0307-j2segc.html`, 2003.

29. http://docs.python.org/tut/node16.html. Floating Point Arithmetic: Issues and Liminations.

30. http://perl-xml.sourceforge.net/perl sax/. Perl SAX (Simple API for XML Page.

31. http://twistedmatrix.com/. Twisted Matrix Laboratories.

32. http://www.activestate.com/. Activeperl User Guide (see the documentation for the Tk module).

33. http://www.w3.org/TR/2004/REC-xml 20040204. Extensible Markup Language (XML) 1.0 (Third Edition), 2004.

34. http://www.w3.org/TR/ws arch/. Web Services Architecture, 2004.

35. http://www.w3.org/TR/xmlschema 0/. XML Schema Part 0: Primer Second Edition, October 2004.

36. Capers Jones. *Programming Language Table, Release 8.2.* `http://www.spr.com/library/0langtbl.htm`, 1996.

37. Richard Jones. *Garbage Collection Bibliography.* `http://www.cs.kent.ac.uk/people/staff/rej/gcbib/gcbibG.html`, 2007.

38. Richard Jones. *Garbage Collection Page.* `http://www.cs.kent.ac.uk/people/staff/rej/gc.html`, 2007.

39. Richard Jones and Rafael Lins. *Garbage Collection, Algorithms for Automatic Dynamic Memory Management.* John Wiley and Sons, 1996.

40. Avinash C. Kak. *BitVector-1.3: A Pure Python Memory-Efficient Packed Representation for Bit Arrays.* `http://cheeseshop.python.org/pypi/BitVector/`.

41. Avinash C. Kak. *Programming With Objects, A Comparative Presentation of Object-Oriented Programming with C++ and Java.* John Wiley & Sons, New York, 2003.

42. Per-Ake Larson. Dynamic hashing. *BIT*, 18 (2):184–201, 1978.

43. Per-Ake Larson. Dynamic hash tables. *Communications of the ACM*, 31 (4):446–457, April 1988.

44. Steve Lidie and Nancy Walsh. *Mastering Perl/Tk.* O'Reilly, 2002.

45. Witold Litwin. Linear hashing: A new tool for file and table addressing. *Proceedings of the 6th Conference on Very Large Databases*, pages 212–223, March 1980.

46. Fredrik Lundh. *An Introduction to Tkinter.* `http://www.pythonware.com/library/an-introduction-to-tkinter.htm`, 1999.

47. Mark Lutz. *Programming Python (3rd Edition).* O'Reilly Media, 2006.

48. G. N. N. Martin. Spiral storage: Incrementally augmentable hash addressed storage. *Technical Report CS-RR-027*, 1979.

49. Steven McDougall. *Representing Sets in Perl.* `http://world.std.com/~swmcd/steven/perl/pm/set.shtml`, 1999.

50. David Mertz and Michele Simionato. *Metaclass programming in Python: Pushing object-oriented programming to the next level.* `http://www.ibm.com/developerworks/linux/library/l-pymeta.html`.

51. John K. Ousterhout. *Scripting: Higher Level Programming for the* 21st *Century.* IEEE Computer Magazine, March 1998.

52. Lutz Prechelt. *An Empirical Comparison of C, C++, Java, Perl, Python, Rexx, and Tcl for a Search/String-Processing Program.* `http://wwwipd.ira.uka.de/EIR`, 2000.

53. Santonu Sarkar, Avinash C. Kak, and Girish M. Rama. Metrics for measuring the quality of modularization of large-scale object-oriented software. *To appear in IEEE Transactions on Software Engineering*, 2008.

54. Santonu Sarkar, Girish M. Rama, and Avinash C. Kak. API-based and information-theoretic metrics for measuring the quality of software modularization. *IEEE Transactions on Software Engineering*, 33:14–32, 2007.

55. Randal Schwartz. *Web Techniques Column 34 — Anonymizing Proxy Server.* `http://www.stonehenge.com/merlyn/WebTechniques/col34.html`, 1999.

56. Randal Schwartz and Tom Phoenix. *Learning Perl.* O'Reilly, 2001.

57. Matt Sergeant. *XML::SAX::Intro.* `http://search.cpan.org/dist/XML-SAX/SAX/Intro.pod`.

58. John Shipman. *Tkinter Reference, A GUI for Python.* `http://infohost.nmt.edu/tcc/help/pubs/tkinter.pdf`, 2007.

59. Michele Simionato. *The Python 2.3 Method Resolution Order.* `http://www.python.org/2.3/mro.html`, 2003.

60. Kevin Smith, Jim Jewett, Skip Montanaro, and Anthony Baxter. *Decorators for Functions and Methods.* `http://www.python.org/dev/peps/pep-0318/`, 2003.

61. Sriram Srinivasan. *Advanced Perl Programming.* O'Reilly, 1997.

62. Lincoln D. Stein. *Network Programming with Perl.* Addison-Wesley, 2002.

63. W. R. Stevens. *Advanced Programming in the UNIX Environment.* Addison-Wesley, 1993.

64. Ivo Timmermans. *Abstract Methods/Classes.* `http://aspn.activestate.com/ASPN/Cookbook/Python/Recipe/266468`, 2004.

65. Guido van Rossum. *Unifying Types and Classes in Python 2.2.* `http://www.python.org/download/releases/2.2.3/descrintro/`.

66. Guido van Rossum. *Python Tutorial.* `http://docs.python.org/tut/`, 2006.

67. Guido van Rossum and Raymond Hettinger. *Conditional Expressions.* `http://www.python.org/dev/peps/pep-0308/`, 2003.

68. Larry Wall, Tom Christiansen, and Jon Orwant. *Programming Perl.* O'Reilly, 2000.

69. Guang Yang. *Build Your Own Lightweight XML DOM Parser.* `http://www.devx.com/xml/Article/10114`, 2002.

70. Moshe Zadka and Guido van Rossum. *Changing the Division Operator.* `http://www.python.org/dev/peps/pep-0238/`, 2001.

71. Ilya Zakharevich. *Package for Overloading Perl Operations.* `http://search.cpan.org/~nwclark/perl-5.8.8/lib/overload.pm`.

Index

A

B

C

D

E

F

G

H

J

K

L

M

N

O

P

Q

R

S

T

U

V

W

X

Z

Printed in the USA/Agawam, MA
February 22, 2021

770543.111